Rural Planning and Management

Managing the Environment for Sustainable Development

Series Editors: R. Kerry Turner
Professor of Environmental Sciences at the School of Environmental Sciences and Director of CSERGE and the Centre for Environmental Decisionmaking, University of East Anglia, UK
Ian J. Bateman
Reader in Environmental Sciences at the School of Environmental Sciences and Senior Research Fellow of CSERGE and the Centre for Environmental Decisionmaking, University of East Anglia, UK

1. Urban Planning and Management
    Kenneth G. Willis, R. Kerry Turner and Ian J. Bateman

2. Rural Planning and Management
    Joe Morris, Alison Bailey, R. Kerry Turner and Ian J. Bateman

3. Water Resources and Coastal Management
    R. Kerry Turner and Ian J. Bateman

Future titles will include:

Environmental Risk Planning and Management
Simon Gerrard, R. Kerry Turner and Ian J. Bateman

Environmental Ethics and Philosophy
John O'Neill, R. Kerry Turner and Ian J. Bateman

Waste Management and Planning
Jane C. Powell, R. Kerry Turner and Ian J. Bateman

Wherever possible, the articles in these volumes have been reproduced as originally published using facsimile reproduction, inclusive of footnotes and pagination to facilitate ease of reference.

For a list of all Edward Elgar published titles visit our site on the World Wide Web at
http://www.e-elgar.co.uk

Rural Planning and Management

Edited by

Joe Morris

Professor of Resource Economics and Management
Institute of Water and Environment, Cranfield University at Silsoe, UK

Alison Bailey

Lecturer in Environmental Economics
Institute of Water and Environment, Cranfield University at Silsoe, UK

R. Kerry Turner

Professor of Environmental Sciences at the School of Environmenal Sciences
and Director of CSERGE and the Centre for Environmental Decisionmaking,
University of East Anglia, UK

and

Ian J. Bateman

Reader in Environmental Sciences at the School of Environmental Sciences
and Senior Research Fellow at CSERGE and the Centre for Environmental
Decisionmaking, University of East Anglia, UK

MANAGING THE ENVIRONMENT FOR SUSTAINABLE DEVELOPMENT

An Elgar Reference Collection
Cheltenham, UK • Northampton, MA, USA

Published by
Edward Elgar Publishing Limited
Glensanda House
Montpellier Parade
Cheltenham
Glos GL50 1UA
UK

Edward Elgar Publishing, Inc.
136 West Street, Suite 202
Northampton
Massachusetts 01060
USA

A catalogue record for this book is available from the British Library.

ISBN   1 84064 220 3

Printed and bound in Great Britain by MPG Books Ltd, Bodmin, Cornwall

Contents

PART III RURAL SECTOR ISSUES

A Agriculture

B Protected Areas

C Forestry

D Energy

Acknowledgements

The editors and publishers wish to thank the authors and the following publishers who have kindly given permission for the use of copyright material.

Academic Press for articles: Michael Redclift (1995), 'The Environment and Structural Adjustment: Lessons for Policy Interventions in the 1990s', *Journal of Environmental Management*, **44**, 55–68; Allan Curtis and Terry De Lacy (1996), 'Landcare in Australia: Does it Make a Difference?', *Journal of Environmental Management*, **46**, 119–37; Colin Kirkpatrick and Norman Lee (1997), 'Market Liberalisation and Environmental Assessment in Developing and Transitional Economies', *Journal of Environmental Management*, **50**, 235–50.

Deryke Belshaw for his own article: (1995), *Rural Development Strategies in Low Income Countries: Poverty Reduction, Productivity Gains and Decentralisation*, A Revised Version of a Paper Presented at the Annual Conference of the Agricultural Economics Society held at Girton College, Cambridge in April 1995, 1–21.

Frank Cass & Co. Ltd for article: Frank Ellis (1998), 'Household Strategies and Rural Livelihood Diversification', *Journal of Development Studies*, **35** (1), October, 1–38.

Walter De Gruyter GMBH & Co. KG for article: Daniel W. Bromley and Ian Hodge (1990), 'Private Property Rights and Presumptive Policy Entitlements: Reconsidering the Premises of Rural Policy', *European Review of Agricultural Economics*, **17**, 197–214.

Elsevier Science for articles: Cleophas Lado (1992), 'Problems of Wildlife Management and Land Use in Kenya', *Land Use Policy*, **9** (3), July, 169–84; Paul Selman (1993), 'Landscape Ecology and Countryside Planning: Vision, Theory and Practice', *Journal of Rural Studies*, **9** (1), January, 1–21; Jan Diek van Mansvelt and Jessie A. Mulder (1993), 'European Features for Sustainable Development: A Contribution to the Dialogue', *Landscape and Urban Planning*, **27**, 67–90; Philip Lowe, Jonathan Murdoch, Terry Marsden, Richard Munton and Andrew Flynn (1993), 'Regulating the New Rural Spaces: The Uneven Development of Land', *Journal of Rural Studies*, **9** (3), July, 205–22; Kevin D. Bishop and Adrian A.C. Phillips (1993), 'Seven Steps to Market – The Development of the Market-Led Approach to Countryside Conservation and Recreation', *Journal of Rural Studies*, **9** (4), October, 315–38; Mark Shucksmith, Polly Chapman, Gill Clark and Stuart Black (1994), 'Social Welfare in Rural Europe', *Journal of Rural Studies*, **10** (4), October, 343–56; Merylyn McKenzie Hedger (1995), 'Wind Power: Challenges to Planning Policy in the UK', *Land Use Policy*, **12** (1), 17–28; D.O. Hall and J.I. House (1995), 'Biomass Energy in Western Europe to 2050', *Land Use Policy*, **12** (1), 37–48; David Wood (1995), 'Conserved to Death: Are Tropical Forests Being Over-protected From People?', *Land Use Policy*, **12** (2), April, 115–35; Kevin Bishop, Adrian Phillips and Lynda Warren (1995), 'Protected for Ever? Factors Shaping the Future of Protected Areas

Policy', *Land Use Policy*, **12** (4), 291–305; Nigel Berkeley, David Clark and Brian Ilbery (1996), 'Regional Variations in Business Use of Information and Communication Technologies and their Implications for Policy: Case Study Evidence from Rural England', *Geoforum*, **27** (1), 75–86; Stephen D. Nutley (1996), 'Rural Transport Problems and Non-car Populations in the USA: A UK Perspective', *Journal of Transport Geography*, **4** (2), June, 93–106; Anne-Mette Hjalager (1996), 'Agricultural Diversification into Tourism: Evidence of a European Community Development Programme', *Tourism Management*, **17** (2), 103–11; Paul Cloke, Paul Milbourne and Chris Thomas (1996), 'From Wasteland to Wonderland: Opencast Mining, Regeneration and the English National Forest', *Geoforum*, **27** (2), 159–74; Colin C. Williams (1996), 'Local Purchasing Schemes and Rural Development: An Evaluation of Local Exchange and Trading Systems (LETS)', *Journal of Rural Studies*, **12** (3), 231–44; Paul Selman (1997), 'The Role of Forestry in Meeting Planning Objectives', *Land Use Policy*, **14** (1), 55–73; Neil Ward and Kate McNicholas (1998), 'Reconfiguring Rural Development in the UK: Objective 5b and the New Rural Governance', *Journal of Rural Studies*, **14** (1), 27–39; Karen A. Poiani, Jeffrey V. Baumgartner, Steven C. Buttrick, Shelley L. Green, Edward Hopkins, George D. Ivey, Katherine P. Seaton and Robert D. Sutter (1998), 'A Scale-Independent, Site Conservation Planning Framework in The Nature Conservancy', *Landscape and Urban Planning*, **43**, 143–56; Paul Milbourne (1998), 'Local Responses to Central State Restructuring of Social Housing Provision in Rural Areas', *Journal of Rural Studies*, **14** (2), April, 167–84; Keith D. Wiebe and Ruth Meinzen-Dick (1998), 'Property Rights as Policy Tools for Sustainable Development', *Land Use Policy*, **15** (3), 203–15; Clive Potter and Philip Goodwin (1998), 'Agricultural Liberalization in the European Union: An Analysis of the Implications for Nature Conservation', *Journal of Rural Studies*, **14** (3), July, 287–98; David J. Brunckhorst (1998), 'Creating Institutions to Ensure Sustainable Use of Resources', *Habitat International*, **22** (4), December, 347–54; Matt Lobley and Clive Potter (1998), 'Environmental Stewardship in UK Agriculture: A Comparison of the Environmentally Sensitive Area Programme and the Countryside Stewardship Scheme in South East England', *Geoforum*, **29** (4), 413–32; Nick Hanley, Martin Whitby and Ian Simpson (1999), 'Assessing the Success of Agri-environmental Policy in the UK', *Land Use Policy*, **16** (2), April, 67–80; Jules Pretty and Rachel Hine (2000), 'The Promising Spread of Sustainable Agriculture in Asia', *Natural Resources Forum*, **24** (2), May, 107–21; John Bryden and Ray Bollman (2000), 'Rural Employment in Industrialised Countries', *Agricultural Economics*, **22**, 185–97.

Journal of Agricultural Economics for articles: Martin Whitby and W. Neil Adger (1996), 'Natural and Reproducible Capital and the Sustainability of Land Use in the UK', *Journal of Agricultural Economics*, **47** (1), January, 50–65; Bill Slee, Helen Farr and Patrick Snowdon (1997), 'The Economic Impact of Alternative Types of Rural Tourism', *Journal of Agricultural Economics*, **48** (2), May, 179–92; Paul Webster (1999), 'The Challenge of Sustainability at the Farm Level: Presidential Address', *Journal of Agricultural Economics*, **50** (3), September, 371–87.

Taylor & Francis Ltd for article: B.J. Gleeson and K.J. Grundy (1997), 'New Zealand's Planning Revolution Five Years On: A Preliminary Assessment', *Journal of Environmental Planning and Management*, **40** (3), May, 293–313.

University of Wisconsin Press for article: Elizabeth G. Katz (2000), 'Social Capital and Natural Capital: A Comparative Analysis of Land Tenure and Natural Resource Management in Guatemala', *Land Economics*, **76** (1), February, 114–32.

Every effort has been made to trace all the copyright holders but if any have been inadvertently overlooked the publishers will be pleased to make the necessary arrangement at the first opportunity.

In addition the publishers wish to thank the Library of the London School of Economics and Political Science, the Marshall Library of Economics, Cambridge University, B & N Microfilm, London and the Library of Indiana University at Bloomington, USA, for their assistance in obtaining these articles.

Managing the Environment for Sustainable Development: Rural Environmental Management and Planning

Joe Morris and Alison Bailey

The complexity of the links among the social, economic and environmental issues implied in the concept of sustainable development is particularly evident in the rural sector. It is here that natural resources and the environment clearly provide the context and mechanisms for the social and economic activities necessary to support not only rural communities themselves, but also urban communities that derive benefit from productive and ecologically stable and resilient rural areas. This introductory essay and the papers that follow capture some of the key themes in the debate on managing the rural environment for sustainable development. While there are considerable differences in context between developed, transitional and developing countries, there are common themes in the search for sustainable livelihoods and vibrant communities. There is also commonality and convergence in the approaches to sustainable development, notably the emphasis on market mechanisms, institution building and participation.

Defining Rurality

'Rural' is a relative term used to describe geographically based characteristics, circumstances and practices which are not urban. By comparison, 'urban' refers to that commonly found in towns and cities. Rural implies landscapes characterized by open space, vegetation and natural physical features, land use characterized by farmed land and a relatively low incidence of built property and infrastructure. Rural also implies human socio-cultural norms captured in labels such as 'conservatism' and 'traditionalism', with social attitudes and behaviour strongly influenced by the patterns of natural processes and a shared sense of heritage and belonging. Thus rurality is often perceived, especially by external observers, as the rustic idyll of a community in equilibrium with itself and nature (McInerney, 1996). This is often in contrast to the perceived disequilibrium, unpredictability and ephemeralism of urbanity. Underlying this, the idea commonly prevails that rural is more natural and urban is more artificial, in both physical and human attributes.

It has also been convenient to distinguish rural in terms of particular demographic, economic and social characteristics (Countryside Agency, 1999). Rural population densities are relatively low, settlements are dispersed and relatively isolated, and the size and structure of the population have been strongly influenced by the carrying capacity of locally available resources and opportunities for outward migration. The stereotypical rural economy is that in which land is the key resource, and access to land the key determinant of prosperity at an individual and community level. Farming and related activities provide the dominant economic base and source of employment: in the peasant rural economy as the basis for subsistence and self-sufficiency; in the commercial agricultural economy as the basis for exchange with the urban industrial economy.

In reality, there are many 'ruralities' (Allanson *et al.*, 1995), within countries, within regions and within communities. These can vary in characteristics, circumstances and practices, evident in the diversity of physical conditions, natural resource endowments, activities, incomes, employment, access opportunities, ease of mobility, social norms, customs and preferences, cultural pursuits, political systems, degrees of involvement and quality of life within the rural sector. Whereas, in industrialized countries, rural living is an ambition of many high income urban dwellers, in many developing countries, rural living is associated with grinding poverty such that migration to urban areas seemingly offers better life chances.

Rural Development

Development describes the process whereby improvements or beneficial change are achieved in conditions which determine the welfare of society, and in the characteristics of society itself in terms of attributes and behaviour. Definitions of development, and the indicators to measure it, have varied over time (United Nations Development Programme (UNDP), 1999; Todaro, 2000). Some emphasize economic parameters, others address broader issues of standards of living, the distribution of development impacts, and the extent to which development is inclusive of society as a whole.

Development is often taken as synonymous with economic development, whereby increased societal welfare is achieved by continued growth in production and consumption goods and services now and into the future. At a global level, the challenge is to meet, subject to limited resources, the increased demands of the relatively well off in pursuit of higher material standards of living and, at the same time, the essential needs of the rising number of absolutely poor people (1.3 billion in 1999) which have not yet been met (United Nations Environment Programme (UNEP), 1999). The vast majority of the world's poor are located in rural areas, and are largely dependent on agriculture and the natural environment for their sustenance.

The rural sector, and within this the agricultural sector in particular, has historically been seen as an important engine of wider economic development: generating tradable surpluses, releasing resources for use in other sectors, providing a market for non-agricultural goods and services, and enabling those that remain in the agricultural sector to enjoy a fair share of the benefits from overall development (Lewis, 1954; Johnston and Mellor, 1961; Schultz, 1964). While the rural and agricultural sectors may achieve significant improvements through increased productivity and structural change, the main perceived contribution was that of underpinning development and growth in the urban sector. This led to conclusions that agriculture was inevitably a declining sector (Kuznets, 1966), could not in itself provide the basis for a modern, prosperous economy, and, in countries which had not already industrialized, was less worthy of support than infant industrial sectors. Thus, in developing countries where agriculture remained dominant, there was a tendency to neglect it (Timmer, 1992). For countries which have successfully industrialized, however, the agricultural sectors retain a powerful political lobby whereby the past favours are returned in the form of subsidies and protectionist measures, reducing the incentive for economic diversity in the rural sector.

In the absence of assistance, and for reasons discussed below, a rural sector dependent on crop and livestock production alone is likely to experience relative decline, unless rural populations have income generation opportunities beyond the farm (McInerney, 1994). In situations where opportunities in the industrial sector are limited, the rural sector must be relied upon to absorb its own population increase. It is here that rural development, funded by governments and international development agencies and partners, has taken a broader, strategic, integrated view, simultaneously developing agriculture and other primary production and processing, rural industry, infrastructure and services, and developing the capacity of rural institutions to manage the development process (Belshaw, 1995). This approach, once top-down technology transfer, now bottom-up participation, has not been without its disappointments (Murray and Greer, 1992). Nevertheless, it interesting to note that in Europe there is now a perceived need for integrated rural development planning, focused at the regional level (Lowe and Ward, 1998).

Rural Environment

'Environment' refers to the media of land, water, air and their associated physical, chemical and biological processes and systems. These can be described in terms of indicators which show the condition of the environment and changes over time, such as the quantity and/or quality of the media and the size and diversity of the ecological systems which occupy them (e.g. Organization for Economic Co-operation and Development (OECD), 1997; Cornforth, 1999). The interest in environmental measurement has grown because of concerns about the impact of human activity and economic development (Hartwick and Olewiler, 1998). This concern may be driven by an ethical commitment to protecting the integrity of the natural world for its own sake, a realization that environmental quality is an important aspect of social welfare, or concern that natural resource and environmental degradation will result in the failure of the economic system, with consequences for human society (Perman *et al.*, 1999).

These concerns are particularly apparent in the rural sector, where social and economic welfare predominantly depend on the use of natural resources and processes. These links between environment and development in a rural context are evident in the economic functions provided by the environment (Turner *et al.*, 1994), namely:

* As a source of renewable and non-renewable resources, such as soil and water, fishing and forestry, mining and quarrying, and water resources;
* As a carrier or location for human-, land- and water-based activity such as farming;
* As a sink for waste arising from rural- and urban-based activities;
* As a provider of environmental goods and services (amenities) associated with natural and biological systems which deliver benefits to society in 'use', such as the hydrological

processes delivered by wetland areas, or in 'non-use'; that is, just because they exist now and into the future, such as irreplaceable species and habitats.

As economic activity increases, so does the pressure on the rural environment (Tietenberg, 1996). Natural resources are exploited, wastes are generated, and natural and ecological features and processes are damaged or destroyed. The characteristics of many environmental functions (external, uncompensated, untraded and unpriced goods (and bads) with high consumer surplus (or deficit), public goods, ill-defined property rights, inter-generational, cumulative and uncertain impacts) mean that environmental issues are often inadequately accounted for in the decisions of individuals, businesses and policy makers (see, for example, McDonald, 1989). In other words, markets and policies often fail to include environmental aspects.

At the margin of development, environmental degradation can significantly compromise social welfare, justifying constraints on further development and/or the commitment of resources to substitute for polluting activities, or to carry out remedial or defensive works. Where economic growth is the political imperative, source and carrier functions associated with farming, harvesting and extractive industries tend to receive policy priority. Where broader definitions of development find support, sink and amenity functions, in so much as they are perceived to be both valuable and vulnerable, receive greater policy attention.

Sustainable Development

Concern about the negative impacts of economic development, especially on people, communities and the natural environment, have encouraged the concept of 'sustainable development'. Bruntland's definition puts people at the centre: 'meeting the needs of the present generation without compromising the ability of future generations to meet their own needs' (World Commission on Environment and Development (WCED), 1987). The 1992 Rio Conference, the Earth Summit, gave a commitment to devising 'environmentally sustainable economic development strategies to halt and reverse the negative impacts of human behaviour on the physical environment' (United Nations, 1993). Sustainable development has thus emerged as an integrating concept with 'a focus on welfare considerations broader than just economic growth' (OECD, 1998), with an 'emphasis on the links between the key components of sustainability, namely the social, economic and environmental dimensions, and balancing these where there are conflicts'.

From an economic perspective, sustainability implies a number of conditions (Perman *et al.*, 1999), namely that:

- levels of consumption do not decline;
- production capabilities of future generations do not decline;
- the stock of renewable natural resources does not decline;
- society is organized and acts in a way to ensure that development is sustainable.

Thus sustainable development implies improvements in standards of living which endure over time. It is essentially concerned with human activity, is people and community centred, and contains a commitment to equity, participation and democratic processes. In this respect it has an important political dimension, explicitly requiring subsidiarity; that is, local stewardship and control.

This holistic approach to development considers the quantitative and qualitative aspects of the flow of goods and services (including environmental quality) enjoyed by society, and the stock of 'capital' which generates these flows. Capital is taken in the broadest sense to include natural (e.g. land, water, air and bio systems), man made (e.g. roads and dams), human (knowledge and skills) and social (social cohesion, community, institutions, civil society) capital (see Katz, 2000 in this volume; Pretty, 1998; Pretty and Ward, 2001). There is increasing emphasis on the latter as a key factor determining the quality of human life and the sustainability of a community-based development process.

The concept of sustainability has been adopted by governments as a framework for development strategies which aim to reconcile social, economic and environmental objectives. The UK government's strategy for a Better Quality of Life (Department of the Environment, Transport and the Regions (DETR), 1999) is an example. The vision is of a prosperous, inclusive society, with a better quality of life for everyone associated with the 'maintenance of high and stable levels of economic growth and employment', achieved through 'prudent use of natural resources' and ensuring 'effective protection of the environment'. Economic growth remains the underlying development paradigm. To suggest otherwise would be politically naïve, at least at the level of national or regional government accountable to an electorate, although a public accounting system which accommodates the 'other capitals' would better promote the sustainability argument.

Sustainable Rural Development

The concept of sustainable development has obvious relevance to the rural sector, where the links between environmental qualities and the functions and performance of social and economic systems are readily apparent. Rural livelihoods such as farming, fishing and forestry are very much dependent on the flow and stock of natural resources, the arrangements which determine access and control, and the distribution of benefits and costs associated with their use. Harvesting beyond the regenerative capacity of renewable systems, and the generation of waste beyond the capacity of natural processes to absorb potential pollutants, degrades the stock and its subsequent flow capability and threatens rural livelihoods (Perman *et al.*, 1999). There are major implications here for the design and promotion of management systems and technologies which can protect and enhance the condition or performance of natural resource systems, through 'sustainable' agriculture, fishing and forestry practices (see, for example, Redclift, 1990).

These linkages and vulnerabilities are apparent in the UK 1997 White Paper on Development (Department for International Development (DFID), 1997), which focuses on the alleviation of rural poverty in low income countries through sustainable livelihoods based on improved management of natural resources. They are also apparent in the debate in high income countries where the challenge is to protect environmental quality for the general good, while ensuring that rural dwellers enjoy similar standards of living to the rest of society (DETR, 1999).

The search for sustainability is further complicated by possibilities of climate change: the balance of evidence suggests a discernible human influence on global warming. Climate change is likely to affect primary sectors such as agriculture and forestry more than other secondary or tertiary sectors such as manufacturing or retailing, and it is likely to have relatively greater adverse impacts on more marginal or poorer areas. In this respect rural environmental management must include assessment of the impacts and adaptations of climate change (Parry, 1990, 2000; Ministry of Agriculture, Fisheries and Food (MAFF), 2000a).

Sustainable Agriculture

Much of the debate on sustainability has focused on farming systems (e.g. Whitby and Adger, 1996; Marsh, 1997; Smith and McDonald, 1998; and van Mansvelt and Mulder, 1993; Webster, 1999; and Pretty and Hine, 2000 in this volume), with attempts to define indicators to express degrees, rather than absolute levels, of sustainability (OECD, 1997; MAFF, 1998). The aforementioned sustainability criteria apply with respect to soil quality, air, energy and water issues, pollution risk associated with agro-chemical use, and protection of wildlife and landscape. However, there is also growing interest in human and social capital aspects, in implications for benefits to local economies and communities, and in product quality and safety for consumers (Pretty, 1998). While the issues are now well rehearsed, policy has been slow to respond, primarily due to short-term vested interests in non-sustainable systems (see van Mansvelt and Mulder, 1993; and Pretty and Hine, 2000 in this volume). The conflicts between market forces and local interests are apparent in the current World Trade Organization wranglings (Pearce, 1999; *The Economist*, 1999a, b). It seems unlikely that the market itself will deliver sustainable solutions without a degree of policy intervention, although there are signs that the more enlightened corporate organizations are taking sustainability seriously (Unilever, 1999).

These issues and policy responses are further elaborated in the following sections drawing on European and developing country perspectives.

Rural Development: The European Perspective

The Agricultural Imperative

Rural has for the most part been taken to be synonymous with farming and agriculture, and rural development and rural prosperity synonymous with that of the agricultural sector (see, for example, Bryden, 1994). This is apparent throughout the world, where farming occupies the greater part of the managed, non-built land surface. Thus farming interests and related institutions, such as those that define property rights and responsibilities, exert a dominant influence on the control of physical resources and the environment (Bateman, 1989; Whitby, 1990; and Bromley and Hodge, 1990 and Weibe and Meinzen-Dick, 1998 in this volume).

The dominance of agricultural policy over rural policy is apparent in Europe (Bryden, 1994; Lowe and Ward, 1998 in this volume) where rural policy has taken one of two forms: first, direct support to agriculture, and second protection of agricultural, and to a lesser extent other rural land use, against urban encroachment (Gardner, 1996; Ritson and Harvey, 1999). This twin-track approach is apparent in Britain.

First, declining fortunes in farming in Britain in the 1930s encouraged the establishment of Producer Marketing Boards, whose main function was to secure financial returns through centrally managed commodity-marketing regimes. In the post-World War II era, the 1947 Agriculture Act provided a framework to create a stable and efficient agricultural industry, producing food for the nation at minimum prices consistent with proper remuneration to farmers, workers and capital invested. This was largely funded by taxpayers rather than food consumers, involving grants for structural adjustment, infrastructure investment, incentives for intensification and increased productivity, and guaranteed payments for output. The result of the Act was thus to initiate a suite of support and interventions over the following 25 years until accession into the European Economic Community (EEC) in 1973.

Second, the 1947 Town and Country Planning Act provided for the control by local authorities of land use change in accordance with pre-defined development plans. The Act legitimized the concept of land use planning and related interventions, and asserted the critical if not primordial role of a large agricultural industry in the definition of rural futures: a prosperous farming community would secure the future of valued, albeit managed, landscapes and vibrant rural communities. Thus, in Britain, as in many other industrialized countries, rural social and economic policy was subsumed within a complex of land use control and agricultural support. Agriculture itself was relieved of many of the controls and conditions placed on other industrial activities. Incomes and jobs in the rural space were tied to the fortunes of agriculture, which were critically dependent on a continued commitment to government intervention.

Agriculture: A Declining Sector

Economic growth and national prosperity are associated with relative agricultural decline, if only because as average incomes rise there is a tendency to spend a smaller relative proportion of that increase on food. As a result, there tends to be a negative correlation between national average per capita income and the relative size of the agricultural sector. Thus, the argument goes, if farming and, by implication, the rural economy wish to enjoy standards of living similar to the national average, productivity in farming must rise in line with overall economic performance and people must leave farming (Brassley, 1997). In the longer term, the farming sector will structurally adjust downwards. Any attempts to prop up incomes in the short term will prove unsustainable. Ideally, those previously engaged in agriculture will find employment elsewhere in the rural or urban sectors. If this is not the case, the immobility of resources, whether labour or physical assets, will impede structural adjustment, resulting in falling incomes, rising rural poverty and deprivation.

The income problems of agriculture are further exacerbated by short-term supply variation due to climatic and biological factors which, combined with low price elasticity of demand, can generate wild variations in prices and incomes to farmers. Hence farmers 'cry famine over a golden harvest'. Although efforts to iron out seasonal fluctuations in commodity prices can help both producers and consumers, actions to protect the general level of farm incomes through farm commodity price support are likely to prove counter-productive in the absence of structural change. Ironically, over-dependence on agriculture is the Achilles' heel of the rural sector. A rural policy which ties development solely to the fortunes of farming is likely to fail in the long term.

All of this is apparent in the British case (MAFF 1999a, b). Downward pressure on commodity output prices relative to input prices has diminished the real terms of trade for farmers during the last 30 years in particular, resulting in the underlying decline in average farm incomes. This is in spite of high levels of price support, the decline in farm numbers, and the rise in the degree of enterprise specialization and the average size of farm holding. Productivity increases in British farming have been impressive by any standards, whether the measures are output per unit of land or labour. Land-augmenting technologies which increase yields per hectare (such as improved genetic material, pest control, field drainage, irrigation and management practices) have been encouraged by guaranteed prices and markets and publicly funded research and extension services. Labour-saving technology in the form of mechanization has encouraged larger farm size in pursuit of economies of scale.

Across the whole of Europe, a common response by farmers to declining real (albeit protected) output prices, given the lack of mobility of farm resources, was to increase output as a means of protecting farm income. Given the limits on the domestic market, this has led to unwanted surpluses and burgeoning agricultural support costs and, subsequently, increasing recognition of the need for structural adjustment.

In terms of European agricultural policy, this need was recognized as early as 1968 in the EEC Mansholt Plan. This focused on getting farmers out of farming and on production re-strictions, but strong farming lobbies resisted the proposals. Although it had been the intention to spend 90 per cent of Common Agricultural Policy (CAP) funds on structural change and 10 per cent or so on price support, for much of the 1970s the converse applied. It was not until much later that the financial non-sustainability of CAP eventually led to policy changes, including the introduction of quotas and co-responsibility levies in the early 1980s, and payments to set land out of production and the 'de-coupling' of farm income support from commodity pricing in the early 1990s. More recently the concept of 'modulating' or targeting support to vulnerable farmers groups has emerged.

Simultaneously, the unprotected vegetable and horticultural sectors have faced fierce competition from international suppliers in a British domestic market now dominated by a few powerful food retailers who are able to seek out least-cost sources.

In short, the CAP and national agricultural policies have long provided the centrepiece of rural policy in spite of their inability to deliver viable, sustainable rural communities. Although there have been productivity improvements on the farm, these have not been sufficient in themselves to arrest the decline of the farm-based economy. Furthermore, they have also had, through trade diversion and impact on world markets, negative repercussions for rural com-munities beyond Europe (Heidensohn, 1995; Hitiris, 1998).

The Changing Rural Scenes and Roles

During the last 30 years, agricultural structural adjustment, together with planning constraints on rural non-farm development, have forced outward migration of the rural workforce. Except in the most remote areas, the voids have been filled by counter-migration from cities to rural areas by a relatively wealthy and mobile middle class of commuters, retirees and weekend dwellers seeking relief from urban pressures. Between 1981 and 1991, the English rural population, for example, rose by 7 per cent (Countryside Agency, 1999). However, this has sometimes threatened the balance and vitality of rural settlements (see, for example, Shucksmith,

1990 and Milbourne, 1998 in this volume in relation to the housing issue). The new rural dwellers retain their links with their urban origins, immunize themselves from some of the common disadvantages of rural living (relatively low wages, immobility and inaccessibility to essential services) (see Shucksmith *et al.*, 1994 in this volume) and seek to embalm the rural space in a formaldehyde of antidevelopment. Those remaining rural dwellers who depend on the rural economy for work and services may face a declining quantity and quality of provision (Errington, 1995), although opportunities have arisen (see Williams, 1996 in this volume). The local shop, the post office, the bank, the bus service and the primary school are potential victims of this demographic change, much of which reflects the lack of a strategic vision for a living countryside and policies tailored accordingly (see, for example, Banister and Norton, 1988; Nutley, 1988; Stokes, 1995; and Nutley, 1996 in this volume).

Policy Response: Emerging Rural Policy

Recognition that the countryside delivers benefits and serves functions other than food production, and concern about the impact of intensive agriculture and development on the natural environment, have led to the introduction of legal powers or duties to protect and enhance specific landscape features, habitats, natural species and public access (Waters, 1994). More recently, attention has also focused on the importance of sustaining vibrant, balanced rural communities.

In Britain, as in most countries, the policy response has been piecemeal and sequential, reflecting increased pressures on, and the declining state of, the rural environment, and the effectiveness of a growing environmental lobby. The response has thus comprised a mix of controls on development, the creation (initially) of protected areas and landscapes, and then (successively) species and habitats (see Bishop *et al.*, 1995 in this volume), incentives to farm in environmentally sensitive ways (Hodge, 1991; Crabtree and Chambers, 1994; Swales, 1994; and Hanley *et al.*, 1999 in this volume), voluntary codes of practice (MAFF, 1998a, b, c) and, more recently, mandatory regulation of farming and other land- and water-using industries (Archer, 1992; Tunney, 1992; Gouldson and Murphy, 1998).

Early emphasis on valued landscapes and public access came in the form of the 1949 National Parks and Access to the Countryside Act, which laid down mechanisms for designating National Parks (Crabtree, 1991; Warren, 1998), Areas of Outstanding Natural Beauty, Sites of Special Scientific Interest (SSSIs) (Adams *et al.*, 1992; Spash and Simpson, 1993), Nature Reserves (Box, 1991) and public rights of way (Whitby, 1997). The 1968 Countryside Act (1967 Scotland) gave local authorities the power to create country parks and established the Countryside Commissions for England and Wales, and Scotland to promote environmental, mainly landscape, protection and recreation. The 1981 Wildlife and Countryside Act consolidated earlier legislation, but gave much greater emphasis to the protection of specific species of animals, plants and habitats, the designation of SSSIs and the public right of way network (Lomas, 1994; Ross and Stockdale, 1996).

The links between agriculture and the environment were made explicit in the 1986 Agricultural Act, which created the Environmentally Sensitive Area (ESA) schemes, areas containing landscape and wildlife attributes of national or regional importance (Potter, 1988; Baldock *et al.*, 1990; Dixon, 1992; Froud, 1994; Whitby and Lowe, 1994; Morris *et al.*, 2000a; and Lobley and Potter, 1998 in this volume). Within ESAs, farmers and landowners voluntarily agree to operate and maintain their farms and property in order to deliver specified, locally defined environmental objectives in return for financial rewards (or compensation, depending on perspective). These include payments to convert arable to grassland, reduce grassland intensity, establish hedgerows, and repair historic farm buildings and structures.

In line with the growing international debate, the UK government in its 1990 White Paper, *This Common Inheritance* (Department of the Environment *et al.*, 1990) recognized the links between environment and development and flagged key issues such as global warming, land use, the countryside and rural economy, landscape and wildlife, towns and cities, heritage, air quality (local and global), noise, water, hazardous substances, and waste and recycling.

This debate was of particular relevance to agriculture where intensive farming systems were perceived to be unsustainable across the spectrum of social, economic and environmental criteria (Waters, 1994; Whitby and Lowe, 1994; Whitby *et al.*, 1996). In 1991, the Countryside Commission launched its Countryside Stewardship programme for the wider countryside (Bishop and Phillips, 1993; Harrison-Mayfield *et al.*, 1998; Morris *et al.*, 2000b; and Lobley and Potter, 1998 in this volume), providing financial inducements to farmers to protect or enhance the environmental quality of the wider countryside. Provision for increasing access was also included (Crabtree, 1997). In 1995, the MAFF took control of the scheme.

The issues facing the rural sector in the European post-productivist agricultural era are apparent in the policy statements (White Papers) produced by the UK government variously entitled *Rural England: A Nation Committed to a Living Countryside* (Department of the Environment and MAFF, 1995), *Rural Scotland: People, Prosperity and Partnership* (Scottish Office, 1995) and *The Working Countryside for Wales* (Welsh Office, 1996). The intended broader perspective is implicit in the titles of the reports. To a large extent these reports reviewed the current position and issues of concern rather than focusing on future policy direction (Hodge, 1996, 1997b). They confirmed the importance of agriculture, farming and farmers in the rural economy and society, but also pointed to farming's declining role as a provider of income and jobs. In the UK, farming occupies 80 per cent of land use, but provides only 1.5 per cent of GDP and 2 per cent of jobs. Even in remote areas, less than 10 per cent earn their living from the land. Of course, the industries supplying agriculture and processing its outputs can account for a much larger proportion of total rural employment, up to 17 per cent in some rural areas of eastern England, for example. Alongside the decline in agricultural employment, jobs in other primary sectors, such as mining and quarrying, have also declined substantially. However, this has been counterbalanced to a degree by a rise in manufacturing and service sector jobs in rural areas (see Bryden and Bollman, 2000 in this volume), which in England now account for about 31 per cent and 25 per cent of the national totals, respectively.

The White Papers also identified key areas for new policy initiatives, with reduced focus on agriculture for food production, although exactly how these are to be pursued is not made clear, especially within a European context in which the agricultural lobby retains considerable political clout. Diversification strategies (Lowe *et al.*, 1993 in this volume; Crocker, 1986; Cloke and McLaughlin, 1989; Byrne and Ravenscroft, 1990; Shucksmith and Winter, 1990) identify prospects for non-food crops, such as energy bio-mass (Hall and House, 1995 in this volume) and forestry (Bullock *et al.*, 1994; Cloke *et al.*, 1996 and Selman, 1997 in this volume; Burgess *et al.*, 1999); other forms of energy production (Coles and Taylor, 1993; and Hedger, 1995 in this volume); ongoing extractive industries (Horne and Frost, 1991; Jones, 1992; Plowden, 1992; Johnson, 1994); environmental protection and enhancement programmes, such as protected area schemes (see Potter and Goodwin, 1998 in this volume); rural industry, craft, recreation and tourism sectors (Slee *et al.*, 1997; and Hjalgar, 1996 in this volume); IT-based telecottage industries (Berkeley *et al.*, 1996 in this volume); and direct or indirect public sector employment. These opportunities, it is suggested, would be promoted by a range of monetary and fiscal instruments, regulation (and deregulation), infrastructure investment, education and training, and relevant national and regional regeneration programmes (see, for example, Lowe *et al.*, 1993 and Bishop and Phillips, 1993 in this volume). What is important about these policy papers, produced jointly by government departments or offices separately responsible for agriculture and environment, is the signs of decoupling agricultural and rural policy and fortune, and an attempt at 'joined up' rural governance.

Rural Development Regulation

Under the aegis of the Agenda 2000 round of CAP reform (MAFF, 1999c), the EC introduced the Rural Development Regulation (May 1999) (MAFF, 1999d). This further promotes the theme of a competitive, diverse, outward-looking agriculture, providing food and non-food commodities for the market, and environmental goods and services for either private or public benefit. Inadvertently referred to by the UK Minister of Agriculture as the 'stump' of policy reform, later corrected to 'sapling', no doubt to ensure its future, its broad aim is to produce a 'comprehensive, multi-functional agricultural sector in the context of a comprehensive integrated strategy for rural development'. More specific objectives are to encourage an efficient farming sector independent of subsidy, improve the competitive advantage of rural areas to engage in a broad spectrum of economic activities, and protect and enhance environmental quality. The new policy involves a switch of farm spending away from production aids to support the broader rural economy, including Countryside Stewardship, organic farming and woodlands. The announcement in December 1999 of an extra £1.6 billion over a seven year period mainly for agri-environmental and rural diversification schemes in England caught the rural sector somewhat by surprise, and heightened interest in a more strategic approach to policy management.

The implementation of the Rural Development Regulation requires that all measures provided be programmed in the context of a national Rural Development Plan covering the period 2000 to 2006. Individual 'Regional Chapters' profile and set strategic objectives for the social, economic and environmental elements of their various areas. In the English case (MAFF, 2000b), these Chapters were developed in a participatory process with key statutory partners, such as local government, English Nature, the Countryside Agency, Forestry Commission, English Heritage and the Environment Agency. Rather suddenly, it appears, there is both opportunity and resources to address the anachronisms and incongruities of an agriculturally biased rural policy. It does require a different complement of skills and processes to achieve this integrated approach, especially those which can reconcile the interests and influences of the variety of stakeholders anxious to participate. In particular, it emphasizes the importance of partnership and good governance in its broadest sense.

Rural Futures

Current rural issues and themes are evident in the debate which preceded the publication of the EU's Agenda 2000, and the resultant Rural Development Regulation and member state plans.

In the UK, further debate has ensued prior to the publication of the new Rural White Paper which was published in November 2000 (DETR/MAFF, 1999; DETR/MAFF, 2000).

The debate recognizes the great diversity of rural areas and 'ruralities' referred to previously. Both the EU and UK government want to make agriculture more market oriented, internationally competitive and technologically advanced. At the same time, they want to relieve pressure on and protect the natural environment, increase public access to enjoyment of the countryside, and encourage the development of alternative sustainable non-agricultural enterprises. The ultimate aim is for a living and working countryside in which thriving and prosperous communities benefit from and secure high standards of environmental quality. Within this, there is recognition of the mutually beneficial interdependence between town and country, alongside the potential for conflicts to arise at the rural/urban interface associated with the spillover effects of urban land use, lifestyles and values. The overall vision is underpinned by the principles of sustainable development, strong communities, inclusive society and stakeholder partnership.

The emerging debate resulting from this vision suggests that the two main lobbies in the countryside, namely environment and farming, may not in themselves deliver what is required. For example, local government planning policies which interpret sustainable development predominantly in terms of environmental protection or the provision of special protection to high quality agricultural land could reduce options for meeting rural economic needs. This suggests that sustainable development must be adequately defined if it is to be useful, with social, economic and environmental indicators which reflect quality of life in rural communities, methods for screening the suitability of development options, and mechanisms for engaging rural populations in the development process.

Within agriculture itself, CAP reform and reduced production support for conventional output are threatening family farm businesses unless they can diversify into alternative crop and livestock products, add value by moving up the supply chain, and/or improve their competitive position *vis-à-vis* the large-scale food processors/retailers. Initiatives such as local area produce networks, localized farm product brands, direct and internet marketing, quality assurance schemes and farmer-owned marketing companies/co-operatives are examples. Concentration in the food retail sector has led to accusations of exploitation of farmers, but there are signs that the supermarkets are becoming sensitive to criticisms of the way they manage supply chain relationships and the impact on rural livelihoods.

The future will also require farmers to demonstrate compliance with higher standards of environmental protection, food safety and quality, and animal welfare. While in the longer term this can be potentially beneficial to producers through market advantage and reduced inputs or waste, in the short term the industry could be competitively disadvantaged because of the costs of compliance. The new Integrated Pollution Prevention and Control obligations placed on the EU pig, poultry and food-processing sectors are examples. Technical assistance and economic incentives can help to support this transition (Gouldson and Murphy, 1998).

For conventional farming, there are heated and somewhat polarized arguments over whether bio and engineering sciences in the form of genetically modified organisms and satellite-controlled 'precision' farming will or will not contribute to sustainable development. At present, these new farming methods appear to be driven more by supply side, technology push rather than demand side, market pull factors. Given the characteristics of demand for food and agricultural products, most of the benefits of these technological changes are likely to accrue beyond, and not within, the farm and rural sectors themselves.

As previously stated, there is a growing awareness of the need to improve the sustainability of farming systems through integrated pest management, organic methods, energy and water conservation, reduced waste and protection of bio-diversity (see, for example, Vereijken, 1992; Holland *et al.*, 1994; Wibberley, 1995; Lampkin, 1996; Jordan, 1998). Emerging evidence suggest that this can be done without substantially compromising yields, value added and rewards, especially if potential costs savings and internalized external impacts are taken into account (see, for example, Bailey *et al.*, 1999; Pretty *et al.*, 2000). Policy interventions, through regulation, economic incentives, voluntary codes and technical assistance, which discriminate in favour of sustainable farming, will increase the pace of adoption (Marsh, 1997).

Away from agriculture, a key element of the rural futures debate is the maintenance of strong communities, through ensuring access to services and supporting community involvement. In England, for example, 70 per cent of parishes have no permanent shop, 83 per cent have no permanent medical practitioner and 75 per cent have no daily bus service (Rural Development Commission, 1997). Location and small populations make it expensive to deliver village services, but access and mobility are critical indicators of quality of life. The provision of primary education, the village school, is an example of a local institution which creates a community identity among young families, with many benefits beyond the delivery of the national curriculum.

The challenge is how best to deliver essential services which critically influence the quality of rural life in a cost-effective manner: education and training, health, housing, transport and communications, social services, cultural pursuits, community safety and support for local businesses. In recent years in the UK, as in many other countries, there has been greater diversity in delivery and funding mechanisms, especially partnerships involving local government and the private and voluntary sectors. Strengthening the capacity of institutions in rural communities is central to this process (Barker and Selman, 1990; Clark *et al.*, 1997).

The greatest threats to sustainability of rural communities are the loss of critical mass and demographic balance, evident in declining populations or lack of diversity in social composition. Although many parts of rural Britain are extremely prosperous, and living in or retiring to the country is a desirable goal, there are pockets of severe rural deprivation, sometimes hidden by the camouflage of the thatched roof, affecting young families and the aged in particular. More general relative poverty is apparent in rural areas dependent on primary, mainly extractive, industries such as fishing, mining and quarrying. In these areas, rural communities and economies have proved especially vulnerable to the declining fortunes of these sectors. In response, European Objective 5b funding has targeted these areas (see Ward and McNicholas, 1998 in this volume; Whittaker *et al.*, 1999).

In terms of economic diversification, there are prospects for developing small and medium-scale enterprises operating in high technology and IT sectors which do not require geographical proximity to urban centres, and for which a rural location can offer advantage to employers and employees as a place to work and live. Local authority-sponsored business parks, innovation centres and industrial units can help to provide necessary infrastructure and critical mass. Tourism, recreation and conservation management offer further opportunities, but these can be seasonal and lowly paid. There is also scope for adding value to farm produce through locally branded products.

All of this calls for a sustainable rural policy which goes well beyond agriculture and which can reconcile the diverse economic, social and environmental dimensions of rural development. The participation of key stakeholders to formulate an integrated rural development strategy for the geographically defined rural areas is fundamental to the design of relevant policy instruments. Subsequent planning criteria and development controls, encompassing employment-generating activities and housing, should also be explicitly designed to protect and enhance the vitality and balance of rural communities, subject to environmental safeguards, rather than being entirely driven by the interests of existing dominant groups. Strategic assessment is an important aspect of this process, but the key is to achieve integration across the variety of organizations and processes in place.

In the UK, the links among local government organizations, regional/national organizations (such as the Environment Agency, non-government organizations (NGOs) and central government agencies) and their functions are often fragmented and unclear. There are examples of good practice, such as the Environment Agency's Local Environment Area Plans which review development objectives and resources within defined water catchments and compile a strategy for environmental management. These could be extended and more fully integrated with other social and economic factors to provide a framework for sustainable development at a local level. Lessons can also be learnt from practices in other countries (see, for example, Curtis and de Lacy, 1996; Gleeson and Grundy, 1997; and Brunckhorst, 1998 in this volume). Land use planning approaches (van Lier, 1998; de Haas *et al.*, 1999; Bosshard, 2000; and Selman, 1993 and Poiani *et al.*, 1998 in this volume) may also be appropriate. The new England Rural Development Plan goes some way towards the integrated approach, but there remain question marks over the dominance of the agricultural perspective.

Developing Country Perspectives

Rural Poverty

Low income countries are characterized in the main by a relatively large rural population whose predominant economic activity is farming: agriculture is often the largest sector in terms of share of GDP and total employment. Most of the world's very poor people live in rural areas, two-thirds of them involved in subsistence farming, many of the remainder involved in petty trading and menial labouring in rural areas or on the peri-urban fringe. In Africa and Asia, the rural poor account for about 80 per cent of all poor people, in Latin America, for about 50 per cent (UNEP, 1999; Todaro, 2000). The key rural challenge in developing countries is the alleviation of the causes and consequences of poverty. It is dangerous to generalize, because circumstances vary considerably, but an interrelated complex of low resource endowment, gross inequity of wealth distribution, technology and human resource limitations, low productivity, high population growth rates, institutional and infrastructural deficiencies, economic marginalization and political instability perpetuate the poverty trap and serve to exacerbate the vulnerability of countries, regions, communities, ethnic groups, families, and women and children. This is especially evident when epidemics and natural disasters wreak havoc.

Approaches to Rural and Agricultural Development

With agriculture as the dominant sector, much of rural policy has focused on agricultural development, attempting to mobilize small peasant farmers on the one hand, while simultaneously promoting large-scale modern farming on the other, often in the state sector. The impact of both strategies has been on the whole disappointing. In the 1950s and 1960s rural development was perceived to be a mainly technological challenge which could be solved by the transfer of technology and the provision of infrastructure, extension and marketing services. Disappointment with this encouraged a farming and rural systems approach, promoted in the 1970s by green revolution development organizations such as Centro Internacional de Mejoramiento de Maiz y Trigo (CIMMYT) (Byerlee and Collinson, 1980) and others (Collinson, 1972), which attempted to understand the circumstances and practices of rural people in relation to technology needs and uptake. The technological bias inherent in the systems approach continued largely to exclude the resource poor. It was apparent (Chambers, 1983; Chambers *et al.*, 1989) that large parts of the rural poor were unable to articulate their needs and participate in the development process. Indeed, as the language of development implies, there has subsequently been a switch in emphasis from a project- to a process-based approach, from a technological to an institutional focus (Scoones and Thompson, 1994) and to a better understanding of the links between livelihoods and environmental stability (Hudson and Cheatle, 1993; Scoones, 1995). This people-based approach has engendered a plethora of 'socio-economic methodologies' for observing rural phenomena and achieving the participation of 'stakeholders', and a realignment of development activities to improve the relevance to beneficiary needs (Okali *et al.*, 1994; Farrington, 1997; Garforth and Usher, 1997; Grimble, 1998; Sutherland, 1998). The people-based approach is at the heart of sustainable development, and this has found expression in the current emphasis on sustainable livelihoods (see Ellis, 1998 in this volume) evident in the programmes of international development agencies such as UK DFID and International Bank for Reconstruction and Development (IBRD).

Changing perceptions of rural development challenges have obvious implications for perceptions of appropriate solutions. The technology bias favoured large-scale projects funded and managed mainly through government organizations. The people bias has favoured smaller-scale activities delivered through NGOs. The latter has been a response to the disappointment and frustrations associated with the former, further promoted by economic reform and liberalization at an international level. NGO-based programmes have facilitated greater diversity and flexibility of development support. They have also been seen as a way to bypass monolithic, ineffective and corrupt government bodies. However, a predominantly NGO-based approach can run the risk of fragmented, selective and, in some cases, exclusive provision, which leaves government institutions behind, further weakening their competency and the prospects of improved leadership and governance in public institutions.

Structural Adjustment and Market-Oriented Policies

The governments of many low income countries have been rendered bankrupt by an inability to service international debts arising from borrowing for consumption, or for development programmes which have not paid off. The solution by the international community has been to offer debt rescheduling in return for specified 'structural adjustments'. These include liberalization of the economy, reduced government intervention and expenditure, and removal of restrictions on international financial and trade flows. The purpose is to achieve market-led, sustainable economic growth. The pursuit of economic efficiency, however, may not be compatible with the social and environmental dimensions of sustainable development (see Belshaw, 1995; Redclift, 1995; and Kirkpatrick and Lee, 1997 in this volume). Devaluation of local currency, reduced government budgets and public services, and export- and market-oriented development policies can discriminate against the poorest people and regions. There are increased pressures to exploit natural resources for export or import substitution, or to support a rural poor that has limited other options. Attempts to protect environmentally sensitive areas (see, for example, Potier, 1991 regarding 'debt for nature swaps') may further discriminate against local people and transfer the pressures on to non-protected locations or resources (see Lado, 1992; Bishop *et al.*, 1995; and Wood, 1995 in this volume). And while low income countries could exploit their comparative rural advantage by exporting agricultural and related manufactured commodities, such as textiles, to high income countries, they find that these are the most protected and inaccessible markets (Todaro, 2000).

The question remains whether market-oriented development policies which emphasize economic growth relieve the fundamental problem of poverty, and especially rural poverty, in developing countries. There are obvious moral and ethical arguments to justify the alleviation of rural poverty. But there are strong economic and environmental reasons for targeted poverty alleviation programmes, which can exploit opportunities for creating incomes and employment, and avoid the hidden and external impacts associated with people's inability to satisfy basic human needs on a sustainable basis. The widely held view is that market forces in themselves cannot be relied upon to resolve rural poverty, and that interventionist and redistributive strategies which protect and enhance natural resources, lessen urban–rural imbalance, deliver basic needs, promote sustainable livelihoods, and provide safety nets for the most vulnerable are necessary and justified. Aligned to this is a reaffirmation that agriculture, especially smallholder-based farming, has a central role to play in this process (Timmer, 1992; Pretty, 1995).

Summary

The above discussion confirms the key role of agriculture; in low income countries as the provider of sustenance, income and employment to a large proportion of the population, and in high income countries as a provider of a diverse range of goods and services to a predominantly urban population. Furthermore, a distinguishing characteristic of the rural sector is the interdependence of social and economic welfare and the endowment and quality of natural resources and the environment. In addition, the rural sector is relatively vulnerable to urban influences and determinations, in terms of flows of goods, services and resources, development opportunities and constraints, and even rural policy itself. There are signs, however, of a new rural agenda in both high income and low income countries focused around the concept of sustainable development, raising awareness of the need for a new institutional framework to facilitate the participation of rural communities in delivering sustainable rural futures.

Selected Papers in Rural Planning and Management

The volume is presented in four parts which address the rural challenge, concepts and approaches, rural sector issues and institutional factors. Key themes are those of diversified rural economies, rural and urban interdependence, the impact on rural economies of major shifts in policy, and the conflicts of interest inherent in sustainable rural development. The papers consistently identify the need for a holistic, integrated, strategic vision of the rural space and its communities, and for policies and institutional mechanisms which can help deliver this.

Part I: The Rural Challenge

EUROPE

Part I begins with an overview of rural issues in the context of developed, mainly European, countries and developing countries. With respect to Europe, Shucksmith *et al.* (1994) review the trends in, and causes of, rural disadvantage, confirming that much social deprivation in rural areas is associated with low wages and old age, compounded by lack of mobility and poor housing. Focusing on rural employment in OECD countries, Bryden and Bollman (2000) consider the changing context for rural development, as affected by globalization and liberalization: international capital movements, global division of labour and market adjustments. The most rapid employment growth has been in urban communities within rural regions, whereas remote areas have suffered greater decline. Lowe *et al.* (1993) report the demise of state-supported agriculture and how this has promoted greater diversity of activity within and between rural areas. Using the examples of minerals, farm diversification and golf, the authors suggest that, in future, land use will reflect greater local and regional, rather than national, regulation and market conditions.

Potter and Goodwin (1998) consider the likely impact on nature conservation of the withdrawal of support and protection for agriculture post-CAP reform. While it is widely assumed that the environment will benefit from liberalization and the de-coupling of agricultural commodity prices and farm incomes support, the extent to which it will benefit depends on the ability to 're-couple' support to broader social and environmental policy objectives.

DEVELOPING COUNTRIES

With respect to a developing country perspective, while there is little dispute about the existence of rural poverty, there is controversy over the best means of its alleviation. In particular there is debate as to whether structural adjustment strategies to deliver economic efficiency can simultaneously protect the interests of the poorest and most vulnerable groups. Belshaw (1995) reviews the way in which poverty alleviation can assist long-term economic growth, and potentially reduce the risk of environmental degradation and protect renewable natural resources. However, it is questionable whether a decentralized, market- and NGO-led approach to rural development is sufficient to deliver this.

Ellis (1998) reviews the livelihood and coping strategies of rural families in their efforts to survive and improve their quality of life, confirming the importance of non-farm income. Policies which affect diversification have impacts for poverty alleviation and income distribution, and also have gender implications. Ellis identifies a number of policy initiatives, reaffirming that raising agricultural productivity and farm incomes remains a central theme for rural development in low income countries.

 Part II: Concepts and Approaches

PROPERTY RIGHTS

The nature and distribution of property rights define access and entitlement to use and draw benefit from land and other natural resources. Bromley and Hodge (1990) explain how for historical reasons landowners often presume rights to use land as they see fit, and that this may conflict with the rights of society to be free of the unwanted effects of land use. In industrialized nations farmers have been successful in translating property rights into 'policy rights', in the form of income protection and enhancement. Wiebe and Meinzen-Dick (1998) trace the development of tenure systems in the USA, especially more recent intervention by the state and NGOs in pursuit of environmental objectives. This has been achieved by the acquisition of partial interests in land which may define that the land be used in particular ways, often in return for financial payment. Such mechanisms require considerable institutional infrastructure which may not be in place in developing countries.

SOCIAL AND NATURAL CAPITAL

Using an example from Central America, Katz (2000) explores the links between social capital, the 'glue' that holds societies together, and natural resource management. She shows how social capital can substitute for formal, legally defined property rights and tenure regimes, and can help to avoid degradation of natural capital. Whitby and Adger (1996) define sustainability in terms of stocks of natural capital at a national level. Examining land use in Britain, they argue that declining stocks associated with greenhouse gas emissions, soil degradation and habitat loss are evidence of declining sustainability in the British land use sector.

CONSERVATION PLANNING

Landscape and ecology are two main elements for capturing the natural characteristics and conservation aspects of countryside management, and there is a large science to underpin the processes of classification, measurement and intervention. Rather than trying to preserve existing landscapes in the countryside, Selman (1993) provides a theoretical framework for reconstructing new functional landscapes using the principles of landscape ecology. While the approach is essentially scientific, it is, he argues, possible to combine it with socio-economic parameters. In this way it is possible to provide a planning frame to reconcile economic activities with a diverse and heterogeneous landscape which meets ecological, visual and hydrological objectives. Using a North American example, Poiani *et al.* (1998) provide a practical, site-level conservation planning framework which combines conservation biology, ecosystem management and stakeholder participation.

MARKET-LED APPROACH

A range of policy mechanisms has been used to integrate conservation and recreation with farming, namely promotion of voluntary best practice, regulation and control, and financial instruments. Bishop and Phillips (1993) review the emergence of a market-led approach to countryside conservation and recreation, whereby the public sector 'buys' environmental goods and services from landowners and farmers in the form of management prescriptions. These schemes have met with popular support in areas where they fit well with dominant farming practices such as livestock production. However, they have been criticized for their selectivity and 'dead weight': paying farmers for things that they would do anyway.

DEVELOPMENT AND ENVIRONMENT

Two papers cover issues linking environment and development in less developed economies. Redclift (1995) examines the impact of structural adjustment policies promoted by international development agencies such as the International Monetary Fund (IMF) and IBRD. He makes the case for including environmental management in rural development policy, but argues that unless this is accompanied by the participation and empowerment of poor people, the objective of sustainable development will be frustrated.

In a similar vein, Kirkpatrick and Lee (1997) examine the potential environmental consequences of market-oriented policies in developing and transitional economies, and how these can be captured in planning techniques such as cost–benefit analysis and environmental impact analysis. In particular they call for a high level, strategic approach to assessing the likely environmental impacts of development policies and instruments.

Part III: Rural Sector Issues

This part examines selected sustainable development issues in the rural sector.

AGRICULTURE

With respect to agriculture, Webster (1999) traces the developments in the theory of sustainability and applies them at the level of the farm business. Although there is an emerging consensus about the issues and themes associated with sustainability at the policy level, this is less so at the level of the individual farm business.

Van Mansvelt and Mulder (1993) debate sustainability at the European rural sector level. They define sustainability in terms of contribution to food security, incomes and employment, conservation and participation. The performance of alternative agricultural systems is assessed against these criteria, particularly that of organic farming, which they argue has the potential to deliver sustainable agriculture and rural development.

Pretty and Hine (2000) offer a broad-based model of agricultural systems which combines physical, financial, natural, human and social capital. They report on the successful promotion and adoption of sustainable agriculture in Asia, which has improved food security and rural welfare, even though consistent policy support is lacking.

In Europe, agri-environmental schemes have become the dominant policy mechanism for reconciling social, economic and environmental objectives in farmed areas. These schemes adopt a management agreement model in which it is assumed that society has no prior property rights to environmental outputs and therefore must pay farmers to produce them. Lobley and Potter (1998) review the two main UK schemes which differ in their objectives and methods: the ESA programme and the Countryside Stewardship Scheme. They classify and explain the motivation and participation behaviour of farmers, distinguishing between conservation-oriented farmers, those driven by financial inducements and those resistant to scheme membership.

Given the growing significance of these schemes as a policy mechanism for rural sustainability, Hanley *et al.* (1999) evaluate agri-environmental schemes in terms of effectiveness and efficiency criteria. They review selected policy options, including the setting of environmental targets, payment rates, and the auctioning or trading of environmental contracts.

PROTECTED AREAS

Two papers draw attention to the conflicts of interest that arise between externally imposed conservation objectives and the needs of the indigenous human population in protected areas. It is apparent that the policy mechanisms have become outdated and less relevant to the new realities, especially in so much as they have been insufficiently integrated with other development policies.

Bishop *et al.* (1995) review the international and UK experience of protected area policy, pointing to external problems associated with failure to integrate with other aspects of public policy such as tourism or transport, and internal problems associated with specific site management issues such as inadequate funding or expertise. New initiatives suggest a move from protection to creative conservation, towards consideration for entire landscapes, towards networks rather than isolated areas, reconsideration of development objectives, and a recognition of the policy and planning hierarchy from global and EU down to local level.

Many of these issues are apparent in the example of wildlife conservation and management in Kenya provided by Lado (1992). He draws attention to the conflicts inherent within conservation management and between conservation management interests and the livelihoods of local people. He argues that improved agricultural productivity is needed to prevent farm encroachment into wildlife areas, but also that indigenous people need to be directly involved in conservation management and derive benefit from it. Integration of protected area policy into other aspects of development policy is clearly required to sustain wildlife resources.

FORESTRY

Turning to non-agricultural land use, Selman (1997) examines the multi-purpose benefits of forestry and demonstrates how forestry has been used by planning authorities to reconcile environmental and socio-economic objectives. The example provided by Cloke *et al.* (1996) demonstrates how multi-purpose forestry can provide opportunities for sustainable development on landscapes scarred by extractive industries, enhancing landscape ecology and assisting economic revival. Both of these papers point to the challenge of integrating forestry with the local planning process.

The paper by Wood (1995) turns the focus to tropical forestry, arguing that continued human use of tropical forests is a more effective and sustainable conservation policy than protection alone: imposed conservation impoverishes the local population. A better approach, he maintains, is by dynamic management through utilization; the mosaic management of small areas rather than strict protection of large forest areas.

ENERGY

Renewable energy sources offer scope for rural diversification through the production of energy from biomass and from wind farms. Hall and House (1995) examine the potential for bioenergy in western Europe, concluding that it has the potential to produce between 17 and 30 per cent of total energy needs by 2050. The extent to which this is realized depends on market conditions, relative prices of fossil fuels, other land use options and environmental issues associated with energy crop production.

Hedger (1995) explains that wind power can offer an economically attractive source of renewable energy but because of its visual intrusion in wild or open areas meets with considerable resistance from conservation bodies. This conflict, he argues, once again points to the lack of strategic vision and integration between a specific sector, in this case energy, and land use planning and policy.

TOURISM AND RECREATION

Tourism has been promoted as a vehicle for economic diversification in rural areas, exploiting potential linkages between urban and rural communities. Slee *et al.* (1997) model the economic impact of tourism in the Highlands of Scotland and draw distinction between soft/green tourism embedded in the local economy and hard tourism characterized by externally owned enclave developments. They argue that economic analysis of alternative tourism strategies can lead to better informed choices about sustainable rural futures.

Using a Danish example, Hjalager (1996) considers the impact on farm holdings of Objective 5b funding for rural tourism. The majority of funds are spent on new or refurbished accommodation and, in common with findings in other parts of northern Europe, the returns on labour and capital from farm-based tourism are low. Hjalager identifies a need for marketing and inter-organizational networks to support agro-tourism.

RURAL ENTERPRISE, HOUSING AND TRANSPORT

The remaining papers in Part III cover current issues in rural enterprise development, housing and transport. Rural areas stand to benefit from location-neutral information and communication technologies. Berkeley *et al.* (1996) examine the awareness, take-up and use of information and communication technologies in rural areas and find them to be generally low and variable, reflecting gaps in the provision of infrastructure and services.

Sustainability at a local level may be enhanced by maximizing community multiplier effects and reducing leakage from the local economy. In this context, Williams (1996) reviews the role of Local Exchange and Trading Systems as a means of simultaneously achieving economic and community development objectives. Such systems can provide a framework within which social networks develop to provide work and credits for those who might otherwise be excluded.

Inadequate housing for lower income groups in rural areas has been associated with deprivation, in some cases due to purchases by high income urban commuters. Milbourne (1998) considers the provision of social housing in rural areas of Wales. There is now a greater diversity of providers, such as housing associations, which often include 'localness' and 'affordability' in their allocations criteria. Nevertheless, social housing has become a residual sector with relatively low income occupiers.

Immobility and remoteness are commonly reported disadvantages of rural lifestyles. Nutley (1996) reviews and compares rural transport issues in the USA and the UK. In the USA, universal car ownership appears to solve the rural transport problem for all but a few. In the UK, however, further car ownership marginalizes the 'have nots', who are likely to be old, poor or disabled. Nutley points to a greater awareness of the issues in Europe, which together with relatively dense rural populations retains a commitment to publicly or community funded transport.

Part IV: Institutions for Rural Development: Joined-up Governance

The final Part examines the institutional dimensions of sustainable rural development, especially regarding local mechanisms for achieving consensus on the definition and implementation of sustainable development strategies.

Brunckhorst (1998) argues that society must make a fundamental change in the way it views and uses natural resources if it is to ensure an ecologically supportable future. There is too little understanding of the relationship between citizenry and ecosystems. He identifies key capacities for resource governance: the ability to define and identify functions, co-ordinate policy, adapt to changing circumstances and enforce rules. These systems need to suit particular local circumstances, whether industrialized or traditional societies, and resource governance systems need to be crafted accordingly.

The institutional dimension of sustainability has found expression in the emergence of partnership organizations which bring together a 'community of interest' with respect to subject-, area- or people-based issues. Curtis and de Lacey (1996) report on the Australian Voluntary Landcare Groups, which address a variety of issues affecting agricultural productivity and bio-diversity, such as water resources, soil erosion and vegetation management. While such local organizations can promote local action, they may have limited impact unless there is a strategic, regional framework for resource management.

Gleeson and Grundy (1997) evaluate New Zealand's radical change in development environmental planning which reflected an uneasy compromise between pressure for deregulation, liberalization and the use of market principles on the one hand, and calls by the environmental movement to ensure ecological values were explicit in development control on the other. The new regime emphasizes control of environmental effects rather than activities. But the experience casts doubt on the wisdom of subsuming the social and economic aspects of development planning under a predominantly environmental management regime. Gleeson and Grundy argue strongly for the retention of a spatial planning regime, as deregulation may increase social and economic risks without the benefits of efficiency gains in administration.

Access to funds can itself spur institutional development and facilitate participation beyond those formally elected political bodies to include voluntary organizations, businesses, mass media and supra-national organizations. Ward and McNicholas (1998) identify a new form of governance emerging in remote areas as a consequence of projects promoted and funded by EU structural adjustment programmes. Rural communities now have to 'think themselves into existence as a precursor to state intervention', suggesting that the term 'community' has come to replace 'society' as a new focus for governance.

General Summary and Conclusion

The preceding essay and review of papers demonstrate the eclectic nature of the sustainable development challenge in rural areas. Furthermore, economic reform and liberalization have exposed the conflicts of interest and perspective between globalization and local stewardship as they affect the rural sector. It is apparent, however, that these changes have, if anything, created greater awareness of the importance of a strategic, integrated vision of rural areas and communities, and of institutional mechanisms which can engage rural people in the process of mapping out and delivering these futures. The preceding review also shows that, although there are common themes and principles, the context-specific nature of the development challenge requires that local solutions must be found. General panaceas are unlikely to prove sustainable.

References

Adams, W.M., Bourn, N.A.D. and Hodge, I. (1992), 'Conservation in the wider countryside. SSSIs and wildlife habitat in eastern England', *Land Use Policy*, October:235–248.

Allanson, P., Murdoch, J., Garrod, G. and Lowe P. (1995), 'Sustainability and the rural economy: an evolutionary perspective', *Environment and Planning*, 27:1797–1814.

Archer, J.R. (1992), 'UK nitrate policy implementation', *Aspects of Applied Biology*, 30:11–18.

Bailey, A.P., Rehman, T., Park, J., Keatinge, J.D.H. and Tranter, R.B. (1999), 'Towards a method for the economic evaluation of environmental indicators for UK integrated arable farming systems', *Agriculture, Ecosystems and Environment*, 72:145–158.

Baldock, D., Cox, G., Lowe, P. and Winter, M. (1990), 'Environmentally sensitive areas: incrementalism or reform?', *Journal of Rural Studies*, 6(2):143–162.

Banister, D. and Norton, F. (1988), 'The role of the voluntary sector in the provision of rural services – the case of transport', *Journal of Rural Studies*, 4(1):57–71.

Barker, A.J. and Selman, P.H. (1990), 'Managing the rural environment: an emerging role for planning authorities', *Journal of Environmental Management*, 1:185–196.

Bateman, D.I. (1989), 'Heroes for present purposes? A look at the changing idea of communal land ownership in Britain: presidential address', *Journal of Agricultural Economics*, 40(3):269–289.

Belshaw, D.G.R. (1995), *Rural Development Strategy in the 1990s: Poverty Alleviation, Productivity Gains and Decentralisation*, Cambridge: Agricultural Economics Society Annual Conference.

Berkeley, N., Clark, D. and Ilbery, B. (1996), 'Regional variations in business use of information and communication technologies and their implication for policy: case study evidence from rural England', *Geoforum*, 27(1):75–86.

Bishop, K. and Phillips, A. (1993), 'Integrating conservation, recreation and agriculture through the market place', *ECOS*, 14(2):36–46.

Bishop, K., Phillips, A. and Warren, L. (1995), 'Protected for ever? Factors shaping the future of protected areas policy', *Land Use Policy*, 12(4):291–305.

Bishop, K.D. and Phillips, A.C. (1993), 'Seven steps to market – the development of the market-led approach to countryside conservation and recreation', *Journal of Rural Studies*, 9(4):315–338.

Bosshard, A. (2000), 'A methodology and terminology of sustainability assessment and its perspectives for rural planning', *Agriculture, Ecosystems and Environment*, 77:29–41.

Box, J. (1991), 'Forty years of local nature reserves', *ECOS*, 12(3):40–43.

Brassley, P. (1997), *Agricultural Economics and the CAP: An Introduction*, Oxford: Blackwell.

Bromley, D.W. and Hodge, I. (1990), 'Private property rights and presumptive policy entitlements: reconsidering the premises of rural policy', *European Review of Agricultural Economics*, 17:197–214.

Brunckhorst, D.J. (1998), 'Creating institutions to ensure sustainable use of resources. Guest Editorial', *Habitat International*, 22(4):347–354.

Bryden, J. (1994), 'Prospects for rural areas in an enlarged Europe', *Journal of Rural Studies*, 10(4):387–394.

Bryden, J. and Bollman, R. (2000), 'Rural employment in industrialised countries', *Agricultural Economics*, 22:185–197.

Bullock, C.H., Macmillan, D.C. and Crabtree, J.R. (1994), 'New perspectives on agroforestry in lowland Britain', *Land Use Policy*, 11(3):222–233.

Burgess, P.J., Brierley, E.D.R., Morris, J. and Evans, J. (eds) (1999), *Farm Woodlands for the Future*, Oxford: Bios Scientific Publishers Ltd.

Byerlee, D. and Collinson, M.P. (1980), *Planning Technologies Appropriate to Farmers: Concepts and Procedures*, Mexico: CIMMYT.

Byrne, P.J. and Ravenscroft, N. (1990), 'The role of diversification in restructuring farms and rural estates', *J. RASE*, **151**:51–65.

Chambers, R. (1983), *Rural Development: Putting the Last First*, London: Longman.

Chambers, R., Pacey, A. and Thrupp, L.A. (eds), (1989), *Farmer First*, London: Intermediate Technology Publications.

Clark, G., Bowler, I., Shaw, A., Crockett, A. and Ilbery, B. (1997), 'Institution, alternative farming systems, and local reregulation', *Environment and Planning*, A **29**:731.

Cloke, P. and McLaughlin, B. (1989), *Politics of the Alternative Land Use and Rural Economy* (ALURE) *Proposals in the UK. Crossroads or Blind Alley?*, Land Use Policy, **6**(3):235–248.

Cloke, P., Milbourne, P. and Thomas, C. (1996), 'From wasteland to wonderland: opencast mining, regeneration and the English National Forest', *Geoforum*, **27**(2):159–174.

Coles, R.W. and Taylor, J. (1993), 'Wind power and planning. The environmental impact of windfarms in the UK', *Land Use Policy*, July:205.

Collinson, M.P. (1972), *Farm Management in Peasant Agriculture: A Handbook for Rural Development Planning in Africa*, New York: Praeger.

Cornforth, I.S. (1999), 'Selecting indicators for assessing sustainable land management', *Journal of Environmental Management*, **56**:173–179.

Countryside Agency (1999), *The State of the Countryside, 1999*, Cheltenham: Countryside Agency.

Crabtree, J.R. (1991), 'National park designation in Scotland', *Land Use Policy*, July:241–252.

Crabtree, J.R. (1997), 'The supply of public access to the countryside – a value for money and institutional analysis of incentive policies', *Environment and Planning*, A **29**:1465–1476.

Crabtree, J.R. and Chambers, N.A. (1994), 'Economic evaluation of policy instruments for conservation', *Land Use Policy*, **11**(2):94–106.

Crocker, S.A. (1986), 'Diversification: pitfalls or profits?', *J. RASE*, **147**:26–33.

De Haas, W., Kranendonk, R. and Pleijte, M. (1999), 'Valuable man-made landscapes (VMLs) in the Netherlands: a policy evaluation', *Landscape and Urban Planning*, **46**:133–141.

Curtis, A. and de Lacy, T. (1996), 'Landcare in Australia: does it make a difference?', *Journal of Environmental Management*, **46**:119–137.

Department of the Environment and MAFF (1995), *Rural England: A Nation Committed to a Living Countryside*, CM 3016, London: HMSO.

Departments of the Environment, Trade and Industry; Health, Education and Science; Scottish Office; Department of Transport and Energy; Northern Ireland Office; MAFF; Department of Employment; Welsh Office (1990), *This Common Inheritance. Britain's Environmental Strategy*, London: HMSO.

DETR (1999), *A Better Quality of Life: A Strategy for Sustainable Development for the UK*, London: DETR.

DETR/MAFF (1999), *Rural England: A Discussion Document*, Department of the Environment, Transport and the Regions and Ministry of Agriculture, Fisheries and Food.

DETR/MAFF (2000), *Our Countryside: The Future. A Fair Deal for Rural England*, CM4909, London: HMSO.

DFID (1997), *Eliminating World Poverty, A Challenge for the 21st Century*, London: HMSO.

Dixon, J. (1992), 'Environmentally sensitive farming – where next?', *ECOS*, **13**(3):15–19.

Ellis, F. (1998), 'Household strategies and rural livelihood diversification', *Journal of Development Studies*, **35**(1):1–38.

Errington, A. (1995), *Rural Employment Trends and Issues in the Peri-urban Fringe*, Cambridge: paper presented to the Conference of the Agricultural Economics Society, Girton College.

Farrington, J. with Shaxson, J. and Gordon, A. (1997), 'Editorial introduction', *Agricultural Systems*, Special Issue, Socio-Economic Methods in Renewable Natural Resources Research, **55**(2):145–153.

Froud, J. (1994), 'The impact of ESAs on lowland farming', *Land Use Policy*, **11**(2):107–118.

Gardner, B. (1996), *European Agriculture, Policies, Production and Trade*, London: Routledge.

Garforth, C. and Usher, R. (1997), 'Promotion and uptake pathways for research output: a review of analytical frameworks and communication channels', *Agricultural Systems*, **55**(2):310–322.

Gleeson, B.J. and Grundy, K.J. (1997), 'New Zealand's planning resolution five years on: a preliminary assessment', *Journal of Environmental Planning and Management*, **40**(3):293–313.

Gouldson, A. and Murphy, J. (1998), *Regulatory Realities: The Implementation and Impact of Industrial Environmental Regulation*, London: Earthscan.

Grimble, R. (1998), *Stakeholder Methodologies in Natural Resource Management: Socio-economic Methodologies Best Practice Guidelines*, Chatham: Natural Resources Institute.

Hall, D.O. and House, J.I. (1995), 'Biomass energy in Western Europe to 2050', *Land Use Policy*, **12**(1):37–48.

Hanley, N., Whitby, M. and Simpson, I. (1999), 'Assessing the success of agri-environmental policy in the UK', *Land Use Policy*, **16**:67–80.

Harrison-Mayfield, L., Dwyer, J. and Brookes, G. (1998), 'The socio-economic effects of the Countryside Stewardship Scheme', *Journal of Agricultural Economics*, **49**(2):157–170.

Hartwick, J.M. and Olewiler, N.D. (1998), *The Economics of Natural Resource Use*, Harlow: Addison-Wesley.

Hedger, M.M. (1995), 'Wind power: challenges to planning policy in the UK', *Land Use Policy*, **12**(1):17–28.

Heidensohn, K. (1995), *Europe and World Trade*, London: Cassel.

Hitiris, T. (1998), *European Union Economics*, London: Prentice Hall.

Hjalgar, A.-M. (1996), 'Agricultural diversification into tourism', *Tourism Management*, **17**(2):103–111.

Hodge, I. (1991), 'Incentive policies and the rural environment', *Journal of Rural Studies*, **7**(4):373–384.

Hodge, I. (1996), 'On penguins on icebergs: the rural white paper and the assumptions of rural policy', *Journal of Rural Studies*, **12**(4):331–337.

Hodge, I. (1997a), *Towards a Broader Perspective*, London: Agricultural Economics Society. One-Day Conference: Designing Agri-Environmental Policy Mechanisms: Theory and Practice.

Hodge, I. (1997b), 'The rural white papers in Great Britain', *Journal of Environmental Planning and Management*, **40**(3):375–403.

Holland, J.M., Frampton, G.K., Cilgi, T. and Wratten, S.D. (1994), 'Arable acronyms analysed – a review of integrated arable farming systems research in Western Europe', *Ass. Applied Biology*, **125**:399–438.

Horne, R. and Frost, S. (1991), 'Opencast coal mining in England and Wales. A review of legislation and policy', *Land Use Policy*, January:29–35.

Hudson, N. and Cheatle, RJ. (1993), *Working with Farmers for Better Land Husbandry*, UK: Intermediate Technology Publications/ World Association of Soil and Water Conservation.

Johnson, A. (1994), 'What's super about big quarries?', *ECOS*, **15**(3/4):35–42.

Johnston, B.F. and Mellor, J.W. (1961), 'The role of agriculture in economic development', *American Economic Review*, **51**:566–593.

Jones, K.B.C. (1992), 'Opencast coal mining and land restoration – best present practice', *J. RASE*, **153**:89–100.

Jordan, V.W.L. (1998), 'Less intensive integrated arable crop production and environmental protection', *J. RASE*, **159**:56–69.

Katz, E.G. (2000), 'Social capital and natural capital: a comparative analysis of land tenure and natural resource management in Guatemala', *Land Economics*, **76**(1):114–132

Kirkpatrick, C. and Lee, N. (1997), 'Market liberalisation and environmental assessment in developing and transitional economies', *Journal of Environmental Management*, **50**:235–250.

Kuznets, S. (1966), *Modern Economic Growth*, New Haven: Yale University Press.

Lado, C. (1992), 'Problems of wildlife management and land use in Kenya', *Land Use Policy*, July:169–184.

Lampkin, N. (1996), *Impact of EC Regulation 2078/92 on the Development of Organic Farming in the European Union*, Working Paper no. 7, Aberystwyth: The University of Wales, Welsh Institute of Rural Studies.

Lewis, W.A. (1954), 'Economic development with unlimited supplies of labour', *Manchester School for Economic and Social Studies*, **22**:139–191.

Lobley, M. and Potter, C. (1998), 'Environmental stewardship in UK agriculture: a comparison of the Environmentally Sensitive Area programme and the Countryside Stewardship Scheme in South East England', *Geoforum*, **29**(4):413–432.

Lomas, J. (1994), 'The role of management agreements in rural environmental conservation', *Land Use Policy*, **11**(2):119–123.

Lowe, P. and Ward, N. (1998), 'Regional policy, CAP reform and rural development in Britain: the challenge for New Labour', *Regional Studies*, **32**(5):469–479.

Lowe, P., Murdoch, J., Marsden, T., Munton, R. and Flynn, A. (1993), 'Regulating the new rural spaces: the uneven development of land', *Journal of Rural Studies*, **9**(3):205–222.

MAFF (1998), *Development of a Set of Indicators for Sustainable Agriculture in the United Kingdom*, London: MAFF.

MAFF (1998a), *Code of Good Agricultural Practice for the Protection of Air*, London: MAFF; Welsh Office Agriculture Department.

MAFF (1998b), *Code of Good Agricultural Practice for the Protection of Soil*, London: MAFF; Welsh Office Agriculture Department.

MAFF (1998c), *Code of Good Agricultural Practice for the Protection of Water*, London: MAFF; Welsh Office Agriculture Department.

MAFF (1999a), *Restructuring of Agricultural Industry*, Working Paper 1, A Discussion Document prepared by the Economics and Statistics Group of the MAFF, August, London.

MAFF (1999b), *Reducing Farm Subsidies – Economic Adjustment in Rural Areas*, Working Paper 2, A Discussion Document prepared by the Economics and Statistics Group of the MAFF, August, London.

MAFF (1999c), *Agenda 2000 CAP Reform, CAP Reform Agreement, An Information Document*, Produced by the MAFF, London

MAFF (1999d), *Agenda 2000 Rural Development Regulation, Consultation on Implementation in England*, Produced by the MAFF, London.

MAFF (2000a) *Climate Change and Agriculture in the United Kingdom*, London: MAFF.

MAFF (2000b), *England Rural Development Plan 2000–2006. A Summary*, London: MAFF.

Marsh, J.S. (1997), 'The policy approach to sustainable farming systems in EU agriculture', *Ecosystems and Environment*, **64**:103–114.

McDonald, G.T. (1989), 'Rural land use planning decisions by bargaining', *Journal of Rural Studies*, **5**(4):325–335.

McInerney, J.P. (1994), 'Duality – the future face of farming', *J. RASE*, **155**:25–33.

McInerney, J.P. (1996), 'Agriculture and rural infrastructure', *Farm Management*, **9**(7):324–335.

Milbourne, P. (1998), 'Local responses to central state restructuring of social housing provision in rural areas', *Journal of Rural Studies*, **14**(2):167–184.

Morris, J., Gowing, D.J.G., Mills, J. and Dunderdale, J.A.L. (2000a), 'Reconciling agricultural economic and environmental objectives: the case of recreating wetlands in the Fenland area of eastern England', *Agriculture, Ecosystems and Environment*, **79**:245–257.

Morris, J., Mills, J. and Crawford, I.M. (2000b), 'Promoting farmer uptake of agri-environmental schemes: the arable options of the Countryside Stewardship Scheme', *Land Use Policy*, **17**:241–254

Murray, M.R. and Greer, J.V. (1992), 'Rural development in Northern Ireland: policy formulation in a peripheral region of the European Community', *Journal of Rural Studies*, **8**(2):173–184.

Nutley, S.D. (1988), '"Unconventional modes" of transport in rural Britain: progress to 1995', *Journal of Rural Studies*, **4**(1):73–86.

Nutley, S.D. (1996), 'Rural transport problems and non car populations in the USA', *Journal of Transport Geography*, **4**(2):93–106.

OECD (1997), *Environmental Indicators for Agriculture*, Paris: OECD Publications.

OECD (1998), *Co-operative Approaches to Sustainable Agriculture*, Paris: OECD Publications.

Okali. C., Sumberg, J. and Farrington, J. (1994), *Farmer Participatory Research: Rhetoric and Reality*, London: Intermediate Technology Publications/ODI.

Parry, M.L. (1990), *Climate Change and Agriculture*, London: Earthscan.

Parry, M.L. (ed.) (2000), *Assessment of Potential Effects and Adaptations for Climate Change in Europe: The Europe ACACIA Project*, Norwich: Jackson Environmental Institute, University of East Anglia.

Pearce, F. (1999), 'Free for all', *New Scientist*, 27 November, pp. 16–17.

Perman, R., Ma, Y., McGilvray, J. and Common, M. (1999), *Natural Resource and Environmental Economics*, 2nd edition, Harlow: Longman.

Plowden, B. (1992), 'Sustainability criteria for minerals planning', *ECOS*, **13**(4):22–26.

Poiani, K.A., Baumgartner, J.V., Buttrick, S.C., Green, S.L., Hopkins, E., Ivey, G.D., Seaton, K.P. and Sutter, R.D. (1998), 'A scale independent site conservation planning framework in The Nature Conservancy', *Landscape and Urban Planning*, **43**:143–156.

Potier, M. (1991), 'Debt-for-nature swaps', *Land Use Policy*, July:211–213.

Potter, C. (1988), 'Environmentally sensitive areas in England and Wales', *Land Use Policy*, July:301–313.

Potter, C. and Goodwin, P. (1998), 'Agricultural liberalisation in the European Union: an analysis of the implications for nature conservation', *Journal of Rural Studies*, **14**(3):287–298.

Pretty, J. (1995), *Regenerating Agriculture: Policies and Practice for Sustainability and Self-Reliance*, London: Earthscan.

Pretty, J. (1998), *The Living Land*, London: Earthscan.

Pretty, J. and Hine, R. (2000), 'The promising spread of sustainable agriculture in Asia', *Natural Resources Forum*, **24**:107–121.

Pretty, J. and Ward, H. (2001), 'Social capital and the environment', *World Development*, **29**:209–227.

Pretty, J.N., Brett, C., Gee, D., Hine, R.E., Mason, C.F., Morison, J.I.L., Raven, H., Rayment, M.D. and van der Bijl, G. (2000), 'An assessment of the total external costs of UK agriculture', *Agricultural Systems*, **65**:113–136.

Redclift, M. (1990), 'Developing sustainably. Designating agroecological zones', *Land Use Policy*, 7(3):202–216.

Redclift, M. (1995), 'The environment and structural adjustment: lessons for policy interventions in the 1990s', *Journal of Environmental Management*, **44**:55–68.

Ritson, C. and Harvey, D.R. (1999), *The Common Agricultural Policy*, Wallingford: CABI.

Ross, A. and Stockdale, A. (1996), 'Multiple environmental designations: a case study of their effectiveness for the Ythan Estuary', *Environment and Planning C: Government and Policy*, **14**:89–100.

Rural Development Commission (1997), *Survey of Rural Services*, London: Rural Development Commission.

Schultz, T.W. (1964), *Transforming Traditional Agriculture*, Newhaven: Yale University Press.

Scoones, I. (1995), *Living with Uncertainty: New Pastoral Development in Africa*, London: Intermediate Technology Publications/IIED.

Scoones, I. and Thompson, J. (eds) (1994), *Beyond Farmer First*, London: Intermediate Technology Publications.

Scottish Office (1995), *Rural Scotland: People, Prosperity and Partnership*, CM 3014, Edinburgh: HMSO.

Selman, P. (1993), 'Landscape ecology and countryside planning: vision, theory and practice', *Journal of Rural Studies*, **9**(1):1–21.

Selman, P. (1997), 'The role of forestry in meeting planning objectives', *Land Use Policy*, **14**(1):55–73.

Shucksmith, M. (1990), 'Rural housing in the UK. Current policy issues', *Land Use Policy*, July:283–286.

Shucksmith, M. and Winter, M. (1990), 'The politics of pluriactivity in Britain', *Journal of Rural Studies*, **6**(4):429–435.

Shucksmith, M., Chapman, J.P., Clark, G. and Black, S. (1994), 'Social welfare in rural Europe', *Journal of Rural Studies*, **10**(4):343–356.

Slee, B., Farr, H. and Snowdon, P. (1997), 'The economic impact of alternative types of rural tourism', *Journal of Agricultural Economics*, **48**(2):179–192.

Smith, C.S. and McDonald, G.T. (1998), 'Assessing the sustainability of agriculture at the planning stage', *Journal of Environmental Management*, **52**:15–37.

Spash, C.L. and Simpson, I.A. (1993), 'Protecting Sites of Special Scientific Interest: intrinsic and utilitarian values', *Journal of Environmental Management*, **39**:213–227.

Stokes, G. (1995), 'Rural transport policy in the 1990s', *Proceedings of the Institution of Civil Engineers Transport*, **111**:245–253.

Sutherland, A. (1998), *Participatory Research in Natural Resources. Socio-economic Methodologies: Best Practice Guidelines*, Chatham: Natural Resources Institute.

Swales, V. (1994), 'Incentives for countryside management', *ECOS*, **15**(3/4):52–57.

The Economist (1999a), 'Storm over globalisation', 27 November, pp. 17–18.

The Economist (1999b), 'After Seattle, a global disaster', 11 December, pp. 21–22.

Tietenberg, T. (1996), *Environmental and Natural Resource Economics*, New York: Harper Collins College Publishers.

Timmer, C.P. (1992), 'Agriculture and economic development revisited', *Agricultural Systems*, **40**:21–58.

Todaro, M.P. (2000), *Economic Development*, Harlow: Longman.

Tunney, H. (1992), 'The EC nitrate directive', *Aspects of Applied Biology*, **30**:5–10.

Turner, R.K., Pearce, D. and Bateman, I. (1994), *Environmental Economics: An Elementary Introduction*, London: Harvester Wheatsheaf.

UNDP (1999), *Human Development Report*, UNDP, New York: Oxford University Press for the United Nations.

UNEP (1999), *Global Environmental Outlook 2000*, UNEP, London: Earthscan for and on behalf of the United Nations Environment Programme.

Unilever (1999), *Growing for the Future: Unilever and Sustainable Agriculture*, Rotterdam: Unilever.

United Nations (1993), *Agenda 21 Programme of Action for Sustainable Development. Rio Declaration on Environment and Development. Statement of Forest Principles*, United Nations Conference on Environment and Development 1992, Rio de Janeiro.

Van Lier, H.N. (1998), 'The role of land use planning in sustainable rural systems', *Landscape and Urban Planning*, **41**:83–91.

Van Mansvelt, J.D. and Mulder, J.A. (1993), 'European features for sustainable development: a contribution to the dialogue', *Landscape and Urban Planning*, **27**:67–90.

Vereijken, P. (1992), 'A methodic way to more sustainable farming systems', *Netherlands Journal of Agricultural Science*, **40**:209–223.

Ward, N. and McNicholas, K. (1998), 'Reconfiguring rural development in the UK: objective 5b and the new rural governance', *Journal of Rural Studies*, **14**(1):27–39.

Warren, C. (1998), 'National parks for Scotland: the other side of the coin', *ECOS*, **19**(2):62–70.

Waters, G.R. (1994), 'Government policies for the countryside', *Land Use Policy*, **11**(2):88–93.

WCED (1987), *Our Common Future*, WCED, Oxford: Oxford University Press.

Webster, P. (1999), 'The challenge of sustainability at the farm level: presidential address', *Journal of Agricultural Economics*, **50**(3):371–387.

Weibe, K.D. and Meinzen-Dick, R. (1998), 'Property rights as policy tools for sustainable development', *Land Use Policy*, **15**(3):203–215.

Welsh Office (1996), *The Working Countryside for Wales*, CM 3180, Cardiff: HMSO.

Whitby, M. (1990), 'Multiple land use and the market for countryside goods', *J. RASE*, **151**:32–43.

Whitby, M. (1997), 'Countryside access: a traditional asset but growing fast?', *Countryside Recreation*, October:4–8.

Whitby, M. and Adger, W.N. (1996), 'Natural and reproducible capital and the sustainability of land use in the UK', *Journal of Agricultural Economics*, **47**(1):50–65.

Whitby, M. and Lowe, P. (1994), 'The political and economic roots of environmental policy in agriculture', in Whitby, M. (ed.) *Incentives for Countryside Management. The Case of Environmentally Sensitive Areas*, Wallingford: CABI, 1–24.

Whitby, M., Hodge, I., Lowe, P. and Saunders, C. (1996), 'Conservation options for CAP reform', *ECOS*, **17**(3/4):46–55.

Whittaker, J.M., Hutchcroft, I.D. and Turner, M.M. (1999), *Fostering Partipatory Rural Development – Lessons from the Objective 5b Programme in South West England*, Agricultural Economic Society Conference Belfast, 26–28 March.

Wibberley, J. (1995), 'Cropping policy and farming systems: integrity and intensity in international perspective', *J. RASE*, **156**:43–55.

Williams, C.C. (1996), 'Local purchasing schemes and rural development: an evaluation of Local Exchange and Trading Systems (LETS)', *Journal of Rural Studies*, **12**(3):231–244.

Wood, D. (1995), 'Conserved to death. Are tropical forests being over-protected from people?', *Land Use Policy*, **12**(2):115–135.

Part I
Rural Challenge

A
European Perspectives

[1]

Pergamon

Journal of Rural Studies, Vol. 10, No. 4, pp. 343–356, 1994
Copyright © 1995 Elsevier Science Ltd
Printed in Great Britain. All rights reserved
0743–0167/94 $7.00 + 0.00

0743–0167(94)00052–2

Social Welfare in Rural Europe

Mark Shucksmith, Polly Chapman, Gill Clark and
Stuart Black

Department of Land Economy, University of Aberdeen, St Mary's, Kings College,
Aberdeen, U.K.

Abstract — Rural development has been identified by EU leaders as one of the priorities of European structural policies, and as one of the objectives of cohesion policy. Yet despite this commitment, we are very poorly informed about how ordinary people live across the rural areas of Europe, their incomes and quality of life, and their perceptions of policies and economic and social change. This paper argues that greater attention should be devoted to issues of poverty, disadvantage and social exclusion in rural Europe by both policymakers and researchers. This is particularly crucial at the present time as rural Europe is subject to major structural changes deriving both from changes in rural economy and society and from policy initiatives such as the Maastricht Treaty and the Single European Act. These are over and above the wider trends operating throughout Europe in relation to employment, fiscal crisis and ageing, for example. A central requirement is for the articulation of policies for tackling economic and social exclusion (e.g. Poverty 3, Exclusion 1), on the one hand, with those directed towards rural development (e.g. Leader 2), on the other. Fundamental household survey work is required to increase our understanding of what constitutes rural disadvantage, which client groups are affected, and how policies can contribute towards relieving their disadvantage, preferably through client-based instruments rather than less appropriate area-based approaches. The last part of this paper presents preliminary results of such a survey, focusing on issues of employment, housing, poverty and quality of life.

Introduction

Rural areas account for 80% of the territory of the European Union (EU) and nearly 50% of the population. According to the EC Commission's 1988 paper, "The Future of Rural Society", these facts demand that the EU take the proper action to ensure the development of rural society. In recognition of this, the Treaty on European Union agreed at Maastricht identifies the development of the EU's rural areas as one of the objectives of cohesion policy, and at Lisbon European leaders subsequently confirmed that rural development should be one of the priorities of EU structural policies.

Yet despite this commitment, we are very poorly informed about how ordinary people live across the rural areas of Europe, their incomes and quality of life, and their perceptions of policies and economic and social change. Such systematic information as exists, other than about farmers, tends to be urban-oriented or derived from secondary sources such as the national population census, rather than from primary surveys of rural living conditions and social exclusion. There has been no comparative survey across EU member states of the experience of living in rural society, although those involved in the rural projects in the Poverty 3 programme met for a series of cross-national seminars to analyse issues of social and economic exclusion. Notwithstanding these seminars, which inevitably focused on local concerns, the lack of information remains, and continues to hamper attempts to formulate an effective strategy for tackling rural exclusion and for promoting rural cohesion.

Lowe (1994) has argued that "while social polarisation and exclusion in urban areas are attracting growing attention (CEC, 1990), the equivalent phenomenon in rural areas is largely ignored in policy circles". He illustrates this by quoting from the EU's 4th Framework Programme which proposes to fund research on social exclusion in the cities because "Urban areas are the focus for the appearance of new forms of social exclusion" (EC Framework Programme 4 Working Document, p.

344   Mark Shucksmith *et al.*

195). This may be unintentional but it is indicative of the lack of awareness of rural living conditions amongst European policymakers.

It is particularly crucial at the present time that such knowledge is collected and an effective strategy developed for addressing exclusion in rural areas. For, as the EU approaches the turn of the century, rural Europe is subject to major structural changes of unprecedented scale, both as a result of changes in rural economy and society and as a consequence of the Maastricht Treaty, the Single European Act, the reform of the CAP, the GATT agreement, and the further enlargement of the EU. Mernagh and Commins (1992) point to:

- transition to an era of production limitations in agriculture;
- decoupling of income supports from food production programmes;
- reorganisation of industrial production to the possible disadvantage of rural areas (e.g. through processes of global restructuring of capital);
- growth of the service sector in urban areas;
- centralisation tendencies as a consequence of the single market;
- continuing depopulation from many rural areas;
- the expansion of information technologies, tourism and leisure industries.

To this list might be added:

- counterurbanisation tendencies in several northern European states;
- increasing environmental demands placed on the countryside;
- ageing rural populations;
- declining service provision and fiscal constraints on public provision;
- changing conceptions of the countryside itself.

Mernagh and Commins indicate correctly that these trends have different implications for differently situated rural areas (e.g. remote or accessible) and that they will have uneven impacts on different social groups. "Several groups face the risk of economic and social exclusion . . .". Yet at this crucial juncture we still know very little about the specific forms and processes of exclusion which

operate within rural economies and societies, still less how these will be modified by the trends listed above.

In order to develop effective policies both for tackling economic and social exclusion in rural areas (e.g. under the proposed Exclusion 1 programme) and for achieving rural development objectives (e.g. through LEADER 2 and through the Structural Funds), the EU needs information about the forms and processes of exclusion in rural areas of Europe and how these will be modified by the structural changes affecting rural society. Without this knowledge, any strategy is likely to fail to take account of how rural exclusion is experienced, and will be based instead on policymakers' assumptions (perhaps false) about the nature of rural exclusion. Given the urban orientation of most surveys of social exclusion, there is a danger that the strategy adopted will be more suited to urban than to rural circumstances. Furthermore, it will be a top-down approach, rather than one informed by a knowledge of people's experience and perspectives.

What is meant by rural exclusion and disadvantage?

There has been much discussion in the academic literature about the meaning of phrases such as rural disadvantage, rural deprivation and social exclusion. Like "rural", "disadvantage" is a concept engendering endless terminological debate and confusion. Moreover, it appears to be a concept which is emphasised in the U.K. while other European countries have other terms and traditions[1]; social exclusion on the other hand is an attempt at a common denominator. It is therefore necessary to begin with some discussion about what is meant by disadvantage and how this differs from the related concepts of poverty, deprivation and social exclusion.

The concept of poverty implies comparing household (or personal) incomes either against an arbitrarily defined minimum standard of living (absolute poverty) or against some measure of average incomes (relative poverty). Townsend (1979) elaborated the latter conception to suggest that poverty is a financial inability to participate in the everyday styles-of-living of the majority. The EC Council of Ministers (1984) similarly define "the poor" as "persons, families and groups of persons whose resources (material, cultural and social) are so limited as to exclude them from the minimum acceptable way of life in the Member States in which they live". Deprivation is a less precise concept, but it is generally agreed that it means "something more than just the lack of material resources" and that it

---

[1] In France, for example, there is a concept of "insertion" implying social as well as economic integration, as the converse of exclusion. In the Netherlands an official report on social renewal, and in Denmark the discussion of a "two-thirds society" also recall the phenomenon of social exclusion, as does the debate in Spain on the social integration of marginalised and excluded groups (Robbins, 1993, pp. 9–10).

"is essentially a normative concept, incorporating value-judgements about what is morally acceptable and what is not" (Garner, 1989). According to a Scottish Office study (Millar, 1980):

A household may be said to be deprived when its welfare falls below some generally agreed standards. The concept goes beyond the single notion of financial poverty . . . to encompass other aspects of welfare observed from or influenced by the activities of the state, for example, the provision of health care, education, housing and recreational provision.

Similarly, Townsend (1987) defines deprivation as:

A state of observable and demonstrable disadvantage relative to the local community or the wider society or nation to which an individual, family or group belongs

Deprivation can also be relative and multi-dimensional, although difficulties surround attempts to measure it in practice. A further distinction may be made between the concepts of deprivation and disadvantage. The term "deprivation" has become associated in the U.K. with emphasis on the individual's own failings, rightly or wrongly, in contrast to the notion of disadvantage whereby individuals or households are seen as systematically disadvantaged by economic and social restructuring and by the exercise of power in society.

Deprivation may at times be due to personal failings, the accidents of birth or sheer bad luck. But disadvantage is the outcome of the systematic applications of handicaps in access to life chances . . . The disadvantaged are those who are consistently exposed to the highest risk of being deprived. Disadvantage is demonstrably a consequence of the structure of society (Brown, 1983; p. 5).

This distinction, while it may appear trivial, is fundamental to our attitudes to poverty/deprivation/disadvantage: for an emphasis on personal failings leading to deprivation can lead to measures to reduce payments to the undeserving poor ("social security scroungers"); while the notion of disadvantaged groups bearing the brunt of social, economic and political forces outside their control suggests their entitlement to some reparation. Either way, poverty may be both a predisposing factor and an outcome of deprivation or disadvantage. *In this paper the term "disadvantage" is used to describe an inability of individuals or households to share in styles of life open to the majority*: it does not imply any failing on their own part.

This is very close to the concept of **social exclusion**, developed during EC discussions of poverty and disadvantage, to emphasise that it is the exercise of systematic power in society which disadvantages or

excludes people. Robbins (1993) explains how EC concern at new forms of disadvantage arose during the late 1980s and led to the concept of exclusion.

The balance of factors contributing to the experience of exclusion varied for individuals, and varied between Member States. Long-term unemployment was a source of concern throughout the Community; but for Germany, reunification had intensified anxieties about the levels and consequences of unemployment. Homelessness was recognised as a problem in most countries; but public concern had become especially acute in France and the U.K. Major reforms of the social welfare system in Spain and Portugal highlighted issues which were being felt in older, long-established systems: questions surrounding the care of frail elderly people, for example. And in every country, demographic change, changes in the family, and new demands on social protection systems were causing increasing strain and a search for ways of limiting expense.

Despite all these differences in context, the sense that these people were being "locked out" of society, left out in the cold — not always the same people, nor necessarily in the same way — became steadily clearer (Robbins, 1993; p. 7).

Accordingly, in 1989 the Council of Ministers passed a resolution relating to social exclusion, which drew attention to the processes creating social exclusion and called for national and community policies for coherent, coordinated development and to ensure access for everyone to decent living conditions. The resolution specifically noted that "the process of social exclusion is spreading in a number of fields, resulting in many different types of situation affecting various individuals and groups of people in both rural and urban areas".

Trends in poverty, disadvantage and social exclusion: a brief review

There are limited data available with which to review trends in Europe, and the analysis must perforce be mainly restricted to financial circumstances. As the CEC (1992) have noted, "satisfactory statistics on the scale of, and trends in, social exclusion are not available. However, work carried out in the field of *low incomes* suggests that poverty increased at the end of the seventies and then *stabilised at a high level*. The findings also show that a number of individual situations are *very precarious*, as reflected in the existence of a highly fluid population hovering on the fringes of the poverty line" (CEC's emphases).

Room (1993) reviews the principal trends in relation to European poverty, according to two different definitions: these are the number of people falling below a given poverty line; and the numbers receiving social assistance benefits.

He notes that O'Higgins and Jenkins (1989) derived estimates for the CEC on the numbers of people living in poverty in each EC country, according to a criterion whereby poverty was defined as being those households with a disposable income less than half that of the mean disposable income in the country. This indicated that in the EC12, the number of people in poverty increased slightly from 38.6 million in 1975 to 39.5 million in 1980, but then jumped rapidly to 43.9 million (14%) in 1985. The highest rates of poverty were to be found in the poorest countries (Greece, Portugal, Ireland and Spain) with between 20 and 25% of their populations living in poverty in the mid-1980s. In other words, it is in the poorest countries that the highest rates of inequality exist. The least inequality was in the Benelux countries.

Subsequent work by Eurostat (CEC, 1990) has focused on household expenditure rather than income data, defining a household as poor when it spends less than 50% of the national average household expenditure. This method produced higher rates of poverty for the EC as a whole (49 million people in 1980 and 50 million in 1985), but a similar pattern of inter-country variation. The principal differences relate to Denmark, which had less inequality than in the O'Higgins and Jenkins study, and Netherlands and the U.K., which had more. The study showed important changes between 1980 and 1985 in individual member states. The number of poor persons fell significantly in France, Spain, West Germany and Greece, but rose substantially in the U.K., Italy and the Netherlands, as shown in Table 1.

More recent statistics have been collected by the Erasmus University Rotterdam (1993) in a report on the living conditions of the least privileged in the EC. These are compiled on the same basis, but give the percentage of households below not only the

Table 1. Poverty incidence in 1980 and 1985 according to household expenditure

Country	1980	1985
	%	%
Belgium	7.1	5.9
Denmark	7.9	8.0
West Germany	10.5	9.9
Greece	21.5	18.4
Spain	20.9	18.9
France	19.1	15.7
Ireland	18.4	19.5
Italy	14.1	15.5
Netherlands	9.6	11.4
Portugal	32.4	32.7
U.K.	14.6	18.2
EC12	15.5	15.4

threshold of 50% but also of 40% and 60% of average household expenditure. The data relate to varying years from 1987 to 1990, and are presented in Table 2, together with the average annual expenditure per adult in each country expressed in its national currency. While perhaps less reliable than the figures shown in Table 1, they do reveal the large numbers just above the 50% poverty threshold who may be regarded as living on the margins of poverty.

In relation to poverty according to the numbers receiving social assistance, during the 1980s increasing numbers were receiving such assistance. As Room (1993) points out, this may be a misleading measure of poverty in so far as cuts in benefit levels would have the perverse effect of making it appear that the population of the poor had fallen; and moreover many of those eligible to claim benefits fail to apply for assistance. Nevertheless, trends in such numbers can give some indication of dependency on state assistance, and the increase in these numbers in the 1980s gave cause for concern. In almost every country the trend in numbers of

Table 2. Households in poverty in Europe, 1987/90

Country	Year	Av. income	%<40%	%<50%	%<60%
Belgium	88	327 058	2.6	6.7	15.3
Denmark	87	80 570	1.3	3.6	10.1
West Germany	88	22 782	4.7	10.8	19.7
Greece	88	832 188	13.0	20.6	29.7
Spain	88	674 331	8.6	16.7	26.2
France	89	73 084	6.5	14.0	23.1
Ireland	88	5130	8.4	16.9	27.0
Italy	88	11,548,338	11.2	20.6	30.4
Luxembourg	87	516 846	3.5	8.8	17.2
Netherlands	88	20 736	1.1	4.3	12.1
Portugal	90	556 118	15.7	25.2	34.4
U.K.	88	5683	5.8	14.2	25.2
EC12					

Social Welfare in Rural Europe 347

Table 3. Incidence of poverty amongst English rural households, 1980

Poverty standard	Essex	Yorkshire	Suffolk	Shropshire	Northumberland	All
Absolute:						
100–139% SB[1]	15.2	15.6	13.1	15.4	18.8	15.6
<100% SB	9.7	10.2	8.3	9.5	8.5	9.3
Relative:						
50–79% mean income	32.1	41.3	34.5	28.4	35.2	34.3
<50% mean income	11.5	14.4	16.7	23.1	18.2	16.8

[1] Supplementary Benefit.

recipients of minimum benefits is upwards (Room, 1993; p. 12), especially in Belgium, Portugal, Germany and Spain. The principal exception, the U.K., arises from changes in the social security system.

Rural disadvantage: existing knowledge

This review of statistical information on trends in poverty, disadvantage and exclusion has been unable to disaggregate between rural and urban areas, of course. For information on specifically rural poverty, disadvantage and exclusion, the problems of comparability of data and the large areas for which data are collected confound attempts at analysis. Instead, one must rely on individual studies of particular areas.

(1) *Rural poverty*

Two major studies of rural deprivation and rural lifestyles in England, commissioned by the Department of the Environment and others, are illuminating. In 1980, households were surveyed in five study areas (see McLaughlin, 1986a, 1986b, 1986c; Bradley, 1987). Subsequently, in 1990, over 3,000 households in 12 study areas were surveyed (Cloke *et al.*, 1994). Table 3 shows the incidence of poverty found in the former study.

In terms of absolute poverty, 25% of rural households overall were found to be living in or on the margins of poverty (i.e. incomes up to 139% of their supplementary benefit entitlement): this represented 20% of the rural population (McLaughlin, 1986c; Bradley, 1987). The most significant element of this group was the elderly, with 35% of these households consisting of elderly people living alone (predominantly elderly widows). The other main element was the low-paid, manual worker's household.

In terms of relative poverty, 17% of households in rural areas earned less than half the mean local household income, and a further 34% earned less

than 80% of this average. Thus, 51% of the households surveyed were in or on the margins of poverty by this definition. According to McLaughlin (1986c), rural incomes are highly polarised with more rich as well as more poor households, so emphasising the degree of relative poverty.

The full extent of the rural poor's marginalisation is underlined by the patterns of inequality in the distribution of household income. In contrast with the national pattern identified by Townsend (1979) in which 11% of households had gross disposable incomes of at least three times their SB (supplementary benefit) eligibility level, the corresponding rural aggregate was 26%.

Generally, better-paid individuals tended to earn more than similar individuals elsewhere, while low-paid individuals earned even less: thus Table 4 shows the average gross weekly earnings for various categories of employment for individuals living in the rural study areas and for Britain. It can be seen that non-manual earnings by individuals living in rural areas comfortably exceed the national average, while manual earnings are appreciably lower in rural areas. Furthermore, the disparity between male and female earnings is also greater in rural areas. It should be noted that many of the non-manual workers may commute to work elsewhere, despite being resident in the rural areas: indeed Newby *et al.* (1978) have argued that it is the influx of relatively affluent commuters into such areas which has increased the relative deprivation of local, non-propertied households.

Table 4. Average gross weekly earning (£) full-time, 1980

	Rural areas of England	Britain
Non-manual		
Male	215.2	163.1
Female	104.1	96.7
Manual		
Male	117.2	121.9
Female	66.3	74.5

While acknowledging that the majority of the poor in rural areas are elderly households, living on state pensions as their sole source of income, McLaughlin (1986c) concludes from these figures that "the most important factor determining the poverty status of other households is income poverty derived from low wages". He supports this conclusion by demonstrating that 24% of all male manual workers and 78% of all female manual workers in the rural study areas earned below the then low-pay threshold of £80/week.

Moreover, the data exploded the myth that a wide range of fringe benefits make up the real wages of low-paid rural workers: on the contrary, free boots were no match for the company cars, occupational pensions and BUPA membership of non-manual groups.

Recent research by Cloke *et al*. (1994) reveals that these findings still apply in the 1990s. Their 1990 data are not directly comparable with McLaughlin's 1980 figures, but Cloke *et al*. are able to conclude that rural poverty is significantly high in many areas in the 1990s.

> It has been argued that issues of poverty and deprivation are somehow phenomena of a previous time-period, becoming anachronistic in the 'prosperity' of the 1980s. Our findings suggest that the issue is not only very significant and important in our 1990 surveys but is also being reproduced by paterns of in-migration to particular places . . . It is those case study areas where aggregate incomes are lowest, and poverty indicators most significant, that figure most strongly as reception of low-income in-migrant households (Cloke *et al*., 1994; s.6.18).

Table 5 shows the proportions of households in Cloke's study areas characterised as in or on the margins of poverty according to three widely used indicators of poverty.

These are:

(1) households with less than 79% of the mean household income for that area — by this indicator, the extent of poverty ranges from 62% of households in North Yorkshire to 44% in Northamptonshire: this compares with an average of 51% in the 1980 survey areas;
(2) households with less than 79% of the median household income for that area — this ranges from 47% in Devon to 35% in Northamptonshire; and
(3) households whose income is less than 140% of income support entitlement — this stricter definition of poverty gives a range of from 39% in Nottinghamshire to only 6% in West Sussex, compared to an average of 25% in the 1980 survey areas. Using this last indicator, nine out of the 12 study areas contained 20% or more households in or on the margins of poverty.

The study also gives details of the characteristics of households experiencing poverty. The findings largely endorse those of previous studies in so far as

> elderly people were found to be most prone to experience difficulties associated with rural poverty, although in some specific areas (for example Northumberland and Nottinghamshire) the problem is also seen to affect younger households. Although normally associated with rented housing, low income households occupied a range of tenure types.

Although survey data of this quality have been lacking for Scotland, the literature has generally accepted that the conclusions of the English research apply equally to Scottish rural households. For one thing, rural Scotland has a similarly "top-heavy demography": Knox (1985) has noted that in rural Scotland "a disproportionate number of the poor are elderly, and a disproportionate number of the

Table 5. Alternative indicators of poverty in rural study areas, 1990 (Cloke *et al*., 1994)

	Mean	Median	Income support
Cheshire	46	44	13
Devon	50	47	34
Essex	53	44	30
Northamptonshire	44	35	15
Northumberland	61	38	26
North Yorkshire	62	41	22
Nottinghamshire	59	41	39
Shropshire	51	35	22
Suffolk	45	43	26
Warwickshire	48	39	23
West Sussex	46	46	6
Wiltshire	49	37	25

elderly are poor", and he suggests that the incidence of multiply-deprived pensioner households is higher in rural than in urban Scotland, and accounts for well over 50% of multiply-deprived households in rural Scotland. Furthermore, Burbridge and Robertson (1978) have demonstrated that the proportion of households in low socio-economic groups is higher in rural than urban Scotland, suggesting, together with Mackay Consultant's analysis of the occupational structure of the Highlands and Islands, that rural areas contain a disproportionate number of people in low-paid occupations. Agriculture and tourism are particularly notable in this respect (Mackay Consultants, 1985).

(2) Rural deprivation

Some detailed survey work has been conducted on rural deprivation in the HIDB area (Cottam and Knox, 1982) and special tabulations of micro-data from the 1981 Census have also been analysed in terms of rural and urban deprivation (Knox, 1985). Further area studies have been undertaken by Midwinter and Monoghan (1990) for COSLA, but these involved no household surveys and relied largely on information from local authorities. Even where surveys have been conducted, however, little research has addressed the causal explanations of particular forms of disadvantage, with most authors content to rely on Census-derived indicators of deprivation, the meaning and interpretation of which is not always clear.

Cottam and Knox (1982) analysed a number of secondary indicators for HIDB statistical areas and found that multiple deprivation centred around low incomes, lack of a car and poor housing, and it was highest in Barra (42% of households deprived on three or more criteria) and Harris (22%). There is considerable doubt about the indicators used to measure deprivation, and particularly about the lack of a car, which in any event was duplicated in two of the criteria. This said, the incidence of deprivation was concentrated among households whose head was semi-skilled or unskilled, and was particularly prevalent among elderly households. This confirms the pattern found in England in relation to rural poverty: deprivation too appears to be closely associated with low-wage earners and the elderly poor.

Knox's (1985) work relied not on surveys but on special tabulations of household data from the 1981 Census, commissioned by SDD. This has obvious advantages over the analysis of area data at the ED level in terms of identifying the characteristics of disadvantaged households. Again, it may be argued

that this study relies upon flawed indicators and double-counting which introduce an urban bias. Notwithstanding this, the findings are instructive. Knox devotes some space to a discussion of rural–urban differences:

> Altogether, 76.5% of all the multiply-disadvantaged households in Scotland are in urban areas, compared to 15% in semi-rural and 8.5% in rural areas [as defined by the Registrar-General for Scotland]. Given that semi-rural and rural areas contain 16.6% and 11.3% of all Scottish households, respectively, these figures go some way towards putting the 'rural deprivation' issue into perspective: it is of minor importance, both relatively and absolutely, compared with urban deprivation. Yet the existence of 29,570 multiply-disadvantaged households in rural areas and 52,120 in semi-rural areas is clearly not an insignificant issue.

Knox also relates the incidence of multiple-deprivation to tenure and other household characteristics. Housing tenure is related to multiple-deprivation quite differently in rural and urban areas. In urban areas, multiply-deprived households are overwhelmingly concentrated in the public sector, whereas in rural areas the incidence is much higher in the privately-rented and owner-occupied sectors. The composition of multiple deprivation is also shown to differ between rural and urban areas, with rural disadvantage characterised by low socioeconomic status and pensioner households.

> In general, the more urban a settlement, the less multiple disadvantage is dominated by the combination of low socioeconomic status and pensioner households, and the more it is characterised by combinations involving low socioeconomic status, unemployment/sickness/disability, overcrowding, and single parent families (Knox, 1985; 421).

This difference in itself is sufficient to call into question the suitability of the indicators used (many of which are clearly biased towards features of urban deprivation) for the identification of rural deprivation. Even using these indicators, it is nevertheless clear that substantial numbers of disadvantaged households do exist in rural areas of Scotland.

A consistent picture emerges therefore of a rural incidence of poverty and disadvantage which is closely associated with elderly households and with low-paid occupations, and which may be as prevalent as urban disadvantage. Yet the existence of rural disadvantage is largely unrecognised, for reasons discussed by Shucksmith (1989). One of these reasons is the use of urban-derived indicators of deprivation to measure rural disadvantage.

(3) Causes of rural disadvantage and exclusion

Poverty is a predisposing factor for rural deprivation, and the causes of rural poverty are therefore to some extent the causes of rural deprivation. However, deprivation is more than poverty alone: there is at the heart of policymakers' concern a notion of cumulative causation, "that deprivation, by its very nature, will perpetuate itself through some 'cause and effect' mechanism" (Garner, 1989). It is necessary, then, to explore ways in which poverty is perpetuated in a rural context if deprivation is to be properly understood. This will certainly differ from the urban causality, through which poor people are likely to be "sorted" into ghettoes of poverty in which the area effects of urban deprivation are all too apparent, with poor housing, poor education, poor employment opportunities and poor services. In contrast, it is unlikely that there will be any such "sorting" process in a rural context (other than out-migration to urban areas), so that poor households in rural areas are unlikely to be concentrated, and area effects similar to those arising in urban concentrations of poverty are unlikely to be present. This is not to say that cumulative disadvantage is absent in rural areas, but merely to note that these processes are unrelated to area concentrations and are therefore more complex to observe. "For the rural poor, disadvantage is as much a matter of interlocking deprivations as it is for the underclasses of the British inner-cities" (Bradley, 1987).

A number of suggestions have been proposed concerning the cumulative processes behind rural poverty and disadvantage. Newby *et al*. (1978), for example, found in Suffolk that an elite of landowners and incomers sought to exclude alternative employers in the name of conservation, and so maintained a low-wage local economy to their own benefit. There is no doubt that an increased demand for labour from rural employers, so bidding up wages, is the fundamental solution to problems of low-wage poverty, and this is a clear objective for rural economic policy.

Another approach was suggested by Shaw (1979) in a model of "the rural deprivation cycle". This related "household deprivation" to "mobility deprivation" and "opportunity deprivation". Low incomes were seen to lead not only to poor housing but also to the inability to afford a car or public transport (if it existed), and so to inaccessibility to jobs, education, health and recreation. This "opportunity deprivation" then leads in turn to perpetuation of low income, so reinforcing the cycle of deprivation. However, as Bradley *et al*. (1987) have pointed out, 'opportunity' and 'mobility' deprivations merely constitute two sides of the same problem: mobility ceases to be a problem if facilities are close to residence, but if they are distant then lack of opportunity becomes the problem of mobility".

Unfortunately, "both Shaw's concept of 'opportunity deprivation' and Newby's sociological theory have remained undeveloped lines of enquiry" (Bradley *et al*., 1987), and instead the simplistic view that rural deprivation equals decline in services has dominated thinking.

The most fully researched study of the causality of rural deprivation was undertaken on behalf of the Department of the Environment by Bradley and McLaughlin, as noted above. Bradley (1987) has discussed some of their conclusions, although the processes described may relate more to England than to the Scottish context.

(4) Sources of poverty

Unemployment was not found to be an extensive cause of poverty in rural England, with unemployment rates of around 1–3% in the areas surveyed, compared to a national average then (1981) of 12%. This finding would certainly not apply to rural Scotland, however. In the HIDB area, for example, unemployment rates in April 1986 ranged from as high as 26% in the Forres area, with Skye and Wester Ross, Easter Ross, Lochaber and Sutherland all above 20%, down to Thurso at 12%, compared to a Scottish average of 16%. Only Shetland had a low rate of unemployment (6%). Unemployment rates in areas such as the Western Isles have risen sharply since then, causing real poverty.

Low wages were found to be typical of family-farming areas, such as the uplands, where the low returns to family labour in agriculture set a yardstick for general wage-rates in the local economy. In other (lowland) areas, where planning policies permitted, employers had invested to take advantage of cheap labour and available land, and this had raised wage rates. Of course, even in the latter areas some wages remained very low, such as those of farm workers. Large areas of rural Scotland would be characterised as family-farming areas, with dominant ideologies of localism and familism, and so would be subject to the same forces observed by Bradley in north Northumberland and the Yorkshire Dales. Low wages are likely to be prevalent in these areas, particularly amongst those employed on the land or in tourism and catering, and those self-employed in small businesses.

The most significant source of poverty, however, was old age. Between 40% and 67% of single elderly men, and between 45% and 85% of single elderly women, were living in or on the margins of poverty.

Table 6. The probability of poverty by household type

	Essex	Yorkshire Dales	Suffolk	Shropshire	Northumberland
Elderly	0.69	0.47	0.62	0.40	0.53
Families	0.18	0.20	0.11	0.29	0.18
Adults only	0.06	0.08	0.06	0.11	0.10

Households composed of elderly people were far and away the most vulnerable to poverty, as shown in Table 6. This finding is likely to be equally applicable to rural Scotland, and relates to the earlier discussion of the findings of Knox (1985) and Knox and Cottam (1981a, 1981b).

(5) *Social isolation and deprivation*

Bradley's work is particularly illuminating, however, in its discussion of the elderly people concerned. Elderly households in the lowlands were mainly from local families, isolated amongst a sea of newcomers, with the majority living almost entirely on their state pensions and other welfare benefits. Substantial replacement of the local working class by an incomer middle class had taken place as a result of housing market forces, and this had effectively diluted and stretched traditional kinship networks, leaving elderly people without the support of family and friends. Many of the elderly households in the uplands, on the other hand, were newcomers who had retired there as relatively affluent couples in the 1960s and early 1970s: many had since suffered the bereavement of a spouse and were living on quite inadequate incomes, with few assets, and again with no connection with local social networks.

> Thus, at one extreme, social spaces are produced where isolated elderly newcomers reside within close-knit small-scale labour areas, dominated by local familism. At the other end of the continuum, an older and more dependent, indigenous population has become isolated within a belt of relatively affluent, mobile newcomers, . . . Many of the upland newcomer population, in our samples, expressed feelings of intense social isolation from what they perceived to be an inhospitable local community. Ethnically local people in many of the lowland villages shared similar feelings, although for them it originated in a sense of local dispossession. Thus, social changes have meant that, whether as a local or a newcomer, growing old in a village often involves coping with loneliness and perceived relative deprivation (Bradley, 1987).

Isolation in this very real sense has little to do with accessibility to services, which is the stereotypical view of rural deprivation, but concerns rather the very limited "degree and quality of their involvement in face-to-face interactions, reciprocity and personal relationships". Such loneliness may face not only elderly households in rural areas, but also

the high proportion of local men in remote areas in mid-life who have never married (15–25% of men aged 25–64).

There are other aspects of rural exclusion which Bradley does not go into, concerning education, health care and training, as well as the lack of choice of both employment and housing. Chapman (1987), for example, points out that for many children in remote areas secondary education involves weekly boarding "so that the experience of family life (or lack of it) during adolescence is unlike that of young people growing up in a city neighbourhood". Midwinter and Monaghan (1990) describe poor access to health and social work services. Bradley touches briefly on the lack of advice services in rural areas which leaves the poorest households relying on "families, friends and employers for advice on benefits and welfare rights".

Bradley's work is therefore very helpful in illuminating some crucial aspects of rural deprivation in England, especially in relation to the social isolation experienced by elderly and single households, and in relation to the principal sources of rural poverty. Nevertheless, even at the end of this study, Bradley concludes that:

> the most important questions, which relate (a) to the causes of deprivation; (b) to how it is actually experienced and perceived within localities; and (c) to priorities of social policy, remain to be researched.

Much empirical work therefore remains to be done before policies can be properly related to an adequate understanding of rural deprivation.

The discussion in the previous section, while highlighting the extent to which rural disadvantage is still imperfectly understood, nevertheless does suggest some factors which are associated with rural disadvantage. On the basis of these insights it will be possible to construct crude indicators of the areal incidence of disadvantage, and to use these to identify the areas within which people are most likely to experience poverty and poor housing, and within which rural disadvantage is therefore most likely to arise. However, the earlier discussion of elderly local people experiencing rural disadvantage through their social isolation and poverty in the most

352   Mark Shucksmith *et al.*

affluent commuter areas highlights the shortcomings of such an identification of areas. Most households suffering rural disadvantage will not live in priority areas identified through the use of such indicators. People, not areas, suffer rural disadvantage. Consequently, an area-based approach may be inappropriate.

Many of the authors of studies of rural disadvantage, referred to in this report, have emphasised the need for a client-based approach to rural disadvantage to complement area-based action. Such an approach to rural poverty and rural disadvantage is less easy to achieve, administratively or politically. Area-based approaches are more convenient, not only because they correspond to administrative territories, but also because they do not challenge the fundamental processes which structure disadvantage.

For all their shortcomings, the studies of disadvantage in Scotland reviewed above (and especially the survey work of Knox and Cottam), together with Bradley and McLaughlin's work in rural England, do offer some insights into the nature of rural disadvantage. In rural Scotland it seems that the most disadvantaged are likely to be poor pensioners, low-paid workers and unemployed people. Their distribution can be inferred from cross-tabulations of Census small area statistics, and assistance targeted on the areas identified. However, more direct assistance could often be given by identifying and ameliorating the causes of their disadvantage: for example, care and repair schemes have made a major contribution to the housing conditions of poor pensioners in certain areas and further advice services would also be helpful; again, low-cost housing initiatives might be tailored specifically to suit low-wage earners and the unemployed. If the dimensions of rural disadvantage can be understood, and those affected can be identified, then it may be more effective to target policies at those groups and the problems which face them, rather than at the areas in which they (and many others) live. More fundamental household survey work is required to increase our understanding of what constitutes rural disadvantage, which client groups are affected, and how policies can contribute towards relieving their disadvantage, preferably through client-based instruments rather than less appropriate area-based approaches. The remaining section of this paper reports current research which attempts to understand rural disadvantage and exclusion from the perspective of those living in rural areas and experiencing rural life, therefore, from the bottom-up.

Recent research in rural Scotland

Research on the perceptions and needs of people living in rural Scotland has been commissioned by Rural Forum (Scotland) with financial support from the Joseph Rowntree Foundation, Scottish Homes, the Royal Scottish Agricultural Benevolent Institution and the Scottish Consumer Council. The project began in January 1993 and was completed in August 1994 (see Shucksmith *et al.* 1994).

The research was conducted in four case study areas. These areas (Harris, Wester Ross, Angus and North Ayrshire) were selected to include a range of types of rural areas in relation to remoteness, population density, strength of local labour market, and other social and cultural variables. The areas were tightly defined so that their total populations were less than 5000 in each case. Within each locality, a common research design was employed. This involved three elements, combining local contextual information with quantitative data on the extent of rural poverty and disadvantage and with qualitative insights into the nature of disadvantage.

The qualitative accounts of respondents interviewed in depth provide a dramatic testament to the economic forces that have driven demographic and social change in rural areas. A distinction may be drawn between patterns of employment in the lowland communities studied (Angus and North Ayrshire) and the scattered communities (Wester Ross and Harris). Opportunities and options were severely constrained in the scattered communities, whereas the access to urban centres provided a favourable range of employment opportunities to respondents in the lowland areas. In both scattered and lowland communities, there was a recognition that very limited work options were now a fact of rural life. Individuals who chose to stay in rural areas did so in the knowledge that they would be facing low-paid, insecure jobs, and those who chose to migrate there generally had strategies to enable them to survive economically — such as teleworking or artisan work in remote areas, or commuting from lowland areas.

Lack of youth employment choice and options was perceived to be the most serious problem facing rural communities, and youth unemployment was blamed for an increase in crime and vandalism in Angus and North Ayrshire. School leavers were further disadvantaged by limited public transport which prevented their journeying to workplaces outwith their home areas. Beyond employment issues, however, the aspirations of young people are changing, and not only lack of jobs but also the socially limiting rural environment and the *type* of jobs may be affecting their migration away from rural areas. Graduate employment options were seen as non-existent in Wester Ross and Harris, for example, and parents accepted that by encouraging their children in school and university they were in fact educating their children "out" of the area. "Educating out" was viewed with a mixture of pride and regret.

Women respondents felt that their role and position in rural society had changed considerably in recent years, and many felt that this had come with increased involvement in the wage economy and changing expectations of women's role in the work-force. In scattered communities, women's main involvement in the workforce was tourism-related work, notably B&Bs, but in the lowland areas access to urban employment greatly improved the range of jobs available — even so, work tended to be in the caring professions or the service industry. The majority of women felt that women's aspirations had to take second place to male employment, given the better pay and greater security accorded to men in rural employment. Even these aspirations were limited by woefully inadequate childcare provision: this did not matter so much in the scattered communities where jobs were lacking anyway; but in lowland areas women considered themselves to be more disadvantaged in terms of childcare provision because they perceived that there were jobs avail-able for them in nearby urban labour markets.

Respondents expressed great concern over high levels of housing costs, both for house purchase and for assured tenancies. The reasons for high housing costs varied from area to area. The consequence was perceived to be that certain groups are excluded from the market for house purchase, and that altenative housing options for these groups were few. Either concealed homelessness would result (e.g. caravans, winter lets, living with parents), or the household would be forced to leave the locality. Young families and single person households were frequently seen as being groups with the most restricted housing choice in rural areas. Respon-dents were anxious that young families should remain in their area because they represented reproduction of the community, and justified the survival of the school with its importance as an arena for social interaction.

Poverty is widespread in rural Scotland, when measured in terms of relative incomes. Sixty-five per cent of heads of households surveyed had incomes below the Low Pay Unit Poverty Threshold of £200/week. This compares with a figure of 55% for Britain as a whole. Moreover, 49% of the sample had incomes below half the median Scottish wage (below £150/week). Some groups were particularly likely to be on a low income: these were the elderly,

especially those relying only on a state pension, and those in low-wage occupations such as agriculture and tourism, as well as the unemployed. Self-employed workers may also receive low incomes.

The uptake of state benefits was found to be very low in all areas, and lower than would be expected given the levels of low income, especially in Wester Ross. Less than half the respondents received any state bnenefits. Respondents were often confused about the benefits that are available and their entitlement. Access to advice in urban centres is problematic, with DSS offices seen as highly intimidating quite apart from the social stigma of claiming benefit.

Previous surveys have documented the extent to which the cost of living is higher in rural areas, Transport costs are higher and a car is a necessity. The costs of heating and fuel, food and shopping, and housing were all perceived to be higher in rural areas. While higher costs affect all rural residents, those affected most are low income groups. Cost differentials were seen as growing, due to the trends towards shopping away from the rural location.

The combination of a low income with a high cost of living has pervasive consequences, restricting choices and opportunities in many areas of life. Travel becomes problematic, restricting choice of food and other goods, and limiting access to leisure and entertainment facilities. Access to training or further and higher education may also be precluded. Many respondents, especially the elderly, felt socially isolated because of the distances and costs involved in travelling to family and friends. Some could not afford a phone. For those people on low incomes that are unable to afford a car, there is a feeling of a loss of independence.

Despite these disadvantages and forms of exclusion, most respondents felt that the benefits of living in a rural area outweighed the disadvantages. They often regarded themselves as "rich in spirit, poor in means". Many rural residents placed a high value on non-monetary aspects of rural life. Values are changing rapidly, however, in all areas, as material expectations rise and community values are eroded. Almost all looked back to a point in the past when poverty had been much more commonplace and obvious: rather than comparison being made with the lifestyles of the majority, people compared their situation with lifestyles of the past, when conditions were much harsher. For this reason very few said there was much, if any, poverty in their area. Respondents identified some groups who might potentially be poor (single parents, the elderly, the unemployed and farmworkers), but members of these groups did not consider themselves to be poor or deprived (or would not admit to it). There is thus a considerable gulf between objective and subjective disadvantage.

These are only some of the preliminary results arising from the current research in Scotland, but they help to illustrate both the types of disadvantage and exclusion which may exist in rural areas of Europe and the lines of enquiry which might be pursued. Problems of employment, housing, low incomes, high costs, and transport and access to services are more apparent than some other subtle, but important aspects of exclusion, such as isolation, lack of childcare options, and loss of young people. The full report of this research (Shucksmith *et al.*, forthcoming) examines such matters in much more detail.

Conclusion

This paper has argued that greater attention should be devoted to issues of poverty, disadvantage and social exclusion in rural Europe by both policy-makers and researchers. This is particularly crucial at the present time as rural Europe is subject to major structural changes deriving both from changes in rural economy and society and from policy initiatives such as the Mastricht Treaty and the Single European Act. These are over and above the wider trends operating throughout Europe in relation to employment, fiscal crisis and ageing, for example. A central requirement is for the articu-lation of policies for tackling economic and social exclusion (e.g. Poverty 3, Exclusion 1), on the one hand, with those directed towards rural develop-ment (e.g. Leader 2), on the other.

Exclusion and disadvantage are often thought of as predominantly urban phenomena, and studies based on urban indicators of deprivation (such as over-crowding, lack of a car and multi-storey dwelling) have concealed the existence of large numbers of disadvantaged households in rural locations. Rural disadvantage tends not to be concentrated, in the manner of urban disadvantage, but dispersed. Indeed, one of its dimensions is frequently that of social isolation. This makes rural advantage less visible and less obviously tractable. We do have some knowledge of the incidence and causes of rural poverty, however, and these may be summarised as follows:

- poverty arises from unemployment, particularly where job opportunities are lacking over a long period;
- poverty arises from the low wages typical of many

rural areas, where the low returns to family labour in agriculture set a yardstick for general wage-rates in the local economy;
- poverty arises most significantly from an in-adequate income in old age.

Households composed of elderly people are far and away the most vulnerable to poverty, according to the British studies. However, this may not be the case in other rural areas of Europe, and many people may experience social exclusion without being poor. How exactly these sources of poverty are related to cumulative rural exclusion in different areas of Europe is a subject for further research, and this must begin with an understanding of how poverty and exclusion are experienced in rural areas.

A number of difficulties arise in seeking to identify the rural incidence of exclusion and disadvantage. Partly these stem from our lack of understanding of the nature of rural disadvantage and exclusion, and the difficulty of operationalising concepts such as isolation and quality of life. Partly they stem from the inadequacy of the data available at a sub-district level, particularly in relation to income, wealth and employment. To some extent, social indicators may be used to identify the area incidence of, for example, pensioners from low socioeconomic groups, low wage-earners and the unemployed, who appear to be the principal disadvantaged groups. However, more fundamental household survey work is required to increase our understanding of what constitutes rural disadvantage, which client groups are affected, and how policies can contribute towards relieving their disadvantage, preferably through client-based instruments rather than less appropriate area-based approaches.

The last part of this paper presented preliminary results of such a survey, focusing on issues of employment, housing, poverty and quality of life. These help to illustrate both the types of disadvan-tage and exclusion which may exist in rural areas of Europe and the lines of enquiry which should be pursued. Problems of employment, housing, low incomes, high costs, and transport and access to services are more apparent but must not obscure other subtle, but important aspects of exclusion, such as isolation, lack of childcare options, and loss of young people. If the dimensions of rural disadvan-tage and exclusion can be understood, and those affected identified, then it will be more feasible to target policies at those groups and at the problems which face them, and to adjust policies which contribute to such exclusion.

Cloke *et al.* (1994) have gone beyond this to argue for community-level involvement in the response to disadvantage and exclusion (through rural community action workers), so as to enable a connection to be made between material help and the localised experience of living and coping with rural change. Certainly, such a proposal would be one means of achieving the necessary articulation of EC and national policies to combat social exclusion with those promoting bottom-up rural economic development.

References

Bradley, A. (1987) Poverty and Dependency in Village England. In *Disadvantage and Welfare in Rural Areas*, Lowe, P., Bradley, A. and Wright, S. (eds) pp. 151–174, Geo Books, Norwich.

Bradley, A., Lowe, P. and Wright, S. (1987) Introduction: Rural Disadvantage and the Welfare Tradition. In *Disadvantage and Welfare in Rural Areas*, Lowe, P., Bradley, A. and Wright, S., pp. 1–39. Geo Books, Norwich.

Brown, M. (1983) *The Structure of Disadvantage*. Heinemann, London.

Bryden, J. and Black, S. (1987) *Estimates prepared for the HIDB*, unpublished.

Buchanan, S. (1989) *Defining Rural Areas and Rural Disadvantage*. NCVO Rural Unit, Resource Paper 2. NCVO, London.

Burbridge, V. and Robertson, S. (1978) *Rural Indicators Study*. Scottish Office Central Research Unit, Edinburgh.

CEC (1990) Inequality and poverty in Europe 1980–85. Eurostat Rapid Reports, Statistical Office of the European Communities, Luxemburg.

CEC (1992) Towards a Europe of Solidarity: intensifying the fight against social exclusion, fostering integration. COM(92) 542. CEC, Brussels.

Chapman (1987).

Chapman, P., Clark, G., Shucksmith, M. and Black, S. (1994) *Life in Rural Scotland Today*. Report awaiting publication.

Cloke, P. (1977) An index of rurality for England and Wales. *Regional Studies* **11**, 31–46.

Cloke, P. (1978) Changing patterns of urbanisation in rural areas of England and Wales 1961–71. *Regional Studies* **12**, 603–617.

Cloke, P. and Edwards, G. (1985) Rurality in England and Wales 1981; a replication of the 1971 Index. *Regional Studies* **20**, 289–306.

Cloke, P. (1987) Rurality and change: some cautionary notes. *Journal of Rural Studies* **3**, 71–76.

Cloke, P., Milbourne, P. and Thomas, C. (1994) *Lifestyles in Rural England*. Rural Development Commission Rural Research Report 18, RDC, London.

Clout, H. (1984) *A Rural Policy for the EEC?* Methuen, London.

Cottam, M.B. and Knox, P.L. (1982) *The Highlands and Islands — A Social Profile*. Report to the HIDB, Inverness.

CRU (1984) *The Urban Programme in Scotland: Results of a Monitoring Exercise*. Scottish Office Central Research Unit, Edinburgh.

Duguid, G. and Grant, R. (1983) *Areas of Special Need in Scotland*. Scottish Office Central Research Unit.

Erasmus University Rotterdam (1993) Living conditions of the least privileged in the EEC: research on poverty statistics based on micro-data for the Member States of Europe, report to the CEC, Brussels.

Fife Regional Council (1987) *Housing Market Area Study*. Fife RC, Kirkcaldy.

Folkesdotter, G. (1987) Research and Policy for Rural Housing in Sweden. In *Rural Housing in Scotland: Recent Research and Policy*, MacGregor, B., Robertson, D. and Shucksmith, M. (eds) pp. 167–182, Aberdeen University Press, Aberdeen.

Garner, C. (1989) *Does Disadvantage Damage?* Centre for Educational Sociology, Edinburgh University.

Knox, P.L. (1985) Disadvantaged households and areas of disadvantage: microdata from the 1981 Census of Scotland. *Environment and Planning* **A17**, 413–415.

Knox, P.L. and Cottam, M.B. (1981a) A welfare approach to rural geography: contrasting perspectives on the quality of Highland life. *Transactions of the Institute of British Geographers* **6**, 433–450.

Knox, P.L. and Cottam, M.B. (1981b) Rural disadvantage in Scotland: a preliminary assessment. *Tijdschrift voor Economische en Sociale Geografie* **72**, 162–175.

Low Pay Unit (1983) *Low Pay in Scotland*. Low Pay Unit, Glasgow.

Lowe, P. (1994) *Social Exclusion in Rural Europe*. Unpublished paper to Conference on Meeting the Challenge of Exclusion in Peripheral Rural Areas, Clifden, Ireland.

Mackay Consultants (1985) *Incomes and Earnings in the Highlands and Islands of Scotland*. Report to HIDB, Inverness.

McCleery, A., McDonald, C.C., Peat, J.A. and Walker, C.A. (1987) *Economic and Social Change in the Highlands and Islands*. Scottish Office, ESU Research Paper No. 13.

McLaughlin, B.P. (1986a) Local Approaches to Rural Disadvantage — the Growing Dilemma. *Local Government Studies* **12**.

McLaughlin, B.P. (1986b) Rural policy in the 1980s — the revival of the rural idyll. *Journal of Rural Studies* **2**, 81–90.

McLaughlin, B.P. (1986c) The rhetoric and the reality of rural disadvantage. *Journal of Rural Studies* **2**, 291–307.

Mernagh, M. and Commins, P. (1992) *Europe 2000: Meeting the Challenge of Exclusion in Peripheral Rural Areas*. Poverty 3 RDU, Dublin.

Midwinter, A., Mair, C. and Moxen, J. (1988) *Rural Disadvantage in Scotland* Department of Administration, University of Strathclyde.

Midwinter, A. and Monaghan, C. (1990) *The Measurement and Analysis of Rural Disadvantage*. Report to COSLA, February 1990. COSLA, Edinburgh.

Millar, A. (1980) *A Study of Multiply Deprived Households in Scotland*. Scottish Office Central Research Unit, Edinburgh.

Newby, H., Bell, C., Rose, D. and Saunders, P. (1987) *Property, Paternalism and Power*. Hutchinson, London.

O'Higgins, M. and Jenkins, S. (1989) Poverty in Europe, paper presented to a seminar on poverty status in Noordwyk, under the sponsorship of the CEC.

Pacione, M. (1984) *Rural Geography*. Harper and Row.

PIEDA (1985) *Housing Demands in Scotland* Report to SDD, Edinburgh.

Randall, J. (1985) Economic trends and support to economic activity in rural Scotland. *Scottish Economic Bulletin* **31**, 10–20.

Robbins, D. (1993) Towards a Europe of solidarity: combating social exclusion. *Social Europe* Supplement 4/93, Commission of the EC (DGV).

356   Mark Shucksmith *et al.*

Room, G. (1993) *Anti-Poverty Action-Research in Europe.* SAUS, Bristol.

SDA (1989) *Rural Development in Scotland — a Review of Trends and Issues.* SDA Rural Development Unit, Edinburgh.

Shaw, M. (1979) Rural Deprivation, Geo Books, Norwich.

Shucksmith, M. (1984) *Scotland's Rural Housing: A Forgotten Problem.* Rural Forum, Perth.

Shucksmith, M. (1989) *Rural Poverty.* Paper to the Jubilee Conference of the Citizens' Advice Service, Erskine Bridge, Glasgow.

Shucksmith, M. (1990) *The Definition of Rural Areas and Rural Disadvantage.* Research Report No. 2, Scottish Homes, Edinburgh.

Shucksmith, M. (1991) *Rural Disadvantage.* Report to COSLA, HIE, SE and Scottish Homes, COSLA, Edinburgh.

Shucksmith, M., Chapman, P., Clark, G., Black, S. and Conway, E. (1994) *Disadvantage in Rural Scotland: A Summary Report.* HMSO, Edinburgh.

Shucksmith, M., Chapman, P., Clark, G., Black, S. and Conway, E. (forthcoming) *Rural Scotland Today: The Best of Both Worlds?* HMSO, Edinburgh.

Townsend, P. (1979) *Poverty in the United Kingdom.* Penguin, Harmondsworth.

Townsend, P. (1987) Disadvantage. *Journal of Social Policy* **16**, 125–146.

Townsend, P. (1989) *Slipping Through the Net.* The Guardian, 6 December 1989.

[2]

ELSEVIER

Agricultural Economics 22 (2000) 185–197

AGRICULTURAL
ECONOMICS

www.elsevier.com/locate/agecon

Rural employment in industrialised countries [☆]

John Bryden[a,*], Ray Bollman[b]

[a]The Arkleton Centre, St. Mary's, Kings College, University of Aberdeen, Old Aberdeen, AB24 2UF Scotland, UK
[b]Statistics Canada, Ottawa, Ont., Canada, K1A OT6

Received 26 January 1999; received in revised form 12 October 1999; accepted 13 November 1999

Abstract

This paper assesses the recent changes in rural employment in the OECD countries, highlighting the growing role of employment in services and, in some cases, manufacturing activity. In many, but not all, rural areas the secular decline in agricultural employment has been more than counterbalanced by growing employment in these other sectors. However, the diversity of employment growth within and between rural areas is stressed, as are the implications of this diversity for policy. A range of explanations for the relative economic success of some rural areas is explored. These include the impacts of globalisation; restructuring of the labour market; new 'consumption' demands on the rural areas; and human mobility. The paper concludes that traditional theories do not explain the diversity of outcomes in rural areas. New approaches are needed. Recent analyses under the banner of 'the new economic geography' has advanced our understanding of the pre-conditions for rural development to occur, but understanding the diverse pattern of rural employment outcomes within the same kind of geography remains a challenge which needs to be addressed by inter-disciplinary approaches and methods. © 2000 Elsevier Science B.V. All rights reserved.

Keywords: Rural employment; Rural development; OECD countries

1. Introduction

This paper was inspired by a collection of papers which, as editors and contributors, we put together in a book, *Rural Employment: An International Perspective*, recently published by CAB International (Bollman and Bryden, 1997). The papers were presented at a conference held in the rural town of Coaticook, Quebec, in October 1995, and seven of the 30 chapters report comparative research undertaken within the OECD rural development programme. For the first time, albeit only for the OECD countries, a reasonably comprehensive body of comparable data analysing the trends and patterns in rural employment is available. This marks a considerable step forward from the usual focus on agricultural employment, and the generally gloomy prognostications about the impact of declining agricultural employment on rural economies.

Although we obviously acknowledge the work of our colleagues at the Coaticook conference and the benefit of the stimulating discussions there, we have

---

[☆] Based on a paper presented at the Rural Employment Symposium at the IAAE XXIII Conference, Sacramento, 10–16 August 1997.

[*] Corresponding author. Tel.: +44-1224-273-901; fax: +44-1224-273-902.

186   *J. Bryden, R. Bollman / Agricultural Economics 22 (2000) 185–197*

tried to go beyond the scope of the book and ask what explanations might underpin observed changes in rural employment.

1.1. The changing context for rural development

The attention given to rural development in OECD countries has steadily increased over the past decade, a period of considerable change at both global and European levels. Liberalisation and globalisation are driving global trade and capital movements and the global division of labour and significant market adjustments follow from this. Partly linked with these trends, major changes in policy frameworks affecting rural areas are occurring. These market and policy changes mean major challenges, as well as some new opportunities, for rural populations. The capacity of rural people to respond to potential opportunities and threats by creating new sources of income and employment to replace declining employment in agriculture, other primary industries, some services (e.g. banking, telecommunications, wholesaling) and manufacturing is a critical issue both for rural people and for policy makers and rural development agencies.

The evidence of the recent past in OECD countries is that some rural areas are 'better placed' than others to adapt to these processes of 'opening up' and the consequential exposure to external forces, although the causal factors are not obvious. Amongst the explanations of rural success we can find those focusing on factor endowments, factor prices, entrepreneurial capacities, good luck, 'social' capital, amenities, proximity to wealthy urban populations with increasing lifestyle demands on rural areas, etc.

Rural areas differ markedly in their economic structure and activity, their natural and human resources, the peripherality of their location (and hence market potential and transport costs), their demographic and social circumstances, in other words, their general 'initial conditions'. Therefore, they are affected in different ways, and to differing extents, by the external forces with which they interact. Policies and support structures for rural areas must increasingly recognise this diversity of conditions and outcomes. It follows that knowledge and understanding of the processes involved, and local responses to them, becomes a crucial element in the improvement of policy and local action.

Increasingly, rural areas are expected to develop their own analyses of their strengths, weaknesses, opportunities and threats, and evolve their own strategies and action plans to deal with them. This is a general tendency, caused by the lack of detailed knowledge and solutions at the 'centre' as well as by fiscal constraints. A critical question for local actors is the dual one: how can they best minimise adverse effects of globalisation and how can they best take advantage of new opportunities? A related question is what room for manoeuvre do they have in an era where the big levers often seem to be beyond their control?

2. Trends in rural employment

2.1. Introduction

In order to identify and analyse trends in rural development, the OECD established a territorial scheme in which 2000 regions, covering the entire territory of the OECD countries, are identified. These regions are grouped into three types according to their share of population living in rural communities:

- Predominantly rural regions: over 50%
- Significantly rural or 'intermediate' regions: 15–50%
- Predominantly urbanised regions: below 15%

By grouping regions in this way, each type of region contains some rural and some urban communities, although to different degrees (Meyer, 1997). It is this OECD classification which is used throughout this paper.

2.2. General trends

The declining relative importance of agriculture in rural areas is continuing largely due to adoption of new technology and the growth of other sectors. The OECD work on territorial indicators of rural employment showed that in only three OECD countries did agriculture account for over 25% of the labour force in predominantly rural regions in 1990. By contrast, industry accounted for more than 25% of employment in such regions in seventeen countries, whilst services accounted for more than 25% of employment in all of them, and over 50% in 18 (OECD, 1996, p. 46).

J. Bryden, R. Bollman / Agricultural Economics 22 (2000) 185–197   187

Table 1
Employment change in dynamic and lagging labour markets, Canada[a]

	Number of regions	Employment 1991 (%)	Employment change 1981–1991	
			Total 1981 = 100	Difference to national
National	266	100	116.5	0.0
Predominantly rural regions	209	30	114.1	−2.4
Dynamic	68	11	129.3	12.8
Lagging	141	19	107.0	−9.5
Significantly rural regions	38	23	126.0	9.5
Dynamic	21	14	138.6	22.1
Lagging	17	8	109.2	−7.3
Predominantly urban regions	19	47	113.9	−2.6
Dynamic	12	21	129.6	13.1
Lagging	7	26	104.0	−12.5

[a] Source: von Meyer (1997) Table 2.2.

The same OECD studies also showed that between 1980 and 1990 the rates of growth of employment in predominantly rural regions exceeded those in predominantly urbanised regions in three of the 15 countries for which data was available (Huillet, 1997, p. 342). More recent work which disaggregates these rural regions shows clearly that even amongst the most 'rural' types of rural region, some have experienced growing employment whilst others have experienced declining employment (and sometimes population). For example, Cunningham and Bollman (1997) show that 'there is a wide variation in employment growth among the different regions of Canada, *independent of their degree of rurality*', with rates of employment growth in predominantly rural regions ranging from −20 to 70% (p. 57). Schindegger and Krajasits (1997) show a similar pattern of growth in Austria, where rates of employment growth range from −19 to 14% in the rural regions (p. 174). Table 1 summarises the data for Canada, which is not atypical.

Although this evidence is both surprising and encouraging, two caveats are required. First, it remains true in most countries that employment has grown faster in predominantly urban regions than in predominately rural regions, and that, in general, it is the significantly rural regions which have experienced the most rapid employment growth. In the rural regions only the urban communities are growing — rural communities are losing both population and employment. According to Irmen (1997)

"rural communities within predominantly rural regions are the losers in spatial development ...

These rural communities lose population and employment, whereas the rural communities in other types of regions (predominantly urban and intermediate) gain in national importance" (p. 28).

In urbanised regions, 'rural' communities are growing because they are situated in an urbanising environment and benefit from it. Second, there has also been a continuing employment deficit in many rural areas of the richer countries — reflected in a net commuting balance with urban areas. Rural areas often continue to be net suppliers of labour to urban areas (Schindegger and Krajasits, 1997, p. 168).

Other labour market changes worth briefly commenting on include: a fall in annual hours worked per person; an increase in self-employment and part-time work especially among women; a rise in long-term and youth unemployment; and the feminisation of the labour force — women are playing an ever larger role in the labour force. Although general trends, they are also evident in rural areas.

The main points to note at this stage are:

1. We cannot generalise about the development or growth experience of rural regions. We cannot assume that they will inevitably experience declining employment and population — the evidence is that some will prosper and others will even grow faster than the fastest growing urban region. Peripheries are not doomed to be perpetually lagging areas in economic terms, nor are centres destined to be perpetually in the lead.
2. Differential outcomes within broad regions are not

188   *J. Bryden, R. Bollman / Agricultural Economics 22 (2000) 185–197*

generally attributable to policy differences — in many cases the same policy regime produces very different outcomes in different localities — real processes of economic, technical and social change are involved which are often independent of policy or even in spite of policy (for example, in the EU the growth of farm household pluriactivity in the 1980s was not encouraged by policy). That is not to say that policy changes and implementation are insignificant factors, especially when they are coherently combined with market and community forces and are flexible enough to cope with varied rural conditions.

3. Some rural areas demonstrate considerable capacity to adapt to rapidly changing external conditions, despite well-known handicaps.
4. At least in terms of direct employment, rural people now work in the manufacturing and the service sectors in almost all of the EU. However, some areas may 'depend' on agriculture (the major export base) even though few are directly employed in it.

In Europe, restructuring is occurring in agriculture, agri-food and food retailing and distribution sectors. There is also a general shift to a service-based economy in which the information and knowledge based industries play an increasing role. Linked with this is a de-materialisation of production (i.e. any good one buys has a higher 'services' component than in earlier decades), a de-linking of economic growth from consumption of raw materials, a dissociation of financial sphere from the 'real economy', and an internationalisation of savings-investment flows and of relations in commercial and knowledge spheres. Although many of these are not new features of rural economies (for example, rural areas have always been open to savings/investment flows to cities), new elements concern the globalisation of these flows, the reduced power of regions and nation states to influence them and the intensifying internationalisation of relations in commercial and knowledge spheres which both threatens many local commercial and knowledge based activities and provides them with new (non-local) opportunities.

De-materialised production (in the sense that consumer demand is shifting from goods consumption to services consumption) in the form of tourism and recreational industries have been particularly important in the richer countries and much of this is based on new 'consumption' uses of the countryside. However, this is not to argue that production activities do not remain important both in terms of their economic significance and in terms of perceptions of rural people.

2.3. There is a steady and long term decline in agricultural employment

The long term and generalised decline in agricultural employment is well documented. In the 1980s annual rates of decline were between 3 and 4% in Japan, Finland, and Austria. In the EU, agricultural employment has declined by around 2–3% per annum over the past decade (Post and Terluin, 1997, p. 310). In 1990, agricultural employment was less than 10% of total employment in all EU countries except Greece (23%), Portugal (20%), Ireland (15%) and Spain (11%) (op. cit., p. 308). Furthermore, in all countries the extent of agricultural employment is exaggerated because the figures include pluriactive farmers and farm families for whom agriculture may provide but a small portion of household income. In the EU-12, a sample of 7000 farm households indicated that just under half of all farm households earned more than half of their household income from agriculture in 1987 (Bryden et al., 1994). Nevertheless, it is clear from differential productivity data that there is still considerable room for further labour savings in agriculture even without major reforms to the CAP. Moreover, in the 10 Central and Eastern European Countries (CEECs) which have applied to join the EU, a quarter of the labour force is still engaged in agriculture (9.5 million people) generating only 8% of GDP: if the CEECs approach the average productivity of the present EU-15, then about 3 million people would leave agriculture over a period of years. It is not beyond the bounds of possibility, based on past experience, that in East, West and Central Europe as a whole more than 6 million people could leave agriculture in the next decade.

The purpose of stating this is to raise the question, if not in farming, where are the jobs in rural areas going to come from; and how might policy best assist in the process of change?

J. Bryden, R. Bollman / Agricultural Economics 22 (2000) 185–197   189

Table 2
Employment in tourism compared to agriculture as percentage of total employment, 1990[a]

Country	Employment in tourism (%)			Employment in agriculture (%)		
	P.R.[b]	S.R[c]	All[d]	P.R.	S.R.	All
Germany	5.2	4.4	4.0	1.5	1.5	1.0
Austria	17.7	21.0	21.8	13.3	4.1	6.2
Canada	9.3	9.3	9.7	10.9	3.3	4.6
US	10.5	11.3	11.2	5.9	2.4	3.3
Finland	11.0	4.2	8.3	16.0	5.3	8.5
France	6.5	7.4	7.9	10.8	5.5	5.7
UK	9.8	4.9	8.3	10.3	4.2	2.4
Switzerland	18.7	11.7	14.9	9.5	6.3	4.1

[a] Source: OECD, 1996.
[b] Predominantly rural regions.
[c] Significantly rural regions.
[d] All regions.

2.4. Employment in rural tourism has been increasing

In several OECD countries, employment in tourism exceeds that in agriculture in all types of region. This is the case in the predominantly rural regions of Austria, US, Germany and Switzerland (see Table 2). Moreover, tourism employment has been growing in all types of rural region (with the exception of Finland) throughout the 1980s; annual growth rates of 3% or higher were recorded in Germany, Spain and Switzerland (Bontron and Lasnier, 1997, p. 436).

2.5. Mixed experience with other services

In all OECD countries employment in services has been growing. This trend is reflected in the predominantly rural regions where most employment growth during the 1980s was due to net increases in the service sector (Meyer, 1997). In all rural regions the growth of most services parallels that at national levels. The main exception is business services (including knowledge and information based services); this tends to be the high value-added, high-wage element of the service sector, and is heavily under-represented in rural areas (Cunningham and Bollman, 1997). Some observers expect such services to dominate all employment after 2000; for example, projections in Finland in 1995 suggested that by the year 2000, 93% of all work would be 'information work' (Bryden, 1997 p. 448). However, questions remain about the linkages between this type of work with other sectors, and about its precise definition.

Public services, including education, health and public administration, are important employers in many rural areas. These sectors grew rapidly during the 1980s, but that growth appears to have been curtailed or even reversed in many regions in the 1990s. Employment trends in other consumer services, especially retailing and personal services, tend to be linked to population levels and changes.

A critical question is whether rural areas can participate in the growth in employment in services. In principal this should be facilitated by the rapidly increasing access to, and significant cost reductions in, digital telecommunications, linked in turn to the 'Information Highway'. However, evidence on the adoption of these technologies by rural actors, and especially of the content and impacts of their use, is rather scarce. Bryden (1997) identifies a number of cases where investment in Information and Communications Technology (ICT) has created employment opportunities in rural areas. The emphasis is placed upon *opportunities* rather than job creation per se as it is the impact of ICT on the competitiveness of rural enterprises in general and the impacts on employment of ICT adoption and use which is important for the future of rural areas. A main point seems to be that significant employment losses as well as gains can be linked to ICT and, at least in some cases, gains may exceed losses. Public policies at both national and local levels can make a difference to the direction of these net effects. For example, the intervention of the Highlands and Islands Development Board (HIDB) and later the Highlands and Islands Enterprise (which succeeded HIDB) in investments in digitalising the telecom network, and targeting new types of enterprise which could utilise the network, appears to have had positive impacts (see Sproull et al., 1996). This supports evidence of profitable relocation of telecommunications-intensive enterprises in rural America (Salant and Marx, 1995).

3. Explanations of rural employment changes

The changes in rural employment in OECD countries are of more than passing interest. They are the opposite of what was expected, if not in terms of agricultural employment, then certainly in terms of growth in manufacturing and services employment in many areas. Moreover, there has been a surprising variability in outcomes. They are not consistent with the predictions of core-periphery models or, indeed, neo-classical models, of development dynamics. The 'New Economic Geography' models have generated scenarios where rural development will take place (Krugman, 1993, 1999; Kilkenny, 1993, 1998, 1999) but the problematique remains — how to explain differential economic performance among rural localities with similar features of geography, settlement and peripherality with respect to metropoles. Although Kilkenny's recent work in particular opens up important new questions, new information, and theory, is needed to explain the loss of competitive advantage in some rural areas, and its accretion in others.

Some of the key explanatory chapters in the book deal with issues such as education levels, niche markets, networks and lifestyle choices as a means of exploring the differential performance of rural regions. In many cases, the findings are similar and point to the need to view rural employment changes both within a set of global and national changes, commonly termed 'restructuring', which have specific rural impacts and with reference to micro-regional characteristics. For example, in their work McGranahan and Kassel (1997) conclude that, despite the long standing emphasis put upon workforce education as a key to economic advancement, high regional education levels offer a limited advantage. Economic development may be just as dependent upon local circumstances such as proximity to industrial districts or expanding urban centres, favourable climate and amenities as local education levels. Through examining lifestyle choices and rural job creation, Persson et al. (1997) identify three factors which lead to increasing differentiation: internationalization and organization of economic activity; diversity of lifestyles and mobility patterns among people; and policy formation and practices (p. 146).

Basically there are three main groups of explanations of rural employment change. The first group relates to the impacts of globalisation and restructuring, and the second to new 'consumption' functions of the countryside in the richer countries. These two groups both relate to external demand forces. The third group of factors is the local 'swift-footedness' (either public or private entrepreneurship) in some communities that is not well understood or measured. Clemenson and Lane (1997) identify the establishment of niche markets as a means of exploiting the potential benefits of each of these groups. Niche markets can both respond to the external demand forces, encouraging a re-examination of the opportunities offered by any one locality and utilise local entrepreneurship to create a successful marketing strategy.

3.1. Impacts of globalisation

Although the internationalisation of economic activity has been occurring for centuries, globalisation[1] is a recent phenomenon which has intensified during the 1980s and '90s. Whereas internationalisation refers mainly to trade in goods and services the production of which was organised within national economies, globalisation involves 'functional integration between internationally dispersed economic activities' (Dicken, 1992). Although much attention has been paid to the globalisation of manufacturing activities, it is evident that globalisation has also occurred in important business services such as banking, insurance, advertising and communications.

Globalisation is marked in part by the reduction of the cost of space due to the reduction in the cost of transportation and communication. Before the onset of globalisation, high transportation and communication costs protected some rural workers from competition, and similarly were protected from competing in metropolitan markets by the same high costs. New technology has caused significant reductions in the costs of transportation and communication. Although technological change is not new, it is the focus on transportation and communications that makes globalisation impact significantly on rural areas.

While internationalisation was greatly boosted in the late 19th century by the development of transport technology (steam ships, railways, refrigeration), globalisation has been facilitated by the reduction in

---

[1] This section draws in part on Chapter 1 in Bor et al. (1997).

J. Bryden, R. Bollman/Agricultural Economics 22 (2000) 185–197 191

average tariffs and other trade barriers after the Second World War[2], by the development of ICT, and linked with the growth in trans-national corporations (TNCs). These changes mean that capital can, in principle at least, be assembled wherever the costs of production are the lowest and where social and environmental restrictions are least. The component parts of a product (or service) can increasingly be manufactured in different international locations and assembled at one spot, either through the growth in TNCs or by outsourcing and 'just-in-time' techniques of the new production system and forms of 'flexible specialisation' (Piore and Sabel, 1984). Although such economic links are established and maintained in many and various ways, the essential features of global economic restructuring are considered to be its 'post-Fordist' nature, flexibilisation, and the international scale of the production and manufacturing processes (Gertler, 1988; Bernat, 1993; Cappellin, 1994).

A second and to some extent related feature of economic life today is the rapidity of change and associated turbulence and uncertainty, although western Europe has gone for more than 50 years without a major war. Sources of turbulence and uncertainty include the separation of the 'real economy' from the 'symbol economy' of international financial flows and transactions[3]; the dramatic changes in the USSR and Eastern Europe which have altered the nature of European space; political instability in the Middle East and Africa; changes in the global environment linked to atmospheric pollution and the 'greenhouse effect'; and continuing trade disputes (Dicken, 1992).

---

[2] In 1940, the average tariff (taxes levied on imports) on goods was about 40%; after the GATT Uruguay round of trade talks (1986–92) it was about 5%. There has at the same time been a growth in non-tariff barriers to trade such as quotas, import licences, and various regulatory devices.

[3] According to Drucker (1986) both visible (goods) and invisible (services) trade are much larger than ever before — US$ 2.5 to US$ 3 trillion a year 'But the London Eurodollar market .... Turns over US$ 300 billion each working day, or US$ 75 trillion a year, a volume at least 25 times that of world trade. In addition there are the foreign exchange transactions in the world's main money centres, in which one currency is traded against another. These run at around US$ 150 billion a day ... 12 times the world-wide trade in goods and services'.

3.2. Why does globalisation matter for rural areas and people?

Why does this matter for rural areas? First and foremost because it has implications for employment and enterprise. Because capital is increasingly mobile internationally, while labour remains relatively immobile and tied to place, at least two tendencies can be observed. First of all, there is downward pressure on real wage rates, especially in low-skill segments of the economy which tend to be over-represented in rural areas. Secondly, there is a relative shortage of investment capital in high cost producing countries and regions which are unable to maintain their competitive edge internationally. Thus, some rural areas are increasingly being seen as sources of labour; labour that is low cost, reliable and unorganised (Glasmeier, 1993), whilst some industrial labour markets such as those concentrated in early industrialised regions are being by-passed by the current processes of production (Urry, 1984).

The processes of globalisation and restructuring have impacted on almost all areas of economic life, public and private, and are generally recognised in the downsizing, re-structuring and rationalisation of businesses, institutions and organisations in recent years — and changing labour market conditions have followed from this.

3.3. Restructuring of the labour market

The restructuring of the labour market has had common effects in most industrial nations, although the impact on rural areas has been differentiated by greater dependence on fishing, forestry, mining or agriculture and the degree to which capital had already penetrated the local economy. Common elements include the rise of unemployment and the changing nature of work (Pahl, 1984). An increasing number of jobs are contract-based, short-term, and casual, such that an increasing proportion of the workforce has two or more income-earning activities that are part-time and provide limited social benefits. As heavy industry declines and information-based activities expand, the nature of work is changing, with a distinct rise in employment opportunities in the service sector, even in rural areas, and a decline in manual labour. Despite this, manufacturing is still important in terms of local employment. Much deskilling has taken place and

192   *J. Bryden, R. Bollman / Agricultural Economics 22 (2000) 185-197*

where reskilling has occurred it has been selective and particular to favoured locations (Newby, 1987). In this massive shift in labour market structures the participation of women has generally increased which, together with the growth of feminism, has contributed to an important shift in gender relations and household maintenance (Barthez, 1982; Whatmore, 1990). For most aspects of labour market change, there is an equivalent effect in rural areas.

3.4. The changing role of the state

Globalisation is also changing the role of the nation State. National borders are less relevant in a world of international finance and global liberalisation of trade, the laws of which are determined collectively at the international level rather than by single countries. Governments are increasingly called upon to ensure participation in world affairs by upgrading communications and transportation infrastructures, agreeing to international environmental accords and programs, and reconciling legal and technical difficulties between trading partners. The pressure to remain 'competitive' in the global economy has led to pressure to reduce taxes and other burdens on the corporate sector, and new demands for increased human capital investment. Governments appear to be shifting some of their responsibilities while shedding others, in an effort to balance the budget in a time of fiscal crisis (OECD, 1993). The ageing of the population and high levels of unemployment have added to pressures on public budgets in many OECD countries. Common responses involve the restructuring of defence, social welfare, health and education, as well as efforts to move away from granting permanent subsidies to declining sectors (agriculture, heavy industry) towards an 'investment approach' through which people, sectors and regions can be assisted to improve their competitive position. The role of governments is increasingly to facilitate development rather than to direct it, to collaborate with other nations for trade purposes, and to initiate partnerships with local groups, including local government and private enterprise, to stimulate economic development that is locally driven and cost-shared. The scope for centralised, uniform policies and rural development measures is limited. Rural community development can no longer (if it ever could) be produced as a standardised item of mass

production. Policy must be flexible to complement and stimulate local capacities and entrepreneurship.

3.5. The pervasive impacts of globalisation and restructuring

Changes due to globalisation and economic restructuring, either causal or responsive, are evident in all sectors of the economy and in most walks of life. Most corporations, institutions, state bodies, and non-governmental organisations are being restructured in some way. Both the rapidity of change and its unpredictability and complexity lead to turbulence and uncertainty. We do not know whether to consider global restructuring in all its manifestations as a disjunctive or a quantum leap in the progress of capitalism (Drucker, 1986; Campanella, 1990). Some contemporary philosophers liken it to romanticism, a stage in communal life which integrates both traditional values and progress (Hall and Jarvie, 1992). To Giddens (1991) globalisation is a form of advanced modernism, while others, such as Gellner, suggest that it may be post-modern (Gellner, 1988; Harvey, 1989). Whatever one's view of the nature and significance of global restructuring, it comprises a set of external factors which seem likely to go on influencing developments in rural areas and opportunities for rural people for some time to come.

3.6. Summary of globalisation impacts

The most important general impacts of globalisation can therefore be summarised briefly as:

- the impact on employment and work;
- the shrinking of distance through lower costs, and increasing efficiency, of transfer and communications, counterbalanced by increased consciousness of cultural groups and communities[4];

---

[4] Robertson (1992) refers to this aspect of globalisation as both the compression of the world and the intensification of consciousness of the world as a whole,' but points out that globalisation is not simply a world of converging societies. Accelerated globalisation is counterbalanced by increased consciousness of cultural groups and communities, which is one of the main contradictions of restructuring. The notion of 'global culture' advanced by Featherstone (1990) involves increased global consciousness, heightened awareness of the individuality of culture groups, reflecting the notion of the 'global village' forecast by McLuhan and advanced by Sachs (1993) as 'cosmopolitan localism'.

J. Bryden, R. Bollman / Agricultural Economics 22 (2000) 185–197 193

- the changing role of the nation state;
- the new role for communities and localities;
- the stress on competitiveness and 'flexibilisation' as main features of entrepreneurial and policy responses.

3.7. Rural impacts of globalisation

Particular impacts of globalisation on people in rural and peripheral areas include:

- global movements of capital and finance, leading to a shortage of external investment capital;
- the decline in agricultural employment and in the relative economic importance of food production, accompanied by structural changes in the farming industry;
- increasingly global penetration of local markets and increased opportunity for local producers to penetrate global (niche) markets, exposure to increased competition, and the related restructuring of capitalism;
- growing inter-dependence between areas and activities which are physically distant from each other;
- increasing efforts to internationalise the terms under which trade takes place, and remove economic and other barriers to trade, including most notably agricultural production subsidies, for example through the GATT and now the WTO;
- the standardisation of many (mass market) products, harmonisation of regulations and standards (ISO 9000 etc.), lowering of trade barriers;
- the introduction and spread of new technologies, especially ICT and biotechnology;
- global cultural flows (e.g. through mass media), evident in mass consumer products;
- demographic changes including increased personal mobility;
- a new international division of labour in which many unskilled jobs and associated production are moving to the Newly Industrialised Countries.

It is not so much the nature of globalisation forces driving change or their general consequences which distinguishes rural from urban areas, but rather the specific forms which these forces take in areas we perceive as 'rural'. We focus on them because rural areas have become progressively less self-sufficient and self-contained, and ever more open to the wider forces (economic, social, political) shaping European and global development.

3.8. Public goods and new demands on the countryside

A second major explanatory factor for rural employment changes is the emergence of new perceptions of the countryside in rich countries with a high population density (e.g. northern European countries), and the emergence of new uses and functions which are linked to these new perceptions.

The economy is comprised of both private (market) and public (non-market) goods and services. For example, food products and pharmaceuticals are private goods of the agricultural sector while pleasant landscapes, clean water (also now a private good) and air, biodiversity and culture are all public goods. Public goods are those which cannot be directly traded as it is difficult or impossible to exclude non-payers from their benefits. However, a further feature concerns the important of public perception of 'rurality' and the social construction of the countryside in general — Newby's 'village in the mind'.

In many cases public goods are critical resources in creating indirect trading activities, for example, they underpin the development of tourism and recreation, and the perceived desirability of rural living. They are also vital for human welfare in both rural and urban areas. The fact that public goods such as a pristine environment or beautiful landscape cannot be traded directly creates the difficulty of valuing tradable versus non-tradable goods which, in the end, places heavy demands on political processes. If a good cannot be traded, should it be protected or preserved merely as a natural amenity? Since non-tradable goods cannot be de-localised, how important are they in (indirectly) establishing local competitive advantages? Who should pay for their maintenance and enhancement, and how should it be financed?

Because of the strong link between public goods and new urban consumption demands on rural space in richer regions/countries with high population densities, they are a vital influence on both the nature and extent of new rural economic activities. For example, urban consumers increasingly see rural areas as important for rest and recreation, for fresh air and clean water, as offering lifestyles with advantages over those in urban areas, as having cheaper and more spacious housing, with positive features of culture and heritage which are worth preserving, and so on. Thus, public goods have an increasingly important influence on the relative competitiveness of different rural areas and offer scope for local action in a range of diversified economic, social, cultural and environmental activities.

3.9. Human mobility

Movements of people are a key aspect of rural change and development. In-migration, out-migration, retirement, the retention or loss of young people, the return of diaspora, commuting, recreation and tourism are all dimensions of this movement. So too are issues of personal and public transport, the location of services (increasingly centralised), the location of employment and housing need, provision and cost. Both out-migration and in-migration have consequences for local people, local societies, local economies, local politics and local cultures. In-migration can offer both threats and opportunities.

The movement of people (and indeed enterprises) into rural areas is not only determined by the availability of work and other economic opportunities, but also by the new values placed on rural space — clean environment, community life, space for leisure, pleasant landscapes, healthy 'lifestyles', rural culture, etc., as well as, in some cases, availability of redundant buildings and lower cost housing.

Previous studies have indicated two types of migration from urban to rural areas: job related migration and residential migration. Much of the literature on urban to rural migration has assumed that these two types of migration are closely related and that occupational change implies a change in residence. Blanc and Tahar (1997) suggest that there are different factors influencing job related and residential migration and the two types of migration should be looked at separately. Drawing on a 1985 INSEE survey, they assess the relationship between occupational and residential migration and indicate that the two types of migration are not interrelated. The analysis suggests a one-way correlation between occupational and residential mobility: i.e. although occupational mobility influences residential mobility, the reverse is unlikely to be true.

Lower population densities in rural areas mean that it is difficult for people moving to a new location to find work and people starting a new job to find housing. However, the rural housing market is in general easier to access than the rural labour market. Three reasons are given for this:

- building one's own house is easier than creating a paid job for oneself;
- vacant houses are not uncommon in the countryside after the long period of rural exodus;
- a person's skills are more specific than housing preferences, and finding a match when there is a shortage is easier on the real estate market than on the job market.

This argument is substantiated by Persson et al. (1997) who focus on the decreasing influence of rural employment availability on individuals' decisions to move to rural areas. They suggest that lifestyle choices are increasingly important in maintaining rural populations, both in encouraging people to move to rural areas and in creating jobs in the area in which they live. A survey of in-migrants in rural Sweden illustrated that employment was not the main reason for their move, and reasons such as moving back to their roots, searching for a sense of community and a non-metropolitan lifestyle were identified. A survey in southern Canada indicated a large proportion of families having diversified their sources of income to maintain particular lifestyle choices such as taking holidays, to benefit children or to sustain family consumption patterns.

Persson et al. use the concept of the 'Arena Society' to illustrate the diverse nature of rural labour markets, the increasing importance of lifestyles in rural areas, and the supply of entrepreneurs able to work at home, provide business, education and health services. They also develop the concept of 'reach' — broadly defined as 'the capacity to compromise the surrounding world in one's sphere of influence' (p. 155). For example, *physical reach* in the form of links with larger population centres is important in rural development, but also important are the dimensions of social reach, time reach, knowledge reach and economic reach in understanding the differences between rural households, and the effects of new technologies. In essence, this concept highlights the importance of different kinds of 'networks' in transcending the boundaries of local space and local markets.

J. Bryden, R. Bollman/Agricultural Economics 22 (2000) 185-197 195

Contemporary lifestyles are influenced by global trends and the pluralistic characteristics of 'footloose' labour markets. Persson et al. make the point that more individualistic lifestyles are developed through a better educated workforce and the emergence of knowledge and information based small production units with flexible working conditions. It is increasingly possible to make choices about where to live and work based on considerations other than just employment opportunities. They predict that the search for quality of life will have a significant impact on settlement patterns.

Persson et al. go on to suggest that the place given to employment creation in rural planning is of less importance today, and that planning at local level is the most appropriate way to assist rural communities to develop their own advantages. 'Public policy should pay as much attention to micro-regional character as is paid to expensive job-creation programmes' (op. cit. p.161).

Errington (1997) also observes that opportunities for rural employment are no longer the essential mandate in keeping populations in rural areas. The concern of policy in rural areas to counteract depopulation has to a certain extent been superseded by a growing outflux of populations from urban to rural areas. However, Errington argues that there is still a case for government intervention in rural employment because of the contribution that local employment opportunities make to achieving balanced (i.e. sustainable) rural communities. He illustrates this point through his study of the village of Lambourn in Berkshire, England, focusing attention on the extent of car use in and around the village. Errington's survey indicated that levels of car ownership were similar for those who worked in the village and those who commuted, but the weekly distance travelled by commuters was two and a half times greater than those who worked in the village. He suggests that more local employment opportunities would reduce the environmental and social costs of commuting, thereby contributing to a more sustainable rural society. This is, of course, an intermediate rural area, close to the southeast England metropolitan area.

Other elements explaining employment changes include:

- neo-classical arguments relating to factor prices;

- impacts of new technology (distance-shrinking effects);
- human capital (not just education, but also lower labour force turnover, loyalty etc.);
- 'social capital' (Putnam, 1993), including institutional effectiveness and propensity of local actors to co-operate;
- flexible networks, linked to previous co-operative structures in agriculture (Piore and Sabel, 1984; Zacchia, 1986; Beccatini, 1990).

The scope for local actors to encourage activities based on these factors is largely beyond the scope of this paper. However, it is clearly influenced by a set of less 'tangible' resources or capacities which may be more, or less, present in local societies. They include effective 'governance' and propensities of local actors in private, public and voluntary spheres to co-operate, as well as material conditions, influence over other 'public goods', resource markets such as those for land and minerals, labour and knowledge, as well as a range of networks and the relationship between these and communications infrastructure. This suggests a new field for cross-disciplinary research which can penetrate the reasons for wide differences between the medium and long term performance of rural localities in similar policy and geographical locations. These issues are further explored in Dawe and Bryden (1999) and Bryden and Dawe (1998).

4. Conclusion

There are many different forces at work leading to a restructuring of rural economy, society and labour markets. What is surprising in a sense is the consistency of many rural employment changes — the inexorable decline in agricultural employment, the increase in services employment, especially that linked to tourism and recreation — and their coherence with changes in urban labour markets (feminisation, shift to part-time and casual work etc.). However, it is clear that rural labour markets are still biased by low-skill, low paid work, that they face tremendous potential changes as the growth in knowledge and information work begins to dominate the labour market, and that new technology and its creative use in rural contexts, as well as human resource development and attention to less 'tangible' resources including 'social capital' in its various guises will be very important in future transformations.

Existing theories, either of the neo-classical or core-periphery school, are of little help in terms of understanding differential economic performance between rural areas, even those in geographical peripheries. They do not account for the differential performance within such peripheries, nor do they consider important aspects of social or environmental capital or the new 'consumption' demand on rural space. We suggest that a new field of cross-disciplinary research is opened up, dealing with the multi-faceted factors which appear important for such explanations. In developing new methods for examining the phenomenon of differential performance between rural areas, more attention needs to be paid to the residual term (R) in the production function. An unpacking of 'R' necessarily involves paying attention to less 'tangible' and hence less easily measurable factors such as institutional performance and culture, and thus implies the need for inter-disciplinary approaches and methods.

Acknowledgements

The authors are grateful for comments at the IAAE Symposium and especially to Albert Valdez and Alan de Janvry. Jackie Cornish is also gratefully acknowledged for her editing assistance in preparing this paper for publication. Two anonymous referees also provided helpful comments.

References

Barthez, A., 1982. Famille, Travail et Agriculture. Economica, Paris.

Beccatini, G., 1990. In: Pyke, F., Beccatini, G., Sengenberger, W. (Eds.), The Marshallian Industrial District as a Socio-Economic Notion. Industrial Districts and Inter-firm Co-operation in Italy, ILO, Geneva.

Bernat, A.G., 1993. Manufacturing restructuring in nonmetropolitan U.S. In: Fuller, A.M., Rounds, R.C. (Eds.), Stimulating Rural Economies for the 2000's: the Challenge for Rural Manufacturing and Tradeable Services. Proceedings of the 4th Annual ARRG Conference, Goderich, Ontario. ARRG Working Paper Series No. 4, Rural Development Institute, Brandon University, MB, pp. 35–41.

Blanc, M., Tahar, G., 1997. The relationships between occupational and residential urban-to-rural migration. In: Bollman, R.D., Bryden, J.M. (Eds.), Rural Employment: An International Perspective, CAB International, Wallingford, pp. 177–192.

Bollman, R.D., Bryden, J.M. (Eds.), 1997. Rural Employment: an International Perspective. CAB International, Wallingford.

Bontron, J., Lasnier, N., 1997. Tourism: a potential source of rural employment. In: Bollman, R.D., Bryden, J.M. (Eds.), Rural Employment: an International Perspective, CAB International, Wallingford, pp. 427–446.

Bor, van den W., Bryden, J.M., Fuller, A.M., 1997. Rethinking Rural Human Resource Management: the Impact of Globalisation and Rural Restructuring on Rural Education and Training in Western Europe. ManSholt Studies 10, Wageningen Agricultural University, The Netherlands.

Bryden, J., 1997. Rural employment and the information highway. In: Bollman, R.D., Bryden, J.M. (Eds.), Rural Employment: an International Perspective, CAB International, Wallingford, pp. 447–459.

Bryden, J.M., Dawe, S.P., 1998. Development strategies for remote rural regions: what do we know so far? OECD International Conference on Remote Rural Areas - Developing Through Natural and Cultural Assets, Albarracín, Spain, 5–6 November 1998.

Bryden, J.M., Bell, C., Gilliatt, J., Hawkins, E., MacKinnon, N., 1994. Farm household adjustment in Western Europe 1987–91. Final Report of the Research Programme: Rural Change in Europe, Farm Structures and Household Pluriactivity, European Commission.

Campanella, M.L., 1990. Globalization: process and interpretations. World Futures 30, 1–16.

Cappellin, R., 1994. The internationalization of regional economies and the role of interregional cooperation in Europe: changing spatial advantages of rural areas. In: Reid, J.N., Mazie, S.M. (Eds.), Conceptual Frameworks for Understanding Rural Development: an International Dialogue, The Aspen Institute, Queenstown, Maryland, pp. 105–118.

Clemenson, H.A., Lane, B., 1997. Niche markets, niche marketing and rural employment. In: Bollman, R.D., Bryden, J.M. (Eds.), Rural Employment: an International Perspective, CAB International, Wallingford, pp. 410–426.

Cunningham, R., Bollman, R.D., 1997. Structure and trends of rural employment: Canada in the context of OECD countries. In: Bollman, R.D., Bryden, J.M. (Eds.), Rural Employment: an International Perspective, CAB International, Wallingford, pp. 36–58.

Dawe, S., Bryden, J., 1999. Competitive advantage in the rural periphery: re-defining the global-local nexus. In Lithwick, H and Gradws, Y. (1999). Urban Development in Frontier Regions Kluwer Academic Publishers. The Netherlands.

Dicken, P., 1992. Society and Nature. Temple University Press, Philadelphia.

Drucker, P.F., 1986. The Changed World Economy. Foreign Affairs, March, pp. 768–791.

Errington, A., 1997. The vitality of small and medium enterprises (smes) in rural Québec. In: Bollman, R.D., Bryden, J.M. (Eds.), Rural Employment: an International Perspective, CAB International, Wallingford, pp. 255–266.

Featherstone, M. (Ed.), 1990. Global Culture: Nationalism, Globalization and Modernity. Sage, London.

Gellner, E., 1988. Plough, Sword and Book: The Structure of Human History. Collins Harvill, London.

Gertler, M.S., 1988. The limits to flexibility: comments on the post-fordist vision of production and its geography. Trans. Inst. Brit. Geog. 13, 419–432.

Giddens, A., 1991. Modernity and Self-Identity. Polity Press, Cambridge.

Glasmeier, A., 1993. Global stakes: peripheral regions in an era of globalization. In: Fuller, A.M., Rounds, R.C. (Eds.), Stimulating Rural Economies for the 2000's: the Challenge for Rural Manufacturing and Tradeable Services. Proceedings of the 4th Annual ARRG Conference, Goderich, Ontario. ARRG Working Paper Series No. 4, Rural Development Institute, Brandon University, MB, pp. 51–57.

Hall, J.A., Jarvie, I.C. (Eds.), 1992. Transition to Modernity. Cambridge University Press, Cambridge.

Harvey, D., 1989. The Condition of Postmodernity. Blackwell, Oxford.

Huillet, C., 1997. Trends in rural policy: the employment issue. In: Bollman, R.D., Bryden, J.M. (Eds.), Rural Employment: an International Perspective, CAB International, Wallingford, pp. 338–345.

Irmen, E., 1997. Employment and population dynamics in OECD countries: an intraregional approach. In: Bollman, R.D., Bryden, J.M. (Eds.), Rural Employment: an International Perspective, CAB International, Wallingford, pp. 22–35.

Kilkenny, M., 1993. Rural/urban effects of terminating farm subsidies. Am. J. Agric. Econ. 75, 968–980.

Kilkenny, M., 1998. Transport costs and rural development. J. Regional Sci. 38(2), 293–312.

Kilkenny, M., 1999. Explicitly spatial rural-urban computable general equilibrium. Am. J. Agric. Econ. 81, 647–652.

Krugman, P., 1993. First nature, second nature and metropolitan location. J. Regional Sci. 33(2), 129–144.

Krugman, P., 1999. The role of geography in development. Int. Regional Sci. Rev. 22(2), 142–161.

McGranahan, D.A., Kassel, K., 1997. Education and regional employment in the 1980s: comparisons among OECD member countries. In: Bollman, R.D., Bryden, J.M. (Eds.), Rural Employment: an International Perspective, CAB International, Wallingford, pp. 74–84.

Meyer, von, H., 1997. Rural employment in OECD countries: structure and dynamics of regional labour markets. In: Bollman, R.D., Bryden, J.M. (Eds.), Rural Employment: an International Perspective, CAB International, Wallingford, pp. 3–21.

Newby, H., 1987. Economic restructuring and rural labour markets in Europe: current policy options. In: Summers, G.F. (Ed.), Agriculture and Beyond: Rural Economic Development, Proceedings of Seminar, University of Wisconsin-Madison, pp. 41–54.

OECD, 1993. Creating Rural Indicators - Framework, Figures, Findings. C/RUR/(93) 11. OECD, Paris.

OECD, 1996. Territorial Indicators of Employment: Focusing on Rural Development. OECD, Paris.

Pahl, R.E., 1984. Divisions of Labour. Basil Blackwell, Oxford.

Persson, L.O., Westholm, E., Fuller, T., 1997. Two contexts, one outcome: the importance of lifestyle choice in creating rural jobs in Canada and Sweden. In: Bollman, R.D., Bryden, J.M. (Eds.), Rural Employment: an International Perspective. CAB International, Wallingford, pp. 136–163.

Piore, M.J., Sabel, C.F., 1984. The Second Industrial Divide: Possibilities for Prosperity. Basic Books, New York.

Post, J., Terluin, I., 1997. The changing role of agriculture in rural employment. In: Bollman, R.D., Bryden, J.M. (Eds.), Rural Employment: an International Perspective, CAB International, Wallingford, pp. 305–326.

Putnam, R.D., 1993. Making Democracy Work: Civic Traditions in Modern Italy. Princeton University Press, Princeton, NJ.

Robertson, R., 1992. Globalization: Social Theory and Global Culture. Sage, London.

Sachs, W., 1993. Global Ecology: a New Arena of Political Conflict. Zed Books, London.

Salant, P., Marx, J., 1995. Shifting Tides: Trends and Opportunities in Rural Development. Northwest Report, 2/95. The Aspen Institute, Washington, DC.

Schindegger, F., Krajasits, C., 1997. Commuting: its importance for rural employment analysis. In: Bollman, R.D., Bryden, J.M. (Eds.), Rural Employment: an International Perspective. CAB International, Wallingford, pp. 164–176.

Sproull, A., Bryden, J.M., Black, S., 1996. Telematics, rural economic development and SMEs: some demand-side evidence. Informationen zur Raumentwicklung, Ländliche Räume: Ländliche Entwicklung im internationalen Vergleich, Heft 11/12, pp. 755–775.

Urry, J., 1984. Capitalist restructuring, recomposition and the regions. In: Bradley, T., Lowe, P. (Eds.), Locality and Rurality: Economy and Society in Rural Regions. Geobooks, Norwich.

Whatmore, S., 1990. Farming Women: Gender, Work and Family Enterprise. Macmillan, Basingstoke.

Zacchia, C., 1986. The possibilities and constraints of endogenous industrial development. In: Bassand, M., Brugger, E., Bryden, J.M., Freidmann, J., Stuckey, B. (Eds.), Self-Reliant Development in Europe, Gower, Aldershot.

Journal of Rural Studies, Vol. 9, No. 3, pp. 205–222, 1993
Printed in Great Britain

0743–0167/93 $6.00 + 0.00
Pergamon Press Ltd

Regulating the New Rural Spaces: the Uneven Development of Land

Philip Lowe,* Jonathan Murdoch,* Terry
Marsden,† Richard Munton‡ and Andrew Flynn†

*Department of Agricultural Economics and Food Marketing, Centre for Rural
Economy, University of Newcastle-upon-Tyne, U.K.; †School of Geography and
Earth Resources, University of Hull, U.K.; ‡Department of Geography,
University College London, U.K.

Abstract — With the demise of agricultural productivism, that set of economic and
political arrangements which made food production the overriding aim of rural
policy, new forms of regulation have come into existence. These are linked to new
patterns of development in rural areas which have arisen as economic actors seek to
exploit the opportunities presented by the crisis in agriculture. Both development
and its regulation have become *localised* — that is, detached from the *national*
regime associated with productivism. This is leading to increased differentiation.
We examine three land development sectors — minerals, farm building conversion
and golf — to illustrate how the processes of differentiation are driven by a variety
of economic, political and social actors. These are assessed using the notion of
'arenas of representation'. Two arenas are identified — those of the market and
regulation — showing how uneven development of the countryside can be
understood as arising from action-in-context. Such differentiation, or the emergence of new rural *spaces*, is inevitable in the post-productivist era.

Introduction

Change in Britain's countryside can only be understood in the larger context of the revised roles that
rural space is playing in national and international
restructuring (Marsden *et al.*, 1993). This is not
simply to acknowledge the growing importance of
transnational policy-making and regulation and new
patterns of investment in a more globalised economy
but also the significance of the changed relations
between the economic and the political that have
followed the widespread adoption of neo-liberal
approaches to macro-economic management during
the 1980s. Born out of dissatisfaction with Keynesian, welfarist ideas, such approaches have
encouraged the greater mobility of capital, the
adoption of more diverse production methods, more
clearly articulated consumer interests, and the deregulation of many centralised political structures.
These tendencies have particular repercussions for
the countryside. New consumption demands and
work patterns are promoting new rounds of uneven
development and providing the social and political
basis for more diversified patterns of economic

restructuring. While the neo-liberal political
rhetoric across Europe demands 'level playing fields'
to break down past rigidities in fixing capital and
exploiting labour, processes associated with spatially
distinct constellations of social, political and
economic interests are leading in practice to more
differentiation. The weakening of centralised
political regulation combined with economic restructuring is thus yielding new types of uneven
development within and between nation states.

Of particular significance to the redefinition of the
countryside has been the demise of the state-
supported model of agricultural development which
placed an overriding priority on the production of
food. Its demise has opened up new political and
economic opportunities and uncertainties at a time
when there has been a substantial growth in demand
for rural space for amenity, recreation, conservation
and residential purposes. In response, new activities
have arisen to exploit these opportunities including
pluriactive farming, alternative crops, conservation
land management, leisure complexes and novel
forms of housing and retail outlets. Additional

possibilities have also thereby been created for new social groups to pursue their demands both in the market place and in the political system. Local planning has begun to reflect these changing conditions, as it adapts to the variable pressures for rural diversification and environmental protection in the post-productivist era.[1]

The shift to a more differentiated countryside is, in many areas, resulting in increased competition for rural resources from a variety of economic actors. Some localities remain closely linked to the food industries; others have their amenity and environmental functions reinforced; and others experience shifts in economic structure accompanied by increased population mobility. Where little social change has occurred, the continuance of established political interests — for instance, the dominance of farming and landowning groups and/or entrenched service class groups — may maintain traditional power structures. However, mounting consumer and environmental concerns have re-oriented the traditional axes of political contestation in many localities. Where such concerns are weakly represented or organised but where traditional corporatist structures associated with food and fibre production have been eroded, there is often a particular vulnerability to the siting of new installations associated with minerals and other digging, dumping and blighting activities (Blowers, 1993).

These divergent development trajectories challenge the conventional modernist conception of 'progress' which tended to envisage increased homogeneity across rural space. In this paper we wish to consider some of the implications of these changes for the regulation of the new rural spaces. In what follows we show first how differentiation is linked to the complex social, political and economic processes which have begun to shape the post-productivist era. Then, with reference to selected land developments (minerals, aspects of farm diversification, and golf courses), we attempt to demonstrate how the regulation of rural areas both reflects and moulds these processes.

Rural differentiation in the post-productivist era

(i) Uneven development

Rurality is currently being redefined by secular changes to many of the key processes which have traditionally given it shape. Of critical importance is the food sector. Food industries have become less reliant upon land-based agriculture, but they demand agricultural practices which are cost-efficient and consistent in the timing and quality of supply. Farming capitals are thus being selectively incorporated by food distributors and processors. At the same time, the altered sourcing policies of the major transnational food corporations, which have accompanied the globalisation of the food sector, have undermined the viability of nationally and regionally based accumulation regimes in agriculture. Support for farmers has seemed increasingly anachronistic to national governments, especially those espousing neo-liberal policies, although the sheer inertia of the Common Agricultural Policy has undoubtedly slowed the abandonment of 'welfarist' rural policies within the European Community [see, for example, the debates arising from the European Commission (1988, 1991)]. The continued political influence of European (and Japanese) farming lobbies, moreover, has ensured new support measures linked to production control and diversification and delayed progress in the GATT talks towards a more deregulated global trading system in agricultural commodities (see Grant, 1993). The retreat from agricultural productivism has been varied. Some farming areas continue to experience intensification of production; others face new types of productivism linked to other external capitals, for example through bio-crop production; while others are experiencing a partial decoupling from the high-tech model through various forms of extensification and diversification and reintegration into local and regional economies (Bye and Fonte, 1991). In these ways, the status of agriculture as a distinct sector is being eroded.

But the crisis of agricultural productivism is only one side of the story. Of at least equal significance in the British countryside are the increasing demands placed on rural space by reconstituted 'urban' capitals in terms of new manufacturing and service industries and the particular demands made for living and recreational space by the employees of those industries. So far, most studies of rural restructuring have separated these interlinked components focusing either on the growing 'service class' orientation of the countryside or the urban–rural shift in manufacturing and services [although for a preliminary analysis which seeks to bring these two components together, see Thrift (1987)]. These partial perspectives obscure the general repositioning of rural space and its resources in which increasing emphasis is placed on what opportunities rural areas can offer in order to meet new demands. Delivery is hampered by the growing competition between a widening range of economic, social and political actors, associated with both the production and consumption of a broadening range of goods and services, such as exclusive housing, up-market leisure and recreation pursuits, sensitive landscapes and habitats, and high-tech firms set in prestigious locations. These are exemplified by the processes of counter-urbanisation and the undermining of traditional forms of settlement planning, as well as revised forms of (commoditised) consumption. Indeed, the social significance of 'the rural' is as powerful beyond its boundaries as it is within them. The widenlng range of demands on the countryside arise, in part, from the development of the service sector (both public and private), the search for more 'flexible' production methods that can be provided by small, spatially dispersed, but extensively networked firms, and the growth of new entrepreneurial elites who are driven by what we might term the 'treadmill of positionality'. The attainment of quality in the production of rural goods, be they agricultural or associated with amenity, reinforces social and political distinctiveness for those who participate in their production and consumption. Uniqueness and authenticity become key considerations in the reconstruction of the countryside and increasingly the local planning system is assessed in terms of its ability to protect and reproduce these positional goods.

Within this overall redefinition of rural space come new types of spatial interdependencies and competitiveness associated with the location of different 'quality' goods, services and (social and material) environments. 'Preserved' pieces of the countryside depend on other regions being less opposed to incoming industrial, mineral or waste-dumping activities; and actors in different localities negotiate with economic institutions and compete with each other for inward investment, value added and market share. While such competition has traditionally been associated with the comparative advantages of national agricultural interests (e.g. Danish versus British bacon, French versus British lamb, Spanish versus southern French wine and olive oils) current contestation has been extended to a wide range of consumption and production concerns and their local specificities. Local appellations, whether for wines (see Moran, 1993), cheeses, rural crafts or water supplies, are actively promoted and challenged as part of marketing strategies and legitimation processes fundamental to local accumulation strategies.

(ii) Regulation

In the past, rural policy was dominated by agricultural productivism and supporting planning policies. The crisis in productivism has been associated with the decline of agricultural corporatism which formed the keystone not only of sectoral (i.e. agricultural) policy but also of spatial policy (i.e. rural planning).

At the pinnacle of the post-war rural planning hierarchy was the MAFF, which watched over a series of subsidiary agencies, including local planning authorities, water authorities, the Nature Conservancy, national park authorities and the Forestry Commission, to ensure that in their land-use planning functions the needs of agriculture were safeguarded. The retreat from this emphasis on agricultural protection has led to considerable uncertainty in land-use management, and to a policy and political vacuum. A wish to wean farmers off their dependence on price supports and Ministers' deregulatory instincts coincided in the 1980s with efforts to free-up the statutory planning system and to open up the countryside to new forms of investment. The consequence, though, has been neither a more liberal planning system nor the demise of corporatism in the countryside (see Marsden *et al.*, 1993).

Other interests (minerals, housebuilding, waste disposal, leisure, forestry and environmental) have sought to exploit the vacuum resulting from the decline of agricultural corporatism, directly, by gaining access or control over rural land, and indirectly, through efforts to establish or break into various corporatist structures (see Fig. 1). Indeed, there would seem to be a persistent tendency for major economic interests in land to seek to colonise local or central government agencies, in order to control the markets for their products, thus leading to an incipient corporatism. As Fig. 2 indicates, however, the partial spatial corporatisms that currently prevail are distinct from the spatial/sectoral corporatism of post-war agricultural policy. For the latter, regulation of output markets was achieved sectorally, while spatial corporatism regulated both the supply of land and labour for agriculture. In contrast, current spatial corporatist arrangements make no effort to regulate labour supply, but instead seek to regulate the supply of land and through this to achieve some management of output markets. This places a considerable onus on the planning system, but varies from region to region.

As well as the efforts of land-based production interests to manage their output markets new social groups have moved into positions of social and political leadership in many rural areas (the 'service class') and have asserted amenity and environmental considerations to great effect. Local and regional political and economic interests have thus taken advantage of the 'opening up' of the countryside to establish localised forms of regulation through the planning system. In general, therefore, efforts to liberalise rural planning have produced the opposite effect, and the planning system has been strengthened not weakened as a result.

Annual Review of Agriculture: pre-EC entry, consisted of a collation of June Census Returns from farms to enable government pricing of commodities in negotiation with farming unions. Subsequently, it has become a more general statistical assessment and review of the state of agriculture, involving a wider range of agricultural interest groups.

Regional Aggregates Working Parties: seen as a key part of aggregates mineral planning since the early 1970's. Membership drawn from local authorities, the minerals industry and central government. They prepare national and regional guidelines for aggregates provision, to assist mineral planning authorities and the Secretary of State and to ensure the safeguarding and availability of aggregates for the construction industry.

Housing Land Availability Studies: one of the key aims of the Government's planning policies is to ensure an adequate and continuous supply of land. Local authorities and builders undertake joint studies of land available for housing under the guidance of the DoE, to establish a context for plan making and development control decisions on housing.

Regional Planning Fora: county council-led conferences to assemble advice for the Secretary of State on appropriate considerations to be included in Regional Planning Guidance (see Figure 6). The conferences involve other local authorities, relevant government departments, business organisations, development interests and bodies representing agricultural and conservation interests.

Regional Forestry Advisory Committees: appointed by the Forestry Commission for each of the seven Conservancies under the Forestry Act 1967, to assist in reconciling differences of opinion over planting and felling proposals. Under a Chairman, they comprise four members representing forestry interests and four representing respectively environment, agriculture, planning and trade unions.

Figure 1. Corporatist structures in rural management.

Post-War Agricultural Policy.

Control	Spatial Corporatism	Sectoral Corporatism
Output markets	-	+
Supply of land/ natural resources	+	-
Supply of labour	+	-

Contemporary Aggregates/Housing/Forestry Policy.

Control	Spatial Corporatism	Sectoral Corporatism
Output markets	+	-
Supply of land/ natural resources	+	-
Supply of labour	-	-

Figure 2. Changing Patterns of Corporatist Control.

The past few years, indeed, have seen the most profound extension of the planning system to the countryside since 1947, including a broadening of the scope of statutory rural planning, additional regulatory powers and a proliferation of plan-making, as part of a shift towards a plan-led system. For example, as well as such themes as housing, leisure and conservation, structure plans are now required to have general policies on the rural economy, by no means a traditional planning concern. The additional powers include controls over excavations and tippings on agricultural land, restrictions on the siting of intensive livestock units, regulation of the siting, design and appearance of new farm buildings and proposed protection for hedgerows. Plan-making now encompasses the revival of a form of regional planning, reprieved but streamlined structure plans, mandatory district-wide local plans, continued reliance on special area or topic plans (for example, to cover an expanding town), and a requirement on county councils to produce plans for minerals and waste disposal (see Fig. 3). Finally, the long-standing presumption within statutory planning in favour of development has been subordinated to the principle that the plan should be paramount, or in the wording of the 1991 *Planning and Compensation Act*, that development control decisions 'shall be made in accordance with the plan unless material conditions indicate otherwise'.

The move towards a plan-led system is occurring in the absence of the sort of overall strategy that agricultural productivism once provided. Despite attempts to impose some consistency, there remains a lack of any specific mechanism to achieve the kind of plan-making hierarchy whereby one plan conforms to the one above in a system where local, district and structure plans all nest within statements of regional guidance. Instead, they simply overlay one another. Real power may continue to lie with the district councils, now the main planning and

development control authorities, especially if this level of administration also proves to be the focus of local government reorganisation.

This trend places a considerable onus upon rural district councils. Realistically, one must ask whether they have the capacity to respond. Many district planning authorities are ill-equipped and the quality of their staff is variable. Experience of development plan work is often limited. The training of planners does not in general cover the fields for which new responsibilities are emerging, such as agricultural buildings, the rural economy, waste disposal and minerals. The changing functions of the countryside and the widening range of interests and values held by rural residents, moreover, make local planning more contentious. They will require sophisticated negotiating and managerial skills if planning staff and their political leaders are to achieve consistency and social justice in arbitrating development proposals. Agreement may readily be reached where the case for development is based on meeting small-scale local needs, but the planners' negotiating skills may be tried to the limit over large or extraneous schemes if confronted by local objection on the one hand and insufficient guidance on strategic priorities on the other.

Overall, we would characterise the shift in rural policy of the past decade as one from a strong

---

In non-metropolitan areas, the 'development plan' is not a single document but includes all those plans referred to below. Planning Policy Guidance Note 12 also states that all plans are specifically to include policies to conserve the natural beauty and amenity of the land. (Planning and Compensation Act 1991; PPG 12 1992).
Local Plans: the mandatory plan which contains detailed policies and proposals for development and the use of land, including improvements to the physical environment and traffic management. (Town and Country Planning Act 1990).
District Plans: district-wide local plans to be prepared by non-metropolitan district councils or park-wide local plans prepared by National Park Authorities. (Planning and Compensation Act 1991).
Structure Plans: a single document for the whole (shire) county which provides the strategic policy framework for planning and development control locally, consistent with national and regional guidance and compatible across county boundaries. (Town and Country Planning Act 1990).
Mineral Local Plans: prepared by county councils in England (policies contained in district plans in Wales) to carry forward policies which provide for the supply of minerals, the safeguarding of reserves, and measures for environmental protection in mineral working, disposal of mineral wastes and site restoration and aftercare. (Planning and Compensation Act 1991).
Waste Disposal Plans: provide local plan coverage of development involving the depositing of refuse or waste materials, other than mineral waste. They contain detailed land use policies for the treatment and disposal of waste and the need for and location of sites and facilities and criteria for them. (Planning and Compensation Act 1991).
Regional Planning Guidance: issued by the Secretary of State in consultation with local planning authorities, taking account of national planning policies, to provide a framework for structure plan preparation. Guidance covers the "broad development framework for the region over a period of 20 years or more". (PPG 12 1992).

Figure 3. Rural plan-making.

national strategy/weak local framework to a weak (or non-existent) national strategy/strong local framework. The up-grading of rural planning and the move towards a plan-led system are to be welcomed in themselves. But to make district planning authorities the focus for resolving the many policy contradictions and social conflicts that re-structuring has engendered is asking too much. The risk is that the development of rural areas is cast in the doldrums of an ever more constricted and parochial planning framework lacking any overall sense of direction. We now turn to examine some of the consequences of this shift in the regulatory framework for rural land development.

The rural land development process

It is clear from the above that the active part that local interests take in the development of their localities cannot be ignored. Local action may be constrained by its broader context but it cannot be simply 'read off' from some notion of 'structural' change (a shift from Fordism to post-Fordism, for example). It is evident that while local differen-tiation is being encouraged by certain economic tendencies (such as more 'flexible' systems of pro-duction, the growing scale and range of con-sumption-led demands for rural resources, the changing nature of 'farming' which is itself opening-up new business opportunities, and the deregu-latory instincts of central government) it is equally true that these pressures face different degrees of local resistance and support. These differences are largely the result of a changing mix of local resident populations, the historical pattern of land ownership and capital investment, and local environmental endowments; and their roles have to be empirically examined and built into any analysis of change. A top-down causal argument, which portrays local areas as merely the passive recipients of general movements of capital (governed by 'laws' of uneven development), is inadequate.

Elsewhere we have argued that rural land develop-ment processes direct our attention to the forces of capitalist reconstruction and the new ways in which these are reliant upon social and political represen-tations, as well as economic tendencies (Marsden *et al.*, 1993). The significance in rural areas of land development as an arena of contestation arises from the social and political roles that access to, and control over, property rights continue to sustain, as well as the obvious importance of land to key economic activities. Certain forms of land develop-ment are restricted to rural space, including agri-cultural intensification, mineral extraction and golf course construction, while others — such as housing

— tend to have distinct rural forms. But with the widening range of demands on rural areas, requiring the overt recognition and assessment of the oppor-tunities for the multiple use of land, it is the changing relations between different uses that are of particular importance to our analysis and which, indeed, fuel public concern over the physical trans-formation of rural space.

In what follows we wish to explore these rather abstract considerations in more detail. In particular, we focus on the changing nature of 'regulation' in the rural context using three types of land develop-ment — minerals extraction, barn conversions and golf course construction — as vehicles of analysis.[2] Each of these exemplifies different constellations of interests within the development process and shows the variable and uneven nature of local policy responses. Each has its own distinct market and regulatory arenas (see next section) and this allows us to investigate a range of economic, social and political actors as they operate within the rural domain. The emphasis here is on how economic activities are subject to new forms of regulation in the post-productivist era and we explore the policy context in some detail below. We conclude with some general observations on the differentiated countryside.

(i) Minerals development

A useful starting point is an industry which is a traditional user of rural land but which now finds itself operating in changed circumstances. Minerals development is also interesting because it has become surrounded by a quite elaborate regulatory framework.[3] Separate structures and procedures have evolved because of the distinctive character-istics of the minerals land development process which set minerals planning apart from the general-ity of land-use planning. This is evident in the following respects:

(i) Minerals and waste disposal are the only subjects where development planning and development control are the sole responsibility of county councils. For all other subjects, in non-metropolitan areas, responsibility for plan-making is divided between county and district authorities, and the districts have responsibility for development control. Thus, not only is decision-making on minerals development institutionally separate, but it is also handled by authorities which are unitary, embracing plan-making and implementation.

(ii) The distinctiveness of these arrangements is recognised in official terminology with specific references (in legislation and circulars) to mineral planning authorities (MPAs). In non-metropolitan areas the MPA is the county planning authority. In metropolitan areas the responsibility lies with the borough or district planning authority.

(iii) While the general statutory framework for mineral planning is provided by the town and country planning legislation, particular and detailed provisions apply to minerals, which also have their own distinct body of legislation [e.g. *Minerals Working Act* 1951 and the *Town and Country Planning (Minerals) Act* 1981]. The main topics on which statutory rules for minerals differ significantly from land-use planning more generally include requirements to avoid sterilising mineral resources by other forms of development; the validity (including the time limit) of planning permissions; the conditions which can be attached to permissions and other regulations allowing authorities to exercise control over the actual workings of minerals; and conditions covering the restoration and after-care of sites.

(iv) A distinct body of policy relating to minerals planning has evolved, codified at the local level in minerals plans and at the national level in the series of Minerals Policy Guidance Notes (MPGs) begun in 1988. This is the only industry to receive such formal, separate policy treatment within the planning system. The 1991 *Planning and Compensation Act* takes the exceptional position another step forward. It requires all county planning authorities to draw up a separate minerals plan and precludes district authorities from including any policies in respect of the winning and working of minerals in the plans they prepare.

(v) A distinct professional sub-culture has evolved in relation to minerals planning. Many authorities have set up minerals sections, and staff tend to specialise in this field. Many have a training in geology which distinguishes them from most mainstream planners. Relations with the industry are close, and there is a degree of movement of specialist staff between the public and the private sectors. There are also specialised communication networks and publications, such as the quarterly journal *Mineral Planning* and the monthly *Mine and Quarry Journal*.

A standard explanation of this distinct status refers to the peculiar nature of minerals working as a form of development. Although the legal definition of development as a basis of statutory planning embraces mining or other operations in, on, over, or under land, in an ontological sense minerals working is not the development of land but its exploitation. Although such working yields a valuable resource, it is not an end in itself but is a destructive and disruptive activity which renders the land less valuable than before. As Marx reminds us:

> in mining, payment (of rent) is made for land not because it is the element in which production is to take place, as in agriculture, not as one of the conditions of production as in the case of a building site, but because it is a reservoir containing the use values to be exploited (Marx, 1964, p. 245).

While the particular mineral to be exploited is rarely spatially ubiquitous, the social and political constraints applied to its exploitation lead to even higher levels of relative scarcity. These, in turn, have to be regulated. As a result, the rules and procedures of the planning system have had to be adapted and refined to take account of the 'peculiar' nature of minerals working.

Not only does the locationally specific nature of minerals reserves confer a natural monopoly on the owner of minerals rights, it also introduces a critical role for the planning system to secure the necessary conditions to exploit such rights. Planners, therefore, have sought to protect these place-specific reserves and the rights associated with their exploitation against other forms of development, under shifting conditions of absolute and relative scarcity. Equally, the growth of amenity and other consumption concerns has forced minerals planning authorities into the greater regulation of the operation, including the restoration and aftercare of minerals sites, and a greater sensitivity towards the choice of available sites to be exploited. However, the authorities must also be sensitive to the demand for minerals so as to allow the industry flexibility to follow market oscillations. In the words of the Government, 'for the economic well-being of the country it is essential that the construction industry is provided with an adequate and regular supply of the minerals it needs' (DoE, 1989, p. 2). Minerals planning must take a long-term view, due to the long lead times and considerable investment needed to develop new minerals reserves and the long life-time of many minerals operations.

Planning authorities and minerals operators develop the 'long-term view' in tandem, within an institutional framework of Regional Aggregates Working Parties (RAWPs) established for this purpose, which consist of representatives from the MPAs, mineral companies, the DoE, and invited clients, such as the Ministry of Transport. A major tension, however, frequently develops between the needs of the planners and the mineral companies to plan strategically about the location and scale of mineral exploitation and the markedly cyclical nature of demand from the corporate building and construction industries. The disparity in the production times required to exploit minerals and to build houses cross-cuts with the spatial heterogeneity implicit in the absolute and relative scarcity of mineral reserves. The inability of either the mineral companies' or the development industry to co-ordinate these temporal and spatial disjunctures (between production and consumption) leaves the planning system with a crucial role.

At the apex of the framework for minerals planning are forecasts of aggregates demand made every four years. Until recently, they were drawn up by the Department of the Environment (DoE) and the National Coordinating Group (comprising the Chairmen of the RAWPs). Since 1988 the Government has used a firm of consultants (ECOTEC). The central element of the methodology used to forecast future demand is the level of construction activity in the economy:

> The level of construction activity in the long-term is closely related to the long-term level of economic activity . . . thus the forecasting methodology must embrace forecasts of economic and construction activity as the basis of the forecast of the long-term trend in the demand for aggregates (Medhurst, 1991).

The forecasts are essentially a 'trend projection' of recent minerals demand moderated by predictions about future economic growth, on the assumption of an unchanging ratio between demand and growth. The national forecasts thus derived are then translated into regional forecasts by the 10 Regional Aggregates Working Parties (RAWPS) in England and Wales and via a similar process in Scotland. The regional forecasts are, in turn, distributed amongst the counties and become incorporated into minerals plans.

The demand forecasts are crucial in keeping MPAs locked into a system of provision from which they might otherwise wish to escape. According to a representative of British Aggregates Construction Materials Industries (BACMI), if there were no forecasts 'mineral planning authorities might become increasingly unwilling to grant additional or new consents and a growing share of applications would have to go to appeal' (Phillipson, 1991). Because the mineral companies need to keep extensive equipment and workforces operating and to maintain supplies to their customers, the delay and uncertainty involved in a planning-by-appeal approach would be highly disruptive. The system, therefore, allows the industry a relatively stable environment in which to develop long-term plans. At the same time, the forecasts determine to a large degree the amount of aggregate that will be ex-

tracted, and it is not surprising that criticism of the minerals planning regime has often focused upon the role and accuracy of the forecasts (e.g. Adams, 1991). This criticism came to a head with the publication of revised forecasts produced by the DoE in Minerals Planning Guidance Note 6 of 1991. These estimated that demand for construction aggregates would rise to 505 million tonnes per annum by 2011, representing an average annual growth rate of 2.5% from the 300 million tonnes in 1989. The revised figures contained in MPT 6 came about because the DoE's demand forecast 'did not fully reflect the rapid increase in economic activity seen in the late 1980s' (DoE, 1991, p. 2). But by 1991 the construction industry had passed into its deepest post-war slump. The counter-cyclical nature of the forecasts made them look absurd.

The Council for the Protection of Rural England (CPRE) capitalised on this absurdity, arguing that the principle of resource conservation through demand management should be placed at the heart of minerals planning policy. It was suggested that

> the real choice we face is between business as usual, with ever-more aggregates extraction, used for an ever-more extensive motorway network, ever-more-out-of-town shopping centres, power stations and reservoirs on the one hand; and on the other, the recognition that we have to organise our lives to allow the constraints imposed by finite and irreplaceable environments (Plowden, 1991).

The CPRE was critical of a minerals planning regime established to ensure the supply of aggregates to match unfettered demand. However, maintaining such levels of supply had steadily brought to the fore the social and environmental costs of this level of mineral extraction and by the end of the 1980s the increase in public concern and opposition was evident to all involved in the industry:

> It is clear that aggregates demand will rise and national needs will come into conflict with local interests. Before winning new approvals to extract, aggregates companies are increasingly going to have to demonstrate to affected communities that vital national needs are being served, and the utmost care is being taken — short and long term — of the environment (*New Civil Engineer*, 2 May 1991).

Such pressures were most acute in the South East region, the area which was the main focus of demand pressures. Here demand for aggregates had long outstripped supply and since 1975 government had accepted that the region could not meet its own needs but instead should be required to maintain historic levels of supply. If a similar approach of making provision supply-led were to be adopted for other regions then the regime could properly be seen as one of demand management; as it is, the South

East simply externalises its development needs and its growing shortfall in supply is made up from imports from other regions. Initially the South West and East Midlands bore the brunt of development activity, but as constraints tightened in these areas too, so the search for suitable supplies extended further afield.

A major problem is the growing difficulty in achieving consents, given the likely environmental impact, in those areas supplying the South East. Resistance to the opening up of new reserves is inevitable if the supplies are to be exported to a region which will not exploit its own minerals for fear of the environmental impact. In response to these worries the DoE commissioned a project to identify alternative sources of supply. According to the Parliamentary Under-Secretary of State for the Environment, the project was to examine

> the possibilities offered by large-scale coastal quarries, such as at Glensada in Scotland. It will examine the potential areas of supply, which include Scotland, and indeed Ireland, Norway and the Iberian peninsula. The consultants will also investigate the environmental and economic consequences of providing aggregates to the South East from such sources (*Hansard*, 9 May 1991, p. 904).

Already the aggregates industry is hoping to open seven coastal 'super-quarries' in Scotland to provide aggregates for the South East. Redland Aggregates, which has sought to extract 600 million tonnes of rock within a 'national scenic area' in the Western Isles, claims that coastal super-quarries are 'the only realistic solution' to the problems posed by environmental constraints on English quarries (*The Guardian*, 7 June 1991).

The choice of Scotland reflects the level of concern about local employment opportunities as opposed to environmental considerations there. This contrasts with the almost overriding concern in the rural South East with the quality of the environment. Employment concerns are not made explicit so the jobs associated with mineral extraction can be exported elsewhere. What this points to is the variation within the U.K. of not just the deposits but also local and regional attitudes towards mineral extraction and the forms of regulation surrounding the industry in different regions. In certain areas protection of the environment matters more than the creation of employment opportunities. For instance, in the 1988 British Social Attitudes Survey respondents were asked whether they felt 'the countryside should be protected from development, even if this sometimes leads to fewer jobs', or that 'new jobs should be created, even if this sometimes causes damage to the countryside'. The results are shown in Table 1:

Table 1. Attitudes to rural development

	Countryside should be protected	New jobs should be created
Region (%)		
Scotland	45	51
Wales	51	42
North	54	40
Midlands	63	32
South	68	26

The forms of regulation are likely to reflect this patterning of concern, although the socio-political concerns of *some* localities (notably those in the South East) seem to translate rather more easily into national forms of regulation than others.[4]

The outcome is unevenly developed and unevenly conserved areas with contrasting environments. While the residents of the South East are likely to seek to further displace extraction activity to other areas, the residents of those areas will have to live with additional minerals workings. However, the requirement under the 1991 *Planning and Compensation Act* for all county planning authorities to formulate minerals plans will at least present local residents and amenity groups with the opportunity to challenge the prevailing assumptions which underpin the mineral planning policies. To what extent these opportunities are taken remains to be seen. It seems likely that levels of representation, tied as they are to the abilities and resources of particular social groups, will also be unevenly distributed throughout the regions and this will further ensure the differentiation of rural environments with regard to mineral working.

(ii) Farm diversification

Attempts to relax planning constraints over agricultural *land* have been strenuously resisted by rural conservation interests and planning authorities. But relaxation of constraints over the re-use of agricultural buildings has found much wider acceptance, on planning, landscape and preservationist grounds. Unlike mineral workings, land-fill or large-scale industrial developments, the conversion of farm buildings promises certain kinds of continuity with the past in the British countryside; their scale is acceptable, they help maintain population and economic activity, and they do not intrude upon the landscape. Farm building conversions have thus become a peculiar focus of rural restructuring in Britain [for instance, 80% of the projects supported under the farm diversification grant scheme involved the re-use of farm buildings — Kneale *et al.* (1992)].

Figure 4 shows the level of planning permissions for such conversions between 1985 and 1989.[5]

The distribution of planning permissions by types of re-use is given in Fig. 5.

The composition of permissions shows pronounced regional variations, as shown in Table 2. Housing is the overwhelming re-use in the North, Yorkshire and the Midlands. Authorities in the South East tend markedly to give proportionally fewer con-

versions for housing but many more permissions for industrial uses. Likewise, the South West has many more conversions for holiday accommodation than the other regions. Finally, the North and the South East account for the bulk of the permissions for stables.

These different pressures reflect variations in regional demands and industrial structures. Thus, the prevalence of accommodation re-uses in the South West reflects the strength of the tourist

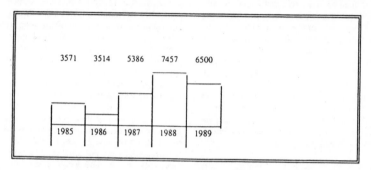

Figure 4. Planning permissions for farm building conversions in England, 1985–1989.

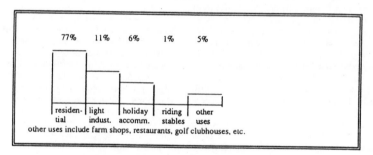

Figure 5. Planning permissions by types of re-use.
Source: Kneale *et al.* (1992).

Table 2. 1989 regional breakdown of farm building conversions by use classes (%)

Region	Housing	Industry	Accommodation	Stables	Other
North	81	6	6	4	3
Yorkshire/Humber	82	11	2	2	3
North West	74	9	4	1	13
East Anglia	78	13	5	0	4
East Midlands	87	9	3	0	1
West Midlands	81	8	6	2	3
South East	69	20	2	2	5
South West	74	7	16	1	2
Total	77	11	6	1	5

Source: Kneale *et al.* (1992), appendix 2.

market in that region. Likewise, the high levels of industrial re-use in the South East and East Anglia occurred in regions with high proportions of small firms and high rates of business formation and hence (until recently) buoyant demand for small business premises. The North, the region with the lowest level of industrial re-uses, has the inverse industrial structure and therefore much less demand for out-of-town, small business premises.

Central government guidance on the re-use of farm buildings has been both positive and largely unconditional, thus attracting criticism for not prescribing sympathetic uses and appropriate design controls. But local planning policies tend to be hedged with variable restrictions and conditions. The local policy instruments that offer most scope to shape permission rates and the types of permissions granted include specifying acceptable new uses (whether residential, light industrial, etc.), design restrictions and agricultural redundancy conditions. Opportunities to diversify are, therefore, heavily dependent on the local economic and planning context, and are very variable geographically.

Unlike the case of minerals development, where supply is highly regulated within a *national* framework and markets are highly localised, levels of barn conversions are determined by *both* local systems of planning regulation and spatially variable markets. They are thus even more indicative of the differential directions that rural areas and regions are taking. These divergent tendencies will no doubt be accentuated as the dispersed development that has taken place, in turn, generates its own pressure for additional development. Such pressures will be difficult to resist. In any case, the government's broadening of the Use Classes in 1987 (in particular, the creation of the combined business and leisure classes) has provided developers with much more flexibility to change use outside the planning system. The consequence is to reduce the scope for local planning authorities to influence the diversification process, once that process has been initiated.

Given the range of factors governing the conversion process, the current emphasis in policy on the provenance of the buildings (i.e. their former use), rather than their future use, seems quite misplaced. While this raises the wider question that if it is desirable to have certain new uses in the open countryside, why should these not be accommodated in purpose-built units appropriately sited, it should also stimulate a more selective and deliberate approach to the choice of which farm buildings should be allowed to be converted, and to which uses. Many buildings, by virtue of their structure or

siting, are not suited to certain (or perhaps any) re-uses. Moreover, there seems to be no general case for allowing the re-use of modern, industrial farm buildings, even if they have become redundant.

Conversely, the overwhelming concern amongst local planning authorities with agricultural redundancy would also seem to be misguided in many instances. After all, if a new use is appropriate at a certain location, why should local planning authorities insist on the maintenance of the existing use (i.e. agriculture)? And if that use is inappropriate, then what difference does it make whether the site or structure is or is not redundant to agriculture? In certain areas, particularly those with good land and consolidated farming structures, it might be deemed generally inappropriate for alternative uses to be allowed to intrude upon the area's agricultural production potential. In which case, there should be a presumption against the re-use of farm buildings even if redundant. A less backward-looking stance towards rural diversification would require local planning authorities to give greater weight to the social and economic needs of rural areas and how their resources and potential might be developed to meet these needs. This would mean paying greater attention to how end-use markets are structured, and the demands to which they respond.

As it is, with the orientation to former use, there is an implicit partiality towards a certain user. Indeed, it is difficult to escape the conclusion that farm building conversion policies are directed more towards the needs of a particular social group (i.e. farmers) than to prospective users, and that much of what has been allowed in the open countryside would not have been permitted under other circumstances. Not surprisingly, therefore, environmentalists have demanded, and been given, a say in the siting of new agricultural buildings (the redundant farm buildings of the future!). None the less, the case of barn conversions suggests that a basic tenet of British planning has been challenged, if not overturned — namely that planning law should discriminate between users but not between uses. As it stands, agrarian property owners are being accorded a key role in determining the pace and direction of rural restructuring, and although agricultural productivism may be in decline, its retreat is casting a long shadow over contemporary developments in rural Britain.

Pressures to intensify production emphasise farmers' vertical links with the food sector, while pressures to diversify emphasise their horizontal links with the local economy (Marsden and Murdoch, 1990). These pressures are creating a bifurcation between the role of the farmer as specialised primary pro-

216   Philip Lowe *et al.*

ducer and the role of the farmer as small rural businessman. There are incipient conflicts between these two roles which means that diversification may ultimately prove to be of limited significance as a means of *production* regulation. More important may be the fact that barn conversions have helped decant a middle-class population into the deep countryside, with significant implications for the changing pattern of social conflicts. This has led to farmers facing new challenges to their authority actually on the farm, over such matters as pollution incidents and access disputes (Ward *et al.*, 1993).

Thus the capital-realisation strategies that diversification encourages may constrain future production possibilities in quite unexpected ways. In itself, this is not necessarily a bad thing. Indeed, it is one of the deliberate aims behind such measures as long-term set-aside and farm woodlands. However, the diversification of social and economic activities in rural areas and their divergent development paths do call for greater orchestration of the process of change at the local and regional levels to ensure compatibility between new and existing uses. This demands the more effective integration of spatial and sectoral planning for rural areas, as the case of golf course development amply illustrates.

(iii) *Golf course development*

As we have argued above, the declining fortunes of agriculture have opened up opportunities for other forms of development leading a wide range of non-agricultural interests to seek access to rural land. As a result, there has been a distinct shift in the balance of outlook amongst those who own rural land between seeing it as a productive asset and a capital asset. This has removed many of the barriers to the potential exploitation of rural land by non-agri-

cultural interests. One consequence is renewed tension between landowners and tenants, and another the erosion of succession as a key motive in family farming (Fig. 3). In the productivist period, business security was seen to lie in continuity of land occupancy. Now, with the emphasis on maintaining the *mobility* of capital, and more sensitively identifying and monitoring its fixity and reducing the risks of its investment, there is greater emphasis on flexibility of ownership and the development of innovative forms of property relations (e.g. options, various forms of short-term leases and contracts, novel and divisible rights) associated with new types of capital with an interest in rural land.

In the late 1980s, for example, golf courses became an attractive response to the problems created by agricultural overproduction, for both farmers and policy-makers (Murdoch *et al.*, 1992a). Until the mid-1980s the planning context in which applications for new golf courses were placed was predominantly determined by agricultural concerns. Any new course involved a significant land-take, equivalent to a medium-sized farm, and, it was often impossible to get the agreement of MAFF, a statutory consultee under the development control process, to the conversion of farmland to golf courses. However, agricultural overproduction, budgetary pressures on levels of state support and declining farm incomes, resulted in the Ministry's attitude to golf development undergoing a fundamental shift. The inter-departmental Alternative Land Use and Rural Economy (ALURE) working party, established in the mid-1980s, led to official recognition of farm diversification as the main solution to the problem of declining farm incomes. New courses seemed to be one appropriate option.

This was compounded by talk in the golfing world of an under-supply of courses. The Royal and Ancient

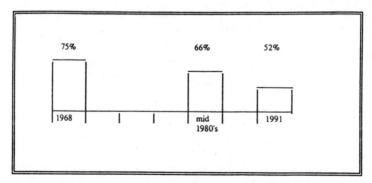

Figure 6. The proportion of farmers planning succession. *Sources*: Harrison (1975); Munton *et al.* (1987); National Westminster Bank (1992).

published a report in 1989 — *The Demand for Golf* — recommending that all regions of the U.K. should achieve a level of provision equivalent to one course per 25,000 head of population, 'an unambitious provision level' in comparison with other 'mature' golfing countries (R&A, 1989, pp. 18–19). This level of provision would require the construction of a further 700 courses by the year 2000. The report, together with articles in the golfing and farming press, argued that levels of provision were a 'problem' because long waiting lists to join clubs suggested considerable unmet demand. Indeed, one of the aims of *The Demand for Golf* was to highlight the 'great opportunities for new business and enterprises as well as established contractors and suppliers to the golfing community' (pp. 1–2) and its publication created considerable excitement amongst developers and golfers.

Planning authorities were quite unprepared for the wave of golf course applications that ensued, and their traditional concern to protect agricultural land in general could no longer be employed except for the best grade (1, 2 and 3a) land following the publication in 1987 of the DoE Circular *Development Involving Agricultural Land*. With the absence of any coherent policy for land coming out of agricultural production emanating from central government, the first golf policies at the local level often relied on assessments of local demand and supply, such as the Sports Council's norm of 18 holes per 30,000 head of population, to determine how many new courses might be needed. Where there was already an excess of facilities the planning authorities felt able to refuse further applications, but more positive approaches were often absent. Furthermore, the ensuing boom was unlike previous expansions in the number of courses which had occurred during periods of low land values. On this occasion, it was the coincidence of the availability of agricultural land and the *perceived* popularity of the game that stimulated the increased supply of courses. Prior to 1987 there had been virtually no market interest in golf development, but subsequently there was rapid recognition of the potential for development, not only for courses and clubhouses but also for other leisure facilities and housing units associated with them. Soon, a kind of gold-rush mentality set in, and, by 1991, some 1400 applications had been submitted.

Lacking policies, local planners responded by relying heavily upon the representations of the land-owning/development/golfing agencies. Some authorities gave consent for up to 30 courses in their districts and were faced with a massive shift in the character of the countryside. Only belatedly did they come to concern themselves with the qualitative

effects this might have on the landscape or the implications for public access to the countryside. By 1992 it appeared that local authorities were beginning to take a tougher stance. As one land agent complained:

> Approvals are becoming increasingly difficult to achieve . . . partly because of a more sophisticated and critical approach by planning authorities. They generally require more detailed applications involving outline layouts, environmental impacts, highway requirements and landscaping proposals . . . planning authorities are going too far in demanding feasibility studies or assessments of demand and supply (*Farmers Weekly*, 12 June 1992).

By this time, in any case, it was generally conceded that the boom had come to an end with *The Guardian* reporting in mid-1992 that 'the golfing boom has been bunkered' (30 May). What may, after all, prevent the wholesale shift of rural land into this new use is the economic vulnerability of the golfing sector. Many of the proposals have proved unviable during the recession. High land costs and, until recently, high real interest rates, combined with falling demand, have radically altered the financial returns for most golfing ventures.

What the golf boom demonstrated, however, is the extent to which the interests of landowners and developers can still lead the planning system to marginalise most other claims on the countryside. At the same time, there has been a substitution of public and domestic sources of capital in the development of rural land and resources, by finance capital. Thus there is increasing volatility in rural land development processes through their growing subjection to money markets and through the use of the property market by government in its overall economic management. This volatility threatens to undermine the long-term planning and management of rural resources and their development. Discontinuity in land occupancy is often associated with radical land management and landscape changes (Marsden and Munton, 1991). The assumptions of stability and continuity that used to underpin rural planning can no longer be maintained. Regulatory bodies need to be flexible; otherwise they will find themselves repeatedly reacting to development events that continually undermine forward plans.

Arenas of representation

It is clear from the preceding analysis that any assessment of the new rural spaces must take account of the range of actors and the contexts in which they operate. We would like to conclude our analysis with a consideration of how these contexts are structured. We propose the notion of 'arenas of representation' as a means of conceptualising the relationships between actors and contexts. We need to focus on the complex processes which give rise to development outcomes. Within these (economic, social and political) processes various actors are attempting to achieve outcomes commensurate with their aims. They *represent* themselves using whatever (economic, social and political) means are at their disposal in various arenas. Thus we term these 'arenas of representation'.

The two main themes of this paper are differentiation and regulation. The first of these was seen to arise from the breakdown of the productivist regime in food production and the competition for rural space from a variety of economic and social actors. The second was characterised as the attempt by these actors to steer this competition in particular directions using the frameworks of regulation. For analytical purposes, therefore, we distinguish two 'arenas' of contestation in which the new rural spaces are taking shape — those associated with the market and those associated with regulation. It is our argument that fundamental changes in the productivist regime have, firstly, 'opened the door' for various (non-agricultural) economic interests to assert claims on rural land and, secondly, created a vacuum in rural policy-making which competing policy 'communities' (i.e. state agencies, quangos and private sector interest groups) have sought to fill. This has resulted in uneven processes of economic development and uneven processes of regulation — both between sectors *and* places.

Different sectors exhibit distinct market/regulation relationships and these are variable across rural space. By analytically separating the arenas of the market and the arenas of regulation (in practice, of course, they are intermingled) we can uncover the means whereby the various actors *represent* themselves both 'economically' (market arena) and 'politically' (arena of regulation). The notion of 'arena' being deployed here is derived from the work of van der Ploeg (1990). In the course of his characterisation of agricultural practices as 'heterogeneous', van der Ploeg argues for a conception of the market as a politically and socially constructed 'arena' where 'farmers find themselves face to face with the state, traders, agribusiness and their advocates' (p. 267). Heterogeneous farming patterns result in part because farmers have different degrees of room for manoeuvre within these arenas; they may vary in their access to resources and in their objectives and they will be caught in differing sets of external relations. Other market sectors can be analysed in these terms. This amounts to a 'sociology

of the market place' where we see market outcomes as resulting from patterns of *interaction* as certain participants attempt to consolidate sets of (power) relations in the exchange of goods and services. The same perspective may be brought to bear upon the arena of regulation [what Clark and Lowe — (1992, p. 22) — have referred to as 'arenas of struggle' and van der Ploeg terms 'power arenas' — (p. 277)] where policy-makers must negotiate with a range of other actors and where the outcomes derive from interaction within the policy process as certain actors attempt to consolidate (power) relations within forms of regulation. If we return to our three case studies we can illustrate how these arenas operate and intersect.

(i) *The market arena*

In the case of minerals extraction we saw how the market is tightly structured by a specialised planning regime. Nevertheless, the market arena is relatively straightforward, with landowners entering into agreements with minerals companies to allow the exploitation of land, usually to service local or regional markets for construction materials (although the development of super-quarries extends the range of certain suppliers). As minerals reserves are depleted existing reserves become more valuable, particularly in 'restrictive' areas such as the South East. Landowners would seem to be increasing their strength in these markets, reflected in the greater use of leasing linked to royalty payments rather than the acquisition of sites by the mineral companies.

The simplicity of the market arena in this sector is mainly due to the structure of the industry. Once a minerals company has secured access to a site it can usually muster internally the resources to extract, process, transport and market the product. However, the very factors which allow the market arena to function in this way (access to sites, size of firms, the ability of firms to take 'the long view', levels of capital investment) need to be underwritten by a strong regulatory framework (see below).

The market in converted farm buildings is more complex. Farmers wishing to 'add value' to their assets adapt farm buildings to either industrial, residential or amenity uses. The demand for such uses will be spatially variable. However, the 'market' here has resulted from the crisis of productivist agriculture and the search by farmers and landowners for other sources of income. There are similarities with golf course development. This too has resulted from the crisis of productivism as farmers and landowners have sought new uses for their land. Again the market seems to have been created by the increased supply of sites although, as we saw, there has been much talk nationally of 'untapped demand' for golfing facilities. In both these cases farmers and landowners find themselves in new and unfamiliar market arenas where they are usually heavily dependent on external expertise (for market intelligence, planning and building regulations, conversion skills, etc.) and external sources of finance. Often they are obliged to enter into partnerships or other forms of agreement with developers if they do not sell out completely. In any case a whole range of other actors will be involved in individual developments (estate agents, planning consultants, solicitors, accountants, bankers, etc.) who are all busily 'making' markets (Murdoch *et al.*, 1992a).

(ii) *Arenas of regulation*

The case of minerals shows how markets can be structured by regulatory regimes. A list of the various participants in the minerals planning arenas would be extensive. However, the key players include the forecasters (setting the targets which flow via the regulatory framework down to the counties), the DoE minerals division, the Regional Aggregates Working Parties, industry interest groups (BACMI and the Sand and Gravel Association), the mineral planning authorities, developers, national environmental groups (including CPRE and the RSPB) and local action/residents groups. At each stage of the planning process one or other of these actors are involved and we can only make sense of their actions by reference to the others. This regulatory arena is complex. It came into existence in order to protect sites and allow the extraction of sufficient minerals to feed national demand, but has become a forum in which various interested parties are attempting to contest many of the underlying assumptions on which the regime is based.

In the case of barn conversions the regulatory regime is much less centralised (now that MAFF has relinquished its hold on the nation's farming assets) and takes place almost exclusively at the local level, within a planning policy framework set down by the DoE and a MAFF policy of encouragement for farm diversification. At this level the planning authority will put forward criteria for conversion to the various uses and may adopt plans which encourage or discourage this type of development (see Marsden *et al.*, 1991). Golf course development also became regulated at the local level once the Ministry of Agriculture withdrew its effective veto over the conversion of farmland to non-agricultural uses. However, this left local planning authorities unclear

as to how they *should* regulate this form of development and patterns of regulation were, perhaps, unduly lax.

By distinguishing these two arenas we can gain some insight into the complexity of the processes which are forging the new differentiated countryside. As we have seen, there are a number of different actors, operating in a variety of local and regional contexts, seeking to achieve a range of outcomes. Differentiation is not caused by the unleashing of market forces — markets are being 'made' — and the institutions of regulation are not simply standing aside to let such forces run 'free'. The types of rurality that are coming into existence are being made by various actors as they seek to impose *their* representations of the rural over others.

However, not all representations are equal. Where a strong regulatory framework exists, such as in minerals or as in the productivist agricultural regime, then the 'key' actors, those who are able to become 'passage points' for the representations of others (the 'gatekeepers' of the development process), tend to be public sector planners or other state agencies (for instance, ADAS). Where the regulatory framework is weak or has broken down and land is being switched *between* sectors, as in the cases of barn conversions and golf courses, then the key actors become a set of intermediaries who are able to exploit the uncertainties of the new regulatory arena. These 'exchange agents' are often knowledgable actors in *both* the arenas identified here, combining an understanding of the policy world (the 'transfer rules' — Flynn *et al.*, 1990) with awareness of local development opportunities. They specialise in combining market and regulatory know-how which allows them to both facilitate planning permission and negotiate the development process. They are often key intermediaries in interpreting local planning policies, in bringing together land-owners and external developers, and in guiding them through a local planning system with which they may be unfamiliar. These 'exchange agents' thrive in the uncertainties of the post-productivist era and must be seen as key actors in the development of the new rural spaces.

Clearly more work is needed in the 'sociology' of rural land development. We have demonstrated that patterns of land development are governed by complex economic, social and political processes operating at a variety of spatial scales. The notion of 'arenas of representation' has been suggested as a means of focusing attention on the interactions between key participants within these processes and how these are 'structured' by the contexts in which they take place (these contexts are, in turn, restructured by these interactions). Thus, the uneven development of rural space can be understood as the *outcome* of actions-in-context (see Marsden *et al.*, 1993, for a fuller account).

Conclusion

In the post-productivist countryside there is a heightened differentiation of land uses and more varied regulatory responses to those uses. These have resulted from increased local pressure on the planning system to safeguard local environments (derived in part from patterns of social change in the countryside) and from the policy vacuum in central government following the breakdown of the productivist regime. The new uses of rural land are now determined much more by the regional context — the structure of the economy, patterns of social change, politics and planning — than was the case under agricultural productivism when, in effect, land use was largely determined by a 'national' demand for increased food production. It is now becoming clear that the countryside is unlikely again to be subject to a national regime of regulation, at least for the foreseeable future. However, as the minerals case study demonstrates, simply leaving regions and localities to determine their own levels of development can have profound implications for development patterns in *other* regions and localities. New patterns of regional interdependency and competition become important concerns. While it would be an exaggeration to claim that, without some national system of co-ordination, the South East countryside could become dominated by golf courses while the north is scarred by extractive industries, this does at least reflect the trajectories of countryside change in certain of their localities. None the less, an increasingly differentiated countryside would seem to be the inevitable outcome of these trends.

The shift to a more differentiated countryside will, in many areas, result in increased competition for rural resources from a variety of economic actors, while in others it may mean an increased reliance upon traditional rural industries. In spite of the overall decline in the importance of agriculture, there can be no doubt that some localities will continue to be even more closely linked to the food industry or to biomass production, where, in all probability, new biotechnologies will be deployed in order to retain the industry's international competitiveness. Other localities will retain a more traditional farming character where the social composition of the population may remain relatively unaltered, while in others a shift in the economic structure may be accompanied by increased social mobility, especially

where more general diversification in the rural economy is linked to the in-migration of a commuting population. Likewise, these changes can also be expected to be reflected in the types of politics practiced, creating a contrast with those localities where a lack of economic and social change may allow the continuance of more locally specific political forms, such as corporatism and clientelism.

However, it is likely, in all rural areas, that the success with which certain social groups are able to pursue their political aims will be determined, to some extent, by their access to, and use of, property rights. With the recombination of agricultural property rights we can expect other production and consumption rights to be vigorously asserted. Property rights thus reveal the varied ways in which individuals, social groups and institutions secure, defend and challenge access to land and natural resources and continuously redefine them in terms of their monetary and non-monetary values. Given the spatial fixity of property rights, it follows that the local construction of these values is an important arena of contestation, leading, as we have seen, to the uneven development of various markets for rural goods, such as minerals, housing, recreational activities and certain types of environment.

The political struggle around rural property rights is now being waged by a well-entrenched middle class, a debt-laden farming sector and a range of other development interests (the rural working class has for long been a marginalised participant). A key arena within which this is being conducted is the planning system. Although central government may set parameters, through the issue of circulars and guidance notes, these must be interpreted and implemented locally. Thus local actors may be able to exert sufficient influence at this level to protect their property interests. Where middle-class actors, concerned with the positional status of their rights, win out we can expect particular forms of *re-regulation* to take place. Much development, judged to have adverse environmental consequences, will be deflected from the locality. In other places, where the protection of positional goods is secondary to employment or development considerations, the regulatory system will tend to uphold the rights of landowners and developers. The trajectories of development in these areas will be markedly different. Certain rural localities will, therefore, achieve a more exclusive 'positional' status, meeting the consumption demands of the middle class, while others will be cast in the role of development zones.

To summarise, local actors mobilise around certain conceptions of place, often defined by their ownership of, or access to, property rights, and through the planning process attempt to establish local policies and modes of decision-making which reinforce these conceptions. These, in turn, influence the networks between local actors and external actors representing, *inter alia*, economic interests, finance capital and state agencies, and the ways in which particular rural spaces are evaluated in developmental terms. Thus, in spite of the increasing global tendencies evident in economic organisation, environmental concern, information flow, and political structures, the nation-state (in the U.K. at least) is confronted by growing local and regional disparities which demand, in turn, that centralised systems of regulation give way to local and regional systems. It is, therefore, hardly surprising that no coherence can be identified in the post-productivist phase of rural development. Local unevenness is its quintessential and necessary feature.

Notes

1. By productivism we mean a commitment to an intensive, industrially driven and expansionist agriculture with state support based primarily on output and increased productivity. The concern was for 'modernisation' of the 'national farm', as seen through the lens of increased production. By the 'productivist regime' we mean the network of institutions oriented to boosting food production from domestic sources which became the paramount aim of rural policy following World War II. These included not only the Ministry of Agriculture and other state agencies but the assemblage of input suppliers, financial institutions, R&D centres, etc., which facilitated the continued expansion of agricultural production.

2. The studies of the land development process were undertaken as part of the ESRC's Countryside Change Initiative and were conducted between 1989 and 1992. They consisted of a series of in-depth interviews with key actors at the national level and in three English localities — Aylesbury Vale in Buckinghamshire, Allerdale in Cumbria, and East Devon — across a range of rural land development processes. These were housing, minerals, waste disposal, industrial development and golf. We present three studies here to illustrate our general argument concerning 'differentiation'.

3. We are concerned here mainly with sand and gravel extraction which has a distinct planning framework distinct from those governing other forms of extraction such as open-cast coal mining (see Murdoch *et al.*, 1992b).

4. It has come to our attention in the course of our local studies that concerns expressed over development in the countryside in the South East seem to feed very quickly into 'national' debates. This may be as a result of spatial proximity to London, the social composition of the countryside in this region, and/or the political importance of these areas to the ruling (Conservative) party.

5. The analysis of barn conversions is based on data collected by the Council for the Protection of Rural England as part of their response to the initial draft of *The Countryside and the Rural Economy* (PPG 7, December 1989). A letter was sent to every English

planning authority outside Greater London in May 1990, asking for details of the permission rate for barn conversion applications and the numbers of such permissions granted since 1985, broken into five land-use categories: residential, holiday accommodation, light industrial/office, riding stables, and 'other'. Where longitudinal data were not available, the authorities were asked to send the figures for 1989. A total of 134 authorities replied in some form or other; about one-quarter sent permission data for five years, while around two-fifths sent data for permissions in 1989 only. We decided to concentrate on one year (1989) to improve the accuracy of the data, while using the 1985–1989 time-series data to identify any national trends. Of the 139 authorities, 108 were useful for our purposes (see Kneale *et al.*, 1992, for details).

References

Adams, J. (1991) *Determined to Dig: the Role of Aggregates Demand Forecasting in National Minerals Planning Guidance.* CPRE, London.

Blowers, A. (1993) Politics, power and periphery: the creation of environmental inequality. Paper presented to the Institute of British Geographers Conference, Royal Holloway and Bedford New College, January 1993.

Bye, P. and Fonte, M. (1991) Technical change in agricultural and new functions for rural spaces in Europe. Paper presented to the Annual Meeting of the American Sociological Association, Cinncinnati, U.S.A., August 1991.

Department of the Environment (1989) *Guidelines for Aggregates Provision in England and Wales: Minerals Policy Guidance Note 6.* DoE, London.

Department of the Environment (1991) *Guidelines for Aggregates Provision in England and Wales: Review of Minerals Policy Guidance Note 6.* DoE, London.

European Commission (1988) *The Future of Rural Society*, Comm (88) 601. Commission of the European Communities, Brussels.

European Commission (1991) *The Development and Future of the Common Agricultural Policy.* Commission of the European Communities, Brussels.

Flynn, A., Lowe, P. and Cox, G. (1990) The rural land development process. ESRC Countryside Change Working Paper Series 6, Department of Agricultural Economics and Food Marketing, University of Newcastle-upon-Tyne, U.K.

Grant, R. (1993) Against the grain: agricultural trade policies of the U.S., the European Community and Japan at the GATT. *Political Geography* **12**, 249–262.

Harrison, A. (1975) Farmers and farm businesses in England. Miscellaneous Study 62, Department of Agricultural Economics, University of Reading, U.K.

Kneale, J., Lowe, P. and Marsden, T. (1992) The conversion of agricultural buildings: an analysis of variable pressures and regulations towards the post-productivist countryside. ESRC Countryside Change Working Paper Series 29, Department of Agricultural Economics and Food Marketing, University of Newcastle-upon-Tyne, U.K.

Marsden, T. and Munton, R. (1991) The farmed landscape and the occupancy change process. *Environment and Planning A* **23**, 663–676.

Marsden, T. and Murdoch, J. (1990) Agriculture in retreat: implications for the changing control of rural

222   Philip Lowe *et al.*

land. ESRC Countryside Change Working Paper Series 9, Department of Agricultural Economics and Food Marketing, University of Newcastle-upon-Tyne, U.K.

Marsden, T., Murdoch, J., Lowe, P., Munton, R. and Flynn, A. (1993) *Constructing the Countryside*. UCL Press, London.

Marsden, T., Murdoch, J. and Williams, S. (1991) From farmers to developers: contested transitions in the development of small industrial units on farms in a prosperous region. ESRC Countryside Change Working Paper Series 22, Department of Agricultural Economics and Food Marketing, University of Newcastle-upon-Tyne, U.K.

Marx, K. (1964) *Theories of Surplus Value (Volume 2)*. Lawrence and Wishart, London.

Medhurst, J. (1991) The New Aggregate Forecast: is it realistic? Paper presented to the RTPI/BACMI Seminar, 27 June, London.

Moran, W. (1993) Rural space as intellectual property. *Political Geography* **12**, 263–277.

Munton, R., Marsden, T. and Eldon, J. (1987) *Occupancy Change and the Farmed Landscape: Final Report*. Countryside Commission, Cheltenham.

Murdoch, J., Flynn, A., Lowe, P. and Marsden, T. (1992b) Uneven regulation and the development process: a comparative analysis of minerals planning in three English regions. ESRC Working Paper Series 35, Department of Agricultural Economics and Food Marketing, University of Newcastle-upon-Tyne, U.K.

Murdoch, J., Kneale, J., Lowe, P. and Marsden, T. (1992a) Making a market: the case of the 1980s golf course boom. ESRC Countryside Change Working Paper Series 34, Department of Agricultural Economics and Food Marketing, University of Newcastle-upon-Tyne, U.K.

National Westminster Bank (1992) *Nat West Farm Survey: Summary Report*. National Westminster Bank Agricultural Office, Coventry.

Phillipson, R. (1991) The Revised Aggregate Forecast: an industry view. Paper presented to the RTPI/BACMI Seminar, 27 June, London.

Plowden, B. (1991) Are the forecasts realistic? The view of the Council for the Preservation of Rural England. Paper presented to the RTPI/BACMI Seminar, 27 June, London.

Royal and Ancient Club of St Andrews (R&A) (1989) *The Demand for Golf*. R&A, St Andrews.

Thrift, N. (1987) Manufacturing rural geography. *Journal of Rural Studies* **3**, 77–81.

van der Ploeg, J. (1990) *Labour Markets and Agricultural Production*. Westview, Oxford.

Ward, N., Lowe, P., Seymour, S. and Clark, J. (1993) Rural restructuring and the regulation of farm pollution. *Environment and Planning A* (forthcoming).

[4]

Pergamon

Journal of Rural Studies, Vol. 14, No. 3, pp. 287–298, 1998
© 1998 Elsevier Science Ltd
Printed in Great Britain. All rights reserved
0743-0167/98 $19.00 + 0.00

PII: S0743-0167(97)00057-0

Agricultural Liberalization in the European Union: An Analysis of the Implications for Nature Conservation

Clive Potter and Philip Goodwin

Wye College, University of London, Environment Department, Wye, Ashford,
Kent TN25 5AH, UK

Abstract — The liberalization of agricultural policy is a more realistic prospect today than ever before. Following the Uruguay Round Agriculture Agreement of 1993, European policymakers are committed, at least at the level of rhetoric, to the further progressive decoupling of agricultural support in order to increase the exposure of Europe's farmers to world markets. There are compelling reasons to believe that, by the turn of the century, policymakers will come under mounting pressure to further liberalize the CAP. The environmental implications of this policy shift are profound. According to some commentators, the rural environment stands to benefit from a double dividend: once when the reduction in prices brings about an extensification of production, and again when resources previously committed to price support are reinvested in agri-environmental schemes. This paper considers the validity of this important idea. It examines the assumptions behind the extensification effect and discusses the willingness and ability of policymakers to plough substantial sums of public money into fully decoupled agri-environmental programmes. The paper suggests that the first round effects of a withdrawal of support may not be unambiguously good for the European countryside, while the 'green recoupling' of support could prove more complicated politically than is often assumed. © 1998 Elsevier Science Ltd. All rights reserved

Key words: agricultural liberalization, nature conservation, green recoupling, CAP, WTO

Introduction

Trade liberalization dominates the international political agenda. McCalla (1993) observes that supporters of free trade have been pressing their case for at least two centuries and since 1945 have been building institutions like the General Agreement on Tariffs and Trade (GATT), and now the World Trade Organization (WTO), to achieve the goal of a world trading system free of barriers or restraint. Until the recent Uruguay Round, however, agriculture had largely escaped GATT disciplines, enjoying levels of protection, particularly in the European Union (EU) and Japan, unmatched in almost any other industrial sector (Ingersent *et al.*, 1993; Grant, 1993; Grant, 1995). The Uruguay Round Agriculture Agreement (URAA) of 1993 was consequently a watershed event. For the first

time, it committed industrial countreis to a concerted reduction in agricultural protection in the interests of freer world trade. There is now in place a common strategy for improved market access through tariffication, the gradual replacement of price support with 'decoupled' income payments (that is, payments not linked to the amount a farmer produces) and the phased elimination of export subsidies. The Agreement puts the agricultural policies of industrial countries on converging paths, subject to the same internationally agreed rules and procedures. It also raises the stakes of domestic agricultural policy reform, for as Rausser and Irwin (1989) observe, a failure to continue the liberalization process will now be seen as a threat to progress towards freer trade in other fields under future Rounds. Commentators differ in their assessment of the implications for the EU's Common Agricultural

288 Clive Potter and Philip Goodwin

Policy (CAP). Rieger (1996) predicts an increasingly defensive response from European policymakers and their agricultural clients and resistance to the vision of a globalized agricultural which is enshrined in the institution of the WTO. Agricultural economists like Harvey (1995) and Swinbank (1996), on the other hand, point to the limits on further export subsidization written into the URAA and to the momentous (and unsustainable) budgetary implications of extending an unreformed system of agricultural support to farmers in the newly acceding Central and Eastern European Countries (CEECs). As Swinbank (Swinbank, 1996, p. 407) puts it 'The Agreement arranged the straitjacket around the CAP. The next Round will tighten the cords and begin the painful process of dismantling CAP support'.

If this latter analysis is correct, then rural Europe is about to experience one of the most important policy shifts of the last forty years. Having spent most of the past two decades critiquing a CAP rooted in protectionism, conservationists, amongst others, are discovering they need to engage with an entirely different policy debate, in which the eventual abolition of the CAP in its present form, not merely its continued reform, is firmly on the agenda. There is now a large body of evidence documenting the impact of the CAP on the rural environment. Most experts agree that, while causation is complex, high levels of 'coupled' price support have interacted with technological change in agriculture to bring about the intensification, specialization and concentration of production that has been the immediate cause of habitat loss and a decline in biodiversity throughout the European countryside (Baldock, 1990; Stanners and Bourdeau, 1995). Observing these effects, some commentators have long argued that 'the single most important change in agricultural policy from the viewpoint of conservation [...] would be a reduction in the level of agricultural support' (Bowers and Cheshire, 1983, p. 10). This is chiefly because the resulting cost–price squeeze would be expected to reduce profits and intensity, leading to a general extensification of production and reduced pressure on the nature conservation resource (Whitby and Harvey, 1988). Others, such as Jenkins (1990) go further in envisaging a double dividend for the rural environment from the liberalization process: once when price support is withdrawn, and again when farm support expenditure is reallocated in favour of fully decoupled environmental programmes set up to deal more directly (and, presumably, more efficiently) with any environmental problems that remain once the distortions caused by price support have been removed. As Bowers (Bowers, 1995, p. 1241) puts it 'the abandonment of agricultural support through

the price mechanism will yield substantial consumer surpluses, part of which might in principle be captured through taxation to pay for alternative support through direct (environmental) payments'. Although an attractive idea, well supported by theory (see below), this largely optimistic view of the likely environmental impact of agricultural liberalization deserves careful analysis in a European context, where the 'first round' nature conservation effects of a withdrawal of price support are more complicated, and the political feasibility of switching substantial amounts of farm support into environmental schemes more uncertain, than is often assumed. This paper considers the validity of the double dividend thesis in the light of these qualifications. It discusses some of the nature conservation repercussions of a withdrawal of price support and assesses the willingness and ability of policymakers to set up the fully decoupled agri-environmental programmes that would appear to be needed to ensure the continued conservation management of Europe's countryside.

The double dividend

It could be argued that the CAP is already set on a path towards liberalization and has been since the MacSharry reforms of 1992 (Josling, 1994). These measures achieved a partial decoupling of arable and livestock support by cutting price guarantees and offering farmers area and headage based payments in their stead. More expediently, they also imposed on larger producers a requirement to set arable land aside in order to receive compensation payments (for a summary and review of the MacSharry reforms, see Winter, 1997). Josling's (Josling, 1994) assessment is that market exposure had been increased, albeit only modestly. The Arable Area Payments Scheme (AAPS), in combination with reduced price guarantees, for instance, means that the link between subsidies and yields is much weaker than it was before, giving farmers a reduced policy incentive to intensify production by applying more inputs to cropped land (though the farmer still has an incentive to maintain the 1992 arable area in order to continue receiving the payments). A similar partial decoupling of support has been achieved in the livestock sector, where new direct producer aids have been introduced that are subject to quotas, ceilings and stocking rate limits. Although payments depend on current livestock numbers being maintained, there is now technically no policy incentive to expand above these levels unless warranted by market prices. All this being said, the case for many of these compensation payments being decoupled from production in the original GATT meaning of the term is a moot

one. As Harvey (1995) (p. 210) observes 'the passing of the present comepnsation arrangements as within the green box (*sic*), and thus non trade distorting, is widely understood to be a convenient fiction for the purposes of the current Agreement only.' Under the terms of the Blair House agreement between the US and the EU, the area and headage payments introduced with the MacSharry reforms have been placed in the so-called 'blue box' and are consequently deemed not to count towards the 'Aggregate Measure of Support' (AMS) that is the main object of liberalizers' concern. The only constraint in this connection is that these domestic support measures 'do not grant support to a specific commodity in excess of that decided during the 1992 marketing year' (quoted in Swinbank, 1996, p. 397).

Nevertheless, most commentators expect the MacSharry compensation schemes to come under renewed assault when the next round of negotiations is convened in 1999 (see Swinbank and Tanner, 1996). Passage of the 1996 Federal Agricultural Improvement and Reform (FAIR) Act in the United States strengthens that country's claim to have decoupled its agricultural support and weakens its commitment to the blue box. As Tangermann (1992) points out, governments throughout the world are moving to decouple and thus liberalize their agricultural support policies. In its 'Agenda 2000' paper setting out spending plans and proposals for long-term CAP reform, the EC acknowledges the need to further decouple support, both to prepare the Union for the next WTO round and to improve its position as a major world exporter of agricultural commodities (European Commission, 1997).

The environmental implications of the further decoupling and liberalization of the CAP, to which all this points, are profound. It is widely agreed that what Rausser (1982) describes as the defining weakness of the CAP — its attempt to maintain the incomes of poorer farmers by offering all farmers 'coupled' price support — has been a significant, if not the only, factor in the intensification of European agriculture over the last forty years (Potter, 1996). Specifically, farmers appeared to have responded to high price guarantees by increasing their use of agricultural resources, particularly land, in an effort to boost output. Since land is in fixed supply, the result has been a steady inflation in land values and rents and a greater incentive to farm land more intensively by using increased quantities of 'land saving' inputs like fertilizers and pesticides. The incentive to reclaim land through drainage, conversion and improvement has also increased. The result, in nature conservation terms, has been the removal of wildlife habitat and ecological

decline throughout the intensively farmed parts of the countryside (Barr *et al.*, 1993). By removing, or at least scaling down, price support it might be expected that this trend would go into reverse. To start with, the profitability of farming would decline. It is generally accepted by economists (Phipps *et al.*, 1990; Ronningen and Dixit, 1991; Tyers and Anderson, 1991) that, while world market prices will probably rise following the withdrawal of support, the improvement will not be sufficient to compensate farmers completely for the loss of price subsidies. A recent estimate for the UK suggests that agricultural incomes would be reduced by between £2 and £4 billion within the first 10 years of price support being withdrawn (MAFF, 1995). Because land is still fixed in its supply, economic theory predicts that most of the fall in profits resulting from the drop in prices will be captured in the value of land (Anderson, 1992a,b). This in turn should lead to a general extensification of production as farmers find they have less incentive to economize on their use of the land input by applying more fertilizers and pesticides to each hectare of crops and by putting more stock onto every hectare of grass.

It is widely assumed (see Whitby and Harvey, 1988; Jenkins, 1990; Abler and Shortle, 1993) that such an extensification of production will be good for the environment, reducing surface water and groundwater pollution problems, eliminating overgrazing and easing the pressure to reclaim land from the wild. It is further argued by advocates of the 'double dividend' like Jenkins (1990) that resources previously tied up in price support would also now be available to be reinvested in environmental schemes expressly designed to address any market failures which remained once price support has been removed. Theoretical support for this action comes from the economic theory of public goods, which identifies a case for continued government intervention and subsidization where there are environmental services (in this case, the management of habitats and landscapes for their amenity and nature conservation value) that would be underprovided if left to the market. It is further claimed that governments will be able to achieve such a substitution of expenditure, because paying farmers to protect the environment is likely to be a politically more defensible policy than one designed to maintain their incomes *per se*. As a UK Minister of Agriculture recognized some time ago (Gummer, 1993, p. 22), 'we are (increasingly) in the business of helping farmers directly but those payments must be in return for environmentally acceptable agriculture …There is now no longer any justification in the argument that a farmer must be paid because he is a farmer.'

Few conservationists would disagree with this last statement. Indeed, achieving the double dividend is arguably what most long-term campaigns to 'green the CAP' are increasingly about (see, for example, recent campaign statements from the Netherlands Society for Nature and Environment, 1995; and the UK's Royal Society for the Protection of Birds, 1996). Nevertheless, uncertainty surrounds both sides of th double dividend equation, particularly in a European context, where the first-round environmental benefits of a withdrawal of price support may be less decisive, and the green recoupling of support to environmental goals more difficult to achieve, than is often assumed in the literature. The eventual environmental outcome will be determined by the balance between passive changes in land use and farming practice triggered by price cuts and the ability of the European Commission and Member States to retain funding for measures (not necessarily all directed at farmers) which ensure the continued management of the countryside. This question is worth further consideration in order to identify some of the choices policymakers may have to face in dealing with the nature conservation effects of agricultural liberalization in the Europe Union.

The extensification effect

To take the extensification effect first, this is heavily predicated on a series of linked assumptions, many of which are in need of further empirical research (Harold and Runge, 1993). One is that farmers will respond to a change in relative factor prices by making cuts in fertilizer and pesticide use that are sufficient to have an environmental effect. This depends, *inter alia*, on the elasticity of substitution between land and these other factor inputs and on the relationship between the level, pattern and intensity of fertilizer and chemical use and environmental damage. As Crabtree (1992) comments, estimates of the elasticity of demand for inputs with respect to product prices vary widely, with programming models usually assuming fertilizer use to be less price sensitive than econometric models. Abler and Shortle's (Abler and Shortle, 1992, 1993) prediction of a 60–85% reduction in fertilizer and chemical use following the decoupling of the CAP is considerably more optimistic than Becker's (Becker, 1992), for instance. Observations of the farmer response to the more moderate price cuts instituted by the MacSharry reforms suggest that, in the short term, elasticities may be rather low (Brouwer and van Berkum, 1995). Even assuming input use falls significantly, the precise nature of the environmental benefit being predicted by these models is often still unclear. Burt *et al.* (1993) point out that a reduction

in nitrogen use (for example) does not automatically mean an improvement in environmental quality as it is losses to the environment through leaching and run-off that determines whether any pollution damage is incurred. In this respect, much depends on the starting point from which reductions in, say, fertilzer use are being made. The Dutch farmer who reduces his fertilizer applications from 700 kg/hectare (the country average for The Netherlands in 1992) to 500 kg/hectare will have achieved a substantial cut in input use, but is unlikely to have done enough to eliminate environmental damage due to run-off or leaching if the rate of nitrogen uptake by the crop is only 150 kg/hectare (Harold and Runge, 1993). As Delpeuch (Delpeuch, 1994, p. 41) puts it 'a reckless driver who reduces his speed from 120 to 100 miles an hour would not deserve any recognition from society, so why should we reward or recognize farmers who do much the same thing?' Furthermore, the environmental value of an input reduction depends on where it takes place, 'the way in which pollutants move through the soil and hydrological system (determining) the damage caused' (Hodge, 1992, p. 68). The EU's concept of 'nitrate vulnerable zones', for example, recognizes that there are specific riparian environments where the risk of nitrate contamination is especially high. As Baldock *et al.* (1993) point out, if the aim is to improve groundwater quality by reducing nitrate pollution, targeting for substantial reductions in nitrogen fertilizer use at these environmentally vulnerable locations, such as arable land overlying aquifers, is likely to be a much more effective strategy than the wide but shallow extensification of production implied by models such as Abler and Shortle's (Abler and Shortle, 1992, 1993).

The nature conservation effects of any extensification of production brought about by the withdrawal of support are largely neglected in the studies reported above. The tendency in Abler and Shortle's work, for instance, is to equate environmental problems in agriculture with pollution and soil erosion and to understate the concern, traditionally more important in Europe than in the US, with the proper management of the farmed countryside to maintain biodiversity and prevent desertification or the abandonment of land. Anderson's (Anderson, 1992b) assessment of the land use effects of liberalization is limited to a discussion of the implications for deforestation in developing countries of a rise in the world market price of agricultural products. While it is easy to see that reduced price support, and the decline in land values and rents which this is expected to bring about, will ease the pressure to reclaim semi-natural vegetation, drain wetland and remove hedgerows, it is less clear what the implications of a cost–price squeeze will be for the active management of wildlife habitat on farms or the long-term survival of high natural value farming systems (Baldock and Condor, 1985).

Most commentators agree that the visual quality and biodiversity of many of Europe's agricultural landscapes depend on the continuation of farming and the management and upkeep of components like hedges, drystone walls, woodland, heather moorland and other types of semi-natural vegetation. As Bowers (Bowers, 1995, p. 1235) puts it 'current farming practices have a crucial role to play in the conservation of genetic diversity, landscapes and archaeological sites. Landscape quality is judged to be dependent on patterns of diversity in farming systems and in field structures.' For Webster and Felton (1993) undermanagement of the conservation resource is arguably already as great a threat to the nature conservation interest of large parts of the farmed countryside in a country like the UK as intensification and overexploitation. Moreover, it is increasingly recognized (and concretely expressed in the form of agri-environmental schemes offering support) that there are certain high natural value farming systems which need to be maintained in order to ensure the proper management of larger tracts of semi-natural vegetation, especially in southern Member States (Beaufoy *et al.*, 1994; Bignal *et al.*, 1996). Research across the EU suggests that low intensity farming systems, such as the dehesas of southern Spain, the montados in Portugal, agro-pastoralism in the Black Forest and traditional hill sheep production in the UK uplands, are critical factors in explaining important distributions of plants, animals and biotopes there (see Garcia, 1992; Vieria, 1993; Bignal, 1996; Luick, 1996). Their high nature conservation value is a function of, first, the ecological stability provided by the continuity of management, and second, the predictability of the dynamics and disturbances associated with traditional patterns of human interference (Bignal *et al.*, 1996). By definition, such systems are already economically marginal, employing 'practices which have been out of fashion for many years and techniques which are not generally part of modern agriculture' (Bignal *et al.*, 1996, p. 31). Other things being equal, the withdrawal of price support could be expected to put their survival at risk, for as Bowers (Bowers, 1995, p. 1238) comments, 'there is no reason to suppose that these less intensive techniques would be profitable at market clearing prices', given their marginal profitability at current supported prices. Amalgamation could likely bring with it extensification of a kind few conservationists desire, as farms are taken over and managed in a less labour intensive way or even abandoned entirely. The result, according to Beaufoy *et al.* (1994), may be a series of changes in

land use and vegetation which will reduce biodiversity throughout the EU.

In the Causse Mejan in France, for example, traditional, low intensity producers are responding to an increasingly competitive market by changing their mix of enterprises and increasing output of sheep's milk for Roquefort cheese. Through a process of farm amalgamation and a concentration of production onto the best land, over 1000 hectares have been abandoned since the mid-1980s (Beaufoy *et al.*, 1994). With this comes a series of ecological changes as species rich grassland is replaced by coarse herbaceous vegetation, scrub and, eventually, forest. Similarly, in the Black Forest region of Baden-Würrtemberg, the continued economic marginalization of extensive cattle production is having serious effects on the landscape and its conservation value, colonization by scrub and pine creating habitats of lower diversity than the grassland vegetation they replace (Luick, 1996). In Sweden, Vail *et al.* (1994) report a significant reversion of farmland to forest due to a fall in agricultural returns following that country's partial liberalization of its agricultural policy in 1990. In southern Member States, the risk of exposure to soil erosion and fire can be expected to significantly increase as terracing practices decline and understocking exacerbates the fire hazard by encouraging the invasion of scrub on grazing land (Baldock, 1996).

The environmental, and particularly the nature conservation, effects of significantly reducing price support do not all run in the same direction, suggesting a strong need for counterbalancing measures which would be deployed to offset, and not merely complement or speed up, some of the first round repercussions of CAP reform. The case for special assistance to keep high natural value farming systems in place would seem to be particularly strong, for it could (and will) be argued that without this, liberalization may wipe out much of the human capital necessary for the effective conservation of the European countryside. The UK's Country Landowners Association (Country Landowners Association, 1994, para. 165) recently opined that 'concerted efforts will need to be made as CAP reform proceeds to prevent the loss of sympathetic land management systems through intensification and abandonment…These systems will need to be protected, sustained and encouraged.' There will also continue to be calls for government action to tackle a countryside management and farm pollution problem likely to be only marginally affected by the shallow extensification of production induced by price cuts alone. In short, obtaining a favourable and environmentally sustainable outcome from the liberalization of agricultural policy will depend heavily on the ability and willingness of policy-makers to recouple support to broader social and environmental policy objectives under the umbrella of a European Rural Policy.

Green recoupling

Achieving this is largely a political question, though there are very good reasons in principle to expect some sort of 'green recoupling' and rebalancing of support will gradually take place. According to an evolutionary model of farm policy change, the decoupling process, once begun, puts mounting pressure on policymakers to find new ways of justifying agricultural support. This is because substituting income compensation payments for market price support increases the visibility and transparency of government transfers, shifting the burden from consumers to taxpayers and engendering a debate about why farmers should continue receiving public support. As Rausser and Irwin (Rausser and Irwin, 1989, p. 363) observe 'consumers are generally less vocal about policies that affect them only slightly, while the taxpayers' burden is more obvious not only to the taxpayer but also to his elected representatives who impose taxes and authorize expenditures.' Given that paying farmers to produce environmental goods is likely to be a more publicly defensible position than supporting them simply because they are farmers (see Gummer's remarks above), it might be expected that expenditure would be switched into agri-environmental programmes as time progressed. In support of this, advocates of the double dividend can point to the immunities enjoyed by green payments under the URAA. By placing such payments in the 'green box', negotiators signalled recognition of their likely future importance as a non-trade distorting source of support to farmers and encouraged governments to begin to substitute them for the more controversial blue box compensation schemes. Any green payments which result must, according to the Subsidies Code, be: (a) part of a clearly defined government programme; (b) non- or minimally trade distorting; and (c) limited to subsidizing the added cost or lost income from the practices adopted or the technology shift accomplished. An OECD analysis of the Agreement (OECD, 1995), comments that the criteria for the exempted measures provide a guide for the development of an agricultural policy capable of targeting problems in a trade neutral way.

In practice, achieving this full green recoupling of agricultural support is likely to be a politically fraught process, very much dependent on the ability

of environmentalists and others to articulate a case for redirecting public money away from agricultural and in favour of broader rural social and environmental objectives. The first sign that this idea is being taken seriously by policymakers would be an expansion in funding for agri-environmental programmes. Theory would suggest that the assumed income boost from liberalization will increase demand for environmental quality among European citizens. This is a version of the argument that free trade is good for the environment because it generates the economic growth which increases the demand for environmental protection as well as providing the resources necessary to achieve it (Ekins *et al.*, 1994). Recent reviews of the evidence on the relationship between income growth and environmental concern, however, suggest that the income elasticity of environmental improvement may be less than one (Office of Technology Assessment, 1995). So far as the demand for agri-environmental services specifically is concerned, Whitby and Saunders (1994) point out that there is presently no objective measure of taxpayers' willingness to pay for an expansion of agri-environmental programmes and no necessary reason why, in aggregate, this should equal existing levels of agricultural support. A decision to switch large amounts of public money into agri-environmental programmes is ultimately a judgement to be made by policymakers themselves. Experience to date suggests that EU Member States are still more concerned to ensure that farmers are compensated for any price reductions achieved than they are to expend large sums of money on agri-environmental policy. The conservation dividend from the MacSharry reforms of 1992 was very small, with less than 4% of the total 1996 farm budget being invested in the EU's newly established Agri-Environmental Programme (AEP). By comparison, the partially decoupled 'blue box' compensation payments absorbed over 43% of the annual farm budget (European Commission, 1997). The resulting policy mix — weakly decoupled compensation schemes in combination with what some regard as seriously underfunded agri-environmental measures — is suboptimal from an environmental point of view, because the new compensation schemes often cut across what many AEP measures are trying to achieve (Winter, 1997). For instance, arable producers, required to set aside a proportion of their cropped land in order to qualify for compensation under the AAPS, can be expected to be more reluctant to find additional land for environmental schemes. At the same time, there is evidence that while the total volume of inputs applied to arable land has (obviously) declined, application rates on land still under crops have marginally increased (Winter, 1997). Brouwer and van Berkum's (Brouwer and Berkum, 1995) assessment is that the partial decoupling of policy represented by the MacSharry reforms is having complex effects, not all of them beneficial to the environment.

Taking a pragmatic line, conservation groups, especially in the UK (Dixon and Taylor, 1990), have argued for environmental conditions to be attached to the direct payments farmers will increasingly receive. At present, the level of 'cross compliance' built into the MacSharry compensation measures is rather low. Groups such as the UK Royal Society for the Protection of Birds have mounted a long campaign to persuade agriculture departments to attach more conservation strings to all compensation payments. The speed with which this idea has been taken up by farm groups (see National Farmers Union, 1994) and now, apparently, the European Commission in its Agenda 2000 proposals (European Commission, 1997), attests to its perceived political as well as environmental advantages. Cross-compliance solves the legitimation problem which partial decoupling creates (by allowing farmers to claim they are delivering publicly demanded environmental services in return for government payments received), and blurs the line between temporary compensation and semi-permanent policy entitlements. The problem is that blue box payments are by definition transitory. Their eventual scaling down will eliminate the leverage cross-compliance is designed to exploit and, incidentally, may sweep away any environmental investments and improvements that have been made meantime.

This has led many to refocus their attention on the need to recouple support directly to environmental and social goals. A question which must then be confronted is how politically feasible is it to put in place systems of payments that are exclusively environmental in the way they are designed and delivered to farmers. Advocates of the double divi-

dend, it should be recalled, appear to envisage a strict green recoupling of support whereby market support is abolished and replaced with a lightly engineered system of environmental payments organized on a purchaser-provider basis (see Table 1). According to the standard formulation, environmental payments must be fully decoupled from both production and the support of farmers' incomes and recoupled to measurable environmental targets if 'rent seeking' by agricultural interests is not to occur (Rausser and Irwin, 1989). Unless this separation is achieved, by targeting schemes or by linking payment to the delivery of definite environmental improvements or products, measures may be prone to adverse selection because farmers will claim blanket payments for undertaking (or resisting) changes that would have (not) taken place anyway. This increases the risk that green subsidies may be abandoned at some later date by a disgruntled public who come to see them as disguised (and thus, in this new policy environment, illegitimate) income payments. According to Jenkins (Jenkins, 1990, p. 7) 'expenditure on such supports can only be justified if they ensure the provision of specific environmental goods.' The House of Lords Select Committee on the European Communities (House of Lords, 1991, p. 48) specifies that 'payments, which should not be restricted to farmers alone, should be graduated according to the environmental interest of the land, the sophistication of the management demanded or the resultant changes in farming practice.' Buckwell (1990, p. 159) further argues that 'in each case it is not only necessary to identify targets but also to define criteria for monitoring the success or otherwise of policy changes designed to achieve specific targets.' The selective enrolment of farmers and land would also seem to be required to ensure maximum environmental value for money and to break the link with farm income support.

Table 1. Degrees of recoupling

Action	Mechanisms for environmental improvement	Agri-environmental policy configuration
Full green recoupling	The double dividend: price-induced extensification; direct reallocation of money into environmental schemes	Strictly decoupled environmental management schemes, payments calculated with reference to environmental outputs achieved
Moderate recoupling	Maintaining sufficient farming activity to ensure production of joint products; additional improvements engineered through top-up payments	Bottom tier hectarage payments and voluntary set aside, upper tier environmental payments offered on a discretionary basis
Weak recoupling	Voluntary enrolment in ELMS; application of cross-compliance to producer subsidies and compensation	ELMS together with pragmatic use of conservation compliance

Source: Potter (1998).
Note: ELMS = Environmental Land Management Scheme.

Judging by the present configuration of the EU's AEP, however, this desideratum, as some see it, is still some way off. Rather than setting up schemes that are designed to maximize the environmental return on every ECU spent, many Member States have sought to adopt a rather permissive approach, laying down minimal entry conditions and management requirements that are often close to existing good agricultural practice (Potter, 1998). The most egregious case of this is the French 'Prime a l'herbe' scheme, which offers any grassland farmer who will take it an annual payment in return for an agreement to maintain a stocking rate of 1.4 livestock units per hectare or less. Similarly in Austria, the ÖPUL scheme operates as a support line to livestock farmers who may otherwise be tempted to intensify production following Austria's recent accession to the EU. Having examined the operation of the much vaunted 'MEKA' scheme in Baden-Württemberg, Wilson (Wilson, 1995, p. 157) has 'the impression that the importance of the environmental element is overshadowed by considerations regarding agricultural markets, production and the survival of the farm household.' Critics like Tangermann (Tangermann, 1992, p. 20) deduce from all this that there is 'a strong tendency to argue for all sorts of measures which are called environmental policies, but whose objective essentially is to find new ways of channelling money to agriculture.' Wilkinson (1994) goes further, seeing in the AEP a faintly disguised set of income aids designed to sweeten the bitter pill of market reform.

These are harsh judgements on a policy at such an early stage in its development; the approach being followed at least has the merit that it brings large numbers of farmers into schemes and maximizes coverage, even at the risk of some adverse selection. It also maximizes the opportunities for policy learning, for as Nelson and Soete (1988) remark, policy evolution from a broad base offers more scope for engaging in experimentation and learning from feedback. The increasingly widespread introduction of tiered payments in all Member States is an example of this because it exploits the current situation of widespread but essentially shallow participation to reward farmers who subsequently agree to undertake more restrictive operations and agree to be brought 'deeper' into schemes (Potter, 1998). Policymakers must tread a fine line between setting up voluntary schemes that are restrictive enough to effect an environmental improvement or prevent a deterioration, and yet also permissive enough to attract sufficient farmers and land to make a difference. There may thus be a good case for policymakers adopting a second best approach in this area of policy, initially establishing a large variety of schemes but then winnowing out those which do not

deliver the environmental product specified. Whitby's (Whitby et al., 1997) view is that over time an evolution in the public's appreciation of what agri-environmental policy is supposed to be about will exert its own pressure for further improvements in policy design and delivery. With the conservation interest on farms coming to be seen as a growing stock of environmental capital that has been paid for out of public funds, policymakers can be expected to adopt arrangements which will define more precisely the product to be delivered and lock farmers into schemes for the longer term.

At the same time, however, it must be recognized that, for many Member States, conflating environmental protection with supporting the incomes of small family farmers is regarded as a perfectly legitimate way of proceeding. A guiding assumption of many continental Europeans is that an economically viable and beautiful countryside is one managed by large numbers of farmers and that a principle concern of rural policy should be to keep farmers on the land. As Hodge (Hodge, 1992, p. 71) points out, on this view the support of farmers' ioncomes and environmental protection are inextricably linked 'such that proposals for reducing prices appear inescapably to imply a denial of environmental values.' This view was widely aired at the landmark Cork conference, concerned by the European Commission in 1996 to debate the future shape of European rural policy. The Irish Minister for Rural Development, for instance, declared that 'agriculture continues to be the lifeblood of rural areas…the pressures on agriculture should be used to encourage policymakers to formulate measures that ensure the maintenance of the maximum number of farm families' (Deenihan, 1996, p. 7). The Commissioner for Agriculture amplified this when he argued that 'rural society is a socio-economic model in its own right which must be preserved in the interests of European society as a whole' (Fischler, 1996, p. 12). Commentators like Berlan-Darqué (1993) and Baudry and Laurent (1993) detect continuing popular support for policies which are designed to maintain the perceived link between farmers, the environment and rural society.

Pressure will thus continue to be exerted to ensure that any money released from price support is used to ensure the continued occupancy of rural land. Indeed, according to the Commissioner for Agriculture, it should be an explicit policy goal to 'guarantee a reasonable income for our farmers and keep the countryside in the Union under cultivation' (Fischler, 1997, p. 3). Proposals were made some time ago for replacing market support with a system of 'producer entitlement guarantees' to enable Member States to retain a broad base of agricultural support in the least trade-distorting way. Under this arrangement, farmers would be allocated an entitlement to an annual government subsidy calculated as a percentage of the output of their farms in the recent past, agricultural output above this level being sold on an unsupported market (Harvey, 1990). According to Harvey (Harvey, 1990, p. 212), 'if there are real social benefits from a more economically secure farming population than the free market would provide, then some annual payments may well be justified.' A more current idea, informed by the same precautionary philosophy, is to offer all farmers who will take it a hectarage payment, again in the form of a permanent policy entitlement (Josling, 1994). These would be moderately decoupled to the extent that they are permanently tied to the land but they could be 'greened' in two ways. First, by linking eligibility to the observation of safe minimum environmental standards. Such standards are already in the process of being defined and legislated for in various member states (see for example The Danish Ministry of the Environment, 1994). They could be further refined, and tailored to local circumstances, in order to define farming practices and precautions which farmers would have to observe and/or implement in order to continue qualifying for payment. Further greening could be achieved by offering additional top-up payments where recipients agree to make improvements or take precautions over and above the baseline. This would give scope for rewarding good practice and for compensating for the costs incurred in undertaking environmental management work in a way that is most compatible with WTO rules (see criteria listed above). While such a system is some way from the full green recoupling envisaged by Jenkins (1990) and others, in which targeted environmental payments are only ever given for a specified product, it could be argued that it is more in line with the broader socio-environmental priorities of the Member States of the European Union as a whole and thus more conceivable within the context of a European Rural Policy. Moreover, by maximizing policy 'reach', enabling policymakers to influence farming practice on a larger number of farms than might be possible under a targeted system of free-standing environmental management payments, it may help realize 'ecological economies of scale' that would be otherwise hard to achieve. At issue here is what, for want of a better description, might be called the 'joint product' view of agri-environmental interaction in which valued cultural landscapes are seen to be the result of widely flung patterns of agricultural activity and occupancy. In the UK, such thinking is beginning to find expression in the idea of protecting and enhancing 'countryside character' (see Gummer,

1993) but it has always been strong in Germany and France where today it translates into a requirement to retain a sufficiently broad base of government support to sustain a strong agricultural presence in rural areas. The proposal in Agenda 2000 to transform support in Less Favoured Areas into 'low input farming supports' (European Commission, 1997) is rooted in precisely this assumption. If such thinking continues to prevail, the challenge of policymakers will be to balance the need to decouple agricultural support in order to meet their future WTO obligations with the desirability of maintaining sufficient agricultural protection to sustain the social and environmental fabric of the European countryside. Public debate on this critical question is only now beginning to take place.

Conclusion

The idea that withdrawing farm support under the CAP will be doubly beneficial for rural environments, first in terms of a price induced extensification of production, and again when funds are released for re-investment in agri-environmental schemes, is currently enjoying wide support. It suggests that improving agricultural competitiveness and boosting environmental protection can be complementary policy goals at a time when the liberalization of agricultural trade is closer than ever before. In a European setting, however, there are grounds for caution concerning this double dividend equation. To begin with, the nature conservation effects of any extensification of production induced by price cuts may not all run in the same direction, the pollution benefits of de-intensification in some locations possibly being offset by a reduction in biodiversity and landscape values caused by a decline in countryside management elsewhere. While these latter effects may be dealt with through a compensating expansion in environmental subsidies, it is unclear how willing or able European policymakers will be to achieve the complete 'green recoupling' of agricultural support advocates of the double dividend appear to have in mind. Despite a seemingly good 'first best' case, at least in a northern European context, for transitional compensation for price cuts giving way to a lightly engineered and fully decoupled system of environmental payments, the reality is likely to be more complicated. Judging by recent pronouncements and policy actions, there will continue to be a strong argument for retaining a broad base of agricultural support in order to prevent the risk of desertification and threats to countryside character which price cuts are perceived to create. The line between farm

296   Clive Potter and Philip Goodwin

income support and environmental protection may
be further blurred as new measures are introduced,
particularly in southern Member States, in an effort
to maintain high natural value farming systems by
keeping marginal producers on the land. A second-
best strategy could be emerging, in which policy-
makers seek through trial and error to discover how
decoupled agricultural support actually needs to be
to sustain Europe's cultural landscapes in a freer
trading world.

Acknowledgements — The desk research on which this
paper was based was funded by English Nature. The
authors are grateful to Mark Tilzey and to two anonymous
referees for comments on an earlier draft of this paper.

References

Abler, D. and Shortle, J. (1992) Potential for Environment and Agriculture Policy Linkages under Reforms in
the European Commission. *American Journal of Agricultural Economics* **74**(3), 775–781.

Abler, D. and Shortle, J. (1993) Environmental and farm
commodity policy linkages in the US and the European
Commission. *European Review of Agricultural Economics*
19, 197–217.

Anderson, K. (1992a) Agricultural Trade Liberalisation
and the Environment: a Global Perspective. *The World
Economy* **15**(1), 153–171.

Anderson, K. (1992b) *Agricultural Policies, Land Use and
the Environment*. Granta Editions, Cambridge.

Baldock, D. (1990) *Agricultural and Habitat Loss in
Europe*. World Wide Fund for Nature, London.

Baldock, D. (1996) Marginalisation of Farming Systems in
Europe: an Overview. In *The Common Agricultural
Policy and Environmental Practices*, proceedings of a
seminar organised by the EFNCP, ed. K. Mitchell. Institute for European Environmental Policy, London.

Baldock, D. and Conder, D. (1985) *Can the CAP Fit the
Environment? The Environmental Implications of Future
EEC Farm Price Policies*. Council for the Protection of
Rural England, Institute for European Environmental
Policy and Worldwide Fund for Nature, London.

Baldock, D., Beaufoy, G., Bennett, G. and Clark, J. (1993)
*Nature Conservation and New Directions in the EC
Common Agricultural Policy*. Institute of European
Environmental Policy, London.

Barr, C., Bunce, R., Clark, R. *et al.* (1993) *Countryside
Survey 1990: Main Report*. Department of the Environment, London.

Baudry, J. and Laurent, C. (1993) Paysages ruraux et acti-
vités agricoles. In *Agricultures et Societie: Pistes Pour la
Recherche*, ed. C. Courtet, M. Berlan-Darqué and Y.
Demarne. Association Descartes, Paris.

Beaufoy, G., Baldock, D. and Clark, J. (1994) *The Nature
of Farming: Low-Intensity Farming Systems in Nine European Countries*. Institute for European Environmental
Policy, London.

Becker, H. (1992) Impact of Taxes and Quotas on Fertilizers and Requirements of Direct Income Payments
within Agricultural Regions of the European
Community. Unpublished paper presented to the 30th
EAAE Seminar, Chateau-d'Oex, Switzerland.

Berlan-Darqué, M. (1993) Preface. In *Agricultures et Societie: Pistes Pour la Recherche*, ed. C. Courtet, M. Berlan-
Darque and Y. Demarne. Association Descartes, Paris.

Bignal, E. (1996) Mixed Livestock Farming in the Highlands and Islands of Scotland. In *The Common Agricultural Policy and Environmental Practices*, proceedings of
a seminar organised by the EFNCP, ed. K. Mitchell.
Institute for European Environmental Policy, London.

Bignal, E., Baldock, D. and Tubbs, C. (1996) *European
Union: the EU's Agri-Environment Regulation No.
2078/92 — Examples of Environmental Benefits*. Paper
given to the OECD Seminar on Environmental Benefits
from a Sustainable Agriculture: Issues and Policies,
Helsinki, 10–13 September 1996.

Bowers, J. (1995) Sustainability, Agriculture and Agricultural Policy. *Environment and Planning A* **27**,
1231–1234.

Bowers, J. and Cheshire, p. (1983) *Agriculture, the Countryside and Land Use*. Methuen, London.

Brouwer, F. and van Berkum, S. (1995) *CAP and the
Environment in the European Union: Analysis of the
Effects of the CAP on the Environment and an Assess-
ment of Existing Environmental Conditions*. Agricultural
Economics Research Institute, The Hague.

Buckwell, A. (1990) Economic Signals, Farmers' Response
and Environmental Change. *Journal of Rural Studies*
5(2), 149–160.

Burt, T., Heathwaite, A. and Trudgill, S. (1993) *Nitrate:
Processes, Patterns and Management*. Wiley, Chichester.

Country Landowners Association (1994) *Focus on the
CAP: a Discussion Paper*. CLA, London.

Crabtree, B. (1992) A More Environmental CAP? Unpub-
lished paper to the Agricultural Economics Society
Conference: 'Reform of the CAP in Relation to
GATT'. London, 10 December 1992.

Danish Ministry of the Environment (1994) *The Danish
Environmental Strategy*. Ministry of the Environment,
Copenhagen.

Deenihan, J. (1996) Address at the opening of the Euro-
pean Conference on Rural Development 'Rural Europe
— Future Perspectives', 7–9 November 1996, Cork,
Ireland.

Delpeuch, B. (1994) Ireland's Agri-Environment Programme in the European Context. In *Agriculture and the
Environment*, proceedings of a conference on the integration of EC environmental objectives with agricultural
policy, ed. M. Moloney, 9–11 March 1994, Agricultural
Conference Proceedings No. 2, Royal Dublin Society,
Dublin.

Dixon, J. and Taylor, J. (1990) *Agriculture and the
Environment: Towards Integration*. Royal Society for the
Protection of Birds, Sandy.

Ekins, P., Folke, C. and Costanza, R. (1994) Trade,
Environment and Development: Issues in Perspectives.
Ecological Economics **9**, 1–12.

European Commission (1997) *Twenty-sixth Financial
Report Concerning the European Agricultural Guidance
and guarantee Fund, 1996 Financial Year*, COM(96)504
final. Office for Official Publications of the European
Communities, Luxembourg.

European Commission (1997) *Agenda 2000 for a Stronger
and Wider Union*, COM(97)2000. Office for Official
Publications of the European Communities,
Luxembourg.

Fischler, F. (1996) *Europe and its Rural Areas in the Year
2000: Integrated Rural Development as a Challenge for
Policy Making*. Opening speech to the Cork Conference
on Rural Development: 'Rural Europe — Future Perspectives', 7–9 November 1996.

Fischler, F. (1997) Keynote address, Agra-Europe Outlook Conference, London.

Garcia, A. (1992) Conserving the Species-Rich Meadows of Europe. *Agriculture, Ecosystems and Environment* **40**, 219–232.

Grant, R. (1993) Against the Grain: Agricultural trade policies of the US, the European Community and Japan at the GATT. *Political Geography* **12**(3), 247–262.

Grant, W. (1995) The Limits of the CAP Reform and the Option of Renationalisation. *Journal of European Public Policy* **2**(1), 1–18.

Gummer, J. (1993) Agriculture, the Environment, and Trade — A British Perspective. In *Agriculture, the Environment, and Trade — Conflict or Cooperation?* ed. C. Williamson. International Policy Council on Agriculture and Trade, Washington, DC.

Harold, C. and Runge, F. (1993) GATT and the Environment: Policy Research Needs. *American Journal of Agricultural Economics* **75**, 789–793.

Harvey, D. (1990) *The CAP and Green Agriculture*. Institute for Public Policy Research, Green Paper 3, London.

Harvey, D. (1995) EU Cereals Policy: an Evolutionary Perspective. *Australian Journal of Agricultural Economics* **39**(3), 193–217.

Hodge, I. (1992) Supply Control and the Environment: The Case for Separate Policies. *Farm Management* **8**(2), 65–72.

House of Lords Select Committee on the European Communities (1991) *Development and Future of the CAP. 16th Report*, Session 1990–91. HMSO, London.

Ingersent, K., Rayner, A. and Hine, R. (ed.) (1993) *Agriculture in the Uruguay GATT Round*. Macmillan, London.

Jenkins, T. (1990) *Future Harvester: the Economics of Farming and the Environment*. Council for the Protection of Rural England, London.

Josling, T. (1994) The Reformed CAP in the Industrial World. *European Review of Agricultural Economics* **21**(3), 513–527.

Luick, R. (1996) High Nature Value Cattle Farming in the Black Forest Region in Baden-Württemberg — a Case Study for the Impact of EU Agricultural Policy on Less Favoured Areas in Germany. In *The Common Agricultural Policy and Environmental Practices*, proceedings of a seminar organised by the EFNCP, ed. K. Mitchell. Institute for European Environmental Policy, London.

MAFF (1995) *European Agriculture: the Case for Radical Reform*. Ministry of Agriculture, Fisheries and Food, London.

McCalla, A. (1993) Agricultural Trade Liberalisation: the Ever Elusive Grail. *American Journal of Agricultural Economics* **75**, 1102–1112.

National Farmers Union (1994) *Real Choices: A Discussion Document*. NFU, London.

Nelson, R. and Soete, L. (1988) Policy Conclusions. In *Technical Change and Economic Theory*, ed. G. Dosi, C. Freeman, G. Silverberg and L. Soete. Pinter, London.

Netherlands Society for Nature and Environment (1995) *A Revised Agriculture Scheme for the European Union: a proposal for an improved European Union policy instrument for the integration of agriculture, nature and environment*. Stichting Natuur en Milieu, Utrecht.

OECD (1995) *Agricultural Policies, Markets and Trade, Monitoring and Outlook Report 1995*. OECD, Paris.

Office of Technology Assessment (1995) *Agriculture, Trade and Environment: Achieving Complementary Policies*. OTA, Washington, DC.

Phipps, T., Rossmiller G. and Meyers W. Decoupling and Related Farm Policy Options. In *Agricultural Policies in a New Decade*, ed. K. Allen. Resources for the Future, Washington, DC.

Potter, C. (1996) *Decoupling by Degrees? Agricultural Liberalisation and its Implications for Nature Conservation in Britain*. English Nature Research Reports No. 196. English Nature, Peterborough.

Potter, C. (1998) *Against the Grain: Agri-Environmental Policy Reform in the US and EU*. CAB International, Wallingford.

Rausser, G. (1982) Political Economic Markets: PERTs and PESTs. *American Journal of Agricultural Economics* **64**(5), 821–833.

Rausser, G. and Irwin, D. (1989) The Political Economy of Agricultural Policy Reform. *European Review of Agricultural Economics* **15**, 349–366.

Rieger, E. (1996) The Common Agricultural Policy. In *Policymaking in the European Union*, ed. H. Wallace and W. Wallace. Oxford University Press, Oxford.

Ronningen, V. and Dixit, P. (1991) *A Single Measure of Trade Distortion*. IATRC Working Paper. United States Department of Agriculture, Washington, DC.

Royal Society for the Protection of Birds (1996) Memorandum to House of Commons Select Committee on Agriculture, *Environmentally Sensitive Areas and Other Schemes Under the Agri-Environmental Regulation*, Second report, 1996–97 Session. HMSO, London.

Stanners, D. and Bourdeau, P. (1995) *Europe's Environment: the Dobris Assessment. An Overview*. Office for Official Publications of the European Communities, Luxembourg.

Swinbank, A. (1996) Capping the CAP? Implementation of the Uruguay Round Agreement by the European Union. *Food Policy* **21**(4/5), 393–407.

Swinbank, A. and Tanner, C. (1996) *Farm Policy and Trade Conflict: the Uruguay Round and the Common Agricultural Policy*. University of Michigan Press, Ann Arbor.

Tangermann, S. (1992) *Reforming the CAP: In for a Penny, In for a Pound?* Institute of Economic Affairs, London.

Tangermann, S. and Josling, T. (1995) *Towards a CAP for the Next Century*. European Policy Forum, London.

Tyers, R. and Anderson, K. (1991) *Global Effects of Liberalising Trade in Farm Products*. Harvester Wheatsheaf, London.

Vail, D., Per Hasund, K. and Drake, L. (1994) *The Greening of Agricultural Policy in Industrial Societies: Swedish Reforms in Comparative Perspective*. Cornell University Press, London.

Vieira, M. (1993) Environmentally Sensitive Areas in Portugal. In *A Future for Europe's Farmed Countryside*, ed. J. Dixon, A. Stones and I. Hepburn. Royal Society for the Protection of Birds, Sandy.

Webster, S. and Felton, M. (1993) Targeting for nature conservation in agricultural policy. *Land Use Policy* **10**(1), 67–82.

Whitby, M. and Harvey, D. (1988) Issues and Policies. In *Land Use and the European Environment*, ed. M. Whitby and J. Ollerenshaw. Belhaven Press, London.

Whitby, M. and Saunders, C. (1994) *Estimating the Supply of Conservation Goods*. Centre for Rural Economy, Working Paper 10. University of Newcastle-on-Tyne, Newcastle.

Whitby, M., Hodge, M., Lowe, P. and Saunders, C. (1997) Conservation Options for CAP Reform. *ECOS: A Review of Nature Conservation* **17**(3/4), 46–54.

Wilkinson, A. (1994) Renationalisation: An Evolving Debate. In *Renationalisation of the Common Agricultural*

298   Clive Potter and Philip Goodwin

Policy?, ed. R. Kjeldahl and M. Tracy. Institute of Agricultural Economics, Copenhagen.

Wilson, G. (1995) Farmer Environmental Attitudes and ESA Participation. *Geo-Forum* **27**(2), 115–131.

Winter, M. (1998) The CAP and the Environment. In *The Reform of the Common Agricultural Policy*, ed. A. Rayner, K. Ingersent and R. Hine. Macmillan, London (in press).

B
Developing Country Perspectives

[5]

RURAL DEVELOPMENT STRATEGIES IN LOW INCOME COUNTRIES: POVERTY REDUCTION, PRODUCTIVITY GAINS AND DECENTRALISATION[1]

DERYKE BELSHAW[2]

1. INTRODUCTION

That the great majority of the world's poorest people – defined in relation to some professionally acceptable poverty line – live in the rural areas of developing countries is a 'stylized fact'[3]. Generally accepted too is the expectation of rapidly rising total numbers of poor people in Sub-Saharan Africa, especially, and also in the Middle East/North Africa and Latin America/Caribbean regions but with the opposite trend occurring in developing countries in south, south-east and east Asia (see, for example, World Bank, 1999). On the questions of poverty causality and the choice of poverty-reducing development strategies, however, there is much less unanimity. During the 1990s the dominant group of multi- and bilateral donors (which included the World Bank, the IMF, USAID and UK's ODA/DFID) saw the open growth-oriented strategies pursued successfully by the newly-industrialising countries (the NICs) as a universally applicable model, the benefits of which could be brought to less successful countries under appropriate strategies of the Structural Adjustment Programme (SAP) type. These are typified by macro-economic stabilisation measures (elimination of macro-economic price distortions) and structural reforms involving market liberalisation, privatisation and significant reductions in the developmental role of the state. Ensuing high rates of economic growth were expected to benefit the poor through 'trickle down' or 'spread effects' operating in factor and product markets. Direct poverty-focused investment should be limited to employment-based safety nets and to the charitable activities of non-governmental organisation (NGOs) as set out in the World Bank's 'New Poverty Agenda' (see

---

[1] A revised version of a paper presented at the Annual Conference of the Agricultural Economics Society held at Girton College, Cambridge in April 1995.

[2] Professor Emeritus of Development Studies, University of East Anglia and Visiting Scholar, Wolfson College, Oxford.

[3] "…while urban poverty is a growing phenomenon, the rural poor still account for over 80 percent of the total number of poor people in … 114 developing countries" Jazairy et al. (1992).

World Bank, 1990; Wilmshurst et al., 1992, Lipton and Maxwell, 1992). Efficiency, therefore, need not be sacrificed in the pursuit of equity.

This view has been strongly contested, however, on three main grounds: firstly, in the light of evidence that the state did play a decisive early role in the transformations of the NIC economies; secondly, on the lack of evidence that the economic and institutional preconditions for successfully emulating NIC performance are yet in place in the poorest developing countries; and, thirdly, robust evidence that in the latter countries large concentrations of poor people are bypassed by market forces and that the resulting socio-political instability counters or reduces the rate of market-led growth elsewhere.

At the centre of this debate is the following question: "Can deliberately rural poverty-focused development strategies – i.e. appropriate rural development strategies – be designed and implemented which will combine positive gains in equity without sacrificing economic growth, achieving a win-win outcome?" Many development agencies were still committed to such an approach in the 1990s (see for example, IFAD 1994; Commonwealth Secretariat, 1993;GTZ, 1993; Netherlands Development Cooperation, 1992 and most, if not all, development NGOs). But rural development itself as a poverty alleviation strategy has a mixed record starting with the show case integrated projects of the 1960s (see Lele, 1975) and their widespread adoption in the 1970s, especially by the World Bank (see World Bank, 1975).

The interpretation of the record of this 'first generation' of interventions and an assessment of the currently dominant paradigm are the primary tasks of this paper. Its purpose is to provide a succinct overview of the rural development record and the accompanying debate. In discussing this agenda it is hoped that the need for the use of a broad framework of economic, social and technical analysis, which the agricultural economics profession is traditionally familiar with and capable of, will become apparent. The next section of the paper examines the important relationships between rural development and the macro-economic dimension. Section 3 identifies the main approaches employed in the 'first generation' period (1965-90) and section 4 critically examines the highly-decentralised approach to poverty alleviation which is still in fashion at the turn of the century. The main implications for policy are summarised in the final section.

2.   MACRO-ECONOMIC ASPECTS OF RURAL DEVELOPMENT

Keith Griffin's seminal study (1989) of the empirical country-level experience of economic development identified six alternative strategies which had been put into effect for periods long enough to evaluate their impacts. While rural development was not amongst them, the broader category labelled 'redistributive strategies', with the key objective of increasing equity through achieving a direct impact on the poorest, can accommodate it alongside similar strategies, such as 'basic needs provision' and 'redistribution with growth'. Nevertheless, suspicion is widespread amongst economists that a rural development strategy is pure populism i.e. it panders to the political demands of a large segment of the (voting) population for the immediate satisfaction of wants – for increased consumption of private and public goods. Certainly much of the literature emanating from other cooperating disciplines strengthens that impression by neglecting to relate the design of a rural development strategy to an economy's long-term transformation path.

At least six possible ways in which rural poverty alleviation strategies may assist long term economic growth can be identified. Firstly, in situations where rural poverty can be alleviated in a cost-effective way by improving access by the poor to under-utilised parts of the natural resource base to produce larger marketed surpluses using more productive technology and/or higher value products, the familiar neo-classical balanced growth model is relevant (Johnston and Mellor, 1961). This strategy usually implies the implementation of some combination of land reform, land tenure codification, assisted land settlement, profitable technological innovation packages, improved marketing arrangements and/or rural physical infrastructure.

Secondly, where 'urban bias' has prevailed in the past (Lipton, 1977) a positive redressing of the imbalance in productive investment and social infrastructure provision could contribute to overall national efficiency and equity objectives simultaneously.

3

Thirdly, in a more constricted environment, a low-income economy may be inhibited from growing 'normally' through the switchback effects of domestic food supply instability (typically dominated by fluctuating surpluses from poor farm households). Diversions of foreign exchange into food imports, foreign financial aid into food aid and national budget expenditures into consumer food subsidies are typical hazards to be avoided. Improved food security would help the poorest families directly and reduce the welfare diversions of resources from economic investment and growth.

Fourthly, continued neglect of the non-monetary subsistence sector under rapid population growth can lead to accelerating natural resources degradation and still greater diversion of resources into relief and re-employment activities (Cleaver and Shreiber, 1994; for an Ethiopian case study see Constable and Belshaw, 1989). Reducing these contingencies in a cost-effective fashion will be beneficial to economic growth elsewhere in the economy.

Fifthly, while in extreme degradation situations formerly productive areas can only be abandoned, in many apparently 'low-potential' areas, severe neglect of technological and infrastructural provision in the past may allow cheap labour-intensive investments, e.g. in micro-irrigation, agro-forestry or feeder roads, to create site specific comparative advantage in tradables production, thus contributing positively to the growth objective as well as to poverty reduction.

Sixth and finally, diversion of resources into rural poverty alleviation could be justified on growth grounds by reducing future social welfare expenditures. For example: (a) avoiding excessive rural:urban migration rates which would have increased urban infrastructure and agglomeration costs (additional commuter transport costs, air and water pollution costs, etc); (b) lower levels of fertility in the rural population i.e. reducing the pension-substitute demand for children by poor rural parents, and (c) raising the capacity of the rural economy to share public social service costs and to fund civil society institutions' welfare activities, reducing the net burden on public expenditure and the risk of excessive rates of inflation across the economy as a whole. More empirical studies and carefully monitored pilot projects are required in these areas.

4

In most situations, therefore, an appropriately designed rural development strategy should not only be capable of making positive contributions to both the efficiency and equity objectives, but also be able to reduce the rate of degradation of, or enhance the protection of, renewable natural resources. At the core of the strategy, there must be food security improving and/or income generating activities utilising the comparative advantages deriving from poor people's low subsistence costs and, in the case of the younger generation at least, their keen motivation to create improved livelihoods and life chances. The implication of this discussion is that a strategy with a welfarist or 'hand out' emphasis, quite apart from facing problems of financial non-sustainability or continued donor/government dependency, will be most unlikely to deliver efficiency benefits to the economy as a whole.

In practice, the size and structure of a rural development strategy which an economic planning mission or adviser could recommend to the government of a given country at a particular time are matters for pragmatic judgement rather than generalised assertions.   But such advice should reflect the ability to identify and design interventions which are likely to contribute to economic growth and environmental objectives as well as to rural poverty alleviation per se.

3.   TYPES OF RURAL DEVELOPMENT INTERVENTIONS: LESSONS FROM THE FIRST GENERATION

Table 1 summarises eight approaches to rural development which have been widely adopted or advocated since the 1950s. Single sector programmes or projects and various kinds of land reform activity (redistribution of land, land tenure codification/modification, land resettlement schemes, assisted rural migration, etc.) have been omitted from the table because, however necessary for achieving significant impact on rural poverty, they have rarely been incorporated into or classified under rural development projects or programmes. Table 2 provides an evaluative framework consisting of eleven criteria; the subjective scoring pattern can be replaced or modified by scores based on alternative experiences.

5

Rural Planning and Management

TABLE 1: MAJOR ALTERNATIVE INSTRUMENTS FOR IMPLEMENTING RURAL DEVELOPMENT STRATEGIES

Strategy emphasis or key instrumentality	Agencies particularly associated with strategy	Key planning concept(s)	Typical plan components
1. Self-help community development	Ministries and departments of Community Development; NGOs	Local participation and small group self-help with technical and in-kind assistance	Small-scale production and social service activities outside main sectoral programmes
2. Rural development funds	Rural Development Ministries or Local Governments	Self-help and assistance in kind	Community infrastructure or production activities identified by rural communities or their leaders
3. Administrative area-based public investment plans	Government Departments in provinces, districts, etc. horizontally coordinated by administrative officers	Project 'shopping lists', physical plans	Government buildings, roads, water supply, power, land settlement, etc.
4. Local-scale rural 'equity institutions'	Governments with strong rural equity ideology (Maoist China, Israel, etc.)	Economies of scale; cooperation; mechanisation; modernisation; mobilisation and control	Collective farms, communes, state farms, village councils, etc. sometimes incorporating diversification (non-agricultural) activities
5. Rural employment creation	ILO, WFP, UNIDO assisted	Local-level development projects to diversify rural economy and create out-of-season wage employment or permanent self-employment	Diversification projects including crafts and small-scale industry; physical infrastructure through labour-intensive methods; grants/credit for self-employment of poorest
6. Integrated Rural Development	e.g. GTZ, SNV donor agency implemented or NGO assisted	Multi-sectoral area-based plans; horizontal integration; participation; self-determination	Multi-sectoral development plans with strong agricultural components based on family farms
7. Poverty alleviation via small farm productivity gains	IFAD assisted	'Agriculture plus' projects; target groups below $x per capita; small farmer rationality and efficiency	Agricultural projects for small farmers, usually cash crop based, with supporting infrastructure
8. Basic needs provision	ILO initiated; NGOs	Target groups below thresholds for nutrition, income, housing, etc.; participation; self-help	Comprehensive planning with multiple sectoral targets, including social services (health, education, water, housing)

Abbreviations:

ILO	International Labour Office
WFP	World Food Programme
UNIDO	United Nations Industrial Development Organisation
GTZ	Gemeinschaft für Technische Zusammenarbeit
SNV	Netherlands Development Cooperation
NGO	Non-governmental organisation
IFAD	International Fund for Agricultural Development

TABLE 2: SUBJECTIVE EVALUATION OF MAJOR ALTERNATIVE RURAL DEVELOPMENT INSTRUMENTS, BY ELEVEN CRITERIA

	Local level/ Intra-Instnl equality	Natnl level/ Inter-Instnl equality	Decentral- isation of economic planning	Popular partici- pation	Integration & coordination across sectors	Focus on production & income gains	Area relevance & coverage	Influence on national resource allocation	Reduction in 'blue- print' plans	Suitable for NGO implement- ation	Simplicity of imple- mentation
	1	2	3	4	5	6	7	8	9	10	11
1 CD	?	X	X	-/	?	-/	-/	X	?	-/	-/
2 RDF	X	X	?	?	X	?	-/	X	-/	?	-/
3 PIP	X	X	?	X	X	X	-/	X	X	X	-/
4 REq	-/	X	?	X	-/	-/	-/	X	X	?	
5 RECr	-/	-/	?	?	?	?	-/	?	?	-/	-/
6 IRD	-/	-/	-/	-/	-/	-/	?	?	-/	?	?
7 SSAg	?	?	-/	?	?	-/	?	-/	?	-/	-/
8 BN	-/	-/	?	-/	?	X	-/	X	X	-/	?

Key: -/   generally positive, unproblematic
        ?   mixed evidence or weak contribution
        X   generally negative, problematic

Significant changes in the frequency of use of each approach occurred across the first generation period. The major changes have been:

(1)   the abandonment by the public sectors of community development as the major approach to rural development by the mid-1960s (Holdcroft, 1984), but its taking up on an increasing scale by development NGOs from the 1980s – especially as increasing volumes of donor funds became available in the later period;[4]

(2)   the provision of non-earmarked rural development funds in the public sector budget has been discredited in practice due to political or bureaucratic manipulation and corruption; for the case of Kenya's District Development Funds see, for example, Alila (1988) and Rutten in Simon (1990);

(3)   the most significant change has been the almost universal abandonment of collective 'equity institutions', the approach to rural development most favoured in socialist countries (for a comparison with the rival and now dominant 'equity measurement' approach, see Table 3). This change was heralded by the post-Mao shift in China after 1978 from the rural commune/brigade/work team hierarchy of institutions to the 'household responsibility system' i.e. family smallholdings (for an assessment, see Longworth, 1989). In Africa the collapse of 'eastern bloc' influence probably has been the main cause of a similar flight from collective rural institutions;

(4)   the use of labour-intensive public works schemes as 'safety nets' for the rural poorest (Gaude and Watzlawick, 1992) is an accepted component in the World Bank's 'New Poverty Agenda'. The wider use of counterpart funds generated from food aid has been recommended to meet domestic currency costs of such public works programmes, as well as their

---

[4] NGOs implementing community development projects sometimes seem to have parallels with an episode in the cartoon strip featuring Garfield (the cat). Owner: 'Garfield, why did you destroy the sofa?' Garfield: 'It's something I happen to be good at'. Questions shout the sustainability of these projects by local communities are usually answered less convincingly.

TABLE 3: TWO APPROACHES TO RURAL POVERTY ALLEVIATION

A: The 'Equity Institutions' Approach	B: The 'Equity Measurement' Approach
Stage 1: Adopt (design) equity institutions to be replicated	1: Identify activities promising to meet needs of identified target population
2: Identify outputs generally consistent with national growth	2: Check against private profitability criterion (financial appraisal)
3: Design programme scale, content etc. to be consistent with equity institutions (and vice-versa)	3: Identify concomitant production infrastructure investment required (if any)
4: Provide government resources to institutions	4: Check 2 and 3 against growth and equity criteria (economic and equity appraisals)
5: 'Persuade' etc. private individuals to join institutions	5: Extend programme resources to: (a) production infrastructure agencies (b) individuals willing to use them.
6: (a) control through: from below (b) inspection of institutions from above	6: Evaluate impact of official programmes on private income distribution
7: Reward/penalise institutional officials or change institutional design	7: Change profitability structure or change programme content or change target population

Source: Belshaw (1974)

9

extension onto private land (and into private asset formation[5]) in the cases of micro-irrigation, water-harvesting and agro-forestry investments (see Maxwell and Belshaw, 1990; Belshaw, 1992). The provision of credit and/ or grant funds to secure access to assets for self-employment, on the other hand, as in the case of the very large Integrated Rural Development Programme in India (which has been in operation since 1979) has become a more controversial matter; problems have arisen over the accuracy of targeting the poor ('leakage' to non-poor groups) and over credit repayment (Maithani, 1993).

(5)   Reliance in the 1970s on 'integrated rural development projects' (not to be confused with India's IRDP) was adversely evaluated by the World Bank and other agencies in the aftermath of the international shock of the late 1970s and early 1980s (Blackwood, 1988; World Bank, 1988). The reliability of these evaluations is discussed in section 4 of this paper. An unnecessary source of confusion was provided by the word 'integrated'. This was frequently taken to mean 'comprehensively multi-sectoral' (Livingstone, 1979; EC 1993). It often resulted in excessively complex projects which were difficult to implement effectively. The alternative view that 'integrated' should refer primarily to the analysis of poverty causation and to the identification and design of problem solutions i.e. to the processes of rural development planning (Belshaw, 1977) has also found support (e.g. Conyers et al. 1988, Netherlands Development Cooperation, 1992). This view justifies, for example, a series of single-sector projects (including approach no.7) each clearly focused so as to alleviate a set of layered constraints in sequence;

(6)   Finally, the 'basic needs' approach (ILO 1976) rapidly ran into the clash between rising demand for public expenditures of a welfarist type based on redistributive taxation, on the one hand, and falling public sector revenues as a result of both international shocks and the resulting SAPs on the other. Nevertheless, development NGOs have frequently taken up the role of provider to rural communities of missing social service infrastructure

---

[5] The use of public funds for private capital formation has been defended on grounds of externalities, in the case of natural resource protection across catchments and hillsides, and future public relief expenditures avoided in all livelihood-protecting or creating outcomes.

10

(primary education and primary health care buildings and equipment, and domestic water supply, typically).

Overall, the main choices for future strategies are between approaches 5, 6 and 7 in Tables 1 and 2, with smaller contributions coming from NGOs espousing approaches 1 and 8. A few NGOs have implemented area-based projects of types 6 and 7, but this often requires closer cooperation with governments and official aid donors than is acceptable to the majority of NGOs.

4.   THE NEW RURAL DEVELOPMENT PARADIGM: AN ASSESSMENT

The approach to assisting rural development followed by several major donors – the World Bank, USAID, the UK's ODA/DFID and FAO, in particular – has undergone significant change in the course of the 1990s. Earlier public sector project-based approaches have been rejected in favour of an emphasis on grassroots level activity in support of local or peoples' organisations and NGOs. 'Empowering the rural poor', long a slogan amongst NGOs, has become part of the official terminology of major donors.

The New Poverty Agenda (NPA) has been systematically developed by the World Bank in a series of documents elaborating and operationalising the ideas originally advanced in the *World Development Report* of 1990 which was entitled 'Poverty'. This has succeeded in injecting an equity focus into the efficiency orientation of Structural Adjustment Programmes with minimal change in the composition of the latter. In essence, the NPA adds a concern with livelihood creation on a sustainable basis to the three main goals of structural adjustment i.e. sound macro-economic policy, expansion of tradable goods production and a switch in the private sector/public sector roles in economic development in favour of the former. In order to achieve accelerated livelihood creation, four components were added to the usual SAP configuration. These are:

(1) An emphasis on the use of labour-intensive techniques in the tradable production sectors;

(2) Investment in human capital formation, especially in primary education and preventative medicine/public health measures;

11

(3) The provision of anti-poverty safety nets, as far as possible on employment-based lines (public works offering unskilled jobs at self-targeting wages);

(4) Transfer of donor funding to those NGOs which are implementing poverty alleviating micro-projects at local community level.

As Lipton and Maxwell (1992) pointed out, this left a number of gaps and weaknesses in the poverty alleviation agenda (see Appendix 1). Of particular concern in achieving an adequate magnitude of rural development activity is the de-emphasis on labour-intensive and anti-poverty measures at sector and project level (rows 3 and 7).

De-emphasising large area-based projects, as previously pursued by major donors in the 1970s, in favour of a radical decentralisation to the level of localised community-based institutions, raises a number of important questions:

(1) How reliable a guide to the design of future rural development strategies can be obtained from review of experience of poor countries, especially those in Sub- Saharan Africa, in the 1980s? And how sound were the evaluation methodologies?

(2) What is new about a highly decentralised set of development activities undertaken at grass-roots level? Even if NGOs have replaced the state, has not the wheel merely returned full circle to the community development approaches of the 1950s and 1960s, with their well-documented weaknesses?

(3) While 'empowerment' of the poor at local level may be a necessary condition for rural poverty alleviation to occur, will it be a sufficient condition when, so often, adverse macro-policy, missing sectoral programmes and inadequate physical infrastructure are contributory causes of the persistence of rural poverty?

(4) Since (i) there are many linkages and externalities between a local community and its neighbours, and between them and the nearest urban service centres, and (ii) market forces which could stimulate investment in shared physical infrastructure are weakest in regions where the poorest are concentrated, is there not a need to install public sector planning capability at this middle level – the region, the district, the province?

(5) Why should local institutions attempting to meet the pressing needs of poor members of the current generation place much weight on the protection of the

12

environment on behalf of generations yet to be born? Will the state not have to facilitate a set of location-specific decisions – as well as play a general policy role – in environmental conflict of interest situations?[6]

It seems necessary to explore these questions to ascertain how far the dominant approach to rural development is truly learning from experience, or is being blown off-course by the winds of development ideology (populist, nationalist and anti- statist currents being prevalent across the 1990s).

In relation to the first question raised above, in 1979 FAO convened the World Conference of Agrarian Reform and Rural Development (WCARRD) which summarised the public sector project approach to rural development. But that same year ushered in the negative macro-economic, trade and indebtedness impacts which seriously affected the majority of poor developing countries throughout the 1980s. Many of the existing rural development and small-scale agriculture projects were undermined by adverse domestic terms of trade or the collapse of public sector budgets, rather than internal design weaknesses.[7] Since careful counter- factual analyses, of the 'with and without project' type, have rarely been made, evaluations have often drawn 'wrong sign' conclusions by ignoring the negative effects of the external variables. It is a truism that in Africa the late 1970's were the least favourable time since World War II to introduce a strongly equity-focused programme. This was the period when increasing rates of economic growth, from which the bulk of resources and jobs for the poor had to be redistributed, went into reverse. But a closed attitude to the case for restarting projectised rural development is built upon the belief that this approach has been a proven failure on the grounds of the evidence of the 1980s.

The second question suggests both differences and parallels between the present donor patronage of large numbers of openly competitive national and international NGOs and the fashion for public community development departments thirty years

---

[6] These questions were used originally to assess FAO's new rural development strategy in Belshaw, 1993.

[7] It is relevant to note that the World Bank's main rural development evaluation concluded that rural development project success rates had been significantly better in Asia, where international shocks were less severe, than in Africa (World Bank 1988).

previously. Similar doubts arise about (i) the limited capacity of the NGO sector to 'scale-up to handle sector-wide problems; (ii) the doubtful commitment of many individuals and organisations to sustain the lengthy effort required in most rural development activity – as opposed to short-term emergency/relief work; (iii) innate conflicts between the more 'value-driven' NGOs over the priority of different ends and means; (iv) the lack of enthusiasm by activists for investment in information systems and monitoring and evaluation procedures to ensure progress up a 'learning-by-doing' curve.

The third issue concerns situations where local community empowerment is not sufficient to resolve a poverty-perpetuating situation. This usually relates to a local dearth of sustainable income-generating opportunities. This may be due, for example, to lack of appropriate technology, to missing physical infrastructure (irrigation, transport, etc.), to persistently unfavourable domestic price terms of trade or to individuals' lack of entitlement to productive assets. National and sectoral policy frameworks, and more complex strategic mixes of policies, projects, programmes and institutional capacity building, often need to be designed and implemented to secure the required improvement. A strong opportunity for rural poverty alleviation is usually present in small-holder agriculture, whether the upstream and downstream linkages are under cooperative, farmer-association, or contract farming arrangements. Where agricultural sector policies and projects are missing from the poverty alleviation strategy, however, rural development often degenerates into non-sustainable welfarist or 'hand-out' approaches where the beneficiaries are 'disempowered' and are prey to the dependency syndrome. The archaic term 'social analysis' as distinct from economic analysis is sometimes used to protect this separation of function. Current economics and agricultural economics analysis, however, has developed techniques to incorporate equity as well as efficiency objectives More importantly, locking poverty alleviation into an economics-free 'social zone' is a recipe for minimising the influence of equity-focused proposals in the key economic policy-making arenas.

The fourth question highlights the risk of isolating through extreme decentralisation the rural periphery from the centre of the national economic and political processes. One FAO discussant (Meliczek, 1993) referred to 'the need for a strong government commitment to rural development, preferably in the form of a national plan'. While such commitment is important, the presence of strong working links between central ministries and local development agencies, is not guaranteed by rhetoric in the form of a national plan document. Even in medium-size countries, a central ministry is unable to comprehend the key features of site-specific problems or opportunities in the rural areas; blanket policy-making prevails. The case for middle-level institutional capacity which can reinforce local initiatives and relay policy-reforming information upwards can only be mentioned here; space precludes detailed discussion (for a recent overview of this area, see Belshaw 2000). Certainly, the successes of state and district-level schemes in India, such as Operation Flood and the guaranteed employment schemes, should provoke more thought on the choice of level at which to site different poverty alleviation functions.

Lastly, there is a growing recognition of the often very local problems of environmental degradation, especially of the soil, water and energy resources on which the rural poor subsist. Here, the main need is to raise the productivity of subsistence agriculture at the same time as reducing the rate of exploitation of the resource base. The market can see no profit from this, while the traditional engineering and timber monoculture practices espoused by many NGOs throw increased costs onto the poor through reducing resource productivity in the short term. Fortunately, potential is usually present for achieving both aims through agro-forestry, micro-irrigation and other intensified cropping practices (green manuring, intercropping, etc.).

The (often-overlooked) incentive for undertaking such investments is the future cost - to national governments and donors – of emergency relief or alternative employment creation for people whose current rural livelihoods are destroyed through environmental degradation. This non-market perspective is consistent with an ongoing state-led role in identifying preventive investment projects though middle-down planning studies.

15

5.   CONCLUSIONS

There appear to be strong grounds for viewing the current approach to poverty alleviation and rural development, reflecting a 'rolling back' of the responsibilities of state agencies, as, to use the title of a book by Tony Killick (1989), 'a reaction too far'. The fear is that the next set of evaluations of the impact achieved by the new approach will be disappointing due to (i) NGOs' partial and 'spotty' coverage of still growing rural poverty; (ii) its inability to address causes of poverty located at the national, sectoral and regional levels of economy and society; and (iii) its failure to resolve situations where the short-run survival needs of the rural poor for food and energy are damaging or even destroying the natural resource bases of their livelihoods.

This is not to advocate an unthinking return to the approaches of the 1970s. Greater simplicity of design, public accountability and participatory engagement with intended beneficiaries are high priorities if rural development project performance is to achieve its potential. At the same time, hitherto separate discourses on land reform, food security, rural technology, rural infrastructure and rural social services delivery need to be incorporated into rural development policy. This should lead to greater location-specificity in development strategy choice at national and sub-national levels, leading to more focused and simpler programmes capable of achieving a quantum improvement in the reduction of mass poverty. This requires a selectively strengthened state role and development capacity in the poorest developing countries. The New Poverty Agenda seems likely to leave unmet the needs of the majority of the rural poor and to result in a lower rate of economic growth, the risk of continuing damage to the natural environment, and continued exclusion of the poorest from education and health services where cost-sharing prevents their access.

In the tasks of designing development strategies for the rural sector which will achieve improved impact on growth, equity and environmental protection objectives, multi-disciplinary studies should provide appropriate analytical frameworks for diagnosis and prescription. Understanding the inter-relatedness between natural resource potential and use, agricultural systems, economic variables and rural peoples' structures, institutions and values is a prerequisite for success. In addition,

16

the ability to identify and prioritise the key constraints and opportunities prevailing at each pertinent level – farm household, gender, farming system, factor and product market, rural region, sector, national and international – is vital if strategy design is not to be overwhelmed with excessive detail on the one hand and undermined by serious omissions on the other.

APPENDIX 1

STRENGTHS AND GAPS IN THE NEW POVERTY AGENDA

Strengths	Gaps and weaknesses
1. A new emphasis on livelihoods, livelihood strategies and sustainability.	1. 'Good governance' and relations between communities, NGOs, state and the private sector.
2. Practical procedures to measure and develop poverty profiles.	2. Relieving external barriers to labour-intensive growth.
3. Linkage of poverty reduction to labour-intensive growth.	3. Issues of labour-intensive growth in agriculture: farm size, organisation, and land reform; rural credit, 'resource-poor' areas; agricultural research, especially for stagnant areas; 'fallacy of composition'.
4. Emphasis on potential of 'human capital' for poverty reduction.	4. Reducing urban and off-farm poverty.
5. Analysis of safety-nets against shocks.	5. Content (and cost) of pro-poor health education, and population policies.
6. A realistic approach to targeting.	6. The thorny issue of redistribution.
7. Awareness of sustainability issues.	7. Anti-poverty strategies at project level.
8. A balanced approach to the role of the state.	8. Gender issues.

Source: Lipton and Maxwell (1992)

18

References

Alila, P. (1988) Rural Development in Kenya: a review of past experience, Regional Development Dialogue, 9, 2 142-165.

Belshaw, D.G.R. (1974) Dynamic and Operational Aspects of the Equity Objective in Rural Development Planning in East Africa. In Amann,.V.F. (ed) Agricultural Employment and Labour Migration in East Africa. Pp 1-22. Kampala: Makerere Institute of Social Research.

Belshaw, D.G.R. (1977) Rural Development Planning: concepts and techniques, J.Agricultural Economics, 27, 3, 279-292.

Belshaw, D.G.R. (1992) The Macro-economics of Counterpart Funds: the case for food-for-hunger prevention in Ethiopia, IDS Bulletin, 23, 2, 46-49.

Belshaw, D.G.R. (1993) FAO's New Approach to Rural Development: micro-activity in a strategy vacuum? Entwicklung und Ländlicher Raum, 27, 2.

Belshaw. D. (2000)Decentralised Governance and Poverty Reduction: comparative experience in Africa and Asia. In P. Collins (ed.) Applying Public Administration in Development: guideposts to the future. Chichester: Wiley.

Blackwood, J. (1988) World Bank Experience with Rural Development, Finance and Development, Dec., 12-15.

Cleaver, K.M. and Schreiber, G.A. (1994) Reversing the Spiral: the population, agriculture and environment nexus in Sub-Saharan Africa. Washington, D.C.: World Bank.

Commonwealth Secretariat (1993) Action to Reduce Poverty. London.

Constable, M. and Belshaw, D.G.R. (1989) The Ethiopian Highlands Reclamation Study: major findings and recommendations. In Belshaw, D.G.R. (ed) Towards a Food and Nutrition Strategy for Ethiopia. Addis Ababa: ONCCP.

Conyers, D. et al. (eds) (1988) Integrated Rural Development: the lessons of experience. Manchester Papers on Development, 4, 1.

European Commission (1993) Principles of Development Design. Brussells.

Gaude, J and Watzlawick, H. (1992) Employment Creation and Poverty Alleviation through Labour-intensive Public Works in Least-developed Countries, International Labour Review, 131, 1.

Griffin, K. (1989) Alternative Strategies for Economic Development. London/Paris: Macmillan/OECD.

GTZ (1993) Regional Rural Development: RRD Update. Eschborn.

Holdcroft, L.E. (1984) The Rise and Fall of Community Development, 1950-65. In Eicher, C.K. and Staatz, J.M. (eds) Agricultural Development in the Third World. Baltimore: Johns Hopkins U.P.

IFAD (1994) The Challenge of Rural Poverty: the role of IFAD. Rome.

ILO (1976) Employment, Growth and Basic Needs: a one-world problem. Geneva.

Jazairy, I. et al. (1992) The State of World Rural Poverty. London: IT for IFAD.

Johnston, B.F. and Mellor, J. (1961) The Role of Agriculture in Economic Development, American Economic Review, 51, 566-93.

Killick, T. (1989) A Reaction Too Far: economic theory and the role of the state in developing countries. London: ODI.

Lele, U. (1975) The Design of Rural Development: lessons from Africa. Baltimore: Johns Hopkins U.P.

Lipton, M. (1977) Why Poor People Stay Poor: a study of urban bias in world development. Canberra/London: Australian National U.P./Temple Smith.

Lipton, M. and Maxwell, S. (1992) The New Poverty Agenda: an overview, IDS U. of Sussex Discussion Paper, No. 306.

Livingstone, I, (1979) On the Concept of 'Integrated Rural Development Planning', J.Agricultural Economics, 30.

Longworth, J.W. (ed) China's Rural Development Miracle, with International Comparisons. St. Lucia: U. of Queensland Press for the IAAE.

Maithani, B.P. (1993) Poverty-specific Approaches: the Indian experience. In Easter, C. (ed.) Strategies for Poverty Reduction: technical papers from a Commonwealth Consultation on rural poverty alleviation. London: Commonwealth Secretariat.

Maxwell, S. and Belshaw, D.G.R. (1990) New Uses for Food Aid: Report of the WFP Mission to Ethiopia. Rome: World Food Programme.

McNamara, R.S. (1973) Speech given to the Meeting of Governors of the World Bank, Nairobi (September).

Meliczek, H. (1993) FAO's Approaches and Concepts for Rural Development, Entwicklung und Ländlicher Raum, 27, 2.

Netherlands Development Cooperation (1992) The Sector Programme for Rural Development. The Hague: Operations Review Unit.

20

Shaw, D.J. and Crawshaw, B. (1995) Overcoming Rural Poverty – thirty years of World Food Programme experience. In Mullen, J. (ed.) <u>Rural Poverty Alleviation: international development perspectives</u>. Aldershot: Avebury.

Wilmshurst, J. et al. (1992) Implications for UK Aid of Current Thinking on Poverty Reduction, IDS U. of Sussex <u>Discussion Paper</u>, No. 307.

World Bank (1975) <u>Rural Development: sector policy paper</u>. Washington, D.C.

World Bank (1988) <u>Rural Development: World Bank experience, 1965-86</u>. Washington, D.C.

World Bank (1990) <u>World Development Report 1990: Poverty</u>. Oxford: Oxford U.P. for the World Bank.

World Bank (1993) <u>Implementing the World Bank's Strategy to Reduce Poverty: progress and challenges</u>. Washington, D.C.

World Bank (1999) <u>World Development Report 1998/99: Knowledge for Development</u>. Oxford: Oxford U.P. for the World Bank.

[6]

Survey Article

Household Strategies and Rural Livelihood Diversification

FRANK ELLIS

This article reviews the recent literature on diversification as a livelihood strategy of rural households in developing countries, with particular reference to sub-Saharan Africa. Livelihood diversification is defined as the process by which rural families construct a diverse portfolio of activities and social support capabilities in order to survive and to improve their standards of living. The determinants and effects of diversification in the areas of poverty, income distribution, farm output and gender are examined. Some policy inferences are summarised. The conclusion is reached that removal of constraints to, and expansion of opportunities for, diversification are desirable policy objectives because they give individuals and households more capabilities to improve livelihood security and to raise living standards.

I. INTRODUCTION

The orthodox view of processes of economic change is that they involve transitions between states of economic structure or performance that can be distinguished from each other. An important component of this view is that sectors are compartmentalised. Rural is contrasted with urban, agriculture is contrasted with industry, and people are interpreted as making complete transitions from one type of activity to another as development proceeds.[1]

Frank Ellis, School of Development Studies, University of East Anglia, Norwich NR4 7TJ, UK. This article results from an ongoing research project on the Policy Implications of Rural Livelihood Diversification, funded by the Economic and Social Committee for Research (ESCOR) of the Department for International Development (DFID). The views expressed are those of the author and not of DFID. The article has benefited from constructive comments by Neil Adger, Piers Blaikie, Debbie Bryceson, Barbara Harriss-White, Gillian Hart, Catherine Locke, Carole Rakodi, Ben Rogaly, Jim Sumberg, Steve Tabor and an anonymous referee, and the author is grateful for the work that each of them put into reading the draft version.

The Journal of Development Studies, Vol.35, No.1, October 1998, pp.1–38
PUBLISHED BY FRANK CASS, LONDON

2   THE JOURNAL OF DEVELOPMENT STUDIES

This view is buttressed by the not always explicitly stated idea that specialisation and division of labour are essential ingredients for the transformation of national economies.[2]

Diversification as an individual or household level survival strategy does not fit well into the conventional picture. Many of its attributes stand in contrast to straitened notions of sectors, specialisation and transition. The received wisdom is that diversification is merely a transient phenomenon [e.g., *Saith, 1992*] or one associated with the desperate struggle for survival in declining economies. Yet diversification may not be so transient, and it may be associated with success at achieving livelihood security under improving economic conditions as well as with livelihood distress in deteriorating conditions [*Collier, 1988*; *Preston, 1989*].

This article undertakes a review of ideas, propositions and policy inferences surrounding diversification as a livelihood strategy of rural families in developing countries. A number of recent articles in development studies journals have examined aspects of diversification, utilising case study evidence [*Reardon et al., 1992*; *Chandrasekhar, 1993*; *Adams, 1994*; *Bigsten, 1996*; *Dercon and Krishnan, 1996*; *Taylor and Wyatt, 1996*; *Carter, 1997*], or have put forward more general interpretations of rural change in which diversification is regarded as a central feature [*Bernstein et al., 1992*; *Bryceson, 1996*; *Heyer, 1996*]. In addition, several researchers have undertaken comparative reviews of empirical evidence on rural household income portfolios, derived from household surveys [*von Braun and Pandya-Lorch, 1991*; *Sahn and Sarris, 1991*; *Sahn, 1994*; *Reardon, 1997*].

Rural livelihood diversification cuts across a number of typically self-bounded arenas of policy discussion in development studies including rural poverty [*Jazairy et al., 1992*], household risk strategies [*Carter, 1997*], household coping strategies [*Davies, 1996*]; intrahousehold relations [Hart, 1995], rural growth linkages [*Hazell and Haggblade, 1993*], rural non-farm activity [*Fisher et al., 1997*], and rural–urban migration [*Stark, 1991*]. While overlaps occur between these arenas, they each tend to bring rather partial insights to bear on the causes, opportunities, effects and policy implications of diversification.

The fragmentation of insights into diversification means that the literature abounds with conflicting propositions about its meaning. Diversification may occur both as a deliberate household strategy [*Stark, 1991*] or as an involuntary response to crisis [*Davies, 1996*]. It is found both to diminish [*Adams, 1994*] and to accentuate [*Evans and Ngau, 1991*] rural inequality. It can act both as a safety valve for the rural poor [*Zoomers and Kleinpenning, 1996*] and as a means of accumulation for the rural rich [*Hart, 1994*]. It can benefit farm investment and productivity [*Carter, 1997*] or impoverish agriculture by withdrawing critical resources [*Low, 1986*].

It is not the intention of this article to attempt to resolve conflicting interpretations of diversification. There is no need to do so because the causes and consequences of diversification are differentiated in practice by location, assets, income, opportunity and social relations; and it is not therefore surprising that these manifest themselves in different ways under differing circumstances. Nevertheless a useful purpose is served by disentangling different strands in the arguments and evidence concerning diversification. In many sub-Saharan African countries structural adjustment has initiated the widespread dismantling of the sectoral layer of state intervention (for example, agricultural policies) that used to act as an interface between the macro-economy and rural household decision-making. With the phasing out of these so-called meso-level policies, the only way of connecting macroeconomic policies with micro-level interventions is through a better understanding of household strategies [*Berry, 1986; Lipton and Ravallion, 1995*].

The article has several aims. The first aim is to pull together into a single discussion a moderately inclusive cross-section of the literature that examines aspects of diversification as a central or major theme. The let-out clause 'moderately inclusive' is inserted here because livelihood diversification crosses so many boundaries of development discussion that its pursuit at the margins could make its treatment quite intractable.[3] The second aim is to set out the different and sometimes contradictory interpretations of livelihood diversification in the areas of its determinants and its implications for poverty, income distribution, agricultural performance and gender relations. The third is to summarise the implications for policy that have been advanced in studies of livelihood diversification.

It is appropriate to remark in passing that livelihood diversification is neither just a rural nor only a developing country phenomenon. It is well-documented as a survival strategy of urban dwellers in developing countries [*Baker and Pedersen, 1992; Maxwell, 1995; Rakodi, 1995; de Haan, 1997; Moser, 1998*]; and is becoming increasingly prevalent amongst farm families in developed countries as agricultural price and other supports to farming are removed [*Benjamin, 1994; Kelly and Ilbery, 1995; Hearn et al., 1996*]. It is also an emerging feature of labour markets more generally in the industrialised countries, being associated with the rise of part-time and home-based working patterns. This article restricts its scope, however, to diversification in the rural economy of developing countries, and particularly to the experience of sub-Saharan Africa on which much of the recent literature is focused.

The article proceeds in the following way. The next section elaborates the concept of livelihood diversification, its social dimensions, and the income categories that are utilised in economic studies of income portfolios. The third section briefly reviews the empirical investigation of livelihood diversification, including sources that contain evidence on rural income portfolios in sub-Saharan Africa in the 1980s and 1990s. The fourth section considers approaches to, and explanations of, the determinants of livelihood diversification. The fifth, sixth, and seventh sections examine, respectively, the relationships of livelihood diversification to poverty and income distribution; farm technology and agricultural performance; and gender dimensions. The eighth section briefly reviews some policy implications of diversification.

II. CONCEPTS OF LIVELIHOOD DIVERSIFICATION

In this article livelihood diversification is defined as the process by which rural families construct a diverse portfolio of activities and social support capabilities in their struggle for survival and in order to improve their standards of living.

Several components of this definition merit elaboration. First, a livelihood is more than just income [*Lipton and Maxwell, 1992*]. Income refers to the cash earnings of the household plus payments in kind that can be valued at market prices. The cash earnings component of income include items like crop or livestock sales, wages, rents, and remittances. The in-kind component of income refers to consumption of own farm produce, payments in kind (for example, in food), and transfers or exchanges of consumption items that occur between households in rural communities.

A livelihood encompasses income, both cash and in kind, as well as the social institutions (kin, family, compound, village and so on), gender relations, and property rights required to support and to sustain a given standard of living. Social and kinship networks are important for facilitating and sustaining diverse income portfolios [*Berry, 1989*; *1993: Ch.7*; *Hart, 1995*; *Bryceson, 1996*]. Social institutions are also critical for interpreting the constraints and options of individuals and families distinguished by gender, income, wealth, access and assets. For example, differential access rights to land are often the key determinant of distinct livelihood strategies pursued by poor compared to better-off rural households. Likewise, social proscriptions on permissible courses of action of women can make big differences to the livelihood options available for women compared to men [*Dwyer and Bruce, 1988*; *Davies and Hossain, 1997*].

A livelihood also includes access to, and benefits derived from, social and public services provided by the state such as education, health services, roads, water supplies and so on [*Lipton and van der Gaag, 1993*; *Blackwood and Lynch, 1994*]. An oft-stated finding of poverty research is the tendency

HOUSEHOLD STRATEGIES AND RURAL LIVELIHOOD DIVERSIFICATION   5

for public service provision to be biased towards the better off and more accessible locations, communities, and social groups, thus exacerbating the material deprivation already experienced by the poor as a result of inadequate levels of assets and income [*World Bank, 1990; Lipton, 1996*].

Livelihood diversification is therefore not synonymous with income diversification.[4] Nevertheless, many, but not all, economic studies of diversification focus on different income sources and their relationship to income levels, income distribution, assets, farm output and other variables [e.g., *Reardon et al., 1992; Adams and He, 1995*]. The term income diversity refers to the composition of household incomes at a given instant in time; diversification, on the other hand, interprets this as an active social process whereby households are observed to engage in increasingly intricate portfolios of activities over time. Lack of comparable evidence across intervals of time means that it is rarely possible to state firmly whether household livelihoods are more diverse now than they were, say, ten or twenty years ago [*Heyer, 1996; Reardon, 1997*]; nevertheless, and certainly for sub-Saharan Africa, there seems to be an informed consensus that diversity has been increasing in recent history [*Bryceson, 1996*], and a few intertemporal case studies seem to bear out this contention [*Valentine, 1993*].

Economic studies distinguish between several different categories and sub-categories of income source when referring to diverse income portfolios. Such distinctions are not arbitrary; they refer to different labour markets with different features of seasonality, sustainability, barriers to entry, location, potential income growth and so on [*Reardon, 1997*]. Different individuals and families are likely to possess different potential access to different income sources, and, therefore, participation in these sources will have different impacts on poverty and income distribution.

The primary categories are farm, off-farm, and non-farm income sources [*Saith, 1992*]. Farm income includes livestock as well as crop income and comprises both consumption-in-kind of own farm output and cash income from output sold.[5] Off-farm income typically refers to wage or exchange labour on other farms (i.e. within agriculture). It also includes labour payments in kind, such as the harvest share systems and other non-wage labour contracts that remain prevalent in many parts of the developing world.[6] Non-farm income refers to non-agricultural income sources. Several secondary categories of non-farm income are commonly identified. These are (i) non-farm rural wage employment, (ii) non-farm rural self-employment,[7] (iii) property income (rents, etc.), (iv) urban-to-rural remittances arising from within national boundaries, and (v) international remittances arising from cross-border and overseas migration.

Not all investigators follow the same conventions for categorising

6 THE JOURNAL OF DEVELOPMENT STUDIES

income sources. In a detailed study in rural Pakistan, for example, Adams and He [*1995*] have the six major income categories of agricultural, non-farm, livestock, rental, domestic remittances and international remittances. In this scheme, wage labour in agriculture is included with own-farm income in the agricultural category; livestock is taken separately from crop income; and non-farm income covers wages, salaries and self-employment outside agriculture, but excludes rents and remittances that are assigned their own categories.[8]

The social and economic characteristics of non-farm income sources tend to be examined in separate literatures. Thus the rural non-farm literature [e.g., *Saith, 1992*; *Fisher et al., 1997*] has different preoccupations from the migration and remittance literature [e.g., *Stark, 1991*]. The former is concerned with stimulating non-agricultural activities in rural areas with a variety of social and economic goals in view. The latter tends to be preoccupied with the motives underlying migration, the rate of urbanisation, and the amount and effects of the remittances sent home.

Most research into income diversification utilises the household as the unit for empirical investigation. The household may be conceived as the social group which resides in the same place, shares the same meals, and makes joint or coordinated decisions over resource allocation and income pooling [*Meillassoux, 1981*; *Ellis, 1993: Ch.1*]. Alternatively, some version of the idea that the household represents a coalition of players committed by choice or custom to act as one unit vis-à-vis the rest of the world can be invoked [*Stark, 1991*; *Preston, 1994*]. There are many instances where these definitions fail to capture important attributes of individual and collective welfare, including spheres of individual decision-making, power relations in the social unit, and constraints on permissible courses of action by gender [*Folbre, 1986*; *Guyer and Peters, 1987*; *Bruce, 1989*].

The farm household economic model treats the household as a single decision-making unit maximising its welfare subject to a range of income-earning opportunities, and a set of resource constraints [*Hymer and Resnick, 1969*; *Nakajima, 1970*; *1986*; *Singh et al., 1986*; *Ellis, 1993*]. This yields a baseline economic proposition, ignoring social institutions and risk factors, that the household will allocate its labour time so that the marginal returns per unit of labour are the same across different activities, whether on-farm, off-farm or non-farm. Intra-household economic approaches based on bargaining theory do not necessarily yield different predictions about patterns of engagement by household members in different labour markets [*Haddad et al., 1997: Ch.1*].

Many researchers recognise that the study of livelihood diversification requires a more spatially extended understanding of the household than the conventional definition. The role of non-resident family members in

HOUSEHOLD STRATEGIES AND RURAL LIVELIHOOD DIVERSIFICATION   7

contributing to the well-being of the resident group requires explicit recognition. Households with members working away in urban centres or abroad are often referred to as 'split families', and their livelihood strategies are described as 'straddling' the rural and urban sectors [*Rempel and Lobdell, 1978; Murray, 1981; Stichter, 1982; Heyer, 1996*]. Urban migrants are commonly observed to continue to maintain strong rural family connections, even after several generations of urban residence [*Lucas and Stark, 1985; Stark and Bloom, 1985; Valentine, 1993; Hoddinott, 1994*]. Circular migration, in which family members work for periods in the urban economy then return to their family farms, is noted in several studies [*Bigsten, 1988; 1996; Lageman, 1989; Andrae, 1992*]. Seasonal migration related to cyclical work opportunities in different locations is also common [*Agarwal, 1990; Breman, 1996*].

The extended definition of the household can be used to capture diversity of social interactions as well as diversity of location. The household or family social unit has been described as a 'multipurpose unit' [*Bryceson, 1996*], the members of which have 'multiple social identities' [*Bangura, 1994*], and the livelihoods of which involve continual processes of renegotiation and redefinition of family, gender, power, and property relations [*Berry, 1993; 1997; Hart, 1995*].

Reviewing the literature, there is a temptation to draw up typologies of diversification. In particular, some branches of the literature are predominantly concerned with diversification as a matter of survival, emphasising the reasons for diversification born of desperation (poverty, lack of assets, vulnerability, disaster). Other branches of the literature focus, by contrast, on diversification as a matter of choice and opportunity, involving proactive household strategies for improving living standards. Along these lines, for example, 'diversification for survival' has been contrasted with 'diversification for accumulation' [*Hart, 1994: 48*].

While such typologies are superficially attractive as a means of distinguishing different motives and opportunities to diversify, they also lend themselves to inaccurate and misplaced generality that fails to engage with the complexity of local circumstances. For example, in some societies income-generating options for women are more socially circumscribed in better-off than in poorer households. More generally, diversification obeys a continuum of causes and motivations that vary across families at a particular point in time, and for the same families at different points in time. Some causes may be location-specific (semi-arid zones highly prone to drought) or disaster-specific (droughts, cyclones, floods, earthquakes), and thus warrant special sets of concepts in order to formulate appropriate policy responses.

An interesting distinction has been made between families within which

8   THE JOURNAL OF DEVELOPMENT STUDIES

each member is involved in many different part-time income generating activities; and those for which individual family members are able to engage in full-time specialised occupations [*Unni, 1996*]. Again this points in the direction of a typology of diversification, this time along the lines of types of work – that is, full-time, part-time, seasonal, casual – rather than the preceding focus on proximity of the household to minimum survival. However, again here, in practice there are infinite gradations and variations in the mixtures of these different types of income sources for households of different total income levels, so that typifying households by type of off-farm or non-farm work is unlikely to prove very insightful for policy purposes.

III. EMPIRICAL INVESTIGATION OF INCOME DIVERSITY

While remaining aware that a rural livelihood is described not only by its income dimensions, this section of the article is concerned with the availability and adequacy of data on household income portfolios, and it therefore puts to one side social aspects for the moment.

The composition of rural household incomes is relatively poorly researched compared to other aspects of rural livelihoods in many developing countries, especially in sub-Saharan Africa [*Ravallion, 1992*]. In particular, there is an almost total lack of data sets that are comparable across time intervals greater than two or three years, and most available evidence is from small-scale, location specific, sample surveys that are not representative of aggregate populations. Added to this, there appears to be little consensus across surveys concerning the definitional categories of income components, so that individual income streams may be assigned to different sub-categories in the data analysis of different surveys.

There are plenty of reasons for this state of affairs. National level income and expenditure surveys have been infrequent in most sub-Saharan African countries, sometimes with such long intervals between their occurrence that definitions and sampling frames are radically altered across surveys. Due to inadequate resourcing or low prioritisation in government statistical offices, some of the surveys that actually get undertaken fail to be subsequently data processed or receive cursory treatment in data analysis and publication.[9]

In parallel with these problems, the emphasis of much living standards research has been on expenditure rather than income data. Indeed some recent large-scale, donor-assisted, household surveys in African countries have chosen to exclude income data collection altogether and concentrate solely on expenditure data and other proxies of household well-being.[10] This follows in part from the well-known axiom in poverty research that material wellbeing is best measured by household expenditure per capita adjusted for

HOUSEHOLD STRATEGIES AND RURAL LIVELIHOOD DIVERSIFICATION   9

the age and gender composition of the household [*World Bank, 1990*; *Glewwe and van der Gaag, 1990*; *Greeley, 1996*; *Lipton, 1996*].

Household income as a welfare indicator is considered prone to several flaws [*Glewwe and van der Gaag, 1988; 1990*; *Lipton and Ravallion, 1995*]. Income in rural households varies from year to year depending on the outcome of farm production and the prices obtained for output sales. Income also varies seasonally, causing practical difficulties for the timing of sample surveys and the accuracy of recall of crop sales and prices. Problems of recall apply more generally to irregular and intermittent income sources over time periods preceding survey interviews. Problems of measurement occur with respect to both farm activities and non-farm self-employment for which the derivation of net income requires data on costs as well as on output and prices.

The upshot of these problems of measurement is that in the absence of first-hand knowledge of individual case-study data sets, most published information on the composition of rural household incomes needs to be treated with circumspection. Reardon [*1997*] reviews data from 31 different surveys in 18 sub-Saharan African countries. The share of non-farm income in total income in these surveys varies from 15 per cent to 93 per cent. This wide variation between survey averages is superimposed, of course, on high inter-household variation in the underlying data sets from which the sample averages were originally calculated.

The wide variations in farm-non-farm income shares for sub-Saharan Africa are corroborated by an earlier comparative review of 15 surveys across eight sub-Saharan African countries by Haggblade, Hazell and Brown [*1989*] and by evidence on 15 surveys across nine sub-Saharan African countries compiled by Sahn [*1994*]. The results cited by Sahn display large differences across surveys in the income shares of individual non-farm sources (such as wages, remittances and so on), but less variability for non-farm income taken in aggregate. Another source of comparative evidence, as well as individual country income surveys, is von Braun and Pandya-Lorch [*1991*] which examines income composition in relation to proneness to malnutrition across 16 surveys in 12 countries, of which two are in Latin America, five are in Asia, and five in sub-Saharan Africa. There is some overlap of coverage between the surveys compiled and compared in these different sources.

These comparative reviews do reveal some discernable patterns. Within sub-Saharan Africa, the role of remittances and transfers is notably higher in countries bordering South Africa than elsewhere on the continent. Rural households in Asia appear to exhibit a greater reliance on non-farm income sources than is generally true in Africa; perhaps in the average order of a 40:60 per cent farm:non-farm income split as compared to the reverse

10   THE JOURNAL OF DEVELOPMENT STUDIES

proportions on average in Africa.[11] This difference is consistent with other
evidence suggesting that the roots of rural poverty differ between Asia and
Africa [*Heyer, 1996*]. Whereas in Asia, a prevalent feature of rural poverty
is near or actual landlessness so that poor households must rely on off-farm
and non-farm income sources for survival; in Africa, the main factors
contributing to rural poverty are locational and reflect not so much lack of
access to land, but location-specific lack of access to an array of services
and opportunities (roads, schools, market services, input supplies, power,
non-farm activities), as well as environmental constraints.

Various points emerge from these comparative reviews of available
evidence. First, non-farm income sources are beyond doubt critical for
describing the living standards of farm households in developing countries.
In sub-Saharan Africa it would appear that 30–50 per cent reliance on non-
farm incomes is commonplace, and in some instances the average
proportion is much greater.[12] Second, data collection on income sources
needs to converge towards an accepted set of categories and definitions; the
surveys reviewed in the sources cited appear to vary tremendously in their
coverage and assignment of income sources. A particular problem is the
assignment of off-farm agricultural wage earnings to farm income in some
surveys and to non-farm income in others. Third, it is not possible to infer
trends in income diversification from the available household-level
evidence; at least not for sub-Saharan Africa, with rare exceptions.[13]

Bryceson [*1996; 1997*] takes a different approach to capturing intertemporal changes in rural livelihoods in sub-Saharan Africa by examining
time-series data on the sectoral composition of national income. The
evidence appears to support the hypothesis, entitled deagrarianisation, that
rural SSA is becoming steadily less agrarian as manifested by rising reliance
on non-farm income sources in rural areas. The review by Reardon [*1997*]
concludes that non-farm wage labour predominates over agricultural wage
labour, non-farm self-employment, and remittances as income sources in
many African settings. However, southern African countries, including
South Africa itself, differ markedly in this regard with remittance and
transfer incomes typically dominating over other off-farm or non-farm
income sources [*May, 1996; Baber, 1996*].

IV. DETERMINANTS OF DIVERSIFICATION

In what follows, the emphasis is placed on the economic logic of household
strategies, utilising the unitary concept of the household described earlier
which is the approach most often encountered in this literature. This has
some disadvantages, not the least of which is the fondness of economists to
consider almost all decision-making as a matter of freely-made choices,

albeit subject to economic constraints (resources, assets, skills, incomes and so on). Social and familial constraints also, of course, apply, and not only what people do, but their capability to change what they do, is influenced by their social context (family, kin, caste, ethnic group, community, belief systems and so on). For example, the social institutions through which livelihoods are mediated may act to suppress opportunities for some members of a community (for example, landless, women, low caste) while enhancing those of other members [*Davies and Hossain, 1997*]. This 'social-embeddedness' [*Rogaly, 1997*] of individual or household actions needs to be kept in mind in interpreting economic propositions in this area.

The literature identifies a range of different motives and pressures that contribute to explaining why diversification occurs and the patterns of diversity that are observed. Some main determinants of diversification are seasonality, differentiated labour markets, risk strategies, coping behaviour, credit market imperfections, and intertemporal savings and investment strategies.

All rural households confront seasonality as an inherent feature of their livelihoods [*Chambers, Longhurst and Pacey, 1981; Chambers, 1982; Sahn, 1989; Agarwal, 1990*]. Seasonality on its own explains many of the patterns of diversity in rural household incomes, especially those involving on-farm diversity and off-farm agricultural wage earnings. In economic terms, seasonality means that returns to labour in both on-farm activities and off-farm labour markets vary during the year, causing seasonal changes in occupation as labour time is switched from lower to higher return activities [*Alderman and Sahn, 1989*]. Note that this can occur without having to invoke risk as a consideration. While in practice risk and seasonality are closely related, conceptually it is useful for some purposes to separate them, and diversification that obeys different opportunities in different seasonal labour markets does not require risk as an explanatory argument for its occurrence.

Seasonality means that continuous household consumption needs are mismatched with uneven income flows. Leaving aside risk and market imperfections, this would not constitute a problem provided that total income was sufficient to cover annual consumption requirements.[14] Crop storage, output sales and savings could be used to convert unstable income into stable consumption. In practice, of course both risk and market imperfections abound in the rural economy [*Alderman and Paxson, 1992*]. Income instability and consumption smoothing are real problems confronted by households, and therefore an important motive for income diversification associated with seasonality is to reduce income instability. This requires income earning opportunities the seasonal cycles of which are not synchronised with the farm's own seasons. Seasonal migration to other agricultural zones may be one option, circular or permanent migration of one or more family members to non-farm occupations, another [*Alderman and Sahn, 1989*].

Seasonality is one particular instance of rural labour markets that are differentiated by location, time, skills, gender and cultural proscriptions. The economic motivation for diversification cited in relation to seasonality applies more generally; when the marginal return to labour time in farming for any individual falls below the wage rate or the return to self-employment attainable off the farm, then the household is better off switching that individual into off-farm or non-farm activities. Work opportunities vary according to skills (for example, in trading, vehicle repair, brick making), education (for example, for salaried jobs), and by gender (for example, male wage work in construction or mines vs. female opportunities in trading or textile factories). Economic considerations of labour allocation may be overlaid and modified by social rules of access both within the family and in the community, and these rules may result in the 'social exclusion' of individuals and households from particular income streams [*Davies and Hossain, 1997*].

Aside from considerations of static comparative advantage in the deployment of labour time, rural households are observed to take a longer term strategic view of future income sources. Investment in social networks is one manifestation of this [*Berry, 1989*]. Investment in education, often linked to migration and remittance behaviour, is another [*Stark, 1982; Stark and Bloom, 1985*].

Risk is often cited in the literature as the primary motive for income diversification [e.g. *Bryceson, 1996*]. However, there are many different strands to the risk argument, and there is a lot of room for confusing risk arguments with coping arguments, and voluntary decisions with involuntary actions [*Dercon and Krishnan, 1996*].

Risk is the subjective probability attached by individuals or by the household towards the outcomes of the various income generating activities in which they are engaged [*Anderson et al., 1977*]. When definite outcomes in relation to income streams are replaced by probabilities of occurrence, the social unit diversifies its portfolio of activities in order to anticipate and to mitigate the threat to its welfare of failure in individual activities [*Alderman and Paxson, 1992*]. In terms of the static allocation of labour time across different activities, it is then the risk-discounted marginal returns to labour that determine the patterns of engagement and specialisation by household members.

Income diversification as a risk strategy is usually taken to imply a trade-off between a higher total income involving greater probability of income failure, and a lower total income involving smaller probability of income failure [*Roumasset et al, 1979*]. In other words, households are risk averse, and they are prepared to accept lower income for greater security. Research into on-farm diversity has sometimes demonstrated that this is not strictly true; that diverse on-farm cropping systems such as mixed cropping and field fragmentation take advantage of complementarities between crops, variations in soil types and differences in micro-climates that ensure risk spreading with little loss in total income [*Norman, 1974; 1977; Walker and Ryan, 1990; Blarel et al., 1992*].

Whether or not risk spreading involves a fall in income, one of the critical features of income diversification for risk reasons is the achievement of a portfolio with low covariate risk between its components. A characteristic of rural livelihoods in developing countries is that most of the income earning opportunities open to poor households, that is, own farm production and agricultural wage labour, exhibit high correlations between risks attached to alternative income streams; in other words, if there is a drought or flood in a particular locality, all income streams are adversely affected simultaneously. While on-farm diversity can take some advantage of differences in the risk-proneness of crops or crop mixes to adverse natural events, the protection this affords is only partial. Diversification into non-farm incomes, by contrast, can result in low risk correlations between livelihood components.

Household risk strategies are prone to confusion with coping behaviour, since some researchers treat coping as an aspect of risk behaviour, as in the phrase 'risk coping strategies' [*World Bank, 1990: 90–91; Alderman and Paxson, 1992: 2*]. This blurring of risk and coping is imprecise as a guide to policy in areas such as poverty reduction or famine prevention [*Davies, 1996*]. It confuses voluntary with involuntary actions; planned responses to potential threats to household wellbeing with unplanned reactions to unexpected livelihood failure.

The distinction between risk and coping as determinants of diversification can be resolved by distinguishing *ex-ante* risk management from *ex-post* coping with crisis [*Webb et al., 1992; Carter, 1997*]. Risk management is then interpreted as a deliberate household strategy to anticipate failures in individual income streams by maintaining a spread of activities [*Walker and Jodha, 1986*]; while coping is the involuntary response to disaster or unanticipated failure in major sources of survival. A complementary way that risk and coping have been distinguished is to interpret risk as *ex-ante* income management and coping as *ex-post* consumption management in the wake of crisis [*Carter, 1997*].

Following this distinction, coping includes tactics for maintaining consumption such as drawing down on savings, using up food stocks, gifts from relatives, community transfers, sales of livestock, other asset sales,

14   THE JOURNAL OF DEVELOPMENT STUDIES

and so on. Several researchers have described the sequential phases which characterise coping behaviour as the adverse impacts of a disaster such as drought intensify [e.g., *Corbett, 1988*]. These sequences typically seek first to protect the future income generating capability of the household, even if current consumption is compromised. It is only as a last resort that assets critical for future survival are sold or abandoned to stave off starvation.

This interpretation may seem to exclude coping as a determinant of income diversification; however, unplanned responses to crisis may involve searches for new income sources in the early stages, and, at a later stage, enforced asset sales may irrevocably alter the future livelihood patterns of the family. Therefore, the term coping can be used to encompass distress and crisis reasons for the emergence of new livelihood patterns, and these differ conceptually and in practice from risk management determinants of livelihood patterns.

A literature pertinent to the concept of coping is that concerned with the vulnerability of rural families to livelihood collapse in the face of disaster such as drought, floods, cyclones and so on [*Blaikie et al., 1994*]. The focus in this is especially on human interactions with natural resource systems, and on ways of describing the robustness of livelihoods confronted by erosion of the natural resource base or sudden shocks [*Campbell, 1990*]. Vulnerability is defined in this context as a high degree of exposure to risk, shocks and stress; and proneness to food insecurity [*Chambers, 1989*; *Davies, 1996*].[15]

The notion of vulnerability is further captured by reference to the resilience and sensitivity of the livelihood system, where resilience means the ability of the system to absorb change or even utilise change to advantage; while sensitivity refers to the susceptibility of the natural resource base to change following human interference [*Blaikie and Brookfield, 1987*]. According to these ideas the most robust livelihood system is one displaying high resilience and low sensitivity; while the most vulnerable displays low resilience and high sensitivity. For example, livelihood systems in the Sahel in West Africa are highly sensitive, that is, prone to natural resource changes, but surprisingly resilient due to the ability of human populations to adapt to their natural environments [*Davies, 1996*].

A further concept that arises in the context of coping behaviour is that of adaptation. Livelihood adaptation has been defined as the continuous process of 'changes to livelihoods which either enhance existing security and wealth or try to reduce vulnerability and poverty' [*Davies and Hossain, 1997: 5*]. Adaptation may be positive or negative: positive if it is by choice, reversible, and increases security; negative if it is of necessity, irreversible, and fails to reduce vulnerability [*ibid.*]. Negative adaptation occurs when the poor can no longer cope with adverse shocks.

HOUSEHOLD STRATEGIES AND RURAL LIVELIHOOD DIVERSIFICATION   15

Adaptation is evidently closely related to diversification but the two are not synonymous. Diversification explicitly draws attention to a variety of dissimilar income sources (farm, non-farm, remittances etc.) as its chief characteristic. This is one potential outcome of adaptation but not the only one; new ways of trying to sustain the existing income portfolio are also forms of adaptation. Adaptation may result in the adoption of successively more vulnerable livelihood systems over time [*Davies, 1996*]. By contrast, the prime motive and consequence of successful diversification by the poor is to reduce vulnerability.

Some researchers have linked income diversification with credit market failures in the rural economy of developing countries [*Binswanger, 1983; Reardon, 1997*]. These failures include low credit availability in African rural settings [*Bigsten and Kayizzi-Mugerwa, 1995*], and personalised lending associated with interlocked transactions in Asian rural settings [*Bell, 1988*]. Governments and NGOs have, of course, for years tried to overcome these market failures [*Johnson and Rogaly, 1997*], but their success at doing so has tended to be intermittent and uneven. By engaging in non-farm activities, farm households can generate cash income to substitute for the absence or high cost of credit, thus permitting them to purchase cash inputs into production, or to make farm investments. Credit market considerations also illustrate how closely interrelated in practice are the different determinants of diversification. Cash generated to overcome a credit squeeze also contributes to mitigating the seasonality problem of managing unstable income, and this in turn may help to reduce risk-aversion in farm production decisions [*Eswaran and Kotwal, 1989; 1990*].

Interestingly enough the basic farm household economic model [*Barnum and Squire, 1979; Singh, Squire and Strauss, 1986*] separates production from consumption decisions in such a way that non-farm income can only enter the household as an increase in income available for consumption, not as an investment in farm production leading to higher farm productivity in the future [*Taylor and Wyatt, 1996*].

Clearly not all diversification represents the unrelenting struggle for survival of the poor, and households that are on an upward path away from poverty, or that are already somewhat better off, may have other motives for diversification than those already cited. In particular, above a certain standard of living, it is likely to become ambiguous whether savings and investment are for farm or for non-farm accumulation, and the spatial locus of household activity may shift to small towns or to cities, even while a farm component is kept in the livelihood portfolio. As noted earlier, Hart [*1994: 48*] makes the distinction that larger landowners diversify to accumulate, while the landless and near-landless diversify to survive. Accumulation may become the motive of diversification once survival and risk loom less large on the horizon of the rural household.

A danger of seeking to isolate separate determinants of diversification is that a rather one-dimensional view of the forces shaping rural livelihoods is conveyed. These determinants – seasonality, labour markets, risk, coping, credit, accumulation – may be conceptually distinct but are rarely separable in practice. All such determinants are mediated through social institutions, including ties of community and kinship [*Berry, 1989; 1993*], property rights and obligations [*Berry, 1997; Bromley, 1989; 1991; Platteau, 1992*], and gender relations within the household [*Hart, 1995*]. In addition, they are shaped by interactions with the physical environment, and by changes over time in the larger economy, including the impact on income-earning opportunities of structural adjustment and market liberalisation policies.

Finally, some interesting insights into the determinants of livelihood diversification are obtained from the literature on migration. Migration decisions have been viewed variously as individual choices [*Todaro, 1969; Harris and Todaro, 1970*] and as intertemporal family contracts [*Stark, 1980; Stark and Bloom, 1985; Stark and Lucas, 1988*]. The former interpretation focuses on income differentials adjusted for job search probabilities as the prime determinant of migration, and this version continues to receive support [*Bigsten, 1996; Larson and Mundlak, 1997*]. The latter interpretation emphasises risk spreading [*Stark and Levari, 1982; Katz and Stark, 1986*] and imperfections in rural capital markets [*Stark, 1980; Collier and Lal, 1986*] as reasons to migrate. Remittance income exhibits the key attribute that it is uncorrelated with both seasonal cycles and risk factors in agriculture.

Critical to these propositions is that migrants maintain a flow of remittances to their families, and several reasons of migrant self-interest are advanced to explain why this occurs; namely, the need for a fall back position if urban income sources collapse, and the protection of land and other assets to which the migrant has claim back home, including assets expected at inheritance [*Lucas and Stark, 1985; Hoddinott, 1994*]. Empirical studies generally show that the majority of migrants (between 80 and 90 per cent) do indeed send remittances home, although the proportion of income sent and its frequency display wide variation across individual migrants [*Rempel and Lobdell, 1978; Hoddinott, 1994*]. In the family contract model, remittances are part of a long-term implicit contract between parents and children that includes investment in education, migration, remittances and inheritance [*Hoddinott, 1994*].

The migration literature has dwelt on both 'pull' and 'push' reasons for migration to occur. Income differentials are seen as the major 'pull' factor; while seasonality, risk, market failures, erosion of assets (for example, land subdivision at inheritance), landlessness, and disasters leading to livelihood collapse are seen as 'push' factors. Evidence supporting both forces are found in the literature, for example, Bigsten [*1996*] finds that the pull of high wages is more important than the push of land scarcity in explaining migration decisions in Kenya; while Adams [*1993*] finds precisely the reverse in a study of the factors explaining international migration from rural Egypt.

The notions of push and pull are similar in descriptive intent to the earlier juxtapositions of involuntary versus voluntary and desperation versus choice as ways of broadly categorising alternative sets of circumstances resulting in livelihood diversification. While it is on occasions useful to dichotomise cause and effect in this way, the ease of so doing should not be confused with the accuracy of the description thus achieved. In practice, individuals and households are influenced by a multiplicity of factors determining the livelihood changes they undergo. While on occasions a single factor may dominate over all others for an entire community or location, more often a cumulative combination of factors will represent variable pressures and opportunities for different individuals and households within the community.

V. DIVERSIFICATION, POVERTY AND INCOME DISTRIBUTION

The relationships between diverse income portfolios, levels of income, and income distribution are fairly complicated, and like many other facets of livelihood diversification they are somewhat prone to unhelpful generalisation rather than being placed in specified contexts.

Some of the more straightforward effects of diversification on incomes follow from the preceding discussion of its determinants. Diversification might be expected (a) to reduce the risk of income failure overall, by diluting the impact of failure in any single income source; (b) to reduce intra-year income variability, by diluting the effect of seasonality in farm-based income streams; and (c) to reduce inter-year income variability resulting from instability in agricultural production and markets. These effects must be regarded as broadly beneficial for poor and rich alike, subject to the caveat that the desperation-led diversification of the very poor may sometimes result from the accumulation-led diversification of the rich (such as might occur, for example, with land consolidation by the rich in order to use capital-intensive methods in new branches of agricultural production). Nevertheless, capability to diversify is likely to be particularly important for poor families that have little or no margin to withstand unexpected shortfalls in the annual level of income required for survival.

These effects have been noted in empirical studies [e.g., *Reardon et al., 1992*]. They play a significant food security role at household level, by enabling the household to maintain food consumption in the deficit season before the harvest. Clearly different income sources will achieve these ends with variable effectiveness. Off-farm wage income is likely to be correlated with the same seasonal and risk factors as own-farm production, and is therefore less able to play a role in smoothing unstable income streams. Local non-farm wage employment and some types of non-farm self-employment will also exhibit seasonal patterns similar to those experienced in agriculture; for example, marketing, food processing, input supply, farm machinery repair and so on. On the other hand rural small-scale industries [*Kilby and Liedholm, 1986*; *Islam, 1987*] may be able to play a counter-cyclical role, and remittances from urban areas are likely to be independent of seasonal cycles in agriculture.

A number of sources concur that the capability to diversify incomes is critical for the survival capabilities of the rural poor [*Matlon, 1979*; *Haggblade et al., 1989*; *Hazell and Haggblade, 1993*]. This is partly because poor households are more vulnerable to seasonal and risk factors than better off households. It is also because poor households lack assets; they may be landless or near landless, and possess few or no livestock. Without the capability to produce enough food on own account, the poor must diversify income sources in order to survive [*Zoomers and Kleinpenning, 1996*].

Increasing the survival options of the rural poor is the major reason that rural sector diversification is regarded by many researchers as an important goal of development policy. One strand of thinking which is examined more fully in the next section of this paper is the rural growth linkage approach which sees non-farm growth being stimulated by agricultural innovation [*Haggblade et al., 1989*; *Haggblade and Hazell, 1989*; *Hazell and Haggblade, 1993*]. Another strand is the active promotion of rural non-farm enterprise [*Saith, 1992*; *Fisher et al., 1997*] and rural small-scale industries [*Chuta and Sethuraman, 1984*; *Liedholm, McPherson and Chuta, 1994*].

Enabling the rural poor to earn enough in order to survive is one thing, reducing income disparities between poor and rich quite another [*World Bank, 1990*]. One view is that diversification has a broadly equalising effect on rural incomes [*Haggblade and Hazell, 1989*], and this is supported by studies suggesting that it raises the incomes of the poor relative to the rich [*Valentine, 1993*; *Adams, 1994*]. However, this may be a function of specific contextual conditions, since two different zones in one African country displayed opposing results in this regard [*Reardon et al., 1992*]. The effect may be indirect, by enabling poor households to overcome credit and risk constraints on agricultural innovation [*Taylor and Wyatt, 1996*]. In a study conducted by the latter authors, non-farm income sources were found to have a disproportionately beneficial indirect impact on small farm output compared to large farm output.

An opposing view is that diversification has a disequalising effect on rural incomes, in other words it exacerbates rural differentiation. Several studies have demonstrated that richer households derive a higher proportion of their incomes from non-farm sources than poorer households [*Collier and Lal, 1986; Evans and Ngau, 1991; Webb et al., 1992: 40; Reardon et al., 1992*]. Note that this does not have to be inconsistent with the critical role of income diversification for poor families; it merely states the obvious which is that better off families are able to diversify in more favourable labour markets than the poor. Important reasons for this effect are the lack of assets of the poor and their exclusion from the more highly remunerated labour markets due to skill and education constraints [*Dercon and Krishnan, 1996*]. Indeed, education may be a major explanatory cause of cumulative processes of rural differentiation [*Francis and Hoddinott, 1993*].

A case study of rural Pakistan described by Adams and He [1995] is instructive on the income distribution question. It demonstrates that some income sources have equalising, and others disequalising effects, on rural incomes. Specifically, livestock, non-farm wages, non-farm self-employment, and domestic remittances were found broadly to have an equalising impact on rural income distribution; while agriculture (cropping), rental income and international remittances had a disequalising impact. This occurred in part because crop income was correlated with highly unequal land ownership, while livestock income was not correlated in this way. Note also that international migration involves barriers to entry (travel and visa costs) that make it more accessible to better off than to poorer households, hence the difference in effects between domestic and international migration.

VI. DIVERSIFICATION, FARM PRODUCTIVITY AND NON-FARM GROWTH

One particular paradigm has governed a large proportion of the policy discussion for the past 20 years concerning the relationship of farm to non-farm rural activity. This is the rural growth linkages model, originating in the mid-1970s in the work of certain influential writers on rural development [*Johnston and Kilby, 1975; Mellor, 1976*], and applied to the study of rural growth, employment and incomes in Asia and Africa [*Bell et al., 1982; Hazell and Roell, 1983; Haggblade et al., 1989; Delgado et al., 1994*]. This approach is relevant to the study of livelihood diversification due to its emphasis on rising farm productivity as the source of diversification of income earning opportunities in rural areas.

While there are variations in emphasis within the rural growth linkages approach, its central tenet is that growth in agriculture itself provides the stimulus for the growth of rural non-farm activities in developing countries [*Haggblade and Hazell, 1989*; *Hazell and Haggblade, 1993*]. This is said to occur due to the rising expenditure of farm households on locally-produced non-farm commodities and services, including consumer goods and services (expenditure linkages), inputs and services to agricultural production (backward linkages), and processing and marketing services related to farm outputs (forward linkages). The significance and magnitude of these linkages have been explored in a number of sources [*Ranis and Stewart, 1987*; *Ranis, 1990*; *Bagachwa and Stewart, 1992*].

Empirical studies utilising the growth linkages approach have appeared to demonstrate big multiplier effects in the rural economy resulting from growth in agricultural output. Studies in Asia concluded that $1 extra value added in agriculture created $0.80 additional non-farm income [*Bell, Hazell and Slade, 1982*; *Hazell and Ramasamy, 1991*]; while a review of evidence for sub-Saharan Africa suggested a lower multiplier of the order of $0.50 growth in non-farm income for each $1 extra agricultural income [*Haggblade et al., 1989*]. However, by altering certain assumptions in the models that produce these figures, some researchers have estimated higher multipliers, ranging between $0.95 and $1.90 non-farm growth per $1 farm growth, for selected sub-Saharan African countries [*Delgado et al., 1994*].[16]

Studies of rural growth multipliers mainly concur that consumption linkages tend to dominate over forward and backward linkages in explaining total linkage effects [*Hazell and Haggblade, 1993*].[17] In other words, labour-intensive non-farm output growth is purportedly stimulated especially strongly by consumption expenditure, reflecting demand by farm households for locally-produced products and services. Controversially, some studies found that these consumption linkages were higher for larger farmers than for smaller farmers [*Hazell and Roell, 1983*; *Haggblade and Hazell, 1989*], leading to the potential policy inference that larger farms should be favoured above small and poor farmers in promoting higher farm productivity in order to achieve balanced growth within the rural sector.[18]

The direction of causality in the growth linkage model is always from farm growth to non-farm growth, not the other way round. This implies that the primary focus of anti-poverty policy should be growth in farm output. This helps to explain the emphasis on technological change in agriculture in much writing on rural development in the 1980s. It also explains the preoccupation of some authors in the 1990s with the supposed 'failure' of the green revolution in Africa; the logic being that unless farm yields and output rise steadily in African agriculture, the growth linkage multipliers will fail to occur and the non-farm rural economy will stagnate as well [*Delgado et al., 1994*].

Concomitantly, the rural non-farm sector according to this viewpoint has little dynamic of its own and would be unlikely to take a leading role in employment and income growth in the rural economy. In the succinct words of Saith [*1992: 114*] 'the tail cannot wag the dog'.

The growth linkage approach has been criticised for relying on unrealistic assumptions about the responsiveness of local non-farm output to increasing demand by farmers, and for ambiguity in the definition of what constitutes local supply and tradables, allowing for wide variation in multiplier results according to the definitions adopted [*Harriss, 1987; Hart, 1989; 1993*]. These assumptions as well as other internal characteristics of the models may result in exaggeration of the multiplier effects of agricultural growth in the local economy [*Haggblade et al., 1991; de Janvry, 1994*].

A study of intertemporal employment and output patterns in India concluded that diversification into non-farm activities was more likely to have occurred as a result of stagnation in agriculture or post-green revolution shedding of labour by farmers who are substituting capital for labour than from farm yield growth itself [*Chandrasekhar, 1993*]. In other words, the existence of an excess labour supply unable to secure agricultural jobs may have been a stronger stimulus to non-farm investment than farm growth. In similar vein, the location and vigour of rural non-farm activity may be due to its own cost and competitiveness characteristics rather than to farm output growth. Fisher *et al.* [*1997*] demonstrate that the most dynamic growth areas in the rural non-farm sector in India rely heavily on urban and export demand, and possess negligible links to agriculture. In some sub-Saharan African countries agricultural linkages have been found to be very weak [*Valentine, 1993; Tschirley and Weber, 1994*].

A focus on the household rather than the sector results in preoccupations that are different to the growth linkage emphasis on the leading role of farm output growth. The key question becomes whether or not the withdrawal of resources from the farm household that occurs with diversification damages the growth prospects of agriculture. In particular, it is typically the younger, more innovative, better educated members of farm families that leave the farm to engage in rural non-farm activities or to undertake distance migration. In doing so they may also divert scarce capital from the farm into rural self-employment or job search funding for would-be migrants.

Several researchers have concluded that livelihood diversification has adverse effects on farm investment and output. A first argument is that investment in the social and kinship networks required to support diverse livelihoods diverts resources from investment in agriculture [*Berry, 1989: 46–51*]. A second is that in some instances it may be farm profits that are invested in non-farm enterprise rather than the other way round [*Pottier,*

1983]. A third is that non-farm diversification withdraws able-bodied and skilled labour from farm production [*Lipton, 1977; 1980; Low, 1986*]. A fourth is that remittances are invariably utilised by the household for consumption purposes rather than productive investment [*Rempel and Lobdell, 1978*]. In a study in Indonesia, written up under the title 'too busy to farm', Preston [*1989*] found that the non-farm occupations of farm household members resulted in the gradual withdrawal from cultivation of the less productive arable areas on farms.

These findings portray a different sequence of events from the growth linkage approach. They relate to situations where buoyant non-farm labour markets cause an exodus of certain types of labour from the farm. The non-farm labour markets may be in cities, export processing zones, general manufacturing or mining industries. The jobs on offer may be gender differentiated or require particular skills or levels of education. The effect is to cause agriculture to stagnate, and in sub-Saharan Africa rural non-farm activity plays little role in the processes under observation.

A contrary household-level view is that the advent of non-farm income sources has a net beneficial impact on agriculture at the household level. Remittances from migrant family members are used for agricultural investment [*Lucas and Stark, 1985*]. In doing this, they can be interpreted as relieving a credit constraint caused by credit market failures [*Stark, 1982; Savadogo et al., 1994; Taylor and Wyatt, 1996*]. Alternatively, non-farm income can be viewed as a substitute for insurance, enabling the farm household to carry out risky innovations [*Evans and Ngau, 1991*]. One well-known case study appears to demonstrate massive long term benefits arising from the investment of urban earnings in environmental recovery and agricultural innovation [*Tiffen and Mortimore, 1992; Tiffen et al., 1994*].[20]

Note, however, that the logic of this position is indeed that the 'tail wags the dog'. Non-farm income sources become the agent of positive change in agriculture, rather than agriculture being the agent of rural non-farm growth. Furthermore, whereas in the growth linkage model it is rising farm productivity that enables labour to be released to the non-farm sector in a virtuous circle of rural growth, in the instances cited it is the prior release of labour from a stagnant agriculture that sets up a reverse chain of causality in which the alleviation of capital constraints becomes the catalyst of farm output growth.

These apparently irreconcilable interpretations of the relationship between farm productivity, agricultural growth, intra-rural diversity, and household level income diversification may merely reflect the distinct temporal and spatial contexts to which they apply. The growth linkage approach is associated with the period in Asia when green revolution technologies were achieving unprecedented increases in yields and output for the food grains, rice and wheat. The approach was formulated in part as a rebuttal of earlier pessimistic prognoses about the distributional impacts of the new technologies [e.g., *Griffin, 1979*]. The context of the models was agrarian economies containing many landless or near landless labour and rural labour markets offering an elastic supply of labour at the going wage.

Sub-Saharan Africa has been unable to reproduce anything like the farm growth of that era in Asia, and nor is it likely to do so given that climate, cropping systems, soils and so on are vastly more heterogeneous and risk-prone than the Asian case. Nor, with few exceptions, do sub-Saharan African countries possess rural labour markets of the type prevalent in Asia; on the contrary rural Africa is prone to seasonal and locational labour shortages in agriculture.[21] Most income diversification in Africa has been not just non-farm but non-rural in character.

The different findings concerning the impact of diversification on farm output are spatially and temporally specific. The stagnation of farming in the southern African periphery in the 1970s and 1980s was due to the adjacency of a booming labour market and low food prices [*Low, 1986*]. These conditions are unlikely to be replicable on the same scale at other times in other places. Likewise the 'greening' of Machakos District adjacent to Nairobi as a result of the reverse investment of urban earnings [*Tiffen and Mortimore, 1992*; *Tiffen et al., 1994*] may not possess the generality it tries to convey. In the end, the direction of resource allocation by family members will reflect real comparative returns to different activities in different locations, modified by considerations of risk and the long term social security of the family.

VII. DIVERSIFICATION AND GENDER

The spatially-extended concept of the household is the social arena around which most economic work on livelihood diversification has been undertaken. The strength of this approach is its recognition of the joint circumstances in which household members find themselves; its weakness is its neglect of the determinants and effects of diversification differentiated between women and men.

It is not proposed here to take on board the vast literature on gender and rural development. However, it is appropriate to consider the additional insights into diversification that are afforded by a more disaggregated approach to the household. Intrahousehold aspects of diversification can be pursued only to a limited degree within the context of the unitary household model, the predictive capabilities of which are restricted to patterns of intrahousehold specialisation that correspond to gender differentiated work opportunities and wage rates in different labour markets.

Collective models of the household based on individual welfare maximisation and bargaining theory provide more scope for examining how the social status and independent decision-making capabilities of women are affected by changing their access to work and income outside the home [*Ellis, 1993: Ch.9; Haddad et al., 1997*]. However, these models remain somewhat economistic in approach, and they need supplementing by an understanding of the social institutions that shape individual and family behaviour [*Hart, 1995*]. This recalls a previous comment about the 'social-embeddedness' of economic courses of action. Individuals may do things because they have no choice, as well as doing things because they are exercising choices.

Taking gender to mean the socially-defined roles of men and women, gender will often be found to constrain the patterns of income diversification pursued by the household [*Davies and Hossain, 1997*]. Such constraints may be direct, due, for example, to the total or partial prohibition of women working outside the home; or they may be indirect, resulting, for example, from girls being permitted less access to schooling than boys. Even without explicit constraints of this kind, the widespread social assignment of women to domestic duties means that their ability to participate in income earning opportunities outside the household or farm is likely, in most cases, to be more circumscribed than is the case for men.

A significant feature of income diversification in sub-Saharan Africa has been the so-called 'feminisation of agriculture', caused by the predominantly male involvement in long distance migration to cities, mines and plantations [*Low, 1986; Berry, 1989; Hart, 1994*]. As discussed in the preceding section, it is generally thought that this process has an immiserising effect on agriculture due to the loss of labour, the heavy domestic obligations of the women left behind, the lack of innovation and farm investment, and the logical use of remittance income to purchase food shortfalls [*Low, 1986*]. The predominance of males, and often younger males, in many different types of seasonal and circular migration has been noted by many researchers [*Agarwal, 1990; Bigsten, 1996; Breman, 1996*].

Gender thus affects diversification options, in terms of which income earning opportunities are taken up and which are discarded; and also affects diversification patterns, as manifested by unequal male and female participation rates in different branches of non-farm activity.

Gender also affects diversification outcomes for the welfare and status of family members as individuals. Some research findings suggest that a greater share of cash income accruing to women results both in more of the household budget being spent on food and in improvements to family nutrition [*Hoddinott and Haddad, 1995; Quisumbing et al., 1995*].

Engagement in independent income sources may raise the social status of women within the household, and improve their negotiating position across a range of household decisions, although these outcomes are not guaranteed merely from the fact of women's engagement in non-farm income-generating activity [*Wolf, 1990*]. For these reasons, gaining a better understanding, in different contexts, of the gender differentiated impacts of alternative income sources within the household could result in improvements in the design of local-level policies intended to ameliorate or reduce poverty, improve nutrition, and enhance the ability of individuals to improve their own living standards [*IFPRI, 1992; Bourguignon and Chiappori, 1992; Alderman et al., 1995*].

VIII. DIVERSIFICATION AND POLICY

One policy implication that arises from livelihood diversification is that the arena for household survival is spatially wider than the local sites often chosen by NGOs and aid donors as focal points for resource management policies [*Painter et al., 1994*]. Another is that different sources of income represent opportunities to different individuals or to families possessing different incomes and assets, therefore poverty reduction and income distribution are affected by policies that, intentionally or not, promote or downgrade alternative income generating activities [*Adams and He, 1995*].

Subject to the foregoing point, the removal of constraints to, and expansion of opportunities for, diversification are desirable policy objectives because they give households more capabilities to improve their livelihood security [*Jazairy et al., 1992*]. Market liberalisation can play a potentially positive role in this respect, by reducing the profile in the economy of state and parastatal agencies that formerly curtailed diversity and constrained opportunities and outcomes.[22] A meticulously conducted participatory study done in a cross section of Tanzanian villages in the early 1990s discovered that increased options for non-farm income generation were regarded by villagers as the single most significant change in their lives resulting at that point from new economic policies [*Booth et al., 1993*].

Arising from the literature, a number of policy areas are identified as having relevance either for the survival portfolios of the poor or for diversifying the income-earning options of individuals and households in rural areas. These are described briefly as follows:

(a) *Targeting:* The purpose of targeting is to provide safety-net support beneath the incomes of those social groups that are most vulnerable to events or shocks that could lead to insufficient food or destitution [*Lipton and Ravallion, 1995*]. There are two main types of targeting. Indicator targeting works by identifying the social groups (landless, old, disabled, etc) thought most likely to require support. Self-targeting works by providing wages or food in return for work at levels that can enable the poor to survive, but that are not so high as to be interesting for the better off. In effect, self-targeting provides a diversification option for those needing to diversify to survive. Successful targeting requires adequate information on the locational and seasonal incidence of food insecurity and deprivation.

(b) *Reduce Risk:* Risk is closely related to market failure, and market failure is related to high transaction costs, political and social instability, lack of rule of law, poor information, poor infrastructure and so on. Market failure will always be with us, but initiatives that improve freedoms of exchange and movement, increase information, facilitate labour markets, ensure transparency and accountability on the part of state agencies, and improve infrastructural facilities (see below) are likely to help.

(c) *Microcredit:* Lack of credit is widely acknowledged as a constraint on potential diversification, and there are several well-known examples of the success of small-scale group lending schemes in enabling individuals and households to widen their income earning options [*Hulme, 1990*] There are now many different models and experiments in micro-credit provision from which to adapt and to choose appropriate elements for local solutions [*Hulme and Mosley, 1996; Johnson and Rogaly, 1997*].

(d) *Rural Services:* In many circumstances the service sector can play a larger role in employment and income generation than is conventionally thought to be the case [*Haggblade et al., 1989; Reardon et al., 1992*]. The service sector includes orthodox services to agriculture such as marketing, input supply, machinery repair and so on; but also covers a diverse range of services in the consumption sector that are often poorly represented or absent in rural areas.

(e) *Rural Non-farm Enterprise:* This strand of policy has been popular in the literature for a long time and comes in different guises in different eras, for example, rural small-scale industry (RSSI) and microenterprise (ME). At least one major review of this sector is dubious of its long term potential, calling it a 'bargain basement sector' which has been encouraged in the past merely to avoid tackling difficult issues such as land reform or in a misguided attempt to slow the pace of rural–urban migration [*Saith, 1992*]. It has also been termed 'the forgotten sector', only in this instance from the contrary view that it does (in India) and can play a most important role in income-generation, employment and growth [*Fisher et al., 1997*]. The latter source contains a detailed discussion of facilitating and enabling roles of government towards the rural non-farm sector.

(f) *Rural Towns:* Rural towns have latterly tended to be neglected as potential focal points for economic growth, and in many countries municipalities have played a subordinated role down to vanishing point in determining the sites, incentives and infrastructure for non-farm investment. Several researchers in the diversification literature note the importance of rural towns as focal points of non-farm income generating possibilities [*Haggblade et al., 1989; Evans and Ngau, 1991*].[23]

(g) *Infrastructure:* The enabling role of infrastructural facilities is a recurring theme throughout the literature on diversification [e.g., *Lipton and Ravallion, 1995: 2630*], and indeed has more history than this because it is one of the few priorities that belongs both in the 1960s era of dinosaur development projects and in the 1990s era of participatory community development. In participatory exercises improved road access is one of the most frequently cited desirable items on village wishlists. Improved rural roads reduce the costs of all types of spatial transaction, including labour, output, input and consumer markets. Power supply also makes a big difference to feasible options for rural output growth. Access to mains electricity is a prerequisite for the location in rural areas of many types of manufacturing industry.

(h) *Education:* All studies that have looked into the matter concur that education is a great facilitator of livelihood diversification. Lack of education has been identified as a critical constraint inhibiting diversification by several researchers [*Evans and Ngau, 1991; Dercon and Krishnan, 1996*]. Since poverty is closely associated with low levels of education and lack of skills, education is also a key factor contributing to the greater ability of better off families to diversify compared to poorer families. It follows that targeting of education and skills training towards poor village households is likely to have a relatively large impact on their ability to diversify income sources.

The foregoing list does not contain the conventional number one rural policy priority of raising farm productivity. This is partly because farm policy is such a large topic in its own right [e.g., *Ellis, 1992*]; and partly because its relationship to the theme of diversification contains several strands which are worth elucidating separately.

First, farming or livestock husbandry is still the majority income source for the largest proportion of poor people in low income countries, and therefore the continued pursuit of productivity increases in developing country agriculture remains an important goal. Meanwhile, the accepted means of stimulating agricultural innovation have changed since the mid-1980s. Price policies, that is, minimum prices, stable prices, subsidised input prices, low interest credit and so on, and the associated state agencies that implemented them, have been dismantled or greatly reduced in scope in many countries. This implies that agricultural research systems and their interactions with farmers through extension and participation have changed from being one of several different means of promoting innovation to being the main way of doing so.

Second, agriculture itself can play a role in diversification options, and indeed, new cropping or crop-livestock systems in agriculture can make important contributions to income diversity. The key feature here is to take advantage of new markets for different outputs, created by economic growth and changes in trade regimes. Rapid growth in the production of high value fruit and vegetable crops for urban and international markets has been achieved in some sub-Saharan African rural areas [*Jaffee and Morton, 1995*]. Similar trends have occurred in milk supplies to towns based on zero grazing regimes in intensive agricultural systems [e.g., *Mdoe, 1996*]. These trends are market driven but can be facilitated by NGOs and governments via market research, credit schemes, and enabling environments, especially where export trade in concerned.

Third, there is the rural growth linkage contention that farm growth itself acts as the stimulant for the emergence of more diverse opportunities in the rural economy [*Hazell and Haggblade, 1993*]. The likelihood that sub-Saharan Africa will experience the kind of tidal wave yield and output growth that Asia experienced in the era from the early 1970s to the mid-1980s seems increasingly remote. This is not meant to convey undue pessimisism; it is merely accepting that achievements of this kind in Africa will continue to occur in a dispersed and uneven way in the future as they have done in the past. Therefore, rural diversity is unlikely to result from massive spillovers of agricultural growth in the African context, even if it arguably had this effect in parts of Asia. The rural growth linkage view of rural development policy seems increasingly beside the point in both Africa and Asia.

The current popularly advocated practice for the conduct of rural policy is to enable rural communities to determine their own priorities through participatory methods of information gathering, consultation, and collaboration with agencies, such as NGOs and government organisations, that have goals of improving rural livelihoods [e.g., *Chambers, 1997*]. This no doubt has its attractions as an antithesis to the allegedly heavy handed rural development practice of the past, but it will only ensure its validity in the future if priorities so identified are then facilitated or acted upon by the catalysts of the discussion. If members of rural communities keep identifying rural roads as a key priority for improving their lives, then they may be forgiven for becoming rather cynical about participation if assistance with rural road construction and maintenance persistently then fails to materialise.

IX. CONCLUSIONS

This article has reviewed livelihood diversification as a phenomenon that characterises the survival and income strategies of individuals and families in rural areas of developing countries. There is a widespread view, difficult to substantiate due to the lack of comparable intertemporal data sets, that diversity has increased over time in general and may be accelerating in the current phase of rural development in sub-Saharan Africa. There are many reasons for this, amongst which changing incentives and labour markets, risk strategies, impact of disasters and civil strife, and saving and investment behaviour, all contribute with different force in different settings.

It is tempting to seek generalisations concerning the causes and effects of livelihood diversification, and, indeed quite a few of the contributions reviewed here purport to demonstrate *the* critical determinant or implication of greater degrees of household income diversity. Clearly an advantage of discovering generalisable causes and consequences of diversification is that policies of wide applicability can then be devised either to tackle its causes (if it is considered bad) or to stimulate it further (if it is considered good) or to channel it in particular directions in order to enhance the opportunities it represents for particular groups (women, the landless, the poor, the risk-prone and so on).

A first conclusion of this article is that such generalisation is neither desirable nor necessary in order for an awareness of diversity to inform local policies. Diversification is an infinitely heterogeneous social and economic process, obeying a myriad of pressures and possibilities in the rural economy. It is differentiated in its causes and effects by location, demography, vulnerability, income level, education and many other factors. Recognition of this heterogeneity is not to advocate neglecting diversification as an important research and policy topic. Rather it emphasises the importance of local contexts and therefore of tailoring local policies to local circumstances.

A second conclusion is that sheer capability to diversify income sources signifies an improvement in the livelihood security and income-increasing capabilities of the rural household. Therefore policies that reduce constraints to diversification and widen its possibilities are in general desirable. Policies that act in this direction are those related to targeting, risk reduction, micro-credit, rural services, rural non-farm enterprise, rural towns, infrastructure and education. Diversification within agriculture to take advantage of new markets is also a desirable policy emphasis.

Finally, there is a need for more systematic knowledge of livelihood strategies and their links to macroeconomic policies. The last decade has seen the uneven dismantling in many countries of the middle-level policy apparatus that used to act as an interface between the macroeconomy and the rural household. Macro-policies are pursued with little more than guesswork as to the changes in rural livelihood systems that they provoke, and therefore little opportunity is afforded to invigorate beneficial trends or to ameliorate adverse ones. Moreover, a better understanding of diversification is needed to underpin social safety net and poverty reduction policies. Amidst the generalised retreat, often in disarray, of big government from the rural economy, the least that needs to be put in place are household monitoring systems that can inform researchers, policy advisers and policy-makers of the livelihood adaptations occurring as a consequence of the policies being pursued. The devising of low-cost and effective livelihood monitoring systems represents a significant methodological challenge for the future.

final version received December 1997

NOTES

1. This compartmentalisation permeates conventional development economics [e.g., *Nafziger, 1997; Todaro, 1997*]. It also informs the collection of most government statistics which is oriented towards counting and classifying full-time jobs (or 'main occupations') and follows clearly demarcated sectoral classifications for employment, wages, outputs and so forth.
2. The proposition that economic progress depends on specialisation and division of labour can be traced back to Adam Smith's *Wealth of Nations* (1776) which contains the famous pronouncement that 'the division of labour is limited by the extent of the market' [*Smith, 1970: 121*]. An explicitly stated rural development version of this proposition is articulated in Tomich *et al.* [*1995: 36–65*].
3. An important branch of enquiry in this area not examined in the article is the inter-relationship of diversification strategies with natural resource management and the environment.
4. In the Indian literature, the term 'occupational diversification' is often used to describe diversification of income sources [*Sadangi and Singh, 1993; Unni, 1996*].
5. Cash income from crop or livestock sales refers to the gross value of sales less the cost of purchased inputs, including seasonal wage labour, used in production [*Brown, 1979*]. The use of livestock as a store of wealth as well as for recurrent sales or consumption makes evaluation of the livestock contribution to income quite difficult in practice [*Sarris and van den Brink, 1993: 67–71*].
6. For example, the bawon system for harvesting rice which is still prevalent in Java [*Hart, 1986; Ellis et al., 1992*], and many different types of labour contract observable in India [*Rogaly, 1997*].

7. Non-farm rural self-employment is referred to as 'business income' in some sources.
8. These differences in categorisation, while valid within the logic of individual studies, cause difficulties for making comparisons across studies utilising secondary data, and indeed many such comparisons are invalidated by the different procedures employed in distinguishing income sources in different studies.
9. This has occurred, for example, with several largescale household surveys undertaken in Kenya [*World Bank, 1995*].
10. This is the case, for example, with the World Bank funded Human Resource Development Survey in Tanzania [*World Bank, 1996*].
11. These are sweeping generalisations that are admittedly indefensible statistically. They result from the dubious procedure of calculating crude averages across non-comparable surveys as published in the sources cited.
12. For example figures cited by Reardon [*1997*] on Lesotho give a sample average of 78 per cent reliance on non-farm sources.
13. One exception in the sub-Saharan Africa literature is the paper by Valentine [*1993*] which compares income sources in rural Botswana between 1973/74 and 1985/86, demonstrating a large increase in non-farm income sources between those two dates.
14. Taking into account interest payments on loans or advances made for consumption purposes.
15. For a different definition of vulnerability – dependence on unreliable non-farm sources of food – see Reardon and Matlon [*1989*].
16. Achieved principally by deciding to include more items in the category of nontradable rural outputs, the production of which are supposedly stimulated by farm household expenditure [*Delgado et al., 1994*]
17. This predominance of consumption linkages did not manifest itself in a study of growth linkages in the Indian State of Tamil Nadu in the mid-1980s [*Hazell and Ramasamy, 1991*].
18. As pointed out with some force by Harriss [*1987*]. Not all writers within the rural growth linkage tradition have concurred on this point [e.g., *Bell et al., 1982*].
19. The two key assumptions are a perfectly elastic supply of locally-produced non-tradables; and local supply defined by point of purchase, not point of origin.
20. The site of this case-study was the previously degraded Machakos District in Kenya, which is close to the capital city, Nairobi.
21. These are, of course, rough generalisations. Seasonal labour shortages can be observed in Asia, just as they may not always be a dominating factor in Africa.
22. The downside is that it may also increase inequality, as plenty of observers have been quick to point out [e.g., *Gibbon, 1992*]. On the other hand much commentary on structural adjustment and its impact in Africa has been premature and thinly supported by evidence; exhibiting a tendency to exaggerate the speed of change in African economic structures resulting from the initial adoption of structural adjustment programmes in the mid-1980s.
23. An earlier literature promoted rural towns as growth poles, but this in the 1970s context of extensive central government involvement [e.g., *Richardson, 1979*].

REFERENCES

Adams, R.H., 1993, 'The Economic and Demographic Determinants of International Migration in Rural Egypt', *The Journal of Development Studies*, Vol.30, No.1, pp.146–67
Adams, R.H., 1994, 'Non-Farm Income and Inequality in Rural Pakistan', *The Journal of Development Studies*, Vol.31, No.1, pp.110–33
Adams, R.H. and J.J. He, 1995, *Sources of Income Inequality and Poverty in Rural Pakistan*, Research Report No.102, Washington, DC: International Food Policy Research Institute.
Agarwal, B., 1990, 'Social Security and the Family: Coping with Seasonality and Calamity in Rural India', *The Journal of Peasant Studies*, Vol.17, No.3, pp.341–412
Alderman, H. and D.E. Sahn, 1989, 'Understanding the Seasonality of Employment, Wage, and Income', Ch.6 in D.E. Sahn (ed.), *Seasonal Variability in Third World Agriculture: The Consequences for Food Security*, Baltimore, MD: John Hopkins Press, pp.81–106

Alderman, H. and C. Paxson, 1992, 'Do the Poor Insure? A Synthesis of the Literature on Risk and Consumption in Developing Countries', *Policy Research Working Papers*, No.1008, Washington, DC: World Bank.

Alderman, H., Chiappori, P., Haddad, L., Hoddinott, J. and R. Kanbur, 1995, 'Unitary Versus Collective Models of the Household: Is it Time to Shift the Burden of Proof?' *World Bank Research Observer*, Vol.10, No.1.

Anderson, J.R., Dillon, J.L. and J.B. Hardaker, 1977, *Agricultural Decision Analysis*, Ames, IL: Iowa State University Press.

Andrae, G., 1992, 'Urban Workers as Farmers: Agro-links of Nigerian Textile Workers in the Crisis of the 1980s', in J. Baker and P.O. Pederson, *The Rural Urban Interface in Africa: Expansion and Adaption*, Uppsala: Scandinavian Institute for African Studies in co-operation with Centre for Development Research, Copenhagen.

Baber, R., 1996, 'Current Livelihoods in Semi-Arid Rural Areas of South Africa', Ch.11 in M. Lipton, F. Ellis and M. Lipton (eds.), *Land, Labour and Livelihoods in Rural South Africa Volume 2: Kwazulu-Natal and Northern Province*, Durban: Indicator Press, pp.269–302.

Bagachwa, M.S.D. and F. Stewart, 1992, 'Rural Industries and Rural Linkages in Sub-Saharan Africa: A Survey', Ch.5 in F. Stewart, S. Lall and S. Wangwe (eds.), *Alternative Development Strategies for Sub-Saharan Africa*, Basingstoke: Macmillan, pp.145–84.

Baker, J. and P.O. Pedersen (eds.), 1992, *The Rural Urban Interface in Africa: Expansion and Adaptation*, Uppsala: Scandinavian Institute of African Studies.

Bangura, Y., 1994, 'Economic Restructuring, Coping Strategies and Social Change: Implications for Institutional Development in Africa', *Development and Change*, Vol.25, pp.785–827.

Barnum, H.N. and L. Squire, 1979, *A Model of an Agricultural Household: Theory and Evidence*, Washington, DC: World Bank, Occasional Paper No.27.

Bell, C., 1988, 'Credit Markets and Interlinked Transactions', Ch.16 in H. Chenery and T.N. Srinivasan, *Handbook of Development Economics Volume 1*, Amsterdam: North Holland, pp.763–830.

Bell, C., P. Hazell and R. Slade, 1982, *Project Evaluation in Regional Perspective*, Baltimore, MD: Johns Hopkins.

Benjamin, C., 1994, 'The Growing Importance of Diversification Activities for French Farm Households', *Journal of Rural Studies*, Vol.10, No.4, pp.331–42.

Bernstein, H., Crow, B. and H. Johnson, 1992, *Rural Livelihoods: Crises and Responses*, Oxford University Press.

Berry, S., 1986, 'Macro-Policy Implications of Research on Rural Households and Farming Systems' in J.L. Moock (ed.), *Understanding Africa's Rural Household and Farming Systems*, Boulder, CO: Westview Press.

Berry, S., 1989, 'Social Institutions and Access to Resources', *Africa*, Vol.59, No.1, pp.41–55.

Berry, S., 1993, *No Condition is Permanent: The Social Dynamics of Agrarian Change in Sub-Saharan Africa*, Madison, WI: University of Wisconsin Press.

Berry, S., 1997, 'Tomatoes, Land and Hearsay: Property and History in Asante in the Time of Structural Adjustment', *World Development*, Vol.25, No.8, pp.1225–41.

Bigsten, A., 1988, 'A Note on the Modelling of Circular Small Holder Migration', *Economics Letters*, Vol.28, pp.87–91.

Bigsten, A., 1996, 'The Circular Migration of Smallholders in Kenya', *Journal of African Economies*, Vol.5, No.1, pp.1–20.

Bigsten, A. and S. Kayizzi-Mugerwa, 1995, 'Rural Sector Responses to Economic Crisis in Uganda', *Journal of International Development*, Vol.7, No.2, pp.181–209.

Binswanger, H.P., 1983, 'Agricultural Growth and Rural Non-farm Activities', *Finance & Development*, June, pp.38–40.

Blackwood, D.L. and R.G. Lynch, 1994, 'The Measurement of Inequality and Poverty: A Policy Maker's Guide to the Literature', *World Development*, Vol.22, No.4, pp.567–78.

Blaikie, P. and H. Brookfield (eds.), 1987, *Land Degradation and Society*, London: Methuen

Blaikie, P.M., Cannon, T., Davis, I. and B. Wisner, 1994, *At Risk: Natural Hazards, People's Vulnerability and Disasters*, London and New York: Routledge.

Blarel, B., Hazell, P., Place, F. and J. Quiggin, 1992, 'The Economics of Farm Fragmentation: Evidence from Ghana and Rwanda', *World Bank Economic Review*, Vol.6, No.2, pp.233–54.

Booth, D., Lugangira, F. *et al.*, 1993, *Social, Cultural and Economic Change in Contemporary Tanzania: A People-Oriented Focus*, Stockholm: SIDA.

Bourguignon, F. and P-A. Chiappori, 1992, 'Collective Models of Household Behavior: An Introduction', *European Economic Review*, Vol.36, pp.355–64.

Breman, J., 1996, *Footloose Labour: Working in India's Informal Economy*, Cambridge: Cambridge University Press.

Bromley, D.W., 1989, 'Property Relations and Economic Development: The Other Land Reform', *World Development*, Vol.17, No.6.

Bromley, D.W., 1991, *Environment and Economy: Property Rights and Public Policy*, Oxford: Basil Blackwell.

Brown, M.L., 1979, *Farm Budgets: From Farm Income Analysis to Agricultural Project Analysis*, World Bank Staff Occasional Papers No.29, Baltimore, MD: Johns Hopkins.

Bruce, J., 1989, 'Homes Divided', *World Development*, Vol.17, No.7.

Bryceson, D.F., 1996, 'Deagrarianization and Rural Employment in Sub-Saharan Africa: A Sectoral Perspective', *World Development*, Vol.24, No.1, pp.97–111.

Bryceson, D.F., 1997, 'Deagrarianization in Sub-Saharan Africa: Acknowledging the Inevitable', Ch.1 in D.F. Bryceson and V. Jamal (eds.), *Farewell to Farms: Deagrarianisation and Employment in Africa*, Research Series No.1997/10, Leiden, Netherlands: African Studies Centre, pp.3–20.

Campbell, D.J., 1990, 'Strategies for Coping with Severe Food Deficits in Rural Africa: A Review of the Literature', *Food and Foodways*, Vol.4, No.2, pp.143–62.

Carter, M.R., 1997, 'Environment, Technology, and the Social Articulation of Risk in West African Agriculture', *Economic Development and Cultural Change*, Vol.45, No.3, pp.557–91.

Chambers, R., 1982, 'Health, Agriculture, and Rural Poverty', *The Journal of Development Studies*, Vol.18, No.2, pp.217–37.

Chambers, R., 1989, 'Editorial Introduction: Vulnerability, Coping and Policy', *IDS Bulletin*, Vol.20, No.2, pp.1–7.

Chambers, R., 1997, *Whose Reality Counts?: Putting the First Last*, London: Intermediate Technology Publications.

Chambers, R., Longhurst, R. and A. Pacey (eds.), 1981, *Seasonal Dimensions to Rural Poverty*, London: Frances Pinter.

Chandrasekhar, C.P., 1993, 'Agrarian Change and Occupational Diversification: Non-Agricultural Employment and Rural Development in West Bengal', *The Journal of Peasant Studies*, Vol.20, No.2, pp.205–70.

Chuta, E. and S.V. Sethuraman (eds.), 1984, *Rural Small-Scale Industries and Employment in Africa and Asia*, Geneva, ILO.

Collier, P. and D. Lal, 1986, *Labour and Poverty in Kenya, 1900–1980*, Clarendon Press: Oxford

Collier, W.L., 1988, *A Preliminary Study of Employment Trends in Lowland Javanese Villages*, Bogor, Indonesia: Agency for Agricultural Research and Development.

Corbett, J., 1988, 'Famine and Household Coping Strategies', *World Development*, Vol.16, No.9, pp.1099–112.

Davies, S., 1996, *Adaptable Livelihoods Coping with Food Insecurity in the Malian Sahel*, London: Macmillan Press.

Davies, S. and N. Hossain, 1997, *Livelihood Adaptation, Public Action and Civil Society: A Review of the Literature*, IDS Working Paper No.57, Brighton: Institute of Development Studies, July.

de Haan, A. (ed.), 1997, 'Urban Poverty: A New Research Agenda', *IDS Bulletin*, Vol.28, No.2.

de Janvry, A., 1994, 'Farm-Non-farm Synergies in Africa: Discussion', *American Journal of Agricultural Economics*, Vol.76, pp.1183–5.

Delgado, C., Hazell, P., Hopkins, J. and V. Kelly, 1994, 'Promoting Intersectoral Growth Linkages in Rural Africa Through Agricultural Technology Policy Reform', *American Journal of Agricultural Economics*, Vol.76, pp.1166–71.

Dercon, S. and P. Krishnan, 1996, 'Income Portfolios in Rural Ethiopia and Tanzania: Choices and Constraints', *The Journal of Development Studies*, Vol.32 No.6, pp.850–75.

Dwyer, D. and J. Bruce (eds.), 1988, *A Home Divided: Women and Income in the Third World*, Stanford, CA: Stanford University Press.

34   THE JOURNAL OF DEVELOPMENT STUDIES

Ellis, F., 1992, *Agricultural Policies in Developing Countries*, Cambridge: Cambridge University Press.
Ellis, F., 1993, *Peasant Economics: Farm Households and Agrarian Development*, 2nd Edition, Cambridge: Cambridge University Press.
Ellis, F., Trotter, B. and P. Magrath, 1992, *Rice Marketing in Indonesia: Methodology, Results and Implications of a Research Study*, Marketing Series No.4, Chatham, UK: Natural Resource Institute.
Eswaran, M. and A. Kotwal, 1989, 'Credit as Insurance in Agrarian Economies', *Journal of Development Economics*, Vol.31, pp.37–53.
Eswaran, M. and A. Kotwal, 1990, 'Implications of Credit Constraints for Risk Behaviour in Less Developed Economies', *Oxford Economic Papers*, Vol.42, pp.473–82.
Evans, H.E. and P. Ngau, 1991, 'Rural-Urban Relations, Household Income Diversification and Agricultural Productivity' *Development and Change*, Vol.22, pp.519–45.
Fisher, T., V. Mahajan and A. Singha, 1997, *The Forgotten Sector: Non-farm Employment and Enterprises in Rural India*, London: IT Publications.
Folbre, N., 1986,'Hearts and Spades: Paradigms of Household Economics', *World Development*, Vol.14, No.2.
Francis, E. and J. Hoddinott, 1993, 'Migration and Differentiation in Western Kenya: A Tale of Two Sub-Locations', *The Journal of Development Studies*, Vol.30, No.1, pp.115–45.
Gibbon, P., 1992, 'The World Bank and African Poverty, 1973–91', *Journal of Modern African Studies*, Vol.30, No.2, pp.193–220.
Glewwe, P. and J. van der Gaag, 1988, 'Confronting Poverty in Developing Countries: Definitions, Information and Policies', *Living Standards Measurement Study, Working Paper*, No.48, Washington, DC: World Bank.
Glewwe, P. and J. van der Gaag, 1990, 'Identifying the Poor in Developing Countries: Do Different Definitions Matter?', *World Development*, Vol.18, No.6, pp.803–14.
Greeley, M., 1996, 'Measurement of Poverty and Poverty of Measurement', *IDS Bulletin*, Vol.27, No.1, pp.50–8.
Griffin, K., 1979, *The Political Economy of Agrarian Change: An Essay on the Green Revolution*, 2nd Edition, London: Macmillan.
Guyer, J.I. and P.E. Peters, 1987, 'Conceptualising the Household: Issues of Theory and Policy in Africa', *Development and Change*, Vol.18, No.2.
Haddad, L., Hoddinott, J. and H. Alderman (eds.), 1997, *Intrahousehold Resource Allocation in Developing Countries: Models, Methods, and Policy*, Baltimore, MD: Johns Hopkins.
Haggblade, S. and P. Hazell, 1989, 'Agricultural Technology and Farm-Non-farm Growth Linkages', *Agricultural Economics*, Vol.3, pp.345–64.
Haggblade, S., Hammer, J. and P. Hazell, 1991, 'Modeling Agricultural Growth Multipliers', *American Journal of Agricultural Economics*, May, pp.361–74.
Haggblade, S., Hazell, P. and J. Brown, 1989, 'Farm-Non-farm Linkages in Rural Sub-Saharan Africa', *World Development*, Vol.17, No.8, pp.1173–201.
Harris, J.R. and M.P. Todaro, 1970, 'Migration, Unemployment and Development: A Two Sector Analysis', *American Economic Review*, Vol.60, pp.126–42.
Harriss, B., 1987, 'Regional Growth Linkages from Agriculture', *The Journal of Development Studies*, Vol.23, No.2, pp.275–89.
Hart, G., 1986, *Power, Labor, and Livelihood: Processes of Change in Rural Java*, Berkeley, CA: University of California Press.
Hart, G., 1989, 'The Growth Linkages Controversy: Some Lessons from the Muda Case', *The Journal of Development Studies*, Vol.25, No.4, pp.571–5.
Hart, G., 1993, *Regional Growth Linkages in the Era of Liberalization: A Critique of the New Agrarian Optimism*, World Employment Programme Research Working Paper No.37, Geneva: International Labour Office.
Hart, G., 1994, 'The Dynamics of Diversification in an Asian Rice Region' Ch.2 in B. Koppel *et al.* (eds.), *Development or Deterioration?: Work in Rural Asia*, Boulder, CO: Lynne Reinner, pp.47–71.
Hart, G., 1995, 'Gender and Household Dynamics: Recent Theories and Their Implications', in M.G. Quibria (ed.), *Critical Issues in Asian Development: Theories, Experiences and*

Policies, Oxford and New York: Oxford University Press.

Hazell, P.B.R. and Roell, A., 1983, *Rural Growth Linkages: Household Expenditure Patterns in Malaysia and Nigeria*, Washington, DC: International Food Policy Research Institute 1983.

Hazell, P.R. and C. Ramasamy, 1991, *The Green Revolution Reconsidered: The Impact of High-Yielding Rice Varieties in South India*, Baltimore, MD, Johns Hopkins.

Hazell, P. and S. Haggblade, 1993, 'Farm-Non-farm Growth Linkages and the Welfare of the Poor', Ch.8 in M. Lipton and J. van der Gaag (eds.), *Including the Poor*, Proceedings of a Symposium Organized by the World Bank and the International Food Policy Research Institute, Washington, DC: World Bank, pp.190–204.

Hearn, D.H., McNamara, K.T. and L. Gunter, 1996, 'Local Economic Structure and Off-Farm Labour Earnings of Farm Operators and Spouses' *Journal of Agricultural Economics* Vol.47, No.1, pp.28–36.

Heyer, J., 1996, 'The Complexities of Rural Poverty in Sub-Saharan Africa', *Oxford Development Studies*, Vol.24, No.3, pp.281–97.

Hoddinott, J., 1994, 'A Model of Migration and Remittances Applied to Western Kenya', *Oxford Economic Papers*, Vol.46, pp.459–76.

Hoddinott, J. and L. Haddad, 1995, 'Does Female Income Share Influence Household Expenditure Patterns? Evidence from Côte d'Ivoire', *Oxford Bulletin of Economics and Statistics*, Vol.57, No.1, pp.77–96.

Hulme, D., 1990, 'Can the Grameen Bank be Replicated? Recent Experiments in Malaysia, Malawi and Sri Lanka', *Development Policy Review*, Vol.8, pp.287–300.

Hulme, D. and P. Mosley, 1996, *Finance Against Poverty*, Vol.1, London: Routledge.

Hymer, S. and S. Resnick, 1969, 'A Model of an Agrarian Economy with Nonagricultural Activities', *American Economic Review*, Vol.59, No.4.

International Food Policy Research Institute, 1992, *Understanding How Resources are Allocated within Households*, IFPRI Policy Briefs 8, Washington, DC: IFPRI.

Islam, R. (ed.), 1987, *Rural Industrialisation and Employment in Asia*, New Delhi: International Labour Organisation.

Jaffee, S. and J. Morton (eds.), 1995, *Marketing Africa's High-Value Foods: Comparative Experiences of an Emergent Private Sector*, Dubuque, IA: Kendall/Hunt for World Bank.

Jazairy, I., Alamgir, M. and T. Panuccio, 1992, *The State of World Rural Poverty: An Inquiry into its Causes and Consequences*, London: IT Publications for the International Fund for Agricultural Development (IFAD).

Johnson, S. and B. Rogaly, 1997, *Microfinance and Poverty Reduction*, Oxford: Oxfam.

Johnston, B.F. and P. Kilby, 1975, *Agriculture and Structural Transformation*, New York: Oxford University Press.

Katz, E. and O. Stark, 1986, 'Labor Migration and Risk Aversion in Less Developed Countries', *Journal of Labor Economics*, Vol.4, pp.134–49.

Kelly, C. and B. W. Ilbery, 1995, 'Defining and Examining Rural Diversification: A Framework for Analysis', *Tijdschrift voor Economische en Sociale Geografie*, Vol.85, No.2, pp.177–85.

Kilby, P. and C. Liedholm, 1986, *The Role of Non-farm Activities in the Rural Economy*, Employment and Enterprise Development Policy Analysis, Discussion Paper No.7, Cambridge, MA: Harvard Institute for International Development.

Lageman, B., 1989, 'Recent Migration Flows and the "Net Reallocation of Labour" Between Rural and Urban Sectors in Nigeria', *African Development Patterns Yearbook*, pp.525–45.

Larson, D. and Y. Mundlak, 1997, 'On the Intersectoral Migration of Agricultural Labour', *Economic Development and Cultural Change*, Vol.45, No.2, pp.295–320.

Liedholm, C., M. McPherson and E. Chuta, 1994, 'Small Enterprise Employment Growth in Rural Africa', *American Journal of Agricultural Economics*, Vol.76, Dec., pp.1177–82.

Lipton, M., 1977, *Why Poor People Stay Poor: Urban Bias in World Development*, London: Temple Smith.

Lipton, M., 1980, 'Migration from Rural Areas of Poor Countries: The Impact on Rural Productivity and Income Distribution', *World Development*, Vol.8, pp.1–24.

Lipton, M., 1996, 'Comment on "Research on Poverty and Development Twenty Years after *Redistribution with Growth*" ', in M. Bruno and B. Pleskovic (eds.), *Annual World Bank Conference on Development Economics 1995*, Washington, DC: World Bank, pp.73–9.

36   THE JOURNAL OF DEVELOPMENT STUDIES

Lipton, M. and S. Maxwell, 1992, 'The New Poverty Agenda: An Overview', *IDS Discussion Paper*, No.306, August.

Lipton, M. and M. Ravallion, 1995, 'Poverty and Policy', in J. Behrman and T.N. Srinivasan (eds), *Handbook of Development Economics Vol.IIIB*, Amsterdam: Elsevier, 1995, pp.2551–657.

Lipton, M. and J. van der Gaag (eds.), 1993, *Including the Poor*, Proceedings of a Symposium Organized by the World Bank and the International Food Policy Research Institute, Washington, DC: World Bank.

Low, A., 1986, *Agricultural Development in Southern Africa: Farm Household Theory and the Food Crisis*, London: James Currey.

Lucas, R.E.B. and O. Stark, 1985, 'Motivations to Remit: Evidence from Botswana', *Journal of Political Economy*, Vol.93, No.5, pp.901–18.

Matlon, P.J., 1979, *Income Distribution among Farmers in Northern Nigeria: Empirical Results and Policy Implications*, African Rural Economy Paper No.18, East Lansing, MI: Michigan State University, Department of Agricultural Economics.

Maxwell, D.G., 1995, 'Alternative Food Security Strategy: A Household Analysis of Urban Agriculture in Kampala', *World Development*, Vol.23, No.10, pp.1669–81.

May, J., 1996, 'Assets, Income and Livelihoods in Rural Kwazulu-Natal', Ch.1 in M. Lipton, F. Ellis and M. Lipton (eds.), *Land, Labour and Livelihoods in Rural South Africa Volume 2: Kwazulu-Natal and Northern Province*, Durban: Indicator Press, pp.1–30.

Mdoe, N., 1996, 'Constraints to Milk Marketing in the Kilimanjaro Highlands of Hai District', *TSAP Proceedings*, Vol.20, pp.247–56.

Meillassoux, C., 1981, *Maidens, Meal and Money: Capitalism and the Domestic Community*, Cambridge: Cambridge University Press.

Mellor, J.W., 1976, *The New Economics of Growth*, Ithaca, NY: Cornell University Press.

Moser, C.O.N., 1998, 'The Asset Vulnerability Framework: Reassessing Urban Poverty Reduction Strategies', *World Development*, Vol.26, No.1, pp.1–19.

Murray, C., 1981, *Families Divided*, Cambridge: Cambridge University Press.

Nafziger, E.W., 1997, *The Economics of Developing Countries*, 3rd Edition, London: Prentice-Hall.

Nakajima, C., 1970, 'Subsistence and Commercial Family Farms: Some Theoretical Models of Subjective Equilibrium', in C.R. Wharton (ed.), *Subsistence Agriculture and Economic Development*, London and Portland, OR: Frank Cass.

Nakajima, C., 1986, *Subjective Equilibrium Theory of the Farm Household*, Amsterdam: Elsevier

Norman, D.W., 1974, 'Rationalising Mixed Cropping under Indigenous Conditions: The Example of Northern Nigeria', *The Journal of Development Studies*, Vol.11, No.1.

Norman, D.W., 1977, 'Economic Rationality of Traditional Hausa Dryland Farmers in the North of Nigeria', R.D. Stevens (ed.), *Tradition and Dynamics in Small-Farm Agriculture*, Ames, IA: Iowa State University Press.

Painter, T., Sumberg, J. and T. Price, 1994, 'Your *Terroir* and My 'Action Space': Implications of Differentiation, Mobility and Diversification for the *Approche Terroir* in Sahelian West Africa', *Africa*, Vol.4, No.64.

Platteau, J.P., 1992, *Land Reform and Structural Adjustment in sub-Saharan Africa: Controversies and Guidelines*, FAO Economic and Social Development Paper No.107, Rome: FAO.

Pottier, J., 1983, 'Defunct Labour Reserve?: Mambwe Villages in the Post-Migration Economy', *Africa*, Vol.53, No.2, pp.1–22.

Preston, D.A., 1989, 'Too Busy to Farm: Under-utilization of Farm Land in Central Java', *The Journal of Development Studies*, Vol.26, No.1.

Preston, D.A., 1994, 'Rapid Household Appraisal: A Method for Facilitating the Analysis of Household Livelihood Strategies', *Applied Geography*, Vol.14, pp.203–13.

Quisumbing, A.R., Brown, L.R., Feldstein, H.S., Haddad, L. and C. Pena, 1995, *Women: The Key to Food Security*, Food Policy Report, Washington, DC: International Food Policy Research Institute.

Rakodi, C., 1995, 'The Household Strategies of the Urban Poor: Coping with Poverty and Recession in Gweru, Zimbabwe', *Habitat International*, Vol.19, No.4, pp.447–71.

Ranis, G., 1990, 'Rural Linkages and Choice of Technology', in F. Stewart, H. Thomas and T. de Wilde, *The Other Policy: The Influence of Policies on Technology Choice and Small Enterprise Development*, Washington, DC: IT Publications.

Ranis, G. and F. Stewart, 1987, 'Rural Linkages in the Philippines and Taiwan', Ch.5 in F. Stewart (ed.), *Macro-Policies for Appropriate Technology in Developing Countries*, Boulder, CO: Westview Press.

Ravallion, M., 1992, 'Poverty Comparisons: A Guide to Concepts and Methods', *Living Standards Measurement Study, Working Paper*, No.88, Washington, DC: World Bank.

Reardon, T., 1997, 'Using Evidence of Household Income Diversification to Inform Study of the Rural Non-farm Labor Market in Africa', *World Development*, Vol.25, No. 5, pp.735–47.

Reardon, T. and P. Matlon, 1989, 'Seasonal Food Insecurity and Vulnerability in Drought-Affected Regions of Burkina Faso', Ch.8 in Sahn [*1989: 118–36*].

Reardon, T., Delgado, C. and P. Matlon, 1992, 'Determinants and Effects of Income Diversification Amongst Farm Households in Burkina Faso', *The Journal of Development Studies*, Vol.28, No.2.

Rempel, H. and R.A. Lobdell, 1978, 'The Role of Urban-to-Rural Remittances in Rural Development', *The Journal of Development Studies*, Vol.14, No.3, pp.324–41.

Richardson, H.W., 1979, 'Rural Growth Centres and National Development: A Defence', *Review of Regional Studies*, Vol.123.

Rogaly, B., 1997, 'Embedded Markets: Hired Labour Arrangements in West Bengal Agriculture', *Oxford Development Studies*, Vol.25, No.2, pp.209–23.

Roumasset, J.A., Boussard, J.M. and I. Singh (eds.), 1979, *Risk, Uncertainty and Agricultural Development*, New York: Agricultural Development Council.

Sadangi, B.N. and R.P. Singh, 1993, 'Understanding Profiles of the Self-Employed Rural Youth for Promoting Occupational Diversification', *Journal of Rural Development*, Vol.12, No.1, pp.57–75.

Sahn, D.E. (ed.), 1989, *Seasonal Variability in Third World Agriculture: The Consequences for Food Security*, Baltimore, MD: John Hopkins Press.

Sahn, D.E., and A. Sarris, 1991, 'Structural Adjustment and the Welfare of Rural Smallholders: A Comparative Analysis from Sub-Saharan Africa', *World Bank Economic Review*, Vol.5, No.2, pp.259–89.

Sahn, D.E., 1994, 'The Impact of Macroeconomic Adjustment on Incomes, Health and Nutrition: Sub-Saharan Africa in the 1980s', Ch.13 in G.A. Cornia and G.K. Helleiner (eds.), *From Adjustment to Development in Africa: Conflict, Controversy, Convergence, Consensus?*, London: Macmillan.

Saith, A., 1992, *The Rural Non-Farm Economy: Processes and Policies*, Geneva: International Labour Office, World Employment Programme.

Sarris, A.H. and R. van den Brink, 1993, *Economic Policy and Household Welfare during Crisis and Adjustment in Tanzania*, New York: New York University Press.

Savadogo, K., Reardon, T. and K. Pietola, 1994, 'Farm Productivity in Burkino Faso: Effects of Animal Traction and Non-farm Income', *American Journal of Agricultural Economics*, Vol.76, Aug., pp.608–12.

Singh, I., Squire, L. and J. Strauss (eds.), 1986, *Agricultural Household Models*, Baltimore, MD: Johns Hopkins.

Smith, A., 1970, *The Wealth of Nations* (1776), Harmondsworth: Penguin.

Stark, O., 1980, 'On the Role of Urban-to-Rural Remittances in Rural Development', *The Journal of Development Studies*, Vol.16, pp.369–74.

Stark, O., 1982, 'Research on Rural-to-Urban Migration in Less Developed Countries: The Confusion Frontier and Why We Should Pause to Rethink Afresh', *World Development*, Vol.10, pp.63–70.

Stark, O., 1991, *The Migration of Labor*, Cambridge, MA: Basil Blackwell.

Stark, O. and D. Levhari, 1982, 'On Migration and Risk in Less Developed Countries', *Economic Development and Cultural Change*, Vol.31.

Stark, O. and D.E. Bloom, 1985, 'The New Economics of Labour Migration', *American Economic Review*, Vol.77, pp.173–5.

Stark, O. and R.E.B. Lucas, 1988, 'Migration, Remittances, and the Family', *Economic Development and Cultural Change*, Vol.36, pp.465–81.

Stichter, S., 1982, *Migrant Labour and Capitalism in Kenya*, London: Longman.

Taylor, E. and T.J. Wyatt, 1996, 'The Shadow Value of Migrant Remittances, Income and Inequality in a Household-Farm Economy', *The Journal of Development Studies*, Vol.32, No.6, pp.899–912.

Tiffen, M. and M. Mortimore, 1992, 'Environment, Population Growth and Productivity in Kenya: A Case Study of Machakos District', *Development Policy Review*, Vol.10, pp.359–87.

Tiffen, M., Mortimore, M. and F. Gichuki, 1994, *More People, Less Erosion: Environmental Recovery in Kenya*, Chichester: John Wiley.

Todaro, M.P., 1969, 'A Model of Labor Migration and Urban Unemployment in Less Developed Countries', *American Economic Review*, Vol.59, No.1, pp.138–48.

Todaro, M.P., 1997, *Economic Development*, 6th Edition, London: Longman.

Tomich, T.P., Kilby, P. and B.F. Johnston, 1995, *Transforming Agrarian Economies: Opportunities Seized, Opportunities Missed*, Ithaca, NY: Cornell University Press.

Tschirley, D.L. and M.T. Weber, 1994, 'Food Security Strategies Under Extremely Adverse Conditions: The Determinants of Household Income and Consumption in Rural Mozambique', *World Development*, Vol.22, No.2, pp.159–73.

Unni, J., 1996, 'Diversification of Economic Activities and Non-Agricultural Employment in Rural Gujarat', *Economic and Political Weekly*, Vol.31, No.33, pp.2243–51.

Valentine, T.R., 1993, 'Drought, Transfer Entitlements, and Income Distribution: The Botswana Experience', *World Development*, Vol.21, No.1, pp.109–26.

von Braun, J. and R. Pandya-Lorch (eds.), 1991, *Income Sources of Malnourished People in Rural Areas: Microlevel Information and Policy Implications*, Working Papers on Commercialization of Agriculture and Nutrition No.5, Washington, DC: International Food Policy Research Institute.

Walker, T.S. and N.S. Jodha, 1986, 'How Small Farm Households Adapt to Risk', in P. Hazell, C. Pomareda and A. Valdes (eds.), *Crop Insurance for Agricultural Development*, Baltimore, MD: Johns Hopkins, pp.17–34.

Walker, T.S. and J.G. Ryan, 1990, *Village and Household Economies in India's Semi-Arid Tropics*, Baltimore, MD: Johns Hopkins.

Webb, P., von Braun, J. and Y. Yohannes, 1992, *Famine in Ethiopia: Policy Implications of Coping Failure at National and Household Levels*, Research Report No.92, Washington, DC: International Food Policy Research Institute.

Wolf, D.L., 1990, 'Daughters, Decisions and Domination: An Empirical and Conceptual Critique of Household Strategies', *Development and Change*, Vol.21, No.1.

World Bank, 1990, *World Development Report 1990: Poverty*, New York: Oxford University Press for World Bank.

World Bank, 1995, *Kenya Poverty Assessment*, Report No.13152-KE, Washington, DC: World Bank.

World Bank, 1996, *Tanzania The Challenge of Reforms: Growth, Incomes and Welfare Vols.I–III*, Report No.14982-TA, Washington, DC, World Bank.

Zoomers, A.E.B. and J. Kleinpenning, 1996, 'Livelihood and Urban–Rural Relations in Central Paraguay', *Tijdschrift Voor Economische en Sociale Geografie*, Vol.87, No.2, pp.161–74.

Part II
Concepts and Approaches

A
Property Rights

[7]

Private property rights and presumptive policy entitlements: reconsidering the premises of rural policy

DANIEL W. BROMLEY* and IAN HODGE*

University of Wisconsin–Madison; University of Cambridge

Summary

Private property in land gives agricultural producers a presumptive claim to certain policies that may be more costly than necessary, and may not achieve their intended results. In this paper an alternative specification of property rights in land is explored, and it is shown how this different structure opens up new options for governments to influence the visual and economic attributes of rural areas. Under existing property regimes farmers must be induced with financial concessions to use land in socially desired ways. Under an alternative property rights specification farmers would have to pay for the right to modify certain land-use practices.

1. The problem setting

Since the decline of feudalism in Europe land ownership has been character-ised by a wide range of property rights residing with the individual. This ownership structure was carried to the new world and its productive success in agriculture needs no elaboration here. The conceptual support for this atomisation of control of land and its related natural resources dates at least from Adam Smith. Implicit in the Smithian celebration of possessive individualism — both in consumption and in production — is the presump-tion that all valuable commodities carry socially appropriate prices to permit

* We are grateful to John Braden, George Peters, Glen Pulver, Harald von Witzke, and Martin Whitby for helpful comments on an earlier version of the paper. Two anonymous reviewers offered helpful comments. Finally, special thanks go to the Editor, Arie Oskam, for his suggestions to improve the manuscript.

Euro. R. agri. Eco. 17 (1990) 197–214

198   *Daniel W. Bromley and Ian Hodge*

socially optimal outcomes from millions of independent choices. Pigou
(1912, 1920) was the first systematically to challenge this optimism regarding
the wisdom of autonomous choice. His work gave theoretical content to the
obvious human and environmental costs of Britain's industrial revolution.
The externality theory derived from his work has always been somewhat of a
problem.

On the one hand externalities were seen as interesting theoretical embel-
lishments to the standard theory of the firm, suggesting corrective measures
that would restore 'efficiency'. On the other hand these corrective measures
implied an all knowing *deus ex machina* in the form of an omniscient
government whose actions contradicted Smith's vision. The irony is important for economic policy; the alleged 'efficiency' of atomistic choice required
the intervention of that opponent of atomism — the state. Coase (1960) has
argued that under certain (unreasonable) assumptions[1] it would not matter
for efficiency which party to externalities had the original property right.
That is, the government need do no more than be sure that *someone* had
clear property rights, and then simply step aside so that atomistic choices
might proceed. While seeming to salvage *laissez faire*, adherence to the
Coase's position simply upheld the dominance of the status quo in economic
policy. That is, since it appears not to make any difference on efficiency
grounds which party has the property right, there can be little benefit to
altering those rights. But of course in the real world it matters very much
who has property rights, since a property right gives the legal ability to
ignore the wishes of those without such rights.[2] Much of public policy —
including agricultural and environmental policy — therefore reduces to
political struggles over which parties can enlist the state in their behalf
(Bromley, 1989a; Schmid, 1987).

With respect to agricultural and rural policy, the property rights in
question pertain to land and related natural resources. In the industrialised
world these rights — either *de jure* or presumed on the part of the owner —
are subject to challenge by those whose interests are in some way adversely
affected by a particularly offensive land-use. Those who seek a change in
practices that *seem to be protected* by some sort of 'right' will suggest that the
political struggle is biased in favour of those who own land. Historically,
property rights in land and the associated agricultural production have been
strongly upheld in order to meet the economic pressures for greater
quantities of food and fibre. North (1984) argues that sedentary agriculture
necessitated a set of exclusive property rights over land, animals and plants.[3]
More generally, private property in land is said to constitute the foundation
of democracy, individual freedom, and a bounteous market. These traditional property rights remain largely intact — and rarely challenged —
today, even though economic conditions and relative scarcities are quite
different from those prevailing when modern agriculture first began to
develop.[4] Specifically, income elasticities of demand in the industrialised

countries for rural amenities such as improved environmental quality (including pleasing landscapes), and viable rural communities are higher than they are for increased food and fibre production. In spite of these changed circumstances, existing property rights in land remain the product of an earlier time when the greatest priority was given to the production of food and fibre.

More significantly for our purposes, contemporary agricultural policy in the industrialised world is predicated upon this property rights structure. Today, when agricultural practices give rise to the undesirable side effects we call technological externalities, the state is faced with a difficult task. When the agricultural sector (including producers as well as the agricultural business sector which sells chemicals and equipment to producers) resists efforts to alter the prevailing property rights position then a struggle occurs between the presumed 'right' of a landowner to do as he/she wishes, and the 'right' of other members of society to be free from the unwanted effects of agricultural land use.[5] The state will be under pressure to reflect the interests of those adversely affected by the externalities.[6] But, given the apparent sanctity of property rights in land, any negotiations with the agricultural sector will start from a position of political weakness.

When those concerned about the environmental externalities of agriculture are successful in bringing about a change in agricultural practices, negotiations typically result in two possible — but not mutually exclusive — outcomes. Either there will be some form of 'regulation' in which specific quantitative goals will be set, or there will be financial inducements from the government to obtain compliance from the agricultural community. Extensive political negotiations will accompany the selection of either policy instrument.

The existing structure of property rights in land implies that the owner (or operator) can — within limits — grow any product in the amounts desired.[7] The fact that farmers produce an abundance of some products in the face of inelastic demand means that agricultural incomes become a political issue as well. Invariably, and with various rationalisations, the public purse is then made available to maintain prices and/or to protect incomes. Notice how the presumed *property rights in land* become translated, through the political process, into *presumptive entitlements in the policy arena*. The modern industrial state has been willing to support incomes for farmers who, for a variety of reasons, have succeeded in resisting virtually all conditions on their producing behaviour — whether that behaviour results in redundant commodities, in chemical contamination of food and rural water supplies, in accelerated soil erosion, or in rural landscapes cleared to make way for larger machinery. Any change in the status quo production domain of the farmer must inevitably be purchased by the state with bribes, subsidies, or concessions at other places in the policy arena.[8] In short, farmers in the industrialised nations deal with their governments from a position of strength — such strength arising from unquestioned property 'rights' in land, with those property rights then successfully transmitted through the political process into a presumptive entitlement for favoured treatment at the hands of policy makers.[9]

We find an example in the financial guidelines for paying compensation to farmers for land-use management agreements in the United Kingdom under the Wildlife and Countryside Act of 1981; such agreements attempting to bring about more favourable treatment of the British landscape. In calculating the payment, an amount is included for the value of any capital grants which the management agreement prevents the farmer from taking up. This clearly implies that farmers have a 'right' to these grants for which they must be compensated if they agree to forego a claim against that right. A *presumptive entitlement* has been politically created that *compensates farmers for grants that they will no longer be able to acquire by dint of agreeing to treat land in a socially desired manner.* Similar examples could be found in other settings.

Let us recount the argument thus far. The conventional approach in both theory and practice regards land as an input into agricultural production. That land is held by the farmer under some considerable latitude and authority. The use of that land, and the results of that use, are thought to be of scant concern to the state. Only when externalities seem persistent, and of potential serious harm, is a collective role taken by governments. Economists talk of *market failure* and mention several policy instruments such as regulation, or fees/charges. In fact, the few policy initiatives to gain acceptance have been accompanied by bribes and other policy concessions; such inducements being necessary to modify the behaviour of a reluctant agricultural sector. The over-production problem is dealt with by complex programmes to support incomes when unwanted commodities accumulate in government storage.

On this evidence we conclude that farmers (and land owners more particularly) in the industrialised nations have been successful in two distinct forms of capitalisation. First they have been able to capitalise the value of agricultural programmes into their land values. More importantly for our purposes, they have managed to 'capitalise' their property rights in land into large, and sometimes embarrassing, agricultural programmes. Policy options to address these matters seem to have reached a dead end for the simple reason that the property rights upon which this elaborate structure rests have never been questioned. That is, economists and policy makers continue to search for ways to induce farmers to grow less of certain redundant commodities, and to employ land uses that are not socially detrimental — if not actually socially beneficial.

We turn now to an alternative model of agricultural property rights and land use that will be seen to suggest novel policy instruments for dealing with the over-production trap of most agricultural policy. This new perspective will also address the increasing problems associated with a larger collective interest in the quality of the rural environment.

2. An alternative property rights regime

We start with a model that sees land *not* as an input into agriculture for the production of food and fibre, but instead regards agriculture as an economic activity that produces a rural milieu and a rural economy of a particular character. This rural milieu would include not only visual attributes, but other environmental quality considerations such as drinking water purity, and wildlife habitat. Moreover, we have in mind economic attributes that relate to the continued viability of small rural communities. We will call these *countryside and community attributes* (CCA). Such attributes are taken to include the positive contributions that certain forms of agriculture can make both to rural communities and to the nature of rural environments. Thus, rather than modelling the use of land by farmers to produce food and fibre, we posit a model in which there is a *prior* relationship of economic interest — that relationship being one in which 'society' uses farmers to produce a particular vector of countryside and community attributes, and also to produce food and fibre of a certain quality. This model differs from the standard approach that regards land, labour, capital, and management as the inputs of agriculture, with CCA as an incidental 'side-effect'.

Consider the following. For the full sweep of human history food and fibre have been the abiding scarce commodities, with the bulk of human energy devoted to their production. Conversely, countryside and community attributes were certainly not scarce nor much valued; urban people had not yet come to appreciate the landscape qualities of rural areas, agricultural practices were devoid of modern chemicals and so did not threaten public health, and the economic vitality of rural areas had not become an object of public concern. However, it cannot, in honesty, be said that food and fibre are currently scarce in the industrialised nations under consideration here. Indeed, we note that many agricultural problems in the industrialised world are concerned with an embarrassing abundance of food and fibre. But it is increasingly obvious in the industrialised nations that certain desired countryside and community attributes are indeed scarce. Soil erosion, agricultural chemicals in food and rural drinking water, the widespread destruction of landscape to allow the use of ever-larger implements and to gain more land for cropping, and the social concern over the changing character of small rural towns and villages suggest that there is an abiding collective interest in the quality of rural areas that, at the margin, transcends the collective interest in the volume of food and fibre produced.

Some may suggest that countryside and community attributes are difficult to quantify. Moreover, it will be said that they defy monetary assignments

202   *Daniel W. Bromley and Ian Hodge*

which will facilitate comparison with market-valued goods and services and that, therefore, they are of limited significance. But of course this is not true. Most would agree that some rural landscapes are very attractive while others are of little social moment. Moreover, well-recognised techniques exist to estimate monetary values of different types of rural amenities (Anderson and Bishop, 1986; Nash and Bowers, 1988). Perceptions of the value of rural amenities will change over time, but then the relative value of food and fibre changes over time in response to changing tastes and preferences. Beef, once a highly valued product of rural areas has fallen in consumer esteem as a result of concern for cholesterol. The same might be said of eggs and some dairy products. Cotton, a once-prized rural product, has lost some edge to synthetic fabrics.

The use of this alternative model simply requires that we specify a slightly different objective function, and the related specification of production processes that follow therefrom. Agriculture becomes a central input into that production process, for in the absence of agriculture rural areas would become depopulated, and the landscape would revert to overgrowth, or grass prairies, or a forested mass that would fail to satisfy the varied environmental conditions that seem to be in demand. We hypothesize that the type of rural area sought by the citizens of the industrialised countries is one containing picturesque farms, a managed landscape, some 'natural' vegetation and wildlife, and thriving small towns. These aspects would be impossible in the absence of agriculture. People residing in rural areas and contributing to its appearance and economic viability are a central part of the sought-after attributes of the countryside.

The objective of the model proposed here would be to provide an understanding of a *particular* physical and economic environment in rural areas, and the appropriate policy instruments could then be chosen accordingly. Recall that under the status quo property rights structure, a vector of countryside and community attributes arises as a by-product of agriculture. The alternative property rights structure discussed here would imply a very different approach. First, the desired level of countryside and community attributes would be determined through collective action at the local level, but with wider oversight if the domain of concern transcended the locality. This might be defined in a plan for a particular area that would specify the constraints over land use required to achieve the desired level of environmental quality. Farmers would then remain free to choose enterprises and methods of production so long as the final result does not violate the plan. Thus it is the collective interest that specifies the level of countryside and community attributes that will result from agriculture. Put somewhat differently, the property rights to determine the attributes that shall exist in the rural landscape would now reside not with the farmer, but with the collective.

However, the plan is flexible. If a particular farmer should wish to undertake a form of production that would detract from the defined level of countryside and community attributes, then it is the farmer who must be willing to pay into the public purse for the right to deviate from the plan. Notice how, with the shift in property right, the burden of proof has shifted from the general citizenry to the farmer. That is, no longer would individuals, through the state, need to bribe the farmer to adopt a set of agricultural practices that did not violate the interests of the collective. Now the farmer must bribe the state (as a representative of interested parties) to undertake a form of production at variance with the wishes of the collective. When farmers wish to deviate from the accepted plan in order to achieve a greater income, this new income potential offers the source of the payments that would flow to the state. Notice that the payments to deviate from the status quo would flow in the opposite direction from at present.

Some might question the feasibility of this alternative property right position. Indeed, while conceptually the notion is quite straightforward, it would, in practice, require a considerable administration in terms of specifying the appropriate constraints for various regions of a country, and in terms of assuring compliance. This complexity arises from the characteristic of CCA, which comprises a range of separate qualities that must be supplied in a variety of combinations, depending upon climatic, topographical, and historical factors. There is no single measure of environmental quality. In some other industries such an alternative property rights specification might simply require that producers do not cause air or water pollution. The vector of elements comprising countryside and community attributes renders the determination more difficult, but not impossible. This difference in practice, however, makes no difference to the principle of considering the alternative position suggested here.

3. A model of alternative property rights use

Consider the following model of the change in property rights in land and related natural resources. Under the status quo property rights structure we can envision a demand for increased countryside and community attributes (CCA); this is shown in Figure 1 as D. The curve shows the aggregate willingness to pay for increased levels of CCA. We can also portray a curve that depicts the willingness of farmers to supply greater levels of CCA. Under the status quo property rights structure, the collective will be able to acquire greater rural amenity only by purchasing it from a reluctant population of farmers. As indicated earlier, this is precisely what has been done over the recent past; the purchase price (P) represents a combination of payments and policy concessions. The willingness of the agricultural community to supply greater CCA has carried a price that can be depicted along the curve S. Under these assumptions, the current level of countryside and community attributes being provided is CCA in Figure 1.

204   *Daniel W. Bromley and Ian Hodge*

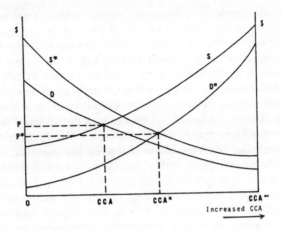

Figure 1.   *Alternative property rights and 'efficient' outcomes*

When the property rights in land are altered to one in which landowners do not have the automatic right to use land as they wish, several things change accordingly. In Figure 1 we depict point CCA ~ as some increased level of CCA specified in a region's agricultural and land-use plan. Thus, CCA ~ becomes the starting point for negotiations under the new property rights structure. S* shows the willingness of the collective to supply less — that is, to accept reductions from CCA ~, but that this provision of reduced CCA will require that farmers pay a price. Farmers' willingness to pay to be allowed to produce less CCA is shown by D*.

Why does the demand curve for greater CCA (D) differ from the supply curve for less CCA (S*)? A number of factors contribute to this divergence. Recall that the demand for greater CCA (D) is a collectively articulated demand brought to bear on the state, which is then required to pay farmers to provide more CCA. The position of D thus depends upon the collective willingness to pay for CCA. In contrast, S* depends upon the collective willingness to accept compensation for less CCA. It is now well recognised that there is a significant disparity between these two measures of value and that this difference is not just an artefact of the procedures used to value them. Individuals typically demand far greater sums in order to be induced to give up a good than they are prepared to pay to acquire it (Knetsch and Sinden, 1984). Further, the different allocation of property rights will cause a different incidence of transaction costs between the parties involved (Bromley, 1986, 1989a). With property rights in land (and, indirectly, countryside and community attributes) allocated to farmers, the initiative will need to be taken by those who prefer a different bundle of CCA. This pressure will then compel the state to bear the costs of collecting information, of initiating and negotiating contracts, and of enforcing contracts that have been struck.

Conversely, with property rights over countryside and community attributes initially allocated to the state, the initiative must be taken by the farmers to seek a reduction in the level of CCA; they will thus bear the necessary transaction costs under this alternative rights regime.

Also, the status quo property rights structure requires that the collective — taxpayers via the state — pay farmers to produce more CCA. This means that the size of the public purse is an important factor in how much CCA can be purchased. This brings us to the difference in Figure 1 between the supply curve for greater CCA (S) and the demand curve for less CCA (D*). The curve S shows the willingness of farmers to supply increased levels of CCA. It shows, in other words, what they would require in compensation to forego the higher level of food and fibre production that less CCA makes possible. Under the alternative property rights regime, where CCA ~ is the starting point, the question becomes one of the willingness of farmers to pay to have less CCA (and hence greater production of food and fibre). This willingness to pay is depicted in D*. Here too, the disparity between willingness to pay and willingness to accept compensation — as well as the incidence of transaction costs — will cause these two curves to diverge.

We see that when the alternative property rights structure introduces a new starting point (CCA ~), the negotiations will proceed along D* and S* towards a new 'socially optimal' point of CCA*. This contrasts with the previous 'optimal' point of CCA. The switch in property rights has produced a different 'optimal' level of CCA from that prevailing under the status quo property rights regime. It is important to note that neither of the two possible property rights structures — and their respective outcomes — is in any sense 'correct'. The nature of the status quo structure of property rights is largely a result of historical conditions. However, beyond the consequences for the environment, an equally pressing question concerns the incentives to produce food and fibre, and the persistent problem of rural incomes. The 'correct' outcome — and hence the 'correct' property rights structure — is a function of the de facto social welfare function which indicates, in a crude fashion, whose interests shall count (Bromley, 1989a). Under the status quo property rights regime it is rural landowners (especially farmers) whose interests have the sanction of the state. Those concerned to increase the level of CCA must either purchase it in whatever markets exist, or they must pressure politicians to pay more attention to their interests. Under the alternative property rights regime it will be the interests of those who place great significance on CCA that will have protection under the status quo. Then farmers and their allies must pay for — or encourage — the state to give greater weight to their interest. Irrespective of the initial property rights regime there will be an 'efficient' outcome. Economic efficiency will not suggest which is the 'correct' property rights structure, for the 'correct' property regime will depend upon one's assessment of whose interests ought to be protected by the state (Bromley, 1989a). It should

206   *Daniel W. Bromley and Ian Hodge*

perhaps be noted, that in practice, given government and market failures, the actual outcome may not be 'efficient' at all.

4.   Rural policy and the production of food and fibre

The above change in property rights in land would also imply a change in the implicit entitlements in the policy arena. Under the new property regime the nature and scope of agricultural production would, of necessity, be more consistent with a desired constellation of countryside and community attributes. The implicit right to pollute rural water supplies, to destroy wildlife habitat, to allow accelerated soil erosion, or to demand public monies to stop these outcomes would no longer exist. The prevailing policy instruments that give financial incentive for farmers to modify their actions would disappear. Rather, agricultural production would be governed by careful consideration of requests for certain environmental changes — land clearance, drainage, building construction, close confinement of large numbers of livestock, increased chemical use — which might threaten important countryside and community attributes. This situation would not prevent all growth in agricultural production, nor would it interfere with needed technological change — it would simply realign the relevant incentives. Some production changes have no adverse environmental impact — the use of a new seed variety or of a genetically superior animal strain.

Governments will still have an interest in protecting their citizens from drastic swings in food and fibre supplies (and prices). It will also remain important to insulate farmers from the more serious income swings that can occur in agriculture. It will, in other words, be necessary to ensure that agriculture remains an attractive economic endeavour. But these two policy objectives can be quite consistent with a collective specification of the desired physical and economic attributes in the countryside. Once that desired condition has been determined, agricultural producers are free to produce within those constraints, or to negotiate — and pay for — changes.

It must be anticipated that without product price increases, farm income levels would be lower under this alternative property rights regime. This would occur because many of the transfers to agriculture, necessary to purchase compliance with collectively determined preferences for certain land uses, would no longer exist. However, over time, the inflated value of agricultural land — now reflecting the capitalisation of these transfers — would come down; the resulting net income position of farmers is indeterminant and would vary between them depending upon their asset positions. It is hypothesized that the current incentives to 'overproduce' would be dulled by this change in property rights in land. Thus, in some instances output prices may be higher and the 'need' for price/income supports could diminish as well. We do not see any immediate prospects that the political interest in income stabilisation in agriculture will disappear. It might be found politically more acceptable to adopt income-smoothing — or even income-supporting — schemes that are not directly linked to agricultural production.

Agricultural producers would come to be regarded as land managers as much as they would be regarded as farmers. There is little reason to suppose that production shortages would result. The price mechanism would continue to suggest which commodities ought to be produced in greater quantities. If food and fibre prices become marginally higher because we are at CCA* rather than CCA in Figure 1, then this simply represents a tax on consumers of food and fibre for the production of a greater level of CCA. This differential represents an estimate of the social costs of current agricultural practices; the environmental externalities of the existing agricultural system would have been internalised. We see no reason why this tax need be any greater in total magnitude than the current financial burden placed on citizens of the industrialised nations by current agricultural policies. Indeed, we see some hope that it will be considerably less. More important for efficiency reasons, the tax will be paid as an increment on the price of food and fibre so that those whose demand stimulates the environmental changes would pay the full price. There may be concern that a country's international comparative advantage in traded commodities would be compromised in this process. With the major agricultural producers now dealing with each other on an oligopolistic basis — and with the intervention of GATT — it seems unlikely that any one country would be seriously disadvantaged. This is particularly so if the kinds of property rights changes under discussion here are phased in simultaneously in the industrialised countries.

The alternative property rights regime would also require a restructuring of the agricultural bureaucracy to implement land-use plans and to ensure compliance. It is not clear that the programmatic demands are any greater than those in place under the status quo.

5. Shifting preferences and shifting entitlements

The proposal under discussion is simply a reflection of new tastes and preferences, and new scarcities relating to the agricultural sector and its use of land and natural resources. However, when institutional changes are considered, those well served by the status quo will protest. Proposals for change will often be met with appeals to presumed 'rights' for a certain kind of health care, for a certain education, for a military pension of current magnitude, or for a comfortable retirement. However, none of these appeals can begin to rival the emotional strength and popular allure that farmers can muster with a reference to the property rights in 'their' land. Indeed, it is the emotional value of this appeal to property rights in land that has permitted

208   *Daniel W. Bromley and Ian Hodge*

the elaborate and expensive constellation of policy instruments in agriculture.

Interestingly, the existing structure of property rights in land is a rather recent historical occurrence. These individual rights arose to serve a particular purpose as Europe was embarking on a major social and economic restructuring in response to new opportunities, new scarcities, and new technological possibilities. Few would suggest that the subsequent institutional changes in land-related property rights failed to accomplish most of what was promised for them. However, neither can many deny that the associated social costs of complete atomisation of control over land have become high.

Our discussion has proceeded on the premise that there are two possible starting points for an analysis of property issues in agriculture: one with rather complete property rights allocated to the landowner as at present, and the other with rather complete property rights in land allocated to the state as an agent for others (including future generations).[10] In practice, the level of CCA will be determined by actions that are subject to a wide range of alternative property rights, some of which can be — and now are — held by the landowner, and some of which can be — and now are — held by the state. Within this range, there is widespread agreement as to where some rights should properly be lodged. For instance, landowners do not now have the right to dump persistent carcinogenic chemicals into watercourses, and they receive no compensation for being denied this opportunity. On the other hand, while the substitution of capital for labour in agriculture may have undesirable impacts on the economic and social life of rural communities, few would deny that farmers should have the right to select their own mix of capital and labour. Between these extremes, the assignment of a whole range of specific property rights will continue to be a divisive issue; examples include those that relate to: (1) allowing soil to erode; (2) draining bogs and marshes; (3) burning crop residues; and (4) applying chemical fertilisers and pesticides.

A general agreement to allocate one particular bundle of rights to the landowner and the other bundle to the state determines a particular *reference point* (Hodge, 1989). This point then defines the particular allocation of individual property rights, and hence the level of responsibility which landowners are required to adopt with regard to the wider implications of their choice of land use. There is thus a continuum of possible reference points ranging between the two extremes of allocating all rights to the landowner, or allocating all rights to the state. Following from this, there is a range of 'optimal' levels of CCA as illustrated in Figure 2.

Note that CCA, broadly similar to the same point in Figure 1, represents the 'optimal' level of CCA arising from the allocation of rights to the landowner. CCA* represents the 'optimal' level of countryside and community attributes associated with allocating property rights to the state.

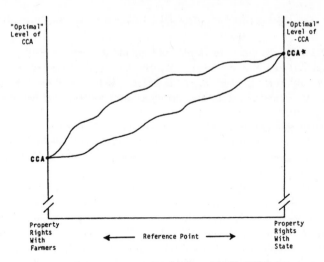

Figure 2. *Alternative property rights and 'optimal' CCA*

Between these two extremes lies the continuum of possible reference points. The figure shows a range within which the 'optimum' falls. The difference between the upper and lower bounds arises from the possibility of different mechanisms for resolving disputes — private negotiation or state regulation — and consequently a different incidence of transaction costs between landowners, those affected by the various outcomes, and taxpayers. There is a further elaboration to the argument in that the choice of reference point might vary spatially, particularly reflecting local environmental quality. Landowners in attractive environments might be expected to make greater efforts to preserve and to enhance the quality of their local area. This leads us towards policies based on some form of local designation or zoning.

How do shifts in the allocation of property rights come about? Numerous individual rights have been withdrawn in favour of the collective interest — non-smoking areas in aeroplanes and restaurants, the prohibition of potentially dangerous chemicals, and the protection of certain wild plants and animals. The determinants of such institutional changes are complex and efforts are still underway to explain institutional change. One way to view such institutional changes is to regard them as examples of a *reallocation of economic opportunity* to a different segment of the populace (Bromley, 1989a). Under the status quo property structure it is farmers who are well served. Under an alternative property rights structure it would be another group of citizens that are well served.

Clearly, shifting preferences among the citizenry have a major influence on changes in the allocation of property rights. As demonstrated here, these changing preferences lead to a change in the 'optimal' level of environmental

210   *Daniel W. Bromley and Ian Hodge*

quality, but they do not identify the means by which this environmental quality should be achieved. Also, technology is an important determinant. As indicated earlier, new technological possibilities may well trigger latent concerns that had hitherto been irrelevant; chemical pesticides are a case in point. The important issue for the economist is to understand the ways in which shifts in social values and priorities become translated into shifts in property rights.

A further element, less often considered by economists, is the question of fairness. Kahneman et al. (1986) have used survey evidence to indicate the influence of community standards on perceptions of fairness concerning activities in the market place. They argue that participants in transactions have an implicit entitlement to the terms of the *reference transaction*, and that firms are entitled to their *reference profit*. The reference transaction represents the widely accepted conditions under which exchanges have taken place, while the reference profit is the firm's profit associated with these conditions. Kahneman et al. emphasize that the reference transaction forms a basis of fairness because it is *normal*, not necessarily because it is *just*. If this notion of 'reference points' is taken with respect to the change in property rights and the associated introduction of controls which limit the actions of farmers, it implies that compensation would be paid in order for the controls to be seen as fair.[11] But changes will often occur in the allocation of property rights in which compensation is not paid. This can occur in either of two possible contexts.

First, and most simply, regulation might constrain activities which are not regarded as 'normal'. A new chemical process might be banned without compensation because its use is not yet part of the standard modus operandi. Second, shifts of presumed property rights for activities regarded as 'normal' may occur only after a long period of struggle between interested parties. A variety of traditional resource uses in the United States are currently the focus of such struggles (Batie, 1984). A first stage in this process is the definition of rights, and perhaps some form of voluntary scheme to encourage landowners to make adjustments to their farming practices (Braden, 1982). This has now been taken further in the United States with the notion of cross-compliance where the right to participate in certain commodity price support programmes is contingent upon practicing soil conservation. Similar changes are underway in Europe as well, and while they are generally marginal with regard to agricultural and environmental policy, political pressure continues in this direction.

The gradual redefinition of rights in land may be followed by a more fundamental shift of rights, perhaps accompanied by a one-time compensation payment. An example of this is found in the 1947 Town and Country Planning Act in the United Kingdom. This Act transferred the rights to develop land to the state. Development was widely defined to include building, engineering, mining or other operations in, on, over or under land,

and the making of any material change in the use of any buildings or other land. However, agriculture and forestry were excluded from the definition of development, so that these changes did not have a great impact on the form of agricultural production. The 1947 Act followed a period during which incremental changes had been made in the rights of urban land users. It is perhaps notable, though, that this major legislative change occurred soon after the Second World War, and hence at a time when many aspects of daily life were undergoing fundamental reassessment.[12] Similarly, many of the major successful land reforms in other countries have also been enacted after periods of major upheaval. Such a period often acts both to allow the development of pressures for change, and to weaken the resistance of those groups whose presumed 'rights' are thereby threatened.

This process of shifting entitlements is consistent with the view of fairness. Constraints are initially introduced over actions where, because of shifting values, social costs are regarded as exceeding private benefits. Where those actions are regarded as 'normal' compensation will be paid. Once the constraints become regarded as normal — and especially where the level of environmental quality is still regarded as sub-optimal — the rationale for compensation becomes weaker and may no longer be accepted.

This type of change can also be applied to the question of policy entitlements. Initial constraints over a farmer's freedom to choose a desired level of production might be accompanied by some form of compensation. But, if the constrained position comes to be regarded as normal, then the bargaining position of the farm lobby becomes weakened and the state will increasingly expect a greater return for agricultural support, possibly in the form of an enhanced physical environment. Alternatively, this might involve some shift in the balance of the agricultural support debate whereby the farm lobby might be willing to make some concessions, perhaps accepting the introduction of production quotas, in return for an assurance that an existing level of support will continue into the future. This represents some degree of attenuation of the underlying property rights position.

6. Conclusions

Landowners have enjoyed a wide range of actual and presumptive property rights which have undergirded both environmental and agricultural policy. This arrangement automatically places the burden of proof — and of possible compensation — on the state when there is a need to: (1) improve the environmental implications of agriculture; (2) constrain agricultural output in the face of expensive surpluses; or (3) modulate swings in agricultural incomes. The location of this burden of proof has been largely ignored in traditional analyses of agricultural policy. Beyond this, the allocation of property rights in land and related natural resources has determined the level of environmen-

212   *Daniel W. Bromley and Ian Hodge*

tal quality which is regarded as 'optimal'. The presumption of an absolute right to produce food and fibre creates an open-ended agricultural policy in which the state — and its treasury — has become a captive of the sanctity of private rights in land, the political power of farmers, and the technological prowess of modern agriculture. If farmers are on a 'technological treadmill', the industrialised state is surely on a 'fiscal treadmill'.

The generally secure position which landowners enjoy, however, has no immutable legitimacy — though its political legitimacy is another matter. Institutional arrangements are social creations, fashioned to serve collective objectives. The status quo property rights arrangements which serve agriculture so well exist for historical reasons and may not necessarily be appropriate for the future. It is possible to sketch out an alternative property rights position for agriculture in the western world and we have begun to do this. Such a preliminary sketch illuminates several important issues concerning the premises of rural policy in the industrialised nations of the world. It is important to recognise that the current assignment of entitlements in land — and by extension, in the policy arena — are simply artefacts of previous scarcities and priorities, and of the location of influence in the political process. To assume that these entitlements are necessarily pertinent and socially advantageous to the future is unwarranted. Shifting values and changing perceptions of the role of agriculture will surely bring about at least marginal shifts in property rights and policy entitlements. The analysis undertaken here seeks to inform that discussion.

NOTES

1. His assumptions require that transaction costs between (among) affected parties be zero, and that there be no income (wealth) effects as a result of changes in property rights. Notice that with his assumptions externalities cannot exist. Hence while Coase did have an interesting insight regarding property rights, it is an observation with absolutely no policy relevance whatsoever. While Coase seems to have understood the serious limitation of his assumption, those pleased by the *laissez faire* implications have been less circumspect; the Coase 'Theorem' has taken its place in economic folklore. For a discussion of the Coase Theorem see Randall (1974), or Bromley (1986).
2. For elaboration of these points see Bromley (1978, 1989a) and Randall (1972, 1974).
3. He has even argued that 'civilisation' and agriculture as we know it required the development of private property (North and Thomas, 1977). This logic — and reading of history — has been questioned elsewhere (Runge and Bromley, 1979).
4. For a discussion of the changing instrumental value of private property rights in urban areas see Sax (1983).
5. We use the term 'landowner' throughout even though in many instances the direct land user — the farm operator — may not be the owner. We assume that few tenants use land and related natural resources in a manner that differs significantly from the wishes of the land's owner and so little is lost in the convention followed here.
6. For simplicity we will speak primarily of those currently affected by externalities, although the state must also represent the concerns of future generations as well.
7. The production of cannabis (marijuana) and other contraband is a notable exception. And,

some countries do indeed tie supply control into the receipt of income support; dairy products in Canada being one example. Dairy quotas represent an exception to this within the European Community. Some alternative controls limit certain inputs (especially land) without directly limiting the volume of production, such as potatoes in the UK.

8. We use the term 'bribe' to convey the idea that some extraordinary inducement is called for in order to change behaviour; we do not thereby imply illegality. The concepts of 'bribes' and 'charges' has a long history in environmental economics.

9. When commentators speculate on this phenomenon it is usually said that farmers have political power out of all proportion to their numbers; the blame (or credit, depending) will usually be laid at the feet of 'effective lobbying' or 'financial clout'. These reasons are, unfortunately, circular and beg the ultimate question. Our thesis is that this dis-proportionate influence stems from the social sanctity of private land, the differentiation of food from other commodities in the mind of the public, and a small dose of rural romanticism.

10. See Bromley (1989b).

11. Proposals exist in Great Britain for the control of nitrate contamination of water supplies. Participation in the scheme will be voluntary and farmers will be paid compensation for reductions in nitrogen applications from a reference point defined as 'good agricultural practices'. The precise definition of such 'good practices' is open for negotiation, but it will certainly be some level of nitrogen applications approaching those now in effect. At present 'good agricultural practices' do not imply a very low level of nitrogen applications such that the chances for contamination of water supplies are non-existent. That is, the reference point will almost certainly *not* be one of 'no pollution' (or 'optimal pollution') since there would then be no basis to bribe farmers not to pollute drinking water, and a policy change would be difficult in the face of certain agricultural opposition.

12. We acknowledge the observation of George Peters that subsequent governments have modified the original provisions and so the situation is clearly one of 'shifting entitlements' as successive governments balance conflicting interests and claims regarding who exactly possesses property rights in land and its incremental value.

REFERENCES

Anderson, Glen D. and Bishop, Richard C. (1986). The Valuation Problem. In Daniel W. Bromley (ed.) *Natural Resource Economics: Policy Problems and Contemporary Analysis.* Boston: Kluwer. 89–137.

Batie, Sandra. (1984). Alternative Views of Property Rights: Implication for Agricultural Use of Natural Resources. *American Journal of Agricultural Economics* 66: 814–818.

Braden, John B. (1982). Some Emerging Rights in Agricultural Land. *American Journal of Agricultural Economics* 64: 19–27.

Bromley, Daniel W. (1978). Property Rules, Liability Rules, and Environmental Economics. *Journal of Economic Issues* 12: 43–60.

— (1986). Markets and Externalities. In Daniel W. Bromley (ed.) *Natural Resource Economics: Policy Problems and Contemporary Analysis.* Boston: Kluwer. Chapter 2.

— (1989a). *Economic Interests and Institutions: The Conceptual Foundations of Public Policy* Oxford: Basil Blackwell.

— (1989b). Entitlements, Missing Markets, and Environmental Uncertainty. *Journal of Environmental Economics and Management* 17: 181–194.

Coase, Ronald (1960). The Problem of Social Cost. *Journal of Law and Economics* 3: 1–44.

Hodge, Ian D. (1989). Compensation for Nature Conservation. *Environment Planning A* 21(7).

Kahneman, Daniel, Knetsch, J.L., and Thaler, R. (1986). Fairness as a Constraint on Profit Seeking: Entitlements in the Market. *American Economic Review* 76: 728–741.

Knetsch, J.L. and Sinden, J.A. (1984). Willingness to Pay and Compensation Demanded:

214   *Daniel W. Bromley and Ian Hodge*

Experimental Evidence of an Unexpected Disparity in Measures of Value. *Quarterly Journal of Economics* 99(3): 507–5 21.

Nash, C.A. and Bowers, J.K. (1988). Alternative Approaches to the Valuation of Environmental Resources. In R.K. Turner (ed.) *Sustainable Environmental Management: Principles and Practice* London: Bellhaven Press. 118–142.

North, Douglass C. (1984). Transaction Costs, Institutions, and Economic History. *Zeitschrift fur die gesamte Staatswissenschaft* 140: 7–17.

— and Thomas, Robert Paul (1977). The First Economic Revolution. *The Economic History Review* 30: 229–241.

Pigou, A.C. (1912). *Wealth and Welfare* London: Macmillan.

— (1920). *The Economics of Welfare* London: Macmillan.

Randall, Alan (1972). Market Solutions to Externality Problems: Theory and Practice. *American Journal of Agricultural Economics* 54: 175–183.

— (1974). Coasian Externality Theory in a Policy Context. *Natural Resources Journal* 14: 35–54.

Runge, Carlisle F. and Bromley, Daniel W. (1979). *Property Rights and the First Economic Revolution: The Origins of Agriculture Reconsidered* Madison: University of Wisconsin, Center for Resource Policy Studies, Working Paper No. 13, January.

Sax, Joseph (1983). Some Thoughts on the Decline of Private Property. *Washington Law Review* 58: 481–496.

Schmid, A. Allan (1987). *Property, Power, and Public Choice* New York: Praeger. Second edition.

Daniel W. Bromley
Department of Agricultural Economics
University of Wisconsin-Madison
Taylor Hall
Madison, Wisconsin 53706
U.S.A.

[8]

Pergamon

PII: S0264-8377(98)00014-3

Land Use Policy, Vol. 15, No. 3, pp. 203–215, 1998
Published by Elsevier Science Ltd
Printed in Great Britain
0264-8377/98 $19.00 + 0.00

Property rights as policy tools for sustainable development

Keith D. Wiebe and Ruth Meinzen-Dick

Introduction

The emergence of land markets in developing countries sometimes concentrates property rights in individual 'owners,' restricting the rights held by other claimants under customary tenure systems. By neglecting livelihood and environmental externalities, this may undermine the objectives of sustainable development. This paper draws lessons from the United States' experience using property rights as policy tools to accommodate multiple interests in resource use and conservation without incurring the political costs of regulation or the full financial costs of land acquisition. The benefits of such tools must be weighed against potentially significant costs, including those of monitoring and enforcing complex property arrangements over time. Published by Elsevier Science Ltd

Key words: Property rights, sustainable livelihoods, environmental policy

Recent years have seen growing interest in the identification and encouragement of economic development strategies that are environmentally and socially sustainable (Serageldin, 1996; Vosti and Reardon, 1997). Along with this interest has grown the recognition that sustainable development, and the efficient and equitable use of resources on which it is based, depends critically on the ways in which property rights are defined and distributed (World Bank, 1997). Yet policies to influence the definition and distribution of property rights have produced decidedly mixed results. In particular, trends toward privatization and land market creation have been associated in many developing countries with a reduction in the number of stakeholders who can lay claim to the use of a given piece of land, with potentially harmful economic and environmental consequences.

There is a temptation to blame such consequences on the emergence of land markets *per se*, when in fact markets only perform as well as the institutional context in which they function. In the case of sustainable development, market performance depends critically on the ways in which traditional rights of multiple stakeholders are accommodated as rights to property become more formally defined. This paper seeks to inform the discussion of property rights as policy tools for resource use and conservation with an examination of lessons from the United States' recent experience with 'partial interests' in land. Partial interests—the individual sticks in the complex bundle of rights that constitutes land ownership—can be identified and traded separately, providing a means of formally valuing and protecting the diverse interests of multiple stakeholders in a particular parcel of land (Wiebe *et al.*, 1996). Lessons from the United States' experience, carefully considered, are valuable in this context because of the scarcity of well-documented examples of statutory tenure arrangements involving market transactions that accommodate multiple uses and users in developing countries (Meinzen-Dick *et al.*, 1997), and because such lessons have not yet been brought to the attention of the wider audience interested in sustainable development.

Keith D Wiebe is with the USDA Economic Service, Room 4202, 1800 M Street, NW, Washington, DC 20036-5831, U.S.A. Tel.: 202-694-5529; Fax: 202-694-5774. Ruth Meinzen-Dick is with the International Food Policy Research Institute (IFPRI), 2033 K Street, NW, Washington, DC 20006, U.S.A. Tel.: 202-862-5600; Fax: 202-467-4439.

In practice, in the process of formalizing tenure arrangements, the bundle of rights that constitute land ownership are often consolidated—whether deliberately or unintentionally—in the hands of a single 'owner', and many of the subtleties which historically allowed other right-holders to access, use, or influence the disposition of land are lost. This process is observed in both explicit privatization policies (such as land titling programmes) and in the undirected evolution of land markets and property rights (for example, under conditions of rising population pressure or market integration). Indeed, the process is sometimes viewed as a necessary and inevitable condition for the development of efficient markets.

The problem with simple (or simplistic) concepts of land 'ownership' is that the nominal landowner is not generally the only person affecting or affected by the use of the land. Two types of side effects, or externalities, are especially important. First, other individuals or households may depend on the resource for their *livelihoods*, and may be threatened economically by exclusion from historic patterns of access to resources. For example, pastoralists may depend on the stubble from cultivated fields as a seasonal source of food for their herds, and may have difficulty feeding their animals if denied traditional access to such fields (Williams, 1997). The livelihoods of fisherwomen in coastal areas may be threatened if they are prevented from using traditional beach areas to dry their fish (Kendrick, 1996). The livelihood effects of such exclusion are exemplified as far back as the Enclosure Movement in England, when fields and forests were enclosed and traditional access by local communities was restricted, causing enormous upheaval as many customary claimants were dispossessed (Baland and Platteau, 1996).

The second type of externality is seen when land use imposes *environmental* burdens on neighbours or society at large. Tenure systems that disregard the interests of these other parties give the landowner no incentive to consider the off-site consequences of his or her use of the land. Examples include air pollution downwind or changes in the quantity or quality of surface water, declining fish stocks, or reservoir siltation downstream. These latter types of externalities have received increasing attention in recent years, in both developed and developing countries. The result has often been the imposition of government regulations restricting certain land uses in order to reduce environmental degradation. In fact, sustainable development requires attention to both the environmental and the livelihood aspects of tenure systems because growth, poverty alleviation, and environmental sustainability are intricately interlinked (Vosti and Reardon, 1997).

A closer look at the experience of the United States is revealing because it shows that this stylized process of simplifying tenure arrangements to individual ownership, and then influencing behaviour by imposing regulations, is not necessarily optimal or even necessary. Instead of simplifying and streamlining the rights of various individuals, interest groups, or society at large, it is possible to use more refined and flexible approaches. This requires us to focus on partial interests in land—the individual sticks in the bundle of rights that constitutes land ownership, such as the rights to draw water, graze livestock, produce crops, or build houses. Such rights may, in general, be held and exchanged separately, providing a mechanism for recognizing a range of claimants on a resource even within a system of formalized tenure. By allowing voluntary acquisition and conveyance of specific rights for specific uses, partial interests offer a more refined alternative to establishing or trading full ownership rights as a package.

Property Rights as Policy Tools: K D Wiebe and R Meinzen-Dick

While they may be equally complex, partial interests in the United States differ from those in many developing countries in various ways, principal among them being that in the United States they are typically more formally codified. This has the important result that in the United States such interests can potentially be traded more easily across a wider pool of market participants than would otherwise be possible. This result becomes important because the acquisition and conveyance of partial interests allows public agencies and private non-profit conservation groups to influence the use of public and private land without incurring the political costs of land regulation or the full financial costs of outright land acquisition.

Section 2 of this paper presents a discussion of property rights and natural resource management, with particular attention to partial interests in land. Section 3 provides an overview of the evolution of land tenure and natural resource policy in the United States, with special reference to policies that rely on partial interests in land to limit environmental externalities such as the loss of farmland to urban uses, the loss of topsoil and wildlife habitat on environmentally sensitive lands, and the loss of wetlands to agricultural use. Section 4 examines the applicability of these concepts in developing countries, where externalities include the potential loss of livelihoods as well as environmental effects. This section also deals with the institutional requirements and costs associated with such an approach to natural resource management, and addresses some of the hurdles that would be faced in extending such an approach in developing countries. Conclusions are summarized in Section 5.

Property rights and resource management

The nature and distribution of property rights are critical in determining how resources are used and conserved. By property rights we mean the formal and informal institutions and arrangements that govern access to land and other resources, as well as the resulting claims that individuals hold on those resources and on the benefits they generate (Bromley, 1997; McElfish, 1994). Property rights determine *who* can do *what* with a particular resource, such as a parcel of land, and sometimes also *when* and *how* they can do it.

Property rights arise from law, custom, and the operation of markets. Public agencies play a central role in shaping property rights. First, public agencies help establish the initial distribution of rights in (or access to) resources within a community or society. Second, they influence the ways in which these rights can be traded between members of society. And third, public agencies may themselves participate in markets for rights in land and other resources.

Because of their role in shaping how income and wealth are generated and distributed, it is not surprising that property rights are the subject of controversy and debate in any but the most static of situations. The United States is no exception, but the United States' experience in this regard is unusual, and perhaps unique, in the extent to which the debate over property rights is depicted in terms of black and white (with respect to the extreme positions that are sometimes taken regarding the nature of property rights). Because of the unique and relatively recent historical experience of United States westward expansion and settlement—during which vast lands were essentially swept clear of their existing inhabitants and thrown open in great abundance to new occupants and owners—some landowners have come to feel that their property is truly their private domain, over which they have complete sovereignty to do as they wish. In effect, the 'what', 'when', and 'how' dimensions of tenure are overlooked in the conventional focus on 'who' and 'where', resulting in expanded claims for compensation of landowners when government agencies restrict the use of land to accomplish public (and especially environmental) purposes. (For a recent sampling of the vast literature on this so-called 'takings' issue, see Bromley, 1997; Goldstein and Watson, 1997; Segerson, 1997; and Stroup, 1997.)

The sharpness of this supposed delineation of private property in the United States stands in marked contrast to the situation in many developing countries, where complex and dynamic tenure systems may consist of multiple rights by multiple parties to a variety of actions on any single parcel of land. One person might have the right to produce crops on a particular parcel of land in a certain season, for example, but others might have the right to graze livestock there after harvest, and still others may have the right to collect fruit or firewood from trees at other times of the year. These tenure systems are further complicated by overlapping (and sometimes conflicting) statutory and customary rights, many of which are not subject to market transfer, or which may be transferable only under certain restrictive circumstances (Bruce and Migot-Adholla, 1994). Even many older industrialized countries retain complex overlaying systems of rights (e.g. public rights of way across private fields in various European countries).

In fact, upon closer examination, property rights in the United States resolve into partial interests in land that can be fully as intricate and complex as those in developing countries. Partial interests are the building blocks of land tenure systems, including rights to use land and other resources in specified ways. Partial interests in a particular resource, such as a parcel of land, can be held simultaneously by multiple parties, and may be organized in a variety of ways to accommodate a variety of objectives. As interests in particular resources may be held privately, publicly, in common, or by no specified party, so may tenure systems be characterized by a mix of state, private, common property, and open access resources. Such systems are inevitably complex, and indeed many of the most interesting problems of resource use and environmental degradation arise when such systems are incompletely specified, or when the rights to particular resources are not clearly defined.

Such situations defy simple attempts to predict the potential consequences of emerging land markets or other changes in tenure, both in terms of equity and in terms of the efficiency of agricultural production. But such attempts are essential to a better understanding of the implications of changes in land tenure, whether directed or undirected, and whether in a developed country or a developing one. Our intent here is to sharpen the resolution of the conventional black and white delineation of private property in the United States, substituting instead a more realistic picture made up of distinct shades of grey (Section 3), and to consider the policy implications of these shades of grey in the tenure systems of developing countries as well (Section 4).

The evolution of land tenure and natural resource policy in the United States

Between Independence (in 1776) and 1867, the federal government acquired ownership of about 80% of the current area of the United States.

Property Rights as Policy Tools: K D Wiebe and R Meinzen-Dick

To encourage westward expansion and settlement, most of this land was given away or sold on concessional terms to State governments, railroad companies, and homesteaders by the end of the nineteenth century. These grants were generally conditioned on the land being cleared, drained, plowed, or otherwise made suitable for productive use.

The results have been two-fold. First, about two thirds of United States land is now privately owned. And second, due in part to past federal policies, much of that land has been used in ways that cause environmental problems. For example, the conversion of wetlands and highly erodible lands for agriculture increases the runoff of soil and water into streams and rivers, reducing water quality and increasing the likelihood of flooding downstream. About half of the wetlands that existed at the time of European settlement have since been converted, most of them for agricultural production. Similarly, inappropriate cultivation of marginal lands was one cause of the 'Dust Bowl' of the 1930s.

Recognition of these environmental consequences led to the gradual withdrawal of public incentives for land settlement and conversion over the first half of the twentieth century, followed in the 1970s by the introduction of new laws and regulations protecting wetlands and endangered species' habitat. These laws and regulations in turn provoked a backlash from some landowners, who saw them as an unwarranted intrusion on their private property rights. This backlash reached a peak in Congress in 1995, including a number of proposals to expand financial compensation requirements for any landowner whose property values were diminished by federal actions, including environmental protection policies.

Wary of the political costs of environmental regulations, the federal government has simultaneously pursued a more voluntary approach to influencing land use, by offering landowners and farmers financial incentives for environmental conservation, restoration, and preservation. In many cases, these incentives amount to the acquisition of partial interests in land, essentially representing the voluntary conveyance by the landowner or farmer, to the federal government, of the rights to use land in certain ways. For example, the federal government might rent from a farmer the right to use a certain parcel of land in a way that causes excessive soil erosion. The point is not that the government itself wishes to cultivate the land in an erosive manner, but that it wishes the farmer to relinquish the right to do so. Accordingly, the rental agreement would require the farmer either to keep the land idle for a certain period of time or to cultivate it in a manner that causes less erosion to occur. The farmer gains a rental payment for the partial interest conveyed to the government, and the government gains a public amenity, such as cleaner water, that the land provides when used less intensively.

These tools were first established with respect to highly erodible soils and wetlands in the 1950s. But it is only in the 1980s and 1990s that they have become as central to United States conservation policy as they are today. Today they are used by both public and private agencies at the national as well as the state and local levels (Table 1). Private agencies have protected about 14 million acres (6 million hectares) of environmentally sensitive land in the United States to date through the voluntary acquisition of partial interests (Wiebe, 1995). By far the largest such federal programme today is the Conservation Reserve Program (CRP), through which as many as 36 million acres (15 million hectares) of highly erodible land have been rented by the federal government at an average rate of US$ 50 per acre (US$ 124 per hectare) per year, for a total cost of almost US$ 2 billion per year (Table 2). The farmer or landowner agrees

Rural Planning and Management

Table 1. Agencies involved in acquisition of partial interests

	National	State & Local
Public	**Federal government agencies** (for example, the Natural Resources Conservation Service, the Forest Service, the Fish and Wildlife Service, and the National Park Service)	**State & local government agencies** (for example, the Maryland Agricultural Land Preservation Foundation and the Lancaster County Agricultural Preserve Board)
Private	**National nonprofits** (for example, The Nature Conservancy, the Trust for Public Land, the Conservation Fund, and the American Farmland Trust)	**Land trusts** (for example, the Trust for New Hampshire Lands, the Maine Coast Heritage Trust, the Iowa Natural Heritage Foundation, and the Montana Land Reliance)

Source: Wiebe et al. (1996).

Table 2. Participation in selected easement and easement-like programmes

Region[1]	Conservation Reserve Program		Wetlands Reserve Program (inc. Emergency Signups)		State and Local Farmland Protection Programs	
	Acres[3]	$/acre/year	Acres[3]	$/acre	Acres[3]	$/acre
Appalachia	1 158 124	54	18 514	n.a.	1 255	1422
Corn Belt	5 603 333	74	115 621	n.a.	0	—
Delta States	1 248 403	44	148 667	n.a.	0	—
Lake States	3 008 337	59	18 664	n.a.	0	—
Mountain	6 687 264	40	3410	n.a.	1904	1709
Northeast	226 411	59	6383	n.a.	337 092	1666
Northern Plains	9 664 110	46	25 254	n.a.	0	—
Pacific	1 791 182	50	27 910	n.a.	56 435	1725
Southeast	1 692 580	43	5257	n.a.	0	—
Southern Plains	5 342 989	40	21 798	n.a.	0	—
Total[2]	36 422 733	50	391 478	600	396 686	1674

[1] Appalachia = KT, NC, TN, VA, WV; Corn Belt = IL, IN, IA, MO, OH; Delta States = AR, LA, MS; Lake States = MI, MN, WI; Mountain = AZ, CO, ID, MT, NV, NM, UT, WY; Northeast = CT, DE, ME, MD, MA, NH, NJ, NY, PA, RI, VT; Northern Plains = KS, NE, ND, SD; Pacific = CA, OR, WA; Southeast = AL, FL, GA, SC; Southern Plains = OK, TX.
[2] Excludes Alaska and Hawaii.
[3] One acre = 0.4 hectares.
Source: Wiebe et al. (1996).

to keep the land idle and under a conservation cover of grass or trees for 10 years.

A much smaller programme is the Wetlands Reserve Program (WRP), which is like the CRP in that it acquires partial interests from private landowners for conservation purposes, but which differs from the CRP in several ways. First, it targets wetlands rather than highly erodible soils, although there is certainly some overlap between the two resources. Second, instead of simply *renting* cultivation rights, the WRP may also *purchase* cultivation rights from landowners in perpetuity in the form of conservation easements. As a result, instead of annual rental payments, the WRP offers one-time payments calculated as the difference between the market value of the land in agricultural production and the market value of the land as a restored wetland. Not surprisingly, the loss of cultivation rights represents a major portion of the value of such lands. However, in a third difference from the CRP, the WRP allows landowners to graze livestock and harvest timber, as long as the wetland is preserved, so some economic value remains with the landowner. Wetland easement payments currently average about US$ 600 per acre (US$ 1482 per

Property Rights as Policy Tools: K D Wiebe and R Meinzen-Dick

hectare), with about 400 000 acres (162 000 hectares) enrolled so far (Table 2).

A third policy context in which partial interests are used is that of slowing the loss of farmland to more intensive uses, especially urban development. A number of states in the United States have established farmland protection programmes since the 1970s, buying agricultural conservation easements for an average of about US$ 1700 per acre (US$ 4199 per hectare) from willing landowners who agree to keep their land permanently in agricultural production rather than develop it. Such programmes originated in the densely populated northeastern United States, and have spread more recently to the west coast and to the Rocky Mountain states (Table 2). A federal farmland protection programme was established for the first time in 1996.

While we have focused so far on public acquisition of partial interests in private lands, partial interests are also relevant in the management of common property resources. Common property resources combine features of both public and private goods (Ostrom, 1994; Dasgupta and Mäler, 1994). They are like public goods in that it is costly to develop institutions to exclude potential beneficiaries. The resource in question might be mobile (such as air), for example, or it might be spread over a wide area (such as rangeland). On the other hand, common property resources are like private goods in that those resources used or consumed by one party (such as forage or water) are not available to others. When rights to common property resources are imperfectly defined or enforced, such resources are in effect free goods, open to access (and thus potentially subject to overexploitation) by all.

In the case of publicly owned rangeland in the western United States, open access prevailed at the turn of the century, contributing to overgrazing and environmental degradation. In response, the federal government established grazing permits—a form of private interest in public lands—which allow (indeed require) ranchers to graze a specified number of livestock in a particular area for a specified period of time. Continuing debate about the effectiveness of these permits in accommodating multiple demands on rangeland resources, including both livestock grazing and wildlife habitat preservation, has led a wide spectrum of observers to suggest the establishment of transferable forage rights—partial interests in federal rangeland that would be allocated on a competitive market basis between ranchers, environmental groups, and other interested parties (Nelson, 1996; Council of Economic Advisers, 1997).

We have introduced the examples above with a deliberate focus on particular partial interests in each case. It is important to note, however, that each partial interest discussed represents only one stick in the bundle of rights that characterizes each resource in question, and that the remaining rights may themselves be held by multiple stakeholders. In the case of the CRP, for example, the federal government negotiates rental contracts for enrolled parcels, while the landowners retain title. Still others may hold rights to hunt on CRP land. On WRP land, third parties may acquire rights to hunt, graze livestock, or harvest timber. Similar nuances characterize farmland protection programmes, while public lands are typically managed to accommodate multiple interests, including (in some areas) the traditional hunting and fishing rights of Native American communities.

Despite the variety of these examples, partial interests have been used as policy tools in the United States primarily to deal with environmental externalities (although there are many examples, such as mineral rights or water rights, of partial interests that are defined and traded to accomplish private economic objectives). In developing countries, by contrast, livelihood externalities may represent more immediate policy concerns, requiring mechanisms to accommodate and protect the interests of multiple individual users.

Policy considerations for developing countries

The partial interests in land that are represented by these rental agreements and conservation easements are the shades of grey that blur the conventional delineation of private property in the United States. They are means by which public agencies or private non-profit conservation groups can influence the use of private land without incurring the political costs of regulation or the full financial costs of outright land acquisition. Precisely because of their flexibility and the variety of resource situations in which they can be applied, they involve potentially significant transactions costs.

By their nature, partial interests in land represent complicated relationships between multiple parties having different and possibly conflicting objectives with regard to a particular parcel of land. The process of trading partial interests requires a general acceptance of who holds what rights to begin with, negotiation of what rights are to be conveyed, and agreement about what those rights are worth. Furthermore, even after a partial interest in land is conveyed, it requires ongoing monitoring, and potentially enforcement as well, to ensure its continued effectiveness over the longer term.

Land tenure systems in many developing countries have been moving in the opposite direction—from complicated patterns of 'grey', where customary systems accommodate the use rights (not necessarily transferable) of multiple parties—toward nominally simpler 'black and white' systems which accord full (and transferable) ownership rights to a single individual. This has often been associated with titling programmes, privatization, and development of land markets (Maxwell and Wiebe, 1998). In the process, many customary rights of access or use (such as grazing animals on crop residues, taking fallen branches for firewood, or collecting medicinal plants from hedgerows) are disregarded (Rocheleau and Edmunds, 1997; Meinzen-Dick *et al.*, 1997). Although these rights may be very important for livelihoods, especially those of poor households, they are often seen as a necessary casualty in the drive toward market development.

What the United States' experience shows is that complex partial interests can be defined and protected even within a relatively highly developed land market. Not all rights need be held by a single individual, and partial interests can be transferred independently of each other. As the constituent elements of land tenure systems, partial interests are not tied to any particular tenure regime. The rights can be held by individuals, communities, interest groups (such as environmental NGOs), corporations, or the government. For example, a private company may hold specific rights to harvest from a community woodlot, or a community may hold rights on public lands.

Partial interests can potentially be defined and conveyed within a wide range of tenure systems, whether the system as a whole draws its authority from community norms and traditions, or from a formal legal system established by the state, or from a combination of the two—as long as its authority is recognized by all parties to the transaction. Partial interests offer a means by which rights can be exchanged, and multiple objectives

Table 3. Relative costs of alternative land policy strategies*

Item	Regulation	Partial interest acquisition	Land acquisition
Negotiation	Low	High	Medium
Acquisition	Low	Medium	High
Monitoring	Medium–high	Medium–high	Low
Enforcement	Medium–high	Medium–high	Low
Political	High	Low	Low

Note: relative magnitudes are intended to be comparable across columns, but not across rows.
*Each strategy may also have additional costs not included here. Regulation, for example, may involve unintended environmental costs, as when concern about possible future designation as endangered species habitat induces landowners to clear habitat or harvest timber prematurely (Stroup, 1997). See also Hanson (1996).
Source: Wiebe et al. (1996).

pursued, even in the process of transition between customary and statutory or market-based land tenure systems.

Nevertheless, because of the complexity involved in acknowledging diverse claimants on a single piece of land, partial interests do require a well-functioning institutional infrastructure for ongoing monitoring and enforcement. In the United States, where institutional infrastructure is the domain of government agencies and lawyers, it is not surprising that the steps involved in conveying partial interests in land are costly (Table 3). Data are scarce, but limited evidence suggests that the costs of easement negotiation and appraisal, for example, are small relative to the cost of acquisition itself, perhaps on the order of 10% or less. On the other hand, experience with conservation easements in the United States is still too short to allow us to know much about the long-term costs of monitoring and enforcement. These are potentially quite high, particularly as easement-encumbered land is acquired or inherited by individuals who were not party to the original conveyance, and may thus be less likely to understand or respect the terms of the original agreement. Table 3 suggests that, while partial interests may offer advantages over a regulatory approach in terms of political costs, and over outright land acquisition in terms of acquisition costs, the costs of negotiation, monitoring, and enforcement leave the overall ranking of the three policy strategies ambiguous.

In many developing country contexts, the institutional infrastructure of customary tenure regimes may accommodate multiple claimants (e.g. Williams, 1997; Rocheleau and Edmunds, 1997), but government agencies and court systems have been less adept in this regard. However, many of the regulatory approaches to dealing with environmental externalities (e.g. erosion control regulations or prohibitions on forest use) have also been ineffective. The partial interests approach requires negotiation among all parties with a stake in the resource, and this process of negotiation increases the likelihood that all users are aware of and will abide by their part of the agreements. It is important to recognize that all users may not be equally able to articulate and protect their interests in such negotiations, and that in some cases, assistance may be necessary to ensure that stakeholders are adequately included (Leach *et al.*, 1997).

Such tools may be appropriate in other common property contexts as well, although the problem becomes more complicated in developing countries when poverty and subsistence thresholds introduce additional constraints on the behaviour of resource users (Perrings, 1989; Larson and Bromley, 1990). Dasgupta and Mäler (1991) distinguish between local and global common property resources, noting that the institutional costs of establishing adequate property rights to a global common property resource, such as the Earth's atmosphere, are prohibitive (although partial interest-based mechanisms are among those being considered in ongoing multilateral discussions about global climate change). By contrast, Dasgupta and Mäler argue that the interests of those most dependent on *local* common property resources may well be best served in an equitable and sustainable fashion simply by placing (or restoring) control in local hands.

Zimbabwe's Campfire programme provides one of the most notable examples of this approach. Local communities have been accorded rights over wildlife on their lands, and receive a share of the income from hunting and tourism. Instead of relying solely on government enforcement of bans on poaching, this approach attempts to give local communities a stake in the resource, so that they have a greater incentive to protect it over the long term (Murphree, 1993). Accommodating the livelihood needs of local residents may prove to be a more effective means of protecting wildlife biodiversity and other environmental interests than externally imposed regulations (Wells *et al.*, 1992).

Two additional and very important policy considerations should also be noted here. First, the use of partial interests as policy tools addresses the distribution of rights and opportunities within an economic system that is itself part of a larger system, the natural ecosystem (Daly, 1991). Questions of the optimal scale of economic activity, though beyond the scope of this paper, are also central to the issue of sustainable development.

And second, the fact that voluntary exchange of partial interests occurs between willing sellers and willing buyers, and that there is no shortage of interested participants (at least in the United States thus far), does not guarantee that such programmes are universally popular among others who are not parties to the exchange. Most of the programmes described in Section 3 are designed to address environmental externalities of private land use, such as sedimentation and habitat loss. As such, they are intended to provide environmental benefits beyond the boundaries of the participating properties. Nonetheless, market solutions may themselves impose other externalities on neighbouring communities that are dependent on traditional patterns of resource use for their livelihoods, or even on more distant communities (including those in developing countries) that are affected by food-price responses to large-scale public and private land retirement programmes.

It is interesting to note that such concerns are analogous to those noted by Amartya Sen in his work on entitlement and deprivation (e.g. Sen, 1981). Sen argued that people suffer deprivation not because markets fail, but because markets, operating through a given system of property rights and legal relations, work 'with a vengeance' (p. 166) to exclude those who lack an effective voice. Poor households (especially those without formal land ownership) offer the clearest example of those who may be excluded. Even within landed households, women may have limited ability to protect their interests under market systems because they lack control over cash, or because titles are registered under the male head of household (Lastarria-Cornhiel, 1997; Meinzen-Dick *et al.*, 1997). The challenge for policy makers who would use property rights as tools to accomplish a broad range of sustainable development policy objectives is to define and distribute those rights in such a way that all interested parties can participate effectively in the markets that will operate as a result.

Conclusion

The process of market development has often been accompanied by simplification of tenure into systems where all rights are held by a single 'owner'. But other potential users, and society at large, have a stake in the ways in which land and other resources are held and used, and simple ownership systems have often generated negative externalities on the environment or the livelihoods of neighbours. The interests of other stakeholders, which may be accommodated in customary tenure systems, are often lost in the transition to statutory tenure systems. Partial interests in land offer a more refined alternative to simple ownership. Even within the formal legal structures that characterize property rights in the United States, partial interests have proven to be flexible, popular, and effective tools for land use and conservation policy involving lower political costs than a strictly regulatory approach and lower acquisition costs relative to outright land purchase. This suggests the potential for wider application of partial interests as policy tools for a broad range of objectives associated with sustainable development.

But partial interests also require considerable institutional infrastructure and involve potentially significant transactions costs, including monitoring and enforcement obligations over the longer term. This raises the question of whether appropriate institutional infrastructure exists—either through the courts or through customary institutions—to accommodate and protect the interests of multiple claimants on resources in developing countries. If market mechanisms are used to allocate and trade partial interests, it raises the further question of whether some claimants will remain excluded. This is especially critical where basic needs of the poor are at stake. Sustainable development requires more than market-led growth; it also requires attention to maintaining the environment and the livelihoods of all members of society. The establishment and distribution of partial interests in land and other resources—and the fundamentally political choices that such actions represent—are critical in defining the path that development will follow.

Acknowledgements

We would like to thank three anonymous reviewers for their helpful comments, and William Whichard of IFPRI for his assistance in preparing this manuscript.

References

Baland, J.-M. and Platteau, J.-P. (1996) *Halting the Degradation of Natural Resources: Is There a Role for Rural Communities?* Clarendon Press, Oxford.

Bromley, D. W. (1997) Constitutional political economy: property claims in a dynamic world. *Contemporary Economic Policy* 15(Suppl.4), 43–54.

Bruce, J. W. and Migot-Adholla, S. E. eds (1994) *Searching For Land Tenure Security In Africa*. Kendall/Hunt (for the World Bank), Dubuque, Iowa.

Council of Economic Advisers (February, 1997) *Economic Report of the President, Together With The Annual Report of the Council of Economic Advisers*, U. S. Government Printing Office, Washington, DC.

Daly, H. E. (1991) Elements of environmental macroeconomics. In *Ecological Economics: The Science and Management of Sustainability*, Chapter 3. Columbia University Press, New York.

Property rights as policy tools: K D Wiebe and R Meinzen-Dick

Dasgupta, P. and Mäler, K.-G. (March, 1994) *Poverty, Institutions, and the Environmental Resource Base*. World Bank Environment Paper, No. 9.

Dasgupta, P. and Mäler K.-G. (1991) The environment and emerging development issues. *Proceedings of the World Bank Annual Conference on Development Economics, 1990*.

Goldstein, J. H. and Watson, W. D. (1997) Property rights, regulatory taking, and compensation: implications for environmental protection. *Contemporary Economic Policy* **15**(Suppl.4), 32–42.

Hanson, N. (1996) Family-owned forests in an era of regulatory uncertainty. *Proceedings of the Symposium on Non-Industrial Private Forests: Learning From the Past*. Prospects for the Future, Washington, DC.

Kendrick, A. (1996) Comments on Fisheries. Submission to Gender and Property Rights E-mail Conference, January 16, International Food Policy Research Institute, Washington, DC.

Larson, B. A. and Bromley, D. W. (1990) Property rights, externalities, and resource degradation: locating the tragedy. *Journal of Development Economics* **33**, 235–262.

Lastarria-Cornhiel, S. (1997) Impact of privatization on gender and property rights in Africa. *World Development* **25**(Suppl.8), 1317–1334.

Leach, M., Mearns, R. and Scoones, I. (1997) Institutions, consensus and conflict: implications for policy and practice. *IDS Bulletin* **28**(Suppl.4), 90–95.

Maxwell, D. and Wiebe, K. (1998) *Land Tenure and Food Security: A Review of Concepts, Evidence, and Methods*. University of Wisconsin Land Tenure Center Paper No. 129, Madison, Wisconsin. January.

McElfish, J. M. Jr. (1994) Property rights, property roots: rediscovering the basis for legal protection of the environment. *Environmental Law Reporter* **24**, 10231–10249.

Meinzen-Dick, R., Brown, L. R., Feldstein, H. S. and Quisumbing, A. R. (1997) Gender, property rights, and natural resources. *World Development* **25**(Suppl.8), 1303–1315.

Murphree, M. W. (1993) *Communities as Resource Management Institutions*. Gatekeeper Series, No. 36, International Institute For Environment and Development, London.

Nelson, R. H. (1996) *How to Reform Grazing Policy? Creating Forage Rights on Federal Rangelands*. Competitive Enterprise Institute, Washington, DC.

Ostrom, E. (1994) Neither Market Nor State: Governance of Common-Pool Resources in the Twenty-First Century. Lecture Series, International Food Policy Research Institute, Washington, DC.

Perrings, C. (1989) Optimal path to extinction? Poverty and resource degradation in the open agrarian economy. *Journal of Development Economics* **30**, 1–24.

Rocheleau, D. and Edmunds, D. (1997) Women, men and trees: gender, power, and property in forest and agrarian landscapes. *World Development* **25**(Suppl.8), 1351–1371.

Segerson, K. (1997) Government regulation and compensation: implications for environmental quality and natural resource use. *Contemporary Economic Policy* **15**(Suppl.4), 28–31.

Sen, A. (1981) *Poverty and Famines: An Essay on Entitlement and Deprivation*. Clarendon Press, Oxford.

Scrageldin, I. (1996) Sustainable development: from theory to practice. *Finance and Development* **33**(Suppl.4),

Stroup, R. L. (1997) The economics of compensating property owners. *Contemporary Economic Policy* **15**(Suppl.4), 55–65.

Vosti, S. A. and Reardon, T, eds (1997) *Sustainability, Growth, and Poverty Alleviation: A Policy and Agroecological Perspective*. The Johns Hopkins University Press, Baltimore.

Wells, M., Brandon, K. and Hannah, L. J. (1992) *People and Parks: Linking Protected Area Management with Local Communities*. World Bank, World Wildlife Fund, USAID, Washington, DC.

Wiebe, K. (1995) Land Trusts Protected 14 Million Acres as of 1994. *Agricultural*

Resources and Environmental Indicators Update No. 13. Economic Research Service, U.S. Department of Agriculture, Washington, DC.

Wiebe, K., Tegene, A. and Kuhn B. (1996) *Partial Interests in Land: Policy Tools for Resource Use and Conservation.* Agricultural Economic Report No. 744. Economic Research Service, U.S. Department of Agriculture, Washington, DC.

Williams, T. (1997) Multiple Uses of Common Pool Resources in Semiarid West Africa: A Survey of Existing Practices and Options for Sustainable Resource Management. Environment and Production Technology Division Workshop Summary Paper No. 5, International Food Policy Research Institute, Washington, DC.

World Bank (1997) *Five Years After Rio: Innovations in Environmental Policy.* Environmentally Sustainable Development Studies and Monographs Series No. 18 (June).

B
Social Capital

[9]

Social Capital and Natural Capital: A Comparative Analysis of Land Tenure and Natural Resource Management in Guatemala

Elizabeth G. Katz

ABSTRACT. *This paper argues that the existence of social capital can substitute for well-defined legal property rights in both private and common property resource tenure regimes. A comparative analysis of two regions in Guatemala suggests that, where significant social capital exists among natural resource users, it fosters a sense of ownership and respect for boundaries, and provides the foundation for use rules, monitoring, and enforcement mechanisms which help preserve the natural resource base. In contrast, an absence of social capital in a situation where property rights are poorly defined can lead to resource mining in both private and common property regimes.* (JEL Q15)

I. INTRODUCTION

It is well known that the incentives for resource allocation vary with property rights systems. In particular, individual, private property regimes can be expected to differ substantially from common property regimes (CPRs), in terms of the bundle of rights available to users, and the corresponding investment and extraction decisions that maintain or deplete natural capital. There is substantial disagreement, however, over which type of land tenure regime is most conducive to long-term sustainable natural resource management. There are those who argue that only well-defined, individual rights in land can restrain over-exploitation and induce conservation-related investment, while others counter that common property resources can be sustainably managed if certain design principle criteria are met.[1]

The growing literature on common property resource regimes (CPRs), has begun to make use of the notion of "social capital"—networks of social relationships that can be drawn upon to improve individual and collective well-being—in describing the conditions under which successful natural resource management can occur. An extension of this idea to the relationship between property rights and natural resource management would be to see whether and to what extent

The author is assistant professor of economics, St. Mary's College of California, Moraga, California. The author would like to thank the team of researchers who contributed to the World Bank's Guatemala Land Tenure and Natural Resources Management Report (No.14553-GU), from which much of the empirical material in this paper is drawn: John Beavers, César Castañeda, Claudio Cabrera, Silvel Elías, David Kaimowitz, María Teresa Robles, and Ronald Strochlic. The useful comments of Chris Barrett, Michael Baxter, Shelton Davis, Michael Goldman, Jolyne Melmed-Sanjak, Denise Stanley, Bill Thiesenhusen, and two anonymous reviewers on earlier drafts of this article are also very much appreciated. Responsibility for the article's analysis and conclusions rest solely with the author.

[1] Wachter (1992, 20) summarizes the "property rights" argument: "Without clear and enforced property rights, everyone is afraid that neighbors will reap the fruits of one's own restraint in resource use, so user costs (the present value of possible future profits foregone by using a resource unit today) are ignored. By contrast, a resource user who has a secure, long-term property right over the resource will take into account any possible future utility from the resource. When user costs figure in the decision making of a rational economic agent, a race to exploit the resource is avoided and conservation objectives are served." Feder and Onchan (1987, 311) claim that ownership security affects both investment incentives and the availability of resources to finance investment. On the common property side, Wade (1987) identifies six types of variables that influence "the likelihood of successful organization" in the commons: the nature of the common property resource; the technology used in its exploitation and to define its boundaries; the relationship between the resource and the user group; the characteristics of the user group itself; noticeability of use rule violation; and the relationship between the users and the state. Similarly, Ostrom (1994) discusses a series of "design principles" which characterize sustainable CPR institutions: clearly defined boundaries; congruence between appropriation and provision rules and local conditions; collective-choice arrangements; monitoring; graduated sanctions; conflict resolution mechanisms; and minimal recognition of rights to organize.

social capital interacts with a variety of both individually and collectively based resource tenure systems in determining incentive structures and the resulting management and investment practices. This paper addresses such a generalization by arguing that the existence of historically and ethnically based social capital can, in certain circumstances, substitute for well-defined legal property rights in both private and common property resource tenure regimes. By allowing natural resource users to overcome barriers to collective action such as negative externalities, underprovision of public goods, information asymmetries, and moral hazard, social capital can mitigate against the sorts of unsustainable natural resource management practices associated with property rights insecurity. Specifically, a respect for customary law and viable local institutions, based on sustained interactions among resource users over time, can enforce respect for private property boundaries and regulate exploitation of common property resources.

In addition to generalizing the argument about the role of social capital to include individual as well as collective tenure regimes, this article addresses the relative paucity of empirical research on property rights and environmental management in a Latin American context. Perhaps because indigenous land tenure regimes have been more comprehensively displaced by colonial and postcolonial states than in Africa and Asia, the Latin American region has been largely neglected in the common property literature, and the history of land reform and titling has generally ignored informal property rights systems among small farmers. Guatemala, an ethnically heterogeneous country with a profoundly unequal[2] and complex land tenure system, significant deforestation, and land degradation problems, is an excellent site to explore these issues in a Latin American context. Comparative analysis of two distinct regions, the largely indigenously populated Western Highlands and the agricultural frontier of El Petén, provides an opportunity to examine differences both between property rights regimes within a given socio-economic-ecological environment, as well as within a given tenure system across re-

gions exhibiting contrasting levels of social capital.

Section 2 of this article, discusses the concept of social capital and its application to the analysis of property rights and natural resource management. Section 3 describes the principal features of the private and common property resource management regimes in the two study regions and develops an analysis of the differences within and between regions and property regimes in terms of social capital and resource management outcomes. Section 4 concludes and discusses the policy implications of the analysis.

II. SOCIAL CAPITAL

Although relatively new in the lexicon of economists, social capital is one of the most hotly debated concepts in modern sociology (Coleman 1990; Putnam 1993). The basic idea is that relationships among individuals give rise to something valuable. This intangible value—social capital—can then be drawn upon to improve individual and collective well-being. As Coleman (1990, 302–5) explains it, "social capital is defined by its function . . . [which is] . . . the value of those aspects of social structure to actors, as resources that can be used by the actors to realize their interests." Social capital may have its foundations in shared history, ethnicity, religion or other group membership, and is manifest in collective knowledge (including environmental knowledge), respect for group rules and norms, and the creation and maintenance of self-governing institutions.

Several features distinguish social capital from its natural, human, and produced counterparts:

1. *Investments in social capital are often a byproduct of activities engaged in for other reasons rather than intentionally undertaken for material gain.* Because it arises out of human interactions and relationships, social capital is most of-

---

[2] The Gini coefficient for land distribution was .86 in 1979, the year of the last Agricultural Census (USAID 1981). This is high even relative to other Latin American countries, most of which have indicators in the .6–.7 range (Theisenhusen 1995).

ten created outside of the market sphere. Common examples include religious or ethnic group affiliation, extended (real and fictive) kinship ties, and other voluntary and ascribed associations to which people do not normally belong with the explicit intention of investing in something from which they can materially profit. This characteristic gives social capital a public good aspect, with all of the attendant problems of incentives for adequate provisioning (Coleman 1990, 315–18). Of course, not all interactions give rise to information-based trust that can be drawn upon in other spheres. Attending church or coaching soccer may simply be ends unto themselves, under some circumstances. On the other hand, if it is observed over time that certain social activities are having spillover benefits for participants, it is quite possible that at least some people will begin to participate with the explicit intention of using the interaction to further themselves—corporate golf is an example here.[3] Among the interesting implications of the nature of social capital-building activities is that if they *do* produce a flow of benefits, the conventional lines between labor and leisure, investment and consumption, are substantially blurred. Methodologically, this means that an inter-disciplinary approach is called for, in which non-economic affiliations and activities are treated as potentially important sites for the production of an economically valuable resource, and transactions that appear purely economic in nature are recognized as possibly incorporating social capital investment.[4]

2. *The existence of social capital can have qualitative impacts on the nature of economic transactions.* By mitigating information costs and moral hazard concerns, strong social relationships between trading partners can affect price, relative risk aversion, and contract choice (Schmid and Robison 1995). Platteau (1994) goes so far as to make the case that social capital, em-

bodied in moral norms and private and public institutions, is the bedrock of a functioning market economy. His argument goes beyond the idea that economies are "embedded" in social relations (Granovetter 1985) to establish the specific informational, behavioral, and enforcement functions provided by these relations, without which market economies would be unable to operate.

3. *Using social capital contributes to, rather than depletes its stock.* Ostrom (1994) contends that reaping the benefits of strong social ties—engaging in successful collective action, for example—reinforces the bonds within a group that permit future such action.[5] In other words, not only is social capital a renewable resource, the stock is actually augmented by "consuming" the flow. Conversely, "if unused, social capital deteriorates at a relatively rapid rate."[6]

In order to be a useful concept, social capital must be distinguishable from other social phenomena which may also influence economic processes and outcomes. As Dasgupta (1997) puts it, "there is a temptation to use 'social capital' as a peg on which to hang all those engagements we like and care for." In particular, in the case of property rights and natural resource management, it is important to differentiate between social capital and so-

---

[3] The economic literature on repeated games (Friedman 1986, chapter 3) has contributed to a formalization of this phenomenon.

[4] Robison and Hanson (1995, 48) note that "investments in social capital may lead to transactions that may occur at nonmarket prices and outside of formal markets. These exchanges . . . may not be examples of market failures but instead represent investments in social capital."

[5] It is worth noting that this notion is valid within, but not necessarily across groups of social actors. Reinforcing ties with one group may involve sacrificing the trust of another . An extreme example of this (provided by a referee) would be active membership in the NAACP by a white supremacist.

[6] Here there is an important parallel with human capital, which can also rapidly deplete if unused. Some forms of natural capital can also be augmented by limited consumption, for example selective tree harvesting.

cial norms. Social norms refer to a set of beliefs about acceptable and unacceptable behavior. Coleman (1987) argues that social norms constitute a form of social capital insofar as they "allow [for those] affected by externalities to gain . . . partial control of the action," and thus "result in higher levels of [social] satisfaction." Another way of thinking about the relationship between social norms and social capital is that the latter is what allows the former to be effectively communicated and enforced—the material "base" of the normative "superstructure." For our purposes here, it is the presence or absence of sustained interaction over historical time that determines groups' differential abilities to develop, utilize, and adapt a set of norms—which in some cases take the form of explicit rules and sanctions. It is the value of the interaction itself that gives rise to the rules that we refer to as social capital, even though the rules (norms) themselves are the more observable manifestation of its existence.[7]

How is the concept of social capital relevant to the analysis of property rights and natural resource management? Both private and common property theorists emphasize the importance of well-defined rights—tenure security—to restrained exploitation and long-term, productivity-enhancing investments. What is argued here is that in the absence of a formal, legal system that can guarantee resource tenure rights for either individuals or groups of users, social capital can substitute for this system by providing a non-market solution to the negative externality, information asymmetry, and moral hazard problems that can be expected to arise when property rights are not well defined.[8] If we think of social capital narrowly as communication, for example, it is how information about property boundaries, group membership, resource stocks, flows, heterogeneity, and returns gets shared among potential users. In this sense, social capital can provide the basis for essential non-market signals regarding the rights, duties, and behavior of all members of the resource management regime—information which, if it were not available, might well lead to unsustainable use. If we define social capital more

broadly as trust based on long-term networks of relationships among natural resource users, it can provide the foundation for people to participate in and abide by social norms governing resource use, and to care about (receive disutility from) sanctions which may be purely moral (i.e., non-material) in nature. Thus, social capital can, to some extent, substitute for the costly monitoring, supervision, and enforcement of the rules governing property rights and resource use in both private and common property regimes.

III. RESOURCE TENURE REGIMES IN GUATEMALA

El Petén

The first region in which we will consider the interaction of land tenure, social capital, and natural resource management is El Petén, Guatemala's northernmost province (Department), covering over 36,000 km² of originally low-altitude moist tropical forest eco-

---

[7] Another distinction is that between social capital and what Hayami and Ruttan (1985) call "cultural endowments." The latter is a broad concept, incorporating religion, ideology, morality, and traditional patterns of cooperation which "make some forms of institutional change less costly to establish and impose severe costs on others" (Hayami and Ruttan 1985, 109). Berkes and Folke (1994) develop a similar notion of what they call "cultural capital," which includes "people's views of the natural world and the universe, and the *source* of these values or cosmology; environmental philosophy, values, and ethics, including religion; and local and personal knowledge of the environment, including traditional ecological knowledge." These constructs essentially borrow language from anthropology ("culture") to describe what social capital theorists mean when they argue for the inherent value of sustained communication among social actors.

[8] The existence of social capital may also reduce transactions costs insofar as multiple contracts governing specific relationships and transactions can be replaced by "credible commitments and . . . generalized forms of reciprocity." (Ostrom 1994, 25–26). Platteau (1993, 802) makes a similar point with respect to enforcement costs: "inasmuch as they act as a substitute for, or as a reinforcement of, state-engineered rules or control mechanisms, [moral] norms allow a society to reduce enforcement costs and the mistakes unavoidable (given asymmetric information) in any process of (central) law implementation."

systems.[9] El Petén has served as the country's agricultural frontier since the reversal of national land reform in the 1950s, and as an important site for large-scale ranching, mining, and timber extraction operations. Since planned migration to El Petén (colonization) began in the 1960s, population growth has exceeded 9% per year and changes in land use have been dramatic.[10]

It will be argued that the migratory nature of the population, itself a function of ecological conditions and insecure land tenure arrangements, has largely prevented the formation of the sort of social capital necessary to stabilize natural resource exploitation in both private and common property situations. In the case of individual migrant farmers, this means that defensive clearing serves to mark plot boundaries, shortening or even eliminating the grow-back periods necessary for sustainable rotational agriculture, and a reluctance to invest even in simple fertility-conserving techniques, such as green manure. For users of common municipal lands, a lack of group identity, and a lack of respect for local authorities has meant that, while agricultural plot boundaries are well-defined, access is frequently granted through an active black market to newcomers with little knowledge of local ecological conditions, and residents have shown little interest in conserving the forest that remains. In other words, the region's transient residents have failed to develop alternative mechanisms to assure mutual respect for informal property rights and overcome collective action problems, with devastating consequences for the natural environment.

Migrant smallholders. Most scholars and policymakers agree that one of the greatest threats to the fragile ecosystems of Guatemala's northern lowlands is the migration of thousands of landless and land-poor peasants to the region. Initially under Government sponsorship, and now spontaneously,[11] rural Guatemalans fleeing land scarcity in the rest of the country come to El Petén in search of agricultural land for subsistence production. However, since this agricultural frontier is eminently unsuitable for intensive agriculture, after several years of planting crops on sites cleared of tropical forest, agricultural

output begins to fall, and migrants move and begin anew along the expanding frontier.[12] Uncertainty over land tenure rights and individual benefits, lead farmers to produce crops with short growing cycles that require little investment, and extension activities geared toward the adoption of sustainable agriculture and agroforestry technologies are routinely frustrated by smallholders' lack of long-term investment incentives (Robles 1994).

---

[9] Such ecosystems are characterized by the fact that most nutrients are stored in the vegetation, and a continual recycling of these nutrients between the soil and the biomass. It is because of this characteristic that the elimination of the vegetative cover brings about a fall in the fertility and the productive potential of these ecosystems.

[10] In 1964, the total population of El Petén was 26,562. Nine years later, it had more than doubled to 64,114, and by 1981 the census indicated a population of 131,927. According to the most recent statistics (1990), the current population of El Petén is over 300,000, the majority of whom are still concentrated in the southern part of the Department and 75% of whom live in rural areas. Southgate and Basterrechea (1992) estimate the population immigration rate at 5.5%. Average population density is 26 per square mile (Sader et al. 1994). Conservative estimates of deforestation imply that between 1976/8 and 1987, the region lost 300,000 hectares of forest, and during the following six years the loss of high and medium density forests rose to 42,000 hectares per year, with an additional 26,000 hectares per year of low density and pine forests also cleared in this period (AHT/APESA 1992). Between 1987 and 1993, land in pasture increased by 36,000 hectares and in crops by 267,000 hectares. Perhaps most dramatically, representing as it does the end of the nutrient mining cycle, 111,000 hectares of cropland were abandoned in this period (Kaimowitz 1994). Sader et al. (1994) report an average annual clearing rate of .4% in the protected Maya Biosphere Reserve, with much higher rates (up to 21.5%) along the southern and western borders of the park, and along major roads.

[11] Government-promoted land colonization in El Petén began in earnest after the military coup in 1954 and the subsequent dismantling of the nascent agrarian reform. The opening up of the agricultural frontier was a way for the new military governments to increase agricultural and livestock production and provide an escape valve for land-hungry peasants, while not compromising their fundamentally anti-redistributional politics. After a brief respite during the violence of the early 1980s, migration to El Petén picked up again after the return to civilian rule in 1985, with levels of approximately 18,000 people annually approaching those of internal migration to the capital city (AHT/APESA 1992).

[12] Currently, in a given year, approximately 12% of the total population in El Petén move internally within the region.

The ethnic and socio-economic heterogeneity of the migrant smallholders, in combination with the itinerant nature of their settlement, and their lack of familiarity with their ecological surroundings, provides a weak foundation for the construction of social capital.[13] In what is essentially an open access situation, neighbors are more likely to be seen as potential trespassers than as co-users of the forest and land resources, and defensive clearing to mark "property" boundaries is rampant. The cycle of soil depletion in the absence of appropriate farming techniques ensures that residence in a particular place will be only temporary, rendering difficult the accumulation of trust and knowledge-sharing that comes with interaction over time, and setting up a viscous circle in which farmers with the most insecure tenure engage in the most unsustainable natural resource management practices, practices which drive continued human settlement of fragile tropical forest.

This relationship between tenure security and land use can be illustrated by the choice of farming systems among Petén smallholders. Migratory agriculture, an ecologically sustainable practice in which a plot of land is cultivated for up to several seasons and then left to natural regeneration, requires a relatively low-population density and the assurance that fallowing lands will not be encroached upon, and therefore is pursued more frequently by farmers in situations of secure property rights. Rotational or shifting farming systems, where the same plot of land is not allowed to lie fallow for much more than double the period of cultivation, appeal to farmers in higher population density areas where possessionary rights over land have to be continually re-established by showing active use. Finally, semi-permanent, smallholder agriculture, in which the land is continuously cultivated with only short or occasional fallow periods, is now more common in El Petén, thanks to the introduction of *frijol abono* (*Mucuna utilis*), a green manure which substitutes for natural periods of fallow, preventing the loss of soil fertility and recovering land invaded by grasses. However, while the farmers with the most to gain from this new technology are those with the smallest plots and the most insecure tenure

arrangements (and therefore the greatest need to demonstrate occupancy), adoption rates have been highest among those with relatively secure tenure who are willing to undertake the additional investment involved (Secaira 1992).[14]

The natural resource management implications of the lack of social capital among heterogeneous and transient smallholders in El Petén is thus mediated by the failure to develop informal solutions to the problem of legal land tenure insecurity. In the absence of local customs, understandings, and institutions that give migrants some assurance that their property boundaries will be respected, their choice of farming system—not to mention their incentives for maintaining forest reserves—is driven by a logic of demonstrating occupancy rather than ensuring the sustainability of the resource base.

Municipal ejidos. The problem of low social capital stocks facing migrant smallholders in El Petén is also manifest in the region's most important common property regime, the municipal *ejido*. Each of El Petén's twelve municipalities has jurisdiction over their own *ejido*—land which is normally rented out to municipal residents for agricultural and livestock production, but may also include a public forest reserve. Poor farmers of varied ethnic backgrounds take advantage of the inexpensive lands to grow subsistence crops, primarily corn and beans, and engage in small-scale livestock production. Table 1 summarizes data on *ejidos'* coverage, users, rental costs, and overlap with other tenure regimes.

---

[13] Ladinos (Spanish-speaking, ethnically non-indigenous Guatemalans) from the dry, steep Eastern Highlands make up nearly half of migrants to El Petén. Q'eqchí Indians from the provinces just south of El Petén account for another 20% of in-migrants. While the former group is primarily oriented towards small-scale cattle ranching, the Q'eqchí can be characterized from a natural resources management perspective as migrant subsistence agriculturalists, sometimes in combination with non-wood forest product extraction (*xate*, *chicle*, and *pimienta*) (Early 1982; Secaira 1992).

[14] While the cited study of green manure adoption (Secaria 1992) did not control for human capital differences among farmers, there is no a priori reason to believe that, given the arbitrary nature of the land adjudication process in the region, titled landholders have higher levels of education than their migratory counterparts.

120 Land Economics February 2000

TABLE 1

MUNICIPAL *EJIDOS* IN EL PETÉN, GUATEMALA

Municipality	*Ejido* Area (has.)	Number of *Ejidatarios*	Observations
Dolores	11,284	700	Approximately 11% forest cover; average parcel size is 13 ha.; active market in rental rights taxed by municipality.
Flores	11,468	n.d.[a]	High levels of illegal occupation and deforestation. Current forest cover approximately 23%.
La Libertad	12,260	n.d.	Rental payment compliance is high because municipality requires proof of "municipal solvency" in order to carry out any municipal transaction.
Melchor de Mencos	12,736	200	40–50% forest cover, high levels of illegal extraction.
Poptún	10,732	n.d	*Ejido* is mostly savanna pasture with dispersed pine. Current municipal policy is to privatize *ejido* parcels.
Santa Ana	12,185	n.d	In coordination with a local NGO, every *ejiditario* who paid municipal rent in 1994 received 5 pounds of *frijol abono*.
San Andrés	11,685	25	The municipality has good knowledge of its lands and has developed relatively strict rental laws with assistance from the National Municipal Development Institute (INFOM).
San Benito	8,900	n.d	None.
San Francisco	11,358	200	The municipality does not rent forested lands.
San José	11,535	800	An NGO-sponsored project has obtained a 3,600 ha. concession within the *ejido* to promote non-wood forest extraction activities.
San Luis	11,789	970	Population pressure has led to the subdivision of the *ejido* into small parcels (1 ha.) and the intensification of agriculture via the use of *frijol abono*.
Sayaxché	11,593	500	Greatest forest cover of all municipal *ejidos* in El Petén, approximately 30% in one section and 95% in another, due to difficult access and relatively low demand for public agricultural land. Current logging license for the extraction of 400,000 bf of commercial timber may be revoked due to non-compliance.
TOTAL	137,525	5,820	

Source: Cabrera Gaillard (1995).
[a] n.d. = no data.

The *ejidos* of El Petén can be considered as largely unsuccessful CPRs on at least two counts: (1) the collectivity of users does not reap the maximum benefits from the system; and (2) the institutional arrangement is not providing incentives for long-term preservation of the resource base, especially forest resources. On the first point, despite being one of the few sources of local fiscal revenue, most Petén municipalities are unaware of the exact location, extension, boundaries, or number of *ejiditarios* using municipal lands. Moreover, practically no effort has been made to increase the fees (currently a nominal US$1–US$4 per hectare per year) or improve the collection of municipal land rental payments, and municipalities generally fail

to benefit from an active black market in rights to *ejido* parcels (which range from 1 to 20 hectares in size).

With regard to natural resource management on the *ejidos*, there are two separate but related issues: the incentives for sustainable agricultural practices, and the provisions for forest conservation and management. Many municipalities prohibit the cultivation of permanent crops or discourage this sort of long-term use with a rental surcharge (Cabrera Gaillard 1995).[15] While the boundaries be-

[15] The discouragement of permanent crops and pastures may also be an attempt on the part of the municipalities to tacitly demonstrate their ownership of the land. Clearly, the overall resource-pricing policy places an extremely low value on the land.

tween *ejido* parcels are well-defined, thus eliminating the need to demonstrate occupancy with continued cultivation, annual rental contracts act as a disincentive for undertaking conservation-related investment and accumulating the knowledge of the microenvironment that can make rotational agriculture relatively sustainable. The resulting low fertility of municipal lands reinforces the tendency for *ejiditarios* to view their land tenure status as temporary, a "way station" for new migrants until they are ready to stake our their own larger, more fertile parcels elsewhere.

With a couple of exceptions, forest cover does not exceed 30% on most *ejidos* in El Petén, and the majority of the remaining forest is severely degraded by years of legal and illegal timber extraction. Consistent with their election-cycle driven time horizon, municipalities have made a practice of entering into short term contracts with logging companies in which valuable forest resources are exchanged for minimal fees, road construction, and other infrastructure development, while longer-term investments in forestry concessions and reforestation are rarely undertaken (Beavers 1995). As for the *ejiditarios* themselves, the usual disincentives to smallholder forest management (small parcel size, poor market access, high discount rates) are exacerbated by the unstable group membership discussed above.

Municipal *ejidos* in El Petén are thus largely failing to preserve both the agricultural and forest natural resource base. This is because, on the one hand, a significant disjuncture exists between users and decision makers (the municipal government), so that the former lack the sense of collective ownership and control that can facilitate restrained use and conservation-related investment. Perhaps even more importantly, the normally temporary nature of *ejido* residence in El Petén does not lend itself to the development of the sort of social capital that would allow farmers to gain detailed local environmental knowledge, or to engage in successful collective action to sustainably exploit their common property forests.

Western Highlands

In stark contrast to El Petén, the Western Highlands of Guatemala, covering approximately 18% of Guatemalan territory and home to over 30% of the national population, is a region characterized by long term, permanent settlement, relative ethnic homogeneity at the local level, and a rich history of collective action around land tenure issues. Ecologically, the Western Highlands are important because they constitute the source of the principal watersheds of 80% of all of Guatemala's rivers, and the habitat for native plant and animal species, some of which are unique to the region (Castañeda Salguero 1995). Seventy percent of the soil is considered apt for forest; the Highlands have the greatest distribution and diversity of conifers, oaks, birch, and poplar in Central America; and the pine forests of the region constitute an essential source of firewood for rural households, almost 80% of which rely on fuelwood for their energy needs.[16]

In the Highlands, both smallholder agricultural lands and common property forests suffer from a lack of formal property rights in the form of a legally registered title. However, because traditional boundaries are generally respected, and the land has not been of significant interest to people from outside the region, resource mining has not occurred, nor has the demand for conservation-related investment been stunted. This is not to say that important natural resource management problems such as soil erosion, pesticide contamination, and deforestation do not exist, or that pressures such as land hunger and population growth which undermine historically accumulated social capital are not significant. However, tenure insecurity is not the principal cause of unsustainable natural resource management practices, and where social capital has been more successfully maintained,

---

[16] The average rural household is estimated to use the equivalent of two to three trees per month, or approximately 25–30 trees per year for fuelwood purposes. Of that, approximately half is estimated to be gathered in the form of dry wood and branches, while the other half comes from felled trees. Firewood accounts for 68% percent of total national energy consumption in Guatemala (Cabrera Gaillard 1991).

one also notes the most successful examples of natural resource conservation in the region.

Minifundio in the Western Highlands. The Western Highlands of Guatemala have long served as a reservoir for smallholding Mayan agriculturalists. First the Spanish colonizers and then a series of national modernizing reformers pushed the native population out of the coastal regions in order to dedicate these lands to export crops. The most recent Agricultural Census data indicate that over 40% of all farm units are located in the Western Highlands, nearly 95% of them (240,000 farms) smaller than 7 hectares and nearly half of these less than 0.7 hectares (Cambranes 1992).[17] Land use in the *minifundio* sector is based on the cultivation of maize and beans, normally in association with one another, sometimes with various species of squash. Taken together, nearly two-thirds of *minifundio* land in the Western Highlands is dedicated to annual crops, which, given the steep slopes of many parcels, is associated with high levels of land degradation, particularly soil erosion. While most plots are too small to accommodate a true forest reserve, Highland farmers frequently keep trees scattered among their crops, around their houses and along the boundaries of their parcels (Castañeda Salguero 1995).[18]

Table 2 illustrates the distinct bundles of land-related rights and restrictions exercised by smallholders under the four principal tenure regimes in the region: private ownership, rental, usufruct, and the tutelage of the government agrarian reform agency (INTA). It is clear that privately held parcels—even those with dubious legal documentation such as unregistered title, municipal declarations, and private documentation of various types—afford the user the greatest management and transfer rights. In the other three categories, the smallholder is limited by the rules established by the true owner: the landlord in the case of tenants, the lender in the case of usufruct, and the government in the case of INTA beneficiaries.

However, land tenure security, in the sense of lack of reasonable fear of eviction, for smallholders in the Western Highlands is not limited to those who hold registered

title. Much of the land in *minifundio* in the region is of no interest to powerful large landholders. Municipal authorization of land rights, while holding little value within the national legal system, is usually sufficient at the local level to stave off competing claims (Strochlic 1994). Most conflicts are between smallholders—many times family members—and communities, and are as often boundary disputes as competing claims over the same property. In many rural areas, informal conflict resolution mechanisms exist to mediate these land tenure disputes, which function as long as all parties are willing to respect customary law. In this sense, lack of formal property rights would not seem to affect the demand for investment (in both long-term productive and conservation activities), but rather only the supply of credit to finance such investments insofar as the capital market requires registered title as loan collateral.

The location specificity of these informal property rights thus illuminates both the strengths and weaknesses of social capital as a substitute for formal legal land tenure security. On the one hand, such arrangements appear to be more than adequate for dealing with informational and externality problems that may exist among the community of natural resource users: property boundaries are respected and individual holders have confidence that they will reap the benefits of long-term investments. On the other hand, the same geographic proximity that allows for the development and maintenance of the network of social relationships that permit informal solutions to these problems also limits their usefulness when it comes to interacting

---

[17] In Guatemala, as in the rest of Central America, land is commonly measured in *manzanas* (1 manzana = 7,000 m² = .7 hectares). Nationally, farms smaller than 10 *manzanas* (7 hectares), commonly referred to as *minifundio*, make up approximately 88% of the number of farms and 16% of the acreage under cultivation; of these, 35% are "microfarms" under 1 *manzana* (.7 hectares) in size (Cambranes 1992).

[18] The size of private forest reserves appears to increase with the size of landholdings, attesting to the fact that trees are considered an important resource when sufficient land is available. Approximately 20% of the small farm land in the Highlands is covered in forest and brush.

TABLE 2

BUNDLES OF RIGHTS UNDER DIFFERENT SMALLHOLDER LAND TENURE REGIMES IN THE WESTERN HIGHLANDS OF GUATEMALA

Nature of Right	Private Property	Rental	Usufruct	INTA
Acquisition	Purchase, inheritance or municipal/*parcialidad* concession	Contract for specific use with individual or municipality	Personal or municipal decision	Adjudication
Transfer	Full rights to bequest, sell, rent, or transfer usufruct rights[a]	No transfer of rental rights, usufruct or subrental	No inheritance, sale, rental, or usufruct transfers	No transfer, division, rental, or mortgaging; Bequest permitted only to previously indicated heirs; Exploitation must be direct (i.e., by beneficiary); Provisional or final title
Management[b]	Free, including improvements	May be limited by rental contract provisions	Free, including improvements	
Legal documentation	Escritura publica (may be registered in the RGP), private document, municipal act, document from the President of the *Parcialidad*	Verbal or written contract, municipal act	Municipal act	

Source: Castañeda Salguero (1995).

[a] In the case of former municipal lands, authorization is sometimes required for sale. In the case of private property that has been carved out of *parcialidades*, transfer is often limited to other members of the *parcialidad*.

[b] In the case of parcels under the prior or current jurisdiction of the *parcialidad*, some management norms may be set. All smallholders must obtain permission from the National Forest Service (DIGEBOS) for non-personal forest exploitation.

with non-group members. These limitations take on more importance, the greater the pressures are on users to deal with the "outside world." For example, with the introduction and adoption of high-value export crops in many Western Highland communities, regional factor markets have been activated to an extent that places farmers with informal tenure arrangements at a clear disadvantage relative to those with formal title (Barham, Carter, and Sigelko 1995). This suggests that social capital-based property rights may be more sustainable under conditions of relative economic isolation and less so where rapid integration with the larger market economy is occurring.

The principal environmental problems facing *minifundistas* in the Highlands—topsoil erosion, reduced farm-level biodiversity, and agrochemical contamination—are a reflection of the overintensification of their farming systems, and not resource mining or underinvestment, as is the case in El Petén. Small farmers in the Highlands invest quite heavily in non-capital intensive improvements such as leaving trees to stand, crop interplanting, careful working of the soil, terracing, live barrier cultivation, and frugal use of agrochemicals in domestic food crops. Their willingness to undertake these labor-intensive investments is due to the existence of informal social recognition of property rights—a manifestation of social capital—at the community level, which effectively replaces formal legal title, at least on the demand side. The real problems facing Highland small farmers, in terms of sustainable natural resource management, are their credit-constrained position in the rural capital market, the small size of their parcels, and the paucity of non-agricultural earning possibilities—daunting problems all, but not related to well-defined property rights in the usual sense.

Communal forests. The same historically and ethnically based social capital that serves to informally guarantee private property rights among Highland smallholders has enabled the co-owners of the region's remaining common property regimes to preserve large tracts of forest for subsistence

use and environmental functions.[19] Forests owned and managed by local communities (*bosques comunales*) and lineage groups (*parcialidades*) have in general been more successful than Highland municipalities at administering their common pool resources. More localized management of communal forests seems to be more effective in terms of the formulation and enforcement of use rules and sanctions, with consequences for the conservation of the resource for subsistence and commercial exploitation. Insofar as the village and not the municipality is the primary unit of social organization and identity, and it becomes more difficult to create and maintain social capital the larger and more heterogeneous the population, it is at the local level that CPR management is the most sustainable.[20]

Although there are no reliable data on the number and coverage of remaining communal lands in the Western Highlands of Guatemala, the most complete inventory to date (Elías Gramajo 1994) indicates the existence of some 94 communal forests in the 7 Highland Departments, with a total extension of 113,883 hectares. Legally, most communities claim ownership of their lands by virtue of the original colonial-era titles, some of which are registered in the National Property Regis-

[19] Veblen (1978) was the first to conjecture that, in contrast to other densely populated areas in Guatemala, the extraordinarily slow rate of contraction in the patchwork of communal forests belonging to several villages and kinship groups in the southwestern Quiché Maya region might be linked to the form of tenure governing their use. Subsequent case studies (Castellon 1992; Pisano de Valenzuela et al. 1991; Elías Gramajo 1994) have supported these findings and detailed the social, institutional, and ecological aspects of Highland communal forest management, which have been remarkably resilient in the face of significant population and land pressure. Landsat imagery from 1988 indicates that the forest area remains relatively stable, and that the minimal deforestation that has taken place is limited for the most part to parcels at lower elevations away from the large areas of contiguous forest, where the clearing of private woodlots for agriculture is a likely explanation (Castellon 1992).

[20] This supports Ostrom, Gardner, and Walker's (1994) finding that compliance with endogenously developed rules is higher than with rules imposed by outside authorities who are not themselves appropriators of the common property resource.

try or its predecessor, the Central American Archives.[21] Colonial titles and customary law use right recognition, however, are poorly validated outside the community, with negative implications for communities' ability to effectively utilize the formal, national credit and criminal justice systems. Nor does the current Forestry Law explicitly treat the case of communal forests.[22] Entering into contracts for forest management, including the establishment of plantations and reforestation, has proven to be easier for communities with registered title, since outside institutions frequently require this for legal transactions.

In economic terms, communal forests provide the rural poor with a secure source of firewood, organic fertilizer, and other products which they would otherwise have to obtain on the market.[23] Communal forests also play a key role in biodiversity conservation in the Highlands; many endangered species, such as the *Abies guatemalensis*, and other rare food and medicinal plants, have been preserved almost exclusively under this tenure regime (Elías Gramajo 1994). Most Western Highland communities engage in some sort of communal forest management, including reforestation, pruning, treatment of plagues and diseases, various preventative measures to protect the forest from fire, and protection of seed-producing trees and rare species. However, increasing demand for, and the existence of, few formally established norms governing the felling of whole trees has led to the selection of the largest and healthiest trees for this purpose, reducing the quality, density, and volume of the forest biomass (Ibid.). Large investments, such as the implementation of a forest management plan or the installation of a mill, are rare in these communal forests—with the important exception of the *parcialidades*, which tend to have a more developed level of internal organization and better-documented, formal property rights than other community-based groups. Authority over communal forest management is vested in a committee of local leaders who oversee maintenance activities, grant permission to fell trees, and represent the community in its dealings with outsiders. These committees form a part of the permanent structure of village life and are integrated with religious, civic, and political institutions that lie largely outside of the national government system.

Table 3 summarizes the possession, use, and transfer rights exercised by individuals within communal forest property regimes in the Western Highlands, and the restrictions and sanctions associated with these rights. Note that use rights in these regimes are both specific and exclusive. For example, many communities allow unrestricted access to community members for the collection of branches, fallen trees, stumps, and dry trunks, but the cutting of a live tree requires prior authorization.[24] Only members of the community may make use of the communal land's goods and services; community membership is usually defined by descendence from one of the established families, and strangers are easily identified.[25] To enforce this exclusivity, most communities have for-

---

[21] Any individual parcelization or other changes in the size and boundaries of these properties that may have occurred over the years tends to be recognized only within local customary law and not legally documented, so that communal lands formally retain their integral character.

[22] On the one hand, subsistence forest extraction is exempt from the licensing requirement; on the other, because of the large size of many communal forests, the Forestry Service (DIGEBOS) does in practice insist on prior authorization and the law does not guarantee community autonomy in this regard (Strochlic 1995).

[23] One recent study of the economic value of communal forests found that, even accounting for the opportunity cost of their time, rural families on average save US$170 per year by gathering their firewood instead of purchasing it (Gonzalez et al. 1994). The savings are even greater in the case of wood for construction or furniture making; while local authorities rarely charge more than US$10 for the right to cut down a mature tree, the market value of equivalent amount of wood could easily be five times that amount.

[24] Some communities only authorize cuttings during the dry season, so as to not affect natural regeneration. In others, saplings are explicitly protected, as are the areas around springs.

[25] In some communities, use rights are further limited to those community members who show an active interest in community affairs, for example, by belonging to one of the various committees, commissions, or other forms of local government. Others exclude family members who live outside the community. In the *parcialidades*, membership is clearly delimited in the organization's legal statutes.

TABLE 3

BUNDLES OF RIGHTS UNDER COMMUNAL FOREST REGIMES IN THE
WESTERN HIGHLANDS OF GUATEMALA

Nature of Right	Specifications	Restrictions and Sanctions
Acquisition	Inheritance or concession (generally made in perpetuity)	Cannot freely use communal land for agricultural purposes, nor sell to outsiders
Access	All community members have free access to communal forest	Access restricted for non-members of the community
Transfer	(1) Allocation of family plots for agricultural production	Transfer of individual rights to non-members of the community implicitly or explicitly prohibited
	(2) Sale, rental, or inheritance among community members	
	(3) Sale of communal lands, normally limited to distress sales to meet outstanding community obligations or debt	
	(5) Sale or rental of partial rights, such as grazing, logging concessions, or water sources.	
Firewood	For family consumption only	Authorization necessary for felling. Per family allowances normally governed by an annual quota. Accumulation and sale, especially outside of the community, are prohibited
Other wood	For construction and carpentry	Authorization necessary. Community may temporarily prohibit altogether to allow forest to recuperate
Plants	For medicines, adornments, and food	Restrictions regarding excess harvesting and sale
Hunting	Community members only	Sanctions applied to community members who facilitate the entry of non-members for hunting
Pasture	In pre-specified areas	Cannot enter forested areas
Organic litter (*broza*)	For use in compost piles or directly on crops	Restricted when natural regeneration is affected
Water	For human consumption	Springs come under community control

Source: Elías Gramajo (1994).

est guards and other forms of vigilance. Some communities also charge a fixed annual fee for the use of the forest.

While the detailed nature of the rules governing Highland communal forest use suggest a highly evolved CPR, it is important to note that these rules and their enforcement are normally quite informal, and sanctions are almost exclusively moral in character. This means that communities rely on socialized knowledge of, and respect for, a fairly restrictive set of use rights in order to preserve the resource. It is only insofar as the stock of social capital is sufficient to maintain this sense of collective responsibility, and to render effective purely moral sanc-

tions, that such an informal system can sustain itself and its natural resource base.

There are currently a number of internal and external pressures on communal forests which threaten these longstanding CPRs. Internally, population growth and land hunger, in the absence of national-level agrarian reform, have led to overexploitation of the forest resource, social pressure to parcel communal holdings, and intra-community conflicts between competing forest users. Externally, and also reflective of population pressure and land scarcity, as well as the failure of other land tenure regimes to conserve sufficient pine forest resources, communal forests are threatened by property disputes with neighboring landowners, invasions, and illicit extractions.[26]

In the face of these pressures, it may no longer be possible for Highland communities to rely exclusively on informal understandings, structures, and sanctions to guide the governance of their common property forests, and to practice such conservative forest management. This raises the controversial issue of whether there exist forms of intervention that can strengthen local governing institutions and formalize use rules and sanctions without threatening the "organic" nature of those institutions and rules as they have evolved historically. Here it seems important that such interventions recognize social capital as the basis for successful natural resource management and thereby focus on supporting activities that increase interaction and mutual trust among the relevant community of natural resource users, as opposed to targeting the resource management system itself via formal legislation and technological change. That is not to say that an significant part of conserving social capital does not lie in increasing the economic returns to sustainable resource management—it is clear that rewards to collective action act as an incentive for further such action. However, augmenting the value of the resource without commensurate "investment" in strengthening the bonds between common property managers runs the risk of contributing to the private incentives for overappropriation.

Municipal forests. As with communal lands, information on the extent of Highland municipal forests is hard to come by, and the few studies that exist are widely divergent in their estimates (CATEC 1993; Carrera and Contreras 1994). Under Guatemalan law, municipalities are considered "autonomous state entities," with rights over their own property, however, the exact legal status of these holdings is ambiguous.[27] Municipal forests are managed as common property regimes in the sense that residents have exclusive and specific use rights over the range of forest products. However, unlike the local communities that administer communal forests, municipalities are unable to draw on close-knit, long-term relationships (social capital) that

facilitate effective self-monitoring and enforcement of those use rights; nor have they successfully replaced these informal mechanisms with official incentives and sanctions for sustainable forest management.

Table 4 summarizes the use right specifications and sanctions that regulate municipal forest reserves in the Western Highlands. As with communal forests, access to municipal forests is limited to residents, and in many cases to full-time residents only. Even when access to or control over municipal forests is decentralized among the villages that belong to the municipality, revenues from licenses, fees, and the like accrue to the municipal seat (*cabecera*). Municipal forest management is limited to reforestation efforts, generally carried out with assistance from the Government Forest Service or NGOs, or by private companies interested in taking advantage of tax incentives for reforestation. While there is often considerable initial community support for these reforestation efforts, with large turn-outs to plant seedlings, enthusiasm often wanes when it comes to caring for the saplings; neither local reforestation committees nor forest guards take responsibility for post-reforestation maintenance (Strochlic 1995).

As in communal forests, specific use rules exist for the various products that can be ex-

---

[26] Several trends have also at least partially counterbalanced this increased pressure: greater reliance on chemical fertilizers has led to decreased use of forest litter as an organic fertilizer; the expansion of smallholder coffee production, with its associated shade trees, has increased private forest cover and reduced reliance on common property forests; and shepherding, an important cause of deforestation in some areas, is declining, due to increased use of synthetic fabrics and greater job possibilities in some Highland urban centers (Strochlic 1994).

[27] The current Forestry Law only entitles municipalities to authorize felling in forests lying within urban limits for quantities of wood under 25 m³ per year. Forest Service licensing is required for all other extractions for "non-personal use," including forest concessions on municipal land. The legal vacuum regulating the felling of trees for personal use (i.e., firewood) in municipal forest reserves located beyond urban limits has in fact been filled by the municipalities themselves, who regularly authorize such use. Unlike in El Petén, Highland municipalities rarely cede forest lands to individuals for conversion to farmland.

TABLE 4

BUNDLES OF RIGHTS UNDER MUNICIPAL FOREST REGIMES IN THE
WESTERN HIGHLANDS OF GUATEMALA

Nature of Right	Specifications	Restrictions and Sanctions
Forest access	Municipal residents only	Violators are conveyed to the courts or their own municipalities for sanctions
Firewood access	Unlimited collection of dry wood and branches for personal use. Tree felling by permit only, usually limited to 1–2 trees per year per household	Sanctions generally apply only for felling entire trees without a permit or for gathering dry wood more than the equivalent of one tree; violators may be charged the assessed value of the wood and/or a small fine
Access to wood for construction	Prohibited for personal use in most cases, with exception of communal projects and sometimes for the very poor	Same as for firewood
Access to wood for commercial purposes	Prohibited in virtually all cases	Violators may be fined the assessed value of the illegally acquired wood by the municipality or prosecuted in court. Contraband wood is generally confiscated, for sale by the municipality or distribution to community members
Grazing	Permitted in most cases, with some restrictions in recently reforested areas	No sanctions are generally applied for violations
Gathering *broza*	Few restrictions for personal use; charge for commercial use	No sanctions are generally applied for violations
Gathering resin, ocote and bark	Permitted on a limited scale in most places, as long as it does not kill the tree	Few sanctions for gathering resin and ocote; removing bark is a more serious offense, and can result in remittance to the courts
Conversion of forest land to farmland	Prohibited in virtually all cases	Few sanctions, since the process is gradual and generally unnoticed
Other uses—hunting, gathering fruits and medicinal plants, pine needles, etc.	No restrictions on other uses	

Source: Strochlic (1995).

tracted from municipal forests.[28] Most municipalities charge only nominal fees for permits to fell trees, and there is normally no charge for non-wood forest products. Community participation in the decision-making process regarding use rules is minimal; the mayor and the municipal council (posts which are often dominated by Ladinos) administer the forests in a fairly top-down fashion.

The monitoring and enforcement of use rules in municipal forests is generally weak, and infractions are common. Municipalities commonly have a few, unpaid forest guards who are on the whole ineffective in combating use rule violations, and residents rarely monitor or ''denounce'' one another for infractions of use rights in municipal forests. Unlike communal forests, where control and management are more localized, municipal forest users sense a lack of authority to take actions against intruders; the municipality is often seen as an antagonistic ''other,'' creating a sense of complicity among residents (Ibid.). Sanctions for use rule violations consist primarily of confiscation of the illegally

[28] For example, while dry wood and branches, *broza* (forest litter used as organic fertilizer), fruits, edible and medicinal plants may be gathered as needed, special permission must be obtained to extract entire trees for firewood or construction purposes, and restrictions may exist on products such as kindling, resins and bark, so that their extraction does not harm the tree.

felled wood or payment of its assessed value—equivalent to the cost of a permit but significantly below market value—and nominal fines.

Thus, while there is a well-defined set of rules regulating user behavior and restraining resource use on municipal lands, the social organization of the formulation and monitoring of these rules does not correspond to the realities of Highland social organization, which is based much more on the community (village) than on the municipality. Within municipalities, there is a strong urban-rural divide (often overlaid by a Ladino-Indian divide) which, when combined with a centralization of control over common property resources, inhibits the social cohesion necessary for sustainable management of those resources. Municipalities may therefore not be meaningful units for resource management regimes that rely on shared interests and collective decision-making (social capital); in the Western Highlands, natural resource management at the municipal level is probably not local enough.

IV. CONCLUSION AND POLICY IMPLICATIONS

This article has argued that social capital should be treated on par with property rights as a determinant of natural resource management practices. It has shown that where the legal status of natural resources (here, land and forest) is insecure or ambiguous, as it is in much of the developing world, informal mechanisms can evolve among the users of those natural resources to counteract externality problems and create the appropriate incentive structure for sustaining natural capital. In the case of individualized tenure, this involves recognition of, and respect for, property boundaries, a customary legal system strong enough to support inter-generational and other intra-community transfers, as well as the absence of the threat of external expropriation. In the case of common property resources, social capital facilitates the establishment of viable governing organizations, use rules, and sanctions. And in both systems, interaction among natural resource

users generates shared environmental knowledge that can be used to adapt natural resource management practices to the local ecosystem.

The Guatemalan case study, which draws on previously unpublished field-based data, illustrates the importance of social capital in both private and common property regimes. Comparing migrant farmers in El Petén with subsistence Highland agriculturalists, we have seen that both groups of smallholders face some common obstacles to sustainable natural resource management: their scale of production and level of poverty, which mitigate against many natural resource management practices requiring either additional factors of production or relatively low discount rates, their limited technological options to overcoming what are essentially ecological constraints, and the inherent linkage of their situation to the national agrarian problem of unequal land distribution. At the same time, important historical differences distinguish the degree to which small farmers in El Petén and the Western Highlands can draw on social capital to counteract the effects of their insecure land tenure.

The Highlands, which have served as a reservoir of the rural, mostly indigenous population since the colonial period, is characterized by relative ethnic and socio-economic homogeneity, long-term settlement in microregions and individual communities, and significant land scarcity. These characteristics have led to the development of a customary legal system which exists primarily at a local level and serves to guarantee property boundaries and intra-group transfers, as well as the accumulation of detailed environmental knowledge which has allowed small farmers to intensify their land use as population pressures have increased. In contrast, migrants to El Petén are socio-economically heterogeneous, recent arrivals struggling with an unfamiliar ecosystem, and prone to short-term tenure on any given plot of land, in part due to the nature of the ecosystem and in part to the perception of continued land availability. All these factors, in combination with the strong role of the national government in defining smallholder tenure status and use rights, have inhibited the formation of local social institutions, which in turn has encouraged boundary-marking and resource mining practices.

Common property regimes in the two regions are similarly affected by the distinct histories and resulting discrepancies in social capital. In the municipal lands of El Petén, the transient nature of *ejiditario* status has contributed to the failure of the governing bodies to control deforestation and land degradation, and to benefit from resource rents. In the Highlands, communal natural resource management regimes, based on highly local forms of social identification and well-established social norms, have been key to the preservation of the region's pine forest ecosystem.

Of course, social capital should not be treated statically; just because a high degree of social cohesion has evolved historically does not mean that it is impervious to atomizing pressures, and similarly, historically atomized groups may face conditions in which they begin to interact and undertake some form of collective action. In the Guatemalan case, it is clear that Highland smallholders and CPR users face the significant challenge of maintaining their customary legal structures, informal arrangements, and local institutions in the face of rapidly appreciating land and forest product values brought on by commercialization, population pressure, and land hunger in the absence of national-level agrarian reform. Meanwhile, as the agricultural frontier reaches its limits in El Petén, settlers will increasingly seek out ways to extend the productive life of their farms, which may put them into greater contact with their neighbors and begin the slow process of social capital formation.

The implications of this analysis for policy are twofold. First, where resources to regularize land tenure for natural resource management improvement purposes are scarce, it makes sense to prioritize areas with weak social capital stocks where informal solutions to externality problems are not forthcoming. In the Guatemalan case, this means that the net social benefits (at least in environmental terms) to, for example, a land titling campaign, would be higher in El Petén than in

the Highlands. In agricultural frontier areas like El Petén, the likely effect of formal title would be a reduction in defensive land clearing and greater incentives for demographic stability. This could in turn contribute to the development of more stable networks of social relationships, reinforcing the titling impact. In long-settled areas characterized by intensive agriculture, in contrast, the principal effect of land tenure formalization is collateralization, which will only increase farmers' access to capital (some proportion of which may be invested in natural resource conservation) insofar as informational, transaction cost and other credit market constraints are not more important determinants of limited credit access.

The second policy implication is that investments in social capital should go hand in hand with investments in natural capital. In places where a relatively strong social infrastructure linked to natural resource management already exists, like the Western Highlands, this may mean providing resources for institutional strengthening to help local groups adapt to internal and external pressures, along with policies to alleviate those pressures, such as substantive land reform. In places like El Petén, the challenge to policy makers is to facilitate the conditions for the initial formulation of social capital, which may involve closing off the agricultural frontier as well as providing appropriate incentives for collective action solutions to shared natural resource management problems.

References

AHT/APESA (Agrar-Und Hydrotechnick GMBH– Asesoría y Promoción Económica S.A.). 1992. *Plan de Desarollo Integrado de Petén: Programa de Emergencia de Protección de la Selva Tropical, Diagnóstico General del Petén Vol. 1.*

Barham, Bradford, Michael R. Carter, and Wayne Sigelko. 1995. "Agro-export Production and Peasant Land Access: Examining the Dynamic Between Adoption and Accumulation." *Journal of Development Economics* 46 (1): 85–107.

Beavers, John. 1995. *Natural Resource Tenure and Forest Exploitation in the Petén and*

Franja Transversal del Norte Regions of Guatemala. Consultant's Report to the World Bank.

Berkes, Fikret, and Carl Folke. 1994. "Investing in Cultural Capital for Sustainable Use of Natural Capital." In *Investing in Natural Capital: The Ecological Economics Approach to Sustainability,* ed. AnnMari Jansson, Monica Hammer, Carl Folke, and Robert Costanza. Washington, D.C.: Island Press.

Cabrera Gaillard, Claudio. 1991. "El manejo de los bosques naturales en el trópico húmedo, algunas consideraciones para su viabilidad económica. *Tikalia* 8 (1/2): 127–40.

———. 1995. *Estudio Sobre Tenencia y Uso de Recursos Naturales en la Franja Transversal y Departamento de Petén, Componente Ejidos Municipales y Areas Protegidas.* Consultant's Report to the World Bank.

Cambranes, Julio Castellanos. 1992. *500 Años de Lucha Por la Tierra.* Guatemala: Facultad Latinoamericana de Ciencias Sociales.

Carrera C., Jaime A., and Byron H. Contreras M. 1994. *Estudio de la capacidad instalada en las municipalidades para la producción y manejo de información registral-catastral.* Consultants' Report to USAID Guatemala.

Castañeda Salguero, César. 1995. *Tenencia y Manejo de los Recursos Naturales en los Minifundios del Altiplano Occidental Guatemalteco.* Consultant's Report to the World Bank.

Castellon, Michael J. 1992. *Communal Forest Preservation in Totonicapán, Guatemala.* Master's thesis, University of Wisconsin-Madison.

CATEC, S.A. 1994. Manejo y utilización sostenible de bosques naturales de coníferas en Guatemala. Consultant's Report to PROCAFOR (Programa Regional Forestal Para Centro América).

Coleman, James S. 1987. "Norms as Social Capital." In *Economic Imperialism: The Economic Approach Applied Outside the Field of Economics,* ed. Gerard Radnitzky and Peter Bernholz. N.Y.: Paragon House.

———. 1990. *Foundations of Social Theory.* Cambridge: Harvard University Press.

Dasgupta, Partha. 1997. "Economic Development and the Idea of Social Capital." In *Social Capital: Integrating the Economist's and the Sociologist's Perspectives,* ed. P. Dasgupta and I. Serageldin. Washington, D.C.: The World Bank.

Early, J. D. 1982. *The Demographic Structure and Evolution of a Peasant System: The Guatemalan Population.* Boca Raton: University Press of Florida.

Elías Gramajo, Silvel. 1994. *Tenencia y manejo de los recursos naturales en las tierras comunales del altiplano guatemalteco.* Consultant's Report to the World Bank.

Feder, Gershon, and Tongroj Onchan. 1987. "Land Ownership Security and Farm Investment in Thailand." *American Journal of Agricultural Economics* 69 (2): 311–20.

Friedman, James W. 1986. *Game Theory with Applications to Economics.* N.Y.: Oxford University Press.

Gonzales, G. et al. 1994. "Estudio de consumo de leña y potencialidades del astillero municipal de San Andrés Itzapa Chimaltenango." Informe de Cursos Especializados, Facultad de Agronomía, USAC.

Granovetter, M. 1985. "Economic Action and Social Structure: The Problem of Embeddedness." *American Journal of Sociology* 91 (3): 481–510.

Kaimowitz, David. 1994. *Land Tenure, Land Markets, and Natural Resource Management by Large Landowners in the Petén and the Northern Transversal of Guatemala.* Consultant's Report to the World Bank.

Ostrom, Elinor. 1994. "Neither Market nor State: Governance of Common-Pool Resources in the Twenty-First Century." Lecture presented at the International Food Policy Research Institute, June 2, 1994. Workshop in Political Theory and Policy Analysis, Indiana University, Bloomington: Indiana University.

Ostrom, Elinor, Roy Gardner, and James Walker. 1994. *Rules, Games and Common-Pool Resources.* Ann Arbor: University of Michigan Press.

Pisano de Valenzuela, Ileana, con la colaboración de Ing. César Castañeda y Lic. Carlos Mendoza. 1991. "La Dinámica Social de la Deforestación en Totonicapán (Guatemala)." United Nations Research Institute for Social Development (UNRISD).

Platteau, Jean-Philippe. 1994. "Behind the Market Stage Where Real Societies Exist – Part I: The Role of Public and Private Order Institutions." *Journal of Development Studies* 30 (3): 533–77.

———. 1994. "Behind the Market Stage Where Real Societies Exist—Part II: The Role of Moral Norms." *Journal of Development Studies* 30 (4): 753–817.

Putnam, Robert. 1993. *Making Democracy Work: Civic Traditions in Modern Italy.* Princeton: Princeton University Press.

Robles, Teresa. 1994. *Smallholder Migrants in El Petén.* Consultant's Report to the World Bank.

Robison, Lindon J., and Steven D. Hanson. 1995. "Social Capital and Economic Cooperation."

Journal of Agricultural and Applied Economics 27 (1): 43–58.

Sader, S.A., T. Sever, J. C. Smoot, and M. Richards. 1994. "Forest Change Estimates for the Northern Petén Region of Guatemala—1986–1990." *Human Ecology* 22 (3): 317–32.

Schmid, A. Allan, and Lindon J. Robison. 1995. "Applications of Social Capital Theory." *Journal of Agricultural and Applied Economics* 27 (1): 59–66.

Secaira, Estuardo. 1992. Conservation among the Q'eqchi'-Maya: A Comparison of Highland and Lowland Agriculture. Master's thesis, University of Wisconsin–Madison.

Southgate, D., and M. Basterrechea. 1992. "Population Growth, Public Policy and Resource Degradation: The Case of Guatemala." *Ambio* 21 (7): 460–64.

Strochlic, Ronald. 1994. *Preliminary Report on Factors Associated with Tenure Insecurity Among Smallholders in Guatemala*. Consultant's Report to the World Bank.

———. 1995. *Natural Resource Tenure and Management of Municipal Forest Reserves in the Guatemalan Highlands*. Consultant's Report to the World Bank.

Theisenhusen, William C. 1985. *Broken Promises: Agrarian Reform and the Latin American Campesino*. Boulder: Westview.

USAID. 1981. *Land and Labor in Guatemala: An Assessment*. Washington, D.C.: USAID.

Veblen, Thomas. 1978. "Forest Preservation in the Western Highlands of Guatemala." *The Geographical Review* 68 (4): 417–34.

Wachter, Daniel. 1992. Land Titling for Land Conservation in Developing Countries? Divisional Working Paper No. 1992–28. Policy and Research Division, Environmental Department, The World Bank.

Wade, Robert. 1987. "The Management of Common Property Resources: Collective Action as an Alternative to Privatisation or State Regulation." *Cambridge Journal of Economics* 11 (2): 95–106.

C
Natural Capital

[10]

NATURAL AND REPRODUCIBLE CAPITAL AND THE SUSTAINABILITY OF LAND USE IN THE UK

Martin Whitby and W. Neil Adger*

The article reviews the relevant concepts in assessing sustainability at the sector level for British agriculture and forestry. It notes that the use of reproducible capital is not sustainable in the sector as depreciation has exceeded gross fixed capital formation for some years, although that retrenchment may, however, be an appropriate response to expected lower farm prices and increased efficiency in the use of capital. It then exemplifies the problems of measuring the sustainability of use of natural capital by reference to specific problems, namely the release of global pollutants from agriculture and forestry, the economic cost of soil erosion and the economic cost associated with damage to Sites of Special Scientific Interest (SSSI). On the basis of a wider review of the context of these changes, it is concluded that the sustainability of primary land use, as currently practised, must await substantial research before positive claims can be made for its overall sustainability.

1. Introduction

The intergenerational equity arguments for sustainable development, popularised by the Brundtland Commission (World Commission on Environment and Development, 1987), have led economists to focus on maintenance of capital stocks as an indicator of whether welfare will be sustained over future time periods. The environmental aspect of sustainable development has thus led to the definition of the natural resource base as environmental capital, to distinguish it from reproducible or man-made capital, and to the re-estimation of aggregate income and welfare measures (Lutz, 1993, for example). The land use sector utilises and has impacts on substantial natural capital. For the UK it has previously been estimated that the land use detector contributes more to aggregate welfare (modified Net Product) than is shown in traditional measures, due to the non-marketed services provided by that sector (Adger and Whitby, 1993). However, who

* Martin Whitby is Professor of Countryside Management in the Centre for Rural Economy, University of Newcastle, Newcastle upon Tyne, NR1 7RU and Neil Adger is a Senior Research Associate in the Centre for Social and Economic Research on the Global Environment, University of East Anglia, Norwich, NR4 7TJ, and University College London. An earlier version of this paper was presented at the Agricultural Economics Society Conference, *Problems and Prospects for a Sustainable Rural Economy*, Royal Society, London, 13th December 1993. The authors thank Paul Allanson, Robert Evans and David Harvey for helpful comments on an earlier version, though responsibility remains with the authors alone.

NATURAL AND REPRODUCIBLE CAPITAL AND THE SUSTAINABILITY OF LAND USE 51

should receive the credit for such additions to welfare depends on whether they arise in spite of land use activity or because of it. It has been argued that income measures are incapable of representing welfare more generally, and that the only feasible adjustments are therefore associated with capital stock changes, thereby retaining the original Hicksian concept of income (Mäler, 1991; Common, 1995).

In this paper, a rigorous definition of sustainability in the land use sector is adopted and illustrative estimates are made of the value of changes in the resource base for the late 1980s. The approach is necessarily national in scale and is not concerned with the financial or environmental sustainability of particular production systems. One reason why sustainability has become widely used as a concept is that it can be applied at all levels of argument. Thus, as pointed out by Buttel (1993), chemical companies have no difficulty in promoting increased use of inputs as adding to the "financial sustainability" of farming. The definition applied here, however, is deliberately narrow, focusing on renewable and non-renewable resources as stocks of natural capital at the national level.

The paper begins by briefly setting out the relationship between the stock of capital and sustainability in an economic framework. In the agricultural sector the changing rates of capital formation and depreciation are examined over recent decades. The paper then considers three resource stocks for the UK as examples of the resource stock measurements which should feature in a sustainability indicator; the stock of carbon in soils, plants and related global pollutants; the aggregate value of soil erosion losses in an area where the greatest losses are occuring; and the value of degradation of Sites of Special Scientific Interest; assessing their changing annual value in recent years. Finally it presents tentative conclusions regarding the sustainability of production from the land base.

2.   A Capital Depreciation Indicator of Sustainability

The familiar economic definition of sustainability as requiring a non-declining capital stock over time stems from the Bruntland Commission's criterion as that which allows future generations to meet their own needs (WCED, 1987). To derive an economic definition of sustainability which then leads to a set of rules for environmental management, it is necessary to treat the environment as a stock of natural capital. This is not controversial when non-renewable natural capital, such as oil and coal reserves, are the focus. For renewable resources, such as many associated with the agricultural and forestry sectors, again there is no conceptual difficulty with sustainability criteria which require that these stocks should not decline over time, except to the extent allowed by increased efficiency of utilisation.

However, the rules of non-declining capital vary in their applicability. Potentially there will be trade-offs between different types of capital: indeed models of economic growth have traditionally been based on the non-exploitive use of non-renewable resources for the building-up of the reproducible capital base. So, if sustainability can be maintained even while depleting renewable or non-renewable resources, how are the net changes to be valued? Non-renewable resources are often not traded in markets and are therefore difficult to price. It is the adaptation of surrogate prices to value changes in these capital stocks which cause controversy and which limit the reproducibility of an annual accounting system for environmental change in the capital account (Atkinson, 1994).

Given changes in the stocks of renewable and non-renewable resources, a test for sustainability in the capital account is to examine whether net additions to the total capital stock are greater than zero. Additions to the stock of reproducible capital come through investment being greater than depreciation. So, for the stock to be non-declining over time requires that:

$$I - \delta_m K_m - \delta_n K_n > 0 \tag{1}$$

where I = investment
  δ = rate of depreciation of capital stock
  K = capital
  n = natural
  m = reproducible

Some qualifications are needed here. First, this definition assumes that natural and reproducible capital are perfect substitutes for each other. This is the weakest definition of sustainability (Turner, 1993). In practice, the substitutability of natural capital is the key question, one which depends in the long run on factors such as irreversibility and technological change. So, in the context of land resources, a weak definition of sustainability would allow depletion of the quality or quantity of wildlife habitat, so long as the development resulted in an overall increase in the total stock of capital. Second, if a stronger definition of sustainability were adopted, one in which irreversible changes to critical natural capital were deemed unsustainable, then such quantitative or qualitative changes would immediately render the sector unsustainable. Ultimately the decision as to what constitutes critical natural capital is outside the realm of economic analysis and would be based on criteria such as the resilience of ecosystems and the threshold levels of pollutants. A third complication arises in the case of renewable and recyclable natural resources (McInerney, 1976) where some rate of extraction is sustainable . Renewables might be handled by counting only destruction or exploitation which exceeded the natural rate of regeneration or would risk reducing future annual increments. This is most relevant to the quantity and quality of habitats discussed below.

3. Reproducible Capital in UK Agriculture

The minimum requirement for sustainability in the agricultural sector is for the total capital stock to grow at the same rate as output, after allowing for changes in technical efficiency. Changes in the stock of reproducible capital, allowing substitution of inputs, labour and other capital, means that agricultural output can be produced at less resource cost. During the fifteen years prior to 1992, as shown in Figure 1, the formation of new reproducible capital in agriculture has fluctuated, as a percentage of gross product, though tending generally downwards throughout the period. By contrast the industry's depreciation bill has fluctuated less, as befits an accounting aggregate embodying the accumulated rate of capital formation over several previous years, and has generally trended upwards in the first part of the period and turned down since the late 1980s.

This analysis of reproducible capital would imply that previous levels of agricultural production were not sustainable unless offset by productivity improvements through technical and structural change. Another interpre-

NATURAL AND REPRODUCIBLE CAPITAL AND THE SUSTAINABILITY OF LAND USE 53

Figure 1   Agricultural Gross Capital Formation and Depreciation: 1972-1992

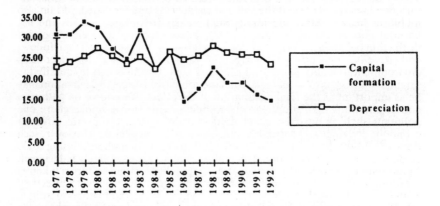

Source: MAFF (1994)

tation would be that the industry's planned output is declining in the medium term and that its optimal capital stock is therefore also on a downward path. In practice both of these arguments are likely to apply. However, decreasing capitalisation of agriculture at the industry level does not necessarily reduce the local environmental impact of particular practices. Indeed it is still the case that the use of reproducible capital and current inputs are a substantial source of degradation of natural capital. Examples are the draining of wetlands and the removal of traditional field boundaries (Barr *et al.*, 1993). The extent of natural capital degradation is explored through three major impacts later.

Valuation of the environment changes to the stock of natural capital in the land use sector applied here relate to non-renewable, non-priced assets, such as amenity, wildlife, soil degradation and global pollutants. In addition to consistent definitions of natural capital it is necessary to identify all the relevant items of capital to be assessed. One might begin by recognising a Ricardian concept of natural capital as constituting the "original and indestructible powers of the soil". However, this should be extended to include recreational capacity, habitats, wildlife and, even livestock and growing crops, which are not included in conventional definitions of reproducible capital. The impact of acidification on soils and waters, mainly through acid rain, is a source of natural capital loss which is barely attributable to land use practices and would be assigned to the natural capital accounts for manufacturing industry or the energy sector. Other possible inclusions would be the drawdown and quality change in rivers, lakes and aquifers. Extending into the hydrological system would bring further additions including the quality of surface and marine waters for human use and direct consumption.

The case for treating the effects of acid rain, aquifer depletion and at least a major part of water quality deterioration within the accounts of other sectors, emphasises the particular problem of analysing natural capital degradation which is not easily treated within the conventional sectors of the national income accounts. The general problem would appear to be that we have to focus on the common property attributes (Dorfman, 1974) of land, air and water to identify these issues. Dorfman stresses the role of common property resources in transmitting externalities from one economic agent to another. Thus land receives acid rain generated from power stations and other sources, this increases the acidity of the soil and changes its fertility. The acid rain also mobilises heavy metals and assists their transport to water courses and has harmful impacts on trees (Innes, 1992). These cases point to the important distinction between the originator of an externality, the pathway it then follows and its final receptor. If corrections are to be made for decreased environmental quality in sectoral accounts then it is important to identify the origin: if damage is to be assessed then the route from origin to destination may be as important as the final destination of the effect. If we focus on pathways and destinations then problems of multiple origins (for example where one pollutant such as nitrogen is released into the system by several different economic activities and natural systems) have to be recognised. However, such a line of reasoning serves to divert research into a situation where nothing could be done until the whole national income accounts were completely redesigned. In this paper, the difficulty in allocating externalities within sectors is taken as requiring caution in offering generalisations about the aggregate effects of capital degradation through land using activities. If the externalities identified are all negative it may be possible to reach tentative conclusions about the direction of damage and the requirements for further research.

The elements of environmental externalities listed above may be grouped into:—

> changes in the global public nature of environmental resources, such as air and sea;
>
> changes in quality or quantity of renewable natural resources, such as soil, water and natural forests;
>
> changes in quality or quantity of recreational and other amenities, such as landscape;
>
> changes in ecological indicators for wildlife habitats, such as hedgerows, ancient woods and semi-natural grasslands.

The quantity of each of these types of capital may be affected in several different ways and as a list they present diverse problems of monetary quantification, not least being the availability of quantitative data as to the scale, time distribution and impact of the changes. Three case studies for analysis as indicators of the types of measurement problem encountered are illustrated in the following section. The first is damage to the global environment through emissions of greenhouse gases; the second is soil erosion and the third is damage to wildlife habitats. These adjustments to the value of the capital stock are indicative of the much broader effects requiring analysis if sustainability is to be a serious objective of policy. The article ends with some discussion of future research implications.

4.   Natural Capital Depreciation in the UK Land Use Sector

Land Use as a Global Polluter

On a global scale, land using activities, and especially the global trends of land use change, contribute to the increasing atmospheric concentrations of greenhouse gases, in the range of 15 to 30 per cent of the total annual increase of gases from all sources (Edmonds *et al.*, 1992). The global trends towards loss

NATURAL AND REPRODUCIBLE CAPITAL AND THE SUSTAINABILITY OF LAND USE 55

of forests and to the draining of wetlands both contribute to the observed atmospheric concentrations (Houghton *et al.*, 1990). Although there is great uncertainty as to the consequences of these increases, it is clear that the impacts will be sea level rise affecting the low-lying regions of the world; changes in ecosystems and agricultural productivity due to changes in temperature and precipitation; and changes in the frequency of extreme climatic events. Other economic consequences of the greenhouse effect will impact on energy demand and the availablity of water.

The main sources in agriculture and forestry which generate net emissions of greenhouse gases are, methane from ruminants and from stored livestock waste; nitrous oxide emissions from the use of fertilisers; and the carbon stock changes due to changes in the standing biomass and soil carbon pools. Estimates of the annual fluxes of the various gases for the UK for the late 1980s are given in Table 1. The estimates of carbon storage are derived from Adger *et al.* (1992) where the stock changes in soil and biomass are estimated from a database of changes in land use in Great Britain in the period 1947-1980 and assumed to be constant throughout the 1980s. The estimated 21 million tonnes (mt) CO_2 which is sequestered by the UK land use sector, derives mainly from land retained in the same use, where the soil carbon pool (and above ground biomass in forestry) has been accumulating. The trends in land use in the UK, primarily the loss of broadleaved woodland and afforestation with coniferous species, increased arable cultivation, and the loss of upland semi-natural habitat, generate a net emission of carbon dioxide annually. CH_4 and N_2O are also emitted from the land use sector: CH_4 from livestock directly and from stored manures, and N_2O from application of fertilisers at a rate of 0.5–2.0 per cent of total applications. What then is the cost of these emissions, which are stock changes in one form of natural capital?

Table 1   Estimating the Damage Cost of Greenhouse Gas Emissions from the UK Land Use Sector.

Greenhouse Gas	Net Annual Emission (Million tonnes)	Global Warming Potential	Equivalent Annual Emissions (mt C Equivalent)	Unit Damage Cost (£ per t C)	Total (£ million)
(1)	(2)	(3)	(4)	(5)	(6)
CO_2					
—sequestrations	−25.026	1	−6.819	13	−88.6
—emissions	3.314	1	0.903	13	11.7
CH_4	1.395	17-32	6.468-12.174	13	84.1-158.3
N_2O	0.065	320	4.782	13	62.2
Total	—	—	6.225-11.931	—	80.9-155.1

Sources and Notes: In column 2, +ve = emissions, −ve = sequestration.

Emissions: CO_2 based on Adger *et al.*, (1992), CH_4 and N_2O based on Adger and Brown (1993).

Global Warming Potential (GWP) is the "time integrated commitment to climate forcing from the instantaneous release of 1 kg of a trace gas relative to that from 1 kg of CO_2," (Watson *et al.*, 1990, p.58). The GWPs reported are based on direct only relative climate forcing apart from CH_4 which includes indirect effects and is based on a lagged response time (see Houghton *et al.*, 1995).

Damage Costs: Based on monetary estimate of global warming damage avoided. Fankhauser (1995) puts this value (for present emissions) at approximately \$20 per tC, which is £13 per tC (or £47.7 per t CO_2) used here.

The stock adjustment can be estimated as the social cost of the environmental externality. This is derived in Table 1, first by converting emissions of the different greenhouse gases to tonnes of carbon-equivalent, weighing each by their global warming potential (column 3); the emissions are then costed with a monetary estimate of the social cost of the impact of global climate change; to arrive at the damage estimate range of £80.9 to £155.1 million in column 6 of Table 1. The range reflects uncertainty surrounding the role of methane as a direct and an indirect greenhouse gas (Houghton *et al.*, 1995).

The impacts of global warming are likely to be skewed geographically and vulnerability to them will be related to the availability of adaptive options and the distribution of resources. Policies or activities which reduce or postpone the impacts of climate change have a global social value. Various studies have attempted to estimate economic (and hence lower bound) damage costs, based on the economic costs of the mentioned impacts (Cline, 1992; Fankhauser, 1995; Nordhaus, 1992). The economic estimates are based on welfare changes: for example, if agricultural production is reduced in western Europe due to climatic factors, this may have welfare benefits to countries outside Europe (see Kane *et al.*, 1992).

The estimate used to value the physical quantities in Table 1 is that of Fankhauser (1995) of £13 per tC for present emissions. The aggregate estimate for CO_2 is negative damage, reflecting the fact that agriculture and forestry are net sequestrators of carbon on an annual basis. This estimate should be qualified by the argument that much of the carbon fixed within the sector is sold as food which is quickly returned to the environment through human and animal digestive systems. Methane, arising mainly from livestock, is damaging because of its potency as a greenhouse gas. Nitrous oxide emissions as a result of fertiliser use are a primary anthropogenic source of total emissions (amounting to 40.6 per cent of total). Total N applications in the UK for 1988 amounted to 1.53 million tonnes of N. This generates emissions of 0.0225 to 0.0915m tonnes N_2O, the range depending on management practices and soil types. A central estimate of 0.065 tonnes of N_2O is given in Table 1.

Collectively these calculations give a lower bound estimate of the monetary value of global warming damage, primarily because the unit value on which they are based does not include the non-market costs of damage (for example those to natural ecosystems) but also because it is calculated within the national income accounting convention that the accounts record events within a sector, ignoring the obvious spillovers to other parts of the economy (as in the case noted above). The results here show that between £80 and £155 million of damage per year is attributable to the UK emissions of greenhouse gases from the land use sector. Even then, emissions are relatively small in comparison with the other sectors of the UK economy, the sequestration of CO_2 amounting to only 0.72 per cent of total UK emissions in 1988 (Adger and Brown, 1993).

Soil Degradation

Soil degradation results in loss of soil productivity and the eroded material may generate off-site costs where it is deposited. For example, wind eroded soil may also reduce crop germination if it is deposited on newly planted land. Degradation is not a widely recognised phenomenon in the UK but it may become problematic in particular locations. One such location is the peatlands of Cambridgeshire where there has been rapid degradation of rich peat soils following drainage. The process here is wider than erosion, including shrinkage, consolidation and aerobic breakdown, as well as wind erosion.

NATURAL AND REPRODUCIBLE CAPITAL AND THE SUSTAINABILITY OF LAND USE 57

The loss of eighty per cent of these soils over 30 to 40 years implies an annual compound loss of peatland which is equivalent to some 1.7 per cent per year. Valuation of this loss, as natural capital, can be undertaken by capitalising the difference between the value added from cropping peatlands and that from the soil types remaining after the peat has been degraded. In practice there are several different possibilities for such soils after they have lost their peat, depending on the nature of the subsoil on which they lie (Evans, 1981). Some sub-soils may mix with the remaining peat to produce higher yields than the original peat; others, particularly those on lighter land will suffer losses in productivity. Where the sub-soil is clay, timeliness of cultivations may become problematic and costs increase. Some changes in cultivation practice may ameliorate the loss of peat; for example deep ploughing when the peat depth becomes sufficiently thin may, by incorporating mineral subsoil, slow down the rate of loss. Maintaining water tables as high as possible may also help to retain peat, as may increasing the proportion of grass in the rotation. Lack of knowledge about the rate of change of farming practices in the Fens makes it difficult to predict what rate of loss is currently occurring and what will be the post-degradation level of production per hectare obtainable on this land.

If we assume that one level of productivity will gradually be transformed to another over a future period, then the rate of loss may be taken as a constant compound proportion of the initial stock and the loss in year n will be:

$$\delta S = [(1-i)^n - (1-i)^{n+1}] * S \qquad (2)$$

where S = original stock and
       i = the annual compound rate of loss.

Starting from 30,855 ha in 1970, with i at 1.7 per cent per annum, the 1992 value of the stock would be 17,002 ha and the annual disappearance from this would be 289.0 ha. Valuation of this loss is then the annual cost of the difference in value added, in this case between Fen Arable land and East Anglian Cereal Farms. Over the four years 1988/9 to 1991/2 (Murphy, 1991 to 1993) this difference has averaged £261.3 (indexed to 1992 using RPI) for the two sub-samples. No detail of the breakdown of value added by size is given, but it is reported that the average size of sampled cereal farms was 189.0 ha for 1990/91 whilst for fen arable farms it was 128.1 ha. There were more farms in the cereal group than in the fen arable group and, although a breakdown of net farm income by area of farm is reported, this tells us little or nothing about whether there are important differences in input costs between these two groups of farms. To proceed beyond this point it is necessary to assume that the two samples are on the flat portion of the average cost curve, so that scale differences will be small enough to ignore.

There is also a particular problem with projecting current levels of value added forward over long periods. The introduction of arable area payments in 1993 as compensation for support price reductions, cannot be seen as part of value added. The future stream of value added may also fall under the impact of lower farm gate prices made acceptable by rising productivity and the low income elasticity of demand for foods at the farm gate. It therefore seems inappropriate to assume that present rates of value added may be projected into the long term future. Evidence in favour of falling rates of value added may be projected into the future. Both of these are known to have occurred over some decades although the appropriate rates for these types of farm is not known. In the absence of quantitative evidence we fall back on assumptions.

First, we discount the difference in gross value added between the two groups of farms at 6 per cent over 50 years and 100 years, which gives differences in the value of soil loss of £4,366 to £4,603. Alternatively, discounting at 7 per cent — equivalent to a 6 per cent discount rate increased by 1 per cent — to allow for the long term decline in value added per hectare gives somewhat lower present values. Complete 'decoupling' of farm gate prices and a return to world prices may, in due course, further reduce the value of soil losses.

According to Evans (1993a), before widespread drainage of the Fens, there were about 160,000 hectares of peat soils in East Anglia and this has now diminished to some 30,500 hectares. Applying the average rate of change (1.7 per cent per year) to 1991/2 and valuing this loss in the same way would suggest an estimate for East Anglia lying between £1.26 million and £1.33 million, discounting at 6 per cent and £1.11 million and £1.14 million when allowing for a further 1 per cent annual fall in value due to price changes as shown in Table 2. Soil degradation occurs on numerous other sites in Britain (see for example: Boardman, 1990; Boardman *et al.*. 1994; and Evans 1993b), from both wind erosion and water run-off.

However, this estimate of the rate of erosion ignores important problems of continuing degradation of peatlands before they reach the threshold of conversion to 'non-peat' status. As the peat thins the range of crops it will grow begins to narrow, acid conditions may appear, water-logging introduces problems of root harvesting and bog oaks may rise to the surface. There are also important clean-up costs which have to be met elsewhere in the system — such as filtering water to make it drinkable. Further problems on remaining peat areas, where the falling water table draws down that of the residual peat islands are also important. The loss of productivity and additional costs imposed by these events are not easily quantified but are taken as evidence that the loss calculated here is very much a lower bound estimate.

Table 2 Estimated Value of Degeneration of Fen Arable Land 1991/2

Discount Period	Discount Rate per cent	NPV of Gross Loss of Value Added £ per ha	Aggregate Value of Soil loss £million 1991/2
50 years	6	4,364	1.26
100 years	6	4,603	1.33
50 years	7	3,832	1.11
100 years	7	3,958	1.14

There is an important conceptual difference between Tables 1 and 2. Whilst Table 1 relates to annual degradation of the environment, valued at opportunity costs, Table 2 values annual depletions of the land resource in terms of its stream of value discounted over 50 or 100 years.

The impacts of erosion excluded from these calculations should also be noted. There is also soil erosion proceeding at a slow rate due to water and this has been measured, using different methods, by Evans (1993b). He shows that up to 14 per cent of the arable area of some countries showed some rill erosion, with measured rates varying with soil type and topography. The next step in converting that to estimates of value is to assess the impact of such erosion on productivity. Degradation of water quality from agricultural run-off may result in a variety of economic costs: sediments, nutrients and pesticides may seriously affect aquatic ecosystems reducing recreational fishing. Sediments may also cause damage to water distribution infrastructure. In the US, Clark *et al.* (1985) estimated off-site damages of soil erosion in the region of $2.2 billion, although Holmes (1988) found this difficult to replicate for the costs of sediment discharge in the water industry. Boardman *et al.* (1994), reviewing the evidence for northern Europe, point out that non-agricultural development may also result in increased risk of flooding, as well as changes in land use, the intensification and extent of arable production and other agricultural changes.

Productivity loss from soil erosion constitutes the lower bound of the loss of natural capital from soil though this loss may be made good to the extent that nutrients may be replaced from other sources. However, where top soil is stripped, the capacity of the remaining soil to support plants may also be impaired as its water holding capacity is reduced (Evans and Catt, 1987). Although the social external costs may be high, the private decision to invest in soil conservation is only justified on marginal sites. An empirical study of these private costs of conservation, through introducing grass into arable rotations and changing to spring sown crops (Frost *et al.*, 1990) finds that in general the costs of effective soil conservation measures greatly exceeded the private benefits to farmers. This emphasises the dichotomy between aggregate indicators of sustainability and policy prescriptions. Although productivity losses are the correct measure of environmental changes, the phenomenon is not perceived as critical, or the soil as critical natural capital, until some threshold is reached.

Damage to SSSI

Losses of natural capital due to the degradation of highly prized landscapes and habitats are difficult to value because of the lack of evidence on the extent of such damage. Such data have been published for designated SSSI and those data form the basis of the estimates here. The damage data separates it into two categories of loss (partial and total) and long and short term damage. To convert such data to value terms requires an estimate of value over a substantial period, knowledge of the appropriate periods and of the appropriate discount rate.

The basic value comes from travel cost estimates of the value of visits to three SSSI (Willis and Benson, 1988) which yielded a starting estimate of £41.97 per hectare per annum based on interviews conducted in 1986 on three SSSI in England. The use of these estimates requires the assumption that they are representative of Wales and Scotland as well as England but also omits Northern Ireland from the calculations as they do not have this conservation designation. Estimation of changes in capital value from changes in SSSI quality requires first, that the 1986 estimates be projected forward to the year in question and, second, conversion of the single year estimate to a stream, allowing for increase in its value due to income growth before discounting it to a present value. Forward projection of the 1986 estimate was made on the basis of assumed 1 per cent per annum increase in per capita real incomes and an assumed income elasticity of demand for environmental goods. The latter was derived from Deaton (1975) who estimated an income elasticity for recreation goods of 1.99: in the absence of other estimates this was taken as the appropriate elasticity. Combining that with income growth at 1 per cent would indicate annual growth in value of environmental goods, in the absence of a substantial increase in supply, of 1.99. Finally, all values were indexed forward from 1986 to 1988-1992 to convert them to the relevant price base.

Discounting this projected stream combines two stages by using a composite discount rate which both embodies the opportunity cost of the natural capital loss and allows it to increase with rising incomes. In other words the raw

Table 3   Estimated Value of Damage to SSSI, 1988 to 1991

Newly Recorded Physical Damage (Hectares)	1988	1989	1990	1991
Loss, total or partial	146	115	13	700
Long term damage (40 years)	2,061	2,307	1,417	4,800
Short term damage (10 years)	31,843	89,258	35,061	26,500
Total	34,050	91,680	36,491	32,000
Value of Damage	£ million	£ million	£ million	£ million
Loss	0.18	0.16	0.02	1.19
Long Term Damage	1.78	2.10	1.34	4.71
Short Term Damage	11.33	33.02	13.48	10.59
Total Damage: 6 per cent Discount Rate	13.29	35.28	14.84	16.49
Total Damage: 3 per cent discount rate	23.51	53.89	22.02	31.34

Source: English Nature (various years) and DoE (various years)

discount rate is divided by the annual growth in consumption value. This is used to modify the official discount rate of 6 per cent, reducing it to 3.99 per cent. The sensitivity to discount rate is tested by applying a lower rate of 3 per cent, reduced to 0.99 per cent, to allow for growth in demand. The other issue to be resolved was the duration of long and short term damage: advice from English Nature led to the assumption of 10 years for short and 40 years for long term damage. The results of these calculations are reported in Table 3.

The resulting estimates, based as they are on a unit value derived from a travel cost study, will omit all elements of non-use value which are likely to be particularly important for such goods. Several studies which estimate relative use and non-use values for natural habitats suggest that non-use values are significant and that ignoring these clearly leads to underestimates of the values of countryside resources (see for example Willis *et al.,* 1993; Walsh, *et al.,* 1984). However, it is difficult to produce reliable estimates of non-use values because of the many problems surrounding contingent valuation and the way in which the analyst is obliged to extend small estimates of value to very large populations, thus magnifying the influence of errors of estimation. Willis (1989) produced contingent valuation estimates of value of the same three SSSI as he examined in his travel cost study and found very large values compared with use values. His results showed use values accounting for only 10 to 12 per cent of the general public's evaluation of these sites and it was only increased to 14 to 19 per cent of total value by sampling only amongst scientists. These results led him to conclude that "option values can be measured using contingent valuation techniques but their reliability is questionable . . ." (Willis, 1989, p255). Non-use values have not, therefore, been incorporated in the arguments here.

Discussion

The results placed above are limited in their scope but illustrate important methodological and policy issues. For example the sectoring problem has been resolved by dealing as far as possible with the agricultural and forestry sectors together as these are "primary land users" which account for the majority of the open space in Britain. The results here do not recognise the central importance of water as a common property resource both in transmitting pollutants and as

NATURAL AND REPRODUCIBLE CAPITAL AND THE SUSTAINABILITY OF LAND USE 61

a source of recreation and amenity benefits in its own right. Similarly, the estimates of SSSI damage reported have numerous causes, of which only a proportion derive directly from agriculture and forestry. If the other losses, such as urban or road development were estimated separately, then by the accounting conventions adopted here, this irreversible damage to natural capital should be recorded as a charge against those sectors. This problem is recognised throughout this land use sectoral account, where non-urban land acts as both a source and as a sink for pollutants, and for numerous environmental impacts from other sectors of the economy.

Another limitation on the measurement of natural capital losses lies in the requirement for annual measures. Whilst data are available for SSSI, there are no annual estimates of the rate of environmental degradation in the National Parks, although such effects are reported over longer periods (Countryside Commission, 1991). Whilst designation of new conservation areas would produce benefits which would grow over a number of years, it is not obvious that they would necessarily produce any benefits in their first year of designation. Complete annual estimates of soil erosion losses would require more precise data than presently available and the estimation of greenhouse gas emissions from several sources is difficult without more annual data on land use change. One approach to this problem would be to use indices of change to revise the estimates each year. Another would be to make more use of the more frequently available data from sources such as the ITE's Countryside Survey, although the latest of these reports relates to a six-year period ending in 1990 (Barr *et al.*, 1993).

As indicated in the introduction, strong and weak definitions of sustainability differ in the extent to which substitution between reproducible and natural capital is allowed. The examples of natural capital degradation presented here differ fundamentally in degree of reversibility and hence in the sustainability of the impacts of their loss, and the possibility for technological solutions which would substitute reproducible for natural capital lost.

Thus the production of gases which promote global warming could be argued to be of little significance to agricultural output or reproducible capital requirement. Because the volume of these emissions is closely linked to outputs and current inputs, it cannot be claimed that increasing investment of reproducible capital would reduce the damage they do to the atmosphere. Only changes in the mixture of outputs and in the level of intensity of inputs would bring that about, within current technology. The impacts of global warming are inherently irreversible, at least in the present state of knowledge and the explicit incorporation of precautionary action in the international policy response to global warming indicates that uncertainty of future impacts assigns the atmosphere to the category of critical natural capital. However, much economic activity, including that from agriculture and forestry, leads to greenhouse gas emissions. It is the scale of this activity which is unsustainable and which requires action to minimise present and future emissions.

Soil erosion represents both a loss of productive potential and the degradation of natural capital. But, it is not possible to identify on-site reproducible investments which might limit this rate of loss. Some changes in agricultural practices may have this effect but these would usually imply some extra cost. If the argument is broadened to include reproducible capital investment on other sites, as an offset to natural capital losses, then substitution of reproducible and natural capital loss does become possible.

Further, the damage to SSSI is subject to the argument that each site is unique so that we are considering irreversible degradation. However, not all damage to SSSI is irreversible: in particular the short-term damage recorded which might be caused by over-stocking of natural pastures, for example, is reversible by appropriate management practices. Also it may be possible to offset damage by designating alternative sites in some cases.

These reflections would emphasise the conclusion that sustainability is not solely to be investigated through the capital account. In the case of primary land use, inputs and the mixture of outputs profoundly influence environmental impacts as well as reproducible capital investments. All of these aspects therefore require examination in assessing sustainability.

5. Conclusions

This paper has given a general rule for the land use sector related to its sustainability: that degradation of natural capital reduces the ability to generate welfare in the future. It has tested this for the UK land use sector, finding that current practices do have negative impacts on environmental assets and that the rate of investment in reproducible capital, compared with depreciation, has been negative for some years. The reduction in reproducible capital would cause concern if there was a demand for agricultural expansion, but in the present state of world and European markets it need not necessarily do so. More fundamental are the losses of natural capital exemplified. These show that degradation is an automatic consequence of agricultural production at present levels.

Research requirements for sustainablity are of two types: first the data needs for assembling natural capital accounts and secondly the modes of analysis necessary. Some improvements on the low information base, which have recently been undertaken, include the ITE Countryside Survey series (Barr *et al.*, 1993) now beginning to appear regularly and the Countryside Commission sponsored study of damage to National Parks (Countryside Commission, 1991). These studies have both applied remote sensing methods which have particular strengths in detecting the types of change which require recording. Adequate data on changes in air and water quality are also needed as are accurate energy accounts for the economy as a whole.

More problematic are the questions surrounding the valuation of changes in natural capital stocks. In the three examples above three different approaches have been used. For greenhouse gases estimates of future costs of impacts have been taken from another study (Fankhauser, 1995). For soil loss, changes in productivity were estimated from the difference in value-added for the two relevant types of land. For damage to SSSI, and estimates of the future value of the various categories of annual loss was assembled from a travel cost study and discounted in perpetuity.

The temporal dimension of such assessments is critical in providing comparability. For example in projecting agricultural losses, only a notional allowance was made for the long-run downward tendency of food prices under the impacts of productivity and a low income elasticity of demand. However, SSSI damage was assumed to have an income elasticity of demand of 1.99 in contrast with the widespread survey evidence that the income elasticity of demand for environmental goods appears to be low (Kriström and Reira, 1995). Where calculations involve the discounting in perpetuity of income streams, the size of which is subject to variation due to income effects, the income elasticity becomes a critical parameter in estimation. The question of the appropriate discount rate to use also remains open and unresolved (Price, 1993).

NATURAL AND REPRODUCIBLE CAPITAL AND THE SUSTAINABILITY OF LAND USE 63

The usefulness of the concept of critical natural capital is important in the context of sustainability. As recognised above the means of identifying and defining critical capital is not amenable to economic proof. The concept can be applied at different temporal and spatial scales, and hinges on the concept of the irreversibility of environmental changes. Yet irreversibility and the degree of criticality of capital are complex issues. Irreversibility can be defined in terms of "unacceptable" cost of recovery rather than "impossible to reverse" (Hodge, 1984). Similarly, the definition of a critical landscape resource is necessarily dependent on "how values are expressed and measured, whether they are widely shared and how to act when they are not" (Owens, 1994).

We conclude that sustainability is a complex concept and that economic indicators give only partial insight into the current sustainability of land using activities in this country. The negative adjustments to the stocks of natural capital considered here show that sustainablity cannot be claimed for these activities. We infer that strong claims about the sustainability of existing policies in the UK (HM Government, 1994) should receive critical attention.

References

Adger, W. N. and Whitby, M. C. (1993). Natural resource accounting in the land-use sector: theory and practice, *European Review of Agricultural Economics*, **20**, 77-97.

Adger, W. N., Brown, K., Shiel, R. and Whitby, M. C. (1992). Carbon dynamics of land use in Great Britain, *Journal of Environmental Management*, **36**, 117-133.

Adger, W. N. and Brown, K. (1993). UK greenhouse gas inventory: on estimating anthropogenic and natural sources and sinks, *Ambio*, **22**, 117-133.

Atkinson, G. (1994). *Towards 'Nature Conservation' Extensions to National Accounts: Some Possible Directions*: A Report for English Nature, Centre for Social and Economic Research on the Global Environment (CSERGE), University College London and University of East Anglia.

Barr, C. J., Bunce, R. G. H., Clarke, R. T., Fuller, R. M., Furse, M. T., Gillespie, M. K., Groom, G. B., Hallam, C. J., Hornung, M., Howard, D. C. and Ness, M. J. (1993). *Countryside Survey 1990*. Institute of Freshwater Ecology and Institute of Terrestrial Ecology, Countryside 1990 Series, Volume 2, HMSO, London.

Boardman, J. (1990). *Soil Erosion in Britain: Costs, Attitudes and Policies*, John Wiley, Chichester.

Boardman, J., Ligneau, L., de Roo, A. and Vandaele, K. (1994). Flooding of property runoff from agricultural land in Northwestern Europe, *Geomorphology*, **10**, 183-196.

Buttel, F. (1993). Environmentalism and greening: origins, processes and implications, in Harper, S. (ed.) *The Greening of Rural Policy: International Perspectives*, Belhaven Press, London.

Clark W. R., Haverkamp, J. A. and Chapman, W. (1985). *Eroding Soils: the Off-Farm impacts*, The Conservation Foundation, Washington, DC.

Cline, W. R. (1992). *The Economics of Global Warming*, Institute for International Economics, Washington DC.

Common, M. (1995). *Sustainability and Policy: Limits to Economics*. Cambridge University Press, Cambridge.

Countryside Commission (1991). *Landscape Change in the National Parks*, Countryside Commission CCP 359, Cheltenham.

Deaton, A. S. (1975). The measurement of income and price elasticities, *European Economic Review*, **19**, 261-273.

Department of the Environment (1989). *Digest of Environmental Protection and Water Statistics*, Governmental Statistical Service, HMSO, London.

Dorfman, R. (1974). The technical basis for decision making, in Haefele, E. T. (ed.), *The Governance of Common Property Resources*, Johns Hopkins University Press for Resources for the Future, Baltimore.

Edmonds, J., Callaway, J. M. and Barns, D. (1992). Agriculture in a comprehensive trace-gas strategy, in Reilly, J. M. and Anderson, M. (eds) *Economic Issues in Global Climate Change: Agriculture, Forestry and natural resources*, Westview Press, Boulder, Colorado.

English Nature (various years), *Annual Report*, English Nature, Peterborough.

Evans, R. (1981). Assessments of soil erosion and peat wastage for parts of East Anglia in England, in Morgan, R. P. C. (ed) *Soil Conservation; Problems and Prospects*, John Wiley, Chichester.

Evans, R. (1993a) *personal communication.*

Evans, R. (1993b). Extent, frequency and rates of rilling of arable land in localities in England and Wales, in Wichereck S. (ed.) *Farm Land Erosion in Temperate Plains Environment and Hills*, Elsevier, Amsterdam.

Evans, R. and Catt, J. A. (1987). Causes of crop patterns in Eastern England, *Journal of Soil Science*, **38**, 309-324.

Fankhauser, S. (1995). *Valuing Climate Change: the Economics of the Greenhouse*, Earthscan, London.

Frost, C. A., Spiers, R. B. and McLean, J. (1990). Erosion control for the UK: strategies for short-term costs and benefits, in Boardman, J., Foster, I. D. L. and Dearing J. A. (eds) *Soil Erosion and Agricultural Land*. Wiley, Chichester.

HM Government (1994). *Sustainable Development: the UK Strategy*, CM 2426, HMSO, London.

Hodge, I. (1984). Uncertainty, irreversibility and the loss of agricultural land, *Journal of Agricultural Economics*, **35**, 191-202.

Holmes, T. P. (1988). The off-site impact of soil erosion on the water treatment industry, *Land Economics*, **64**, 356-366.

Houghton, J. T., Meira Filho, L. G., Bruce, J., Lee, H., Callander, B. A., Haites, E., Harris, N. and Maskell, K. (eds.) (1995). *Climate Change 1994: Radiative Forcing of Climate Change and an Evaluation of the IPCC IS92 Emission Scenarios*. Cambridge University Press, Cambridge.

Houghton, J. T., Jenkins, G. J. and Ephraums, J. J. (1990). *Climate Change: The IPCC Scientific Assessment*, Cambridge University Press, Cambridge.

Innes, J. L. (1992). Forest condition and air pollution in the United Kingdom, *Forest Ecology and Management*, **51**, 17-27.

Isaksen, I. S. A., Ramaswamy, V., Rodhe, H. and Wigley, T. M. L. (1992). Radiative forcing of climate, in Houghton, J. T. Callander, B. A. and Varney, S. K. (eds), *Climate Change 1992: the Supplementary Report of the IPCC Scientific Assessment*, Cambridge University Press, Cambridge.

Kane, S., Reilly, J. and Tobey, J. (1992). An empirical study of the economic effects of climate change on world agriculture, *Climate Change*, **21**, 17-35.

Kriström, B. and Riera, P. (1995). Is the income elasticity of environmental improvements less than one?, *Environmental and Resource Economics*, in Press.

Lutz, E. (ed.) (1993). *Toward Improved Accounting for the Environment*, World Bank, Washington, DC.

Maff, (1994). *Agriculture in the United Kingdom, 1993*. HMSO, London.

Mäler, K. G. (1991). National accounts and environmental resources, *Environmental and Resource Economics*, **1**, 1-15.

McInerney, J. (1976). The simple analytics of natural resource economics, *Journal of Agricultural Economics*, **27**, 31-52.

Murphy, M. C. (1991-1993). *Report on Farming in the Eastern Counties of England*, Deparment of Land Economy, Cambridge.

Nordhaus, W. D. (1992). An optimal transition path for controlling greenhouse gases, *Science*, **258**, 1315-1319.

Owens, S. (1994). Land, limits and sustainability: a conceptual framework and some dilemmas for the Planning System. *Transactions of the Institute of British Geographers*, **19**, 439-456.

Price, C. (1993). *Time Discontuing and Value*. Blackwell, Oxford.

Turner, R. K. (1993). Sustainability: principles and practice, in Turner, R. K. (ed.) *Sustainable Environmental Economics and Management: Principles and Practice*, Belhaven Press, London.

Walsh, R. G. Loomis, J. and Gillman, R. (1984). Valuing option, existence and bequest demands for wilderness, *Land Economics*, **60**, 14-29.

Watson, R. T., Rodhe, H., Oeschger, H. and Siegenthaler, U. (1990). Greenhouse gases and aerosols, in Houghton, J. T., Jenkins, G. J. and Ephraums, J. J. (eds.) *Climate Change: the IPCC Scientific Assessment*, Cambridge University Press, Cambridge.

Willis, K. G. (1989). Optimum value and non-user benefits for wildlife conservation, *Journal of Rural Studies*, **5**, 245-256.

Willis, K. G. and Benson, J. F. (1988). Valuation of wildlife: A comparison of user benefits and costs at three nature reserves, *Regional Studies*, **22**, 417-428.

NATURAL AND REPRODUCIBLE CAPITAL AND THE SUSTAINABILITY OF LAND USE 65

Willis, K. G., Garrod, G. D. and Saunders, C. M., (1993). *Valuation of the South Down and Somerset Levels Environmentally Sensitive Area landscapes by the General Public; Summary Report,* Centre for Rural Economy, The University of Newcastle upon Tyne.

World Commission on Environment and Development (1987). *Our Common Future,* Oxford University Press, Oxford.

D
Conservation Planning

[11]

Journal of Rural Studies, Vol. 9, No. 1, pp. 1–21, 1993
Printed in Great Britain

0743–0167/93 $6.00 + 0.00
Pergamon Press Ltd

Guest Editorial

Landscape Ecology and Countryside Planning: Vision, Theory and Practice

Paul Selman

Department of Countryside and Landscape, Cheltenham and Gloucester College
of Higher Education, Swindon Road, Cheltenham GL50 4AZ, U.K.

Abstract — Landscape planners are beginning to recognise the need for a strategic response to countryside change, but lack an appropriate theoretical framework. Landscape ecology is proposed as a basis for planning at a variety of scales. A number of key concerns of landscape ecology are identified, which help to explain the functioning of present and future ecosystems. These centre upon population dynamics, characteristics of habitat patches, movements between patches, visual cohesion and hydrological structures. Despite the complex relationships between biophysical and socio-economic systems, some broad principles are emerging which can be used to underpin landscape plans. Several implementational mechanisms are available which might help to convert these plans into reality. A set of strategic landscape planning principles is proposed, as a basis for further discussion.

Introduction

Ageing commentators on the rural scene can describe graphically the transformation of their childhood haunts. One particularly recurrent image is the demise of the former estates, as their component units passed into owner occupation. Broader landscape features, which had unified the whole estate, but which made an aesthetic or sporting contribution rather than a directly agricultural one, were removed or fell into neglect. The sense of a broader estate, providing visual structure and ecological interconnection, is one that landscape planners are now often unwittingly attempting to regain. We are starting to recognise the need for a strategic perspective on landscape change, transcending the mere design of sites and localities.

It is the contention of this editorial that the vigour and scale of planned change must match the external forces of environmental transformation. These forces principally comprise farm intensification, regional agricultural specialisation, extensive commercial afforestation and climate modification. Other countryside activities, though environmentally significant, have caused mainly local impacts. The major consequences of strategic change have been loss and fragmentation of semi-natural wildlife habitat, nitrification of ground and surface waters, and the loss of scenic distinctiveness.

Whilst extensive landscape transformation may be easy to describe, it is intractable to remedy. The policy commitment to 'countryside management' initiatives from the early 1970s has resulted in a number of effective actions, but ones which are focused on local and pragmatic projects. Community involvement and 'getting things done' have taken precedence over strategic vision. Countryside management projects are also sparingly funded and staffed — especially when considered on a 'per hectare' basis — with paltry powers of enforcement and a rapid turnover of inexperienced assistant officers on insecure contracts. The response to landscape attrition has in no way matched the scale of the problem.

To respond more effectively will require purposeful policy measures but also, equally importantly, a body of theory which provides a rationale for strategic landscape planning. Essentially, the need in Britain is for the creation of extensive lowground, mixed species, multi-purpose discontinuous forests in landscapes with a long history of land management and ecosystem disturbance. None the less, whilst woodland is frequently the favoured prospective land cover, it is equally clear that many areas must be safeguarded from re-forestation. The overall framework must also accommodate the requirements both of natural environmental processes and of cultural and economic activities. It

1

2   Paul Selman

must also be sufficiently flexible and adaptive to respond to modifications in the original design, given the lack of public sector controls to steer private land use in a particular direction. A major opportunity to translate this hypothesised need into reality is currently afforded by the promotion of farm woodlands throughout the EC, especially the promulgation of community forests.

Britain and many other developed countries have a long heritage of purposeful modification of the rural scene. During the eighteenth and nineteenth centuries estate plans took into account a wide range of considerations. Pre-eminent was agricultural improvement, but other objectives included visual satisfaction, game cover (coincidentally valuable for much other wildlife), drainage and associated planting of willows, microclimate improvement, and timber production for a variety of uses. This broader perspective became difficult to sustain with the progressive break-up of estates, and the modern attrition of cohesive landscape features is merely the continuation of a longer historical process. Four criteria would have to be met before a comprehensive reversal of this trend could take place and a broad 'rural estate' could become re-established. These comprise: adequate powers of statutory or economic intervention in rural land use; a realistic accommodation of the varied psychology of the farming community, and farmers' likely responses to various inducements and exhortations; a comprehensive policy of large-scale habitat re-creation, including commensurate financial commitments; and a theoretical basis for the reconstruction of functional new landscapes. Much literature has focused on the first two of these. This paper focuses on the last, in the context of the third.

Landscape ecology as a framework

Current developments in British, and to some extent European, countryside policy are facilitating a broader response to landscape regeneration (e.g. Dessylas, 1990). Environmentally Sensitive Areas (and a variety of similar, locally operated schemes) encourage retention and re-creation of traditional features within extensive areas, on the basis of whole farm plans. The Countryside Stewardship initiative supports the maintenance and re-establishment of critical habitat types, whilst Community Forests (including the new National Forest and Central Scotland Woodland) promote the development of large multi-purpose woodlands [Countryside Commission (1989a, b, 1991)]. The idling of land under set-aside also provides some scope for alternative land use, although EC provisions fall well short of the U.S. 'Conservation Reserve' in this respect

(Potter, 1991), and currently fail to provide opportunities for long-term habitat establishment. Despite the fact that all of these measures have been subject to justified criticism, it is still realistic to presume that a policy context now exists for the re-establishment of broad structural features in our countryside. Since the vision and patronage of the wealthy landowner cannot be prevailed upon to provide a strategic landscape design framework for the twenty-first century, we must seek a defensible and coherent scientific basis upon which to regenerate a habitat network. The author has elsewhere advocted landscape ecology, a rather unfamiliar body of theory to the British audience, as the most promising basis for this task (Selman, 1988).

It must be admitted that landscape ecology is the subject of much scepticism within certain quarters of the scientific community. In its totality, it is bewilderingly complex and appears to act as a portmanteau for many disparate strands of ecological research. There is controversy over whether it offers anything more than a re-packaging of traditional ideas, or whether it is merely a trendy title in search of a convincing body of theory. This excessive caution, however, appears to be a mainly British reserve, which may be evaporating with the recent establishment of a U.K. chapter of the International Association of Landscape Ecology. The present review attempts to cut a swathe through the jargon and conflicting terminology of landscape ecology, and to identify its key themes which are of potential interest to practical countryside planning. It is a selective interpretation, looking primarily at land use planning applications and skewed towards the creation of new woodlands.

Ecological models dating from the 1960s have emphasised island biogeographic theory, in which species diffuse from a mainland source to an island in proportion to the distance of hostile habitat (i.e. water) to be crossed and the land area of the island (MacArthur and Wilson, 1967; Simberloff, 1976). Eventually, an equilibrium will be established in which extinctions are matched by incoming colonists. This principle was subsequently extended to terrestrial fragments of natural or semi-natural habitats (Harris, 1984), in which the species diversity of 'island' remnants (e.g. native woodlands) could be related to the extent of hostile matrix (e.g. intensively farmed arable land) surrounding them and, more controversially, to the network of interconnecting corridors (e.g. hedgerows). This initial theory has been progressively replaced by a more complex scheme of patch dynamics, in which remnant fragments ('isolates') support species populations which interact with those of other isolates in a number of ways (cf. Pickett and White, 1985). These fragments are conventionally termed 'patches' in America and Britain and 'ecotopes' in continental Europe. Landscape ecologists have extended these notions to broader areas within which 'metapopulations' are assumed to exist, that is, accumulations of adjacent populations which overlap via predation, reproduction, gene flow, local stochastic extinctions and re-invasion. Thus, the pattern is more complex than one in which a single source of colonists invades and replenishes an isolated island habitat, and requires to be explained in terms of habitat supply analysis. However, a broadly comparable dynamic equilibrium is established in the (rare) absence of disturbance. Means of communication between isolates clearly involves animals, birds, insects and plants crossing matrix areas by a variety of processes including, for some species at least, diffusion along linear corridors.

Whereas patch dynamic theory now has an international currency, its extension to landscape ecology is more controversial. This situation has not been assisted by somewhat separate strands of research in North America and Europe, which have become associated with inconsistent terminology and differing foci of interest. It is useful, therefore, to summarise the main areas of concern within landscape ecology and establish their relevance to large-scale planning. At the outset, two major hallmarks are evident. First, it incorporates explicitly the human role in ecological change, and is thus eminently suited to programmes of integrated, multi-objective rural land use change. It combines a study of human ecology (food, water, health, shelter, fuel and cultural cohesion) with biophysical health (plant productivity, bio-diversity, minimal erosion, nutrient conservation and clean water) (Forman, pers. comm., 1990). Second, by definition, it adopts as its macroscopic framework the broad (at least several kilometres-wide) landscape (Noss, 1983; Naveh and Lieberman, 1984; Forman and Godron, 1986). This entails specific recognition of the inherent land use diversity of the cultural countryside, which is seen as a driving force rather than an inconvenient complication. Thus, the landscape is viewed as a heterogeneous land area comprising a cluster of interacting ecosystems which is repeated in similar form throughout its overall extent (Forman and Godron, 1986). Spirn (1988, 1989) has also suggested that there is a 'deep structure' within the environment, which provides a foundation for all ecological and cultural landscape processes.

The nature of landscape ecology

Landscape ecology is the study of the spatial relationships and functional interactions between the component patches of an extensive and heterogeneous land area, and how these bring about changes of structure and function in the ecological mosaic over time. Thus, the emphasis is on structure, function and change, alternatively (but not entirely comparably) expressed by some authors as heterogeneity, landscape and disturbance (e.g. Risser, 1987). Anthropogenic features are explicitly included, with human actions responding to, and having reciprocal effects on, ecological processes. It also emphasises *inter-scale* relationships between landscapes, patches and organisms — integrating these into a hierarchical system (Allen and Starr, 1982; Urban *et al.*, 1987) and assuming that change at one level drives changes at others. Functional studies focus on energy, species, water and nutrient fluxes amongst landscape elements; some authors would add transport of materials by humans, and human movements, to these natural cycles and cascades.

The apparent clarity and distinctiveness of landscape ecology as a subject conceals its diversity of purposes and approaches. Opdam (1989) has drawn attention to the ways in which researchers on both sides of the Atlantic have been influenced by the nature of their home environments. Thus, early studies originated in Europe as a fusion between the functional (ecosystem) approach of ecology and the spatial approach of geography, enabling landscapes to be described and mapped as extensive areas characterised by a particular heterogeneity of geomorphic, soil and vegetation features (cf. Vink, 1983). This subsequently developed into a more functional approach, exploring the presumed biotic and abiotic fluxes between the geographic subunits. Thus, in the substantially modified, fragmented and densely settled landscapes of Europe, studies have emphasised the role of patches, corridors and matrix (e.g. Agger and Brandt, 1988). Fragmentation effects are investigated by focusing on what is for most species an inhospitable matrix. By contrast, in parts of the world where biomes are extensive, there may be no apparent repeating pattern of spatially well-defined subunits. Thus, landscape ecology focuses on heterogeneity and scale, in particular the mapping of land use or conservation values over land facets which are much less obviously apparent than their European counterparts. Models often tend to test if landscape patterns deviate from random expectation, and may provide insights into the influence of disturbances such as wildfire. Latterly, both schools of thought have been strongly influenced by the modelling and analytical capabilities of geographic information systems (GIS), which have facilitated studies of ecological processes associated with patchiness and heterogeneity, instead of holistic treatments of landscapes.

4   Paul Selman

Dennis (1991) describes this more recent focus as ecology practised within a geographical context and with a consideration of human impacts. It could also be argued that GIS-based approaches provide an opportunity for the more practical application of emergent theories.

Island biogeography theory confirms that geographical isolation can reduce species richness, since some species are poor dispersers or are restricted to specific habitat types and their associated microclimates. Under fragmented conditions, a species can become locally (or ultimately, wholly) extinct due to chance processes. The situation clearly becomes more complex when considering the interaction of sub-populations in fragmented landscapes, where viability can be sustained by metapopulation processes which maintain adequate numbers and genetic variation (overall and within local populations) (Quinn and Hastings, 1987; Hanski, 1989; Dennis, 1991). The size of the metapopulation and the effective genetic breeding unit will be controlled by the degree of fragmentation and patchiness (heterogeneity). The traditional biological emphasis on natural selection, acting on individuals via reproductive success, may also be integrated into the study of landscape configurations, the latter being seen to constrain the behaviour and demographic fortunes of a hierarchy of reproductive units (cf. Slatkin, 1987; Merriam, 1991). Thus, grain of spatial scale — from whole landscape to an organism's foraging area — can be related to life-cycle and daily patterns of behaviour, and to survival strategies from the metapopulation to the individual.

Five key concerns of landscape ecological theory — population dynamics, patch characteristics, interpatch movements, visual cohesion and hydrological structure

Population dynamics

Where habitat islands are under the strong influence of a large source habitat, island biogeographic models may be appropriate. However, this is typically not the case in the highly fragmented landscapes of developed countries where local populations are in demographic and genetic disequilibrium, but with a stable metapopulation (Olivieri *et al.*, 1990). Here, the 'persistence time' of a metapopulation will increase exponentially with the number of island populations, assuming free dispersal in a landscape supporting several fragments of the same habitat. This supposition is confirmed by models which consider birth, immigration, death and emigration (BIDE models) as processes taking place on an inter-patch (or 'source' and 'sink') basis

(Pulliam, 1988). Most of the literature has tended to focus on woodland habitats and on a restricted range of small mammals (Middleton and Merriam, 1981; Adler *et al.*, 1984; Henderson and Merriam, 1985; Merriam, 1988; Merriam and Lanoue, 1990; Wegner and Merriam, 1990), insects (Wallin and Ekbom, 1988; Asselin and Baudry, 1989; Burel, 1989; Saville *et al.*, 1992; Woiwood and Thomas, 1992), birds (Moore and Hooper, 1975; Ambuel and Temple, 1983; Arnold, 1983; McCollin *et al.*, 1984; Opdam and Schotman, 1984; Opdam *et al.*, 1984; Urban and Shugart, 1986; Askins *et al.*, 1987; Saunders and Ingram, 1987; Shaw, 1988) and plants (Baudry, 1988a, b; Usher *et al.*, 1992).

Theories of inter-patch movement must obviously take into account the need for species to cross a matrix, and three basic processes have been proposed for this, all of which have varying degrees of relevance to particular situations. First a 'stepping stone' (or landscape 'porosity') hypothesis assumes the matrix to be completely hostile, so that traversal occurs only where suitable habitats are found within a directly accessible radius around the source habitat. Certain densities of favourable habitat may be necessary for organisms to 'percolate' (O'Neill *et al.*, 1988), and these densities will vary between species (Stauffer, 1985). Second, the matrix may be deemed partially usable by the diffusing species (landscape 'permeability'), even though it fails to provide a desired level of cover or cater for all life-cycle requirements. Third, 'connectivity' models emphasise the role of corridors of suitable habitat between patches, which supposedly afford movement, foraging and breeding opportunities. These must be treated as idealised viewpoints, as much of the detailed discussion tends to focus on definitions of what represents a viable corridor or an acceptable distance between stepping stones. In diversified landscapes, such questions are frequently academic: many species seem to move quite freely, and attention then turns towards appropriate measures of detail design and habitat management. Broad structure cannot be overlooked, however, either from an ecological or aesthetic standpoint.

A major reason for landscape ecologists' concern with population dynamics in fragmented environments is the likelihood of local extinctions, and the potential for repopulation (Gilpin and Soule, 1986; Opdam, 1988). The desirable population size is likely to be above the minimum breeding unit, in order to compensate for genetic drift: populations of woodland birds, for instance, tend to experience genetic deterioration where the demographic unit comprises less than about 50 pairs. Ideally, therefore, large patches should be provided, but where this is unfeasible inter-patch distances should be minimised and corridor connections maximised to facilitate migration. Since the commoner species tend to perform well under a variety of conditions, attention has increasingly centred on those species associated with the interior of habitats. Temple and Carn (1988) considered that interior species were likely to become extinct in severely fragmented landscapes and also doubted whether migration from larger islands would occur even if such islands survived in close proximity. Migration rates for several species to small isolated woodlands are found to be too low to compensate for extinctions, the rates themselves being sensitive to distance (Opdam *et al.*, 1985).

However, there is some evidence that small islands near mainland forests do support habitat interior species not found on more isolated islands (Whitcomb *et al.*, 1981). Other (generalist and edge) species are clearly less inflexible in their requirements, and Middleton and Merriam (1985) found similar species distributions in patchy landscapes to those in continuous forest. They suggest that dispersal mechanisms which were evolved to cope with patchy species distributions within continuous forest are also suited to dispersal in patchy habitat conditions. Overall, however, it does seem likely that certain species associated with habitat interiors will be sensitive barometers of landscape quality.

In fragmented landscapes, it is clear that demographic stochasticity will lead to fluctuation in numbers of small populations, producing an area-dependent extinction rate. This 'area effect' has substantial implications for nature conservation management, whose main purpose is to assure the survival of target populations (Diamond, 1975; Margules *et al.*, 1982; Soule and Simberloff, 1986). As well as minimising extinctions of desired species, this also requires controlling invasive species which are especially problematic in habitats with high edge to area ratios. Merriam (1991) suggests that conservation objectives can be conceived as preventing local patch extinctions from accumulating into landscape, then regional, then subcontinental extinctions. If the demographic units of the species function as metapopulations, prevention of extinctions can be simplified to maintaining or increasing connectivity for the species, so that the rate of local extinctions does not exceed the rate of recolonisation of empty patches.

These principles have found application in nature reserve design, especially with regard to the SLOSS (single-large-or-several-small) debate, which seeks to affirm whether a single large reserve is superior to a mosaic. Maximisation of species richness tends to favour 'several small' reserves, but this may conflict with longer-term planning as it increases extinction probabilities and external perturbations (Burkey, 1989). Thus, a 'tiered' approach may be preferable. For survival of rare species in fragmented areas inter-patch migration should be improved by corridors, always bearing in mind the potential of corridors to be vectors for disease, fire and biological invasions. For conservation of communities a similar approach may be adopted, but with close consideration to the needs of 'key' species and area-sensitive species with low population densities. For conservation of diversity a high level of habitat heterogeneity should be sought, but constrained by an analysis of the highest species extinction rates after isolation of the smallest fragments (Dennis, 1991; Burkey, 1989; Simberloff and Cox, 1987).

Patch characteristics

Although landscape ecology has tended to emphasise the role of large-scale heterogeneity and ecological fluxes, it has also dwelt upon the size and qualities of individual patches. Treatment of scale is also crucial, since each species views a landscape differently, and what appears as a homogeneous patch to one may represent a heterogeneous patchy environment to another (Lord and North, 1990). Risser (1987) observes that investigations undertaken at a given scale may treat such features with unequal resolution.

There is extensive evidence for the importance of patch size, mostly in relation to woodlands, and generally confirming a positive species-area relationship. With respect to woodland birds (Rafe *et al.*, 1985; Atkins *et al.*, 1987), species richness and abundance of individuals are both positively correlated with patch area for forest interior birds, though species diversity and abundance of edge species appear unrelated. There is no clear evidence on the optimum upper size of a wood, though it is likely that value simply continues to increase with increasing size, and that in Britain the ideal size is unfeasibly big. Some commentators suggest that a law of diminishing returns operates beyond 100 ha, and there is some consensus that 50 ha is a realistic minimum block size to support an interesting variety of species, including those associated with woodland interiors. Very large habitats are clearly necessary to protect a comprehensive range of species, but in more fragmented areas an alternative objective may be for patches to be of sufficient size to enable their populations to be self-perpetuating and ensure local survival of habitat interior species (Westmacott, 1991). Woodlots over 4 ha appear to be able to perform this function in urban areas, and those as small as 0.2 ha are found to retain fairly diverse

6   Paul Selman

populations of edge species of birds (Levenson, 1981).

As well as size, the shape of a patch may be important. Various studies suggest that patch size and shape may have significant ecological effects in soft-edged habitats, but not in hard-edged, insular ones (Dennis, 1991; Stamps *et al.*, 1987; Drake, 1988). With respect to soft-edged habitats, Game (1980) showed that the equilibrium theory of island biogeography dictates shape as an important influence over species number at equilibrium. Where immigration contributes significantly to the species number, non-circular patches would be better, whereas in more isolated habitats or those noted for sessile organisms (where immigration is extremely slow or unimportant) the optimal shape is large and circular to minimise extinction. When it is necessary to enhance immigration, large patches should be broad and perpendicular to the direction of species movement (i.e. non-circular); this design may further promote species richness by providing greater habitat heterogeneity and soil diversity.

Edge convolutions generally appear conducive to increased immigration: Collinge *et al.* (1991), for instance, found that convoluted areas had much higher usage of elk and deer than rectilinear plots. However, increased edge effects can also assist invasive species and other disturbances from the surrounding matrix (Andren and Angelstram, 1988). There is a well-documented 'peninsula effect' as a patch extends in narrow linear form from its core: reductions in woodland plant (Milne and Forman, 1986) and bird (Opdam *et al.*, 1985) species have been recorded along such peninsulas. Compact (closer to circular) patches are therefore often favoured.

Internal structure is undoubtedly important, but relatively under-researched by landscape ecologists, a principal reason being that studies tend to address areas with patches of similar structure, so that this can be held constant and research can focus on spatial effects. However, Askins *et al.* (1987) did find that forest interior birds favoured woods with dense ground vegetation and high diversity of trees, whereas forest edge birds preferred woods with small trees, high diversity and dense cover of shrubs and a low basal area of living trees. Lynch and Wigham (1984) similarly observed that forest interior bird species were influenced to a large extent by the percentage cover of the herb layer and by the basal area of trees. Bird species diversity was also correlated with herb diversity. Evidence is accumulating of various treatments to enrich edge and ground layer habitats — by additional planting, scalloping, management regimes, and permitting

old-growth — in order to benefit birds and invertebrates (Peterken *et al.*, 1992; Saville *et al.*, 1992; Francis *et al.*, 1992).

Of all patch characteristics, it would appear that size is the dominant one, whereas little empirical evidence has been presented for woodland shape and orientation as crucial factors. In a study of vascular plants, for instance, Usher *et al.* (1992) found that 63% of variance in the number of species was accounted for by area, whilst shape of the wood had no significant effect either on the total number of species in a wood or on the number found in the wood margin. Isolation also appeared to have no effect on the number of species. These unusually striking results were perhaps associated with the fact that the study sites were all recent farm woodlands, a point which is of particular interest in the current context. The results also firmly favoured several small, rather than one large, woodland patch, with 5 ha emerging as the threshold above which a 'woodland ecosystem' started to function.

Inter-patch movements

Many landscape ecological studies have focused on the role and quality of corridors, and the spatial arrangements whereby patches are connected. The emphasis has been heavily upon wooded features such as shelterbelts, hedgerows, treelines and fence-rows, and the ways in which these inter-connect larger wooded landscape elements. The role of inter-patch movement along corridors, and even the effects of isolation itself, remain controversial though of continuing fascination for those concerned with macro-scale landscape structure. It is likely that individual species do display some characteristic mean maximum movement length which we could call the normal inter-patch distance in a particular landscape type (Harris and Gallagher, 1989). It is also reasonable to assume that this distance might be extended by the existence of suitable connecting corridors, especially where these fulfil habitat requirements rather than merely a conduit role. Some degree of connectivity is required to permit metapopulations to perform inter-patch movements, though physical corridors are not always necessary.

In general terms, research studies are concerned with the proximity of habitats to each other, the density of similar habitats within an area, and the connectedness of those habitats (van Dorp and Opdam, 1987; McDonnell and Pickett, 1988). Computer models of corridors have tended to simplify ecological processes, taking into account either mortality alone, or mortality plus reproduction, and have typically only considered whether a patch is connected or isolated (Levkovitch and Fahrig, 1985). In real life, the situation is much more complicated. Corridor quality will be highly variable, and multiple life-cycle processes will take place in different corridors (Noss, 1987; Henein and Merriam, 1990). Different animal, plant and insect species clearly have such varied dispersal capabilities that simplified models can only ever tell part of the story.

Some studies suggest that isolation (and hence corridors) have little effect on number of species. Hobbs (1988), for instance, confirmed size of woodland as the best single indicator of avian diversity and found no significant relationship between species richness and distance of patches to each other. Fritz (1979), however, showed that spruce grouse (*Canachites canadensis*) occupied remnant patches of spruce forest more often the closer together these patches were situated. Dennis (1991) shed some light on the complex relationships which might arise. In a study of arthropod presence and fitness in beech woodlands, he found that area, rather than isolation, influenced beech weevil (*Rhynchaenus fagi*) fitness, but that for gall midges (*Hartigiola annulipes*) there were clear differences in numbers for isolated, connected and source types of woodlands. Hedgerow links were found to be important, and there was also some evidence that porosity and orientation of woodlands were important aids to the reception of wind-dispersed individuals.

Although a good deal of debate still surrounds the function of landscape corridors, it is generally acknowledged that physical linkage ('connectedness') does not necessarily imply functional usage ('connectivity') (Fahrig and Merriam, 1985). Equally, connectivity is not necessarily a function of linear corridors, though corridors may serve to combine small patches into a single larger one or to reduce the effective distance between habitat patches. The concept of connectivity represents, at the landscape scale, the degree of linkage within and between metapopulations. Forman (1991) has identified five potential functions of corridors, namely those of conduit, barrier, source, sink and habitat.

Connectivity (use of corridors) is a behaviourally determined species-specific parameter. For instance, some species may require different habitats at different stages in their life-cycles: some may adapt more readily to increasing fragmentation, enabling them to assemble vital resource patches and access them along interconnections (Merriam, 1991). A corridor may be readily passable for a relatively vagile species, for instance, but too long for a more sedentary or vulnerable species and may even be a

demographic 'sink' draining individuals from attached patches. Considerable differences clearly exist in the extent and method of corridor use by different species; in respect of small mammals, Hansson (1988) notes that whilst some are highly dependent on core patches, others previously thought to be dependent on woodland or hedgerows have demonstrated remarkable adaptability to new habitats. The role of isolation is best documented in relation to the distribution of forest birds in woodlots. Usually the amount of, or distance to, forest patches in the surrounding landscape is found to correlate with species number or with the probability of occurrence of particular species.

Confirmation of the role of physical linkages in enhancing connectivity is controversial, and such evidence as exists is clearly taxon specific, making generalisation problematic. With regard to carabid beetles, Burel (1989) showed that hedgerows were generally ineffective as conduits, although a small minority of species did move along them. Several studies confirm that small mammals — white-footed mice (*Peromyscus leucopus*) and chipmunks (*Tamias striatus*) — and birds use hedgerows (e.g. Wegner and Merriam, 1979), but for birds it is unclear whether hedges represent transit corridors or whether movement is simply from wood to hedge and back again. Asselin and Baudry (1989), studying spiders in agricultural land, concluded that inter-parcel flows were unimportant and that, whilst well-protected patches might accelerate colonisation of adjacent patches, this could not adequately be confirmed from empirical evidence. One of the few projects to consider plant movement (reported in Forman and Godron, 1986) found that no forest species extended continuously for more than 50 m from a woodlot along an attached hedgerow, a distance which could be related to microclimatic influence from the woodlot edge. Beyond 50 m, forest interior herbs were essentially limited to hedgerows over 12 m in width and network intersections or nodes. Merriam (1991) suggests that plant species do not appear to spread progressively along corridors, although certain types of species such as autochores and zoochores may do so. Saltatory movement, involving plant colonisation, reproduction and further colonisation may be common. Nodes where links intersect may assist dispersal by animals or wind, and thus influence the probability of plant migration. Human agencies may also be more significant than geographical factors in dispersing plant propagules (le Duc *et al.*, 1992).

It is important to affirm the 'habitat' role of corridors which often become key conservation resources in their own right, contributing a valuable proportion of a region's remnant vegetation (Hobbs *et al.*, 1989). This is despite the management problems arising from external disturbances associated with high edge to area ratios. Intensity of use of hedgerows as wildlife corridors may in fact be as much a function of their dissimilarity from surrounding croplands (i.e. contrasting habitat) as it is of their similarity to the woodlands which they connect (e.g. Merriam, 1984).

Modelled results suggest (Soule and Gilpin, 1991) that width is a critical feature, with narrow corridors constraining movements and speeding individuals towards their goal, but increasing the rate of mortality because of minimal safe (interior) habitat. A very wide corridor, conversely, has a high occupancy and relatively low mortality rate but permits relatively unconstrained movement, and individuals may spend a lot of time simply wandering from side to side. As width increases incrementally, marginal increase in habitat value lessens. Optimum width depends on edge effects, so that small predation-prone birds or mammals may require a wider corridor than a large predator or herbivore. Shape may also be important, with rectangular forms outperforming 'funnels' which over-concentrate or scatter users. Dog-leg shapes appear to reduce corridor capability, the vertical 'wall' acting as a barrier and temporarily stopping most animals.

There is a broad consensus with regard to corridor width that 'wider is better', and indeed some of the widths advocated seem remarkable by British standards. Evidently, tracts 30 m wide tend to be dominated by processes characteristic of forest edges, whereas sites 250 m from the forest edge resemble the interior of larger forests, suggesting that a corridor 500 m wide would possess a central strip allowing passage of interior species. Baudry (1988a) and Baudry and Merriam (1988) similarly showed that large hedges (over 8 m wide) contained significantly more plant species than hedges 4–8 m wide and were effectively used by more species as dispersal corridors. Increasing the number of high quality corridors between patches also had a positive effect on metapopulation size and vice versa, but the addition to a metapopulation of a patch connected by low quality corridors had a negative effect. Geometrically isolated patches connected by low quality corridors were, understandably, most vulnerable to extinction.

Caution must be exercised in adding or substituting low quality corridors into a landscape. 'Death traps' may be installed and, even where corridor predation or other mortality does not occur, behavioural isolation by low quality connections can effectively reduce metapopulation survival. Some linear features of hostile ecotopes may act as barriers to species dispersal (e.g. major roads restricting movement of toads to and from breeding ponds) (Mader, 1984; Merriam *et al.*, 1989; Mader *et al.*, 1990). As with user-friendly corridors, perceptions of barriers such as roads and rivers will be behaviourally determined, and what for some species will be a hazard or death trap will for others be a conduit or food source.

Visual cohesion

Although the main body of theory of landscape ecology has concerned scientific aspects of metapopulations, its distinguishing hallmark is that of integration of the scientific and cultural dimensions. In terms of landscape design, it is clearly essential to consider the more qualitative and subjective matter of visual aesthetics. Ahern (1990, 1991) also notes that public support for wildlife corridor planning is more likely to be forthcoming if it provides compatible benefits of recreational trails, scenic conservation and protection of rural character. Government subsidy is similarly more probable if visible benefits accrue. Landscape structure is thus most appropriately conceived as part of a comprehensive planning effort, including consideration of land use development, open space provision and scenic resource management. Hall (1991) even suggests that the cultural components of landscape — symbolic, ethical, phenomenological or perceptual aspects — are as truly ecological as nutrient cycling or water flows. Other writers have likewise proposed a 'landscape ecological aesthetic', based on the overall health of a landscape in terms of its air quality, availability of high quality water from minimally disrupted hydrological cycles, conservation of soils, intact plant and animal associations and self-motivated cultural continuity (Thorne and Huang, 1991; Berger, 1987). At the very least, from the point of view of practical planning, it is important to confirm that ecological and visual objectives are not incompatible.

A substantial amount of research has been undertaken into the classification of landscape and the expression of the resultant classes in terms of subjective desirability. Other research, drawing on psychological theory, has sought to establish fundamental human preferences in landscapes, and to relate these to design principles (Zube *et al.*, 1984; Berleant, 1988). This latter line of inquiry seems more relevant to the present study, although it is probable that future research could integrate it with landscape attributes identified by quantitative ecological and scenic classifications. Of particular concern has been the loss of spatial definition in open space and the need to reconstruct sites which are coherent and comprehensible. Experimental results confirm that open space occupied by vegetation is preferred to unvegetated sites (perhaps partly associated with green colours), and that open space of higher visual complexity is favoured over homogeneous green areas (Calvin *et al.*, 1972; Kaplan and Kaplan, 1978; R. Kaplan, 1983; S. Kaplan, 1988). It also appears that landscapes which show obvious stewardship are preferred by local observers to those where obvious stewardship is lacking. Nassauer (1988) argues that by formalising landscape configurations to provide for run-off and erosion control, species movement and cultural continuity, the ecologic aesthetic can provide a coherent sense of stewardship.

One of the most persistent and persuasive notions has been prospect-refuge theory, proposed by Appleton (1975, 1988). This presumes that modern humans have a remnant ability to distinguish between environments in which their evolutionary forebears could survive and reproduce with relative ease and those in which they could not (Orians, 1986). Although Appleton's theories have been criticised, they continue to shed useful light on humans' environmental responses. Some evidence indicates that selection of a biologically favourable environment by many species is based on the distinctive conspicuous features of a habitat rather than the presence or absence of specific features assisting survival. If the 'symbolic' approach to habitat selection is extendable to humans then this provides the basis for an aesthetic. Analysis of the landscape in terms of 'prospects' and 'refuges' is thus compatible with the need of early humans to see without being seen. Subsequent analysis has indicated that the most pleasing vistas are either prospect-dominant or refuge-dominant. This basic hermeneutic is compatible with other hypotheses which emphasise the need for balance. Designers tend to seek balance between parameters such as: complexity and coherence, or mystery and legibility, in which sections of the landscape are emphasised by texture, colour, brightness, etc.; voids and masses; light and dark; and between landscape tracts arising from different patterns of human activity.

Legibility of view in both urban and rural scenes is often associated with massing of elements so that they are sufficiently grouped to be coherent and positive, but not so dominant as to overwhelm natural detail or be insensitive to human scale. Afforestation guidelines (Forestry Commission, 1989) emphasise primary principles of shape and scale, and their derived principles of visual force, diversity and mystery. Visual force and shape are associated with major landforms which may, through concealment of enclaves, enhance mystery;

presumably they also assist reinforcement of prospects (e.g. spurs) and refuges (e.g. valleys). Diversity requires the presence of a coherent but varied landscape mosaic, with high levels of admixture being acceptable provided one element is dominant. Again, this is compatible with the hypothesised need for either prospect- or refuge-dominant landscapes, each having a proportion of the other. Scale considerations require that expansive landscapes seen from a distance should be designed on a larger scale than those seen close up. In coarse grain landscapes, large-scale features can be acceptable even where they override traditional patterns, and habitat patches (small woodlands, for instance) may need to be clustered for visual strength. Where both long and short views are to be catered for, it may be appropriate to impose an irregular edge design on a larger scale curved outline.

Burel's (1991) observation that there is no antagonism between aesthetic and functional landscape approaches, even if they usually ignore each other, may be a considerable understatement. Traditional frictions between visually pleasing 'tidy' vistas and 'unimproved' wildlife havens are likely to diminish as tastes become more educated and naturalistic. Ecological principles suggest that landscape elements should be large and internally complex, basically isodiametric in shape, but possessing lobes and convoluted boundaries to aid inter-patch dispersal and to maximise edge usage by wildlife. Elements should link together into a coherent whole by connections allowing movement between patches, and these networks should operate at nested scales, with wide corridors linking all key areas and narrow corridors found throughout. Aesthetic principles similarly indicate the division of landscape into recognisably different areas, each of which is internally complex but which share certain common features to provide overall unity. Use of appropriately shaped patches and corridors to provide inter-scale linkages is common to both ecological and aesthetic viewpoints. Change through time is also mutually important, with the progression of seasons, ages, species and densities transmitting sensory messages, underpinning ecological rhythms and emphasising stewardship. There appears, therefore, to be considerable potential correspondence between scientific and cultural landscape planning principles, both of which favour comparable designs and the promotion of 'stable change'.

Hydrological structure

Although most landscape ecological research has centred on biological factors, a growing number of studies have focused on the physical environment, most notably ground- and surface-water hydrology. This reinforces the notion of 'deep structures' underlying the surface manifestation of landscapes. Hydrological landscape structure can be deemed to comprise:

- groundwater flow systems
- parts of groundwater flow systems on either side of the groundwater catchment boundary
- infiltration and related exfiltration zones
- surface water catchment areas (of different orders)
- parts of the surface water catchments of either side of a stream
- upstream and downstream areas in surface water catchments.

Within this, shallow groundwater systems appear and disappear depending on precipitation, whilst deeper systems and their exfiltration zones have a more permanent character. Surface water flow is closely related to the groundwater (van Buuren, 1991).

According to van Buuren (1991), landscape disturbance can be arrested by re-establishing a stabilising hydrological framework in which sustainable management can be practised. This framework should be based on the major physiographic elements and their associated water flows. He argues that hierarchically ordered and superimposed groundwater flow systems can be identified, each with its particular infiltration zone and one or more exfiltration zones. These systems vary in their chemical and physical properties, leading to a differentiation of environmental conditions throughout the landscape. Similarly, de Smidt *et al.* (1991) claim that landscape gradients in river plains are caused by the interaction of different water types associated with regional and local groundwater systems, surface water systems and local rainwater bodies. Their qualitative and quantitative differences influence vegetation patterns, producing ecologically rich transition zones associated with shallow, local groundwater flows.

Temporal and spatial variation in the physico-chemical properties of flow systems is caused by numerous factors, including human activities such as land drainage, forestry and agriculture. With regard to groundwater, the chemical composition in infiltration zones is 'atmospheric', resembling rainwater, but during its passage underground mineralisation and other processes lead to a more 'lithospheric' composition in exfiltration zones. The extent of these changes is influenced by residence times, rock and soil composition and human impacts. Wetland habitats are of major conservation importance, but are also highly sensitive to human interference in flow systems. Upland bogs rely solely on precipitation to maintain saturated conditions, the direction of water flow being radially outwards from the centre. Land drainage or peat extraction on adjacent land will increase outflow at the margins, lowering water levels across a wide area. In fens, water balances rely on groundwater inflow and water from neighbouring high ground, and reduction of these inputs by drainage or groundwater abstraction can cause rapid drying out. Buffer zones can help reduce these impacts, but their delimitation is difficult.

A major hydrological impact in recent decades has been pollution by agricultural nitrate applications. This is especially important in cool temperate climates where intensive arable and livestock enterprises are conducted on soils overlying exposed aquifer recharge zones (Strebel *et al.*, 1989; H. Cook, 1991). Farm woodlands may also have significant effects, especially when newly established. Whiteley (1990) suggested that in the early years of woodland establishment, drainage volumes would probably be higher because of reduced transpiration from exposed soils, and nitrate leaching could be increased by mineralisation of soil organic matter. On experimental plots, Whiteley and Rushton (1991) confirmed the high levels of mineralisation and nutrient flows in young plantations, with arable plots, permanent grassland and mature woodlands showing progressively smaller drainage volumes and nitrate leaching. Part of this effect will clearly be due to mature woodland reducing the amount of hydrologically effective rainfall; smaller woodlands (such as those on farms) will often be disproportionately effective because of their greater edge effects and associated evaporative losses. Removal of sediments and nutrients by woodland establishment and grass filter strips in aquifer recharge zones and river ecotones has been widely documented and offers a landscape ecological opportunity to reduce nitrate leaching (cf. Bleuten and de Wit, 1991; Gilliam *et al.*, 1991; Descamps, 1991).

Hydrological systems may provide a valuable framework for ecological planning, with corridor systems based on river ecotones. Stream order also provides a natural framework on which to base inter-scale connections and assists open space allocations, with buffer size varying according to order. In practice, landscape plans may entail the reconstruction of historic hydrological regimes, given the anthropogenically induced tendency to either dry or eutrophic conditions in developed countries. Attempts to do this have been based on qualitative interpretations of geology, hydrology, soils, groundwater, topography, land use and vegetation, occasionally supplemented by computer simulations (van Buuren, 1991).

Modelling of landscape ecology

Much of the recent interest in landscape ecology has centred on the construction of mathematical indices or models, with the hope that these can aid the development of a cogent and distinctive theoretical basis to the subject. Broadly speaking, two types of model exist: those seeking to simulate dynamic processes between organisms and their environment (*process* models), and those providing summary measures of landscape structure (*pattern* models). The latter are sometimes thought of as 'high level' spatial models of distribution, and the former as smaller-scale models relating metapopulations and local populations to land use. All have been strongly influenced by the widespread adoption of GIS.

One of the most genuinely landscape ecological approaches has been to summarise corridor structure by topological measures. The best known are the gamma index of connectivity (proportion of the possible links in a network to those which it actually contains) and the alpha index of circuitry (alternative routes of flow) (Forman and Godron, 1986):

$$\gamma = \frac{L}{L_{max}} = \frac{L}{3(V-2)}$$

$$\alpha = \frac{\text{actual circuits}}{\text{maximum circuits}} = \frac{L - V + 1}{2V - 5}$$

where L = number of links in network, and
V = number of nodes in network.

Together these may be taken as an indication of the degree of network complexity. However, they are abstractions and do not contain important ecological information such as actual distances, direction of links or precise locations of nodes. Heterogeneity may also be used as a synoptic measure, to obtain an overview of how intimately mixed are the constituents of a landscape. One means of expressing this is via the diversity of patch size — especially important for those creatures which depend on visiting several separate patches to satisfy their life-cycle needs. Baudry (1984) has proposed the Shannon Index (*SI*) as a summary measure of the heterogeneity of grain size.

$$SI = \sum P(i) \cdot \ln P(i)$$

where $P(i)$ = the frequency of grain size class i estimated by the distance between two consecutive hedgerows on a transect.

Other measures attempt to convey the notion of traversibility of landscapes. Schaffer and Knaapen (1990), for instance, relate traversibility to habitat isolation from a source area and the characteristics of the interjacent matrix. To account for the latter, they propose a measure of 'minimal cumulative resistance' (MCR) based on beneficial matrix elements (e.g. habitats suitable for foraging and resting) or pathways (corridors), and on adverse physical or psychological barriers to dispersing creatures. Given enough information on the characteristics of a species, and a classification of landscape patches, it should then be possible to hazard at least an intelligent guess as to the resistance of different landscapes to dispersal. Probability of a trajectory being successfully covered is assumed to decrease with distance travelled and the user-unfriendliness of the matrix. This probability is expressed as a monotonically decreasing function of the integral of all landscape resistances experienced over the travelled distance:

$$P = f \sum_{i=1}^{i=n} (d_i \cdot r_i)$$

where p = probability of successful coverage of the whole trajectory
f = some unknown but monotonically decreasing function
d_i = distance travelled through landscape type i, and
r_i = resistance of landscape type i.

The cumulative resistance provides an indication of the relative difficulty of migrating along a complete trajectory, and an algorithm may be written to search for the route with the least simulation steps, that is, the MCR. The principal problem with this approach is our limited understanding about the correct form of the function f (Knaapen *et al.*, 1990). Thus, rather than yielding accurate quantitative predictions, it is more suited to providing insights into the comparative impacts of different landscape alterations and the effects of severing particular patches or corridors. Equally, it can be used to evaluate the accessibility of a new habitat and its contribution to the accessibility of previously isolated patches.

Further insights into landscape structure have been assisted by models based on fractal geometry. Here, the fundamental characteristic of interest is the consistent manner in which patch density, forage biomass, patch edge length and shape vary as a function of the resolution (scale) at which measurements are made (Wiens, 1989; Milne, 1991). As previously noted, a landscape pattern will be perceived differently by different species, depending on the scale at which they operate. Each of the quantitative measures of a landscape, such as peri-meter to area ratio of patches, are predicted to vary as a function of the length scale used, according to the general fractal scaling relation:

$$Q(L) = kL^D$$

where $Q(L)$ = quality measured using a length
scale L
k = a constant, and
D = the fractal dimension of the quality.

If animals and plants are conceived as operating at different scales (e.g. due to differences in home range area or dispersal distance), this equation will describe how a species' perceptions of a resource will vary with scale type (Milne *et al.*, 1989; Wiens and Milne, 1989; Milne, 1991). Interactive modelling can be employed to produce fractal designs which, in contrast to the mechanistic qualities of natural fractal patterns, fortuitously resemble plausible eco-system patterns. Despite the attractive nature of fractal models in exploring potential land use con-figurations, they share the limitation of other spatial models in failing to maintain the structural relation-ships of real landscapes.

Models of dynamic landscape ecological processes are numerous, and much of the previously reviewed evidence has been derived from modelled results. The most useful approaches can be related to what Merriam *et al.* (1990) describe as 'doubly dynamic' models in which elements of changing landscape patterns interact in time and space with demograph-ically and spatially dynamic populations. Many other researchers have similarly alluded to the importance of recognising the 'shifting mosaic', or perpetual change taking place in habitats. Thus, models may elucidate ways in which organisms match their dynamics to the fluctuations of vital life-cycle re-sources or, equally, means whereby conservation strategies may make available a spatio-temporal array of resources suited to particular organisms. Model categories broadly comprise:

- *corridor models*, where connectivity (or the extent and quality of corridors) is assumed to be the key element affecting demographics
- *non-corridor models*, used particularly for bird species, which disperse on a broader front
- *pool models*, in which dispersal may take place indirectly through a pool of potential immigrants. These tend to ignore conventional metapopulation and habitat considerations and are based primarily on time and chance, emphasising the link of con-nectivity to species behaviour and the individual ways in which habitat fragmentation affects different species

- *mixed pool/corridor models*, where species are assumed to use a landscape matrix as a subdivisible pool with an overlay of directed corridor movement.

The major limitation to the use of landscape ecological models is probably data input, as there continues to be a scarcity of reliable information about detailed environmental needs or behaviour of individual species.

From modelling to planning

An ideal basis for modelling a future landscape would include comprehensive information on its species and their habitat requirements. This species-specific approach is clearly impractical and leads to a 'Nero dilemma', inducing inaction because of un-certainty (Soule, 1986). The other extreme would be a 'black box' approach in which only broad measures such as connectivity and porosity were considered. However, such a generalised method could be opposed on the grounds that actual landscapes do not in reality satisfy all species' requirements, rendering a 'grapeshot' approach invalid (cf. van Selm, 1988). A compromise position seems to be to establish clear planning objectives, based on the known requirements of key organisms such as rare species, indicator species and pollinators. Merriam (1991) argues that the appropriate land (planning) unit should be that which satisfies the minimum habitat quantities and combinations necessary for the demographic and genetic survival of a given species. Key parameters would then be the maximum normal distance and area that the species moves through, and the habitat and corridor types used. It would also be necessary to ensure the user-friendliness of corridors and stepping stones in facilitating sufficient delivery of the target species to the recipient habitat patches, and the presence of a satisfactory source of colonists.

Landscape ecological planning must not only con-sider the appropriate spatial arrangement of eco-logical features, but also the temporal dynamic of landscape change. Ideally, this should permit the rotation of habitats of different successional stages through space over time. Conscious management, especially of non-climax patches, is needed to introduce the disturbance regimes essential to sus-taining a mosaic of ecological patches. Piecemeal approaches to species and land management can distort the integrity of ecological units, resulting in severe changes to vital processes (Merriam, 1991; Pickett and White, 1985).

Since practical planning cannot accommodate the

whole range of needs for all likely species, a number of studies have sought to highlight indicator species occupying a core habitat which can be used to anchor land use planning strategies. A major opportunity to test this has been with the Randstadt 'green structure' in which new woodlands are being established at a distance accessible to migrating species from existing woodlots. Experimental results had demonstrated a strong area effect, with most woodland bird species displaying a minimum size threshold for survival (Harms and Opdam, 1990). Presence of forest birds (i.e. those restricted to forest habitat) was correlated with area but not with isolation variables. However, residual variance for forest-interior (i.e. mature woodland) species was explained by a combination of regional difference, total woodland area within 1 km of core habitat and density of hedgerows. The most distinct isolation effects (i.e. greatest dependence on connecting wooded corridors) were displayed by the green woodpecker, marsh tit and nuthatch, which could be taken as sensitive indicator species. Results indicated an area effect, with minimum threshold size set at 10 ha, and 50 ha proposed as a locally appropriate size to ensure healthy populations. Scheffer and Knaapen (1990) likewise evaluated potential forest sites for groups of mammals, birds and butterflies, each group comprising a few representatives of a larger class associated with similar habitat. Landscape resistance was related to interforest distances (exceeding 1 km), lack of hedgerows and trees, and distinct linear features likely to behave as barriers (such as broad rivers/canals, dual carriageways).

Ahern (1990, 1991) utilised landscape ecology as a means of underpinning 'sustainable' plans for open space, in which spaces were explicitly conceived as an integrated system. Several other studies have advocated or implemented greenway networks to perform various supposed functions. Wildlife corridors and timber production are perhaps the most common, but recreation (e.g. Groome, 1990), local climatic amelioration, and a number of hydrological functions such as flood control, river pollution filtering and reduction of bank erosion have been noted (E. Cook, 1991a, b). Bridgewater and Woodin (1990) also suggest that interconnecting open space networks can assist species to adjust to climatic change — an increasingly important issue in land use planning (cf. DoE, 1992) — by enabling them to respond to new distribution ranges. A popular design principle emphasising the variety of functions of open space is the multiple-use-module (MUM), comprising a well-protected habitat of sufficient size to support interior species, and with a concentric buffer subject to increasing influences away from the interior (Noss and Harris, 1986).

Ahern's approach was to devise an extensive open space system (EOSS) within which patches and corridors shared sufficient connectivity to function inter-dependently as a network. It thus marked a departure from direct ownership and management of designated conservation sites towards an extensive concept of land management emphasising the context and configuration of greenways. The primary determinants of the EOSS were topographic and drainage features, which typically were geographically continuous and unsuited to development. Consequently, much emphasis was placed on maintaining or creating stream buffers. Similarly, de Buuren (1991) has indicated that hydrologically based plans might include belts of trees and shrubs along major streams in upland reaches, or meander and inundation zones in lowland reaches. Purification marshes may also be useful in agricultural areas. The main components of the EOSS were then linked to broader landscape patches through corridors, so that the EOSS became a skeleton to which adjacent habitats could be attached. Planners are warned against giving undue emphasis to recent land use elements (such as hedgerows and forest patches) at the expense of the deeper structure, though other research (e.g. Bunce and Peters, 1991) stresses the value of retaining hedgerows as these host much of the remaining reservoir of species in intensively farmed areas.

A pragmatic basis for an EOSS may be to use a management region (e.g. watershed, political unit) as the operative top-level zone, and within this to have a nested hierarchy of landscape management elements at several ecologically meaningful scales. It is also practical to limit the rationale for EOSS design to certain 'indicator species', and to assume that these represent habitat types in which a larger community of species is known to exist. In Ahern's study, the otter (*Lutra canadensis*) and fisher (*Martes pennanti*) were selected: both are fragmentation intolerant, have relatively specific habitat requirements and possess complementary needs (otter is riparian and fisher is upland). Thus, it could be assumed that the establishment of an otter–fisher wildlife corridor network would be inclusive of many other species' needs.

Plan production and implementation

The first step in the production of any plan is to obtain comprehensive survey information. This should comprise both ecological resources (landscape structure and potential source populations) and socio-economic information on productive rural land uses and landownerships. Selman and Doar (1991, 1992), for instance, obtained information on forestry potential, habitat types, selective patch and corridor extent and condition, per cent broadleaf composition and age classes of woodlands, various management practices, farm viability, and farm boundaries. Ahern similarly mapped the bio-physical, socio-cultural, visual-aesthetic, and development potentials of his pilot region. In both of these studies, data were fed into a geographic information system (GIS) as feature-coded layers.

Having constructed an acceptable information base it then becomes possible to move towards an overall design. Master plans for *remembrements* in Belgium (Froment and Wildmann, 1987) and France (Baudry and Burel, 1984) have been produced, on the basis of rather qualitative criteria, aimed at allowing free movement of fauna and regulating water and soil flows. In general terms, the main features of a landscape which planners can seek to manipulate will be its basic structural characteristics (size, shape, number, type and configuration of patches, corridors and matrix) and the disturbance regimes to which they are subjected. More detailed proposals may also be appropriate: for instance, in areas subject to clearfelling, retention of windfirm woodland edges may help provide continuity of age classes in the broader landscape, 'low warmth' for game birds, and visual cover (Selman, 1990a).

Given the unacceptability of grapeshot landscape plans, proposals must be based on objectives and policies which guide plan production along particular lines. In the context of farm woodland promotion within their central Scotland study area, Selman and Doar (1991, 1992) sought to: conserve moorland birds (effectively delimiting 'no go' areas for forestry), conserve woodland birds, mix age classes and species, and balance coniferous and

deciduous planting according to ecological, cultural and managerial considerations. A more comprehensive hierarchy of aims, objectives, policies and proposals was adopted, based on the maintenance of sustainable ecological processes and socio-economic viability (Table 1). Although these policies were diverse in nature and intent, they can be illustrated by the proposal to mass woodland adjacent to the periphery of farm units. This was intended to create a 'forest experience' and a more viable ecological unit, to enable adjacent farms to share a degree of shelter for stock (one of the principal motives for farmers to plant trees), and hopefully to minimise the economic fragmentation of the remaining agricultural land.

An element of qualitative choice had to be retained as a high degree of precision was impossible. Thus, since an infinite number of corridors could be devised, these were not located or evaluated on a quantitative basis, but were included in detailed designs according to policy assumptions. Elements such as matrix width (inter-patch distance) and the topology of nodes and edges were measured and used to discriminate between alternative designs, though absolute quantification proved difficult because of ambiguities in potentially measurable properties. However, marked improvements in parameters of patch shape, size and isolation were observed, whilst analysis of circuitry and connectivity demonstrated the benefits to be gained from concentrating on the quality rather than merely the quantity of corridors. Land use planning and economic factors were reflected in the selection of part and whole farms for afforestation. The economically marginal conditions of the area suggested that the smallest farms would be most vulnerable and thus relatively likely to be converted outright to

Table 1. Objectives and policies for central Scotland pilot area

Objectives
- avoid harm to sites of existing conservation value
- minimise adverse effects of planting on species characteristic of open habitats which are already present in the landscape
- promote woodland interior species and species requiring both woodland and open habitat
- increase aesthetic value of the landscape
- operate within specified socio-economic constraints

Policies
- identify and protect sites of conservation interest with surrounding buffer zones
- avoid planting bog areas and pay special attention to their buffer zones
- seek to maintain connectivity, width of connections and presence of loops in the open matrix
- plant woodland blocks as large as possible, with a few smaller outliers
- maintain at least two options for movement between every pair of woods via the landscape's network of field boundaries
- aim to create and/or maintain large, structurally complex hedgerows which are linked to as many woods as possible
- woods should be approximately isodiametric in shape, but with some boundary irregularities and a tendency towards curved edges, following landform where appropriate
- plant land near to access routes and towards the periphery of land units
- where possible, do not plant class 3 agricultural capability land or better
- where possible, do not plant class 5 forestry capability land or worse

forestry, whilst farms with the most favourable cash flows were assumed to be able to invest in integrated plantations. Landownership and farm business data assisted in the identification of appropriate holdings. Local planning objectives proposing alternative targets of 5% individual farm woodland cover and 30% total woodland cover in the area were then used to guide the production of two hypothetical landscape ecological plans.

Ahern (1990, 1991) was faced with the reverse situation of protecting existing woodlands at risk from attrition and fragmentation, and thus selecting the most suitable areas to retain in an open space strategy. His approach was to identify broad swathes within which specific barriers and assets to wildlife could be sought, and then to define the EOSS within these corridors on the basis of presumed species requirements. These aimed to incorporate the shortest routes between principal nodes. Corridors were located mainly on existing public land and undevelopable land, so as to minimise sterilisation of development prospects. At a qualitative level at least, the corridors could be tested for types of linkage appropriate to different fauna: this is consistent with previous observations about circuitry (loops) and connectivity.

Some species, for instance, require circuits to be present to permit return to base following foraging ('travelling salesmen' networks) whilst others may prefer to move progressively through a landscape to new territories ('Paul Revere' networks). Planning objectives sought to retain 100 m wide corridors with additional 15 m limited use buffers either side, maximum amount of habitat linkage, shortest average length of linkages, and least numbers of parcels covered.

In both Ahern's and Selman and Doar's studies, the actual landscape proposals were somewhat arbitrary, leading to recommendations for adaptive and flexible planning approaches supported by GIS. Adaptive environmental assessment and management (AEAM) has been advocated (Holling, 1978; Walters, 1986) as a means of coping with activities which are subject to uncertainties during pre-planning, implementation and operation and for which a combination of flexible data input, interactive modelling, and expert brainstorming is appropriate. GIS, despite the initial time-consuming investment in data entry, becomes a valuable tool not just for initial plan design but also for rapid reassessment of the consequences of unforeseen modifications. This is particularly appropriate to the circumstances of landscape planning, where planners exercise little control over detailed outcomes.

Powers to implement landscape plans are highly variable, but broadly comprise land acquisition, use regulation and voluntary mechanisms (Ahern, 1990). Perhaps the strongest and best financed programme is that of the Randstadt green structure, which will include many specific landscape ecological principles. In Denmark, conservation orders have been introduced which enable protection of existing habitat through restrictions on management practices, as well as landscape restoration (Primdahl, 1990, 1991). An initiative of exceptional promise in Britain has been the initiation of community forests. These are to be based on indicative plans (cf. Selman, 1990b) which could potentially incorporate an ecological framework. The mechanisms underpinning them are fundamentally weak, however, and supplementary financing is modest. In contrast to the Randstadtgroenstructuur, there is no power to acquire and trade land. The expectation is that they can be implemented through a combination of existing measures, including farm woodland grants, planning obligations, restoration of mineral workings and derelict land, and other amenity planting grants. Woodland planting on publicly owned land is likely to be an important early feature of community forests, but declining thereafter. However, Bishop (1991, 1992) has amassed a considerable amount of evidence that reliance on these means is likely to meet with limited success. Only the creative after-use of mineral extractions, guided by firm planning policies, appears to hold promise.

Nevertheless, recent fundamental reform of EC agricultural policy might make farm woodland options preferable, especially if the Farm Woodland Premium can be enhanced and the immediate economic pressures on farmers alleviated. Key capabilities of a community forest development company would then be to advise and assist farmers in making grant applications, and perhaps offer additional top-up funds and co-operative services. Given an effective means of implementation, community forest plans offer an outstanding opportunity for strategic landscape ecological planning to create an extensive and coherent rural estate.

Conclusion

Most commentators on the countryside now acknowledge that it is insufficient simply to conduct rearguard actions against ecological losses. Research and practice since the 1970s have recognised the need to create new agricultural landscapes, rather than preserve eighteenth-century ones. Serious responses, however, have lacked both a clear theoretical base and a *modus operandi*. We have

Table 2. Emergent landscape ecological planning principles

1. Define management region — e.g. watershed, political unit, countryside project area
2. Survey area for ecological, socio-economic and landownership patterns, especially:
     location and quality of existing habitats
     hydrological structure
     current land use and forward planning proposals
     farm boundaries
     farm profitability
     forestry land capability potential
3. Identify small range of indicator species on which to base landscape design
4. Ascertain inter-patch dispersal distances, and user-friendly qualities of patches and corridors, for named species
     (inter-patch distances typically 1 km for large blocks and 50–100 m for small patches or corridor nodes)
5. Identify sources of colonists of named species
6. Demarcate protected buffers (e.g. 100 m) and limited use buffers (e.g. additional 15 m) around rivers
7. Aim for large forest blocks (e.g. 50 ha), many smaller blocks (but not <5 ha), and wide hedgerows and shelterbelts
     (e.g. over 8 m for conduit role and up to 500 m for 'interior' habitat conditions)
8. Integrate hierarchical plan design, possibly based on stream order
9. Integrate ecological, visual and recreational measures within multiple use modules, with varying degrees of intensity
     appropriate to local objectives
10. Produce management guidelines to promote a 'stable change' of key habitats and minimise user-unfriendliness of
     matrix areas
11. Create GIS model of plan area to facilitate adaptive responses to future land use changes
12. Monitor future changing distributions of wildlife species, alongside development of 'process' models

been constructing a countryside of fragments, rather than shaping a rural estate whose whole is greater than the sum of those parts.

Several new policy measures are now available which at least offer an initial prospect of extensive landscape reconstruction. It has been proposed here that the emergent discipline of landscape ecology can provide a practical and theoretical framework for broad-scale countryside design. Although the theories are predominantly scientific, the hallmark of landscape ecology is its readiness to integrate biophysical and socio-economic parameters. It is thus able to integrate the disturbances created by economic land uses with ecological processes in heterogeneous landscapes. Despite the fact that the explicit study of landscape ecology is barely a decade old, there is already a growing consensus about the principles upon which appropriate planning policies can be based. In the fullness of time we must hope that process models and behavioural studies can help refine the rather crude assumptions which must presently be made. However, it is unlikely that the blunt instruments of countryside policy and planning can ever accommodate fine levels of detail and rigid design criteria. A shopping list of emergent planning principles — offered as a basis for debate and constructive criticism, rather than a definitive statement — is proposed in Table 2.

Examples have been reviewed of embryonic practical applications. These indicate that, whilst valid design strategies can be produced, the control framework, and landowners' or developers' responses, can be difficult to predict. Consequently, a flexible, adaptive approach to planning must be adopted. GIS models are thus likely to be pivotal both to the original design stage, and to the revision and testing of subsequent modifications to the basic framework. An outstanding opportunity for the application of landscape ecological planning is currently presented by the policy programme and indicative framework plans for community forests. Planners involved in these and similar exercises must take seriously their responsibility as custodians of the regional landscapes of the twenty-first century, and not simply be guided by opportunism.

Acknowledgement — This paper arises from a study funded by the Forestry Research Co-ordination Committee (which formed part of their Special Topic Programme in Farm Forestry), and by the Cheltenham and Gloucester College of Higher Education.

References

Adler, G.H. and Tamarin, R.H. (1984) Demography and reproduction in island and mainland white-footed mice (*Peromyscus leucopus*) in South-Eastern Massachusets. *Canadian Journal of Zoology* **62**, 58–64.

Agger, P. and Brandt, J. (1988) Dynamics of small biotopes in Danish agricultural landscapes. *Landscape Ecology* **1**, 227–240.

Ahern, J. (1990) Wildlife corridor planning in central Massachusets. In *Proceedings of the 1990 ASLA Annual Meeting*, pp. 31–47, Ahern, J. and Fabos, J.G. (eds). American Society of Landscape Architects, San Diego, California.

Ahern, J. (1991) Planning for an extensive open space system. *Landscape and Urban Planning* **21**, 131–146.

Allen, T.F.H. and Starr, T.B. (1982) *Hierarchy: Perspectives for Ecological Complexity*. University of Chicago Press, Chicago.

Ambuel, E. and Temple, S.A. (1983) Area dependent changes in the bird communities and vegetation of

South-Eastern Wisconsin forests. *Ecology* **64**, 1057–1068.

Andren, H. and Angelstam, P. (1988) Elevated predation rates as an edge effect in habitat islands: experimental evidence. *Ecology* **69**, 544–547.

Appleton, J. (1975) *The Experience of Landscape.* John Wiley, London.

Appleton, J. (1988) Prospects and refuges re-visited. In *Environmental Aesthetics: Theory, Research and Applications*, pp. 27–44, Nasar, J.L. (ed.). Cambridge University Press, Cambridge.

Arnold, G.W. (1983) The influence of ditch and hedgerow structure, lengths of hedgerows and area of woodland and garden on bird numbers on farmland. *Journal of Applied Ecology* **20**, 731–750.

Askins, R.A., Philbrick, J. and Sugeno, D. (1987) Relationships between the regional abundance of forest and the composition of forest bird communities. *Biological Conservation* **39**, 129–152.

Asselin, A. and Baudry, J. (1989) Les araneides dans une espace agricole en mutation. *Acta Ecologica* **10**, 143–156.

Baudry, J. (1984) Effects of landscape structure on biological communities: the case of hedgerow network landscapes. In *Methodology in Landscape Ecological Research and Planning. Proceedings of the 1st International Seminar of the International Association of Landscape Ecology*, Vol. 1, pp. 55–65, Brandt, J. and Agger, P. (eds). Roskilde Universitetsforlag, Roskilde.

Baudry, J. (1988a) Structure et fonctionnement ecologique des paysages: cas des bocages. *Bulletin on Ecology* **19**, 523–530.

Baudry, J. (1988b) Hedgerows and hedgerow networks as wildlife habitat in agricultural landscapes. In *Environmental Management in Agriculture: European Perspectives*, pp. 111–124, Park, J.R. (ed.). Belhaven, London.

Baudry, J. and Burel, F. (1984) Landscape project *remembrement*: landscape consolidation in France. *Landscape Planning* **11**, 235–241.

Baudry, J. and Merriam, G. (1988) Connectivity and connectedness: functional versus structural patterns in landscapes. In *Connectivity in Landscape Ecology. Proceedings of the 2nd International Seminar of the International Association of Landscape Ecology*, pp. 23–28, Schreiber, K.-F. (ed.). Munstersche Geographische Arbeiten, Munster.

Berger, J. (1987) Guidelines for landscape synthesis: some directions old and new. *Landscape and Urban Planning* **14**, 295–311.

Berleant, A. (1988) Aesthetic preceptions in environmental design. In *Environmental Aesthetics: Theory, Research and Applications*, pp. 84–97, Nasar, J.L. (ed.). Cambridge University Press, Cambridge.

Bishop, K. (1991) Community forests: implementing the concept. *The Planner* **77**(18), 6–10.

Bishop, K. (1992) Creating community forests: problems and opportunities. *Tree News* (Summer), 14–16.

Bleuten, W. and de Wit, N.H.S.M. (1991) The buffering of nutrient pollution of groundwater related to spatial position, soil type and land use. Paper presented to the World Congress of Landscape Ecology, International Association for Landscape Ecology, University of Carleton, Ottawa, 21–25 July 1991.

Bos, E.M. and Bleuten, W. (1991) Restoration of valley bog ecosystems surrounded by agriculture. Paper presented to the World Congress of Landscape Ecology, International Association for Landscape Ecology, University of Carleton, Ottawa, 21–25 July 1991.

Bridgewater, P. and Woodin, S.J. (1990) Role of greenways in helping species adjust to climatic change. *Land Use Policy* **7**, 165–168.

Budd, W.W., Saunders, P.R. and Coen, P. (1987) Stream corridor management in the Pacific North-West 1: determination of stream corridor widths. *Environmental Management* **11**, 587–597.

Bunce, R.G.H. and Peters, J.C. (1991) The incorporation of ecological principles into planning in Great Britain. Paper presented to the World Congress of Landscape Ecology, International Association for Landscape Ecology, University of Carleton, Ottawa, 21–25 July 1991.

Burel, F. (1989) Landscape structure effects on carabid beetles' spatial patterns in Western France. *Landscape Ecology* **2**, 215–226.

Burel, F. (1991) Concurrence between landscape ecology and landscape aesthetics in Brittany, France. Paper presented to the World Congress of Landscape Ecology, International Association for Landscape Ecology, University of Carleton, Ottawa, 21–25 July 1991.

Burkey, T.V. (1989) Extinction in nature reserves: the effect of fragmentation and the importance of migration between reserve fragments. *Oikos* **55**, 75–81.

van Buuren, M. (1991) A hydrological approach to landscape planning. The framework-concept elaborated from a hydrological perspective. *Landscape and Urban Planning* **21**, 91–107.

Calvin, J.S., Dearinger, J.A. and Curtin, M.E. (1972) An attempt at assessing preferences for natural landscapes. *Environment and Behaviour* **4**, 447–470.

Collinge, S.K., Forman, R.T.T. and Smith, D.S. (1991) The influence of boundary form on habitat usage by elk and mule deer. Paper presented to the World Congress of Landscape Ecology, International Association for Landscape Ecology, University of Carleton, Ottawa, 21–25 July 1991.

Cook, E.A. (1991a) Urban landscape networks: an ecological planning framework. *Landscape Research* **16**(3), 7–15.

Cook, E.A. (1991b) Ecosystem modeling as a method for designing synthetic fluvial landscapes: a case study of the Salt River in Arizona. *Landscape and Urban Planning* **20**, 291–308.

Cook, H. (1991) Nitrate protection zones: targeting and land use over an aquifer. *Land Use Policy* **8**, 16–28.

Correll, D.L., Jordan, T.E. and Weller, D.E. (1991) Nutrient dynamics in coastal plain agricultural watersheds: the role of riparian forests. Paper presented to the World Congress of Landscape Ecology, International Association for Landscape Ecology, University of Carleton, Ottawa, 21–25 July 1991.

Countryside Commission (1989a) *Forests in the Community.* The Countryside Commission, Cheltenham.

Countryside Commission (1989b) *A New National Forest in the Midlands.* The Countryside Commission, Cheltenham.

Countryside Commission (1991) *Countryside Stewardship.* The Countryside Commission, Cheltenham.

Dennis, P. (1991) Fragmentation of farm woodland: processes affecting the distribution and fitness of arboreal arthropod species. Research note (43 pp.), Institute of Terrestrial Ecology, Edinburgh, U.K.

Department of the Environment (1992) *Local Plans. Planning Policy Guidance Note 12* (revised). HMSO, London.

Descamps, H. (1991) The ecology of fluvial landscapes. Paper presented to the World Congress of Landscape

Ecology, International Association for Landscape Ecology, University of Carleton, Ottawa, 21–25 July 1991.

Dessylas, M.D. (1990) The adaptation of social and structural policy of the EEC to the changed market situation: the protection of the countryside. *Landscape and Urban Planning* **18**, 197–207.

Diamond, J. (1975) The island dilemma: lessons of modern biogeographic studies for the design of natural reserves. *Biological Conservation* **7**, 129–146.

van Dorp, D. and Opdam, P. (1987) Effects of patch size, isolation and regional abundance on forest bird communities. *Landscape Ecology* **1**, 59–73.

Drake, J.A. (1988) Biological invasions into nature reserves. *Trends in Ecology and Evolution* **3**, 186–187.

Fahrig, L. and Merriam, G. (1985) Habitat patch connectivity and population survival. *Ecology* **66**, 1762–1768.

Forestry Commission (1989) *Forest Landscape Design Guidelines*. The Forestry Commission, Edinburgh.

Forman, R.T.T. (1990) Personal communication.

Forman, R.T.T. (1991) Landscape corridors: from theoretical foundations to public policy. In *The Role of Corridors*, pp. 71–84, Saunders, D.A. and Hobbs, R.J. (eds). Surrey Beatty and Sons, Chipping Norton, Australia.

Forman, R.T.T. and Godron, M. (1986) *Landscape Ecology*. John Wiley, New York.

Fritz, R.S. (1979) Consequences of insular population structure: distribution and extinction of spruce grouse populations. *Oecologica* **42**, 57–65.

Froment, A. and Wildmann, B. (1987) Landscape ecology and rural restructuring in Belgium. *Landscape and Urban Planning* **14**, 415–426.

Game, M. (1980) Best shape for nature reserves. *Nature* **287**, 630–632.

Gilliam, J.W., Daniels, R.B. and Parsons, J. (1991) Vegetated buffers for nutrient and sediment removal. Paper presented to the World Congress of Landscape Ecology, International Association for Landscape Ecology, University of Carleton, Ottawa, 21–25 July 1991.

Gilpin, M.E. and Soule, M.E. (1986) Minimum viable populations: processes of species extinction. In *Conservation Biology*, pp. 19–34, Soule, M.E. (ed.). Sinauer, Sunderland, Massachusetts.

Golley, F.B. (1987) Introducing landscape ecology. *Landscape Ecology* **1**, 1–3.

Greenbie, B.B. (1988) The landscape of social symbols. In *Environmental Aesthetics: Theory, Research and Applications*, pp. 64–73, Nasar, J.L. (ed.). Cambridge University Press, Cambridge.

Groome, D. (1990) 'Green corridors': a discussion of a planning concept. *Landscape and Urban Planning* **19**, 383–387.

Gulinck, H., van den Berghe, I. and Abts, E. (1988) Dynamics, interactions and connectivity of linear elements in rural landscapes in central Belgium: planning opportunities. In *Connectivity in Landscape Ecology. Proceedings of the 2nd International Symposium of the International Association of Landscape Ecology*, pp. 89–91, Schreiber, K.-F. (ed.). Munstersche Geographische Arbeiten, Munster.

Hall, D.L. (1991) Landscape planning: functionalism as a motivating concept from landscape ecology and human ecology. *Landscape and Urban Planning* **21**, 13–20.

Hanski, I. (1989) Metapopulation dynamics: does it help to have more of the same? *Trends in Ecology and Evolution* **4**, 113–114.

Hansson, L. (1988) Dispersal and patch connectivity as species-specific characteristics. In *Connectivity in Landscape Ecology. Proceedings of the 2nd International Symposium of the International Association of Landscape Ecology*, pp. 111–113, Schreiber, K.-F. (ed.). Mustersche Geographische Arbeiten. Munster.

Harms, W.B. and Opdam, P. (1990) Woods as habitat patches for birds: applications in landscape planning in The Netherlands. In *Changing Landscapes: an Ecological Perspective*, pp. 73–97, Zonneveld, I.S. and Forman, R.T.T. (eds). Springer, New York.

Harris, L.D. (1984) *The Fragmented Forest: Island Biogeographic Theory and the Preservation of Biotic Diversity*. Yale University Press, New Haven.

Harris, L.D. and Gallagher, P.B. (1989) New initiatives for wildlife conservation: the need for movement corridors. In *Preserving Communities and Corridors*, pp. 11–34. Defenders of Wildlife, Washington, D.C.

Henderson, M.T., Merriam, G. and Wegner, J. (1985) Patchy environments and species survival: chipmunks in an agricultural mosaic. *Biological Conservation* **31**, 95–105.

Henein, K. and Merriam, G. (1990) The elements of connectivity where corridor quality is variable. *Landscape Ecology* **4**, 157–170.

Hobbs, E.R. (1988) Species richness of urban forest patches and implications for urban landscape diversity. *Landscape Ecology* **1**, 141–152.

Hobbs, R.J., Hussey, B.M.J. and Saunders, D.A. (1989) Nature conservation: the role of corridors. *International Association of Landscape Ecology Bulletin* **7**, 21–23.

Holling, C.S. (ed.) (1978) *Adaptive Environmental Assessment and Management*. Wiley, Chichester.

Jacobs, P. (1986) Sustaining landscapes — sustaining societies. *Landscape and Urban Planning* **13**, 349–358.

Kaplan, R. (1983) Dominant and variant values in environmental preference. In *Proceedings of a Conference on Environmental Preferences in Landscape Management*, pp. 21–23, Connecticut College, New London.

Kaplan, R. and Kaplan, S. (1978) *Humanscape: Environments for People*. Duxbury Press, Duxbury, U.S.A.

Kaplan, S. (1988) Perceptions and landscape: conceptions and misconceptions. In *Environmental Aesthetics: Theory, Research and Applications*, pp. 45–55, Nasar, J.L. (ed.). Cambridge University Press, Cambridge.

Knaapen, J.P., Scheffer, M. and Harms, W.B. (1990) Estimating isolation by means of simulation: an application. Winand Staring Centre, Wageningen (Mimeo).

Le Duc, M.G., Morton, A.J. and Boorman, L.A. (1992) Predicting potential colonisers of new woodland plantations. *Aspects of Applied Biology* **29**, 41–48.

Lefkovitch, L.P. and Fahrig, L. (1985) Spatial characteristics of habitat patches and population survival. *Ecological Modelling* **30**, 297–308.

Levenson, J.B. (1981) Woodlots as biogeographic islands in South-Eastern Wisconsin. In *Forest Island Dynamics in Man-dominated Landscapes*, pp. 13–39, Burgess, R.L. and Sharpe, D.M. (eds). Springer, New York.

Lord, J.M. and Norton, D.A. (1990) Scale and the spatial concept of fragmentation. *Conservation Biology* **4**, 197–202.

Lynch, J.F. and Wigham, D.F. (1984) Effects of forest fragmentation on breeding bird communities in Maryland. *Biological Conservation* **28**, 287–324.

MacArthur, R.H. and Wilson, E. (1967) *The Theory of Island Biogeography*. Princeton University Press, New Jersey.

Mader, H.J. (1984) Animal habitat isolation by roads and agricultural fields. *Biological Conservation* **29**, 81–96.

Mader, H.J., Schell, C. and Kornacker, P. (1990) Linear barriers to arthropod movements in the landscape. *Biological Conservation* **54**, 209–222.

Margules, C., Higgs, A.J. and Rafe, R.W. (1982) Modern biogeographic theory: are there any lessons for nature reserve design? *Biological Conservation* **24**, 115–128.

McCollin, D., Tinklin, R. and Storey, R.A.S. (1984) Woodlands in an arable landscape — bird habitat requirements. In *Methodology in Landscape Ecological Research and Planning. Proceedings of the 1st International Seminar of the International Association for Landscape Ecology*, Vol. 4, pp. 143–146, Brandt, J. and Agger, P. (eds). Roskilde Universitetsforlag, Roskilde, Denmark.

McDonnell, M.J. and Pickett, S.T.A. (1988) Connectivity and the theory of landscape ecology. In *Connectivity in Landscape Ecology. Proceedings of the 2nd International Symposium of the International Association of Landscape Ecology*, pp. 17–19, Schreiber, K.-F. (ed.). Munstersche Geographische Arbeiten 29, Munster.

Merriam, G. (1984) Connectivity: a fundamental ecological characteristic of landscape pattern. In *Methodology in Landscape Ecological Research and Planning. Proceedings of the 1st International Seminar of the International Association of Landscape Ecology*, Vol. 1, pp. 5–15, Brandt, J. and Agger, P. (eds). Roskilde Universitetsforlag, Roskilde.

Merriam, G. (1988) Modelling woodland species adapting to an agricultural landscape. In *Connectivity in Landscape Ecology. Proceedings of the 2nd International Symposium of the International Association of Landscape Ecology*, pp. 67–68, Schreiber, K.-F. (ed.). Munstersche Geographische Arbeiten, Munster.

Merriam, G. (1991) Corridors and connectivity: animal populations in heterogeneous environments. In *The Role of Corridors*, pp. 133–142, Saunders, D.A. and Hobbs, R.J. (eds). Surrey Beatty and Sons, Chipping Norton, Australia.

Merriam, G., Henein, K. and Stuart-Smith, K. (1990) Landscape dynamics models. In *Quantitative Methods in Landscape Ecology*, Turner and Gardner (eds), pp. 399–416. Springer, New York.

Merriam, G., Kosakiewicz, M., Tsuchiya, E. and Hawsley, K. (1989) Barriers as boundaries for meta-populations and demes of *Peromyscus leucopus* in farm landscapes. *Landscape Ecology* **2**, 227–235.

Merriam, G. and Lanoue, A. (1990) Corridor use by small mammals: field measurements for three experimental types of *Peromyscus leucopus*. *Landscape Ecology* **4**, 123–131.

Middleton, J. and Merriam, G. (1981) Woodland mice in a farmland mosaic. *Journal of Applied Ecology* **18**, 703–710.

Middleton, J. and Merriam, G. (1985) Distribution of woodland species in farmland woods. *Journal of Applied Ecology* **20**, 625–644.

Milne, B.T. (1991) The utility of fractal geometry in landscape design. *Landscape and Urban Planning* **21**, 81–90.

Milne, B.T. and Forman, R.T.T. (1986) Peninsulas in Maine: woody plant diversity, distance and environmental patterns. *Ecology* **67**, 967–974.

Milne, B.T., Johnson, K. and Forman, R.T.T. (1989) Scale-dependent proximity of a wildlife habitat in a spatially neutral Bayesian model. *Landscape Ecology* **2**, 101–110.

Moore, N.W. and Hooper, M.D. (1975) On the number of bird species in British woods. *Biological Conservation* **8**, 239–250.

Nassauer, J.F. (1988) Landscape care: perception of local people. In *Landscape and Land Use Planning*, Vol. 8, pp. 27–41. American Society of Landscape Architects, Washington, D.C.

Naveh, Z. and Lieberman, A. (1984) *Landscape Ecology: Theory and Application*. Springer, New York.

Noss, R.E. (1983) A regional landscape approach to maintaining landscape diversity. *Bioscience* **33**, 700–706.

Noss, R.F. (1987) Corridors in real landscapes: a reply to Simberloff and Cox. *Conservation Biology* **1**, 159–164.

Noss, R.F. and Harris, L.D. (1986) Nodes, networks and Multiple Use Modules: preserving diversity at all scales. *Environmental Management* **10**, 299–309.

Olivieri, I., Couvert, D. and Gouyon, P.H. (1990) The genetics of transient populations: research at the meta-population level. *Trends in Ecology and Evolution* **5**, 207–210.

O'Neill, R.V., Milne, B.T., Turner, M.G. and Gardner, R.H. (1988) Resource utilisation scales and landscape pattern. *Landscape Ecology* **2**, 63–69.

Opdam, P. (1988) Populations in fragmented landscapes. In *Connectivity in Landscape Ecology. Proceedings of the 2nd International Symposium of the International Association of Landscape Ecology*, pp. 75–77, Schreiber, K.-F. (ed.). Munstersche Geographische Arbeiten, Munster.

Opdam, P. (1989) Landscape ecology in Europe and North America: a personal impression. *International Association of Landscape Ecologists Bulletin* **7**(2), 3–6.

Opdam, P., van Dorp, D. and ter Brakk, C.J.F. (1984) The effect of isolation on the number of woodland birds in small woods in The Netherlands. *Journal of Biogeography* **11**, 473–478.

Opdam, P., Rijsdijk, G. and Hustings, F. (1985) Bird communities in small woods in agricultural landscapes: effects of area and isolation. *Biological Conservation* **34**, 333–352.

Opdam, P. and Schotman, A. (1984) Bird communities in small woods in agricultural landscapes: effects of area and isolation. In *Methodology in Landscape Ecological Research and Planning, Proceedings of the 1st International Seminar of the International Association of Landscape Ecology*, Vol. 3, Brandt, J. and Agger, P. (eds), pp. 145–146. Roskilde Universitetsforlag, Roskilde.

Orians, G.H. (1986) An ecological and evolutionary approach to landscape aesthetics. In *Landscape Meanings and Values*, pp. 3–22, Penning-Rowsell, E.C. and Loewenthal, D. (eds). Allen and Unwin, London.

Peterken, G.F., Ausherman, D., Bucknell, M. and Forman, R.T.T. (1992) Old-growth conservation within British upland conifer plantations. *Forestry* **65**, 127–144.

Pickett, S.T.A. and White, P.S. (1985) *The Ecology of Natural Disturbance and Patch Dynamics*. Academic Press, New York.

Potter, C. et al. (1991) *The Diversion of Land: Conservation in a Period of Farming Contraction*. Routledge, London.

Primdahl, J. (1990) Heterogeneity in agriculture and landscape: from segregation to integration. *Landscape and Urban Planning* **18**, 221–228.

Primdahl, J. (1991) Agricultural and landscape change in Denmark: centralised policy-making and local effects. Paper presented to the World Congress of Landscape Ecology, International Association for Landscape Ecology, University of Carleton, Ottawa, 21–25 July 1991.

Pulliam, R.H. (1988) Sources, sinks and population regulation. *American Naturalist* **132**, 652–661.

Quinn, J.F. and Hastings, A. (1987) Extinction in sub-divided habitats. *Conservation Biology* **1**, 198–208.

Rafe, R.W., Usher, M.B. and Jefferson, R.G. (1985) Birds on reserves: the influence of area and habitat on species richness. *Journal of Applied Ecology* **22**, 327–335.

Risser, P. (1987) Landscape ecology: state of the art. In *Landscape Heterogeneity and Disturbance*, pp. 3–15, Turner, M.G. (ed.). Springer, New York.

Saunders, D.A. and Ingram, J.A. (1987) Factors affecting survival of breeding populations of Carnaby's cockatoo *Calyptohynchus funereus latirostris* in remnants of native vegetation. In *Nature Conservation: the Role of Remnants of Native Vegetation*, pp. 249–258, Saunders, D.A., Arnold, G.W., Burbidge, A.A. and Hopkins, A.J.M. (eds). Surrey Beatty and Sons, Chipping Norton, Australia.

Saville, N.M., Corbet, S.A. and Marrs, R.H. (1992) Bumblebees and farm woodlands. Paper presented to the Forestry Research Co-ordination Committee, Special Topic Conference on Farm Forestry Research, Royal Geographical Society, London, 30 September–1 October 1992.

Scheffer, M. and Knaapen, J.P. (1990) Estimating isolation by means of simulation: theoretical considerations. Winand Staring Centre, Wageningen (Mimeo).

van Selm, A.J. (1988) Ecological infrastructure: a conceptual framework for designing habitat networks. In *Connectivity in Landscape Ecology. Proceedings of the 2nd International Symposium of the International Association of Landscape Ecology*, pp. 63–66. Munstersche Geographische Arbeiten 29, Munster.

Selman, P.H. (1988) Rural land use planning — resolving the British paradox? *Journal of Rural Studies* **4**, 277–294.

Selman, P.H. (1990a) *Workshop Report: Landscape Ecology as a Basis for Structured Farm Woodland.* Summary of Proceedings, Department of Environmental Science, University of Stirling, U.K.

Selman, P.H. (1990b) Forestry and land use planning: a case for indicative strategies. *Arboricultural Journal* **14**, 53–59.

Selman, P.H. and Doar, N.R. (1991) A landscape ecological approach to countryside planning. *Planning Outlook* **34**, 83–88.

Selman, P.H. and Doar, N.R. (1992) An investigation of the potential for landscape ecology to act as a basis for rural land use plans. *Journal of Environmental Management* **35**, 281–299.

Shaw, P. (1988) Factors affecting the numbers of breeding birds and vascular plants on lowland farmland. NCC Chief Scientist Directorate, Commissioned Research Report No. 838, NCC, Peterborough.

Simberloff, D. (1976) Species turnover and equilibrium island biogeography. *Science* **194**, 572–578.

Simberloff, D. and Cox, J. (1987) Consequences and costs of conservation corridors. *Conservation Biology* **1**, 63–71.

Slatkin, M. (1987) Gene flow and the geographical structure of natural populations. *Science* **236**, 787–792.

de Smidt, J.T., Wassen, M.J., Schot, P.P. and Barendregt, A. (1991) Landscape gradients in freshwater wetlands. Paper presented to the World Congress of Landscape Ecology, International Association for Landscape Ecology, University of Carleton, Ottawa, 21–25 July 1991.

Soule, M.E. (1986) Conservation biology in the real world. In *Conservation Biology*, pp. 1–18, Soule, M.E. (ed.). Sinauer, Sunderland, Massachusetts.

Soule, M.E. and Gilpin, M.E. (1991) The theory of wildlife corridor capability. In *Nature Conservation: the Role of Corridors*, pp. 3–8, Saunders, D.A. and Hobbs, R.J. (eds). Surrey Beatty and Sons, Chipping Norton, Australia.

Soule, M.E. and Simberloff, D. (1986) What do genetics and ecology tell us about the designing of nature reserves? *Biological Conservation* **35**, 19–40.

Spirn, A.W. (1988) The poetics of city and nature: towards a new aesthetic for urban design. *Landscape Journal* **7**, 108–126.

Spirn, A.W. (1989) Deep structure: on process, form and design in the urban landscape. In *Proceedings of the 4th Annual Landscape Ecology Symposium*, p. 40. Fort Collins, Colorado.

Stamps, J.A., Buechner, M. and Krishnan, V.V. (1987) The effects of edge permeability and habitat geometry on emigration from patches of habitat. *American Naturalist* **129**, 534–552.

Stauffer, D. (1985) *Introduction to Percolation Theory.* Taylor and Francis, London.

Strebel, O., Duynisweld, W.H.M. and Bottcher, J. (1989) Nitrate pollution of groundwater in Western Europe. *Agriculture, Ecosystems and Environment* **26**, 189–214.

Temple, S.A. and Carn, J.R. (1988) Modelling dynamics of habitat interior bird populations in fragmented landscapes. *Conservation Biology* **2**, 340–347.

Thorne, J.F. and Huang, C.-S. (1991) Toward a landscape ecological aesthetic: methodologies for designers and planners. *Landscape and Urban Planning* **21**, 61–79.

Urban, D., O'Neill, R. and Shugart, H. (1987) Landscape ecology: a hierarchical pattern can help scientists understand spatial patterns. *Bioscience* **37**, 119–127.

Urban, D.L. and Shugart, H.H. (1986) Avian demography in mosaic landscapes: modeling paradigm and preliminary results. In *Wildlife 2000: Modeling Habitat Relationships of Terrestrial Vertebrates*, pp. 273–279, Verner, J., Morrison, M. and Ralph, C.J. (eds). University of Wisconsin Press, Madison.

Usher, M., Brown, A.C. and Bedford, S.E. (1992) Plant species richness in farm woodlands. *Forestry* **65**, 1–13.

Vink, A.P.A. (1983) *Landscape Ecology and Land Use.* Longman, London.

Wallin, H. and Ekbom, B.S. (1988) Movement of carabid beetles (Coleoptera: Carabidae) inhabiting cereal fields: a field tracing study. *Oecologia* **77**, 39–43.

Walters, C. (1986) *Adaptive Management of Renewable Resources.* Macmillan, New York.

Watkins, C. (1991) *Nature Conservation and the New Lowland Forests.* Nature Conservancy Council, Peterborough.

Wegner, J.F. and Merriam, G. (1979) Movements by birds and small mammals between a wood and adjoining farmland habitats. *Journal of Applied Ecology* **16**, 349–357.

Wegner, J. and Merriam, G. (1990) Use of spatial elements in a farmland mosaic by a woodland rodent. *Biological Conservation* **54**, 263–276.

Westmacott, R. (1991) Scale economics: ecological theory and planning practice in urban landscapes. *Landscape and Urban Planning* **21**, 21–29.

Whitcomb, R.F., Robbins, C.S., Lynch, T.F., Whitcomb, B.L., Klimkiewicz, M.I.C. and Bystrak, D. (1981) Effects of forest fragmentation on avifauna of the eastern deciduous forest. In *Forest Island Dynamics in Man-dominated Landscapes*, pp. 125–205, Burgess, R.L. and Sharpe, D.M. (eds). Springer, New York.

Whiteley, G.M. (1990) Extensive re-afforestation of arable farmland in Eastern England: the potential for groundwater protection in Nitrate Sensitive Areas. *Belowground Ecology* **Summer**, 10–11.

Whiteley, G.M. and Rushton, K.M. (1991) Effects of age and species composition of farm forestry on soil hydrology and nutrient leaching to an exposed magnesium limestone aquifer. Research note, University of Leeds, January 1991 (11 pp.).

Wiens, J.A. (1989) Spatial scaling in ecology. *Functional Ecology* **3**, 385–397.

Wiens, J.A. and Milne, B.T. (1989) Scaling of 'landscapes' in landscape ecology, or landscape ecology from a beetle's perspective. *Landscape Ecology* **3**, 87–96.

Wilcove, D.S. (1986) Habitat fragmentation in the temperate zone. In *Conservation Biology*, pp. 237–256, Soule, M.E. (ed.). Sinauer, Sunderland, Massachusetts.

Woiwood, I. and Thomas, J. (1992) The ecology of butterflies and moths at the landscape scale. Paper presented to the International Association of Landscape Ecology-U.K., *Landscape Ecology in Britain*, Nottingham University, 22–23 September 1992.

Zube, E.H., Sell, J.L. and Taylor, J.G. (1984) Environmental perceptions and behaviour. *University of Chicago Reporter* **209**, 60–83.

[12]

ELSEVIER

Landscape and Urban Planning 43 (1998) 143–156

LANDSCAPE
AND
URBAN PLANNING

A scale-independent, site conservation planning framework in The Nature Conservancy

Karen A. Poiani[a,*], Jeffrey V. Baumgartner[b], Steven C. Buttrick[c], Shelley L. Green[d],
Edward Hopkins[1,d], George D. Ivey[d], Katherine P. Seaton[e], Robert D. Sutter[e]

[a]*The Nature Conservancy, Department of Natural Resources, Cornell University, Ithaca, NY 14853, USA*
[b]*The Nature Conservancy, 2060 Broadway, Suite 230, Boulder, CO 80302, USA*
[c]*The Nature Conservancy, 201 Devonshire St., 5th Floor, Boston, MA 02110, USA*
[d]*The Nature Conservancy, 1815 North Lynn St., Arlington, VA 22209, USA*
[e]*The Nature Conservancy, PO Box 2267, Chapel Hill, NC 27515, USA*

Received 11 April 1997; received in revised form 23 October 1997; accepted 23 October 1997

Abstract

Site conservation planning in The Nature Conservancy is a scale-independent process that defines the landscape within which conservation targets (i.e., species and communities of concern) can persist. The process integrates more traditional preserve design and land acquisition activities with newer conservation biology and ecosystem management concepts into a single dynamic framework. Site conservation planning can be thought of as a series of questions, which if answered would constitute the major components of a plan. These questions are: (1) What are the significant conservation targets and long-term goals for those targets? (2) What biotic and abiotic attributes maintain those targets over the long term? (3) What are the basic characteristics of the human communities at the site? (4) What current and potential activities interfere with the survival of conservation targets and maintenance of ecological processes that sustain them? (5) Who are the organized groups and influential individuals at the site (i.e., stakeholders), what impacts will the goals have on them, and how might they help or hinder us in achieving those goals? (6) What can we do to prevent or mitigate threatening activities, and how can we influence important stakeholders? (7) What are the areas on the ground where we need to act? (8) What kinds of actions are necessary to accomplish our goals, who will do them, how long will they take, and how much will they cost? (9) Can we succeed in our goals, based on assessment of both ecological and human concerns and programmatic resources? (10) How will we know if we are making progress toward our goals and if our actions are bringing about desired results? Site conservation planning is best accomplished with an interdisciplinary team consisting of scientists, planners, and implementers. We recommend revisiting plans periodically to update and revise information, particularly threats to major ecological processes sustaining conservation targets and strategies that address those threats. © 1998 Nature Conservancy. Published by Elsevier Science B.V. All rights reserved.

Keywords: Site conservation planning; Biodiversity; Landscape design; The Nature Conservancy; Applied conservation; Ecosystem-based management

---

*Corresponding author. Tel: +1-607-255-2810; fax: +1-607-255-0349; e-mail: kpoiani@tnc.org.
[1]Present address: 5432 Connecticut Ave, NW, #4004, Washington, DC 20015, USA.

0169-2046/98/$19.00 © 1998 Nature Conservancy. Published by Elsevier Science B.V. All rights reserved.
PII: S0169-2046(97)00086-8

144   *K.A. Poiani et al./Landscape and Urban Planning 43 (1998) 143–156*

1. Introduction

Conserving biodiversity entails many diverse activities including site selection and design, conservation planning, land protection, and in many cases, long-term management. The scientific literature has focused considerably on management issues, particularly because many agencies and organizations have now embraced ecosystem and multiple-use management (Hansen et al., 1993; Christensen et al., 1996). Conservation biologists have discussed and debated preserve design, but primarily in the context of 'SLOSS' ('single large or several small' reserves; Simberloff and Abele, 1982; Murphy and Wilcox, 1986). Proactive conservation planning has received less attention but is becoming increasingly important as greater and more widespread threats to biodiversity are combined with more limited financial resources (Rookwood, 1995). Because we must deploy limited resources more effectively and efficiently, many states and regions are taking a proactive approach by conducting and implementing large-scale planning activities (Soulé, 1991; Scott et al., 1993; Cox et al., 1994; Reid and Murphy, 1995).

In the recent past, conservation planning within The Nature Conservancy has encompassed three primary activities: site identification, preserve design, and management. We primarily have focused on and protected rare species and communities by acquiring their immediate and surrounding areas (i.e., preserves and buffers) (Noss, 1987a). Following recent advances in understanding the dynamic nature of ecological systems (Pickett et al., 1992; Turner et al., 1995), the Conservancy is expanding its focus from preserves and buffers to protecting biota and landscape-level processes that sustain them (Noss, 1987a; Mohan, 1993; The Nature Conservancy, 1996). This shift requires additional protection tools including sustainable resource use, compatible development, and community education. It also demands a new and comprehensive site planning framework. The framework needs to be applicable to sites of any spatial scale or level of complexity and to provide a standardized mechanism for evaluating site integrity. A comprehensive planning procedure will insure that on-the-ground conservation actions are directed wisely and that they specifically address maintenance or restoration of critical ecological processes that sustain bio-

diversity (Wyant et al., 1995). Such a framework should encompass ecosystem-based management concepts and be able to provide specific direction for adaptive management decisions and activities.

To address the need for a comprehensive planning framework, The Nature Conservancy formed a national Site Design Working Group. The group drew on the experience and knowledge of many members of the Conservancy's staff to formulate the current site planning process. Thus, authorship of the process itself belongs to the entire organization. The authors of this paper are part of a second organizational team, that includes members from the first, charged with implementing the process, including sharing information to a wider non-Conservancy audience.

The objective of this paper is to provide an introduction to site conservation planning as outlined for The Nature Conservancy. We discuss individual planning components and illustrate major parts of the process with a hypothetical site example. The example is relatively simple for purposes of illustration but conveys the general principles we advocate.

It should be noted early in this paper that the framework is now employed widely by Conservancy staff, particularly at sites where we play a prominent conservation role. Because the framework is relatively new, we have no examples of it's success in protecting biodiversity over the long term. We do know from recent experience, however, that the process is a powerful planning tool and works extremely well for determining conservation and management actions at specific sites. Only long-term monitoring of conservation entities of concern will demonstrate the ability of the process to truly succeed in protecting biodiversity.

Other landscape conservation planning frameworks in the literature exist, but many focus on theoretical aspects of design or education methodology (Giliomee, 1977; Steinitz, 1990; Rookwood, 1995). For example, Steinitz (1990) outlines a series of questions associated with landscape alteration primarily geared toward educating environmental design professionals. His questions range from those focused on decision making (e.g., How will we know if we have the best design?), to landscape process (e.g., How well do we understand how the landscape works?), to change (e.g., What would happen without design intervention?). Our framework shares theoretical

K.A. Poiani et al./Landscape and Urban Planning 43 (1998) 143–156   145

underpinnings with many of these studies (Noss, 1987b; Marusic, 1993), but we go beyond theory to offer a practical, efficient method for conservation planning that is applicable at all spatial scales and levels of complexity.

2. Overview of site conservation planning

Site conservation planning in The Nature Conservancy (Fig. 1) is a scale-independent process that defines the landscape or 'site' within which conservation targets (i.e., species and communities of concern) can persist. The process integrates more traditional preserve design and land acquisition activities with newer conservation biology and ecosystem management concepts into a single dynamic framework (Mohan, 1993). The level of detail in planning is consistent with the scale and conservation value of a site and anticipated level of activity, resource commitment, and financial exposure expected. We can apply the process to large, complex sites as well as smaller areas of interest, including existing preserves.

The flow of site planning is important, and individual components are integrated and interrelated (Fig. 1). The process defines a series of questions, and answers to these questions constitute the major components of a plan (Table 1). Ideally, planning for a given site is accomplished by an interdisciplinary team consisting of scientists, planners, and implementers. First, a team identifies conservation targets, sets goals for those targets, and determines the ecological and human setting in which the targets exist. Next, the team elucidates threats to the targets and key ecological processes that maintain the targets, and evaluates major community stakeholders present at the site. They then develop conservation strategies to address identified threats and stakeholders, and map areas on the ground to indicate where and what kind of actions are necessary to accomplish specified goals. Finally, the team outlines specific actions needed to implement conservation strategies. They also must assess overall feasibility and determine short- and long-term monitoring benchmarks indicative of progress. We recommend revisiting plans periodically to update and revise information, particularly threats and resulting strategies that address those threats.

As mentioned previously, Conservancy staff currently employ site conservation planning at all high priority sites. In the short time we have been using this process, we have found the framework successful and valuable for a variety of reasons. First, it views the ecological system as a whole and focuses on key driving variables and processes necessary to maintain conservation targets. Second, it explicitly defines the interface between socio–economic issues and those

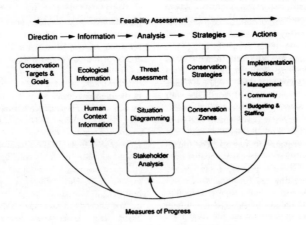

Fig. 1. Flow diagram of site conservation planning.

Table 1
Questions asked in site conservation planning

Planning component	Component question
Teams	Who should be included in the planning process and implementation of the plan?
Targets and goals	What are the significant conservation targets and long-term goals for those targets?
Ecological information	What biotic and abiotic attributes maintain the targets over the long term?
Human context information	What are the basic characteristics of the human communities at the site?
Threats	What current and potential activities interfere with the survival of the conservation targets and the maintenance of ecological processes?
Stakeholders	Who are the organized groups and influential individuals at the site, what impacts might we have on them, and how might they help or hinder us in achieving our goals?
Conservation strategies	What can we do to prevent or mitigate threatening activities, and how can we influence important stakeholders?
Conservation zones	What are the areas on the ground where we need to act?
Implementation	What kinds of actions are necessary to accomplish our goals, who will do them, how long will they take, how much will they cost?
Feasibility	Can we succeed in our goals, based on assessment of ecological and human context concerns and programmatic resources?
Measures of progress	How will we know if we are making progress toward our goals and if our actions are bringing about desired results?

critical ecological processes, and seeks to find conservation and management strategies that take both into account. Third, actions developed through the process are linked back directly to the conservation targets; thus, they are justified and defensible scientifically. In this regard, the process prioritizes actions and deploys resources more efficiently and effectively. Finally, site conservation planning uses a team approach that ensures a diverse perspective, promotes organizational buy in, and encourages partner involvement where appropriate from the start.

We also stress the planning framework is meant to provide *guidelines* for conservation action and management. Because ecological systems are highly complex and unpredictable, we cannot be sure the approaches we specify through the process will produce results we ultimately desire. Thus, it is critical to view the product of site planning as an 'experimental' framework within which we work at a particular site. We therefore must outline explicit monitoring protocol and benchmarks that will provide information on resulting changes to the ecological system and biota and feedback to our strategies at the site (Fig. 1 and see Section 3.6.2).

3. Individual planning components

3.1. Define direction

3.1.1. Conservation targets and goals

To begin site planning (Fig. 2), we must first articulate our direction and goals (Hansen et al., 1993). Why

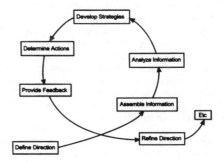

Fig. 2. Major components of site conservation planning, illustrating iterative nature.

K.A. Poiani et al./Landscape and Urban Planning 43 (1998) 143–156   147

do we want to protect an area? What is our long-term vision for the system or site? What are our specific conservation targets and goals for those targets?

We advocate selecting a relatively short list of specific conservation targets on which to focus and direct planning. Within The Nature Conservancy, conservation targets typically consist of rare or common communities and species, but also can be subspecies, assemblages of species like functional guilds, or broad habitat types. Selection of conservation targets will have a major impact on the entire process and conservation effort, and is a key to all other planning that follows (Mohan, 1993). It is the conservation targets that ultimately dictate site boundaries by defining broad-scale ecological processes that maintain those species and communities over the long term.

Choosing specific conservation targets can be challenging because sites typically have many species and communities of interest and importance. Several strategies for selecting conservation targets include: (1) choose those species and communities for which the site is particularly noted; (2) consider those species and communities that if lost, would cause you to stop working at the site; (3) choose species and communities for which it is feasible to meet meaningful goals; (4) use strategically chosen habitat types if they can meet the needs of a wide diversity of communities and species (Jenkins, 1976; Hunter, 1991; Walker, 1992); (5) group species into functional groups or guilds (Boutin and Keddy, 1993; Dale et al., 1994) and choose representative groups or highly sensitive groups; or (6) choose several targets that encompass multiple levels of organization and various spatial and temporal scales (Noss, 1990; Grumbine, 1994). In the case of functional guilds, groupings can be based on many relevant characteristics, including area requirements, gap-crossing ability, dispersal strategy, trophic status, etc. (Dale et al., 1994). For 'noted' species and communities, deciding characteristics might include rarity, quality of occurrence, or degree of threat. Examples of conservation targets for several types of sites are illustrated in Table 2.

After selecting conservation targets, we must articulate and identify specific conservation goals and objectives (Noss, 1993). Goals direct the planning effort and minimize misdirected efforts. In addition, clearly outlined goals provide the framework from

Table 2
Examples of conservation targets for several types of sites

Site	Conservation targets
Great Lakes dunes	Great Lakes sand dunes complex of fen types (rich, medium, poor) buckmoth (*Hemileuca* sp.)
Hawaiian rainforest	native vegetation native birds
East Coast riverine	pocosin wetlands coastal marshes canebreak rattlesnake (*Crotalus horridus atricaudatus*)
Midwest deciduous forest	interior songbirds mosaic of forested, woodland, and open-canopy communities aquatic insects
Hypothetical example in text	rare prairie flower aquatic mussels

which to measure progress (Schroeder and Keller, 1990; Henry and Amoros, 1995). Goals should be clear and concise and set early on. Goals that are flexible and adaptable with measurable results are most useful. We must refine and revise our goals periodically as new information becomes available and as we begin to implement conservation strategies and assess feasibility (Fig. 2).

The hypothetical example we use throughout the paper illustrates selection of conservation targets and development of goals. There are two conservation targets in this example, a rare prairie flower and several important aquatic mussel species. The site has one large population of the rare plant and multiple locations of high quality mussel populations. A map of the site is shown in Fig. 5. The prairie flower depends on periodic disturbance (fire or controlled grazing), and the mussels depend on clean, cool stream water. Cool temperatures are maintained by intact streamside trees and vegetation. Exotic invasive weeds are a problem in the prairies due to suppression of fire, loss of habitat from encroaching development, and general degradation by human influences. The goals developed for the two conservation targets include: (1) maintain at least one high quality occurrence of the rare prairie flower. Ensure that prairie habitat is burned at least once every 5–8 yr to sustain native grasses and eliminate shrub encroachment; (2) reduce the abundance of aggressive, noxious weeds within prairie habitats, focusing on spotted knapweed; (3) maintain and restore permanent native vegetative cover in watershed, especially within 100 m of all streams, reduce sediment inputs to the stream by 20% and increase number of individual mussels in each population and number of populations by 10% over the next 20 yr; (4) ensure the natural range of variation for riverine hydrologic processes that result in disturbances like overbank flooding and channel scouring.

3.2. Assemble information

3.2.1. Ecological information

The next step in the process is assembling relevant information (Fig. 2). This encompasses both ecological information and information on human context (see Section 3.2.2). Ecological information includes life history characteristics and major biological and ecological patterns and processes operating at multiple spatial and temporal scales (Wyant et al., 1995). During this phase, we must discern *key* biotic and abiotic attributes maintaining targets over the long term and provide a basis for understanding threats to their viability. This is not an endless exploration for data, but rather a search for essential properties of the system or system components (Keddy and Drummond, 1996).

We have found that conceptual ecological diagrams or 'models' are useful tools for summarizing complex biological information. An ecological model is a conceptual or mathematical representation of a natural system, component, or process (Barrows, 1996). It provides a framework for understanding and evaluating complicated systems (Maddox et al., 1997), and is necessarily a simplification or abstraction of the real world. In The Nature Conservancy, we often construct simple, conceptual state/transition diagrams (Fig. 3). As more and more data and knowledge are obtained,

we can use the ecological model to predict state changes as processes operate over time (van der Valk, 1981; Keddy, 1992). Ecological models or diagrams are excellent for organizing and communicating ideas visually (Fig. 3), generating research hypotheses, and elucidating areas of system behavior that are not well understood (Barrows, 1996; Maddox et al., 1997). The conceptual model for the rare prairie flower at our example site shows key processes critical to healthy populations (i.e., periodic disturbance from fire or grazing) (Fig. 3).

3.2.2. Human context information

We next must understand the human context in which the conservation targets are embedded (Brunson, 1996). This includes a broad overview of social, economic, land use, fiscal, and cultural information for a site (Fig. 1). Such information will provide an analytical basis for understanding the socio–economic forces influencing the land use of an area (Wyant et al., 1995; McCool, 1996). Again, data collection should be a targeted information search (Table 3).

Human context information can include many different types of data.

1. demographic profile (e.g., population growth, household structure)
2. economic profile (e.g., unemployment rates, cost of living)
3. land profile (e.g., ownership, zoning regulations, land use)
4. fiscal/government profile (e.g., politics, local government)
5. cultural attitudes and values (e.g., social values, conservation values)

Information can encompass status and trend statistics gleaned from Department of Census and Labor documents. We can discover more locally based information like cultural attitudes and beliefs through

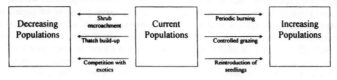

Fig. 3. Conceptual model of rare prairie flower population dynamics and key processes.

K.A. Poiani et al. / Landscape and Urban Planning 43 (1998) 143–156   149

Table 3
General human context information for hypothetical example

Socio and demographic	Economic	Land use	Fiscal and government	Community attitudes
27,000 people in town of Minnieopolis	agriculture accounts for 10% of economic activity	terrestrial landscape is 52% agriculture	the State Department of Natural Resources is active player	residents want primarily recreational development
bigger metro areas are experiencing high population growth	services account for majority of economic activities	residential development is increasing, especially near urban areas	watershed consists of twelve townships, two counties, two state senate districts	scenic characteristic of streams and intact prairie is important to property owners
county grew by 4% over last decade	tourism is important part of economy	most landholdings are 40 to 120 acres	county boards develop zoning regulations	majority of residents see a need for zoning
rural population more likely to work within county	farmers typically earn less income than surrounding areas	soils are excellent, mostly plant row crops	state regulatory agency oversees dam operation	residents favor nature preserves and farming land uses
projections indicate sustained growth in urban areas	Megapolis Power Company employs 5000 people in the watershed, mostly in the city of Megapolis	farmers generally employ good management practices but add considerable amounts of fertilizer and pesticides	development pressure is strongly influenced by public decisions in Metropolis and Megapolis	general openness to implement best management practices

informal means (opinion surveys, attending local events, polling community members). We will use such human context information later in the planning to evaluate important stakeholders at the site, assess threats, and develop strategies to address those threats.

3.3. Analyze the information

Once we have assembled the basic ecological and human context information, we use several assessment tools to further understand conservation needs at the site: threat assessment, situation diagrams, and stakeholder analysis. Although we present these components in that order, they are highly interactive and often are performed concurrently or in an order that suits a particular site or planning team.

3.3.1. Threat assessment

Formal methods for analyzing stresses to species, communities, or ecosystems have been used in a number of environmental fields in different capacities. They include: (1) environmental impact assessments (Westman, 1985); (2) decision analysis (Maguire, 1986); (3) ecological risk assessment (Norton et al., 1992). These methods are decision-making tools that provide a framework for explicitly identifying and

analyzing stresses at a site. They assess a wide range of impacts, but differ in their focus, information requirements, and level of complexity.

Threat assessment in The Nature Conservancy's site planning process attempts to address all known threats and impacts of those threats. It is simple, easy to implement, independent of spatial scale, cost-effective, and adaptive. Threat assessment consists of identification, evaluation, and ranking of current and potential stresses and sources of stress to conservation targets. This includes threats that alter processes (suppression of fire, elimination of native herbivores, alteration of hydrologic regimes), and impact conservation targets directly (plant collection, grazing) or indirectly (fragmentation resulting in isolation of populations). Stresses are those processes or events with direct deleterious ecological or physiological impacts on conservation targets (e.g., sedimentation, direct mortality, habitat loss). Sources of stress are actions or entities from which a stress is derived, or agents driving decline of targets (e.g., agriculture, second home development, road building).

A formal threat assessment can be performed using several approaches including: numeric with weighted scores and tables (Table 4), non-numeric tables where ranking is based on qualitative assessments like 'high', 'medium', or 'low' (Table 5), or visual dia-

Table 4
Numerical stress analysis for aquatic mussels

Stress	Severity	Geographic scope	Score
Sedimentation	4	4	8.0
Altered hydrology	4	2	6.0
Stream habitat alteration	2	4	6.0
Toxics	0.5	1	1.5
Nutrients	0.5	1	1.5
Competition from exotics	0.5	0.5	1.0
Draining/filling wetlands	0.5	0.5	1.0

Table 5
Ranking of sources of stress for top three stresses from Table 4

Source	Top three stresses		
	Sedimentation	Altered hydrology	Habitat alteration
Development	H	M	H
Roads	H	M	M
Hydroelectric dam	L	H	L
Irrigation	L	M	L
Industry	L	M	M
Agriculture	H	M	M

grams. Possible criteria for evaluating and ranking stresses and sources of stress include:

1. severity (potential impact),
2. scope (geographic scale of impact),
3. immediacy (current or potential),
4. likelihood (probability of occurring),
5. reversibility (restoration potential),
6. frequency (chronic or intermittent).

It is important to consider both direct and indirect stresses as well as proximate and ultimate sources of stress. Situation diagrams, discussed fully below, help separate and identify direct and indirect stresses and proximate and ultimate sources of stress. Threat

assessment for our example site focuses on the aquatic mussel target. It shows that highest priority stresses to mussels are sedimentation, altered hydrology, and stream habitat alteration (Table 4). Top-ranked sources of these stresses include development and associated roads, a hydroelectric dam, and agriculture (Table 5).

3.3.2. Situation diagrams

Situation diagramming is the development and visualization of interrelationships among ecological and human components including stresses and sources of stress (Fig. 4). Situation diagrams clearly illustrate component linkages. As appropriate (i.e., a relation-

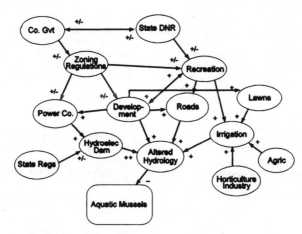

Fig. 4. Situation diagram for altered hydrologic regime stress (see Table 4).

ship exists or is assumed), a cause–effect arrow links any two components, and is directed from causal to affected component. The arrow is characterized as '+' or '−', depending on whether the causal component has a positive or negative impact on the affected component.

Situation diagrams are an excellent precursor for developing conservation strategies. A situation diagram will show those site components that can be targeted precisely by specific strategies. In the example situation diagram, it is clear that altered hydrology in the stream is caused by a variety of sources, some of which potentially can be influenced at the county or state government level (Fig. 4). Most diagrams are developed by analyzing high-priority stresses as defined in the threat assessment. Sometimes single-stress diagrams can be combined to show the overall situation at the site.

3.3.3. Stakeholder analysis

Stakeholder analysis explicitly addresses and evaluates organized groups and influential individuals that may affect conservation efforts at a site. It is a critical step in building more powerful constituencies, participating more effectively in local decision-making, and avoiding potential pitfalls. This analysis also can elucidate potential negative effects conservation work will have on local communities. Taking time to understand the community has been critical to the success of many Nature Conservancy projects, while neglecting to learn about human context has led to significant setbacks in some cases.

It should be possible for a site planning team to identify basic information on stakeholders in a relatively short time. An initial analysis can be performed in a one-day session. More sophisticated understanding of public opinion and local political decision-making can be identified as future needs, and strategies can be developed to address those needs.

Stakeholder analysis consists of several steps which together provide an overall view of the human components at a site.

Step 1: Identify stakeholders

1. Who is causing the sources of stress?
2. Who would benefit from work at this site?
3. Who would be hurt?
4. Who could shape public opinion?
5. Who has authority to make decisions?

Step 2: Assess each stakeholder

1. What effects/potential effects will goals have on stakeholder?
2. What effects/potential effects will stakeholders have on goals?
3. What is known/unknown about stakeholder?

Strategies and actions to address stakeholder issues are developed later in the planning. A partial stakeholder analysis for the hypothetical example is shown in Table 6.

3.4. Develop strategies

3.4.1. Conservation strategies

Conservation strategies are broad action paths that mitigate stresses or address critical concerns regarding stakeholders. Strategies are solution-oriented. They are sometimes straightforward and simple, other times innovative and creative. This is the point in the process

Table 6
Example of stakeholder analysis for example site

Stakeholder	Effect on stakeholder	Stakeholder effect	What we know/do not know about stakeholder
Megapolis Power Company	Prohibiting further dam construction or regulating operations may limit hydro-electric power output.	Company is politically powerful— could lobby state politicians.	Output is sufficient to meet current needs.
		Interest in appearing 'green' to the public could be a benefit.	What are feelings about different operations schedules? Would they fund a study on the effects of hydrologic regimes on mussels?

where our understanding of ecological and human context merge to direct our conservation work. Every site has a unique combination of strategies, and developing conservation strategies for a site ideally is accomplished by a broad-based team.

There are many different types of conservation strategies that fall into several generalized areas.

1. land protection (legal rights, acquisition, easements)
2. management and restoration (of biological or human effects)
3. community relations (education, regulation, partnerships)
4. programmatic (fundraising, staff, equipment)
5. research (natural systems, species, threat effects)

Conservation strategies are different from goals and action plans. Goals define a desired ecological condition, and strategies are broad paths that illuminate how to get there. Actions break strategies into specific units necessary to accomplish strategies (see Section 3.5.1). Specific steps to develop conservation strategies include: brainstorm all possible strategies; prioritize list of strategies according to importance; run through a first-cut feasibility assessment of list and revise accordingly. We show a partial list of strategies for our example site (Table 7). Each strategy is clearly focused on meeting the

goals and eliminating high priority threats (see Tables 4 and 5).

3.4.2. Conservation zones

Conservation zones depict the geographic location of land-based conservation strategies (Rookwood, 1995). Strategies that can be mapped include land protection, management and restoration, and some community relations. Ideally, zones represent different points on a continuum of active conservation management, ranging from outright management to only influence of management activities. A planning team can identify as many zones as are appropriate for a particular site. Different sites will vary in number, type, and arrangement of zones.

Fig. 5 illustrates conservation zones for the hypothetical example. The planning team determined that to meet their ecological goals they would carry out the following highest-priority strategies: (1) conduct prescribed burning in prairie habitat; (2) eliminate development in prairie habitat; (3) prevent loss of riparian vegetation adjacent to best mussel populations; (4) reduce sediment and nutrient inputs to all reaches of the river; (5) educate local communities on importance of ecological resources and effects of farming practices (Table 7).

The team determined the best places on the ground to implement these strategies. *Zone A* designates the

Table 7
Partial list of strategies (by goal) for hypothetical example

Goals	Strategies
1. Maintain at least one high quality occurrence of the rare prairie flower; ensure that prairie habitat is burned	a. reintroduce fire in high priority prairie areas b. eliminate development in high priority prairie areas c. develop public outreach program on importance of rare prairie flower and prescribed fire
2. Reduce abundance of noxious weeds within prairie habitats	a. remove noxious weeds each year using various mechanical and/or chemical methods b. educate horticultural industry about sale of nuisance species
3. Maintain permanent cover adjacent to streams: reduce sediment inputs by 20%; increase populations of freshwater mussels	a. work to implement agricultural best management practices within 100 m of stream b. reintroduce mussels to areas in which they were once common
4. Insure natural variation in hydrologic processes	a. determine natural variation in key hydrologic processes prior to dam construction b. work with state regulators and power company to operate dam releases to mimic natural variability

K.A. Poiani et al./Landscape and Urban Planning 43 (1998) 143–156   153

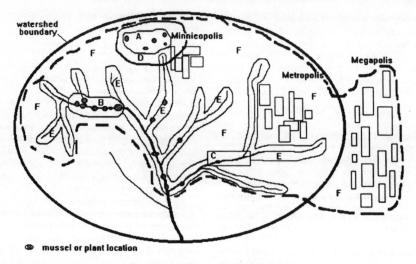

Fig. 5. Conservation zones for hypothetical site.

only high quality prairie at the site (near the city of Minnieopolis) where prescribed burning and elimination of development are critical (Fig. 5). Acquisition or conservation easements are appropriate for this zone. *Zone B* is an area along the river (left side of map, Fig. 5) with the highest quality and largest mussel population in the region. Conversion of riparian vegetation in this area must be prevented and thus, acquisition or easements also are appropriate. A riparian area easily accessible from Metropolis (*Zone C*) is a third area that should be acquired for development of a nature trail to educate the public. *Zone D* designates a 1/2 mile smoke buffer needed to burn the prairie patch (Fig. 5). Acquisition may not be necessary for this zone; an easement or management agreement may be appropriate. To reduce nutrient and sediment inputs to mussels, a forested buffer along the river and major streams was determined to be necessary (*Zone E*). Conservation tools for this zone could be a combination of easements, registries, regulation, and management agreements. Finally, the team determined that strategy 5 was best accomplished throughout the watershed and in the city of Megapolis (county seat where zoning decisions are made) and designated this area *Zone*

F. Outreach and education would be the primary tools in this zone.

3.5. Outline actions

3.5.1. Implementation

Implementation outlines how we will accomplish high priority conservation strategies. Implementation breaks larger projects into manageable, measurable actions, that are directed toward our stated conservation goals. Implementation addresses programmatic implications like: *How, What, When, Who,* and at *What Cost.* It not only states how and what will be done, but provides information on how to measure progress in accomplishing strategies and achieving goals. Issues to consider include: staff and volunteers, research and monitoring, capital, fundraising, and budgets. An initial estimate of the resources required for site conservation is part of this step. Implementation provides important information that feeds back to annual planning and feasibility.

Implementation analysis and its resulting list of actions and tasks is: (1) best performed hierarchically (from general to specific); (2) brief enough to be usable; (3) prioritized by importance; (4) updated

154   *K.A. Poiani et al./Landscape and Urban Planning 43 (1998) 143–156*

Table 8
Examples of actions for hypothetical site

Strategies	Actions
Reintroduce mussels to areas in which they were once common	1. determine potential reintroduction areas 2. contract laboratory to culture mussels 3. design pilot reintroduction project 4. monitor results of pilot project
Develop public outreach program on importance of rare prairie flower and prescribed fire	1. hire public education coordinator 2. develop 'high-tech' presentation materials on prescribed fire 3. develop high-school intern program focusing on field projects like monitoring rare prairie flowers, shrub encroachment, etc.

regularly. Level of detail for this component depends on scale and conservation value of the site and to some degree, inclinations of the planning team. Implementation actions for selected conservation strategies for the hypothetical example are shown in Table 8.

3.6. Provide feedback

3.6.1. Feasibility analysis

Feasibility analysis focuses on assessing overall potential for success at a site, or revealing potential fatal flaws. Feasibility should be assessed for all aspects of site conservation planning as components are completed (Fig. 1). It also is valuable to assess overall feasibility once a draft plan has been completed. As appropriate, the following issues should be considered when assessing feasibility.

1. Ecological goals

    1.1. Given sufficient resources, can biological needs of the targets be met?
    1.2. Can we reasonably expect to succeed over the long term in meeting ecological goals?

2. Conservation strategies and zones

    2.1. Can all or most of the damaging stresses be eliminated or moderated?
    2.2. Can we expect to gain needed level of control and influence?
    2.3. Will we be able to overcome socio–economic, political, or regulatory hurdles?
    2.4. What constraints are imposed by existing or potential land use zoning and landownership patterns?

3. Stakeholder risks

    3.1. Can we take these (or any) actions without destroying essential credibility and trust among our supporters, or building harmful opposition among our detractors?
    3.2. How will we test community response to the plan, if necessary?

4. Financial/staff resources

    4.1. Do we have staff resources to implement actions?
    4.2. Can we expect to raise the money needed?
    4.3. Can we expect to develop necessary partnerships?

5. Opportunity costs

    5.1. Is this the best use of our resources, or could we accomplish more with fewer resources at a different site?
    5.2. How will implementation impact the program's ability to accomplish other strategic goals?

3.6.2. Measuring progress

At some point in the planning and after sufficient implementation of conservation strategies, progress must be assessed. Are current actions bringing about desired results? To this end, measures of progress, or benchmarks, must be developed to help monitor progress toward our goals. These should include direct biological measures (e.g., are populations increasing?), abiotic measures (e.g., is the stress reduced?), conservation action measures (e.g., have we implemented the strategies?), and organization or capacity measures (e.g., has the money been raised?). Changes in biological parameters are the most direct assessment of project success, but are most difficult actually to measure. Organizational measures are least direct, but are easiest and quickest to measure. We should use such information to adapt management and conservation actions.

Measuring progress includes both short- and long-term evaluations. Long-term benchmarks are big milestones or long-term visions for the site. Short-term benchmarks can help determine whether we are making progress toward our long-term goals. At our hypothetical site for example, we want to reduce siltation to the river by 20% in the long-term, so we might determine a short-term benchmark of 5% reduction within 2 yr. Similarly, we also might choose to monitor riparian vegetation cover every 5 yr using aerial photographs, and presence of exotic species, prairie flowers, and mussel populations every other year. Based on our priority strategies, we might focus on organizational measures such as hiring an outreach coordinator, developing an education program, and tracking number of farmers contacted vs. number implementing best management practices.

4. Challenges, constraints, and conclusions

Organizations will vary in their ability and willingness to do site planning. One constraint is that we often misconceive site planning as too time consuming and burdensome. As stated previously, the level of detail in any particular plan should be consistent with scale and conservation value of a site and anticipated level of activity, resource commitment, and financial investment. Site plans can be complex if necessary, but for some sites, plans may be completed informally within a day. In addition to planning at new sites, the planning process also can be applied to existing protected lands to determine what strategies and actions should be implemented to meet ecological and programmatic goals. Taking time to set goals for existing sites is sometimes an overlooked activity in itself, the benefits of which cannot be overestimated.

Other challenges exist in site conservation planning. It often is time consuming to use teams in planning, but the added benefits of a broad-based perspective are critical to many components. Inclusion of fundraising, land protection, science staff, and selected partners insures that conservation strategies will encompass many viewpoints and that goals and strategies (both ecological and programmatic) are realistic. Such a team more likely will take ownership of efforts and generate more interest in implementing agreed-upon actions. In addition, a team can help overcome organizational constraints and may foster better internal and external communication and cooperation.

Constraints to site conservation planning also include inexperience with planning and underappreciating the conservation and business-related value of the products. We believe, however, that the benefits of site planning will become obvious at all levels of conservation activities once we experience direct and tangible results. Within The Nature Conservancy, site planning under the new, comprehensive framework outlined in this paper has been well received and quickly is becoming a high priority. We believe that in a time of diminishing resources and increasing threats to biodiversity, effective and efficient use of limited money and staff as directed by site conservation planning can make the difference between success and failure at protecting natural systems over the long term.

References

Barrows, C.M., 1996. An ecological model for the protection of a dune ecosystem. Conserv. Biol. 10, 888–891.

Boutin, C., Keddy, P.A., 1993. A functional classification of wetland plants. J. Vegetation Sci. 4, 591–600.

Brunson, M., 1996. Integrating human habitat requirements into ecosystem management strategies: a case study. Nat. Areas J. 16, 100–107.

Christensen, N.L., et al. 1996. The report of the Ecological Society of America committee on the scientific basis for ecosystem management. Ecol. Appl. 6, 665–691.

Cox, J., Kautz, R., MacLaughlin, M., Gilbert, T., 1994. Closing the gaps in Florida's wildlife habitat conservation system. Office of Environmental Services, Florida Game and Fresh Water Fish Commission, Tallahassee, FL.

Dale, V.H., Pearson, S.M., Offerman, H.L., O'Neill, R.V., 1994. Relating patterns of land-use change to faunal biodiversity in the Central Amazon. Conserv. Biol. 8, 1027–1036.

Giliomee, J.H., 1977. Ecological planning: method and evaluation. Landscape Planning 4, 185–191.

Grumbine, R.E., 1994. What is ecosystem management? Conserv. Biol. 8, 27–38.

Hansen, A.J., Garman, S.L., Marks, B., Urban, D.L., 1993. An approach for managing vertebrate diversity across multiple-use landscapes. Ecol. Appl. 3, 481–496.

Henry, C.P., Amoros, C., 1995. Restoration ecology of riverine wetlands: I. A scientific base. Environ. Manage. 19, 891–902.

Hunter, M., 1991. Coping with ignorance: the coarse-filter strategy for maintaining biodiversity. In: Kohm, K.A. (Ed.), Balancing on the Brink of Extinction—the Endangered Species Act and Lessons for the Future. Island Press, Washington, DC, pp. 256–281.

Jenkins, R.E., 1976. Maintenance of natural diversity: approach and recommendations. Trans. of the 41st North American Wildlife Conference. Wildlife Management Institute, Washington, DC, pp. 441–451.

Keddy, P.A., 1992. Assembly and response rules: two goals for predictive community ecology. J. Vegetation Sci. 3, 157–164.

Keddy, P.A., Drummond, C.G., 1996. Ecological properties for the evaluation, management, and restoration of temperate deciduous forest ecosystems. Ecol. Appl. 6, 748–762.

Maddox, D., Poiani, K.A., Unnasch, R., 1997. Evaluating management success: using conceptual ecological models to ask the right monitoring questions. In: Johnson, N. (Ed.), Ecological Stewardship Project Reference. In Review.

Maguire, L.A., 1986. Using decision analysis to manage endangered species populations. J. Environ. Manage. 22, 345–360.

Marusic, J., 1993. Conservation planning within a framework of landscape planning in Slovenia. Landscape Urban Planning 23, 233–237.

McCool, S.F., 1996. Wildlife viewing, natural area protection, and community sustainability and resiliency. Nat. Areas J. 16, 147–151.

Mohan, J., 1993. An autecological site design model for nature reserves. Master's Thesis, School of the Environment, Duke University, Durham, NC.

Murphy, D.D., Wilcox, B.A., 1986. On island biogeography and conservation. Oikos 47, 385–387.

Norton, S.B., Rodier, D.J., Gentile, J.H., van der Schalie, W.H., Wood, W.P., Slimak, M.W., 1992. A framework for ecological risk assessment at the EPA. Environ. Toxicol. Chem. 11, 1663–1672.

Noss, R.F., 1987a. From plant communities to landscapes in conservation inventories: a look at The Nature Conservancy (USA). Biol. Conserv. 41, 11–37.

Noss, R.F., 1987b. Protecting natural areas in fragmented landscapes. Nat. Areas J. 7, 2–13.

Noss, R.F., 1990. Indicators for monitoring biodiversity: a hierarchical approach. Conserv. Biol. 4, 355–364.

Noss, R.F., 1993. A conservation plan for the Oregon Coast Range: some preliminary suggestions. Nat. Areas J. 13, 276–290.

Pickett, S.T.A., Parker, V.T., Fiedler, P.L., 1992. The new paradigm in ecology: implications for conservation biology above the species level. In: Fiedler, P.L., Jain, S.K. (Eds.), Conservation Biology: The Theory and Practice of Nature Conservation Preservation and Management. Chapman & Hall, New York, pp. 66–88.

Reid, T.S., Murphy, D.D., 1995. Providing a regional context for local conservation action. BioScience Supplement S-84–S-90.

Rookwood, P., 1995. Landscape planning for biodiversity. Landscape Urban Planning 31, 379–385.

Schroeder, R.L., Keller, M.E., 1990. Setting objectives—a prerequisite of ecosystem management. NY State Museum Bull. 471, 1–4.

Scott, J.M., Davis, F., Csuti, B., Butterfield, B., Groves, C., Anderson, H., Caicco, S., Derchia, F., Edwards, T.C., Ulliman, J., Wright, R.G., 1993. GAP analysis: a geographic approach to protection of biological diversity. Wildlife Monogr. 123, 1–41.

Simberloff, D., Abele, L.G., 1982. Refuge design and island biogeographic theory: effects of fragmentation. Am. Naturalist 120, 41–50.

Soulé, M.E., 1991. Land use planning and wildlife maintenance: guidelines for conserving wildlife in an urban landscape. J. Am. Planning Assoc. 57, 313–323.

Steinitz, C., 1990. A framework for theory applicable to the education of landscape architects (and other environmental design professionals). Landscape J., 136–143.

The Nature Conservancy, 1996. Conservation by design: a framework for mission success. The Nature Conservancy, Arlington, VA.

Turner, M.G., Gardner, R.H., O'Neill, R.V., 1995. Ecological dynamics at broad scales. BioScience Supplement S-29–S-35.

van der Valk, A.G., 1981. Succession in wetlands: a Gleasonian approach. Ecology 62, 688–696.

Walker, B.H., 1992. Biodiversity and ecological redundancy. Conserv. Biol. 6, 18–23.

Westman, W.E., 1985. Ecology, Impact Assessment, and Environmental Planning. Wiley, New York.

Wyant, J.G., Meganck, R.A., Ham, S.H., 1995. A planning and decision-making framework for ecological restoration. Environ. Manage. 19, 789–796.

E
Market-Led Approach

[13]

Journal of Rural Studies, Vol. 9, No. 4, pp. 315–338, 1993
Printed in Great Britain

Seven Steps to Market — the Development of the Market-led Approach to Countryside Conservation and Recreation

Kevin D. Bishop and Adrian A.C. Phillips

Environmental and Countryside Planning Unit, Department of City and Regional
Planning, University of Wales College of Cardiff, P.O. Box 906, Cardiff CF1 3YN,
U.K.

Abstract — Fifty years of interplay between farming, environment and politics are
reviewed within the context of the search for policy tools which reconcile the need
for conservation and access to the countryside with the needs of those who own or
manage the land. Seven main policy instruments which have been used to reconcile
conflicts between the various interest groups representing farmers and landowners,
conservationists and recreationists are identified and their strengths and weaknesses analysed. The significance and initial impact of the seventh of these policy
tools — the incentives or market-led approach — is considered in greater detail.

Introduction

The past half-century has witnessed profound
changes in the countryside as the agricultural industry has pursued policies that until recently were
aimed at maximising production. The consequences
for the environment of modern farming practices
have been well documented. Surveys by statutory
agencies (Nature Conservancy Council, 1984;
Countryside Commission, 1986) have shown, for
example, that between 1947 and 1980:

- 22% of all hedgerows were removed (110,000
  miles, or nearly four times round the world);
- 40% of broadleaved woodlands were lost;
- 95% of lowland hay meadows have been
  destroyed; and,
- 25% of semi-natural vegetation lost.

These and other figures record the destruction of
much of the ecological, visual and historic value of
the countryside. This was accompanied by neglect of
rights-of-way and the loss of open country (to
improved agriculture or afforestation) which reduced its recreational value as well.

As a result, there has been a public policy debate for
a number of years on the relationship between
agriculture on the one hand, and on the other the
conservation of the wildlife, scenic and historic

qualities of the farmed countryside. A central
concern has been the search for policy tools which
reconcile the need for conservation and access to the
countryside with the needs of those who own or
manage land. These tools can be viewed as a means
of mediation between two interest groups, whose
relative status has changed over the years (Cox and
Lowe, 1983).

The aims of this paper are to:

- provide an overview of agricultural, environmental and political influences on this policy area
  over the last 50 years;
- identify the six main policy instruments which
  have been used to reconcile conflicts between the
  interest groups representing farmers and landowners, conservationists and recreationists; and,
- consider in greater detail the significance and
  initial impact of the seventh of these: the incentives or market-led approach.

Part 1: 50 years of interplay between farming, environment and politics

Agricultural fundamentalism

The general philosophy of countryside policy in the
post-war period was largely shaped by the con-

clusions of the 1942 Scott Committee's investigations into land utilisation in rural areas: 'It is not too much to say that in the 40 years odd since its publication the Scott Report has been responsible for some of the best and many of the worst things that have happened to the British countryside since the last war' (Wibberley, 1985, p. 13). The report was written in the middle of World War II, at a time of acute food shortages, and when memories of the great agricultural depression were still fresh and the Land Utilisation Surveys had illustrated significant agricultural land losses to urban development. It reflected an attitude that has been termed 'agricultural fundamentalism' — that is, the ethos of farming first and the assumption that all other considerations in the countryside should take second place. The Scott Committee concluded that protecting agricultural land from development and providing an appropriate framework of price support for farmers would produce an efficient agricultural sector and an attractive rural environment. Central to the conclusions of the Scott Committee was the notion of custodianship (Winter, 1990). Given that the landscape characteristics of the much treasured British countryside were man-made and that 'it must be farmed to retain these features', it was a logical conclusion at the time to assume that farmers were the natural custodians of the countryside and that a prosperous agricultural sector would automatically ensure the conservation of and access to the countryside.

In this consensus there was one dissenting voice. Professor Dennison produced a minority report which challenged the assumptions of the majority of the Committee and correctly anticipated the course of post-war agriculture. Dennison argued that agricultural prosperity depended on efficiency which would only be achieved by specialist farming and reducing the number of agricultural workers. He suggested that farmers could be paid to conserve the landscape as 'landscape gardeners and not as agriculturalists' — an idea that is only now, some 50 years on, being adopted. However, Dennison's advice was ignored and the conclusions of the rest of the Committee were to provide the framework for post-war countryside policies. So it came about that the countryside environment was to be shaped more by the powerful economic elements of agricultural policy than by the regulatory powers of the new town and country planning system.

Since World War II, agriculture has been subject to a period of unparalleled and sustained government intervention (Hodge, 1990). The Agriculture Act 1947, described by Gilg (1978) as 'one of the most successful and long standing pieces of major legislation in British parliamentary history' (p. 26), provided a system of price support and import protection. The aim of the Act was to create a stable and efficient agricultural industry. There was no mention of environmental aims; if these were considered at all, they were assumed to be compatible with an efficient agricultural sector. The framework of agricultural control and support established by the 1947 Act proved to be enduring and enjoyed widespread public support.

In contrast to the adversarial politics that shaped urban land use policy in the post-war period (Cox, 1984), there was near-political consensus over countryside policies from 1945 to the early 1970s (Flynn, 1986). Despite the land nationalisation arguments advanced in the Labour Party Research Department's document 'Labour and Land Owners' (1944) and the Party's close association with the access movement (Blunden and Curry, 1990), once in power the post-war Labour Government shelved its policies for land nationalisation. The Town and Country Planning Act 1947 excluded the use of land and buildings for agriculture and forestry from the definition of development. The agricultural policy developed by the post-war Labour Party was conditioned by Labour's campaign for rural support; the controls that were introduced were not aimed at environmental protection but at increasing agricultural production (Flynn, 1986).

Agriculture and conservation: growing recognition of a problem

It was only in the 1960s that the consensus about agricultural fundamentalism started to be questioned seriously — and with it the assumed compatibility between an efficient, modern agricultural sector and countryside conservation. In particular, the 'Countryside in 1970' conferences focused attention on the landscape changes attributable to modern farming practices (Cox *et al.*, 1990), and Rachel Carson's '*Silent Spring*' (1963) highlighted the ecological impact of modern farming, notably, the contamination of food chains by agricultural pesticides. However, until the late 1970s, the Government was unwilling to recognise the extent of the damage, even when the Nature Conservancy Council's surveys (NCC, 1977) and the Countryside Commission's New Agricultural Landscapes reports (Westmacott and Worthington, 1974) documented the changes and projected these into the future with even more disturbing predictions. Ministers, echoing the farmers' leaders, would claim that the countryside as we know it is the creation of the farmers and that it could be safely left in their good hands — an attitude which was also implicit in the Common Agricultural Policy (CAP) that the U.K. had joined in 1972. The accusation that U.K. government and European Community policy, with its emphasis on increasing food production at almost any cost, was to blame for the environmental degradation in the countryside was either denied — or it was argued that this was a necessary price to pay for agricultural progress. The question of the loss of public access was largely ignored.

By the end of the 1970s such arguments became harder to sustain as the evidence mounted of widespread environmental destruction in the countryside. Research by the Countryside Commission and NCC, and *cause célèbres* such as moorland reclamation on Exmoor, forced a change in government perception of the relationship between agriculture and conservation. Some farmers, alarmed by the environmental impact of modern farming techniques, argued that farmers needed to talk to conservationists; they believed that, given advice and education, many farmers could be persuaded to adopt more environmentally friendly practices requiring relatively minor adjustments in land management regimes. The establishment of the Farming and Wildlife Advisory Group (FWAG) in 1969 reflected that view (Cox *et al.*, 1990). The Countryside Commission's 10 demonstration farms (Cobham *et al.*, 1984), where conservation practices were tested, costed and promoted within a variety of typical farming systems, were another example.

Implicit in this 'voluntary approach' was an assumption that there was no inherent conflict between agriculture and conservation and that such difficulties as did arise could be resolved by goodwill and common sense. However, the limits of the voluntary approach soon became evident. Some farmers were ready to respond to the advice of FWAG, but they were usually those who could afford to invest in conservation — and would have done so in any case. Frequently, the environmental benefits of projects promoted in this way — typically pond digging or field corner planting — were offset by intensification elsewhere on the farm. And of course, for most farmers, FWAG's call went unheeded; financial pressures and a traditional view, promoted by government policy, about the need to increase production were far more compelling considerations in determining land management. In particular, those who were intent on destroying valued habitats to increase yields could not be stopped, even if they were farming land of the highest ecological or landscape value. Marion Shoard (1980) captured the sense of anger among many which such conduct provoked. The title of her book, '*The Theft of the Countryside*', expressed a view that people other than farmers and landowners also had a legitimate interest in the way in which land was managed.

The political consensus between the Labour and Conservative parties over the purpose and implementation of agricultural policy finally broke down over how to implement the conclusions of Lord Porchester's inquiry into 'Land Use Change in Exmoor'. The 1974–1979 Labour Government had intended, through its Countryside Bill, to introduce controls over agricultural practices in environmentally sensitive areas. In particular, the Bill contained clauses that would allow Ministers to designate specific areas of open moor or heath within which national park authorities would have been able to make moorland conservation orders to prevent agricultural 'improvements' detrimental to the environment. When the Conservative Government came to power in 1979 it rejected moorland conservation orders, planning controls or any other form of compulsion to enforce conservation policies. Instead, it made the voluntary approach the centrepiece of the Wildlife and Countryside Act 1981. Yet there were some contradictions: while Ministers were at pains to stress that their approach enshrined the voluntary principle, in fact the Act introduced a power of last resort to protect SSSIs (but not National Parks).

Labour's Countryside Bill, and the Conservative-promoted Wildlife and Countryside Act 1981 which replaced it, provided the first evidence that central government at last recognised a conflict between modern farming practices and environmental objectives. However, the dominant perception remained one of agricultural fundamentalism, with environmental concerns still secondary. The 'culture' of farming was still one that did not question that the basic purpose of the operation was to grow two ears of corn where one grew before.

The 1984 watershed

Change came suddenly in 1984. The abrupt introduction of milk quotas signified a crisis in European agricultural policy and the dawn of a new era of continuing agricultural policy reform. Increasingly the prevailing concern was to cut food surpluses and the costs of the CAP (MAFF *et al.*, 1987). This view was in line with the Thatcher Government's enthusiasm for market forces and the non-interventionist stance of the influential New-Right (Bracewell-Milnes, 1988). Since the mid 1980s, government policy, tempered by membership of the EC, has been to reduce and redirect state support for agriculture. New support schemes have been developed that aim to curb production, diversify the rural economy and conserve the countryside. The Government's approach has largely been conditioned by their enthusiasm for market forces and desire to reduce state intervention. For example, MAFF has emphasised that farmers need to adopt new scientific and technological advances so as to compete effectively in the market place (MAFF *et al.*, 1991) and also highlighted an 'opportunity to create a market place for environmental goods' (MAFF, 1990, p. 3).

With the dethroning in the mid-1980s of the philosophy of agricultural fundamentalism, a new perception has emerged in which conservation has moved to the centre of agricultural policy. The first indication of this came in 1984 with the formation of an 'Environmental Co-ordination Unit' within MAFF. The passage of the Agriculture Act in 1986 'greened' the remit of MAFF: it was no longer solely concerned with the promotion of a stable and efficient agricultural industry but had to endeavour to achieve a reasonable balance between: agricultural considerations; the economic and social interests of rural areas; conservation and enhancement of the natural beauty and amenity of the countryside; and promotion of the enjoyment of the countryside by the public. MAFF had promoted the Bill in the belief that the integration of environmental considerations within its remit would: strengthen its position at a time when there were calls for a new 'Ministry of Rural Affairs'; and provide a new, politically acceptable rationale for supporting agriculture (Winter, 1990). The greening of agricultural policy gathered momentum as publicity increased about the costs of the CAP, the levels of surplus production, the prospects of surplus agricultural land and the environmental damage wrought by modern farming practices. Drawing on the experience of the Broads Grazing Marshes Conservation Scheme, the Government lobbied for the adoption of an EC regulation allowing for the designation of Environmentally Sensitive Areas (ESA) (see part 2). Under the terms of the ESA scheme, farmers were, for the first time, offered financial encouragement from agriculture departments not to increase production but to continue traditional farming practices which would ensure protection of areas of 'national environmental significance'. The passage of the Agriculture Act 1986 and establishment of ESAs signified official recognition of the role of agricultural policy in the protection, enhancement and enjoyment of the countryside. A more recent government statement on agricultural policy (MAFF *et al.*, 1991) continues the trend of emphasising the environmental benefits of state support for agriculture, arguing that 'environmental concerns lend a new urgency to the already weighty case for removing the distorting effects of the present system of CAP support' (p. 2). It also outlines the Government's commitment to developing 'farming systems which will help to protect the landscape, wildlife and historic interests, and which recognise the value of traditional local rural practices' (p. 22).

Politics and the environment in the 1980s

The 1980s witnessed the greening of British politics and society (McCormick, 1991), with environmental issues moving from the periphery to the centre of the public policy debate. Some authors have suggested that environmental policy development during the Thatcher administration can be divided into two phases (McCormick, 1991). In the first, the Government attempted to reduce 'over sensitivity to environmental considerations'; in the second, the Conservatives actively promoted themselves as the 'green party'. In terms of the integration of agricultural and environmental policy, the change in policy stance seems to date from 1984. However, a distinction has to be drawn between policies developed for nationally important landscapes and policies that evolved for the rest of the countryside (Lowe and Flynn, 1989).

Throughout the 1980s the Conservative Government promoted policies that were based on the facilitation of the free market and a desire to reduce State intervention whilst retaining a strong State. These neo-liberal ideas are clearly witnessed in countryside planning and management with continued Conservative commitment to the voluntary principle: conservation through persuasion. However, in contrast to the weakening of general planning controls (Thornley, 1991), the same Government extended the scope of environmental policy in rural conservation and heritage protection — areas closest to traditional Tory paternalism (Lowe and Flynn, 1989). The result has been the evolution of what some have described as a two-tier system of countryside protection (Cloke and McLaughlin, 1989): areas of national environmental importance (national parks, for example) have been excluded from the relaxation of planning controls and even granted extended regulatory safeguards; whilst in the rest of the countryside a more market orientated and less community responsive planning system has evolved. This gradual development of a dual countryside planning system came to a head over the debate about the draft circular on 'Development Involving Agricultural Land' (Cloke and McLaughlin, 1989).

The appointment of Chris Patten as Secretary of State for the Environment in 1989 marked an important change in the Conservative approach to environmental policy. The pursuit of unadulterated market forces (for example, Nicholas Ridley's proposals to privatise nature reserves), were replaced by enthusiasm for market mechanisms for environmental protection and enhancement. Patten's specialist advisor, Professor David Pearce, advocated a market-based approach to sustainable development with consumers and industry given clear signals about the costs which will be imposed upon society by given levels of pollution (Pearce *et al.*, 1989). Pearce's ideas were readily accepted by Chris Patten who stated that market-based instruments offered an 'efficient and flexible response to environmental concerns' (Patten, 1990). The Government's commitment to the so-called market-based approach to the environment was outlined in the White Paper on the Environment (HM Government, 1990): 'In the Government's view, market mechanisms offer the prospect of a more efficient and flexible response to environmental issues, both old and new' (p. 14). This emphasis on market mechanisms is the closest the Government has come to a distinct political philosophy on environmental policy.

In 1989, proposals to greatly extend the scope of permitted development rights on agricultural land were abandoned by Chris Patten. More recently, the Major Government has started to rebuild the standing of planning in its concern to establish the place of government as the guardian of the environment. Thus the Planning and Compensation Act 1991, and the revised Planning Policy Guidance Notes 1 and 12 (DoE and Welsh Office, 1992a; DoE, 1992a), put a new emphasis on a plan-led approach to development and place planning at the centre of the pursuit of sustainable development. The present Government continues to concentrate on the market-based approach to environmental policy, although indicating a willingness to introduce new closely targeted controls where necessary (DoE and Welsh Office, 1992b).

The international dimension

International considerations increasingly influence government policy in this sphere, in particular, through our membership of the EC. In recent years the EC has become a new source of environmental initiatives and ideas with an emphasis on fixed standards and codification rather than the administrative discretion often associated with British law (Baldock, 1989). Between 1980 and 1991 the EC adopted over 250 items of environmental legislation (DoE, 1992b). Although most were concerned with environmental pollution, the EC has had an important influence on British countryside policy. For example, the Birds Directive created a special category of SSSI, the Directive on Environmental Assessment has influenced land use planning and Directives on nitrates in drinking water have led to

the creation of Nitrate Sensitive Areas. The Habitats Directive, adopted in May 1992, aims to establish a pan-European ecological network to be called 'Natura 2000' and will bring increased protection for scarce habitats and threatened or endangered species of plants and animals. The recent adoption of the Community's Fifth Environment Action Programme (Commission of the European Communities, 1992a) marks a pan-European move towards a broader range of policy instruments and, specifically, economic instruments (such as the much debated carbon tax) to get environmental protection working within the grain of the market (DoE, 1992b). The CAP is starting to demonstrate green tinges with member States required, under the 'Agri-Environment Regulation' (Commission of the European Communities, 1992b) to develop agricultural production methods compatible with the protection of the environment and maintenance of the countryside.

Conclusion

The above analysis of agriculture and conservation policy during the last 45 years reveals the ebb and flow of three important forces which influence policy as it affects the resolution of conflicts between conservation and farming:

- the status of agriculture
- concern about environmental problems
- the macro political context.

These forces provide the setting within which the various policy instruments have been developed and explain why, at different stages over the years, different approaches have found favour and progressed further than others.

Part 2: six policy instruments

In the first part of this paper we have analysed the underlying considerations — agricultural, environmental and political — which bear on the debate about farming and conservation. In this part, we consider policy instruments which have, in various ways, contributed to the solution of conflicts between these two interests. As illustrated in Fig. 1, there are broadly three types of mechanism for integrating agriculture/conservation policy: regulation; advice and information; and financial instruments.

Regulation

There are three types of direct environmental

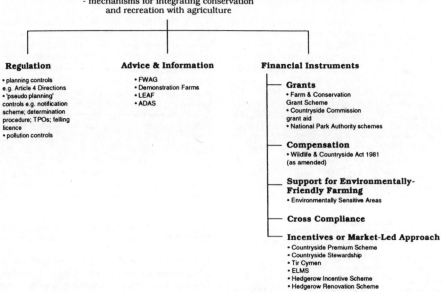

Figure 1. Countryside tools: mechanisms for integrating conservation and recreation with agriculture.

regulations or controls over agricultural and forestry activities: planning; 'pseudo-planning' and pollution control. Whilst successive governments have remained committed to the voluntary principle, there has been a general increase in the range of controls over rural land uses in recent years.

Planning controls

The Town and Country Planning Act 1947 introduced the first comprehensive system of land use planning into this country. Following the Scott Committee's conclusions, the Act was designed to protect the countryside, and agricultural land in particular, from urban encroachment. The planning system not only sought to contain urban development in order to safeguard agricultural land, it also imposed minimal controls on agricultural and forestry enterprises. The use of land and buildings for agriculture and forestry is excluded from the definition of development contained in the 1947 Act, and all successive Acts; hence there is no need to obtain planning permission for agriculture or forestry operations. Also, most building or engineering operations carried out for agriculture or forestry purposes are classified as permitted development

under the General Development Order (GDO), Schedule 2. The Government has resisted pressure from amenity and conservation interests (CPRE *et al.*, 1990) to extend planning controls over a variety of farming activities. Although controls over agricultural developments were tightened in the 1980s, these reforms were normally operationally specific, geographically based and/or in the form of 'pseudo planning' controls (see below). For example, the GDO was amended in 1986 to limit excavations on farmland to legitimate farming operations, in 1988 further restrictions were imposed on the building of livestock units and in 1992 the permitted development rights of agricultural holdings of less than 5 ha were restricted. Some of the controls that have been implemented have originated from Brussels rather than Whitehall. For example, the environmental assessment regulations as they apply to proposed afforestation schemes and certain agricultural operations are a direct result of EC environmental policy rather than a U.K. initiative.

Article 4 Directions provide local planning authorities with a last resort power to remove specified permitted development rights altogether and require an application to be made for planning permission for otherwise exempted development. For example,

Mendip District Council have used an Article 4 Direction to control landscape change through fencing in certain parts of the Mendip Hills Area of Outstanding Natural Beauty. More recently, the Secretary of State for the Environment approved an Article 4 Direction for the Swainswick Valley, near Bath, which will require developers of new agricultural buildings to obtain planning approval. There are, though, several limitations to the use of Article 4 Directions (Land Use Consultants, 1990; National Housing and Town Planning Council *et al.*, 1990). Local authorities are liable for compensation if permission for development is refused. Such Directions cannot be retrospective, meaning that local authorities have to be constantly vigilant to potential rather than actual changes. Directions are subject to Secretary of State approval and the consequent delay often means that development will occur in the interim period without control.

'Pseudo planning' controls

By 'pseudo planning' we mean:

- controls that are implemented under planning legislation but do not question the principle of development (prior notification systems, for example); and/or,
- land use regulations introduced under non-planning legislation (for example, limestone pavement orders, nature conservation orders, potential hedgerow management orders and grant notification).

The range of pseudo planning controls has increased considerably since 1980 as the Government illustrated a willingness to introduce specific restrictions on farming activities but resisted calls for a general extension of planning controls.

The notification procedure, first introduced in 1950 in areas of special landscape significance under the Landscape Areas Special Development Order (LASDO), provided local planning authorities in (and near) parts of the Lake District, Peak District and Snowdonia National Parks with a discretionary control over the siting, design and external appearance of farm and forestry developments subject to permitted development rights. This system was extended in 1986 and 1989 to cover all national parks in England and Wales and the Broads Authority area, respectively. More recently, changes to the GDO which came into force in January 1992 have extended this system of pseudo planning control to agricultural and forestry buildings constructed throughout England and Wales. Under the amended GDO, permitted development cannot be exercised unless the farmer/developer has applied to the local planning authority for a determination as to whether their prior approval will be required for certain details: siting, design and external appearance of farm and forestry buildings, roads, waste disposal facilities exceeding 0.5 ha and fish tanks. The 'determination procedure' does not impose full planning controls — the principle of development is not relevant (DoE and Welsh Office, 1992b).

The agricultural grant notification system operated in national parks since 1980 is another form of pseudo planning control. Under this scheme, farmers seeking agricultural grant aid for development or land improvement from MAFF or WOAD were required to notify the appropriate national park authority before approval for grant aid could be given.

Other pseudo planning measures have been proposed, for example, Landscape Conservation Orders (LCO) or Hedgerow Management Orders (HMO). These would offer protection backed by sanctions to conserve important landscape features. In practice, they would operate in the same way as Tree Preservation Orders are currently used. The Government did include a commitment to introduce LCO procedures in national parks in the 1987 Conservative election manifesto but formally abandoned this in September 1988. More recently, the Government, responding to figures from the Institute for Terrestrial Ecology that illustrated continued and accelerated hedgerow loss, promised to introduce legislation for a hedgerow notification scheme when time permits (DoE, 1992c). A private members bill designed to protect hedges of historical, wildlife or landscape value was introduced in Parliament but recently failed to complete the report stage and third reading.

Limestone Pavement Orders are another example of a closely targeted control introduced by the Conservative Government. Section 34 of the Wildlife and Countryside Act 1981 makes provision for the protection of limestone pavements. Under this section the Secretary of State or county planning authority can make a Limestone Pavement Order when it appears that the character and appearance of a limestone pavement is likely to be adversely affected by the removal of limestone. Such orders make it a criminal offence for any person to remove or disturb limestone on a limestone pavement unless planning permission is obtained from the local planning authority first. The effect of such Orders is to give protection to limestone pavements in perpetuity and without compensation.

The Wildlife and Countryside Act 1981 (Section 29)

also provides the Secretary of State with the power to make a Nature Conservation Order for the following purposes:

- to ensure the survival in Great Britain of any kind of animal or plant; or
- to comply with an international obligation; or
- where the land is of national importance, to ensure the conservation of any of its flora, fauna, geological or physiographical features.

The Order will specify operations which the Secretary of State considers likely to damage or destroy the special interest of the land and makes it an offence for any person to carry out such operations without prior written approval of the relevant conservation agency. The owner or lessees of land affected by a Nature Conservation Order may be entitled to compensation.

Licences provide another form of pseudo planning control. For example, the Forestry Commission operate a system of felling licences to control the felling of trees in Great Britain (Forestry Commission, 1987). The Countryside Commission for Scotland (1987) proposed a similar system of licences for planting schemes, under which proposed afforestation schemes above a certain size would require a licence in order to be eligible for public subsidies (then in the form of planting grants and tax relief). Such a scheme would not be statutory and its success would depend on the importance of public subsidy to the economics of the proposed afforestation.

Pollution control

As agricultural practices have 'industrialised' so agriculture has become increasingly prominent as a source of pollution, especially pollution of water. Howarth (1992) argues that in 1988 agriculture was the most damaging single activity in relation to water quality. The Control of Pollution Act 1974 did not apply the 'Polluter Pays Principle' in full to farming. Under the 1974 Act farmers had been exempt from prosecution if their actions were in accordance with 'good agricultural practice' — a reference to the MAFF code of good agricultural practice. Although in practice an infrequent defence, this 'loophole' attracted considerable criticism from bodies such as the House of Commons Environment Committee and was closed by enactment of the Water Act 1989. The 1989 Act signalled the introduction of a stricter policing of water quality. The National Rivers Authority established by the Act has proved to be more active in prosecuting farmers than previous authorities (Howarth, 1992). The maximum fines for

pollution have also been increased from £2000 to £20,000 on summary conviction.

The Water Act 1989 also signified increased attention on the role of precautionary regulations. Although provision to enact precautionary regulations has existed for some years, it is only since passage of the 1989 Act that such powers have been exercised (Howarth, 1992). The 1989 Act provides for the designation of Nitrate Sensitive Areas where there is pollution of watercourses and bodies by leaching of nitrate. When a Nitrate Sensitive Area is designated, the relevant Minister can prevent or control the entry of nitrate into controlled waters by voluntary agreements with farmers in the area affected or through mandatory orders. In all, 10 Nitrate Sensitive Areas have been designated since 1990. The Government has adopted a voluntary approach and indicated that it will only introduce compulsory measures if voluntary arrangements are ineffective. Other examples of precautionary regulations include the power under the Water Resources Act 1989 to designate water protection zones — a mechanism to protect areas that are particularly vulnerable to water pollution — and the Control of Pollution (Silage, Slurry and Agricultural Fuel Oil) Regulation 1991 which establishes controls and sets standards for construction of silage stores, slurry installations and agricultural fuel oil tanks in England and Wales. Generally, the strengthening of pollution control measures over agriculture has often been initiated by the requirement to implement an EC directive and introduced in association with grants for the instillation of pollution control machinery. However, public opinion can also be a powerful force: the ban on the burning of stubble and straw which (with limited exceptions) took effect after the 1992 harvest provides an example of the importance of public opinion.

Advice and information

As quantifiable evidence of landscape change caused by modern farming practices increased during the 1970s, so the farming community began to argue that farmers needed to talk to conservationists, and that — given advice and education — many farmers could be persuaded to adopt more environmentally friendly farming practices. The establishment of the Farming and Wildlife Advisory Group (FWAG) in 1969 reflected that view. FWAG was essentially an exercise in compromise politics: it was established to provide a forum where conflicting interests could meet to work towards a compromise (Lowe *et al.*, 1991). FWAG operates through a series of county farm conservation advisers whose purpose is to provide realistic and practical advice to farmers on

Development of the Market-led Approach   323

ways in which modern farming can be carried on with due regard to wildlife and landscape features.

The Countryside Commission has been active in promoting advice, often in association with grant-aid, as a means of influencing landowners and managers to adopt conservation practices and the Commission's most recent policy statement on this issue highlights the role of technical advice and support as integral to the success of payment schemes (Countryside Commission, 1993a). The experimental New Agricultural Landscape Projects were based on the practice of employing a project officer who offered advice, practical assistance and limited financial aid. The Countryside Commission's Demonstration Farms experiment (Cobham *et al.*, 1984) is another example of advice being used as a tool to integrate conservation objectives into agricultural practices. The Demonstration Farms project was established in 1975 on commercial farms to illustrate how modern farming practices could be made compatible with countryside conservation and thus influence the prevailing attitudes of land-owners, farmers and public agencies towards better practice (Cobham *et al.*, 1984). During the 1980s, the Countryside Commission's advisory efforts were mainly pursued through FWAG; it supported the Group in the employment of county conservation advisers.

A more recent initiative based on the provision of advice and dissemination through demonstration is the LEAF project (Linking Environment And Farming) funded by the European Crop Protection Association. LEAF was launched in 1991 with the aim of developing and promoting integrated crop management (Drummond, 1992). General guide-lines on farm management have been developed and six demonstration farms established for growers and the public to visit (Abel and Hill, 1993). LEAF focuses on a whole farm approach and the emphasis is on utilising efficient production methods to grow safe and wholesome food using lower inputs. The emphasis is on wider environmental concerns than the Countryside Commission's Demonstration Farms Project, although maintenance and improve-ment of local habitats and landscape features are included amongst the aims of LEAF. A common element between LEAF and the Countryside Com-mission's Demonstration Farms Project is that neither focus on access to the countryside.

Farmers have also traditionally received advice from the state through the Agricultural Development Advisory Service (ADAS). Until the 1980s this advice concentrated on improving agricultural pro-ductivity but as awareness of the environmental costs of modern farming increased, so conservation considerations started to figure more prominently amongst ADAS's advisory services. Despite the provisions of the Agriculture Act 1986, which allow ADAS to charge for services and advice to farmers, the initial provision of conservation advice is still treated as a public good and provided free of charge.

A review of countryside adviser policy for the Countryside Commission (Broom *et al.*, 1989) found that, in the case study areas examined, two-thirds of farmers interviewed followed up some or all of the advice provided. The study highlighted the inability of advisers to promote a whole-farm approach as a major weakness of current practice; in part this reflects the link between advice and grant-aid, and the feature-focused nature of most conservation grant schemes. The Government's preference for market forces is evident in the recent evolution of advice and demonstration schemes. For example, the Countryside Commission has agreed to hand over responsibility for Demonstration Farms to the farming industry (Countryside Commission, 1992a); the LEAF project is looking to funding through independent and corporate membership when the three-year funding from European Crop Protection Association ceases; and ADAS now operates in the commercial sector.

Financial instruments

Grants

Traditionally, government advice to farmers has been closely associated with the provision of government grants but while grants to encourage farm efficiency and maximise production have a long history, the widespread availability of grants for conservation is of more recent origin. Conservation grants are normally either fixed level payments for specific works or are offered to cover a stipulated proportion of the cost of the works.

Grants for landscape conservation have been offered by local authorities, statutory agencies and, more recently, government departments. The Countryside Commission pioneered the provision of grants for landscape conservation as part of its statutory duty to 'conserve and enhance the natural beauty and amenity of the countryside'; it offers grants to local authorities, public bodies and voluntary organis-ations for employing conservation project officers, countryside advisers and operating their own land-scape conservation programmes. Countryside Commission grants to farmers and landowners are normally administered by local authorities and offer assistance for planting trees and small woods, managing existing trees and small woods and con-serving or creating other landscape features.

Grants for conservation works also became widely available from agriculture departments in 1989, when the Farm and Conservation Grant Scheme (FCGS) replaced the Agricultural Improvement Scheme. The introduction of the FCGS marked an important shift in policy. After more than four decades of production-led grant schemes, the provisions of the new scheme concentrate on pollution prevention and conservation rather than any further stimulation of food production; indeed measures that might increase production on most farms are specifically excluded from the new grant scheme.

As Colman *et al.* (1992) note, grant aid has the advantage of encouraging recipients to seek the lowest cost method of undertaking the work given that they will be bearing a proportion of costs. However, grant-aid schemes can result in comparatively high administration costs; and they encourage a feature-based response to landscape conservation. For example, between 1974 and 1985 the Countryside Commission spent over £9 million on amenity tree planting (Sykes and Briggs, undated). This is not a problem when the grants are responding to the loss of a particular feature, as with the grants offered by Task Force Trees following storm damage (Countryside Commission, 1989a), but is an inappropriate means of securing a whole farm approach to conservation. The development of initiatives such as Countryside Stewardship (see below) and the availability of grants for landscape enhancement from other sources have led the Countryside Commission to reduce the amount of resources that it devotes to conservation grants (Countryside Commission, 1991a, 1992a).

National park authorities have used grant schemes to encourage environmentally friendly farming. For example, Exmoor National Park Authority have operated a Landscape Conservation Scheme under which they can top-up grants made to farmers by MAFF; the Farm Conservation Scheme operated by the North York Moors National Park Authority offered an income source to farmers for maintenance of wildlife and landscape features; and in the Peak District National Park, the Peak Board, utilising EC finance, pioneered an integrated grant scheme that paid by results; payments for the care of herb-rich meadows, for example, were based on the number of species retained or reintroduced.

Compensation

Compensation came into being with the passage of the Wildlife and Countryside Act 1981 as a response to increasing public concern about the damage done by farming to treasured landscapes and wildlife —

for example, to national parks and SSSIs. Compensation payments were to be paid for profits foregone, in return for the farmer or landowner giving undertakings, as part of a formal management agreement, not to carry out certain prescribed environmentally destructive practices: not to drain wetlands or to desist from applying fertilisers to hay meadows, for example. There were many who criticised the legislation on the grounds that it created a potential for blackmail. It contrasted with the principles underlying the operation of the planning system, under which compensation is not normally payable for the withholding of planning permission. And it appeared to reward those who wanted to destroy the countryside rather than the farmers and landowners who conserved nature and landscape at a cost because of their sense of stewardship. Others were concerned that it gave protection only to the special areas, notably SSSIs. The principle of compensation for profit foregone also means that the subsidy paid from one area of public spending (agricultural policy) can inflate the level of compensation to be paid from another (environmental policy) (Marsden *et al.*, 1993). The Act, incidentally, did nothing to encourage farmers to provide public access to their land, although there were some powers to clarify the law as it relates to rights-of-way.

Support for environmentally friendly farming

Compensation arrangements under the 1981 Act did help to check the pace of destruction, especially in SSSIs, but the critics were able to point to many shortcomings; in particular some of the six-figure compensation payments. However, it seems likely that the next shift of policy came about so soon not because of conservation fears but because the outlook for farming had changed. The arrival, overnight, in 1984, of milk quotas had the effect of signalling to farmers and others the painful news that surpluses had arrived. Henceforth, farm policy was going to be less about growing more — and more about growing less.

This was the context in which the row over the Halvergate Marshes took place. Conservationists — like soldiers — rarely have the luxury of choosing the ground upon which they must fight. Halvergate was an improbable battleground: flat, Norfolk grazing marshes between the Yare and the Bure, with a somewhat esoteric landscape appeal. However, the rarity value of such places was undeniable and the marshes were important for wildlife. Almost from the moment that the area was identified as critical to the conservation of the Broads and its landscape, it was under threat from drainage and conversion to cereal cropping. 'Arabalisation' was the word for an ugly process, but one which made economic sense for farmers who could get capital grants for drainage and better, CAP-inflated prices for barley than for the grazing of cattle.

Efforts by one of the farmers concerned to drain and plough his marshland at Halvergate encountered demonstrations by the Friends of the Earth: the publicity was embarrassing to government and there was much scurrying around to find a way out of the impasse. Late in 1984, Ministers announced a three-year experiment to safeguard the grazing marshes. The legal basis was the experimental powers of the Countryside Commission (Section 4 of the 1968 Countryside Act and Section 40 of the 1981 Wildlife and Countryside Act) which allow the Commission to carry out 'experimental schemes designed to facilitate the enjoyment of the countryside or to conserve or enhance its natural beauty or amenity'.

The experiment, in which the Commission was supported by MAFF, DOE and the Broads Authority, was based on a new approach: payments to support the traditional grazing economy. In return for undertakings about the use of fertilisers, the maintenance of water levels and the dates for the first cut of grass, graziers were to receive a standard payment per hectare; extra payments were available to those who chose to convert the land back from arable to pasture. Payments for access were not part of the scheme.

The Broads Grazing Marshes experiment was successful in halting the loss of grazing marshes in the area. More importantly, it became the model for the proposals advanced by the Ministry of Agriculture in its negotiations in the EC, from which emerged Environmentally Sensitive Areas. The first six ESAs were designated in 1987.

ESAs marked a fundamental shift in policy. Instead of compensation as under the 1981 Act — an approach which in effect assumed an irreconcilable conflict between conservation and agricultural aims — they offered financial support for traditional forms of farming which brought environmental benefits. The funds came from the agricultural budget. For the first time the NCC and the Countryside Commission were to play a formal role in advising the Ministry of Agriculture (on the selection of the areas and the suitable conservation regimes). The ESAs covered areas of not only wildlife but also landscape and archaeological importance.

ESAs have been considerably expanded since, a testimony to their popularity among both farmers and conservationists, and to their compatibilty with the new priorities of agricultural policy in the U.K. and Europe as a whole. However, they have been criticised (Lobley, 1989; Orme, 1992; Rowe, 1987; RSPB, 1991; Sinclair, 1986), in particular, for:

- Bringing benefits only to limited areas and a few farmers.
- Placing too much emphasis on supporting the status quo and not enough on environmental rehabilitation.
- Doing nothing for access. This criticism may soon be answered as MAFF, and other agriculture departments, have issued a consultation paper on 'New Public Access in ESAs' (MAFF, 1993a) as part of their obligation under EC Regulation 2078/92 (the so-called Agri-Environment Regulation) which gives MAFF, for the first time, the legal powers it needs to pursue access aims.
- Excluding any element of discretion; since ESAs are made as part of an EC structural measure, the Government is required to accept any applicant who can implement the guidelines.

Cross-compliance

The principle of cross-compliance is that support for agricultural production should be conditional upon compliance with certain stipulated forms of environmentally sensitive farming practice. Farmers deciding not to farm in an environmentally friendly manner would not receive price support.

There are at least two forms of cross-compliance (Colman *et al.*, 1992). The first has been described as the 'red-ticket approach' and would mean that participation in certain government programmes is conditional on farmers' attainment of specific conservation standards. The second method, described as the 'green-ticket approach', would enable benefits of farm support programmes to increase as farmers improved conservation standards and public good outputs. The red-ticket approach is probably more efficient in terms of administration costs but the green-ticket approach could deliver more substantive environmental benefits (Colman *et al.*, 1992).

Cross-compliance policies have operated in the U.S.A. since 1985 when legislation was introduced to discourage production on highly erodible land. If farmers contravene the cross-compliance provisions they risk forfeiting eligibility for federal farm support (Taylor and Dixon, 1990). The Food Security Act 1985 established three compliance measures: conservation compliance, sodbuster and swampbuster (Ervin *et al.*, 1991). The conservation compliance stipulates that farmers with highly erodible land obtain an approved conservation plan by 1990 and implement it fully by 1995. If producers do not comply with the provisions of the conservation plan, they forfeit state support in the form of deficiency payments, government loans, price support, etc. The sodbuster provisions deny farm programme benefits to farmers who plough up highly erodible land afer 23 December 1985 unless they adopt and implement a conservation plan. The swampbuster provision in the Food Security Act 1985 denies agricultural programme benefits to any farmer producing on wetland (swamp) converted since 23 December 1985. This system of cross-compliance was amended, in the light of experience, by the Food, Agriculture, Conservation and Trade Act 1990 (FACTA). FACTA extended the compliance requirements to cover currently set-aside or diverted lands; it increased the range of programme benefits that producers could lose; and it refined the penalties to allow for inadvertent misdemeanours (Ervin *et al.*, 1991). It is difficult to evaluate the U.S. experience of cross-compliance because the schemes will not have been fully implemented until 1995. However, as Potter *et al.* (1991) note, the cross-compliance provisions mark an important shift in farm policy away from the interests of farmers towards those of society as a whole.

The EC, through its 1992 reforms to the CAP, has introduced an element of cross-compliance (farmers wishing to qualify for area payments for arable crops must set-aside 15% of the total area for which they are claiming), but this is linked to budgetary and surplus production considerations rather than environmental objectives. Although there is no widespread system of cross-compliance linking agricultural support packages with environmental objectives, several existing conservation schemes include elements of cross-compliance. For example, acceptance for Tir Cymen payments is conditional upon the whole farm being managed according to the Tir Cymen code of good agricultural practice (see below) and Countryside Stewardship payments (see below) are conditional on the maintenance of rights-of-way in a good condition. The system of tax relief for outstanding scenic land also demonstrates elements of cross-compliance. Owners of land of 'outstanding scenic, historic or scientific interest' can apply for exemption from Inheritance Tax and Capital Gains Tax. If the land is deemed to be of exemptable quality, owners wishing to obtain exemption must agree the detailed steps necessary to maintain the land, to preserve its character and secure reasonable access; these conditions and management prescriptions are normally detailed in a Heritage Landscape Management Plan (Countryside Commission, 1990). Exemption from the specified

tax will be lost if owners depart from these undertakings.

Responding to growing calls for cross-compliance to be used to link farming practice, environmental objectives and price support within Britain and the EC (Association of National Park Officers, 1988; NCC, 1990; RSPB, 1992; Taylor and Dixon, 1990), the Government announced in 1991 that 'farmers can expect that the principle of cross-compliance, under which the receipt of payments is conditional upon protection of the environment, will become a normal feature of future agricultural support schemes' (MAFF *et al.*, 1991, p. 25). The first steps towards implementing this commitment came with recent reforms to the Hill Livestock Compensatory Allowances (HLCAs) which added an ecological definition of 'overgrazing' to the stipulation of maximum stocking rates eligible for HLCA payments.

The advantage of cross-compliance is that it would harness the power of price support for food production by making it act as a dual support for environmental protection as well (Taylor and Dixon, 1990). It would avoid the problem of output price support inflating conservation payments — a basic problem of ESAs (Colman *et al.*, 1992). Potential problems could include a complex administration; and the general reductions in agricultural support subsidies that the EC has instigated, together with the uncertainty about the future development of the CAP, may reduce the leverage element necessary for cross-compliance to work.

Part 3: the market-led or incentives approach

Partly in response to the shortcomings of ESAs (see above), there has emerged support in recent years for the market approach. The principle here is the creation of a market in environmental and related recreational services which can be 'acquired' from farmers and landowners. Incentives are offered from the public sector to farmers and landowners to manage their land according to certain prescriptions, who are thus able to market their role as custodians and managers of the countryside. Unlike ESAs or the compensation arrangements under the Wildlife and Countryside Act 1981, the public sector 'buyer' of environmental and recreational services is not obliged to come to an agreement; they can pick and choose in order to get the best value for money. Discretion, therefore, is an important part of the concept.

To date, the market approach has taken five forms:

- locally based schemes;
- the Countryside Premium Scheme on set aside land (now closed to new applications);
- the Countryside Stewardship Scheme operational in England;
- the Tir Cymen scheme (operational in Wales); and,
- the Hedgerow Incentive Scheme (operational in England) and the Hedgerow Renovation Scheme (operational in Wales).

Though these various schemes share certain principles, they differ importantly in detail. One important feature of all the approaches (except those concerned with hedgerows), however, is that public access for informal recreation is regarded as a marketable product. While it has not, in general, been practicable to find ways of charging people directly for this service, the arrival of publicly funded schemes, run by local government or central government agencies, has created a market in access.

Local environmental land management schemes

The idea of landowners and farmers selling an environmental land management service was contained in the Country Landowners Association (CLS) report on 'Enterprise in the Rural Environment' (Greenwell, 1989). The Greenwell report responded to the challenge of the Government's ALURE document (1987) which had enjoined farmers and landowners to be more enterprising in the marketing of a whole range of goods and services from their land, not only food. It envisaged landowners and farmers acting as independent businessmen, taking the initiative to draw up an environmental plan for all or part of their land. The decision to prepare such a plan would be voluntary and not as a result of a designation imposed by government. The plan would be negotiated, and a contract drawn up, between the owner/occupier concerned and central or local government. An owner/occupier might also negotiate with other public or private organisations.

The CLA called this approach the Environmental Land Management Scheme (ELMS). It envisaged that certain elements of ELMS contracts, such as provision of public access, would be applicable nationwide; other elements would reflect local environmental features.

Devon County Council have pioneered the development of a local market or incentive-led approach to conservation and recreation. The central aim of the Devon Environmental Land Management Scheme is to contribute to 'the protection and improvement of the Devon environment, and recreational use of it, through the establishment of partnership agreements with the owners and managers of land' (Devon County Council, 1990). The scheme aims to encourage landowners and occupiers to implement projects which not only maintain and improve the landscape and wildlife habitats but also enhance facilities for informal recreation. The Devon scheme is for one-off capital grants, though the eligible costs may include the projected annual maintenance costs over an agreed period such as 10 years. The budget (£204,000 for 1992/1993) is targeted at priority areas:

1. *Landscaping or tree planting*
The management of prominent landscape features and assistance with the restoration, planting and management of traditional orchards — particularly those managed by, and for, the benefit of local people — under the Devon Orchards Initiative.

2. *Nature conservation*
The management and conservation of existing features and habitats, or the creation of new habitats. In particular, Culm grassland and habitats valuable to cirl buntings.

3. *Informal recreation and access*
The facilitation of access to the countryside through footpaths, bridleways and cycleways; assistance with the provision of informal recreation areas, nature trails and picnic areas or car parking, and the provision of facilities for the elderly or disabled.

4. *Environmental awareness*
The provision of interpretation and information facilities in connection with 1–3 above.
(*Source*: Compiled from Devon County Council, 1992).

The ELMS scheme is being used by Devon County Council as a means of implementing various rural initiatives. For example, the 'Devon Orchards Initiative' and the 'Devon Action for Tourism and the Environment' programme. A total of 28 projects were supported from the first year's budget of £199,000, and in the second year of operation 33 projects were agreed from a budget of £212,800. Agreements are normally secured utilising powers under Section 39 of the Wildlife and Countryside Act 1981.

Although there has been no thorough evaluation of the scheme, it would appear to have been successful in integrating conservation and recreation. For example, one ELMS agreement provides for the development of a conservation area of about 2 ha

328   Kevin D. Bishop and Adrian A.C. Phillips

with disabled access; another agreement near Tiverton provides for the establishment of a wildlife conservation area on approximately 3 ha for educational purposes; a third agreement at Hatherleigh gives local people access to a traditional orchard.

Adoption of the ELMS concept by other local authorities would not appear likely because of the financial costs and the development of various national schemes, such as Countryside Stewardship and Tir Cymen (see below). For example, Gwent County Council seriously considered the adoption of an ELMS along the lines advocated by the CLA. However, a bid to the relevant county council committee in October 1991 proved unsuccessful because of the cost of offering such a scheme and knowledge that Tir Cymen (see below) was forthcoming.

The Countryside Premium Scheme

The Countryside Premium Scheme, launched in 1989, provided incentives to farmers for positive management of land entered into the Set-aside Scheme, for the benefit of wildlife, the landscape and the local community. It was developed in response to criticism that the set-aside arrangements, introduced in the late 1980s in response to EC rules, did nothing for the conservation and enjoyment of the countryside. The scheme, which was operated by the Countryside Commission under its experimental powers, was available only in seven

counties in eastern England (Bedfordshire, Cambridgeshire, Essex, Hertfordshire, Norfolk, Northamptonshire and Suffolk). To be accepted into the scheme, applicants must have already applied for, and been accepted into, the former MAFF Set-aside Scheme and only land set-aside as permanent fallow was eligible for additional Countryside Premium payments.

Under the terms of the scheme there were five management options (see Fig. 2). Acceptance of an application was at the discretion of the Countryside Commission, which operated the scheme, and payments were made annually in arrears for as long as the set-aside agreement had to run.

The meadowland option (see Fig. 2) was the only management option which specifically aimed to integrate conservation and recreation. Under the terms of the meadowland option applicants agreed to create new areas of grassland for the benefit of wildlife and quiet enjoyment by the local community.

The Countryside Premium Scheme was open for applicants for three years; during those three years the meadowland option proved to be the most popular management option. The Scheme resulted in the provision of over 3500 ha of new grassland areas available for quiet enjoyment by the public at over 140 sites (Countryside Premium Unit, pers. comm.). The popularity of the meadowland option would appear to indicate the willingness of rural

Option	Objectives of Management	Payment (£ per ha)
Wooded margins	To manage existing hedgerows to improve or create valuable habitats for wildlife. To create new hedgerows and belts of broadleaved trees and shrubs	75
Meadowland	To create new areas of grassland for the benefit of wildlife and for quiet countryside enjoyment by the local community	110
Wildlife fallow	To create a habitat attractive to ground nesting birds and encourage the growth of wildflowers on arable land by allowing controlled growth of natural vegetation on light, well-drained soils.	45
Brent Geese pasture	To create winter grazing for Brent Geese in selected areas as a means of minimising grazing damage to winter cereal crops elsewhere	80
Habitat restoration	To restore certain valuable wildlife habitats	varies

Source: Countryside Commission, 1989.

Figure 2. Countryside Premium Scheme management options.

Development of the Market-led Approach   329

landowners/occupiers to allow people onto their land on a concessionary basis in return for a modest income.

Although the three-year results appear impressive there has been no comprehensive study of the costs and benefits of the scheme. However, research for the Countryside Commission indicates that such sites are being used by a high proportion of those local people who participate in countryside recreation and also yields landscape and wildlife benefits. A survey by Land Use Consultants (1993) found that a range of 17–33% of local households were making use of meadowland sites which was equated to 33–92% of all potential users.

The Scheme closed to new applicants in 1992 following the agreement reached on reforms to the CAP and the introduction of the Arable Area Payments Scheme, which replaced the Set-aside Scheme. Proposals published in spring 1993 to implement the so-called 'Agri-environment Regulation' (Commission of the European Communities, 1992b) are based on the experience gleaned from the Countryside Premium Scheme and start to address the commitments in the Environment White Paper (HM Government, 1991, 1992) to introduce national environmental set-aside arrangements. As part of MAFF's proposed package of measures, supplementary payments would be offered to farmers who voluntarily offer public access to land set-aside under the Arable Area Payments Scheme on a non-rotational basis; also, conservation management proposals have been suggested for rotational and non-rotational set-aside land (MAFF, 1993b). The 'Agriculture and England's Environment' package also contains proposals for a 'Habitat Improvement Scheme' (MAFF, 1993c) which would offer farmers who withdraw agricultural land from production for at least 20 years for purposes connected with the environment (for example, the creation of biotope reserves or natural parks for the protection of hydrological systems) annual payments.

Countryside Stewardship

The White Paper on the Environment — 'This Common Inheritance' — publicised the Government's invitation to the Countryside Commission to develop a 'new national countryside initiative in England which might offer landowners, managers and farmers incentive payments to manage or recreate landscapes particularly valued by the public while at the same time providing access to the public' (HM Government, 1990, p. 103). The result, Countryside Stewardship, was launched in 1991 and builds upon the Commission's experience of operat-

ing the Countryside Premium Scheme. Like the Halvergate experiment and Countryside Premium Scheme, Countryside Stewardship is a pilot scheme operated by the Countryside Commission under its experimental powers. Through it, the Commission aims to demonstrate that 'conservation and public enjoyment of the countryside can be combined with commercial land management through a national system of incentives' (Countryside Commission, 1991b, p. 1). It also hopes to 'develop a basis for a comprehensive scheme to achieve environmental and recreation benefits as an integral part of agricultural support' (Countryside Commission, 1991b, p. 1).

Countryside Stewardship operates only in England and in its first year applied to five distinct landscapes and their wildlife habitats:

- chalk and limestone grassland;
- lowland heath;
- waterside landscapes;
- coastal land; and,
- uplands.

As part of the Government's 'Action in the Countryside' package (DoE, 1992c), two new target landscapes were introduced for the second year of the scheme:

- historic landscapes; and,
- meadow and pasture (Culm grasslands of mid-Devon and grasslands of Hereford and Worcester).

Countryside Stewardship aims to conserve the target landscapes by encouraging positive conservation management — to sustain, or return to, traditional management practices, or to adopt practical modern equivalents that produce the qualities for which the target landscapes are values. The scheme combines four elements:

- *Landscape* — developments in agriculture have improved productivity but have tended to impose uniformity. Countryside Stewardship offers opportunities to restore characteristic qualities and features to our diverse landscape.

- *Wildlife* — all landscapes support an important, and sometimes unique, wildlife. The scheme offers opportunities to improve and restore typical habitats.

- *History* — the landscapes all contain important historical and archaeological remains, and can provide glimpses of an ancient countryside and the activities of those who lived there. The scheme offers opportunities to protect and maintain important sites.

• *Access* — the scheme will create opportunities for people to enjoy the landscapes through the sensitive provision of new access, help to farmers and landowners in managing land under visitor pressure, and through existing rights-of-way.
(*Source*: Compiled from the Countryside Commission, 1991c).

The scheme is voluntary. It is open to anyone who is responsible for managing suitable land and able to enter into a 10-year management agreement. For each landscape type there are two or three manage-

ment tiers (see Fig. 3) with annual payments and management guidelines which vary to suit the individual qualities of the landscapes. Applicants choose a combination of the measures specified for each landscape, from the 'menu' (see Fig. 3) and propose a 10-year agreement. In addition to payments for conservation management, payments are also offered for allowing access. The payment for land made available for quiet, informal access is £50.00 per ha, fixed across all target landscapes. Payments for access routes (paths, bridleways and paths for disabled persons) and land used by educational establishments were introduced for the second year of the scheme (see Fig. 3). It is a general

ANNUAL PAYMENTS	£/ha
Chalk & limestone grassland	
Conservation of chalk & limestone grassland	£50/ha
Creation of chalk & limestone grassland	£210/ha
Lowland heath	
Base payment	£20/ha
For measures to improve the quality of the heath	£30/ha
Re-creation of lowland heath on improved land	£250/ha
Waterside landscapes	
Conservation of existing waterside landscapes	£70/ha
Creation or restoration of waterside landscapes	£225/ha
Coastal land	
Conservation of salt-marsh	£20/ha
Conservation of coastal grazing marsh	£70/ha
Conservation of coastal vegetation on cliff tops and sand dunes	£50/ha
Establishment of coastal vegetation on improved land	£225/ha
Uplands	
Regeneration of heather on enclosed moorland	£15/ha
PLUS:	£50/ha for first five years
Regeneration of heather on agriculturally improved land	£50/ha
PLUS:	£50/ha for first five years
Restoration and management of:	
• hay meadows	£80/ha
• additional payment on small hay meadows of 5 ha or less	£50/ha
• in-bye pasture	£50/ha
• intake or allotment rough pasture	£20/ha
Historic landscapes	
Conservation of existing historic features	£70/ha
Restoration of land to permanent pasture or other suitable vegetation	£225/ha
Restoration of old orchards	£250/ha
Old meadow and pasture	
Conservation management of old meadow and pasture	£70/ha
Access	
On land made available for public access	£50/ha
For the creation of new permissive paths, bridleways and paths for the disabled	£100/agreement
PLUS: Paths	£0.10/metre
Bridleways	£0.20/metre
Paths for the disabled	£0.20/metre
On land used by educational establishments	£25/ha
Supplements	
Supplements for initial restoration or re-creation works on chalk and limestone grassland, waterside landscapes, coastal land or pasture and meadows	£40 first year payment
Supplement for initial work needed to conserve historic features	£40 for up to five years
Supplement for special heather regeneration works	£50 for first five years

CAPITAL PAYMENTS		PAYMENT
Scrub management:	scattered scrub under 25%	£100/ha
	scrub between 25-75%	£250/ha
	scrub more than 75%	£500/ha
Pond restoration:	first 100 sq. metre	£2/sq. metre
	thereafter	£0.50/sq. metre
Pond creation:	first sq. metre	£3/sq. metre
	thereafter	£0.50/sq. metre
Creation of scrapes		£1.25/sq. metre
Sluice for water level control:	soil bund	£40
	timber	£140
	brick, stone or concrete	£400
Stone wall:	repair	£7.50/sq. metre
	restoration	£15
	step-over stile	£20
	step-through stile	£30
Top wiring of stone wall		£0.60/sq. metre
Stone faced hedge banks:	repair	£10/metre
	restoration	£25/metre
Earth banks restoration		£3/metre
Tree and shrub planting:	whips and transplants	£0.65/plant
Planting maiden fruit tree in old orchards		£3/tree
Planting standard fruit tree in old orchards		£7/tree
Planting standard parkland or hedgerow tree		£6/tree
Tree guards:	rabbit guard	£0.20/guard
	tube	£0.50/tube
	parkland	£30/guard
	orchard	£1.50/guard
Coppicing bankside trees		£12.50/tree
Pollarding		£17.50/tree
Tree surgery/major pruning		£40/tree
Frameworking of old fruit trees		£30/tree
Fruit tree pruning and restoration		£8/tree
Hedge planting		£1.75/metre
Hedge laying		£2/metre
Hedge coppicing		£1.50/metre
PLUS:		
Hedge supplement for laying or coppicing hedges over 1.5m wide at base		£0.50/metre
Hedge supplement for wire and post removal to aid laying or coppicing		£0.50/metre
Bracken control:	mechanical	£50/metre
	chemical	£85/ha
Clearance of eyesores		£120
Field gate		£125
Bridle gate		£100
Kissing gate		£130
Kissing gate for disabled		£200
Stile		£30
Ladder stile		£40
River gate		£125
Footbridge		£125
Culvert		£40/metre
Ditch, dyke, rhyne restoration		£2/metre
Post for sign or waymarking		£4
Sign with map of agreement land		£20
Interpretation board		£80
Bench		£30
Car parks/hardstandings		£5/sq. metre
Construction of path for disabled		£7.50/metre
Advice/application preparation		£100
Management plan preparation		£300
The following payments are available only for work that is essential to achieving good environmental management		
Fencing:	post and wire	£0.80/metre
	sheep fencing	£1.20/metre
	rabbit or sheep netting	£0.40/metre
For historic parks/deer parks only:		
Deer fencing		£3.50/metre
Continuous iron rail fencing		£6/metre
Water:		£0.40/metre
	supply	
	trough	£25

Figure 3. Types of Countryside Stewardship payments.

Development of the Market-led Approach   331

condition of entry to the scheme, whether or not use is made of the access option, that all rights-of-way on the land are in good order (i.e. it contains an element of cross-compliance). The market approach is also being extended to the provision of conservation advice, with participants being offered capital grants of £100 to purchase advice from any source and a payment of £300 to purchase advice on management plan preparation (see Fig. 3).

Applications are processed by Countryside Stewardship advisers in each of the Countryside Commission's regional offices. These staff are also available to provide technical advice and information free of charge. If sites are accepted into the scheme, payments are made annually in arrears.

A key aspect of the scheme is its flexibility: 'The Countryside Commission is concerned to achieve results and will not impose set guidelines where alternative local practice and traditions are more appropriate' (Countryside Commission, 1991c, p. 1).

Under normal circumstances, applicants will be expected to fulfil contractual obligations for the full 10 years of the agreement. However, the Countryside Commission may amend or terminate an agreement if there are mitigating circumstances, for example where agreement land becomes subject to a

Compulsory Purchase Order. The Commission will also consider written applications to terminate an agreement if justified on the grounds of economic hardship or good land management. If agreement land is sold or let, the new occupier may take on the agreement. If the new occupier does not wish to continue with the agreement, the original applicant may be liable to repay a proportion of payments already received. Land already subject to funding for environmental management will not usually qualify for Countryside Stewardship, for example land managed under agreement with English Nature. However, the Countryside Commission may, at its discretion, offer elements of Countryside Stewardship within an ESA that are not covered by the ESA scheme, the prime example being access payments.

During the first operational year of the Countryside Stewardship Scheme (1991–1992) agreements were signed covering a total of 29,534 ha throughout England (see Fig. 4). The results from the first year of the scheme would seem to indicate a high willingness amongst applicants to accept or encourage the quiet enjoyment of their land if suitably recompensed. Thus access payments cover 7013 ha or 24% of the total agreement area; they have been particularly biased towards chalk and limestone grassland landscapes. In the second year of the scheme agreements were signed covering an

Landscapes	Area covered by agreements secured in 1991 (ha)	Area covered by agreements secured in 1992 (ha)
Chalk and limestone grassland	7,817	4,657
Lowland heath	2,867	3,401
Waterside landscapes	7.305	7,049
Coastal land	3,540	3,284
Uplands	8,005	7,809
Historical landscapes	N/A	3,161
Old meadow and pasture	N/A	677
Open access	7,013	4,563
Linear access	N/A	183.4 km
Educational access	N/A	3157

Source: Data supplied by Countryside Commission

Figure 4. Countryside Stewardship agreements by area (1991–1992).

additional 30,038 ha with open or educational access on 7720 ha (26%) and the creation of 183.4 km of new linear access routes.

The examples of Stewardship agreements cited in Table 1 are not intended to be representative of the range of agreements concluded in the first year; rather the agreements were chosen to illustrate the positive way in which Countryside Stewardship would appear to combine conservation management with promotion of informal countryside recreation. They illustrate that Countryside Stewardship has the advantage of being a comprehensive support package (albeit limited to seven target landscapes), acceptance of all or part of a proposed agreement is entirely discretionary and dependent upon the advisers' judgement and the scheme is open to all types of rural landowner and occupier.

Tir Cymen

Tir Cymen is a new scheme to provide for con-

servation and quiet enjoyment of the Welsh countryside. The scheme was launched in the summer of 1992 and fulfils the Secretary of State for Wales's commitment to implement such a scheme as part of the Government's environmental strategy (HM Government, 1991). Tir Cymen has been introduced by the Countryside Council for Wales (CCW) as a market-based approach to the management of the farmland of Wales. It is operated under the Council's experimental powers and the scheme is being piloted in three areas: the districts of Meirionnydd, Dinefwr and Swansea. Tir Cymen is a voluntary scheme combining annual payments with capital grants on a discretionary basis with agreements to last for 10 years.

There are a number of important differences between Countryside Stewardship and Tir Cymen. Unlike Countryside Stewardship, which is open to all owners and occupiers of land within the seven target landscapes, Tir Cymen is open only to farmers who manage registered holdings (and to common land graziers provided that an application is made by

Table 1. Examples of Countryside Stewardship agreements that integrate conservation and recreation

---

Example 1: Upland Access, Cornwall
This Stewardship agreement covers 12 ha of upland formerly used for sheep grazing. Under the terms of the agreement, the area is to be restored to traditional pastures and hay meadows and access will be allowed over the whole site. The site is particularly valuable for access because of its archaeological value - a number of stone hut circles are visible as are the original stock compounds which would have accompanied the huts. The intention is to develop a visitor attraction through a comprehensive interpretation scheme. The annual cost of the agreement is approximately £1,200, 50% of which is for access provision.

Example 2: Waterside Access, Somerset
Under the terms of this agreement 1.42 ha of grassland adjoining the River Frome is to be managed as town conservation area open to the public. The parcel of land is owned by a town council and the example illustrates the benefits of Stewardship as a comprehensive support package not just limited to traditional rural landowners and managers.

Example 3: Coastal Access, Cornwall
Two Stewardship agreements cover an area of rugged and dramatic cliff scenery typical of the Cornish coastline and popular for walking. The agreements cover over 100 ha under the coastal and heathland options with access to most of this area. Under the terms of the agreement, arable areas will be returned to heathland and permanent grassland. The creation of a substantial access area will help disperse recreational pressure. The agreement also includes the creation of a permissive waterside walk which will link the coastal path, existing rights of way and the newly created access areas - thus illustrating the potential to use Stewardship payments as a mechanism for creating access networks including circular routes as well as areas.

Example 4: Waterside Access, Shropshire
This agreement covers an area of 43.8 ha for which revenue payments are being made to encourage traditional management of riverside meadows. As well as securing wildlife and landscape benefits, the agreement also provides for the provision of a 3km permissive access path linking existing rights of way and development of a car park for recreationists.

all the graziers), within the three pilot areas. Another important distinction between Countryside Stewardship and Tir Cymen is the requirement that applicants for Tir Cymen must enter the whole farm. In line with the Countryside Council's integrated constitution, which combines the duties of the old Nature Conservancy Council and those of the Countryside Commission, Tir Cymen takes a holistic view of the environment. The whole farm approach has been adopted so as to avoid the problem of intensification of farming on land not covered by an environmental agreement. Providing incentives for the conservation of heather moorland, for example, many encourage the farmer to improve semi-natural grassland elsewhere on the farm to accommodate the sheep he has had to remove from the moor — thus quite possibly resulting in a net environmental loss. Such problems have been encountered in some ESAs and the criticism might apply to Countryside Stewardship with its emphasis on target landscapes. The whole farm approach may also prove to be more effective in terms of negotiating new countryside access, since the provision of new access will not be tied to presence of a particular landscape type.

There are essentially four elements to a Tir Cymen agreement:

1. A basic requirement that the whole farm is managed according to the *Tir Cymen Code of Good Environmental Practice*, rights-of-way are kept free of obstruction and water pollution is avoided — an element of cross-compliance. This code is designed to maintain all existing landscapes and habitats of value and prevent further intensification of agricultural production on these areas. In return for this base level of environmental husbandry, applicants will receive £20 per hectare per annum from a minimum of £500 to a maximum of £5000.

2. Applicants will be *required to follow positive management guidelines*, in return for additional annual payments per hectare (or metre) for all moorland and heathland, all broadleaved woodland, all unimproved coastal land, all unimproved grassland (except grass leys or reseeded pasture) and selected stone walls, hedges, earth banks and slate fences of particular landscape, historic or wildlife value.

3. Applicants *may choose to enter other land* as arable field margins managed for wildlife, winter grazing for wild swans and geese and new permissive access paths. Such features will attract annual payments per hectare or metre, as appropriate.

4. There are specified *capital payments* for major repair or restoration work required to bring landscapes or habitats up to a standard where they would then qualify for maintenance payments; and grants towards expenditure essential for new access or for tree planting. In certain circumstances the CCW might also consider grant aiding projects that offer real environmental benefits such as the construction of artificial otter holts or the provision of small car parks or picnic areas for visitors.

(*Source*: Derived from CCW, 1992a).

In the first year of the Tir Cymen scheme, 201 agreements were secured covering 24,897 ha (approximately 14% of total eligible land in the three pilot areas). These agreements included 28 km of new permissive paths and over 12,000 ha of open access (a condition of agreements for land entered under the heather moorland and upland grassland management options) (CCW, pers. comm.).

The market approach applied to hedgerows

Responding to research by the Institute for Terrestrial Ecology (Barr *et al.*, 1991) that illustrated widespread decline in the quality and number of hedges, the DoE and the Welsh Office have initiated schemes to slow the decline in the practical care and quality of management of hedges, both of which follow the market or incentives-led approach and include an element of cross-compliance.

The Hedgerow Incentive Scheme was launched in 1992 by the Countryside Commission in collaboration with MAFF, English Nature and English Heritage (Countryside Commission, 1992b). The Scheme offers a range of financial incentives for measures necessary to restore hedgerows and their associated features (see Fig. 5), with funds targeted towards hedgerows that meet at least one of four criteria and are over 100 m in length (Countryside Commission, 1993c). Applicants propose a programme of work to restore the hedgerows they wish to enter into the scheme from a menu of works and incentives (see Fig. 5). If accepted, this restoration programme forms the basis of a 10-year agreement. Under the terms of the agreement, restoration is completed in the first five years in order to achieve 'healthy, vigorous hedgerows on the holding by the tenth year' (Countryside Commission, 1993c). The scheme includes an element of cross-compliance: in addition to hedgerows identified for restoration all applicants will be required to protetct and manage sympathetically all other hedgerows on the holding. The scheme is discretionary and the Countryside Commission will 'only accept proposals that offer

334 Kevin D. Bishop and Adrian A.C. Phillips

HEDGEROW INCENTIVE SCHEME (ENGLAND): PAYMENTS

ITEM	INCENTIVE
Hedge laying	£2.00/m paid on length laid
Coppicing	£1.50/m paid on length coppiced
PLUS: on hedges over 1.5m wide	£0.50/m
PLUS: supplement for removal of old fence posts and fence wires in hedgerow to be restored	£0.50m
Gapping up	£1.75/m paid on length planted
In all cases a second stage payment 5 years after satisfactory completion of initial stages of restoration	£1.00/m paid on length laid, coppiced or gapped-up
Ancillary works:	
Protective fencing	
3 line wire for cattle fence	£0.80/m
Woven wire fencing for cattle and sheep	£1.20/m
Rabbit netting - additional to fencing for sheep and/or cattle	£0.40/m
Spiral guard	£0.20 each
Trees	
Pollarding	£17.50/tree
Tree surgery	£40.00/tree
Planting standard hedgerow trees	£0.65 each
Tube for standard trees only	£0.50 each
Hedge banks	
major restoration of earth banks	£3.00/m
Minor restoration of stone-faced banks	£10.00/m
Major restoration of stone-faced banks	£25.00/m
Advice and plan preparation	£100.00

HEDGEROW RENOVATION SCHEME (WALES): PAYMENTS

ITEM	INCENTIVE
Hedge laying	£1.75/m
Coppicing	£1.00/m
Re-planting	£2.00/m
Protective fencing	
Post and wire - softwood	£1.00/m
Post and wire - hardwood	£1.20/m
Supplement for stock fencing	£0.40/m
Post and rail - softwood	£9.00/m
Post and rail - hardwood	£11.00/m
Stone-faced banks, earth banks, gapping and restoration	£12.00/m
Hedgerow tree planting, plant, tube, stake and tie	£2.00/m
Spiral rabbit-guards for shrubs	£0.30/m
Gates and stiles	
Field gate - softwood	£110.00 each
Field gate - hardwood	£130.00 each
Bridle gate - softwood	£100.00 each
Bridlegate - hardwood	£120.00 each
Kissing gate - softwood	£110.00 each
Kissing gate - hardwood	£130.00 each
Stile	£4.00 each
Pollarding or tree surgery	- to be agreed for individual cases as a special capital payment
Management costs (payment for biennial trimming capitalised over the ten-year agreement)	£1.20/m

Figure 5. The incentives or market-led approach applied to hedgerows.

potential for environmental improvement and public benefit' (Countryside Commission, 1993c).

The Hedgerow Renovation Scheme is the Welsh equivalent to the English Hedgerow Incentive Scheme and is operated by the Countryside Council for Wales in conjunction with WOAD and Cadw. The objective of the scheme is similar to that in England: 'to bring back into good management selected hedgerows in Wales that are in particularly poor condition' (CCW, 1992b, p. 2). Under the terms of the Scheme payments are available for specific management operations (see Fig. 5). Applicants suggest an agreement to the CCW by selecting from the menu of works and incentives offered those which they can provide (see Fig. 5). The works eligible for grant aid and level of payment differs from the Hedgerow Incentive Scheme (see Fig. 5), reflecting regional variations in costs, management practices and hedgerow characteristics. As with the Hedgerow Incentive Scheme there are criteria to aid the selection of hedgerows, acceptance of a proposed agreement is discretionary and there is an element of cross-compliance, though it differs in detail relating only to the retention, by agreement, of an overall pattern of hedgerows on the holding and not specifically mentioning management (CCW, 1992b). The Hedgerow Renovation Scheme is also different from the English Hedgerow Incentive Scheme in that applicants in possession of an agreement under the Tir Cymen scheme (see above) are not eligible because Tir Cymen already contains provisions for payment for similar works.

Conclusions

Public policy towards the integration of conservation and access with farming has developed greatly over the past few years, partly because of public and political concern over environmental matters and partly because of the food surpluses in Europe. After a long period of political consensus about the importance of State support for food production in the national interest, the 1980s initiated a period of important reform. The post-1979 Conservative Government has been committed to the free market and reducing state intervention. Thus, although regulation of the agricultural industry for environmental purposes has increased during the 1980s, the emphasis has been on voluntary control and positive initiative stimulated by financial incentives such as tax relief and capital grants. For example, the White Paper on the Environment (HM Government, 1990) states that the Government's policies for the countryside are based on the philosophy of steward-ship and that wherever possible 'the Government

works in partnership with its owners and managers to protect it through voluntary effort' (HM Govern-ment, 1990, p. 96). Nevertheless, an analysis shows that during the 1980s the policy context for the voluntary approach to the resolution of agriculture/conservation conflicts changed. In the early part of the period, the voluntary approach had to work within a policy framework still promoting agri-cultural production as a primary aim. By the end of the decade, the pursuit of food production was increasingly constrained by environmental objectives. As a result, these environmental factors have begun to be incorporated into the culture of farming in a way that was unimaginable only a few years ago.

The shortcomings of certain policy instruments (notably the compensation arrangements under the Wildlife and Countryside Act 1981 and ESAs), the Government's support for market mechanisms and lobbying of the powerful of landowning interests has led, in recent years, to the development of the market approach to countryside conservation and recreation. Under schemes such as Countryside Stewardship and Tir Cymen a market is being created in environment and related recreation services, with incentives offered to farmers who manage their land according to certain prescriptions. The schemes allow farmers to identify relevant environmental services and goods which they can provide and the opportunity to market these and promote their role as custodians and managers of the countryside. Unlike ESAs or compensation arrange-ments under the Wildlife and Countryside Act 1981, the rules of the market operate. The public sector 'buyer' is not obliged to come to an agreement — like any discerning customer, officials select on the basis of value for money. Payment is not for the process but for the product. Such an arrangement mirrors the way payments are made for most other agricultural products; it provides an incentive to produce the environmental product at lowest cost; and it encourages managerial and entrepreneurial flair. This should lead to diversity of environmen-tally friendly management practices and a greater understanding of the process involved (Countryside Commission, 1993a; Hodge, 1991).

Although the various market approach schemes are still in their infancy, they appear to have been well received. Early results would seem to indicate that once the provision of conservation and access on farmland become the subject of payment, the attitudes of many farmers appear to change from suspicion to enthusiasm. It is especially significant that access appears to hold out less terrors for farmers and other rural land managers than had often been assumed. However, it is important that the agencies concerned evaluate and publicise the impact. In particular, there is a need for a comparative study of the experience in England and Wales. In this way, the separate approaches of the new independent English and Welsh countryside agencies could be turned to advantage.

The development of the incentives or market-led approach, and in particular the operation of Countryside Stewardship and Tir Cymen, raise a number of policy and research issues which will need to be addressed:

* *Targeting*: doubts have been raised about some aspects of these schemes. For example, the Ramblers' Association (1993) has argued that Countryside Stewardship provides new access in areas that are inaccessible or where demand is low. If incentive schemes are to meet the criterion of good value for public money, then the 'buyers' will need a well-developed knowledge of the kind of environmental and recreation goods that are in 'demand', in order that they can target payments where they will produce the best returns. Information is needed on: landscape and wildlife character trends; and, actual and potential demand for access and recreation.

The Countryside Commission's New Map of England project is designed to help in this, by producing regional statements of landscape characteristics. Likewise, county recreation, landscape and nature conservation strategies will help. None the less, at present information upon which to target environmental and recreation incentives is still limited.

* *Cost Information*: the efficient operation of any market assumes good knowledge on the part of the suppliers of the costs of producing goods and services, and on the part of the purchasers of acquiring them. More needs to be known about the real costs of providing selected environmental goods to ensure that incentive levels are set at the right level to attract sufficient uptake, but not so high that public funds are used inefficiently.

* *Publicity*: The Ramblers' Association has also been critical of the Countryside Commission for giving insufficient publicity to the access provision made through the Countryside Premium and Stewardship Schemes. There is clearly a need to ensure that the public receive value for money by being properly informed of the access and environmental benefits that have been purchased in their name.

* *Restoration Ecology*: the thrust of the incentives approach is moving away from landscape and habitat protection towards restoration. The techniques for much of this work are still poorly developed. Several years — even decades — may be needed before the success of the various approaches can be demonstrated conclusively. Much research is needed on the methods for restoring former vegetation types, for example meadows or chalk grassland; and when the information is available, it needs to be delivered to the land managers in an accessible and easily understood format. Clearly the development and application of this information has a bearing on questions of value for money achieved through incentive schemes.

References

Abel, C. and Hill, P. (1993) Environment link sympathetic to farm and wildlife. *Farmers Weekly* **118**, 38–40.

Association of National Park Officers (1988) *National Parks — Environmentally Favoured Areas?* Association of National Park Officers, Lake District Special Planning Board, Kendal.

Baldock, D. (1989) The European Community and conservation in the Thatcher decade. *ECOS* **10**, 33–37.

Barr, C., Howard, D., Bunce, B., Gillespie, M. and Hallam, C. (1991) *Changes in Hedgerows in Britain Between 1984 and 1990*. Institute for Terrestrial Ecology, Grange-over-Sands.

Blunden, J. and Curry, N. (1990) *A People's Charter?* HMSO, London.

Bracewell-Milnes, B. (1988) *Caring for the Countryside: Public Dependence on Private Interest*. Social Affairs Unit, London.

Broom, C., Curry, N., Lowe, P., Richardson, C., Rowe, J., Watkins, C. and Winter, M. (1989) *Review of Countryside Adviser Policy*. Centre for Rural Studies, Royal Agricultural College, Cirencester.

Carson, R. (1963) *Silent Spring*. Hamish Hamilton, London.

Cobham, R., Matthews, R., McNab, A., Stephenson, E. and Slatter, M. (1984) *Demonstration Farms*. Countryside Commission CCP 170, Cheltenham.

Colman, D., Crabtree, B., Froud, J. and O'Carroll, L. (1992) *Comparative Effectiveness of Conservation Mechanisms*. Department of Agricultural Economics, University of Manchester, U.K.

Commission of the European Communities (1992a) *Towards Sustainability: a European Community Programme of Policy Action in Relation to the Environment and Sustainable Development*. COM (92)23, Volume II. Commission of the European Communities, Brussels.

Commission of the European Communities (1992b) Council Regulation No. 2078/92 on Agricultural Production Methods Compatible with the Requirements of the Protection of the Environment and the Maintenance of the Countryside. *Official Journal of the European Communities* **L215**, 85–90.

CPRE (1990) *Building Responsibilities: the Case for Extending Planning Control Over Agricultural and Forestry Buildings*. Council for the Protection of Rural England, London.

Countryside Commission (1986) *Monitoring Landscape Change.* Countryside Commission, Cheltenham.

Countryside Commission (1989) *Task Force Trees — Two Years On.* Countryside Commission CCP 280, Cheltenham.

Countryside Commission (1990) *Capital Tax Relief for Outstanding Scenic Land.* Countryside Commission CCP 204, Cheltenham.

Countryside Commission (1991a) *Annual Report 1990–1991.* Countryside Commission CCP 350, Cheltenham.

Countryside Commission (1991b) *Countryside Stewardship: an Outline.* Countryside Commission CCP 346, Cheltenham.

Countryside Commission (1991c) *Handbook for Countryside Stewardship.* Countryside Commission CS 1, Cheltenham.

Countryside Commission (1992a) *Annual Report 1991–1992.* Countryside Commission CCP 385, Cheltenham.

Countryside Commission (1992b) *Handbook for the Hedgerow Incentive Scheme.* Countryside Commission CCP 383, Cheltenham.

Countryside Commission (1993a) *Paying for a Beautiful Countryside.* Countryside Commission CCP 413, Cheltenham.

Countryside Commission (1993b) *Countryside Stewardship: an Outline.* Countryside Commission CCP 346 (revised edition), Cheltenham.

Countryside Commission (1993c) *Hedgerow Incentive Scheme.* Countryside Commission CCP 393 (revised edition), Cheltenham.

Countryside Commission for Scotland (1986) *Forestry in Scotland: a Policy Paper.* Countryside Commission for Scotland, Battleby.

CCW (1992a) *Tir Cymen: a Farmland Stewardship Scheme.* Countryside Council for Wales, Bangor.

CCW (1992b) *Hedgerow Renovation Scheme.* Countryside Council for Wales, Bangor.

Cloke, P. and McLaughlin, B. (1989) Politics of the Alternative Land Use and Rural Economy (ALURE) proposals in the U.K.: crossroads or blind alley? *Land Use Policy* **6**, 235–248.

Cox, A. (1984) *Adversary Politics and Land.* Cambridge University Press, Cambridge.

Cox, G. and Lowe, P. (1983) Countryside politics: goodbye to goodwill? *Political Quarterly* **54**, 268–282.

Cox, G., Lowe, P. and Winter, M. (1990) *The Voluntary Principle in Conservation: the Farming and Wildlife Advisory Group.* Packard, Chichester.

Devon County Council (1990) *Environmental Land Management Scheme.* Engineering and Planning Department, Devon County Council, Exeter.

Devon County Council (1992) *Environmental Land Management Scheme.* Engineering and Planning Department, Devon County Council, Exeter.

DoE (1992a) *Planning Policy Guidance Note 12: Development Plans and Regional Planning Guidance.* HMSO, London.

DoE (1992b) *Protecting Europe's Environment: the Environmental Policy of the European Community.* HMSO, London.

DoE (1992c) *Action for the Countryside.* Department of the Environment, London.

DoE and Welsh Office (1992a) *Planning Policy Guidance Note 1: General Policy and Principles.* HMSO, London.

DoE and Welsh Office (1992b) *Planning Policy Guidance Note 7: the Countryside and the Rural Economy.* HMSO, London.

Drummond, C. (1992) LEAF (Linking Environment and Farming). *European Environment* **2**, 22.

Ervin, D., Heimlich, R. and Osborn, T. (1991) Cross-compliance and set-aside programmes for environmental improvement: preliminary lessons from U.S. experience. In *Implementation of Agri-environment Policies in the EC*, Bladock, D. (ed.). IEEP, London.

Flynn, A. (1986) Agricultural policy and party politics in post-war Britain. In *Agriculture: People and Policies*, Cox, G., Lowe, P. and Winter, M. (eds), pp. 216–237. Allen & Unwin, London.

Forestry Commission (1987) *Control of Tree Felling.* Forestry Commission, Edinburgh.

Gilg, A. (1978) *Countryside Planning: the First Three Decades 1945–76.* Methuen, London.

Greenwell, E. (ed.) (1989) *Enterprise and the Rural Economy.* Country Landowners Association, London.

HM Government (1990) *This Common Inheritance*, Cm 1200. HMSO, London.

HM Government (1991) *This Common Inheritance: the First Year Report*, Cm 1655. HMSO, London.

HM Government (1992) *This Common Inheritance: the Second Year Report*, Cm 2068. HMSO, London.

Hodge, I. (1990) The changing place of farming. In *Agriculture in Britain: Changing Pressures and Policies*, Britton, D. (ed.), pp. 34–45. CAB International, Wallingford.

Hodge, I. (1991) Incentive policies and the rural environment. *Journal of Rural Studies* **7**, 373–384.

Howarth, W. (1992) Agricultural pollution and the aquatic environment. In *Agricultural Conservation and Land Use: Law and Policy for Rural Areas*, Howarth, W. and Rodgers, C.P. (eds), pp. 52–73. University of Wales Press, Cardiff.

Ilbery, B.W. (1992) From Scott to ALURE — and back again? *Land Use Policy* **9**, 131–142.

Land Use Consultants (1993) *Countryside Premium Scheme Monitoring and Evaluation Report.* Unpublished research report to the Countryside Commission, Land Use Consultants, Rugby.

Land Use Consultants, Countryside Planning and Management and Pryor and Ricketts Sylviculture (1991) *Permitted Development Rights for Agriculture and Forestry.* HMSO, London.

Lobley, M. (1989) A role for ESAs? *ECOS* **10**, 27–29.

Lowe, P. and Fynn, A. (1989) Environmental planning and the Thatcher Government. *ECOS* **10**, 22–29.

Marsden, T., Murdoch, J., Lowe, P., Munton, R. and Flynn, A. (1993) *Constructing the Countryside.* UCL Press, London.

MAFF (1993) *Agriculture and England's Environment: Consultation Document.* MAFF, London.

MAFF (1993a) *Agriculture and England's Environment: New Public Access in ESAs.* MAFF, London.

MAFF (1993b) *Agriculture and England's Environment: Set-aside Management.* MAFF, London.

MAFF (1993c) *Agriculture and England's Environment: Habitat Improvement Scheme.* MAFF, London.

MAFF, DAFS, DANI and WOAD (1987) *Farming U.K.* MAFF, London.

MAFF, DANI, SOAFD and WOAD (1991) *Our Farming Future.* MAFF, London.

McCormick, J. (1991) *British Politics and the Environment.* Earthscan, London.

National Housing and Town Planning Council, CPRE and Association of District Councils (1990) *Planning Control over Farmland: Reforming Permitted Development Rights in the Countryside.* National Housing and Town Planning Council, London.

NCC (1984) *Nature Conservation in Great Britain.* Nature Conservancy Council, Peterborough.

NCC (1990) *Nature Conservation and Agricultural Change.* Focus on Nature Conservation No. 25, NCC, Peterborough.

Orme, E. (1992) *Environmentally Sensitive Areas: Assessment and Recommendations.* Friends of the Earth, London.

Patten, C. (1990) The market and the environment. *Policy Studies* 11, 4–10.

Pearce, D., Markandya, A. and Barbier, E.B. (1989) *Blueprint for a Green Economy.* Earthscan, London.

Potter, C., Burnham, P., Edwards, A., Gasson, R. and Green, B. (1991) *The Diversion of Land: Farming in a Period of Contraction.* Routledge, London.

Ramblers Association (1993) *Countryside Stewardship Access Schemes — Dismal Picture According to Ramblers Association Survey.* Press release issued by the Ramblers Association, London.

Rowe, F. (1987) ESAs — are they the answer? *Tarn and Tor* No. 12, pp. 14–15.

RSPB (1991) *A Future for Environmentally Friendly Farming.* Royal Society for the Protection of Birds, The Lodge, Sandy.

RSPB (1992) *Our Countryside, Our Future.* RSPB, The Lodge, Sandy.

Shoard, M. (1980) *The Theft of the Countryside.* Temple Smith, London.

Sinclair, G. (1986) Environmentally Sensitive Areas or green fig-leaves? *ECOS* 7, 12–15.

Sykes, J.M. and Briggs, D.R. (n.d.) *An Assessment of Amenity Tree Planting Schemes.* Countryside Commission, Cheltenham.

Taylor, J.P. and Dixon, J.B. (1990) *Agriculture and the Environment: Towards Integration.* RSPB, The Lodge, Sandy.

Thornley, A. (1991) *Urban Planning Under Thatcherism: the Challenge of the Market.* Routledge, London.

Webster, S. and Felton, M. (1993) Targeting for nature conservation in agriculture policy. *Land Use Policy* 10, 67–82.

Westmacott, R. and Worthington, T. (1974) *New Agricultural Landscapes.* Countryside Commission, Cheltenham.

Wibberley, G. (1985) The Famous Scott Report — a text for all time? *The Planner* 71, 13–20.

Winter, M. (1990) Land use policy in the U.K.: the politics of control. *Land Development Studies* 7, 3–14.

F
Development and Environment

[14]

Journal of Environmental Management (1995) **44**, 55–68

The Environment and Structural Adjustment: Lessons for Policy Interventions in the 1990s

Michael Redclift

Environment Section, Wye College, University of London, Wye, Kent, TN25 5AH, U.K.

Received 1 *April* 1994

Considerable attention is currently being given to the effects of structural adjustment policies on rural development and poverty in India (Iyer, 1991; Agarwal, 1993; Hauff, 1993; Ranadive, 1993; Von Urff, 1993). In particular, consideration is being given to the alleged effects of such policies on the environment (Reed, 1992; Chossudovsky, 1992; Hauff, 1993). This paper argues, from Latin American material, that the situation of the poor has certainly worsened under structural adjustment policies, but that reduced sustainability needs to be seen against a longer-term perspective. In countries such as Mexico, the current environmental crisis reflects longstanding development priorities, including economic liberalization.

One of the most important consequences for the environment, and the increased participation envisaged under Agenda Twenty One, is the progressive disempowerment of the poor. New policies emanating from the World Bank, and other international development agencies, attempt to include environmental management within their compass. However, they do not facilitate the necessary transfer of control, and responsibility, for the management of local resources, without which sustainable development cannot be achieved. At the global level, structural adjustment could be better applied to the developed countries as well as the developing, in an effort to transform their economies in a sustainable direction, and to close the gap which exists between the conditions of life for the majority in the North and the South.

Keywords: structural adjustment, environment, environmental management, sustainability

1. Introduction

When structural adjustment policies were first introduced in the 1980s, little attention was paid to their environmental consequences. This paper charts the growth of interest in this dimension, and, building upon the experiences, particularly those of Mexico, in the 1980s it suggests some of the lessons for the 1990s.

It is important to acknowledge that structural adjustment policies did not arrive in a political vacuum. There are also a series of very important issues with implications

55

0301–4797/95/010055 + 14 $08.00/0

for the environment which concern the link between the "democratization" of societies and policies of economic liberalization. The perspective on this relationship varies according to which part of the globe is being considered (Cornia *et al.*, 1987; Commander, 1989; Bishop, 1991; Boyd *et al.*, 1991; Panayotou and Sussangkarn, 1991; Stein and Nafzign, 1991; IIED, 1990; Cruz and Repetto, 1992). In the case of Latin American countries, the promotion of "free market" policies and deregulation accompanied the return of many governments to civilian rule during the 1980s. In many parts of Asia, economic liberalization, which is already "successful" in terms of orthodox economic indications, has usually been associated with authoritarian government (whether or not the state has been interventionist in economic policy). The question remains central: structural adjustment policies carry implications for the organization of civil society and the distribution of power that are in turn linked to the achievement of environmental objectives. These issues are returned to later in the paper.

Since 1991, India has embarked on a series of structural adjustment policies. It is suggested in the literature that such policies arise from a "deep crisis" of which those in Government are well aware (Iyer, 1991). It is also suggested that the effects of structural adjustment will be unequally spread, affecting the working class (Veerashekerappa, 1992) and poor households in general, most severely (Ranadive, 1993). Opinions differ over the desirability of restructuring in the agricultural sector (Von Urff, 1993) and in Indian industry. However, most commentators appear to agree with Anil Agarwal, in spirit if not in the letter: "... Indian industry is powerless to draw from the global economy, and it will turn to increase the pressure on the country's own ecological base" (Agarwal, 1993, p. 1).

Latin America first experienced structural adjustment policies almost a decade ago. Against a background with some similarities with India (import substitution industrialization), Latin American economies were by degrees subjected to the full rein of market forces. To what extent can we assign responsibility for Latin America's environmental problems to the onset of structural adjustment?

To answer this question, we need to review the policy context in which restructuring was undertaken in Latin America, and to examine the relationship between human poverty and environmental degradation. But we need to begin by considering the paradigms which are employed to understand environmental problems in developing countries.

2. Environmental problems and structural problems

Environmental problems in developing countries are usually viewed in one of two ways:

1. They are looked upon as the consequences for human societies of "natural" disasters, prompted by forces over which we exert little control. Environmental problems are therefore problems of a scientific nature, amenable to scientific analysis and, occasionally at least, solution. From this standpoint, the principal issue over which we have control is that of population increase. Broadly speaking, this is the Neo-Malthusian scenario.

2. An alternative perspective places more emphasis on policy intervention. This approach views environmental problems as the consequence of a failure to "get the prices right". That is, we have failed to assign the real costs of environmental degradation to the development process. The challenge to policy, which can play a major role according to this perspective, is to design policy instruments which guide

human behaviour, and encourage people to act more sustainably. This is the Managerialist approach.

Both these models of environmental change contain important insights. To some extent, our ability to cope with environmental problems depends upon the "carrying capacity" of resource systems, and their sustainability is linked to their ability to withstand shocks and abrupt changes. However, in this paper, it is argued that human agency should be accorded a much more important place than this approach concedes, and human behaviour cannot be reduced to demographic factors, however important they are.

Similarly, the urgency of environmental policy intervention, designed to shift human behaviour, should not blind us to the sources of that behaviour. The way that groups of people manage their environment is itself a cultural process, and policy needs to engage with the practices of specific groups and societies, without having recourse to abstract notions of "rationality" and economic behaviour, largely derived from developed market economies. We need to assign the real costs of environmental losses to the development process, but the process itself also needs to be investigated. Economic growth frequently fails to accommodate to conflicting human aspirations, and environmental costs are then a necessary consequence (ERL, 1989; Ierland, 1990; Jayawardena, 1990; Davies *et al.*, 1991).

This paper examines a third perspective on the relationship between development and the environment: environmental problems are the necessary structural consequence of the development process, not simply a failure to recognize "natural" imperatives or evidence that policy instruments require greater refinement. In rising to the challenge of global environmental management, post UNCED, we need to be informed by human needs, not abstract "global environmental" ones. We also need to do much more than invent new tools for better management. What is required is a better understanding of the way human purposes can be married to environmental objectives, at both a local and an international level. This, in turn, means serious consideration of human agency as a way of shifting and challenging the international economic system. It means taking an uncomfortable look at the assumptions behind the new environmental agenda, which places conditionality at the forefront of its claims to relevance.

3. Poverty and the environment

We can begin with consideration of the linkages between poverty and the environment. In their study of this relationship in developing countries, Leach and Mearns (1991) make the following points:

- Poor people in developing countries are represented as both the victims and the unwilling agents of environmental degradation. The two-way links between environmental change and impoverishment are not, however, direct ones.
- Rather, these links are mediated by a diverse set of factors that affect the decisions poor people make. Environmental entitlements mediate poor people's interactions with particular environments, while macro-level processes structure these interactions.
- At the micro-level, the environmental entitlements of individuals (households, villages) depend on a range of factors, including natural resource tenure arrangements, labour processes, social relations (including gender), capital endowments and technology.

- At the macro-level, wider processes involving markets, trade and technologies, favour some social groups and geographical areas over others.
- Environmental degradation may impose very severe costs on the poor as the result of declining resource availability, and the absence of alternative, more sustainable, development options.
- Current approaches to reducing poverty pay insufficient attention to the underlying effects of environmental change, implying a need for additional policy interventions to address specific environmental problems in particular locations.
- The major objective of policies to reduce poverty and to ensure sustainable environmental management should be to widen the range of choices available to the poor.
- Differences in the physical environmental properties of different areas mean that such policies need to be tailored to resource-poor and resource-rich areas, including "enhancement areas" with development potential. Consideration needs to be given to the fact that the most vulnerable poor people often live in ecologically fragile regions.

The analysis provided by Leach and Mearns (1991) of the specificities in the linkages between poverty and the environment should alert us to the dangers of setting environmental policy objectives in a vacuum. The environment, the principal source of livelihood for the poor, cannot be accessed "over the heads" of the poor. As Ranadive (1993) points out, for India, the household falls outside the policy ambit of most regimes, notably during periods of structural adjustment. Similarly, an emphasis on the role people can play in managing their own environments more sustainably (primary environmental care) will work best if it is supported by changes in macro-economic policy.

If we examine the effects of structural adjustment policy in the 1980s, and the later addition of "environmental" weighting to these policies, we can appreciate how difficult it is to achieve environmental benefits when the social fabric itself has been damaged. Restoring the social fabric, through an attack on poverty, is the *sine qua non* for effective environmental action.

3.1. THE ENVIRONMENTAL AND STRUCTURAL ADJUSTMENT

Structural adjustment lending in the 1980s did not incorporate environmental factors for several reasons. These include:

- The World Bank and other multilateral development banks (MDBs) did not view the environment as a priority investment at the time.
- Borrowing countries had not requested financial support to deal with environmental problems.
- Public concern with global environmental problems had not reached the point at which policy changes were considered necessary. In the 1980s, environmental costs were seen, on balance, as a natural consequence of economic growth.
- The connection between economic policy instruments and their environmental impacts was only poorly understood by the World Bank. Often it was thought necessary to "get the prices right" and no more.
- Environmental spending appeared to require more budgetary outlays—increased public expenditure, which ran counter to the whole thrust of adjustment lending (Reed, 1992).

The link between structural adjustment and the environment has acquired urgency for both methodological and, essentially, political reasons.

The lesson of the 1980s experiences in Latin America was that a failure to appreciate the environmental consequences of adjustment policy was linked to the view taken of economic policy reform itself. Environmental issues were left out of this policy reform. This in turn presented a problem: *if the environment was left out of economic calculations, then, adjustment policy could be held responsible for unforeseen consequences.* As conditions have worsened in the region, so this was attributed to the absence of environmental considerations in the framing of structural adjustment interventions. There was also growing evidence that the supposed economic benefits of adjustment policy would be undermined by population increase which, in the context of reduced resource carrying capacity, was likely to exacerbate the social and political tensions which adjustment policy brought in its train. Economic policy reform was likely to leave the poorest social groups more exposed and this, in turn, carried environmental consequences one stage further. Clearly, economic policy reforms needed to be refashioned in such a way that increased sustainability became an object of the reform process itself. Experience since 1990 of the Global Environment Facility suggests only the first steps have been taken. A later section of this paper discusses whether this re-orientation in development thinking has borne fruit, and the factors likely to determine future success.

4. The genesis of the problem

The links between adjustment policy and the environment can be traced to the early 1970s. The 1973/4 oil shock left developing countries with significant trade imbalances, which the International Monetary Fund (IMF) sought to address, through stabilization policies.

By the mid 1970s, the IMF's role increased—for example, through extended fund facilities—while the commercial banks increased their lending to less developed countries (excluding oil exporters) *sixfold* to $220 billion between 1973 and 1981.

These commercial banks had little development expertise and poor control of lending policy, compared with that of the IMF.

Also, by the 1970s, LDC commodity prices were beginning to fall, and this, together with the second oil shock (1978–80), had negative effects on their terms of trade. In addition, under President Reagan, U.S. remilitarization pushed up interest rates to previously unheard of levels. As global interest rates rose, most LDCs were forced to allocate a rising proportion of their dwindling foreign exchange to servicing their debts.

The economic crises of the 1980s led many LDCs to reduce their imports significantly while seeking to stimulate export earnings against the tide of negative terms of trade. Domestically, their policies made greater inroads on capital investment in the early 1980s than on public expenditure *per se*. One of the consequences was that the majority of the poor, especially the rural poor, were unprotected at a time of fiscal discipline. To varying degrees, social spending fell in virtually all developing countries during the early 1980s. One consequence of this, especially in Latin America, was deep mistrust of the economic packages imported from without. To some extent, this mistrust probably stimulated the democratization process, and military regimes in the region made way for civilian ones. However, positive political change did not extend to the resolution of broader economic policy, which still foundered on servicing the external debt and removing the protection of the state from a sizeable proportion of the population partly as a consequence of the austerity programmes encouraged by the International Monetary Fund (IMF). As the Latin American response to Brundtland made clear, *Our Own Agenda* (IBRD, 1989) was as far from being enacted at the end of the 1980s as it was a decade earlier.

The difference between the stabilization policies encouraged largely by the IMF in the 1970s, and the adjustment policies encouraged by the World Bank in the 1980s, was that the latter were supposed to rest on enhancing the supply side, through institutional reform and economic growth. Increasingly, stabilization was associated with demand management, and it was left to the World Bank to provide the alternative economic package.

In its efforts to do so in the early 1980s, the World Bank sought to reduce export taxes and to remove import quotas, which had previously impeded competitiveness on world markets. The Bank also sought to reform public enterprises. Without the expectation of a revival in the global economy, which had been set back by Mexico's default on its commercial debt obligations in 1982, the attention of the Bank switched to institutional reforms in the South, particularly sectoral adjustment loans. The reform agenda included reforming the manufacturing sector during the late 1980s, and, as privatization spread, reforming the financial sector in the hope of attracting foreign capital.

The negative effects of the IMFs earlier adjustment policies on the poor produced some important responses from within the U.N. system. First among these was the U.N. Children's Fund, which provided carefully documented cases of the impact of adjustment on children in developing countries. Despite some misgivings, the World Bank still insisted that, during the transitional period, adjustment could be expected to carry heavy costs, particularly for the poor, which only long term improved economic performance could mitigate. In particular, as Ranadive (1993) points out, demand measures act much faster than supply side measures, seriously prejudicing the poor. One of the lessons of this period, of enormous consequence for meeting future environmental objectives, was the late recognition that countries needed to "own" their adjustment programmes, if they were to prove at all effective.

During the 1980s, most developing countries were therefore vulnerable to increased pressure from the North, consequent upon both escalating military expenditure, and the increased economic dependence of the South. In the wake of the Cold War, the major challenge facing North–South relations is to improve the environmental security of the South, and to reschedule military spending towards increasing domestic sustainability. This will require *structural adjustment in the North*, as well as the South, to bring the economic malaise in the developed world closer to a basis for global sustainability. The measures signalled at the Rio Summit in 1992 could form the basis of this new global partnership.

5. Structural adjustment and the environment: exploring connections

In a recent paper, Mearns (1991) discusses the analytical problems which have accompanied the growing doubts about the efficacy (and, for some, the equity) of structural adjustment policies. He rightly points out that the deficiencies in supply-side management, which were not always apparent to World Bank economists (Lipton, 1987), were mirrored by growing anxieties about "externalities" (environmental costs) over the longer-term, of policies designed to meet relatively short-run problems. In my view, the recent attempt to develop environmental economics, notably in the World

Bank itself, represents an inadequate response to the crisis generated by economic policy reforms in the early 1980s (Redclift, 1993). In addition, as Hauff (1993) contests, structural adjustment policies which envisage "compensation" for social groups that are adversely affected, do not extend their remit to environmental considerations. To do so would imply, in my judgement, a major redirection of economic policy rather than the addition of a series of tools for better environment management.

There are several ways in which adjustment policies, by changing the relative prices of inputs through the elimination of subsidies, and through changes in import tariffs and export taxes, affect the resource base on which economic development rests. The cumulative effect of decisions about what to produce, and what to consume, has an important, if indirect, effect on the environment.

The importance of this environmental impact depends on the fragility of the stock of natural capital, in itself dependent on the extent to which existing patterns of resource use place burdens on the ecological system. As Harvey (1979) noted, the stock of natural capital determines the capacity of the environment to continue to carry out its source, sink and service functions. This capacity is influenced, critically, by technological change, the distribution of resources and the overall scale of resource use. Whether adjustment policies stimulate more sustainable practices, particularly in agriculture, depends upon the way that prices affect the management practices associated with specific crops, and the conservation of biotic resources by farmers and others. The extent to which new production technologies and practices are environmentally detrimental is an essentially empirical question from this point of view.

Another way in which structural adjustment policies have an indirect effect on the environment is through shifts in the pattern of government expenditure. Some economists, such as Hansen (1990), have argued that cuts in public investment have often had environmentally beneficial consequences, such as fewer access roads in tropical forest areas. Others have argued that "this is manifestly not the case in instances where logging products constitute a high percentage of exports, as in Ghana" (Mearns, 1991, p. 11) and adjustment policies have stimulated this production. On the negative side, too, allocations to protect the environment and manage resources more sustainably are often a casualty of adjustment policies, as Latin American critics, in particular, have argued (Sunkel and Gligo, 1981). Similarly, the ability of developing countries to make their own decisions over research and development, is likely to be hampered by cuts in public investment. However, the development and transfer of cleaner technologies, especially in the energy sector of developing countries, is a key element in achieving longer-term sustainability.

The economic literature on the relationship between structural adjustment and the environment pays little attention to one consideration of enormous importance. This is the extent to which economic reforms have induced social changes in the developing countries which make the achievement of sustainable development more difficult. With the exception of some robust, but polemical, writing (see Chossudovsky, 1992 on India and George, 1988), the wider social impact of adjustment on the *context of environmental policy* has received little attention. The premise of both the Second World Conservation Strategy (IUCN, 1991) and much of the post-UNCED deliberations, in marked contrast, emphasizes the need to democratize and empower the poor in the cause of more sustainable development. It is argued in these documents that, without widespread popular participation and "ownership" of the new environmental agenda, policy advances in the South will be slow. (Incidentally, the same observation can be made about industrial countries which have been subjected to structural changes, and in which the problems of civil society increasingly defy easy solutions: unemployment, increasing crime and the breakdown of the nuclear family).

6. The experience of structural adjustment and the Mexican environment

The principal criticisms of structural adjustment have laid emphasis on the short-term and often sweeping policy measures which paid insufficient attention to the long-term trends in declining terms of trade between North and South. Ishikawa (1993) suggests that where potential market economies are relatively underdeveloped "... and mixed with various forms of customary economy as well as customary political culture", structural adjustment policies are not usually successful (Ishikawa, 1993, p. 169). Critics of adjustment policies make the following points.

- The time in which some countries, especially in Africa, were supposed to reduce demand and improve supply responses, was far too short.
- Rural economies proved unable to respond to incentives to undertake production for export, given their scarce foreign exchange and severe infrastructural bottle-necks.
- Adjustment policies have undermined the food security of the rural and urban poor, and increased imbalances in domestic income distribution.
- The emphasis on export growth has served to increase the marginalization of many poor people from the economy, and with it their ability to meet local needs. The implication of growing poverty for women and children were highlighted in a UNICEF study, which obliged international lending institutions to consider adjustment's social dimensions.

The World Bank's response to those criticisms was to belatedly institute more pro-grammes of "social mitigation", often through compensation to the most adversely affected groups. By the end of the 1980s, one third of all adjustment loans addressed social aspects of the process. However, critics have argued that such programmes have limited effect. They should be seen, rather, as designed to co-opt the poor during the political transition that accompanies economic reforms. There is still an absence of clearly defined social objectives in structural adjustment programmes. Changing the balance of power within a developing country's élites, although one of the most potent effects of economic policy reforms, has failed to provide a democratically arrived-at political consensus, and has suppressed, rather than assisted, social mobilization (Re-petto, 1988; Sebastian and Alicbuscan, 1988; World Bank, 1989, 1990; Rauscher, 1990). In his analysis of the impact of adjustment programmes on the environment, Reed (1992) asserts that "... at virtually no point during the 1980s was there a focused effort to understand the impact of World Bank macroeconomic lending on the natural resources sector.." As I have argued, in the absence of any contextual understanding of environmental decision-making, which can only be provided by locating this decision-making within the context of poverty and human entitlements, such a conclusion is not surprising. The Mexican experience merely underlines the fact that the environmental "management" practised by international lending institutions pays little or no attention to the environmental practices of the poor.

In Mexico, the effects of adjustment on the environment are extremely difficult to calculate. The conditions prior to adjustment were not auspicious. Environmental problems were stimulated by subsidies to wasteful resource exploitation, and the profligate use of revenues from petroleum. Urban households, which now account for three-quarters of the total, have benefited from food and transport subsidies and the availability of relatively cheap energy. At the same time, peasant farmers have been encouraged by the artificially high price of staples, notably maize, to cultivate marginal land and to remove forest cover. Water policy has been an area of continuous distortion as supplies were channelled to urban areas and, in cities, towards the better-off population. The long term effects of soil erosion, deforestation and the pollution of irrigation systems have never been satisfactorily calculated.

Although adjustment policies cut public revenues, and with this investment in environmental protection, Mexico's record suggests that periods of economic "boom" such as the late 1970s were also periods in which environmental standards (air pollution, water quality and waste disposal) were very low. In this respect, Mexico, as a middle income country, has exhibited the environmental sores of development, as well as those of underdevelopment. The reliance on large-scale projects, often financed in ways which accelerated the debt burden, and further impoverished the poor, have left environmental degradation in their wake. The world is reminded of these every time an oil installation explodes, or more or less futile attempts are made to control urban air pollution by taking cars off the road. Mexicans experience appalling environmental standards as a fact of everyday life: *la vida cotidiana*, from which there is no escape.

We can appreciate the scale of Mexico's problems if we take some current statistics. Estimated total reserves of water, per inhabitant, are expected to halve between 1993 and 2010 (from 1000–2000 cubic metres to 500–1500 cubic metres per person per year). Currently, the supply of water to the Federal District is between 200 and 300 litres per person per day. The average citizen of Mexico City now uses more water than anybody else in the globe. Within this area, over 15% of the water is lost. For each 60 cubic metres per second that enters the city, nine cubic metres are lost: enough to supply the needs of a large city like Guadalajara. Where maintenance is poorer, losses can be much higher: up to 40% in some cases (Mexican National Commission for Water, 1993; quoted in *Nexos*, 1993).

Statistics on deforestation generate a similar scene of impending crisis. The annual rate of deforestation in Mexico is probably one of the highest in the world: a significant proportion of the 6·2 million hectares lost from the ten most critical countries. Of the 12 million hectares of tropical forest that once grew in Mexico, only 500 000 hectares remain. The rate of deforestation for areas like Los Tuxtlas in Veracruz suggest 4% annual losses. Reforestation programmes have been very modest by comparison: only about 5% of the area lost has been replanted (Toledo and Carahas, 1989; Arizpe and Carabias, 1992). The principal cause of tropical deforestation in Mexico, like most of Latin America, has been cattle-raising. In Latin America as a whole, between 1971 and 1986, three-fifths of the tropical forest losses can be attributed to cattle-ranching.

The loss of tropical forests also carries implications for biodiversity. The majority of natural species live in the tropics, where it is estimated that one quarter of the natural species of flora will have been lost by 2023. Mexico is a key country in this respect. Within thirty key tropical ecosystems, approximately two thousand species (of a total in excess of thirty thousand) are threatened with extinction in the next thirty years (Arizpe and Carabias, 1992).

The gravity of Mexico's environmental problems is not in doubt. To what extent is this reflected in public unease and official government action? During the last two decades, Mexico has begun to experience the birth of an environmental movement. At the same time, legislation has been enacted on an unprecedented scale, and both public and private sectors have expressed increasing concern (Provencio, 1992).

However, during the early part of 1992, events demonstrated how inadequate has been the official response. Evidence emerged of widescale pollution in the Valley of Mexico, and much attention was given to the catastrophe in Guadalajara on 22 April, when an oil depot exploded. Alarm was also sounded that nuclear waste was being housed near the border with the United States and that toxic waste processing plants were also being established on a large scale. Reports in July 1993 that the World Bank was planning a four billion dollar (U.S.) loan to Mexico for environmental "projects" along the U.S.–Mexican border, over a ten year period, have done little to stifle fears. Critics of the planned loan from within Mexico have argued that the disclosure is part of an effort to appease growing internal opposition to the North American Free Trade Agreement (NAFTA). It was suggested that the World Bank loan would be used for sewage, water treatment and industrial waste processing in the border region. Estimates for the cost of addressing the current problem vary widely, but at least 10 billion dollars would be needed. This compares with the Bank's two major loans for environmental purposes to Mexico in 1992: 50 million dollars for Mexico's central environmental agency and 220 million dollars to improve air quality in the Federal District. Organizations like the Sierra Club have argued that such expenditure is wasted, and that it would be better to set up an environmental fund to guarantee bonds, loans and grants to pay for environmental investments, using a transaction fee of goods, services, and investment as the main source of funding. An estimated \$21 billion (U.S.) could be raised in this way, and directed to areas other than the politically sensitive border.

`According to Provencio (1992) the establishment of new legal bodies, such as the National Commission for the Use of Biodiversity and the discussion surrounding the environmental implications of NAFTA enshrined in the Integrated Environmental Plan for the Border, have had little practical effect. The programme to reduce industrial pollution in Mexico City published in the *Ecological Pact* of 24 April 1992 will have no effect on the main source of air pollution, which is road transport. However, public reaction to recurring environmental "disasters" is beginning to have an impact on the authorities. Opposition to the proposed construction, by American Companies, of nuclear waste plants near the border was *strengthened* by the publicity given to NAFTA and the call for a liberalization of trade. Permission was cancelled for the operation, by Chemical Waste Management (a U.S. company) for the incineration of toxic wastes in Tijuana. These actions were prompted by much more international collaboration between environmental groups throughout North America, itself stimulated by the UNCED deliberations. Mexico's almost "routine" environmental problems are increasingly perceived within a more "global" context, and cannot be so easily disguised. The links between the United States, Canada and Mexico, over agrochemical impacts, toxic waste disposal, industrial contamination and the loss of marine resources, have begun belatedly to assume importance in the political agenda of the region. For these reasons, environmental problems themselves, so neglected during the economic adjustments of the 1980s, have become the focal point for misgivings about the direction of Mexican development in the 1990s. They have done so because of longstanding structural problems, rather than because of the effects of adjustment policies. Recurrent, almost daily, environmental "disasters", together with longer-term problems of water supply and soil erosion, are no longer seen as separable from social distress and poverty. The environmental agenda in Mexico, prompted it must be said by the attention given to global environmental issues at Rio, has underlined the failure to address poverty and inequality in the aftermath of the debt crisis 10 years ago.

7. The way forward: participation, pluralism and environmental management

The current confusions surrounding the revision of adjustment policies, to incorporate "environmental" considerations, strike at the very limits of reductionist economics (Mearns, 1991). Environmental economics has reached a point of ascendancy within development policy circles, if not within the discipline of economics itself, because of its promise to lead development institutions out of the cul-de-sac of short-term policy formulation. However, the authority of a perspective must be judged by whether it works and it is not at all clear that environmental economics can deliver on its promises. The question we need to ask is will the growing sophistication in modelling environmental factors within neo-classical economic theory contribute towards achieving greater sustainability?

Once this question has been asked, we are immediately called upon to acknowledge that people, including poor rural people, utilize environmental resources according to social and cultural principles: they are "allocative resources" in Giddens' (1984) terms. People are influenced in their behaviour by a number of different "rationalities" depending on the roles they play, and their social objectives. Mearns provides an example in the case of a woman farmer in Malawi:

"... The small holder in Malawi with less than half a hectare of land, who as a result of policy reforms under structural adjustment in the early 1980s found that she could no longer afford the fertiliser essential for self-provisioning food products, is unlikely to regard higher grower prices as much of an incentive to intensify efforts at soil conservation on her land, when much of her income ... is derived from non-farm activities or labouring on someone else's farm. For her, the 'solution' could be cheaper fertiliser but it could also be better access to relatively lucrative non-farm employment or a shift in the power balance within the farm employment market. Only by acknowledging plural problem definitions can they be reconciled: a possible policy option in this hypothetical instance, for example, could be to provide such employment in an activity that is environmentally benign, and as part of a structural adjustment programme". (Mearns, 1991, p. 61).

The idea of "plural rationalities" (Thompson *et al.*, 1986) which explains behaviour differently depending on who you are, and where you stand in a society, is impossible to accommodate within the kind of environmental economics that wishes to make environmental concerns an addition to adjustment policies. But it is an essential precondition for the wider participation in sustainable development envisaged by Agenda 21 and incorporated, in principle, in national submissions to the Commission for Sustainable Development. Without widespread "ownership" of environmental objectives, against a background of the struggle against poverty and an extension of human rights, the rights of future generations will remain an impossible goal, clouded in technical obscurity. Structural adjustment policies, in Mexico as in India, have taken no account of the need to incorporate the cultural practices and epistemologies of the poor in their management of their environments. This is a major consideration for policy that has hardly been remarked upon in the literature.

8. Conclusion

This paper began by describing the way in which criticism of structural adjustment policies in India is being increasingly related to environmental problems. It went on to identify two dominant perspectives within the current policy discourse on environment and development: Neo-Malthusianism and Environmental Managerialism. It was suggested that a third *structural* perspective helped to illuminate the relationship between poverty and environmental degradation, particularly at the international level. The analysis suggested a rather different, and more complex, relationship between structural policies and the environment. This relationship was examined in the light of Mexican experience.

1. It is increasingly recognized that economic development rests upon viable and sustainable systems of resource use. However, most leading agencies did not recognize this fact until after the stabilization and adjustment policies of the 1980s had been framed. One of the consequences is that long term sustainable development objectives have been added to short term market reforms in a contradictory fashion, without examining the most appropriate avenues through which such reforms might be pursued.

2. Structural adjustment programmes like those of the World Bank, have tended to undermine the social fabric of many developing countries. This has implications for the success of environmental policies designed to mobilize poor people around sustainable development. The "ownership" of sustainable development policies requires a more collaborative and reflexive approach to the poor on the part of leading agencies.

3. The solutions to environmental problems lie in structural reforms which assist the poor in acting more sustainably. Technical interventions and population programmes which seek to arrest the declining carrying capacity of the resource base are no substitute for such reforms. Nor are the sophisticated assessments of environmental costs, favoured by many environmental economists, a substitute for local empowerment and an actively collaborative approach to environmental management. Environmental policy objectives should not be set in a vacuum, ignoring the specific relations between poverty and resource degradation which govern the use of resources in the South.

4. Since UNCED was held in Rio de Janeiro in July 1992, the discussion surrounding Agenda 21 has served to emphasize the role of public participation in achieving sustainable development goals. Such participation should begin by recognizing that different "stakeholders" in the environment often possess different epistemologies, which need to be given weight within the paradigms that govern development. Neither of the dominant paradigms, Neo-Malthusianism and Environmental Managerialism, do this.

5. Future environmental policy in the South needs to begin by recognizing global responsibilities for environmental problems through linking environmental issues with trade negotiations, technology transfer and commodity prices. A start has been made by recognizing the role of many tropical countries as carbon sinks and as the location of natural capital stocks, especially of biodiversity. However, since UNCED, the global account needs to be widened to include responsibility for the processes which undermine sustainability. We need more theoretical attention to be given to global processes under which "sinks" are created, similar to that which we have given to the creation of global "sources". Structural "adjustment"—towards increased sustainability—needs to be identified as a policy goal for the North, and a necessary pre-requisite for more global sustainable development. Environmental goals need to be seen as the objective of future structural policy reforms, rather than as a consequence of past failures in economic management.

This paper has benefited from the suggestions and advice of participants at the *Seminar on Structural Adjustment Policy in India*, held in Bangalore from 10–12 October 1993. Their help, and that of the British Council in attending the meeting, is gratefully acknowledged.

References

Agarwal, A. (1993). CSE Round Table on the Environmental Impact of India's Economic Liberalisation Policy, Centre for Science and Environment, New Delhi, May.

Anderson, D. (1990). *Environmental Policy and Public Revenue in Developing Countries.* Washington, D.C.: World Bank.

Arizpe, L. and Carabias, J. (1992). Mexico ante el cambio global. *Antropologicas*, No. 3, UNAM, Mexico.

Bishop, J. (1991). *The Debt Crisis, Structural Adjustment and the Environment. Discussion of Case Study Results.* Cote D'Ivoire: WWF/LEEC.

Boyd, R., Hyde, W. F., Krutilla, K. (1991). *Trade Policy and Environmental Accounting: A case study of structural adjustment and deforestation in the Philippines.* Unpublished manuscript.

Chossudovsky, M. (1992). India Under IMF Rule. *The Ecologist*, **22** (6) 215–230.

Commander, S. (ed.) (1989). *Structural Adjustment & Agriculture. Theory and Practice in Africa and Latin America.* ODI in conjunction with James Currey, London and Heinemann, Portsmouth.

Cornia, G. A., Jolly, R. and Stewart, F. (1987). *Adjustment With a Human Face. Protecting the Vulnerable and Promoting Growth.* Oxford: Oxford University Press.

Cruz, W. and Repetto, R. (1992). The Environmental Effects of Stabilization and Structural Adjustment Programs: The Philippines Case. Washington: The World Bank.

Davies, S., Leach, M. and David, R. (1991). *Food Security and the Environment: conflict or complementary.* IDS Discussion Paper 28S Sussex.

ERL (1989). *Natural Resource Management for Sustainable Development. A study of feasible policies, institutions and investment activities in Nepal with special emphasis on the hills.* Final Report and Data Review Report for the World Bank.

George, S. (1988). *A Fate Worse Than Debt.* London: Pelican.

Giddens, A. (1984). *The Constitution of Society.* Oxford: Politics Press.

Hansen, S. (1990). Macroeconomic policies: incidence on the environment. ODI Conference on *The Environment, Development of Economic Research.* London, March, 1990.

Harvey, D. (1979). Population, resources and the ideology of science. In *Philosophy in Geography.* (S. Gale and G. Olsson, eds). New York: Rockwell.

Hauff, M. (1993). The transformation process and the structural adjustment program in India—a few ecological consequences. Research Workshop on *Agriculture, Poverty and the Environment after Structural Adjustment.* Bangalore, India, 10–12 October.

IIED/LEEC (1990). The Debt Crises, Structural Adjustment and the Environment. *Final Report IIED/LEEC.* World Wildlife Fund.

Ishikawa, S. (1993). Structural adjustment in China, Egypt and India. In *Development and Change* (P. Bardham, M. D. Chaudhuri and T. N. Kishuan eds. Bombay: Oxford University Press.

IUCN (1991). *Caring For The Earth,* Second World Conservation Strategy, Gland, Switzerland.

Iyer, R. (1991). The Economic crisis: issues before the new Government, Research Workshop on *Agriculture, Poverty and the Environment after Structural Adjustment.* Bangalore, India, 10–12 October.

Jayawardena, L. (1990). *The Macroeconomics of Sustainable Development.* WIDER, United Nations University, Tokyo.

Leach, M. and Mearns, R. (1991). *Poverty and the Environment in Developing Countries.* ESRC/ODA., London.

Lipton, M. (1987). Limits of price policy for agriculture: which way for the World Bank? *Development Policy Review* **5(2)** 197–215.

Mearns, R. (1991). *Environmental Implications of Structural Adjustment: reflections on Scientific Method.* Institute of Development Studies, University of Sussex. Discussion Paper 284.

Nexos. (1993). *La Escasez de agua,* No. 187, July. Mexico City, Mexico.

Panayotou, T., Sussangkarn, C. (1991). *The Debt Crisis, Structural Adjustment and The Environment: The Case of Thailand.* WWFN. (Paper prepared for WWFN's project on the Impact of Macroeconomic Adjustment on the Environment.)

Platteau, J. P. (1990). *Land Reform and Structural Adjustment in SubSaharan Africa: Controversies and Guidelines.* Food and Agricultural Organisation (Faculté des Sciences Economiques, Facultés Universitaires Notre-Dame de la Paix, Namur, Belgium).

Provencio, E. (1992). La crisis ambiental en 1992: algunas implicaciones, *Antropologicas* No. 3. UNAM, Mexico.

Ranadive, J. (1993). The role of the household in structural adjustment programmes: a special focus on the PDS in India and its implications for women. In *Development and Change.* (P. Bardham, M. D. Chaudhuri and T. N. Kishuan eds). Bombay: Oxford University Press.

68   **The environment and structural adjustment**

Rauscher, M. (1990). 'The optimal use of environmental resources by an indebted country. Universitat Konstanz'. (Forthcoming in *Journal of Institutional and Theoretical Economics.*)

Redclift, M. (1993). Sustainable development: needs, values, rights. *Environmental Values* **2(1)** Spring, 3–20.

Reed, D. (1992). *Structural Adjustment and the Environment.* Boulder, Colorado: Westview Press.

Repetto, R. (1988). 'Economic Policy Reform for National Resource Conservation'. World Bank, Washington.

Sebastian, I., Alicbuscan, A. (1989). *Sustainable Development: Issues in Adjustment Lending Policies.* Washington, D.C.: The World Bank Environment Department.

Stein, H. and Nafzigu, E. W. (1991). Structural adjustment, human needs and the World Bank agenda. *The Journal of Modern African Studies* **29(1)**, 638–652.

Sunkel, O. and Gligo, N. (1981). *Estilos de Desarrollo, modernization y medio ambiente en la agricultura Latinoamericana.* Santiago, Chile: CEPAL.

Thompson, M., Warburton, M. and Hatley, T. (1986). *Uncertainty on a Himalayan Scale.* London: Milton Ash Editions.

Toledo, V. and Carahas, J. (1989). *La produccion rural en Mexico: alternativas ecologicas.* Fundacion Universo Veintiuno: Mexico.

Veerashekerappa, N. (1992). Impact of structural adjustment on the working class. *Indian Journal of Labour Economics* **35(4)**, 328–333.

Von Urff, W. (1993). Structural adjustment and agricultural policy: implications for poverty alleviation and sustainability. Research shop on *Agriculture, Poverty and the Environment after Structural Adjustment.* Bangalore, India, 10–12 October.

World Bank/IMF (1989). *World Bank Support For The Environment.* A Progress Report. Washington, D.C.: World Bank/IMF.

World Bank (1989). *Adjustment Lending. An Evaluation of Ten Years of Experience.* Country Economics Department. Policy and Research Series 1, Washington, D.C.: World Bank.

World Bank (1990). *Making Adjustment Work for the Poor: A Framework for Policy Reform in Africa.* Washington, D.C.: The World Bank.

World Bank (1990). *How Adjustment Programs Can Help The Poor.* World Bank Discussion Paper No. 71. Washington, D.C.: The World Bank.

[15]

Journal of Environmental Management (1997) **50**, 235–250

Market Liberalisation and Environmental Assessment in Developing and Transitional Economies

Colin Kirkpatrick* and Norman Lee†

Institute for Development Policy and Management and † School of Economic Studies, University of Manchester, Manchester, U.K.

Received 30 *March* 1996; *accepted* 17 *November* 1996

The paper examines the relationship between market-liberalising economic policies and environmental assessment procedures, in developing and transitional economies. The current scope of market liberalisation measures is reviewed, and the possible environmental impacts of market liberalisation policies are discussed. The various types of policy instruments that may be used to address these environmental impacts are considered and, in particular, a comparative analysis of cost–benefit analysis and environmental impact assessment, as investment appraisal instruments, is presented. The final part of the paper identifies several areas for further research.
© 1997 Academic Press Limited

1. Introduction

Post-Rio, there is a widely held view that governments should take environmental considerations into account within the development process. Concurrently, the past decade has seen the widespread adoption of more market-oriented strategies for economic growth in both developing countries (LDCs) and countries in transition (CITs). However, the precise means by which environmental considerations are to be integrated within market-based development policies and practices is often unclear.

The objective of this article is to explore the relationship between the market liberalisation measures proposed to promote development through more efficient resource utilisation, and the environmental assessment provisions proposed to promote sustainability through the more systematic integration of environmental considerations within the development planning and implementation process. It focuses particularly on two questions:

(1) Is market liberalisation, and in particular, privatisation, good for the environment, or not?
(2) What are the implications of market liberalisation for the choice of environmental policy instruments and, more particularly, for the effectiveness of environmental assessment measures?

0301–4797/97/070235 + 16 $25.00/0/ev960107

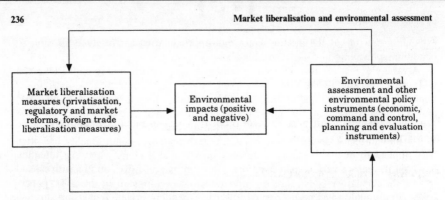

Figure 1. Marker liberalisation and environmental assessment linkages.

Environmental assessment (EA) procedures may be applied to market liberalisation measures with a view to reducing any resulting negative environmental impacts. However, market liberalisation measures may also modify the regulatory framework within which environmental assessment procedures are applied and, as a result, modify their effectiveness (see Figure 1).

These linkages between market liberalisation and EA have received little attention in the research literature and official governmental studies until very recently. Increasingly, however, during the 1990s a number of major international bodies have begun to examine market liberalisation–environmental quality linkages; these include the World Bank, United Nations Conference on Trade and Development (UNCTAD), United Nations Economic Commission for Europe (UNECE), Organisation for European Cooperation and Development (OECD), and certain non-government organisations (NGOs) such as World Wildlife Fund (WWF) and International Institute for Environment and Development (IIED) (Anderson and Blackhurst, 1992; Reed, 1992, 1996; UNECE/UNDP, 1994; Munasinghe and Cruz, 1995; OECD, 1994a; 1996a; UNCTAD, 1995; Abaza, 1996; Potier, in press). Nevertheless, the number of completed studies is still relatively small and several important empirical and policy questions remain unresolved.

The remainder of the paper examines the main elements of these linkages according to the following structure. Section 2 reviews the scope of market liberalisation measures in LDCs and CITs. Section 3 discusses the possible environmental impacts of market liberalisation measures. The fourth part considers the different types of policy instruments that may be used to address these environmental impacts (including, particularly, environmental assessment measures), and Section 5 provides a comparative analysis of the effectiveness of cost–benefit analysis (CBA) and environmental assessment procedures (EIA and its strategic level counterpart, SEA) as instruments of investment appraisal, in the context of market liberalisation. The final part of the paper contains the conclusions and identifies several areas for follow-up investigation and research.

2. The scope of market liberalisation measures

Market liberalisation policies and programmes contain a heterogeneous and varied collection of measures whose overall objective is to promote economic growth and development through the more efficient use of resources, which is to be achieved by expanding the role of the private sector and approximating as closely as possible to conditions prevailing in competitive markets.

A variety of market liberalisation measures have been promoted in both LDCs and CITs since the late 1970s, often with strong encouragement from the international financial institutions and aid agencies (notably the International Monetary Fund, IMF, and World Bank), each of which have made their financial assistance to these countries, in part at least, conditional upon the adoption of these policy measures (IMF, 1996; World Bank, 1996b). In the case of LDCs, this policy-based conditionality has often been applied through structural adjustment programme lending, where the intention has been to remove various perceived distortions in market prices and incentives, and to ease the regulatory constraints on private sector development. In the CITs, policy-based conditionality has been oriented towards expanding private ownership through the privatisation of state-owned assets, and creating the institutional structures and stable macro-economic environment within which private ownership may develop.

These market liberalisation measures (combined, in certain cases, with macro-economic stabilisation measures) can be grouped into two broad categories: correction of market distortions; and privatisation of state-owned enterprises.

2.1. CORRECTION OF MARKET DISTORTIONS

The overall purpose of these measures is to correct "distortions" in factor and product markets. Here, a "distortion" refers to a deviation between actual prices and opportunity costs to the economy of the items concerned. This divergence can result from "inappropriate" policy interventions, or from market imperfections. However, market liberalisation measures are generally concerned only with the former case (other sources of market imperfections are assumed to be non-significant or to be corrected by additional but separate policy measures).

Policy reforms are designed to create a more competitive domestic market environment through the removal or reduction of market interventions and controls. The distortionary impact of both tariff and non-tariff measures on the efficiency with which traded goods are produced has been studied extensively in LDCs, where countries have adopted a strategy of import-substituting industrialisation behind high protective barriers. Trade liberalisation measures have featured prominently in LDCs' structural adjustment programmes, and are intended to correct trade related distortions in relative price incentives for tradable goods (Kirkpatrick, 1995). Similarly, the distortions caused by intervention in factor markets—foreign exchange, labour, capital—have been identified as constraints on efficient resource allocation and use. Controls on price, output, sales, market entry and exit, and regulatory burdens on enterprises (licensing and permitting procedures) are additional causes of resource misallocation costs. The issue of regulatory burden is also of potential significance when considering the effects on EIA effectiveness when deregulation takes the form of reducing or simplifying licensing and permitting procedures (see Section 4 for a further discussion of this issue).

2.2 PRIVATISATION OF STATE-OWNED ENTERPRISES

The term "privatisation" is used to describe a range of policy measures which share the common aim of reducing the state's control over the use of productive assets. These policy measures may initially take the form of a privatisation policy, plan or programme covering many enterprises but, in the most common usage of the term, the majority-ownership of individual enterprises is transferred from the public to the private sector. The transfer of ownership can be affected in a variety of ways, including public flotation, private sale, management (and employee) buyout, voucher distribution. The method of privatisation will, in turn, have implications for the ownership pattern—that is, on the extent to which domestic ownership is spread over a large number of small investors or is concentrated in a few, monopolistic enterprises—and for the degree of foreign ownership and control.

The pace of privatisation in LDCs has accelerated in recent years, with the developing countries' share of world privatisation sales increasing from less than 10% in 1988 to 40% in 1992 (Cook and Kirkpatrick, 1995). In the CITs, privatisation has been the main means of creating a market economy. Much of the early privatisation activity was concentrated on small scale enterprises, often in the services sector, but in more recent years there has been significant privatisation of large scale industrial enterprises (Cook and Kirkpatrick, 1996).

3. Environmental impacts of market liberalisation measures

The environmental impacts of market liberalisation measures are extremely diverse for two main reasons. First, the market liberalisation measures themselves are diverse. Second, there is also great diversity in the "country context" in which these measures are applied, notably in those variables (e.g. definition and distribution of property rights, pre-existing environmental controls and their practical efficacy, etc.) which may exercise a more fundamental influence, in their own right, on the extent of environmental impacts and on the degree to which these are "internalised" in decision-making within the liberalised markets. In the cases of LCDs and CITs, which are the types of economies that are of primary concern in this paper, the significance of the second set of factors is likely to be particular great.

This diversity, both in the market liberalisation measures themselves and in the country-specific conditions within which the measures are applied, may account, at least in part, for the limited information that currently exists for answering the first of the two basic questions with which this paper is concerned, namely, is market liberalisation good for the environment or not? The current literature which addresses these issues comprises a mixture of theoretical reasoning, indirect "proof by association" evidence, and some case studies.

3.1. MARKET LIBERALISATION AND ENVIRONMENTAL IMPACT

Any change in the policy framework is likely to have some environmental consequences through the output and resource use effects that follow from changes in economic incentives, after market liberalisation.

However, structural adjustment loan agreements have not normally included specific conditions relating to environmental concerns. Therefore, where it has occurred, the environmental impacts of structural adjustment lending, and policy-reform lending more generally, have not been identified and assessed on a systematic basis. Instead, considerable personal judgement has been exercised in identifying those loan conditions whose environmental effects might be significant. For example, a recent review of the environmental effects of adjustment lending identifies changes in agricultural output prices (producer prices and export tax adjustments), changes in agricultural input prices (input subsidy changes and reduction in import duties), energy sector policy measures, trade and industry sector reforms (import liberalisation and export promotion), and institutional reforms, as the types of policy changes which are likely to have significant environmental effects (Warford *et al.*, 1994). Most of these effects were considered, in this review, to be beneficial. Further, the frequency with which market liberalisation measures affecting these areas were included in loan agreements was found to have increased over the period 1988–1992, as compared to 1979–1988 (Warford *et al.* 1994).

The failure to conduct thorough, systematic environmental assessments of market liberalisation reforms has been rationalised by some observers on the grounds that the liberalisation–environmental impact relationship is invariably a "win–win" situation, a view which was strongly reflected in the World Bank's 1992 *World Development Report* on Development and the Environment. A more recent statement of this position is provided by Warford *et al.* (1994): "Even in the past, where there was limited concern over the environment, the resulting neglect was not necessarily bad. On the contrary, good economics, particularly as it emphasises efficient use of resources, is often good for the environment too. There remain, due in large part to government policy failure, many opportunities for 'no regrets' policies—i.e. those which satisfy both economic and environmental objectives" (p. 14–15).

The study of Munasinghe and Cruz (1995), on behalf of the World Bank, uses a range of country case studies to identify the environmental impacts of economy-wide reforms. The conclusions drawn from the study are: (i) removal of price distortions, promotion of market incentives and relaxation of other constraints generally contribute to both economic and environmental gains; (ii) unintended adverse side effects occur when economy-wide reforms are undertaken while other neglected policy, market or institutional imperfections remain; (iii) such undesirable impacts may be mitigated by extra measures that address the specific imperfections underlying the environmental problems; (iv) macro-economic stabilisation measures will generally yield environmental benefits but may also have unforeseen adverse short-term impacts on the environment; and (v) economy-wide policy changes will have additional longer term effects on the environment through employment and income distribution changes.

Some other empirical studies and case study surveys are rather more critical but again demonstrate mixed results (Cromwell and Winpenny, 1993; Reed, 1992, 1996; Abaza, 1966; Richardson, 1996; Kitetu and Rowan, in press; Potier, in press). For example, Cromwell and Winpenny's study of the environmental consequences of the economic reform programme in Malawi in the 1980s found that agricultural price changes resulting from reform were environmentally damaging in terms of encouraging a switch to more erosive crops such as cotton and tobacco, and by increasing the intensity of cultivation. The reforms, which aimed at increasing output of tradable goods, provided no incentives for tobacco estates to change from the extensive, environmentally wasteful production methods typically used, and small holders were unable to change their production techniques because of their limited access to capital equipment and external inputs such as fertiliser (Cromwell and Winpenny, 1993 p. 645).

3.2. PRIVATISATION AND ENVIRONMENTAL IMPACT

It is common, in environmental analysis, to distinguish between two different forms of impact: on stocks and flows. Pollution stocks include inherited hazardous waste and other deposits of contaminated materials (e.g. in the form of contaminated land) which pose a continuing threat to environmental quality and human health. In the privatisation context, the issue of liability for environmental costs resulting from existing pollution stocks has been a major concern for policy-makers. The question of responsibility for any environmental damage which arises after privatisation, but is the result of pre-privatisation activity, is at the core of the issue (Goldenman, 1995). On the one hand, uncertainties over the possibility of new private owners becoming liable for environment damage caused by the earlier activities of the public enterprise have been seen as a major constraint to the inflow of foreign direct investment for privatisation sales in the CITs (United Nations Economic Commission for Europe, 1994; World Bank, 1994). On the other hand, the exemption of the new private owners from this liability in their privatisation contracts may leave responsibility for environmental clean-ups and compensation payments unresolved, particularly if part of the privatisation proceeds are not allocated for this purpose.

The determination of environmental liabilities arising from inherited pollution stocks at the time of enterprise privatisation is a matter for environmental (liability) auditing (World Bank, 1994). The determination of the impacts of privatisation on subsequent environmental flows is a matter of environmental assessment, which is examined more fully below.

Privatisation may take many different forms and consequentially have different environmental consequences. It may simply involve a change of ownership, where the enterprise continues to operate in the same way as previously. In the earlier privatisations in most CITs, for example, a number of enterprises were transferred to the existing management and workforce, and there was little immediate change in operations. However, the more likely outcome, especially with the passage of time, is that there will be a significant change in the output level and technology of the privatised enterprise, and, as a consequence, a change in its environmental impact.

As with market liberalisation, the environmental impact of privatisation may be positive or negative. The net effect will be determined by a complex of factors which include, *inter alia*, type of activity, degree of competition, existing regulatory requirements and technology choice. Privatisation may produce positive environmental effects, such as increased efficiency in the use of natural resources, better housekeeping practices and more rapid adoption of cleaner technologies. Privatisation may bring with it secure and transferable property rights and greater incentives to invest in the maintenance of the natural resources stocks which the private owner acquires. If privatisation increases profitability, this can lead to more investable funds which, in part, may be used for increased investment in pollution abatement. Where privatisation takes the form of liquidation of certain activities or enterprises, then some negative environmental flows may be terminated.

However, privatisation may lead to any of the following negative environmental impacts (World Bank, 1994). First, there may be a stronger financial incentive to pollute the environment or exhaust natural resources. In the absence of an appropriate regulatory framework, privatisation may increase a firm's incentive to maximise profits on existing activity levels, by avoiding the costs of reducing pollution or by over-extraction of natural resources. Delays in implementing privatisation and land restitution policies can, as in certain CITs, increase uncertainties over property rights and contribute to further degradation of the environment. Second, privatisation may be accompanied by a regulatory relaxation or freeze. Less rigorous environmental standards may be imposed on private firms, whether locally or foreign owned. Privatisation may also lead to a freezing of environmental standards which blocks further strengthening of the environmental regulatory framework. Finally, there may be a recapitalisation effect which counterbalances the liquidation effect mentioned above. Privatisation may revive an enterprise that would otherwise go out of business and lead to an expansion of activity, which results in higher pollution flows.

Case study findings relating to the environmental impacts of privatisation are also mixed. For example, since the early 1990s, two forms of privatisation have been taking place in Estonia—privatisation of enterprises and housing stock, and the restitution of land to its former private owners—alongside other market liberalisation measures. Their environmental consequences are quite complex and not easily interpreted (United Nations Economic Commission for Europe, 1996). On the one hand, substantial environmental improvements have resulted from the closure of heavily polluting enterprises and the reduced use of fertilisers and pesticides. On the other hand, the unauthorised exploitation of certain natural resources has increased and the provision of local environmental services has been seriously disrupted. At the same time, there have been welcome policy initiatives to address certain of the environmental problems associated with the privatisation process—the regulatory requirements for environmental liability auditing and the environmental assessment of privatised enterprises are being strengthened and it has been agreed to allocate 5% of the proceeds from privatisation to environmental audits and environmental clean-ups.

In Cubatao, Brazil, the major industrial area of São Paulo state, it has been found that state-owned enterprises tend to be more air and water pollution intensive than privately owned plants, even after size and age are taken into account. The state-owned enterprises fail to comply with pollution standards, by using their bureaucratic connections to avoid regulatory control. The proposed privatisation of the state-owned enterprises has been welcomed by the state pollution control agency, which anticipates fuller compliance by private firms (World Bank, 1996c, p. 41).

Thus, in response to the basic question "is market liberalisation good for the environment or not?" and at the risk of some simplification, we can distinguish three viewpoints: optimistic, pessimistic and pragmatic, which are summarised below.

3.3. THE OPTIMISTIC VIEWPOINT

Market liberalisation has a number of consequences which will frequently, if not universally, lead to environmental improvements. For example, it is argued that the correction of price-related distortions (e.g. by setting more appropriate prices for energy or water) and removing taxes or subsidies on particular commodities or factors of production will stimulate the more efficient use of resources (and economic development) and enhance environmental protection and natural resource conservation (e.g. Munasinghe and Cruz, 1995).

Where unfavourable environmental consequences do occur, it is argued that they are not due to the market liberalisation measures themselves but to other pre-existing and continuing sources of market failure (e.g. the absence of a clearly defined system of property rights, absence of satisfactory economic instruments for pollution control). This being so, the remedy to these environmental problems does not lie in diluting the marked liberalisation measures but in ensuring that the other sources of market failure are effectively addressed.

3.4. THE PESSIMISTIC VIEWPOINT

It is argued, on the basis of case studies, supplemented by simple analysis and more anecdotal evidence, that negative environmental consequences have followed from the implementation of specific market liberalisation measures (sometimes accompanied by market stabilisation measures) in particular countries (e.g. Reed, 1992, 1996; Abaza, 1996). For example, where a price rise occurs (e.g. in one form of energy) it may reduce *its* consumption and environmental impacts but lead to substitution effects which are more environmentally damaging (e.g. greater use of fuel wood—whose use is not effectively regulated by the existing system of property rights—leading to deforestation, land erosion, river silting and flooding, etc.).

Such increased environmental pressures may occur particularly (but not exclusively) in poorer countries, both in LDCs and CITs. Market liberalisation may increase the country's overall growth rate but reduce the standard of living within the poorest section of society whose response is to engage in the kinds of informal sector activities which can be particularly damaging to the environment. Market liberalisation may also change trade patterns such that economies become more dependent on natural resource extracting and exporting, or the growth of other "dirty" industries including toxic waste disposal (Low, 1992). These also are often the countries which are least capable of handling additional environmental pressures—their property rights are not well-defined, environmental regulations are very weak or non-existent, institutions for regulation enforcement are very defective—and there is no realistic short- or medium-term prospect of them correcting these weaknesses.

3.5. THE PRAGMATIC VIEWPOINT

The theoretical analysis of the environmental effects of market-liberalising measures is relatively straightforward where we can safely assume that the measures will lead to a situation in which private entrepreneurs populate markets which approximate to perfectly competitive markets, and in which environmental externalities are internalised. However, the analysis of liberalising measures which move markets in that direction but stop well short of the ideal (and where shifts between public and private ownership are occurring simultaneously), is much more complex. In the latter situation we have to face up to the uncertain environmental consequences of changes in enterprise objectives, the indeterminances of imperfect markets and the complexities of identifying second best solutions. This suggests that it may be more prudent to look for greater insights into the market liberalisation–environmental impacts relationships through case specific, rather than through general theoretic, analysis.

Good quality, *ex-post*, empirical studies of the environmental impacts of specific market liberalisation measures are still very few in number. Also, their findings often conflict—because they are not strictly comparing like with like, or because of differences in the underlying assumptions built into the analysis, or because of differences in the quality of data used, modelling and other analytical techniques employed (see reviews by Abaza, 1996; Reed, 1992, 1996; and Potier, in press, for further details).

Ex-ante empirical studies (i.e. studies of the likely environmental impacts of specific market liberalisation measures *prior* to their adoption) are also very sparse (see, example, studies of the likely environmental impacts of the North America Free Trade Agreement). Also, their findings are sensitive to the assumptions that are made about the timing of other measures relevant to environmental protection relative to the timing of market liberalisation measures (e.g. is it assumed that environmental protection measures are in place *before* market liberalisation measures are introduced or at some unspecified date *after* market liberalisation measures are in place?).

The provisional conclusions that are drawn in this article are that the pragmatic viewpoint is probably the most tenable at the moment and, if this is accepted both for policy and research purposes, then new *ex-ante* and *ex-post* case studies of the environmental impacts of market liberalisation measures will need to be undertaken to complement any future use of more general analysis.

4. Environmental policy instruments and market liberalisation measures

Let us assume that market liberalisation measures may have some significant negative environmental impacts, if they are not preceded by (or at least not accompanied by) certain environmental policy measures. Then, with reference to the second question with which this article is concerned, what forms should these measures take? For present purposes these will be grouped into three categories:

(1) economic instruments (charges, taxes, subsidies, etc.);
(2) direct regulations—command and control instruments (permits, licences, etc.);
(3) planning and evaluation instruments (EIA, CBA, etc.).

4.1. ECONOMIC INSTRUMENTS

Economic instruments are understandably the economists' first-choice method for achieving optimal resource pricing and to internalise environmental pollution externalities. However, it is necessary to be realistic about what can be achieved by such instruments in the near future, especially in LDCs and CITs. The obstacles to their becoming major instruments of environmental policy are formidable: valuation problems (e.g. relating to pollution damages (see Hearne, 1996; Winpenny, 1996), pollution control costs, discounted resource values); problems associated with their practical implementation (charging the polluter for a comprehensive array of pollutants—with all the risks of distortions to relative prices if the system is not comprehensive); problems of political acceptance (charges, in particular, are not popular); problems associated with ambiguities over property rights (though these are not peculiar to economic instruments); and problems due to distortions in charges systems where they have been captured to serve other purposes (e.g. for tax revenue raising purposes). The net result is that, in all countries, economic instruments are still only applied to a very small proportion of polluting and other environmental activities and in most cases the levels and structures of the charges and subsidies are not consistent with either efficiency or cost-effectiveness criteria (OECD 1994c, 1996a).

4.2. DIRECT REGULATIONS

Direct regulations (command and control instruments) are the predominant instruments of environmental policy in all countries despite their widely acknowledged deficiencies (e.g. they are not closely related to efficiency objectives, they are not cost-effective, and there are serious problems of non-compliance especially in LDCs and CITs; Dasgupta *et al.*, 1995; Pargal *et al.*, 1995). Another problem with regulations is that they can be counterproductive, in so far as they ignore the underlying economic incentives that lead to environmentally damaging behaviour and, in some situations, may even exacerbate it (e.g. bans on log exports may accelerate deforestation and bans on trade in ivory may decrease the elephant population). However, given their greater political acceptability, it is likely to be more practical in the short-term to achieve improvements in environmental performance through direct regulations than economic instruments but unrealistic to assume that entirely satisfactory performance can be achieved by such means alone.

4.3. PLANNING AND EVALUATION INSTRUMENTS

If all environmental externalities were internalised and all decision-makers were rational and perfectly informed, then planning and evaluation instruments would be unnecessary or, at most, be of limited significance. Given that these conditions do not apply, they have a potentially useful supportive role to play, in conjunction with regulatory and economic instruments, in achieving environmental policy objectives.

For present purposes, the main concern is how environmental considerations are to be integrated into the preparation, approval and implementation of market liberalisation policies, plans and programmes (which eventually translate into the implementation of individual projects). The current thinking (given the imperfections already mentioned in the case of economic instruments and direct regulations), is to use planning and evaluation instruments to (a) encourage the more systematic consideration of environmental impacts in the early stages of preparing policies, plans, programmes and projects; (b) integrate the resulting environmental assessment findings into the approval procedure for those policies, plans and programmes; and (c) ensure that the monitoring of their implementation takes place and that appropriate remedial action is taken where there is non-compliance or unexpected environmental impacts occur for other reasons. The next section considers, therefore, the relationship between environmental planning and evaluation instruments and market liberalisation, and the implications of the latter for the effectiveness of the former.

5. Cost–benefit analysis, environmental assessment and market liberalisation

5.1. COST–BENEFIT ANALYSIS

Economists understandably turn first to cost–benefit analysis (CBA) as the primary tool of investment appraisal at the project level. The underlying logic of taking all social costs and benefits into account across generations is hard to challenge. However, there are continuing debates over the detailed methods by which this is achieved (Kirkpatrick and Weiss, 1996). One of these, which is of primary interest, concerns the monetary valuation of environmental benefits and disbenefits. Here, also, it is necessary to be realistic—despite the advances over the last 25 years (e.g. in contingent valuation/ stated preference techniques), there are many environmental impacts for which the valuation method and the resulting findings are not sufficiently widely accepted so that, for example, they will stand up to successful cross-examination in a public enquiry (Abelson, 1996; Winpenny, 1996). The state of the art is such that for project appraisal purposes, environmental impacts often have to be ignored or they have to be expressed in their physical form. Given that the former is unsatisfactory, acceptance of the latter means logically that appraisal based on a single value NPV (net present value) has to be abandoned and be replaced by an evaluation framework or approach (involving multi-criteria or multi-objective analysis) in which the NPV is only one of the inputs (Lee and Kirkpatrick, 1996; Newton, 1995).

Additionally, it should be noted, the scope for applying social cost benefit analysis may be sharply reduced in a privatised market system since private enterprises may only feel obliged to take private benefits and costs into account in project appraisals. Also, CBA is primarily a project-level appraisal technique—practical experience in its use at the policy, plan and programme level is much more limited.

5.2. ENVIRONMENTAL ASSESSMENT

This leads on to the consideration of the nature and role of the environmental assessment (EA) of projects. This is both a method of project appraisal and a process for integrating environmental considerations into the project cycle. As a method its purpose is to assess the significant environmental impacts which may result from a proposed project. There is no restriction on the form in which those impacts may be expressed (physical, monetary, or both)—the choice is to be determined by the state of knowledge, the use to which the information is to be put and its likely political acceptability for this purpose. The methods used are drawn from different social science and scientific disciplines and there are, at the project level at least, fairly standard methodological steps through which the analysis proceeds—describing the project and highlighting those of its features which may give rise to environmental impacts, describing the base-line environmental conditions, predicting the magnitude of the changes that are expected to occur to the base-line conditions, evaluating the significance of those changes and integrating these into the overall project evaluation (Canter, 1996). In order to focus these assessment activities, screening methods are used to help in deciding which projects should be submitted to EIA and scoping methods are used to help in identifying particular types of impacts which are likely to require assessment.

However, EIA is also a process whose main components are now typically regulated by law (unlike CBA). All OECD countries now have their own EIA legislation, and virtually all of the major international and bilateral donor agencies and banks have their own EIA procedures which make aid loans and grants conditional upon conformity with those procedures (Lee, 1995; OECD, 1996b). A significant and rapidly increasing number of LDCs and CITs also have their own EIA procedures, although many are very recent and some are not yet functioning very effectively (Fisher, 1994; EIA Centre, 1995). These procedures and regulations contain provisions relating to screening, scope of assessments, responsibilities for their preparation, publication of EISs (environmental impact statements), provisions for consultation and public participation, integration of EIS and consultation findings into decision-making (e.g. permit approvals), mitigation, monitoring and management plans. Their overall purpose is to try to ensure that EIA is not a "stand-alone" study which fails to be integrated into the project planning, decision-making and implementation cycle.

5.3. STRATEGIC ENVIRONMENTAL ASSESSMENT

A relatively new development, which is at a much earlier stage in its evolution, is the use of a more strategic-level environment assessment process and method (SEA) for application at earlier stages in the planning process than the individual project authorisation stage, (see Figure 2 which illustrates the underlying similarities between EIA and SEA processes) (Lee and Walsh, 1992). A UNECE Working Party recommended in 1992 the adoption of such an approach for policies, plans and programmes (PPPs) that might give rise to significant environmental impacts and outlined a set of guiding principles and procedures for such a system (UNECE, 1992). The EU is developing its own proposal for a directive on SEA to complement its existing

246   **Market liberalisation and environmental assessment**

<u>Principal stages in the process</u>

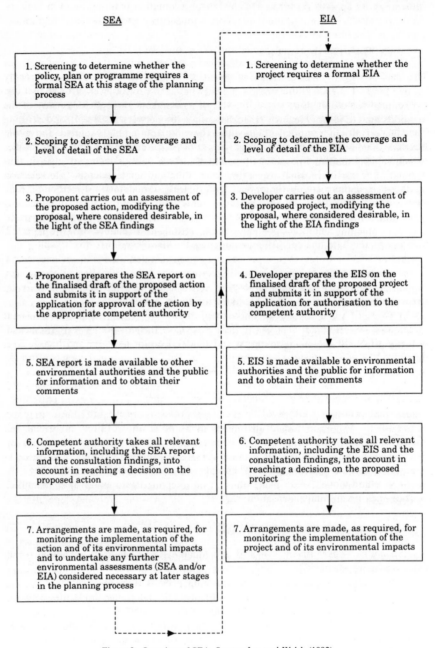

Figure 2. Overview of SEA. Source: Lee and Walsh (1992).

directive on EIA at the project sector level which was approved in 1985. A case study, illustrating its application in the Dutch transport situation is to be found in Niekerk and Arts (1996). Its application in relation to Structural Adjustment Programmes (SAPs) is described in Abaza (1996). The case for its more extended future use is presented in Sadler (1995) and Sadler and Verheem (1996).

Wood and Djeddour (1992) have identified a range of different assessment methods that may be used to undertake each of the tasks in the SEA process. These are broadly of two kinds. First, there are methods already in use in project-level EIA but that can be adapted for use at more strategic levels of assessment. These include many of the methods used to identify impacts (checklists, matrices, network analyses), for describing base-line conditions, for predicting pollution impacts from multiple sources, and so on. Second, there are those methods already used in policy analysis and planning studies which can be adapted for use in SEA. These include various forms of scenario and simulation analysis, regional forecasting and input–output techniques, site selection and land suitability analysis, geographical information systems (GIS), systems modelling (for instance, for traffic networks, energy systems, water resource systems), policy and programme evaluation techniques (such as multi-criteria analysis, goals achievement analysis, planning balance sheet approaches, cost–benefit analysis, constrained cost minimisation analysis, sensitivity analysis, and other techniques for handling uncertainty).

A number of individual countries have begun to adopt an embryonic form of SEA for certain of their PPPs. Both the U.S.A. and Canadian Governments, for example, have prepared EISs (or their equivalent) for the North American Free Trade Agreement (NAFTA) and the Uruguay Round of the GATT Agreement, and environmental assessment is increasingly reflected in the Country Assistance Strategies (CASs) which are the principal statements of the World Bank's overall development strategy in a borrowing country (World Bank, 1995).

5.4. Environmental assessment of market liberalisation measures

Given the widespread adoption of environmental assessment procedures, they are a potentially important policy instrument to apply in the planning, approval and implementation of those market liberalisation measures which may have significant environmental impacts. First, since most of these measures are initially introduced at the policy, plan or programmes level, it is likely that SEA rather that EIA will be the form of environmental assessment which is more commonly applied. If so, it will be necessary to ensure that the "state of the art" of SEA is sufficiently developed for this purpose.

Moreover, their practical effectiveness is likely to be strongly influenced by the process of market liberalisation and de-regulation, which may reduce the impact of SEA and EIA procedures. In some cases, reducing the regulatory burden may entail simplifying authorisation procedures or exempting enterprises from environmental permitting requirements (Anon, 1994). In other cases, in order to speed up the privatisation process, EIA procedural requirements may be waived or commenced too late in the approval process. Different EIA provisions may be applied for public and private enterprises; privatisation may therefore diminish (though it could extend) the overall area of application of EIA. A further possibility is that market liberalisation measures, combined with macro-economic stabilisation measures, may reduce government expenditure levels leading to staffing cuts in environmental ministries which diminish their capability to direct and manage the EIA system. Finally, if property rights and associated environmental obligations are not clarified as part of the process of land privatisation, the responsibilities for inherited and future environmental liabilities will be unclear and this could seriously reduce the potential benefits from using EA instruments.

In principle, however, these difficulties could be avoided by carefully checking that the form taken by market liberalisation measures does not undermine the effectiveness of the EA instruments and other environmental regulations which are in place.

6. Conclusions and follow-up work

Three main issues arise from the above review, to which the following provisional answers may be given: First, should market liberalisation measures be subject to some form of environmental assessment? The short answer is that they should if their implementation is likely to give rise to significant environmental impacts. Since many of these measures will be at the strategic level of policies, plans and programmes, SEA is likely to be the more common requirement although EIA (possibly incorporating an environmental audit component to address concerns over environmental liabilities, particularly in CITs) will also be needed for some, more specific, privatisation schemes. Among the desirable mitigating measures which EA should highlight are any corrections for market imperfections and other policy failures which may contribute to the occurrence of significant negative environmental impacts. Second, can environmental assessment procedures be satisfactorily applied in a liberalised market system? As indicated in Section 5, the answer given is a qualified "yes"—provided the necessary corrective measures are taken to ensure their continued effectiveness and to avoid any weakening of this as an unintended side effect of particular forms of privatisation and de-regulation. Third, can SEA be satisfactorily applied to market liberalisation measures in the LDC/CIT context? Here also a qualified positive answer can be given—provided certain additional measures are taken.

At the political level, increased awareness and acceptability of the value of SEA as a policy instrument is needed. This can be helped by demonstrating, in the form of real case examples, how SEA can work satisfactorily in practice. Some examples already exist (see, for example, de Boer and Sadler, 1996; Sadler and Verheem, 1996; Therivel and Partidario 1996) but additional SEA case studies, undertaken in different types of economy, are also needed (Cassios, 1995).

At the procedural level, the primary need is to identify the most appropriate ways in which to link SEA procedures to existing market liberalisation policy, plan or programme procedures and to tackle sensitively any concerns over confidentiality which may arise in doing so.

At the methodological level, the basic requirement is to identify and develop the most appropriate ways in which to link and analyse the key relationships between two systems—the economic development system and the environmental system (Munasinghe and Cruz, 1995; Reed, 1996). There is an existing body of scientific and technical knowledge which needs to be carefully evaluated for use in the environmental assessment of market liberalisation measures. Particular attention should be given to three issues: the level of detail at which different types of SEA may need to be undertaken; the likely availability of data in typical LDC and CIT situations; and the most appropriate ways in which to handle the substantial uncertainties which arise in this type of assessment work.

The follow-up work which is most urgently needed in these three areas can be deduced from the conclusions already reached. It should include: (i) a review of the principal ways in which market liberalisation measures may weaken the effectiveness of EA procedures and of the most appropriate actions which might address such problems; (ii) a review of the principal technical requirements in linking and analysing relationships between economic development/trade systems and environmental systems, and of the extent to which existing knowledge can meet these requirements; and (iii) *ex-antelex-post* EA case studies of the application of market liberalisation measures in different LDC and CIT contexts.

Thanks are due to David Glover, and participants at the conference on *Development Projects: Issues for the 1990s*, University of Bradford, April 1995 and to two anonymous referees, for helpful comments on an earlier version of the paper.

References

Abaza, H. (1996). Integration of sustainability objectives in structural adjustment programmes through the use of strategic environmental assessment. *Project Appraisal* 11, 217–228.

Abelson, P. (1996). *Project Appraisal and Valuation of the Environment.* Basingstoke: MacMillan Press.

Anderson, K. and Blackhurst, R. (eds) (1992). *The Greening of World Trade Issues,* London: Wheatsheaf.

Anon (1996). Deregulation cuts into environmental assessment. *ENDS* 230, 34–35.

Beghin, J., Roland-Holst, D., van de Mensbrugghe, D. (1994). A survey of the trade and environmental nexus: global dimensions. *OECD Economic Studies* 23, 167–192.

de Boer, J. and Sadler, B. (eds) (1996). *Strategic Environmental Assessment: Environmental Assessment of Policies.* Briefing Paper on Experience in Selected Countries, no. 54, Ministry of Housing, Spatial Planning and the Environment, The Hague.

Canter, L.W. (1996). *Environmental Impact Assessment,* 2nd edn. New York: McGraw Hill.

Cassios, C. (ed.) (1995). *Environmental Impact Assessment Methodology and Research.* Third EU Workshop on Environmental Impact Assessment. Brussels: European Commission.

Cook, P. and Kirkpatrick, C. (1995). *Privatisation Policy and Performance: International Perspectives.* London: Harvester-Wheatsheaf.

Cook, P. and Kirkpatrick, C. (1996). Privatisation in transitional economies: East and Central European experience. In *International Business and Europe in Transition* (F. Burton, M. Yamin and S. Young, eds), pp. 168–183.

Cromwell, E. and Winpenny, J. (1993). Does economic reform harm the environment? A review of structural adjustment in Malawi. *Journal of International Development* 5, 623–650.

Dasgupta, S., Mody, A., Roy, S. and Wheeler, D. (1995). Environmental regulation and development: a cross-country empirical analysis. Mimeo. Washington DC: World Bank.

EIA Centre (1995). *EIA in Developing Countries.* Leaflet 15. Manchester: Department of Planning, University of Manchester.

Fisher, D. (ed.) (1994). *Environmental Impact Assessment Legislation.* Graham and Trotman (for European Bank for Reconstruction and Development) London.

Goldenman, G. (1995). *Environmental Liability and Privatisation in Central and Eastern Europe.* A Report for the Environmental Action Programme for Central and Eastern Europe OECD/World Bank, Paris and Washington DC.

Hearne, R.R. (1996). A review of economic appraisal of environmental goods and services in development projects. *Project Appraisal.* 11, 255–260.

International Monetary Fund (IMF) (1996). *Annual Report.* Washington DC: IMF.

Kirkpatrick, C. (1995). Does trade liberalisation assist third world industrial development? Recent experience and lessons. *International Review of Applied Economics* 9, 22–40.

Kirkpatrick, C. and Weiss, J. (eds) (1996). *Cost Benefit Analysis and Project Appraisal in Developing Countries.* Cheltenham: Edward Elgar.

Kitetu, J. J. and Rowan, J. S. (in press). Integrated environmental assessment applied to river sand harvesting in Kenya. In: *Sustainable Development in a Developing World: Integrating Socio-Economic Appraisal and Environmental Assessment.* (C. Kirkpatrick and N. Lee, eds). Cheltenham: Edward Elgar.

Lee, N. and Walsh, F. (1992). Strategic environmental assessment: an overview. *Project Appraisal* 7, 126–136.

Lee, N. (1995). Environmental assessment in the European Union: a tenth anniversary. *Project Appraisal* 10, 77–90.

Lee, N. and Kirkpatrick, C. (1996). The relevance and consistency of EIA and CBA in project appraisal. *Project Appraisal* 11, 229–236.

Low, P. (ed.) (1992). *International Trade and the Environment*. World Bank Discussion Paper no. 59. Washington DC: World Bank. 126–136.

Munasinghe, M. and Cruz, W. (1995). *Economy-wide Policies and the Environment: Lessons from Experience*. World Bank Environmental Paper No. 10. Washington: World Bank.

Newton, J.A. (1995). *The Integration of Socio-Economic Impacts in Environmental Impact Assessment and Project Appraisal* MSc dissertation, University of Manchester, Manchester (*mimeo*).

Niekerk, F. and Arts, F. (1996). Impact assessments in Dutch infrastructure planning: towards a better timing and integration. *Project Appraisal* **11**, 237–246.

OECD (1994a). *The Environmental Effects of Trade*. Paris: OECD.

OECD (1994b). *Methodologies for Environment and Trade Reviews*. Paris: OECD.

OECD (1994c). *Managing the Environment: the Role of Economic Instruments*. Paris: OECD.

OECD (1996a). *Coherence in Environmental Assessment: Practical Guidance on Development Co-operation Projects*. Paris: OECD.

OECD (1996b). *Integrating Environmental Economy: Progress in the 1990s*. Paris: OECD.

Pargal, S., Hettige, H., Singh M. and Wheeler, D. (1995). Formal and informal regulation of industrial pollution: evidence from Indonesia and the U.S. *Mimeo*. Washington DC: World Bank.

Potier, M. (in press). Environmental assessment of trade liberalisation: an OECD perspective. In *Sustainable Development in a Developing World: Integrating Socio-Economic Appraisal and Environmental Assessment*. (C. Kirkpatrick and N. Lee, eds), Cheltenham: Edward Elgar.

Reed, D. (1992). *Structural Adjustment and the Environment*. London: Earthscan.

Reed, D. (ed.) (1996). *Structural Adjustment, the Environment and Sustainable Development*. London: Earthscan.

Richardson, J.A. (1996). *Structural Adjustment and Environmental Linkages*. London: Overseas Development Institute.

Sadler, B. (1995). *Environmental Assessment in a Changing World: Final Report*. International Study of the Effectiveness of Environmental Assessment. Hull, Quebec: Canadian Environmental Assessment Agency.

Sadler, B. and Verheem, R. (1996). *Strategic Environmental Assessment: Status, Challenges and Future Directions*, no. 53. The Hague: Ministry of Housing, Spatial Planning and the Environment.

Therivel, R. and Partidario, M. (1996). *The Practice of Strategic Environmental Assessment*. London: Earthscan.

UNCTAD (1995). *Comparative Experiences with Privatisation: Policy Insights and Lessons Learned*. Geneva: United Nations.

United Nations Economic Commission for Europe (1992). *Application of Environmental Assessment Principles to Policies, Plans and Programmes*. Geneva: UNECE.

United Nations Economic Commission for Europe/United Nations Environment Programme (1994). *Guidelines on Environmental Management in Countries in Transition*. New York: United Nations.

United Nations Economic Commission for Europe (1996). *Environmental Performance Reviews: Estonia*. New York: United Nations.

Warford, J., Schwab, A., Cruz, W. and Hansen, S. (1994). *The Evolution of Environmental Concerns in Adjustment Lending*. Environment Working Paper No. 65. Washington DC: World Bank.

Winpenny, J. (1996). Economic valuation of environmental impacts: the temptations of EVE. *Project Appraisal* **11**, 247–254.

Wood, C. and Djeddour, M. (1992). Strategic environmental assessment: EA of policies, plans and programmes. *Impact Assessment Bulletin* **10**, 3–22.

World Bank (1994). *Environmental Assessment Sourcebook Update: Privatisation and Environmental Assessment: Issues and Approaches* (No. 6). Washington DC: World Bank.

World Bank (1995). *Mainstreaming the Environment*. The World Bank Group and the Environment since the Rio Earth Summit. Washington DC: World Bank.

World Bank (1996a). *Environmental Sourcebook, Update: Regional Environmental Assessment* (No. 14). Washington DC: World Bank.

World Bank (1996b). *World Development Report: From Plan to Market*. Oxford and New York: Oxford University Press for the World Bank.

World Bank (1996c). *Bureaucrats in Business: The Economics and Politics of Government Ownership*. World Bank Policy Research Report. Washington DC: World Bank.

Part III
Rural Sector Issues

A
Agriculture

[16]

Journal of Agricultural Economics — Volume 50, Number 3 — September 1999 — Pages 371-387

The Challenge of Sustainability at the Farm Level: Presidential Address

Paul Webster

*T*he sustainability of farming systems is currently under debate. There is concern that technological and other changes have long-run consequences, which may compromise future levels of desired outputs from agricultural and other resources. The paper traces developments in the theory of sustainability and discusses their application at the farm level. Findings include firstly, that sustainability should be regarded as an emergent property of an agricultural system. Its operational definition at the farm level thus may not apply at other levels in the hierarchy. Secondly, whilst individual farmers may attach value to "sustainability" goods, they are unlikely to adopt socially optimal levels without regulation or incentive. Finally, since sustainability issues at the farm level are usually long-run, dynamic and have social dimensions, a central task for farm management researchers lies in investigations which allow tradeoffs between different sustainability criteria to be determined and then optimised according to society's norms.

1. Introduction

This paper deals with the implications at the farm level resulting from a change of emphasis in the demands placed upon agriculture by society at large. The unpriced outputs of agricultural systems, both positive and negative, have become of increased importance as compared with conventional marketed outputs. In addition, there is concern that, whilst technical changes have brought major benefits to consumers in terms of reduced food prices, some developments have taken us into uncharted waters. Society, sensitised by problems of pollution, health and other issues arising from earlier technical developments, appears less ready to accept change, which may involve consequences which might be damaging and irreversible. Hence the need for caution and reappraisal. Such concerns underlie the move to a spectrum of production systems ranging from "organic", "alternative", and "integrated" farming systems. The long-term sustainability of our farming systems is thus under debate. The question is "how can we induce progress towards farming systems which are sustainable and how might we measure that progress?"

Whilst much of this debate goes on at the aggregate level, it is the individual farmer or manager who makes the major land use decisions and who chooses what he or she

■ Paul Webster is Professor of Agricultural Business Management at Wye College, University of London. Acknowledgements are due to John Lingard, Uwe Lohmann, John Nix and Nigel Williams for helpful comments on an earlier draft of this paper, which was the Presidential Address at the Society's Annual Conference in Belfast in March 1999.

regards as the appropriate technology with which to operate. Furthermore, in a small, crowded country such as the UK, the farmer often feels that he or she takes the blame if things go wrong. A recent development has been the proposal of indicators to measure sustainability. But the question is whether there is a logic to their specification or whether they are merely arbitrary selections of characteristics of particular interest to their author. My aim is to review the theory and principles underlying sustainability and thus to try to place in context the application of the concept at the farm level.

As far as indicators per se are concerned, it is the case that farmers are well used to managing their business on the basis of financial indicators. Moreover, they have long recognised the ability of others, with property rights to parts of their business, to influence decisions on the basis of such indicators. Their bank managers may take great interest in such indicators of financial sustainability as net worth, percentage equity and other ratios. At the same time, those with long memories will recall the use of survey-constructed indicators of performance in the 1950s and 1960s known as farm standards. One of the criticisms of the approach at the time was that there was no direct or theoretical relationship between the levels of these indicators and the wider maximisation of returns to the farmer (Candler and Sargent, 1961). It is a lesson worth remembering today in the context of sustainability indicators.

The next section reviews some recent economic theory relating to sustainability in order to clarify the basic concepts and to illuminate some of the current debates about the applicability of such concepts. The paper then points out the need for recognition of the hierarchical nature of agricultural systems when attempting to produce operational definitions of sustainability. Given that many of the components of sustainable systems involve unpriced outputs and inputs, the mechanisms by which sustainability might be promoted are then reviewed, and their consequences analysed at the farm level. Finally, the paper attempts to draw a few conclusions.

2. Economic Concepts of Sustainability

Maintenance of Utility Over Time

Nix (1990) pointed out that the idea of sustainability is central to attempts to define farm income. He quoted Hicks (1946) who defined income as that which could be consumed in a given period leaving the consumer as well off at the end of the period as at the start. Since those days, the definition as to what constitutes capital has widened. Recent theories of economic growth have built upon neoclassical foundations (Solow, 1992) and recognise that aggregate capital (K) consists of manmade capital, K_m, plus natural capital, K_n, plus human capital, K_h, and social capital K_s, such that

$$K = K_m + K_n + K_h + K_s \tag{1}$$

The quantity and quality of this capital determines the level of provision of utility for humankind on a year by year basis (Pearce, 1998). The notion of sustainability arises when it is required that the capacity of K to produce utility from one period to the next does not decline. Important modifiers to K include technological change, which may be regarded as endogenous or exogenous, and population growth, which may have positive or negative impacts on the components of capital.

Strong or Weak Sustainability

The distinction between "weak" sustainability and "strong" sustainability hinges upon whether substitution is permitted between the components of K in equation 1 (Turner, 1993). Weak sustainability implies that substitution may take place in order to maintain K. In other words, rates of substitution or elasticities are assumed to exist. In contrast, strong sustainability does not permit substitution between components of K and the emphasis is placed on conserving K_n (and each of its separate sub-components) at all costs. Arguments for such an approach include the irreversibility of some changes in natural capital (e.g., species extinction) and evidence of "kinked" utility functions for consumers who may attach a higher value to losses as compared with gains (Tversky and Kahneman, 1981). A more basic argument for strong sustainability is the view that natural capital is impossible to value by whatever means. A consequence of this view is that without a numeraire of any sort, no trade-offs could be made within K_n, or any level of subdivision of K_n, (for example at the individual species or community), thus ensuring no reduction in any natural characteristic or consequent increase in another. Such an approach would be highly restrictive for the farm manager, to say the least.

However other writers (e.g., van der Hamsfoort and Latacz-Lohmann, 1998) have argued for strong sustainability on the basis of the second law of thermodynamics (the entropy law) which implies a limit to the stock of energy available to mankind for transforming low-entropy natural capital through manufactured capital to high-entropy waste products. Given this limit, it is argued that K_m and K_n should be complements rather than substitutes. There are clear implications for energy production and use at the farm level.

The operational consequences of the strong sustainability view have been developed by Costanza and Daly (1992) who suggested that the total value of human welfare should be limited to the carrying capacity of the existing stocks of capital. Likewise, technological progress should only be applied to maintaining current levels of welfare, and in order to reduce dependence on manufactured capital or enhance the value of natural capital. Renewable natural capital should only be used up to the point where harvest rates are less than regeneration rates and where waste products are limited at levels below the natural assimilative capacities. Finally, recognising the difficulty of implementing a strict rule against *any* depletion of non-renewable natural capital, they suggested that extraction of such capital be restricted to the rate at which renewable substitutes could be developed. It seems clear that major shifts in social objectives amongst farmers as well as the rest of society would be needed if such precepts were to be adopted.

Social Capital

Whilst the notions of man-made capital and human capital are well known in the economics literature, the concept of social capital and its influence upon human utility is more recent (e.g., Putnam, 1993). Social relationships can engender trust between individuals, leading to reduced search times for information, reduced transactions costs and reduced need for policing costs. Community membership could mean a reduction in the costs of externalities if the norms of those communities suggested particular courses of action to members (Colman, 1994). Examples relating to agriculture might include the existence of machinery rings or landcare groups (OECD, 1998). At the same time there may be negative effects on aggregate welfare if such communities engaged in anti-competitive practices, "crony" capitalism, "mafia" type activities and so on. This is a new area for research but would seem to be a fruitful topic, given the importance of remoteness and isolation in many farming communities (e.g., Copus and Crabtree, 1996).

3. Application of these Concepts at the Level of the Farm

"Farm as though you would live for ever"

With the forgoing theoretical background in mind, we now turn to the application of these concepts at the farm level. The preponderance of decisions about the use of land, a major component of natural capital, are made by farmers and their families who have access to specific amounts of various types of capital, and have to cope with a decision environment shaped by natural, social and political and, of course, economic considerations.

The general idea that the farming system must be sustainable over a long period is, of course, well known to farmers and is encapsulated in such aphorisms as "live as though you would die tomorrow but farm as though you would live forever". But this view does suggest an economic, social and scientific environment which changes but slowly: one in which the consequences of actions in the long run are well known, predictable and therefore avoidable if the consequences are negative. The speed of technological change in the latter half of the twentieth century means that this assumption can no longer be relied upon. In developed agricultures, technological development in the form of the application of new scientific knowledge has often been used to attempt to maintain sustainability of farm incomes in the face of declining product prices (Willard Cochrane's well-known technology trap).

Table 1 lists the main subcategories of the four types of capital referred to earlier and which are available to farmers. Whilst the concern at the aggregate level is to sustain the flow of utility to society, the farmer's aim is to sustain the flow of utility to his or her family. The farmer's task is to allocate his or her capital to those activities which maximise the flow of utility in a sustainable manner. Farmers are expected to take advantage of education and of social networks. Many in the UK are now concerned as to how they as a group should interact with the rest of society which, of course, constitutes the vast majority of the population. Problems arise for society as a whole when, either by choice, ignorance or other means, the sustainability of the farmer's utility flow, or that of others in the community, is compromised by his or her own activities (Pearce and Tinch, 1998; Batie, 1989).

In the case of the use of man-made capital, social capital and human capital, it will often be the case that there will be few conflicts between the maximisation of a farmer's utility

Table 1 A Classification of Types of Capital Available to Farmers

Man-made	• Buildings, machinery and equipment
	• Livestock and related technology, breeds, feeds, promoters etc.
	• Crop technology; seeds, fertiliser, sprays etc.
	• Landscape microfeatures; hedges, field sizes and margins, etc.
Natural	• Land and soils quality
	• Natural environment; air, water, flora and fauna
	• Landscape macrofeatures
	• Energy
Human	• Management and labour force
	• Knowledge, skills and expertise
Social	• Community and group membership
	• Institutions, etc.
	• Social relationships

and society's utility. But it is in the interactions of these three types of capital with the fourth, namely natural capital, that the problems lie. In particular, the main sources of conflict relate to the interactions between man-made and natural capital.

Sustainability as a Social Construct

One of the difficulties of the concept of sustainability is that, ultimately, it is a social construct. Like truth, beauty and courage, its precise definition depends to some extent on the standpoint of the observer (Norgaard, 1994; Bell and Morse, 1999). In practice, at least three types of questions need to be answered (Lele and Norgaard, 1996):

(i)   What is to be sustained, at what scale and in what form?

(ii) Over what time period and with what level of certainty?

(iii) Through what social process and with what trade-offs against other social goals?

Attempts to produce such answers will entail the reconciliation of major differences in the world-view of the participants, their value judgements and the status of the knowledge used to inform the debate. It is clear that definitions must emerge as a result of some form of "political" process to which the various sectors of society, informed about the problems and possibilities, can contribute (Pannell and Schillizzi, 1997; Bell and Morse, 1999). The need for agreement does create the requirement for social institutions whereby such agreements can be generated. It is not clear that such institutions yet exist in the UK, despite the efforts of many limited-issue pressure groups.

A Hierarchy of Sustainability Definitions

The recognition of agricultural systems as a hierarchy may help us to clarify issues of concern at various levels (Kruseman *et al.*, 1996).

The concept is of a global system consisting of independent yet interdependent nations. Each nation's agriculture consists of a number of groups of farmers embedded within a

376   *P. Webster*

Table 2   A Means-Ends Hierarchy Relating to Agricultural Sustainability

Level	Ends	Means
Global	Maintenance of global human welfare (e.g., WCED, 1987)	WCED, WTO, International Treaties, etc.
National	e.g., "Food Security", "Vibrant Countryside", etc. (MAFF, 1991)	Agri-environmental and other policies implemented by national governments
Regional/ Community	e.g. Maintenance of local employment, markets, communities, landscapes (OECD, 1998)	Regional policies, Agenda 21 plans, implemented by Regional and local bodies, e.g., Landcare Groups, Regional Development Agencies
Farm	Farm family goals, etc., within the existing economic and regulatory framework (e.g., McGregor, *et al.*, 1996)	Selection and combination of farm and other enterprises
Enterprise	Contribution to "fixed" costs, subject to interactions with other farm and non-farm enterprises (e.g., Barnett *et al.*, 1995)	Selection and use of cultural and other techniques

community. Farmers, with goals of their own, choose from a variety of enterprises as production systems in order to fulfil those goals. Concerns about sustainability appear at each level and, whilst exhortations to "think globally and act locally" are laudable, the farmer or manager cannot be expected automatically to take account of higher level goals when deciding what technology to adopt.

Table 2 shows such a hierarchy. Definitions of sustainability at a higher level only have meaning for a lower level if there are no interactions between the lower level systems. Since such interactions will normally exist, any operational definition of sustainability can only be regarded as an emergent property of a particular level within the hierarchy of agricultural systems. Thus to define the concept at one level and to attempt to apply it at another level may lead to confusion. What may be regarded as unsustainable at the individual farm level may, when all farms are taken into account, indeed be sustainable at the national level. Micro-conditions on one farm, when aggregated with micro-conditions on another, may produce a different picture at the community level. The same is true at higher levels. Does variability of natural populations matter within countries if aggregate populations are maintained across countries? Information must move up and down the hierarchy in order to achieve workable, local solutions and institutions are needed to facilitate this process (Lowe *et al.*, 1998).

4.   Achieving Sustainability at the Farm Level

The Production of "Sustainability Goods"

One view of the problem would hold that higher level ends are not automatically maximised by lower level ends because property rights have not been clearly defined. The policy implication of this weak sustainability position would be to assign property rights and to develop markets in the commodities so created. It is clear that there are such possibilities for some types of pollution and landscape features (e.g., Spash and

Simpson, 1994). The alternative view, involving a stronger definition of sustainability, would hold that some goods defy monetisation and must therefore involve regulation. These differences of view account for those who look for "root and branch" changes in society's attitude to natural capital and the more gradualist approach favoured by others (Schaller, 1993).

A simple product-product diagram serves to illuminate some of the problems surrounding farm management involving sustainability considerations. Figure 1 shows the situation of the utility maximising farmer whose utility function, UU, has two arguments, namely money income from marketed agricultural production and psychic income derived from the production of what McInerney (1986) called CARE goods and are here referred to as sustainability goods. Sustainability goods comprise those characteristics which go to make up the non-marketed aspects of sustainability, as defined by the social process referred to earlier.

With a given stock of resources at his disposal the farmer faces a production possibility curve, RSTV, such that over a restricted range, production of the two goods is complementary. Starting at point R in the diagram, very low levels of marketed output are insufficient to sustain a farm family, let alone perhaps, a community. Increased levels of sustainability are achieved with more marketed output. Beyond maximum sustainability at point S, the farmer moves to higher levels of agricultural production up to a maximum at V, but there is competition for resources such that production of sustainability goods is reduced. Such goods are therefore joint products only over a restricted range of the agricultural production function. At the farmer's utility-maximising point T, the farmer's psychic income will only include his own willingness to pay for sustainability goods and not that of the rest of society. Since they are not marketed, these goods will usually be under-produced.

Figure 1 Production Possibility Curve for a Hypothetical Farm

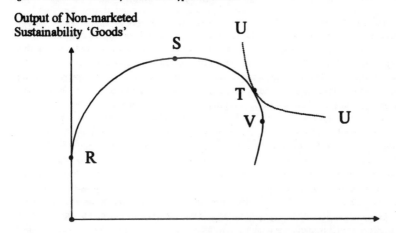

Output of Non-marketed
Sustainability 'Goods'

Output of Marketed Agricultural Products

This simple analysis does raise a number of important issues. The non-linear two-dimensional utility function recognises that many farmers do take account of non-financial aspects (Burton *et al.*, 1999, McGregor *et al.*, 1996). It also points out the distinction between firstly, the role of the market and society, via product prices and agri-environmental incentives, in fixing the position and slope of the farmer's indifference curve and secondly, the role of the farmer whose task is to understand the nature of the production surface. His or her task includes understanding the consequences of movement along the production surface or, in the case of technological developments such as precision farming (Cain *et al.*, 1997), from one surface to another.

Mechanisms for Enhancing Sustainability

Where society determines that sustainability goods are under-produced, there are a number of mechanisms by which the decision environment of the farmer can be modified. These include:

(i)   Subsidies on positive sustainability goods

(ii)   Taxes on negative sustainability goods

(iii) Regulatory measures to enforce maximum or minimum limits on specific characteristics

(iv)   Indicators as means of education and persuasion

The literature relating to the theory of environmental pricing and of regulatory instruments is extensive (e.g., Bromley, 1995; Laffont and Tirole, 1993). The literature relating to its application to agriculture in the search for appropriate instruments is also massive and increasing by the day (e.g., Hanley, 1991; Moxey and White, 1994; Pan and Hodge, 1995; Russell and Fraser, 1995; Wu and Babcock, 1996).

The subsidy or tax approach can be expected to work well where there is a direct relationship between the sustainability good being produced and the mechanism used to price it. If particular features, such as hedgerows or numbers of a particular type of bird, emerge from the social process as being highly valued then payments per unit of the desired feature would give clear signals and objectives to farmers and managers. Bearing in mind their preferences for gains as compared with aversion to losses (Tversky and Kahneman, 1981), farmers can be expected to react more favourably to positive incentives rather than restrictions on their activities. However, if benefits or damage are less direct, problems may arise. For example, pesticides include very many active ingredients with different degrees and types of effects on the environment (Ecotec, 1997). Each active ingredient has its own specific use and recommended dosage rate but without the smooth, differentiable response function required to give meaning to the concept of elasticity. Thus a blanket tax on all pesticides or even on pesticides grouped into a few categories is unlikely to deliver the expected environmental benefits, since the damage is only indirectly being approached. Milton Friedman's advice to "question the assumption, which is made *a priori* by economists, that no economic series or distribution ever has a discontinuity in the first derivative" is perhaps worth heeding (Friedman and

Friedman, 1998). The situation becomes more complex when it is recognised that many environmental problems of pesticides arise from their indirect effects on cropping systems and food supplies of natural fauna (Campbell and Cooke, 1997).

A further point about incentives relates to the discussion in the previous section concerning the production frontier. Lump sum payments, while perhaps easy to administer, provide no incentive for the farmer to explore his immediate production possibilities for the provision of sustainability goods at least cost. If effort is put into the design of policies which identify and provide payments based on quantity supplied, the skills, creativity and local knowledge of the farmer will be put to use in the search for ways of providing such goods. Lump sum payments may waste these valuable resources.

Suffice it to say here that the interest in sustainability indicators may arise from a perceived inadequacy of policy tools to deal satisfactorily with sustainability issues.

The Development of Indicators of Sustainability

On the basis of the theoretical concepts referred to earlier, various attempts have been made to define and measure sustainability at the aggregate economy level (Victor, 1991; Pearce and Atkinson, 1993). The World Bank (1997) has produced estimates for a number of countries and has shown that some economies, whilst sustainable when measured in conventional national accounting terms, have shown lack of sustainability when environmental and natural resource depletion is accounted for.

At the agricultural sector level, considerable effort is being expended in the search for appropriate indicators of sustainability (Brouwer and Crabtree, 1999). OECD (1997), using a "driving force state - response" framework, identified a series of 13 "priority issues". For each "issue", a number of potential indicators were suggested, based on such criteria as policy relevance, analytical soundness and measurability. The declared aim was to provide information to improve the targeting, monitoring and assessment of agri-environmental schemes.

This initiative has been followed by the publication of a consultative document by the UK government (MAFF, 1998). Proposals were set out for a series of 34 individual indicators based on 13 "themes". These are listed in Table 3. There is broad agreement between many of OECD's "issues" and MAFF's "themes". But it is interesting to note a greater emphasis in the OECD document upon the adoption of farm management practices (relating to nutrients, pests, irrigation and soils) and farm financial viability. In the MAFF document, there is more direct reference to the use of energy crops. Both documents emphasise the use of indicators for policy purposes.

Table 4 presents the interactions between man-made and natural capital in terms of the MAFF proposed themes. As expected, the emphasis is upon technology and its effects on natural capital. Gaps in the table, of course, may exist not necessarily because of the absence of interactions, but also possibly because of difficulties of measurement or perceived lack of current importance to the community.

The development of indicators at the policy level suggests that it is unlikely to be long before they are used at the individual farm level. Indeed, work is proceeding apace on a

Table 3   Issues and Themes for Agricultural Policy Indicators

OECD "Issues"	MAFF "Themes"		MAFF Proposed Indicators
Nutrient use	Nutrient losses to freshwater	1	N losses in selected catchments
	Soil P levels	2	P losses in selected catchments
	Nutrient management practices	3	Percentage land sampled for P Slurry storage and timing of application Nutrient application techniques
	Ammonia emissions	4	Quantity emitted
Greenhouse gases	Greenhouse gas emissions	5	CH_4 emissions NO emissions
Pesticide use	Pesticide use	6	Pesticides in rivers Pesticides in groundwater Quantity of active ingredient "Spray area" treated Number of wildlife "incidents" Residues in food
Water use Water quality	Water use	7	Storage capacity as percentage of irrigated use Economic value of irrigated crops
Soil quality	Soil protection	8	Topsoil organic matter content Topsoil heavy metal content Soil management practices
	Agricultural land resource	9	Area lost to non-agricultural development Area restored following mineral extraction or landfill
Land use and conservation Landscape Biodiversity Wildlife habitats	Conservation value of agricultural land	10	Area under environmental conservation Area under organic production Length of hedgerows and walls Population of key farmland birds Area of semi-natural grassland Area of field margin under environmental management Upland management
Farm management	Environmental management systems	11	Adoption of environmental management systems by farmers
Socio-cultural issues Farm financial resources	Rural economy	12	EU producer subsidy equivalent Environmental payments as percentage of CAP expenditure Agricultural productivity Rural unemployment
	Energy	13	Area planted with energy crops

Source: OECD, 1997; MAFF, 1998.

number of different aspects of the farm decision environment (e.g., Levitan *et al.*, 1995; Syers *et al.*, 1995; van Mansfelt, 1997; Tisdell, 1996; Girardin *et al.*, 1996; Duelli, 1997). The challenge is to ensure that the manager is equipped with enough knowledge about the consequences of alternative cropping regimes or techniques so that his decisions can be taken with a reasonable degree of certainty as to likely impacts on indicator levels (Yiridoe and Weersink, 1997). An ambitious development has been reported by Bockstaller *et al.* (1997) who, having identified seven sustainability objectives (relating to the protection of the quality of soil, water, air, non-renewable resource, biodiversity and landscape quality), proceeded to specify indicators regarded as under the direct control

Table 4 Indicators Relating to Interactions of Man-made and Natural Capital

Natural Capital	Man-made Capital			
	Buildings and Machinery	Livestock and Related Technology; Feeds, Breeds, Enhancers, etc.	Crop Technology; Seeds, Fertilisers Pesticides, Feed, Vet. and Medicine	Landscape Microfeatures: Hedges, Field Sizes and Margins, etc.
Air		4, 5	4, 5	
Water	7	1, 3, 5, 11	1, 5, 6, 11	
Soil	3, 8	3, 8, 11	2, 3, 8, 11	
Flora and fauna		11	6, 11	10, 11
Landscape macrofeatures		11	11	10, 11
Energy	13	11, 13	11, 13	

Note: The numbers in the cells refer to MAFF (1998) "Themes", as listed in Table 3.

Figure 2 Example "Amoeba Diagram" Showing the Use of Agro-ecological Indicators at the Farm Level

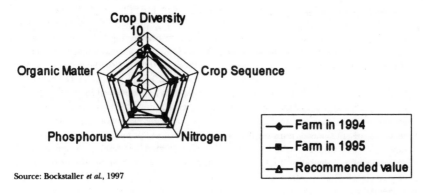

Source: Bockstaller *et al.*, 1997

of the farmer via his management practices. A technical research programme was proposed in which models of various types would be used to predict the effect of changes in the indicator levels upon the objectives. Values of the indicators were then scaled (1-10) with an expert-defined "acceptable" level specified as seven. The results for an individual farm were displayed as an "amoeba" diagram.

Figure 2 shows a prototype version with just five attributes. The aim was to advise the farmer as to how his system was performing in terms of the attributes. With developments in measuring and analysis techniques for some water pollutants (e.g., Pearce, 1999), together with increasing possibilities for remote communications, it seems likely that over the next decade or so we may see close monitoring of some specific indicators.

5. Some Issues Relating to the Application of Indicators

Strong or Weak Sustainability Revisited

The uncomplicated application of indicators would seem to imply no trade-offs and hence the adoption of the strong sustainability position. But if the chosen indicators are, as they must be, a subset of all possible indicators of the real state of the system, some trade-off will be implied between the specified indicators and those not quantified. Thus the extreme version of strong sustainability is avoided. But particular types of display, as for example the diagram shown in Figure 2, may imply unconscious (equal) weighting of the limited set of indicators. The scales chosen may also imply a particular set of weights. Attempts to produce an overall index of sustainability must be viewed with the utmost caution because of these issues.

Who Determines their Levels?

The question arises as to who should choose the identities, scales of measurement and levels to be adopted. If, as argued earlier, sustainability is an emergent property and relates to a particular level within the hierarchy, then groups of stakeholders representing the various levels should be involved. Bell and Morse (1999) have suggested processes by which system indicators (SI's) might be generated. Whilst their proposals were developed in the context of projects and community development, they clearly have application to rural issues. Mayhew and Alessi (1998) report an attempt to develop sustainable pesticide uses. For farmers and others to "buy in" to the concept of rural sustainability, they must be involved in the process by which indicators are developed. Foltz *et al.* (1995) report the use of opinion survey data to specify weights for components of sustainability. *Ex cathedra* statements of sustainability indicators from single-issue groups, whilst clearly a start to the process, are unlikely to be enough to persuade all sections of the rural community. Nevertheless, proposals are being made for management strategies whose application is regarded as making progress in the direction of sustainability. Table 5 lists examples from both developed and developing country agricultures. Many of these strategies are unexceptional, but some involve tradeoffs between particular dimensions of sustainability and where their consequences are less easy to predict. In particular, the impacts upon "upstream" and "downstream" industries must not be ignored (Webster, 1997).

Table 5   Strategies Frequently Associated with Sustainability

Self-sufficiency through preferred use of on-farm or locally available "internal" resources to purchased "external" resources

Reduced use or elimination of soluble or synthetic fertilisers

Reduced use or elimination of chemical pesticides by substituting integrated pest management practices

Increased or improved use of crop rotations for diversification, soil fertility and pest control

Increased diversity of crop and animal species

Maintenance of crop or residue cover on the soil

Reduced stocking rates for animals

Source: Hansen (1996); see also Pretty (1998).

The Generation of Farm-Level Recommendations

The supply of information for management decisions remains important. Increasingly the debate is being focussed on the effects of changes in cropping areas on natural populations. New technologies may be problematic, not necessarily because of their direct impacts on particular plant or animal species, but because they enable changes in farming systems which may alter the food supplies of these species. Agronomic experiments (e.g., Jordan and Hutcheon, 1993), designed to capture the longer-run interactions with environmental variables have potential. But the approach may suffer because of lack of adequate controls, lack of baseline data as unexpected changes emerge, restricted numbers of treatments, leading to "counterintuitive" results (e.g., Bailey *et al.*, 1999, p.155) in addition to heavy costs and lack of timeliness. Many of the questions can only realistically be addressed by using a modelling approach (e.g. Jacobsen *et al.*, 1998). It is here that many of the major challenges for our profession lie.

Firstly, the aim must be to avoid partial analyses of sustainability issues in optimisation models. Omitted variables lead to biases in the decision variables and overestimates in the objective function. Secondly, whilst the regional or subregional nature of sustainability issues are recognised, the challenge is to recognise the variability of individual resource-endowment within the region and to avoid treating the region as a single decision-making unit. Furthermore, the variability of individual resource-endowment at the farm level means that recommendations for one farm will not necessarily hold for others - the well-known problem of the representative farm. Thirdly, the long-run nature of many of these issues may entail the use of predictive crop-growth models (e.g., EPIC, GLEAMS) to evaluate large numbers of individual points on the multivariate production function before any attempt at optimisation can occur. Such models can become very complex and may run the risk of becoming black boxes whose assumptions become hidden and whose results are therefore difficult to appraise.

Sustainability Indicators as a Basis for Compliance

At present, indicators are generally being proposed as advisory. It is suggested that changes in the variables in appropriate directions are all that is required (Pretty, 1998). But, as the expected developments in the identification and measurement of indicators take place, it seems only a matter of time before proposals are made for farm support programmes to become linked in some way with certain specified indicators.

The difficulties are clear. Farms may start from very different levels of the quantities being measured and their differing resource bases may provide a wide range of potential for change, for a given amount of managerial effort or income forgone. Sometimes little or no change in profit maximising plans will be needed to achieve change, whereas in other situations major reductions in income may occur if movement of indicators is to take place (see, for example, Lingard and Barron, 1999). Quantities of inputs needed to implement change may not be easily visible to society's monitors, even if the outputs are measurable. Management agreements for some agri-environmental schemes can take account of these problems. But it is difficult to see the approach being applied over very extensive areas since the cost of setting up the agreements and their monitoring would be prohibitive. Nevertheless farmers and managers must expect to see such developments over the coming years.

6. Conclusion

Over the past decade, a theoretical basis for the concept of sustainability has developed. Sustainability is recognised to be a social construct and therefore some degree of relativism is inevitable. Different views will generally exist and informed negotiation is needed to get coherent definitions. Despite disagreements over values and analyses, sufficient consensus is now beginning to exist about the need for discussion concerning operational definitions in specific circumstances. We are at the early stages of that process. Institutions to allow the process to take place - at the various levels identified earlier - need to be developed and nourished. Given the importance of agricultural policy in transmitting society's wants and desires back to the farmer, we need open-minded policy makers and politicians, informed by these institutions, but who are not swayed by narrow self-interested single-issue pressure groups.

The farmer's decisions remain central to movements toward sustainability. It is important to understand his decision processes and to ensure that he is well informed as to the consequences of his decisions. The knowledge-base concerning the longer-term effects of changes in farming systems with respect to natural capital is itself changing rapidly. Society has an interest in supporting the dissemination of that knowledge. The location-specific nature of the endowment of natural capital means that any farm-level definition of sustainability must to some degree be determined locally. Policy design should provide incentives for farmers to explore and exploit their own specific circumstances in the provision of sustainability goods.

The development of the knowledge-base poses challenges. Real-time observations and experiments are necessary to provide basic data, but are of limited help in predicting the effects of changes in systems at the level of the farm or region. The aim for farm management economists must therefore be to combine theory with empirical data to support the sustainability debate with timely, relevant and objective analyses using whatever models are appropriate for the purpose.

References

Bailey, A. P., Rehman, T. U., Park, J., Keatinge, J. D. H. and Tranter, R. B. (1999). Towards a Method for the Economic Evaluation of Environmental Indicators for UK Integrated Arable Farming Systems. *Agriculture, Ecosystems and Environment,* **72,** 145-158.

Barnett, V., Payne, R. and Steiner, R. (eds.) (1995). *Agricultural Sustainability: Economic Environmental and Statistical Considerations.* Chichester: John Wiley.

Batie, S. S. (1989). Sustainable Development: Challenges to the Profession of Agricultural Economics. *American Journal of Agricultural Economics,* **71(5),** 1083-1101.

Bell, S. and Morse, S. (1999). *Sustainability Indicators: Measuring the Immeasurable.* London: Earthscan.

Bockstaller, C., Girardin, P. and van der Verf, H. M. G. (1997). Use of Agro-ecological Indicators for the Evaluation of Farming Systems, *European Journal of Agronomy,* **7,** 261-270.

Bromley, D. W. (ed.) (1995). *The Handbook of Environmental Economics.* Oxford: Basil Blackwell.

Brouwer, F. and Crabtree, R. (1999). *Environmental Indicators and Agricultural Policy.* Wallingford: CAB International.

Burton, M., Rigby, D. and Young, T. (1999). Analysis of the Determinants of Adoption of Organic Horticultural Techniques in the UK, *Journal of Agricultural Economics,* **50(1)**, 48-63.

Cain, P. J., Yule, I., Miller, J. and Evans, E. (1997). Precision Farming in the Arable Enterprise, *Farm Management,* **9(8)**, 370-382.

Campbell, L. H. and Cooke, A. S. (eds.) (1997). *The Indirect Effects of Pesticides on Birds.* Peterborough: The Joint Nature Conservation Committee.

Candler, W. V. and Sargent, D. (1961). Farm Standards and the Theory of Production, *Journal of Agricultural Economics,* **15,** 282-298.

Colman, D. R. (1994). Ethics and Externalities: Agricultural Stewardship and Other Behaviour, *Journal of Agricultural Economics,* **45(3),** 299-311.

Copus, A. K. and Crabtree, J. R. (1996). Indicators of Socio-economic Sustainability: An Application to Remote Rural Scotland, *Journal of Rural Studies,* **12(1),** 41-54.

Costanza, R. and Daly, H. E. (1992). Natural Capital and Sustainable Development, *Conservation Biology,* **6(1),** 37-46.

Duelli, P. (1997). Biodiversity Evaluation in Agricultural Landscapes: An Approach at Two Different Scales, *Agriculture, Ecosystems and Environment,* **62,** 81-91.

Ecotec (1997). *Economic Instruments for Pesticide Minimisation.* Birmingham: Ecotec Research and Consulting Ltd.

Foltz, J. C., Lee, J. G., Martin, M. A. and Preckel, P. V. (1995). Multiattribute Assessment of Alternative Cropping Systems, *American Journal of Agricultural Economics,* **77(2),** 408-420.

Friedman, M. and Friedman, R. (1998). *Two Lucky People.* Chicago: University of Chicago Press.

Girardin, P., Bockstaller, C. and van der Verf, H. M. G. (1996). Evaluation of the Sustainability of a Farm by Means of Indicators, in Behl, R. K., Gupta, A. P., Khurana, A. L. and Singh, A., *Resource Management in Fragile Environments.* New Delhi: CCS HAU, Hisar and MMB, 280-296.

Hanley, N. (ed.) (1991). *Farming and the Countryside.* Wallingford: CAB International.

Hansen, J. W. (1996). Is Agricultural Sustainability a Useful Concept? *Agricultural Systems,* **50,** 117-143.

Hicks, J. R. (1946). *Value and Capital.* Second Edition, Oxford: The Clarendon Press.

Jacobsen, B. H., Petersen, B. M., Berntsen, J. B., Boye, C., Sorensen, C. G., Sogaard, H. T. and Hansen, J. P. (1998). *An Integrated Economic and Environmental Farm Simulation Model (FASSET),* Report No. 102. Copenhagen: Danish Institute of Agricultural and Fisheries Economics.

Jordon, V. W. L. and Hutcheon, J. A. (1993). Less Intensive Integrated Farming Systems for Arable Crop Production and Environmental Protection. Proceedings No. 346, London: The Fertiliser Society.

Kruseman, G., Ruben, R., Kuyvenhoven, A., Hengsdijk, H. and van Keulen, H. (1996). Analytical Framework for Disentangling the Concept of Sustainable Land Use, *Agricultural Systems,* **50,** 191-207.

Laffont, J.-J. and Tirole, J. (1993). *A Theory of Incentives in Procurement and Regulation.* Cambridge, MA: MIT Press.

Lele, S. and Norgaard, R. B. (1996). Sustainability and the Scientist's Burden, *Conservation Biology,* **10(2),** 354-365.

Levitan, L., Merwin, I. and Kovach, J. (1995). Assessing the Relative Environmental Impacts of Agricultural Pesticides: The Quest for a Holistic Method, *Agriculture, Ecosystems and Environment,* **55,** 153-168.

Lingard, J. and Barron, N. (1999). A Linear Programming Model of a Pennine Dales Farm in an Environmentally Sensitive Area, *Farm Management,* **10,** 6.

Lowe, P., Ray, C., Ward, N., Wood, D. and Woodward, R. (1998). Participation in Rural Development: A Review of European Experience, Centre for Rural Economy Research Report, Newcastle: University of Newcastle upon Tyne.

MAFF (1991). *Our Farming Future.* London: Ministry of Agriculture, Fisheries and Food.

386   P. Webster

MAFF (1998). *Development of a Set of Indicators for Sustainable Agriculture in the United Kingdom: A Consultation Document.* London: Ministry of Agriculture, Fisheries and Food.

Mayhew, M. and Alessi, S. (1998). Unravelling the Stakeholder Dialogue of Pest Management in Vorley, W. and Keeney, D., *Bugs in the System.* London: Earthscan, 136-169.

McGregor, M., Willock, J., Dent, J. B., Deary, I., Sutherland, A., Gibson, G., Morgan, O. and Grieve, B. (1996). Links Between Psychological Factors and Farmer Decision Making, *Farm Management,* **9**(5), 228-239.

McInerney, J. P. (1986). *Agricultural Policy at the Crossroads,* in Gilg, A. W. (ed.), *Countryside Planning Yearbook.* Norwich: Geo Books, **11,** 44-75.

Moxey, A. and White, B. (1994). Efficient Compliance with Agricultural Nitrate Pollution Standards, *Journal of Agricultural Economics,* **45**(1), 27-37.

Nix, J. S. (1990). Aspects of Farm Profitability: An Outmoded Concept? *Journal of Agricultural Economics,* **41**(3), 265-291.

Norgaard, R. B. (1994). *Development Betrayed: The End of Progress and a Coevolutionary Revisioning of the Future.* London: Routlege.

OECD (1997). *Environmental Indicators for Agriculture.* Paris: OECD Publications.

OECD (1998). *Co-operative Approaches to Sustainable Agriculture.* Paris: OECD Publications.

Pan, J. H. and Hodge, I. (1995). Land Use Permits as an Alternative to Fertiliser and Leaching Taxes for the Control of Nitrate Pollution, *Journal of Agricultural Economics,* **45**(1), 102-112.

Pannell, D. J. and Schillizzi, S. (1997). Sustainable Agriculture: A Question of Ecology, Equity Economic Efficiency or Expedience? Working Paper 97/01, Sustainability and Economics in Agriculture Project, University of Western Australia.

Pearce, F. (1999). *Light Fantastic: Laser Sensors Will Help Keep Waterways Clean.* New Scientist, **161,** No. 2177, 13th March, p.23.

Pearce, D. W. (1998). *The Contribution of Economics to a Sustainable Society.* Paper to the International Conference on Sustainability in Agriculture, October 1998, Stuttgart: IER Institute.

Pearce, D. W. and Atkinson, G. (1993). Capital Theory and the Measurement of Sustainable Development: An Indicator of Weak Sustainability, *Ecological Economics,* **8,** 103-108.

Pearce, D. and Tinch, R. (1998). The True Price of Pesticidies in, Vorley, W. and Keeney, D. (eds.), *Bugs in the System.* London: Earthscan, 50-89.

Pretty, J. (1998). *The Living Land.* London: Earthscan.

Putnam, R. D. (1993). *Making Democracy Work: Civic Traditions in Modern Italy.* Princeton, NJ: Princeton University Press.

Russell, N. P. and Fraser, I. M. (1995). The Potential Impact of Environmental Cross-Compliance in Arable Farming, *Journal of Agricultural Economics,* **46**(1), 70-79.

Schaller, N. (1993). The Concept of Environmental Sustainability, *Agriculture, Ecosystems and Environment,* **46,** 89-97.

Solow, R. (1992). *An Almost Practical Step Towards Sustainability.* Washington, DC: Resources for the Future.

Spash, C. L. and Simpson, I. A. (1994). Utilitarian and Rights-based Alternatives for Protecting Sites of Special Scientific Interest, *Journal of Agricultural Economics,* **45**(1), 15-26.

Syers, J. K., Hamblin, A. and Pushparajah, E. (1995). Indicators and Thresholds for the Evaluation of Sustainable Land Management, *Canadian Journal of Soil Science,* **75,** 423-428.

Tisdell, C. A. (1996). Economic Indicators to Assess the Sustainability of Conservation Farming Projects: An Evaluation, *Agriculture, Ecosystems and Environment,* **57,** 117-131.

Turner, R. K. (1993). *Sustainable Environmental Economics and Management; Principles and Practice.* London: Bellhaven Press.

Tversky, A. and Kahneman, D. (1981). The Framing of Decisions and the Psychology of Choice, *Science,* **211,** 453-458.

Van der Hamsfoort, C. P. M. and Latacz Lohmann, U. (1998). Sustainability: A Review of the Debate and an Extension, *International Journal of Sustainable Development and World Ecology,* **5,** 1-12.

Van Mansfelt, J. D. (1997). An Interdisciplinary Approach to Integrate a Range of Agro-landscape Values as Proposed by Representatives of Various Disciplines, *Agriculture, Ecosystems and Environment*, **63**, 233-250.

Victor, P. A. (1991). Indicators of Sustainable Development: Some Lessons from Capital Theory, *Ecological Economics*, **4**, 191-213.

Webster, J. P. G. (1997). Assessing the Economic Consequences of Sustainability in Agriculture, *Agriculture, Ecosystems and Environment*, **64**, 95-102.

WCED (1987). *Our Common Future.* World Commission on Environment and Development, Oxford: Oxford University Press.

World Bank (1997). *Expanding the Measure of Wealth: Indicators of Environmentally Sustainable Development.* Washington, DC: World Bank.

Wu, J. J. and Babcock, B. A. (1996). Contract Design for the Purchase of Environmental Goods from Agriculture, *American Journal of Agricultural Economics*, **78**, 935-954.

Yiridoe, E. K. and Weersink, A. (1997). A Review and Evaluation of Agroecosystem Health Analysis: The Role of Economics, *Agricultural Systems*, **55**(4), 601-626.

[17]

Landscape and Urban Planning, 27 (1993) 67–90
Elsevier Science Publishers B.V., Amsterdam

European features for sustainable development: a contribution to the dialogue

Jan Diek van Mansvelt*,a, Jessie A. Mulder[b]

[a]*Department of Ecological Agriculture, Wageningen Agricultural University, Haarweg 333, NL-6709 RZ Wageningen, Netherlands*
[b]*Mulder Bio-Agro-Consultancy, Zwolseweg 11, NL-7412 AA Deventer, Netherlands*

Abstract

Within the framework of agricultural policy-making, the world-wide demands for sustainable development in general are related to the sustainable development of rural areas in particular. According to the definitions of sustainability, four fundamental aspects are considered: (1) food security; (2) employment and income generation; (3) environmental and natural resource conservation; (4) people's participation and empowerment. Different priorities may be set in the implementation of these aspects, expressing different attitudes toward nature, society and the ethical decisions involved. In line with these differences, different strategies for agricultural development are favoured, each with specific consequences for rural development. In this paper, we consider some of the basic features of the above-mentioned problems, focusing on technical aspects but touching upon some underlying social and ethical issues as well. We compare basic requirements of sustainable development with some features of recent strategies, such as integrated agriculture (integrated pest management and integrated plant nutrition systems) and low external input sustainable agriculture (LEISA). Special attention is given to the principles underlying autonomous ecosystem management (AEM), as applied in organic types of agriculture (OA). By aiming for the multi-purpose efficiency of the agro-ecosystem and its subsystems, OA complies with the requirements for a sustainable use of natural resources. Its impact on the environment, nature and landscape meet the requirements of European Community (EC) and national policies. Its economic performance is remarkably similar to that of comparable conventional farms. Yields tend to be somewhat lower than those of high external input agriculture (HEIA), but enough to meet the EC's efforts to diminish overproduction, and OA seems to meet society's need for sufficient good-quality food. Also, higher labour demands in organic agriculture, labour diversification and upgrading at the farm, and the social networks between farmers and consumers make a significant contribution to sustainable social development. This presentation of various development perspectives can widen the options for choices. Far from offering a blueprint or turnkey solution, these considerations are meant as a contribution to a challenging dialogue on agriculture's role in sustainable rural development.

Introduction

The invitation to this conference states: "It is widely recognised throughout the world that one of the greatest problems facing humanity is to provide food for the fast-growing population, without harmful effects on nature and the environment." In this statement, the first part reflects the agro-policy of almost a century. The last part reflects the problems arising from the high external input agriculture (HEIA, or green

---

*Corresponding author.

Revolution) approach, as has become increasingly obvious during recent decades. Altogether, this statement leads to the demand for "New Strategies for Sustainable Rural Development", as mentioned in the title of this conference. Against this background, the challenge to all efforts in favour of a sustainable development is to identify roads that merge the benefits of the environmentally sound extensification approach with the benefits of the high external input food production strategy. A strategy to optimize the relationship between quality and quantity, and between food and

68 *J.D. van Mansvelt, J.A. Mulder / Landscape and Urban Planning 27 (1993) 67–90*

environment, is the considerable challenge at stake here.

In this paper, we will look for some of the basic features of the above-mentioned problems, focusing on technical aspects but touching upon some underlying social and ethical issues as well. Subsequently, we will consider some basic features of recent strategies, such as integrated agriculture (integrated pest management and integrated plant nutrition systems), rural development and low external input sustainable agriculture (LEISA) These strategies will be compared with the basic requirements of sustainable developments as indicated by the Food and Agriculture Organization's Declaration and Agenda for Action and Sustainable Agriculture and Rural Development (FAO's SARD) and Agenda 21 of the UN Conference on Environment and Development (UNCED). Special attention will be given to the principles underlying autonomous ecosystem management (AEM), as applied in organic types of agriculture (OA). We will explain how OA cultivates the benefits of diversity, to provide more better quality food. Data on the agro- and economic production of OA will be presented, including environmental, nature and landscape production and some indications on regulatory aspects. The food trade, being the info-junction in the food chain, will then be touched upon. A fair sharing of the profits made in the food chain between all its participants will provide strong support for the socio-economic sustainability of the chain. Finally, perspectives for the sustainable development of rural areas by OA and other strategies will be mentioned, to widen the options for choices.

Concepts of sustainability in agriculture

"Humanity has the ability to make development sustainable—to ensure that it meets the needs of the present without compromising the ability of future generations to meet their own needs." Since this was stated in the Brundt-

land report (World Commission on Environment and Development, 1987), sustainable development has become a major issue in development policy. This definition clearly shows the concern for the (a)biotic environment, and at the same time it underlines the need for sufficient food to feed the world population. In the wake of the sustainability concept as phrased by Bruntland (1992) many researchers have defined implementations of this concept for agriculture.

Different definitions and different concepts of agriculture have different implications for farming in practice as well as for the design of farming systems (Altieri, 1989; Food and Agriculture Organization (FAO), 1992; International Federation of Organic Agricultural Movements (IFOAM, 1992; Neher, 1992; Schultink, 1992; Vereyken, 1992; Van Mansvelt and Mulder, 1992). The most fundamental issues, shared by various perceptions of sustainable agriculture, are present in the main goals stated by the FAO (1992) (see Table 1). These regard the basic motives of humans, identified as far back as the 1950s, as ranging from food security to self-realization (Maslow, 1968), but now include the notion that the viability of the environment is a prerequisite for human survival. As presented, they largely comply also with the main goals of the UNCED Agenda 21 (Chapter 14), which was based on the FAO–SARD preparatory papers (UN, 1992).

The choice for the roads that will lead to these goals is strongly influenced by the values, expressed as priorities, that policy-makers give to each of these issues (Wetenschappelijke Raad voor het Regeringsbeleid, 1992). Generally, HEIA and integrated agriculture (IA) give priority to food production, whereas LEISA and OA try to give more balanced attention to all values. This expresses an integrative approach in the latter movements, whereas the former believe in the power of a segregational approach.

Evaluation of farming systems, in the inter-

J.D. van Mansvelt, J.A. Mulder / Landscape and Urban Planning 27 (1993) 67–90   69

Table 1
Objectives for sustainable rural development

Objectives for Sustainable Rural Development	
Basic values and interests of sustainability, as phrased by FAO [1992] (human motivations)	Specific objectives of sustainability, as mentioned for example by: Altieri 1989; Vereyken 1992; FAO 1992; van Mansvelt 1992; Schultink 1992.
Food security (physical survival)	Self-sufficient supply of good quality food
Employment and income generation in rural areas (social survival)	Diversification of income, Labour demand in rural areas, Social equity, Socially and culturally acceptable technology.
Natural resource conservation and environmental protection (earth's survival)	Biodiversity, Regenerative potential of nature, Stability, Use of local resources Health and well-being of the ecosystem, Local landscape values
People's participation and human resource development (ethical survival)	Human Resource Development, Self-promoting and self-help potential, Farmer's and community's empowerment

est of the farm's management as well as that of external validation, needs feasible specification of the FAO–SARD goals for sustainability. For every farming sub-system, special objectives can be formulated that eventually lead to 'checkpoints' at farm level. So, for example, Altieri (1989), FAO (1991), Vereyken (1992) and others formulated more specific objectives for the comparison of farming systems with regard to their sustainability. Using such sources, more specific objectives derived from FAO's values and interests are listed in Table 1. In the following we will consider some features of modern segregationist and post-modern integrationist strategies for transition to-

wards sustainable rural development and matching types of agriculture.

Some basic features of modern strategies (IPM & IPNS)

Potential harvest

Here we will give some consideration to the integrated agriculture approach, which aims for the highest possible production within a science-based concept of 'best technical means' (Rabbinge et al., 1990; De Wit, 1992). The basis frame of reference for the appreciation of agricultural production in this strategy is the 'potential harvest', which is defined on the basis of the 'solar energy to carbohydrate (and protein) conversion potential' of the photosynthetic system (De Wit, 1992). This energy conversion concept is a basically abstract, theoretical and generic one. Its validity has been established elegantly in micro-systems, by growing micro-organisms or single-crop species under laboratory conditions. However, when this model is translated into practical conditions, the potential harvest levels of any crop are not met.

Underlying values and consequences for practice: ecology and economy

Ecology
In the models underlying the integrated agriculture approach, the almost 75% gap between potential and real production is explained in an interesting sequence of natural constraints. These range from production-defining factors (local radiation, temperature and physiological features of the crop variety) via production-limiting factors (locally available water and nutrients) to production-reducing factors (incidence of pests and diseases) (Lövenstein et al., 1992). This approach basically perceives nature's reality as a default situation in which environmental conditions and ecosystem interactions are competing with

J.D. van Mansvelt, J.A. Mulder / Landscape and Urban Planning 27 (1993) 67–90

farmers' and societies' economic interests.

For science-advised farming practice this approach obviously enhances efforts to improve these conditions by technology, so as to make them meet the requirements for the highest-return crop. Consequences of this perception are narrowing rotations leading to single-crop production systems and fully controlled off-soil conditions (hydroponics). This model brought into full practice in a radical green revolution style eventually contributes to ruining the soil, ecosystem and the rural social structures (Lampkin, 1990; Oldeman et al., 1990; Hildyard, 1992; De Wit, 1993; Brown et al., 1992).

This conceptual attitude contrasts considerably with that of researchers from all over the world, such as Dokuchayev (1892), Steiner (1924), Howard (1943), Albrecht (1975), Koepf (1980), Chaboussou (1985) and Vogtman (1985). They advocate a strategy of working with nature, as a comprehensible ecosystem or organism, instead of fighting against it (Naess, 1975; Lovelock, 1979; Bockemühl, 1984; Devall, 1985; Baars, 1990). From their point of view, a harvest's quality reflects the farmers' management capacities. Also, the incidence of pests and diseases is mainly an indicator of mismanagement, from which farmers can learn (Kenmore, 1991). Here, the actual discussion starts from whether the modern, science-directed agro-technology should be regarded as mismanagement or as farming by the best technical means (Hildyard, 1991; Kenmore, 1991; Greenpeace, 1992; Vereyken, 1992).

Economy

In the same way, the basic opposition between economy and ecology, which is part of today's orthodox economic theory and political practice of decision-making, is an ideological, conceptual one. It is rooted partly in the self-understanding of modern society in a competitive relationship with nature. According to this, nature is regarded as nothing but a commodity, completely at the mercy of human high-handedness. Only the instrumental value of nature is being considered, and any intrinsic value is denied (Sheldrake, 1990)

As far as the economic growth-mania is concerned, it can be realized that it is rooted in an over-emphasized attention to one of the development phases. Over-emphasis on the ego-oriented physical growth of the youth phase can easily contribute to disregard or at least depreciation of the following development phases: flowering, fructification and ripening. These phases of limited or even diminishing physical growth offer an extensive amount of short-term and long-term 'nutritive values' to a wide range of ecosystem partners. It is interesting that in these phases integrated complexity is found in physiology and morphology. However, besides the obvious similarities, a keen awareness of the differences in the development of material and socio-cultural systems should be warranted. At the moment, the actual idea of moderating physical commodity consumption is widely sensed as limiting continuing mental growth (ethical development or self-realization). This might be seen as indicating a misidentification of physical and mental development (Maslow, 1968; Schumacher, 1973; Boulding, 1978; Lievegoed, 1979; Bockemühl, 1984; Meadows and Randers, 1992). Understanding this over-emphasis and misidentification might contribute to the attitudinal shift that is a prerequisite for the changes needed in global policy (Choudhury, 1991; Gore, 1992).

Hierarchies of interdependent networks of vital relationships between eco-partners, including humans, on the global scale of our home planet, require substantial human responsibility for our common future. Thus, a concept of fraternal economy must be developed, based on cultural efforts to share commodities world-wide, as well as to adapt human physiological needs to match the natural limitations of global resources. This fraternal economy contrasts with the classical 'competitive' economy, originating from a social-Dar-

J.D. van Mansvelt, J.A. Mulder / Landscape and Urban Planning 27 (1993) 67–90   71

winistic view of human relations (George, 1985; Van Mansvelt, 1991).

To facilitate these urgently needed developments, both in ecology and economy, extensive reflections on current concepts and reconsiderations of ethics are required. Technical implementations can only contribute to globally sustainable resource management when they are conceived from appropriate images and used within appropriate attitudes (Van Mansvelt, 1988; Daly et al., 1990; Blatz, 1991; Von Mallinckrodt, 1991).

Some prerequisites and impacts of model use

An obvious strong point of the abstract theoretical approach is that it allows, in principle, for precise analyses and subsequent mathematical modelling of a set of cause–effect relationships in the agro-ecosystems under study. (It should be kept in mind, however, that modelling of the complete set is more of a theoretical than a practical possibility, even when 'all' is restricted to the relevant factors (Dillon and Anderson, 1990).) However, even when we disregard the considerable time and labour input needed to fill all the links of the models with legitimate data (locally, the management system and crop-specific data), there is still the perceptional/attitudinal aspect of the model to be taken into consideration. This attitude consists of three interrelated parts. First, the presumption of the potential production level is a theoretical and abstract one; strictly speaking, it is a purely ideal goal, which as such can never be reached (except perhaps under artificial, extremely controlled laboratory conditions). Second, it simultaneously implies that all features of the real world (agriculture in practice) are detrimental to the potential production. Thus, nature is perceived as a chaotic, disruptive nuisance (Sheldrake, 1990; Gore, 1992). Third, this approach disregards the many interconnections between these sets of 'limiting' factors. Altogether, agriculture is seen basically as an art to outsmart nature by means of

single-factor-directed technology. The efficiency of the system is perceived as the (external) input or resource efficiency (Hayami and Ruttan, 1985; Brinks and Van Mansvelt, 1992). Generally speaking, the HEIA, IPMS and IPNS concepts are in line with this approach (FAO, 1992). In terms of sociological and anthropological trends, this radical reductionist approach contributes to an alienation from nature (Boulding, 1978; Koepf, 1980; Van Mansvelt, 1988; Van Mansvelt and Verkley, 1991). (Needless to say, this controversy is mainly one of streams of perception, schools of thought and policy, not a personal one.)

In conclusion, we can say that, in spite of the obvious strong points, the outlined scientific approach seems to lack the conceptual means and instruments either to develop or to validate the multipurpose efficiency of agricultural systems. These systems are soil-bound and empirically based on the practice of minimal non-renewable resource inputs. Such practical systems of autonomous ecosystem management (AEM), such as LEISA and OA, are derived from the concept of co-evolution and an understandable co-operative nature (Lampkin, 1992; Sattler and Von Wistinghausen, 1992; Reijntjes et al., 1992). They comply with the majority of the FAO's SARD requirements (FAO, 1992; Hiemstra et al., 1992; Van Elzakker et al., 1992). We will discuss these options and their performances in more detail below.

Consequences for policy

Segregation

In political decision-making, the merging of a scientific agro-technical attitude and a 'homo economicus' approach can easily lead to proposals of segregation between agriculture and 'other' forms of land use in rural areas, whereby the modern, rational trend is supposed to be a concentration of agricultural production in the zones of high potential yield (fertile soils and favourable humidity conditions) (WWR,

1992). This stand, however, tends to disregard the economic, social and cultural importance of appropriate land management in all the regions of a country. The rural area's viability, the protection of the environment and nature, together with an appropriate agricultural production level, require an integrated approach instead of a segregationist one, whereby factors such as regional infrastructure, knowledge, attitude, national price policies and (other) financial incentives should be conspicuously included in the studies (De Zeeuw and Van der Meer, 1990; Centraal Plan Bureau, 1992).

Uniformity

A leading principle in modern agricultural policy has been the perception of a basically homogeneous population of farmers. Farmers were supposed to differ only in the dimension 'advanced' vs. 'conservative'. This biased point of view is misleading and should be replaced by a more accurate, differentiated one. For example, in sociological research, quality-oriented farmers have been distinguished from quantity-oriented farmers, and capital- and/or technology-intensive farming from labour- and/or knowledge-intensive farming (Van der Ploeg and Ettema, 1990). Here, not only the local differences (natural and infrastructural) but also those in style of farm management (mental and psychological) are taken into account (Van der Ploeg and Roep, 1990; Roep et al., 1991; De Bruin et al., 1992). Labour diversification on farms and job diversification in the region might be post-modern solutions by which farmers can enhance ecological and social sustainability as well as economic viability. Empowerment of regional specificity and increased access to appropriate education in the region are key issues in the development of diversified management of agriculture and related crafts (Anosike and Coughenour, 1990; FAO, 1991; Evans and Ngau, 1991). Shifting away from the idea of generic uniformity to that of structural diversity will most probably

favour a more flexible, sustainable policy-making.

Intensification

In recent decades, the merged concepts of an economically competitive agriculture have intensified tremendously. Farmers were supposed to work towards economic optimization, led by technology (Anosike and Coughenour, 1990). Agriculture was aiming at the highest unit product output per unit labour input, which has lead to intensive use of capital and commodity inputs (Hildyard, 1991; Kenmore, 1991). At the same time as this approach generated the desired increase of products output, it brought about undesired outputs of waste and labour. It thus contributed unintentionally to the degradation of soils, ecosystems, landscapes and rural societies, inside as well as outside the countries (National Research Council, 1989; Oldeman et al., 1990; Brown et al., 1992; Greenpeace, 1992). How much these 'side'-effects will in the end appear to be inherent to the applied system approach and its implementation in research models is a matter for further evaluation (Bartussek, 1982; Merril, 1983; Van Mansvelt, 1988; Gore, 1992).

Basic concepts of organic types of agriculture

Autonomous Ecosystem Management

Like all types of agriculture, organic types of agriculture are implementations of a basic concept, model or mental map. In organic types of agriculture, the conceptual common denominator can be defined as autonomous ecosystem management (AEM). This includes such notions as optimizing the primary production efficiency of agro-ecosystems, in compliance with the local soil and climate conditions (carrying capacity) and the social needs of the region. In view of the management requirements, these types of agriculture demand an attitude in favour of an exchange of eco-in-

J.D. van Mansvelt, J.A. Mulder / Landscape and Urban Planning 27 (1993) 67–90   73

telligence for non-renewable inputs. Agriculture, in this concept, is more a policy for land use in general, including agro-, sylvi- and aquaculture in mixed or integrated agro-ecosystems. Pest prevention and well-balanced mineral flows and sustainable resource management result in low external inputs (chemical fertilizers and non-renewable energy).

This basic conceptual framework of agricultural systems management can be traced back in many countries' agronomic literature. Together with many of the aspects indicated in the following sections, they have been explained by researchers such as Dokuchayev (1892), Steiner (1924), Howard (1943), Albrecht (1975), Draghetti (1991) and Boehnke (1992). In the following paragraphs, we will abstain from specific literature references for each item, and will simply list the critical notions of the organic approach to agriculture as derived from the study of the researchers listed above.

Cultivating multi-purpose efficiency

Introduction

To optimize the production of agro-ecosystems in the framework of AEM, it is important to cultivate the multi-purpose characteristics of the relevant kingdoms of nature—the eco-partners of the system. Overstressing any single production aspect of any subsystem might easily lead to the deterioration of the balanced efficiency of the whole system. Orchestrating the benefits of diversity (Van Elzakker et al., 1992), or optimizing the soil–crop–animal interactions, is therefore the foremost challenge of OA (Van Mansvelt and Verkley, 1991). This strategy includes using animals to upgrade the non-foods produced with the foods, and manuring the soils for food and feed production (Lampkin, 1990). Within this framework, some aspects of the multi-purpose efficiency of each eco-subsystem can be listed as follows.

(1) Soils (mineral–clay–humus complexes; sandy, loamy or peaty) merge various pur-

poses: (i) source and store or buffer of nutrients (i.e. organic and inorganic nutrients, water) for crops; (ii) biotope for general waste feeders (for C/N balance, nutrient transformation and waste recycling) (here it becomes obvious that the idea of waste/garbage as non-useful matter is largely a lack of consistent thinking; once this is understood, it becomes a challenge to make sure that the matter that is recycled fits the eco-subsystem that it returns to, so soil digestibility might become a useful prerequisite for manure–slurry–compost–silt application); (iii) basis of the agricultural production (sustainable soil fertility, sustainable land use, land regeneration and/or improvement).

(2) Crops (mainly floriferous plants) merge various purposes: (i) human food and fibre producers (carbohydrates, oils and proteins, fuel, shelter, building and clothing materials); (ii) animal feed producers (energy and protein, shelter and bedding); (iii) soil organic matter and structure producers (leguminous and bacterial N fixation, edaphon feed/energy input, soluble minerals (nitrogen) trapping, soil structure and mineral mobilization) (so, in this case, the N input in the system goes intrinsically together with an input of structure (root action) and an input of energy for the edaphon (phases in root decay)); (iv) water harvesters (water uptake through root canals, dew or air moisture interception by crops or treetops, and reduction of evaporation); (v) climate regulators (micro-, meso- and macro-climate, wind shielding, shadow casting, temperature moderating and rain catching).

(3) Husbandry (mainly vertebrates, but also fowl, fish and bees) merges various purposes: (i) human food and fibre producers (milk, meat, honey, hair, wool, hides and wax); (ii) roughage feeders (non-food to food transformation, waste feeders instead of competitors for human food) (ideas on dairy feed regimes have recently been adapted away from overemphasizing the importance of protein to reappreciation of energy (carbohydrates); in

this way, the gradual degradation of the food has become important as well, to optimize intestinal digestion); (iii) manure production (N recycling and redistribution and stabilizing of soil aggregates); (iv) intelligent traction (low external energy input; efficiency dependent on infrastructure); (v) pollinators.

(4) Climate (sunshine, rain, temperature and wind) merges various purposes: (i) provides time-scale and regulation (long-time, seasonal and diurnal cycles which trigger the phases of development; (ii) source of external energy input for primary (plant) production.

Aspects of soil management

In agreement with farming tradition in many regions, organic types of agriculture regard soil improvement, by means of well-balanced stewardship, as a key issue of its professional ethics. Regeneration and conservation of the soil's fertility are basic requirements as well as a challenge to the farmers' craftsmanship. In this framework, making the successor a better soil is the ultimate goal. Appropriate liming, and rock-dust applications are accepted as medication of soils in need of special care (as a result of nutrient deficiencies). Consideration of non-renewable energy and other resource depletions are therefore critical, stressing the need for minimal input strategies. On-site nutrient mining by deep rooting crops, improvement of nutrient availability with mycorhizas and optimal nutrient recycling are components of the multi-purpose approach. Within the agro-ecosystem, specific crop rotation and manuring strategies for different soil types, structures and exposures are part of the craftsmanship.

Aspects of crop rotation

Within the framework of multi-purpose efficiency of crop production, crop rotation is instrumental in orchestrating the complementary characteristics of various crops in their mutual and plant–soil relationships. Intercropping, after-cropping, alley-cropping and

mixed cropping are examples of spatial and temporary alternations, always chosen according to crop- and soil-specific cycles, needs and gifts. Sophisticated crop rotations also appear to be instrumental in biological pest prevention (fungi, insects and weeds). Additional multipurpose aspects of crops, to be considered when designing rotations, are, for example:
—legumes as N-fixers and protein food or feed producers;
—leguminous ley-grasslands as N-fixers, feed producers and weed suppressors;
—corn as a producer of (staple) food and feed, animal housing and an N-absorbent material for all kinds of manures (maintaining the soils C/N ratio at appropriate levels);
—vegetables (food diversification) as vitamin and mineral sources;
—roots as (staple) food, feed and silage
—fruits (fresh and staple);
—herbs (for teas, spices and medicine);
—flowers;
—seeds (for propagation, growth and oils);
—hedges and woodlands (for feed, shelter, housing, fuel, landscaping, soil stabilization and humidity regulation).

Aspects of mixed husbandry

Within the framework of multi-purpose efficiency of animal husbandry, cultivation of animal-specific characteristics is instrumental. As before, implementation always depends on the actual farm situation, soil and climate conditions, and inter-species interactions of local or adapted breeds. The multi-purpose approach for animals focuses on manure production and roughage, and the waste-to-food conversion capacity of cattle and other animals. This is an important key to avoiding competition for human food in a world of limited resources (Meadows, 1992; Meadows et al., 1992).

Cultivation cycles and development phases

To optimize or 'orchestrate' the multi-purpose potential of the above-mentioned eco-

J.D. van Mansvelt, J.A. Mulder / Landscape and Urban Planning 27 (1993) 67–90   75

subsystems, the whole scale of different qualities of developmental phases, seasons and other cycles must be taken into account. The features to be considered include the following.

(1) Specific properties of the seedling, growing, flowering, ripening, decaying and dormant phases in crops; (i) selective cropping for food, feed, fuel and timber in forestry (including crops for green manuring which are harvested before flowering and special after-sowing of crops for nitrate trapping); (ii) seed production (on-farm and/or local).

(2) Specific properties of the young, adult and mature phases in animals; (i) meat vs. reproduction; (ii) dairy vs. traction; (iii) breeding for health and long-life.

(3) The alternating consumption of plant-food in the growing season and animal-food in the 'hunger' season.

(4) Anticipating bio-meteorological cycles (such as sunspots and locust plagues, lunar cycles and cassava planting).

Farm management: privatization and associative co-operation

Reflecting on the listed options and considering the requirements for professional craftmanship, it will become clear that agriculture in general, and OA in particular, is a field which demands great knowledge and ability. Those who are familiar with its practice will probably agree that most farms in the western parts of Europe, although described as family farms, are run by one person, and clearly show that person's preferences in scale and emphasis on vegetable or arable crops, small or large livestock, fruits or whatever.

This situation is often perceived as a deadlock within either professional farming, albeit highly specialized, or within mixed farming, although this is relatively unprofessional. Both would structurally exclude the options of multiple-purpose efficiency as presented. To overcome this conceptual deadlock, the establishment of associative forms of co-operation between farmers might be seen as an interesting tool, which would be instrumental in helping the farmers to profit from from the benefits of diversity. On the one hand, it can give the farmers a larger say in the agro-business complex: it will make them, as a community, a stronger, more independent partner. The accompanying increase in economic importance of the enterprise will result in a greater volume for trade and services and improve the value of capital provision by the banks. On the other hand, it could serve the appropriate task division within the mixed, multi-purpose types of agriculture discussed. This is important because co-operation helps to combine individual aptness with the demand for professional craftmanship in all parts of the complex agro-ecosystem's management (Groh and Mac-Fadden, 1990; Bader, 1992; Hermannstorfer, 1992). In practical farming such associations have the potential to adapt more flexibly to fluctuations in work load, allowing for some internal task diversification and holiday stand-in services.

It seems evident that when on-farm up-grading of the products is realized, the number of tasks per farm will increase accordingly. This will contribute to the buffering capacity of the association or co-operative. In the list of options for diversification, the option of external job diversification should be added as well.

In our opinion, such associative community farming, could, altogether, considerably increase the sustainability of rural life. By providing a critical mass for renewed rural community building, it sets an end to the isolation of farmers, the spread of which is a key issue in rural degradation (Klett, 1990; Gengenbach and Limbacher, 1991; De Bruin et al., 1992; Hiemstra et al., 1992). In view of the actual East–West polarity, it could be argued that the post-modern farmer should overcome the alienating phase of emancipation and enter into a post-emancipatory type of associative co-operation. He would then be able to take full responsibility as an individual professional, but willing to co-operate with others in a team to

76   *J.D. van Mansvelt, J.A. Mulder / Landscape and Urban Planning 27 (1993) 67–90*

manage the full scale of benefits from a sound farming system's diversity (Kampfraath, 1990).

Performance of OA

Introduction

Some data from the relevant literature will be presented to give some indications of what happens when the above-mentioned principles are implemented. We will not give a detailed discussion here on their specific or general validity; the data are intended to be indicative of the relevant order of magnitude, and are open to further study (Greenpeace, 1992; Rijksinstituut voor Volksgezondheid en Milieuhygiene, 1993).

The following will be dealt with in succession: some examples of the impact on the environment (pesticides and nitrogen losses); some of the effects on nature conservation (diversity of the levels of species, habitats and landscapes); some data on food security (yields and food autonomy) and on income generation and employment (farm economy and market potential). People's participation

and human resource development will also be touched upon. Other data on each of these issues and other important parameters such as food storage and consumption quality, mineral balances, pest incidence, energy efficiency, labour conditions and socio-economic impact are important but are beyond the scope of this paper.

Pesticide inputs and nitrogen losses (environmental protection)

As chemical pesticides are excluded from use in organic types of agriculture, it is not surprising that the main pesticide problems are those of ubiquitous stress, in-soil remnants of times before the conversion, and drifting sprays from neighbours.

As far as nitrogen leaching is concerned, more mineral balance accounting than comparative monitoring has been done. Here we present the data available from Dutch research (Table 2). The data in the upper part of the table are from a research farm on clay soil (Zadoks, 1989), and the remaining data are a comparison of organic, mixed and conventional, practical farms on sandy soils (Van der Werff, 1992). On the clay soil, the nitrogen

Table 2
Losses of nitrogen in organic agriculture
Clay soils: development of farming systems (November 1982–April 1983) (Zadoks, 1989)

	Organic (BD)	Integrated	Conventional
Total N in drain (mg l^{-1})	6.4	14.6	21.4
Total N loss (kg ha^{-1} year^{-1})	29	67	98

Sandy soils: testing of emissions of organic mixed farms in the Netherlands on sandy soils (September 1990–April 1991) (Van der Werff, 1992)

	Organic farms in the research project					Nature conservation areas	EC norm for drinking-water (35 mg l^{-1} NO$_3$)	Dutch soils including agriculture
	1	2	3	4	5			
Total N in soil moisture (mg l^{-1})	11	15	12	15	31	2–10	11.3	15–60
Total N loss (kg ha^{-1} year^{-1})	18	19	18	31	39	14	–	5–200

BD, biodynamic.

J.D. van Mansvelt, J.A. Mulder / Landscape and Urban Planning 27 (1993) 67–90 77

level in the water matched the European Community (EC) level; on sandy soils they were close, and well below the Dutch drinking-water level. Considering additional denitrification on the way to water intake points, these data indicate the potential for drinking-water production on organic farms even on sand soils. The total N losses per year in OA were much lower than in conventional agriculture, on sandy soils as well as on clay soils. (It should be realized that the averages on farmed lands are higher than the mean for all clay and all sandy soils (agriculture and other land use).)

Species, habitat and landscape diversity (natural resource conservation)

Species diversity

Increasing numbers of agro-policy-makers realize that agriculture produces not only foods and fibres, but also environment and landscape (nature) (Van Mansvelt, 1988; De Zeeuw and Albrecht, 1990; Struik et al., 1991; WRR (1992). Originally, as a measure of the quality of nature production generally, the diversity of plant and animal species was chosen. More recently, as well as species diversity, biotope or habitat diversity is included, as a meta-parameter of species diversity (Latour and Groen, 1993). Here, even fewer data from monitoring are available than for the environmental performance. Considering the basic concepts of OA as described above, it seems rather obvious to suppose that a multi-purpose or bio-diversity management approach leads to more species per plot and more plots per farming system. To establish the data needed to support these suppositions, a literature survey is under way in the framework of the above-mentioned policy document by Latour and Groen (1993) (Braat, 1992; RIVM, 1993). For the time being, beetles and earthworms, as representatives for soil fauna diversity, are found to range from 200% to 2000% more individuals in organic soils and orchards than in conventional farms; additional plant species

(weeds) are found to range from 133% to over 700% more species under organic management; butterflies, bees and bumblebees are represented by 700% more species under organic management, and spiders by 50% fewer to 300% more species (Table 3) (Braat, 1992).

Habitat and landscape diversity

The description and definition of values of nature over and above those of species and sometimes habitats is still in a preliminary phase (Terwan, 1992). Recently, two landscape students carried out a pilot study on how to identify and describe the contribution of agriculture to those landscape values. They selected four biodynamic farms and compared them with their neighbours who implemented conventional types of agriculture. The farms were located in Sweden (1), Germany (2) and the Netherlands (1) (Hendriks and Stroeken, 1992). In their study, 'Differences in appearances' (authors' translation), they found that the biodynamic farms they visited, as compared with their neighbours, showed the following features:

(1) more harmony between land use and natural subsoil;

(2) a more clearly interwoven structure of land use;

(3) a larger number of land uses;

(4) a larger number of human participants in the production;

(5) a greater labour diversity (including a greater diversity of on-farm processing);

(6) a greater diversity in biotopes (arable crops, vegetables, fruit and brambles;

(7) a greater diversity in husbandry;

(8) a larger surface percentage planted up with a larger number of shrub and tree species, which were better integrated in the farm management structure;

(9) a greater diversity in 'wild' flora (in addition to (6) and (8);

(10) a greater overall range of sensory perceptions (sense-information, recreative impressions). (See Table 3 (C).)

Table 3(A)
Number of beetles and earthworms (individuals) (100% represents value on conventional farm)

Species	Country and year of research	Author	Type of research	Numbers compared with conventional agriculture
Beetles	Germany, 1987	Von Ammer et al. (1988)	Number of individuals; organic compared with conventional	200%
	Germany, 1990	Schweigl (1990)	Comparison of organic and conventional agriculture; numbers in apple orchards	1000%
	Netherlands, 1981–1987	Wijnands (1991–1992)	Numbers in biodynamic and conventional agriculture on the OBS	~200%
Earthworms	Germany, 1990	Schweigl (1990)	Comparison in apple orchard	2000%
	Denmark, 1982	Rasmussen and Haas (1985)	Comparison of conventional and biodynamic neighbours	200–400%

Table 3(B)
Number of species (fauna) (100% represents value on conventional farm)

Butterflies, bees, bumblebees	Germany, 1987	Von Ammer et al. (1988)	Hardly any butterflies, bees or bumblebees on conventional sites	> 700%
Spiders	Germany, 1987	Von Ammer et al. (1988)	Comparison in grainfields	> 700%
	Germany, 1990	Schweigl (1990)	Comparison of species in apple orchards	50%
	Netherlands, 1981–1985	Vereyken (1986–1988)	Mean of various crops	200–300%

Table 3(C)
Number of weed species (100% represents value on conventional farm)

Weeds in crops	Germany, 1983–1984	Hermann et al. (1986)	Comparison of organic and conventional agriculture; in potatoes, wheat, corn, fodder beet	> 200%
	Germany, 1984–1985	Braunewell et al. (1986)	Mean number of species in organic farming compared with conventional	~200%
	Germany, 1987	Von Ammer et al. (1988)	Organic compared with conventional practice	200%
	Germany, 1986, 1988	Von Eisen (1989)	Mean number of species	centre > 700%; sides 150%
	Austria, 1988	Schütz (1983)	Biodynamic compared with conventional	200–300%
Weeds in meadows	Switzerland, 1978	Manintveld (1979)	Organic compared with conventional	~200%
	Netherlands, 1980	Baars et al. (1983)	Dairy farms; organic compared with conventional	133%

Table 3(D)
Landscape values of four biodynamic farms, as compared with their neighbours

Biodiversity	Social diversity	Coherence of functions
More types of land use	More on-farm labour; land use and processing	Harmony between subsoil quality and land use
More biotopes	More non-farm labour; training, extension	Harmony between subsoil quality, climate and farm management
Greater diversity in crops, husbandry, plantation, brambles and wild flora	More people living on the land	Better structured farm management
Larger area of plantation and brambles		Better structured land use
		More structured plantation

J.D. van Mansvelt, J.A. Mulder / Landscape and Urban Planning 27 (1993) 67–90   79

Table 4
Vegetables and spring wheat (100% represents conventional yield)

Crop	Country and year of research	Author	Type of research	Yield compared with conventional agriculture
Carrots	Netherlands, 1985–1991	Results from DLV (1993)	Organic practice compared with conventional practice (DLV–LEI)	83%
	Germany, 1983 (Baden Württemberg)	Böckenhoff et al. (1986)	All farms in the district	96%
	USA 1976–1980 (Maine)	Stanhill (1990)	Research experiment	95%
	Germany, 1978–1990	Lindner (1991)	Research experiment	90%
Beetroot	Netherlands, 1985–1991	Results from Mulder (1992)	Organic practice compared with conventional practice (DLV–LEI)	73%
	Germany, 1983 (Baden Württemberg)	Böckenhoff et al. (1986)	All farms in the district	92%
	Germany, 1978–1990 (Rheinland)	Lindner (1991)	Research experiment	90%
Spring wheat	Netherlands, 1985–1991	Results from DLV (1992)	Organic practice compared with conventional practice (DLV–LEI)	82%
	Sweden, 1970–1974	Stanhill (1990)	Research experiment	83%
	Germany, 1983 (Baden Württemberg)	Lampkin (1990)	200 holdings, biodynamic and conventional	72%
Winter wheat	Germany, 1984–1990	Agrarbericht (1985–1991)	Organic farms compared with conventional average	67%
Potatoes	Germany, 1989	Agrarbericht (1991)	Organic farms compared with conventional average	65%
	Germany, 1990	Agrarbericht (1992)	Organic farms compared with conventional average	56%

In view of these observations, it was concluded that, in principle, biodynamic/organic types of sustainable agriculture have a remarkable potential for landscape enrichment. Obviously, this pilot study complements the interesting evidence of the findings mentioned above on biodiversity. This potential is also important for the implementation of the MacSharry proposal on positive extensification in the framework of the Common Agricultural Policy of the EC (Commission of the European Communities (CEC), 1991). This topic seems to be well worth thorough large-scale monitoring, to determine its general validity.

Yields and national food autonomy (food security)

As the whole set of agro-chemical inputs developed over recent decades was intended to boost yields, it is not surprising that yields in OA tend to be lower. However, for a scientifically sound comparison, each level of observation involves it own demands. Comparisons at scientific plot level are different from those in practice, and experimental input levels, as well as those in practice, differ considerably depending on the country and region. Here we show a few data to indicate the magnitude of the differences found between high external input conventional (100%) and OA (56% for potatoes to 96% for beetroots) (Table 4). It goes without saying that the lower the external inputs in the region's conventional agriculture, the closer OA comes to 100% or higher (Van Elzakker et al., 1992). In studies on national or regional scales, the differences between farms and farmers within each group often come close to the differences between the groups, complicating the conclusions some-

J.D. van Mansvelt, J.A. Mulder / Landscape and Urban Planning 27 (1993) 67–90

Table 5
Summary of research projects on the possibilities of agricultural self-sufficiency in the Netherlands, Germany, Finland, the UK, Switzerland and Sweden

Country and source Type of research	Agricultural presumptions of research[1]	Estimated yield levels of organic types of farming used in research	Dietary presumptions of research	Is agricultural self-sufficiency possible? (With conditions for self-sufficiency)
Netherlands Nauta, 1978, Scenario study	1. No mineral N 2. Organic farming	70% of conventional yield	Less meat (minimum), sugar (20%), potatoes (20%), dairy produce (20%)	Yes; With different diet, organic farming can feed the Netherlands for at least 20–50 years (long-term research needed)
Germany (Henze, 1980) I. Descriptive research II. Research-based estimation	I 1. No feed imports 2. Agricultural self-sufficiency II 1. No mineral N	75% of conventional yield	Normal	Yes, but based on fertilizer import II. Organic agriculture if no imports at all
Netherlands (Bakker, 1985) Scenario study	1. No mineral N 2. Self-sufficient food supply	–	Normal Healthy Minimal	Yes; The Netherlands can be self-sufficient in crises; the method of farming will then change towards organic farming
Finland (Kettunen, 1986) Descriptive research	1. No imports 2. Agricultural self-sufficiency	–	Vegetable diet	Yes, but self-sufficiency in Finland will always need energy inputs (fuel); organic farming can meet a large part of this energy demand
Germany (Bachmann, 1987) Scenario study	1. Standards of organic farming	Actual yields of organic farming in 1986 in Germany	Normal Healthy; less meat (40%), less sugar	Yes, organic farming can feed Germany is 40% less meat is consumed; also in the future (2050)
UK (Lampkin, 1989) Arithmetic method	1. Standards of organic farming 2a. 10% organic farming 2b. 100% organic farming	Actual yield level of organic farming in 1986 in UK	Normal	Yes; 10% conversion gives no problems with food supply; 100% conversion is also possible (conclusion from extrapolation)
Switzerland (Meyer, 1990) Arithmetic method	1. Standards of organic farming	Average yields in organic farming in 1989 in Switzerland	Normal	Yes; overall conversion to mixed organic farming with stocking rate of 1.3–1.6 labour units ha^{-1}; more feasible with healthy diet
Sweden (Granstedt, 1990) Descriptive research	1. No mineral N resulting in standards of biodynamic farming	–	Healthy; less meat, less sugar	Most probably yes

[1] 1, Main presumption; 2, additional presumption.

what (Reijntjes et al., 1992; Van Elzakker et al., 1992).

One of the most frequent and fair questions, raised in discussions on the feasibility of OA is the question of whether it can feed the increasing world population. Up till now, and as far as we know, the data on OA have not been included in global modelling of agriculture. This

J.D. van Mansvelt, J.A. Mulder / Landscape and Urban Planning 27 (1993) 67–90   81

situation will change in the near future, but results are not yet available. However, in several European countries national surveys on this question have been carried out. Their results are summarized in Table 5. Their common message is that, when consumption complies with recent concepts of healthy nutrition, these countries could very well produce enough for their own people. Thus avoiding widespread over-consumption, especially of meat and sugar, is a key issue for both a healthy nutrition and agriculture.

Farm economy and market share (employment and income generation)

Validation strategies in economy

As regards the economic feasibility of OA, it should be realized that prices are largely a product of policy, on locally, nationally and internationally interacting levels. It is only within this framework that farmers and their partners in the food chain can adjust their balance between input and output of goods and money, i.e. economy (Kampfraath, 1990; Daly et al., 1990; Hueting et al., 1992). Each of the steps on each of these levels includes a certain amount of free choice, subject to priority decisions by those responsible: farmers, traders, consumers and authority on each level. It is only within the framework of such considerations that comparisons on farm or national economy are possible, because, hard as any set of data on economy might be, these data are but the reflection of a soft system, a set of interlinked validations made by society or its representatives (Brinks and Van Mansvelt 1992).

The most obvious debate on prices in conventional agriculture deals with the lack of environmental and social accounting, which sets these prices lower than those in organic production. This makes a big difference, because conventional agriculture has externalized the social and environmental impact on the national budget, whereas organic agriculture has

included it within its own farm budget. Thus, the competition between conventional and organic (alternative, sustainable) produce on the market is regarded as unfair from this point of view (Van Mansvelt,1988; MacRae et al., 1989; Conway and Barbier, 1990; Greenpeace, 1992).

Farm economy

For this paper we have selected some data on economic performance on the farm level focusing on farm income (gross profit) and labour income per person (full labour unit) (Table 6). Organic and conventional farms in different countries and regions are compared. As in the section on yields the results show a remarkable deviation within each group, mainly as a result of the different management qualities of the farmers. As this deviation often comes close to the differences between the paired groups, conclusions are difficult. On top of this, there is a considerable difference between the years. In studies over longer periods,the differences between the systems diminish, but averages over these periods cover up improvement tendencies.

Generally, farm income in organic farming is slightly higher than or equal to that in conventional agriculture, whereas the labour income per person tends to be lower in organic farming. Premium prices and reduced input costs can partly offset lower yields and higher labour input. Increased farm and crop diversity, however, are not covered by the premium price. Longer rotations with fewer cash crops are a basis for organic management, which means that, especially in the conversion period, income problems can arise. Here the MacSharry farm income support could be a solution. Besides income support, an equitable environmental accounting system can also support fair competition in a truly sustainable agriculture at large (CEC, 1991).

Market share

Estimates have been made of the potential penetration of organic produce in the retail

82 J.D. van Mansvelt, J.A. Mulder / Landscape and Urban Planning 27 (1993) 67–90

Table 6
Financial performance of organic farms (100% represents farm income of conventional farm)

Country	Source	Type of research	Farm income (gross profit) (%)	Labour income (per labour unit) (%)
Switzerland, 1979–1981	Steinman (1983	Organic farms compared with conventional partner	104	82
		Organic farms compared with regional average	107	92
Denmark, 1988	Dubgaard et al. (1990)	80 organic farms compared with conventional partners	164	123
		80 organic farms compared with average conventional farms	136	105
Switzerland, 1986–1988	Mühlebach and Näf (1990)	Organic farms compared with conventional partners	96	92
Germany, 1987–1990	Priebe (1990) (after Agrarberichten (1986–1990))	Organic test farms (n=33–81) compared with conventional test farms (n=9531–8884) in the same region	117–104 99–87	–
Germany, 1989–1990	Rosenow	Organic and conventional practice	130	136
Germany, 1990–1991	(after Agrarbericht (1991))		109	115

food market during the 1990s. A figure of 5–10% of vegetable sales has been widely quoted. A recent study of the Agriculture Economic Institute in the Netherlands on the prospects of organic products is moderately positive, more specifically for the export market (Landbouw Economisch Instituut, 1990; Baggerman and Hack, 1992). The turnover of organic products in the Netherlands has increased 15 times over the last 8 years. In 1984, it made up 0.2% of the market share, in 1988 it was 0.5% of the market share and last year it was 3.0% (Hack et al., 1993). This tendency will probably continue in future, as political acceptance and consumer demand increase (Tate, 1991).

Linking producers and consumers (people's participation)

Farmer's initiatives

Organic farmers set up farmers' associations with various intentions. They wanted not only to work out their agricultural ideas, but also to elaborate on social and ethical questions. We will here mention some practical results of their efforts.

Associations in various countries formulated standards for methods of production, to be able to communicate a common way of farming to consumers by reliable labelling. To allow for equally reliable international trade, they had to decide on a set of norms acceptable to their counterpart organizations in other countries. Therefore a process of interprofessional expert discussions was set up by the International Federation of Organic Agricultural Movements (IFOAM), the umbrella organization of organic agricultural and related (sympathizing) associations (IFOAM, 1992; IFOAM, PEC, 1992). The IFOAM Standards are explicitly basic or minimum standards and should be regarded as the legal text of the moment (Schmidt and Haccius, 1992). They can in no way be used as a textbook for organic agriculture. Organic agriculture is not a fixed blueprint, but a post-modern way of farming. It is continuously to be developed in practice, with increasing scientific support, in the sense or spirit of the basic principles explained above.

In the Netherlands, the two farmers' associations (the Biodynamic Farming Association and the Association of Organic Farmers) are working together in the national organization BIOLOGICA to promote organic products. This co-operation makes them an important partner in discussions with the trade and retail companies, organic or conventional. The Platform of Organic Agriculture and Food (an umbrella organization of 10 NGOs) has likewise become a structural discussion partner in Dutch agro-policy. It played an important role in the compilation of the policy document on organic agriculture released by the government (LNV, 1992).

On- and off-farm labour diversification

Another way to re-establish a conscious connection with society is agricultural diversification. On-farm product up-grading is one of the most striking examples of this: making cheese from one's own and/or one's friend's cattle's milk or baking bread oneself and/or from one's friend's grains, for house consumption or as a regional specialty.

Starting a farm shop, going to local markets or working with a 'subscription' system provides direct links between producers and consumers. The subscription system has been invented on horticultural farms to sell the products directly to local people The consumers take a subscription and every week receive a fair amount of a selection of vegetables, according to the season. This relationship, which started as a marketing option,has deepened in several cases where consumers now help with the farmwork, packaging and distribution. Restoring the relationship between producers and consumers means opening the farm gate and letting people in to work, visit and ask for information.

A pleasant landscape can also, however, be considered as a product of agriculture. This implies that establishing holiday facilities on the farm is a way of product up-grading too. It can be extended by student and/or consumer summer-help actions to carry out special projects and/or solve peak-labour problems. A new

awareness of mutual needs and offers is thus established in associations of community-supported farms/farm-supported communities (Groh and MacFadden, 1990).

In line with these examples, it is clear that the farm's fence becomes less and less of a strict limit to agricultural labour. On-farm product upgrading has already been mentioned. On-farm- and farmer-participatory research, extension, retaining and development are becoming increasingly acknowledged as crucial for a sound and sustainable future for agriculture and the rural areas (MacRae et al., 1989; Van Mansvelt, 1992; Hiemstra et al., 1992). However, as part-time labour becomes accepted as necessary and profitable for a flexible economy, all kinds of off-farm jobs can be combined with some on-farm jobs if the leading team of farmers acquires appropriate management capacity (Klett, 1990; Gengenbach and Limbacher, 1991).

Here we clearly touch again on the human motivation for continuing self-development or permanent education mentioned at the start of this paper. With Choudhury (1991) and the other researchers cited, we presume that empowerment of the farmers, enhancing their capacities for autonomous ecosystem management, together with those of post-emancipatory co-operation, is the most fundamental prerequisite for structurally sustainable rural development (FAO, 1991; Bruntland, 1993).

Conclusions

It has been shown in this section that organic types of agricultural have a remarkable potential for efficient and sustainable land use. Attention has been paid to the values and interests formulated by the FAO (1992) for sustainable development in the practice of organic agriculture. The principles for farm management drawn up by the IFOAM (1992) are completely in line with the FAO's development goals (see Table 7).

In seeking sustainable options for agricul-

J.D. van Mansvelt, J.A. Mulder / Landscape and Urban Planning 27 (1993) 67–90

Table 7
Objectives for sustainable rural development

Objectives for Sustainable Rural Development		
Basic values and interests of sustainability, as phrased by FAO [1992] (human motivations)	Specific objectives of sustainability, as mentioned for example by: Altieri 1989; Vereyken 1992; FAO 1992; van Mansvelt 1992; Schultink 1992	Principles for farm management as phrased by the IFOAM [1992] (+ standards in charge) (* standards in preparation)
Food security (physical survival)	Self-sufficient supply of good quality food	Diversified and balanced local or regional farming systems Proper handling of agricultural products. (+)
Employment and income generation in rural areas (social survival)	Diversification of income, Labour demand in rural areas, Social equity, Socially and culturally acceptable technology	Agricultural producers earn a living according to UN human rights that cover their basic needs. They obtain an adequate return and satisfaction from their work including a safe working environment. (*)
Natural resource conservation and environmental protection (earth's survival)	Biodiversity, Regenerative potential of nature, Stability, Use of local resources, Health and well-being of the ecosystem, Local landscape values	Maintenance of genetic diversity, Prevention of erosion (rotation, green manure), Local manure supply, Maximum stocking rate, Natural enemies encouragement, Energy saving, Closed nutrient cycles, prevention of leaching and volatilization, Mechanic and thermic weed management, Diversification of the agro-ecosystem to prevent pests and diseases and gain landscape values, Harvesting or gathering without negative impact on the ecosystem, Species-specific animal housing. (+)
People's participation and human resource development (ethical survival)	Human Resource Development, Self-promoting and self-help potential, Farmer's and community's empowerment.	Associations, Labels, Standards, Training, excursions. (*)

ture, the governments of many countries examine OA. The Dutch government has stated (LNV, 1992): "Organic agriculture complies to most of society's and the EC's requirements for the environment, nature and animal welfare. It thus serves as a model for sustainable agriculture." The New Zealand government has formulated its policy as follows (Ministry of Agriculture and Fisheries (MAF), 1991): "The Ministry of Agriculture and Fisheries should provide encouragement and support to organic farming to realise the improved sustainability of farming systems and increased market revenues." In the field of legislation, conversion subsidies and extensification programmes, national governments pay attention to OA (Lampkin, 1991). This type of agriculture, developed in and by agricultural practice, has acquired a place in the agricultural policy of tomorrow.

J.D. van Mansvelt, J.A. Mulder / Landscape and Urban Planning 27 (1993) 67–90   85

Some remarks on rural development

Features of AEM relevant to rural development

Looking back now on the relevance of the points presented above for rural development, the following can be noted: the concept of autonomous ecosystem management (AEM), as implemented in the organic types of agriculture (OA), includes the guiding ideas of (1) the multi-purpose efficiency of the agro-eco-system and its sub-systems as a tool to optimize resource use; (2) the benefits of diversity as a tool to merge ecological with economic performances; (3) the individualization of research as a tool to use science to help the farmers in the implementation of (1) and (2).

Although these ideas as presented are largely developed on farms, in practice they have always been perceived as intended for agriculture as such. They are in no way limited to small farming or otherwise dependent on any metric scales. The only limiting factor is that of the responsible peoples' consciousness and management capacities. Here it should be stressed that the concept of the benefits of diversity applies as much on the level of task division within a farm's human capacity management as it does in the management of agro-eco-capacities.

Another issue of OA is the system of accredited bio-labelling. This, together with several systems of community-supported agriculture (Groh and MacFadden, 1990), offers a range of opportunities for consumers to express their co-responsibility for the rural development in general and AEM in particular. On-farm recreation, for leisure and/or co-working, has become an option of increased interest. It both requires and contributes to a viable rural community life. Landscape and farm-life have thus become 'products of agriculture' with an increasing value in money and social value.

Instruments for implementation of potential

To implement the up-scaling from farm level to the level of rural areas and nations, upgrading and transport can be identified as two interlinked and critical technology issues. Here, regional and national policy could consider instruments to enhance multi-scale food processing and reduce bulk transport. The objective could be to minimize overall waste production and energy demand in the food chain. Decentralized upgrading would, for example, create more jobs in the agricultural production region, enhance recycling of organic matter (including nutrients) and limit bulk transport. Such a policy would obviously require an appropriate adaptation of economic relationships (costs and prices). It could thus be important to realize that prices are 'only' reflections of socio-political validations. With such rules in place, profits now made in excessive transportation will not completely vanish but will shift to other parts of the chain. With a decentralized reallocation of processing, and a diversification of product lines, flexible adaptation to changes in production and demand can be enhanced. Here, as in strictly agricultural production, the economy can be redirected to increase the benefits of diversity (Van Elzakker et al., 1992).

Regional food autonomy, at least as far as the bulk of staple food is concerned, is another demand that has been repeatedly expressed as a prerequisite to achieve sustainable development in all countries (Djigma et al., 1990; FAO, 1991). This is not to be taken in a dogmatic way, but seen as a tool to minimize the irrational and counterproductive impact of unfair competition, based on power-biased access to markets, capital, knowledge and other facilities. Imports and exports of regional specialty products, provided their prices include the environmental and social production costs in an acceptable way, need not be a problem. They can be seen as a basic tool for co-operation and a way of meeting other cultures (Fuchs, 1991; Harkaly, 1991; Pedersen, 1991).

Conclusions

Considering the concepts of AEM and the experiences of OA in practice as presented, they seem to indicate the following options for sustainable rural development:

(1) by choosing the multi-purpose efficiency of the agro-ecosystem and its subsystems, OA complies with the requirements for a sustainable use of natural resources.

(2) Regarding the contribution of OA to the ecological and economic aspects of sustainable rural development, we could indicate that: (i) its yield per hectare are lower than those of HEIA, although they are sufficient to meet the EC's efforts to reduce overproduction, and to meet the requirements for eventual national food autonomy. OA therefore seems to meet society's needs for sufficient good quality food; (ii) its impact on the environment, nature and landscape seem to meet the requirements of EC and national policies; (iii) its economic performance per farm, under the actual policy conditions and prices, is remarkably similar to that of comparable conventional farms.

Therefore the physical performance of OA indicates that it could be an environmentally sound and economically viable option, fulfilling several of the actual agro-policy demands.

(3) Regarding the contribution of OA to the social aspects of sustainable rural development, we should indicate that its tendency to (i) higher labour demands per hectare, (ii) product upgrading on the farm, (iii) labour diversification within the farm, (iv) job diversification from farming, (v) building of farmer's associative co-operatives, and (vi) emphasis on the importance of links with consumers (through labelling, excursions, visits and holidays) increases the number of people living on and linked to farms or farming enterprises. This again could contribute to an in-

crease in the rural population and to the viability of rural life.

(4) Regarding the contribution of OA to the ethical and attitudinal aspects of sustainable rural development, it could be supposed that (i) its basic attitude of co-operation with nature, (ii) its professionally applied care and respect for the living soil and the environment, (iii) its emphasis on the needs for human development, could play a role in the cultural shift toward a common future.

(5) For science, the challenge seems to be to develop a strategy of serving the interests of sustainable agriculture. This might very well include the development of strategies for the individualization of science, so as to meet the demands of particular regions and farmers. The science of agro-ecosystems will remain open for and even in need of generic understanding; however, this generic understanding should facilitate rather than limit diversified application, which complies with the farmer's style of management, the ecosystem's capacities and the consumers' demands.

Acknowledgements

We thank Frans Verkley, Darko Znaor and Jelmer Buys from the Department of Ecological Agriculture, Wageningen Agricultural University, for constructive criticism.

References

Albrecht, W.A., 1975. The Albrecht Papers. Acres U.S.A., Raytown, MO, 401 pp.

Altieri, M. (Editor), 1992. Special Issue 'Sustainable Agriculture'. Agric. Ecosystems Environ., 39 (1–2).

Altieri, M.A., 1989. Agroecology: a new research and development paradigm for world agriculture. Agric. Ecosystems Environ., 27: 37–46.

Anosike, N. and Coughenour, C.M., 1990. The socioeconomic basis of farm enterprise diversification decisions. Rural Sociol., 55(1): 1–24.

Baars, T., 1990. Het bos-ecosysteem als beeld voor het bedrijfsorganisme in de biologisch-dynamische landbouw. Louis Bolk Instituut, Driebergen, 32 pp.

Baars, A., van de Klundert, A.F. and Reyer, A.W.J., 1983. Vegetatie, bodem, mineralenbalans en energieverbruik van

J.D. van Mansvelt, J.A. Mulder / Landscape and Urban Planning 27 (1993) 67–90

enkele gangbare en alternatieve agrarische bedrijven in Noord Holland, RUL.

Bader, U., 1992. Engagement in der Regionalgruppe—wozu? Bioland, 6: 34–35.

Baggerman, T. and Hack, M.D., 1992. Consumentenonderzoek naar biologische produkten: hoe het marktaandeel vergroot kan worden. (Consumer investigation of organic products: how to increase the market share; English summary.) SWOKA/LEI-DLO, Meded. 463. LEI, Den Haag, 110 pp.

Bakker, Th.M., 1985. Eten van eigen bodem, een modelstudie. LEI, Den Haag, 225 pp.

Bartussek, H., 1982. Probleme der Massentierhaltung aus ganzheitlicher Sicht. In: R. Kikuth (Editor), Die oekologische Landwirtschaft. Müller, Karlsruhe, 205 pp.

Bechmann, A., 1987. Landbau-Wende Gesunde Landwirtschaft-Gesunde Ernährung. Fischer-Verlag, 288 pp.

Blatz, V. (Editor), 1991. Ethics and Agriculture. University of Idaho Press, Moscow. ID.

Bockemühl, J., 1984. In Partnership with Nature. Biodynamic Literature, WY.

Böckenhoff, E., Hamm, U. and Umhau, M., 1986. Analyse der Betriebs- und Produktionsstrukturen sowie der Naturalertrage im Alternativen Landbau. Ber. Landwirtsch., 64: 1–39.

Boehnke, E., 1993. Basic principles of organic animal husbandry. Paper presented at Conference on New Strategies for Sustainable Rural Development, Gödöllő University of Agricultural Sciences, Gödöllő, 22–25 March 1993.

Boulding, K.E., 1978. Ecodynamics: A New Theory of Societal Evolution. Sage, 368 pp.

Braat, R., 1992. Bio-diversiteit in de biologische landbouw. RIVM, Bilthoven.

Braat, R.H. and Vereyken, F.H.M., 1993. Het effect de biologische landbouw op natuur en landschap: een literatuurstudie. RIVM, Bilthoven.

Braunewell, R., Busse, J. and Martens, S., 1986. Der Biologische Landbau: auch eine Alternative für Flora und Fauna. Bioland, 6: 25–26.

Brinks, G. and van Mansvelt, J.D., 1992. The influence of market and government policies on resource use and environment in agriculture. Paper for UNCTAD (presented for expert consultation).

Brown, L.R., Flavin, C., Postel, S. and Starke, L., 1992. The State of the World. Worldwatch Institute, Washington, DC.

Brundtland, G.H., 1987. Our common future. World Commission on Environment and Development, Oxford University Press.

Bruntland, G.H., 1992. Statement at the opening of the Conference on Environment and Development, Rio de Janeiro, 3 June.

Chaboussou, F., 1985. Santé des Cultures: une Revolution Agronomique. La Maison Rustique, Paris, 126 pp.

Choudhury, K., 1991. Intervention at the FAO–SARD Conference. Den Bosch, Netherlands.

Commission of the European Communities (CEC), 1991. Communication of the Commission to the Council: the development and future of the CAP. COM (91)100. CEC, Brussels, 1 February 1991, 238 pp.

Conway, G.R. and Barbier, E.B., 1990. After the Green Revolution: Sustainable Agriculture for Development. Earthscan, London, 205 pp.

CPB, 1992. Scanning the Future. A Long-Term Scenario Study of the World Economy, 1990–2015. SDU, Den Haag.

Daly, H.E., Cobb, J.B. and Cobb, C.W., 1990. For the Common Good: Redirecting Community, the Environment and a Sustainable Future. Green Print, London, 482 pp.

De Bruin, R., Oostindie, H. and van der Ploeg, J.O., 1992. Verbrede plattelandsontwikkeling in de praktijk. Studierapporten van de Rijksplanologische Dienst No. 54. Ministerie van VROM, Den Haag, 69 pp.

De Lange, H. and van Mansvelt, J.D., 1991. Organic Agriculture: a source-directed policy to prevent pesticide's pollution. Department of Ecological Agriculture, Wageningen. Agricultural University Commissioned by Greenpeace International, Amsterdam.

De Wit, C.T., 1992. Resource use efficiency in agriculture. Agric. Systems 40: 125–151.

De Zeeuw, D. and Albrecht, W.G., 1990. Duurzaam samengaan van landbouw, natuur en milieu. Manifest en rapport van de gelijknamige wijkgroep, Amsterdam, 18 pp.

De Zeeuw, D. and van der Meer, W., 1992. Grond voor keuzen — suggesties voor vervolg. Spil, 5: 29–34.

Devall, B. and Sessions, G., 1985. Deep Ecology, Living as if Nature Mattered. George Sessions Layton Smith, USA, 267 pp.

Dillon, J.L. and Anderson, J.R., 1990. The Analysis of Crop and Livestock Production, 3rd edn. Pergamon, Oxford, 251 pp.

Djigma, A., Nikiema, E., Lairon, D. and Ott, P. (Editors), 1990. Agricultural alternatives and nutritional self-sufficiency. Proc. 7th Int. Sci. IFOAM Conference, IFOAM, 2–5 January, 1989, Tholey-Theley, Germany.

DLV, 1993. Biokwint, quantitative information on organic yield performance (in preparation).

Dokychayev, V.V., 1892. In Kashtanov, A.N., 1992; Nauchnoye naslediye V.V. Dokuchayev i yevo razvitye v sovremennom lanschaftnom zemledelii. (The scientific heritage of V.V. Dokuchayev and its meaning for present agriculture.) Keynote paper presented at the Scientific Conference of the Russian Academy of Agricultural Sciences, Voronezh, Russia.

Draghetti, A., 1991. Principi di Fisiologia dell'Azienda Agraria. Edagricole, Bologna, 416 pp.

Dubgaard, A., Olsen, P. and Sørensen, N., 1990. Okonomien i okologisk jordbrug- en regnskabusundersogelse. (Profitability of organic farming in Denmark.) Landbrugsministeriet, Statens Jordbrugsokonomoske Institut, Rep. 54 (with an English summary).

Evans, H.E. and Ngau, P., 1991. Rural–urban relations, household income diversification and agricultural productivity. Dev. Change, 22: 519–545.

Food and Agriculture Organization (FAO), 1991. The Den Bosch Declaration and Agenda for Action on Sustainable Agriculture and Rural Development. Report of the Conference and Main Document No. 1. FAO/Netherlands

88 J.D. van Mansvelt, J.A. Mulder / Landscape and Urban Planning 27 (1993) 67–90

Conference on Agriculture and the Environment, 's-Hertogenbosch, Netherlands, 15–19 April 1991. FAO, Rome, 29 pp.

FAO, 1992. FAO Policies and Actions; Stockholm 1972–Rio 1992. FAO, Rome, 88 pp.

Fuchs, H., 1991. EFTA's assessment of fair trade. In: B. Geier, C. Harst and A. Pons (Editors), 2nd Int. IFOAM Conf. Trade in Organic Foods, 11–13 November 1991, Vienna, Tholey Theley, Germany, p. 8.

Gengenbach, H. and Limbacher, M., 1991. Kooperation oder Konkurs? Verlag Freies Geistesleben, Stuttgart, 170 pp.

George, S., 1985. How the Other Half Dies. Penguin, Harmordsworth, UK, 352 pp.

Gore, A., 1992. Earth in Balance. Forging a New Common Purpose. Earthscan, London, 407 pp.

Grandstedt, A., 1990. Kann die Schwedische Landwirtschaft ohne Mineraldünger arbeiten? Lebendige Erde, 4: 262–269.

Greenpeace, 1992. Green Fields, Grey Future, EC Agricultural Policy and the Crossroads. Greenpeace International, Amsterdam, 98 pp.

Groh, T. and MacFadden, S.S.H., 1990. Farms of Tomorrow, Community-supported Farms, Farm-supported Communities. Biodynamic Farming and Gardening Association, Kimberton, USA, 169 pp.

Hack, M.D. et al., 1993. De groothandel en verwerking van biologische produkten, de mogelijkheden van het gangbare naast het biologische kanaal. LEI–DLO, Den Haag, 74 pp.

Harkaly, A., 1991. Is there a way out for the (small) farmer in developing countries? In: B. Geier, C. Harst and A. Pons (Editors), 2nd Int. IFOAM Conf., Trade in Organic Foods, 11–13 November 1991, Vienna. IFOAM, Tholey Theley, Germany, pp. 73–78.

Hayami, Y. and Ruttan, V.W., 1985. Agricultural Development. An International Perspective. John Hopkins University Press, Baltimore, MD, 506 pp.

Hendriks, K. and Stroeken, F., 1992. Verschil in Verschijning, een vergelijkende studie naar biologische en niet-biologische landbouwbedrijven. Vakgroep Ruimtelijke Planvorming, Landschapsarchitektuur en Vakgroep Alternatieve Landbouw, Wageningen Agricultural University, 109 pp.

Henze, A., 1980. Zur Sicherung der Nahrungsmittelversorgung in der Bundesrepublik. Agrarwirtschaft, 29(11): 333–339.

Hermann, G., Hampl, U. and Bachtaler, G., 1986. Unkrautbesatz und Unkrautentwicklung; ergebnissbericht von Regulierungsmassnahmen bei oekologischer und konventioneller Wirtschaftsweise. Bayer. Landwirtsch. Jahrb., 63(7): 795–805.

Hermannstorfer, U., 1992. Wege zum partnerschaftlichen Wirtschaften. Demeter Bl., 52: 15–17.

Hiemstra, W., Reijntjes, C. and van der Werf, E., 1992. Let Farmers Judge. Intermediate Technology, UK, 208 pp.

Hildyard, N., 1991. An open letter to Edouard Saouma, Director-General of the FAO. Ecologist, 21(2).

Howard, A., 1943. An Agricultural Testament. Oxford University Press, London, 253 pp.

Hueting, R. et al.,1992. Methodology for the Calculation of Sustainable National Income. 's-Gravenhage, CBS, 64 pp.

International Federation of Organic Agricultural Movements (IFOAM), 1992. Basic Standards of Organic Agriculture. IFOAM General Secretariat, Tholey Theley, Germany, 32 pp.

IFOAM PEC, 1992. The IFOAM Evaluation Programme of Certifying Organisations. IFOAM PEC, Darmstadt, 4 pp.; The IFOAM Accreditation Programme, Operating Manual, Draft No. 7. IFOAM AC, Darmstadt, 57 pp.

Kampfraath, 1990. Integratie, het vraagstuk van de jaren negentig. Afscheidsrede, Wageningen Agricultural University.

Kenmore, P.E., 1991. Indonesia's Integrated pest Management—a model for Asia, how rice farmers clean up the environment, conserve biodiversity, raise more food, make higher profits, FAO Inter-Country Programme for Integrated Pest Control in South and Southeast Asia, Manilla, 56 pp.

Kettunen, L., 1986. Self-sufficiency of agriculture in Finland in 1970–1983. J. Agric. Sci. Finland, 58(4): 143–150.

Klett, M., 1990. How can we liberate agriculture from its industrial prison? In: Growing Together ... Why Should We Bother? Int. Biodynamic Initiative Group, Hartfield, UK, 52 pp.

Koepf, H.H., 1980. Landbau: Natur- und Menschen gemäss. Verlag Freies Geistesleben, Stuttgart, 270 pp.

Lampkin, N., 1990. Organic Farming. Farming Press, Ipswich, UK, 701 pp.

Lampkin, N., 1991. Organic farming and agricultural policy in Europe. Ecol. Farming, 2: 4–7.

Lampkin, N., 1992. The economic implications of conversion from conventional to organic farming systems. Ph.D. Thesis, Department of Economics and Agricultural Economics, University of Wales, Aberystwyth.

Latour, J.W. and Groen, C.L.G., 1993. Environmental quality assessment in multifunctional regions. RIVM, Bilthoven (in preparation).

LEI, 1990. Productie en afzet van BD- en EKO-produkten. Band 2. Meded. 425, LEI, Den Haag, 89 pp.

Lievegoed, B.C.J., 1979. Phases. Rudolf Steiner Press, London, 120 pp.

Lindner, U., 1991. Dreizehnjähriger Vergleichsversuch zwischen konventionellen und ökologischem Gemüsebau. Garten Organisch, 4: 24–29.

LN&V, 1992. Beleidsnota Biologische Landbouw. Ministry of Agriculture, Nature Management and Fisheries, Den Haag, 36 pp.

Lovelock, J.E., 1979. Gaia, a New Look at Life on Earth. Oxford University Press, 157 pp.

Lövenstein, H., Lantinga, E.A., Rabbinge, R. and van Keulen, H., 1992. Principles of Theoretical Production Ecology. Revised Course Book, Department of TPE, Waningen Agricultural University, 111 pp.

MacRae, R.J., Hill, S.B., Henning, J. and Mehuys, G.R., 1989. Agricultural science and sustainable agriculture: a review of the existing scientific barriers to sustainable food production and potential solutions. Biol. Agric. Hortic., 6: 173–219.

Manintveld, K., 1979. Vielzahl von Kleinlebewesen und

J.D. van Mansvelt, J.A. Mulder / Landscape and Urban Planning 27 (1993) 67–90   89

Pflanzenwelt auf Dauerwiesen. Lebendige Erde, 4: 131–134.

Maslow, A.H., 1968. Motivation and Personality. Harper and Row, New York, 411 pp.

Meadows, D.H., 1992. No, you don't need to be afraid of sustainability. Int. Herald Trib., 29/4, p. 7.

Meadows, D.H. and Randers, J., 1992. Beyond the Limits. Earthscan, London, 300 pp.

Merril, M.C., 1983. Eco-agriculture: a review of its history and philosophy. Biol. Agric. Hortic., 1: 181–210.

Meyer, A., 1990. Wieviel Boden brauchen wir? Zum Beispiel, 1: 11–13.

Mühlebach, J. and Näf, E., 1990. Die Wettbewerbsfähigkeit des biologischen Landbaus. Eine betriebs- und arbeidswirtschaftliche Analyse des biologischen Landbaus. Rep. 33, Swiss Federal Research Station for Farm Management and Agricultural Engineering, FAT, Tänikon.

Ministry of Agriculturel and Fisheries (MAF), 1991. A proposed policy on organic agriculture. MAF Policy Paper 111. MAF, Wellington, New Zealand.

Naess, A., 1975. Science between culture and counterculture. In: C.I. Dessaur, A. Naess and E. Reimer (Editors), Science between Culture and Counterculture, paper of a Congress, University of Nijmegen.

National Research Council, Committee on the Role of Alternative Farming, 1989. Alternative Agriculture. Washington National Academy Press, Washington, DC, 448 pp.

Nauta, R.S., 1979. Landbouwkundige produktie in Nederland bij natuurlijke Stikstofvoorziening. Meded. 79-18, Wageningen Agricultural University, 58 pp.

Neher, D., 1992. Ecological sustainability in agricultural systems: definition and measurement. Am. J. Sustainable Agric., 2(3):51–61.

Organization for Economic Co-operation and Development (OECD), 1992. Agents for Change. Summary Report from the OECD Workshop on Sustainable Agriculture Technology and Practices, 11–13 February, Paris, 132 pp.

Oldeman, L.R., Hakkeling, R.T.A. and Sombroek, W.G., 1990. World map of the status of human-induced soil degradation; world map, an explanatory note and annex 5. International Soil Reference and Information Centre, UN Environment Programme in co-operation with The Win- and Staring Centre, The International Society of Soil Science, Food and Agricultural Organization of the UN and the International Institute for Aerospace Survey and Earth Science, 34 pp.

Pedersen, B., 1991. Ethical trade and organic agriculture. In: B. Geier, C. Haest and A. Pons (Editors), 2nd Int. IFOAM Conf., Trade in Organic Foods, 11–13 November 1991, Vienna. IFOAM, Tholey Theley, Germany, 149 pp.

Priebe, H., 1990. Ergebnisse ökologische Wirtschaftsweise. Lebendige Erde, 3: 162–167.

Rabbinge, R., Rossing, W.A.H. and van der Werf, W., 1990. The bridge function of production ecology in pest and disease management. In: R. Rabbinge F. Goudriaan and H. van Keulen (Editors), Theoretical Production Ecology: Reflections and Prospects. Pudoc, Wageningen, 301 pp.

Rasmussen, J. and Haas, H., 1985. Sammenligning af unkrudsfloraen i biodunamisk og konventionelt landbrug. KVL.

Reijntjes, C. et al., 1992. Farming for the Future, An Introduction to Low-External-Input and Sustainable Agriculture. ILEIA, Leusden, Netherlands, 250 pp.

RIVM, 1993. Basis document natuur en milieu effecten van biologische vormen van landbouw en hun economische haalbaarheid. RIVM, Bilthoven (in preparation).

Roep, D., van der Ploeg, J.D. and Leeuwis, C., 1991. Zicht op duurzaamheid en kontinuïteit; bedrijfsstijlen in de Achterhoek. Wageningen, 207 pp.

Sattler, F. and von Wistinghausen, E., 1992. Biodynamic Practice. BDAA, Stourbridge, UK, 33 pp.

Schmidt, H. and Haccius, M., 1992. EG-Verordnung "Ökologischer Landbau". Alternative Konzepte 81, Stiftung Ökologie und Landbau, Müller, Karlsruhe, 452 pp.

Schultink, G., 1992. Evaluation of sustainable development alternatives: relevant concepts, resource assessment approaches and comparative spatial indicators. Int. J. Environ. Stud., 41: 203–224.

Schumacher, E.F., 1973. Small is Beautiful. Blond and Briggs, London.

Schütz, P., 1983. Der biologische Landbau in Österreich: eine kritische und zeitgemässe Betrachtung. Ludwig-Boltzmann Forschungsstelle für Biologischen Landbau, Wien, Heft 3.

Schweigl, U., 1990. Vergleichungsuntersuchungen zwischen biologischen und konventionellen Landbau. Obstbau–Weinbau, 27(4): 114–116.

Sheldrake, R., 1990. Rebirth of Nature. Ryder, London, 215 pp.

Stanhill, G., 1990. The comparative productivity of organic agriculture. Agric. Ecosystems Environ., 30: 1–26.

Steiner, R., 1924. Geisteswissenschaftliche Grundlagen zum gedeihen der Landwirtschaft. Rudolf Steiner Verlag, Dornach, 258 pp.

Steinmann, R., 1983. Der biologische Landbau—ein betriebswirtschaftlicher Vergleich. Rep. Swiss Federal Research Station for Farm Management and Agricultural Engineering, FAT, Tänikon.

Struik, P.C., van Niejenhuis, J.H. and de Hoogh, J., 1991. Problematiek en vooruitzichten van de Nederlandse akkerbouw. Wageningen Agricultural University, 35 pp.

Tate, W., 1991. Organic Produce in Europe. The Economist Intelligence Unit, London, 178 pp.

Terwan, P., 1992. Boeren met natuur: een verkenning van kansen voor natuur op landbouwbedrijven. CLM, Utrecht, 98 pp.

UN, 1992. Agenda 21 of the Earth Summit. UN Conference on Environment and Development, Rio de Janeiro, UN Department of Public Information, New York, 124 pp.

Van der Ploeg, J.D. and Ettema, M., 1990. Het kwaliteitsvraagstuk in de landbouw: een inleiding. In: J.D. van der Ploeg and M. Ettema (Editors), Tussen Bulk en Kwaliteit: Landbouw, Voedselproduktie en Gezondheid. Van Gorcum, Assen/Maastricht, 149 pp.

Van der Ploeg, J.D. and Roep, D., 1990. Bedrijfsstijlen in de Zuidhollandse Veenweidegebieden; nieuwe perspectieven voor beleid en belangenbehartiging. Wageningen/Haarlem, 98 pp.

Van der Werff, P.A. (Editor), 1992. Toetsing en nadere ontwikkeling van milieuvriendelijke bedrijfsvoering en bepaling van milieuemissies van biologische gemengde bedrijven in Nederland op zandgronden. Interimrapport over de periode 1 juli 1990–1 juli 1991. Wageningen Agricultural University, 136 pp.

Vereyken, P., 1986–1988. Verslagen over het proefbedrijf OBS 1982–1985 (Nos. 3–5). Nagele.

Van Elzakker, B., Witte, R. and van Mansvelt, J.D., 1992. Benefits of diversity, an incentive towards sustainable agriculture. UNDP, Environment and Natural Resources Division, New York.

Van Mansvelt, J.D., 1988. The role of lower-input technologies in the future. In: M. Whitbey and J. Ollerenshaw (Editors), Land-Use and the European Environment. Belhaven Press, London, 189 pp.

Van Mansvelt, 1991. Opening Address. In: B. Geier, C. Haest and A. Pons (Editors), 2nd Int. IFOAM Conf. Trade in Organic Foods, 11–13 November 1991, Vienna. IFOAM, Tholey Theley, Germany, pp. 19–24.

Van Mansvelt, J.D., 1992. Vers une agriculture renouvenable et durable. Rev. Tiers Monde, XXXIII(130): 311–328.

Van Mansvelt, J.D. and Mulder, J.A., 1992. Basics and performances of organic agricultural production, considerations on the role of trade and the IFOAM programme evaluation and accreditation system. Paper presented at the Int. Policy Council Conf., Agriculture, the Environment and Trade—Conflict or Cooperation, Noordwijk, Netherlands, 6–8 September 1992.

Van Mansvelt, J.D. and Verkley, F., 1991. Society's steps toward sustainable agriculture. Paper presented for the UNESCO International Forum on Sustainable Development, 23–25 September, Paris, p. 36.

Vogtmann, H. (Editor), 1985. Oekologischer Landbau, Landwirtschaft mit Zukunft. Pro Natur Verlag, Stuttgart, 159 pp.

Von Ammer, U., Utschik, H. and Anton, H., 1988. Die auswirkung von biologischem und konventionellem Landbau auf Flora und Fauna. Forstwiss. Zentralbl., 107(5): 274–291.

Von Eisen, T., 1989. Ackerwildkraut Bestände biologisch-dynamisch und konventionell bewirtschafter Hackfruchttäcker in der Niederrheinischen Bucht. Lebendige Erde, 4: 277–281.

Von Mallinckrodt, F., 1991. More efficient agriculture without losing the physical and moral foundation. UNDP, New York.

World Commission on Environment and Development (WCED), 1987. Our Common Future. Oxford University Press, 383 pp.

Wijnands. F.W., 1991–1992. Verslagen over het proefbedrijf OBS 1987–1988 (Nos. 8 and 9), Nagele.

Zadoks, J.C. (Editor), 1989. Development of Farming Systems: Evaluation of the Five Year Period 1980–1984. PUDOC, Wageningen, 90 pp.

[18]

PERGAMON

Natural Resources Forum 24 (2000) 107–121

Natural Resources
FORUM

www.elsevier.com/locate/natresfor

The promising spread of sustainable agriculture in Asia

Jules Pretty[a], Rachel Hine[b]

[a]*Director, Centre for Environment and Society, University of Essex, Colchester, UK. E-mail address: jpretty@essex.ac.uk*
[b]*Research Officer, CES, University of Essex, Colchester, UK*

Abstract

Despite great successes in increasing food production, Asia still faces enormous food security challenges. Most commentators agree that there will have to be increases in food production from existing agricultural land, but many are pessimistic about the future, judging likelihood of success on the basis of past performance of 'modern' agricultural development. Sustainable agriculture, though, offers entirely new opportunities, by emphasising the productive values of natural, social and human capital, all assets that Asian countries either have in abundance or that can be regenerated at relatively low financial cost.

This paper sets out an assets-based model of agricultural systems, together with a typology of eight approaches for sustainable agriculture improvements. In the 16 projects/initiatives spread across eight countries that are analysed, some 2.86 million households have substantially improved total food production on 4.93 million hectares, resulting in greatly improved household food security. Proportional yield increases are greatest in rainfed systems, but irrigated systems have seen small cereal yield increases combined with added production from additional productive system components (such as fish in rice, vegetables on dykes). The additional positive impacts on natural, social and human capital are also helping to build the assets base so as to sustain these improvements in the future.

This analysis indicates that sustainable agriculture can deliver large increases in food production in Asia. But spreading these to much larger numbers of farm households will not be easy. It will require fundamental policy reform. © 2000 United Nations. Published by Elsevier Science Ltd. All rights reserved.

Keywords: Food production; Sustainable agriculture; Asia; Food security; Social assets; Agro-ecosystems

1. The scale of the challenge

Despite several decades of remarkable agricultural progress, the world still faces a massive food security challenge. The world population passed 6 billion people in late-1999, and the UN Population Division (1998) predicts increases to 7.5 billion by 2020 and to 8.4 billion by 2050. By that time 84% of the world's population will be in those countries that currently make up the 'developing' world. Already, though, there are an estimated 830 million people lacking adequate access to food, of whom 31% are in East and South-East Asia (258 million), 31% in South Asia (254 million), 25% in Sub-Saharan Africa (210 million), 7.6% in Latin America and the Caribbean, and 5% in North Africa and Near East (Pinstrup-Anderson and Cohen, 1999).

Asia faces particular challenges. Even though food production per capita has risen by some 30% since the 1960s, it still has the largest absolute numbers of hungry people. It also has the two most populous countries in the

world, China and India. The pressure on the food system also grows with increasing prosperity as consumption of livestock products (meat, eggs and milk) will grow. Delgado et al. (1999) indicate that per capita consumption in all developing countries was 21 kg of meat and 41 kg of milk in 1993, and predicts an increase in demand to 29 and 63 kg by 2020. Extra livestock would appear to mean some increased consumption of cereals for feed.

Most commentators, therefore, agree that food production will have to increase, and that this will have to come from existing farmland (cf. IFPRI, 1995; FAO, 1995, 1996; Leach, 1996; Conway, 1997). Many predictions are gloomy, indicating that the gap between demand and production will grow. But solving these problems is not simply a matter of developing new agricultural technologies. Most hungry consumers are poor, and so simply do not have the money to buy the food they need. Equally, poor producers cannot afford expensive technologies. And if they cannot afford them, no amount of 'modern' technology developed by external organisations seeking to make a financial return

108   *J. Pretty, R. Hine / Natural Resources Forum 24 (2000) 107–121*

will make any difference for them. They will have to find solutions largely based on existing resources.

This paper reviews recent evidence on sustainable agriculture in Asia. Such sustainable agriculture offers two types of new opportunities: (i) substantial increases in food production in precisely those regions that have missed out in the past; and (ii) transitions to more diverse and environmentally sensitive agro-ecosystems in those areas that have seen substantial food productivity increases, but at some cost to environmental and human health. Instead of having to rely on costly external inputs (which of course can be effective, but only if farmers can afford them and national systems can deliver them), the improvements are based on improved configurations and uses of natural, social and human capital assets.

An assets-based model of agricultural systems describes the fundamental changes needed, together with a typology of eight improvements that are currently in use in sustainable agriculture projects, initiatives and programmes.

2. An assets-based model for agricultural systems

Agricultural and rural systems at all levels, from farms, livelihoods and communities to national economies, rely for their success on the total stock of natural, social, human, physical and financial capital (Coleman, 1990; Putnam et al., 1993; Putnam, 1995; Costanza et al., 1997; Daily, 1997; Carney, 1998; Pretty, 1998; Pretty and Ward, 2000). These consist of the following:

1. Natural Capital, nature's free goods and services. These comprise: food (both farmed and from the wild); wood and fibre; water regulation and supply; waste assimilation, decomposition and treatment; nutrient cycling and fixation; soil formation; biological control of pests; climate regulation; wildlife habitats; storm protection and flood control; carbon sequestration; pollination; and recreation and leisure.
2. Social Capital, the cohesiveness of people in their societies. This comprises relations of trust that lubricate co-operation; the bundles of common rules, norms and sanctions for behaviour; reciprocity and exchanges; connectedness and social institutions.
3. Human Capital, the quality or status of individual persons. This comprises the stock of health, nutrition, education, skills and knowledge of individuals; access to services that provide these, such as schools, medical services, adult training; the ways individuals and their knowledge interact with productive technologies; and the leadership quality of individuals.
4. Physical Capital, or local infrastructure. This includes housing and other buildings; roads and bridges; energy supplies; communications; markets; and air, road, water and rail transportation.
5. Financial Capital, or stocks of money. These comprise: savings; access to affordable credit; pensions; remittances; welfare payments; grants and subsidies.

These five assets are transformed by policies, processes and institutions to give desirable outcomes, such as food security, jobs, welfare, economic growth, clean environment, reduced crime, better health and schools, and so on. If achieved, these desirable outcomes then feed back to help build up the five capital assets. In general, when outcomes are undesirable, resulting in pollution or deforestation, increased crime or social breakdown, they reduce the asset base.

The basic principle is, therefore, that sustainable systems accumulate stocks of these five assets. They increase the capital base over time. But unsustainable systems deplete or run down capital, spending it as if it was income, liquidating assets and leaving less for future generations.

The assets-based model described in Fig. 1 shows how farms and rural livelihoods take inputs of various types, including renewable assets, and transform these to produce food and other desirable outputs. These can be processed for home consumption, transformed through value-added processes for sale, or sold directly as raw product. The inputs are shown as:

- Renewable natural capital—soil, water, air, biodiversity, etc.
- Social and participatory processes—including both locally embedded and externally induced social capital, and partnerships and linkages between external organisations.
- New technologies, knowledge and skills—both regenerative (e.g. legumes, natural enemies) and non-renewable (e.g. hybrid seeds, machinery).
- Non-renewable or fossil-fuel derived inputs (e.g. fertilisers, pesticides, antibiotics).
- Finance—credit, remittances, income from sales and grants.

Availability and access to these five inputs is shaped by a wide range of contextual factors (on the far left of Fig. 1). These include unchanging factors (at least over the short-term), such as climate, agro-ecology, soils, culture; and dynamic economic, social, political and legal factors shaped by external institutions and policies. These contextual factors are an important entry point for shaping and influencing agricultural systems (such as national policies, markets, trade).

Agriculture, though, does more than just produce food. It has a profound impact (positive or negative) on many other aspects of local, national and global economies and ecosystems. A fundamental principle of sustainable systems is that they do not deplete capital assets, whilst unsustainable ones deplete them (Butler-Flora, 1998; Goodland, 1998). More sustainable agricultural systems, therefore, tend to have a positive effect on natural, social and human capital whilst also producing food, fibre, oil, etc. A vital feedback

J. Pretty, R. Hine / Natural Resources Forum 24 (2000) 107–121   109

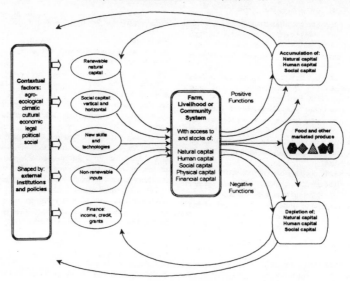

Fig. 1. Assets-based model of agricultural systems.

loop occurs from outcomes to inputs: agricultural systems impact on the very assets on which they, together with many other sectors of economies, rely for inputs.

For example, an agricultural system that depletes organic matter or erodes soil in order to produce food external-ises costs that others must bear. One that sequesters carbon in soils through organic matter accumulation both contributes to the global good by mediating climate change and to the private good by enhancing soil health. Equally, a diverse agricultural system that protects and enhances on-farm wildlife for pest and disease control contributes to wider concerns about biodiversity and genetic conservation, whilst simplified systems that eliminate wildlife do not.

Agriculture is, therefore, fundamentally multi-functional (FAO, 1999). It delivers many unique non-food functions that cannot be so efficiently produced by other economic sectors. A key policy challenge is to find ways to enhance food production, whilst seeking both to improve the positive functions and to eliminate the negative ones. This will not be easy, as past agricultural development has tended to ignore both the multi-functionality of agriculture and the external costs (Conway and Pretty, 1991; Altieri, 1995; Pretty, 1998). Fortunately, there has emerged much evidence to illustrate that it is indeed possible to produce more food and more natural, social and human capital. Ironically, though, much of this has occurred without significant or intentional policy support.

3. Agricultural modernisation and types of transformation

The process of agricultural modernisation during the 20th century has produced three distinct types of agriculture: industrialised country, Green Revolution, and all that remains—the pre-modern, 'traditional' or 'unimproved' (Chambers et al., 1989; Pretty, 1995a). The first two types have been able to respond to modern technological packages, producing highly productive systems of agri-culture. Their conditions were either like those where the technologies were generated, or else their environments could easily be homogenised to suit the technologies. These systems tend now to be endowed with access to roads and urban markets, modern crop varieties and live-stock breeds, inputs, machinery, marketing infrastructure, transport, agro-processing facilities, credit, and water supply.

Most agricultural systems in industrialised countries are high-external input systems, save for steadily increasing numbers of organic farmers and remnants of traditional, low-intensive systems. In Europe, for example, there were 2.26 million ha of organic farming in 1997 (1.7% of utilised agricultural area), and 56 million ha of traditional agriculture (Bignall and McCracken, 1996; Lampkin, 1999). In developing countries, modern high-input systems tend to be monocrop and/or monoanimal enterprises geared for sale, and so include lowland irrigated rice, wheat and

110   J. Pretty, R. Hine / Natural Resources Forum 24 (2000) 107–121

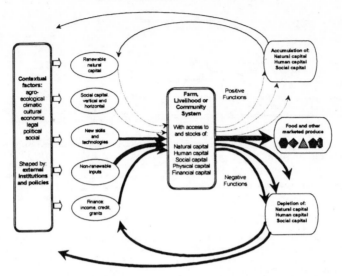

Fig. 2. Assets-based model of agricultural systems—flows and outcomes in modernised systems.

cotton; plantations of bananas, pineapples, oil palm, sugar cane; market gardening near to urban centres; and intensive and extensive livestock rearing and ranching.

The third type of agriculture comprises all the remaining 'pre-modern', 'traditional' or 'unimproved' agricultural systems. Farming systems are complex and diverse, and cereal yields are low—typically only 500–1500 kg/ha. They are remote from markets and infrastructure; located on fragile or problem soils; and are unlikely to be visited by agricultural scientists and extension workers or studied in research institutions. The poorest countries, in particular the low income food deficit countries, have higher proportions of these agricultural systems. In the mid-1990s, some 30–35% of the world's population, about two billion people, were still directly supported by this third type of agriculture (Pretty, 1995a).

Fig. 2 illustrates the emphasis on the assets-based model for industrialised systems. Those systems have become efficient transformers of technologies, non-renewable inputs and finance to produce very large amounts of food, but with substantial negative impact on capital assets (e.g. reduced natural capital, diminished labour) and large leakage of value from local systems.

So what is it that constitutes success? Wheat yields in India and Pakistan grew from 1.2 to 2.5 and 1.8 t/ha, respectively, from 1970 to 1995; rice yields in China grew from 3 to 5 t/ha, in India from 1.6 to 2.8 t/ha, and in the Philippines from 2.2 to 4 t/ha; and maize yields in Latin

America as a whole grew from 1.5 to 2.5 t/ha (Conway, 1997). In Europe, per hectare yields of wheat, barley and other grains, potatoes and sugar beet have tripled over 50 years, while milk yields have more than doubled (Pretty, 1998).

It would be misleading to imply that these kinds of improvements have resulted only in benefits. Environmental and health problems associated with agriculture have been increasingly well documented (cf. Balfour, 1943; Carson, 1963; Conway and Pretty, 1991; EEA, 1996, 1998), but it is only recently that the scale of the costs has come to be appreciated. There have been several recent studies on the external costs of modern agriculture in Germany, Netherlands, UK and the USA (Steiner et al., 1995; Pimentel et al., 1995; Evans, 1995; Waibel and Fleischer, 1998; Pretty et al., 1999). These have put the external costs at some US$20–200 per hectare of arable and permanent pasture, a very significant proportion of net farm income.

Modern rice cultivation has proven to be costly. IRRI researchers investigated the health status of Filipino rice farmers exposed to pesticides, and found statistically significant increased eye, skin, lung and neurological disorders (Rola and Pingali, 1993; Pingali and Roger, 1995). The health costs of these pesticide problems were calculated, and the economics of various pest control strategies compared. The so-called 'complete protection' strategy, with nine pesticide sprays per season, had lower returns per hectare than the other two control strategies, and cost the most in terms of ill-health. Any expected positive

J. Pretty, R. Hine / Natural Resources Forum 24 (2000) 107–121   111

Table 1
Benefits and health costs of pest management strategies in lowland irrigated rice, Philippines. *Source:* Rola and Pingali 1993

Pest management strategy	Agricultural returns, excluding health costs (Pesos/ha)	Health costs (Pesos/ha)	Net benefit (Pesos/ha)
'Complete' protection: nine applications of pesticide per season	11,846	7500	4346
Economic threshold: treatment only when threshold passed, usually no more than two applications used	12,797	1188	11,609
Natural control: pest control emphasises predator preservation and habitat management, alternative hosts and resistant varieties	14,009	0	14,009

production benefits of applying pesticides were over-whelmed by the health costs (Table 1).

4. Opportunities for making the transition to sustainable agriculture

What then do we understand by sustainable agriculture? And how then can we encourage transitions in both 'pre-modern' and 'modernised' systems towards greater sustain-ability? Sustainable farming seeks to make the best use of nature's goods and services whilst not damaging the environment (Altieri, 1995, 1999; Thrupp, 1996; Pretty, 1995a, 1998). It does this by integrating natural processes such as nutrient cycling, nitrogen fixation, soil regeneration and natural enemies of pests into food production processes. It minimises the use of non-renewable inputs (pesticides and fertilisers) that damage the environment or harm the health of farmers and consumers. And it makes better use of the knowledge and skills of farmers, so improving their self-reliance and capacities (see Fig. 3).

Sustainable agriculture is multi-functional within land-scapes and economies—it produces food and other goods for farm families and markets, but it also contributes to a range of public goods, such as clean water, wildlife, carbon sequestration in soils, flood protection, and landscape qual-ity. It delivers many unique non-food functions that cannot be produced by other sectors (e.g. on-farm biodiversity, urban to rural migration, social cohesion).

A desirable end-point for both modern and pre-modern agricultural systems is clearly some design that enhances both the private benefits for farmers and the public benefits through other functions. Transitions in agriculture are often conceived of as requiring sudden shifts in both practices and values. But not all farmers are able or willing to take such a leap. However, everyone can take small steps, and small steps added together can bring about big change in the end (MacRae et al., 1993; Pretty, 1998).

But where do we start? Drawing on the assets-based model and on empirical evidence from the field, a typology of eight improvements has been developed to illustrate where adjustments towards sustainability can be made (Pretty, 1999a) (see Table 2).

Farmers can choose to make improvements that increase sustainability by drawing on externally derived finance (credit, grants, increased sales, or tourism), or by making better use of non-renewable inputs (precision-farming, low-dose sprays, slow-release fertilisers). They can choose from three types of improvement to natural capital:

- They can focus on better use of available natural resources (Type 3), such as through water harvesting, irrigation management, or rotational grazing.
- They can intensify a single sub-component of their farm, while leaving the rest alone, such as through double-dug beds, adding vegetables to rice bunds, or digging a fish pond (Type 4).
- They can diversify the whole agroecosystem by adding new regenerative components, such as legumes, fish in rice, agroforestry and livestock (Type 5).

Type 6 improvements focus on social and participatory processes that lead to social capital increases, so improving people's capacity to work together on common resource management problems, forming groups for pest, irrigation, watershed, joint forest or credit management. Finally Types 7 and 8 focus on adding value to produce, either by proces-sing to reduce losses and increase returns, or through direct marketing of produce to consumers.

Any one or combinations of these eight types of improvement can produce benefits for farmers and rural economies. Some sustainable agriculture projects/initiatives focus on one or two of these types of improvement; others on a larger number. Although evidence suggests that adopt-ing one of these types of improvement can result in substan-tial benefits, this may not alone be enough to say that a system is now sustainable.

For example, water harvesting in dryland areas may produce greater yields, but result in a net loss of nutrients. Precision-farming technologies can result in substantial reductions in pesticide and fertiliser use in modern systems, largely through reduced wastage, but may have little long-term effect if farmers assume this is all they have to do to become sustainable. Reducing waste is clearly a step towards sustainability, as negative impacts have been reduced, but this is not the same as making a positive impact on natural capital.

112   *J. Pretty, R. Hine / Natural Resources Forum 24 (2000) 107–121*

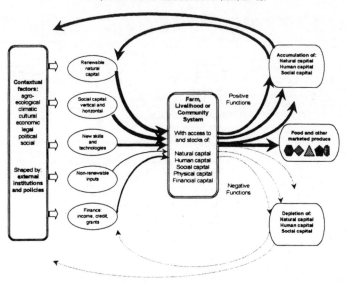

Fig. 3. Assets-based model of agricultural systems—flows and outcomes in sustainable systems.

However, it is also clear that there can be reinforcing relationships between these types of improvements, and in some cases synergistic outcomes may result from the application of several or all at once.

5. Sustainable agriculture in Asia: preliminary review of the evidence

Some have grave doubts that sustainable agriculture can deliver the necessary improvements in food production (cf. Crosson and Anderson, 1999). Others have sought to redouble efforts to increase adoption of modern technology and inputs (cf. Borlaug, 1994; Sasakawa Global 2000, 1993–1998). The argument is that farmers simply use too few fertilisers and pesticides, and the rhetoric is strong. Borlaug (1992) said that agriculturalists "must not be duped into believing that future food requirements can be met through continuing reliance on… the new complicated and sophisticated 'low-input, low-output' technologies that are impractical for the farmers to adopt".

It is self-evident that 'modern' technologies can and do improve productivity. But the key questions are, given current levels of poverty, economic instability and lack of foreign exchange, are countries and farmers of Asia really likely to be able to take on or continue with this model? And

if they do, what would be the external environmental and health costs? These pessimists would have us believe there are no alternatives—but evidence increasingly suggests otherwise.

This paper draws upon new information currently being collected to investigate sustainable agriculture alternatives across both developing and industrialised countries. The University of Essex SAFE-World research project (The Potential for Sustainable Agriculture to Feed the World) is drawing together some 250–300 case studies of sustainable agriculture, and will report on these during the year 2000. Not all projects submitted to the database have been classified as making a contribution to renewable assets—i.e. that they were on a path towards sustainability. The Asia case studies of 'success' can be divided into two broad groups according to natural resource endowments and past approaches to agricultural modernisation:

- the so-called Green Revolution lands, particularly intensive rice, wheat and cotton systems, which have seen substantial increases in yields since the 1960s, but where environmental health damage is threatening these successes;
- the complex and diverse agro-ecosystems largely missed by agricultural development, where yields remain low and systems largely unimproved, and where much rural poverty still exists.

J. Pretty, R. Hine / Natural Resources Forum 24 (2000) 107–121   113

Table 2
Typology of improvements for sustainable agriculture. *Source:* Pretty, 1999a,b

Type	Description	Elements
Type 1	Finance	Access to credit, grants, subsidies
		Increased returns on sales of produce
		Attract new sources of money for natural capital (e.g. eco-tourism, hunting of wildlife)
Type 2	Better use of non-renewable inputs and technologies	Precision-farming: patch spraying, targeted inputs and slow-release for pesticides and fertilisers
		Low dose (and non-toxic) sprays
		Veterinary services
		Pheromones, sterile males
		Resistant crop varieties and livestock breeds
		Machinery, handtools, ploughs
		New cash crops, including energy crops
Type 3	Better use of available renewable resources (natural capital)	Water harvesting
		Soil and water conservation—e.g. contour cropping, terraces, minimum tillage, grass strips
		Composting, livestock manures
		Irrigation scheduling and management
		Restoration of degraded or abandoned land
		Rotational grazing
		Habitat management for pest-predators
		Drainage systems and sub-soiling
		Raised beds or chinampas
		Bio-pesticides and bio-fungicides
Type 4	Intensification of single sub-component of farm system	Double-dug beds
		Vegetables on rice bunds
		Kitchen gardens
		Fish ponds
		Micro-environments, e.g. gully cropping, silt traps
Type 5	Diversify by adding new productive natural capital and regenerative components	Legumes in cropping systems (cover crops, green manures) and pastures
		Integrated livestock (e.g. poultry, stall-fed ruminants)
		Fish in rice fields; Azolla in rice
		Trees in cropping systems, including woodlots
		Natural enemy releases for pest control
		Habitat management, e.g. hedgerows, beetle banks, flowering strips
Type 6	Social and participatory processes leading to group action for making better use of existing resources and development of new skills	Farmers' research and experimentation groups
		Resource management and users' groups (e.g. forest protection, fisheries, irrigation, watersheds)
		Credit groups
		Horizontal partnerships between external sectoral agencies (e.g. government and NGOs; private and public)
Type 7	Add value by processing to reduce losses and increase returns	Post-harvest technologies
		Processing primary produce before sale (e.g. dried fruit, chutney, oil press, sawmills)
		Fuel-efficient stoves
Type 8	Add value by direct or organised marketing of produce to consumers	Farmers' markets, box schemes, farm shops and direct mailing and community supported agriculture
		Producer groups for collective marketing
		Rural roads and infrastructure

We have taken a purposive sample of the Asian projects to illustrate the types of improvements to both assets and agricultural productivity that are already occurring. These 16 cases in eight countries cannot yet be said to be representative. What is clear from these cases, however, is that the growth in the extent and outcomes of sustainable agriculture has been remarkable in the past decade in both contexts.

The first eight programmes are those occurring in irrigated cereal (mainly rice) growing regions, where cereal productivity is already high (3–5 t/ha per season); the second eight are from rainfed regions where yields start from a lower base (typically 0.5–1.5 t/ha per season). Table 3 summarises the findings.

6. Sustainable agriculture project summaries

6.A. Irrigated systems

6.A1. National integrated pest management for rice programme, Bangladesh

Integrated Pest Management (IPM) for rice in Bangladesh

is being implemented through three projects (INTERFISH, NOPEST and GOLDA) that are supported by DFID and the EU and implemented by Care (Desilles, 1999). They involve farmers attending farmer field schools ('schools without walls') during a whole rice season. They meet each week to learn new agro-ecological principles and concepts relating to rice, pest and predator management. Some 6000 farmer field schools have been completed, with about 150,000 farmers adopting more sustainable rice production on 54,000 ha. The programmes also emphasise fish cultivation in paddy, and vegetable cultivation on rice field dykes. Rice yields have improved by 5–7%, and costs of production have fallen owing to reduced pesticide use—some 80% of farmer field school participants no longer use pesticides. The fish–rice–vegetable systems have been shown to produce synergistic benefits: additional income from fish is US$156/ha, from vegetables on dykes US$23/ha, but fish and vegetables together bring an additional US$250/ha.

6.A2. China: fish in rice programme, Jiangsu province

Jiangsu province in China has more than 2 million ha of rice fields, among which one-third are suitable for rice–fish culture (Li Kangmin, 1998). The extension of large-scale, high-yielding, highly effective techniques of rice aquaculture project was launched by the provincial government in the mid-1990s. There has been rapid growth of rice aquaculture: from about 5000 ha in 1994 to 117,000 ha of rice–fish, rice–crab and rice–shrimp systems. Rice yields have increased by 10–15%, but the greatest dividend is in proteins: each mu (one fifteenth of a hectare) can produce 50 kg of fish. Additional benefits come from reduced insecticide use, and measured reductions in malaria incidence have resulted from fish eating mosquito larvae.

6.A3. China: wheat–maize double cropping programme, Hebei plain

The Wheat–Maize Double Cropping System project is located on Hebei Plain, northern China (Liang Weili, pers. comm, 1999). It began in 1996 and is financially supported by the provincial government, Xinji County government, and the Science and Technology Committee of Hebei Province. After successful field trials, the wheat–maize double cropping system was extended through model farms, videos and printed materials. Some 224,000 households have since adopted the technology on about 100,000 ha. Yields have improved by about 10%, water use has been reduced by 30%, and fertiliser use reduced by 20%. As a result, net returns have improved by 30%.

6.A4. India: national integrated pest management (IPM) programme

As in a range of other Asian countries, the national IPM programme in India uses farmer field schools (FFS) to build farmer capacity and knowledge on agro-ecology (Eveleens et al., 1996). Some 77,000 farmers have been trained in 2600 FFS on rice, cotton, sugarcane and oilseeds. A further 12,400 demonstrations have been conducted after FFSs to help spread the concepts and practice of IPM. FFSs are also being used to address wider soil, water and nutrient management issues. In Tamil Nadu, for example, farmers are experimenting with row planting, planting distance, bio-fertilisers (*Azospirillum, Azolla*), organic manures and basal fertiliser applications. Farmers' adoption of biocontrol agents (e.g. *Trichogramma*, neem) means that conventional pesticide use has fallen by 50% on average. Incomes have increased by Rs. 1000–1250/ha, and rice yields have increased by 250 kg/ha.

6.A5. Indonesia: national IPM for rice programme

In 1986, a Presidential Decree banned 56 brands of pesticide on rice and established a national IPM programme, with the aim of making farmers experts in their own fields through the use of farmer field schools (van der Fliert, 1993; Eveleens et al., 1996; Kenmore, 1999). One million farmers have now attended about 50,000 FFSs, the largest number in any Asian country. The programme is supported by the Food and Agriculture Organisation of the United Nations (FAO), the World Bank and US Agency for International Development (USAID), and operates in 12 of the 26 provinces, including all six rice-bowl provinces. The impacts have been substantial: one survey of 2000 farmers found that rice yields had increased by 0.5 t/ha on average, with lower variation in year-to-year yields. At the same time, the number of pesticide applications had fallen from 2.9 to 1.1 per season, with dramatic reductions in the use of banned products. On average, 25% of all farmers are now applying no pesticides, rising to 50% in some villages. Many of the FFSs have continued to be active as farmer IPM groups, meeting to discuss farming problems; monitor pest and predator populations in their villages; conduct village wide campaigns to control rats; extend IPM to neighbouring villages; and run savings and credit programmes.

6.A6. Sri Lanka: national integrated pest and crop management programme

This project is an IPM extension programme working in a wide range of agro-ecological zones of Sri Lanka (Jones, 1999). It is implemented by Care International, with funding from the European Union and the UK Department for International Development (DFID). The project uses farmer field schools to promote IPM, and has trained 4300 farmers in sustainable rice and vegetable production methods. Some 55,000 farm households on about 33,000 ha have now adopted sustainable agriculture, with substantial reductions in insecticide use (2.9–0.5 applications per season for rice). Yields have increased by 12–44% for rice and 7–44% for vegetables, depending on location.

J. Pretty, R. Hine / Natural Resources Forum 24 (2000) 107–121   115

Table 3

Extent and outcomes of Asian sustainable agriculture transformations in 16 projects with either irrigated or rainfed agro-ecosystems. *Notes:* A1–A8: transformations in irrigated systems. B1–B8: transformations in rainfed systems. Original sources: see text. Full case studies are posted at http://www2. essex.ac.uk/ces

System	Number of farm households and extent in million hectares	Types of sustainable agriculture improvements (see Table 2)	Outcomes
Irrigated systems			
Projects A1–A8 in Bangladesh, China, India, Indonesia, Sri Lanka, Viet Nam	2,356,000 households on 1.75 million ha	Mainly 2, 3, 6	Rice yields up 5–10%, sometimes +15%
			Rice yields up 40% when combined with improved crop management
		Some 4	Net incomes substantially up (30–100%), owing to reduced input costs
		Occasional 5	Insecticide use down 50–70%, in some countries large numbers of farmers have completely eliminated pesticides
			Improved efficiency of water use, allowing better scheduling, increased crop intensity and increased equity of water use
			Increased protein for rural families (fish, crab, shrimp) and increased incomes
			Increased vegetable production and consumption
Rainfed systems			
Projects B1–B8 in China, India, Nepal, Philippines	508,000 households on 1.18 million ha	Mainly 3, 4, 5, 6	Sorghum, millet, wheat and maize yields up 40–150%
		Often 1	Non-productive seasons now producing crops through better water harvesting and community management—increases food production and reduces seasonal migration
			Fodder grass and wood production up
			Increased diversification of systems
			Reductions in pesticide use, particularly on vegetables
			Increased livestock production, especially milk

6.A7. Sri Lanka: Gal Oya and Mahaweli participatory irrigation schemes

The participatory approach to irrigation system rehabilitation was pioneered in the Gal Oya scheme, and had the effect of changing many professionals' views about farmer involvement in water management (Uphoff, 1999; Wijayaratna and Uphoff, 1997). At the beginning of the project, Gal Oya was the largest and most run-down scheme in Sri Lanka. The approach was founded on building local institutions for water management, taking groups through a process of problem identification and collective action, leading to formal organisation. Some 33,000 water users' associations (comprising at least 500,000 farmers on 0.5–1 million hectares) were formed in both Gal Oya and Mahaweli. The economic benefits arise mainly from increased water use efficiency, enabling farmers to increase cropping intensity and so raise total production. There were also some increases in rice yields. As farmers took control, so the number of complaints received by the Irrigation Department about water distribution fell to nearly zero. Since project completion, farmers' organisations have maintained themselves, progressed institutionally, and developed their own capacity for dealing with problems.

6.A8. Viet Nam: national IPM for rice programme

Viet Nam has seen spectacular progress with its implementation of the FFS approach, with some 250,000 farmers trained since 1992 (Eveleens et al., 1996). The programme began by focusing on rice, but quickly spread to vegetables, soybean, cotton, tea and rice–fish culture. It works in all 53 provinces, with nearly 9000 FFS organised by the national programme, with about one-third funded by local sources and non-governmental organisations (NGOs). In many villages, IPM graduates form IPM clubs, which meet to discuss IPM, conduct collaborative research, and test new practices (e.g. fish in rice, IPM on vegetables). The programme has seen rice yields increase by about 3%, pesticide expenditure fall by 80%, pesticide application events decline by 79% (from 1.1 to 0.23 per season), and urea use fall by 10%. Farmers have also changed the timing of fertiliser applications, spreading it more evenly throughout the season. Long-term studies show that insecticide applications remain at about 25% of the former level. National policy support has played a vital role, including 1993 legislation on plant protection, a clean vegetable programme for organic production, limits on the import of restricted pesticides, pesticide bans, bans on new pesticide

116   *J. Pretty, R. Hine / Natural Resources Forum 24 (2000) 107–121*

factories, and the establishment of a national cross-ministry IPM Steering Committee.

6. B. Rainfed systems

6.B1. China: East Gansu sustainable agricultural techniques for effective use of rainfall resources project

The East Gansu region is part of the 51 million ha dryland area in the Northwest of China (Fan Tinglu, pers. comm, 1999). This sustainable agriculture project was initiated by the Gansu Academy of Agriculture in 1991 as part of Ninth Five-year National Development Plan aimed at achieving food security and self-sufficiency. It promotes more efficient use of rainfall through run-off collection techniques, water storage tank construction, devices for lifting and conveying water, micro-catchment water conservation with film mulching, and multi-use crop products and bi-products for livestock. The number of farm households adopting sustainable agriculture is now 100,000 on an area of some 70,000 ha. Cereal yields have increased substantially— wheat by 40% (from 3 to 4.2 t/ha), and spring maize by 38% (from 6 to 8.3 t/ha). There is greater availability of both irrigation water and drinking water for people and animals. Additional benefits include reduced soil erosion, decreased pesticide and fertiliser use, increased social capital formation through farmers' mutual aid groups, and increased capacity of women to play a major role in fruit and vegetable management and livestock rearing.

6.B2. India: Indo-German watershed development programme (IGWDP), Maharashtra

The IGWDP is an integrated environmental regeneration programme implemented by village self-help groups in the drought-prone state of Maharashtra. It is assisted by the German development agency GTZ and development bank KfW, and administered by NABARD (the National Bank for Agriculture and Rural Development) and the locally based Watershed Organisation Trust (IGWDP, 1998; Lobo and Korchendorfer-Lucius, 1998). The programme works in partnership with 51 local NGOs and 77 village self-help groups, and has seen sustainable agriculture implemented on some 92,000 ha, with the involvement of about 20,000 farm households. There has been a marked improvement in agricultural productivity (dryland yields up 250%; milk production up) and natural resource productivity (wells wet for more months per year; increased fodder grass production). These improvements have in turn led to increased incomes and food security (household grain production up 40–100%), reduced seasonal migration, increased school attendance, and a wider sense of hope and confidence amongst rural people. Many new village institutions have also been organised by rural people, including grain banks, women's groups, youth groups,

credit unions, dairy cooperatives, and agricultural cooperative societies.

6.B3. India: KRIBHCO Indo-British rainfed farming project (west)

This participatory soil and water conservation project is supported by DFID and is based in upland areas of Gujarat, Rajasthan and Madhya Pradesh (Smith, 1999). Land degradation is severe, soils are poor, and agricultural production is usually inadequate to support most families. The project works with local groups of 15–25 households on water-harvesting, tree planting, and grazing land improvements. There are now 232 groups in 70 villages: funds raised by each group now average Rs. 650, generated mostly from increased agricultural production (giving a total fund base of Rs. 151,000). Basic grain yields (rice, wheat, pigeon peas and sorghum) have improved from 400 to 800–1000 kg/ha. The increased fodder grass production from the terrace bunds is also valued highly. The improved water retention (water tables have risen by 1 m over the past 3–4 years) means that a *rabi* season crop is now possible for many farmers, turning an unproductive season into a productive one, resulting in a sharp decrease in seasonal out-migration.

6.B4. India: government of Rajasthan watershed development programme

The Watershed Development and Soil Conservation Department of the Government of Rajasthan (GoR) was set up in 1991 to implement a participatory approach for integrated watershed development (Krishna et al., 1997; Krishna, 1999). Since the 1940s, groundwater levels had fallen dramatically, forests had become degraded, and community institutions undermined. But despite considerable expenditure on soil conservation, the impacts were poor: "...field observations confirmed... near zero maintenance by the beneficiaries" (Krishna, 1999). The GoR recognised the need to involve local people, and has since facilitated the formation of 15,000 watershed users' groups, with at least three million hectares (possibly as high as 10–15 m ha) under sustainable practices. The technologies are low-cost and based on indigenous and biological technologies, including strips of vetiver and other grasses on the contour; contour bunds and contour cropping; field bunds; drainage line treatment; and regeneration of common lands with shrubs and trees. Sorghum and millet yields have more than doubled to 400–875 kg/ha (without addition of fertilisers); and grass strips have improved yields by 50–200% to 450–925 kg/ha.

6.B5. India: the society for people's education and economic change (SPEECH), Tamil Nadu

SPEECH has been working in Kamarajar District of Tamil Nadu since 1986, and has helped to build and

J. Pretty, R. Hine / Natural Resources Forum 24 (2000) 107–121   117

strengthen local groups and institutions in 45 villages (Devavaram et al., 1999). The region is known for its acute droughts, erratic monsoons, poor services and entrenched socio-economic and cultural divisions. Village groups, or *sanghas*, have adopted a range of sustainable agriculture approaches to make better use of existing resources. Water harvesting has been particularly effective, as it not only brings previously abandoned land into production, but also means sufficient water can be saved for an additional wet rice crop on the small amount of irrigated land. Milk cows have been introduced, bringing particular benefits to women and children. Sorghum and millet yields have doubled, and extra crops and fruit and timber trees are being cultivated. As *sanghas* become more confident, they begin to develop new activities, such as providing for health care, building roads, and running savings and credit schemes. Representatives are elected to a Cluster Level Governing Council, an independent society that provides a platform for local groups to address emerging concerns.

6.B6. Nepal: Jajarkot permaculture programme

This programme promotes sustainable food production in 31 villages of Jajarkot Khalanga, and is supported by ActionAid Nepal (JPP, 1997–1999; Chris Evans, pers. comm. 1999). A community-based process builds on the skills and knowledge of local people and professionals through social capital formation. The main impacts of the programme are increased food production. Some 40% of the 580 participating households, organised into 44 groups, are now entirely food self-sufficient through increased used of regenerative agriculture technologies, including green manures, composting, intercropping and agro-forestry. Increased diversification of farm systems has been achieved through incorporation of fruit trees, bees, sheep, rabbits, cotton and flowers, and intensification of kitchen gardens. The programme also utilises smokeless stoves and pit latrines. It works with community groups for managing local savings and credit system, supporting small businesses, strengthening adult education and providing access to health facilities.

6.B7. Philippines: Contour farming on sloping lands in Claveria

Claveria is in northern Mindanao, and is characterised by acid soils on sloping lands with severe erosion (Garrity, 1999; Fujisaka, 1999). ICRAF and local research and extension agencies worked with farmers on the development of a variety of contour farming technologies. The project began with leguminous trees, but after relatively weak uptake, developed more locally suited methods in the form of natural vegetative strips combined with ridge tillage. A wide range of perennial crops have been tested by the 2000 farmers working in the 80 local groups formed by the project, including fruits, coconut, mulberry and fast-growing timber species. On farms with soil improvement

(some 6000 ha), maize yields have improved 15–25% and land values by 35–50%.

6.B8. Philippines: integrated pest management for highland vegetables

The CABI Bioscience IPM for Highland Vegetables project was set up in 1994 and is funded by the Asian Development Bank. Insecticide resistance and human health problems had become severe, and so the IPM project set up farmer field schools to increase awareness about the harmful effects of pesticides, to increase knowledge of natural enemies, and to encourage discussion on best husbandry practice amongst farmers. The project reached 1719 farmers in 65 FFS groups, with 48 trainers trained, mainly from local government. As a result, a range of alternative pest control methods was developed by farmers. There has been an 80% decrease in pesticide use in the wet season (55% fall in the dry season) and the synthetic fertiliser rate has halved, giving farmers a net rise in income of 17%. Vegetable yields have also increased by about 20%. Farmer field schools are now considered locally to be a good investment by municipal authorities.

7. Accumulating assets offer great promise

What does the empirical evidence tell us about these types of sustainable agriculture improvements? It indicates first that a transition to sustainable agriculture in irrigated systems has to date only delivered a relatively small increase in per hectare grain output (5–10%, but rising if farmers experiment with redesign of nutrient, water and soil management issues). However, whole agricultural systems have become considerably more productive, as they are producing more protein (fish, shrimps, crabs), and more vegetables (on rice bunds and in kitchen gardens). They are also considerably more efficient in their use of water, as well as less polluting.

By contrast, there are much greater cereal productivity increases in the dryland systems (50–100%, sometimes up to 200% increases), though of course per hectare yields are starting from a much lower base. In addition, farmers are increasing total farm production by bringing formerly unproductive lands into cultivation, as well as harvesting enough water for an extra irrigated crop during formerly unproductive seasons.

What we do not yet know is whether a transition to sustainable agriculture, delivering increasing benefits at the scale occurring in these projects, will result in enough food to meet the current food needs of Asia, the future basic needs after continued population growth, and the potential demand following adoption of more meat-rich diets. Even these substantial increases may not be enough. However, there is scope for additional confidence, as the evidence also indicates that productivity dividends can grow with an increasing number of improvements, and that productivity

118   *J. Pretty, R. Hine / Natural Resources Forum 24 (2000) 107–121*

increases steadily over time if natural, social and human capital are accumulated.

Each type of improvement, by itself, can make a positive contribution to raising production. But, the real dividend comes with combinations. Synergistic effects tend not to be captured or appreciated by reductionist methods of analysis that measure the effects of one variable at a time, whilst holding all the others unchanged (the *ceteris paribus* approach). But this misses synergism—where the whole is greater than the sum of the parts (Cornia, 1985; Altieri, 1999; Desilles, 1999; Rosset, 1999; Uphoff, 1999). Thus soil and water conservation that emphasises terracing and other physical measures to prevent natural resource losses is much less effective than combinations with biological methods that seek to increase the productivity of the system (e.g. green manures, cover crops), and finance for credit groups that reduces indebtedness of households. In Bangladesh, for example, fish raised in rice fields increase incomes by US$156/ha; vegetables on dykes by US$23/ha; but together they raise returns by US$250/ha (Desilles, 1999).

The second issue is improvements over time. If agricultural systems are low in assets (either intrinsically low, or have become low because of degradation), then a sudden switch to 'more sustainable' practices that have to rely on these very assets to be productive will clearly not be immediately successful. But as the asset base increases, so does farm performance.

In Cuba, the productivity and efficiency of sustainable agriculture increased over a three-year period—yields increased (number of people fed by one ha up from 4 to 4.8), and energy inputs declined (SANE, 1998, reported in Altieri, 1999). This is also clear in industrialised systems when farmers make the switch to organic farming. This almost always results in a cut in productivity (typically 30–50% for cereals), and economic viability is only maintained through grants from governments and/or receipt of premium prices from consumers. But longitudinal studies show that yields increase over time as soil fertility improves, and as various elements of the system increasingly are able to provide valued services to farmers (Dabbert, 1990; Lampkin and Padel, 1994; see also Drinkwater et al., 1998; Tilman, 1998).

The same principle applies for accumulation of social capital. The past decade has seen the emergence of many thousands of local resource management groups worldwide—for irrigation and watershed management, joint forest management, integrated pest management, and farmers' research (Pretty and Ward, 2000). What is particularly interesting is that when comparisons have been made in the same context (with the same set of technologies in use), between farmers working in groups and those working individually, it is clear that social capital (in the appropriate form) pays—both for private returns to farmers and public benefits to natural resources.

Sustainable agriculture systems also become more productive when human capital increases, particularly in the form of farmers' capacity to innovate and manage actively their farm systems for sustainable outcomes. Sustainable agriculture is not a concretely defined set of technologies, nor is it a simple model or package to be widely applied or fixed with time. It is more a process for social learning. Lack of information and management skills are a major barrier to the adoption of sustainable agriculture. We know much less about these resource-conserving technologies than we do about the use of external inputs in modernised systems. In addition, much less research on resource-conserving technologies is conducted by research institutions.

It is clear that the process by which farmers learn about technology alternatives is crucial (Pretty, 1995a,b). If they are enforced or coerced, then they may only adopt for a limited period. But if the process is participatory and enhances farmers' capacity to learn about their farm and its resources, such as through farmer field schools, then the foundation for redesign and continuous innovation is laid. As Bunch and Lòpez (1996) have put it, "what needs to be made sustainable is the social process of innovation itself".

8. Fundamental policy challenges for spreading sustainable agriculture in Asia

It is clear that sustainable agriculture in Asia, in its form envisaged here, has delivered substantial increases in food production at low cost, as well as benefited natural, social and human capital. In the 16 cases, some 2.86 million farm households have already increased total farm productivity on close to 5 million ha. Were these approaches to be widely adopted across Asia, they would make a significant impact on local and regional food security.

Sustainable agriculture can contribute significantly to natural and social capital, as well as make a significant impact on rural people's food security, welfare and livelihoods. But without appropriate policy support at a range of levels, combined with wider social organisation and alliances, these improvements will remain at best localised in extent or, at worst, will wither away.

Clearly much can be done with existing resources. A more sustainable agriculture will not, however, happen without some external help and money. There are always transaction costs associated with shifting from one way of doing things to another—the costs of learning new knowledge, the costs of developing new or adapting old technologies, the costs of learning to work together, the costs of institutions having to break free from existing paradigms of thought and practice. It will also cost time and money to rebuild depleted natural and social capital.

With some important exceptions, many of the sustainable agriculture improvements seen in the 1990s throughout the world have arisen without significant national and institutional policy reform. Policies framed to deliver increased

J. Pretty, R. Hine / Natural Resources Forum 24 (2000) 107–121   119

food production will have to be changed if they are to help deliver environmental and social benefits as well. Food policies framed to help deliver cheap and abundant food regardless of quality will also have to change. Moreover, rural development policies and institutions focusing on 'exogenous' solutions to the economic and social problems of rural communities are often ill-suited to the needs of community-based and participatory development.

The 1990s have seen considerable global progress towards the recognition of the need for policies to support sustainable agriculture, and this is beginning to be translated into practice. To date only three countries (Cuba, Switzerland and Austria) have given explicit national support for sustainable agriculture—putting it at the centre of agricultural development policy and integrating policies accordingly (Pretty, 1999b).

Some have given significant support to specific sectors, such as to IPM in rice in Indonesia, Viet Nam, Bangladesh, Sri Lanka and India, though a combination of disincentives for pesticide use, support for alternatives, including farmer field school programmes, and national steering committees. Other examples include support for participatory irrigation, such as in Sri Lanka. Some countries have seen significant sub-national or regional policy support, such as in certain provinces in China and states in India.

Most reforms, though, remain piecemeal, with sustainable agriculture still largely at the margins of conventional policy processes and aims. No agriculture minister is likely to say they are against sustainable agriculture, yet good words remain fully to be translated into integrated and comprehensive policy reforms (Pretty, 1999b).

There are additional constraints to overcome. Vested interests in maintaining the status quo will make any reform difficult. Why should fertiliser companies support a transition to legume-based farming or biofertilisers when this could mean this would cost them huge amounts of revenue? Why should a pesticide company be balanced in its presentation of different types of farming, when it knows some types of sustainable agriculture mean that little or none of its products will be used? Such problems will be very difficult to overcome.

Despite the many constraints, it is increasingly clear that sustainable agriculture can bring substantial private and public benefits. National agricultural policies that put sustainable agriculture firmly centre stage, with appropriate support, incentives, and institutional reform, would begin to see nations throughout Asia and their people reap substantial dividends in the coming years.

Acknowledgements

The authors are grateful to three anonymous referees for their constructive and helpful comments on an earlier version of this paper, and for the insights from a wide range of colleagues who have contributed in a variety of ways to this paper and its concepts and findings. This paper arises out of the SAFE-World (The Potential for Sustainable Agriculture to Feed the World) research project conducted by the University of Essex, with funding from the UK Department for International Development, Bread for the World, and Greenpeace (Germany).

References

Altieri, M., 1995. Agroecology: The Science of Sustainable Agriculture. Westview Press, Boulder.

Altieri, M.A., 1999. Enhancing the productivity of Latin American traditional peasant farming systems through an agro-ecological approach. Paper for Conference on Sustainable Agriculture: New Paradigms and Old Practices? Bellagio Conference Center, Italy, 26–30 April.

Balfour, E.B., 1943. The Living Soil. Faber and Faber, London.

Bignall, E.M., McCracken, D.I., 1996. Low-intensity farming systems in the conservation of the countryside. Journal of Applied Ecology 33, 413–424.

Borlaug, N., 1992. Small-scale agriculture in Africa: the myths and realities. Feeding the Future (Newsletter of the Sasakawa Africa Association) 4, 2.

Borlaug, N., 1994. Agricultural research for sustainable development. Testimony before US House of Representatives Committee on Agriculture, 1 March.

Bunch, R., Lòpez, G., 1996. Soil recuperation in Central America: sustaining innovation after intervention. Gatekeeper Series SA 55, Sustainable Agriculture Programme. International Institute for Environment and Development, London.

Butler-Flora, C., 1998. Sustainability in agriculture and rural communities. Paper for Conference Sustainability in Agriculture: Tensions between Ecology, Economics and Social Sciences, Stuttgart, Germany, 28–30 October.

Carney, D., 1998. Sustainable Rural Livelihoods. Department for International Development, London.

Carson, R., 1963. Silent Spring. Penguin Books, Harmondsworth.

Chambers, R., Pacey, A., Thrupp, L.A. (Eds.), 1989. Farmer First. Farmer Innovation and Agricultural Research. IT Publications, London.

Coleman, J., 1990. Foundations of Social Theory. Harvard University Press, Cambridge, MA.

Conway, G.R., 1997. The Doubly Green Revolution. Penguin, London.

Conway, G.R., Pretty, J.N., 1991. Unwelcome Harvest: Agriculture and Pollution. Earthscan, London.

Cornia, G.A., 1985. Farm size, yields and the agricultural production function: an analysis for 15 developing countries. World Development 13 (4), 513–534.

Costanza, R., d'Arge, R., de Groot, R., Farber, S., Grasso, M., Hannon, B., Limburg, K., Naeem, S., O'Neil, R.V., Parvelo, J., Raskin, R.G., Sutton, P., van den Belt, M., 1997. The value of the world's ecosystem services and natural capital. Nature 387, 253–260.

Crosson, P., Anderson, J.R., 1999. Technologies for meeting future global demands for food. Paper for Conference on Sustainable Agriculture: New Paradigms and Old Practices? Bellagio Conference Center, Italy, 26–30 April.

Dabbert, S., 1990. Der Begriff des Betriebsorganismus. Lebendige Erde 90 (5), 333–337.

Daily, G. (Ed.), 1997. Nature's Services: Societal Dependence on Natural Ecosystems. Island Press, Washington, DC.

Delgado, C., Rosegrant, M., Steinfield, H., Ehui, S., Courbois, C., 1999. Livestock to 2020: the next food revolution. IFPRI Brief 61. International Food Policy Research Institute, Washington, DC.

Desilles, S., 1999. Sustaining and managing private natural resources: the way to step out of the cycle of high-input agriculture. Paper for

120 *J. Pretty, R. Hine / Natural Resources Forum 24 (2000) 107–121*

Conference on Sustainable Agriculture: New Paradigms and Old Practices? Bellagio Conference Center, Italy, 26–30 April.

Devavaram, J., Arunothayam, E., Prasad, R., Pretty, J., 1999. Watershed and community development in Tamil Nadu, India. In: Hinchcliffe, F., Thompson, J., Pretty, J., Guijt, I., Shah, P. (Eds.). Fertile Ground: The Impacts of Participatory Watershed Development. IT Publications, London.

Drinkwater, L.E., Wagoner, P., Sarrantonio, M., 1998. Legume-based cropping systems have reduced carbon and nitrogen losses. Nature 396, 262–265.

EEA, 1996. Environmental taxes: implementation and environmental effectiveness. Environmental Issues Series No 1. European Environment Agency, Copenhagen.

EEA, 1998. Europe's Environment: The Second Assessment. Report and Statistical Compendium. European Environment Agency, Copenhagen.

Evans, R., 1995. Soil Erosion and Land Use: Towards a Sustainable Policy. Cambridge Environmental Initiative, University of Cambridge.

Eveleens, K.G., Chisholm, R., van der Fliert, E., Kato, M., Nhat, P.T., Schmidt, P., 1996. Mid Term Review of Phase III Report. The FAO Intercountry Programme for the Development and Application of Integrated Pest Control in Rice in South and Southeast Asia. FAO, Manila and Rome.

FAO, 1995. World Agriculture: Toward 2010. United Nations Food and Agriculture Organisation, Rome.

FAO, 1996. Food, agriculture, and food security: developments since the World Food Conference and prospects. World Food Summit Technical Background Doc 1, Rome.

FAO, 1999. Cultivating our futures: taking stock of the multifunctional character of agriculture and land. FAO, Rome.

Fujisaka, S., 1999. A retrospective on soil conservation in the Philippines. In: McDonald, M., Brown, K. (Eds.), Issues and Options in the Design of Soil and Water Conservation Projects. Proceedings of a workshop held in Llandudno, Conwy, 1–3 February. University of Wales, Bangor.

Garrity, D., 1999. Contour farming based on natural vegetative strips: expanding the scope for increased food crop production on sloping lands in Asia. Paper for Conference on Sustainable Agriculture: New Paradigms and Old Practices? Bellagio Conference Center, Italy, 26–30 April.

Goodland, R., 1998. Environmental sustainability defined for the agricultural sector: leave livestock to the private sector. Paper for conference Sustainability in Agriculture: Tensions between Ecology, Economics and Social Sciences. Stuttgart, Germany, 28–30 October.

IFPRI, 1995. A 2020 vision for food, agriculture and the environment. International Food Policy Research Institute, Washington, DC.

IGWDP, 1998. The Indo-German Watershed Development Programme—programme structure and activities. Ahmednagar, India.

Jones, K., 1999. Integrated pest and crop management in Sri Lanka. Paper for Conference on Sustainable Agriculture: New Paradigms and Old Practices? Bellagio Conference Center, Italy, 26–30 April.

Jajarkot Permaculture Programme (JPP), 1997–1999. Grihasthashram Newsletter, Dec 97, May 98, Dec 98, May 99. JPP, Kathmandu, Nepal.

Kenmore, P., 1999. Rice IPM in Asia. Paper for Conference on Sustainable Agriculture: New Paradigms and Old Practices? Bellagio Conference Center, Italy, 26–30 April.

Krishna, A., 1999. Large-scale government programmes: watershed development in Rajasthan, India. In: Hinchcliffe, F., Thompson, J., Pretty, J., Guijt, I., Shah, P. (Eds.), Fertile Ground: The Impacts of Participatory Watershed Development. IT Publications, London.

Krishna, A., Uphoff, N., Esman, M.J., 1997. Reasons for Hope: Instructive Experiences in Rural Development. Kumarian Press, West Hartford, CT.

Lampkin, N., 1999. Organic farming in Europe. Paper to Soil Association Annual Conference, 8 January, Cirencester.

Lampkin, N., Padel, S. (Eds), 1994. The Economics of Organic Farming: An International Perspective. CAB International.

Leach, G., 1996. Global land and food in the 21st Century. Polestar Series Report, No 5. Stockholm Environment Institute, Stockholm.

Kangmin, Li, 1998. Rice aquaculture systems in China: a case of rice-fish farming from protein crops to cash crops. In: Eng-Leong Foo, Tarcision Della Senta (Eds.), Integrated Bio-Systems in Zero Emissions Applications. Proceedings of an Internet Conference on Integrated Biosystems (http://www.ias.unu.edu/proceedings/icibs).

Lobo, C., Korchendorfer-Lucius, G., 1998. Replication of self-help approaches in watershed development through NGOs. GTZ and KfW, Ahmednagar and Berlin.

MacRae, R.J., Henning, J., Hill, S.B., 1993. Strategies to overcome barriers to the development of sustainable agriculture in Canada: the role of agribusiness. Journal of Agricultural and Environmental Ethics 6, 21–51.

Pimentel, D., Harvey, C., Resosudarmo, P., Sinclair, K., Kunz, D., McNair, M., Crist, S., Shpritz, L., Fitton, L., Saffouri, R., Blair, R., 1995. Environmental and economic costs of soil erosion and conservation benefits. Science 267, 1117–1123.

Pingali, P.L., Roger, P.A., 1995. Impact of Pesticides on Farmers' Health and the Rice Environment. Kluwer Academic Press, Dordrecht.

Pinstrup-Anderson, P., Cohen, M., 1999. World food needs and the challenge to sustainable agriculture. Paper for Conference on Sustainable Agriculture: New Paradigms and Old Practices? Bellagio Conference Center, Italy, 26–30 April.

Pretty, J.N., 1995. Regenerating Agriculture: Policies and Practice for Sustainability and Self-Reliance. Earthscan Publications, London; National Academy Press, Washington, DC; ActionAid, Bangalore.

Pretty, J.N., 1995. Participatory learning for sustainable agriculture. World Development 23 (8), 1247–1263.

Pretty, J.N., 1998. The Living Land: Agriculture, Food Systems and Community Regeneration in Rural Europe. Earthscan Publications Ltd, London.

Pretty, J., 1999. Sustainable agriculture in Africa: an assets-based model. Paper for Conference on Sustainable Agriculture: New Paradigms and Old Practices? Bellagio Conference Center, Italy, 26–30 April.

Pretty, J., 1999. Sustainable Agriculture: A Review of Recent Progress on Policies and Practice. United Nations Research Institute for Social Development (UNRISD), Geneva.

Pretty, J., Ward, H., 2000. Social capital and the environment (forthcoming). Centre for Environment and Society, University of Essex, Colchester.

Pretty, J., Brett, C., Gee, D., Hine, R., Mason, C.F., Morison, J.I.L., Raven, H., Rayment, M., van der Bijl, G., 2000. An Assessment of the External Costs of UK Agriculture (forthcoming). University of Essex.

Putnam, R., 1995. Bowling alone: America's declining social capital. Journal of Democracy 6 (1), 65–78.

Putnam, R.D., Leonardi, R., Nanetti, R.Y., 1993. Making Democracy Work: Civic Traditions in Modern Italy. Princeton University Press, Princeton, NJ.

Rola, A., Pingali, P., 1993. Pesticides, Rice Productivity and Farmers—An Economic Assessment. IRRI, Manila and WRI, Washington.

Rosset, P., 1999. The Multiple Functions and Benefits of Small Farm Agriculture. Food First Policy Brief No 4. Food First/Institute for Food and Development Policy, Oakland, CA.

Sasakawa Global 2000, 1993–1998. Annual Reports. Sasakawa Africa Association, Tokyo.

Smith, P., 1999. Participatory soil and water conservation in India: experiences from the KRIBHCO Indo-British Rainfed Farming Project. In: McDonald, M., Brown, K. (Eds.), Issues and Options in the Design of Soil and Water Conservation Projects. Proceedings of a Workshop held in Llandudno, Conwy, 1–3 February, University of Wales, Bangor.

Steiner, R., McLaughlin, L., Faeth, P., Janke, R., 1995. Incorporating externality costs in productivity measures: a case study using US agriculture. In: Barbett, V., Payne, R., Steiner, R. (Eds.), Agricultural Sustainability: Environmental and Statistical Considerations, Wiley, New York, pp. 209–230.

Thrupp, L.A., 1996. Partnerships for Sustainable Agriculture. World Resources Institute, Washington, DC.

J. Pretty, R. Hine / Natural Resources Forum 24 (2000) 107–121   121

Tilman, D., 1998. The greening of the green revolution. Nature 396, 211–212.

UN Population Division, 1998. World Population Prospects: The 1998 Revision. UN, New York.

Uphoff, N., 1999. What can be learned from the system of rice intensification in Madagascar about meeting future food needs. Paper for Conference on Sustainable Agriculture: New Paradigms and Old Practices? Bellagio Conference Center, Italy, 26–30 April.

Van der Fliert, E., 1993. Integrated pest management: farmer field schools generate sustainable practices. Ph.D. thesis, Wageningen Agricultural University, Netherlands.

Waibel, H., Fleischer, G., 1998. Kosten und Nutzen des chemischen Pflanzenschutzes in der Deutsen Landwirtschaft aus Gesamtwirtschaftlicher Sicht. Vauk-Verlag, Kiel.

Wijayaratna, C.M., Uphoff, N., 1997. Farmer organisation in Gal Oya: improving irrigation management in Sri Lanka. In: Krishna, A., Uphoff, N., Esman, M.J. (Eds.), Reasons for Hope: Instructive Experiences in Rural Development. Kumarian Press, West Hartford, CT.

[19]

Pergamon

Geoforum, Vol. 29, No. 4, pp. 413–432, 1998
© 1998 Elsevier Science Ltd. All rights reserved
Printed in Great Britain
0016-7185/98 $19.00+0.00

PII: S0016-7185(98)00019-0

Environmental Stewardship in UK Agriculture: A Comparison of the Environmentally Sensitive Area Programme and the Countryside Stewardship Scheme in South East England

MATT LOBLEY*† and CLIVE POTTER‡

† Faculty of Agriculture, Food and Land Use, Seale-Hayne University of Plymouth, Newton Abbot, Devon TQ12 6NQ, UK
‡ Environment Department, Wye College, University of London, Wye, Kent TN25 5AH, UK

(Received 30 June 1997; and in revised form 17 April 1998)

Abstract: Research into the adoption of Environmental Land Management Schemes (ELMS) has typically sought to identify the defining characteristics of participants and the 'barriers to entry' that dissuade others from joining. More recently, attention has focused on the motivation of participants and non-participants in helping to understand patterns of participation. This paper compares the pattern of participation in two distinct schemes operating in South East England. Indirect evidence suggests that scheme design and implementation is influencing the type of farmer joining and their motivation for doing so. Results from a survey of farmers also support the idea that the schemes are recruiting from different sections of the farming community. ESA farmers are largely motivated by financial gain, whereas those enrolling land in the Countryside Stewardship Scheme have more clearly defined conservation motives. Although there is also a 'core' of resistant non-participants, further changes to the design and delivery of policy could encourage a large number of 'potential enrolers' to join. © 1998 Elsevier Science Ltd. All rights reserved.

Introduction

The rapid expansion of agri-environmental policy in recent years reflects the growing acceptability of channelling public funds into agriculture on environmental grounds. Although the proportion of total spending devoted is comparatively small in Common Agricultural Policy (CAP) terms (some

3% of the total agricultural budget in 1995), the rate of increase in spending has been rapid and by 1995 an estimated 24% of the agricultural area of the Union was eligible for payments under the Agri-Environment Regulation (CEC, 1996). The significance of this policy development rests as much on its future potential as its current contribution to tackling agri-environmental problems however. Under World Trade Organisation (WTO) rules,

* E-mail: M.Lobley@Wye.ac.uk

413

'green payments' that are decoupled from production enjoy immunity from disciplines designed to eliminate trade distorting agricultural subsidies. It is widely expected that there will be a steady substitution of environmental for conventional support in the years ahead (Swinbank and Tanner, 1996). Aware of this, organisations representing major UK land holding interests such as the Country Landowners Association (CLA) and Scottish Landowners Federation (SLF) have offered proposals aimed at replacing current support mechanisms with ambitious national schemes for the provision of public agri-environmental goods (see CLA, 1994; SLF, 1995). Furthermore, in a demonstration of the degree of consensus which now exists, similar proposals have been put forward independently by academic commentators such as Buckwell (1997), who suggest that agri-environmental programmes covering the entire area of the EU could play a major role in a reformed CAP, redirecting and decoupling support but still able to channel public monies for the support of environmental land management.

Meanwhile, in reaffirming its commitment to Environmental Land Management Schemes (ELMS) in the recent Rural White Paper (DoE/MAFF, 1995) the UK Government has stated that it will continue to expand the use of voluntary incentive led and targeted mechanisms. In England, the vast majority of agri-environmental expenditure is presently channelled through MAFF's two flagship land management schemes, the Environmentally Sensitive Area (ESA) programme and the Countryside Stewardship Scheme (CSS). Together these schemes currently absorb some 87% of GB agri-environmental spending and account for 97% of the total area currently enrolled in GB (MAFF, 1996). While both are based on the same voluntary contractual model, they nevertheless differ in important respects in terms of their genesis, objectives, design and operation. The ESA programme was developed in response to specific land management conflicts arising from the abandonment of traditional management practices and/or intensification of broad tracts of land (see Baldock et al., 1990; Lowe et al., 1986; Potter, 1988, 1998) and has been designed to encourage the enrolment of relatively large areas of land in order (in the first instance) to maintain conservation character and habitat mosaics. This reflects "a recognition that specific tracts or pieces of countryside can often only be effec-

tively conserved by maintaining the traditional systems and styles of farming which lie behind them" (Potter, 1988, p. 301).

In contrast, CSS stems from a recognition that important habitats in the wider countryside, outside designated areas, were becoming increasingly fragmented, isolated and marginalised by the process of agricultural change and that site safeguard alone was unlikely to sustain the conservation value of this 'peripheral' resource (Adams et al., 1994; DoE/MAFF, 1995). By setting up this scheme on an experimental basis in 1991, the Countryside Commission (CC) aimed to bring about the conservation and restoration of habitats and landscapes on a broader front than was possible with ESAs. The approach adopted under CSS differs from ESAs in a number of important respects[1]:

- a greater emphasis on objectives and environmental outputs achieved through flexible management practices
- the use of target landscapes and habitats rather than specifically designated areas
- selectivity in the acceptance of applications (the discretionary principle)

From the start, access provisions were a key feature of the scheme and it was envisaged that a wider cross section of land managers, including institutional owners of land, would be involved. The use of discretion in screening applications in order to ensure that only applications promising a high environmental return would be accepted, was seen as the most innovative feature of this new scheme (Fraser, 1993, 1996). This compares with the more permissive approach adopted within ESAs, where applications are accepted provided they meet entry and eligibility conditions.

At an early stage, these programmes came to be seen as complementary rather than competitive schemes. ESAs, with their management prescriptions tailored to specific landscapes and locations, were largely designed to tackle the 'integral' or 'core' conservation resource such as grassland and semi-natural vegetation in livestock systems (Webster and Felton, 1993). CSS, on the other hand, characterised by a flexible and discretionary approach "has been particularly successful in securing the protection.. of fragmented habitats" in 'peripheral' situations where the conservation interest lies outside the management of agricultural systems (EN, 1996). This was recognised explicitly by

MAFF when, in its consultation paper on ELMS, it stated that "the ESA approach works well where large areas of land of particular environmental value are targeted" on the other hand, where the conservation resource is "small and fragmented... Countryside Stewardship would be a more effective mechanism for conservation and enhancement than ESAs" (MAFF, 1995, p. 18). However, in the absence of research confirming long term patterns of farmer response, and equally, the longer term conservation achievements of the schemes, it is closer to a hypothesis than a description of reality. Despite more than ten years experience with ESAs, agri-environmental policy is still seen as an innovative and experiment approach with current research providing support for both 'sceptics' and 'supporters' (House of Commons, 1997). For instance, it is unclear whether schemes are appealing to different sections of the farming community, or whether they are achieving different levels of farmer engagement or commitment. Although the Countryside Commission has claimed that the "unique value [of agri-environmental policies] is that they can tap into and strengthen farmers' and other land managers' interest in responsible stewardship in the environment to sustain and create public benefits" (CC, 1996, p. 2), it is far from proven that measures like the CSS are having this long term effect. While evidence emerging from environmental monitoring exercises is beginning to establish the environmental credentials of both ESAs and CSS (see below), concerns persist over the interconnected issues of the longevity of ELMS impacts (Whitby, 1994, 1996; Wilson, 1996) and participant commitment to scheme objectives, leading researchers to argue with some force that unless such a commitment can be demonstrated payments will be seen as "temporary bribes, shallow in operation and transitory in their effect" (Morris and Potter, 1995, p. 52).

Against this background, the present paper compares the development and operation of these 'core' schemes, contrasting their approach to targeting the conservation resource and accepting applications for enrolment. It begins by outlining the targeting and operational characteristics of ESAs and CSS and reviews current levels of enrolment. The paper goes on to examine the pattern of ELMS participation in two areas of South East England — the South Downs ESA and CSS on the North Downs of Kent. This analysis assesses how far the schemes can be said to be appealing to different types of farmer in terms of motivation, farm and farm household characteristics. The paper concludes by exploring some of the implications for the future deployment of ELMS in the UK.

The design and implementation of ESAs and the CSS

Agri-environmental policy in general is designed to encourage farmers to modify farming practices to achieve conservation objectives or to maintain those practices that sustain the conservation resource. Designated on the basis of their national conservation significance, ESAs, for example, require the adoption, maintenance or extension of a particular form of management practice to maintain the conservation character of a particular area. While each individual ESA has specific agri-environmental objectives, an overall objective common to all is "to maintain and enhance the landscape, wildlife and historic value of the area by encouraging beneficial agricultural practices" (MAFF, 1994, p. i). ESAs operate on a landscape scale (Hodge et al., 1992; Potter, 1988), with boundaries drawn widely enough to encompass an area of distinct landscape or conservation character within which farmers are offered flat rate area based payments in return for entering into a ten year contract to comply with a series of management prescriptions. Management packages are tailored to individual ESAs, restricting certain practices while encouraging others and a tiering system of payments is employed to encourage a progression from the lowest, entry level maintenance tier to higher, more ambitious enhancement tiers. Experience to date suggests that the emphasis of ESA policy is to restrict potentially environmentally damaging practices rather than stimulate those with an environmentally enhancing effect due to the programme's emphasis on process rather than output (Whitby, 1994; RSPB, 1996a, b). That said, the acceptability of this approach to farmers is readily demonstrated by the rapid increase in the area enrolled and the number of agreements signed under the ESA mechanism. Designated in four stages (the first in 1987 and the last in 1994), by 1996 the 22 English ESAs covered an area of one million hectares with some 427,000 ha (or 4.5% of utilised agricultural land) enrolled in close to 8000 agreements and, as Figure 1 illustrates, each successive tranche of ESAs accompanied a steep rise in the area enrolled.

These figures point to the achievements of ESA policy, at least in terms of enrolment — an important 'proxy' indicator of success in the early stages of policy implementation (see Morris and Potter, 1995). Closer examination of the proportion of individual ESAs under agreement, however, reveals significant variation (Figure 2). For example, while 77% of the eligible area of the Clun ESA was under agreement by the end of 1996, only 17% of the Blackdown Hills and 11% of the eligible area of the Essex Coast ESAs had been enrolled (MAFF, 1996). Such uneven uptake can arise for a number of reasons. Partly it can be related to the passage of time since designation (House of Commons, 1997), while complex patterns of ownership, low payment levels and the relative profitability of other land uses can all have the effect of reducing uptake (EN, 1996). This uneven take up is of concern to conservationists who have called for modifications to management packages and changes to payments rates (the latter have recently been announced, (MAFF, 1997). At the same time, further analysis suggests that the majority of enrolled land is in the basic entry tiers. Estimates (based on data supplied

by MAFF) indicate that approximately 87% of the area under agreement in the English ESAs by 1996 was in these basic maintenance tiers. English Nature confirm this, estimating that 63% of the ESA budget is currently devoted to Tier One payments, which while valuable "in sustaining the broader fabric of the countryside character" leave areas of high conservation value outside of agreements (EN, 1996, p. 2).

There is something of the self-fulfilling prophecy about all this. On the one hand, policymakers have chosen to set relatively undemanding entry conditions in order to recruit enough farmers to make a difference. On the other hand, low tier management agreements often require little from participating farmers in the way of changed management practices. The result is a high level of compliance by farmers in order to receive payment but little evidence of environmental additionality due to the scheme — changes that would not have taken place without the scheme. Researchers such as Hodge et al. (1992) and Froud (1994a) confirm that entry tier ESA management agreements often require little

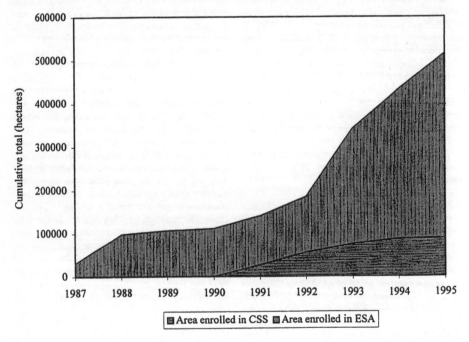

Figure 1. Cumulative enrolment in the English ESA and Countryside Stewardship Schemes. *Source*: MAFF uptake data.

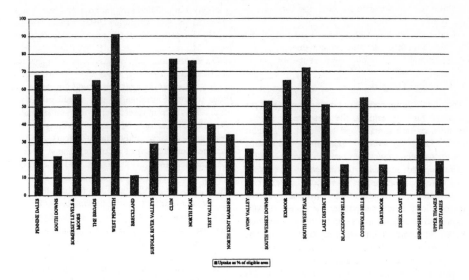

Figure 2. ESA uptake as a proportion of eligible area (management tiers combined). *Source*: MAFF uptake data.

change in management practices and in some cases participants already farm below ESA intensity thresholds. Environmental monitoring of the first five English ESAs between 1987 and 1995 now offers confirmation of the 'maintenance effect' of the ESA model. Although the performance of individual ESAs varies, monitoring highlights the effectiveness of ESA agreements in maintaining the landscape and nature conservation characteristics. MAFF (1996) point to the success of the Somerset Levels, West Penwith and Pennine Dales ESAs in preventing further intensification, and while the CC (1996) note that the Somerset Levels ESA has successfully prevented conversion to arable, it has been less successful in maintaining the quality of existing grassland and that the absence of an arable reversion tier is constraining the potential for enhancement. By contrast, "the single greatest influence of the [South Downs] ESA... has been the success of the arable reversion tiers" involving the conversion of over 5000 hectares of arable land (ADAS, 1996, p. 33). Overall, the South Downs ESA is reported to have been largely successful (in net terms) in maintaining the landscape, wildlife and historical characteristics of the area, while enhancement has been limited. The latter may reflect the longer time period necessary for enhancement effects to materialise as well as technical issues such as the parti-

cular seed mixtures used in arable reversion (ADAS, 1996).

By comparison, the emphasis of CSS is much more on restoration and recreation of wildlife habitat. Established by CC/DoE in 1991 as an experimental pilot programme and handed over to MAFF in 1996, CSS has multiple objectives of sustaining, improving and creating landscapes, habitats and conservation features and improving the public enjoyment of the countryside, reflecting the CC's belief that "... a thriving and diverse countryside... is much more likely to be produced by schemes which reward land managers for clearly defined environmental outputs, rather than for simply following a uniform set of management prescriptions" (CC, 1993, p. 9). In addition to tailoring their own conservation objectives to national and local CSS objectives, aspiring CSS participants are encouraged to offer a combination of environmental benefits in order to receive a higher priority score in the application screening process. Particular emphasis is placed on positive management changes to achieve clear conservation objectives and in this sense CSS places a greater emphasis on enhancement than ESA policy. Each application is judged against four main criteria:

• ability to contribute to national and local priorities
• landscape, wildlife and historical interest of the site (both inherent value and any threats)
• opportunities for public enjoyment (not necessarily access)
• feasibility of proposal

Additional factors considered include proposals for a whole farm agreement, the presence of special features or rare species and the level of support from local conservation organisations. Applicants are encouraged to include documentary support for their proposals such as results of ecological surveys and statements of support from local conservation organisations. Although the precise scoring methodology is not yet publicly available, MAFF expect to accept approximately 75% of applications. Environmental monitoring (LUC, 1996, p. 142) indicates that the discretionary scheme "appears to have achieved a high degree of success in meeting its environmental objectives and providing significant benefits for environmental interests, both individually and in various combinations". Where objectives are not met this frequently results "not so much from non-compliance but rather from agreement holders failing to undertake management in the most appropriate way... poor standards of implementation appear to be due to agreement holders not having a full understanding of what the CSS agreement is seeking to achieve" (LUC, 1996, p. 138). As with ESAs, CSS uptake data point to a rapid increase in the number of agreements and area enrolled (see Figure 1). Sixty-three percent of the total area enrolled by the end of 1995 had been entered in the first two years. The area enrolled at the time of the scheme's transfer to MAFF, just over 97,000 ha, indicates a degree of success in targeting important wildlife habitat and highlights the willingness of land managers to engage with a different policy model. By 1994 it was estimated that 12% of remaining calcareous grass and up to 26% of lowland heath had been entered in addition to major areas of other land of high conservation value (CC, 1996).

Understanding farmer reaction to ELMS

Much research has been conducted into the environmental and socio-economic impact of ELMS, although with some exceptions (e.g. CEAS, 1996; LUC, 1996; Morris and Young, 1997), most of this is largely ESA related (e.g. Hughes and Sherwood, 1992; Moss and Chilton, 1993; Froud, 1994a, 1994b; Russell, 1994; Skerratt, 1994; Whitby, 1994; Morris and Potter, 1995; Wilson, 1996, 1997). A principal concern has been to assess the 'additionality' effects of schemes — their success in bringing about changes that would otherwise not occur (or resisting changes that would otherwise occur). This present researchers with familiar methodological difficulties, because, as Whitby (1994) observes, assessing additionality effects requires accurate identification of a counter-factual or control situation (see also Hughes and Sherwood, 1992). In practice, it may be very difficult to disentangle the scheme influence from that of other policy, business and farm family determinants of farming and land management change. In the absence of data describing long term trends in land management on individual farms, researchers have attempted to infer causation by comparing the situations of participating and non-participating farms (see contributions to Whitby, 1994; Morris and Potter, 1995). At the same time they have examined the motives of participating farmers in order to assess the level of engagement with, and commitment to, scheme objectives — and the likelihood that schemes are stimulating beneficial environmental change. Such work reveals a complex state of affairs. A key determinant of participation for most current participants is the 'goodness of fit' between scheme design and existing farming system. Research suggests that for many, the participation decision was eased by the good fit between scheme requirements and the participant's own farming plans (Hodge et al., 1992; Froud, 1994a, b; Skerratt, 1994; Whitby, 1994; Battershill and Gilg, 1996). This suggests rather low levels of additionality, at least among the existing 'middle majority' of participants, though Whitby argues that as long as the conservation benefits are secure the schemes have gone some way to achieving the successful 'decoupling' of agricultural support (Whitby, 1994). While this may be so, it does raise questions about the longer term impact of such payments and the extent to which participating farmers are engaging with the conservation objectives of the schemes.

Increasing anxiety about the depth and longevity of ELMS effects has stimulated a 'deeper' analysis of the motives for participation (e.g. Morris, 1993; Wilson, 1996) and the way in which farmers themselves understand the conservation value of the farmed landscape and the impacts of their actions (e.g. McHenry, 1996). Wilson (1996) for example, found few participants in the Cambrian Mountains ESA who would continue to meet scheme guidelines in the absence of regular payments, while elsewhere anecdotal evidence suggests some participants may wish to 'improve' their land before re-entering after the expiry of an initial contract (Russell, 1994). The implication is that, to date, ELMS may have only a limited impact in terms of encouraging a positive conservation attitude, analysis of motivation revealing a "surprising extent of passive participation... and the apparent shallowness of... engagement with countryside management goals" (Morris and Potter, 1995, p. 60). Although it is recognised that differences in motivation do exist, much research has tended to view participants as a single coherent group. Recently though it has been proposed that all farmers (including non-participants) can be placed on a "participation spectrum" (Morris, 1993; Morris and Potter, 1995; Wilson, 1996), ranging from the most recalcitrant non-participants through to the most actively committed participants for whom the ELMS is as much a reflection of their own stewardship ethic as it is a reaction to incentive payments. This research suggests that many of those with land enrolled in ESAs are essentially "passive adopters" (Morris and Potter, 1995), with "utilitarian" motivations to join due to the potentially high financial rewards (Wilson, 1996, 1997). A much smaller proportion is concerned with the environmental aspects of participation, often following a history of small scale conservation action on the farm. Despite the suggestion of distinct differences in characteristics, attitudes, motivations and land use between participants, the implications for additionality are less clear. Morris and Potter (1995) suggest that ELMS, at least as currently configured and delivered to farmers, often merely reinforced existing patterns of land use and resource deployment.

Just as treating participants as a single group can obscure important distinctions, differences between non-adopters are also apparent, leading to the identification of a group opposed to the *concept* of ELMS as much as levels of payment. Typically these resistant farmers feel participation in an ELMS is contrary to good agricultural practice and not relevant for their farm (presumably because it would set the farm on a different development trajectory or because they lacked any land of intrinsic

conservation value). In the Cambrian Mountains, Hughes and Sherwood (1992, p. 72) identified non-participants who "gave a wish to maintain their independence as their most important reason" for not joining, although in most cases financial factors dominated. The latter would be among those who have or would consider joining a scheme conditional on changes in scheme characteristics (e.g. level of payments). These farmers can be seen as a reservoir of potential participants to be tapped if offered sufficient payment or if goodness of fit could be improved.

Little is known about the motives and dispositions of participants in the CSS, still less how the participation profile compares with that of ESAs. One hypothesis, already referred to above, is that given the greater selectivity built in to CSS and the greater demands made on potential participants during the application procedure, it is possible that CSS is appealing to a different type of participant, perhaps with more clearly definable countryside management objectives. Is there any evidence that a more discretionary scheme recruits more committed farm participants? If differences exist, how might this affect the ability of first generation ELMS to act as a springboard to propel farmers into more ambitious agri-environmental programmes that may be introduced in the future? Are existing schemes successful in encouraging progression from less to more demanding forms of agri-environmental management on farms? With these questions in mind in 1996 a farm survey was carried out in South East England in order to describe the pattern of participation and investigate the existence of distinct groups of farmers based on their motives for participating in or rejecting ELMS.

The farm survey

Two study areas were selected to represent target areas for ELMS in South East England. These were the South Downs ESA and the North Downs, which is a CSS target area. Although the two schemes have broadly comparable objectives in these areas, CSS places more emphasis on habitat and landscape recreation and restoration. The main objectives of the South Downs ESA is to maintain and enhance the conservation value and landscape quality of chalk grassland through the sensitive management of existing areas and the creation of new areas of permanent grass and chalk grassland. Areas remaining in arable production can be enhanced through increasing the conservation value of arable field margins. Similarly in the North Downs, CSS aims to restore and enhance chalk grassland and reduce the isolation of existing sites through the creation of new grassland with further objectives of enhancing wildlife corridors though the restoration of field boundaries and the creation of uncropped and grass field margins. The sample was drawn from Ordnance Survey maps and Yellow Pages, with CSS participants identified with the assistance of the CC. A randomly selected sample was then contacted by letter to explain the objectives of the survey, followed up with a telephone call. This approach yielded a final sample of 144 respondents spread evenly between the North and South Downs, of these just over half were participating in one of the two schemes (see Table 1). The two study areas are broadly comparable in terms of farm type and size, although a greater proportion of farms in the South Downs are dairy farms while the North Downs contains a greater proportion of small farms.

Patterns of participation: characteristics of participants and non-participants

The 85 participants in the sample had enrolled a total of 5372 ha into the South Downs ESA and CSS. As Figure 3 demonstrates, in both cases close to half the total area enrolled on survey farms by 1996 was entered in the first year of applications, mirroring the rapid rise in the area under agreement nationally (see Figures 1 and 3). However, in proportionate terms, this represents just 12% of the total agricultural area covered by the survey (and

Table 1. Distribution of respondents by study area (numbers in brackets)

	South Downs	North Downs	Total
ELMS participants	69.4% (50)	48.6% (35)	59.0% (85)
Non-participants	30.6% (22)	51.4% (37)	41% (59)
Total	100.0% (72)	100.0% (72)	100% (144)

Source: farm survey.

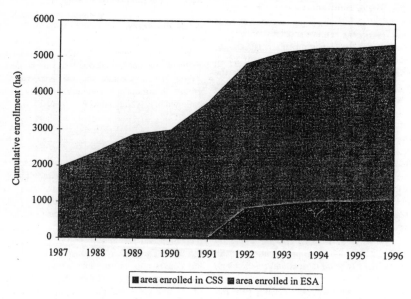

Figure 3. Cumulative enrolment in the ESA and CSS programmes in the North and South Downs. *Source*: farm survey.

18% of the area of participant farms). This pattern varies by study area, with only 6% of the surveyed area in the North Downs enrolled, compared to 17% of the South Downs, confirming the findings of others (e.g. Morris and Young, 1997) that CSS agreements tend to cover only a limited proportion of farmed land. This may be a reflection of the more precisely targeted approach of the CSS, although one result is that only a limited proportion of an individual farm is covered by a CSS agreement. On average, CSS farmers enrolled 16% of their farm compared to 28% for ESA farmers. Figure 4 provides further confirmation, indicating that 43% of CSS farmers enrolled less than 6% of their farm, while 17% had enrolled 26% or more compared to 30% of ESA farmers. This underlines the limited 'reach' of CSS on individual farms. However, in a number of cases, CSS had successfully captured relict habitats and landscape features such as unimproved chalk grassland and old orchards. For example, 38% of CSS agreements included old fruit orchards or cobb nut plantations, some of which had previously been 'derelict'. In the case of cobb nut orchards in particular CSS has played a major

role in helping to maintain this characteristic feature of the Kentish landscape (Game, 1996, personal communication). These fragmented remnants of what would once have been a much more extensive area often necessarily form only a small proportion of a farm. The larger areas enrolled in the ESA on the other hand, is in line with the 'broad but shallow' pattern of participation it is designed initially to promote.

Comparing participants and non-participants for both schemes, initial analysis suggests a wider gap in the case of CSS participants than ESA farmers. As Table 2 indicates, despite the findings of others (e.g. Morris, 1993; Moss and Chilton, 1993), analysis of the age structure of the sample suggests that ESA participants are drawn from all ages. In the case of the CSS, on the other hand, participants are somewhat younger than those who chose not to enter the scheme. They are also more likely to be concentrated at either extreme of the farm size range, compared to non-participants, 37% managing small farms and 29% managing very large farms (Figure 5). ESA participants on the other hand, while less likely to operate small farms, are

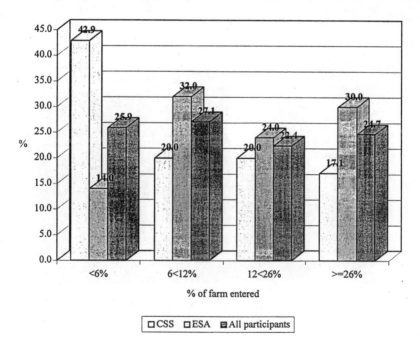

Figure 4. Proportion of farms enrolled in the South Downs ESA and CSS. *Source*: farm survey.

Table 2. The age structure of ESA and CSS farmers

Farmer age group	CSS	ESA	Non-participants
<45	39.4	32.0	25.5
45<55	30.3	28.0	28.8
55<65	21.2	24.0	25.4
¦65	9.1	16.0	20.3
Total (%)	100.0	100.0	100.0

Source: farm survey.

drawn from a range of farm sizes. These findings are not easily reconciled with those of other ELMS researchers who suggest that participants are more clearly defined in terms of age and farm size. In explaining this apparent discrepancy, it should be noted that at the time of the survey the South Downs ESA had been in operation for nine years, achieving a high level of uptake. While the early adopters of the scheme may have had a more distinct identity (and innovation adoption and diffusion theory would support this), energetic promotion of the basic entry scheme achieved wide participation in the study area, with recruitment from a wide cross-section of farmers. Countryside Stewardship's more recent introduction, on the other hand, means that participants to date have tended to be recruited from the ranks of farmers

better networked and also closest in situation to land management configurations demanded by the scheme, while at the same time scheme characteristics themselves may be stimulating a greater degree of self selection among the pool of potential participants.

Further (indirect) evidence for this adoption effect emerges from analysis of household income structure and recent investment behaviour which suggests that while ESA participants are often similar to non-participants, CSS farmers are both more well defined and appear to be following a different business trajectory. Table 3 presents data on the proportion of household income derived from all agricultural sources. Comparing ESA farmers with non-participants, it can be seen that they are largely

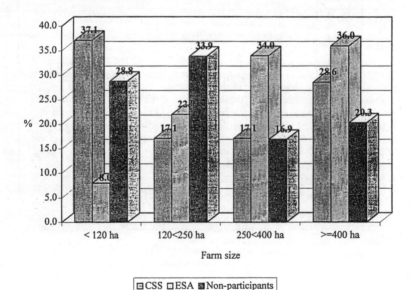

Figure 5. Farm size and participation in ELMS. *Source*: farm survey.

Environmental stewardship in UK agriculture 423

Table 3. Dependency on agricultural income

Agriculture and ELMS	Percentage of household income from		
	CSS participants	ESA participants	Non-participants
<25%	32.3	6.4	8.9
25<75%	19.4	17.0	37.5
75<95%	29.0	31.9	21.4
>95%	19.4	44.7	32.1
Total	100%	100%	100%

Source: farm survey.

dependent on agricultural income sources. CSS farmers, though, are much more likely to be less dependent on agricultural income, with one third gaining less than 25% of household income from agricultural sources (including ELMS payments). This partly reflects differences between the study areas, farmers in the South Downs being more dependent on agricultural income anyway. Nevertheless, in the North Downs, CSS farmers are considerably less dependent on agricultural income than non-participants. In the case of ESA farmers these findings are supported by other research indicating that ELMS participants tend to operate full time farms in the sense of gaining the majority of their income from agriculture (e.g. Moss and Chilton, 1993). Further confirmation of this can be found in the recent investment profiles of the sample (see Table 4). The majority had undertaken recent capital investment with a value of £8000 or more (for a single item) and almost all of these (98%) had carried out agricultural investment. Predictably, fewer had carried out investment associated with diversification, only 26% of ESA farmers and 25% of non-participants. A different pattern emerges for CSS farmers. Although a high incidence of agricultural investment has been recorded, 45% of CSS farmers had also carried out significant investment in diversification, ranging from farm tourist and food processing facilities to investment in off-farm business interests. In some cases enrolment complemented existing land management in

these more diversified business, particularly where there was already some provision for the public (e.g. heritage centres, farm open days etc.) and helped establish a farmer's environmental credentials. As one respondent commented "it's given more publicity to the estate. The access land is adjacent to the village and we've had a lot of favourable comments from the public" (CSS Farmer, North Downs).

Despite the implication that ESA and CSS farmers have been following different business trajectories, their respective recent land management histories are less distinct, or at least point in a similar direction. Table 5 presents data on the recent land management activities of respondents, revealing some important points. Participants in both schemes report a greater incidence of change that could be regarded as positive in a conservation sense, such as converting arable and temporary grassland to permanent grass, reducing stocking density and increasing the overall grazed area of the farm. However, rather than suggesting that participants are following different land management trajectories to non-participants, these changes can largely be seen to reflect effective compliance with the prescriptions of the schemes themselves (although the period covered by the data also includes pre-participation changes). The lower incidence of these (nominally) positive changes among CSS farmers is harder to explain, given the greater emphasis the

Table 4. Investment activities 1985–95 (column %)

	CSS participants	ESA participants	Non-participants
Investment over £8000	82.9	82.0	81.4
Buildings	58.6	53.7	52.1
Food processing facilities	10.3	4.9	4.2
Tourist facilities	20.7	7.3	8.3
Other agricultural equipment	27.6	24.4	18.8
Other non-agricultural investment	31.0	14.6	12.5

Source: farm survey.

Rural Planning and Management

Matt Lobley and Clive Potter

Table 5. Management activities of survey farmers 1985–95 (column %)

	CSS participants	ESA participants	Non-participants
Removed field boundaries (other than fences)	5.7	2.0	11.9
Reduced frequency of hedge trimming	22.9	28.0	13.6
Converted permanent grass to temporary grass/arable	17.1	14.0	18.6
Converted arable/temporary grass to permanent grass	37.1	58.0	6.8
Increased stocking density	17.1	14.0	13.6
Reduced stocking density	31.4	48.0	15.3
Increased grazed area	34.3	46.0	10.2
Increased fertiliser	11.4	20.0	22.0
Reduced fertiliser	22.9	44.0	10.2
Increased pesticide use	20.0	20.0	28.8
Reduced pesticide use	34.3	22.0	18.6

Source: farm survey.

scheme places on active change. The more recent nature of the scheme could be a factor here, although without knowledge of pre-enrolment management it is difficult to comment on the significance of the changes. Additionally, while Table 5 reports the incidence of change, the extent of scheme induced change (i.e. the area involved) could vary, while more subtle changes also remain unrecorded.

The impact of participation

While identifying the typical characteristics of participants is an important first stage in the analysis, a second consideration is the impact of participation on farm management and income. Thus, an important element of 'participation studies' is a concern with the positive additionality effects of schemes, that is the ability of a scheme to bring about a change that would otherwise have not occurred. Table 6 suggests that in terms of the immediate impact on farm businesses, the incidence of scheme-induced change is lower for CSS farmers, notably in terms of the impact on timing of agricultural operations, overall impact on production and the impact on investment plans. This may

reflect scheme design, the CSS being a victim of its own success in targeting land marginal to the main productive function of the farm. The greater reported impact of the ESA on production and investment plans, on the other hand, frequently stems from the conversion of arable to grass, resulting in a reduction in both the volume and value of arable production, and at the same time reducing wear and tear on arable machinery, so lengthening the replacement cycle. Overall though, the impact of participation would seem to be a function of the characteristics of the particular management package adopted and the existing farming system. In encouraging the conversion of arable land, ESA participation can be associated with abrupt land use and land management change, with effects spreading out to the rest of the farm. In the North Downs, although CSS does target some arable land for reversion, many agreements involved the fine tuning of management practices on existing grassland which could help to explain the lower incidence of change. Others have also noted that when 'traditional' farms enrol land few substantial changes are required (Battershill and Gilg, 1996)

Despite these differences, roughly comparable numbers of CSS and ESA farmers reported that

Table 6. Impact of participation on farm and farm business (column %)

	CSS participants	ESA participants	All participants
Impact on timing of operations	26.5	44.0	36.9
Impact on machinery	29.4	34.0	32.1
Impact on production	21.2	48.0	37.3
Impact on farm income	66.7	64.0	65.1
Impact on investment plans	6.1	30.0	20.5
Impact on labour use	45.5	42.0	43.4
Other impact	50.8	30.0	38.1

Source: farm survey.

participation had an impact on labour use and farm income. The former was largely associated with the use of contract labour, particularly for the reintroduction of grazing, confirming the findings of a CSS monitoring evaluation which revealed significant CSS-induced increases in the use of contract labour (CEAS, 1996). The widely reported income effect is also confirmed by previous ESA evaluations which highlighted the positive income effects associated with participation deriving from the ease with which participants could comply with scheme conditions (e.g. GRE, 1995). Indeed, many respondents commented on the financial benefits of the scheme, particularly where few if any changes were necessary for compliance (also suggesting low levels of additionality). The following comment was echoed by a number of participants: "It was already an SSSI which restricted what we could do and it was too steep to fertilise. Therefore we are able to get money for carrying on as before" (ESA farmer). Others recognised a positive income effect but lamented the loss of payments under the Arable Area Payments Scheme (AAPS), or found that the income effect declined with time. One ESA farmer reported that participation "was beneficial to start with, until the early 1990s, but now it has become detrimental, especially with arable aid payments so high. The production of the land has plummeted — I'm surprised at how low its gone, its not something I really foresaw. The grass has become very rough, there's no fertility left and I can't even get up to the allowed stocking rates" (South Downs ESA farmer). Problems like this though were rare, and the overall impression gained from participants was that the ESA had a positive income effect. A similar proportion of CSS farmers also reported a scheme-induced income effect although previous research points to a lower incidence of income effects associated with the scheme (CEAS, 1996). The large proportion reporting a change in income in the present survey could be explained by differences in questioning, with respondents including their own contribution to capital costs in their overall assessment of scheme impact on farm income. Some farmers argued that while in purely income terms participation would often have only a marginal impact, partially funding capital works (especially in the early years of an agreement) left them worse off. That said, the provision of capital grants was for many an important reason for participating, particularly where CSS contributed to existing plans for the reintroduction of grazing for example.

The participation decision: the motives of participants

Previous research into the adoption of ELMS suggests a complex interplay between farm and farmer characteristics and the characteristics of the schemes themselves, and points to only a minority of more traditional or conservation orientated participants (Morris and Potter, 1995; Battershill and Gilg, 1996; Wilson, 1996, 1997). In the current survey, although participation in the two ELMS appears to be steering land management in broadly the same direction, survey evidence suggests that the schemes are appealing to different sections of the farming population in terms of farm and farm household characteristics. Further support for this selectivity effect comes from an analysis of participants motives, indicating that not only are CSS farmers more atypical in terms of certain farm business characteristics, they are also motivationally distinct. As might be expected, participants in Countryside Stewardship were, on average, more emphatic in justifying their participation in conservation terms than those in the ESA. Participants were questioned about their main reason for enrolling and about the importance they placed on a range of motivational influences identified from previous ELMS adoption research. For the sample as a whole two motivationally distinct groups of participants can be recognised: compliers and stewards.

'Compliers', making up 67% of participants, were willing to comply with conservation land management practices in return for what they considered to be reasonable financial compensation. Fifty-three percent reported that the level of payment per hectare was a very important consideration in their decision to join (see Table 7). Contrary to some suggestions, (e.g. Brotherton, 1991) this factor outweighed the emphasis placed on total financial returns from participation. Many indicated that this was less relevant for small areas, although that said, 25% felt that the guaranteed income offered by ELMS did play an important role in their participation decision. At the same time, goodness of fit with existing farming system was seen as an important precondition for entry, and where this criteria was met the attractions of a given level of payment were increased. For compliers then, the decision to participate was largely determined by the interaction between 'goodness of fit' and level of payment

Table 7. The motives of participants*

	Stewards	Compliers	All participants
Level of payment per ha	22.2	52.8	42.5
Total contribution to farm income	11.1	15.1	13.8
Useful source of guaranteed income	14.8	24.5	21.3
Provides useful source of investment funds	3.7	5.7	5.0
Marketing and presentation of scheme	14.8	9.4	11.3
Compatibility with existing farming system	40.7	39.6	40.0
Opportunity to reduce intensity	3.7	5.7	5.0
Support for existing low intensity system	14.8	7.5	10.0
Helps carry out conservation work previously unable to do	22.2	5.7	11.3
Helps extend and improve existing conservation plans	14.8	3.8	7.5
Adds to conservation value of farm	29.6	11.3	17.5

Source: farm survey.
*Proportion stating that motivating factor was 'very important'.

— the type of instrumental reasons stressed by Wilson (1996). Even where ELMS involved an abrupt change in land use and management, this was also often compatible with existing plans as the following example illustrates.

> the arable land had been corn for 20 years, it was on top of the hill with poor soil and yields were very poor so we were going to put it into a ley for the sheep. The scheme provided an income for doing this even though it was for a longer period of time (South Downs ESA farmer).

As with the 'passive adopters' identified by Morris and Potter (1995), few compliers seem to have engaged with the conservation objectives of the scheme, rather they see participation as a means of achieving farming and income goals. Compliers are the dominant group in the South Downs ESA (accounting for 83% of participants). Most operate large farms, and with few having diversified, they are largely dependent on agricultural income.

'Stewards' (representing 41% of all CSS farmers) were more motivationally distinct and noticeably less dependent on agricultural income than the rest of the sample. Stewards justified their participation decision much more in terms of the potential conservation benefits of participation, 30 and 22% respectively reporting that the addition to the conservation value of the farm and injection of funds to carry out conservation work were very important considerations in their participation decision. For stewards operating some of the smallest farms, the former could be particularly important, especially where this enhanced the capital value of the farm if it were to be sold for residential or 'hobby' farming purposes. In their responses to questions about what had prompted them to join in the first instance, stewards were much more likely to identify directly

with the conservation objectives of the scheme, whereas compliers continually and consistently emphasised financial aspects. One farmer commented that:

> I was disenchanted with modern high pressure farming — it lacks an understanding of the complexities of the environment. I'm interested in conservation and wildlife as a hobby and the ESA is a good compromise as I can continue to farm in a less aggressive way while still using the land in a way that set aside wouldn't allow (South Downs ESA farmer).

Similarly, another reported that:

> what primarily attracted me to the ESA is that I can tell myself I'm still farming it and that its properly farmed — unlike set aside. The Downs shouldn't have been ploughed in the first place and having done it [joined the ESA] I'm very pleased (South Downs ESA farmer).

While the survey results suggest that stewards are living up to their name, expressing support for the conservation objectives of ELMS both in their words and deeds, further analysis reveals that this group also has closer ties with the wider conservation community. As Table 8 indicates, for all participants, family and other farmers are relatively unimportant sources of information on the availability of ELMS. Project Officers and promotional literature not unexpectedly played an important role for both stewards and compliers. More notable are the 25% of stewards who first learnt about the scheme from other conservation organisations such as local conservation trusts and countryside projects. A number of stewards reported prior involvement with such organisations, sometimes using them as an advisory source and in other cases using conservation volunteers to carry out small scale conservation projects on their farms. Certainly, recipients of conservation advice tend to have an

Table 8. Source of first advice about scheme

Source of advice	Stewards	Compliers	All participants
Family and other farmers	10.0	5.1	6.3
Farmers Union	5.0	1.7	2.5
Professional advisor	0.0	5.1	3.8
Press and media	30.0	28.8	29.1
Project Officer	30.0	50.8	45.6
Other conservation advisors	25.0	8.5	12.7
Total (%)	100.0	100.0	100.0

Source: farm survey.

existing predisposition towards conservation (Winter et al., 1996). Stewards also found their links with conservation organisations particularly useful in preparing their applications and were often using them in the management of agreement land.

The motives of non-participants

The potential for ELMS to bring about positive environmental change rests as much on the ability of future schemes to recruit from a wider range of farmers as it does from influencing the behaviour of current participants. Further along the so-called 'participation spectrum', distinct groups of farmers can be recognised on the basis of their motives for non-participation. Non-participants were asked if they had ever considered enrolling in an ELMS, and if so, what had influenced their decision not to participate. This led to the identification of two similar sized groups. The first (56% of all non-participants) can be seen as a reservoir of 'potential enrolers', 72% of whom had given serious consideration to enrolling land (indeed some had applied to CSS but had been turned down for a variety of reasons). Motivationally close to compliers, in many ways the reasons reported by this group for not participating mirror those of compliers, with farm and scheme characteristics combining to reduce the attraction of ELMS. Although few were concerned with the length of agreements or additional administration, 54% of potential enrolers reported that the level of payment per hectare was a very important factor in deciding not to enrol land (particularly compared to arable subsidies) while 38% and 23% respectively reported that, on closer examination, the scheme did not fit with their plans for the farm or that they would have difficulty in meeting scheme guidelines. Other influences were also apparent, the following example illustrating the complex interaction between scheme and farm characteristics and farm tenure:

> The farm has a lot of permanent grass and traditional parkland but under tier one you get very little for the restrictions imposed making it unviable. We would also need more land to put stock on at other times as we can't afford to reduce output on our present acreage but the compensation doesn't allow for that and arable reversion is completely unviable on the rents we have to pay (South Downs farmer).

Others were more clearly deterred by scheme characteristics, as the following North Downs farmer observed:

> In response to environmental concerns I thought about putting unfertilised grass in and got close to entering but thought it would be a lot of extra hassle for a negative return. I would have cleared some scrub and also developed hazel coppice but I didn't want access so there wasn't much in it for me (North Downs farmer).

Although granting access has never been a condition for acceptance into CSS, it is included in the priority scoring mechanism and a number of farmers who had considered and rejected CSS explained this in terms of not wanting access. Although it cannot be determined from survey data, it is possible that these were among some of the more marginal CSS applications that had had value added (and therefore stood a greater chance of acceptance) through the creation of access opportunities. It is also worth noting that these farmers were among some of the earliest applicants for CSS and following criticism of access agreement (RA, 1995) project officers may have placed less emphasis on this aspect when dealing with applications.

Motivational differences aside, potential enrolers were not well defined across a range of farm and farmer characteristics although they are slightly more elderly and are more likely to manage smaller farms than compliers for instance. More noticeable is the farm type profile of potential enrolers, 73% managing arable farms compared to 49% of both stewards and compliers. For those with entirely arable operations this was seen as a significant barrier to entry, although the wider policy environment also exerts an influence as the following example illustrates:

> It meant a change of farm policy by introducing livestock and it's not as profitable especially with IACS payments. But without the subsidies the arable wouldn't be viable since it's marginal land and so would definitely revert to grass if the payments were cut (South Downs farmer).

In motivational terms, furthest removed from the steward minded farmers, who enrolled for conservation reasons, are a group of resistant non-participants opposed to the philosophy of ELMS including some who even denied the need for such an approach. As with potential enrolers, they are not particularly well defined in terms of farm or farm household characteristics although they are to some extent concentrated among smaller farms (35% manage small farms). 'Resistors' are the least likely to have sought conservation advice in the past (only 26% compared to 60% for the whole sample), resenting the intrusion into their private decision making. One farmer describing himself as "quite feudal, you know an Englishman's castle... I fundamentally disagree with the scheme and think I do a better job myself. I don't like people telling me what I can and can't do". Others simply saw ELMS as inappropriate management:

> It's a backward move not to fertilise and constitutes bad farming practice. I don't think heavy stocking is anti-conservation and haven't seen a decline in wildflowers here. Looking at my neighbour's land which has been entered it's weed infested and reminds me of scrubland after the war and the struggle to get it back into production (South Downs farmer).

Not surprisingly, this group has the most limited awareness of ELMS and while this no doubt partly reflects their resistance it probably also reinforces it through lack of knowledge of what ELMS seek to achieve. Inevitably they would be the last to enrol land and while some expressed an interest in conservation, at best they would be 'begrudging compliers'.

Discussion and Implications

The results of the survey suggest that the ESA programme and CSS are indeed appealing to different sections of the farming community, and in a motivationally selective way. To an extent this reflects the way the schemes have been conceived, designed and offered to farmers. The ESA operates as a *platform scheme*, drawing farmers from a range of backgrounds into a basic entry level tier aimed at maintaining the conservation character of the area. It elicits *compliance behaviour* from farmers, most participants having carefully assessed the scheme for it goodness of fit with existing farming practice and the financial return. The emphasis ESA farmers place on the financial aspects of the scheme could partly reflect the way the scheme is sold by project Officers (Wilson, 1996). Project Officers' apparent success in recruiting a large number of farmers reflects the close match between current farming conditions and scheme requirements. Although compliance is therefore high, it is less clear how willing participants would be to move into higher tiers. Countryside Stewardship, on the other hand, works as a *sieve scheme*. By offering applicants the opportunity to tailor their own management package, CSS is evidently appealing more to those with existing countryside management objectives. At the same time, an emphasis on applications offering multiple objectives supported by conservation expertise favours steward-minded farmers with an existing interest in conservation and better contacts with local conservation organisations. The difference between the two schemes in the profile of participants is not simply a function of the length of time they have been in operation. One hypothesis might be that stewards are the early adopters of ELMS and, therefore, will inevitably form a large proportion of participants in more recent schemes. However, for both the ESA and the CSS, it is the enrolers in the sample who are early adopters. In the case of CSS then, there appears to be a double selectivity effect operating: first when discretion is exercised by Project Officers and then secondly through a greater degree of self-selection from within the farm population.

Environmental additionality may be limited for both stewards and compliers, but for subtly different reasons. Although stewards align themselves more closely to the conservation objectives of ELMS and have a greater exposure to conservation organisations, the apparent correspondence between scheme objectives and farmers' personal conservation objectives could mean, paradoxically, that 'additions' to conservation value produced by stewards may be just as limited as it is for compliers, as the following examples drawn from the North and South Downs illustrate:

I value our Downland and feel it's a very focal feature of the farm and so any scheme that gave us benefit to continue farming in an environmentally sound way was the right thing. The North Downs Way goes through the land so additional access was no problem and we've have had good positive feedback from locals. It's money for old rope because I'm being paid for what I wanted to do ('Steward', North Downs).

the Project Officer came to look and said that we were doing what was needed anyway so we should join. I like the chalk downland and remember the area before the war when it was all downland. I found it distressing to see it disappear and would like to help bring a bit back ('Steward', South Downs).

By definition, compliers are drawn into schemes requiring little or no change to existing plans. This is actively encouraged by the ESA approach where entry tiers "generally involve prevention of intensification... they are intended to stabilise the environmental status of land on entry into the scheme" (House of Commons, 1997, p. xix). Although it has been argued that entry into lower tiers can lead to enrolment in higher tiers (RSPB, 1996b), discussions with farmers in the present survey suggest that participation was frequently a case of entering marginal arable land to achieve farm management and income objectives, with little appreciation of the environmental objectives.

One way to enhance additionality and improve participant commitment could be to widen the range of ELMS available, not just in terms of objectives but also delivery. Policymakers should be aware that in addition to deploying different types of scheme to tackle different agri-environmental problems, they can appeal to and recruit different sections of the farming community through adjustments to the way schemes are designed and operated. While the two approaches examined here are undoubtedly complementary, further analysis of survey data reveals the willingness of participants and potential enrolers to consider a number of other ELMS models. From Table 9 it can be seen that stewards were the most willing to consider offering

environmental services to other 'purchasers' (85% compared to 67% of compliers) and express a greater interest in some form of management sharing with conservation groups — 72% of stewards would consider this option compared to 49% of compliers. Increasing the range of contracting agencies or purchasers in this way would increase administrative capacity and could provide the means to implement and enforce ELMS on a larger scale (Hodge, 1991). The willingness of stewards to consider this option is perhaps most easily explained by the greater informal contact already taking place between these farmers and conservation groups. Encouraging stewards to enter into contracts for agri-environmental services with these organisations could reinforce the strong self motivation already apparent amongst this groups while also appealing to compliers and potential enrolers. Stewards, compliers and potential enrolers would also be willing to allow conservation volunteers on their farm 93, 91 and 79% respectively), usually with the proviso that they were kept under 'strict control'. Interestingly, a major consideration here was not so much the potential supply of free labour but the beneficial impact of conservation expertise and knowledge.

Table 9 also indicates changes that could increase the appeal of ELMS to potential enrolers, effectively pulling them along the participation spectrum towards enrolment. Although relatively few existing participants were likely to consider tendering as a means of scheme entry, 60% of potential enrolers felt that a tendering system would offer greater flexibility, both in terms of management package and price, claiming that many participants were 'getting money for nothing' and would be exposed under a tendering approach. Another radical proposal, but one receiving a surprisingly high level of support, is that of a local environmental association. This suggestion is based on a model in operation in the Netherlands (Horlings, 1994) where local farmers and conservationists form an environmental

Table 9. The willingness of participants and non-participants to consider alternative policies (column %)

	Stewards	Compliers	Potential participants
ELMS operated by conservation organisation	85.0	60.5	53.3
Using conservation volunteers on farm	92.6	90.6	78.8
Allowing conservation group to manage land	72.4	48.8	40.0
Would consider submitting tender	32.0	44.0	60.0
Join local environmental association	50.0	43.1	54.8

Source: farm survey.

430   Matt Lobley and Clive Potter

association or co-operative, devise local agri-environmental management plans and seek funding from a local purchaser (e.g. Local Authority). Each plan specifies a basic set of landscape elements to be managed for which the farmer would receive payment, individual farmers would then be free to opt for further measures subject to their interests and ability. How much relevance though does this idea have in the British context? Despite the high level of support for the principle, most respondents included a caveat and a warning. The former was that such an association would work only if not dominated by 'incomers' and 'do-gooders', the latter that farmers are not very good at co-operating. Nevertheless, one possibility would be to develop a series of agri-environmental networks comprising farmers, landmanagers and conservation organisations tied to the promotion of 'countryside character'. The network could be used to identify important aspects of the conservation resource (perhaps adopting a tiering system) and in collaboration with farmers could identify suitable farming practices. Groups or individual farms could then apply for the contract to produce these conservation goods, some of which could be sub-contracted to CARTs (Conservation, Amenity and Recreation Trusts, see Hodge, 1988) who could also bid in their own right. Taken together, these findings point to the considerable scope for broadening the delivery and operation schemes and bringing potential enrolers into ELMS. With the policy still at quite an early stage in its evolution, it is clearly important to identify where improvements can be made. Although it is mostly existing participants who are the most willing to consider alternative ELMS mechanisms, large numbers of potential enrolers also responded positively to alternative ELMS models.

Within the existing population of participants, it would be naive to assume that stewards will ever make up the majority of participants in a voluntary ELMS. Nevertheless, their willingness to engage with the conservation objectives of schemes could prove important for the success of more ambitious management regimes on sites of greater nature conservation value. In addition, it has yet to be explored how the actions of this minority, and their ability to reconcile farm management and conservation objectives, could influence other participants and potential enrolers. While Project Officers clearly play a role in encouraging farmers and building on initial interest, mobilising stewards into

a network of ELMS demonstration farms could help cement the foundations of a larger ELMS.

Acknowledgements — The research on which this paper is based was funded under the European Commission's AIR Programme. The authors wish to thank Kaley Hart for her assistance in the farm survey and data analysis.

Note

1. Including the opening up of ELMS to all managers of suitable land, although this is beyond the scope of the present paper.

References

Adams, W., Hodge, I. and Bourn, N. (1994) Nature conservation and the management of the wider countryside in Eastern England. *Journal of Rural Studies* 10(2), 147–157.
ADAS, 1996. Environmental monitoring in the South Downs ESA 1987–95. Report to the Ministry of Agriculture, Fisheries and Food, MAFF, London.
Baldock, D., Cox, G., Lowe, P. and Winter, M. (1990) Environmentally Sensitive Areas: incrementalism or reform?. *Journal of Rural Studies* 6(2), 143–162.
Battershill, M. and Gilg, A. (1996) Traditional farming and agro-environment policy in Southwest England: back to the future? *Geoforum* 27(2), 133–147.
Brotherton, I. (1991) What limits participation in ESAs?. *Journal of Environmental Management* 32, 241–249.
Buckwell, A., 1997. Towards a Common Agricultural and Rural Policy for Europe, European Economy Reports and Studies, 5. Office for Official Publications of the European Communities, Luxembourg.
CEAS, 1996. Socio-economic Effects of the Countryside Stewardship Scheme. CEAS Consultants (Wye) Ltd, Wye.
Commission of the European Communities, 1996. Twenty-Fifth financial report concerning the European Agricultural Guidance and Guarantee Fund, 1995 Financial year COM (96) 504 Final. CEC, Brussels.
Country Landowners Association, 1994. Focus on the CAP: a CLA discussion paper. CLA, London.
Countryside Commission, 1996. Memorandum by the Countryside Commission submitted to House of Commons Agriculture Committee Inquiry into ESAs and other schemes under the Agri-Environment Regulation. Countryside Commission, Cheltenham.
Countryside Commission, 1993. Paying for a Beautiful and Diverse Countryside: Securing Environmental Benefits and Value for Money from Incentive Schemes. Countryside Commission, Cheltenham.
Department of the Environment and Ministry of Agriculture, Fisheries and Food, 1995. Rural England: A Nation Committed to a Living Countryside. HMSO, London.
English Nature, 1996. Memorandum by English Nature submitted to House of Commons Agriculture Committee Inquiry into ESAs and other schemes under the

Agri-Environment Regulation. English Nature, Peterborough.

Fraser, I., 1993. Agri-environmental policy and discretionary incentive mechanisms: the Countryside Stewardship Scheme as a case study. Discussion paper no. 93-05, Department of Economics and Economic History, Manchester Metropolitan University.

Fraser, I. (1996) Quasi-markets and the provision of nature conservation in agri-environmental policy. *European Environment* **6**, 95–101.

Froud, J. (1994) The impact of ESAs on lowland farming. *Land Use Policy* **11**(2), 102–118.

Froud, J., 1994b. Upland moorland with complex property rights: the case of the North Peak. In: Whitby, M. (Ed.), Incentives for Countryside Management. The case of ESAs. CAB International, Wallingford, Oxon, pp. 81–104.

Game, M., 1996. Personal communication.

Gould Rural Environment, 1995. Socio-economic evaluation of the Stage III ESAs in England, baseline study. Unpublished report to MAFF.

Hodge, I. (1988) Property institutions and environmental improvement. *Journal of Agricultural Economics* **39**, 369–375.

Hodge, I. (1991) Incentive policies and the rural environment. *Journal of Rural Studies* **7**, 373–384.

Hodge, I., Adams, W. and Bourn, N. (1992) The cost of conservation: comparing like with like — a comment on Brotherton. *Environment and Planning A* **24**, 1051–1054.

Horlings, I. (1994) Policy conditions for sustainable agriculture in the Netherlands. *The Environmentalist* **14**(3), 193–199.

House of Commons, 1997. Environmentally Sensitive Areas and other Schemes under the Agri-Environment Regulation, vol. 1, Report and Proceedings, Select Committee on Agriculture, Second Report, Session 1996–7. HMSO, London.

Hughes, G., Sherwood, A., 1992. Socio-economic aspects of designating the Cambrian Mountains and the Lleyn Peninsula as ESAs. Department of Economics and Agricultural Economics, University College of Wales, Aberystwyth.

Lowe, P., Cox, G., MacEwen, M., O'Riordan, T., Winter, M., 1986. Countryside Conflicts: The Politics of Farming, Forestry and Conservation. Temple Smith/Gower, London.

Land Use Consultants, 1996. Countryside Stewardship Monitoring and Evaluation, 4th Report. LUC, London.

McHenry, H., 1996. Understanding farmers' perceptions of changing agriculture: some implications for agri-environmental schemes. In: Curry, N., Owen, S. (Eds), Changing Rural Policy in Britain. The Countryside and Community Press, Gloucester, pp. 225–243.

MAFF, 1994. Environmental Objectives and Performance Indicators for ESAs in England. MAFF, London.

MAFF, 1995. Environmental land management schemes in England: a consultation document. MAFF/DOE, London.

MAFF, 1996. Memorandum submitted to House of Commons Agriculture Committee Inquiry into ESAs and other schemes under the Agri-Environment Regulation. MAFF, London.

MAFF, 1997. Expansion of environmentally-friendly farming. News release 40/97.

Morris, C., 1993. Recruiting farmers into conservation: an analysis of farmer participation in agri-environmental schemes in lowland England. Unpublished PhD thesis, Wye College, University of London.

Morris, C. and Potter, C. (1995) Recruiting the new conservationists: farmers' adoption of agri-environmental schemes in the UK. *Journal of Rural Studies* **11**(1), 51–63.

Morris, C. and Young, C. (1997) Towards environmentally beneficial farming? An evaluation of the Countryside Stewardship Scheme. *Geography* **82**, 305–316.

Moss, J., Chilton, S., 1993. Agriculture and the Environmentally Sensitive Area scheme. In: Marry, M., Greer, J. (Eds), Rural Development in Ireland: A Challenge for the 1990s. Avebury, Aldershot, pp. 71–83.

Potter, C. (1988) Environmentally sensitive areas in England and Wales: an experiment in countryside management. *Land Use Policy* **5**, 301–313.

Potter, C., 1998. Against the Grain: Agri-environmental Reform in the United States and the European Union. CAB International, Wallingford, Oxon.

Ramblers' Association, 1995. Countryside Stewardship Scheme Public Access Sites: A Report into the Value for Money and Effectiveness of Purchasing Public Access to the Countryside via a Government Funded Experimental Scheme. Ramblers' Association, London.

Royal Society of the Protection of Birds, 1996a. ESAs and other schemes under the Agri-Environment Regulation, RSPB comments submitted to the House of Commons Agriculture Committee. RSPB. Sandy.

Royal Society of the Protection of Birds, 1996b. Comments submitted by the RSPB to the National Audit Office study of ESAs. RSPB, Sandy.

Russell, N. (1994) Grassland conservation in an arable area: the case of the Suffolk River valleys. In: Whitby, M. (Ed.), Incentives for Countryside Management: The Case of ESAs. CAB International, Wallingford, Oxon, pp. 25–40.

Scottish Landowners Federation, 1995. Supporting the Countryside — Future Opportunities. SLF, Scotland.

Skerratt, S., 1994. Itemised payments within a single system: the case of Breadalbane. In: Whitby, M. (Ed.), Incentives for Countryside Management: The Case of ESAs. CAB International, Wallingford, Oxon, pp. 105–134.

Swinbank, A., Tanner, C., 1996. Farm Policy and Trade Conflict: The Uruguay Round and Common Agricultural Policy Reform. The University of Michigan Press, Ann Arbor.

Webster, S. and Felton, M. (1993) Targeting for nature conservation in agricultural policy. *Land Use Policy* **10**(1), 67–82.

Whitby, M. (Ed.), 1994. What future for ESAs? In: Incentives for Countryside Management: The Case of ESAs. CAB International, Wallingford, Oxon, pp. 253–271.

Whitby, M. (Ed.), 1996. The prospect for Agri-Environmental Policies within a reformed CAP. In: The European Environment and CAP Reform: Policies and Prospects for Conservation. CAB International, Wallingford, Oxon, pp. 227–240.

Wilson, G. (1996) Farmer environmental attitudes and (non) participation in the ESA scheme. *Geoforum* **27**(2), 115–131.

Wilson, G. (1997) Selective targeting in Environmentally Sensitive Areas: implications for farmers and the

432   Matt Lobley and Clive Potter

environment. *Journal of Environmental Planning and Management* **40**(2), 199–215.

Winter, M., Gasson, R., Curry, N., Selman, P., Short, C., 1996. Socio-economic Evaluation of Free Conservation Advice Provided to Farmers in England, Rural Research Monograph Series No. 1. The Countryside and Community Press, Cheltenham and Gloucester College of Higher Education, Cheltenham.

[20]

PERGAMON

Land Use Policy 16 (1999) 67–80

Land Use Policy

Assessing the success of agri-environmental policy in the UK

Nick Hanley[a,*], Martin Whitby[b], Ian Simpson[c]

[a] *Institute of Ecology and Resource Management, University of Edinburgh, Management Kings Building, West Mains Road, Edinburgh EH9 3JG, UK*
[b] *Centre for Rural Economy, Department of Agricultural Economics and Food Marketing, University of Newcastle-on-Tyne, UK*
[c] *Department of Environmental Science, University of Sterling, Sterling FK9 4LA, UK*

Received 21 September 1998; received in revised form 1 December 1998; accepted 8 December 1998

Abstract

This paper considers alternative means for assessing the success of "agri-environmental" policy (AEP), which has become an increasingly-important aspect of agricultural and environmental policy throughout Europe, and which has probably developed more extensively in the UK than elsewhere. After a brief description of the main elements of AEP in the UK, we consider two broad classes of assessment method, those based on efficiency and those based on effectiveness. The latter class of methods has dominated appraisal so far in the UK, primarily through participation measures. We outline the limitations of these, and then consider evidence of policy efficiency gained through cost–benefit analysis techniques. Finally, we suggest how a combined approach could be used to appraise three possible changes to UK agri-environmental policy. © 1999 Elsevier Science Ltd. All rights reserved.

Keywords: Agri-environmental policy; Cost-benefit analysis; Policy reform; Environmental variation

1. Introduction

This paper reviews different means for assessing one particular section of UK land use policy, namely agri-environmental schemes. These schemes have become an increasingly important part of UK agricultural policy, although spending associated with them is still dwarfed by spending on more conventional aspects of farm support. These policies have as their goal the production of environmental benefits, in return for opportunity–cost-based payments to participating farmers, an application of the "Provider Gets" principle for public goods provision (Hanley et al., 1998a). We consider the evolution of these schemes, and the dominant model for their design. Alternative criteria for assessing the performance of these policies are then set out and results from appraisals noted. We concentrate in particular on the increasing use of cost-benefit analysis (CBA) in this respect. Finally, possible reforms of agri-environmental policy are evaluated in the light of these criteria. Evaluations of agri-environmental policy (AEP) in other European contexts may be found elsewhere: see, for example, Dabbert et al. (1998).

* Corresponding author. Tel.: + 44-131-535-4111; fax: + 44-131-667-2601
E-mail address: n.d.hanley@ed.ac.uk (N. Hanley)

0264-8377/99/$ - see front matter © 1999 Elsevier Science Ltd. All rights reserved.
PII: S 0 2 6 4 - 8 3 7 7 (9 8) 0 0 0 4 1 - 6

2. Trends in agri-environmental policy

In this paper, we define as AEP any policy implemented by farm agencies or ministries, for which funding comes out of agricultural support budgets, and which is concerned mainly with encouraging or enforcing the production of environmental goods, as joint products with food and fibre outputs. There are now many examples of such policies within the OECD (see OECD, 1995). In Britain, as in the EU more widely, the late 1980s and 1990s have seen a modest and gradual reform of farm support policy under the Common Agriculture Policy (CAP), as a gradual shift away from output-related support, and towards area-based payments and payments for the supply of environmental goods (Billing, 1998). Area support payments now constitute the largest single component of CAP spending in the UK. Under the most recent CAP reform proposals, *Agenda 2000*, further incremental change is proposed, as reductions in price support for arable crops, beef and sheepmeat, with increasing use of area-based support. In the UK, this may have particularly important impacts in Less Favoured Areas, with movement away from headage payments discouraging excessively high stocking rates in fragile hill upland areas. *Agenda 2000* also promises a "prominent role" for environmental measures under the CAP. This

68   *N. Hanley et al. / Land Use Policy 16 (1999) 67–80*

change in policy direction has been the outcome of three forces: originally, due to the budgetary pressures of surplus production and of increasing community demand for environmental quality, and more recently because of demands from the World Trade Organisation (and the US government) for a reduction in trade-distorting measures.

In 1985, the EU's "Green Handbook" advocated combining environmental policies with agricultural market and income support policies to produce environmental benefits. Expression was given to these sentiments in the UK-proposed Article 19 of the "Structures Regulation" in 1985 (1797/1985). Regulation 1760/87 then allowed member states to claim up to 25% of the compensation paid under such arrangements from the Guidance Section of FEOGA, allowing spending on environmental outputs from national agricultural budgets for the first time. In the UK, this major change was introduced by the 1986 Agriculture Act, followed swiftly by the introduction of the first major element of AEP, the Environmentally Sensitive Areas (ESA) scheme in 1987. In 1992, the EU 5th Action Programme on the Environment set as a priority "…the establishment of a sustainable and environmentally friendly agriculture". Also in 1992, the increasing budgetary costs of the CAP, pressure from the Uruguay round negotiations and the promise of even bigger budgetary pressures from EU enlargement, led to reductions (of up to 30%) in the level of price support, the introduction of area payments and the use of compulsory set-aside.

"Accompanying measures" to these reforms included the Agri-Environmental Regulation 2078/92, which en-

couraged the much wider use of AEP throughout the EU. The standard model put forward was one of a contractual agreement between farmers and the state in return for environmental service provision. Regulation 2078/92 leaves the details of actual policy design up to individual member states, under the subsidiarity principle. In Britain, this led to the introduction of a large number of schemes (detailed below), all based on largely the same design principle: that of voluntary co-operation in return for payments.

Increases in spending on AEP in the UK can be seen by either from total spending or at spending on individual schemes. Total spending, which includes payments to farmers, running costs and monitoring costs has increased from £33 million in 1992/1993 to £86 million in 1996/1997 (Agriculture Committee, 1997). For the largest single scheme (ESAs), spending in England has risen from £2.9 m in 1987/1998 to £33 m in 1996/1997 (see Fig. 1), whilst in Scotland it has increased from £57807 to £6.31 m over the same period. Despite this, for the UK as a whole, spending on AEP is still a very small percentage of total spending on agricultural support: for example, in 1995/1996 it accounted for only 2.5% of total CAP spending in the UK of £2,857 m. In the EU as a whole, spending on AEP was 1.4 billion ECUs in 1996, which was about 3% of total CAP spending of 41.2 billion ECUs in the same year. Regulation 2078/92 allows for a 50% refund to member states of AEP spending, rising to 75% in Objective One areas, but for the UK the Fontainebleau settlement of 1983 means that the EU

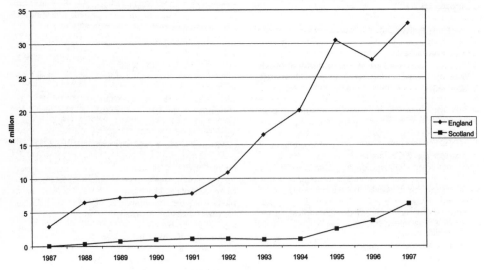

Fig. 1. Spending on ESAs.

N. Hanley et al. / Land Use Policy 16 (1999) 67–80 69

contribution is less, at around 17% of the total costs of the schemes.

3. Agri-environmental policy in the UK

In the UK, the environmental goods which have been targeted by AEP are predominantly wildlife habitat and landscape quality (of course, these are very much jointly produced). There is much less of an emphasis than, say, in the US, the Netherlands or Denmark on the control of non-point source pollution from farming. This may be due to the focus of public concerns regarding farming's impact on the countryside (for example over issues such as hedgerow loss and declines in farmland birds: see Fig. 2); and to the fact that farm-sourced non-point pollution is not viewed as a particularly serious problem in most areas of the UK. All of the habitats covered by the AEP are semi-natural, in that some degree of human intervention/management is necessary to keep them in a "most desired" condition. For example, heather moorland requires a particular grazing and heather management pattern to remain as such, and not revert to either scrub woodland or rough grazing. Again, this is rather different from the wilderness concept of nature in, say, the western US.

The schemes so far implemented in the UK include the following:

- Environmentally sensitive areas
- Countryside stewardship
- Nitrate sensitive areas and nitrate vulnerable zones
- Organic aid
- Habitats
- Countryside access
- Moorland
- Arable incentive
- Scottish countryside premium (which supersedes habitats, heather moorland and set-aside access in Scotland).

The key features of each of these schemes may be summarised as follows:

3.1. Environmentally sensitive areas scheme

Primary benefits: wildlife conservation; landscape effects.

Secondary benefits: water quality; recreation; archaeological benefits.

ESAs are designated in areas of national significance, where the conservation of wildlife and landscape depend on particular farm practices which are changing, or are likely to change, in a way which would damage this interest. There are now 43 ESAs in the UK, covering an area of 3 362 633 ha. The total area entered under contract in 1997, accounted for 1 152 554 ha (34% of the

total)[1] and 14 843 farmers. ESAs cover a wide range of habitat/landscape types, including hay meadows, wet grasslands, lowland heath, chalk downland and heather moorland. Payment rates are aimed at two objectives: preventing a loss of conservation interest (Tier one); and enhancing and expanding conservation interest (Tier two and above). The Primary benefits generated by the scheme are wildlife and landscape conservation. These accrue to visitors, residents (both are use values) and the general public (non-use values). Secondary benefits comprise the protection/enhancement of certain lower-grade archaeological sites; and possible water quality improvements (for example, in river valley grassland management, due to less fertiliser/pesticide use and the creation of buffer strips). In addition, there may be benefits in terms of enhanced recreation opportunities and rural employment.

3.2. Countryside stewardship scheme

Primary benefits: wildlife; landscape.

Secondary benefits: archaeological sites; recreation (access).

The Countryside Stewardship scheme (CS) has developed into the main agri-environmental policy instrument outside of ESAs, as it applies to the "wider countryside". Its objectives are to improve and protect wildlife habitat, landscape beauty and to improve access. A large number of eligible habitat/landscape types are specified, for example, lowland heath and limestone grasslands. Restoration of old farm buildings using "appropriate" methods and materials is also allowable. Standard per ha payment rates are offered, which may be either on-going (per annum) or once-off (capital items). MAFF took over administration of the scheme in 1996, by which time 5 312 agreements covering 96 913 ha of land and 3 640 km of hedgerow restoration had been signed. The CS thus both safeguards existing environmental quality on eligible land, and allows for expansion and enhancement of safeguarded habitats/other sites. Primary benefits are in terms of wildlife protection and landscape quality; secondary benefits are in terms of archaeological site protection, and recreation. Applications to enrol in the CS scheme are currently assessed by a points scoring system within MAFF, since the scheme is over-subscribed.

3.3. Nitrate sensitive areas scheme and nitrate vulnerable zones

Primary benefits: (human health effects); water quality improvements.

---

[1] The lower figure of 2 655 515 ha is given for the "eligible area", total sign ups are 43% of this total.

70 *N. Hanley et al. / Land Use Policy 16 (1999) 67–80*

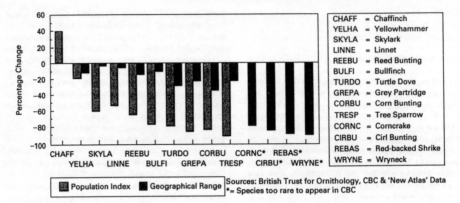

CHAFF	= Chaffinch
YELHA	= Yellowhammer
SKYLA	= Skylark
LINNE	= Linnet
REEBU	= Reed Bunting
BULFI	= Bullfinch
TURDO	= Turtle Dove
GREPA	= Grey Partridge
CORBU	= Corn Bunting
TRESP	= Tree Sparrow
CORNC	= Corncrake
CIRBU	= Cirl Bunting
REBAS	= Red-backed Shrike
WRYNE	= Wryneck

Sources: British Trust for Ornithology, CBC & 'New Atlas' Data
*= Species too rare to appear in CBC

In addition there are several species which have started to show large declines in numbers in the last decade: swallow (−43%) blackbird (−42%), mistle thrush (−39%), moorhen (−37%), sedge warbler (−35%), dunnock (−29%)

Fig. 2. Changes in UK farmland bird populations numbers, 1969–1994 range 1968–1991.

Secondary benefits: habitat protection, landscape protection.

There are 32 Nitrate Sensitive Areas (NSA)s in the UK. By 1996, 24000 ha were enrolled in the scheme, involving 410 farmers. The NSA and Nitrate Vulnerable Zones (NVZ) schemes are motivated by legal requirements under the EU directive (1991/1976) to prevent nitrate pollution in sensitive areas. The Primary benefits of the schemes are thus to reduce nitrate levels in drinking water; and potentially, to reduce eutrophication damages where nitrate is the limiting nutrient. In general, nitrate-limited eutrophication is more likely in marine waters than in freshwaters, where phosphate is typically the limiting nutrient (e.g., Loch Leven in Fife), although some examples of nitrate-related eutrophication exist in the UK (e.g., the River Ythan). The Primary benefit of the NSA scheme is thus to reduce risks to human health. Secondary benefits relate to reduced eutrophication. It may be that there are non-use benefits from less nitrates being present in water courses; this was found in a study in Sweden by Silvander and Drake (1991). Furthermore, since run-off of organic fertilisers (manure) is an important source of biological oxygen demand, water quality benefits in terms of higher-dissolved oxygen levels may be a by-product of the scheme. A further secondary benefit of the NSA scheme relates to some of the management requirements on farmers who join the scheme, which will generate landscape and conservation benefits. For example, farmers must agree to protect hedges and field trees. Some 68 NVZs have been designated in England and Wales, covering 600 000 ha, and one NVZ has been designated in Scotland. Since the mandatory measures to be adopted in NVZs are still under discussion, this paper will restrict its attention to NSAs. However, we note that NVZs constitute the only mandatory element of British AEP.

3.4. Organic aid scheme

Primary benefits: "healthier" food; wildlife habitat.
Secondary benefits: landscape; water quality.

This scheme, which is currently available to those converting from conventional to organic farming, imposes certain cultivational practice requirements on farmers who join, in return for area payments over a five year period. The Primary effects, from an environmental standpoint, would appear to be in terms of improvements in wildlife habitat due to reductions in pesticide use and inorganic fertiliser application. An example of the former is the effects of reduced pesticide use, via increased invertebrate numbers, on grey partridge. An example of the latter might be wildflower meadows, where inorganic fertiliser application and heavy grazing could result in conversion to single species grassland. Water quality (both groundwater and surface water) could benefit too, in terms of reduced chemical contamination; although if farmers increase livestock manure applications, then this could have deleterious effects on water quality. The scheme is also likely to have beneficial effects on landscape quality, through requirements for the protection of natural features such as wetlands and semi-natural woodland. Finally, people might derive utility from the knowledge that more of our food production system is proceeding on an organic basis, rather than an "industrial farming" basis. This might be additional to the price premium they are willing to pay for organic produce.

3.5. Habitat scheme

Primary benefits: wildlife habitat enhancement; landscape benefits.

Secondary benefits: improved water quality; protection of non-scheduled archaeological sites.

This scheme, launched in 1994, has as its primary aim the enhancement of wildlife habitats by taking land out of arable production. Three habitat types are targeted: saltmarsh, water fringe areas, and former set-aside land. A distinguishing feature of the Habitats Scheme is that management agreements are drawn up with farmers over a 20 yr time period, rather than the five and 10 yr agreements in ESAs. In return, farmers receive payments varying from £240 to £525/ha. By 1996, 780 farmers had entered the scheme, enrolling 9 400 ha of land. The Habitats scheme is concerned thus with expanding and enhancing the areas of habitats which it is concerned with, for example by getting farmers to block up drains/ditches to help expand salt marshes. The water fringe area element currently applies in six pilot areas, and allows, for example, for the withdrawal from production of arable land along rivers. Major benefits of the scheme are in terms of wildlife and landscape; secondary benefits are in terms of improved water quality through reduced pollution by nutrients and pesticides; and the protection of non-scheduled archaeological sites.

3.6. Countryside access scheme

Primary benefit: recreational access.
Secondary benefits: none.

This policy, introduced in 1994, had signed up 1 544 ha in 116 agreements by 1996. Payments are made to farmers who agree to make provisions for public access to set-aside land for informal recreation, in five-year agreements. The routes must provide access to, or pass by, attractive landscapes, wildlife sites or archaeological sites. The only benefit from this scheme is thus recreational benefits due to increased access.

3.7. Moorland scheme (England and Wales); Heather Moorland scheme (Scotland)

Primary benefits: wildlife enhancement/conservation; landscape improvement.

Secondary benefits: protection of minor archaeological sites.

Heather moorland is a highly valued habitat, for both wildlife and recreation. Heather moorland can be degraded in quality terms by over-grazing; whilst moorland can be converted, e.g., into upland pasture by re-seeding, fertilising and liming. The scheme works by setting maximum winter and summer grazing limits, over a five year period. "Heather moorland" is defined as moorland with a minimum of 25% heather cover (*Calluna vulgaris*; *Erica tetralix*). Grazing limits are specified in both GLUs and ewes. New drainage, and fertiliser applications, are both banned. The Primary benefit of the scheme is to improve the quality of heather moorland. This benefits wildlife such as Golden Plover, Dunlin, Merlins and Grouse; but might also be expected to enhance landscape quality. Minor clauses on archaeological site protection are also included. By 1996, 18 009 ha had been enrolled in the scheme in the UK, comprising 10 505 ha in England, 7 302 in Scotland and 202 in Wales.

3.8. The arable stewardship scheme

Primary aim: wildlife enhancement.
Secondary aim: reduced chemicals run-off.

This began operation in 1998, as a collaboration between MAFF, the RSPB, English Nature and the Game Conservancy. Farmers in two pilot areas (in Cambridgeshire and the West Midlands) are being offered payments of up to £620/ha to reduce herbicide use, leave stubbles over winter, and leave land fallow, in order to encourage farmland birds.

4. The dominant model

All the elements of AEP in the UK share a common framework, and this is the "management agreement" model (Hodge, 1994). The implicit property rights assumption behind this is that farmers/rural land managers have the right to carry out the most profit-maximising activity on their land, irrespective of the external costs (and benefits) of doing so. If farming in a more environmentally sensitive manner imposes costs on farmers, then society must compensate them for these costs. Society has thus no prior property right (either legal or presumptive) to environmental outputs, but must subsidise farmers to produce them (Bromley and Hodge, 1990). This position is re-enforced by an absence of regulations to restrict/impose environmental performance on farmers, except in a very few cases.[2]

This management agreement model has resulted in a suit of policies whereby farmers are offered payments in return for environmental outputs. These payments may be uniform across the country (as with countryside stewardship); uniform or tiered within certain areas (as with the ESA scheme), but varying across these areas; or individually negotiated (as with management agreements under the Wildlife and Countryside Act). Required environmental outputs may be either uniform or variable, and may operate throughout the country (as in the organic aid scheme) or in designated areas only (as in the nitrate

---

[2] An example of such an exception is recent "due care" requirements on the storage of farm wastes.

sensitive areas scheme). Participation in such schemes is always voluntary, and is not required to qualify for other support payments (that is, no cross-compliance requirements are in place). Finally, management agreements may either be offered to prevent a deterioration of environmental quality below the current baseline (as in Tier one payments in ESAs), or to secure an improvement in quality or quantity terms over the current baseline.

As with any policy which arranges the transfer of property rights, these activities involve transactions costs which must either be born by the state or by the individuals/agencies making the transfer. Obviously, heavy transactions costs of negotiating will, if imposed on landowners, serve as a substantial deterrent to entering schemes. This leaves policy makers with a choice, either they must compensate landowners for these costs or they must take steps to minimise them. In practice both expedients are found. In agreements made under Regulation 2078/92 the compensation paid to landowners and farmers is generally sufficient to cover their costs of making agreements, whilst under the Wildlife and Countryside Act arrangements in SSSIs and earlier arrangements, the state undertakes to re-imburse contractees for these costs. If this is not done then either the rate of response to policies will be lower than desired or the provision of public goods in the countryside will become dependent on the altruism of landowners.

5. Criteria for assessing policy

Two broad classes of criteria for assessment of policy seem appropriate for AEP, being (i) efficiency and (ii) effectiveness based. Efficiency measures include CBA and cost-effectiveness analysis (CEA). CBA has only recently come into use in the assessment of environmental policy in the UK, and we discuss this in detail in the next section. CEA (that is, the calculation of the costs of meeting a pre-defined target) seems to have been little used, although the potential usefulness of CEA in a land-use context has been shown in a recent study of native pinewoods regeneration by MacMillan et al. (1998).

Policy *effectiveness* has been judged on two grounds: participation, and ecological outcomes. Participation-based approaches have dominated appraisal of AEP in the UK. Measures include farmer sign up rates (percent of qualifying farmers entering into the scheme), and area participation (percent of elegible area entered into a scheme). Table 1 gives some details on these participation measures for selected AEPs. However, the fact that many habitats are affected by more than one scheme makes such scheme-related participation measures of limited usefulness, and re-inforces the need for habitat-based measures. These could relate the area of habitat safeguarded under all AEP schemes with the national area of that habitat. Some 28% of neutral grasslands are included within designated ESAs, for example, whilst only 1% (2973 ha) of the total area of moorland (510000) is included (Stewart et al., 1997). Moorland is also protected under Countryside Stewardship (18587 ha) and under the Moorlands Scheme (10505 ha), but this still leaves the great majority of this habitat un-protected.

However, participation approaches are rather indirect measures of the effectiveness of schemes, where the ultimate objective is improvements in environmental conditions, since they measure promised changes in management actions, rather than the consequences of actual changes in actions. It is, after all, perfectly possible to

Table 1
Examples of participation rate measures of scheme success

Scheme	Area entered	Farmers entered	Total "eligible" area (ha)	Area entered as proportion of total area (%)
ESAs: all English	446330		1149902	48
West Penwith	6312	199	6914	91
Clun	40397	950	50500	80
Pennine Dales	15728	801	24000	65
Somerset levels	14996	995	25900	58
South Downs	11264	245	51700	22
Breckland	5659	129	51600	11
Countryside stewardship	92585	5284	*	*
Habitats scheme	5100	301	*	*
Moorland scheme (E)	9026	15	510000	2
Organic aid scheme	4673	101	All farmed area	*
Nitrate sensitive areas: all	19611	*	35089	56
N Lincs	5836	45	8568	68
Aswarby	1777	29	2169	82
Hopwas	15	3	174	9
Broughton	258	8	1407	18

Key: * = missing data.

N. Hanley et al. / Land Use Policy 16 (1999) 67–80 73

explain high participation rates in terms of the generosity of payment rates alone. Moreover, given the uniform payment rates offered, those farmers with the lowest opportunity cost of entering could be expected to do so first. Yet there is no control over whether these farmers provide below-average environmental benefits (indeed, they might well be farmers who can meet the conditions of the management agreement at no extra cost, implying they receive payments for doing nothing). Ecological measures offer a more direct means of assessing policy effectiveness. Such measures are aimed at measuring the ecological performance of schemes, and comparing this with either expected change or baseline conditions. They thus relate to environmental outputs rather than management inputs. Expected changes can be predicted, for example, using vegetation succession models based on the NVC system to predict the number and type of plant communities observed. More direct measuring of changes in the ecological condition of land could also relate to changes in the pressures on environmental systems, such as where reductions in grazing levels are important, as in the case of the Heather Moorlands scheme.

Direct ecological measures of policy impact have been extensive. The largest programme of evaluation has been concerned with ESAs. In England, for example, ecological appraisals take place for each ESA every five years, as part of a formal review process. The 1996–97 round of evaluations found that:

- in the South Downs ESA, landscape quality has been enhanced due to reversion from arable land to grassland;
- declines in meadow diversity have been halted, and in some cases reversed, in the Pennine Dales;
- Bird numbers have increased in the Somerset Levels and Moors ESA, compared with a situation of rapid decline prior to the policy being introduced;
- however, land outwith the ESA boundary and on non-agreement land has experienced intensification in the Somerset levels and Pennine Dales.[3]

The process of identifying ecological improvements in this way is complicated by boundary revisions to ESAs: for example, the Pennine Dales ESA trebled in size after re-designation. Consistent, long-term ecological times series data may thus be unavailable, whilst improvements in some cases have been patchy. It is also the case that in some ESAs, the direction of change in landscape features has been the same for both participating and non-participating farms, implying that environmental change has

not been caused by the ESA. In addition, it is possible to find reports of desirable environmental features declining in both participating and non-participating farms. Examples of both these phenomena are reported for the Somerset Levels and Moors ESA (MAFF, 1991; ADAS, 1996).

Monitoring of NSAs has concentrated on measuring nitrate levels in drain waters of fields entered into the scheme, and comparing these with pre-scheme levels. Groundwater surveys have also been undertaken, although the long length of percolation times means effects are delayed here. In surveys over three winters following the introduction of the NSA scheme, ADAS found that NO_3 concentrations had been significantly reduced by the planting of cover crops and by conversion from arable to grassland. Reductions in leaching under cereals were much lower. In the 10 NSAs monitored, four areas now complied with the EU 50 mg/l limit, and two more were within 10% of compliance. Computer modelling of predicted changes in N in soil water is also undertaken, using survey results from participating and non-participating farms.

A monitoring exercise of the Countryside Stewardship scheme surveyed 120 farms prior to entry in 1991–92, and then re-surveyed them two years later. Ninetyone percent of these farms showed environmental improvements on at least one criterion over this period, with many improving on more than one criterion (for example, wildlife and access). Of the other 11 sites, three showed no change and eight showed damages. A biological monitoring strategy is in place for all three habitats covered by the Habitats scheme, comprising a baseline survey in 1995 (before any farms entered the scheme) and further surveys in 1997–98 and 1998–99. Similar monitoring work has been commissioned for the (Heather) Moorland scheme.

However, it is worthwhile noting that monitoring costs may well be higher for ecological measures in general, compared with participation measures. The *overall* monitoring costs of the ESA programme in 1992/93 were estimated at £3.6 m, or 16% of total scheme costs; this figure had fallen to 5% of total scheme costs of £39 m in 1996/97 (Whitby et al., 1998). For all AEP schemes under Regulation 2078/92, monitoring costs fell from 12.5% of the total costs in 1992–93 to 7.5% in 1995–96. Whitby et al. (1998) speculate that this fall (which was accompanied by a similar fall in running costs, but an increase in payments to farmers) is due to relatively high transactions costs in the early years of a new policy initiative, which reduce as agents get more familiar with the policy and as institutions (such as standard contracts and self-reporting) are established which reduce these transactions costs. It should also be noted that not all environmental effects attributed to individual schemes may be additional, in the sense that they would not have resulted in the absence of the policy initiative. Ensuring that environmental outputs pass this additionality test is

---

[3] In a sense, this is to be expected. Given that the costs of signing up to the ESA vary across farms, and that the payment rate is uniform, one would expect those farms not signing up to be more profitable enterprises.

74   N. Hanley et al. / Land Use Policy 16 (1999) 67-80

clearly important, since otherwise farmers are being paid for a zero environmental gain, but this does involve identifying what would have happened in the absence of the policy being appraised. This alternative state-of-the-world may be quite different to the current situation, due to the dynamic nature of the system. Ecological measures may also fail as an indicator of long-term change, since the time period over which such data is available is very limited. Participation rates might fare better in this regard.

A further problem with cost-effectiveness measures is that there may very easily be long delays in the appearance of intended beneficial policy outcomes. Many ecological processes may require decades to reach a desired state and it is possible that policy contracts will never produce the desired result in some cases. Yet the contracts used in AEP are typically for 10 years (in rare cases for 20 years) and there is virtually no constraint on the farmers' behaviour after the end of the contract. Once the contract has ended the farmer may freely revert to any set of agricultural practices he chooses even if they destroy all the accumulated benefit of several years of conformity with a contract to produce environmental goods. Most of these contracts will ensure the accumulation of natural capital at the taxpayers' expense. It is arguable thus that society may claim some rights over the disposal at the end of contracts, though this is not easy to provide without discouraging farmers from taking up contracts (Whitby et al., 1996).

It is also interesting to note that an opportunity lost in the individual farmer contract based approach is that of influencing strategic land management over substantial areas. By emphasising individual contracts we lose the possibility of managing whole blocks of land in an ecologically homogenious way – for example, to produce wildlife corridors or improve catchment performance. This idea, which comes from MacFarlane and Smith (1997), has been proposed for the Lake District ESA, an ESA which virtually coincides with the National Park designation, where a landscape-scale approach has obvious advantages. Finally, we note that neither of the effectiveness measures address the issue of whether, from a society's point of view, the costs of AEP are justified by the benefits.

6. Efficiency as a criterion: cost-benefit analysis of agri-environmental schemes

In the UK, the use of CBA in the appraisal of policies which impact on the environment has become more widespread within government departments and agencies. A particular spur for this trend was the publication in 1991 of the Department of the Environment's *Policy Appraisal and the Environment* (DoE, 1991). MAFF, WOAD, DANI and SOAEFD, as the government

departments principally responsible for AEP, have made increasing use of the CBA approach, especially in terms of commissioning studies to estimate the monetary value of the environmental benefits, with particular focus on ESAs. These studies have all been carried out ex post, and it would be difficult to make a stronger case than that they have been used to justify government action already undertaken for reasons other than producing a Potential Pareto Improvement. Nevertheless, results have been interesting.

6.1. Types of benefit, and applicable benefit measurement methods

In summary, the AEP schemes discussed above are designed to deliver the following types of benefits:

- Protection and/or enhancement or wildlife habitats. This will generate both use and non-use values in terms of direct utility effects; but will also generate biodiversity protection benefits which are additional to these (for example, in terms of ecosystem resilience).
- Protection/enhancement of landscape quality; this again may be expected to generate use and non-use benefits in terms of direct utility impacts, although it could be assumed that non-use values will take up a smaller percentage of total economic value than use values in the case of landscape, than in the case of wildlife.
- Protection/enhancement of water quality; due to lower pesticide use/run-off, and lower or better managed fertiliser and manure use, possibly generating both use and non-use values.
- Protection/enhancement of minor (unscheduled) archaeological and historical sites, possibly generating both use and non-use values.
- Enhanced access possibilities. This is clearly a use, rather than non-use, value, although a positive option value may also exist for preserving the option of future access.

If estimates of the monetary value of these benefits are desired, then valuation techniques would seem to be applicable in the following manner (Table 2):

6.2. Evidence from empirical studies

Stewart et al. (1997) have summarised results from existing studies of environmental benefits for AEP. As mentioned above, ESA valuation has dominated, with very little work being done on other schemes. The Contingent Valuation Method (CVM) has been used in all the studies reported except one (Foster and Mourato, 1997). CVM is a survey-based method which directly elicits preferences for environmental goods from individuals (see Hanley and Spash, 1994 for a description of the method). Comparison of results across the studies is

N. Hanley et al. / Land Use Policy 16 (1999) 67–80 75

Table 2
Benefit categories and valuation methods

	Contingent valuation method	Choice experiments	Recreational demand models	Hedonic pricing	Dose-response	Avoided costs
Wildlife effects	**	**	*			
Landscape effects	**	**	*	*		
Water quality	**	**	**		*	*
Archaeological sites	**	*	*			
Enhanced access	**	*	**			

Key: ** = Highly relevant; * = somewhat relevant; blank = not relevant.

complicated by a diversity of survey designs (for example, between open-ended and dichotomous choice designs) and beneficiary categories (between, for example, residents, visitors and the general public). Table 3 summarises these results, whilst Table 4 shows more detail for a number of ESA studies.

As may be seen, per person values vary widely, but this is to be expected given the diverse nature of the schemes appraised. Where non-use values are included, aggregate benefit figures rapidly become very large. Aggregation is particularly difficult in the cases of the NSA and Organic Aid schemes, where benefit estimates come from studies not originally targetted at the AEP schemes themselves.[4] Table 3 also reports the exchequer costs of each scheme for each scheme appraised, and as may be seen aggregate benefits outweigh these costs by a very large margin. Given that social costs are likely to be less than exchequer costs due to the presence of price support (see below), this conclusion would become even stronger.

Several problems may be noted in connection with the valuation results reported in Table 3:

1. The very large magnitude of non-use values[5] limits CBA's ability to discriminate between projects (since admitting non-use values mean schemes are almost bound to pass the CBA test);
2. No value estimates exist for a majority of schemes, including the second largest scheme, Countryside Stewardship. There are currently no estimates of Willingness To Pay (WTP) for heather moorland *per se* to be used to appraise the Moorlands Scheme,[6] nor of the specialised habitats covered by the Habitats Scheme.

3. Benefit figures are expressed as per household or per individual, whereas per hectare amounts might be more useful in many cases (for example, if consideration was being given to extending an ESA). Here the well known problem of average values being used to represent marginal values applies. Very few estimates of the marginal value of changes in AEP exist, two exceptions being the study by Moss and Chilton of the Mourne Mountains/Slieve Croobe ESA in Northern Ireland; and in the case of the Farm Woodlands Scheme (Hutchison et al., 1996). Both these studies found evidence of marginal benefits diminishing in value as the area protected increased.

4. The production of environmental benefits following contractual agreement between the farmer and the government regarding promised changes in management actions is typically subject to both uncertainty and time lags. For example, the effect of reducing stocking levels on heather moorland recovery may be both uncertain, and may take many years to occur to a significant level. As Hodge and McNally (1998) note, there is a problem for the researcher in knowing (i) whether land managers *can* meet the terms of ESA-type contracts; (ii) whether they *will* meet these terms after the contract is signed, given asymmetric information; and (iii) whether these management changes will produce the desired outcomes. It is often not clear how CVM researchers put across these uncertainties and time lags to respondents, if at all. In the work by Hanley et al. (1998b) on Breadalbane ESA, respondents were shown photo montages of how the area would look "at maturity" of the scheme, but no explicit mention was made in the survey materials about how long this would take, nor about how likely the changes shown were to occur.[7] This was also the case in the Garrod and Willis (1994) study of the Somerset Levels, where respondents were shown pictures of the landscape "with" and "without" the ESA, but were not told about the likelihood of the "with" scenario actually coming about, nor about how long it would take. If

---

[4] Although in the latter case, the study is concerned with the impact of pesticide reductions on wild birds: a recent MAFF review of the Organic Aid scheme concluded that "...the most important benefit (because it was not delivered by other farming systems) was the virtual absence of pesticides and the impact of that on biodiversity".

[5] Non-use values are values to people who do not directly use the resource, for example by visiting it. Non-use values have proved to be a significant part of total value for many environmental resources, but are relatively problematic to estimate and interpret.

[6] Although an indication of WTP for an increase in heather moorland protection, based on a small sample of Wildlife Trust members in Northumberland is given in Garrod and Willis (1994).

[7] For an example of a CVM study which explicitly incorporates uncertainty over environmental outcomes, see MacMillan et al., 1995.

Table 3
Cost–benefit analysis of agri-environmental schemes

Agri-environmental scheme	Benefit estimate per person	Aggregate benefits	Scheme exchequer costs	Net value	Valuation method
Mourne Mountains and Slieve Croob ESA Moss and Chilton (1997)	Not known	13 090 000	2 042 823	11 047 177	CVM
South Downs ESA Willis and Garrod (1993)	1.98–27.52	263 177–79 835 000	970 000	(−)707 000–78 865 000	CVM
Somerset levels and Moors ESA Willis and Garrod (1993)	2.45–17.53	101 422–52 637 000	1 859 000	(−)1 757 000–50 778 000	CVM
Stewartry ESA Gourlay (1995)	3.00–22.56	371 840–1 825 268	430 000	(−)58 160–1 395 268	CVM
Loch Lomond ESA Gourlay (1995)	2.28–32.8	229 600–3 211 311	70 000	159 600–3 141 311	CVM
Breadalbane ESA Hanley et al. (1996)	22.02–98	92 938–44 100 000	396 796	(−)206 796–43 703 204	CVM
Breadalbane ESA Hanley et al. (1996)	107.55	636 050[a]–4 841 363[b]	396 796	239 251–4 444 567	CE
Machair ESA Hanley et al. (1996)	13.4–378	75 539–26 800 000	101 981	(−)26,442–13 298 019	CVM
Machair ESA Hanley et al. (1996)	23.15	256 039[a]–563 864[b]	101 981	154 058–461 883	CE
Norfolk Broads ESA Bateman et al. (1994)	142–150	Not known	1 821 300	Not known	CVM
NSA Hanley (1990)	16.17	13 506 311[c]	1 500 000	12 006 311	CVM
Organic aid Foster and Mourato (1997)	17.59	17 060 000[d]	419 000	16 640 000	CR

CVM = contingent valuation; CE = choice experiment; CR = contingent ranking.
[a] Residents only.
[b] Residents plus visitors.
[c] East Anglia only.
[d] Based on saving one bird species only; aggregated over RSPB members.
All values are in £ sterling.

benefits are actually uncertain, then households would be willing to pay less than if the outcome was certain: in this case, existing WTP estimates for ESAs are biased upwards.

As Hodge and McNally (1998) have pointed out, there is indeed a general problem with applying CBA to such policies, namely that of correctly identifying the counterfactual: what the landscape and wildlife interest of an area would be without the policy in place. In the Garrod and Willis (1994) study, the assumption was that without the ESA in place, agricultural intensification would continue, leading to a consistent decline in environmental quality. This is hard to predict, especially given current and likely future reforms in farm policy. However, CBA is not the only policy analysis tool to face this counterfactual problem.

5. As some areas of the country (and some habitats) are affected by more than one policy instrument, it can be difficult to disentangle the effects of, say, the ESA scheme

itself distinct from management agreements on SSSIs. Colman et al. (1993) note that in Breckland ESA, conservation benefits may be due more to SSSI designation than to ESA designation. Hodge and McNally make a similar point for the Somerset Levels. The risk is thus that the CBA analyst ends up valuing a landscape/habitat, rather than a policy instrument, since the links between the policy instrument and the public good are complex (Bonnieux and Weaver, 1996).

6. Value estimates also appear to be scheme-specific: this is of interest with respect to benefits transfer. Whilst mixed academic support exists for the practice of benefits transfer[8] (see Bergland, 1995; or Downing and Ozuna, 1996), policy makers in practice must make use of

---

[8] Benefits transfer refers to the practice of using estimates of environmental values gained in one context to predict environmental values in a similar, but different, context.

Table 4
Comparing contingent valuation method estimates for ESAs in the UK (WTP, £/hsld/y)

ESA	Residents	Visitors	General public
Hanley et al. (1998)			
Breadalbane	31.43[a]	73.00[b]	22.02[a]
Machair	13.66[a]	–	13.37[a]
Willis et al. (1993)			
South Downs	27.52[a]	19.47[a]	1.98[a]; 7.47[b]
Somerset levels	17.53[a]	11.84[a]	2.45[a]
Gourlay (1996)			
Loch Lomond	20.60[a]	1.98 per visit[a]	n/e
Stewartry	13.00[a]	2.53 per visit[a]	n/e
Bullock and Kay (1996)			
Southern Uplands	n/e	69.00[b]	83.00[b]

[a] Open-ended CVM.
[b] Dichotomous choice CVM.

benefits transfer in some form to allow environmental valuation to become part of routine policy appraisal (ENDs, 1998). The UK government had appeared to sanction a benefits transfer practice (based on adjusted mean values) for appraising the benefits of water quality improvements (FWR, 1996). However, recent legal rulings have cast a doubt over the appropriate future direction of benefits transfer policy (ENDS, 1998).[9] It may be that valuation methods which more directly address the value of individual landscape/habitat attributes, such as choice experiments or multi-attribute utility models, would perform better with regard to benefits transfer.

7. Finally, each of the value estimates reported in Table 3 were collected for each scheme in isolation. From what we know of nesting effects and part-whole bias in CVM, and more general path dependency problems in CBA, it would not be proper to add individual scheme aggregate values to produce a total "all ESAs" or still less an "all programme" estimate of benefits, since WTP for all ESAs together will be less than the sum of WTPs estimated for individual ESAs.

Estimates of scheme costs are in principle more straightforward, as budgetary records are kept of payments to farmers, as well as some of the transactions costs of the scheme. In the former regard, Whitby et al. (1998) make the point that payments to farmers mis-state the opportunity costs of the schemes to society, since these costs are more correctly valued as the net value of output foregone, priced at shadow prices which exclude compensation (subsidy) amounts. These are net values since

resources (eg fertiliser) are saved by not producing output, or by producing at a lower intensity, and since farmers may well switch to alternative crops. In terms of correcting for subsidy payments, Saunders (1996) shows that the social opportunity costs of lost wheat, barley, and sheepmeat outputs are 91%, 48% and 30% of their exchequer costs, whilst the social opportunity costs of suckler cow outputs is actually negative. Applying such figures to the whole ESA scheme in England, Whitby et al., find that the social opportunity costs of the scheme in 1994/95 (in terms of the net value of lost output) were also negative. With respect to transactions costs, Whitby et al., note that data are only available on the public sector costs of transacting AEP bargains, but that farmers will also face costs (for example, of drawing up farm plans, and negotiating entry to a scheme). From a CBA viewpoint, the value of resources used up in transacting and enforcing bargains are a relevant component of costs; Whitby et al.'s estimate of these transactions costs for UK ESAs is £8 m in 1994/95, and this is the only positive resource cost of the policy. However, if, as planned, farm prices are moved to a lower level and surpluses eliminated, the situation will become significantly different and positive resource costs of agricultural output might begin to feature in the argument.

6.3. Combining measures

However, it is perfectly feasible to combine CBA and environmental effectiveness measures to assess policy. Environmental effectiveness could be regarded as a type of sustainability measure, since it related to physical measures of elements of the natural capital stock, Kn. CBA is an efficiency measure, and is neither a necessary nor sufficient condition for sustainability. But it does offer an (albeit imperfect) means of incorporating citizen preferences into decision making, in a way which is generalisable (especially if the benefits transfer/adding up problems referred to above can be resolved). Citizen preferences should almost certainly contribute to decision making in many cases (Randall, 1997). In the final section of this paper, we indicate how this combined approach could be applied to three possible reforms of AEP.

7. Assessing possible changes to AEP

In this section, we look at possible reforms to AEP (or the conditions under which it is applied), and speculate how each one would perform on both efficiency (CBA) and effectiveness criteria. We discuss CBA outcomes in terms of the likely impact on benefit/cost ratios; and refer to an ecologically based measure of effectiveness, which picks up changes in the composition of the natural capital stock, Kn.

---

[9] Although in fact the objection made relates more to the size of benefitting population for non-use values than the process of mean values adjustment.

78   *N. Hanley et al. / Land Use Policy 16 (1999) 67–80*

7.1. Reducing conflicts with production and income support measures

One of the main features behind the low take-up rate in some AEP schemes is conflicts between the payments offered, and financial rewards under other aspects of the CAP. Many examples exist. Headage payments to sheep grazing, under the HLCA scheme, provide a direct counter-incentive to farmers in Moorland Scheme areas to reduce stocking rates, since each ewe taken off the hill means a loss in headage payments. Farmers might also loose quota entitlements for HLCAs by reducing stocking rates. For the habitats scheme, Wildlife Trust figures show that a farmer entering land into the saltmarsh part of the scheme would suffer a £500/ha loss due to the arable areas payments scheme, whilst on water fringes the net loss would be around £175/ha. In the Countryside Premium scheme, WWF in evidence to the Select Committee of Parliament showed that a farmer in a species rich neutral grassland area in a river valley would receive 10 times as much per ha. for converting to potatoes compared with entering the scheme (Stewart et al., 1997). AEP payment rates are thus too low relative to production-related subsidies, the effect of which is to (i) depress sign-up rates and (ii) increase the apparent costs of conservation.[10]

A reduction in, for example, headage payments for ewes in upland areas would be potentially beneficial on both the criteria referred to above. If headage payments are cut, then, *ceteris paribus*, the minimum necessary payment for the Moorland scheme, to achieve a given reduction in stocking rate, could fall too (for empirical evidence, see Hanley et al., 1998a). If there is no change in stocking rate, environmental benefits are constant whilst scheme costs fall, implying an increase in the B/C ratio. Balanced against this would be the net value, priced at shadow prices, of lost output, but as hinted at above, this amount could well be negative. Alternatively, payment rates could be maintained, which given the fall in opportunity costs would mean more farmers entering the scheme. Benefits should increase (although CVM might not be able to register this), increasing the B/C ratio again. The ecological measure of effectiveness, if it is truly a measure of environmental outputs, traces impacts on the natural capital stock, Kn. In the first case, this would stay constant and in the second case increase. On both criteria, then, such a reduction in headage payments might be approved.

7.2. Redesigning the transfer mechanism

At present, farmers are offered fixed payment rates in return for a given environmental output. As many

authors have noted, this over-compensates all farmers except for the marginal one, assuming that the private costs of producing the environmental output vary across farms. A recent study by the National Audit Office (1997) concluded that there was a substantial element of over-compensation in ESA payments, although some farmers were under-compensated. An alternative design, which has been used in the US for soil conservation since 1986, and which has been recently put forward in the context of AEP by Latacz-Lohmann and Van der Hamsvoort (1997), is to auction conservation contracts. The government specifies a list of environmental outputs which it wishes to achieve. Farmers then bid for these contacts, with the lowest prices being accepted up to either the aggregate environmental target or the budget allocation. Under a fixed-price arrangement, infra-marginal suppliers of the environmental good earn producers surplus, or informational rents, due to the inability/unwillingness of the government to operate a perfectly differentiated payments system. Under the auction, farmers tender sealed bids stating their required minimum payments. Assume for the moment that all environmental outputs covered by the auction are homogeneous. Then, as Latacz-Lohman (1998) shows, bidding reveals the farmers' type (that is, their opportunity costs of participation), and reduces information rents. This means the cost to the government of securing a given level of environmental outputs also falls; or that, for a given budget, a greater level of environmental outputs can be bought. If environmental outputs are heterogeneous, then bids could be weighted by expected environmental benefits, but here the government would need far greater information to conclude the auction, increasing *ex ante* transactions costs.

In terms of our two criteria then the effects depend on the budget allocation. For a fixed budget, more environmental outputs are produced at a constant exchequer cost. The value of increased environmental quality would then be compared with the net social value of any reductions in output and any net changes in transactions costs. Informational rent reductions constitute a transfer from the producer to the tax payer. On ecological effectiveness grounds, the auction under a fixed budget delivers an increase in Kn. If the level of environmental output is held constant, and the budget is reduced, then the effect of Kn depends on whether the environmental output is homogeneous.

However, we should note here that problems of collusion in repeated auctions may reduce their cost-effectiveness; this seems to have been the experience in the US (Latacz-Lohmann, 1998). Moreover, there are no data on the transactions costs of auction systems.

7.3. Focusing on environmental features

Currently, many elements of AEP in the UK are focused on defined areas of the countryside, rather than

---

[10] This "inflation" of policy costs also affects forestry policy, in that planting grants have had to be raised in line with HLCA payments (Whitby and Lowe, 1994).

N. Hanley et al. / Land Use Policy 16 (1999) 67–80 79

defined habitats, or wildlife populations. For example, the ESA scheme (the largest element within AEP) offers payments within a defined geographic area, within which they will be a diversity of farm types and a diversity of habitats, of variable conservation interest and variable quality. A national scheme (which would probably be an extension of the countryside stewardship scheme) which offered payments for target improvements in a range of specified habitats would be a more direct way of achieving environmental goals, and would permit the merging of several current schemes. It would also reduce environmental wastage in current schemes where payments may be made for increases/non-decreases in ecologically less interesting habitats (such as *Molinia-Nardus* rough grasslands). This would have the merit of assisting the UK in fulfilling its obligations under the Habitats Directive. Recent changes to the countryside stewardship scheme have followed in this direction, as additional habitats have been brought within its aegis. However, it would mean an end to the ESA scheme amongst others. Monitoring/reporting would then be carried out on a habitats/species basis, rather than an area uptake basis; results from monitoring could be integrated into the countryside information system database, supplemented by NVC classifications as a measure of diversity/quality (Stewart et al., 1997).

In terms of our criteria, such a reform would produce uncertain effects on the value of environmental benefits, but the best guess would be that benefits would rise, since the scheme would be better targeted at what is valuable (habitats and species) rather than geographic areas. The implications for monitoring and other transactions costs are unknown, but could perhaps be inferred by comparing current data on transactions costs for countryside stewardship with that for ESAs.[11] It is possible that, should a uniform payment rate system be retained, then payment rates would have to rise, if for example including farms from outside ESAs increased the average opportunity cost of participation. Changes to the effectiveness measure (K_n) would seem likely to be positive, since low-quality habitat (e.g., rough grassland within an ESA boundary) would be replaced by high-quality habitat (e.g., Heather Moorland just outside a boundary). Moving to a national scheme from the locally based ESA scheme could increase information asymmetries, and also increase the spread of compliance costs. This might encourage a move away from standard rate payments and towards auctions or variable payment schemes.

8. Conclusions

Both economics and ecology have contributions to make to the assessment of AEP. Economics can address the efficiency of policy, in terms of evaluating its net social benefits through CBA; whilst ecologists can study the effectiveness of schemes in terms of environmental outputs. This can be related to measures of the natural capital stock, and thus to the concept of sustainability (defined here as a non-declining natural capital stock over time). However, there is no need to see the criteria as being mutually exclusive, but rather they are best viewed as complementary in policy assessment. This is important if both criteria are of relevance to policy makers (and indeed, to society at large).

Nevertheless, many significant problems exist with both approaches. For CBA, the issues of aggregation of non-use values, part–whole bias, benefits transfer and calibration complicate issues. The observation can also be made that if including non-use values for UK AEP benefits leads to benefits that always massively exceed costs, then this decreases both the credibility and the attractiveness of the CBA approach to decision-makers, who may perhaps prefer to use it more as a tool for ranking options (that is, only relative benefits are considered reliable). It may also be that CBA has a more useful decision-making role in terms of its ability to marshal arguments for and against a change; and if monetisation of benefits and costs is avoided. Measurement of the social opportunity costs of AEP is also in its infancy, and much work remains to be done if measures of the full social costs of AEP, including transactions costs, are to be provided. Identifying the counter-factual in CBA analyses is also difficult, whilst uncertainty and time lags in the production of benefits need to be better handled. CBA is also of limited use in advising on the best design of AEP, and, as currently conducted, does not on the whole address itself to marginal changes in designation (for example, in increasing the size or changing the required management practices of an ESA). Ecological measures of effectiveness suffer from aggregation problems, from uncertainty over outcomes, potentially high monitoring costs, and the difficulty of quality weighting.

Proposals under *Agenda 2000* seem likely to produce a further re-direction of agricultural budget spending away from production and towards environmental payments and direct income support. The former will imply that AEP expands in scope and coverage in the UK and throughout the EU. We have already shown how a combined method, which uses criteria based on both economic efficiency and strong sustainability, can be used to assess proposed changes in land use policy. However, we have also alluded to remaining problems in implementing this combined approach. Addressing these problems will thus become an increasingly-important task for research.

---

[11] In 1995/1996, £2 m was spent on running costs under countryside stewardship, to maintain a total of 5 284 agreements, implying a per-agreement cost of £378. The equivalent figures for the ESA programme were £7.463 m on 7463 agreements, implying a per-agreement cost of £945 (Agriculture Committee, 1997).

80   *N. Hanley et al. / Land Use Policy 16 (1999) 67–80*

Acknowledgements

We thank Lisa Stewart for research assistance; and HM Treasury and MAFF for funding work on which some of this is based. We have received valuable comments from Dr. Ian Hodge (University of Cambridge), from Dr. Katherine Falconer (University of Newcastle-on-Tyne) and from participants at the World Congress of Environmental and Resource Economists, Venice, June 1998. Responsibility for the opinions reported in this paper lies, however, with the present authors alone.

References

ADAS, 1996. Environmental monitoring in the Somerset levels and Moors ESA, 1987–1995. Report to MAFF, London.

Agriculture Committee, 1997. 2nd Report: ESAs and other schemes under the agri-environment regulation. HMSO, London.

Bateman, I., Willis, K., Garrod, G., 1994. Consistency between contingent valuation estimates: a comparison of two studies of UK national parks. Regional Studies 28(5), 457–474.

Bergland, O., Magnussen, K., Navrud, S., 1995. Benefits transfer: testing for accuracy and reliability. Discussion paper 95-03, Dept of Economics, Agricultural University of Norway.

Billing, P., 1998. Towards sustainable agriculture: the perspectives of the common agricultural policy in the EU. In: Dabbert et al. (Eds.), The Economics of Landscape and Wildlife Conservation. CAB International, Oxon.

Bonnieux, F., Weaver, R., 1996. Environmentally sensitive areas schemes: public economics and evidence. In: Whitby, M. (Ed.), The European Environment and CAP Reform. CAB International, Oxon.

Bromley, D., Hodge, I., 1990. Private property rights and presumptive policy entitlements. European Review of Agricultural Economics 17(2), 197–214.

Colman, D., Froud, J., O'Carroll, L., 1993. The tiering of conservation policies. Land Use Policy 10(4), 281–292.

Dabbert, S., Whitby, M., Dubgaard, A., 1998. The Economics of Landscape and Wildlife Conservation. CAB International, Oxon.

Department of the Environment, 1991. Policy Appraisal and the Environment. HMSO, London.

Downing, M., Ozuna, T., 1996. Testing the reliability of the benefit function transfer approach. Journal of Environmental Economics and Management 30, 316–322.

ENDS, 1998. Environmental Data Services Newsletter. March.

Foster, V., Mourato, S., 1997. Behavioural consistency, statistical specification and validity in the contingent ranking method: evidence from a survey of the impacts of pesticide use in the UK. CSERGE Working Paper 97-09, University of London.

Garrod, G., and Willis, K., 1994. Valuing biodiversity and nature conservation at the local level. Biodiversity and Conservation 3, 555–565.

Garrod, G., Willis, K., Saunders, C., 1994. The benefits and costs of the Somerset levels and moors ESA. Journal of Rural Studies 10(2), 131–145.

Gourlay, D., 1995. Loch Lomond and Stewartry ESAs: a study of public perceptions of policy benefits. Unpublished Ph.D. Thesis, University of Aberdeen.

Hanley, N.D., 1990. The economics of nitrate pollution. European Review of Agricultural Economics (17), 129–151.

Hanley, N., Spash, C., 1994. Cost–Benefit Analysis and the Environment. Edward Elgar, Cheltenham.

Hanley, N., Kirkpatrick, H., Oglethorpe, D., Simpson, I., 1998a. Principles for the provision of public goods from agriculture. Land Economics 74(1), 102–113.

Hanley, N., MacMillan, D., Wright, R.E., Bullock, C., Simpson, I., Parsisson, D., Crabtree, B., 1998b. Contingent valuation versus choice experiments: estimating the benefits of environmentally sensitive areas in Scotland. Journal of Agricultural Economics, 1–15, January.

Hodge, I., 1994. Rural amenity: property rights and policy mechanisms. The Contribution of Amenities to Rural Development. OECD, Paris.

Hodge, I., McNally, S., 1998. Evaluating the environmentally sensitive areas: the value of rural environments and policy relevance. Journal of Rural Studies 14(3), 1998.

Latacz-Lohmann, U., Van der Hamsvoort, 1997. Auctioning conservation contracts: a theoretical analysis and an application. Journal of Agricultural Economics 40(3), 334–345.

Lacatz-Lohmann, U., 1998. Mechanisms for the provision of public goods in the countryside. In: Dabbert et al. (Eds.), The Economics of Landscape and Wildlife Conservation. CAB International, Oxon.

MacFarlane, R., Smith, S., 1997. Implementing agri-environmental policy: a landscape ecology perspective. In: Cooper, A., Power, J. (Eds.), Species Dispersal and Land-use Processes. IALE (UK), Univerisity of Ulster, Coleraine.

MacMillan, D., Hanley, N., Buckland, S., 1996. A contingent valuation study of uncertain environmental gains. Scottish Journal of Political Economy 43(5), 519–533.

MacMillan, D., Harley, D., Morrison, R., 1998. Cost-effectiveness analysis of woodland ecosystem restoration. In: O'Connor, M., Spash, C. (Eds.), Valuation and the Environment. Edward Elgar, Cheltenham, forthcoming.

MAFF, 1991. The Somerset levels and Moors ESA. Draft Report on monitoring. Ministry of Agriculture, Fisheries and Food, London.

Moss, J., Chilton, S., 1997. A Socio-Economic Evaluation of the Mourne Mountains and Slieve Croob ESAs. Queens University, Belfast, Centre for Rural Studies.

National Audit Office, 1997. Protecting Environmentally Sensitive Areas. Stationary Office, London.

OECD, 1995. Amenities for Rural Development: Policy Examples. OECD, Paris.

Randall, A., 1997. Taking benefits and costs seriously. Paper to Landscape Valuation workshop, Agricultural University of Norway, Aas.

Saunders, C., 1996. Financial, exchequer and social costs of changes in agricultural output. Working Paper, Centre for Rural Economy, Univerisity of Newcastle-on-Tyne.

Stewart, L., Hanley, N., Simpson, I., 1997. Economic valuation of the agri-environment schemes in the United Kingdom. Report to MAFF and HM Treasury.

Whitby, M., Saunders, C., Ray, C., 1998. The full cost of stewardship policies. In: Dabbert et al. (Eds.), The Economics of Landscape and Wildlife Conservation. CAB International, Oxon.

Whitby, M.C., Hodge, I.D., Lowe, P.D., Saunders, C.M., 1996. Conservation options for CAP reform. ECOS 17(3/4), 46–54.

Willis, K., Garrod, G., Saunders, C., 1993. Valuation of the South Downs and Somerset Levels ESAs. Centre for Rural Economy, University of Newcastle-on-Tyne.

B
Protected Areas

[21]

Land Use Policy, Vol. 12, No. 4, pp. 291–305, 1995
Elsevier Science Ltd
Printed in Great Britain
0264-8377/95 $10.00 + 0.00

0264-8377(95)00030-5

Protected for ever?

Factors shaping the future of protected areas policy

Kevin Bishop, Adrian Phillips and Lynda Warren

Protected areas – such as national parks and nature reserves – are a well-established tool of conservation policy. At least 24 separate types of protected areas exist in the UK, and more may be added. While protected areas must remain a central feature of international, national and local conservation effort, there are pressures for change and for reviewing the system of protected areas which we have inherited from the past. Any review should take into account some new thinking about the nature of protected area systems. There are five aspects in particular: new proposals for categorizing protected areas by the objectives of their management; the development of the concept of 'networks' of protected areas; the elaboration of a geographical hierarchy of protected areas; the converging policy objectives of different kinds of protected areas; and the broad objective of integrated management of human activities along substantial lines.

Kevin Bishop and Adrian Phillips are with the Environmental and Rural Planning Unit, Department of City and Regional Planning, University of Wales, Cardiff, PO Box 906, Cardiff, CF1 3YN, Wales. Lynda Warren is with the Cardiff Law School, University of Wales, Cardiff, PO Box 427, Cardiff, CF1 1XD, Wales.

[1]See IUCN *Guidelines for Protected Area Management Categories* World Conservation Union, Cambridge, UK (1994)
[2]See McCormack, J *The Global Environment Movement* Belhaven Press, London (1989)

continued on page 292

The International Union for the Conservation of Nature (IUCN) has defined a protected area thus: 'an area of land and/or sea especially dedicated to the protection and maintenance of biological diversity, and of natural and associated cultural resources, and managed through legal or other effective means'.[1] This definition is used in this paper. It embraces nature conservation and the protection of scenic values, as well as heritage values where these are associated with the conservation of biodiversity. Therefore the 'universe' of protected areas covered includes the full range of geographically focused nature and landscape conservation measures used in the UK. Although protected areas designated exclusively for heritage protection (eg Areas of Archaeological Importance) are excluded, the cultural, architectural, archaeological and historical values associated with places like national parks are within the scope of the paper. Indeed, certain principles and issues are common to all protected areas, whether they are established to conserve science, wildlife or heritage values.

Almost all organized human societies identify certain areas under their control for protection, by imposing limitations on access to or the use made of such areas, whether for the public good or for the benefit of an elite. Forest reserves were set up in India 24 centuries ago; medieval rulers declared hunting reserves in many parts of Europe; in Pacific islands *tapu* (taboo) systems, which pre-date the European arrival, give protection to certain areas to this day. However, it is generally accepted that the first modern protected area is the Yellowstone National Park, Wyoming, established by the US Congress in 1872.[2]

In the ensuing 120 years protected areas have been established in nearly every country, and are now being set up on the high seas as well under international agreements.[3] In 1993 there were over 9800 protected areas recognized by the IUCN for inclusion in the so-called 'United Nations List'. This list includes only those areas greater than 1000 ha in extent (or 100 ha in the case of whole islands designated for protection), which also accord with specified management objectives and which are administered by a recognized management agency.[4]

Protected for ever?: K Bishop, A Phillips and L Warren

Table 1. Protected areas in the UK.

Protected areas designated under international treaties and programmes
World Heritage Sites (global)
Ramsar Sites (global)
Biosphere Reserves (global)
Biogenetic Reserves (Council of Europe)

Protected areas created under EU legislation
Special Protection Areas
Special Areas of Conservation
Environmentally Sensitive Areas
Nitrate Sensitive Areas

Protected areas found throughout the UK
Forest Park
Forest Nature Reserve
National Nature Reserve
Marine Nature Reserve
Local Nature Reserve

Protected areas found at the country level
Regional Park (Scotland)
National Heritage Area (Scotland)
National Scenic Area (Scotland)
Marine Conservation Area (Scotland)
Area of Special Scientific Interest (Northern Ireland)
Site of Specific Scientific Interest (England, Scotland and Wales)
Area of Special Protection (England, Scotland and Wales)
National Park (England and Wales)
Heritage Coast (England and Wales)
Area of Outstanding Natural Beauty (England and Wales)
Area of Outstanding Natural Beauty (Northern Ireland)

Note: A distinction is drawn between Area of Outstanding Natural Beauty (England and Wales) and Area of Outstanding Natural Beauty (Northern Ireland) as these are established under separate legislation with differing powers. A similar distinction separates Areas of Special Scientific Interest (Northern Ireland) from Sites of Special Scientific Interest in England, Scotland and Wales.

Together the protected areas on the UN list cover about 926 million ha, or some 5% of the Earth's land surface.

The UK has, of course, been part of this worldwide movement to set up and manage protected areas. Within the UK a complex pattern of protected areas has developed in the past 50 years (see Table 1).[5] The main features of UK protected areas are:

- the separation of nature conservation from landscape protection and enjoyment;
- the evolution of partially different administrative and legal arrangements in each part of the UK;
- the separation of nature conservation at sea from that on land;
- the development of certain protected area types within the system of town and country planning;
- the existence of certain types of protected areas developed and/or promoted by conservation agencies;
- the creation of protected areas to encourage environmentally sensitive management of farm land; and
- the increasing number of protected area types established under European and international agreements.[6]

Strengths and weaknesses of the protected area approach

The importance of protected areas has been recognized in numerous international conferences and reports relating to the environment. For example, the IVth World Congress on National Parks and Protected Areas (Caracas, Venezuela, February 1992) identified that protected areas:

- safeguard places which are outstanding in terms of natural wealth, natural beauty and cultural significance;

continued from page 291
[3]For example, the Southern Ocean Cetacean Sanctuary set up by the International Whaling Commission, Mexico, May 1994
[4]IUCN *1993 United Nations List of National Parks and Protected Areas* World Conservation Union, Cambridge, UK (1994)
[5]For a full explanation of the different types of UK protected area and reasons for the differentiation between the identified types, see Bishop, K, Nicholls, C, Ormerod, S, Phillips, A and Warren, L 'Protected areas in the Welsh countryside, Volume 2: Protected areas – past, present and future' Unpublished report to the Countryside Council for Wales, Bangor (1993)
[6]See Bishop, K, Phillips, A and Warren, L *Protected Areas in Wales* Countryside Council for Wales, Bangor (1995)

- maintain the life-supporting diversity of ecosystems, species, genetic variation and ecological processes;
- protect species and the genetic variation that humans need, especially for food and medicine;
- provide homes for human communities with traditional cultures and knowledge of nature;
- protect landscapes reflecting a history of human interaction with the environment;
- provide for the scientific, educational, recreational and spiritual needs of societies;
- provide benefits to local and national economies and are models of sustainable development to be applied elsewhere.[7]

This, however, is very much a world view of protected areas, which perhaps underplays an aspect which is important in the European context, and specifically in that of the UK: the valuable contribution which protected areas can make to the quality of life where (as in most European parks and reserves) access is permitted. Protected areas offer: opportunities for inspiration and vision; an antidote to stress; scope for peaceful enjoyment; a source of mental, physical and spiritual renewal; and a place of understanding and learning.[8]

Despite their many strengths, however, practical experience with protected areas, here and abroad, has revealed numerous difficulties. It is helpful to distinguish between those which are 'external' and 'internal'. External difficulties derive from a failure to integrate protected areas into other aspects of public policy; internal ones are to do with how the concept has been applied within its own sphere of influence.

The IVth World Congress in Caracas identified the following as the principal external problems facing protected areas:

- the tendency to treat protected areas as 'islands' set apart from the areas around;
- the tendency to see protected areas as an alternative to, rather than one element within, a national strategy for conservation;
- the failure to integrate protected areas requirements into policies for the sectors (eg agriculture, tourism, transport) which affect them;
- the inadequate recognition of the needs and interests of local people upon whose support the long-term survival of protected areas will depend; and
- limited public and institutional support for protected areas.[9]

The internal problems are closely linked to the above, but often occur in the form of 'symptoms' of the limited support given to protected areas, for example limited financial resources, gaps in scientific and other information, inadequate powers to manage the protected areas, and poorly trained staff, with limited skills.

Together, these external and internal factors undermine the effectiveness of protected areas in achieving their stated aims. As a result protected areas attract criticism. The deliberately provocative analysis presented in Table 2 summarizes these. Such criticisms are not about protected areas in isolation but reflect a lack of integration of protected areas into wider policies.

Changing views of conservation

It can be concluded that protected areas are a necessary, but not

[7]IUCN *Parks for Life: Report of the Fourth World Congress on National Parks and Protected Areas, Caracas, Venezuela, February 1992* World Conservation Union, Cambridge, UK (1993)
[8]IUCN *Parks for Life: Action for Protected Areas in Europe* World Conservation Union, Cambridge, UK (1994)
[9]IUCN *op cit* Ref 7

Table 2. Criticism of protected areas.

Protected areas negate the holistic approach. The environment is all-embracing, but the practical effect of too much reliance on protected areas for environmental conservation may be to disaggregate the policy response.

Protected areas encourage the view that conservation is a sector or a land use. Because protected areas are set up for conservation purposes, conservation may be viewed as a sector or land use, ie conservation is an activity pursued only within specifically defined areas.

Protected area boundaries are arbitrary lines on maps. All protected areas must have boundaries, ie lines on the ground or under the water. But subtle gradations of scenery or clines between ecosystems cannot properly be reflected in a line on a map.

Protected areas create a 'boundary effect'. Lines on the ground between policy regimes create problems. The integrity of a protected area cannot be divorced from what goes on around.

Environmental problems do not stop at protected area boundaries. Influences, such as trans-frontier air pollution and polluted rivers flowing into the area, do not recognize protected area boundaries.

Biological phenomena ignore protected area boundaries. Animal migrations, and animal and plant eruptions and dispersals, for example, will cross protected area boundaries.

Protected area systems are getting too complex. Protected areas have been developed to protect differing environmental resources, at different scales, through various agencies, using different mechanisms and employing different names. As a result the 'systems' often evolve *ad hoc* and contain complex, frequently overlapping series of designations with often only subtly different aims.

There is a growing problem of diminishing returns. As the number of protected areas proliferates, it may become more difficult to argue that the areas are 'special' and in need of special policies.

Some new ecological thinking questions the value of protected areas. Established concepts, such as succession and climax, are being challenged by 'new ecology' research which emphasizes the dynamic nature of ecosystems and their capacity to change rapidly to alternate states. This implies that protection to maintain supposedly stable climax conditions may not work.

Physical changes could make protected areas obsolete. It has been assumed that the physical environment is essentially unchanging. But if the climate is changing, then it may be impossible to protect biodiversity within areas.

Protected areas are an inflexible concept. Industry, urban development, agriculture and other uses may have so altered the character of protected areas since designation that it is desirable to redraw boundaries, perhaps even de-designate them – but this is often controversial and hard to do.

Protected areas are too defensive a concept. The focus of protected area policy is often on defence against human-induced threats to the environment, often at the expense of a more dynamic vision of environmental management and conservation of biodiversity.

Protected areas are bound to be too weak and small. Because protected areas are essentially defensive, they involve restrictions; hence they are often opposed by those whose interests they would affect. As a result the political process tends to minimize the area receiving protection and limits the degree of protection.

sufficient, aspect of a conservation policy. Indeed such a conclusion fits well with the changing perceptions of conservation over recent years. For example, the practice of nature conservation has been evolving in the following ways:

- from the protection of species towards the protection of their habitats;
- from the protection of species and habitats towards placing their conservation within the protection of the natural processes upon which they depend;
- from self-contained nature conservation towards its integration into the planning and management of the terrestrial and marine environment as a whole, and into each economic sector;
- from isolated local and national initiatives towards international programmes guided by agreed criteria; and
- from a concern with scientific and aesthetic qualities towards a recognition of the importance of biodiversity (ie ecosystems, species and the variety within species) as a component of sustainable development.[10]

Similar trends in thinking can be detected in the area of landscape conservation:

- from an almost exclusive concern with the protection of the 'best', towards an interest in (a) the diversity of the entire landscape, and (b) local distinctiveness;
- from a concern with 'protection' towards more interest in creative conservation, both to restore lost features and to create new ones; and

[10]See Institute for European Environmental Policy *Towards a European Ecological Network* IEEP, Arnhem (1992); and European Commission *Europe's Environment 1993* CEC, Brussels (1995) Chapter on Nature Conservation

- from an essentially aesthetic approach towards a deeper appreciation of the ecological, historical and cultural values of landscape and the way in which these are interwoven.[11]

Finally, there have been important developments in appreciation of the historic dimensions of the countryside. In particular, archaeologists and historians now lay much more emphasis on the links between heritage and nature conservation, promoting archaeology as a 'green' topic which contributes 'time-depth' to understanding the environment.[12] Thus historic understanding brings new perspectives to protected area issues, and emphasizes the need for multidisciplinary approaches to the planning and management of such areas.

Against such a background of changing perceptions, it is no surprise that there should be a growing interest in many quarters in re-examining the role of protected areas as instruments of conservation policy. Those asking the questions are not only the traditional opponents of protective designations, eg farmers and landowners, but also some in conservation circles. While no one would seriously argue for doing away with the protected areas altogether, many believe that it is time to look across the board at the way in which protected areas policy is developed and implemented – and that this should be done in a multidisciplinary way – rather than reviewing each type of protected area, *ad hoc* and in isolation, as has been the usual practice in the past. Indeed, specific proposals for reviews of this kind were quickly made by the integrated nature conservation and countryside agencies in Scotland and Wales following their establishment in 1991 and 1992 respectively; even the Countryside Commission has floated the idea of reviewing 'the links between the wide variety of designations in the countryside'.[13] In the remainder of this paper some of the current thinking about protected area systems is examined, with a view to identifying pointers to the scope and possible outcome of such reviews of protected areas in the UK.

New thinking on protected area systems

In recent years attention has been given to the characteristics of protected area systems. This has been driven by advances in fundamental knowledge (eg in the biological sciences), in environmental concepts (eg the interest in sustainability as an overarching principle), and by the changing requirements of policy makers (eg protected area priorities respond increasingly to international considerations). Several complementary conceptual approaches have been identified, addressing the question 'how to design systems of protected areas'. They are: management categories, functioning networks, hierarchical systems, converging objectives, and integrated environmental management.

Management categories

Through its Commission on National Parks and Protected Areas, IUCN (the World Conservation Union) has promoted the concept of management categories for protected areas. It first published guidance on this topic in 1978,[14] and has recently updated this in new Guidelines for Protected Area Management Categories.[15] The concept is built around the proposition that protected areas can best be classified by the objectives for which they are managed. Protected areas are, in fact, managed for a variety of objectives. However, in any one area some

[11]See for example Countryside Commission *The New Map of England: A Celebration of the South Western Landscape* CCP 444, Countryside Commission, Cheltenham, UK (1994) as well as other publications by the Commission on landscape assessment over the past 10 years.
[12]See Macinnes, L and Wickham-Jones, C R (eds) *All Natural Things: Archaeology and the Green Debate* Oxbow Monograph 21, Oxbow Books, Oxford, UK (1992)
[13]See Countryside Council for Wales *Threshold 21* Countryside Council for Wales, Bangor (1993); Scottish Natural Heritage *Working with Scotland's People to Care for our Natural Heritage* Scottish Natural Heritage, Battleby (1992); and Countryside Commission *Quality of Countryside: Quality of Life* CCP 470, Countryside Commission, Cheltenham, UK (1995)
[14]IUCN *Categories, Objectives and Criteria for Protected Areas* World Conservation Union, Cambridge, UK (1978)
[15]IUCN *op cit* Ref 1

Protected for ever?: K Bishop, A Phillips and L Warren

Table 3. Objectives/categories matrix.

Objectives	Categories						
	Ia	Ib	II	III	IV	V	VI
Scientific research	1	3	2	2	2	2	3
Wilderness protection	2	1	2	3	3	–	2
Preserve species and genetic diversity	1	2	1	1	1	2	1
Maintain environmental services	2	1	1	–	1	2	1
Protection of special features	–	–	2	1	3	1	3
Tourism and recreation	–	2	1	1	3	1	3
Education	–	–	2	2	2	2	3
Sustainable use of resources	–	3	3	–	2	2	1
Maintenance of cultural/traditional attributes	–	–	–	–	–	1	2

Key:
1 Primary objective
2 Secondary objective
3 Acceptable objective
– Not applicable

objectives are more important than others. The priority given to them determines the different types – or categories – of protected areas (see Table 3).

By identifying the objectives of management in this way, it is possible to classify all protected areas into just six main categories which will have the same broad meaning the world over (see Table 4). Bearing in mind the more detailed information given in the published IUCN guidelines, to date only categories IV and V have been considered relevant to the management objectives of protected areas in the UK. Thus the following appear under the UK entry in the 1993 UN list:

- *Category IV:* Marine Nature Reserves, National Nature Reserves
- *Category V:* Areas of Outstanding Natural Beauty, National Parks, National Scenic Areas

However, management objectives may change over time. As a result, other IUCN management categories could become relevant in Britain in future. In particular, the use of Categories Ia and VI may arise in the UK context.

National Nature Reserves are currently classified under Category IV because habitat management and manipulation are the norm in order to maintain or re-establish the biodiversity values of the site in question. However, there is increasing interest in the creation of certain reserves where the object of management is deliberately not to manage. There are several reasons for this:

- the reduced need to farm marginal land, which makes it possible to contemplate 'land abandonment' as a responsible course;
- the need for scientific monitoring of the effects of climate change and other anthropogenic change in environments that are otherwise not manipulated;
- more speculatively, growing public acceptance that there may be intrinsic merit in the existence of truly wild places in Britain, even if these can never be visited.

Table 4. Categories of protected area.

I	Strict Nature Reserves and Wilderness Areas: areas managed mainly for science and wilderness protection
II	National Parks: areas managed mainly for ecosystem conservation and recreation
III	Natural Monument/Natural Landmark: areas managed mainly for conservation of specific natural features
IV	Habitat and Species Management Areas: areas mainly for conservation through management intervention
V	Protected Landscape/Seascape: areas managed mainly for landscape/seascape conservation and recreation
VI	Managed Resource Protected Area: areas managed mainly for the sustainable use of natural ecosystems

Protected for ever?: K Bishop, A Phillips and L Warren

Thus a new look at protected areas might find room for places which are deliberately left free of human interference. An indication of this is to be found in the Edwards report on national parks,[16] which canvasses the idea of 'experimental schemes on a limited scale (within national parks) where farming is withdrawn entirely and the natural succession of vegetation is allowed to take its course'. This approach, providing it was applied on a fairly large scale – say upwards of 1000 ha – and involved the total exclusion of the public other than for scientific purposes, could qualify as Category Ia, a Strict Nature Reserve, in the IUCN system. The scope for doing so in Scotland would, of course, be greater.

Category VI is new to the IUCN classification system, having been promoted by a number of developing countries which argued that there should be greater recognition that some natural or semi-natural areas are managed to a conservation regime to produce a sustainable flow of natural products and services for people. Examples include the forest reserves of Brazil and Nepal, managed for the sustainable production of nuts, rubber, rattan, game meat, etc, and marine reserves managed as breeding and spawning grounds for commercial fisheries which operate nearby.

In the UK context there are at present no extensive areas where the prime aim of management is to conserve natural or semi-natural ecosystems for a regular, sustainable flow of goods for the well-being of the local community. Our land use patterns are so altered from their natural state and our economy is so integrated that it is probably unrealistic to imagine a situation where large tracts of countryside are managed for local needs in this way. But there are three situations where land or sea management policy could move in this direction.

First, many upland areas are already managed at low intensity for sporting purposes. A Category VI approach to their management would put greater emphasis on conservation of the areas' total biodiversity, rather than a concentration as now on a narrow range of 'products', eg red deer or grouse; and the benefits would accrue more to local people rather than to large landowners and shooting syndicates, for example.

Second, a Category VI approach would signal a deliberate shift in the management of some large forests towards small-scale, locally owned woodland operations which bring employment to local people (along principles already pioneered by the Woodland Trust for small community woodlands, for example) rather than large-scale, contractor-type operations as now.

Third, the application of ecosystem management principles to coastal fisheries could assure long-term productivity for local fishing communities. This would require fishing in traditional ways, abandoning the use of industrial methods which damage both the fishery stocks themselves and other parts of the marine ecosystem.

Whether or not it is practical to establish areas in the UK which satisfy the requirements of Category VI, there is scope for greater application of the principles of sustainable resource management, based upon ecosystem management and bringing benefits to local communities.

[16]See National Parks Review Panel *Fit for the Future: Report of the National Parks Review Panel* Countryside Commission, Cheltenham, UK (1991)

[17]See Quinn, J F and Hastings, A 'Extinction in subdivided habitats' *Conservation Biology* 1987 **1** (3) 198–208; and Gilpin, M E 'A comment on Quinn and Hastings: extinction in subdivided habitats' *Conservation Biology* 1988 **2** (3) 290–292

Functioning networks

In recent years, biologists have argued the conservation merits of a single large reserve against several small ones (the so-called SLOSS controversy).[17] Some have suggested that the conservation of biodiversity would benefit from the creation of corridors between reserves;

297

critics, however, point out that disease, predators and exotic species can use such corridors as well as endangered species.[18]

Such debates have largely focused on the needs of developing regions, where there are still areas of relatively undisturbed forest, but also great pressure on land from fast-growing human numbers. Within Europe – where little remains that is remotely natural, but there is surplus food capacity and therefore the potential to increase nature conservation values in parts of the countryside – a rather different approach is finding favour. Here the emphasis has been placed more on holding on to what natural areas still exist, linking them up, protecting them with surrounding buffer zones in which local communities become partners in conservation, and restoring damaged areas where practicable.

A good example of this approach is the EECONET concept, or the European Ecological Network.[19] This is being promoted by the Government of the Netherlands as a strategic approach to the protection and enhancement of Europe's biological and landscape diversity. EECONET, which was the subject of a governmental conference in Maastricht in November 1993, acknowledges many of the problems with protected areas as they currently operate. It seeks to reverse the fragmentation of habitats into small, isolated islands by establishing and developing a coherent European network of habitats, based on four kinds of action:

- better protection of core areas,
- the development of support zones around these,
- the creation of corridors between these, and
- the restoration of damaged habitats.

In order to achieve EECONET, it is envisaged that: the protection of existing parks and reserves in Europe will be strengthened as the cores or 'nodes' of the network; Natura 2000 sites (see below) and land affected by CAP change (eg set-aside land) will also be used to build the network; some connecting corridors will cross national boundaries; and much more effort will go into the restoration of degraded agricultural and industrial environments. Thus EECONET is about strategic environmental planning, based less on traditional defensive approaches and more on creative and adaptive techniques. It is made possible by the existence of greater international cooperation, food surpluses and spare agricultural capacity in Europe and reflects the need for a dynamic response to possible climate change. The concept also envisages that the same principles will be applied at local levels, where – for example – hedgerows and streams, rather than mountain ranges and large rivers, link locally important areas of landscape and habitat.[20]

EECONET – and especially its emphasis on a strategic vision, developing corridors between protected areas and restoring damaged environments – is a signpost to the way in which protected area systems in the UK might evolve in future. Already certain features of this approach can be detected. For example, several Countryside Stewardship prescriptions, eg the riverside and coastal options, make it possible to assemble the elements of a corridor by restoring damaged habitats. The Countryside Commission has offered incentives to encourage neighbouring owners of land along river valleys and in coastal areas to collaborate in the recreation of landscape features, habitats and recreation provision – all developing along natural corridors.[21]

[18]Bonner, J 'Wildlife corridors under fire' *New Scientist* 1994 **143** (1939) 30–34
[19]Institute for European Environmental Policy *Towards a European Ecological Network* IEEP, Arnhem, the Netherlands (1991)
[20]*The EECONET Declaration* Declaration of the Conference 'Conserving Europe's Natural Heritage: Towards a European Ecological Network', Maastricht, The Netherlands, 9–12 November 1993, IEEP, Arnhem, the Netherlands (1993)
[21]Bishop, K and Phillips, A 'Seven steps to market: the development of the market-led approach to countryside conservation and recreation' *Journal of Rural Studies* 1993 **9** (4) 315–338

Hierarchical systems

In most countries, pressures to establish protected areas were initially focused at the national level. The words 'national park' reflect this. However, over time there have been two parallel developments: upwards, in the sense that action for protected areas has increasingly taken place at the international level, and downwards, in the sense that provincial and even local administrations have become involved in the establishment and management of protected areas. These trends will continue and indeed become more marked. Consider the following developments.

At the global level, there are continuing pressures to strengthen the effectiveness of existing international designations and programmes. Thus, in the context of the Ramsar (Wetlands) Convention[22] there is an emphasis on the production of management plans for all Ramsar sites; this is significant because only a few of the 68 Ramsar sites in the UK can presently fulfil this requirement.[23] Under the World Heritage Convention, the World Heritage Committee takes an increasing interest in monitoring the management of World Heritage Sites, a requirement which could be relevant to the two Natural World Heritage Sites in the UK, St Kilda and the Giant's Causeway.[24] The international network of Biosphere Reserves (developed under the auspices of UNESCO's Man and Biosphere Programme) will be comprehensively reviewed at a conference in March 1995 in Seville, Spain. At that meeting, proposals will be forthcoming to formalize the definition of Biosphere Reserves, introduce criteria for evaluating proposals for additions to the reserves network, formalize a designation procedure and set up a system of periodic review of sites in the network – all of which could have implications for the 13 Biosphere Reserves in the UK.[25]

Another important global development concerns the adoption by the World Heritage Committee of new criteria which make it possible for 'Cultural Landscapes' to be recognized as World Heritage Sites.[26] Hitherto, only natural and cultural sites could be recognized (in the UK context, cultural sites include Stonehenge/Avebury, Ironbridge/Coalbrookdale, Hadrian's Wall and Georgian Bath). However, the addition of the cultural landscapes category should enable the UK to submit other sites for recognition for their 'outstanding, universal qualities'. Examples would include not only great designated gardens (eg Stowe or Stourhead) but also the landscapes of certain of our national parks (eg the Lake District) or other areas (eg the West Penwith peninsula of Cornwall). The process of reviewing candidate areas and submitting them for assessment as possible World Heritage Sites is likely to stimulate interest in landscape as an international resource.

Although the Convention on Biological Diversity, signed at the Earth Summit in Rio and coming into force late in 1993, does not create a new category of protected area, Article 8 – *In Situ* Conservation – requires states to establish a 'system of protected areas, or areas where special measures need to be taken to conserve biological diversity'.[27] The UK can expect greater international attention to be paid to the quality of its stewardship of nature reserves, etc; and the significance of this development will probably grow as there will undoubtedly be pressure on governments to add 'teeth' to the convention in future.

At the European level, the greatest impact is likely to be the establishment of the UK part of Natura 2000. Combining Special

[22]Convention on Wetlands of International Importance especially as Waterfowl Habitat
[23]See, for example, Resolution 5.7 (Management Planning for Ramsar sites and other Wetlands) of the Fifth Meeting of the Contracting Parties to the Ramsar Convention on Wetlands, Kushiro, Japan, 1993
[24]See, for example, 'The monitoring of sites – a vital task for the Committee' in *World Heritage Newsletter* 1993 (1)
[25]Personal communication from the MAB Secretariat of UNESCO, Paris
[26]See for example *World Heritage Newsletter* 1993 (1) 15; 1993 (2) 14; 1994 (4) 15
[27]It is a weakness of the Convention that this requirement is qualified by the words 'as far as possible and as appropriate'. This is an attribute of the broad brush approach of the convention, which contains few specific obligations.

Protection Areas (SPAs) designated under the Birds Directive[28] and Special Areas of Conservation (SACs) under the Habitats Directive.[29] Natura 2000 is intended to be a Union-wide ecological network of sites representative of Europe's diversity of habitats and species. Designated sites must be afforded a degree of protection that is greater than that currently enjoyed by sites in the UK.[30] The government has published draft regulations to implement the directive in Great Britain[31] which build on and strengthen existing site protection legislation, especially in relation to nature conservation orders. For marine sites, however, the existing arrangements are regarded as inadequate[32] and a new framework, based mainly on administrative arrangements rather than legislative changes, is to be introduced. The focus is on the need to manage sites rather than simply to protect them from adverse impacts.

The Birds Directive was a catalyst for the Wildlife and Countryside Act 1981. In view of the deficiencies within this Act, it had been hoped by some that the Habitats Directive would lead to a fresh think and new primary legislation. In the event, however, the government has chosen to implement the directive by regulations issued under the European Communities Act 1972, a decision which precludes the possibility of wider amendment of the 1981 Act. Nevertheless, it seems likely that the high standards set by the Habitats Directive will attract the attention of the courts in testing the UK's approach to implementation.[33]

More speculatively, there are three other areas where a stronger European influence may be felt in future: marine, the coast and landscape. In the marine context, the IUCN has identified a major gap in the provision of protected areas in the North East Atlantic.[34] Whereas the Barcelona and Helsinki Conventions have enabled the development of networks of marine protected areas in the Mediterranean and the Baltic respectively, the comparable 1992 Convention on the Protection of the Marine Environment for the North East Atlantic (the Paris Convention) contains no powers of this kind; hence the IUCN call for a protocol to the convention to establish a network of protected areas for this marine region too. The European Commission has also been following up Council proposals[35] to protect the marine environment from adverse impacts of shipping; member states were invited to identify environmentally sensitive areas with a view to the eventual adoption of some sort of added protection of a type as yet undecided.

In the coastal context, the European Commission is currently developing a Union strategy 'for integrated planning and management of the coastal zone based on the principles of sustainability and sound ecological and environmental practice'.[36] Similar calls are made in the Union's Fifth Environmental Action Plan, *Towards Sustainability*, which sketches out the main elements of such a coastal strategy, including 'higher priority to the environmental needs of coastal zones'.[37] Though the precise implications for protected areas in the coastal zone are not yet clear, a Union strategy in this area is bound to strengthen European interest in the way in which the UK coastal resource is managed.

On the landscape front, a possible long-term development is the successful conclusion of current efforts to develop some kind of European convention (to cover the whole of Europe) on the protection and management of the rural landscape. The argument for such an initiative lies in the international importance of the European landscape resource, the degree to which its future is now threatened by Europe-

[28]Council Directive on the conservation of wild birds (79/409/EEC)
[29]Council Directive on the conservation of natural habitats and of wild fauna and flora (92/43/EEC)
[30]Under Article 6 member states are required to establish the necessary conservation measures and to take appropriate steps to avoid deterioration of habitats. Any proposed plan or project that is likely to have a significant effect upon a designated site must be subjected to an assessment before approval is granted. If the assessment is negative approval may only be given on the grounds of imperative reasons for overriding public interest, including those of a social or economic nature. In such cases compensatory measures must be taken to ensure the overall coherence of Natura 2000.
[31]The Conservation (Natural Habitats, &c) Regulations 1994 (draft)
[32]The Consultation Paper on the implementation in Great Britain of the Council Directive on the conservation of natural habitats and of wild fauna and flora (92/43/EEC), the 'Habitats Directive', dismisses SSSIs, marine nature reserves and marine consultation areas as mechanisms for implementation.
[33]There have already been cases concerning the protection of Special Protection Areas including, most recently, a challenge in the Court of Appeal (unreported) by the Royal Society for the Protection of Birds against a decision to allow development within an estuarine SPA. Leave to appeal to the House of Lords has been granted.
[34]IUCN *op cit* Ref 8
[35]Environment Council, 29 June 1993
[36]Council for Environment Ministers Resolution, 25 February 1992
[37]CEC *Towards Sustainability* Office for Official Publications of the European Community, Luxembourg (1993)

wide forces, and the absence of any European framework for the protection of the landscape. Proposals for a landscapes convention have the support of a number of non-governmental bodies, including that of the IUCN.[38] Though the outcome of this initiative is at present uncertain, it seems probable that, like the new Cultural Landscapes aspect of the World Heritage Convention, the debate around the notion of international instruments to protect landscapes will add to awareness of landscape as a resource for more than national interest.

At the country (ie sub-UK) level, an important development has been the recent establishment of a separate conservation agency each for Wales and Scotland, and two agencies with remits only for England.[39] Legislation for the establishment of conservation agencies includes provisions as to their functions, duties and powers and, in some cases, reference to particular protected areas. Where new protected areas have been devised subsequently, or old ones amended, lead responsibilities have been assigned to one or more of the agencies. Such an arrangement tends to minimize variation between the law and practice for protected areas covered by the same agency. Until very recently, therefore, the system of protected areas for nature conservation was more or less the same throughout Great Britain, which was the extent of the Nature Conservancy Council's remit, whereas separate systems of protected areas for countryside matters evolved in Scotland (with its Countryside Commission for Scotland) and in England and Wales (which together came under the Countryside Commission remit).[40] The establishment of Scottish Natural Heritage, under the Natural Heritage (Scotland) Act 1991, brought with it a new statutory designation, the Natural Heritage Area, and a new appeal mechanism for SSSIs which is not applicable in England and Wales. In England and Wales the substantive law remains unchanged, yet even here there are signs of individuality creeping in. Thus both the Countryside Commission and the Countryside Council for Wales have responded to the need for greater integration of environmental concerns into agricultural practices by using their experimental powers under the Wildlife and Countryside Act (s40) to promote farm management schemes, but the approaches adopted in the Countryside Stewardship Scheme (Countryside Commission) and Tir Cymen (Countryside Council for Wales) are rather different. It is reasonable to suppose that the new administrative arrangements, not least of which is the elevated importance of the Secretaries of State for Wales and Scotland, may give rise to further divergence in approach between countries and proposals for new statutory arrangements for their protected areas.

At the local level, too, there are forces at work which encourage further layers to be developed in the protected areas system. For example, recent research in Wales has calculated that 31.9% of the land surface is covered by special landscape or wildlife interest areas identified in development plans,[41] and at least one authority, Ceredigion, has extended the practice to the marine environment through the establishment of a Marine Heritage Coast. This practice of defining special landscape/wildlife areas, however defined, has been given added impetus by the provisions of the Planning and Compensation Act 1991, which requires all development plans to include policies in respect of the conservation of the natural beauty and amenity of the land. English Nature views structure plans as a way of linking its new concept of 'natural areas' to planning policies.[42]

[38]IUCN *op cit* Ref 8
[39]The case for retaining separate agencies in England has been the subject of recent questions.
[40]National Parks, AONBs and Heritage Coasts in England and Wales; National Scenic Areas and Regional Parks in Scotland
[41]Bloomer Tweedale 'Special landscape and wildlife areas in Wales' Unpublished report to the Countryside Council for Wales, Bangor (1993)
[42]Wright, R 'Natural selection' *The Planner* 19 May 1994, 13

There is also renewed interest in conservation circles in local authorities using the local nature reserve powers contained in the 1949 Act,[43] and many local community groups focus on the creation of small, community-based nature reserves, pocket parks, etc. While such places are not usually regarded as protected areas, many do in fact fit within the broad definition used at the outset of this paper. The point is thus made: the hierarchy of protected areas extends from the global level to the local level.

Converging objectives

Protected areas in the UK have developed from several disciplinary and institutional origins. Thus some have been developed as instruments of nature conservation policy, some for landscape protection (with or without a public enjoyment component) and some for the protection of particular types of habitat or environment (eg the coastal or marine environment). However, in recent years there has been an increasing awareness of the complementarity which exists between the aims of nature, scenic and heritage conservation, and of the extent to which the instruments of one policy can serve the aims of others. In brief, the approaches to conservation have been converging, and this has important implications for the development of protected area systems. At the same time there has been a growing awareness of the drawbacks of separate types of protected area that are too narrowly defined in terms of the powers and duties that go with them. A good example would be a marine nature reserve adjoining a terrestrial national nature reserve, where the legislative powers associated with one cannot be used to complement the powers of the other. Similarly, the provisions for management agreements in the Countryside Act 1968 (s15) restrict their application to purposes directly related to the reasons for notification of an SSSI and do not permit wider countryside matters to be included.

Several examples of this current trend towards greater convergence between previously separate strands of conservation can be identified:

The convergence of the conservation agencies. The importance of CCW and SNH in this context has already been noted. Their establishment as single, unified agencies for conservation, in place of formerly separate nature and countryside bodies, both reflects a growing awareness of the complementarity between the different 'schools' of conservation, and further strengthens the forces of convergence. While the process will not be rapid or straightforward, it seems highly probable that integrated agencies will over time help to create a more integrated approach to conservation in both Wales and Scotland. While there is now no prospect of an early similar institutional change in England, ministers can be expected to bring increased pressure on the Countryside Commission and English Nature for closer working.

The development of integrated types of protected areas. There have been several examples of these recently:

• Natural Heritage Areas (NHA): The origins of this new designation type for Scotland lie in Natural Heritage (Scotland) Act 1991 (s6). This refers to the appropriateness of special protection measures for areas of outstanding value to the natural heritage of Scotland. It defines 'natural heritage' as including 'the flora and fauna of Scotland, its geological and physiographical features, its natural beauty

[43]See Bishop, K and Phillips, A 'A programme for small access areas' Available from the Countryside Council for Wales, Bangor (1993)

and amenity'. Though the Act does not explicitly specify the purposes of NHAs, this wording, subsequent advice from the Scottish Office and the stated policies of SNH all indicate that a wide-ranging approach is envisaged, one indeed which also embraces meeting the economic and social needs of rural populations in a sustainable way. As the Chief Executive of SNH has stated: 'We are at present developing one specific type of designation which could be seen as a model for realising this wider approach to protection, combining both conservation and development.'[44] The NHA concept has attracted criticism on the grounds that it lacks the means to ensure compliance and does not require the setting up of special mangement authorities for the areas (and therefore does not appear to meet the needs of areas like the Cairngorms or Loch Lomond and the Trossachs). However, its innovative aspect in bringing together nature and landscape protection within an overall context of sustainable land use has generally been well received.

- Environmentally Sensitive Areas (ESA): Introduced originally by EC Regulation 797/85, ESAs are 'areas of special landscape, wildlife or historic interest which can be protected or enhanced by supporting specific agricultural practices'.[45] More recently, grants made under ESAs have also been made available to encourage public access to the countryside. ESAs have no direct implication for the operation of the planning system, and entry into an ESA agreement is entirely voluntary. In the context of this paper, however, ESAs mark an important innovation by bringing together nature conservation, landscape protection, care of the historic heritage and public access and countryside recreation. Furthermore, the government departments for agriculture, which are responsible for ESAs, are required under the 1986 Agriculture Act to consult the statutory nature conservation and countryside agencies in the selection of ESAs and the management prescriptions within them; as a matter of policy, they also consult the agencies responsible for the conservation of the built heritage. Here, too, convergence and integration are replacing previously discrete approaches.

- Countryside Stewardship and Tir Cymen: These are schemes developed respectively by the Countryside Commission in England and the Countryside Council for Wales to encourage land managers to care for the rural environment. Countryside Stewardship does not satisfy the definition of a 'protected area' because it does not focus on a particular area, but is a system of incentives available to land managers in particular habitat types; moreover, even though Tir Cymen is geographically targeted, it has been made clear that this is for the pilot stage only, and that CCW hopes eventually that the scheme will operate throughout rural Wales. Nonetheless, the development of both schemes marks a further step in the integrated approach to land management and conservation, since each embraces measures for the protection of nature, landscape and heritage – and provides for public access.

The broadening of the aims of existing protected areas. Finally, there is a trend to broaden the objectives of established protected areas so that they serve a wider range of purposes. For example:

- National parks: The 1949 National Parks and Access to the Countryside Act declares the aims of national parks to be to preserve and

[44]Crofts, R (Chief Executive of SNH) 'The future of protected areas in Scotland' Address to the Federation of Nature and National Parks of Europe, Battleby, Perth, 16–19 September 1993
[45]Department of the Environment, Welsh Office *PPG 7: The Countryside and the Rural Economy* HMSO, London (1992)

Protected for ever?: K Bishop, A Phillips and L Warren

enhance the natural beauty of the areas, and to promote their
enjoyment by the public. The Edwards report on national parks
recommended that these purposes should be redrawn thus: 'to
protect, maintain, enhance the scenic beauty, natural systems and
land forms, and the wildlife and cultural heritage of the area; and to
promote the quiet enjoyment and understanding of the area, insofar
as it is not in conflict with the primary purpose of the area'. Though
there has been some dispute about the implication that enjoyment
and understanding should be a secondary purpose, the broadening of
the conservation purpose of national parks to refer specifically to
'scenic beauty, natural systems and land forms, and wildlife and
cultural heritage' has been widely welcomed. The government in-
tends to bring legislation before Parliament during the 1994/95
session to create independent national park agencies which will
redefine their purposes.

- Heritage coasts: The original objectives of these were to conserve the
natural beauty of the coastline and to facilitate recreational use
consistent with that objective, with a special emphasis on management tools to achieve these ends. However, experience – confirmed
through a review of Heritage Coasts undertaken by the Countryside
Commission concluded in 1992 – has shown that this is too narrow an
approach. Commenting on the review, the government agreed with
the Commission that the objectives for these protected areas should
be 'widened to recognise the need to preserve and enhance important
habitats for flora and fauna, and to protect architectural, historical
and archaeological features' – and also to promote higher standards
of environmental protection generally within such areas (bathing
water standards and litter clearance, for example).[46]

It is thus apparent that there are a number of parallel trends – the
emergence of integrated agencies, the development of new kinds of
integrated protected areas and the widening of the remits of established
protected areas – which together suggest the development of the
protected areas system of the UK will increasingly involve convergence
between a number of previously separate objectives. The speed and
extent to which progress can be made will ultimately depend on how
broadly the governing legislation can be interpreted or amended. Given
the premium on parliamentary time, it is unrealistic to expect a major
revision of protected area legislation in the near future.

Integrated environmental management

Point 4 of the Rio Declaration, made at the UN Conference on
Environment and Development in 1992, states that 'in order to achieve
sustainable development, environmental protection shall constitute an
integral part of the development process and cannot be considered in
isolation from it'. The UK Biodiversity Action Plan, which was produced to meet commitments made at Rio, states that the 'conservation
of biodiversity should be an integral part of Government programmes,
policy and action'. The underlying message is clear: the official perception of conservation is moving away from viewing protected areas in
isolation towards fitting them into part of the jigsaw of sustainability.
The key process is likely to be management, be it of land use, sea use or
sectoral interests, so as to comply with the principles of sustainable
development. The role of protected areas under such a regime is likely
to be rather different from the present situation.

[46]Countryside Commission *Heritage Coasts in England: Policies and Priorities 1992* CCP 397, Countryside Commission, Cheltenham, UK (1992)

The idea of integrated management has been progressed to the greatest extent in the case of coastal zone management where the consequences of failure to coordinate management are particularly obvious because so many different players and interests are involved.[47] In this country, coastal zone management has been championed by the nature conservation non-governmental organizations who have long realized that conservation interests are best met by such an approach.[48] The development of various schemes for coastal management plans[49] is evidence of a widening recognition of the importance of such an approach, and the main thrust of the government's proposed regulations for protecting marine Special Areas of Conservation under the Habitats Directive is integrated management.

Taken to its logical extreme, the integrated management approach would lead to the whole of the UK being included within one or more management plans operating at different geographical scales. While such a possibility may be remote in the current political climate, some eminent conservationists believe that in future it will be necessary to adopt this total approach to the sustainable management of natural resources.[50] In such a scenario, protected areas would be set within a strategy for wider countryside management, involving tools such as spatial and temporal zoning, by-laws and other regulations, complemented by incentives to land managers for environmental care.

If this model for the protection of natural and related resources is developed it could eventually lead to the decoupling of the identification of protected areas from the imposition of special measures for their protection. The main purpose of the protected area would be as a label, identifying the distinct nature of a particular area in accordance with clear, scientific, socioeconomic or other specified criteria. Protection of the designated area would then be achieved by drawing the most appropriate tools from a bank of available mechanisms. Such an approach would have the advantage of introducing flexibility into the system by rationalizing the legislation, thereby overcoming some of the limitations addressed in this paper.

Conclusion

The protected areas system of the UK has grown piecemeal. Not since the second world war and immediate post-war period, with the reports of Dower, Ramsay, Ritchie, Hobhouse and Huxley, has there been a government enquiry into the system as a whole, though individual elements have been examined from time to time. Because a complex functional and geographical pattern has now emerged, only an initiative from central government would bring about such a comprehensive review of the current arrangements. In the current political climate such a move seems unlikely; in its absence, the existing system will continue to evolve *ad hoc* and the current pattern of protected areas will become even more complex.

However, the forces for change outlined in this paper are already considerable. Moreover, the logic of a comprehensive review of the protected areas system in the UK seems likely to become more compelling in future. It is to be hoped that before too long a radically minded government, committed to real progress in the environmental field, will be prepared to seize the nettle. The prize is a much more dynamic, flexible and effective system of UK protected areas, set within a nation-wide policy for sustainability which meets the needs of the 21st century.

[47]See, for example 'A selection of case studies illustrating the need or coastal zone management in the United Kingdom' Submitted in evidence to the House of Commons Environment Committee by Wildlife Link, House of Commons Environment Committee, Session 1991–92, Second Report, 'Coastal Zone Protection and Planning' Vol II, HC 17-II, 125
[48]Early players included the Marine Conservation Society and the World Wide Fund for Nature Conservation who together produced a number of publications, including Gubbay, S *A Future for the Coast?* (1990).
[49]Examples include catchment management plans produced by the National Rivers Authority and estuarine management plans sponsored by English Nature together with various local initiatives.
[50]Martin Holdgate, former Director of IUCN, for example, suggests that almost all areas of land and coastal sea will be used in some way by people and that integrated management of the whole environment will be the norm: see Holdgate, M 'Protected landscapes – an overview' in *Protected Landscapes – Where Next?* Report of the 1992 National Parks Conference, Countryside Commission and Countryside Council for Wales, Cheltenham, UK (1992).

[22]

Problems of wildlife management and land use in Kenya

Cleophas Lado

This article examines the history of wildlife conservation and management in Kenya, and identifies land use practices, innovations and conflicts. Questions of competition for land use, potential threats to wildlife and historical factors of land issues are examined. Problems of wildlife conservation areas are outlined, including ecological considerations and the impact of increasing numbers of visitors leading to conflict between economic and conservation objectives. There is a need for the examination of wildlife management strategies to identify ways that would guarantee sustainable conservation, such as the involvement of local people and consideration of their immediate livelihood strategies, perceptions and values by policy makers and planners.

Dr Lado is Senior Lecturer, Department of Geography, Kenyatta University, PO Box 43844, Nairobi, Kenya.

The broad expanses of savanna and woodland environments provide one of the surviving refuges for the dwindling and untamed herbivores and carnivores in tropical Africa. A powerful scientific and social obligation is required to protect its fauna and habitat. Because scarcity often increases value, wildlife provides an important source of revenue, particularly for the developing countries.

New awareness of conservation issues is mainly focused in Western countries where the environmental impact of 'modern' technology has become obvious. In fact, a perusal of the literature on conservation might lead to the belief that the problems of environmental deterioration are almost entirely confined to the developed nations. However, throughout the world, human activities are altering and degrading the physical environment.

Wildlife conservation in Kenya has a long history which starts in the precolonial period. One of its associated dilemmas has been how to deal with land use conflicts in wildlife areas in a manner that will meet both conservation and human requirements. The present challenge for Kenya in developing and managing the wildlife sector is to find institutions and processes that take into consideration the needs of the local communities and wildlife so as to use the sector effectively and hence alleviate inherent land use conflicts.

Various management strategies and innovations have been adopted to deal with this problem. Initial views and implementation of conservation techniques were based on the US parks systems.[1] This article traces the history of wildlife conservation in Kenya; identifies land use practices, innovations and conflicts associated with the sector; and examines the complex question of competition for land use through temporal and functional approaches.

Increasing human population is a potential threat to wildlife, and competition for land between people and animals is a serious constraint. Historical factors characterizing the land issue in relation to wildlife are examined.

Geographical and wildlife conservation realities in Kenya

Kenya possesses a relatively limited resource base. It lacks major exploitable mineral resources, and good agricultural land is scarce as

[1]Republic of Kenya, Wildlife Conservation and Socio-Economic Development in the 1980s, Proceedings of the First All African Wildlife Conference held at the Kenyatta International Conference Centre, Nairobi, Kenya, 13–19 July 1980.

Wildlife management and land use in Kenya

Table 1. Percentage of total value of Kenya's exports and principal commodities, 1965–73.

Commodity	1965	1967	1969	1971	1973
Coffee (not roasted)	29.9	29.3	26.6	26.8	29.2
Tea	12.9	13.8	17.8	16.2	13.8
Sisal fibre and tow	8.2	3.9	2.7	2.1	3.9
Meat and meat preparations	5.2	5.3	4.1	5.0	3.1
Pyrethrum extract and flowers	4.7	5.4	4.4	4.6	3.0
Hides, skins and furskins, undressed	3.7	3.3	3.0	3.3	4.2
Maize, unmilled	–	2.6	4.4	–	4.6
Wattle bark and extract	1.8	1.7	1.9	1.6	1.0
Pineapples, tinned	1.6	1.0	1.1	1.3	1.2
Cotton, raw	1.6	1.2	1.2	1.6	1.1
Wool, raw	1.2	0.9	0.9	0.4	0.7
Cashew nuts	1.2	1.0	1.1	1.0	0.5
Beans, peas and lentils	1.0	0.6	0.8	0.6	1.0
Oil seeds, oilnuts and oil kernels	1.0	0.7	0.5	0.6	0.4
Butter and ghee	0.6	0.5	0.4	0.1	0.6
Non-agricultural	16.4	18.3	16.3	19.7	12.5
Tourism	9.1	10.5	12.8	15.1	19.2
Total	100.0	100.0	100.0	100.0	100.0

Source: Annual Trade Reports, East African Customs and Excise Department, and adapted from Republic of Kenya, Statistical Abstract.

much of the northern and eastern regions is too dry to support any farming activity except pastoralism. The agricultural sector contributes substantial and reasonably stable export earnings, and is a base for industrial and commercial growth sectors (see Tables 1 and 2), thus minimizing the use of foreign exchange to finance food imports. However, the extreme climatic variations and the continuous worldwide inflationary pressure and devaluation of the Kenyan shilling have not warranted a policy of total self-sufficiency.

Kenya's wildlife is a unique and economically valuable resource. Wildlife has a significant role in a complex ecological system. The interaction of animals with the environment contributes to natural beauty, maintenance of checks and balances, the stability of ecosystems, and useful genetic resources. The economic value of this unique resource is realized through game viewing, mainly by international tourists and visitors.

As shown in Table 2, tourism earned some K£62 million of Kenya's foreign currency in 1979 and K£152 million in 1984. It provided 3.1% of Kenya's gross domestic product (GDP) in 1979 and 4.1% in 1984.[2] In 1987, for example, tourism provided K£292 million in foreign exchange earnings. Indeed, there has been an upward trend between 1960 and 1982, rising from K£25 million at independence in 1963 to a record K£6 billion in 1987.[3]

On the other hand, if harmony between the local people and wildlife could be restored by involving them directly in wildlife management and removing unnecessary restrictions on their lives, they would be able to

[2]Republic of Kenya, *Wanjigi Acts on Tourism*, November 1983.
[3]M. Korir-Koech, 'Evolution of environmental management in Kenya', in A. Kiriro and C. Juma, eds, *Gaining Ground: Institutional Innovations in Land Use Management in Kenya*, African Centre for Technology Studies, Nairobi, Kenya, 1991, pp 21–34.

Table 2. Most important single export items of Kenya, 1979 and 1984.

Item	1979 K£ million	%	1984 K£ million	%
Coffee (unroasted)	110.6	28.7	203.6	27.0
Tea	62.8	16.3	189.5	25.1
Petroleum products	68.1	17.7	131.6	17.4
Pineapples (canned)	9.3	2.4	25.9	3.4
Cement	8.3	2.2	17.5	2.3
Sisal	4.8	1.2	12.6	1.7
Soda ash	5.6	1.5	10.5	1.4
Pyrethrum extract	5.5	1.4	9.7	1.3
Hides and skins	13.8	3.6	7.1	0.9
Other export items	96.7	25.1	146.8	19.4
Total	385.5	100.0	754.8	100.0
Tourism[a]	62		152	

[a]As an invisible asset, tourism does not figure in the export statistics.
Source: Republic of Kenya, Economic Survey, 1981 and 1985.

reap some of the economic benefits of the parks – from tourism through wages and sales of souvenirs, and from game cropping or sale of live animals. Safari hunting would also be controlled by the community and the income – concession fees, trophy fees, meat sales and wages – would accrue to the community, thus reducing unemployment.

In order to provide mechanisms for nature conservation and management, Kenya has formulated its own policy on the environment and established an institutional framework for its implementation. Wildlife management and conservation is very much associated with, and influenced by, policies dealing with overall environmental protection. There is need to protect Kenya's animal species for present and future generations. This calls for global efforts in the protection of endangered animal species such as elephant and rhino. The Kenya government's recent bold act of burning K£60 million (US$3 million) worth of ivory tusks captured from illegal poaching in 1989 demonstrates commitment towards the conservation and management of wildlife.[4]

Wildlife conservation is mainly implemented through an elaborate system of national parks, game reserves and other types of sanctuaries. Although the system would appear to be adequate, there are many constraints on its effectiveness. Chief among these is the increasing competition from other forms of land use.

Kenya's human population is increasing at an estimated rate of 3.5% a year.[5] Most of the people are engaged in smallholder agriculture and, in relation to their limited technologies, are densely settled in zones of relatively rich natural fertility. This expanding population has already begun to come into conflict with wildlife as people move out of the 'traditional' settlement areas in search of new land for cultivation and grazing. Such new areas have long been occupied exclusively by wild animals. In effect, the rapidly increasing population and densities are the characteristics of the peripheral agricultural areas adjacent to the newly designated game sanctuaries. Population pressure is also mounting within the game reserves and national parks, as wide-ranging large ungulates are confined to finite spaces.

Figures 1 and 2 show high population densities ranging from 200–399 persons/km^2 in the Nairobi National Park and Maasai Mara Game Reserve, while there are between 100 and 199 persons in Mount Elgon Nature Reserve and Lambwe Valley Game Reserve. There are also high population concentrations of 50–99 persons/km^2 in Tsavo, Mount Kenya and Meru National Parks.

At the periphery of arable areas, the creation of game sanctuaries has meant larger livestock populations per unit of land, and increasing loss of both pasture and livestock quality to overgrazing. This threatens both people and animals with a devolutionary process of overpopulation and a declining subsistence sector. Combined with an agricultural policy which replaces food crops with export commodities in the more fertile areas, these ecological disturbances have led to more frequent food shortages and high dependence on grain imports, greater rural landlessness (squatting) and socioeconomic inequality and hence higher rates of rural-to-urban migration.

Thus, under the current agrotechnical, political and economic conditions, and with the competition for land between people and animals in some areas of wildlife abundance, Kenya's human carrying capacity may soon be exceeded as population more than doubles within the next 25 years. Unless these conditions improve, the only existing opportunity

[4]Republic of Kenya, 'Conservation', *The Weekly Review*, 20 October 1989, p 43.
[5]Republic of Kenya, *Population Census*, mimeo, Central Bureau of Statistics, 1979.

Wildlife management and land use in Kenya

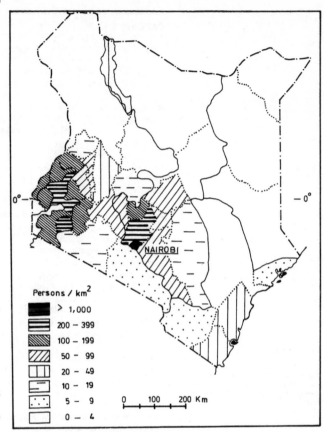

Persons / km^2

> 1,000

200 – 399

100 – 199

50 – 99

20 – 49

10 – 19

5 – 9

0 – 4

0   100   200 K m

Figure 1. Population density in Kenyan Districts, 1979.

Source: Republic of Kenya, statistical abstract, 1980.

for an expansion of subsistence agriculture may have to include opening up new lands, including grassland, bush and forest which are currently preserved for wildlife. However, rapid environmental or ecological destruction can be anticipated from converting these expanses into high-density farms and livestock ranges, culminating in an eventual net loss not only of wildlife but also food production.[6]

Kenya's varied environments support a variety of wild animals, and although wildlife populations have been substantially reduced in recent years, game can still be seen in spectacular abundance in some areas. There are several mammal species such as buffalo, kudu, gazelles and antelopes, lion, leopard, hyena, aardwolf, rhinoceros, elephant and giraffe, as well as a very rich bird life and other small mammals.[7] The most common herbivores may be classified according to their food preferences: the buffalo, zebra, wildebeest and Thomson's gazelle are almost grazers; while giraffe, kudu, bushbuck and black rhinoceros are entirely browsers. Other mixed feeder species (consuming grass and shrubs) include impala, reedbuck, and sable and roan antelopes.

Different wildlife species are limited to particular vegetation types

[6]C. Lado, Agricultural and environmental knowledge: a case study of peasant farming in Maridi District, Southern Sudan', *Malaysian Journal of Tropical Geography*, Vol 13, 1986, pp 7–36.
[7]C.A. Petrides, *Kenya's Wildlife Resource and the National Parks*, Trustees of the Royal National Parks of Kenya, Nairobi, 1955.

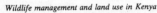

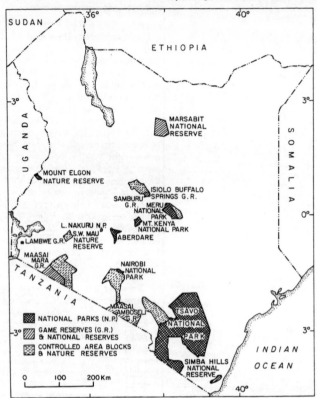

Figure 2. National parks and reserves in Kenya.

Sources: Survey of Kenya, Kenya hunting map, series SK 57B, Ed 1, 1988; Survey of Kenya, Game Policy Committee Map of Kenya, 1988.

such as bushland, savanna and grassland and forest which provide the food and other resources for survival. The dry thorn scrub vegetation in the southeastern part of the country supports elephants, black rhinoceros, impala, oryx, lesser kudu, Grants gazelle and gerenuk. The savanna and grassland is the most productive and supports large herds of zebra, wildebeest, kongoni, topi, gazelles, antelope and giraffe. The forest areas including montane provide habitats for rare bongo and hog, mountain reedbuck, duikers and monkeys.

With the exception of coastal zones and a few other small pockets of high density (including urban centres), the rest of the country is sparsely populated.

Before wildlife came to be viewed as a valuable but endangered natural resource, an unstable but mutually beneficial ecological balance was maintained between indigenous land users and the fauna. Each group helped to prevent the demographic expansion of the other beyond what the physical environment could support. Since the animals' most immediate human competitors lived in scattered and periodic mobile settlements – practising shifting cultivation and semi-nomadic pastoralism at the marginal levels of technology, productivity and ecological disturbance – there has always been room for wildlife movement in the sparsely populated bushland, forests, and dense bush amidst cultivated savanna grasslands shared with the pastoralists' livestock.

The complex problem of land use conflict in Kenya involves land use, land pressure, migration, allocation and other spatially expressed phenomena. It is hardly possible to view the question of land competition without a continuous reference to the political circumstances in a country whose very independence was, to some extent, the result of a crisis over land. Indeed, agricultural land use and game protection and management have long been reciprocal political problems in those African countries with relatively large wildlife populations.[8]

This generates the difficult question of whether the issues raised can be related to some fundamental conceptual constructs in geography in general and 'ecodevelopment' in particular. In fact, Hartshone proposed that political geographers adopt a more functional approach to their problem solving.[9] However, this suggestion lacked a mechanism to include the relevant evolutionary qualities of a functional political region. Jones's field theory model in political geography has wider application in other disciplines.[10]

Within this context, this article outlines the historical forces characterizing the land question as it relates to wildlife conservation. The functional analysis of Kenya's wildlife conservation system, with emphasis on spatial ramifications, is also noted. For a variety of reasons, the administration of wildlife areas is a relatively difficult issue in Kenya; areas set aside for total protection adjoin others where hunting may take place, and hence animals migrate without regard for human boundaries and other socioeconomic priorities and perceptions.

Poaching affects many of Kenya's animals, and the system can only partially cope with it. Destruction of wildlife habitats by squatters penetrating the wilderness poses yet another threat. Superimposed upon this are uncertainties about the appropriateness of population control policies applied to wild animals. Indeed, even the numbers, distribution and migration patterns of some species are uncertain.

In Kenya, land use conflict is the most serious long-term threat to the future of wildlife. More specifically, a set of critical policy problems centred on past agricultural land use practices, wildlife management and conservation, and carrying-capacity crisis are examined.

[8]S.S. Ajayi, 'Wildlife as a source of protein in Nigeria', *Nigerian Field*, Vol 36, 1971, pp 115–127; M.A. Novicki, 'Tourism with a socialist slant', *African Report*, Vol 28, 1983, pp 49–53.
[9]R. Hartshone, 'The functional approach in political geography', *Annals of the Association of American Geographers*, Vol XL, No 2, June 1981, pp 95–130.
[10]S.B. Jones, 'A unified field theory of political geography', *Annals of the Association of American Geographers*, Vol XLIV, 1954, pp 11–23.
[11]R.M.A. Zwanenberg and A. King, *An Economic History of Kenya and Uganda, 1800–1979*, Macmillan, London, UK, 1975; T. Kanogo, *Squatters and the Roots of Mau Mau*, Heinemann, Nairobi, Kenya, 1987.
[12]A. Segal, 'The politics of land in East Africa', *Africa Report*, Vol XII, 1967, pp 46–50.

Colonial land use and wildlife conservation policies in East Africa

The East African states of Kenya, Tanzania and Uganda have reorganized their political structures and economies to reflect new aspirations, perceptions, values and socioeconomic objectives. These nations also have chosen individual directions designed to meet their differing needs and socioeconomic development issues, mainly centred on land policies and ownership. A body of laws and attitudes reflecting European and African objectives have been instituted.

In Kenya the land issue helped to provoke the Mau Mau revolt of the 1950s, thus witnessing the end of racial restrictions on land ownership.[11] In the relatively fertile and productive White Highlands, European estates were vacated and available for African use. Before independence, a successful programme of land reform and consolidation was in progress, and today the country's hopes for agricultural development rest upon a large and productive base of African smallholders.[12]

Rural Planning and Management

Indeed, it was land that drew European settlers to the region, and hence land policies and grievances became the central political issue during the colonial period.[13] It is not surprising that land was a major theme of African politics as the colonial period drew to a close, and the hopes of landless and hungry people were sometimes falsely raised that independence would lead to an immediate solution to existing land problems. Unsympathetic outsiders predicted the reversion of rich and commercially productive Kenya White Highlands to subsistence agriculture, and the destruction of East Africa's magnificent wildlife heritage by the encroachment of local people and their livestock.

Since independence the pressures for farmland, hunting and poaching, and the impact of pastoralism on fragile grasslands, have been severe and damaging. But the administrators have instead strengthened conservation policies, and faced issues which the colonial officials conveniently ignored. In fact, tourism has undergone rapid growth and the East African governments have recognized the great value of wildlife heritage and its conservation strategies. Thus political, socioeconomic and capital investments on the construction of game lodges, roads and park fences have to be made. The encroachment on wildlife reserves has been restricted by force, squatters have been evicted, and poaching and illegal hunting laws made much tighter than during the colonial period.

The emergence of Kenya as an independent state in 1963, with nearly 20% of its territory set aside as wildlife conservation areas, produced two sets of boundary and territorial problems – local and external. The complex origins of Kenya's national parks and game reserves, the decisions that defined and delimited them, their frequent revisions, the disruption of established migration patterns and creation of new ones, and the continuing spatial adjustments resulting from these circumstances will now be examined.

The conservation idea in East Africa received its first official expression in the British East Africa Company's Sporting Licences Regulation of 5 September 1884, which proposed hunting restrictions and regulated the number of kills that might be made on each licence.[14] The first wildlife sanctuaries in East Africa were created in Tanzania. There were two large wildlife conservation areas in German East Africa by late 1896.[15] Figure 3 shows the Northern Reserve extending from the Maasai Steppe south of Mount Kilimanjaro to the present-day Serengeti; and the Southern Reserve coinciding mainly with the Selous Game Reserve.

In British East Africa, it was proposed that 'large wild game preserve areas' should be created and that there should be closed seasons on all species and additional reserves where hunting of any kind would not be permitted.[16] These early conservation ideas demonstrated the lack of knowledge regarding space requirements of truly viable ecological units. More importantly, they showed an apparent lack of concern for the African peoples whose lands were considered for the establishment of wildlife sanctuaries. The complex patterns of natural resource utilization practised by the local populations were not adequately understood and were singled out for eradication.

From idea to decision: the 1900 London Convention

In response to growing concern over the destruction of wildlife in Africa, an international conference was convened in London in 1900

[13]C.G. Rosberg, Jr, and J. Nottingham, *The Myth of Mau Mau: Nationalism in Kenya*, Praeger, New York, NY, USA, 1966; Kanogo, *op cit*, Ref 11.
[14]Korir-Koech, *op cit*, Ref 3.
[15]J.P.B.M. Ouma, *Evolution of Tourism in East Africa*, East African Literature Bureau, Nairobi, Kenya, 1970.
[16]H.J. De Blij, *A Geography of Sub-Saharan Africa*, Rand McNally, Chicago, IL, USA, 1964.

Wildlife management and land use in Kenya

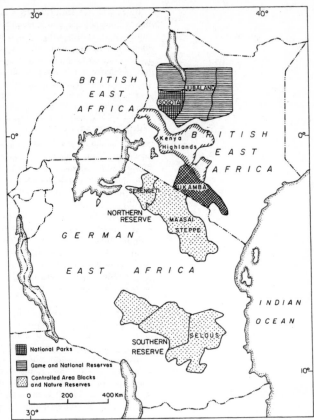

Figure 3. Early wildlife sanctuaries in East Africa.

Sources: For British East Africa: *Parliamentary Papers*, Vol LXXIX, 1906 (*Africa*, No 58), Command 3189, p 39; for German East Africa, *ibid*, pp 2–3 and 34–36.
Note: The modern boundary framework is superimposed for reference.

attended by representatives of the colonial powers with African dependencies. This led directly to the consolidation of a game reserve, and definition and delimitation of others in British East Africa. The newly consolidated reserve included Kenia District of Ukamba Province incorporating a large part of the Akamba and Maasai land (see Figure 3).

The newly delimited conservation areas included Northern Reserve as an extension of the Sogota Reserve unofficially and without sanction.[17] New sanctuaries were also created in the Aberdare and Mount Kenya areas north of Nairobi. The decisions leading to the establishment of conservation areas in East Africa were not often based on an adequate knowledge of the local people and their perceptions. The advice of other Europeans in Kenya was sometimes ignored, leading to conservation problems.

Creation of game sanctuaries led to such consequences as the interference in local hunting rights on 'traditional' grounds and the dividing of settlements by lines demarcated on the ground, and these led

[17]R.F. Dasmann, *African Game Ranching*, Macmillan, New York, NY, USA, 1964.

176

to the revision of the whole conservation idea. While complete protection of wildlife could be achieved in some reserves, other areas existed where wildlife would have to share the land with the local people. Thus the concept of a hierarchy of conservation areas emerged and became a cornerstone of wildlife preservation in East Africa. Consequently Kenya currently has three basic categories of wildlife reserves: the national parks, game reserves and game controlled areas (see Figure 2).[18]

Wildlife conservation decision and movement

Kenya's population is concentrated in the southwestern part of the country, the core area of which stretches north and northwest from Nairobi to Lake Victoria.[19] When the Europeans first penetrated the interior of the country, the Kikuyu dominated the White Highlands, while the Maasai grazed their livestock over wide areas in the south of the country. When the wildlife conservation decisions were implemented, the Maasai realized that they were occupying an area of great interest to the Europeans. The Maasai were not hunters and, although they compete with wildlife for grazing and water, they have never been directly responsible for the large-scale destruction of wild game. With the decision to establish National Reserves, it seemed to the Maasai that further encroachments were being made upon their already shrunken domain.[20]

The political overtones of the conservation issue were prominent during the colonial administration in Kenya. In a country with several ethnic groups and sociocultural diversity, the government cannot impose conservation decisions on one group without arousing the fears of others, arguments about the 'national interest' notwithstanding.

Although the Maasai have been subjected to intense criticism for their failures in the Amboseli Reserve, they have not been alone in their opposition to government conservation policies. The pastoral Samburu, for example, grazed their livestock on the dry rangelands between the northen edge of the Kenya White Highlands and the southern end of Lake Turkana. They objected to the establishment of the national park on their grazing land and the Game Department observed that too strong pressure on the issue might endanger future conservation efforts in the area.[21]

Decisions on the conservation issue have produced other consequences, all with direct or indirect political implications, some of which involved the tourism industry in Kenya. The overwhelming majority of the hotels and other tourist-oriented enterprises were mainly owned and managed by non-Africans, thus leading to the argument that dependence on the above industry leads to status-quo politics.[22] The socioeconomic impact of the tourist industry is evident in the rapid development of Nairobi, where luxurious hotels and travel and safari offices reflect the large number of international visitors. Outside Nairobi the impact of tourism, though less obvious, is felt almost everywhere. The national parks and game reserves alone have an increasing number of foreign tourists.

The wildlife conservation areas in colonial and post-colonial Kenya constitute a relatively large part of the country, and their establishment and maintenance have involved a substantial number of people and institutions with several consequent problems.

[18]Kenya, Colony and Protectorate, *A Game Policy for Kenya*, Sessional Paper No 1 1959/60, Government Printer, Nairobi, Kenya, 1959.
[19]J.J.D. Fair, 'A regional approach to economic development in Kenya', *South African Geographical Journal*, Vol XLV, 1963, pp 55–77.
[20]I. Sindiga, 'European perceptions as a factor in degrading Maasai ecology', unpublished MA thesis, Ohio University, USA, 1981.
[21]Kenya, Colony and Protectorate, *Game Department Annual Reports, 1956–1961*, Government Printer, Nairobi, Kenya, 1982.
[22]Ouma, *op cit*, Ref 15.

Problems with colonial wildlife conservation and management

In Africa the optimal utilization and conservation of wildlife resources directly relates to planning, organization and control processes. Where the exploitation of such resources has gone unchecked or with inadequate control, their expendability was soon reflected by growing lists of extinct animal species. Notwithstanding the richly varied flora and fauna of Kenya, effective conservation practices did not feature until after the second world war.[23] Efforts in this direction had been piecemeal since the establishment of the first wildlife sanctuaries in the early 20th century. But not until the mid-1940s did a practical and integrated approach for large-scale wildlife protection emerge.

The first movement towards a reorganization of wildlife conservation in Kenya was the convening in 1939 of the Game Policy Committee, charged with making recommendations to the government in regard to the establishment of parks and wildlife sanctuaries. However, these deliberations were interrupted by the war, and the Committee was only able to submit a brief interim report in 1942 on the legislation enacted to institute national parks, particularly that the area near Nairobi and Tsavo in the south be made desirable park sites. In 1946 the second interim report was published, and the reorganization of the country's wildlife conservation system developed.

The Game Policy Committee also recommended that 'Park Adjuncts' be created in areas unsuitable for national parks which were administered by National Board of Trustees with complete powers for the management of parkland. The Committee, however, noted that there were some areas of outstanding biological and scenic interest and attraction which should be protected. But permanent human rights precluded the exercise of authority inherent in national parks administration.

The 'Park Adjuncts' created were known as national reserves, and included Amboseli, Mara and Marsabit (see Figure 3). Smaller national reserves, including Ngong Hills near Nairobi, Western Chyulu area, and along the road and railway rights-of-way through Tsavo National Park, were also established.

Initially, there were difficulties with the national reserve idea and it soon became evident that conflicts between human and wildlife conservation and management objectives were inevitable. The National Parks Board of Trustees observed that it could not implement the type of management programmes vital in these areas without some human interference and interests leading to land use conflict.

Such conflicts were particularly severe in the Amboseli Reserve characterized by competition between wildlife and Maasai livestock. To involve the people in the wildlife conservation efforts, local authorities were thus encouraged to assume full responsibility in areas of high faunal interest through the creation of African District Council Game Reserves. In the new reserves, wildlife would still be managed by the Game Department and the Council assumed all other regulations pertaining to the socioeconomic activities.

Problems with post-colonial wildlife conservation and management

Kenya's wildlife conservation areas today are generally meeting their

[23]Kenya, Colony and Protectorate, *Second Interim Report of the Game Policy Committee*, Government Printer, Nairobi, Kenya, 1946.

Wildlife management and land use in Kenya

preservation and management objectives, and have thus become an important economic asset and foreign exchange earner. The economic significance of wildlife-based tourism has prompted the government to support the development and expansion of tourists' infrastructural amenities, especially in the parks and game reserves or sanctuaries. It also encouraged the creation of management institutions dealing with land use regulations to ensure the preservation of valuable areas with wildlife resources. However, there are still serious constraints facing the wildlife conservation and management system in Kenya, as outlined below.

Management problems and conflicts

There are two categories of wildlife conservation problems in Kenya. One of these is of a management nature, including the problems of ecological requirements of game populations, and the necessity to manipulate the environment to achieve as nearly 'natural' conditions as are possible within the confines of game sanctuaries, and those produced by the environmental impact of increasing numbers of visitors in the wildlife viewing areas. The second group of constraints includes conflicts between human and wildlife interests, particularly in areas within or adjacent to game sanctuaries, such as the impact of agricultural land use in pastoral and arable areas.

Management problems involving primarily ecological considerations are particularly well illustrated by the long-standing controversy about the Tsavo elephant population. The Tsavo National Park (see Figure 2) has been subject to large-scale destruction of woody vegetation by the increasing elephant population since the 1960s, and much concern had been expressed in relation to the possible elephant overpopulation.[24]

In fact, conservationists maintained and emphasized that without a sensitive land use programme for animal–habitat interaction, ecological destruction is inevitable.[25] This has already occurred in Tsavo National Park, as confined and expanding elephant populations have transformed a balanced ecosystem into a near desert.[26]

Another significant management problem is the impact of tourism and visitor accommodation on wildlife conservation areas. The increasing numbers of game-viewing tourists have had a deleterious effect on some national parks and game reserves, particularly in Nairobi, Amboseli and along the coastal areas of the country. In the Amboseli Reserve, automobile traffic is accentuating an already serious erosion problem; numerous car tracks accelerate the loss of already very sparse vegetation cover and therefore the erosion process.

Some road improvements have been made, but no effective remedy to the problem of auto-induced erosion had been implemented. Although the problems of visitor impact have not yet become as serious elsewhere as they are in Amboseli, it is likely that many other wildlife areas will begin to suffer from visitor-related disturbance. Visitor accommodation should be sited on the periphery of wildlife conservation areas to reduce the impact of elaborate infrastructural facilities for tourists and management staff.

Conflicting objectives of wildlife conservation and economics

There can be little doubt that the above management policies would have beneficial effects on the natural environments of wildlife conservation areas. But are these policies feasible? Is it possible to place

[24]Ouma, *op cit*, Ref 15.
[25]A.R.E. Sinclair, 'Dynamics of Serengeti ecosystem: process and pattern', in A.R.E. Sinclair and M. Norton-Griffiths, eds, *Serengeti: The Dynamics of an Ecosystem*, University of Chicago Press, Chicago, IL, USA, 1979, pp 180–230.
[26]Ouma, *op cit*, Ref 15.

limitations on the number of visitors entering national parks and game reserves in view of the understandable desire of the private investors and government to maximize the economic benefits accruing from wildlife conservation areas?

In effect, the necessity that wildlife conservation areas produce substantial economic returns to justify their continued existence poses a dilemma to management staff. The objectives of wildlife conservation and economic development are not completely compatible because management plans designed to achieve maximum benefits yield less than maximum economic gains, and management aiming to maximize economic returns will inevitably minimize conservation benefits.[27]

The question of where to locate visitor accommodation is a relatively good case in point. The location of all types of accommodation outside wildlife areas would be an ideal solution from the conservation viewpoint, reducing the impact from day visitors in cars.

However, the vital questions posed relate to whether tourists would accept such accommodation and, more importantly perhaps, whether investors (including government development corporations) would risk capital in the construction of game-oriented hotels and lodges outside the wildlife areas, when more economical and attractive alternatives exist within them. In effect, as tourist pressure increases, there could be a shift in priorities towards visitor limitation and conservation objectives. Such a shift would involve economic sacrifice, requiring difficult decisions from policy makers and planners.

Conflict between human and wildlife interests

Management problems involving basic conflicts between human and wildlife interests are difficult to resolve. For instance, the desire of a poacher for game meat or rhinoceros horn for sale leads to conflicting goals. Farmers need to clear new land for cultivation and protect their crops from the depredations of wild animals. Pastoralists want to see their livestock increase and are not eager to share scarce pastures and water with wild grazing animals.

Game utilization for meat has been the most valuable resource for peasant farmers although it has not been acknowledged by the government due to lack of vital information on the extent of its use and dietary importance. In fact, hunting within the parks and reserves (except that undertaken by the Game Department) has been anathema in the past, but culling might be more successfully achieved if the local people realize and appreciate the value of wildlife conservation.

Poaching or illegal hunting is probably the most widely known human–animal conflict. The direct destruction of animals produces strong public concern and reaction. Unregulated wildlife hunting is important in the reduction of some animal populations.[28] Controlled hunting can replace natural mortality, thus keeping animal populations from increasing beyond the capacity of the environment supporting them.[29]

Illegal hunting is a problem because its pressure cannot be controlled and inflicts serious damage on wildlife populations, and results in complete destruction of species with high trophy values (eg elephants for ivory, rhinoceros for horn and leopard for skin).

The most serious long-term threat to the future of wildlife populations in Kenya is due to the indirect effects on habitat resource destruction or alteration. The habitat requirements of wildlife species vary. Alteration

[27]H.F. Lamprey, 'Ecological separation of the large mammal species in the Tirangire Game Reserve, Tanganyika', *East African Wildlife Journal*, Vol 1, 1963, pp 63–92.
[28]Novicki, *op cit*, Ref 8.
[29]Dasmann, *op cit*, Ref 17; G. Matzke, *Wildlife in Tanzania Settlement Policy: the Case of the Selous*, Mazwell School of Citizenship and Public Affairs, Syracuse University, New York, NY, USA, 1977; R.C. Bigalke, 'Technological problems associated with the utilization of wild animals', *Third World Conference on Animal Production*, Sydney, Australia, 1973, pp 336–346; and J.D. Skinner, 'Technological aspects of domestication and harvesting of certain species of game in South Africa', *Third World Conference on Animal Production*, Sydney, Australia, 1973, pp 119–125.

in the habitat effects changes, either quantitative or qualitative, to the vegetation which in turn affects the capacity of the habitat to support wildlife.

In fact, any change in vegetation may lower or increase the carrying capacity for one species, making the habitat unsuitable for another. Thus vegetation inevitably produces other changes in the composition and density of wildlife populations.[30] The ultimate solution to the problems produced by conflicting objectives and interests probably lies in education and changes in people's values and perceptions of the importance of wildlife.

Agricultural land use and game control

Man is the most significant agent of habitat alteration through effects on vegetation. The impact of agricultural activity is not a new phenomenon in Kenya. Arable farming produces severe alterations of natural ecological systems, involving the removal of natural vegetation cover and the substitution of a few domesticated plants for the original large variety of wild species.

Pastoral agricultural activity and domestic grazing animals (with their specific food preferences) can produce changes in the species composition of grassland vegetation.[31] Other human activities such as the gathering of firewood and wild plants (for food or other uses) may, over a considerable time, have a significant impact on vegetation.[32] Charcoal-making can remove a substantial proportion of trees and larger shrubs in an area in a relatively short time.

As people and their livestock use more land, wildlife habitats degenerate and disappear. There are several areas in Kenya where human use of the land conflicts with the goals of wildlife conservation especially in the pastoral areas due to overstocking and overgrazing of domestic animals leading to deterioration of the range. With the introduction of veterinary services the mortality rates have been drastically reduced, and large livestock numbers became a major concern because of the failure to limit them. The lowering of the land and range carrying capacity for wildlife and domestic livestock is best exemplified by the problems of Amboseli Game Reserve.

The use of land for arable farming produces a severe and long-lasting impact upon wildlife populations. The high human population densities characteristic of many agricultural settlement schemes produce unfavourable conditions for the survival of larger game animals incompatible with agriculture; and in the heavily populated areas of the central highlands and western Kenya large game has been exterminated or reduced to a small proportion in the few remaining patches of natural vegetation cover. Where farming land borders game concentration areas, conflict is direct and often violent. Wildlife destruction of crops is a major problem in many areas and serious injuries and deaths caused by wild animals are common.

The increasing conflict between the human population and wildlife may be attributed to the rapid expansion of agricultural settlement schemes in which, after independence, tens of thousands of people were resettled on new lands often in close proximity to areas of abundant wildlife. The movement of agricultural pioneers into marginal areas is increasingly common. More people are abandoning uneconomic land-holdings and seeking subsistence in the urban centres as wage labourers. The migrants to the arid and semi-arid lands or fringes represent a new

[30]Dasmann, *op cit*, Ref 17.
[31]Ajayi, *op cit*, Ref 8.
[32]W.T.W. Morgan, 'The ethnobotany of the Turkana: use of plants by a pastoral people and their livestock in Kenya', *Economic Botany*, Vol 35, 1981, pp 96–130; and Lado, *op cit*, Ref 6.

and potentially serious threat to Kenya's wildlife resources. The arid bushlands, long the most secure refuge for the nation's wildlife, are coming under serious pressure and threat.

In this context the government has been a major force in utilizing wildlife areas for economic purposes, mainly in the form of tourism. Future policy projections favour the economic development of these areas. This is evident in the recent formation of the Ministry of Reclamation and Development of Arid, Semi-Arid and Wastelands. Politically it is unrealistic to expect the large land masses under national parks and game reserves to maintain their current status when the 'traditional' institutions and sociocultural values do not accept landlessness.

The challenge is to find ways of using the land which benefit the local population, thereby minimizing the potential for encroachment. The separation of wildlife areas from adjacent human settlements provides a solution to conservation and management problems, thus reducing the necessity of destroying relatively large numbers of animals and offering a better attainment of objectives and interests for both humans and wildlife.

Conclusion and policy implications

This article has examined the condition of wildlife in Kenya. The political entity of Kenya has developed as a result of many ideas and decisions, but within the state wildlife conservation areas are expansive enough (involving a sufficient number of people), emerging from a concentrated set of decisions over a long period, to constitute a political arena in their own right. They are represented in Nairobi by their own administrative staff and policed by the Game Department. The boundaries of conservation areas are more than merely administrative; their resources represent one thing to the state, and yet another to the local people living in or near them.

The problems of contemporary wildlife conservation emanate from several conditions, including a variety of organizations and interest groups controlling conservation areas, and in the late emergence of a full-scale conservation effort.

Many government interests have been motivated by a mounting concern for the protection and conservation of wildlife which is being threatened by economic activities and expanding human populations. The most pressing problems relate to land use and human–animal conflict. In pastoral areas in the south of the country, overstocking of domestic animals has been a persistent problem, and the growing conflict between farmers and wildlife is reflected in the high levels of control shooting necessary to protect human life and property in the agricultural areas. Outside the reserves, where wildlife conservation is not a primary objective, and in the game reserves in which human interests take precedence, future land use determines the fate of wildlife.

Although national parks appear to be secure, adjacent lands may also suffer from intensive agricultural land use. In the central highlands, mountain parks, Aberdare and Mount Kenya, which are being threatened and encircled by farming settlements, barriers have had to be erected to separate the human and animal populations. In fact, much of Kenya's remaining wildlife occupies lands that have long been considered marginal and unsuitable for agriculture. But in recent years these lands have been invaded by land-hungry farmers, thus presenting potential threats to the survival of wildlife. Indeed, the long-settled areas of central and western Kenya are even now unable to fully support their burgeoning agricultural populations, as evidenced by the high rates of migration.[33]

These trends carry some implications for agricultural land use and wildlife conservation and management. There is a need for a viable wildlife policy involving a technically and financially subsidized agricultural intensification which reduces population pressure on conservation areas so that tourism can easily be promoted.

The magnitude of the effort to transform 'traditional' agriculture in Kenya suggests that outside assistance may be necessary to provide the technical and financial resources needed for the development programme. Conservation agencies should assist in the development process by reassessing their priorities and directing attention or efforts towards the solution of basic conservation problems and human population growth and its impact. Beyond compensation for any wildlife damage, conservation approaches must respond to the changing needs of society. Conservation must therefore not be considered as a static science seeking only to preserve, but should be dynamic.

A more practical strategy for wildlife protection must accommodate the involvement of local people and other land uses on the boundaries of protected areas. This would transform the sanctuaries into a large ecosystem rather than 'conservation islands'.[34] Rarely can wildlife parks be established so as to include an entire ecosystem, especially in regard to the year-round needs of migratory species. To establish and develop parks without the management of the surrounding land will lead to management problems for the animals and the area. Unless these seasonal habitats of migratory species in the parks are controlled and protected from unnecessary fencing, overgrazing and unplanned cultivation, the herds are likely to be decimated and the migrations hindered or stopped.

Park management must therefore be coordinated with the use of the surrounding lands. The wildlife park must also be culturally and economically valuable to the local people if it is to be a permanent institution, since one of the threats to the park concept is opposition from local people. Harmony would be restored by involving the people directly in management and conservation; livestock and wildlife populations would also be controlled.

Through the District Focus for Rural Development Strategy, the public has an opportunity to help develop management strategies for conservation areas and the surrounding lands. Their participation can be achieved through cooperative societies such as group ranches, local councils and development committees, and ministries dealing with agriculture, livestock, environment, lands, energy, arid and semi-arid areas and regional development.

Protected areas surrounding parks should include locations for intensely developed tourist lodges and associated facilities. Restricted local grazing would be allowed by permit only. Roads would be of a higher standard, and airstrips would be permitted near the lodges. These areas would allow grazing and hunting by the local people, and lodges and game viewing for tourists.

Wildlife management would involve harvesting animals on a sus-

[33]S.H. Ominde, *Land and Population Movements in Kenya*, Heinemann, Nairobi, Kenya, 1968.
[34]W.J. Lusigi, 'Alternative strategies and approaches for the conservation of African wildlife', *Environmental Awareness*, Vol 10, No 1, 1987, pp 60–66.

tained basis, both for sale of meat and hides and to control the herds migrating in and out of the park. Live capture of animals for sale would also be used to control the population, while prescribed burning and water development programmes would be introduced to maintain increases in the carrying capacity of the ranges. The objective would be the preservation of a wildlife ecosystem and unique scenic areas including tourism and game viewing. Only those roads necessary for management and minimum tourist use should be established, and population increase among pastoral peoples should be controlled.

Public participation in wildlife conservation and revenue sharing should be encouraged. Education, research in wildlife utilization, multiple institutional management systems and economic incentives are necessary in bringing about this process. Actual projects in game cropping and sale of subsidized game meat to local communities as in Tanzania, Zimbabwe and Botswana should be established, and the Kenya Wildlife Service could coordinate these projects as a component of wildlife conservation and management. The current wildlife management strategies need to be closely examined to identify ways and means that would guarantee sustainable wildlife conservation.

C
Forestry

[23]

Pergamon

S0264-8377(96)00015-4

Land Use Policy, Vol. 14, No. 1, pp. 55–73, 1997
Copyright © 1996 Elsevier Science Ltd
Printed in Great Britain. All rights reserved
0264-8377/97 $17.00 + 0.00

The role of forestry in meeting planning objectives

Paul Selman

Forestry policy increasingly aims to secure multiple benefits from new and existing plantations or woodlands. This implies that forestry policy needs to become harmonized with wider land use
policy. One means for achieving this is
through the planning system, although it
is commonly the case that forestry operations are exempt from planning control.
This creates a situation in which planning
authorities must use a variety of imaginative measures in order to influence the
future pattern and condition of forest
resources. The present study indicates
that there is a widespread recognition
amongst planning authorities in Britain
of the ways in which forests and woodlands can help contribute to the fulfil-
ment of many environmental and
socioeconomic objectives. Indeed, development plans already contain numerous relevant policies. However, there are
several key issues on which planners can
only exercise indirect influence, and
these are commonly approached by indicative planning, advisory references to
management, and cautious use of planning 'gain'. It is suggested that there is
considerable scope for further official
guidance on the opportunities for positive influence by planners on the development of forests and woodlands.
Copyright © 1996 Elsevier Science Ltd

The author is from the Countryside and
Community Research Unit, Cheltenham and
Gloucester College of Higher Education,
Swindon Road, Cheltenham GL50 4AZ, UK
(Tel: 01242 543313; fax: 01242 532997;
e-mail: pselman@chelt.ac.uk).

This research project took place under contract to the Forestry Commission. The author
gratefully acknowledges the sponsors' permission to publish this paper.

continued on page 56

The condition of forests has become a major issue in the pursuit of
sustainable development. The exploitation of moist tropical forests, the
damage inflicted on northern coniferous forests by industrial pollutants,
and the attrition of temperate hardwoods have emerged as salient topics of
concern. The Earth Summit[1] produced, as one of its principal outputs, a
Statement of Forest Principles[2] which set standards for the sustainable
management of all types of forest. This Statement has been pursued at
various other geographical levels. For example, the Helsinki Conference[3]
established a set of guidelines which related the Rio Statement to
European forests. Countries attending the conference committed themselves to implementing these guidelines, both to ensure sustainable management of the timber resource and to conserve levels of biodiversity. In
the United Kingdom, the Government has published its Programme for
Sustainable Forestry (HM Government, 1994), which affirms the variety of
approaches being adopted towards the improved management and further
development of the country's woodland resource.

In addition to the need to sustain levels of timber production, forestry
policy now generally emphasizes the scope for multiple benefits. Forests
are major reservoirs of biodiversity, key touristic and recreational assets,
and core elements in the conservation of soil, water and air quality. Timber
production also supports substantial levels of direct and indirect employment, often in areas where few alternative economic opportunities exist. In
developed countries, the extension of new commercial plantations over
bare ground also raises more sensitive land use issues of safeguarding
existing landscape, wildlife and archaeological assets. In Britain, forestry
policy now aims equally to achieve the sustainable management of existing
woods and forests, and a steady expansion of tree cover to increase a
number of diverse benefits. References to multiple use have featured in
official forestry policy for many years, but it is probably only in the 1990s
that a more equal partnership is being sought between commercial factors
and broader social considerations.[4]

Despite the widespread desire to obtain maximum benefit, however, few
countries seek to govern the location and design of new forests, nor to
compel the management of deteriorating woodland. Forestry is thus
typically separate from the land-use planning system, and is driven

55

predominantly by commercial factors. Perhaps the most distinctive aspect of land use policy is how to promote forests which optimize the public interest, when the public sector has so little control over their location and condition.

This concern for multiple benefits is particularly significant in Britain where, for various reasons, forestry can rarely be justified on investment grounds alone, and must be supported by public money. Through taxation, the public thus supports the activities of the Forest Enterprise,[5] and grant-aids the private sector. Until the late 1980s, support for private landowners and forestry companies came in a combination of planting grant and tax relief, but now is consolidated into a system of grant aid for planting and management. This benefit is administered by the Forestry Authority through the Woodland Grant Scheme (WGS),[6] which provides differential rates of assistance for planting and management operations. Under certain circumstances, third parties will be consulted on, and may raise objections to, the award of planting grant: for example, where planting affects a Site of Special Scientific Interest, the statutory nature conservation organizations must be consulted. This enables the wider public interest to be at least partially represented in forestry activities, especially as most plantations would be economically unviable in the absence of grant aid. However, it is a rather negative and reactive arrangement, and cannot be expected to drive the pursuit of broader benefits, or wholly to represent public interests.

A further notable consideration is that, following the progressive withdrawal of tax benefits since the late 1980s, planting rates in the uplands (the areas of relatively inexpensive and agriculturally deficient land traditionally targeted by forestry companies) have greatly diminished. Thus, in order to meet the targets set by government, foresters have had to explore new opportunities for expansion. These have increasingly been on lower ground closer to towns and cities, where shifts in agricultural policy (occasioned by food surpluses) have facilitated the release of relatively good quality land. Indeed, there are some explicit policies substantially to extend woodland cover in certain peri-urban areas.

Partly as a consequence of revived agricultural fortunes, however, economic conditions facing forestry in these areas are relatively bleak and positive measures may be necessary significantly to increase the extent of sustainable woodland cover. Lorrain-Smith *et al.* (1995) considered the varied circumstances in which new farm woodland planting might take place, and segmented the British countryside into zones possessing different likelihoods of capturing afforestation. It was clear that in many areas where additional woodland cover was most desirable, planting was relatively unlikely, and that planning authorities would have to 'seek ways of dynamic cooperation' if they were to achieve local targets.

Forestry and land use planning

If governments are to be able to influence the design and location of future forests, this presupposes that some kind of regulatory mechanism is available to them. Public agencies must be able both to react to proposals coming forward from the forestry industry, and to influence positively, whether by direct action or influence on private investors, the future pattern of afforestation. The sustainability, biodiversity, appearance, accessibility and environmental impact of forests are clearly matters of public concern, and democratically accountable bodies can reasonably expect their views to be represented.

In Britain, land use change is typically regulated through a mature system of town planning. However, planning controls only apply to land

continued from page 55
[1]UN Conference on Environment and Development *Agenda 21—Action Plan for the Next Century* (1992)
[2]UN Conference on Environment and Development *Non-legally Binding Authoritative Statement of Principles for a Global Consensus on the Management, Conservation and Sustainable Development of all Types of Forests* (UNCED A/CONF.151/6/Rev.1) (1992)
[3]Ministerial Conference on the Protection of European Forests, Helsinki (1993)
[4]Parliament, House of Commons Select Committee *Forestry and the Environment. Volumes I and II, Session 1992–93* HMSO, London (1993)
[5]The Forestry Commission (the Government Department of Forestry) is divided into the Forestry Authority, responsible for policy and other matters, and the Forest Enterprise, which manages the 'state-owned' forest. It is currently proposed that the Forest Enterprise should be privatized.
[6]The Woodland Grant Scheme is the main source of public grant-aid for private forestry. The basic rates may be added to by various supplements, notably for farm woodlands, community woodlands and planting proposals involving native tree species or located within specific project areas.

use and property changes officially defined as 'development', and agricultural and forestry operations are exempted from this official definition. This situation remains controversial as, in many parts of the country, these types of land use change are the most dramatic which occur.

Despite this exclusion, planning authorities have sought to involve themselves in woodland and forestry matters, through various means. In essence, these are threefold. First, when investors apply for grant aid, their applications are often referred to third parties for comment. In many circumstances, the planning authority is an important consultee. Second, in parts of the lowland countryside, several projects have been instigated in order substantially to extend woodland cover, as a means of regenerating landscape, creating employment, providing an alternative use for 'surplus' farmland, and producing a recreational and touristic infrastructure. These projects are often operated by or in conjunction with local government, and may become enmeshed with more general land use planning policies. Third, on important issues of rural land use change, planners have sometimes sought to become involved through the preparation of 'indicative plans'. These, whilst lacking a statutory basis (since the key land use changes are exempt from planning control), seek to indicate preferred patterns of land use change and management. Though they face many problems of implementation, and are a very limited basis on which to challenge powerful landowning interests, they may exert some influence via consultative, grant-aid and bargaining mechanisms. Influencing forestry through the planning system in Britain thus raises generic issues of land use policy which may be transferable to other situations which lie between state control and pure *laissez faire*.

Aims and method

Given that planners have expressed concern at the type and scale of some upland afforestation, yet are often keen to see expansion of mixed woodland in the lowlands, it has been claimed that there is now a natural convergence of interests between the town planning system and multi-benefit forestry. The aims of the present study were thus to:

- find out the present activities of planning authorities with respect to woodland and forestry;
- assess the level of understanding within the planning profession of the use that can be made of forestry and woodlands to meet planning objectives; and
- identify ways of promoting forestry and woodlands to the planning profession as a means of meeting planning objectives.

The approach involved an extensive appraisal of published documents, coupled with a large number of telephone and face-to-face interviews. This was complemented by an analysis of current legislation and guidance relevant to the interface between planning and forestry. As a starting point, information on current practice was sought from planning authorities throughout Britain to establish a comprehensive baseline of information on current practice. This entailed a circularized request for relevant plan policies, as well as supplementary policy guidance and action plans. Some other recent research projects had also gathered similar evidence from a more restricted range of informants, and planning departments which had responded to these earlier requests were not re-approached. However, the information from these projects was available to supplement the present enquiry. Altogether, responses were secured from 10 national parks, 47 county, regional and island councils, and 299 district councils.

This first stage permitted identification of numerous planning departments whose experience was of especial interest. Some of these were selected for closer examination, on the basis of factors such as experience of preparing forestry strategies, location within forestry project areas, and experience of implementing certain types of forestry policy. Additionally, there were several organizations whose complementary knowledge was relevant to the pursuit of multi-benefit forestry or the outreach strategies which the Forestry Commission might adopt towards planning departments. Consequently, a second investigative stage thus entailed 50 telephone interviews and 25 face-to-face interviews (with non-overlapping samples) to enquire more deeply on specific successes and difficulties.

This resulted mainly in textual and qualitative information, which has been analysed by repeatedly distilling plan, policy and interview statements into synopses and bullet points, with progressive re-working to try and identify consistent themes and ensure that no significant responses were omitted. In addition, an expert steering group met periodically to consider drafts and to add further information. Although the various lines of enquiry yielded information on common themes, textual and verbal sources are presented separately, to differentiate between official policy positions and informal opinion.

The land use framework

In Britain, there is very little formal statutory requirement or authorization for planning departments to consider forestry and woodland matters. The primary legislation [Town and Country Planning Act 1990; Town and Country Planning (Scotland) Act 1972] contains a small number of sections which refer to the planting and protection of amenity trees, but these scarcely equate to mainstream forestry and woodland. Of at least equal significance are more general elements contained in the Planning and Compensation Act 1991 which require development plans to be 'development led' and local plans (in England and Wales) to have geographically comprehensive coverage.

In the context of the present study, an important provision in these Acts is that of enabling either the planning authority or the developer to seek a binding agreement to be attached to a planning consent. This can secure development-related benefits which help overcome planning objections to the proposal but which, for legal reasons, cannot be attached as planning conditions. These agreements are officially referred to as planning obligations, but are informally known as planning gain.

Perhaps of greater relevance than the few legislative clauses is the wider framework of statutory advice and guidance, particularly in the form of Planning Policy Guidance Notes (PPGs) and ministerial circulars, which give supplementary direction on the ways in which government expects law and policy to be interpreted. The most comprehensive item of relevance to the present study is a circular on *Indicative Forestry Strategies* (Scottish Development Department, 1990; Department of Environment/Welsh Office, 1992). This emphasizes the role of indicative planning, namely the production of area-based, non-statutory plans which indicate the pattern of land use change which a democratically elected council would wish to see occur within its area.

Although there are some differences between the Scottish and Anglo-Welsh circulars on indicative forestry strategies (IFSs), their content and purpose are essentially similar. Their intention is broadly to distinguish between *preferred areas* for new planting (with land suitable for growing trees and where there are few competing interests), *potential areas* (containing perhaps one serious constraint, which may be overcome by careful design) and *sensitive areas* (where the number, intensity or complexity of issues renders large-scale afforestation generally undesirable). This is based on a sieve-mapping exercise of constraints imposed by suitability of land for tree growth, agricultural land quality, nature and scenic conservation designations, mineral deposits, public recreation, archaeology and water. The output is a 'schematic strategy map' and a 'supporting statement'.

In addition to the IFS circulars, there are several more informal pieces of guidance issued by public agencies. These include statements by the Countryside Commission[7] on matters such as design or the use of woodland in mineral restoration and, in particular, the creation of community forests. Community forests are a joint venture by the Countryside Commission and Forestry Commission to create forest settings for selected major towns. In the English Midlands, the Countryside Commission is also supporting the new 'National Forest', and a similar project exists in central Scotland. Guidance on these new, mainly lowland, forests seeks to induce woodland-related land use change and to ensure that development proposals in general respect the existing or potential forest setting. The planning system is perceived as a major mechanism whereby these objectives can be secured.

Evidence from development plans

Development plans in Britain are formally adopted documents through which local planning authorities seek to establish policy stances in order to regulate those land use changes which are deemed to constitute 'development'. From the early 1970s, they have been divided into structure plans, which address strategic issues of land use change, and local plans, which depict actual parcels of land where specific changes of use are intended within a relatively condensed time period. This has been accompanied by a mainly two-tier system of local government, where counties (in Scotland, regions) have prepared structure plans, and districts have prepared local plans. Latterly, some cities and their surrounding boroughs (including all the boroughs within Greater London) have been given unitary status (i.e. there is a single local authority, rather than a division of responsibilities between county and district). These boroughs prepare unitary development plans. Since this study was conducted, a unitary system of local government has also been introduced in Scotland and Wales, and a less radical local government review is also underway in England. These distinctions become important in interpreting the results of the present study, and in anticipating the ways in which future changes might take place. In addition to this background of change, it should also be noted that development plans have to undergo a lengthy adoption procedure, so that evidence in the present study may reflect local authorities' draft policy position, rather than one which has the formal support of citizens and elected members.

It was evident from the large sample of structure and local plan extracts obtained that policies on trees, woodlands and forestry were widespread in development plans throughout Britain. Figure 1 gives a very broad summary of the nature and frequency of the main types of policy statement. In general, it may be observed that certain concentrations of policy concern arise in different types of authority and parts of the country. The traditional concern for amenity tree preservation, for example, is most evident in district councils, where there is also a significant emphasis on imposing landscape conditions on developers. It is also notable that counties and national parks state a desire to exercise a more strategic influence over the standard of plantation design, particularly in respect of scenic and ecological impacts. This is also pronounced in Scotland, and

[7]A key piece of guidance from the Countryside Commission, which consolidates many of their views on woodland development, was *England's Trees and Woods* (1993); see also Countryside Commission, *The National Forest: The Strategy, CCP 468* The Commission, Cheltenham (1994)

The role of forestry in meeting planning objectives: P Selman

Policy Topic	Counties						Districts							
	SSE	MID	N	SW	WA	SC	SSE	MID	N	SW	WA	SC	MET	NP
Enhancement														
Preservation														
LA planting														
Landscaping														
Native species														
ASNW														
Retention														
Devel. sites														
Management														
Comm. woods														
Comm. forests														
Encouragement														
Strategic siting														
Access														
Creative value														
Derelict land														
WGS consulting														
Scenic impact														
Ecology impact														
Heritage impact														
Farm impact														
Water impact														
Employment														
Diversification														
Green belts														
Felling														

Other policy topics occurring less frequently

- management (sometimes exemplary) of local authority's own woodland estate
- active discouragement of large-scale planting
- impact of forestry operations on rural transport infrastructure
- use of 'voluntary agreements' between interested land use parties
- use of guidance and advice by local authority
- woodlands as performers of environmental functions (e.g. biodiversity, carbon sinks)
- exploration of new woodland markets (e.g. coppice)
- promoting high standards of woodland design
- use of woodland in screening mineral sites
- promoting 'development-led' forestry (mainly in Community Forests)
- oppositing conifers on existing broadleaved sites
- promotion of education/community use of woodlands.

Key

Frequency of occurrence of policy:

1–10%

11.30%

30+%

Geographical Area:

SSE – south, south-east and eastern England
MID – English Midlands
N – north of England
SW – south-west England
WA – Wales
SC – Scotland
MET – metropolitan or London borough
NP – national park authority

(continued opposite)

(Figure 1—continued)

Policy Topic

Enhancement – promoting trees and woodlands in order to enhance existing landscape (either to improve degraded areas or further enrich the quality of scenic areas)
Preservation – protecting existing trees and woodlands, normally by Tree Preservation Orders
LA Planting – intention by the local authority to undertake and finance its own tree planting/woodland establishment programme
Landscaping – requirement on private developers to undertake tree planting in order to landscape development sites
Native species – expression of preference to use native (usually broad-leaved) tree species
ASNW – commitment to protect areas designated as Ancient and Semi-Natural Woodland
Retention – policy commitment to secure the retention of existing woodland sites
Development sites – protection of trees on sites proposed for development
Management – desire (often very generally worded) to ensure good management and maintenance of existing woodlands
Community woodlands – policy commitment to the establishment of community woodlands
Community forests – support for objectives of formally-designated Community Forest
Encouragement – policy commitment to encourage further woodland/forestry planting in the area
Strategic siting – stated preference for new planting to be located in particular areas, or to avoid particular areas
Access – desire to protect existing woodland access (n.b. other policies aimed to protect existing access rights on unplanted land or to create access opportunities by establishing new woodlands)
Creative value – expressed desire to use new woodlands to create additional visual and ecological assets
Derelict land – proposed use of woodland in the reclamation/after-use of derelict land
WGS consulting – policy background against which to comment on WGS applications referred to the Council for comment
Scenic impact – consideration of new forestry proposals in terms of their visual impact
Ecology impact – consideration of effect of forestry proposals on areas of ecological importance, notably Sites of Special Scientific Interest
Heritage impact – consideration of effect of forestry proposals on areas of historic or archaeological interest
Farm impact – consideration of effect of new forestry on the viability of farming enterprises (especially in marginal upland areas with limited resources of productive land)
Water impact – consideration of effects of forestry proposals on water catchment
Employment – likelihood of future forestry creating direct and indirect employment
Diversification – potential of new woodland planting to contribute to farm enterprise diversification
Green belts – role of woodland in reinforcing and benefiting green belt
Felling – expressed concern over clearfelling, or more general desire to be consulted over felling proposals

Figure 1. Frequency and distribution of types of development plan policy on woodland and forestry.

reflects not only the historical controversy over large-scale planting, but also the advanced state of IFS production. Many planning authorities explicitly state the desirability of retaining existing woodland, and it is also noteworthy how many policies seek to secure good management of woodlands (though this is outside planning control) and, perhaps contrary to the popular image, generally encourage new planting. Especially in counties and national parks, planners state a desire to influence the location of new planting, yet it frequently occurs that these authorities have made no provision, such as an indicative strategy, to influence location in any systematic sense.

Two other general points emerge. One is the effect of introducing specific designations, notably Ancient Semi-Natural Woodlands (ASNW). Although many planners are weary of additional designations, there is no doubt that they have a positive effect on generating favourable policies. The other is the extent of missed opportunity, instanced by the remarkably few references to the role of woodland in derelict land renewal or green belt reinforcement. Indeed, many plans with generally sound forestry and woodland policies often omitted to state the obvious: examples of under-utilized policies include woodland retention, the use of native species, or a planning authority's position relative to WGS consultations.

The most numerous policies related to traditional matters of tree preservation and aboriculture and thus, whilst of great significance to local amenity, were of marginal relevance to the present study. A slightly broader approach was taken by numerous planning authorities, reflecting a wish to strike a balance between woodland protection and expansion. Thus, what might be thought of as a standard approach included policy statements on matters such as tree protection, reparation of storm damage, amenity planting by the local authority or developers, and encouragement of the use of native species. Less regularly, but still commonly, planners encouraged the promotion of woodlands for public access and recreation (noting the need for continued access following privatization), and the pursuit of local tree-planting projects including community woodlands.

In certain parts of the country, there was still a strong concern to improve the standard of commercial plantations. Here, plan policies reflected a legacy of insensitive designs and the limited public benefits associated with some large-scale schemes. Some of these policies were very comprehensive and sought to achieve:

- integration with other land uses;
- high standards of design, especially in special landscape areas;
- retention and incorporation of existing native trees;
- safeguard of nature conservation, archaeological and historic sites;
- traffic levels on rural roads;
- protection of water catchment interests; and
- retention and provision of sport and recreation opportunities.

A few policies appeared to imply that planners could control or require these features, but this is clearly beyond the law: encouragement, negotiation and support would have been more suitable expressions. Surprisingly few plans took the opportunity to develop a position in relation to second rotation forests, where particular scope often exists to influence the Forest Enterprise's forest design plans.

Most regional authorities in Scotland, and some counties (and occasionally districts) in England and Wales have addressed, or are addressing, issues of location and design by means of an indicative strategy. Within Scotland, these normally adhered to the government circular on indicative forestry strategies, but elsewhere the practice was more variable, and many other types of informal strategy have been produced (Table 1). Only one-fifth of the strategies identified by the research were formal, adopted IFSs, conforming closely to official guidance. These, instead of merely including elaborate development plan policies framed to cope with diverse eventualities, were able to set out more general terms for afforestation in the area, and to facilitate a wider consideration of cumulative impacts. They were also intended to guide, focus and simplify the preparation of environmental impact statements which may be required for major planting proposals.

IFSs are usually linked into the development plan (normally the structure plan of the county or region) via a formal policy, and this can give them greater statutory effect. They identify where the planning authority will typically support or oppose planting proposals, and the kinds of measures which are most likely to render proposals acceptable in particular circumstances. In view of the strategic, subregional nature of IFSs, there is a growing recognition of the desirability of guiding land use change on a more intimate basis in certain sensitive areas.

IFSs tend to focus mainly on new commercial woodland, whereas other types of forestry and woodland strategies target more local issues, especially those of regenerating existing woodland and encouraging farm forestry. For example, the Yorkshire Dales National Park Woodland Strategy aims to create a partnership with farmers and landowners to achieve '. . . a landscape more enriched with woodland, better managed than at present, for a variety of different but compatible objectives, and which will provide the basis for a sustainable, local woodland industry in the future'. This broad distinction is, however, very blurred and both formal and informal strategies may share similar intentions.

Some types of plan policy aim more directly to extend woodland cover and improve the condition of local woodlands, perhaps through direct action by the local authority. Thus, some policies refer to ambitious tree-planting programmes instigated by a council and its partners, and the

The role of forestry in meeting planning objectives: P Selman

Table 1. Examples of types of woodland/forestry strategy identified by the study. (NB. The categories are the author's choices, and not necessarily those of the local authorities.)

Type of strategy	'Official' indicative forestry strategies	'Informal' indicative forestry strategy	Forestry/woodland action plans	Woodland projects/initiatives	Community forest plans	Community woodland strategy	Urban forestry strategy	Local forestry frameworks/agreements
Examples								
Counties, regions	Borders, Central, Clwyd (proposed), Dumfries and Galloway, Grampian, Gwent, Highland, Lancashire, Lothian (proposed), Norfolk (proposed), Staffordshire (draft), Strathclyde, Tayside	Buckinghamshire (Countryside Strategy—Forestry)	Bedfordshire, Buckinghamshire (Plan for the Chilterns), Suffolk (County Forest Strategy)	Buckinghamshire (Woodland Management and Marketing Strategy), Oxfordshire Woodland Project	Cleveland	Gloucestershire		West Cumbria (Woodlands Policy)
Districts, cities, boroughs		Bromley	Erewash (Woodland Strategy), Oldham (draft Woodland Strategy), Rochdale, Wakefield (proposed Woodland Strategy), Wycombe	Amber Valley (East Derbyshire Woodland Project), Rossendale ('New Forest' Strategy)		North Kent, Blackburn, Bradford, Braintree, Burnley, Edinburgh, Glanford, Lancaster, Perth & Kinross, Stirling, Banff & Buchan, Gordon	Edinburgh, Glasgow (in preparation), Middlesbrough, Newnham (corporate tree strategy), Stockport	
Other geographic areas—regions, counties, national parks		Yorkshire Dales		New Forest of Arden (Consultation Draft), Marches (Woodland Initiative), Anglia (Woodland Project), Coed Cymru (Welsh Woodlands)	Central Scotland Forest		Black Country	Exmoor (agreement with Forestry Commission) Campsie-Touch Hills

most complex of these may be supported by an Action Plan designed to identify funding and allocate responsibilities. In some instances, these policies are clearly intended to target scarce resources at the most needy areas, though in one instance a local plan inspector recommended a change to a geographically targeted policy as this was felt to be unfair on other parts of the district. Perhaps surprisingly, given the traditional importance of local authority tree-planting programmes, commitments to implement these were rarely contained in formal policy statements, and this doubtless reflects the increasing financial constraints on local authorities. More frequently, policies sought to stimulate private sector funds for new woodland. Thus, plans are typically underpinned by a diversity of potential mechanisms such as:

- securing new planting in association with development;
- providing guidance and advice on planting and management, including sources of grant aid;
- providing top-up financial assistance;
- liaising closely with the Forestry Commission and other agencies likely to undertake planting, but whose actions are not subject to planning control;
- working with town and parish councils;
- maintaining databases of private woodland in their area;
- undertaking extensive tree planting by the council itself; and
- practising good management techniques on trees in council ownership.

A particular contribution is made by national parks who, in their national park plans[8] include many action statements about woodland planting, management and regeneration. It was also noted that national parks authorities are more favourably placed than local authorities in terms of resources available for countryside work.

Many plan policies refer to the need to manage and maintain existing woodlands, and for many authorities the most pressing issue is that of woodland condition, rather than the extension of forest cover. The inclusion of management policies in development plans is, however, contrary to government guidance.[9] Most policies on woodland condition were thus typically bland, stating only a rather pious desire to promote good practice. Some planning authorities have sought to include woodland management statements in their policies, only for these to fall foul of Department of the Environment (DoE) objections at local plan inquiry. The Department does, however, permit management references in the supplementary statements which support policies. A solution adopted in a few plans has been to include a policy encouraging developers and landowners to prepare woodland management plans, though this would rely heavily on co-operation and goodwill. Alternatively, some policies seek to secure commuted payments from developers (via planning obligations) for the maintenance of existing or new woodland.

In some parts of the country, major new woodland projects are taking place, most notably in areas designated as community forests (these comments apply equally to the new National Forest and Central Scotland Forest). As there is no means of enforcing new afforestation in these areas, land use objectives have to rely entirely on existing mechanisms of advice, persuasion, negotiation and grant aid. The teams responsible for promoting the forests thus clearly have to work closely with the statutory planning system, and community forest plans (non-statutory, zonal plans) dovetail with structure and local plans. Planning authorities generally relish inclusion within these areas, recognizing their potential contribution to environmental regeneration and tourism. Thus, whilst a few plan policies are somewhat lukewarm with regard to the ways in which a community forest

[8]National park plans are plans which set out the management and expenditure programmes for each national park; they are not development plans (in contrast to structure, local and unitary development plans) and can thus include many management prescriptions.

[9]Planning Policy Guidance Note 12, *Development Plans and Regional Planning Guidance*, emphasizes that plan policies should refer only to land use, and not to land management, matters (para 5.6). Management references may, however, be included in the supporting text of policies, subject to considerations of the overall length of the plan.

might complement their normal economic development strategy, most are highly affirmative. Policies typically specify ways in which future development should 'respect the forest setting', either by including extensive tree planting or by itself being a 'forest-related development' (e.g. certain types of leisure facility). However, government guidance and decisions indicate clearly that community forests do not constitute grounds for operating a special planning regime, and thus some policies emphasize that 'normal planning considerations' should not be overridden in the pursuit of development-related woodland planting, especially within green belts. Structure plan policies may be elaborated in local plans by site-specific commitments to establish woodlands within the community forest area, usually on derelict land and usually instigated by the council.

An issue of major significance over the past few years has been the new statutory requirement for plans to lead development. During the 1980s the balance of presumption was tipped firmly in favour of the applicant; now the presumption is that a development proposal should be determined in accordance with the adopted plan. One role of plan policies will thus be to define and secure development leading to the type of woodland which, strategically, is most desirable, rather than that which most opportunistically can be obtained. This has most widely, though not exclusively, been adopted in the community forests. A closely related issue is the use of planning gain. Here, policies can anticipate the situations in which extensive tree planting would typically be sought from an applicant for planning permission, and the composition of planting likely to be most suitable locally. Whilst this would generally be required via conditions, planning obligations would be appropriate where off-site planting was sought, or where legal agreements were needed to secure commuted payments. Planning gain poses complex legal issues, and its use in relation to lowland woodland has been particularly controversial, especially as it might be construed to imply a relaxation of normal planning policies in strictly controlled peri-urban areas. Not surprisingly, very few planning authorities have grasped this particular nettle.

Various policies have sought to secure a wide range of environmental benefits from new and existing woodlands. Collectively, these include:

- enhancement of the green belt environment, in ways which enable the green belt to contribute positively to urban regeneration and provision of local amenities;
- community involvement, particularly by assistance to parish councils and support for community woodlands;
- the role of woodland in derelict land reclamation, or as an after-use on mineral extraction sites;
- the potential of short-rotation coppices as an 'alternative' energy source; and
- the 'carbon sink' function of woodlands, in helping to combat global warming.

Although there is great potential for woodland to contribute to wider environmental objectives, relatively few policies of the above type were encountered.

Finally, in relation to plan policies, it is worth recording how few policies on trees and woodland were formally monitored. Only a handful made specific reference to condition surveys or performance indicators, and those which did typically took superficial measures such as number of trees, or area, planted per annum. These measures are notoriously distorted by landscaping practices such as mass planting in the early stages of establishment. Some interesting draft indices have been proposed for the Central Scotland Forest (Central Scotland Countryside Trust, 1994), and these comprise:

- area of land treated;
- area of new woodland established;
- level of public awareness of the Forest;
- length of footpath created;
- private sector investment in all aspects of the Forest;
- increase in the area of native woodland; and
- area of woodland under productive management.

This list is likely to be too ambitious for most local authorities, but the topic of monitoring must be addressed seriously if policy objectives for woodland are to be evaluated other than purely subjectively.

Evidence from interviews

One of the strongest impressions to emerge from the interviews was a recognition of the common ground between forestry and planning. While the relationship between forestry and planning was at times acrimonious during the 1980s, the two activities are now widely seen to possess a common purpose. Nevertheless, a few interviewees also referred to continuing mutual suspicions: some planners feared a re-emergence of unsympathetically designed forestry whilst some foresters suspected a secret agenda to extend planning controls. The more common view, though, was that forestry and planning shared similar long-term timescales, with a need for a clear vision, transcending the exigencies of short-term political needs. This long-term commitment is at the nub of sustainable development, and provides a firm foundation for joint endeavour. Equally, some respondents observed that, as forestry moves on to the lower ground (and as existing lowland woodlands are extended and rejuvenated), it becomes enmeshed much more inextricably in the general land use bargaining framework, which is the essence of planning. By the same token, development plans were seen to be capable of setting out a broad environmental agenda, including the attraction of a new style of forestry, integrated into the wider land use framework in areas adjacent to major centres of population.

In one community forest (CF), associated with a rapidly expanding urban area, one CF officer spoke of 'growing the town in conjunction with the forest', thus emphasizing the coincidence of interests between the two land uses. Elsewhere, it was noted that:

. . . if you are trying to change the way in which the countryside around towns is managed, you are inevitably drawn into the links between statutory planning and the land management framework of community forest plans. Development is a powerful agent, and you have to be prepared to harness this power. The greatest opportunity for landscape gain is at the point of land use change—the community forest plan can help influence whether this change is for the better or worse (CF officer).

Others, however, were far more cautious about the scope for such an explicit pursuit of landscape gain. One respondent felt that:

. . . a development-led approach can bring some benefits, but you must be careful how you unlock the funding. We need to get away from the 'most expensive scheme' mentality (CF officer).

Similarly, it was argued that:

. . . attempts to link planning too overtly to forestry are ill-founded. My experience is that, if woodland is not owned and managed for direct benefit (e.g. timber production), it will not in the long-term be well managed . . . (County Council Forestry Officer).

Generally, an intermediate stance was taken, with officers viewing the CF plan as a framework within which development proposals could be influenced at the detailed design stage, to maximize their congruity with CF objectives. Thus:

. . . by having a positive attitude towards development, the CF will be able to obtain greater leverage on change and ensure that the CF is an increasingly material consideration (CF officer),

and

. . . when the opportunity arises for the use of the planning system to increase planting, the (Forest Framework Plan) would recognize that certain areas or trees must be kept during development or delivered during development, making sure the best opportunities are taken (CF officer).

The capacity of planning departments to devise and implement tree and woodland policies appeared to vary greatly, particularly in terms of the expertise available to them. Most local authorities have at least one of a landscape architect, arborist, tree officer, forester, or planner/countryside officer with an ecological background. Most authorities considered their existing level of expertise to be adequate in relation to their needs and, indeed, some were impressively staffed, though some admitted to being insufficiently competent in this area. Where this admission was made, it was usually within a reasonably appropriately staffed section, and perhaps reflected an honesty borne of having to make specific decisions, or to cope without a former expert who was not replaced.

Many planning officers said that they would routinely go outside their department or authority for specialist advice. Amongst the further sources of expertise cited were the Forestry Authority, the Tree Council, the county/region council (by districts), community forest (in designated areas), Coed Cymru (in Wales) and other local woodland projects (which the local authority may be helping to fund). It was especially interesting to observe the regular use which was made of community forest and other project teams, beyond their primary functions, as a more general source of advice and expertise. Equally, the reduction of local government to a single tier in Wales and Scotland, and in certain parts of England, may well lead to the loss of specialist expertise which existed in the top tier (county or region) at the time of the survey. One respondent was especially worried about the loss of the strategic view:

. . . We believe that the county is the right scale for forestry strategy. Regional Planning Guidance is too weak. A good policy at the strategic scale is crucial (Non-governmental conservation organisation).

Whilst it is clear that a considerable amount of liaison between planners and forestry interests is taking place, there appeared to be no single model of good practice; indeed, much consultation was *ad hoc*. Co-ordination within local authorities may also be poor, and the periodic reference to 'some else in the department' being 'familiar with published guidance' or 'handling WGS consultations' is probably indicative of the low profile of woodland issues in many planning departments. One consequence of the absence of a forestry strategy is that there tends to be no systematic basis on which planners can respond to WGS consultations, and that, arguably, the responses which planners do make are taken less seriously. There was a general impression that planning authorities were unhappy about the extent to which their comments were taken on board, and over the lack of feedback from the Forestry Authority. One county planning official noted that:

. . . objection to WGS is not to be done lightly, so the County tend only to 'comment'; however, there is no feedback and the impression is that the Forestry Authority are inclined to ignore this.

A national conservation agency had likewise recently undertaken an analysis of WGS consultations in one of its regions, and it appeared that their observations, though detailed and knowledgeable, had had little effect on eventual schemes. Equally, planning authorities perhaps tended to be ignorant of the Forestry Authority's limited scope to require modifications to schemes, especially if consultees do not raise formal and valid objections.

However, there were often very positive and active relations with the regional Forestry Authority Conservancy offices, whilst in some areas local commercial and environmental interests were co-ordinated by a woodland forum. It is also noteworthy that councillors (elected members) were generally sympathetic to, and interested in, woodland matters. Instances where planning committees were hostile, indifferent or unduly deferential to forestry, though occasionally in evidence, were extremely rare.

Quite extensive published guidance is now available to planners on aspects of woodland and forestry. In addition to many publications on tree care and planting, there is well-prepared information on woodland design, recreation, restitution of storm damage, urban woodlands, and woodlands on reclaimed and restored land. Widespread awareness, at least of the existence of this information, was claimed by interviewees, and some respondents were able to name specific documents and comment on their contents. There was a general feeling that advice and guidance were fragmented and could usefully be consolidated, and more than one respondent stated that some kind of 'national forest plan' would have helped them to prepare their own indicative strategy in much less of a vacuum. Some planners found a lack of information in relation to specific local needs, such as recognition of tree diseases and the problems of planting on waste disposal sites.

However, two more general issues were notable. First, there was an unexpectedly wide interest in learning more about local forest economies, particularly their structure, viability, employment potential, and range of downstream activities. Second, whilst there was some dissatisfaction with information on technical matters, there was much more widespread unease about planning policy guidance, which was felt to be ambiguous and unclear. Characteristically, one respondent considered that current guidance was

either too general or too obvious . . . it would be better for guidance to give examples of good practice, containing down to earth information backed up with case studies (Metropolitan Borough Council).

This related especially to the kinds of planning regimes which were permissible in community forests for securing 'development-led' forestry.

In the absence of statutory powers of enforcement, a crucial issue is the implementation of woodland strategies and action plans. Given that the elements of a strategy must mainly be encouraged by financial inducement, the most frequently mentioned issue in relation to implementation was, in one guise or another, that of cost. A strong impression was that local authorities' ability to contribute financially was increasingly constrained, and that reliance would have to be placed essentially on advising landowners about WGS opportunities, though grant aid is itself finite. Nevertheless, there were some impressive examples of proactive local authority pump-priming which resulted in high leverage of supplementary income, and a further glimmer of hope is now offered by the Millennium Fund.

In many areas, great hope is being placed on the expansion and creation of farm woodlands, especially in the land between the uplands and the urban fringe. Here again, finance is seen as a serious obstacle. Several interviewees felt that targeted, additional grants for specific community benefits and a simplified grant structure would assist debt-ridden farmers; the announcement in late 1995 to permit woodland establishment on 'set-aside' farmland is also seen as a major bonus. Several other implementation issues arose, such as, the difficulty of identifying the right people to target, the need to instil a tree planting culture among both farmers and the community at large, and the need to obtain real community involvement in establishing and managing local woodlands. Indeed, one respondent saw the primary aim of their IFS as

. . . to increase community woodlands and to galvanise the community (Scottish District Council).

None the less, whilst local authorities collectively contain a great repository of experience in various aspects of community involvement, there were concerns that this was difficult to achieve at more than a superficial level in relation to woodland creation and management:

. . . few opportunities to give the community a real stake in ownership and management. Systems are too traditional—there is a need for a re-think (Community Forest officer).

There is widespread use of supplementary documentation for forestry and woodland, including indicative strategies, woodland and landscape strategies, community woodland plans, urban forestry strategies and community forest plans. The use of supplementary statements was generally perceived as valuable, especially in the context of pressure to keep development plans concise and to exclude management considerations. They also permit the provision of much more extensive advice on woodland and forestry. Many advantages were cited for IFSs, including:

. . . they can be more technical, and give more detailed information and recommendations (Scottish Region);

. . . give a valuable means of differentiating between statutory and non-statutory aspects . . . a more flexible basis for working and responding (Scottish Region);

. . . able to go into a lot more detail; able to use it as a promotional document (Scottish Region);

. . . a promotional document, trying to sell the county as an area for woodland development (English County);

. . . a good way of getting a County Council—and thus hopefully a democratic "county" view on woodland matters—rather than just the *ad hoc* view of individual officers, as might otherwise happen on consultations (English County).

Several references were also made to the very extensive consultations and public participation which often accompanied IFS production, thus affording a more democratic and representative foundation.

These positive views were not universal, however, and a number of planners felt that policy should be consolidated into a single document, and that only the development plan carried real political weight. Indeed, individual respondents generally had a mixed perception of supplementary planning guidance. Thus, for example, disadvantages included:

. . . possible lack of statutory support . . . (Scottish Region);

. . . find it an advantage to keep everything contained in one document . . . (English County);

. . . doesn't have the back-up of a development plan—may lose out at appeal . . . (Scottish Region);

. . . current IFS approach is pointless unless grant aid is limited and targeted (English County);

. . . don't like IFS—we would like to see an approach which focused on more detailed landscape areas. We want to define and use more sub-groups covering precise geographical areas (National Park).

Some saw the circular for England and Wales as having been too strongly influenced by the Scottish Office circular, and inspired by a totally different style of afforestation. For example:

. . . advice is too general. Scottish-size plantations are not relevant . . . average size of woodlands locally is less than 10 hectares (Welsh County).

Thus, many planners (even in Scotland) saw IFSs as too generalized—'like trying to address all the scales of planning in one document'—and inappropriate to the fine-grained and sensitive landscapes of the lowlands. Some departments already claimed to be supplementing broader strategies with more local frameworks.

Finally, there is the issue of whether there is any evidence of improved outcomes where IFSs and other formal collaborative devices had been in existence. Several authorities were willing to venture that this was the case, and none reported a deteriorating situation. Typical observations included:

. . . Over the last five years there has been an improvement in schemes. Possibly some of this is attributable to planning policies—consultations have certainly led to improvements in specific schemes. Quality of submissions has improved—'Forests Design Plans' from Forest Enterprise and some similar practice by private owners (Scottish Region).

Through WGS consultations we are able to influence applicants to increase level of broadleaves (Welsh County).

Evidence that WGS applications are improving in terms of choice of species, appropriateness of planting, shape/layout of planting plans; also policies have had an influence in new planting and felling in relation to landscaping (English County).

Clearly, it will be difficult to corroborate these impressions in the absence of formal performance-monitoring procedures. This is an issue on which more explicit guidance to planners would be very welcome.

The key issue—land use planning without planning powers

It is evident that there is widespread recognition by planners of the ways in which forests and woodland can assist the attainment of a wide range of land use and socioeconomic objectives. However, this positive situation is hampered by the limited statutory basis and, some would argue, inadequate financial input. This is not, of course, necessarily to imply that planning controls should be extended or levels of public subvention vastly increased. Much can be achieved by the clarification of existing powers and more purposeful and concerted planning action. In practical terms, this is presently most likely to be effected by the mechanisms of indicative planning, development-led forestry and improved management.

Indicative planning apparently does yield some benefits. Its advantages include those of extending the democratic input into the afforestation and deforestation of land, of promoting areas for new planting, of guiding large-scale proposals away from sensitive locations, and of providing a context for WGS consultations. Conversely, it may ultimately prove ineffective and, as presently conceived, may be at the wrong scale to induce real improvements to plantation design or locally integrated land use. Much could be done to remedy this situation by re-issuing circular guidance on the production and use of woodland strategies, and the more general ways in which planning objectives can be assisted by new planting.

The issue of development-led forestry and, in particular, of the use of planning 'gain' may be a crucial ingredient in the realization of multi-purpose lowland woods, but its potential application is still far from clear. More than one respondent referred to this aspect of planning policy as being 'totally confused'. One concern of the DoE (echoed by developers) is that some planning authorities may seek costly obligations even where these are only tenuously linked to the application in question. Equally, some applicants may seek to impose an obligation on the planning authority which is so generous that the authority is disinclined to reject it even though the application is apparently at variance with what they would normally approve.

There are specific policies about the circumstances in which planning obligations can be entered into, and these were further clarified by representatives of the DoE during the present study. The essential policies are set out in Circular 16/91 (Department of Environment, 1991) and these, together with recent judgements, indicate that obligations have to be directly related to the application in question, and that the obligation must have more than a *de minimis* connection with the development. Contributions to the creation of woodlands (especially components of community forests) may typically only be loosely related to an individual planning application. It would appear that miscellaneous benefits such as these cannot be demanded and should not (if offered) influence a decision on a planning application. Going beyond the possibilities of normal planning obligations, it has also been suggested that new woodlands may be established through 'enabling development'. Enabling development provides for proposals, which are associated with some planning objections, to be considered because they release funds to facilitate other directly related, beneficial planning objectives. This can only occur when 'very special conditions' are met. Citing what he considers to be a comparable precedent, Pitt (1991) argues that some planning proposals in areas designated as green belt could exceptionally be approved, if they were able to release substantial land and funds for the establishment of community forests. He feels that, occasionally, these could satisfy the 'very special conditions', though this viewpoint is not officially accepted.

Development plan policy references to management are equally problematic, though it is clear that in many areas the condition of existing woodlands is of much greater concern than the expansion of new ones. The principal difficulty which planners have encountered is that of finding an acceptable policy wording, in the light of DoE insistence to include only land use, rather than management, policies in development plans.[10] One draft local plan included policies encouraging the management of commercial and privately owned amenity woods, and the desirability of securing felling and replanting to an agreed programme. At the public inquiry, the Inspector considered both of these to be management statements, which should be either redrafted to form a land use policy or used as the reasoned justification for such a policy (i.e. included only in the supporting text). Eventually, a very different policy emerged, in which management issues were all but neglected. A more general (though still infrequently used, and perhaps weaker) solution has been to encourage woodland owners to prepare management plans, if not already in a WGS scheme. Some planning authorities had pursued the management issue by producing supplementary guidance including, in one county, a woodland owners' database to support their efforts in providing free advice on small, unmanaged woodlands. However, whilst supplementary guidance provides extra flexibility, its status is less than that of a development plan, and its

[10]See footnote 9.

commitments may be more difficult to defend in periods of financial restraint, or when a council's political composition changes.

Conclusion

There is clearly widespread evidence of the actual and potential merging of forestry and planning interests. Recent changes to national policy are leading to a type of forestry which is more closely integrated into the complex land use situation of the lowlands and urban fringe. However, whereas planners and elected members are broadly sympathetic to the positive ways in which woodland can contribute to planning objectives, they often lack clear mechanisms to secure appropriate types of woodland in suitable settings.

Consolidation and clarification of advice by central government and non-departmental government bodies would certainly be of major assistance, both on certain technical matters and on policy stances. The trend of current policy guidance is to dampen expectations about the use of new development to fund woodland creation. Whilst the policy risks and practical difficulties of relaxing normal planning regimes are quite evident, it would nevertheless be helpful if official advice were more constructive and imaginative in helping planners to identify such limited opportunities as are available.

A great deal of reliance has been placed on the production of indicative forestry strategies by planning departments and, where these have been prepared, they have served a purpose in establishing a database, raising understanding and creating a dialogue. However, it is clear that they have been unpopular in England and Wales for various reasons, and that planners have not found the government circular on this topic particularly helpful. One reason is the unsuitability of their schematic zonal approach to the comparatively intimate landscapes of the lowlands. Also, IFSs were inspired by the historic pressures on the uplands during the 1980s and by the need to respond to new planting proposals, whereas much of the concern in the lowlands relates to the use and renewal of existing woodland cover. More sophisticated guidance on the production of woodland and forestry strategies is, therefore, desirable.

Financial restrictions will continue to hamper implementation, but considerable grant aid is available from conventional sources (mainly WGS), and it is becoming permissible in certain areas (via 'locational premia') to target this assistance in order to achieve locally defined land use objectives. It will be important to complement the availability of grant aid with accessible and informed local advice, good local databases on woodland condition and ownership, and well-cultivated relationships between private and public interests. Most of these features can be facilitated by local authorities, provided they have the energy and expertise. Equally, co-ordination and practical activity is often greatly enhanced where a woodland project or community forest team exists, and this is a model worthy of wider emulation.

Although the planning system is one important mechanism through which modern multi-benefit forestry policy can be effected, it is unlikely that planners will take a concerted and unilateral initiative on this. The initiative will have to come from the Forestry Commission, aided by the production of technical advice and policy guidance from central government and non-departmental government bodies. A co-ordinated strategy could help to achieve national forestry policy objectives, and there is much evidence to suggest that it would find a receptive audience amongst planning officers and elected members.

References

Central Scotland Countryside Trust (1994) *The Central Scotland Forest Strategy*. The Trust, Shotts.

Department of Environment (1991) *Circular 16/91, Planning and Compensation Act 1991: Planning Obligations*. HMSO, London.

Department of Environment/Welsh Office (1992) *Indicative Forestry Strategies, DoE Circular 29/1992, WO Circular 61/92*.

HM Government (1994) *Sustainable Forestry: the UK Programme*. HMSO, London.

Lorrain-Smith, R., Bell, M., Bunce, R.G.H. and Goodstadt, V. (1995) *The Potential for Extending Forest Cover in the Lowlands of England and Wales*. Forestry Industry Committee of Great Britain.

Pitt, J. (1991) Community forests, cities of tomorrow. *Town and Country Planning* **60** (6), 188–190.

Scottish Development Department (1990) *Indicative Forestry Strategies, SDD Circular 13/1990*. HMSO, Edinburgh.

[24]

 Pergamon

Geoforum, Vol. 27, No. 2, pp. 159–174, 1996
Copyright © 1996 Elsevier Science Ltd
Printed in Great Britain. All rights reserved
0016–7185/96 $15.00 + 0.00

S0016–7185(96)00006–1

From Wasteland to Wonderland: Opencast Mining, Regeneration and the English National Forest

PAUL CLOKE,* Bristol, U.K., PAUL MILBOURNE,† Cheltenham, U.K. and CHRIS THOMAS,‡ Staffordshire, U.K.

Abstract: In this paper we examine the outcomes of restructuring within the British coal mining industry in the English countryside and an attempt by the Countryside Commission to regenerate an area of the rural East Midlands through a forest project of sustainable development. In this particular area, deep-mine coal production has collapsed resulting in high levels of unemployment and large parcels of derelict land, while an expansion of opencast coal (and other mineral) extraction has led to considerable landscape despoliation. We examine critically the Countryside Commission's project of the National Forest in this area, involving the planting of thirty million trees over an area of almost 200 square miles. The Forest is seen as an example of sustainable development, bringing together economic growth—based around timber production and the encouragement of tourism and 'green' business— and environmental enhancement. However, the National Forest will be planted on private land, some of which is controlled by major mineral companies, with relatively little public ownership of this so-called 'national asset'. The paper draws on recent research carried out by the authors which has explored a series of important land use conflicts surrounding the sustainability of the Forest alongside on-going processes of opencast mining within its boundaries and also tensions associated with public access within a privately-owned forest. Copyright © 1996 Elsevier Science Ltd

Introduction

The words 'industrial' and 'countryside' do not sit comfortably together in the dominant imagery of rural areas. Indeed, popular culture often seems to equate heavy and extractive industrial activities with the urban arena. Nevertheless, such activities have a long history in some areas of rural Britain (china clay extraction in Cornwall; coal mining in the Forest of

Dean; precious metal mining in west Wales—to name just three). This paper explores one such economic activity in the English countryside—coal extraction— and considers how restructuring of the British coal industry over recent years has resulted in a series of local outcomes—economic, socio-cultural and land-based—in many parts of the rural coalfields.

Alongside a general contraction of the deep-mine industry, certain rural areas have witnessed a rapid expansion of opencast coal (and other mineral) production over recent years. Such growth has offset (at least in part) job losses in the deep-mine coal industry, although opencast production has resulted in a series of landscape and environmental conflicts within these areas, particularly in areas of 'high quality' countryside, such as National Parks. These

*Department of Geography, University of Bristol, Bristol, U.K.
†Countryside & Community Research Unit, Cheltenham & Gloucester College of Higher Education, Cheltenham, U.K.
‡Division of Geography, Staffordshire University, Staffordshire, U.K.

conflicting uses of countryside are discussed in greater depth in the second part of the paper. Here attention is given to the development of a new National Forest in an area of the English Midlands which is characterised by previous rounds of extractive capital investment (deep-mine coal production) and on-going rounds of investment (opencast mining). Alongside other objectives—increased timber production, alternative uses for surplus agricultural land and the creation of new wildlife habitats—the National Forest is intended to provide new (leisure-based) employment and enhance the scarred landscape of the Leicestershire and South Derbyshire coalfield area. The Forest is viewed as a project of sustainable development, enabling both environmental enhancement and economic development. However, the fact that 11% of the Forest area is controlled by major mineral companies means that certain development-based activities contradict these other key objectives of tourism and landscape beautification. Moreover, the fact that the development of this National Forest is dependent on the actions of private landowners raises important issues concerning private property rights and public environmental interests.

In the third part of the paper we seek to understand some of the attitudes of local residents towards private property rights, opencast mining and the National Forest by drawing on recent research carried out by the authors with community groups and organisations within the coalfield area of the Forest.

A Restructured Coal Industry: From Deep-mine to Opencast Production

Any consideration of recent processes of restructuring within the British coal mining industry needs to be placed within a wider context of change in the post-war period. Hudson and Sadler (1990), for example, have suggested that, in overall terms, the British coal mining industry has experienced a gradual decline since the late 1950s, with regional planning policies introduced in the 1960s and early 1970s attempting to diversify the local economies of those areas characterised by declining coal mining production. Oil price increases of the early 1970s were seen as offering a new, expanded future for the British coal industry, although the advent to power of the Thatcher Government in 1979 heralded a shift towards market

economics. Moreover, the criteria utilised for determining 'economic' and 'uneconomic' pits became much more stringent, with new financial structures introduced under which British Coal (formerly the National Coal Board) was forced to operate. Such reorganisation resulted in an increased shift towards lower-cost production methods—predominantly the closure of loss-making (or least profitable) deep-mine operations, importation of cheaper coal, and an expansion of British opencast mining activities. Increased opencast mining was also encouraged by central government, particularly when such activities were linked to private operators (Roberts, 1989). Such changes can be viewed from a wider political-economy perspective of coal production within the U.K. since 1979:

> . . . a definite political choice was made to allow market forces a much greater influence in determining the size, shape and geography of the coal industry in the U.K. (Hudson and Sadler, 1990, p. 437).

By the early 1980s, the privatising tendency within the British coal industry was clear (Beynon *et al.*, 1991), both in terms of the increasing use of private contractors in collieries and the growing influence of private sector civil engineering firms involved in open-cast mining activities.

Such trends have, in many ways, been accentuated in the first half of the 1990s with an absolute decline in total British coal output (particularly associated with deep-mined production) and a proportional switch from deep mine to opencast output. In fact, total output fell from 104.5 million tonnes in 1985–1986 to 91.1 million tonnes in 1991–1992 (Trade and Industry Committee, 1993) and opencast output as a proportion of total output increased from 14.6% in 1985–1986 to 22.0% in 1992–1993 (Coalfields Communities Campaign, 1993). Moreover, October 1992 witnessed the Government announcement of a widespread contraction of the deep-mine coal industry—with the proposal to close 31 out of 50 mines within six months. By July 1993 production had ceased at 209 mines and 19,000 men had accepted redundancies (Fothergill, 1993). Finally, following this dramatic contraction of British coal production, the industry was privatised in 1994, with control over the remaining English sites (English Coal[1]) acquired by a single mining company—Doncaster-based RJB Mining—for an estimated price of £815 million (Mining Journal, 1994, 1995).

Expanding opencast coal production: new landscapes for old?

The post-war development of opencast mining. According to Atkin (1993), 'official' organised production began in Britain on two sites in 1941, and by 1944, 419 sites were operating with an annual output of around 8.6 million tonnes. In the immediate post-war period high levels of demand for coal from programmes of reconstruction meant that opencast production totalled around 12 million tonnes in 1950 and the industry employed 9000 persons. A period of stabilisation in the 1960s (production levels of 5–10 million tonnes per year) was followed by a gradual expansion of production over the 1970s. The 1974 *Plan for coal* proposed a growth in annual production to 15 million tonnes, and such a target was reached in 1980–1981 (Mabey, 1994, p. 3). In addition to this absolute growth in production, opencast methods began to account for an increasing proportion of the overall national coal market—rising from 11% of the U.K. coal output in 1979 to 19% by 1989 (Bate *et al.*, 1991).

By 1994 British Coal Opencast was operating 40 sites, with an annual production total of 13.5 million tonnes of coal (1993–1994). Moreover, there were 83 operational private sector opencast mines divided between 48 companies and involving an overall production level of 2 million tonnes (Mineral Planning, 1994a). Table 1 highlights the growth of opencast activities in England and Wales during the 1980s and early 1990s. It can be seen that while both British Coal and private sector production increased considerably over this period, the rise in private production was much more pronounced—increasing its share from 6% in 1983–1984 to 16% of opencast output by 1992–1993. Moreover, production levels on British Coal sites peaked in the period 1988–1992 in the run up to privatisation, whereas private sector production has continued to grow in the early 1990s, and while a slight reduction in production levels was witnessed in 1993–1994, approval was nevertheless granted for 10.7 million tonnes of opencast coal production over these twelve months—involving 1700 hectares of land in Great Britain. Indeed, in the period 1985–1994 planning approvals were granted for an area covering 24,107 hectares—155 million tonnes of opencast coal—and identified reserves increased by 59% over the same period (County Planning Officers' Society, 1994).

Table 1. Opencast production in Great Britain (million tonnes)

Year	British Coal Opencast	Private sector
1984–1985	13.7	1.2
1985–1986	13.9	1.4
1986–1987	12.8	1.8
1987–1988	14.5	1.8
1988–1989	16.1	1.9
1989–1990	16.8	1.8
1990–1991	16.2	2.1
1991–1992	16.1	3.0
1992–1993	14.7	3.2
1994–1995	13.3	2.9

Source: County Planning Officer's Society (1994).

Three key reasons can be suggested for such a growth in opencast activities over recent years. First, the profitable nature of such activities relative to other mining methods. In 1992–1993 the cost of opencast coal was £32 per tonne compared to £38 for coal extracted from deep-mine techniques (British Coal, 1993). However, the cost gap between these two mining activities has narrowed considerably over recent years. Secondly, political pressure to extend opencasting and moves to privatise the coal industry meant that an increasing number of private sector companies became interested in opencast mining in the period prior to the privatisation of the coal industry (see Table 1). Finally, the introduction of Mineral Planning Guidance Note (MPG) 3 in May 1988 placed opencast mining in a privileged position relative to other mineral activities:

> there is a strong case in the national interest for allowing these resources [opencast coal] to be developed unless there are overriding environmental considerations (Department of the Environment, 1988).

This presumption in favour of opencasting resulted in a rapid rise in the number of opencast applications approved by planning departments in the late 1980s and early 1990s (Table 2). Moreover, the number of applications that were decided at appeal rose by 70%, and the success rate of such appeals almost doubled in the five years following the introduction of MPG3.

Opencast coal production and environmental concerns: unsustainable development? Increasing levels of opencast production have not been without their environmental concerns and conflicts, particularly in areas of the British countryside. The Council for the Protection of Rural England (1994), for example,

Table 2. Comparison of the five years before and after the introduction of MPG 3 in England and Wales

	Hectares		
	1983–1988	1988–1993	%age change
Total area in opencast applications (determined by local authorities or at appeal)	15,585	16,689	+7.1
Land approved for opencasting (by local authorities or at appeal)	6540	8676	+32.7
Determined at appeal	3004	5097	+69.7
Allowed on appeal	1104	3288	+197.8
Allowed on appeal as percentage of all appeals	36.8	64.5	
Allowed on appeal as percentage of all approvals	16.9	37.9	

Source: Coalfield Communities Campaign (1993)—based on figures from County Planning Officers' Society.

commenting on the rising scale of production on green field sites, refers to such activities in the following terms:

> ...one of the most environmentally destructive processes going on in the countryside today (p. 19).

Most commentators on the opencast mining industry would agree that there exist a host of problems associated with its operations. Examples which are cited frequently include blasting, noise levels, dust, visual impacts and the intrusion on community life (Bate *et al.*, 1991; Hudson and Cox, 1990). However, most concern has been expressed about the latter two problems. In terms of visual effects, extractive operations are nearly always associated with a dramatic transformation of the local landscape:

> The appearance of the landscape during opencast working can be quite horrific as the countryside can be torn apart, and large sites may be scarred to a depth of hundreds of feet under hundreds of acres (Bate *et al.*, 1991).

and while the actual process of mineral extraction may be relatively short lived, with restoration agreements eventually returning the land to its 'original' state, it has been suggested that such reclamation cannot replace overnight mature woodland landscapes which have taken many years to develop. Moreover, when coal is mined alongside other minerals—such as clay, sand or gravel—temporary stockpiling of these surplus materials may occur which represents a further visual intrusion for local communities. Opencast mining may also bring about a range of conflicts surrounding the interests of local populations and local economic development, in terms of both the ways people perceive their local environment and how the local area is viewed from

without by leisure users and potential (housing and industrial) developers. Indeed, it can be suggested that any new employment created by opencast production may be offset by its potentially detrimental effects on the leisure/tourism industry and on the marketing of the area to potential developers. With regard to the effects of opencast mining on local communities, Bate *et al.* (1991) comment that, with consents for such activities lasting up to ten years, images of childhood may become dominated by scarred and (for children) dangerous landscapes:

> A generation can experience the sensory deprivation of the assault on the local landscape, as buildings, trees, boundaries, habitats, archaeology, historical remains and the immeasurable reminders of past experiences are lost forever (p. 6).

They suggest further that while opencast mining triggers a whole range of negative reactions amongst local communities, many local people have come to accept the despoilment of their everyday landscapes:

> Residents generally do not become inured to the ongoing impacts of opencast mining; rather they continually perceive it but, for the most part, take the view that it is inevitable and therefore scarcely worth complaining about (p. 6).

Alongside such localised problems and conflicts, two important beneficial aspects of opencast mining have often been stressed in areas of declining deep-mine coal production. First, the industry provides new sources of employment (estimates of the national opencast coal mining workforce range between 5000–8000 persons—Trade and Industry Committee, 1993), and secondly, opencast activities on derelict land are often associated with the restoration of such sites without the need for (local) state funding (Glen, 1994; Siddall, 1994). Indeed, following the closure of many deep-mines over the 1980s and early 1990s, large amounts of derelict land have been restored subsequent to being deep-mined using opencast techniques. While such sites are becoming increasingly scarce—the County Planning Officers' Society (1994) has estimated that in 1993–1994 only 17% of approvals for opencast coal mining involved derelict land—opencast mining on these scarred landscapes appears to be welcomed by many local communities given that restoration is often associated with such activities:

> Seen in this light, opencast coal extraction may, in certain situations, cease to be the environmentalist's 'bête noire' and be seen as a positive agency for regeneration of degraded landscapes (Glen, 1994, pp. 29–31).

Moreover, Siddall (1994) suggests that the opencast industry can provide many benefits for greenfield sites, as well as areas of derelict land:

> Restored sites are, of course, new landscapes, but with the careful management we give them during the after-care period and the techniques we have learnt over the years they mature more quickly than might be supposed... More recently restorations are imaginative and varied, with conservation and leisure uses to the fore, such as the Rother Valley Country Park in South Yorkshire, Hauxley nature reserve in Northumberland and the many golf courses on restored opencast sites (p. 34).

Such landscape 'improvements' resulting from opencast production are an obvious example of 'planning gain'. On a wider scale, Thornley (1991) reports that such planning agreements between developers and local planning authorities are now widespread within the development control system. However, while several commentators have recognised the 'planning gain' received by the local authority as a result of a proposed development, considerable disquiet has been raised about such agreements:

> ... concern has been expressed over the secret and undemocratic nature of the process and the potential for abuse whereby permission could be granted to an inherently 'bad' development if sufficient planning gain was offered (*ibid.*, p. 152).

Nevertheless, such agreements represent a method of involving social, economic and environmental 'gains' into planning decision-making (Whatmore and Boucher, 1993), and here public sector policy-makers have begun to envisage the role of opencast mining in creating new landscapes, possibly including public access rights, leisure parks and woodland. Such imaginative after-uses of opencast sites depend, how-

ever, on land ownership. For example, if the land is owned by a farmer then the site might be restored to agricultural land resulting in relatively little benefits for local communities. On the other hand, more imaginative schemes of reclamation may be possible if the site is owned by the mineral operator. Such schemes might involve voluntary organisations, such as local wildlife trusts and the Woodland Trust, together with statutory bodies, particularly local authorities, with longer term land management secured through a nominal levy being placed on minerals extracted (Glen, 1994). However, with the increasing involvement of private operators and the recent privatisation of the industry, fear has been expressed that restoration agreements may be at best satisfied to a minimum standard and at worst be disregarded by future private operators (Bate *et al.*, 1991).

Concern about the rising scale of opencast mining in areas of the countryside in the early 1990s was focused on MPG3, which, it was alleged, placed too much weight on 'the national interest' relative to local environmental considerations within planning decisions. In its response to the consultation process leading to the Coal Industry Bill, the Coalfields Communities Campaign (1994) highlighted three key issues which it felt planning guidance needed to address in order to reduce conflicts surrounding opencast mining:

(i)   that adequate prominence is given to environmental issues;

(ii) that 'national interest' or 'commerical' considerations do not override environmental concerns;

(iii) that the onus for decision-making is placed with the local authorities whose communities are affected by opencast mining proposals.

In 1992, the Department of the Environment conducted a consultation exercise with those groups and organisations involved with opencast mining (see Mabey, 1994), following which the Government announced a revision of MPG3 (Department of the Environment/Welsh Office, 1994). The new MPG3 guidance has removed the presumption in favour of opencast and provided more stringent environmental criteria for the assessment of opencast applications:

> This guidance aims to provide a policy framework for mineral planning authorities (MPAs) and the industry to ensure that the extraction of coal and disposal of colliery spoil can take place in accordance with the full and

proper protection of the environment and the principles of sustainable development (*ibid.*, p. 1).

Here we see an attempt by the Department of the Environment at engaging with recent arguments surrounding sustainable development; that economic development can (and must) be combined with environmental protection. However, there remains considerable confusion surrounding the meaning of sustainable development. As O'Riordan (1988) has highlighted, the concept is capable of being understood and utilised in different ways by developers and environmentalists. There remains a need to explore in greater depth the meanings attached to sustainable development and whether it can be achieved in practice (see Lowe and Murdoch, 1993; Redclift, 1992; Redclift and Benton, 1994).

The remaining parts of the paper explore such issues of sustainable development associated with opencast mining in one particular rural area in the East Midlands. This area, which lies within the Leicestershire and South Derbyshire rural coalfield, is characterised by a recent collapse in deep-mine production and ongoing processes of opencast extraction. The area is also located within the boundary of the new National Forest—a project of sustainable development, involving multi-purpose forestry, which is being funded by the Countryside Commission.

The National Forest: Sustainable Development in Practice?

The concept

> What is being sought is no less than a transformation, involving a major conversion of land use at an exceptional rate. This, in an area that is one of the least wooded in the country, has a generally poor environmental outlook and bears the scars of years of mineral working. Economically the area has also been severely hit by the demise of the deep-mine coal industry. It has relatively high levels of unemployment and is trying to pull itself out of economic decline (Countryside Commission, 1993b, p. 6).

The National Forest was commissioned by the Countryside Commission in a 1987 publication titled *Forestry in the Countryside*. The proposal was for a multi-purpose forest, involving timber production, recreation, landscape enhancement, alternative uses for surplus agricultural land and the creation of

wildlife habitats. In 1989 a shortlist was drawn up of five locations in the English Midlands, and after considerable consultation the Commission announced in October 1990 its selection of a site linking the former ancient forest areas of Needwood in Staffordshire with Charnwood in Leicestershire (Figure 1). The National Forest boundary includes 194 square miles and current proposals involve the planting of thirty million trees, increasing the wooded area from the present level of 6% to one-third (the original target was 40% of the land area). It is intended to alter radically the existing landscape, transforming agricultural, industrial and urban land. The forest is also intended to help regenerate the local economy, particularly in those areas where the mining industry has recently contracted, by creating new employment based around tourism. Thus, the forst could, it is envisaged, help regenerate both local employment and the degraded landscape, as well performing an important environmental purpose (both locally and globally) and contributing to national timber supplies.

Following a three-year development programme which involved the production of a Forest strategy, the Government has announced recently the establishment of a Forest Company in April 1995 to overview the Forest's development. While the Company will receive central government funding of £1 million, the growth of the Forest will be reliant on the benevolence (linked to financial incentives) of private land-owners. It will involve planting on privately-owned land, and access agreements will be negotiated with individual landowners. By January 1995, only 3% of the National Forest tree target had been planted covering an area of 1000 acres.

Implementing the regeneration of a scarred landscape

While improvements to derelict sites and the creation of new (leisure-based) employment need to be placed within this wider remit of the National Forest, it can be suggested that these two objectives are closely linked to the concept of the Garden Festival. Such festivals represented an extremely visual component of government urban regeneration schemes in the 1980s and early 1990s.[2] Their main goals were land reclamation, economic regeneration, environmental enhancement and improvements to the morale of areas which had experienced recent economic decline. Leverton *et al.* (1992) have suggested a series of

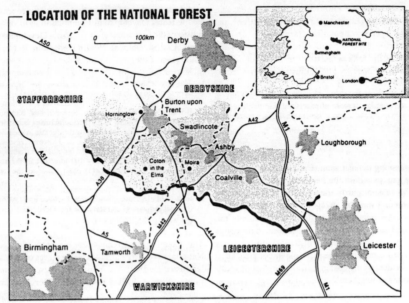

Figure 1. The National Forest Area.
Source: The Countryside Commission (1993b).

short- and long-term benefits associated with such projects, based on study of the Ebbw Vale Festival:

> Short term benefits—environmental improvement of the sites; rapid reclamation of the sites which will make it attractive to new developers; and economic benefits attached to tourism.
> Long term benefits—an improvement of the area's image based on Festival publicity; the site will provide an environmentally attractive area which will enable it to compete more effectively for outside private developers.

Such beneficial outcomes of land reclamation schemes (including the Garden Festival) have also been highlighted by Kivell (1993) in the case of the Potteries region in north Staffordshire:

> The visual impact which this has made upon the local environment is both obvious and dramatic, but it is also measurable in more tangible terms such as a reduction in population out-migration from the urban area, the attraction of new industrial and commercial investment, and an increase in the number of visitors (p. 250).

The National Forest is intended to bring about similar types of improvements to areas of rural landscape despoilment to those initiated by the Garden Festivals in urban locations over previous years. Clearly there are important differences between the two types of project, with the Forest concept interlinking economic (re)development with environmental enhancement to a greater degree than the Festivals (which tended to prepare the sites solely for future industrial and housing developments). Another contrast is the level of central government resources invested into each project. Leverton *et al*. (1992) report that about £50 million was invested into the Ebbw Vale Garden Festival, whereas government funding for the National Forest will not exceed £1 million (Steele, 1995). Nevertheless, the potential impacts of the Forest on the degraded parts of the Midland coalfield are frequently stressed in promotional material and strategy documents:

> The heritage of mineral working is one of the reasons why this area was chosen for the National Forest. It offers the biggest possible challenge in improving the landscape and encouraging economic revival—derelict land and mineral sites providing excellent opportunities for woodland creation (Countryside Commission, 1993a, p. 14).

166   Paul Cloke *et al.*

and such landscape improvements in an area scattered with the remnants of past mining activity and present opencast operations (see Figure 2) have created considerable positive local publicity for the Forest, as the following extract from an editorial in the *Leicester Mercury* (1991) illustrates:

> From wasteland to wonderland—a place to relax, a place to enjoy, a place of peace and tranquillity... you can help create a green haven where slag, shale and stagnant pools once stood.

Regenerating derelict sites. The Forest is viewed by many groups within the Midland coalfield as being able to reclaim partly the interests of the local environment from the ravages of the operations of extractive capital. In fact, the area represents the localised outcomes of the earlier identified processes of restructuring within the British coal industry. It has witnessed a rapid decline in employment associated with the deep-mine coal industry, with a set of socio-economic problems associated with such contraction,

and these problems have been acknowedged recently by the Rural Development Commission in its designation of the coalfield region as a Rural Development Area (Leicestershire and South Derbyshire RDA) in 1993[3] (Figure 2):

> The key feature of the local economy has been the demise of the coal industry with the loss of 8000 jobs. It has been estimated that a further 2000 jobs were lost in British Coal's administration, research and transport functions, and directly related manufacturing industries. The indirect job losses caused by the decline in spending power are more difficult to estimate. However, research commissioned by the Coalfield Communities Campaign has suggested that for every 100 jobs lost in the coal industry, 50 jobs will be lost in other sectors of the local economy. This decline in spending power was particularly felt in the former mining communities where 30% to 50% of economically active males were employed in the coal industry (Leicestershire and Derbyshire Coalfields Rural Partnership, 1994).

The Countryside Commission estimates that the National Forest area includes 500 hectares of derelict land associated with past mining activities, with restoration schemes divided between the Derelict Land

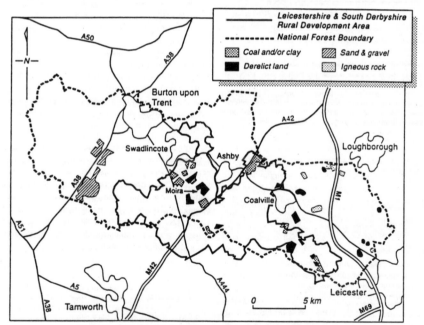

Figure 2. Opencast extraction and derelict land within the National Forest.
Source: The Countryside Commission (1993b) and the Leicestershire and Derbyshire Rural Partnership (1994).

Grant programme and mineral companies satisfying earlier planning agreements. In the coalfield area the Countryside Commission stresses the beneficial effects associated with new woodland in terms of landscape enhancement and improvements to the overall image of the region:

> Extensive areas of dereliction scar much of the landscape and their early planting would be a tremendous physical and psychological boost to the area, and provide focal points for forest activity and access (Countryside Commission, 1993b, p. 69).

The pace of restoration, however, remains determined by the mineral companies, and by RJB Mining (formerly British Coal) in particular, which very often consider the process of restoration as a negotiating tool when attempting to secure new sites for mineral activity. It remains to be seen whether the privatised coal industry will place as much stress on restoration agreements as was the case with British Coal. Indeed, Bate *et al.* (1991) have highlighted that, relative to British Coal, private mining operators are characterised by poorer compliances to planning requirements. Such fears have also been expressed within the National Forest area, as a recent interview with the assistant director of environmental planning at Leicestershire Country Council illustrates:

> As we've moved towards privatisation, it's been increasingly difficult to have a dialogue with anyone at British Coal. They've either retired, been made redundant, or jumped the sinking ship before it sank... There is concern among local authorities that we will have an inheritance of problems, but without the means to deal with them (Steele, 1995, p. 6).

Opencast mining and the National Forest: conflicting land uses? Alongside sites of past mining activity the Forest area also contains considerable on-going mining activity, predominantly involving opencast production methods. Indeed, Derbyshire and Leicestershire represent two of the five counties which accounted for one-half of all opencast coal output in Britain between 1983 and 1988 (Hudson and Sadler, 1990). Mineral companies own or have control over 11% of the forest area (half of which is operational) and RJB Mining (formerly British coal)—the largest landowner within the Forest— accounts for 5% of the total Forest land area. Currently, opencast production extends over an area of 667 hectares and a further 452 hectares are being extracted for both coal and clay (Figure 2). More-

over, RJB Mining has acquired a number of reserve opencast sites which presently do not contain planning consents, and a fear has been expressed by local authorities within the area that applications for mining will follow in the near future. In north-west Leicestershire, for example, there are currently two opencast coal sites in operation, another site is likely to come on stream in the near future, and four new applications are expected for potential sites following the transfer of land assets from British Coal to RJB Mining.

On-going and future opencast mining would seem to represent a major obstacle for the development of the National Forest. However, in one sense, the Countryside Commission (1993b, p. 62), in a similar way to Glen (1994) and Sidall (1994), suggests that such activities may represent an enormous opportunity for establishing the Forest, stressing seven key benefits:

- mineral ownerships constitute a major component of the Forest land area
- land-use change is relatively short term and governed by planning permissions
- restoration costs are relatively small compared to the overall investment on a site
- tree planting represents a cost-effective method of restoration
- restoration provisions provide the opportunity to create multi-use sites
- funding to restore derelict sites may be available through the Dereliction Land Grant programme
- the minerals industry is increasingly recognising the importance of ecological resources and landscaping.

Notwithstanding these potential benefits which opencast mining may offer for the National Forest, such activities clearly question the 'sustainable' components of the Forest project, particularly when local employment is dependent in part on environmentally damaging development. More generally, Redclift (1992) has warned of the employment and social consequences of sustainable development for fractions of the local population:

> Often the poor are alienated from their environment, or depend for their livelihood on practices which are not sustainable. The environment is frequently an arena of conflicting interests and needs. If the concept of sustainable development is to prove useful it must help us make difficult choices rather then simply occupy the high moral ground (p. 398).

and the Countryside Commission recognises that

opencast activities will continue within the Forest area, leading to potential tensions over competing land uses:

> Consideration has to be given as to how to accommodate minerals activity over a long period and how to develop a long-term relationship between what can be complementary, but are at the same time essentially competing, land uses (Countryside Commission, 1993b, p. 63).

Indeed, mineral activity must be seen as a 'complex equation', which in one respect generates local employment and on the other hand results in considerable opposition within the local area. The development of opencast mining remains dependent in many ways on outside forces—market demand for minerals, energy policies and the recent privatisation of the coal industry, and the decisions of private landowners. However, prior to coal privatisation, British Coal had signed a Charter with the National Forest, in which it announced support for the Forest, agreed to prioritise tree planting in its restoration of opencast sites and consult the Forest administration on all future mineral proposals (National Forest/ British Coal, 1993). Such agreements have yet to be secured with private mineral operators. The Countryside Commission (1993b) considers that the future development of the Forest in areas of opencast activities will depend on a more 'enlightened approach to land utilisation' on behalf of such companies:

> If mineral companies . . . see that the Forest proposal could continue to provide them with a long-term supply of raw materials in a more publicly acceptable manner, then much could be achieved (p. 65).

Considerable fear has been expressed locally that opencast companies may use planning gain as a tool to secure new sites. Here the tension between these two conflicting land-uses is most apparent; that the development of the National Forest in the coalfield region may depend partly on the release of additional land for opencast mining. This may be particularly true if public access and imaginative restoration schemes are proposed, and might lead to the development of a zonal Forest. Here we can begin to envisage a situation of on-going mineral activities alongside large-scale planting schemes, as opencast companies search for new deposits:

> It is also unrealistic to assume that the completion of an opencast site will necessarily be the end of the story. Where coal reserves are close to the land surface there will always be an interest in digging them up. If one site closes, the industry will normally want to maintain their

rate of output from the area by means of new sites. A sequence of field after field, landscape after landscape can be damaged in this way. In areas where opencasting took place many years ago, the industry is even returning to the very same sites, using the benefits of modern earth-moving machinery to excavate lower seams of coal that could not be tackled previously, once again moving the soil and the rock and affecting people who thought that they were safe from a repeat experience (Bate *et al.*, 1991, p. 7).

Private property rights and public interest. The concept of the National Forest is very much dependent on the actions of private landowners, given that relatively little public ownership of land is envisaged within the Commission's development plans. Bishop (1992) has suggested that this situation of land ownership results in a public dependence on private interest which will ultimately impede the growth of the Forest:

> The various new forest proposals that have been launched during recent years are heavily reliant on private interest because of the pattern of British land-ownership yet offer little incentive to private landowners to participate in new woodland creation. Indeed, the idea of small woodland creation, especially when linked to increased public access to the countryside is a complete anathema to many private landowners (p. 154).

Clearly, such tensions and conflict are related to more general issues of property rights and the relatively powerful positions of landowners (including farmers) as 'gatekeepers' who are able to influence access to rights such as housing, leisure and economic development in the countryside (Marsden *et al.*, 1993). Indeed, Cox *et al.* (1988) have suggested that such landowners exercise considerable 'power of constraint' which enables their particular visions of environmental protection—linked to compensations for reduced property rights—to dominate discussions. Private landowners can be seen to draw on a 'largely unquestioned presupposition' which tends to present 'a view which privileges their claims upon the rest of society and upon the public and private purse' (Lowe *et al.*, 1993, p. 107). Furthermore, public access to land within Britain has traditionally been based on *de facto* rights (Bonyhady, 1987), with recent attempts at 'commoditising' areas of countryside acting to threaten this customary access:

> On some of the Forestry Commission land and water authority land that has been privatized, for example, there was much informal and customary access. The risk is that the new private owners will look either to terminate such access or to raise revenue from it. With such proposals on the agenda, there is a pressing need to

consider turning certain customary freedoms into rights to moderate the scope of private market power (Lowe *et al.*, 1993, pp. 107–108).

However, public rights of access within the National Forest will remain bound by existing private property rights. This is not to say that an increased level of access is not envisaged by the Countryside Commission, but the emphasis is placed on access that is both sensitive to and negotiated with key local private landowners:

> Commerical farming has been the dominant land use, and the prospect of greatly increased free public access over farmland and forested private land worries the farming and landowning community. Permissive and improved access within management agreements may be acceptable but the compulsory imposition of statutory rights of way or access would be strongly resisted (1993, p. 36).

Sustaining general development within the National Forest. A further aspect of sustainable development in rural areas involves the so-called 'greening' of local business (see Lowe and Murdoch, 1993). Alongside environmental gains on sites of previous mining activities, the Countryside Commission (1993b) has also emphasised the benefits that the National Forest would bring to the image of the area and future economic development:

> The National Forest is intended as a dynamic proposition, and a positive force for regeneration that could bring with it new forms of economic activity, jobs and wealth (p. 59).

In a similar manner to the Garden Festival concept, environmental improvement is seen as encouraging new housing developments, an expansion of leisure and tourist facilities and a growth in 'green' companies. However, such developments need to be restricted to a scale that does not conflict with the growth of the Forest. New commercial development will be encouraged to support the Forest's development through a loose form of planning gain. Within the Forest area there are currently 350 hectares of land allocated for industrial development, mainly along the M42 and A38 corridors (see Figure 1), and 450 hectares have been allocated for residential development. Certain kinds of development are seen by the Countryside Commission (1993b, p. 59) as being associated with (and encouraged by) the Forest's development:

- tourism, recreation and leisure facilities

- derelict land reclamation to woodland, public open space, leisure use and/or created wildlife habitats
- farm diversification
- rural enterprises including visitor attractions, forest enterprises and tree and wildflower nurseries
- commercial business and industry attracted by an improved environment
- increased pressure for residential development within the Forest.

Finally, in addition to attracting new development, the Countryside Commission (1992) is attempting to encourage existing businesses within the region to participate in the Forest's developments, by stressing the advantages of the 'greening' of local industry:

> Companies find that environment projects make good business sense: good environmental practice enhances a company's image; schemes which improve the surroundings of local employees boost morale and corporate pride and contribute to increased productivity; many well-qualified young people actively seek out 'green' employers; politicians and the public look to companies to take an active role in environmental care (p. 1).

Local perceptions of opencast mining and the National Forest

It is important within these schemes of 'land transformation' to gauge the expectations and experiences of local communities which are embedded within this 'land', and we would suggest that such an exploration represents a very necessary component of any understanding of localised changes from *wasteland* to *wonderland*. This third part of the paper is based on a series of group interviews conducted in the village of Moira which is located within the coalfield area of the National Forest (Figure 2). The Moira interviews form part of a wider research project commissioned by the Countryside Commission in 1992 (see Cloke *et al.*, 1993) which explored perceptions of local landscapes and attitudes towards the National Forest in three areas within its boundaries: an 'urban' area—Burton-upon-Trent; an 'agricultural' area—Coton-in-the-Elms; and an 'industrial' village—Moira.

Following a search for local community groups and organisations active within the Moira area, five individual group discussions and one open discussion group were carried out between November 1992–

February 1993.[5] Each discussion group proceeded in a similar pattern, although the practice of using three researchers resulted in slight variations in presentation style and emphasis. After an initial introduction from the research team, discussion was centred around perceptions of local landscapes and awareness of the National Forest project. This was followed by a short slide presentation of the proposed Forest project using information supplied by the Countryside Commission and a more detailed discussion based on the perceived impacts of these proposals for the Moira area.

While we recognise some of the limitations associated with such group discussions, we nevertheless believe that the comments which are outlined below represent a valuable insight into local people's perceptions of their local landscapes, both in terms of mining activities and the development of the National Forest.

Perceptions of local landscapes. Alongside the environmental impacts of opencast mining, both Hudson and Cox (1990) and Bate *et al.* (1991) suggest that attention needs to be given to more subjective experiences of such activities amongst local communities. Perceptions of the local area exhibited considerable variation within our group discussions, although the dominant description related to a landscape tarnished by the scars of previous rounds of deep-mine coal production and on-going opencast coal and other mineral extraction:

> devasted by two separate mines that have been pulled down and we have got a lot of dereliction (Town Council).

> it's been torn apart... by British Coal (Miners' Welfare).

> I think we've got very beautiful countryside round here. The only blot on the landscape—[a] blackspot—is where the coal mines have been (Young Mothers).

Such industrial degradation of the local landscape, however, was viewed as a relatively recent development. In fact, several respondents, particularly within the Darby and Joan group discussion, recounted a countryside of previous years which was characterised by small pockets of bluebell woods, and a tremendous feeling of regret was apparent over the loss to extensive mining operations of these wooded areas:

> [it is] not as good as used to be. The nice walks, nice woods—they've been ruined (Darby and Joan Club).

> Just across the road here, there were fields [and] Willesley Wood, and there were little woods, and they have all gone, apart from the odd one here and there (Darby and Joan Club).

> you used to be able to walk around [the woods] once a day but then the Coal Board took it over and you couldn't go round it (Darby and Joan Club).

> that was a forest—a bluebell wood—I mean they [the Coal Board] dug up all that and they are doing it again (Miners' Welfare).

For such people, the idea of the National Forest, with the re-establishment of 'pockets' of woodland, was viewed overwhelmingly in positive terms, enabling local people to reclaim their local area from the exploitation of major mineral companies. As one elderly discussant commented, the Forest provided the opportunity to 'turn the clock back fifty years' and, in the words of another, return the woods "to like I knew it as a lad".[6] However, while the idea of the Forest was welcomed warmly by most people, the reality of its development was greeted by many with considerable scepticism. Several discussants commented that the interests of the mineral companies, and particularly British Coal[7] would conflict with the development of the National Forest. In an area where the interests of British Coal and the major mineral companies were perceived as taking precedence over ecological, environmental and aesthetic considerations, many persons within our groups feared that the National Forest would always take second place within any planning consideration. Indeed, considerable expressions of anger were evident amongst many local people regarding the attitudes of the mineral companies towards the local countryside. Such companies were seen as 'exploiting' local landscapes and environments, 'stripping' the land of its natural resources, whilst 'ploughing nothing back' into the local community. Feelings of anger were accompanied by expressions of distrust, with one respondent commenting that the interests of the local environment relative to those of major mineral companies represented "... one big battle which goes on continuously". Moreover, the restoration of sites of past opencast mining was considered by many people as merely a negotiation tool on the part of British Coal and the mineral companies, with such companies being accused frequently of satisfying planning agreements to a minimum standard:

> when you look around and see what they've done, and you go down a foot you're in waste, not in the sense of rubbish, but industrial waste. They've sort of covered it over and put grass there (Open Meeting),

the mineral companies want to milk what they have got . . . they say 'well you let us dig it up and we will plant some trees'—which they do. But they have only got a five year restoration period attached to it. In other words, they can put little trees there. They plant them in ground that is more or less shale and then after five years they don't need to look after them anymore. I know of one place locally where within two years there was nearly 50% casualties of trees (Miners' Welfare).

several years ago they opened the land up for ground extraction. They were supposed to restore on completion and that is still lying derelict" (Miners' Welfare).

we have areas of mature woodland. Then they [British Coal] come along [and] dig it up so that not only do the trees disappear but all the floor with it. Because when they put it back all they put back of course is the little young trees, but you have no bluebells, no floor at all. All you have is rye grass and little trees (Miners' Welfare).

Many people within our discussions considered that newly planted trees would not provide any guarantees against future rounds of mineral extraction within the coalfield area. In this sense, our discussants appear to be reiterating the 'field after field, landscape after landscape' progression of opencast mining (Bate *et al.*, 1991). As one group discussant commented:

they will dig those [trees] up like they dig the land up. If they want the coal and clay, and they get planning permission, [then] the trees will come up again (Open Meeting).

For this reason, several people within our groups considered that increased planning powers were needed to ensure that the National Forest could enforce restoration of derelict land and present mineral extraction sites, and prevent future opencast production within the area. Negotiation, compromise and legal agreements between the Forest team and British Coal were seen as desirable, although the [then] uncertainty surrounding the future of British Coal and the profitability of opencast mining made many people within our groups sceptical about the likely success of such agreements—it was 'one battle after another'.

A national asset or private woodland? Public environmental interests and private property rights. It can be suggested that the conflicts surrounding mineral extraction within the Forest boundaries stem, in the main, from the fact that the National Forest—a forest for the nation—is being developed on land which is largely privately-owned. Almost all our discussants equated the notion of the National Forest with open

public access, and considerable disquiet was expressed when each group was informed that this would not be the case. Indeed, while the alleviation of visual blight associated with sites of past mining activities was welcomed almost universally by people within our groups, many demanded more tangible benefits including public access and the provision of footpaths, bridleways, viewing areas, picnic sites and information centres. Such features would represent planning gain for local people, and ensure that they could again walk through small pockets of woodland:

I was under the impression that the National Forest was a forest for the people—to go walking through, and to ride their horses, and take their children for a walk at the weekend. I was under the impression that once it had been established it would be handed to the people (Town Council).

Here the notion of negotiated public access dependant on the decisions of private landowners was seen by many people within our groups as contradicting the raison d'être of the National Forest—a forest for the nation. One person asked whether the National Forest should be renamed the 'Private Woodland' and questioned the benefits which it offered for local communities. Our groups did not merely desire to experience trees in a visual sense but wanted also to physically encounter woodland through a network of public paths. This issue of public access and private property rights within the Forest was also raised by a local landowner (a farmer) in one of our discussions, who argued that public footpaths were not an economic consideration for the landowner. Instead, landowners, he suggested, viewed the Forest and tree planting on their land in relation to available financial incentives:

they are not going to have the population of Derby, Nottingham, Leicester, Birmingham and Sheffield swarming over their doorsteps... (Town Council).

. . . the footpath isn't an economic feature from the point of view of the farmer. The farmer would have to be paid to maintain the footpath, or compensated for wear and tear (Town Council).

New jobs for old land: economic gain and the National Forest. Another key concern expressed at meetings related to the funding of the National Forest, with many people suggesting that a forest planted on predominantly private land and funded through a series of financial incentives to private landowners would inhibit the Forest's development. Many people considered that the 'national' nature of the Forest warranted considerable financial input from central government. Moreover, very few people within our groups felt that the National Forest offered any significant economic benefits for their local area. In fact, with the exception of financial benefits available to farmers, the issue of employment creation was rarely mentioned, and discussion on this topic tended to be initiated by the research team. Most people within our discussions stated that any new employment in the local area would be favoured, although such economic benefits needed to be placed within a wider context of massive mining redundancies over recent years:

> we want to see people set up in a restaurant or a cafe. We want to see people coming in and spending a bit of money. [However,] I wouldn't like to say that this is going to match the loss of 1500 jobs from the mine closures (Town Council).

Others commentated that certain types of new leisure-based employment might not be appropriate for many ex-miners resident in the local area:

> I mean, it might not be much of a job for a man who has been used to tearing lumps of rock out of the ground . . . to make a living with a little bike hiring [business] (Town Council).

while a further group of discussants warned against any large-scale economic developments which might alter dramatically the character of the local area. Such developments mentioned included major house building programmes and a massive growth in tourist-based enterprises, as this final comment illustrates:

> you can see all kinds of little initiatives [and] enterprises being established within it all. But I feel that the minute anybody tries to turn it into a fun park around here, it will be knocked on the head instantly. Nobody is going to turn this patch into Alton Towers (Town Council).

Conclusions

In this paper we have explored some local outcomes of political-economic restructuring within the British coal industry in areas of (post) industrial countryside, highlighting two key processes of change: a collapse of the deep-mine industry, particularly in the early 1990s, and an expansion of opencast mining, linked to policy shifts towards the open market and privatisation. The growth of opencast production methods,

however, has not been without its environmental and landscape concerns and conflicts, particularly where such mining has taken place in areas of open countryside. These two components of restructuring have impinged directly on the (post) industrial countryside within the Leicestershire and South Derbyshire coalfield. Here, the local deep-mine coal industry has collapsed, while opencast production methods have expanded over recent years. Such localised economic restructuring has resulted in a set of employment and socio-cultural problems for many households within the region. Moreover, mining activities have led to a series of landscape and environmental transformations, as the contraction of deep-mine production has left a legacy of derelict sites, and the expanding opencast industry continues to scar a considerable area of the immediate countryside.

While we are not suggesting that the establishment of the National Forest in its present location was determined solely by the presence of these past and present mining landscapes, it seems clear from Countryside Commission literature that this mining component did play an important role in the area's designation. In this sense then, we begin to understand the notion of a 'multi-purpose forest'—a project of sustainable development—as one involving increased timber production, providing new uses for surplus agricultural land and creating new wildlife habitats alongside other objectives of providing new (leisure-based) employment and rehabilitating scarred landscapes. Indeed, we would suggest that the concept of the National Forest follows on closely from the National Garden Festivals of the 1980s and early 1990s.

However, if one of the key factors behind the present location of the National Forest was the presence of scarred mining landscapes, then we would argue that this same mining industry constitutes one of the main threats to its development. In this paper we have highlighted a series of fundamental conflicts surrounding the establishment of the Forest in an area of on-going (and, indeed, expanding) opencast mining activities. Such conflicts have stemmed, in the main, from the fact that the National Forest is being planted on land which is predominantly privately-owned. With relatively limited central government financial investment and only small-scale land purchase, it is difficult to envisage how the ambitious targets stated by the Countryside Commission will be achieved. Indeed, the initial goal of 40% tree cover has been reduced to one-third and only 3% of the tree target has been achieved in the Forest's first three years' development.

The benefits of the National Forest for derelict sites of (past) mining activities have been generally accepted by both the Countryside Commission and local communities within the area, as the first part of this paper's title—taken from an editorial in a local newspaper—demonstrates. In a similar vein to the garden festivals at Ebbw Vale and Stoke-on-Trent, the National Forest is seen as extinguishing landscape despoilment and visual blight from an area previously characterised by traditional heavy or extractive industries. However, on-going opencast mining is recognised—again, by both the Commission and local groups—as a much more complex industrial activity. Here, the Countryside Commission envisages the relationship between this industry and the Forest's development as one of negotiation through planning gain, in that mining may be permitted in return for schemes of regeneration which coincide with other Forest objectives. In this sense then, the National Forest is claiming rehabilitation of mining landscapes as a key part of its rationale, yet at the same time, it is dependent on the exploitation of the local landscape through new or expanded opencast production as 'gain' from more stringent regeneration clauses. Therefore, the National Forest has to accommodate development which then contradicts other parts of its main objectives (tourism, landscape beautification, etc.), and we question whether this will lead to a zonal approach within the Forest area, with an unofficial policy operating within the mining zone of 'cleaning up by making more dirt'—a Forest which is sustainable only in parts.

Our research has also revealed a series of experiences of opencast mining and a set of expectations associated with the establishment of the National Forest within local communities in the coalfield area. We believe that the commentaries which have been highlighted within this paper enrich our understanding of everyday perceptions of local landscapes and the contradictory demands placed on such landscapes from opencast mining and the imposition of forestry. In overall terms, local people within our group discussions appeared to welcome the establishment of the Forest, and the associated potential benefits of improved employment opportunities and enhanced local landscapes. However, it should be noted that many were also aware of a series of underlying (past, present and future) power relations embedded within

the transformations of their familiar landscapes, and the 'on-going battles' between (the now private) extractive capital and local environments. For such people, the interests of coal were viewed as taking precedence over the planting of trees, and any new rights of public access in newly forested areas were seen as being secured only at the 'cost' of increased mining activities. Others were extremely wary about the large-scale nature of the Forest project and the potential alterations to the local area in terms of industrial, residential and tourist developments. In this sense then, local people within our discussions appear to welcome the removal of *wasteland*, but remain sceptical towards any transformation of their familar landscapes to *wonderland*.

Notes

1. English Coal consists of many of the assets of the British Coal Corporation and includes 17 underground coal mines and 16 opencast sites (Mining Journal, 1994). British Coal's assets in Scotland have been purchased by Mining (Scotland) and Celtic Energy has acquired Welsh mines.
2. Garden Festivals were held in the following locations in the 1980s and early 1990s: Liverpool, 1984; Stoke-on-Trent, 1986; Glasgow, 1988; Gateshead, 1990; Ebbw Vale 1992.
3. Prior to its designation as a Rural Development Area, the Leicester and South Derbyshire coalfield had been included within the RDC's Rural Coalfield Areas programme.
4. See Bate *et al*. (1991), p. 7.
5. Meetings were conducted with the Town Council, a young mothers' group; a class of school children; Darby and Joan Club; the Miners' Welfare. In addition, an open meeting was held in the community centre.
6. Both comments are taken from our discussion with the Darby and Joan Club.
7. Reference is made to British Coal within this section since discussions were conducted prior to the privatisation of the coal industry.

References

Atkin, D. (1993) Black gold and sunshine mining, *Town and Country Planning*, July, 182–184.

Bate, R., Rutherford, L., Peart, J. and Cox, R. (1991) *Campaigners' Guide to Opencast Coal Mining*. CPRE, London.

Bishop, K. (1992) Britain's new forests: public dependence on private interest, In: *Restructuring the Countryside: Environmental Policy in Practice*, A. Gilg (Ed.). Avebury, Aldershot.

Bonyhady, T. (1987) *The Law of the Countryside: the Rights of the Public*. Professional Books, Abingdon.

British Coal (1993) *Annual Report and Accounts*. British Coal, London.

Beynon, H., Hudson, R. and Sadler, D. (1991) *A Tale of Two Industries: the Contraction of Coal and Steel in the*

174   Paul Cloke *et al.*

North East of England. Open University Press, Milton Keynes.

Cloke, P., Milbourne, P. and Thomas, C. (1993) *The National Forest Community Study.* Countryside Commission, Cheltenham.

Coalfield Communities Campaign (1994) *Coal Industry Bill Briefing Paper No. 3: Opencast Coal.* Coalfield Communities Campaign, Barnsley.

Coalfield Communities Campaign (1993) *Statistics on Opencast Coalmining and the Planning System.* Coalfield Communities Campaign, Barnsley.

Council for the Protection of Rural England (1994) Coal sores, *Countryside Campaigner,* Autumn, 19.

Countryside Commission (1987) *Forestry in the Countryside.* Countryside Commission CCP 245, Cheltenham.

Countryside Commission (1992) *Business in the Forest.* Countryside Commission, Cheltenham.

Countryside Commission (1993a) *The National Forest.* Countryside Commission CCP 410, Cheltenham.

Countryside Commission (1993b) *The National Forest Strategy.* Countryside Commission CCP 411, Cheltenham.

County Planning Officers' Society (1994) *Opencast Coalmining Statistics 1993–94.* County Planning Officers' Society, Durham.

Cox, G., Lowe, P. and Winter, M. (1988) Private rights and public responsibilities: the prospects for agricultural and environmental controls, *Journal of Rural Studies,* **4**(4), 323–337.

Department of the Environment/Welsh Office (1988) *Minerals Planning Guidance: Opencast Coal Mining.* HMSO, London.

Department of the Environment/Welsh Office (1994) *Minerals Planning Guidance: Coal Mining and Colliery Spoil Disposal.* HMSO, London.

Fothergill, S. (1993) The coal industry after the White Paper, *Town and Country Planning,* July, 169–170.

Glen, M. (1994) The changing role of opencast coal restoration in landscape regeneration, *Mineral Planning,* **38**, 29–31.

Hudson, R. and Cox, A. (1990) *British Coal and Opencast Mining,* Discussion Paper Number 9, source not stated.

Hudson, R. and Salder, D. (1990) State policies and the changing geography of the coal industry in the United Kingdom in the 1980s and 1990s, *Transactions of the Institute of British Geographers,* New Series, **15**, 435–454.

Kivell, P. (1993) Dereliction and environmental regeneration, In: *The Potteries: Continuity and Change in a Staffordshire Conurbation,* A. Phillips (Ed.). Allen Sutton, Stroud.

Leicester Mercury (1991) Editorial, *Leicester Mercury,* November 8th, Leicester.

Leicestershire and Derbyshire Coalfields Rural Partnership (1994) *Rural Development Area Strategy.* Leicestershire and Derbyshire Coalfields Rural Partnership.

Leverton, P., Prescott, G., Delpak, R. and Wang, H. (1992) Fruits from the garden?, *Town & Country Planning,* February, 52–54.

Lowe, P., Clark, J. and Cox, G. (1993) Reasonable creatures: rights and rationalities in valuing the countryside, *Journal of Environmental Planning and Management,* **36**(1), 101–115.

Lowe, P. and Murdoch, J. (1993) *Rural Sustainable Development.* Rural Development Commission, London.

Mabey, R. (1994) Planning guidelines for coal, *Mineral Planning,* **58**, 3–7.

Marsden, T., Murdoch, J., Lowe, P., Munton, R. and Flynn, A. (1993) *Constructing the Countryside.* ULC Press, London.

Mining Journal (1994) Budge completes deal, *Mining Journal,* December 16th, 446.

Mining Journal (1995) British Coal in private hands, *Mining Journal,* January 6th, 15.

Mineral Planning (1994a) British Coal opencast 1993/4, *Mineral Planning,* **61**, 17.

Mineral Planning (1994b) Slate quarrying deferred in National Park, *Mineral Planning,* **61**, 34–35.

National Forest/British Coal (1993) *British Coal and the National Forest—A Growing Relationship.* British Coal Property, Eastwood.

O'Riordan, T. (1988) The politics of sustainability, In: *Sustainable Development Environmental Management: Principles and Practice,* R. K. Turner (Ed.). ESRC, Belhaven, Westview, London.

Redclift, M. (1992) The meaning of sustainable development, *Geoforum,* **23**(3), 395–403.

Redclift, M. and Benton, T. (Eds) (1994) *Social Theory and the Global Environment.* Routledge, London.

Roberts, P. (1989) Coal and the environment: planning and management issues for the future of coalfields, *Environment and Planning A,* **21**, 1285–1296.

Siddall, R. (1994) The opencast coal industry and the Coalfield Communities Campaign, *Mineral Planning,* **59**, 33–37.

Steele, J. (1995) Wooden headed, *The Guardian,* January 25, 6–7.

Thornley, A. (1991) *Urban Planning Under Thatcherism: the Challenge of the Market.* Routledge, London.

Trade and Industry Committee (1993) *British Energy Policy and the Market for Coal,* First Report, HMSO, London.

Whatmore, S. and Boucher, S. (1993) Bargaining with nature: the discourse and practice of 'environmental planning gain'. *Transactions of the Institute of British Geographers,* New Series, **18**, No. 2, 166–178.

[25]

Land Use Policy, Vol. 12, No. 2, pp. 115–135, 1995
Copyright © 1995 Elsevier Science Ltd
Printed in Great Britain. All rights reserved
0264-8377/95 $10.00 + 0.00

0264-8377(94)00003-4

Conserved to death

Are tropical forests being over-protected from people?

David Wood

There are plans to double the area of strictly protected tropical forest. This article suggests that the siting and management of such reserves are based on models of conservation inappropriate to developing countries, and that an ignorance of past and present tropical land use will prevent reserves achieving their major objective of conserving useful biodiversity. Strict preservation could also destroy the indigenous knowledge needed for ecosystem management. Multipurpose management and continued human use of tropical forests is a more effective and sustainable conservation policy for tropical developing countries. Rural communities should be actively and physically involved in the future productive management of tropical forests, rather than being induced or pressured into abandoning their forest heritage.

The author is an environmental consultant for International Germplasm Associates, 12A Prospect Row, Gillingham, Kent, ME7 5AL, UK (Tel: 0634 847255).

The author wishes to thank several anonymous referees for their valuable comments.

[1]McNeely, J A (ed) *Parks for Life: Report of the IVth World Congress on National Parks and Protected Areas* IUCN, Gland (1993)
[2]World Bank *Congo: Wildlands Protection and Management Project Document* Global Environment Facility, World Bank, Washington, DC (1993)
[3]World Bank *Bhutan: Trust Fund for Environmental Conservation* Global Environment Facility, World Bank, Washington, DC (1992)

continued on page 116

'. . . whoever could make two ears of corn or two blades of grass to grow upon a spot of ground where only one grew before, would deserve better of mankind and do more essential service to his country than the whole race of *conservationists* put together.' Adapted from Jonathan Swift, *Gulliver's Travels*, 'Voyage to Brobdingnag'

The debate over land use in tropical regions continues to be polarized. On one hand, conservationists wish to preserve biodiversity in increasingly large protected areas and nature reserves; on the other hand, developing countries wish to exploit their land and biological resources in order to increase national food, timber and export crop production (often under imposed structural adjustment programmes).

As an example of the headlong rush to expand protected areas, the Fourth World Congress on National Parks and Protected Areas recommended that the global network of protected areas be expanded from the current 5% coverage to 10% of each biome by the year 2000.[1] Land alienation for reserves is increasing under the Global Environmental Facility (GEF) programme: for example, in the Congo five forest reserves total 25 660 sq km;[2] in Bhutan 9505 sq km – about 20% of the area of the country – is already protected. Despite a critical shortage of agricultural land (only about 8–10% of the total area) and existing conflicts over land use between people and wildlife there are plans to expand protected areas in Bhutan to 25–30% of total land area 'in order to address the gaps in coverage'.[3]

Alienation of potential agricultural land continues, despite warnings from sociologists that 'parks and forest reserves are likely to be one of the major issues of future rural social conflict in many developing countries'.[4] Conservation insensitive to local needs has led to a situation where the 'majority of local people view wildlife conservation as alien, hypocritical, and as favouring foreigners'.[5] The sustainability of reserves is now in question: it is thought that 'it is inconceivable that networks of protected areas can be maintained indefinitely by what amounts, in some cases, to military force'.[6]

I attempted to bridge the polarity by reviewing evidence that much tropical forest is secondary, the land having been formerly used for agriculture.[7] I suggested that these secondary forests could be preferentially used for future tropical agriculture to reduce pressure on primary forest. My argument that secondary forests could be usefully developed for agriculture has been criticized and rejected.[8] Conservationists demand that 'Conservation is thus an imperative'[9] – forests should be conserved as forests.

This paper is a counter-criticism of the intransigent position of some conservationists on tropical land use. Its theme is that large areas of land which could be used for agriculture and forestry are now being alienated into unproductive 'white elephant' reserves, with the quite unnecessary exclusion of local people. It argues that the siting and management of reserves are based on models of conservation inappropriate to developing countries, and that an ignorance of past and present tropical land use will prevent reserves achieving their major objective of conserving useful biodiversity.

Types of conservation area

There are several international systems for designating protected areas. The most widely used is that of IUCN management categories,[10] which includes eight classes (I–VIII), ranging from Scientific Reserve/Strict Nature Reserve (I), through National Park (II), Natural Monument/Natural Landmark (III), Managed Nature Reserve/Wildlife Sanctuary (IV), Protected Landscape or Seascape (V), Resource Reserve (VI), Natural Biotic Area/Anthropological Reserve (VII), to Multiple-Use Management Area/Managed Resource Area (VIII). In general, the higher the number, the greater the degree of human access is permitted or tolerated. In addition, there are two international conventions for protected sites: the World Heritage Convention for areas of 'outstanding universal value' (not necessarily biological value), and the Ramsar Convention for wetlands. World Heritage Sites can include 'cultural landscapes' for the 'combined works of nature and man' including 'organically evolving landscapes resulting from successive social and economic imperatives and in response to the natural environment' and a 'social, traditional way of life in which the evolutionary process is still in progress'.[11] Although not an international convention, the Unesco 'Man and the Biosphere' programme designates Biosphere Reserves. In most cases the human component is thought to be vital for the functioning of a Biosphere Reserve.

In addition to these international systems, nations have their own criteria for protection of areas under national laws, with a range of conditions from strict protection to controlled use.[12] For example, in addition to National Parks, India has designations for Sanctuary, Game Reserve and Closed Area, under its Wildlife (Protection) Act. Under the Indian Forest Act, designated forests include Reserved forest, Village forest and Protected forest. Terminology may differ dramatically – for example, the legally established English 'National Parks', with towns, farms and road and rail networks, correspond to the IUCN category VIII, 'Multiple-Use Management Areas', or category V, 'Protected Landscape', rather than the 'National Parks' of IUCN category II of protected area.

Rural communities maintain many types of protected areas. For example, the local population of Mount Oku, Cameroon, had very sophisticated norms for managing watersheds, catchment areas and

continued from page 115
[4]Ghimire, K B *Parks and People: Livelihood Issues in National Parks Management in Thailand and Madagascar* Discussion Paper No 29, United Nations Research Institute for Social Development (1992) 34; also published with the same title in *Development and Change* 1994 **25** 195–229
[5]Munthali, S M 'Traditional and modern wildlife conservation in Malawi – the need for an integrated approach' *Oryx* 1993 **27** 185–187
[6]Wells, M P and Brandon, K E 'The principles and practice of buffer zones and local participation in biodiversity conservation' *Ambio* 1993 **22** 162
[7]Wood, D 'Forests to fields: restoring tropical lands to agriculture' *Land Use Policy* 1993 **10** (2) 91–107
[8]Fearnside, P M 'Forests or fields? A response to the theory that tropical forest conservation poses a threat to the poor' *Land Use Policy* 1993 **10** (2) 108–121; Hill, R D 'Letter to the Editor: Forests and fields: comments on a debate' *Land Use Policy* 1993 **10** (4) 330–332
[9]Hill *op cit* Ref 8, 332
[10]IUCN *Protected Areas of the World: A Review of National Systems* Vol 1: *Indomalaya, Oceania, Australia and Antarctic* IUCN, Gland, Switzerland (1992)
[11]*World Heritage Newsletter* February 1993 (1) 15
[12]*Ibid*

[13]Fisiy, C F 'The death of a myth system: land colonization on the slopes of Mount Oku, Cameroon' in Bakema, R J (ed) *Land Tenure and Sustainable Land Use* Bulletin 332, Royal Tropical Institute, Amsterdam (1994) 12–20

[14]Dei, G J S 'A forest beyond the trees: tree cutting in rural Ghana' *Human Ecology* 1992 **20** 57–88, 72–73 for protective myth and tradition

[15]Lucas, R C 'Wilderness perception and use: the case of the Boundary Waters canoe area' *Natural Resources Journal* 1964 **3** 394–411

[16]*Economist* 30 October 1993 prints a letter from the Administrator of the Global Environmental Facility of the World Bank which defends large-scale biodiversity conservation projects on 'previously uninhabited land'.

[17]Braatz, S *Conserving Biological Diversity: A Strategy for Protected Areas in the Asia-Pacific Region* Technical Paper No 193, Asia Technical Department Series, World Bank, Washington, DC (1992)

[18]World Bank *op cit* Ref 2. This candidly admits (p 73) that 'there is growing hostility on the part of the population to the introduction of protection measures'.

[19]For example, the definition of 'virgin forest' as 'forest not previously cleared by nonindigenous immigrants' by Fearnside, P M 'Fire in the tropical rain forest of the Amazon Basin' in Goldhammer, J G (ed) *Fire in the Tropical Biota: Ecosystem Processes and Global Challenges* Springer-Verlag, Berlin (1990) 109. With this kind of definition anything is possible.

[20]Gómez-Pompa, A and Kaus, A 'Taming the wilderness myth' *BioScience* 1992 **42** 271–279

[21]Posey, D A 'The importance of semi-domesticated species in post-contact Amazonia: effects of Kayapo indians on the dispersal of flora and fauna' in Hladik, C M, Hladik, A, Linares, O F, Pagezy, H, Semple, A and Hadley, M (eds) *Tropical Forests, People and Food: Biocultural Interactions and Applications to Development* Man and the Biosphere Vol 13, Unesco, Paris (1993) 63–71

[22]Schüle, W 'Vegetation, megaherbivores, man and climate in the Quarternary and the genesis of closed rain forests' in Goldhammer *op cit* Ref 19, 45–76

[23]Wood *op cit* Ref 7; World Bank *op cit* Ref 3. This notes (p 5) that the project will assist Bhutan to conserve its 'pristine' ecosystems.

[24]McNeely, J A 'Lessons from the past: forests and biodiversity' *Biodiversity and Conservation* 1994 **3** 4. This paper also argues that evidence is growing for the view that very few of today's forests anywhere in the world can be considered pristine, virgin or even primary, and that conserving biological diversity requires a far more subtle appreciation of both human and natural influence.

[25]Bailey, R C, Bahuchet, S and Hewlett, B 'Development in the Central African rain-
continued on page 118

fragile forest ecosystems.[13] Any tract of land that possessed these properties was declared a sacred forest. Individual trees are protected by myth and tradition in Ghana.[14]

Conservationist perceptions of land use

The US Wilderness Bill (1964) regards wilderness as 'an area where the earth and its community of life are untrammeled by man, where man himself is a visitor who does not remain'.[15] This view of wilderness is apparently a driving force behind the Global Environmental Facility of the World Bank,[16] which has a 'Wildlands Operational Note' to govern the framework for protected area projects.[17] However, a GEF project for the Congo with the deceptive title 'Wildlands Protection and Management'[18] will manage reserves with existing large human populations engaged in farming, intensive hunting, timber extraction and even gold mining and oil exploration. Such areas cannot be considered to be wildlands without disrupting the meaning of the word.[19] Yet conservationists continue to ignore or play down past and present use of tropical forest in an effort to attract funding from proponents (now notably the World Bank) of classic Yellowstone-style large national parks and wilderness areas.

The most relevant and detailed criticism of the 'wilderness myth' comes from Gómez-Pompa and Kaus, who suggest that:

The concept of wilderness as the untouched or untamed land is mostly an urban perception, the view of people who are far removed from the natural environment they depend on for raw resources. The inhabitants of rural areas have different views of the areas that urbanites designate as wilderness, and they base their land-use and resource management practices on these alternative visions. Indigenous groups in the tropics, for example, do not consider the tropical forest environment to be wild; it is their home.[20]

'Natural' is also a word subject to romanticized usage. Posey notes that 'Probably much of what has been considered "natural" in the Amazon is, in fact, modified by prehistorical and historical Amerind populations . . .'.[21] In a remarkable analysis of the effects of prehistoric people on forest structure, Schüle suggested that closed-crown forest is not the natural structure of tropical forest, but rather patchwork forest: a closed forest canopy was possible only after man had exterminated the forest megafauna and decimated other vertebrates.[22] The terms 'virgin', 'pristine', 'untouched nature' and the like have been extensively used to justify the protection of 'wilderness'.[23] However, the reality is very different: humans have been a dominant force in the evolution of today's forests.[24] For example, in Central Africa all present-day forests areas are really a patchwork of various successional stages of growth created by people, and no areas are what proposals and reports refer to as 'pristine', 'untouched', 'primary' or 'mature' forest.[25] In short, these forests are human cultural artefacts. The mistaken concept of 'wilderness' prevents continued sustainable management by local communities: reserves are being 'conserved to death'.[26]

Imposed and inadequate models of conservation

By far the most serious impediment to tropical forest conservation is the promotion in developing countries of a particularly inappropriate model: that of North American 'national parks'. The drawbacks of this

Tropical forests – conserved to death?: D Wood

model have been repeatedly noted, yet it still largely determines global conservation funding. National parks in the USA are based on the notions that (a) they are protecting ecosystems that are not materially altered by human exploitation and occupation, and (b) the relevant authority 'has taken steps to prevent or eliminate as soon as possible exploitation or occupation of the whole area'.[27] West argues that, based on such definitions, resident peoples have been displaced or blocked from traditional use of park resources, without any documented proof that they were harming the resources. West notes that the international conservation movement had perhaps too eagerly proselytized the US concept of national parks. Eidsvik had earlier argued that much of the growth of protected areas over the last century had followed from the model of North American national parks where the emphasis was on the protection of nature and where human populations were not of major concern.[28]

Southgate and Clark pointed out that the present conservation paradigm was 'an attempt to transplant national parks, a rich country institution, to an alien setting', and that as 'traditionally defined, a park is a natural area where no people . . . live or work'. Using as an example the Brazilian Amazon, they suggested that nowhere, aside from a few permanent swamps, was truly uninhabited, and that practically any attempt to establish a park would cause people to be displaced.[29] Brower, in a survey of conservation in Nepal, noted that problems arose from the hasty imposition of imported conservation ideology and techniques based on Western models, and that this imposition undermined traditional resource management practices.[30] Bidol and Crowfoot commented on the expansion of the US national park philosophy to developing countries:

The Western world's practices of siting and managing national parks have been implemented by developing nations throughout the world. This tradition of national parks does not allow the local resident peoples to live within the boundaries of the park or to use and extract the park's resources.[31]

As an example of a major conservation initiative, the Global Environmental Facility (GEF) of the World Bank is culpable over the issue of resettlement of rural communities, and has confirmed to the Director of the Kenya Wildlife Service that GEF resources can be use to finance 'voluntary or involuntary resettlement' of people from reserves.[32] The supposition that strictly protected areas are an appropriate land use is particularly misconceived for tropical forests. Yet conservationist organizations – and the donors who support them – continue to insist on strict protection for forests.

Gómez-Pompa and Kaus claim that 'conservationist beliefs have generally held that there is an inverse relationship between human actions and the well-being of the natural environment'.[33] This claim is supported by conservation literature: conservationists have argued that 'human economic or exploitative uses of protected lands are wholly unacceptable if protection of those lands is going to be possible'.[34] IUCN/UNEP suggested that 'Ecologically, as little human interference as possible is desirable in rain forest' and that, for tropical forest, it is 'a matter of urgency to conserve as much as possible now'.[35] As a specific example of the exclusionist philosophy of national park management, a study of the Rio Abiseo National Park (270 000 ha) in Peru noted that 'Protection of the park requires the identification and prevention of human impacts.'[36]

continued from page 117
forest: concern for forest peoples' in *Conservation of West and Central African Rainforests* Environment Paper No 1, World Bank, Washington, DC (1992) 208
[26]Romell, L G 'Man made "nature" of northern lands' *Proceedings and Papers of the Sixth Technical Meeting of the International Union for the Conservation of Nature and Natural Resources* Edinburgh, June 1956 (1957) 52–53
[27]West, P C, 'Introduction' in West, P C and Brechin, S R (eds) *Resident Peoples and National Parks: Social Dilemma and Strategies in International Conservation* University of Arizona Press, Tucson, AZ (1991) xv–xxiv
[28]Eidsvik, H K 'National parks and other protected areas: some reflections of the past and prescriptions for the future' *Environmental Conservation* 1980 **7** 185–190
[29]Southgate, D and Clark, H L 'Can conservation projects save biodiversity in South America?' *Ambio* 1993 **22** 163–166
[30]Brower, B 'Crisis and conservation in the Sagarmatha National Park, Nepal' *Society and Natural Resources* 1991 **4** 151–163
[31]Bidol, P and Crowfoot, J E 'Towards an interactive process for siting national parks in developing nations' in West and Brechin *op cit* Ref 27, 283–300
[32]*Global Environment Facility Monthly Operations Report* February 1992, 8
[33]Gómez-Pompa and Kaus *op cit* Ref 20
[34]This argument for protected areas is noted by Ham, S H, Sutherland, D S and Meganck, R A 'Applying environmental interpretation in protected areas of developing countries: problems of exporting a US model' *Environmental Conservation* 1993 **20** 232–242. In contrast these authors suggest that human use 'is even requisite to sustainable protection'.
[35]IUCN/UNEP *Managing Protected Areas in the Tropics* IUCN, Gland (1986) xvi, 295
[36]Young, K R 'National park protection in relation to the ecological zonation of a neighboring human community: an example from northern Peru' *Mountain Research and Development* 1993 **13** 268

Rural Planning and Management

A recent IUCN statement on forest conservation suggested that the safest way of ensuring the maximum protection of biodiversity in tropical forests was to allocate significant forest areas to national parks and reserves where human interference is minimized.[37] The same paper noted that in 1980 the lowland tropical moist forest biome included 669 reserves of a total of 66 million ha, falling within IUCN categories I–IV of protected areas of which no significant human use was permitted. The intention was to achieve the 'modest' target of 10% total protection of all the moist tropical forest by 1990.

Even for the limited-use 'buffer zones' that surround protected areas, it has been suggested that 'The optimal form of land use outside parks and reserves is near-natural forests under sustainable management for timber or non-timber products.'[38]

The 'anti-resident-peoples' model for national parks derived from the USA is similar to the colonial view of nature conservation. Tendencies for strictly protected areas are rooted historically in colonial systems, particularly in Africa and Asia.[39] The iniquities of the colonial conservation systems have been pointed out several times.[40] McHenry noted the failure of established management structures, generally colonial or post-colonial adaptations of centralized legal and bureaucratic models, to accommodate traditional methods of wildlife usage and provide more flexible means for the conservation of wildlife.[41] The negative effect of protected areas on rural populations has been surveyed by Rao and Geisler.[42]

Local hostility to protected areas is longstanding. Following Norman colonization the royal forests of medieval England quickly expanded and provide an early model for the exclusion of rural people from resource areas. Attempts to farm in these royal forests were dealt with harshly, with the seizure of property and the imposition of substantial fines. There was deliberate depopulation of royal forests. Not surprisingly, these forests were 'bitterly hated and opposed',[43] as they had provided essential resources to rural communities, who often maintained specific forest-feeding varieties of cattle and pigs under sophisticated traditional management. The area of these parks, once a quarter of all England, is now very fragmentary. There are pronounced similarities in central control and in management problems between the royal forests, colonial conservation and the present trends in conservation in developing countries, as rural communities attempt to emulate Robin Hood in the modern equivalent of taking the king's deer. Alcorn notes that reports from the field indicate that few tropical protected areas are likely to survive for another century, much less thousands of years into the future.[44]

Who benefits from conservation?

At their most general, arguments for tropical forest conservation try to demonstrate a wide range of benefits – for example, O'Riordan proposes that genepools and critically endangered habitats should be safeguarded in the interests of science, medicine, minority cultural values and the good of future generations.[45] However, conservationists are realistic in accepting that funds for tropical forest conservation will come predominantly from developed countries.[46] Rubinoff recognized that 'It seems clear that, in the short run, the developed world will not help the developing countries in any appreciable way until the threat for

[37]Sayer, J 'Conservation and protection of tropical rain forests: the perspective of the World Conservation Union' *Unasylva* 1991 **166** 42

[38]Sayer, J A and Whitmore; T C 'Tropical moist forests: destruction and species extinction' *Biological Conservation* 1991 **5** 210

[39]West *op cit* Ref 27. West notes that the IUCN is stimulating tendencies to follow the US national parks philosophy.

[40]Grove, R H 'Colonial conservation, ecological hegemony and popular resistance: towards a global synthesis' in MacKenzie, J M (ed) *Imperialism and the Natural World* Manchester University, Manchester, UK (1990) 15–50; Munthali *op cit* Ref 5; Anderson, D 'Managing the forest: the conservation history of Lembus, Kenya, 1904–63' in Anderson, D and Grove, R (eds) *Conservation in Africa: Peoples, Policies and Practice* Cambridge Unversity Press, Cambridge, UK (1987) 249–268

[41]McHenry, T J P 'Policy and legal tools for the management of wildlife resources' *Unasylva* 1993 **175** 46–50

[42]Rao, K and Geisler, C 'The social consequences of protected areas for resident populations' *Society and Natural Resources* 1990 **3** 19–32

[43]Grant, R *The Royal Forests of England* Alan Sutton, Stroud, UK (1991) x, 246

[44]Alcorn, J B 'Epilogue: ethics, economies, and conservation' in Oldfield, M L and Alcorn, J B (eds) *Biodiversity: Culture, Conservation, and Ecodevelopment* Westview Press, Boulder, CO (1991) 317–349

[45]O'Riordan, T 'On the "greening" of major projects' *Geographical Journal* 1990 **156** 145

[46]Gunawardene, N 'Bridging the gap between perception and reality' *Perspectives* 1993 (11) 13–14

not doing so is immediate and personalized, to the extent that the quality of life in the developed world is immediately at risk or already seriously deteriorated.'[47]

As developed countries provide the main source of funds for conservation, conservationists have attempted to gain funds by demonstrating the value of tropical forests to developed countries. For example,

Genetic resources from tropical forests are an essential part of world economic productivity and play a vital role in supporting human civilizations. Without their contributions to the genetic improvement of crop species and to the location of new biotic resources of industrial and medicinal products, economic productivity will eventually be severely curtailed. Deforestation and conversion of tropical forests are primary causes of such loss.[48]

Myers puts the self-interest argument more bluntly: 'we can expect entire cornucopias of new and improved foods, and whole pharmacopoeias of new medicines, plus vast stocks of industrial raw materials, provided the scientific investigator can get to wild gene pools before the "developer" gets to their habitats'.[49]

Unfortunately, the need to obtain funds from developed countries for tropical forest conservation has led to a vicious circle of conservationist exaggerations and donor expectations.[50] As an example, it has taken 15 years for the conservationist myth that the Amazonian forests were 'the lungs of the world' to be satisfactorily countered in the media.[51] Appeals to the self-interest of developed-world decision makers have concentrated on the expected benefits of developing new medicines from tropical forest organisms. In the emphasis on tropical forests as 'pharmacopoeias', truth has often taken second place to fiction, as in the deceptive promotion of the 'rosy periwinkle' (*Catharanthus roseus*, also known as the Madagascar periwinkle), which produces a valuable anti-leukaemia drug.

The *WWF Atlas of the Environment* claims that the 'rosy periwinkle, a pretty but unremarkable plant discovered in a Madagascan forest, has transformed the prospects of children with leukemia'.[52] A World Bank review claims that 'Many of the species native to tropical rain forests have proved invaluable to humankind: for example, drugs (vincristine and vinblastine) developed in the past two decades from a wild periwinkle found in the forests of Madagascar have dramatically improved the effectiveness of treatment for leukemia . . .'[53] Another source notes the rainforest connection: 'drugs derived from one of the plants unique to the island [Madagascar], the rosy periwinkle, have proved invaluable in treating childhood leukemia and Hodgkin's disease'.[54] A senior conservationist makes a characteristic plea for conserving tropical forest: 'The fact that Madagascar is the only home of the genus *Catharanthus* (Apocynaceae), whose alkaloids provide the basis for a 22-year-old industry yielding well over a hundred million dollars annually, saving thousands of victims of childhood leukemia each year, is a poignant reminder of what we are losing . . .'[55] While this latter may be strictly the truth, it is not the whole truth: the rosy periwinkle is one of the most widespread tropical weeds; it is very drought resistant, and in Madagascar it predominately grows in drier, sandy places and not tropical rainforests; its valuable medicinal properties were discovered by research on samples from Jamaica and the Philippines.

The value of the rosy periwinkle is an excellent justification for human disturbance of tropical ecosystems and continued use of rural

[47]Rubinoff, I 'A strategy for preserving topical forests' in Sutton, S L, Whitmore, T C and Chadwick, A C (eds) *Tropical Rain Forest: Ecology and Management* Blackwell Scientific, Oxford, UK (1983) 474
[48]Oldfield, M 'Tropical deforestation and genetic resources conservation' in *Blowing in the Wind: Deforestation and Long-range Implications* in Studies in Third World Societies No 14, College of William and Mary, Williamsburg, VA (1980) 323
[49]Review by Myers in *Journal of Tropical Ecology* 7 98 of Oldfield, M I *The Value of Conserving Genetic Resources* Sinauer Associates, MA (1989) xvii, 379
[50]Known as the 'magic bullet' syndrome: Vivian, J 'NGOs and sustainable development in Zimbabwe: no magic bullets' *Development and Change* 1994 25 167–193
[51]Moran, E F 'Deforestation and land use in the Brazilian Amazon' *Human Ecology* 1993 21 1–21
[52]Lean, G, Hinrichsen, D and Markham, A *WWF Atlas of the Environment* Hutchinson, London (1990) 127
[53]Mahar, D J *Government Policies and Deforestation in Brazil's Amazon* World Bank, Washington, DC (1989) 2
[54]Wright, M 'The great rain forest rip-off' *Conservation Now* February/March 1991, 56–57
[55]Raven, P H 'A plea to the citizens of the world: live as if earth matters' *Diversity* 1993 9 (3) 50

Rural Planning and Management

Tropical forests – conserved to death?: D Wood

resources. It is remarkable how it has been used by conservationists to justify the opposite approach: the strict protection of forest. Funding gained by conservationists using such spurious arguments will be used to exclude people from forests. Ironically, Ghimire discovered that the internationally reputed panda logo of the WWF was taken as a symbol of ill-fortune in Madagascar, as a result of restricted local access to forest and fines for infringement.[56]

In addition to arguments for conservation based on the fear of loss of resources – for example, forests as the 'lungs of the world' and 'pharmacopoeias' – there are arguments based on the agricultural interests of developed countries. Many significant donors to tropical forest conservation (including the USA, Canada, Australia and the European Community) have considerable agricultural surpluses to export each year. The expanding area of tropical forest reserves represent the alienation of large areas of potential agricultural land. It has been suggested that a minimum size of 400 000 ha is too small for wilderness areas in rainforest, and that 2 million ha ought to be the 'minimum to optimize biodiversity'.[57] A single reserve of 2 million ha of rainforest, if only partly converted to intensive rice production, could readily produce yearly more that the current US rice exports of 2 164 460 t (value $734 983 000, 1992 figures). An expansion of protected areas will reduce the ability of developing countries either to compete in agricultural export markets (Brazil, Thailand, Vietnam) or to reach and maintain self-sufficiency in staple foods (Mexico, India, most of sub-Saharan Africa). Donor support for the conservation of very large protected areas of tropical forest could therefore be regarded as a very low cost mechanism for reducing the future agricultural competitiveness of developing countries, equivalent in effect to 'setaside' in Britain, or the 'Conservation Reserve Program' in the USA, which are costly government programmes to remove land from agricultural production. By arguing for such large and strictly protected reserves, conservationists are exposing themselves to criticisms of being used to protect the agricultural interests of international donors.

The possible link between conservation and reduced agricultural potential is subject to scathing comment by Southgate and Clark, who consider that most conservation organizations are far more interested in seeing Integrated Conservation and Development Projects (ICDPs) and related initiatives funded and implemented that they are in projects to increase overall agricultural productivity.[58]

In addition to promoting tropical forest conservation, some donor agencies are at the same time scaling back agricultural development programmes, perhaps in response to pressure exerted by farm protectionists in North America and Europe, who are loath to make African, Asian and Latin American agriculture more competitive.[59] The hope apparently is that developing countries should conserve forest and import food, while the richer countries should export food. Crossin and Anderson, in a World Bank review of prospects for world cereal production, note the relationship between crop production and demands for environmental protectionism by developed countries. They argue that the costs of forest clearing are believed to be high by what they term 'influential members of the world community', and that widely publicized efforts are underway to persuade the Brazilian and other governments in tropical areas to slow if not halt tropical forest clearing. Significantly, Crossin and Anderson argue that the more

[56]Ghimire *op cit* Ref 4
[57]McCloskey, M 'Note of the fragmentation of primary rainforest' *Ambio* 1993 **22** 250–251
[58]Southgate and Clark *op cit* Ref 29
[59]Von Braun, J, Hopkins, R F, Peutz, D and Pandya-Lorch, R *Aid to Agriculture: Reversing the Decline* IFPRI, Washington, DC (1993) note that US funding for agricultural aid fell from $1402 million in 1980 to $388 million in 1990, apparently due to opposition from farm lobbies; also 'IFPRI: study about "underrated agriculture"' *ATSAF Circular 33* 1993 (4/93) 3–4 noted sharp decline in agriculture support by some development agencies, for example the World Bank and USAID; and according to Petit, M 'Financing agricultural development in the 1990s: toward a World Bank strategy' in Garbue, Pritchard, A and Knudsen, O (eds) *Agricultural Issues in the 1990s: Proceedings of the Eleventh Agriculture Sector Symposium* World Bank, Washington, DC (1991) 251–256, in 1976–80, 30.2% of funding was for agriculture and rural development; by 1986–90 it was 20.5%.

developed countries 'could continue to be important suppliers of grain to the rest of the world, thus taking some of the pressure off the natural resource and environmental base of the LDCs'.[60] It is ironic that both conservationism and the reduction in funding for agricultural development in tropical countries may be driven by the same need for farm protectionism in developed countries. However, this review argues that reduced agricultural research will certainly threaten the environment by permitting extensive and inefficient crop and animal production to continue.

International conservation NGOs are substantial financial beneficiaries from tropical forest conservation. The Global Environmental Facility Cameroon project notes that there are 'about a dozen' international NGOs active in Cameroon at present. Gunawardene advocates sustainable forest management but notes the conflict between rural communities and wildlife conservation:

A number of NGOs have come to defend elephants, but in their haste, they have put more value on elephants than on the needs of local people . . . Championing the cause of elephants is perhaps more lucrative than defending hapless farmers. Due to heavy reliance on external funding support, NGOs have been known to tailor their programmes to be attractive to donors.[61]

To mitigate the economic damage done by denying local communities access to resources in reserves, some attempts are being made to compensate rural communities. This is commonly done through ICDPs, which provide development assistance to displaced communities and to communities that might threaten the integrity of reserves. However, conservation and development are *not* integrated in such projects, but separated, with conservation in protected areas, and attempts at development normally sited in buffer zones around protected areas.

Also, there is no evidence that ICDPs are meeting with general success. Braatz noted that, despite discussion for at least a decade, there have been few initiatives to reconcile the needs of local people with conservation; ICDPs are still experimental, and most have been small and highly dependent on external resources; furthermore, ICDP programmes often involved organizations with little experience in development; in some cases, design and implementation flaws of ICDPs had led to problems similar to those experienced by the earlier generation of integrated rural development projects.[62] Southgate and Clark warned that neither the donors nor the environmentalists should delude themselves into thinking that ICDPs and park protection initiatives alone will yield the desired results.[63] The major thesis of this present review is that the separation of rural communities from areas they have traditionally managed could reduce the conservation value of areas which conservationists are seeking to protect.

It can now be argued that dwellers in tropical forest have not been well served by conservationists, who may be more intent on obtaining funding for pet reserves and research than taking a long-term view of the local environment and the needs of local people. Exaggerations to obtain funds could be excusable if benefits from forest conservation were equally distributed. This is far from the case. There are substantial costs to local communities.

Burdens on the periphery

Protected areas are placing a heavy burden on rural survival.[64] Tropical

[60]Crossin, P and Anderson, J R *Resource and Global Food Prospects: Supply and Demand for Cereals to 2030* Technical Paper No 184, World Bank, Washington, DC (1992)
[61]Gunawardene *op cit* Ref 46; a recent review of the role of environmental NGOs notes that 'NGOs need to learn from the past: continuing the same conservation policies which have failed for seventy years will not be useful': Vivian *op cit* Ref 50, 191
[62]Braatz *op cit* Ref 17, xi; see also Shepherd, G 'Local and national level forest management strategies – competing priorities at the forest boundary: the case of Madagascar and Cameroon' *Commonwealth Forestry Review* 1993 **72** 316–320
[63]Southgate and Clark *op cit* Ref 29; see also Brandon, K E and Welles, M 'Planning for people and parks: design dilemmas' *World Development* 1992 **20** 557–570, which reviews the failings of ICDPs, partly due to the 'desperation to show success'; and Munasinghe, M and Wells, M 'Protection of natural habitats and sustainable development of local communities' in *Conservation of West and Central African Rainforests* Environment Paper No 1, World Bank, Washington, DC (1992) 161–168, which notes the capabilities of implementing organizations for ICDPs are 'modest' in view of their lack of development experience.
[64]For example, Bailey, Bahuchet and Hewlett *op cit* Ref 25; Ghimire *op cit* Ref 4; MacKenzie, J M, 'Introduction' in MacKenzie *op cit* Ref 40, 1–14; Southgate and Clark *op cit* Ref 29, and very many others

Tropical forests – conserved to death?: D Wood

forest conservation now suffers from the 'core/periphery' syndrome well described by Mather for rural Scotland, where people living in and from 'wilderness', at the periphery, will have different perceptions to those living in the 'core' – the cities. Mather argued that there was a need to move away from the classical, 'scientific reserve' protected area to one in which sustainable use based on the goodwill and environmental knowledge of local people could be integrated into the conservation effort.[65] The pressure to address the development needs of the periphery has already led to a radical change in the administrative structure of official conservation agencies in Britain. However, this change was only possible because landowners in northern Scotland were vocal, informed and politically powerful: they could protect their own patch.

This political power is not characteristic of tropical forest people. These communities are doubly peripheral: at the periphery of national decision making, and well to the periphery of international conservation activity. This is unfortunate, as it is now international funding and developed-country policies that determine conservation models for tropical forests. Braatz suggested that 'As people in the communities around protected areas tend to be poor, politically powerless, and lacking in government services, a large part of the costs of conserving biological diversity is being borne by those least able to pay.'[66] Bell noted that 'The international establishment has in the past come to apply a double standard with regards to conservation and development, applying more rigorous constraints to development to the Third World and Africa in particular, than to the developed countries.'[67]

A considerable literature now supports the view that the burden of conservation falls on local communities, and that this burden is unjust; for example:

- the 'interests of indigenous peoples and their land uses and land management were often ignored in the designation of conservation areas imposed on areas of savanna and forest in Africa and India';[68]
- 'In areas where the economy is based on primary activities and sources of sustenance, local people cannot be excluded from resources within previously exploited areas. Instead, protected areas must be managed to benefit local people as well as wildlife and wildlands';[69]
- 'the failure of established management structures, generally colonial or postcolonial adaptations of centralized legal and bureaucratic models, to accommodate traditional methods of wildlife usage and provide more flexible means for the conservation of wildlife';[70]
- wilderness preserves are 'no more than robbing indigenous peoples of their homeland and assigning it to an artificial idealized landscape in which humans have no place';[71]
- self-sufficient populations become impoverished peasants.[72]

Access to resources

In some cases the boundaries of protected areas were drawn *around* existing populations, instantly converting what were once traditional lifestyles into 'illegal activities'.[73] The colonial administrations in Malawi 'were not familiar with the local subsistence economy, which depended on large areas of uncultivated land for the collection of a wide range of food items (game meat, insect larvae and honey) as well as building material, clay for pottery and firewood'.[74] Woodland resources

[65]Mather, A S 'Protected areas in the periphery: conservation and controversy in Northern Scotland' *Journal of Rural Studies* 1993 **9** 371–384
[66]Braatz *op cit* Ref 17, 25
[67]Bell, R 'Conservation with a human face: conflict and reconciliation in African land use planning' in Anderson and Grove *op cit* Ref 40, 89
[68]Mather *op cit* Ref 65
[69]Steinberg, M 'Protecting wildlands through culturally compatible conservation' *Environmental Conservation* 1993 **20** 260
[70]McHenry *op cit* Ref 41
[71]Icamina, P 'Threads of common knowledge' *IDRC Reports* 1993 **21** (1) 14–16
[72]Rao and Geisler *op cit* Ref 42
[73]Ham, S H, Sutherland, D S and Meganck, R A 'Applying environmental interpretation in protected areas of developing countries: problems of exporting a US model' *Environmental Conservation* 1993 **20** 233. This paper wisely notes that human use 'is even *requisite* to sustainable protection'.
[74]Munthali *op cit* Ref 5; perhaps a reasonable response – Bell noted that 11% of the land of Malawi was 'allocated to conservation, most of it arable land . . .': Bell *op cit* Ref 67, 94.

were important to people living in the communal areas of Zimbabwe, allowing risk spreading and diversifying the source of inputs into the farming system. Access to woodland allowed a reliance on manure, leaf litter and soil from termite mounds instead of chemical fertilizer. Diverse sources could prevent the collapse into 'acute hunger'.[75]

The entire economy and livelihood of rural populations may rely on the adjoining forests where agriculture is marginal and people depended on off-season employment potential offered by these areas.[76] The Quiatoni Indians of Mexico survive by diversifying their productive strategies. To them, forestry and grazing are one of many forms of resources that they must manage in order to *marginally* survive.[77] The forest economy of Lembus, in Kenya, was based upon the cultivation of cereals within the forest, and the dynamics of movement between forest glades and the surrounding lowland grazing area.[78] The complementarity of crop production and food gathering specifically in tropical forests is emphasized in another extensive review.[79] There may be a seasonal dependence on forest foods – particularly during the 'hungry' season before harvest, when forest foods complement crops.[80] Alcorn noted that the traditional agroecosystem was a fluid complex of planted fields, fallows, savannas, dooryards, forests, rivers and river banks – the entire range of resource zones that are open for human exploitation.[81] Large protected areas will prevent rural communities continuing with their strategies of diversification of access to resources from different ecosystems.

Pandey argued that declaration of a national park or wildlife sanctuary may immediately restrict access of the local community to biotic wealth traditionally harvested to meet daily requirements.[82] A review of wild foods reports a massive body of evidence on the survival value of wild foods to rural communities, particularly the poorer groups, and within the poorer groups, women and children.[83] The poor could be disproportionately threatened by strictly protected areas. Another recent review established that 100% of rural households were dependent on access to common property resources, that rural poor receive the bulk of their fuel supplies and fodder from common property resources, and that relatively poor households depend more on access to the common property resources represented by forest.[84] The prevention of hunting – a priority target for strictly protected reserves – may critically reduce community access to protein. In the Congo, there is no real alternative to bushmeat for the supply of animal protein to the population.[85] Hunting has been regarded as a 'subsidy from nature' without which many other forest-based activities would not take place.[86]

Lizot suggested that nomadism in tropical forest, mixed with cultivation, constituted a remarkable adaptation to the natural environment by which wild resources are exploited in times of crisis or famine. Zones of Yanomani tribal influence were systematically raked for resources.[87] The possibility of complementarity – access to resources from different ecological zones – governed the use of resources by families in highland Peru.[88]

Chandran and Gadgil related state control of forests in India to a decline in food resources:

A complex landscape of species rich sacred groves of climax forest, supply forests, pastures, fields and fallows in different stages of succession with corridors of rivers, streams, gorges and ridges would have been responsible for the rich wildlife that existed in Uttara Kannada. The maintenance of these

[75]Bradley, P and Dewees, P 'Indigenous woodlands, agricultural production and household economy in the communal areas' in Bradley, P and McNamara, K (eds) *Living with Trees: Policies for Forestry Management in Zimbabwe* Technical Paper No 210, World Bank, Washington, DC (1993) 63–137

[76]Pandey, D P 'Wildlife National Parks and people' *Indian Forester* 1993 **119** 521–529; Toledo, V M 'Pátzcuaro's lesson: nature, production and culture in an indigenous region of Mexico' in Oldfield and Alcorn *op cit* Ref 44, 147–171

[77]Peasant Solidarity Group of Quiatoni and Martinez, E A 'Integrated resource management: a Zapotec community's approach' in Downing, T E, Hecht, S B, Pearson, H A and Garcia-Downing, C (eds) *Development or Destruction: The Conversion of Tropical Forest to Pasture in Latin America* Westview Press, Boulder, CO (1992) 345–352; emphasis in original

[78]Anderson *op cit* Ref 40, 261

[79]Hladik *et al*, *op cit* Ref 21

[80]Katz, E 'Forest food resources in the tropical mountains of the Mixtec Highlands, Mexico' in Hladik *et al*, *op cit* Ref 21, 199–204

[81]Alcorn, J B 'Process as resource: the traditional agricultural ideology of Bora and Huastec resource management and its implications for research' in Posey, D A and Balée, W (eds) 'Resource management in Amazonia: indigenous and folk strategies' *Advances in Economic Botany* 1989 **7** 65

[82]Pandey *op cit* Ref 76

[83]Scoones, I, Melnyk, M and Pretty, J N *The Hidden Harvest: Wild Foods and Agricultural Systems – A Literature Review and Annotated Bibliography* IIED/SIDA/WWF, London (1992) 256, refs 942

[84]Jodha, N S *Common Property Resources: A Missing Dimension of Development Strategies* Discussion Paper No 169, World Bank, Washington, DC (1992); in contrast, Fearnside *op cit* Ref 8, claims that conservation does not harm the rural poor.

[85]World Bank *op cit* Ref 2, 6

[86]Redford, K H 'Hunting in neotropical forests: a subsidy from nature' in Hladik *et al*, *op cit* Ref 21, 227–246

[87]Lizot, J 'Yanomani natural resource use: an inclusive cultural strategy' in Hladik *et al*, *op cit* Ref 21, 479–486

[88]Young, K R 'National park protection in relation to the ecological zonation of a neighboring human community: an example from northern Peru' *Mountain Research and Development* 1993 **13** 267–280. Young noted that grave problems remained with enforcement of park protection at the local level, in part because complementarity is not taken into account.

landscape elements was crucial for the population which also depended on hunting and gathering.[89]

The loss of common resource territories by privatization; encroachment and government appropriation have been the main processes taking resources out of common use. Arnold noted that increasing pressures on what was left have frequently led to its progressive degradation.[90] In Cameroon there was a disastrous impact of government intervention in the traditional but effective conservation strategy of a local community. Local patterns of authority were reduced, thereby destroying local knowledge systems relating to land use and environmental protection.[91] The recent call to double the global network of protected areas[92] will further remove resources from common use.

Local response: encroachment and conflict

Community response to the denial of access to traditional and much-needed resources is perhaps the most serious threat to the integrity of reserves. Community opposition to reserves often takes the form of continuing with their traditional use of resources – widely stigmatized in conservationist literature as 'illegal' activities – which include hunting, woodcutting, grazing, gathering forest products and re-establishing former settlements. This reaction may extend to conflict, and is now a severe threat to the system of strictly protected areas.[93] Colchester noted that national parks established on indigenous lands have denied local rights to resources, turning local people practically overnight from hunters and cultivators to 'poachers' and 'squatters'.[94]

MacKenzie demonstrated that present conservation faces problems of local hostility. The priorities of the park authorities did not match the needs of local inhabitants, and the majority of local people were aware that the interests of park authorities lay in animals and trees, rather than in people:

Conservationist ideas . . . were progressively applied in French and British imperial territories . . . Marginal cultivators and forest dwellers were culturally devalued, particularly in the later nineteenth century, and conservationism destroyed the traditional survival mechanisms of such people.[95]

Tropical forest conservationists are ignoring problems from other areas. A case study in Swaziland discovered a growing resistance of rural people to conservation and showed that rural people saw protected areas as enemies because they take away land and resources. Three demands about reserves were identified by local people: (1) 'nature reserves must not be located on good agricultural land: it is preferable to put them in the mountains'; (2) nature reserves should be small; (3) 'people should be considered before animals' where there is any conflict.[96]

Technical dangers of excluding people from protected areas

There are now substantial threats to the integrity of reserves as a result of conservationist insistence on the total exclusion of local communities. The remainder of this review will argue that, in addition to the social problems and threats, there are serious technical problems generated by exclusion management. The technical assumption behind the conservationist arguments for the strict protection of forests and involuntary resettlement is that human access will in some way damage forests and

[89]Chandran, M D S and Gadgil, M 'State forestry and the decline in food resources in the tropical forests of Uttara Kannada, Southern India' in Hladik *et al*, *op cit* Ref 21, 733–744
[90]Arnold, J E M 'Production of forest products in agricultural and common land systems: economic and policy issues' in Sharma, N P (ed) *Managing the World's Forests: Looking for Balance Between Conservation and Development* Kendall/ Hunt, Dubuque, IA (1992) 439
[91]Fisiy *op cit* Ref 13
[92]McNeely *op cit* Ref 1
[93]For example, in Nigeria conservation policies which oppose local use of resources are almost breaking down: Osemeobo, G J 'Land use policies and biotic conservation: problems and prospects for forestry development in Nigeria' *Land Use Policy* 1990 **7** (4) 314–322. Conservation is at a crossroads in India, with conflicts between conservation and 'sustainable, secure, and dignified livelihoods' for people: Pandey *op cit* Ref 76: local people 'do not see why the government should deny their right to move into forest land that belonged to their forefathers'. Ojany, F F 'Mount Kenya and its environs: a review of the interaction between mountain and people in an equatorial setting' *Moutain Research and Development* 1993 **13** 309. Gadgil, M and Guha, R 'Ecological conflicts and the environmental movement in India' *Development and Change* 1994 **25** 101–136, and other papers in this volume.
[94]Colchester, M 'Sustaining the forests: the community-based approach in South and South-East Asia' *Development and Change* 1994 **25** 69–100
[95]MacKenzie *op cit* Ref 64
[96]Hackel, J D 'Rural change and nature conservation in Africa: a case study from Swaziland' *Human Ecology* 1993 **21** 295–312

lower their conservation value. There is now substantial criticism of this dogmatic position from more enlightened conservationists. It has recently been noted that 'the idea that conservation of natural resources can be achieved by excluding human activity from protected areas is currently being seriously challenged . . .'[97]

By excluding people from reserves, present conservation strategies for tropical forest are failing in four ways:

- They destroy *human knowledge of species utilization* which is a key to productive future use.
- They prevent *experimentation with land use options* which is key to the viable use of scarce land.
- They remove the *anthropogenic disturbance* of ecosystems which may be essential for biodiversity generation and conservation.
- They stop the *historical process* which has been responsible for the present character of tropical forests.

Destruction of indigenous knowledge of species

Many of the arguments used by conservationists on the need to conserve tropical forests emphasize the *global* economic value of tropical species as crops, medicines and a host of economic plants and animals. For example, several important crops (including rice, bananas, sugar cane, oil palm, coffee and cocoa) were domesticated by rural communities in tropical forest. Valuable genetic resources of many crops are still maintained by forest farmers. For example, the Sinharaja Rain Forest, Sri Lanka – now a National Wilderness Area – was earlier this century used by surrounding villagers for food, medicinal, and other requirements. It is now reported that:

Villagers living near the forest are now prohibited from collecting forest products and tapping palms as they used to do before . . . This has already led to the loss of valuable traditional knowledge of forest plants used for food, medicinal and other uses and, in particular, the rural processing technology which has evolved over many generations . . .[98]

Local knowledge of medicinal plants can be of both local and global importance, allowing a close targeting of research to develop new drugs. Schultes lists drugs such as curare alkaloids, cortisone, reserpine, strophanthine and others as resulting from ethnobotanical medical knowledge.[99] Most of the present economic value of species of tropical forest depends on cumulative indigenous knowledge gained over thousands of years of experimentation on tropical species by many millions of human inhabitants. Yet exclusion of rural communities is now a standard feature of protected areas conservation.

In addition to the global value of forest resources, there is now the very widest documentation of the direct *local* value of tropical species to rural communities. Amazonian communities use most of the species in their resource territories. For example, the Ka'apor knew and used 76.8% of the species that occurred on the hectare of rainforest studied. The Chácobo of Bolivia used 74 of the 94 species on the study plot.[100]

The effect on the cultural values of communities may also be great. Wild foods have an enhanced cultural and symbolic significance to communities.[101] Prohibiting access will lead to 'future generations not being able to recognize the food value of these species, or remember the methods of processing and preparing them'.[102] These same authors also

[97] McCabe, J T, Perkin, S and Schofield, C 'Can conservation and development be coupled among pastoral people? An examination of the Maasai of the Ngorongoro Conservation Area, Tanzania' *Human Organization* 1992 **51** 353

[98] Gunatilleke, N I A U and Gunatilleke, S C V 'Underutilized food plants resources of Sinharaja Rain Forest, Sri Lanka' in Hladik *et al*, *op cit* Ref 21, 183–198

[99] Schultes, R E 'Reasons for ethnobotanical conservation' in Johannes, R E (ed) *Traditional Ecological Knowledge: A Collection of Essays* IUCN, Gland (1989) 31–37

[100] Prance, G T, Balée, W, Boom, B M and Carneiro, R C 'Quantitative ethnobotany and the case for conservation in Amazonia' *Conservation Biology* 1987 **1** 296–310

[101] Janowski, M R H 'The symbolic significance of food from the forest among the Kelabit of Sarawak' in Hladik *et al*, *op cit* Ref 21, 651–660

[102] Gunatilleke and Gunatilleke *op cit* Ref 98

note a degradation of vital crop genetic resources which results from a prohibition of human use of forest:

> Prohibition of forest clearance, particularly shifting cultivation, has also led to the gradual disappearance of a number of 'land races' of hill paddy and other food crops which villagers have been cultivating for generations. Ironically, measures taken to conserve rain forest biota have led to the extinction and extirpation of valuable germplasm of traditionally grown crop species.

Crop breeding continues to depend on breeders having access to land races. The continued maintenance of land races of crops by farmers is now recognized as an important conservation strategy.[103]

Without human access to protected areas, the indigenous knowledge that makes species so valuable at the local and global levels will rapidly and irreversibly disappear. Excluding human communities from forests will inevitably destroy this fragile knowledge base and prevent future experimentation, thereby reducing the value of forest species. There may even be a scientific value in allowing people access to forests. The recent discovery of an important new species of large mammal – the Vu Quang ox in Vietnam – depended on local people living and hunting in the forest.[104]

Experimentation with land use options

Indigenous knowledge of individual species is translated into the cultural ability to exploit and even manage ecosystems for greater productivity. Indigenous management can increase the economic value of ecosystems by encouraging useful plants and animals and enhancing ecosystem productivity. Many forest ecosystems have been managed productively by rural communities for long periods of time. In particular, the very widespread system of shifting cultivation or bush fallow has caused profound changes in the structure and composition of tropical forests.[105] Kesavan and Aburu pointed out the advantages of bush fallow:

> The most common crop production system is bush-fallowing for long periods which allows natural vegetation to regenerate. This system has the advantage of minimizing disturbance to the existing natural ecosystems and facilitates hunting and gathering of food from the forests. At the same time, valuable wild species are preserved within a stable community in balance with the environment.[106]

More than 30 years ago Corner stressed the importance of a thorough study of shifting cultivation in understanding tropical forest and tropical soil. He regarded shifting cultivation as an experiment in regeneration, and further noted that it was the 'practice to deprecate shifting cultivation but this is probably another misunderstanding by temperate man of tropical complexity'.[107] The present paper argues that deprecation and misunderstanding continue. Morán noted that the liana forests which covered up to 100 000 sq km of the Amazon basin may have been wholly, or in part, the result of the activities of prehistoric populations of Amazonia and were managed by a 'cornucopia of management practices'.[108]

Strictly protected areas in tropical countries may be very large. Figures from 1980 suggest that reserves average about 1000 sq km each.[109] Such reserves are on a landscape scale, and would normally include a mosaic of different ecosystems and high-potential agricultural land. Exclusion of communities from reserves prevents the build-up of experience on which areas within the diverse ecosystems of the reserve

[103]Altieri, M A and Merrick L C 'Agroecology and in situ conservation of native crop diversity in the Third World' in Wilson, E O and Peter, F M (eds) *Biodiversity* National Academy Press, Washington, DC (1988) 361–369
[104]Dung, Vu Van, Giao, Pham Mong, Chinh, Nguyen Ngoc, Tuoc, Do and MacKinnon, J 'Discovery and conservation of the Vu Quang ox in Vietnam' *Oryx* 1994 **28** 16–21
[105]Wood *op cit* Ref 7
[106]Kesavan, V and Aburu, K 'Conservation of plant genetic resources' in Morauta, L, Pernetta, J and Heaney, W (eds) *Traditional Conservation in Papua New Guinea: Implications for Today* Monograph 16, Institute of Applied Social and Economic Research, Boroko, PNG (1992) 380
[107]Corner, E J H 'Botany and prehistory' in *Symposium on the Humid Tropics Vegetation, Goroka, Papua and New Guinea, September 1960* Unesco, Paris (1960) 38–41
[108]Morán, E F 'Managing Amazonian variability with indigenous knowledge' in Hladik *et al*, *op cit* Ref 21, 753–766
[109]Sayer *op cit* Ref 37

are suitable for agriculture and which are not. Trial and error identification may be better than land capability surveys. Farmers in Europe have this ability: Dudley Stamp insisted that existing land use was a better guide to land worth than capability classifications, not only because it was more objective, but because it reflected what Stamp saw as the British farmer's genius for identifying the true quality of the land.[110] Landscape scale reserves deny tropical farmers the opportunity to identify suitable land for agriculture and to experiment with and improve location-specific systems of production.

Indigenous agricultural and ecological management systems have been shown to be more sophisticated than expected. Forest areas used for agriculture turned into old fields, which were important to the indigenous ecosystem management process, but which are now frequently confused with 'natural' forest.[111] In Amazonia very many species were managed and grown for their economic value. In particular, a range of palms (including *Bactris gasipaes*, *Orbignya phalerata* and *Astrocaryum* spp) is associated with habitats occupied by people.[112] Posey views indigenous use and management of tropical forests as continua between plants that are domesticated and those that are semi-domesticated, manipulated or wild. In addition, there is no clearcut demarcation between natural and managed forest.[113] Such managed areas have not been recognized by conservationists during the alienation of land into protected areas.

I suggest that such areas – now known to be very extensive in tropical regions[114] – cannot be managed as if they were untouched. Conservationists can no longer justify the exclusion of human communities from reserves on technical grounds. With the present inadequate state of knowledge on past tropical land management, decisions on reserve siting and management cannot be made with any certainty of success.

Disturbance and biodiversity

The exclusion of people could have a disastrous effect on the biodiversity of reserves. Bonnicksen argued against the false premise that national parks and wilderness areas were pristine or untouched when they were set aside. Bonnicksen claimed that such areas were not pristine: much of the vegetation and wildlife in park and wilderness areas was profoundly altered due to thousands of years of management and use by aboriginal people. Management was thought to be essential, as 'since human intervention eliminated aboriginal people from national park and wilderness areas, these areas must be deliberately managed now and forever to ensure the existence of natural vegetation mosaics and wildlife populations'.[115] Gómez-Pompa and Kaus argue that for tropical countries the 'current composition of mature vegetation may well be the legacy of past civilizations, the heritage of cultivated fields and forests abandoned long ago'.[116]

It has been argued that the biodiversity of tropical forests is a result of human influence, and that:

current biodiversity in the rainforest is the result of the introduction of exotic species, the creation of new habitats, and manipulation by forest people for thousands of years – indeed, biodiversity exists in central Africa because of human habitation, and if human beings are excluded from large areas of forest, this will not conserve the present biodiversity.[117]

Western and Gichohi query the conservation value of national parks in East Africa, which 'have been the dominant method of conservation for

[110]Hare, F K 'The conservation of resources' in *Land Use and Resources: Studies in Applied Geography* Special Publication No 1, Institute of British Geographers (1968) 45

[111]Posey, D A 'The importance of semi-domesticated species in post-contact Amazonia: effects of Kayapo indians on the dispersal of flora and fauna' in Hladik *et al, op cit* Ref 21, 63–71

[112]Kahn, F 'Amazonian palms: food resources for the management of forest ecosystems' in Hladik *et al, op cit* Ref 21, 153–162

[113]Posey, D A 'A preliminary resport on diversified management of tropical forests by the Kayapo Indians of the Brazilian Amazon' *Advances in Economic Botany* 1984 **1** 112–126

[114]Wood *op cit* Ref 7

[115]Bonnicksen, T M 'Nature vs man(agement)' *Journal of Forestry* 1989 **87** (12) 41–43

[116]Gómez-Pompa and Kaus *op cit* Ref 20

[117]Bailey, Bahuchet and Hewlett *op cit* Ref 25

more than a century, based on the assumption that strict protection from human impact will maintain biodiversity. The assumption is proving too simple . . . What has been overlooked are the negative effects of protected areas . . . impoverishment is slow, seldom monitored and usually attributed to some reason other than the establishment of the park itself'. They further argue that 'The implicit assumption in creating a park is that protection will maintain and most likely enhance biodiversity. In reality, the opposite may be the case. Part of the reason stems from the large role human ecology has played in shaping and maintaining the East African savannas . . .' Western and Gichohi conclude by questioning the relevance of national parks to conserve biodiversity: 'The appeal of parks lies in the premise that if human activity threatens biological diversity, removing all human activity will arrest the deterioration. The biological inadequacy of protected areas has only become apparent in recent years . . .'[118]

Perhaps more importantly, from a conservation perspective, indigenous management provides the controlled disturbance needed for ecosystem diversity and the maximum diversity of species. For example, the index of diversity of species following shifting cultivation in the Amazon was greater than for original forest.[119]

There is now other evidence that human disturbance is at least partly responsible for tropical ecosystem biodiversity. A survey of the 14 300 year history of a lake in Panama showed that the first humans in Central America penetrated and exploited tropical rainforest. The survey concluded that humans may have influenced rates of forest diversification and reduced the likelihood of monodominance by tree species.[120] The wide extent of tropical secondary forests provides substantial evidence for past human disturbance. For example, Rodgers noted the inability to find patches of totally undisturbed forest even within plots which had been specifically preserved by foresters in the Western Ghats of India.[121] Prance suggests that 'a great deal of the Amazon rainforest has been felled at one time or another by the Indians, as is evidenced by charcoal and pottery shards in many soil samples'.[122]

The Fourth World Congress on National Parks and Protected Areas discussed cultural landscapes and adapted natural systems, and drew attention to human communities, 'especially those living in and around protected areas'. The Congress noted that these relationships frequently contribute to biological diversity.[123]

Productivity and diversity may be stimulated by a range of customary conservation practices.[124] In some cases, human disturbance benefits animal populations. For example, elephants in national parks in Sri Lanka prefer to feed in the open, disturbed habitats associated with farming.[125] In Zaire shifting cultivation increased productivity in regrowth areas, enabling a sustained higher level of exploitation than in uncut climax forest.[126] This effect is probably due to the presence of patchy vegetation at differing stages of recovery. This encourages vegetation diversity, provides a wider range of plant products, and thereby attracts game. The essential role of humans in ecosystem maintenance is better understood outside tropical regions.

Ignoring the historical process

Ignorance of past land management makes any attempt at scientific reserve management impossible. This has long been recognized in developed countries. Packard noted that in Illinois the human species

[118]Western, D and Gichohi, H 'Segregation effects and impoverishment of savanna parks: the case for ecosystem viability analysis' *African Journal of Ecology* 1993 **31** 269–281

[119]De Miranda, E E and Mattos, C 'Brazilian rain forest conservation and biodiversity' *Agricultural Ecosystems and Environment* 1992 **40** 285

[120]Bush, M B *et al* 'A 14,300-yr paleoecological profile of a lowland tropical lake in Panama' *Ecological Monographs* 1992 **62** 251–275

[121]Rodgers, W A 'Forest preservation plots in India 1 – Management status and value' *Indian Forester* 1991 **117** 425–433

[122]Prance, G T 'Saving the Amazon – some discussion points' in Jaenicke, H and Flynn, P (eds) *Sustainable Land Use Systems and Human Living Conditions in the Amazon Region* Commission of the European Communities, Directorate General, Science, Research and Development, Brussels (1992) 27

[123]McNeely, J A 'Parks for life: results of the IV World Congress on National Parks and Protected Areas' *Nature et Faune* 1992 **8** (3) 4–12

[124]Cunningham, A B 'Indigenous plant use: balancing human needs and resources' in Huntley, B U (ed) *Biotic Diversity in Southern Africa: Concepts and Conservation* Oxford University Press, Cape Town (1989) 99

[125]Ishwaran, N 'Ecology of the Asian elephant in lowland dry zone habitats of the Mahaweli River Basin, Sri Lanka' *Journal of Tropical Ecology* 1993 **9** 169–182

[126]Wilkie, D S and Finn, J T 'Slash-burn cultivation and mammal abundance in the Ituri Forest, Zaire' *Biotropica* 1990 **22** 90–99

has played an important role in the landscape for thousands of years, and that the loss of people from a natural system in which they have played an essential role could be as destructive to the functioning and survival of that system as the loss of a big predator, pollinator, herbivore or any other key species.[127]

There is substantial evidence of reserve degradation from other well-studied temperate ecosystems. Almost 40 years ago, in a perceptive account of conservation in Sweden, Romell noted that conservationists were making a fundamental mistake in prohibiting the use of land inside national parks: strictly protected areas may suffer a 'conservation to death'. Disturbance was necessary:

the old face of the land had received many of its essential traits from old land uses which had acted as ecological factors since time immemorial, some for thousands of years . . . It is quite clear today that the rural Sweden of olden days owed most of its hospitable features to the work of the scythe and the muzzles of grazing beasts.[128]

Areas set aside as parks were found to suffer from the protection that they were given. Protection from fire and grazing caused some areas to change to the point of being unrecognizable. An unbroken cover of coniferous forest extended over previously treeless or thinly wooded pastures. Further evidence from Europe casts doubts on whether our much poorer knowledge of tropical land is comprehensive enough to allow the rational management of reserves. In Europe, as rural populations declined, forest regenerated on abandoned farmland. This is a well-understood process in Europe, but certainly also happened repeatedly in tropical countries.[129] Several studies in Italy showed the importance of a knowledge of site history, including previous forms of land use and land management practices, in order to understand the dynamics of the forest recolonization process.[130]

Even in well-studied forests in North America, ecologists greatly simplify the history of inferred human impacts on the forest. A detailed historical survey of a forest in New England suggested that the extensive and variable nature of human use of the landscape produced complexity. One striking result of this survey was a realization that little evidence of the prior vegetation, including the original forest, or past land use was apparent in the modern landscape. The study concluded that 'any attempt to understand modern forests and ecosystem processes requires an understanding of this historical past'.[131] We should note that a dynamic view of forest history is only possible with excellent historical records and detailed research: if these are lacking, as for most tropical forest, a more static, unchanging view of forest history has been assumed. This is dangerous for conservation, as it implies that static conservation will suffice to maintain forests in their present form, rather than dynamic management.

A further paper on the same New England forest is yet more relevant to tropical forest management. It argued that the 'changing quality and intensity of human activity resulted in the dynamic vegetation characteristic of this period [1730–1990]' and that the continually dynamic nature of the vegetation pattern in central New England was one of the most remarkable aspects of the post-settlement landscape. It concluded that 'the ramifications of this history in terms of contemporary ecological processes are too great to be dismissed by modern-day ecologists'.[132] Characteristically, the implications of past human use of temperate forests based on detailed historical evidence are being ignored in siting

[127]Packard, S 'Restoring oak ecosystems' *Restoration and Management Notes* 1993 **11** 5–16
[128]Romell *op cit* Ref 26
[129]Wood *op cit* Ref 7
[130]Salbitano, F 'Depopulation and afforestation: sources and methods from 19th century Italy' in Watkins, C (eds) *Ecological Effects of Afforestation: Studies in the History and Ecology of Afforestation in Western Europe* CAB International, Wallingford, UK (1993) 45
[131]Foster, D R, Zebryk, T, Schoonmaker, P and Lezberg, A 'Post-settlement history of human land-use and vegetation dynamics of a *Tsuga canadensis* (hemlock) woodlot in central New England' *Journal of Ecology* 1992, **80** 773–786
[132]Foster, D.R 'Land-use history (1730–1990) and vegetation dynamics in central New England, USA' *Journal of Ecology* 1992 **80** 768

Rural Planning and Management

Tropical forests – conserved to death?: D Wood

and management of tropical reserves. Yet we should note that, for tropical forests, their history has often included periods of intensive human management.[133]

Studies of past disturbance regimes in tropical forests are essential, both to determine where reserves are to be sited and to guide subsequent management. In a strong argument for disturbance studies, Waide and Lugo note that relatively few such studies have occurred in the humid tropics, and that disturbance and the subsequent 'patch dynamics' of the recovery from disturbance play as great a role in community dynamics as competition and predation.[134] A severe problem for subsequent conservation is that the type of disturbance that initiated succession at a site is difficult or impossible to determine through examination of the regenerated mature forest. A review of this problem noted that the natural disturbance regime is unlikely to persist within conservation areas, since fragmentation and human intervention have usually modified physical and biotic conditions.[135] Active management decisions have to be made on what disturbance regime is required. For the highest possible biodiversity, climax and very productive successional stages should be juxtapositioned.[136]

Evidence based on pollen suggests that disturbance of rainforests by people may have been in process in the tropics for much longer than previously believed. Estimates for the age of this disturbance ranged from 3000 BP in West and East Africa, 5000 BP in Fiji, 6000 BP in Sumatra, to 6000–9000 BP in New Guinea.[137]

The history of vegetation, and the danger of excluding people from reserves (known for decades as a problem in European and North American reserve management), are both being ignored by many conservationists arguing for the strict protection of tropical forests.

Sustaining conservation

Notwithstanding the threat that protected areas now offer to rural communities, there is a trend to expand conservation beyond the present concept of protected areas. In a proposal for integrated landscape ecology, it has been argued that conservation management can no longer be concerned only with the landscape patches set aside for conservation, and that conservation biology has to tackle the interconnected nature of the landscape.[138] At the Fourth World Congress on National Parks and Protected Areas there was a request that protected areas should be included in regional development plans, and that aid agencies 'accept international responsibility to help support protected areas'.[139] There is an alarming belligerence to some calls for forest conservation. Schultes argues for 'iron-handed international methods' – presumably foreign intervention – and 'action above the wishes and activities of national governments' to protect what Schultes obviously regards as the 'global commons' of tropical forest.[140]

In contrast to conservationist calls for expansion of protected areas, there are demands for new concepts of management for tropical protected areas, to reduce the social inequity and technical inadequacy of present management. Pandey notes that conservation is at a crossroads, with conflicts between conservation and sustainable, secure and dignified livelihoods for people.[141] Mather saw 'the beginning of a paradigm shift in conservation, away from the classical "scientific reserve" model of the protected area towards one in which "sustainable

[133]Reviewed by Wood *op cit* Ref 7
[134]Waide, R B and Lugo, A E 'A research perspective on disturbance and recovery of a tropical montane forest' in Goldhammer *op cit* Ref 19, 173–190
[135]Hobbs, R J and Huenneke, L F 'Disturbance, diversity, and invasion: implications for conservation' *Conservation Biology* 1992 **6** 324–337
[136]Hansson, L and Angelstam, P 'Landscape ecology as a theoretical basis for nature conservation' *Landscape Ecology* 1991 **5** 198
[137]Flenley, J R 'Palynological evidence relating to disturbance and other ecological phenomena in rain forests' in Goldhammer *op cit* Ref 19, 19
[138]Hobbs, R J, Saunders, D A and Arnold, G W 'Integrated landscape ecology: a Western Australian approach' *Biological Conservation* 1993 **64** 231–238
[139]McNeely *op cit* Ref 1
[140]Schultes, R E 'Amazonia never to be revisited' *Environmental Conservation* 1993 **20** 4
[141]Pandey *op cit* Ref 76

use" and the involvement of local people have more prominent roles'.[142] In another reference to a paradigm shift, it was noted that emphasis should be on 'balance of nature' rather than the 'flux of nature' within which open systems are dominated by episodic, historical and *anthropogenic* factors. It was suggested that the watchwords of this new paradigm were to be 'process and context'.[143] Yet another argument for a paradigm shift emphasized the new 'paradigm of disturbance' and promoted patch dynamics as a 'new concept' in ecology.[144]

In a critique of current conservation, Steinberg argued:

Traditional protected areas, which usually forbid any resource extraction from within their borders, are increasingly incapable at protecting wildlands while at the same time meeting the needs of the growing numbers of rural people . . . conservationists who design and manage protected areas must take into consideration the sustainable need of the local people instead of alienating them by eliminating or severely restricting resource extraction.[145]

Polunin argues that protected areas are an extreme form of conservation, and that other forms of regulated area management may be more appropriate for the management needs of local development.[146] The present review argues that if outmoded concepts of 'wilderness' and repressive reserve management were to be abandoned, future conservation could be based predominantly on those categories of protected areas which accept human use. Examples include the IUCN category VIII (Multiple-Use Management Area), World Heritage 'cultural landscapes' and Unesco Biosphere Reserves.[147]

Sustainable agriculture may represent the most viable land use option for many forest areas at present under strict protection. Agriculture in its many forms is by far the most predominant form of land use in tropical regions. Agricultural management may also benefit conservation. McIntyre *et al* recommend an approach which:

moves away from an obsession with reserves as isolated entities and looks at the integration of human land-use and nature conservation . . . The struggle to maintain biodiversity is going to be won or lost in agricultural systems. Management of agricultural landscapes will be the litmus test of our ability to conserve species . . . most terrestrial biota will eventually have to coexist with human agriculture . . . Integrating human exploitation with conservation through the diversification of types and intensity of land-use is a realistic way of minimizing extinctions . . .[148]

A thorough understanding of traditional agriculture is a prerequisite for any form of tropical forest conservation.

To conserve biodiversity any future conservation of tropical forest must include two key features:

- a disturbance regime of dynamic management associated with human access to and utilization of the ecosystem;
- the strict avoidance of large reserves, and a new emphasis on 'patch' or mosaic management of small areas.

Dynamic management through utilization

Disturbance may be critical to the future management of biodiversity in tropical forests. Hobbs and Huenneke note that ecologists and conservationists have come to recognize that many forms of disturbance are important components of natural ecosystems.[149] This view contrasts with past conservation methodology, which consisted of measures to protect natural communities from disturbance. There was growing

[142]Mather *op cit* Ref 65, 383
[143]Review of Fiedler, P G and Jain, S K *Conservation Biology: The Theory and Practice of Nature Conservation* Chapman & Hall, New York (1992) xxix, 507, in *Global Ecology and Biogeography Newsletter* 2 180
[144]Waide and Lugo *op cit* Ref 134, 174
[145]Steinberg *op cit* Ref 69, 260
[146]Polunin, N V C 'Delimiting nature: regulated area management in the coastal zone of Malesia' in West and Brechi *op cit* Ref 27, 113; Eidsvik *op cit* Ref 28 noted that 'protected areas are but one mechanism for attaining conservation objectives'.
[147]Batisse, M 'The relevance of MAB' *Environmental Conservation* 1980 **7** 179–184; the purpose of Biosphere Reserves is to study scientifically the interactions between resources and peoples; for conservation of genetic material in characteristic ecosystems; and, in buffer zones, to carry out research on various management practices, and to allow monitoring, education and training: see also Gregg, W P 'MAB Biosphere Reserves and conservation of traditional land use systems' in Oldfield and Alcorn *op cit* Ref 44, 274–294.
[148]McIntyre, S, Barrett, G W, Kitching, R L and Recher, H F 'Species triage – seeing beyond wounded rhinos' *Conservation Biology* 1992 **6** 606
[149]Hobbs and Huenneke *op cit* Ref 135, 234

empirical evidence that suggested that moderate frequencies or intensities of disturbance fostered maximum species richness. Hobbs and Huenneke further argued that the natural disturbance regime is unlikely to persist within conservation areas, since fragmentation and human intervention have usually modified physical and biotic conditions. They suggested that active management decisions would have to be made on what disturbance regime is required. Baker noted that a reserve management objective should be to ensure that the essential attributes of the disturbance regime were all perpetuated as well as possible within a reserve.[150] The essential spatial and temporal variation in landscape structure that is a consequence of a fully active disturbance regime was thought to be missing from many reserves. The thesis of the present paper is that past, present and future human management through traditional use is the most appropriate management regime for most tropical forest areas.

Gómez-Pompa and Kaus suggest as a priority:

research on the influence of human activities on past and present environments to understand the influence of all forms of management, whether modern or traditional, intensive or extensive, on the shape and content of the environment.[151]

Hyndman argued that 'Biological and cultural diversity would best be achieved by keeping indigenous people on their homeland and allowing them to employ their own time-tested sustainable resource management.'[152] Toledo suggested that the multiple use strategy of indigenous communities was an effective mechanism for preserving and even increasing biological diversity by increasing habitat heterogeneity.[153] Romell suggested that desired features of the landscape could only be maintained by continuing 'practices associated with age-old use of the land' or by the application of another, ecologically equivalent, treatment.[154] Alcorn noted the continuity over time between forest and agroecosystems.[155]

A Council Directive of the European Community on the conservation of natural habitats and of wild fauna and flora recognizes that 'the maintenance of such biodiversity may in certain cases require the maintenance, or indeed the encouragement, of human activities'.[156] This review argues that tropical conservation has not kept up with the advances in conservation theory and practice in developed countries.

The Unesco 'Man and the Biosphere' Programme seems to have come very close to a rational concept of the dynamic management of ecosystems:

one of the most valuable features of biosphere reserves [is] that they offer an excellent way of integrated conservation with development by building on the knowledge of indigenous people about the sustainable management of their ecosystems and about the properties and values of the plants and animals therein. When this is appropriately supplemented by modern science and technology, such knowledge should enable even better use to be made of those ecosystems while preserving their essential character – and to do this in ways that benefit local people and are acceptable to them.[157]

This programme has been less than fully effective, not from technical failures, but because of the past political opposition to Unesco policies by some major donors. Donors are now actively supporting a far larger but inferior conservation programme – that funded through the Global Environmental Facility of the World Bank.

[150]Baker, W L 'The landscape ecology of large disturbances in the design and management of nature reserves' *Landscape Ecology* 1992 **7** 181–194
[151]Gómez-Pompa and Kaus *op cit* Ref 20, 276
[152]Hyndman, D in Icamina *op cit* Ref 71, 14–16
[153]Toledo *op cit* Ref 76
[154]Romell *op cit* Ref 26
[155]Alcorn, J B 'Process as resource: the traditional agricultural ideology of Bora and Huastec resource management and its implications for research' in Posey and Balée *op cit* Ref 81, 65
[156]*Offical Journal of the European Communities* No L 206/7 of 22.7.92: 'Council Directive' 92/43/EEC
[157]Derkatch, M 'Unesco programme on biosphere reserves as centres for conservation of gene pools of life support species' in Paroda, R S, Kapoor, P, Arora, R K and Mal, B (eds) *Life Support Plant Species* NBPGR, New Delhi (1988) 45

Traditional, sustainable management systems should be carefully nurtured, rather than displaced. Human communities must be encouraged to live with forests, rather than resettled. Past more intensive land management systems should be studied and promoted. Brookfield notes that there has been a major retrogression in agrotechnology since precolonial times. Many former intensive systems for forest agriculture have disappeared. For example, the 'terra-preto-do-Indio' soils of the Amazon were purposely enriched with organic matter from surrounding land.[158] Such soils need to be studied so that we can emulate this increased fertility.[159] Relics of the classic Mayan land management system of Central America still exists and could provide a model for more intensive agriculture.[160]

The study, nurturing and transfer of traditional forest management through agriculture will be a job for development professionals rather than conservationists. A key feature of future tropical forest management will be the acceptance of shifting cultivation, a system generally condemned by conservationists, but a traditional and pantropical response to the periodic need to regenerate both forests and fields. As still practised in the Mayan area of Mexico, traditional systems of shifting cultivation can feed more people than has been assumed, while conserving biological diversity for future use.[161]

Mosaic management of small areas

Tropical protected areas are now too large and too 'anti-people'. Large reserves represent the most damaging and unsustainable type of conservation. In the words of Ewel, 'the community of conservationists must recognize that without land use systems that are economically, socially and ecologically sustainable, the conservation of natural ecosystems cannot be sustained politically'.[162] Large reserves may not even be the best mechanism to conserve biodiversity. It has been noted that the 'argument that single large reserves are preferable to several smaller ones is among the more cherished tenets of island theory as applied to conservation that have fallen by the wayside'.[163]

There are several alternatives to large, strictly protected areas. Gadgil has suggested that reserves in India should take the form of 'a highly dispersed network of tiny protected areas, ranging in size from individual *Ficus* trees to groves of a few hundred m^2 to a few ha in size'.[164] Forests types in India are already represented by small conservation plots, ranging in size from 10 to 50 ha, 187 of which are in natural forest and 122 in plantations.[165] In Britain the large, multi-use National Parks (average size 136 480 ha) are complemented by much smaller areas of strictly protected Nature Reserves (average size 695 ha) and yet smaller Sites of Special Scientific Interest (average size 314 ha).[166] This model may be more appropriate for tropical developing countries than the North American model of national parks.

There is a need for a replacement of major parts of the tropical protected area system by 'mosaic management' to allow multiple use and to reflect the multifaceted abilities and needs of local communities. Baker has suggested that an emerging tenet of landscape ecology is that the patchy structure of landscape is important to ecological functioning at a variety of levels of biological organization, and that this itself was worthy of conservation and management attention.[167] Brown and Lugo note that a mix of ecosystems is required to secure the welfare of tropical peoples. They recommend a balance between the preservation

[158]Brookfield, H 'The human context of sustainable smallholder development in the Pacific' in Pushparajah, E and Elliot, C R (eds) *Soil Management and Smallholder Development in the Pacific Islands* IBSRAM Proceedings No 8 (1989) 189–204

[159]Sombroek, W G, Nachtergaele, F O and Hebel, A 'Amounts, dynamics and sequestering of carbon in tropical and subtropical soils' *Ambio* 1993 **22** 417–426; for an extensive review of changes in Amazonian resource management, see Roosevelt, A 'Resource management in Amazonia before the conquest: beyond ethnographic projections' in Posey and Balée *op cit* Ref 81, 30–62.

[160]Nations, J D and Nigh, R B 'The evolutionary potential of the Lacadon Maya sustained-yield tropical forest agriculture' *Journal of Anthropological Research* 1980 **36** 1–30; Gliessman, S R 'Ecological basis of traditional management of wetlands in tropical Mexico: learning from agroecosystem models' in Oldfield and Alcorn *op cit* Ref 44, 211–229

[161]Gómez-Pompa, A 'Learning from traditional ecological knowledge: insights from Mayan silviculture' in Gómez-Pompa, A, Whitmore, T C and Hadley, M (eds) *Rain Forest Regeneration and Management* Man and the Biosphere Vol 6, Unesco, Paris (1991) 340

[162]Ewel, J J 'The power of biology in the sustainable land use equation' *Biotropica* 1993 **25** 250–251

[163]Bond, W J 'Describing and conserving biotic diversity' in Huntley *op cit* Ref 124, 2–18

[164]Gadgill, M 'Biodiversity and India's degraded lands' *Ambio* 1993 **22** 172

[165]Khullar, P 'Conservation of biodiversity in natural forests through conservation plots – a historical perspective' *Indian Forster* 1992 **118** 327–337

[166]IUCN *Protected Areas of the World* Vol 2: *Palaearctic* IUCN, Gland (1991) xxviii, 556

[167]Baker *op cit* Ref 150

Tropical forests – conserved to death?: D Wood

of mature forest and the complete conversion to intensive systems, with an enhanced role for the management of secondary forest.[168] There is a need for a wide range of management options for land management, to develop an integrated mix of national parks, national forests, biosphere reserves, extractive reserves, community forestry and peasant reserves in a variety of different ecosystems.[169]

Conclusions

The current and widespread strategy of tropical protected area conservation – with the exclusion of human populations – depends on theories and perceptions on the design and management of biological reserves that are now proving irrelevant and inadequate for the needs of tropical countries. Tropical forest conservation is based on misconceptions of past and present tropical land use and of the economic ecology of rural communities. These misconceptions about tropical land use in the designation of reserves could translate into serious errors when it comes to reserve management. Protected area management which assumes it is managing previously uninhabited land is management that will fail.

The major thesis of this review is that the disturbance regime associated with the past productive use of tropical forest areas is a key to the future productive management of biodiversity. Conservationists must accept that nearly all tropical land is or has been productively used – intensively for agriculture and extensively to complement agriculture by gathering wild plants and by hunting. Diversity may depend on disturbance. Any misguided attempt to reduce, change or prevent disturbance by the establishment of strictly protected areas will have unpredictable but probably damaging consequences for the survival of tropical forests in their present form. Strict preservation could destroy biodiversity and also the indigenous knowledge needed for ecosystem management. Management policies excluding rural communities from reserves are not only socially provocative, but counterproductive technically.

It is suggested that multipurpose management and continued human use of tropical forests is a more effective conservation policy for tropical developing countries than the strict protection of large forest reserves. The present system of large strictly protected areas should be replaced with a system more in harmony with the traditional resource management needs and abilities of rural communities. Rural communities should be actively and physically involved in the future productive management of tropical forests, rather than being induced or pressured into abandoning their forest heritage.

[168]Brown, S and Lugo, A E 'Tropical secondary forests' *Journal of Tropical Ecology* 1990 **6** 26
[169]The Oaxaca 67 'The Oaxaca Recommendations' in Downing *et al, op cit* Ref 77, 367–372

D
Energy

[26]

Land Use Policy 1995 **12** (1) 37–48

Biomass energy in Western Europe to 2050

D O Hall and J I House

Presently biomass energy supplies at least 2 EJ/yr (47 Mtoe) in OECD Europe, which is about 4% of total primary energy consumption (54.1 EJ). Estimates of the potential for bioenergy in the next century range from 2 to 20 EJ/yr. This paper estimates a potential of 9.0–13.5 EJ in 2050, which represents 17–30% of projected total energy requirements. This depends on assumptions of available land areas, achievable yields and the amount of recoverable residues utilized. Greater environmental and net energy benefits can be derived from perennial and woody energy crops compared to annual arable crops as alternative feedstocks for fossil fuels. The relative contribution of biofuels in the future will ultimately depend on markets and incentives, on R&D progress and on environmental requirements.

Biomass refers to all forms of plant-based material that can be converted into usable energy, for example wood, sugarcane, crop and forestry residues, and dung. Biomass offers considerable flexibility of fuel supply due to the range and diversity of fuels which can be produced, at small or large scales (from very small scale domestic boilers up to multi-megawatt size power plants), in a centralized or dispersed manner. It is presently burnt directly, converted to liquid fuels for transportation, anaerobically digested to produce biogas, or used to produce electricity via gas or steam turbines. Biomass already supplies 14% of the world's energy and is considered one of the key renewable energy resources of the future.

This paper looks at the potential for bioenergy in Western Europe and the constraints to its production and use, particularly land availability, environmental considerations and economics. We show that the problems are not insurmountable, and should be considered as entrepreneurial opportunities which will allow Western Europe to diversify its fuel supplies (increasing energy security), reduce its CO_2 emissions and provide an economic use for surplus agricultural land.

The authors are with King's College London, Campden Hill Rd, London W8 7AH, UK (Tel: 071 333 4317; fax: 071 333 4500).

Present energy use, land use and subsidies in Western Europe

Total primary energy use in OECD Europe in 1990 was 54.1 EJ (joules $\times 10^{18}$), according to the International Energy Authority (IEA) (Table 1).[1] Predictions of future energy requirements vary considerably according to differences in accounting methodologies and assumptions made (such as population rise, energy efficiency, environmental restraints, etc). For example, the IEA anticipates a 40% increase in primary energy (Table 1) whereas Johansson *et al*,[2] who carried out an assessment for the 1992 Rio Earth Summit, predict a 20% decrease – the discrepancy is about 30 EJ or 724 Mtoe (14.5 million barrels of oil a day). Obviously the fraction of primary energy which biomass could potentially supply in 2050 depends on the degree to which these two predictions represent extremes or not. It is also dependent on other factors such as land availability, environmental constraints, available technology, attainable yields, energy markets and political factors.

Present land use patterns within OECD Europe are shown in Table 2. About 76% (333 Mha) of the total land area is classified here as 'usable', ie it can potentially be used for growing biomass for energy. How much of this 'usable' land could be put to energy cropping will depend on policies regarding food surpluses, energy self-sufficiency and rural economics. The role of agricultural subsidies in particular will be crucial in future land use policies. Presently total subsidies for OECD Europe are about $167 billion (1990) out of a total for all OECD countries of about $320 billion.[3] Whether this level of subsidies will be maintained in the future, and whether they could be shifted away from food production towards bioenergy and other non-food crops, are crucial questions. Just a small fraction of the $167 billion would have a significant effect on stimulating the large-scale development of bioenergies.

0264-8377/95/010037-12 © 1995 Butterworth-Heinemann Ltd

Rural Planning and Management

Biomass energy in Western Europe: D O Hall and J I House

Table 1. Energy supply in OECD Europe, 1990 to 2050.

| | Primary energy supply (EJ) | | | End use supply (EJ) | | | End use by sector (EJ) | |
	1990	2050		1990	2050		1990	2050
Coal	14.0	21.6	Coal	5.4	5.4	Industry	12.0	16.3
Oil	21.6	21.7	Oil	18.5	18.9	Transport	11.7	16.6
Gas	8.8	17.0	Gas	7.2	12.2	Agriculture	1.0	0.9
Nuclear	8.1	11.2	Electricity	7.2	13.8	Commerce	4.7	7.2
Hydro	1.4	2.2	Heat	0.6	1.3	Residential	9.5	10.7
Other renewables	0.1	0.3						
Other	0.1	1.8						
Total	54.1	75.8	Total	38.9	51.6	Total	38.9	51.6

Notes: OECD Europe: Austria, Belgium, Denmark, Finland, France, Germany, Greece, Iceland, Republic of Ireland, Italy, Luxembourg, Netherlands, Norway, Portugal, Spain, Sweden, Switzerland, Turkey, UK. Nuclear power is calculated on the basis of a fossil fuel substitution value (ie the amount of coal needed to produce the same amount of energy at 33% efficiency), whereas hydro is calculated on the basis of a fossil fuel heat value (ie the actual energy content of coal before conversion losses). It can therefore be argued that the hydro values should be multiplied by three to put hydro and nuclear on a comparable basis.

Source: Data from Ybema, J R (ed) *An Energy Scenario for OECD-Europe: 1990–2020–2050*, Netherlands Energy Research Foundation (ECN), IEA, Paris (in press).

Present plant biomass use

Plant biomass is already exploited in a number of ways. Humans have manipulated crops and forests for many centuries for their own needs and desires, including their energy requirements. Traditional uses of biomass for energy – burning wood and agricultural residues – are still widespread throughout much of the developing world, with some countries relying on biomass for over 90% of their energy requirements. However, use of biomass for energy has also been modernized along with agriculture and forestry practices, and there is still great potential for improvement.

Energy

Present biomass use for energy in Western Europe is at least 2 EJ (47 Mtoe) per year, which is about 3.6% of total primary energy consumption (54.1 EJ) (Table 3).[4] This figure is an underestimate since it is based on poor-quality data. Recent studies in the EU, for example in France, have shown that rural and agroindustrial biomass energy use has been inadequately monitored in the past. More systematic data gathering on biomass energy use is now under way in the EU which will put it on a comparable basis to the EFTA countries.

Crops

Cereals dominate crop production in OECD Europe, with 54 Mha (over half total cropland)

producing 220 Mt in 1990. According to the Food and Agriculture Organization's (FAO) annually produced statistics, throughout the whole of Europe (29 countries classified by the FAO) average grain yields increased by 1.0 t/ha (2.5% average per annum) between 1980 and 1990 to 4.5 t/ha. For the OECD countries, yield increases allowed production to rise overall by 31 Mt/yr while land use decreased by 3.4 Mha. Production of 'all crops' increased by 10% between 1980 and 1990 (and per capita production increased by 6%); however, this was not a steady increase since production actually peaked in the mid-1980s then fell somewhat as subsidies were redirected towards lower crop production. Since average yields of 'all crops' have continued to rise at 1% per year (nearly 2% for cereal crops), the area of land used has declined. Agronomic and breeding successes have so far led to huge yield increases for all crops throughout the world – in England, for example, average wheat yields rose from 2.5 t/ha in 1945 to 7.5 t/ha in 1985 – and the impact of biotechnology, which has yet to be seen, may allow even higher yields with lower inputs. It must also be noted that the above figures represent the grain yield only; an equal (or greater) amount of straw is also produced, therefore the UK's total wheat biomass yields in 1985 were over 15 t/ha.

Forestry

Total roundwood production in 1990 was 333 Mm³ on 141 Mha of forest and woodland (2.4 m³/ha), with

Table 2. Land use in OECD Europe (Mha).

	Cropland	Permanent pasture	Forest and woodland	Total = 'usable land'	Total land area
Western Europe	92.0	63.0	121.1	276.1	358.1
Turkey	27.9	8.6	20.2	56.7	77.0
Total OECD Europe	119.9	71.6	141.3	332.8	435.1

Notes: Western Europe: As for OECD Europe (Table 1), without Turkey. 'Usable land' = that classified by this paper to be under the uses of listed in the table.

Source: Data from World Resources Institute *World Resources 1992–3* WRI, Washington, DC (1993)

Table 3. Estimates of biomass energy use in Europe.

| Source | OECD Europe – Energy consumption | | | | EU 12 – Energy consumption | | | |
	Total energy (EJ)	Biomass energy (EJ)	Biomass energy (Mtoe)	Biomass %	Total energy (EJ)	Biomass energy (EJ)	Biomass energy (Mtoe)	Biomass %
Woods and Hall[a]	54.1	1.96	46.7	3.6	48	0.83	19.8	1.7
Johansson et al[b]	56.6	1.20	28.6	2.1				
Palz et al[c]					48	0.93	22.1	1.9

Notes: These estimates are probably quite conservative and based on poor-quality data. More up-to-date data are becoming available, eg from France, which indicate that biomass energy use may be at least 50% greater than previously estimated.
OECD Europe: As Table 1. EU 12: Belgium, Denmark, France, Germany, Greece, Republic of Ireland, Italy, Luxembourg, Netherlands, Portugal, Spain, UK.

Sources: [a]Woods, J and Hall, D O *Bioenergy for Development: Technical and Environmental Dimensions* FAO, Rome (1994); [b] Johansson, T B J et al, 'Renewable fuels and electricity for a growing economy' in Johansson et al (eds) *Renewable Energy: Sources for Fuels and Electricity* Island Press, Washington, DC (1993); [c] Palz, W, Caratti, G and Zerros, A 'Renewable energy development in Europe' Paper delivered to EC Euroforum, Paris (1993)

industrial roundwood accounting for 287 Mm^3 (Table 4). Roundwood imports were 44 Mm^3 and exports 24 Mm^3, resulting in only a small 20 Mm^3 deficit. This figure is very approximate and disguises significant trade in roundwood of greatly different values, eg pulp, sawnwood, paperboard, etc. There is a large deficit in the EU 12, but this is nearly balanced by production in the other seven countries. As Bazett clearly states, 'Europe (includes W & N Europe) is presently in a surplus wood supply situation with annual growth outstripping supply' and 'the European region has the potential to increase long-term sustainable harvest by about 110 Mm^3/ year or some 35% over present levels'.[5] The problem is that FAO demand projections foresee a roundwood deficit of 40 Mm^3 by 2010 and there may be pollution-induced decreases of 85 Mm^3/yr. However, these discussions and scenarios do not include the 'huge resource base' of the CIS forests, which Bazett says have 'an indicated annual surplus of almost 450 Mm^3'. Demand projections for global industrial roundwood use have decreased significantly over the last few years. Changing processing technologies and waste paper recovering (increasing globally from 33% at present to 50% in the future) are predicted to significantly slow consumption growth rates of industrial roundwood. As Bazett summarizes, the 'biggest imponderable is the extent to which the non-industrialized countries will be able to develop economically in the long term' which will have 'a significant effect on roundwood removals'.

Technical potential of biomass energy in 2050

The technical potential for bioenergy production in Western Europe will depend on many factors. Most

importantly, it will depend on the amount of land available for biomass production, and the biomass productivities that can be achieved and that are sustainable in the long term. In the short term the availability of residues and wastes will be important to 'kick-start' the industry, as will the way the public and the energy markets perceive bioenergy, and the support it receives from governments. There is already sufficient technology for the conversion of biomass fuels in an efficient manner, and continued R&D will improve matters further.

Land

A study by the Netherlands Scientific Council for Government Policy on the future of rural areas concluded that in the EU 12 their four scenarios (free market and free trade; regional development; nature and landscape; environmental protection) 'can be put into effect using at least 40 Mha less than the 127 Mha of agricultural land currently in use'.[6] Another EU study has also concluded that 30–40 Mha of agricultural and marginal land could be available for biomass production after 2000.[7] At least 15–20 Mha of good agricultural land (an area the size of England and Wales) is expected to be taken out of production in the EU by the year 2000/2010 (and this could reach over 50 Mha in the next century). This area of land could provide 3.6–4.8 EJ/yr of biomass energy, displacing 90–120 Mt of carbon emissions from coal, 72–96 Mt from oil or 50–67 Mt of carbon emissions from natural gas (7–17% of total EC carbon emissions in 1991).[8]

Present concerns about overproduction of cereals and other foods in the EU, and also in the wider OECD Europe (notwithstanding Eastern European countries' surpluses and potentials), have highlighted the need to seriously address the potential for

Table 4. OECD Europe roundwood production, imports and exports in 1990 (Mm^3).

| | Production | | Imports | | Exports | |
	Industrial	Total	Industrial	Total	Industrial	Total
Western Europe	280.8	317.2	41.3	43.7	23.1	23.6
Turkey	5.7	15.5	0.7	0.7	0.1	0.1
Total OECD Europe	286.5	332.7	42.0	44.4	23.2	23.7

Source: Data from FAO *Forest Products Yearbook 1990* FAO, Rome (1992)

non-food agriculture. This is already happening in relation to oilseed rape and the CAP (Common Agricultural Policy of the EU) and GATT (General Agreement on Tariffs and Trade) restrictions. These restrict the amount of rape that can be produced for food, but there is no restriction on non-food uses. Hence farmers already producing rapeseed are keen to see it being used for biodiesel so they do not have to change their farming practices.

Productivity

Cereal production and yield increases give some indication of the technical potential for increasing biomass yields, although increases in overall biomass yields are more difficult to achieve. Future yield increases could come with lower inputs, resulting in more environmentally acceptable arable agriculture. Research on improving the productivities of biomass energy crops/plantations is still at an early stage compared to agriculture and conventional plantation forestry. Nevertheless significant yield increases have already been recorded[9] and the aim of the EU's biomass programme is to attain average production of 12 OD(oven dry)t/ha (240 GJ/ha; gigajoules = joules × 10^9) in the next century; this is considered feasible but will require greatly enhanced research efforts.[10] This involves ongoing research and monitoring and is not a short process to ensure such average yields over all Europe.

Biomass potential

Numerous estimates have been made in recent years for various definitions of 'potential supplies' of biomass energy in Europe. These are summarized in Table 5 and show a range from about 3 to over 20 EJ

per year. Whether these scenarios come to fruition will depend on numerous factors related to economics, rural and employment policies, public acceptability, agricultural and forestry priorities, and, very importantly, environmental factors. A European workshop has recently addressed many of these issues related to afforestation of agricultural land.[11] For a more global perspective of the biomass energy potential, see the review by Sampson et al.[12]

The present study examines the possibility of using between 10% and 15% of 'usable land' (ie cropland, permanent pasture, and forestry and woodland), at yields of 10 t(200GJ)/ha and 15 t(300GJ)/ha, and with use of 25% of potentially harvestable residues from agriculture, forestry and urban wastes (see Table 6). About the year 2020 we expect that 10% of usable land (33.3M ha) could be used for biomass energy production with an average yield of 10 t/ha, thereby providing 16.6% of present primary energy. This area also represents 28% of cropland alone or 13% of combined cropland and forests/woodlands. By 2050 yields of 15 t/ha might be expected. If so, 10% of usable land could provide 17.8% of the primary energy predicted by the IEA[13] or 29.7% of that predicted by Johansson et al.[14] Naturally, if 15% of usable land was available by 2050 greater proportions of primary energy could be provided by biomass (Table 6).

The question arises as to whether 33 Mha or more could be planted for energy plantations and cropping. At present industrial wood plantations (as opposed to conventional natural forests) occupy about 19 Mha in Europe (25 countries) and about 100 Mha worldwide (total commercial plus natural forests = 2051 Mha).[15] The case of forests in Turkey

Table 5. Estimates of potential biomass energy supplies (not imported) in Europe after 2000 (residues and energy cropping).

Authors	Region	Year	EJ	Remarks
Dessus et al (1992)[a]	Europe	2010	8	'accessible reserves potential' and traditional biomass
Hall et al (1992)[b]	Western Europe (17 countries)	>2000	8.2–15.1	'potential'
Swisher and Wilson (1993)[c]	Western Europe	2030	7.9–9.9	'practical potential' and 'maximum technical potential'
Scurlock et al (1993)[d]	Western Europe (17 countries)	>2000	8.0–10.3	'potential'
Hall et al (1993)[e]	Europe (EC)	>2000	15.2	'potential'
Johansson et al (1993)[f]	OECD Europe	2050	10.5	'supplies'
NUTEK (1993)[g]	Western Europe (19 countries)	>2000	4.2	'potential'
Grassi and Bridgwater (1993)[h]	EU (12 countries)	2030	26.4	'gross technical potential'
ESD (1994)[i]	EU (12 countries)	2010	4.7	'full potential penetration'
Action Plan (1994)[j]	EU (12 countries)	2005–10	2.9	'realistic potential'
This study	OECD Europe	2050	9.0–13.5	'potential'

Sources: [a] Dessus, B, Devin, B and Phrabod, F *World Potential of Renewable Energies* JOUVE, Paris, (1992); [b] Hall, D O, Woods, J and House J I 'Biological systems for uptake of CO$_2$' *Energy Conservation and Management* 1992 **33** (5–8) 721–728; [c] Swisher, J N and Wilson, D 'Renewable energy potentials *Energy* 1993 **18** 440–459; [d] Scurlock, J M O, Hall, D O, House, J I and Howes, R 'Utilising biomass crops as an energy source: a European perspective' *Water, Air and Soil Pollution* 1993 **70** 139–159; [e] Hall, D O, Rosillo-Calle, F, Williams, R H and Woods, J 'Biomass for energy: supply prospects' in Johansson, T B J et al (eds) *Renewable Energy: Sources for Fuels and Electricity* Island Press, Washington, DC (1993) 593–652; [f] Johansson et al, op cit Table 3; [g] NUTEK *Forecast for the Biofuel Trade in Europe* Swedish National Board for Industrial and Technical Development, Stockholm (1993); [h] Grassi, G and Bridgwater, A V 'The opportunities for electricity production from biomass by advanced thermal conversion technologies' *Biomass and Bioenergy* 1993 **4** 339–345; [i] ESD *The European Renewable Energy Study* No 4, 1030/E91-02, Commission of the EC, DG XII, Brussels (1994); [j] Action Plan 'Working group report on energy from biomass and waste' in *An Action Plan for Renewable Energy Sources in Europe* EU, Madrid conference (March 1994)

Table 6. Potential biomass energy production.

1. Land areas needed for energy production from biomass[a]
Current energy use in OECD Europe = 54.1 EJ
Assuming productivity of 200 GJ or 10 t/ha (oven dry) = 0.2 EJ/1.0 Mha
For all energy would need   271 Mha
For 10% energy would be   27 Mha
                          = 8% of all 'usable' land (Table 2)
                          = 23% of cropland (Table 2)
                          = 38% of pasture (Table 2)
                          = 19% of forest and woodland (Table 2)

2. Potential biomas energy production from residues[b]
Potentially harvestable = 9.2 EJ (those residues that could potentially be removed from land)
Recoverable = 2.3 EJ (the proportion of residues that are likely to actually be removed from land = 25% of potentially harvestable residues)

3. Potential biomass energy production from 'usable' land (energy plantations/crops) and residues[a]
(a) About 2020
   10% 'usable' land (33.3 Mha) (with yields of 10 ODt/ha = 200 GJ/ha) = 6.7 GJ
                                            = 12.3% of present energy
   Recoverable residues   = 2.3 EJ
   Total   = 9.0 EJ
                                            = 16.6% of present energy

(b) 2050
   (i) 10% of 'usable' land (yields 15 ODt/ha; residues 3.5 EJ)
   Energy plantations/crops   = 10.0 EJ
   Residues   = 3.5 EJ
   Total   = 13.5 EJ
                                            = 17.8% of ECN 2050 primary energy (75.8 EJ)
                                            = 29.7% of Johansson *et al* primary energy (45.4 EJ)

   (ii) 15% of 'usable' land (yields 15 ODt/ha; residues 4.6 EJ)
   Energy plantations/crops   = 15.0 EJ
   Residues   = 4.6 EJ
   Total   = 19.6 EJ
                                            = 25.9% of ECN 2050 primary energy (75.8 EJ)
                                            = 43.2% of Johansson *et al* primary energy (45.4 EJ)

Sources: [a] This paper; [b] Woods, J and Hall, D O *Bioenergy for Development: Technical and Environmental Dimensions* FAO, Rome (1994)

is interesting because of its large land area and because forests (all types) occupy about 20 Mha, with about half presently being considered as productive.[16] The 'potential area for forestation' is estimated to be a further 5.4 Mha, with planting rates in the 1980s of almost 220 000 ha/yr. If incentives were available in Turkey it is likely that further forestation could take place. These and other studies in, for example, France,[17] Sweden,[18] Germany,[19] the UK,[20] Finland,[21] etc, highlight the point that country and region-specific analyses are essential if estimates of land and suitability for biomass production are to be acceptable for future energy and land use planning.

Economics

It is very difficult to evaluate the overall economic status of any form of biomass energy since regional and site-specific factors determining the cost of delivered biomass (at the conversion facility) can have overriding significance. Direct comparisons of costs of biofuels and competing more-conventional fuels tend to be misleading as they do not consider the environmental costs of fossil fuels or the relative benefits of biomass fuels. They also do not consider all the subsidies given to conventional fuels, both directly and indirectly; ie it is necessary to 'internalize the externalities', and at the same time put all

fuels on a comparable cost basis, ie create a 'level playing field'.

A recent study by the World Bank examined biomass electricity and ethanol costs worldwide on a comparable basis from a total of 114 reports. In the case of electricity it was concluded that 'costs . . . compare well with the costs of fossil-fired generation and even hydro generation in favourable situations; some are as low as 2–4 c/kWh . . . biomass gasification combined-cycle technologies show much promise for reducing costs for large-scale power generation . . .' As for ethanol from biomass, data mostly from the USA and Brazil show that the 'decline in costs since the 1970s has been significant and is attributable to technology improvements and a shift toward cheaper crops . . . The costs of ethanol were beginning to compare well with gasoline until the collapse of oil prices in the mid-1980's.'[22]

The conference proceedings[23] and the reviews by Williams and Larson[24] and Larson[25] are also good summaries of costs of biomass electricity and fuels and comparisons with other energy sources. Elliott concludes that the emerging technology of gasifier/turbines can give electricity at about 5 c/kWh and that the investment costs could be as low as $1300/kW after the tenth plant was installed.[26] Presently two such plants are coming on stream in Sweden and Finland and a 30 MWe plant is planned for Brazil.[27] The EU plans shortly to construct two 8–10 MWe

Biomass energy in Western Europe: D O Hall and J I House

Table 7. Biofuels for transport: summary of energy, CO_2 balances and costs of best case scenarios (ie use of byproducts, efficient technology and high yields).

	Ethanol from wheat	Ethanol from beet	Rape methyl ester	Methanol from wood	Electricity from wood
Net energy yield (GJ/ha)	58.4	200.6	48.9	158.1	209.9
Net energy ratio, energy input:output	4.74	12.21	4.98	13.33	22.85
% gasoline or diesel life-cycle energy use	52	38	43	22	8
Gasoline or diesel substitution (l/ha)	1 695	3 961	885	4 909	–
Net CO_2 abatement (kg/ha)	4 072	13 628	3 722	10 661	9 480
% of gasoline/diesel life-cycle CO_2 emissions	40	28	31	18	9
Cost of gasoline or diesel replaced					
– EU feedstock prices	89–103	92–100	98–136	33–39	6.4–9.5c/kWh
– World feedstock prices	54–62	64–72	50–59	33–39 (USA)	
Cost ratio to gasoline or diesel (EU)	5.1–5.9	5.3–5.7	5.6–7.8	3.4–4.2	1.3–1.9
Net cost (subsidy) required (annual $/t)	1 207–1 444	2 960–3 284	710–1 052	1 068–1 436	142–447
Cost of CO_2 abated ($/t)	424–507	374–415	304–450	186–250	27–86
Net energy yield if 20% of OECD Europe cropland set aside and used in 2050 (EJ)	1.4	4.8	1.2	3.8	5.0

Note: Transport fuel use in 1990 = 11.7 EJ, and predicted in 2050 = 16.6 EJ (see Table 1 also for electricity).
Source: OECD *Biofuels* OECD/IEA, Paris (1994)

plants using short rotation forestry as the feedstock. The economics of short rotation forestry in seven European and North American countries are given in various detail in Ledin and Alriksson's handbook.[28]

A recent report by the OECD has comprehensively synthesized and reanalysed data on biomass liquid fuels (ethanol, methanol, rape methyl ester) and electricity from a cost point of view – besides net energy benefits and CO_2 amelioration potentials (Table 7).[29] The cost of gasoline or diesel replaced by the biofuels varies from 3.4 to 7.8 times the equivalent petroleum fuel using EU feedstock prices but with lower multiples if world feedstock prices are used. At EU prices the subsidies required to make these biofuels cost-competitive vary from $710 to $3284/ha/yr. The obvious question is whether these microeconomic comparisons justify shifting agricultural subsidies away from (surplus) food production towards biomass energy production or whether a more macroeconomic view incorporating environmental and social benefits is justified.[30] The amount of liquid biofuels which could be produced if 20% of cropland was set aside for this purpose varies from 1.2 to 4.8 EJ/yr compared to the present transport fuel use of 1.7 EJ/yr and a 2050 predicted amount of 16.6 EJ[31] or 12.2 EJ (liquids).[32] A general conclusion of these economic analyses so far is that using woody biomass as a feedstock results in the most favourable product costs. However, the use of starch and sugar crops may be a desirable short-term use of biomass if the economic incentives are adequately structured. Other factors such as the environmental benefits of perennial woody biomass compared to annual crops must also be considered (see later).

CO_2 seqestration *v* fossil fuel substitution

Since it was first proposed by Dyson and Marland in 1977, there have been numerous analyses of the potential for forests to mitigate the global CO_2-induced greenhouse effect by sequestering (absorbing) carbon and storing it in their standing biomass. Global estimates of the potential range from 1 to 3 Pg carbon sequestered per annum into the middle of the next century depending on land afforested, enhanced forest management and longevity of the stored carbon.[33] Carbon is absorbed by trees as they grow to maturity over a long period, eg 20–60 years, but then it ceases. To continue carbon uptake, the trees can be harvested and the woody biomass can theoretically be put into permanent storage ('pickled') or can be used as long-lived forest products. However, the storage option is quite costly, while the demand for long-lived wood products may be too small to have a major impact on the global carbon cycle. Alternatively, using biomass produced on available land to substitute for fossil fuels would be more effective in decreasing atmospheric CO_2 than simply using the biomass as a carbon store, and would also provide a wider range of benefits.[34] This will allow the land to be used indefinitely for carbon removal, and since biomass energy crops have relatively high growth rates and higher yields compared to conventional tree cover they can make a larger and more rapid contribution.

Bioenergy can be sold and is competitive in many circumstances, therefore the net cost of offsetting CO_2 emissions by substitution could be near zero or negative. Growing trees as a long-term carbon store will be important where the creation of new forest reserves is deemed desirable for environmental or economic reasons and on low productivity land, but in general, using biomass to substitute for fossil fuels is more advantageous and appropriate. A detailed analysis by Hall *et al* outlined the economic advantages of the fossil fuel substitution route compared to the carbon sequestration alternatives. With advanced biomass electric conversion systems profits could be made (depending on feedstock costs) while

42

decreasing CO_2 emissions to the atmosphere compared to coal electric systems.[35]

Sequestering carbon into biomass would incur costs between $8 and $60/t carbon in the USA in order to offset 25% of current CO_2 emissions.[36] Recent estimates by Nilsson and Schopfhauser for a global afforestation programme over the next century on 335 Mha (total sequestration = 104 GtC) give 'integrated costs of carbon sequestration' at $6.01/tC for the USA, $13.86/tC for Europe and $8.20/tC for the CIS. Tropical Asia, Africa and Latin America have costs of only $1.66 to 2.41/tC.[37] A US study concluded that natural gas and biomass were the two cheapest electricity supply technology options (relative to existing coal plants) for mitigating CO_2 with costs of $32 and $36/t CO_2.[38]

Marland and Marland modelled the most effective strategies for using forest land to ameliorate CO_2 increases in the atmosphere. The options 'depend on the current status of the land, the productivity that can be expected, the efficiency with which the forest harvest is used to substitute for fossil fuels, and the time perspective of the analyses'. Forests with large standing biomass and low productivity should be protected as carbon stores. Deforested land with low productivity should be reforested and managed for forest growth and carbon storage. Productive land could be forested and managed for a harvestable crop which is used with optimum efficiency for long-lived products or as a substitute for fossil fuels. 'The longer the time perspective, the more likely that harvesting and replanting will result in net carbon benefits'.[39] Dewar and Cannell also concluded that short rotations do not achieve high carbon storage and that conifers and broadwood plantations will give different carbon storage benefits at 50 and 100 year time horizons.[40]

To conclude, as did Hall *et al*, 'displacing fossil fuel with biomass grown sustainably and converted into useful energy with modern conversion technologies would be more effective in decreasing atmospheric CO_2 than sequestering carbon in trees'. The extent to which biomass energy would decrease OECD Europe's CO_2 emissions depends on the ability of wood (say) to displace coal. 'Thus if biomass is considered primarily as a substitute for coal using modern conversion technologies for producing either electricity or liquid synfuels, the effect on atmospheric CO_2 would be comparable to what could be achieved with C sequestration, per tonne of biomass produced.'[41]

Net CO_2 and energy benefits

If biomass energy is to be used as a fossil-fuel substitute, particularly if it is to reduce CO_2 emissions, the energy provided should be greater than the fossil fuel energy needed to produce it (energy for land preparation, agrochemicals, transport and conversion). Ledig examined this relationship for 11 differing situations involving biomass from trees, and found that the net energy yield tended to be around 12 times the energy input.[42] More recent estimates for the USA of plantation biomass (including both woody and herbaceous crops) with near-term expected biomass yields (net of harvesting and storage losses) in the range 9–13 dry tonnes per hectare per year give net energy yields in the range 10–15 times the energy inputs for these crops.[43] With projected increases of future yields, these ratios would be somewhat higher. A modelling study in the UK has shown that energy output:input ratios of around 30:1 could be achieved depending on yield and management efficiency.[44]

Several studies have examined liquid fuels in Europe.[45] They show that utilizing starch, sugar and oil crops for liquid fuels can give net energy and CO_2 benefits provided that the agricultural phase is well managed and that the byproducts of grain production, eg straw, are used in the energy conversion processes (which also should be efficient) or that the byproducts offset other energy-requiring processes. The OECD study highlighted in Table 7 shows that, of the liquid fuel options, ethanol from sugarbeet (12:2) and methanol from wood (13:3) show the best energy ratios, with the methanol option giving the greatest gasoline and diesel substitutions (4909 l/ha). In terms of CO_2 abatement the beet/ethanol and wood/methanol options again appear best but the methanol option is the least costly ($186–250/t CO_2). However, the wood/electricity option is the most favourable in terms of energy ratios, fuel substitution and CO_2 abatement costs.[46] As will be discussed below, woody crops (trees and herbaceous plants such as miscanthus) generally have more environmental advantages (especially in the production phase) than annual, arable crops. The use of conventional agricultural practices compared to those in forestry will have to be carefully weighed as arable land is taken out of food production.

Environmental concerns

With the realization that biomass energy could become part of the modern energy economy on a large scale there have been increasing concerns as to the short-term and long-term environmental effects of such a strategy. Fortunately a number of environmental and biomass energy groups acknowledged some time ago that if biomass was to play an important role in future energy policy then its production, conversion and use must be environmentally acceptable and also accepted by the public. These two factors are likely to be the most crucial constraints on future biomass developments and must be addressed in some detail in order for scenario builders to appreciate the opportunities and problems associated with biomass energy production.

These environmental aspects should also have the highest priority in future R&D policy as the authors firmly believe that ensuring environmental sustainability will be the single most important determining factor in future biomass for energy development. Several studies give a more comprehensive coverage of environmental factors than what follows below.[47] The review by Williams on the role of biomass energy in sustainable development should also be consulted.[48]

If plantations were to replace natural forests, there would be destructive environmental effects and negative effects on carbon inventories; this should be avoided. On the other hand, forestry projects established on degraded land or abandoned cropland can have numerous positive environmental effects. Negative environmental effects might include soil compaction and loss of fertility, increased runoff, water pollution from agrochemicals, lowering of water tables in arid areas, loss of biodiversity, exotic species becoming a weed; or introducion of new pests and diseases, uncontrolled forest fires, and construction of roads, buildings and traffic. With careful planning and management these problems can be avoided. The possible positive effects far outweigh these negative effects. Reforestation/afforestation of degraded or agricultural land can improve soil structure, soil organic matter and nutrients, reduce runoff and increase soil water storage, thereby reducing flooding downstream, increase local rainfall and modify local temperatures, increase biodiversity, reduce pressure on natural forests, create windbreaks and, of course, store carbon. In this way afforestation can protect fragile regions by conserving watersheds and aquifers, reducing erosion and preserving wildlife habitats. Furthermore, if the biomass is used to replace fossil fuel it can offset many other environmental impacts.

If biomass plantations are to play major roles in the global energy economy, strategies are needed for achieving and sustaining high yields over large areas and long periods. Despite the embryonic state of understanding of what is required, some general guidelines can be provided, drawing on the limited experience with plantations and much broader experiences with agriculture and forestry. Some specific environmental concerns are discussed below.

Site establishment

In industrialized countries the most likely sites are reasonably good agricultural lands that have been abandoned due to food surpluses. Therefore site establishment is not technically difficult, nor is it likely to create much environmental impact. With many energy crops, planting is far less frequent than for food crops: short-rotation forestry (SRF) crops are only replanted every 15–20 years; for perennial grasses with a three-year cutting cycle, replanting occurs perhaps once a decade. With such energy crops, herbicide applications would be much less frequent than for agricultural crops. Biodegradable agrochemicals should be used when required during establishment.

Species selection

Species selected for the plantations should be fast growing and well matched to the plantation site. This applies, for example, in respect to water requirements and its seasonality, drought resistance, soil pH, nutrition, tolerance of saline soils, as well as susceptibility to herbivores, fire, disease and pests. Consideration must also be given to the crop's potential impact on the surrounding habitat, with care taken to prevent aggressive exotic species from establishing themselves outside the plantation and displacing native flora. Exotic species should be chosen only when they are markedly superior to local species. It may often be feasible to obtain high yields with indigenous species and clones by giving adequate attention to nutrient balances. However, if plantations are established on degraded lands where regeneration of desirable native species is difficult or impossible, an introduced species may be the best option for restoring these lands, and indigenous species could be introduced subsequently.

Soil fertility

Attention must be given to long-term soil fertility, which also involves soil management and enhancing micro and macro fauna in the soil.[49] Nutrients removed during harvesting must either be generated naturally or restored by adding fertilizers. Fertilizers are usually required when establishing plantations on degraded lands and may also be needed to realize high yields even on good sites, but it will often be desirable to reduce fertilizer inputs. For SRF it will usually be desirable to leave leaves and twigs in the field, as nutrients tend to concentrate in these parts of the plant. Also, the mineral nutrients recovered as ash at the energy conversion facilities should be returned to the site. Species can be selected for efficiency of nutrient use; in addition, either selecting a nitrogen-fixing species or intercropping the primary crop with an N-fixing species can make the plantation self-sufficient in nitrogen. The promise of intercropping strategies is suggested by 10-year trials in Hawaii, where yields of 25 t/ha/yr have been achieved without annual N fertilizer additions when *Eucalyptus* is interplanted with N-fixing *Albizia* trees.[50] In the future it may be feasible to reduce fertilizer requirements by matching nutrient applications more precisely to the plant's time-varying need for nutrients.

Pests and diseases

Monocultural single-age plantations can be more vulnerable to attack by pests and pathogens than natural forests or grasslands. The adoption of this practice has led to an increase in the number and severity of diseases and pests, although much of this increase has been associated with land-clearing methods. poor matching of species and clones to sites, or the new ecological conditions arising from intensive management. Thus care in species selection and good plantation design and management can be helpful in controlling pests and diseases, rendering the use of chemical pesticides unnecessary in all but special circumstances. Good plantation design includes: (i) areas set aside for native flora and fauna to harbour natural predators for planation pest control, and perhaps (ii) blocks characterized by different clones and/or species. If a pest attack breaks out in a block of one clone, a now common practice in well-managed plantations is to let the attack run its course and to let predators from the set-aside area help halt the pest outbreak. Species and clones should be selected for resistance to local pests and diseases.

Erosion

The potential for erosion control will be an important criterion in selecting species wherever erosion is a problem. Erosion tends to be significant during the year following planting, therefore tree (SRF) or perennial grass crops, for which planting is infrequent, can provide better erosion control than annual crops. Recent experience with the Conservation Reserve Program of the US Department of Agriculture showed that the erosion rate declined 92% on 14 Mha of highly erodible US cropland taken out of annual production and planted with perennial grasses and trees.

Water pollution

Leaching of agrochemicals can contaminate groundwater and runoff, degrade drinking water supplies and promote algal blooms. These problems can be reduced with better management of agrochemical inputs, erosion control and planned water management. Site design can make optimum use of rainfall in dry areas or allow rapid drainage in wet areas. Irrigation can also be more closely matched to the crops' needs and can be applied efficiently.

Biological diversity

Biomass plantations are often criticized because the range of biological species they support is much narrower than for natural forests. While true, this criticism is only relevant if a biomass plantation replaces a virgin forest; it is not relevant if a plantation and associated natural reserves are established on degraded lands; in this instance the restored lands would be able to support much greater biological diversity than was possible before restoration. If biomass energy crops were to replace monocultural food crops, in most cases the shift would be to a more biologically diverse landscape. Achieving sus-

tainable biomass production while maintaining biological diversity may ultimately require a shift to polycultural strategies (eg mixed species in various planting configurations). It is possible to achieve high yields with a mix of indigenous species and clones, although silviculturally compatible combinations of species are difficult to design and establish because of the tendency of one species to dominate. Monocultures have tended to be favoured for energy crops because management techniques were borrowed largely from agriculture and thus designed for monocultural systems necessary in serving agricultural markets. Yet biomass energy conversion systems can usually accommodate a variety of feedstocks. Polycultural establishment and management techniques therefore warrant high priority in research and development programmes for energy crops.

As already noted, establishing and maintaining natural reserves with plantations can help control crop pests while enhancing the local ecosystem. However, preserving biodiversity on a regional basis will require land use planning in which natural forest patches are connected via a network of undisturbed corridors (riparian buffer zones, shelterbelts, and hedgerows between fields), thus enabling species to migrate from one habitat to another.

Landscape

As Bell has noted, 'landscapes of countryside are highly valued by many people. Energy forestry represents a possible major change to well loved landscapes.'[51] Thus it is essential for biomass energy developers to recognize local and national perceptions from the outset of any large-scale developments. 'Horizon-to-horizon' monocultures are not necessary (or acceptable) since only a relatively small fraction of the landscape needs to be planted to biomass crops. Bioenergy systems favour medium-scale 20–50 MW power plants which can be modular, as opposed to 500–1000 MW fossil fuel plants. Figure 1 shows that a 20 MW plant (45% efficiency), using biomass produced at 10 ODt/ha, would require 7000 ha which represents only 10% of the land within a 14 km radius of the generation plant. For a 50 MW plant with plantation yields of 15 ODt/ha and 11 000 ha requirements with a 15% land use, the radius of the planted area would be 16 km. These two examples correspond to the scenarios used in this paper.

Guidelines

There is a need for the establishment of guidelines which should address the main concerns of environmentalists and the public, while ensuring that the biomass growers are able to operate efficiently and profitably, and that social and other benefits are optimized. Such a balancing act needs careful consideration and planning if long-term benefits are to

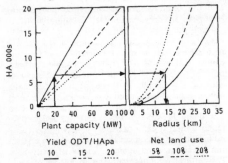

Yield ODT/HApa
10 ___15___ 20

Net land use
5% ___10%___ 20%

Assumes 45% efficiency, 80% load and 18GJ/ODT

Figure 1. Land requirements for biomass power plants.
Source: Booth, R, Shell International Petroleum Co, London, personal communication (1993)

accrue. Biodiversity and land use issues, technologies for production and conversion, and bioenery development policies should all be subject to agreed guidelines established in advance wherever possible. The Shell/WWF 'Guidelines' report sets out to establish 'a general framework of principles within which more detailed guidelines may be developed and assessed'. It deals mainly with plantation forestry and encompasses a range of issues from site and species selection to local involvement and social and business responsibility to sustainability and environmental management.[52] Most publications stress the need for ongoing, good-quality monitoring and the practical feedback to bioenergy policy making. Merely conforming to initial guidelines and thereafter not maintaining the necessary standards could result in environmentally damaging bioenergy production with adverse long-term impacts. A background paper from the Office of Technology Assessment, US Congress recommends that continuing R&D and environmental monitoring is necessary along with long-term and large-scale demonstration programmes.[53] Environmental impacts of biomass production, residue removals and bioenergy use on soil, water and air quality and on habitats, cropping practices and greenhouse gas emissions all need to be fully understood if recommendations on best practice are to be made.

Conclusions

The Electric Power Research Institute (EPRI) of the USA has concluded that 'biomass could become a truly important feedstock for electricity generation in the near term . . .' The main barriers to such an outcome were considered to be the lack of reliable markets, current agricultural policies and a lack of

agreed criteria for environmentally sound development of bioenergy. The main 'stimuli likely to encourage biofuels production' were market and regulatory incentives, constraints on fossil fuel use, and increases in cogeneration opportunities; public pressure could also act as an encouragement.[54] Europe has several good projects, such as those in Austria, Denmark and Sweden, on which to rapidly develop research and demonstrations, and on which policies can be formulated to ensure large-scale take-up of bioenergy. Such policies need to be implemented soon if biomass is to play an important role by 2020 and a significant role in the European energy scene by 2050.

Major expansions in research are needed to provide a sound analytical and empirical basis for achieving and sustaining high biomass yields in environmentally acceptable ways. There is, however, time for such research as well as for extensive field trials, because major bioenergy industries can be launched with residues from the agricultural and forest products industries. If substantial commitments are made to biomass plantation research in the near term, plantation biomass could start to make contributions to energy supplies when residue supplies are no longer adequate to meet the needs of the growing biomass energy industry, perhaps at the beginning of the next century.

Pasztor and Kristoferson have summarized the issues well:

In conclusion, if biomass energy systems are well managed, they can form part of a matrix of energy supply which is environmentally sound and therefore contributes to sustainable development. When compared, for example, to conventional fossil fuels, overall the impacts of bioenergy systems may be less damaging to the environment, since they produce many, but local and relatively small impacts on the surrounding environment, compared with fewer, but larger and more distributed impacts for fossil fuels. It is these qualities which may make the environmental impacts of bioenergy systems more controllable, more reversible and consequently, more benign.[55]

To conclude, biomass energy offers the potential to produce energy in an environmentally acceptable manner providing it is produced sustainably; the development of mutually acceptable guidelines will be important in ensuring this happens. Although bioenergy is already economic in certain cases in comparison with fossil fuels, ongoing development of the industry along with the creation of a more 'level playing field' (internalizing externalities and redistribution of subsidies) will allow it to compete more effectively. Growing biomass is among the cheapest options for CO_2 emissions reduction, particularly if that biomass is used for energy production; it also provides many other benefits over simply growing trees as a carbon store. Land availability does not appear to be a constraint because the predicted surpluses in land and food will lead to larger areas of land being 'set aside'. This paper estimates a potential of 9.0–13.5 EJ of energy could be produced from biomass in OECD Europe in 2050, which represents 17–30% of projected total energy requirements.

References

[1]Netherlands Energy Research Foundation (ECN) *An Energy Scenario for OECD-Europe: 1990–2020–2050* IEA, Paris (in press)
[2]Johansson, T B J, Kelly, H, Reddy, A K N and Williams, R H 'Renewable fuels and electricity for a growing economy' in Johansson, T B J *et al* (eds) *Renewable Energy: Sources for Fuels and Electricity* Island Press, Washington, DC (1993) 1–72
[3]Williams, R H 'Roles for biomass energy in sustainable development' in Socolow, R H *et al* (eds) *Industrial Ecology and Global Change* Cambridge University Press, Cambridge, UK (in press)
[4]Woods, J and Hall, D O *Bioenergy for Development: Technical and Environmental Dimensions* Environmental and Energy Series, FAO, Rome (1994)
[5]Bazett, M D 'Industrial wood' Study No 3 in Shell/WWF *Tree Plantation Review* Shell International Petroleum Co, London (1993)
[6]Rutter, F W *et al*, *Ground for Choices: Four Perspectives for the Rural Areas of the EC* Netherlands Scientific Council for Government Policy, The Hague (1992)
[7]Grassi, G and Bridgwater, A V 'The opportunities for electricity production from biomass by advanced thermal conversion technologies' *Biomass and Bioenergy* 1993 **4** 339–345
[8]Scurlock, J M O, Hall, D O, House, J I and Howes, R 'Utilising biomass crops as an energy source: a European perspective' *Water, Air and Soil Pollution* 1993 **70** 499–518
[9]Hansen, E A 'Poplar woody biomass yields: a look to the future' *Biomass and Bioenergy* 1991 **1** 1–8; Mitchell, C P, Zsuffa, L and Stevens, D J 'IEA Bioenergy Agreement: progress and achievements' *Biomass and Bioenergy* 1992 **2** 1–370
[10]Cannell, M G R 'Physiological basis of wood production' *Scandinavian Journal of Forest Research* 1989 **4** 459–490
[11]Volz, K R and Weber, N (eds) *Afforestation of Agricultural Land* Report EUR 4804, Commission of the EC, Brussels (1993)
[12]Sampson, R N *et al* 'Biomass management and energy' *Water, Air and Soil Pollution* 1993 **64** 139–159
[13]ECN *op cit* Ref 1
[14]Johansson *et al*, *op cit* Ref 2
[15]Bazett *op cit* Ref 5
[16]Ozer, U 'Assessment of uncertainties in the projected concentrations of CO_2 in the atmosphere' *Pure and Applied Chemistry* 1991 **63** 763–796
[17]Chantier, P and Mauguin, P *Rapport Final du Groupe d'Etudes ANVCE/ADEME*, Paris (1993)
[18]Bodlund, B and Bergman, J 'Bioenergy in Sweden: potential, technology and application' *Bioresource Technology* 1993 **46** 31–36
[19]Kaltschmitt, M and Wise, A 'Technical potentials of a bioenergy production in a Bundesland in the Federal Republic of Germany' *Biomass and Bioenergy* 1992 **3** 309–317
[20]Richards, K M, Hall, D O and Maryan, P S 'Prospects for biopower' *Nuclear Energy* 1993 **32** 291–298; de Selincourt, K, Howes, R and Hall, D O 'Europe's home-grown fuel' *New Scientist* 1993 **140** (1985) 22–24; ETSU *An Assessment of Renewable Energy for the UK* Report R82, Energy Technology Support Unit, Department of Trade and Industry, HMSO, London (1994)
[21]Sipila, K 'New power production technologies: various options for biomass and cogeneration' *Bioresource Technology* 1993 **46** 5–12
[22]Ahmed, K *Renewable Energy Technologies: A Review of Status and Costs of Selected Technologies* Energy Series Technical Paper No 240, World Bank, Washington, DC (1994)
[23]*Proceedings of the Bioenergy '93 Conference* VTT Combustion and Thermal Engineering Labororatory, Jyuaskyla, Finland (1993); NREL *Proceedings of the First Biomass Conference of the Americas* Vols I–III, National Renewable Energy Laboratory, Golden, CO (1993); Hall, D O, Grassi, G and Scheer, H (eds) *Biomass for Energy and Industry* 7th EC Conference, Ponte Press, Bochum, Germany (1994)
[24]Williams, R H and Larson, E D 'Advanced gasification-based biomass power generation' in Johansson *et al*, *op cit* Ref 2, 729–786
[25]Larson, E D 'Technology for electricity and fuels from biomass' *Energy and Environment* 1993 **18** 567–630
[26]Elliott, P 'Biomass energy overview in the context of the Brazilian biomass power demonstration' *Bioresource Technology* 1993 **46** 13–22
[27]VTT *op cit* Ref 23; Carpentieri, E, Larson, E D and Woods, J 'Prospects for sustainable, utility-scale, biomass-based electricity supply in Northeast Brazil' *Biomass and Bioenergy* 1993 **4** 149–174; 'Hot air fuels the energy debate' *Financial Times* 19 May 1993, 19
[28]Ledin, S and Alriksson, A *Handbook on How to Grow Short Rotation Forests* Swedish University of Agricultural Sciences, Uppsala (1992)
[29]OECD *Biofuels* ECD/IEA, Paris (1994)
[30]Mauguin, P *Using Biofuels as Additives for Cleaner Fuels Formulation* ADEME, Paris (1993); Sourie, J C 'Stratégies pour le développement des productions non alimentaires et les besions afférents de recherche' Paper presented at EC conference, 'Research, Training and Agriculture in Europe: The New Challenges', Brussels, November 1993
[31]ECN *op cit* Ref 1
[32]Johansson *et al*, *op cit* Ref 2
[33]Dyson, F J and Marland, G 'Technical fixes for the climate effects of CO_2' in Elliot, W P and Machta, L (eds) *Workshop on the Global Effects of Carbon Dioxide from Fossil Fuels* Miami Beach, FL, 7–11 March 1977, CONF/770385, US Dept of Energy, Washington, DC (1979); Breuer, G 'Can forest policy contribute to solving the CO_2 problem?' *Environment International* 1979 **2** 449–451; Houghton, R A 'The future role of tropical forests in affecting the CO_2 concentration of the atmosphere' *Ambio* 1990 **19** 204–209; Marland, G and Marland, S 'Should we store carbon in trees?' *Water, Air and Soil Pollution* 1992 **64** 181–195; Nakicenovic, N 'Long-term strategies for mitigating global warming' *Energy* 1993 **18** (special issue) 401–609; Dixon, R K, Brown, S, Houghton, R A, Soloman, A M, Trexler, M C and Wisniewski, J 'Carbon pools and fluxes of global forest ecosystems' *Science* **263** 185–190
[34]Hall, D O and Rosillio-Calle, F 'CO_2 cycling by biomass: global bioproductivity and problems of devegetation and afforestation' in Lingeman, E W A (ed) *Balances in the Atmosphere and the Energy Problem* European Physical Society, Geneva (1990) 137–179; Hall, D O, Mynick, H, Williams, H and Williams, R H *Carbon Sequestration Versus Fossil Fuel Substitution: Alternative Roles for Biomass in Coping with Greenhouse Warming* Report No 255, Centre for Energy and Environmental Studies, Princeton University, NJ; also *Nature* 1991 **353** 11–12
[35]Hall, Mynick, Williams and Williams *ibid*
[36]Richards, K R, Moulton R J and Birdsey, R A 'The cost of creating carbon sinks in the US' *Energy Conversion Management* 1993 **34** 905–912
[37]Nilsson, S and Schopfhauser, W 'The carbon sequestration potential of a global afforestation program' *Climate Change* (in press)
[38]Rubin, E S, Cooper, R N, Frosch, R A, Lee, T H, Marland, G, Rosenfield, A H and Stine, D 'Realistic mitigation options for global warming' *Science* 1992 **257** 148–266
[39]Marland and Marland *op cit* Ref 33
[40]Dewar, R C and Cannell, M G R, 'Carbon sequestration in trees, products and soils of forest plantations: an analysis using UK examples' *Tree Physiology* 1992 **11** 49–71

Biomass energy in Western Europe: D O Hall and J I House

[41]Hall, Mynick, Williams and Williams *op cit* Ref 34
[42]Ledig, F T 'Silvicultural systems for the energy efficient production of fuel biomass' in Klass, D L (ed) *Biomass as a Non Fossil Fuel Source* Symposium 144, American Chemical Society, Washington, DC (1981)
[43]Turhollow, A H and Perlack, R D 'Emissions of CO_2 from energy crop production' *Biomass and Bioenergy* 1991 1 129–135
[44]Foster, C 'The carbon and energy budgets of energy crops' *Energy Conversion Management* 1993 14 897–904
[45]Colley, R, Fulton, A, Hall, D O and Raymond, W F *The Environmental Effects of Large-scale Bioethanol Production in Europe'* EFOA (European Fuel Oxygenates Association), Brussels (1990); Levy, F *Les Biocarborants* AFME, Paris (1993); POST 'Biofuels for transport' Briefing Note 41, Parliamentary Office for Science and Technology, Houses of Parliament, London (1993); Okken, P A *et al* 'The role of energy crops in the energy system under CO_2 constraints' in Hall, D O *et al* (eds) *Biomass for Energy and Industry* VII EC Biomass Conference, Ponte Press, Bochum (1994) 562–568
[46]OECD *op cit* Ref 29
[47]Ledin and Alriksson *op cit* Ref 28; Pasztor, J and Kristoferson, L A (eds) *Bioenergy and the Environment* Westview Press, Boulder, CO (1990); Beyea, J, Cook, J, Hall, D C, Socolow, R and Williams, R *Toward Ecological Guidelines for Large Scale Biomass Energy Development* National Audubon Society/Princeton University Workshop, Audubon Society, New York

(1991); Ranney, J W 'Environmental considerations in biomass resource management for a greenhouse-constrained society' in Kuliasha, M A *et al* (eds) *Technologies for a Greenhouse-Constrained Society* Lewis Publishers, Boca Raton, FL (1992) 519–546; OTA *Potential Environmental Impacts of Bioenergy Crop Production* Office of Technology Assessment, US Congress, Washington, DC (1993); Shell/WWF 'Guidelines' in Shell/WWF *Tree Plantation Review* Shell International Petroleum Co, London (1993); Gustafsson, L (ed) 'Environmental aspects of energy forest cultivation' *Biomass and Bioenergy* (in press)
[48]Williams *op cit* Ref 3
[49]Makeschin, F 'Soil ecological aspects of arable land afforestation with fast growing trees' in Hall, D O *et al* (eds) *Biomass for Energy and Industry* VII EC Biomass Conference, Ponte Press, Bochum (1994) 534–538; OTA *op cit* Ref 47
[50]See review by Wormald, T J *Mixed and Pure Forest Plantation in the Tropics and Subtropics* Forestry Paper No 103, FAO, Rome (1992)
[51]Bell, S 'Energy forestry in the landscape' *Biomass and Bioenergy* 1994 6 53–62
[52]Shell/WWF *op cit* Ref 47
[53]OTA *op cit* Ref 47
[54]Turnbull, J *Strategies for Achieving a Sustainable, Clean and Cost Effective Biomass Resource* Electric Power Research Institute, Palo Alto, CA (1993)
[55]Pasztor and Kristoferson *op cit* Ref 47

Professor David Hall sadly passed away in August 1999. He will be long remembered for his enthusiasm and hard work to promote the importance of biomass energy and its role in sustainable development.

Land Use Policy 1995 **12** (1) 17–28

Wind power: challenges to planning policy in the UK

Merylyn McKenzie Hedger

Controversy has surrounded the development of windfarms since they started to appear in England and Wales in 1991, and the issues have received considerable media attention. The conflict has taken place within the planning system, site by site. Closer examination suggests that the wind power controversy is a result of the inadequate integration of both the two main bodies of public policy which bear upon the topic: energy policy and land use planning policy. Wind power is being developed within the culture of energy policy with its supply-side bias and its capacity to allow for rapid technological change which is counter to the protective and regulatory approach of planning policy for the upland areas chiefly affected. As a result the existing public policy framework in the UK is failing to address all the strategic issues posed by the development of wind power for the uplands of Britain. This paper starts to analyse the issues involved. The content, application and interactions of the relevant areas of policy are examined and related to the requirements for a strategic approach to wind power.

Increasing polarization and intensification in the wind power debate suggests that there is a dysfunction in the current approach. The main argument advanced in this paper is that the controversy about wind farming reflects over-rapid development in the absence of a strategic framework integrating national energy policy with the mainstream of planning policy.

Great Britain has the best wind resource in Europe.[1] But until recently it was lagging behind Denmark, the Netherlands and Germany, which had more installed capacity and also clear targets for wind power. However, in three years 22 'farms' have been installed, including the largest windfarm outside the USA.[2] Nevertheless, closer analysis of intensified government policy on renewable energy reveals that, for the new technology, old mindsets and cultures prevail. Wind power is being developed with a supply-side bias whereby the rapid exploitation of the energy resource takes precedence over

other considerations such as long-established planning policy.

Windfarms involve varying numbers of turbines which are tall, man-made structures with noise-emitting, moving components, requiring deep foundations and to which permanent, wide access roads are constructed. They need open, exposed areas and thus their visual influence extends over large land areas. Their approval in 'wild' and upland areas effectively constitutes a major reversal of land use policy in places which have, for the most part, been protected from developments other than agriculture and forestry because of their special characteristics. Public policy for these areas has developed over many years, after what at times have been fierce public campaigns, through conflict resolution, consensus-building and partnership. Moreover, because of the increased priority afforded to country-side conservation, successive administrations have amended agricultural and forestry policy over the past 20 years to take account of the need for landscape conservation and enhancement – a trend which is accelerating through the extensions of Environmentally Sensitive Areas (ESAs) and other measures included in the agri-environmental zonal programmes. Thus the present approach on wind power represents a significant shift in policy for the uplands.

Due to their novelty and characteristics, windfarms were likely to generate considerable controversy.[3] While some surveys have indicated strong local support in some areas,[4] as proposals have come forward there have been adverse reactions at local level in many places. A new national organization, Country Guardian, has also been formed to network groups whose chief objective is to oppose windfarms. Once windfarms have become operational, experience of impacts has fuelled opposition and local controversy where noise impacts are of most significance, for example at Llangwyrfon, Ceredigion and Llandinam, Powys, in

Dr McKenzie Hedger is with the Institute of Earth Studies, University of Wales, Aberystwyth, Dyfed, SY23 3DB, UK (Tel: 0970 622606; fax: 0970 622659).

Wales. The disputes have attracted considerable media interest, particularly when well-known names have become involved. Opposition by Sir Bernard Ashley (co-founder of the Laura Ashley shops) to a windfarm funded by the Body Shop in Mid-Wales led to headlines like 'Battle of the Green Giants'.[5] The literary great and good signed a letter to the *Times Literary Supplement* about the proposed windfarm at Flaight Hill and its 'wholesale despoliation' of Bronte country, and this position was supported by a *Times* editorial.[6] These reactions have been mirrored elsewhere in the media. An article on windfarms in the *Economist* in January 1994 was headed 'A new way to rape the countryside'.[7] An article by Matthew Engel in the *Guardian* (March 1993) made an analogy of the development of wind power and the Vietnam War (destroying what it is purporting to save).[8]

The pro-wind lobby has started to blame the media for distorting the situation and using arguments without any factual basis[9] and has been asserting that opponents are pro-nuclear.[10]

Context

Until recently the UK government saw the role of renewable energy as having little impact until the next century, at which point it would be developed, if commercial, primarily for strategic, diversity-of-supply reasons. The wind energy programme of the Department of Energy has received only modest support: between 1978 and 1991 some £35 million was invested.[11] Faced with the need to reduce greenhouse gases to comply with international conventions, reassessments have been made. The Coal Review accepted the recommendation of the Renewable Energy Advisory Group and increased the 1000 MW target of installed renewable capacity by the year 2000 to 1500 MW.[12]

Although there is only a relatively small number of sites operating in England and Wales, there is evidence of a massive explosion of interest in developments in response to the creation of the Non-Fossil Fuel Obligation (NFFO). The Minister for Energy reported that as many as 230 applications have been received under the 1994 NFFO round.[13] In Wales, planning applications for anemometers have been made for 68 different sites, and 33 planning applications can be identified, as can be seen in Figures 1 and 2.[14] The NFFO mechanism was intended to address the high price of electricity generated from nuclear power. The form of obligation enabled campaigners for renewable energy to seize the opportunity to include renewables in the subsidy, although only a small proportion has been diverted to the renewable energy technologies (3% in 1990/91, increasing to 6% in 1993/94). The levy on consumers represents around 10% of final bills, which in 1992/93 raised £1348 million. By early 1994

two orders had been announced, bids for another were underway and others were due in 1995 and 1997.

The government has set no targets for the wind band of the next tranches of NFFO, but even if only 20 windfarms are approved of the 230 submitted, as reported,[15] it is likely to form a substantial proportion of the total 300–400 MW promised for renewables. The emphasis is on achieving convergence with commercial prices, which means that areas of high wind speed are favoured.[16] Effectively the industry is gearing up to large-scale commercial exploitation to provide 10–20% of electricity requirements. There are scenarios in existence which sketch a higher potential role for the wind industry. A study by the Institute of Terrestrial Ecology which allowed for physical, institutional and environmental constraints on the development of windpower, excluding all designated areas, found that 142 912 turbines could potentially be sited in the 'unconstrained' areas with an output of 122 TWh/yr, about half of current energy requirements.[17] The Renewable Energy Advisory Group (REAG) pointed out that onshore wind energy could provide 20% penetration, producing 32 TWh/yr and involving 38 000 330 kW machines in the UK as a whole.[18] The Department of the Environment (DoE) and the Welsh Office judge that 'wind energy is on the verge of commercial exploitation'[19] without specifying what that implies. The latest statement of government policy states that 'onshore wind energy has the potential to make a significant cost effective contribution to UK energy supplies, possibly as much as 10% of electricity generation provided it is given credit for its environmental benefits'.[20]

It can be argued, however, that there is no great need for rapid installation of wind power at this stage in terms of the supply of electricity. With 9 GW of gas-fired capacity currently under construction or recently completed, there is no immediate prospect that generating capacity will be inadequate to meet foreseen demand to the end of the century.[21] Nor will the rapid acceleration materially affect the UK's compliance with the Climate Change Convention. The government's Climate Change Programme,[22] which was published in January 1994, identifies a target reduction of 10 million tons of carbon (MtC) that need be 'saved' to reduce carbon dioxide emissions to the 1990 level by the year 2000. In that document it is calculated that the contribution of *all* renewables to this will only be 0.5 MtC.

It has been the NFFO introduced as part of electricity privatization to secure the future of the nuclear industry which at a stroke rapidly increased resources going into wind power investment and enabled the industry to grow so rapidly from a handful of experimental turbines to commercial reality. This rapid growth can be hailed as a major achievement, as 'the UK is rapidly climbing

Europe's wind energy league'.[23] There seems to be an imperceptible transition from demonstration projects to 'the verge of commercial take-off', with thousands of wind turbines proposed. Yet there has been no opportunity at national and strategic level for considered discussion of the broad impacts, costs and benefits of such a route and alternatives to it. The rapid growth and the way it is being achieved can be seen to rest within the framework and culture of energy policy.

Culture of energy policy

Three features distinguish energy policy: its supply-side bias, its handling of uncertainty and its use of the pricing tool.

Supply-side bias

In so far as it is possible to discern a distinct and coherent energy policy over time, its principal objectives have been to secure adequate supplies of energy at the lowest practicable cost to the nation. Recent administrations have placed more emphasis on market mechanisms to achieve this and more attention has been paid to establishing a framework for environmental protection in which energy supplies are produced and used. But the exigencies of energy policy have consistently taken precedence for many years over other considerations such as the local environment, socioeconomic factors and locational consequences of energy sector developments. The culture of energy planning is rooted in this supply-dominated approach, which has been dubbed 'full steam ahead in all directions'.[24] Thus a recent statement of the main objective of current government policy declared: 'The aim of the Government's energy policy is to ensure diverse and sustainable supplies of energy in the forms that people and businesses want at competitive prices.'[25] Major decisions are not determined in geographical and locational contexts. Energy policy works on national statistics, graphs and tables, not maps. Only macroeconomic aspects are considered, not local or even regional dimensions.

Uncertainty

Another important component of energy policy in recent years has been its capacity to deal with uncertainty. Energy policy makers are now so used to surprises that they have come to expect them.[26] Uncertainty and changeable perceptions and expectations are now in the forefront of energy policy.

There have been major failures in energy planning. The first such failures came in the 1960s with electricity supply. People froze in dark homes in the winter of 1963; then by the end of the decade the forecasters were shown to have overcompensated. The nuclear programmes have also proved problematic to energy planners, as a brief foray into this complex scene reveals:

- While new supplies of uranium have been found, despite fears that its diminution could cause a constraint to the development of nuclear power by the end of the century,[27] this has itself caused unpredicted problems because massive investments in plant assumed otherwise.
- In the first three decades of nuclear power little attention was given to the disposal of nuclear waste.[28] As plans were made to deal with it, opposition grew as no one wants nuclear waste as a neighbour for life.[29]
- Reactor accidents at Three Mile Island and Chernobyl have increased public anxiety about the safety of nuclear power.

The volatility of projections on oil reserves, consumption and oil prices has proved particularly confusing to energy planners in view of the role of oil as the marginal fuel in the energy economy. Indeed, the forecasts for the duration of oil reserves which were made in the 1970s can now be considered at the least as embarrassing. The most pessimistic forecast by the Central Intelligence Agency (in 1977) saw demand as overtaking supply as early as 1983. The considered view of the Department of Energy was that world oil supplies would begin to level off in the late 1980s, reach a peak in the early 1990s, and decline thereafter.[30] A recent review, however, suggests that the world will not run out of oil in the next century but problems with oil will continue to arise as periodic shocks cause demand to adjust within a supply ceiling.[31] Proved reserves for oil and natural gas have almost doubled since the mid-1970s despite increases in consumption.

Such major failures of energy planning have had three principal effects. First, they have undermined the confidence of energy planners to plan. By the mid-1980s, as a commentator has noted, official forecasters and their political mentors were prefacing each prediction with the disclaimer, 'Forecasts are always wrong, including this one.'[32] Second, they have increased the perceived need for diversity of supply for reasons of national security. Third, they have increased reliance on the market mechanism.

Pricing

Pricing has been an important policy tool since 1978. Indeed, it is perhaps surprising in present circumstances that in the early 1970s it was a Conservative administration which kept the price of gas and electricity well below economic levels in the interest of fighting inflation.[33] It was the subsequent Labour government which 'decided that the burden on the taxpayer represented by subsidies should be reduced, and that prices should accordingly be allowed to rise so that they bore a closer relationship to real cost' (costs being costs of supply on a continuing basis with an adequate return on investment).[34] The

Wind power and planning policy in the UK: M McKenzie Hedger

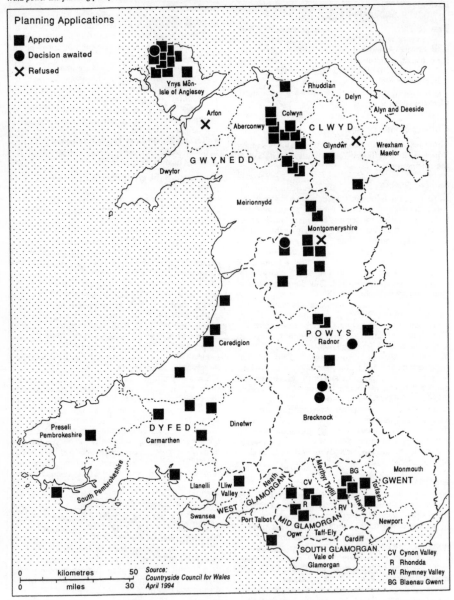

Figure 1. Anemometers: planning applications in Wales.

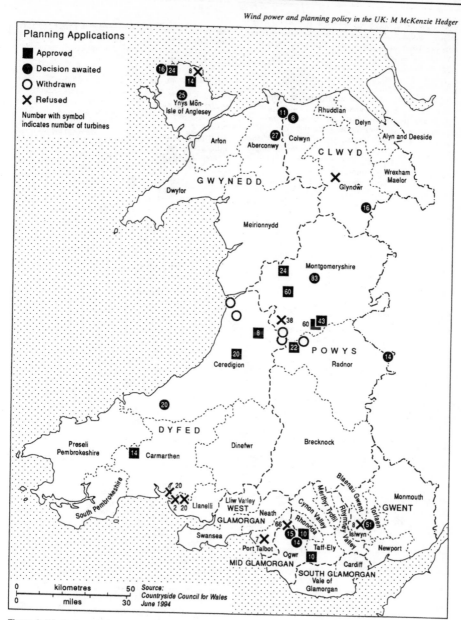

Figure 2. Wind power stations: planning applications in Wales.

oil price hikes accompanied by the exploitation of oil and gas reserves in the North Sea gave increased importance to this policy tool. Once strategic decisions had to be made on fuel mix, as the UK moved to being a four-fuel economy it proved imperative to use this mechanism to handle decision making. 'One of the most important instruments for exerting this influence is the level and structure of energy prices. Prices are important above all because they are all-pervasive, affecting millions of individual decisions over which the Government can have no direct control. They influence demand through consumers' decisions and supply through the industries' finances and investment programmes.'[35]

Energy policy has therefore long been supply-side led. It has become increasingly short-term, flexible, rapidly changing, innovative and influenced by external circumstances, with major reversals in approach due to changes in technology and economics. This culture of uncertainty has reinforced the role of the market. It is the market which provides the certainties. Energy policy is concerned to provide and ensure supply because of its economic importance. Therefore it provides freedom of regulation so that firms can perform efficiently.

Culture of planning policy

Energy planners have grown used to rapid technology changes and the abandonment of sites (and communities) after such change. Apart from the ample evidence of this in the coal sector, at all stages of production and use, there is evidence in the nuclear sector and also in the soil sector relating to offshore platform construction sites. In contrast, planning policy can be characterized by its historical continuity, its regulatory approach and its local focus.

Historical continuity

The origins of planning policy can be traced back to the rapid exploitation of energy resources. Coal fuelled industrial development which led to urbanization, subsequent suburbanization and perceived needs for green space and open country which in turn led to the early development of a town and country planning system. Planning policy has developed as a coherent body of policy over time. It works through incremental modification of past policy. It is closely associated with the mainstream of UK law and it is a body of policy in which concepts of 'precedence' and 'established use' have meaning.

Legalism and regulation

The planning system was born in a time of profound social change in a command and control system. It relies on regulation and the limitation of individual property rights. Initially it involved the capturing of development values, but once that had gone it has

meant the protection of property values. There have therefore been strong motives to preserve the planning system even in a period when deregulation has been favoured.

Local versus national interest

While having the advantage of being effectively controlled by local democratic institutions, the planning system has its own weaknesses as a means of resolving national issues of land use policy. The principal weakness is that it is undertaken by large numbers of administrative units with considerable hegemony in their areas within national planning guidelines which are stated as general principles. There has been little enthusiasm in successive administrations since the immediate post-war period for addressing major land use issues at national level. Nevertheless the planning system has often been the only way of addressing critical issues in energy policy such as opencast coal mining and particularly the development of nuclear power.[36]

Interaction of energy and planning policy

In two key areas of the operation of public policy on wind energy it is possible to perceive the dominance of energy policy: (i) its willingness to accept rapid technological change and its acceptance of uncertainty in the operation of the NFFO system, and (ii) its supply-side bias in the management of the planning system from central government.

Impacts of NFFO and the management of uncertainty

The rapid acceleration of the progress of wind energy has effectively involved an abandonment of the ordered, sequential approach over time of technology develoment, demonstration and diffusion. It is during the demonstration stage that there have been negative effects and short cuts have been taken. It is as if an experimental approach is being adopted at the demonstration/commercialization stage and uncertainty is being managed as a central plank of policy. This has had several effects.

First, rather than continue the process of the steady development of British technology, the pressure to rapidly commercialize has affected the choice of technologies and their siting. There has been implicit pressure for developers to select proven technologies which have been used in other parts of the world. Only 20% of wind turbines in the UK are of British manufacture.[37] Where British technology has been used, unfortunately it is only too clear that there has been compression of the research, demonstration and commercialization stages. The three sites operated by National WindPower which used Wind Energy Group technology were damaged in December 1993[38] and were not fully operational for several months. It is also important to note that concern has been expressed that the increase in funds for demonstration has been accompanied by a decline in funds for basic research.[39]

Second, there has not been a deliberate and open attempt, within the public domain, to select a variety of locations and sites for testing and evaluation so that considered assessments could be made at a strategic level about where, or where not, windfarms should develop. Such basic questions have not even been posed, although it appears from guidance to developers in the statement on the 1994 NFFO made in October 1993 by the Minister of Energy that this type of assessment will be made within the DTI.[40] By far the largest wind resource in the UK is in upland and remote Scotland. It is not clear how the relatively small English and Welsh projects which capture a comparatively patchy wind resource will usefully contribute to developing policy there. Instead the government has indicated that it is the bottom-up, site-by-site approach within the planning system that will prevail, despite the variations in decision making by local authorities.[41] For example, in Ceredigion, Dyfed, the district council has deferred a decision on the Llangwyrfon site until the completion of a comprehensive consultants' report on windpower in Dyfed (to which they had contributed financially), but once it was completed they immediately overlooked its conclusions and approved the site. Some consistency with a bias in favour of windfarm development has been imposed by decisions from the DOE and the Welsh Office following public inquiries, but there is still inconsistency in these.

Third, in the early stages of the NFFO it seemed to be usurping the planning mechanism, particularly as this was a time when government advice to local planning authorities on renewable energy was very limited. Under the Electricity Act 1989 the Director General of Electricity Supply with his staff in the Office of Electricity Regulation (Offer) has to be satisfied that the arrangements made by the regional electricity companies (RECs) are such that they 'will secure', in accordance with the Act, the generating capacity necessary to meet the level set by the Order.[42] The operation of the 'will secure' test undertaken by Offer within the NFFO includes an assessment about the planning status of the application as the facility must be capable of generating the specified capacity for the duration of the contract. Approval under the NFFO can clearly be used to demonstrate government 'approval' for a scheme, and the developers used this as an argument, for example, at the Mynydd y Cemmaes 'test' case inquiry. While there has been a revision of the 'will secure' procedures and Offer now makes it clear that it is not trying to second-guess the planning system, there has been an awkward disjunction between the two different assessment procedures, recognized by the Minister of Energy's statement on 11 March 1994.[43]

Fourth, the NFFO process has introduced commercial confidentiality issues, inhibiting research and planning. For example, in a written answer on 20 April 1993 Sir Wyn Roberts said that although figures on the amount of wind energy produced in Wales had been collected since 1990 they could not be released. A subsequent answer to a question tabled by Jonathon Evans on 14 March 1994 gave aggregate figures for the whole of Wales only. Problems with uncooperative electricity companies refusing to release grid capacity data have been identified by the Welsh Wind Energy Forum.[44] If there is to be a massive scaling up of wind power use, new transmission lines will be required. The impacts of these, the responsibility for their costs and their effect on wind power economics have not yet been raised as a material issue for discussion within the public policy domain.

Fifth, the NFFO has been perceived as providing inflated subsidies which are encouraging development everywhere, even in cherished landscapes. In order to be competitive and successful in the bidding process, developers have consistently chosen the highest wind speed sites. This, combined with government policy expressed through the planning system, has probably contributed to increased polarization. It is evident, for example, that environmental groups such as the Ramblers Association and the Campaign for the Protection of Rural Wales have shifted their position and become more negative.

Negative impacts were anticipated by industry itself and its supporters. For example, in evidence to the House of Commons Select Committee on Energy, the British Wind Energy Association identified that the yardstick of bid price alone put an unnecessary emphasis on high-elevation, hilltop sites.[45] Friends of the Earth (FoE) recognized that forcing wind energy developments onto higher wind speed sites would result in an increase in potential landscape conflicts, generating a negative impression of wind energy development[46] – points they also put to the House of Commons Energy Committee to argue for modifications to the NFFO. In 1990 FoE had also warned of the need to establish criteria to avoid intense conflicts which would prejudice the exploitation of wind energy.[47]

Sixth, no attention has been given to alternative models of development. There is a range of possible models for organizing relationships between investment capital, developers and landowners. Other models would have facilitated the development of community-based windfarms, taking full advantage of the potential of the technology for integrated rural development and minimizing transmission losses. A clear division on this issue is now opening up within the British Wind Energy Association.[48]

Central government, planning and wind power

The production of fuel and the generation of electricity from all sources have land use impacts through their life cycles. There have therefore been complex interactions between energy and planning policy over many years. Indeed, public inquiries in the planning system have served to discuss major national issues of energy policy. However, the exploitation of wind energy on land raises particular problems for planning policy. Past exceptions to planning policy, for example the building of Trawsfynydd nuclear power station in Snowdonia National Park, could possibly have been justified at the time as exceptional cases in the national interest requiring a single site. But large land areas would be involved for wind energy, and these are the areas which have generally been protected from similar industrial, visually intrusive developments. The very fact that the large-scale use of wind energy is being seriously contemplated as a possible strategy suggests to those with a background in planning policy that there is a distinct institutionalized pro-wind bias.

Policy guidance. Planning policy attempts to accommodate and integrate competing demands for space. It takes a long-term perspective and demands a strategic and comprehensive approach. It has a responsibility for regulating the rate at which land is transferred from agriculture, forestry and other rural uses to urban commercial and industrial use.[49] In doing so it has to take account of the need to protect landscape, wildlife habitats and historic features.[50]

Although the recent announcement by the Minister for Energy states that the government places just as much emphasis on the need to protect the local environment as the benefits of wind energy, so far official guidance to planning authorities on renewable energy (PPG 22) reveals the dominance of energy supply objectives over other considerations. New aims are set for the planning system:

(i) to ensure that society's needs for energy are satisfied, consistent with protecting the local and global environment;
(ii) to ensure that any environmental damage or loss of amenity caused by energy supply and ancillary activities is minimised; and to prevent unnecessary sterilisation of energy resources.[51]

PPG 22 recognizes that wind turbines have special features such as the need to site the machines in open, exposed locations, often in rural areas and in attractive landscapes, and the nature of noise emissions from the turbines. The main tenor of the annexe on wind energy is to make it seem that such applications can be handled in a routine and ordinary way and that there are no special features about them which would merit refusals. It states that it is inevitable that most development of commercial windfarms will be in the uplands, on the coast and other exposed regions, without acknowledging that conservation of the countryside and landscape has been an important aim of planning policy for many such areas for many years. It indicates that there is a clear role for windfarms to produce electricity. It does not identify conditions when windfarms should be refused, and the discussion on siting and landscape section focuses on how to minimize visual impacts with positioning, colour and layout modifications so that applications can be approved.

Most surprisingly, in view of their considerable visual impacts, it only envisages that particular care should be given to applications in National Parks and Areas of Outstanding Natural Beauty (AONBs). They are not 'no go areas', in contrast to the recommendations of the House of Commons Energy Committee and the proposals of both the government's statutory advisers on landscape in Wales and England during evidence to that committee.[52] No specific mention is made of Sites of Special Scientific Interest (SSSIs) in the wind annexe, and indeed it envisages that applications to harness wind energy will often be made in areas designated as of ecological importance. It recognizes that the moving blades may have an impact, but points out that the risk of bird collision is minimal. No reference is made to bird disturbance, nor to the possible effects of construction on local hydrology and soil structures.

The Guidance Note states that 'When a wind farm reaches the end of its design life, the turbines can be easily removed and the foundations could be re-used for the installation of new turbines (subject to planning permission) or, if required, the land could be reinstated.'[53] Obviously the removal of a windfarm is easy compared to a Magnox site. But there could be a lot of windfarms with which to deal. Experience shows that the creation of access roads causes irrevocable land use changes and that established use rights will have been secured during the operation of the windfarm. Furthermore, Planning Policy Guidance Note 7 states: 'once agricultural land is developed even for soft uses such as golf courses its return to best quality agricultural use is seldom practicable; once any land is built on the restoration of semi-natural and natural habitats and landscapes features is rarely possible and usually expensive'.

Overall the effect of PPG 22 is to encourage local planning authorities to approve planning applications for windfarms despite the visual impacts. The industry regarded the draft version of the guidance note as 'remarkably sympathetic to the special case of wind farm development'.[54]

Planning decisions. This pro-wind approach has been reinforced by decisions on call-in applications and appeals against refusals of planning consents. A recent check of decisions on public enquiries reveals that eight have been granted and three have been refused. This approach is again regarded by parts of the industry as 'firmly tipped in favour of wind'.[55] In only one case were the possible cumulative impacts mentioned by the Inspector and the small contribution to savings of air-polluting gases recognized. Elsewhere, while the visual impacts have been acknowledged they have not been judged to be sufficient to offset the national 'need' for wind energy.

For example, in the Mynydd y Cemmaes case it was reported in the decision letter that the Secretary of State for Wales had decided that: 'the visual impact of the proposal is such that it constitutes an important planning objection. Nevertheless he has concluded that this objection is not sufficiently compelling to outweigh the need for renewable energy and he therefore proposes to grant planning permission for the development.'[56]

In the case of a proposal for 15 turbines for Kirkby Moor Common in Cumbria, the Inspector appointed by the DoE to consider the application accepted the special quality of the site as an SSSI, an area designated as being of Great Landscape Value within the Cumbria and Lake District Structure Plan and as lying close to the Lake District National Park. Indeed, he reported that he could see no marked difference between the quality of the landscape in the National Park and the south of it and accordingly recommended refusal of the application. Nevertheless, the Secretary of State for the Environment approved the application because it would

not directly affect the Park's appearance or character. It is appropriate to consider the proposal therefore only as one situated in an area designated by the County Stucture Plan as one of Great Landscape Value. Whilst such an area should be protected from inappropriate development, the evidence points to the suitability of such areas in general, and the appeal site in particular, for the purposes of wind energy generation and the conclusion is reached that this form of development should not be regarded as being, by its nature, one which is necessarily inappropriate.[57]

The accumulating approvals and the rewriting of planning policy have concerned professional planners. In Wales the need for a clear national framework for energy policy and wind energy was identified by the Assembly of Welsh Counties.[58] The Welsh Wind Energy Forum wrote in November 1993 to the Secretaries of State for Wales and the Environment and the President of the Board of Trade, suggesting that PPG 22 inadequately covered large windfarms, cumulative effects of visibility and intervisibility and the need for a national policy. There has been outrage about appeal decisions in Cornwall;[59] Northumberland County Council is seeking a review of wind energy because of fears over proliferation generated by the appeal decisions.[60] In an overall review by the Association of County Councils which argues for the need for a national sustainable energy policy, the case of wind energy development in Dyfed is used to demonstrate that the absence of an explicit overall national

energy policy is inhibiting the development of a rational strategic policy for wind energy.[61]

Designated areas. For planners and all those who have been working on landscape conservation, it is perhaps the approach on designated areas which has caused most disquiet. Apart from the direct effects on National Parks, Areas of Outstanding Natural Beauty and Heritage Coasts, this issue has a broader significance. If visually intrusive windfarm developments can be permitted in areas that have been assessed as having the best and better landscapes, how can any area logically be excluded from potential windfarm development? This is of particular concern in Wales where the designation process has ceased, not because of the quality of the landscapes but because of political fears that there were simply too many designated areas. Thus many landscapes outside designated areas possess features of as high a quality as within them.

To exacerbate such fears, it is known that parts of the industry do not even see the need for excluding designated areas: 'My fear is that if areas of visual sensitivity are shut away from renewable energy then wind energy will be concentrated in those areas deemed as not very important. There are plenty of designated areas which could well absorb windfarms.'[62]

National Parks and Areas of Outstanding Natural Beauty have been designated because of the quality of their landscapes, and the point of designation was to develop policy to safeguard their quality. Such policies have been pursued for decades. A recent restatement of the need for special emphasis was given in PPG 7, which states that: 'Conservation of the natural beauty of the countryside should be given great weight in planning policies and development control decisions in National Parks. In general policies and development control decisions affecting AONBs should favour conservation of the natural beauty of the countryside.'[63] These policies have involved, for example in Snowdonia National Park, the use of traditional natural materials – stone and slate – where the increased costs have been justified for landscape conservation. Large tourism-related developments have been refused because of concern for their intrusiveness. There have been battles against communication equipment. Such strictly protective policies had been supported by the government, even to the extent of modifying and withdrawing developments associated with the Ministry of Defence in National Parks.[64]

With windfarms there has been a clear shift. In England, for example, the Secretary of State for the Environment upheld objections by the Park Authority and the Countryside Commission to one 30 m mast in the North York Moors Park in 1987.[65] In 1993, however, the DoE objected to a policy with a presumption against large-scale windfarms in the

Yorkshire Dales National Park Plan (each turbine can be expected to be at least 45 m tall).[66] It indicated that the balance between particular care for National Parks and the government's policy on renewable energy had not been met, despite the fact that in presentation of the policy it was clear that full consideration had been given to all the circumstances.

Discussion and conclusions

The NFFO mechanism has stimulated great interest by developers in the construction of windfarms in England and Wales. The government has created the conditions which encourage this phenomenon. But a major conflict has arisen because, for maximum efficiency, windfarms have to be sited in exposed upland and coastal areas which have for the most part received protection from 'industrial' developments within the planning system over many years. It is clear that government policy is to assert that, because there is 'a national need' to have a renewable energy component to energy supply, wind energy developments must involve a changed approach to the consideration of planning applications, overriding other policies such as on landscape protection. Such an approach is consistent with the operation of energy policy with its supply-side bias and its capacity to deal with rapid technological change. Planning policy, however, has been characterized by its careful accommodation of competing interests and its longer time scale.

There are a number of major questions which have not yet been addressed within this prevailing policy framework. Many analysts claim the cost of electricity from wind power is already competitive, particularly if the external costs of using fossil fuels are defined. The pace of development in the UK has already been impressive, so we could be on the edge of a massive take-off. One of the advantages of wind power is that it can be installed very rapidly: already 100 MW have been installed in the UK in three years.[67] However, it could well be argued that, as with the early nuclear programme, we may be embarking on a programme which is premature, too large and too expensive.[68] The full impacts of the strategy have not been identified, and it seems to be an ideal case for Strategic Environmental Assessment. If wind turbines are to make a useful and significant contribution to UK electricity supply (10–20%), a large number of turbines (perhaps 70 000) would be required. Furthermore there would also need to be major changes in the transmission system. Inevitably these developments would change the character of upland Britain.

The present framework for the development of the industry is not generating discussion of the major issues. There are strategic choices to be made about size and numbers of machines and also whether sites

should be concentrated or dispersed. An area of Britain could be used intensively while others could be 'saved'. Some bodies did not object to the proposed Kielder windfarm in Northumberland (267 turbines) because it was seen as a least bad location and would absorb much of the capacity for the next round of the NFFO. If a dispersed approach is adopted, what is landscape carrying capacity? In any event there is already evidence that elegant studies identifying suitable sites can be ignored by local councillors, who may grant permission in areas zoned as unsuitable or be overturned by local residents who may demand refusal in areas deemed to be suitable for windfarms in such studies.

For those concerned with landscape protection, a new incentive has been given to develop protective designations, an issue which for years had not been thought to be of paramount importance. The best wind resource is in Scotland, where landscape protection systems are less well developed than in England. Problems are already evident in Wales because not all its quality landscapes have protected status. However, the introduction of protective measures might not in fact be effective, and anyway might prove unpopular with landowning interests, if it meant that lucrative turbines were prevented. This might suggest that the protection of upland landscapes has had a free ride for 50 years on the back of low-intensity uses of agriculture and forestry. Alternatively, perhaps windfarms seem to provide economic benefits for these areas because their assets as providers of wildness and remoteness are not yet properly valued in monetary terms.

Economic and social aspects are being inadequately explored within the present framework at a strategic level. There is a range of possible models for organizing relationships between investment capital, developers and landowners. Encouragement of individual and community ownership in Denmark has been crucial to its acceptability so far. Some developers in the UK are now providing compensatory payments to local communities to encourage their acceptance of windfarms. On the other hand there may be basic incompatibilities. Is policy for wind power creating the right policy synergies with tourism and rural development? The Wales Tourist Board recently asserted that while visitors might find one or two windfarms a novelty, large numbers could prove a deterrent, and since the quality of Wales' natural environment is one of the tourist industry's greatest assets, windfarms could threaten the industry.[69]

At present the planning system is the only way in which some of these issues are being addressed, and efforts are being made to undertake regional assessments, such as that undertaken in the South Western Electricity Board Area.[70] Yet the planning system cannot plug all the gaps. Apart from the need for a strategy on wind power, the Association of County

Councils has drawn attention to the urgent need for the government to develop a coherent energy policy at national level for sustainable development.[71] It points to current problems faced by councils with opencast coal sites for which there is no coal market, the paralysis in the nuclear programme, and as a result of privatization of the electricity supply industry the uncoordinated development of combined cycle gas turbine plant, with five component projects being handled at different points in time by three companies.

Clearly these questions argue for a changed interaction between planning and energy policy. There is a need for both a much closer integration of energy policy with the mainstream of planning policy and the development of a coherent energy policy which can take into account land use policy issues.

References

[1]Department of Trade and Industry *Energy Paper 62* HMSO, London (March 1994)
[2]As at June 1994, including those under construction
[3]For a discussion of the debate see Hedger, Merylyn McKenzie 'Wind farms: a case of conflicting values' in Guerrier, Y, Alexander, N, Chase, J and O'Brien, M (eds) *Values and the Environment* Wiley, Chichester, UK (forthcoming)
[4]See for example Energy Technology Support Unit (ETSU) *Attitudes Towards Wind Power: A Survey of Opinion in Cornwall and Devon* ETSU W/13/00354/038/REP, Harwell, UK (1993); Delabole and Chris Blandford Associates *Wind Turbine Power Station Construction Monitoring Study* Report to Countryside Council for Wales, Chris Blandford Associates, Cardiff, UK (February 1994)
[5]*Western Mail* 13 September 1993
[6]*The Times* 19 February 1994
[7]*Economist* 22 January 1994
[8]*Guardian* 11 March 1994
[9]Harper, M 'No wind situation' *New Statesman and Society* 11 March 1994, 30–31
[10]*Cambrian News* 10 December 1993
[11]Bevan, G G, Statement of Evidence to Mynydd y Cemmaes Wind Farm Public Inquiry, Department of Energy, London (April 1991)
[12]Department of Trade and Industry *The Prospects for Coal: Conclusions of the Government's Coal Review* Cm 2235, HMSO, London (1993)
[13]Department of Trade and Industry 'Tim Eggar spells out challenge for wind energy' Press Notice P/94/143 11-03-94, DTI, London (1994)
[14]A comprehensive database for England does not exist.
[15]DTI *op cit* Ref 13
[16]For rounds one and two of the NFFO, a cut-off of 1998 was imposed by the EC because of the nuclear connection. Due to the capital-intensiveness of wind power technology it was the most expensive form of renewable generation: in the 1992 Order the price paid was 11p/kWh compared to 5.7p/kWh for landfill gas and 6.0p/kWh for hydroelectricity.
[17]Bell, G G, Murray, T D, Howard, D C and Bunce, R G H *The Environmental Constraints on the UK Wind Resource for Wind Energy* Institute of Terrestrial Ecology, Merlewood, UK (October 1989)
[18]Department of Trade and Industry *Renewable Energy Advisory Group: Report to the President of the Board of Trade* Energy Paper 60, HMSO, London (1992)
[19]Department of the Environment and Welsh Office *Renewable Energy* Planning Policy Guidance Note 22, HMSO, London and Cardiff (February 1993)

Wind power and planning policy in the UK: M McKenzie Hedger

[20]DTI *op cit* Ref 1
[21]DTI *op cit* Ref 12
[22]*Climate Change – The UK Programme* CM 2427, HMSO, London (1994)
[23]Department of Trade and Industry *Review: The Magazine for Renewable Energy* December 1993 (21) 5
[24]Patterson, W C *The Energy Alternative* Macdonald, London (1990) 67
[25]DTI *op cit* Ref 12
[26]Pearson, P 'Introduction' in *Energy Policies in an Uncertain World* Longman, London (1989) xii–xxx
[27]Department of Energy *Energy Policy: A Consultative Document* Cmnd 7101, HMSO, London (1978)
[28]Boyle, S and Boyle, J *The Greenhouse Effect* Hodder & Stoughton, Sevenoaks, UK (1989)
[29]Fernie, J and Pitkethly, A S *Resources, Environment and Policy* Paul Chapman, London (1985)
[30]Department of Energy *op cit* Ref 27
[31]Eden, R J 'World energy to 2050: outline scenarios for energy and electricity' *Energy Policy* March 1993 **21** 231–237
[32]Patterson *op cit* Ref 24
[33]Department of Energy *op cit* Ref 27
[34]*Ibid*
[35]*Ibid*
[36]As was first highlighted by the Town and Country Planning Association at the Windscale Inquiry; see *Planning and Plutonium* Town and Country Planning Association, London (1978)
[37]According to a written answer by the Minister for Energy (3 March 1994)
[38]*Daily Telegraph* 29 January 1994
[39]*Windpower Monthly* May 1992, 19
[40]Department of Trade and Industry *Information on the Non-Fossil Fuel Obligation for Generators of Electricity from Renewable Energy Sources* Renewable Energy Bulletin No 5, DTI, London (1993)
[41]Written answer from Tim Yeo (25 October 1993)
[42]Non-Fossil Fuel Purchasing Authority *Information Notes for Generators* Non-Fossil Fuel Purchasing Agency, Newcastle, UK (8 October 1993)
[43]DTI *op cit* Ref 13
[44]Letter from Chairman Welsh Wind Energy Forum, M Backhouse, to Secretaries of States for Wales and the Environment and President of the Board of Trade, Montgomery District Council, UK (November 1993)
[45]House of Commons Energy Committee *Renewable Energy* Vols I, II and III, Fourth Report, HMSO, London (1992)
[46]Friends of the Earth *Removing the Windbrakes: Wind Energy, the Landscape and the Government* Friends of the Earth, London (1991)
[47]Friends of the Earth *Developing Wind Energy for the UK* Friends of the Earth, London (1990)
[48]Network for Alternative Technology and Technology Assessment *Renew: Natta Newsletter* 1993 (85) 4
[49]DOE and Welsh Office *The Countryside and the Rural Economy* Planning Policy Guidance Note 7, HMSO, London and Cardiff (1992)
[50]*Ibid*
[51]*Ibid*
[52]House of Commons Energy Committee *op cit* Ref 45
[53]DOE and Welsh Office *op cit* Ref 49
[54]*WindPower Monthly* 1991 **7** (2)
[55]*WindPower Monthly* 1992 **8** (5)
[56]Welsh Office, decision letter on Local Inquiry into 24 Turbines at Mynydd y Cemmaes, P62/546 (19 September 1992)
[57]Decision letter from Department of the Environment on Planning Application for 15 Wind Turbines at Kirkby Moor Common, Cumbria
[58]Assembly of Welsh Counties *Strategic Planning Guidance in Wales: Overview Report* Submission to the Secretary of State for Wales (May 1993)
[59]*Planner* 21 January 1994
[60]*Planning* 22 March 1994

Wind power and planning policy in the UK: M McKenzie Hedger

[61]Association of County Councils *Energy Policy: Delivering a Sustainable Energy Policy* CC Publications, London (1993)
[62]Trinick, Marcus, at British Wind Energy Association Annual Conference 1992, reported in *WindPower Monthly* 1992 **8** (5)
[63]DOE and Welsh Office *op cit* Ref 49
[64]Countryside Commission *Annual Report of the Countryside Commission 1984–1985* Countryside Commission, Cheltenham, UK (1985)
[65]Countryside Commission *Annual Report of the Countryside Commission 1987–1988* Countryside Commission, Cheltenham, UK (1988)
[66]Department of the Environment, Yorkshire and Humberside Regional Office, Objection to Yorkshire Dales Draft Structure Plan (March 1993)

[67]However, in the USA in four years 1000 MW were installed, equivalent to a nuclear power station which would have taken eight or nine years to build after planning and approval stages; World Bank *Guidelines for Assessing Wind Energy Potential* Energy Department Energy Paper 34, World Bank, Washington, DC (1986)
[68]According to Christopher Hinton, when Chairman of the Central Electricity Board; see Patterson *op cit* Ref 32, 62
[69]Wales Tourist Board *Tourism 2000* Wales Tourist Board, Cardiff, UK (1994)
[70]South Western Electricity Plc and Energy Technology Support Unit *Renewable Sources of Electricity in the SWEB Area: Future Prospects* SWEB and ETSU, Bristol, UK (1993)
[71]ACC *op cit* Ref 61

E
Tourism and Recreation

[28]

THE ECONOMIC IMPACT OF ALTERNATIVE TYPES OF RURAL TOURISM

Bill Slee, Helen Farr and Patrick Snowdon*

Rural tourism has become an important part of many rural development strategies in the last decade. However, it has largely been ignored by rural economists. This paper examines the impact of different styles of tourism development on the local economy of Badenoch and Strathspey, in the Highlands of Scotland. Policy changes in tourism and agriculture are reviewed and the proportional multiplier method used in this study is explained. The study contrasts the repercussions on local economies of 'soft', land-based tourism with those arising from 'hard', enclave forms of tourism. The results indicate that soft tourism is more embedded in the local economy and therefore generates higher local income and employment multipliers per unit of visitor spend. However, spend per head is higher for hard tourists, suggesting that development agencies may have to trade off the total volume of visitor spend against locally beneficial effects.

1. Introduction

Tourism has been largely disregarded by rural economists as an arena of enquiry, in spite of the fact that, by almost any definition of rural, there are large areas of Britain where the overall well-being of rural residents is more dependent on tourism than farming. Where tourism has been investigated, it has been largely in relation to farm tourism as a particular form of farm diversification (see for example Davies, 1983; Slee 1987; McInerney *et al.*, 1989), rather than as a separate facet of the rural economy, although farm tourism is, in most parts of Britain, a relatively small part of the rural tourism sector as a whole.

This paper examines the impact of different styles of tourism on the economy of one of six rural areas of Europe, recently investigated as part of a three-country, six-region EC-funded study.† The principal objective of the study was to examine whether small-scale, 'soft', rural tourism has more beneficial economic impacts on rural areas than large-scale 'hard' tourism developments. First, the debate about tourism and rural development is reviewed; second, the principal analytical

* Bill Slee and Patrick Snowdon are Senior Lecturer and Teaching Assistant in the Department of Agriculture at the University of Aberdeen. Helen Farr is now Rural Development Programme Officer for the Cornwall and Isles of Scilly Rural Development Area. The authors gratefully acknowledge the assistance of Dr R. Vaughan and the comments of Professor K. J. Thomson.

† Contract No. AIR3 CT92-0477.

methods deployed in the study are described, and finally some results on the economic benefits of hard and soft tourism are presented from which conclusions are drawn.

2. The Policy Context for Tourism and Rural Development

Interest in rural tourism as a development strategy has grown in the last decade, partly in response to changes in agricultural and rural policy and partly in response to changes in thinking and practice in the tourism industry. As regards the first of these, the reform of European Union (EU) Structural Funds in 1988, the reform of the Common Agricultural Policy (CAP) in 1992 and the Uruguay Round Agreement on Agriculture in 1994 are evidence of redirections in policy which have profound consequences for the rural economy of EU member states.

The reform of the EC Structural Funds in 1988 encouraged the development of more multi-sectoral and integrated policy mechanisms. Funds were made available to assist infrastructure developments, to aid the diversification of farming, to encourage small- and medium-sized enterprises (SMEs), to assist in training schemes and to conserve the environment. In the Highlands and Islands of Scotland, substantial grants were offered to farmers to diversify their enterprises under Structural Fund support in the Rural Enterprise Programme (REP). The European Community's LEADER programme, established in 1991, explicitly supports community development by both social and economic mechanisms, with many schemes including actions relating to tourism and local speciality food production and marketing. Other EU-funded schemes such as LIFE offer potential support for integrated rural development in disadvantaged rural regions.

The reform of the CAP in 1992 represents a distinct shift away from the previous production-centred support to a partially decoupled system. It is anticipated that the agri-environmental payments introduced under the reform will comprise a bigger share of the total public support for agriculture. This may provide an opportunity for the commercialisation of the environment for many farmers, either through uptake of one of the schemes or through exploiting environmental externalities by establishing commercial recreation or tourist enterprises (Slee, 1995).

The 1994 Uruguay Round Agreement on Agriculture reinforces the CAP reforms by reducing the likelihood of a return to policies which have the capacity to encourage overproduction and dumping, thus leading the EU towards particular styles of support. In the long run, further reductions in price support can be anticipated. The use of 'green box' payments to farmers, which do not increase output, reinforces the role of farming in delivering environmental goods and services.

Unlike the agriculture industry, the tourism sector in the UK has been the recipient of only limited intervention by the state. The policy context for tourism derives principally from the Development of Tourism Act of 1969, which established national and regional tourist boards - area (not regional) tourist boards were set up in Scotland - and the British Tourist Authority (BTA). Until the mid-1980s, tourism policy was essentially a form of regional assistance under which discretionary grants were paid in areas designated as disadvantaged under regional policy measures.

Several important changes took place in attitudes towards tourism in the 1980s. First, tourism was increasingly seen as an industry with the ideological credentials (fostering the entrepreneurial spirit, untainted by heavy government subsidy) and the ability to address problems of labour surpluses elsewhere in the economy.

Second, tourism was regarded as a legitimate component of rural restructuring, even in areas with no prior involvement in tourism. Finally, tourism was seen as an industry which would benefit from more co-ordinated policy formation and implementation.

The White Paper *Pleasure, Leisure and Jobs* (HMSO, 1985) expressed a desire to see the tourism sector expand in a more deregulated market. In the same year, responsibility for tourism was transferred from the Department of Trade and Industry to the Department of Employment, emphasising the government's perception of the tourist sector as a prospective provider of new employment. Estimates for the period 1975 to 1985 indicate that between 300,000 and 325,000 new jobs were created in tourism (Williams and Shaw, 1991).

The second change in tourism policy arose from the growing realisation of tourism's role in rural restructuring (and indeed in inner-city economic restructuring). During the 1970s and 1980s, traditional holidaymaking patterns were changing. The traditional seaside resorts were struggling to compete with overseas package holidays, and in a typical holiday region such as south-west England, the rural parts of the region were gaining market share at the expense of the resorts. The Rural Development Commission and the Tourist Boards explored the potential of rural tourism in a number of reports. However, at least two very different styles of tourist development were taking place in rural areas. First, a number of large-scale, rurally located tourist complexes were developed. Such developments became increasingly sophisticated, providing enclaves of tourist accommodation and activity, reaching their apotheosis in Center Parcs holiday villages. Second, traditional rural tourist providers (at least in some areas) recognised the need to upgrade and redefine their tourism product and to develop new forms of marketing.

During the 1980s, academic interest grew in the concept of green/soft/alternative tourism, derived principally from the work of Krippendorf (1987), and a number of pilot projects were implemented (see, for example, Lane, 1988a,b). The principal elements of this alternative model are that tourism:

(i)   is embedded within a diverse local economy;

(ii)   makes use of local products as inputs (crafts, food, etc.);

(iii)   employs local people and yields them satisfaction and enhanced self-esteem;

(iv)   does not place unacceptable burdens on the environment; and

(v)   respects local traditions and ways of life.

Soft tourism contrasts with hard tourism which is characterised by externally owned large-scale developments, which are less locally oriented and tend to create single industry resorts, highly dependent on tourism for their well-being. The soft-hard dichotomy is in reality a continuum (see later).

The scope for soft or green tourism to provide a solution for the problems of both tourism and the rural economy has been questioned (Wheeller, 1991). Nevertheless, rural tourism has come to occupy a prominent position in the debate about rural restructuring (OECD, 1994), partly because of demand changes which favour rural tourism and partly because rural agencies recognise a need to provide economic activities with potential for growth in a rural economy in which traditional providers of rural employment have been shedding labour at a rapid rate.

The final change to occur in tourism policy in the 1980s was the tendency for public agencies to engage in more co-ordinated action such as the Tourism Development Action Programmes which were instigated in many areas (Lavery, 1993). They were established on the basis of area-specific partnerships, including tourist boards, local authorities, national parks and other relevant bodies seeking to develop the tourism industry. In Scotland, the replacement of the Scottish Development Agency and the Highlands and Islands Development Board by Scottish Enterprise and Highlands and Islands Enterprise respectively, and their acquisition of the function of tourism development support from the Scottish Tourist Board, was further evidence of the decline of industry-specific support, although the Scottish Tourist Board remains as a marketing and standard-setting agency.

Additional multi-agency groups have emerged to address the specific problems arising in relation to tourism and the environment. A guide to good practice in rural tourism has been produced for a consortium of countryside agencies in England and Wales, and in Scotland the Scottish Tourism Co-ordinating Group (STCG) commissioned a review on Tourism and the Scottish Environment in 1991. Subsequently in Scotland, a Tourism Task Force was set up in 1992 to support the development of Tourism Management Programmes - with both sectoral and spatial remits - and the STCG produced a report on Tourism and the Scottish Environment (STCG, 1993).

It is thus possible to trace a major change in public and private sector interest and action in relation to rural tourism in the last decade. The growth of rural tourism is rendered even more significant in the light of changes in traditional sectors of the rural economy. However, policy makers are confronted with a difficulty. Green tourism has been advocated for social and environmental reasons but has received limited attention from economists. Although a number of studies have been conducted on economic aspects of tourism, no studies to date have focused specifically on the economic merits of green tourism rather than other forms of tourist development. It is this question that constitutes the core of the present project: i.e. can green/soft/alternative tourism deliver higher levels of benefit than other forms of rural tourist development and thus offer a desirable tourism development strategy?

3. Economic Modelling of Rural Tourism

This section reviews an economic approach to the estimation of the economic effects arising from tourism. Input-output analysis has been used as a technique to identify the impacts on employment and income of an industry. However, the nature of the tourism industry, which includes aspects of the transport, service and catering industries, makes it (almost) impossible to utilise data produced in national input-output tables. Conducting a full input-output analysis from raw data requires data pertaining to each sector of the economy. This normally makes the costs of such analysis prohibitive. Therefore alternative methods have been devised to investigate the regional economic impacts of tourism. Most studies utilise the proportional multiplier methodology generally attributed to Archer (1973) and developed further by Henderson and Cousins (1975) and Vaughan (e.g. 1988; 1994).

In order to obtain an estimate of the economic benefits accruing to an area through tourism, it is necessary to analyse the level of visitor spending and the impacts of that spending on the host economy. The impacts of visitor spending include:

(i)   direct impact: the impact of tourist spending on incomes and jobs at businesses where tourists spend their money;

(ii)   indirect impact: the impact resulting from successive rounds of local business transactions that result from tourist spending;

(iii) induced impact: the impact on incomes and jobs of the spending of income earned as a result of spending by tourists.

The assumptions that are made for proportional multiplier analysis are the same as those required for input-output analysis. The data required to estimate the proportional multiplier fall into three sets:

(i) estimation of the level of visitor spending and the distribution of that spending between different business types;

(ii) estimation of the allocation of business turnover between different expenditures, i.e. inputs, rent, taxation and income to owners and employees;

(iii) estimation of household expenditure in the study areas.

The first set requires information relating to different groups of visitors. The second set requires data to be collected from a variety of business types, including those receiving direct benefit from tourists, and their suppliers. The third set requires estimates of household spending in the study areas across a range of goods and services. The analysis estimates the direct and indirect impacts of tourism spending, using input-output methodology on this reduced set of business sectors. Estimation of the induced impact is analysed using a traditional Keynesian multiplier. The unique feature of the proportional multiplier methodology is in its expression. The multiplier coefficients are expressed as a proportion of the original visitor spending, not as an increment to the direct impact as multipliers are traditionally presented (Vaughan, 1994). This form of analysis is especially useful for policy makers and those institutions which support tourism as it provides guidance as to the injection of spending, i.e. tourism expenditure, which is required to create a given effect, as well as the level of interdependency that exists in the local economy.

Direct Impact

Analysis of the direct impact establishes the proportions of turnover which are allocated as income to owners and employees, and the relationship between turnover and employment. The data used are from tourism businesses within the local area. Income throughout the analysis is income remaining after income tax, corporation tax, and social security payments have been deducted.

Indirect Impact

The indirect effect of visitor spending is a measure of the inter-industry impacts of visitor spending. It calculates the income and employment generated as a result of purchases from suppliers by tourism businesses, and the subsequent purchases by suppliers from other suppliers. The approach used is partial input-output analysis in which transactions between a reduced set of business sectors which are related to tourism are recorded. A transactions matrix is derived using the data from suppliers to tourism businesses. The indirect effect is then calculated using an inverse matrix.

Induced Impact

The induced effect analyses the effects of income earned from tourism on income and jobs. Using a modified form of the traditional Keynesian multiplier analysis, it incorporates the pattern of spending by residents as determined from household expenditure surveys, the income they have earned as a result of visitor spending, and the characteristics of the businesses in which residents spend their money. Only disposable income is considered.

Total Economic Impact

The total impact (including the multiplier) is expressed as a proportion of the original visitor spending and is calculated using the pattern of visitor spending in each type of business. The data from the business surveys, visitor surveys and household expenditure are used in the following equations to calculate the income and employment effects respectively.

In each equation, the first terms in the first square bracket measure the direct effect, the second term in the first square bracket measures the indirect effect, and the term in the second square bracket measures the induced effect.

Income effect:

$$G_y = \Sigma_j N_j Q_j \Sigma_i K_{ji} \, [(\Sigma_d \Sigma_i Y_{id} + \Sigma_i \Sigma_r P_{ri} Y_i) / \Sigma_i T_i] \, [1/(1 - L\Sigma_i X_i Z_i Y_i)]$$

where:

G_y = total local income resulting from spending by visitors

N_j = number of day/nights spent in the local area by the jth type of visitor

Q_j = average spend per day/night by the jth type of visitor

K_{ji} = proportion of spending by the jth type of visitor accounted for by the ith type of business

Y_{id} = direct income generation (d) by the ith type of 'direct business' (those in which visitors spend their money)

P_{ri} = payments for goods and services purchased from the ith type of local business by the rth type of local business

Y_i = income generation coefficient (direct and indirect) of the ith type of local business

T_i = turnover of the ith type of business

L = average propensity to consume

X_i = proportion of spending by local residents accounted for by the ith type of business (local or otherwise)

Z_i = proportion of spending by local residents in the ith type of business that is spent within the local area.

Employment effect:

$$G_e = \Sigma_j N_j Q_j \Sigma_i K_{ji} \, [(\Sigma_d \Sigma_i E_{id} + \Sigma_i \Sigma_r P_{ri} E_i) / \Sigma_i T_i] \, [G_y(\Sigma_i X_i E_i)]$$

where:

G_e = total employment generated within the area from tourist spending

E_{id} = local employment generated directly by the ith type of business

E_i = local employment coefficient (direct and indirect) of the ith type of business

and all other terms remain as previously defined.

Two notes of caution should be made regarding the interpretation of multipliers. Firstly, they do not give an indication of the actual value of tourism to the local economy. This requires data on the multiplicand, i.e. the total value of tourist spending in the area. Thus, although the multipliers relating to one subsection of the industry, e.g. hotels, may be comparatively low, a greater volume of visitors may generate a greater volume of income for the local economy than that arising from bed and breakfast visitors. Secondly, the results produced by the multiplier methodology reflect the characteristics of a particular local economy. It is inappropriate to extrapolate from one geographical area to another.

A number of studies in the UK have utilised the proportional multiplier methodology in a variety of settings including national parks (Coppock *et al.*, 1981), long distance footpaths (Walker and Vaughan, 1992) and regional economies (Henderson and Cousins, 1975; Surrey Research Group, 1993). Where results have differentiated between different types of tourist accommodation, some considerable differences in multipliers can be found (Coppock *et al.*, 1981; Surrey Research Group, 1993).

The proportional multiplier methodology measures the inter-industry linkages that exist in the local economy. This study focuses on a comparison of two styles of tourism development, namely 'hard' and 'soft', which encapsulate the exogenous: endogenous debate in rural development. This is a new application of the proportional multiplier methodology and necessitates disaggregating the tourist market into at least these two component parts. The definitions adopted for this project regard farm tourism, i.e. agricultural holdings providing bed and breakfast, self-catering or camping and caravan pitches, as being 'soft'. Hard tourism is characterised by hotels with over ten bedrooms, holiday villages and timeshare developments.

The geographical areas used for this study were chosen to reflect the diversity of rural tourism developments that exist in the UK. Exmoor National Park in the south-west of England represents an area of well developed soft tourism. Badenoch and Strathspey District in the Highlands of Scotland is relatively less well developed in terms of soft tourism, though it has received considerable investment in hard tourism infrastructure in the past. This paper refers only to the results for Badenoch and Strathspey.

Administrative boundaries were used to delimit the study area. It is recognised that these areas may not be economic entities. Previous studies, including the previous study of Exmoor National Park (Coppock *et al.*, 1981), indicate that multipliers can be low at the park/local level but increase substantially at the sub-regional level. Two levels of geographical analysis were used in this study,: the core area; and the extended area, which covers the area within 25 km of the core area boundary, therefore including important regional service centres.

4. The Case Study: Badenoch and Strathspey District, Highland Region, Scotland

The district of Badenoch and Strathspey lies in the Highland Region of Scotland at the geographical and economic periphery of Britain and the European Union (EU) and covers an area of 2291 square kilometres in the upper valley of the River Spey between Perth and Inverness. The Region was accorded Objective 1 status in 1994 under the EU Structural Fund reforms. The district's population of 11,190 is concentrated in several small towns. Population density is low, at approximately 5 inhabitants per km^2, compared to an average for Scotland of $66km^2$ (Scottish Office, 1992).

Flanked by the Monadhliath and Cairngorm mountains, the district is renowned for its high landscape quality and has developed as a popular destination for summer and winter tourism which has become the mainstay of the local economy

(Getz, 1986). Tourism has evolved around a number of recreational activities, including skiing, fishing, hunting, watersports, climbing and walking. Approximately 70 per cent of employment in the district derives from tourism and service industries. Rothiemurchus Estate, in the centre of the district, receives in excess of 300,000 day visitors per year (Scottish Tourist Board, 1993), and the district as a whole is estimated to receive 323,000 holiday trips per year (Moray, Badenoch and Strathspey Enterprise, 1994). The 'knock-on' effects on the local economy from visitor spending are considerable; for example, skiing in the Cairngorms contributed £10 million expenditure to the local economy of Aviemore in 1986 (Mackay Consultants, 1986).

A further 8 per cent of the work-force is employed in agriculture, comprising mainly extensive stock rearing and a little arable farming. Poor land quality ensures that extensive land management practices predominate. Farm structure is divided between landowners with large sporting estates, and small, often tenanted, family farms and crofts.

The growth of tourism is concentrated around Aviemore, where a large hotel and entertainment centre was constructed in the 1960s. Accommodation is mainly provided in large hotels (average size = 54 bed spaces), holiday villages and timeshare developments. These developments from the 1960s helped to reverse the effects of depopulation in the 1950s by encouraging in-migration, particularly into Aviemore, thereby establishing a more balanced population structure (Getz,1981). However, in recent years the Aviemore Centre has suffered from neglect and decay; a number of facilities have been closed, and the Centre has failed to provide lasting economic and social benefits.

Methodology

Fieldwork for the study took place between June and October 1994. All data were collected through 'face-to-face' interviews, conducted by the two research assistants employed on the project. Interviews were held with approximately 120 tourist-related businesses and 1800 visitors.

Business Surveys

The following stratification of businesses was adopted:

(i)   Hard tourism accommodation

      (a) Hotel with 101+ bedrooms

      (b) Hotel with 51-100 bedrooms

      (c) Hotel with 11-50 bedrooms

      (d) Self-catering accommodation in a holiday village, i.e. 10 or more self-catering houses belonging to the same business, usually with shopping, eating and recreation facilities within the complex

(ii)   Soft tourism accommodation

      (a) Farmhouse on a farm offering serviced accommodation

      (b) Self-catering accommodation on a farm

      (c) Camping and caravan site on a farm

(iii) Other businesses benefiting directly from visitor spending

(iv)   Suppliers to these businesses.

Businesses in the third category included a diverse range of businesses which receive tourist spending, for example, restaurants, cafes, shops, art and craft centres, visitor attractions and public sector facilities. The population base of businesses was obtained from a business directory provided by Moray, Badenoch and Strathspey Enterprise Company and a random selection of ten businesses was made from each business group.

The fourth category of businesses included wholesalers, building contractors, business support services, and office suppliers; five businesses were randomly selected from each sub-group. The population base of suppliers was obtained during interviews with the accommodation providers and the other businesses benefiting directly from tourism. The sample of suppliers was broadened to include businesses within the 'extended area'. This allowed the exploration of business linkages within the regional economy.

In some cases there were small numbers of enterprises in certain groups. In such situations, the aim was to interview two thirds of all firms in that group. The overall response rate to the detailed business questionnaire was 89 per cent. This contrasts favourably with the 38 per cent response rate of a recent Scottish tourism study (Surrey Research Group,1993).

Visitor Surveys

Each visitor questionnaire corresponded to one sampling unit and could comprise an individual or a group of visitors. At least 50 per cent of the total population of hard and soft tourism accommodation establishments were included in the survey as locations at which to interview visitors. Interviews were conducted on every day of the week to eliminate bias from daily variations in visitor spending.

Quota sampling was used to ensure that adequate sample sizes were obtained (for each visitor sub-group) to give statistically significant results. It was intended to obtain a comparable number of questionnaires from visitors staying at soft and hard tourism accommodation, but this was not achieved, due to low numbers of visitors at farm bed and breakfast and self catering establishments.

Following completion of the survey, a weighting procedure was applied to the data to ensure that the number of bednights covered by questionnaires in each accommodation type was representative of the number of bednights sold in each accommodation type during the period of the survey. This removed bias resulting from the gathering of a disproportionate number of bednights from any particular accommodation provider.

5. Results: The Economic Impact of Tourism in Badenoch and Strathspey

Visitor Spending

Table 1 illustrates that visitors staying at accommodation in the hard tourism sector spend more than twice as much per person per day as visitors staying at accommodation in the soft sector. This is due mainly to the low expenditure levels of visitors staying at camping and caravan sites and the higher expenditure levels of visitors at hotels. It also demonstrates that the high and low levels of expenditure at hotels and camp-sites respectively are attributable principally to the accommodation tariffs. Amounts of visitor spending in other expenditure categories are broadly similar in the hard and soft sectors, although expenditure on food and at shops is higher for visitors at soft accommodation than at hotels.

Rural Planning and Management

Table 1   Average Daily Expenditure Per Person of 'Soft' and 'Hard' Accommodation Visitors in Different Types of Expenditure in Badenoch and Strathspey, 1994 (£)

Accommodation Type	Acc.	Food	Shops	Leisure	Other	Total
Farm bed & breakfast/self-catering	13.90	5.54	1.72	1.14	2.25	24.55
Farm camping & caravan sites	3.20	5.55	1.47	1.00	2.97	14.19
Soft tourism	*5.03*	*5.55*	*1.51*	*1.02*	*2.85*	*15.96*
Large/medium hotels	33.00	1.80	0.80	0.78	0.66	37.04
Small hotels	32.30	2.02	2.12	5.91	1.22	43.57
Holiday villages (rented & timeshare)	15.66	9.19	3.86	2.04	1.59	32.34
Hard tourism	*24.83*	*5.27*	*2.42*	*2.11*	*1.17*	*35.80*

Source: Authors' survey.

Table 2   Total Bednights Sold, Average Expenditure Per Person Per Day, and Visitor Spending between June and September 1994 in Badenoch and Strathspey

	Total Bednights Sold	Average Expenditure Per Person Per Day (£)	Total Visitor Spending (£)
Hard tourism	406,784	£35.80	£14,556,534
Soft tourism	138,407	£15.96	£2,208,911

Source: Authors' survey.

Table 2 shows that tourist spending in the local economy is approximately seven times greater in the hard than in the soft accommodation sectors.

Income and Employment Generation

Table 3 gives the income multipliers associated with hard and soft tourism. Spending by tourists staying in soft tourism accommodation contributes over one third more to the local economy per unit of visitor spending. This is a result of a larger proportion of those businesses used by soft tourists, most notably the soft accommodation sector, making their business expenditures in the local and extended areas than those businesses used by hard tourists. In contrast, a larger proportion of the hard sector visitor spend leaks out of the region as it is respent by the business sector.

For both soft and hard tourism, the most significant income effect arises from the direct effect which accounts for 91 per cent and 87 per cent of income for soft and hard tourism respectively in the core area, and 66 per cent and 68 per cent in the core and extended areas together. The indirect effect is enhanced by the inclusion of the extended area indicating the importance of a major service centre, Inverness, as a source of supplies for the district.

Employment multipliers per £100,000 visitor spending for unstandardised and standardised employment in the hard and soft tourism sectors in Badenoch and Strathspey are given in Table 4. Unstandardised jobs represent the actual number of jobs in existence, whether they are full-time, part-time, seasonal or casual. Standardised jobs are the number of unstandardised jobs expressed as full-time equivalents (FTEs).

The results indicate that the soft sector produces a higher number of jobs per unit of visitor spending, mainly from the direct effect. Farm bed and breakfast and farm

Table 3   Income Generation Per £100,000 of Visitor Spending in Hard and Soft Tourism Accommodation in Badenoch and Strathspey, 1994 (£)

	Soft Accommodation		Hard Accommodation	
	Core	*Core and Extended*	*Core*	*Core and Extended*
Direct	26,977	27,511	18,985	20,471
Indirect	2,454	13,856	2,576	9,238
Induced	246	408	210	314
Total	29,677	41,775	21,771	30,023

Source: Authors' survey.

Table 4   Employment Multipliers per £100,000 of Visitor Spending in Hard and Soft Tourism Accommodation in Badenoch and Strathspey, 1994 (£)

	Unstandardised		Standardised	
	Core	*Core and Extended*	*Core*	*Core and Extended*
Farm B&B/SC	10.5	12.7	5.3	6.7
Farm camping	5.1	6.9	3.1	4.2
Soft	*6.3*	*8.2*	*3.6*	*4.8*
Large/medium hotels	3.0	3.7	2.4	2.9
Small hotels	4.2	5.0	2.9	3.4
Holiday villages	5.6	6.8	3.1	3.9
Hard	*4.3*	*5.3*	*2.8*	*3.4*

Source: Authors' survey.

self-catering enterprises together produce the highest figures in terms of unstandardised jobs reflecting a higher proportional of seasonal and part-time employment.

Table 5 compares conventional and proportional multipliers for income generation. Conventional multipliers lead to a focus on the ratio of direct to indirect and induced effects, with the result that hard tourism appears to offer greater benefits to the local economy than does soft tourism. However, the proportional multipliers reflect the overall impact, which overtly takes into account the level of the direct effect, and thus more accurately reflects the overall impact of tourist spending in the local economy. The proportional multipliers are greater for soft tourism than for hard tourism in both the core and the core + extended areas.

Table 6 shows the total economic impact of hard and soft tourism on income and employment in Badenoch and Strathspey district. The results take into account the rate of spend (Table 1), and the actual number of visitors in each type of tourism during the survey period as given in Table 2. Hard tourism dominates the district,

Table 5   Type 2 Conventional and Proportional Income Multipliers for Hard and Soft Tourism Accommodation in Badenoch and Strathspey, 1994 (£)

	Conventional		Proportional	
	Soft	*Hard*	*Soft*	*Hard*
Core Area	1.10	1.15	0.30	0.22
Core and Extended Area	1.52	1.47	0.42	0.30

Source: Authors' survey.

Rural Planning and Management

190   B. SLEE, H. FARR AND P. SNOWDON

Table 6   Total Economic Impact of Soft and Hard Tourism in Badenoch and Strathspey, 1994

| | Soft Accommodation | | Hard Accommodation | |
	Core	Core + Extended	Core	Core + Extended
Income	655,575	922,757	3,155,261	4,251,751
Standarised jobs	99.8	133.2	522.4	644.6

Source: Authors' survey.

and this is reflected in the results. The income generated from this sector is over four times that arising from soft tourism. In terms of employment, hard tourism supports roughly five times more employment than soft tourism.

6. Conclusions

The results of this analysis reveal that Badenoch and Strathspey district (and the region of which it is part) is highly dependent on tourism for its well-being, and that the soft and hard sectors of the tourism industry generate different impacts on the local and regional economy. The area is dominated by hard tourism, and this sector receives the bulk of tourist spending. However, a relatively small soft tourism sector generates a pattern of visitor spending and tourist business transactions that generate a much greater level of local economic activity per unit of visitor spending.

The particular characteristics of the tourist sector of Badenoch and Strathspey represent a rather different adjustment challenge to that experienced in many other parts of the UK, for there are few (if any) examples of an ailing rural resort such as Aviemore. However, in other parts of Europe, spa towns and many mountain sport centres have similar characteristics, and the example chosen is by no means unique at a European level. Indeed, other study areas in this EC-funded project include a spa area in Portugal and an area in France which is heavily used for winter sports.

It is not clear from the foregoing analysis whether a tourism development cycle (Butler, 1980) is discernible. If so, such a cycle would imply that the benefits to the local and regional economies to be derived from soft tourist development are at best interim, and that successful soft tourist development will be transformed over time into hard tourism. Alternatively, it may be possible to build tourism strategies which focus on small-scale tourism providers and enable distinctive niche-market tourism products to be developed by collective action and institutional endeavour. The resultant tourism industry may be more fully embedded in the local economy than the hard tourism alternative, and, as a result, will be likely to generate higher levels of knock-on effects in the local economy.

The data collected from Badenoch and Strathspey also indicate that the transformation of this part of the Highland Region economy and the reversal of depopulation owes more to external capital injection (by government and private sector) than to indigenous enterprise. Even though, per unit of tourist spending, soft tourism outperforms hard tourism in the local and regional economy on a wide range of economic criteria, the overall effect of hard tourism is greater. Development agencies in backward regions are thus confronted by a dilemma: the rapid development of the tourist sector is likely to be associated with external ownership and high rates of leakage of benefits out of the local economy but is likely to have a greater impact on the regional economy than the soft tourism alternative. This study reveals that it is necessary to trade off the total volume of tourist spending against the locally beneficial effects.

The selection of appropriate rural development strategies has become an issue of great importance as the economic significance of the traditional rural industries has declined. However, such strategies should be based on full information on the economic effects of different alternatives. This study has described one way in which economic research can contribute to making more informed choices about rural futures, with particular reference to the debate about appropriate styles of tourist development. Such an approach seeks to avoid the rhetoric that so often surrounds the discussion of tourism and provide information from a number of study areas that yields a better understanding of the tourist industry and its connections with local and regional economies.

References

Archer, B. H. (1973). *The Impact of Domestic Tourism.* University of Wales Press, Cardiff.

Butler, R. (1980). The Concept of a Tourism Area Cycle of Evolution. *Canadian Geographer,* **24,** 5-12.

Coppock, J., Duffield, B. and Vaughan, D. R. (1981). *The Economy of Rural Communities in the National Parks of England and Wales,* **47,** 1-399. Tourism and Recreation Research Unit, University of Edinburgh, Edinburgh.

Davies, E. T. (1983). *The Role of Farm Tourism in the Less Favoured Areas of England and Wales, 1981.* University of Exeter, Exeter.

Getz, D. (1981). Tourism and Rural Settlement Policy. *Scottish Geographical Magazine.* December, 158-168.

Getz, D. (1986). Tourism and Population Change: Long-Term Impacts of Tourism in the Badenoch and Strathspey District of the Scottish Highlands. *Scottish Geographical Magazine,* **102(2),** 113-126.

Henderson, D. and Cousins, L. (1975). *The Economic Impact of Tourism. A Case Study in Greater Tayside.* Tourism Recreation Research Unit, University of Edinburgh, Edinburgh.

HMSO (1985). *Pleasure, Leisure and Jobs: The Business of Tourism.* HMSO, London.

Johns, P. M. and Leat, P. M. (1986). *An Approach to Regional Economic Modelling: The Case of Grampian.* Economic Report No. 44. North of Scotland College of Agriculture, Aberdeen.

Krippendorf, J. (1987). *The Holidaymakers: Understanding the Impact of Leisure and Travel.* Butterworth Heinemann, London.

Lane, B. (1988a). *What is Rural Tourism?* Countryside Recreation Research Advisory Group, Bristol.

Lane, B. (1988b). Small Scale Rural Tourism Initiatives. The Role of a British University, Council of Europe (ed.) *Tourism and Leisure in Rural Areas,* **3,** 1-7. Council of Europe, Strasbourg.

Lavery, P. (1993). A Single European Market for the Tourist Industry, in Pompl, W. and Lavery, P. (eds) *Tourism in Europe. Structures and Developments,* 80-98. CAB International, Wallingford.

Mackay Consultants (1986). Cited in Highland Regional Council (1991) *Structure Plan, 1991.* Highland Region, Inverness, Scotland.

McInerney, J., Turner, M. and Hollingham, M. (1989). *Diversification in the Use of Farm Resources.* Agricultural Economics Unit, University of Exeter, Exeter.

Moray, Badenoch and Strathspey Enterprise (1994). *The 1993 Moray, Badenoch and Strathspey Tourism Survey.* TMS, Edinburgh.

OECD (1994). *Tourism Strategies and Rural Development.* OECD, Paris.

Scottish Office (1992). *Scottish Rural Life - A Socio-Economic Profile of Rural Scotland.* Scottish Office, Edinburgh.

Scottish Tourism Co-ordinating Group (STCG) (1993). *Tourism and the Scottish Environment. A Sustainable Partnership.* Scottish Tourist Board, Edinburgh.

Scottish Tourist Board (1993). *Visitor Attractions Survey, 1993.* Scottish Tourist Board, Edinburgh.

Slee, B. (1987). *Alternative Farm Enterprises.* Farming Press, Ipswich.

Slee, B. (1995). Market Led Provision of Environmental Goods in *Agricultural Externalities in High Income Countries,* Wissenschaftsverlag Vauk Kiel KG, Kiel, 53-67.

Surrey Research Group (1993). *Scottish Tourism Multiplier Study. Volume 1 Main Report.* Scottish Office, Edinburgh.

Vaughan, D. R. (1988). *Tourism in Eastbourne: Visitor Characteristics, the Economic Impact of Visitor Spending and the Businessman's Experience.* Eastbourne Borough Council, Eastbourne.

Vaughan, D. R. (1994). The Impact of Visitor Spending: A Review of Methodology in University of Aberdeen, Institut D'Etudes Politiques de Grenoble, and Universidade de Trás-os-Montes e Alto Douro (eds) *Agrotourism and Synergistic Pluriactivity. First Progress Report,* 31-90, University of Aberdeen, Scotland.

Walker, S. and Vaughan, D. R. (1992). *Pennine Way Survey 1990. Use and Economic Impact.* Countryside Commission, Manchester.

Wheeller, B. (1991). Tourism's Troubled Times. Responsible Tourism is not the Answer. *Tourism Management.* June, 91-96.

Williams, A. and Shaw, G. (1991). *Tourism and Economic Development. Western European Experiences.* Belhaven Press, London and New York.

[29]

Pergamon

0261-5177(95)00113-1

Tourism Management, Vol. 17, No. 2, pp. 103–111, 1996
Copyright © 1996 Elsevier Science Ltd
Printed in Great Britain. All rights reserved
0261-5177/96 $15.00 + 0.00

Agricultural diversification into tourism

Evidence of a European Community development programme

Anne-Mette Hjalager

Science Park, Gustav Wiedsvej 10, 8000 Aarhus C, Denmark

Based on the empirical evidence provided by an evaluation study of the EU Objective 5b programme measures* for the expansion of rural tourism, this article discusses the impact of rural tourism on agricultural holdings. It is shown that the financial returns most often do not measure up either to the expectations of the politicians or to that of the farmers. In some respects rural tourism contributes positively to the innovation of the tourist product since its small scale, 'green' issues and special facilities differentiate the product from others. But the unleashing of real potential is hampered by the fact that farmers tend to give priority to traditional agriculture and by the fact that industrialized agriculture is not easily combined with the commodifying of agricultural traditions for tourism. The community level inter-organizational innovations which are designed to ensure the marketing and quality control of rural tourism are taking place too slowly. Cooperative efforts in the field of tourism are hampered by the fact that the organizations have not been logically placed in the value chain. This article introduces measures to improve the inter-organizational set-up, suggesting that this is essential if rural tourism is to be launched on any large scale.

Keywords: rural tourism, innovations, financial impact

The categorization of rural tourism as a mode of lifting rural areas out of a situation of migration and economic decline is very commonplace: 'Tourism by its very nature draws outside capital into the local community which can lead to positive economic benefits that may be the essential attributes for the survival of a rural community undergoing economic transition. These economic benefits include a diversification of the local industry base, increased public employment, higher incomes, enlargement of the tax base, and business revenue growth.'[1] The success of rural tourism reported by a number of authors is measured in terms of the growth of tourism inflows into the rural areas.[2,3] Envisaging the change of consumer demand away from mass tourism, a number of authors[4-7] forecast further growth in this particular tourism market segment.

Incentive programmes aimed at increasing the rural tourism base and resources have been launched widely in many countries,[8-10] and thus the goals and means relevant in this connection might be considered to have been put to the test rather well. At European Community level, rural tourism is considered crucial,[11] and appropriate policies have been implemented, eg through the Objective 5b and Leader programmes.

In 1994, the European Commission, the Directorate General for Agriculture, initiated an evaluation of the national Objective 5b programmes. This programme includes measures aimed at tourism development in rural districts (agricultural diversification, public investments in tourism infrastructure and training), as well as other measures such as

---

* The author is responsible for the conclusions drawn in this article.

financial support for SMEs and incentives to develop
new crops and production methodologies within
traditional types of agriculture. In relation to the
Danish small islands (the beneficiary region of the
national Objective 5b programme) the evaluation
process produced crucial evidence of the effects and
prospects of the rural tourism concept and the
policies activating it. Selected evaluation data are
included and discussed in this article.

The focus of this article is on the innovation
issues. In the case of rural tourism, innovation can
be analysed from two entirely different angles:

● innovation of the tourist product by expanding
  the scale and scope of *tourist products* based on
  rural resources;
● innovation at community level in the *rural districts* by means of shifting diversifying production
  away from being concentrated entirely on agricultural production and towards gradually more
  leisure-orientated production.

This main emphasis of this article is on the internal
and external push factors leading to these categories
of innovation. The term internal factors refers specifically to resource management within the individual
agricultural holding, which again interacts with external factors such as policy issues, constraints and
opportunities in the market-place, etc. As there is a
widespread tradition for collaborative innovativeness in Danish agriculture, it becomes an essential
task to analyse whether the institutional set-up is
geared to continue its activities in the field of rural
tourism, and whether it is capable of intermediation
in the learning processes going on in the individual
agricultural holdings.

Effects of a development programme: an overview

The Objective 5b programme rural tourism measure
The Objective 5b programme aims to restructure
and to create/maintain jobs in rural areas – in
Denmark defined as 33 islands, the largest of which
has 45 000 inhabitants, and the smallest less than 100
inhabitants.

One of the seven policy measures in the programme included incentives aimed at the creation of
alternative incomes on farm holdings, generated
from tourism accommodation, activities and attractions. During the period 1990–93 a total of 68 farms
received EU and national investment subsidies.
Close to ECU 1 million were granted for this purpose, and national co-financing funds equalled this
amount. The farmers themselves contributed ECU
2.5 million, ie 56% of the investments.

The majority of the funds were spent on the
establishment and renovation of accommodation
facilities, which are concentrated on the following
types:

● bedrooms;
● apartments, particularly self-catering;
● cottages;
● summer houses for rent, some of which are large
  (12–16 persons) and well equipped (pools, spa,
  etc), also suitable for off-season stays;
● primitive camping (low cost, no-frills camping
  sites).

None of these types of facilities is new in the Danish
tourism landscape. But the proprietors are con-
sciously attempting to adapt to a variety of demands,
and at the same time they try to be able to provide a
set of facilities involving substantial flexibility.

As a supplement or as an alternative to accommodation, a number of projects are concerned with
investments in other types of tourist facilities. It is
evident that these particular farms can be claimed to
increase the scope and scale of the local tourism
products by establishing facilities not so far available
at the island destinations in question. The following
list illustrates the products supported by the EU
grants:

● tennis courts;
● guided landscape tours;
● riding facilities, renting of horses;
● shops selling farm products;
● put-and-take fishing lake;
● boats and vessels for hire;
● prairie wagons with horses for hire;
● educational facilities;
● open farm facilities;
● exhibitions;
● farm museums;
● swimming pools;
● wool processing workshops;
● pipe workshop;
● shooting grounds for rent;
● cafés.

Those facilities which can be related to traditional
agricultural activities (wool, honey, geese, meat,
berries, etc) particularly lend themselves to giving
rural tourism a distinctive image not obtainable as
part of other tourist products available in Denmark.

Evaluation methodology

In order to give the most precise information possible on the preliminary effects of the programme, the
collection of information was undertaken by contacting all agricultural holdings which obtained support
from this particular measure of the Objective 5b
programme. Out of 68 possible beneficiaries, 67
answered the questions put in telephone interviews.

In addition, three intermediary organizations
were paid personal visits.

The main objective of this policy measure is to
create alternative sources of income for agricultural

Table 1 Contribution margins* per year (1000 ECUs) before projects and estimated figures post-investment

Contribution margin	Pre-investment	Estimates post-investment
From traditional agriculture	7781	7757
From alternative incomes	15	994
Sum	7796	8751

Note: *Turnover minus materials, services and wages to staff, but before interest and wages to proprietors.

holdings. A number of effects might be of importance in relation to rural development:

- alternative incomes;
- time allocation;
- employment of staff;
- side-effects on local competition.

It should be noted that most of the investments have not yet been fully completed, and the facilities created have not been utilized for long enough to yield a comprehensive evaluation. Wherever possible the real impact is assessed, but in a number of cases the evaluation must rely on the anticipated effects. Nevertheless, this early evaluation does provide farmers and policy makers with crucial information.

Alternative incomes

In *Table 1* the sum of the contribution margins of all of the farm holdings is shown.

The table indicates that the contribution margins achieved through traditional agricultural activities are expected to remain much the same. The slight decrease observed in the estimates reflects the fact that a few farms expect to launch into rural tourism more substantially. Generally, however, the farmers intend not to let the level of farm activities be influenced by the tourism activities.

Before the investments were made, the alternative income contribution was very low; it is expected to rise considerably as a consequence of the investments. The alternative income will then – if realized – account for more than 11% of the total contribution margin.

The contribution margins deriving from alternative incomes vary considerably in the approved projects. Nine farmers expect a contribution margin of ECU 4000 or less per season. This is true particularly of farmers who launched into primitive camping projects. On the other hand, eight farmers calculated that their expected contribution margins would be higher than ECU 25 000 per season. Clearly, it is those farms that already have high contribution margins from traditional agriculture that also take on extensive projects resulting in high contribution margins from alternative incomes.

Thus, a professional farming attitude, larger scale activities and probably greater availability of capital seem to transfer themselves to the alternative income activities.

From the interviews it soon became evident that alternative income sources from jobs outside the farm activities were very common, particularly in cases where the farms only contributed small margins. Farmers in this category also seem less ambitious when it comes to the scale and scope of alternative farm incomes.

At the time of the evaluation, only 18 projects had had a full tourism season (1993) in which to gain experience of the financial impact. Of the 18 farmers, four achieved the expected contribution margin. One farmer achieved slightly more than expected, and 13 less than expected. Most of these 13 looked forward to the 1994 season and hoped it would turn out as expected. They refer to the starting-up of their rural tourism projects as a troublesome period when practical experience had to be gained.

Only one of the farmers found that he had been altogether too optimistic concerning the contribution margin opportunities.

ECU 1 million of Community funds were allocated to this programme, and together with private and national co-financing funds the investments came to a total of at least ECU 4.5 million. A number of interviewees claimed that their own investments ended up being much higher than estimated in their applications. Lack of relevant counselling bodies able to assist during preparation is one essential reason for this.

An average gross return of around 20% on the invested capital must initially be said to be favourable, a point which must, however, be discussed in relation to the time spent on obtaining this extra income.

Time allocation

In their applications, the farmers were asked to estimate the number of hours necessary to obtain the anticipated extra alternative income from rural tourism. *Table 2* shows the estimates as provided by the applicants.

The beneficiaries expected their time consump-

Table 2 Estimated time consumption (hours per year) in relation to obtainable alternative incomes

Time consumption	Pre-investment	Post-investment
In relation to traditional agricultural incomes	197 063	194 540
In relation to alternative incomes	500	43 068
Sum	197 563	237 608

tion on traditional agricultural activities to be slightly lower – in harmony with their expectations of gaining a slightly lower contribution margin. Compared with the extra contribution margin that tourism is expected to earn, these activities will, however, occupy a substantial number of additional working hours. As calculated above, the extra income will account for approx. 11% of the total contribution margin, but the time spent on gaining this extra income will amount to 18%. It may thus be concluded that traditional agriculture is still much more efficient than rural tourism in regard to generating earnings.

The experience that 18 farmers gained in the 1993 season further emphasizes this conclusion. With only one exception, they all claim that they spent longer hours on rural tourism activities than expected. A few of them do, however, expect time consumption to drop again after the running-in period.

Thus analysed, rural tourism activities might be regarded as a fairly sub-optimum way of allocating time and investments. We do, however, have to consider the real alternatives of the rural population before jumping to this conclusion.

The interviews illustrate the fact that farmers consider the prevailing conditions of traditional agriculture to be extremely difficult. For instance, in 1994 the price of pork dropped, leaving even lower contribution margins than anticipated in the applications. This means that farmers have been searching more actively for alternatives than ever before, and are willing to accept lower margins if necessary.

Employment impacts

Another important issue when it comes to the evaluation of the efficiency of rural tourism projects is the fact that these new activities occupy *idle manpower resources* present within the farm households. The activities are made possible as a consequence of a (re)allocation of family labour.

Only the most ambitious projects envisage the employment of additional staff, and in all cases the employment effect generated will be part-time jobs or jobs for sub-contracting cleaners, etc. The norm within rural tourism is that the family – particularly the wife and older children – is the active partner in the rural tourism project.

It can be concluded that in spite of many expectations, rural tourism will not contribute substantially to job creation. But rural tourism may nevertheless be of some importance in maintaining the activities and populations of rural districts.

Displacement effects: rural tourism in the local tourism economy

In Denmark, rural tourism is riding on the crest of a wave of growth in tourism generation. It is fairly

easy to document that this development has also benefited the largest island eligible for the programme, Bornholm;[12] we do, however, not have reliable information about the development in the number of bed-nights on the smaller islands. Growth in demand does not mean that providing accommodation in itself entails no competition problems. Outside the main season excess capacity is substantial.

If it were not for the fact that the tourism industry is experiencing a period of general growth, the new capacity might have caused a competitive situation leading to criticism from the accommodation sector itself.

There are, however, local disparities, which may lead to the conclusion that establishing accommodation facilities should nevertheless be regarded as a favourable measure. Some of the very small islands have a severe lack of accommodation which leads to a situation where tourism is concentrated solely on day trips. In such cases there are strong arguments in favour of providing accommodation. However, it is important to notice that this particular measure was not utilized in any of these very small islands where the need for additional facilities is greatest.

As the excess capacity problem associated with traditional hotel accommodation has become the general rule, it is obvious that farmers will attempt to counter this problem by providing self-catering facilities or other kinds of very flexible accommodation, which will leave them more competitive in relation to hotels. In this respect, the farmers are creating a greater variety in the tourism product, a factor which may appeal to new target groups who would not otherwise have considered rural vacations at all.

Conclusions of the evaluation study

In economic terms the main conclusions are as follows. In the estimation of the applicants, the financial returns that may be earned on the projects are favourable, but still lower than the returns yielded by traditional agriculture. The returns actually achieved during the first season were, however, lower than expected, and it turned out that more manpower than estimated had to be invested. The extra income was thus acquired at a higher 'price' than forecast by the beneficiaries.

Rural tourism creates hardly any extra jobs in the primary sector, but reallocates family work.

Based on the interviews and the application material, it appears obvious that the very competent farmers with high incomes also launch into the most professional and larger-scale tourism projects with greater probabilities of success. The very small-scale projects and attractions, where the utilization of manpower resources is estimated to be substantial, also have bleaker prospects, and the proprietors are often half-hearted about the outlook and continuation of the projects.

The very small islands (often with populations of fewer than 500) are the ones less able to take up the opportunities for rural tourism. This contradicts the fact that they very much lack sufficient facilities to accommodate tourists wanting to stay for more than one day. The incentive programme was particularly well received and more successful on those islands where active intermediaries took the lead. The very small islands isolated from consultants and other intermediaries were most often left out of this process.

Conclusions concerning the early impacts of the programme do to a certain extent contradict the political objectives. However, the Danish evidence is not unique in this respect. Other investigations express reservations about the efficiency of rural tourism in relation to accepted goals concerning the financial benefits that ought to be achieved by individual agricultural holdings.[13,14] For instance: 'It must be stated that outcomes have been modest . . . . Economic returns have not been that significant so far but, with some proper attention to training, standards and marketing, there is potential for larger economic impacts to occur' ([13]p 51). And 'Cloke suggests that while many commentators believe that tourism is a basis for achieving economic and social viability, they fail to question whether the benefits accruing from tourism development mostly favour the sections of the community who are in a position to invest for profit'.[15]

> It appears, however, that one common feature of farm-tourism is that, because it is the economically better-off land-owning families that take up this avenue of accumulation, the practice widens rural income differentials and does little to alter the financial predicament of poorer agricultural households.[16]

In the following section we shall discuss the findings in relation to internal and external change mechanisms, and in relation to the collective inclination to embark on innovations in rural districts.

Innovations in the agricultural production portfolio: push mechanisms for change

In this section the factors of importance in relation to the emergence of rural tourism will be summarized. Furthermore, the factors affecting the occurrence of innovation in the tourism products compared with other tourist products will be investigated.

Push mechanisms for change in the agricultural portfolio

Technology push. This is generally regarded as a very important mechanism inducing change in the manufacturing as well as in the tourism sector.[18] The mechanization of the primary sector has been a continual and ongoing process over the last centuries and decades, some technologies causing heavier impacts than others. The implementation of labour-saving technology in agriculture will probably not cease, in spite of more extensive trends towards organic farming.

The mechanization, automation and computerization of agriculture only affects rural tourism activities in so far as it leaves labour resources idle, resources which may be redirected into other economic activities. On the other hand, the more of an industrialized business, the less attractive the farm may seem for visitors.

Idle labour resources are not primarily channelled into other agricultural activities. The surplus labour in the agricultural sector has been gradually disposed of: in 1993, only 16% of Danish farms employed staff. In addition, working farmers' wives have become the norm rather than the exception.

If they do exist, family labour surpluses have to be invested either in increased production volumes or in diversified activities. The third possibility – wage-earning activities outside the farm holding – is often not available on small islands, hampered as they are by high unemployment rates and considerable travelling distances to mainland job opportunities. The rural tourism option may therefore seem more attractive in island environments.

Agricultural and environmental policy impact on rural tourism. A major external push factor promoting innovation and change in the production portfolio is agricultural policy, particularly, but not exclusively, the one imposed by the European Union. GATT talks and the Common Agricultural Policy (CAP) reform including continually changing intervention prices, levies and compensatory payments obtainable under set-aside schemes, etc will necessarily have some kind of influence on the strategic management of the individual holdings.[18]

CAP restricts the output of traditional agricultural products. Nevertheless and in spite of reductions, the quotas are claimed to be financially more attractive than incomes obtainable from rural tourism. If quotas or other possibilities are available, the average farmers would rather pursue traditional production than rural tourism. Only if quotas are restricted or if time or investment resources are present will the rural tourism option be seriously considered.

Danish environmental policies imply that there should be a balanced relationship between livestock and land on every farm holding. Industrialized pig-breeding farms have increased their acreage by buying neighbouring farms. A general need to consolidate led to the same type of acreage expansions. Very often the only reason for the provision of tourism accommodation is existence of surplus farm-

houses and convertible barns, which would otherwise be unsaleable or unlettable.

In the agricultural community – as elsewhere –
one does not like to leave resources idle. The forced
limits to output pushed other options into the considerations of the individual farmer, thus contributing to structural change of the farm product.

Around 10% of Danish farm holdings have gone
in for rural tourism,[19] which is far less than the 20%
reported by Maude and van Rest[20] for the UK.
Agricultural traditions and income opportunities in
Denmark as well as legislation on the utilization of
land resources may differ slightly from UK conditions, thus resulting in a situation where tourism
facilities are not able to compete with other categories of agricultural activities for capital and manpower resources. Thus, Neate[31] indicates that the land
ownership rules and the rigoristic farm size regulations existing on the Isles of Scilly are important
background factors promoting the intensive development of rural tourism in this particular region.
Such push factors do not exist in Denmark.

In spite of the fact that in Denmark farming is
considered a tough or even unattractive way of
earning a living, the options are broader than in
other countries or regions. Rural tourism is one such
option, but it does not, however, seem to appeal
quite as much to farmers as other diversification
possibilities.

Something new? Or the traditions revisited?

What are the particular features of a rural tourism
product? And how does it fit in with agricultural
production? Earlier in this article, the products were
identified as either accommodation and/or experiences, workshops, leisure facilities, etc.

When analysing the core content of the products,
it becomes evident that the emphasis of the tourism
services offered is nearly always on the typically
female work operations existing on a farm. The
process implies that ordinary household-type activities are 'upgraded' and now become income-
generating work operations. In its simplest form the
provision of accommodation and catering services
may be regarded as an extension of the ordinary
household services to comprise services being made
available also to 'strangers' without introducing particular innovative elements. Things take place on a
larger scale, but are still performed as they used to
be.

Nevertheless, tourists will probably not be treated
as family members, as shown by Bouquet.[23] The
introduction of strangers as users of the comforts
provided by a farming household will change relations from a family-based, long-term mutual dependence into a short-term economic relationship.
In other words, essential elements have changed – in
spite of the fact that the providers of rural tourism

tend to emphasize the importance of the social
element.[8,23] This change of emphasis is a very basic
condition underlying the occurrence of innovations
in the field of rural tourism.

In her analysis of agrarian formations Friedmann[24]
emphasizes that over the years a separation of
commodity relations has taken place in agricultural
households. The home production of various products and services for household use has been replaced by industrialized products and services
bought outside the household. From the point of
view of the core farm production activities this
development is a logical consequence of the economies of scale concept, and of the fact that the farm
workforce has diminished dramatically.

With the exception of a situation where the rural
tourism facilities offered consist exclusively of
accommodation services (for instance self-catering),
a development towards the separation of commodity
relations is only partly compatible with demand
patterns. As is the case with many types of tourist
attractions, the consumer choice of the rural tourism
product should be seen as a response to a need to
immerse oneself in the emotion of nostalgia. The
urbanization of the population, which has taken
place over the last four or five decades, gives rise to
a need to (re)experience one's own childhood or the
lives of not so very distant ancestors. In their hearts,
the Danes are all still rural people, and through their
holiday experiences they wish to become the ethno-
graphers of their own, their parents' or their grandparents' pasts.

However, the modern agricultural community is
not immediately capable of providing the facilities
enabling tourists to experience or re-experience
even the very near past. The complete chain of
processes involved in the production of milk, vegetables or poultry from 'plough to plate' cannot be
observed in any single place. Furthermore, the
separation of commodity relations has led to the
abolition of some of the essential elements of particularly memorable activities, for instance home baking, the conservation of fruit and vegetables, etc;
weaving, knitting, etc.

It is all a question of whether the tourist will want
to face the realities of modern agricultural production. Therefore, the most distinctive innovative
effort involved in developing rural tourism products
is concerned with the reinvention of tradition.[25] As
an example, the concept of establishing outlets
enabling tourists to purchase farm products has
penetrated into a number of rural tourism projects –
no matter whether the product was produced on the
farm or not. It is unlikely that the home production
of these artefacts would ever have been undertaken
if it did not serve the purpose of satisfying the needs
of the tourists and to 'extend' a rural tourism product image to them.

The concept of reinventing tradition is not only

concerned with creating possibilities for purchasing farm products. More interesting is the provision of 'hands-on experiences': participation in pipe production, wool preparation, weaving, milking and feeding and other types of workshop and farm activities – fishing ponds, horse riding facilities, etc. The innovative activity is concerned with the commodification of former household and farming activities. A number of beneficiaries of the Objective 5b programme stated that in order to be able to provide these opportunities and experiences, special workshops and stables had to be established, as most often the experiences demanded by tourists were completely incompatible with modern farming.

The labour input required for producing farm products and guiding and managing hands-on experiences has, however, not decreased in relation to the requirements of earlier days. Therefore, not surprisingly, the farmers claim that even in a commodified form these activities yield very disappointing financial returns.

It may be concluded that as individuals the farmers have begun an innovative process which will lead towards a restructuring of the basic purpose of agricultural production. When agriculture becomes a provider of services, a change in the set-up of the farm will necessarily have to take place, possibly creating internal conflicts along the way.

The internal innovative process – ie the definition of products and services, the rationalization of the production process by means of new technologies and management remedies – has been quite troublesome. The objectives involved in creating something excitingly new (for instance reinventing past agricultural production methods) and those involved in running a profitable business can only be combined with difficulty.

If farmers are to be successful in this respect it will definitely involve changing some farming concepts, ie abandoning the traditional production concepts and moving towards a concept of exclusively catering for tourists. The links to traditional agriculture will then have to be severed. Some farmers will probably choose this road, but it is evident that this option will not be open to all of the 10% of Danish farmers who presently offer accommodation, catering, etc.

Cooperative innovation in rural tourism communities

Peasant households have important communal relations, including local exchange of products and reciprocal sharing of labour. For this reason the village is typically the immediate arena of reproduction. Even asymmetrical relations, such as credit and tenancy, are with particular persons, not banks and corporations, and are not governed by market prices.[34]

These days, the village as a community is withering away, though the exchange of products and services is still essential but has now been extended to take place on a wider spatial scale. The integrative efforts of modernized agriculture are handled by organizations which in some respects still resemble the original community model, but operate at a larger scale. In Denmark, these organizations cover most types of agricultural production, and offer services in relation to the purchasing of raw materials and machinery, production at farm level, processing, marketing, financing, etc. The creation of a multitude of organizations at all spatial levels – a process that began in the late 19th century and has continued until the present – represents the single most important factor when it comes to the competitiveness of Danish agriculture.

However, tourism does not carry any significant weight in the otherwise extensive and tightly knit agricultural networks and services. In relation to tourism, the farmers are mostly individualized providers of products/services.

The inquiry among the beneficiaries of Objective 5b concerning support for rural tourism in Denmark revealed the farmers' reactions to the lack of cooperative facilities in the field of tourism. On the larger islands it was possible to find local 'allies' with whom to exchange business experiences. A joint marketing initiative has been established, but this initiative can by no means be compared to the extremely efficient – in terms of extent and market penetration – cooperative enterprises within, for instance, the pork, beef, cereals, vegetables and other subsectors of agricultural production.

Some rural tourism providers without colleagues in the immediate community chose other marketing channels: the local tourist boards, summer cottage intermediaries, or even other tourist enterprises with complementary products, ie established links outside the agricultural 'family'. The need for advisory services is also often satisfied by outside consultants. More than half of the beneficiaries reported that they had faced severe marketing problems during the first and second years of operation.

The need to 'reinvent' marketing channels has taken the farmers by surprise, and the task of adapting has necessarily been a time-consuming one. The easiest way chosen by a number of holdings is to let the accommodation go into the catalogues of the summer house intermediaries. Hereby marketing becomes efficient, but expensive. The rural tourism organization undertakes the marketing, but less ambitiously than for instance the French 'gites'. This opportunity seems to be considered less attractive by the farmers. Nevertheless some holdings are members of a rural tourism organization. The least expensive method is to put a signboard along the road; this will create some business, but not enough, and the mode of marketing is not appropriate on the very small islands.

Only one group of farmers supported by Objective 5b have gone beyond the traditional methods of marketing. They created a network with farmers in Southern Sweden and printed and distributed elegant brochures. This transborder initiative released funds from other supportive programmes, thus facilitating a more ambitious and innovative approach. The farmers could not have identified the opportunities and adopted this approach without the supportive assistance of consultants.

Why are inter-organizational innovative activities apparently so slowly established in the field of rural tourism? In other words, why do collaborative organizations not attempt to diversify at the same time as their members?

One reason for the lack of inter-organizational networks is the insignificant returns. The running and staffing of joint organizations is essential, but the individual farm holding will weigh its contribution against the scale of its activities. Second, the existing cooperative organizations have not been very efficient in gaining a place in the value chain. The success of traditional cooperative enterprises can to a very large extent be attributed to their ability to earn profits along the way from 'plough to plate'.

Third, and perhaps most important, the tourism product is not a 'bulk' product designed for further processing and marketing. Increasingly, it is becoming a differentiated product relying on the provider for quality and performance. In his analysis of the cooperative food production sector, Søgaard[26] is particularly concerned with the problem of input substitution. 'The competitive advantages of cooperatives are to be found in their ability to improve product quality on a broad basis, i.e. without having to select a small group of "elite" producers in the primary sector. In view of this fact, surprisingly little attention has so far been paid to the possibility of including primary producers in the process of product development.'

Cooperatives are found by Søgaard to be generally disinclined to engage in vertically coordinated product innovation involving primary producers. The reason is the 'Equal treatment proviso'. Differentiated products do not fit into this cooperative concept very well. In this respect tourism issues and organic production envisage identical set-backs *vis-à-vis* the agricultural organizations.

Conclusions: wider ranging organizational innovations needed

Taking into account the increased competition within the tourism sector as a whole and considering the politically expressed need to support the development of rural districts, the need for organizational innovations at community level becomes very clear.

If rural tourism is to become something other than the least attractive diversification option open to the individual farmer, one must launch into 'architectural innovations'.

'Architectural innovations' will disrupt existing linkages and create new ones, and in addition will disrupt or make obsolete existing competences. 'Innovation of this sort defines the basic configuration of product and process and establishes the technical and marketing agenda that will guide the subsequent development. It lays down the architecture of the industry, the broad framework within which competition will occur and develop.[27] Architectural innovations seem to be the necessary preconditions and consequences if rural tourism is to become more than a trivial supplement to diminishing agricultural incomes.

What is lacking if rural tourism is to develop from a trivial matter and into a significant contribution to a changed agenda for community development in rural districts? The following items represent some of the most essential elements of a concept change process:

- a marketing organization with the resources that will enable it to disseminate the product efficiently and to influence consumer attitudes in such a way that a change away from the 'cheap holiday' image and towards an 'experience holiday' image is effected;
- quality monitoring procedures and measures to control basic accommodation and catering facilities;
- a joint organization of the attractions that are offered in connection with the rural tourism product, its commodification and production. This may require the establishment of farms or sites which will exclusively undertake the 'nostalgia' version of farming and where guiding services can be made available. The division of labour may leave some farmers with accommodation as their only option – a solution which many farmers will prefer, as it opens up the choice of concentrating mainly on a core business;
- the efficient linking of the food production sector with tourism in order to utilize tourism as a marketing 'showcase', particularly for niche products. The eating culture is a distinctive feature which is utterly underestimated in the tourism sector in general, and paradoxically so in rural tourism;
- capital provision opportunities related to tourism issues.[31]

These issues are important, but for the reasons mentioned above the shift towards change will not be an easy one. Agricultural and tourism policies may be utilized to assist grass-roots involvement during the difficult transition processes. A remodelling of the Objective 5 support provided by the

European Community and the Danish Government may, for instance, represent a first and necessary step if the organizational and product innovation objectives are to be achieved. Reformulating entrepreneurial potentials is crucially important. A reiteration of the formal (policy initiated) and informal (grass-roots initiatives) strategies is needed in this process.

It must be observed that tourism is not the only issue causing a reopening of the debate concerning agricultural structure after one hundred years of a high level of consensus. Environmental matters too are contributing to this process. These two issues are not entirely incompatible in regard to the aim of ensuring economic activity, jobs and sustainable resource utilization in the rural districts: quite the reverse, in fact.

References

[1]Potts, T D, Backman, K F, Uysal, M and Backman, J 'Issues in rural community tourism development' *Visions in Leisure and Business* 1992 **11** (1) 5–13
[2]Gilbert, D C 'Issues in appropriate rural tourism development for southern Ireland' *Leisure Studies* 1993 **12** 137–146
[3]Grolleau, H *Le tourisme rural dans les 12 Etats membres de la Communauté économique européenne* Commission des Communautés Européennes, TER (1987)
[4]Blunden, J and Curry, N *A Future for our Countryside* Basil Blackwell, Oxford, 1988
[5]Davies, E T and Gilbert, D C 'A case study of the development of farm tourism in Wales' *Tourism Management* 1992 **13** 56–63
[6]Dernoi, L A 'Prospects of rural tourism: needs and opportunities' *Tourism Recreation Research* 1991 **16** (1) 89–94
[7]Lanazpère, J-B 'Tourism at the service of rural development' *LEADER Dossiers* (Bruxelles) 1993
[8]Frater, J M 'Farm tourism in England. Planning, funding, promotion and some lessons from Europe' *Tourism Management* 1983 **4** (3) 167–179
[9]Luloff, A E, Bridger, J C, Graefe, A R, Saylor, M, Martin, K and Gitelson, R 'Assessing rural tourism efforts in the United States' *Annals of Tourism Research* 1994 **21** (1) 46–64
[10]Winter, M 'Private tourism in the English and Welsh Uplands: farming, visitors and property' in Bouquet, M and Winter, M (eds) *Who from their Labours Rest? Conflict and Practice in Rural Tourism* Avebury, Aldershot (1987) 22–35
[11]Commission of the European Community *Community Action to Promote Rural Tourism* COM(90) 438 final, Brussels (12 October 1990)
[12]Holm-Petersen, E, Hjalager, A-M, Framke, W and Ploughmann, P *Turisme fritid – en erhvervsøkonomisk analyse* Erhvervsfremmestyrelsen, Copenhagen (1993)
[13]Keane, M 'Rural tourism and rural development' in Briassoulis, H and van der Straaten, J *Tourism and the Environment. Regional, Economic and Policy Issues* Kluwer, Dordrecht (1992) 43–55
[14]Maude, A S J and van Rest, D J 'The social and economic effects of farm tourism in the United Kingdom' *Agricultural Administration* 1985 **20** 85–99
[15]Keane, M J and Quinn, J *Rural Development and Rural Tourism* Research Report No 5, Social Science Research Centre, University College Galway (1990)
[16]Britton, S 'Tourism, capital and place: towards a critical geography of tourism' *Environment and Planning D: Society and Space* 1991 **9** 451–478
[17]Hjalager, A-M 'Dynamic innovation in the tourist industry' *Progress in Tourism, Recreation and Hospitality Management* Vol 6, Wiley, Chichester (1994) 197–224
[18]Commission of the European Communities *Green Europe: The New Regulation of the Agricultural Markets* Vademecum, No 1 (1993)
[19]Lægaard, J and Larsen, S S *Agronetværk Danmark. Foranalyse* DOR, Århus (1993)
[20]Maude, A J S and van Rest, D J 'The social and economic effects of farm tourism in the United Kingdom' *Agricultural Administration* 1985 **20** 85–99
[21]Neate, S 'The role of tourism in sustaining farm structures and communities on the isles of Scilly' in Bouquet, M and Winter, M (eds) *Who from their Labours Rest? Conflict and Practice in Rural Tourism* Avebury, Aldershot (1987) 9–21
[22]Bouquet, M 'Bed, breakfast and an evening meal: commensality in the nineteenth and twentieth century farm household in Hartland' in Bouquet, M and Winter, M *Who from their Labours Rest? Conflict and Practice in Rural Tourism* Avebury, Aldershot (1987) 93–104
[23]Edwards, J 'Guest–host perceptions of rural tourism in England and Portugal' in Sinclair, T and Stabler, M J (eds) *The Tourism Industry: An International Analysis* CAB, Wallingford (1991)
[24]Friedmann, H 'Household production and the national economy: concepts for the analysis of agrarian formations' *Journal of Peasant Studies* 1980 **7** (2) 158–184
[25]Hobsbawn, E and Ranger, T (eds) *The Invention of Tradition* Cambridge University Press, Cambridge (1983)
[26]Søgaard, V *Farmers, Cooperatives, New Food Products* MAPP Monograph, Aarhus (May 1994)
[28]Abernathy, W J and Clark, K B 'Innovation: mapping the winds of creative destruction' *Research Policy* **14** 3–22
[28]Evans, N J and Ilbery, B W 'A conceptual framework for investigating farm-based accommodation and tourism in Britain' *J Rural Studies* 1989 **5** (3) 257–266

F
Rural Enterprise, Housing and Transport

[30]

 Pergamon

Geoforum, Vol. 27, No. 1, pp. 75–86, 1996
Copyright © 1996 Elsevier Science Ltd
Printed in Great Britain. All rights reserved
0016–7185/96 $15.00 + 0.00

S0016–7185(96)00003–6

Regional Variations in Business Use of Information and Communication Technologies and their Implications for Policy: Case Study Evidence from Rural England

NIGEL BERKELEY,* DAVID CLARK† and BRIAN ILBERY,†
Coventry, U.K.

Abstract: This paper compares the awareness, take-up and use of information and communication technologies in an 'accessible' rural region with that in a 'remote' rural region and assesses the implications for policy. Data are drawn from a survey of small businesses in south Warwickshire and north Lancashire. The findings reveal the overall adoption of information and communication technologies, both basic and advanced, to be low, but especially low in north Lancashire compared with south Warwickshire. The reasons for these patterns are explored. In general, the low take-up rates are a function of a combination of factors: infrastructure; business size; the cost, complexity and relevance of the technology; awareness and training; whilst the observed differences between the two regions reflect differences in business culture. The policy implications of these findings are discussed. It is advocated that local policy intervention is necessary to take account of the differences that exist between rural areas. Copyright © 1996 Elsevier Science Ltd

Introduction

The recent advances in information and communication technologies and their associated implications for regional economic development have been much discussed (Hepworth *et al.*, 1987; Hepworth, 1989). There is a widespread view that information technology and telecommunications will destroy traditional barriers of time and distance, and thus have the potential especially to benefit rural areas (Rural Development Commission, 1989; Commission of the European Communities, 1988). They can be assisted in this respect by programmes and policies designed

to promote take-up and use (Giaoutzi and Nijkamp, 1988; Grimes, 1992). Such arguments, however, tend to be couched in general terms and overlook the wide range of circumstances that exist in rural areas. Much of the literature reflects the experience in America and continental Europe, and the implications for policy are not directly transferable to the United Kingdom where the technological and geographical contrasts are very different (Parker *et al.*, 1989; Schmandt *et al.*, 1991; Gillespie, 1987). Rural England is highly differentiated in terms of spatial and economic structure, as Keeble *et al.* (1992) have shown. A need exists to examine such regional variations and their consequences. This paper contributes to the debate by comparing the take-up and use of information and communication technologies in two very different English rural areas and assessing the implications for policy.

---

*Centre for Local Economic Development, Coventry University, Priory Street, Coventry CV1 5FB, U.K.
†Geography Division of the School of Natural and Environmental Sciences, Coventry University, Priory Street, Coventry CV1 5TB, U.K.

The paper is divided into four sections. The first reviews the recent advances in information technology and telecommunications and their implications for regional economic development. The second presents the findings of a survey carried out in 1993 contrasting the awareness and use of IT/telecommunications technology in small rural businesses in south Warwickshire and north Lancashire. The third attempts to provide explanations for the key findings; and the final section addresses emerging policy issues.

Telematics and their Regional Implications

The past decade has witnessed significant developments in information and telecommunication technologies. These have occurred alongside, and parallel to, the shift to flexible production techniques, the globalization of the economy and the liberalization of the U.K. telecommunications market (Graham, 1991; Robins and Hepworth, 1988). The key technological development has been the convergence of computing and telecommunications (Goddard and Gillespie, 1986; Driver and Gillespie, 1993; Capello and Nijkamp, 1994). This coalescence, referred to as 'telematics', provides businesses with a medium through which they can communicate rapidly and at low-cost. Telematics facilitate business-to-business messaging, document exchange, funds transfer and data transmission. In addition, through networked databases, businesses can access supplier information, as well as market their own products. Well-known telematic applications include electronic mail, electronic data interchange, teleconferencing, and electronic funds transfer. These are available through the public switched telephone network and are being used in most economic sectors (Graham, 1992). More advanced services such as videophones utilize the integrated services digital network (ISDN), whilst cable, broadcast and satellite systems provide tele-shopping and teletext facilities. Telematics networks include local area networks, specific to one building or company, wide area networks for intercity communication, international corporate networks and global telecommunications networks (Gibbs and Leach, 1994; Hepworth, 1987).

Telematics have the potential to bridge distances and, in theory, to reduce economic disparity between core and periphery (Gillespie, 1987; Ilbery *et al.*, 1995). By improving remote access and reducing communication costs, they can significantly enhance the competitiveness of firms in rural areas (Grimes, 1992; Clark *et al.*, 1995) Much of the early thinking on telematics impacts, which was grounded in the somewhat naive belief that rural areas would derive the greatest benefits, has recently been replaced by a recognition that information and communication technologies "in fact constitute new and enhanced forms of inequality and uneven development" (Gillespie and Robins, 1989, p. 7). Spatial impacts are likely to be highly differentiated. Far from eroding the locational disadvantages faced by the periphery, it is possible that telematics will further enhance the dominance of core regions and particularly large firms within them (Graham, 1991). Equally, 'accessible' rural areas of the type identified by Keeble *et al.* (1992) may benefit more than those that are 'remote'. There are several strands to this argument.

The first is that core regions have greater access to both information, and national and international markets, and thus are better placed to take advantage of technological developments. Peripheral regions, by contrast, are hampered by their remoteness from information sources and especially national and international markets (Gillespie and Robins, 1989; Ilbery *et al.*, 1995). Similar differences would be apparent between an 'accessible' rural region and one that is described as 'remote'. By way of example, Moss (1987) remarks on the dominance of global cities in terms of their ability to attract information-based activities. This process is self-reinforcing in that the new advanced technologies will initially gravitate to cities dominated by information-based activities.

Secondly, computer networks, through which much business-to-business communication takes place, are mainly private and operated by large multinational organizations. These are controlled from head offices located mainly within core regions. The restricted access to computer networks provides significant advantages for those that become 'locked in', and significant disadvantages for those 'locked out' (Gillespie and Williams, 1987; Gillespie and Robins, 1989; Grimes, 1992). It has also been suggested that large firms are much more likely to take advantage of new and advanced information and communication technologies than small and medium-sized enterprises (SMEs) that predominate in rural areas (Gibbs and Leach, 1994).

A third argument is that local services in rural areas

could become undermined by cheaper, higher quality services imported via telematics. Benefits are likely to accrue to core-based suppliers at the expense of local providers. The outcome in the long term would be to increase, rather than reduce, the dependency of the peripheral regions on the core (Graham, 1991; Dabinett and Graham, 1994).

Finally, cultural, institutional and psychological barriers may seriously affect the adoption of new and advanced technologies by rural businesses. Significant timelags in the adoption of new technology between core regions and peripheral regions have been observed. Debate concerning infrastructural timelags is not new (Clark, 1979; Goddard and Gillespie, 1986) but the problem still exists. Graham (1992) and the Rural Development Commission (1989) have noted that advanced services and infrastructures will develop first and foremost where investment returns are greatest. This process results in "uneven social and spatial development and the allocation of information and communication technologies according to ability to pay and market potential, not the potential of the technologies to offer genuine social, economic or geographical development benefits" (Graham, 1992, p. 760). The major beneficiaries are thus large firms in primary business centres, whilst SMEs, and especially those in peripheral areas, are 'major losers' (Gibbs and Leach, 1994). Moss (1987) has noted similar developments with respect to the United States.

The possibility that telematics could accentuate rather than reduce regional differences suggests that policies are required to ensure that the benefits afforded by information and communication technologies are realized in rural areas. The need for such intervention has been recognized by the Commission of the European Union in its Special Telecommunications Action for Regional Development (STAR) and more recently Opportunities for Rural Areas (ORA) programmes. The principal objective of STAR was to introduce advanced telematics services into the lagging regions of the E.U., whilst ORA was established to conduct research and development on telematics and the opportunities provided for rural development. A number of individual projects within ORA were commissioned with the aim of awareness-raising, as well as identifying current uses and potentials of telematics applications in terms of promoting rural development. The objective of TYPORA, which is one of the ORA projects, is to identify

differences between rural areas so that policies can be tailored to local circumstances.

The emphasis placed on telematics by the E.U. contrasts sharply with that in the U.K. Here there is only a minimal rural development policy with negligible technology content (Clark *et al.*, 1995). Economic activity in rural areas is encouraged but in the absence of any detailed guidance. The potentials that might arise from telematics are not addressed. Indeed, Morgan (1990, p. 2) suggests that "there is no other country in Europe which comes close to the U.K. in having a government so resolutely committed to market-led strategies of telecommunications development", a factor that arguably contributes to the uneven diffusion of telematics (Gibbs and Leach, 1994). Research undertaken for the Development Board for Rural Wales, Highlands and Islands Enterprise, and Scottish Enterprise, in their respective areas, provides a basis for informed intervention, but elsewhere policies lack specificity (Bryden *et al.*, 1993; Gillespie *et al.*, 1991). Some insights into the ways in which business use of information and communication technologies vary regionally and the implications for policy arose in connection with research carried out in north Lancashire and south Warwickshire as part of an ORA survey of Services and Applications for Rural Business Activities (SARBA).

Regional Variations in Business Use of Telematics

South Warwickshire and north Lancashire were chosen so as to complement the localities studied in the wider SARBA project. They differ significantly in terms of relief and degree of remoteness. The north Lancashire region comprises coastal plain and marginal upland and is far more remote and peripheral than lowland and centrally located south Warwickshire. The south Warwickshire region is a rural enclave within the core area of the south of England. It is surrounded by London to the south and the cities of the West Midlands conurbation to the north (see Figure 1). Using Keeble *et al.*'s (1992, p. 49) terminology, the north Lancashire region could be described as "remote rural" typified by its "remoteness from major urban areas", whilst the south Warwickshire region, being close to "main urban areas", is "accessible rural". Despite these geographical differences, both areas are well served by the public switched

78   Nigel Berkeley *et al.*

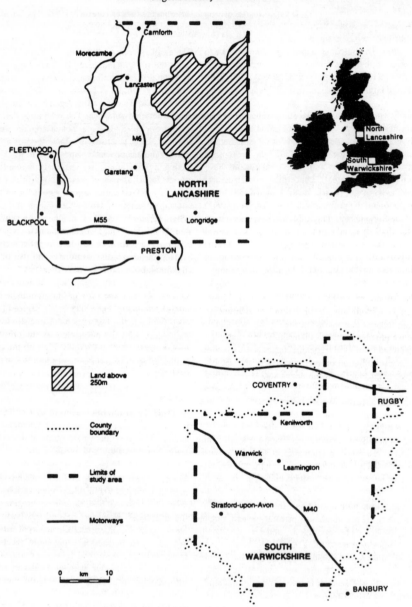

Figure 1. The North Lancashire and South Warwickshire study areas.

Business use of information technology

Table 1. Distribution of companies by business size and region

Region	% of companies by employment size band				
	1–6	7–10	11–25	26–50	51+
North Lancashire	60	12	16	5	5
South Warwickshire	58	13	17	7	5

Table 2. Distribution of companies by customer type and region

Region	% of companies by customer type		
	General public	Other businesses	Both
North Lancashire	31	31	36
South Warwickshire	17	48	35

telephone network. This supports basic telephony, facsimile and a range of teleservices. At the time of survey the Integrated Services Digital Network (ISDN) was available via exchanges in both areas, although there were very few business subscribers.

The survey of SMEs involved contacting, with a postal questionnaire, all non-farming rural businesses from villages and market towns in the two regions with a population of less then 50,000. Businesses, as identified from local trade directories, were asked to supply information on their awareness and use of a range of information technology and telecommunications equipment. Some 928 usable replies were received (541 from Warwickshire and 387 from Lancashire), a response rate of 22%. Some 60 companies were subsequently chosen for further 'intensive' research in order to explore specific business problems and the relevance of telematics in addressing these problems. This second stage was conducted by face-to-face interviews with business managers.

Businesses in both north Lancashire and south Warwickshire are predominantly privately owned, single-site, service sector operations, and are very small. The majority of responding businesses in each region have 10 or fewer employees. Only 5% have more than 50 (Table 1). Businesses involved in service sector activities account for 68% of the total sample, with those in distribution, hotel services, catering and repair forming the largest subgroup. Little difference is observed between the two regions. In terms of ownership, businesses in both regions are controlled predominantly by entrepreneurs who live and work in the areas. Although 39% of all businesses are part of a group, the majority of these groups are locally based

(Clark *et al.*, 1995). However, here the similarities end. Distinct differences between the two regions are observed in respect of customer/supplier networks, and in particular, the awareness and use of information and communication technologies.

Most businesses sell their products and services to other businesses, although there is a degree of difference between the two regions (Table 2). In north Lancashire 67% of businesses sell to other businesses, whilst 31% deal exclusively with the general public. In contrast, only 17% of south Warwickshire businesses serve the general public exclusively. Customer/supplier networks are extensive in both areas, but they are larger in the case of south Warwickshire. Very few businesses (10%) in either region maintain networks via advanced telematic applications. However, the vast majority of those that do are businesses in south Warwickshire.

The survey provided data on the ownership of information technology and telecommunications equipment (Table 3). All businesses in both regions are on the telephone. However, beyond this basic equipment significant differences are apparent with south Warwickshire businesses being more receptive to technology than their north Lancashire counterparts. The table reveals low levels of uptake of all other information technology and telecommunications equipment. Many businesses do not have a fax machine (43% in the 'remote rural' north Lancashire, compared with 26% in the 'accessible rural' south Warwickshire). Similarly, only 40% of the north Lancashire companies use an ansaphone, compared with 54% of those in south Warwickshire. Despite the apparent value to small businesses in using messaging

Rural Planning and Management

Nigel Berkeley *et al.*

Table 3. Business use of information and communication technologies by region

Equipment	% of companies	
	North Lancashire	South Warwickshire
Telephone	99	99
Telex	3	5
Fax	57	74
Ansaphone	41	54
Portable Phone	37	47
Personal Computer	38	57
Mainframe	26	36
Modem	13	23

Table 4. Business use of advanced telematics services by region

Service	% of companies			
	North Lancashire		South Warwickshire	
	Aware of	Using	Aware of	Using
Teleconferencing	44	3	50	6
Teleworking	38	3	45	6
Electronic mail	42	5	49	9
Electronic data interchange	37	7	39	11
Teletext/videotext	36	3	45	2
Electronic funds transfer	41	4	47	10

services, the levels of uptake, particularly in north Lancashire, are low. The opportunities afforded by portable phones would also appear to be under-utilized, especially in the case of north Lancashire businesses.

Equally surprising for a survey conducted in 1993 is the under-use of computers by businesses in the sample. However, there are distinct differences between the two regions. Only 57% of businesses in south Warwickshire have a personal computer, but this figure falls to an even lower 37% in north Lancashire. By way of comparison, a survey of 100 'predominantly small firms' in Manchester showed that 80% of firms used a personal computer (Gibbs and Leach, 1994). Similarly, 36% of the south Warwickshire businesses use a mainframe system (a computer network), compared with only 26% of those in north Lancashire. Very few companies have a modem, an essential device for linking information and communication technology together. Again, the majority of those that do (70%) are in south Warwickshire. The speed at which firms in both regions, but particularly those in north Lancashire, have adopted the basic telecommunications and information technology does not bode well for the adoption of more advanced telematic services. It would

appear that only a dramatic change in culture will alter this position.

The differences between the two regions in the adoption of basic telecommunications and IT infrastructure are compounded when examining the uses that businesses make of their computing equipment. For example, the use of computing technology for functions more advanced than word-processing is significantly higher amongst Warwickshire businesses, especially in the case of financial management/bookkeeping, purchasing and stock control.

The survey also provided data on the awareness and use of a series of more advanced telematics services (Table 4). These are: teleconferencing, teleworking, electronic mail, electronic data interchange, teletext/videotext and electronic funds transfer. Generally, the findings indicate a lack of awareness and use in both regions. However, as with the more basic information technology and telecommunications equipment, south Warwickshire businesses appear to be more receptive. In the north Lancashire study area, for example, teleconferencing is the most commonly reported application, but less than half of businesses are 'aware' of it. Levels of awareness are higher in south Warwickshire, reaching 50% for teleconferencing. The actual use of the more advanced telematics applications is minimal. Some 80% of businesses in the total sample use none of these advanced telematics services. Significantly, of the 171 businesses that do, 69% are south Warwickshire-based. Only 14% of the north Lancashire businesses use one or more of the listed applications, compared with 22% in south Warwickshire. In both regions less than 10% of businesses are using electronic mail. This compares with a figure of 24% for businesses in the Manchester survey (Gibbs and Leach, 1994). In north Lancashire and south Warwickshire the most commonly used application is electronic data interchange.

Explaining the Key Findings

The survey has identified the principal characteristics of business telematics use in two contrasting rural regions of the U.K. Two distinct features can be observed. First, the overall take-up of equipment and services, both basic and advanced, is low; and second, it is especially low in the north Lancashire region, compared with the south Warwickshire region. The objective of this section is to try to explain these patterns. A number of possible reasons are suggested. These include: infrastructure, business size, investment costs, sectoral differences, awareness, training, and business culture.

It has been argued elsewhere that infrastructural difficulties in the U.K. can no longer be used to explain differences in the diffusion of new technology between regions. For example, Grimes (1992, p. 276) states "the problem for diffusing IT is now seen more in terms of inadequate demand for services in lagging areas, rather than any significant deficiency in infrastructure". However, the timelags observed in rural and peripheral areas must have an effect on awareness and uptake of information and communication technologies. By the end of the 1980s, 40% of local telephone exchanges, and predominantly those in rural and peripheral areas, were still based on analogue switching rather than the digital system associated with ISDN (Graham, 1992). Countrywide coverage of ISDN did not occur until the end of 1994.

Goddard and Gillespie (1986) suggest that take-up and use of information and communication technologies are strongly related to business size. This is confirmed by the survey findings. For example, some

91% of those businesses without a facsimile have ten or fewer employees. A minimum number of these micro-enterprises are telematics users (only 10% in north Lancashire and 16% in Warwickshire). By contrast, for those companies employing 26 or more employees the percentage of telematics users is much higher (40% in north Lancashire and 47% in south Warwickshire). The proliferation of micro-enterprises in the sample helps to explain the low take-up rates overall, but it does not account for the regional disparities. The earlier description of business characteristics indicated that the size structure of companies within the sample is almost identical. Moreover, evidence from Goddard and Gillespie's survey work (1986) showed that small businesses in the U.K. core region (the South East) took advantage of new technology much faster than small businesses in the peripheral Northern Region.

A further reason for low adoption rates of information and communication technologies could be the cost of the technology involved (Clark *et al.*, 1995). This was confirmed in the SARBA research in a series of face-to-face 'intensive' interviews with employers in the two regions. Many businesses who have not invested in telematics technology expressed concerns about cost. Comments such as "computer equipment is too expensive" were commonplace. Again, cost would certainly help to explain the low take-up rates in general, but not the spatial contrasts. Evidence from the SARBA research would suggest that many companies are put off by the initial short-term implications without being sufficiently aware of, or convinced by, the longer-term benefits. Companies in north Lancashire are particularly sceptical about computer technology with a number of entrepreneurs expressing a degree of 'techno-fear'. In addition, many companies had been put off by the complexity of the technology, as well as being sold systems that did not live up to expectations. These latter issues were also observed in the Manchester survey (Gibbs and Leach, 1994).

The differences between the two regions in the take-up of information technology and telecommunications equipment might be explained by the sectoral distribution of companies. It is contended, for example, that "information-intensive activities such as the financial services sector are major users of networks" (Grimes, 1992, p. 270). Proportionally, there are many more companies in this sector in south Warwickshire than in north Lancashire (24% compared with 12%). However, evidence of the use of advanced telematics services adds little weight to this argument. Only 12% of advanced telematics users in Lancashire are companies within this sector, compared with 27% in south Warwickshire. Moreover, only 13% of financial service sector companies in north Lancashire are users of these advanced services. The figure for south Warwickshire is 24%.

It can also be argued that low take-up rates for telematics services in peripheral areas can be partly attributed to a problem of awareness (Grimes, 1992). Findings from the SARBA project again support this view, indicating that awareness levels of advanced telematics services in general are low, with no more than 50% of businesses being aware of any of the specified services. Moreover, additional findings suggest that very few companies are aware of the benefits that telematics can bring to the company in terms of improved competitiveness. Again, more south Warwickshire companies than north Lancashire companies see the benefits (29% compared with 24%). Additionally, companies are, on the whole, sceptical about the relevance of telematics to their business, suggesting a cultural barrier to the adoption of new technology. Part of the problem could relate to training. The survey data indicate that formal training received by technology users is minimal. There is a reliance on self-teaching, which could mean that companies are not making the best use of their equipment. They are probably unaware of its potential. The lack of faith in formal training was often put down to cost and the issue of relevance. Many companies in the SARBA survey complained that training courses are far too expensive and too detached from the real needs of the business. However, the reluctance to invest in training creates skill barriers where companies will be left behind by those who are prepared to invest. From an organizational point of view, many rural SMEs are simply too small to employ specialists who can fully exploit the technology available and to afford the initial investment and subsequent training. It is possible that the technology is simply beyond the realms and needs of many rural SMEs.

It would appear from the survey findings that the north Lancashire rural economy is much more 'closed' than that of south Warwickshire. This, it is argued, is one of the principal reasons behind the observed differences between the two regions. On the surface, businesses in the two regions display very

similar characteristics. They are predominantly small, privately owned, service sector operations with a wide network of customers and suppliers. However, more detailed investigation during face-to-face interviews with 60 companies in each region revealed important differences. For example, the business customers of firms in south Warwickshire are much more geographically dispersed than those in north Lancashire. Many more south Warwickshire firms serve national and international markets than do firms in north Lancashire. Similarly, north Lancashire businesses rely much more heavily on local suppliers than their counterparts in south Warwickshire. By way of comparison, Goddard and Gillespie (1986, p. 392), commenting on the lower levels of Prestel penetration in the Northern Region of England in the mid 1980s, suggested that "businesses in the Northern Region are more locally oriented—they do not perceive themselves as operating, nor do they in fact do so in national and international markets". This can be viewed as a problem of business culture.

By operating in a more closed environment, businesses in the north Lancashire region are less likely to deal with multinational enterprises within their customer/supplier networks. These larger companies are more likely to be users of the new technologies and may demand communication via telematics or, by using the services themselves, they may encourage other smaller firms in the network to do so. The south Warwickshire region clearly benefits in this respect from its centrality within the U.K., close to major urban areas. Multinational companies are more attracted to the region because of the combined advantages of rurality, accessibility and proximity to the core.

The explanatory analysis suggests that the low uptake of information and communication technologies is a function of a combination of factors, including infrastructure, business size, the cost and complexity of the technology, awareness and training. The differences observed between the two regions reflect the nature of the two rural economies, particularly the cultural characteristics of businesses. It should be emphasized that such analysis provides a broad overview of factors that have influenced the observed trends. At the level of the individual firm different structures and processes will affect the extent to which new information and communication technologies are adopted. This was revealed during the 'intensive' phase of this research where individual comments included "we are too small a business striving to keep going in a recession to think about such things (telematics)", "we have a computer, but we are not using it anywhere near enough. I am not sure how to get better use out of it", and "I am not convinced that information technology would save us time and money".

Policy Issues

The findings presented in this paper suggest that technology-intensive policies for rural development need to raise the levels of telematics uptake generally, as well as address the problems and potentials that exist in different localities. It is argued here that the most important barrier to overcome is one of awareness, the need to create an environment where companies not only know what telematics services are available but are also aware of the benefits such services can bring. The findings support the view of Gibbs and Leach (1994) that awareness building should be a 'key component of any telematics policy'. In essence, there is a need to engender a technology culture amongst rural SMEs.

Telecottages provide one mechanism to improve awareness, foster a technology culture and stimulate uptake of telematics in rural areas (Grimes, 1992; Gillespie *et al.*, 1991). Examples of experiments where telecottages have succeeded in raising rates of awareness and uptake stand out in several Scandinavian countries (Qvortrup, 1989). Also, in Scotland the Community Teleservice Centres (CTCs) launched as pilot projects in the Highlands and Islands in the early 1990s have "generally succeeded in raising awareness of computer-based and telecom activities, skills and opportunities amongst businesses" (Bryden *et al.*, 1993, p. 26). In mid-Wales a network of Business Service Centres has been established in which basic facilities are available for SMEs, including telematics advice. In Manchester Electronic Village Halls (EVHs) are being developed to give access, raise awareness and provide training in telematics (Gibbs and Leach, 1994). How are such developments funded? In Scotland the pilot CTCs were financed primarily through Highlands and Islands Enterprise, which contributed 66%, and partly through British Telecom. In Manchester the EVHs form a small part of an overall telecoms strategy (the HOST project), which also relies on a combination of public and private funds (the Urban

Programme, British Telecom and European sources). The Scandinavian telecottages are also publicly funded.

These type of developments provide a range of basic information technology and telecommunication equipment on-site. In this way they can significantly reduce the cost barrier that inhibits so many enterprises from being integrated into the information economy. Moreover, by providing on-site training facilities and specialist IT consultants, they help to raise skill levels and overcome barriers to training (Grimes, 1992). By raising skill levels, it follows that users become more aware of the potential benefits of telematics systems such that they may be prepared to invest in their own equipment. Telecottages (EVHs/ CTCs, etc), by providing an environment that can demonstrate the relevance of information technology and telecommunications systems to the users' own requirements, make the transition from awareness to adoption much easier (Goddard and Gillespie, 1986). The key advantage of such developments is that they help to create an environment that is conducive to the uptake and use of technology. However, several difficulties can be noted. In geographically diverse rural regions there needs to be a number of centres to provide access to all potential users. Given the level of public investment required to set up a telecottage, this can be problematical. In mid-Wales, eight Business Service Centres have been established, whilst the pilot CTCs in Scotland involve six centres. Inevitably, not all businesses will have equal access, and this may deter many potential users. Secondly, a strongly proactive approach is required in order to overcome techno-phobia among potential users. If businesses are not convinced of the opportunities afforded by telematics, they may not be willing to spend valuable time at a telecottage.

The research endorses the establishment of locally oriented IT networks as another important strand of policy. The value of such networks that presently exist suggests that their extension to include local authorities, businesses and educational institutions would lead to "more efficient linkages within the local economy and more efficient distribution of information flows and services" (Graham, 1992, p. 765). Moreover, networking enables benefits to be derived from the 'competence embedded in other firms' by creating information channels that encourage inter-firm cooperation in key areas such as marketing and can significantly reduce transaction costs and ultimately improve efficiency and market competitiveness (Grimes, 1992). It is possible that local authorities could take the lead and adapt their own networks to provide the necessary telecommunications infrastructure (Moss, 1987; Graham, 1991).

One difficulty with the establishment of computer networks is that, in order to be viable, they need quickly to attract a 'critical mass' of subscribers. The smaller the network in terms of users, the more difficult it is to convince potential users that it is worth their while joining. However, evidence from the U.S.A. suggests that once the critical mass has been achieved networks can grow very quickly (Gibbs and Leach, 1994). Other difficulties will inevitably include resources; the availability of expertise; and, perhaps most of all, the lack of a culture of cooperation rather than competition between organizations (Graham, 1992).

As the development of telematics infrastructure and services through the 'free market' tends to favour large multi-site firms in core areas, policy-makers have increasingly developed local strategies designed to cater for the needs of SMEs and other disadvantaged groups (Graham, 1991). Such intervention is necessary if SMEs, an integral part of a local economy, are to become more competitive and take advantage of the opportunities afforded by the Single European Market. To appeal to the SME community, it is important that such strategies are accessible, available at low cost and use familiar technology (Gibbs and Leach, 1994). The Manchester HOST project, although urban, provides a good example.

The Manchester HOST is the U.K.'s first local-authority-controlled, citywide telematics network. It utilizes the PSTN to provide a range of applications and services aimed especially at disadvantaged groups such as SMEs, women and ethnic minorities. Registered users only need have a PC, a modem and a telephone line to access the service. The HOST services include electronic mail, fax and telex facilities, and gateways to databases. Monthly costs to users are estimated at £20–£25 per month. It is anticipated that benefits of the system will be fourfold: the enhancement of the city's IT culture; improved economic prospects for the city as a whole; the awareness and benefits of telematics exposed to a greater cross-section of the city; and the improved delivery of council services. Electronic Village Halls will be linked to the host to provide IT services and especially training to disadvantaged groups (see Graham, 1992). Other well documented citywide initiatives include the Edinburgh 'Teleport' aimed at combating the city's peripherality, as well as encouraging local SMEs to compete in global markets, and the Sheffield 2000 Information Group Network aimed at coordinating existing telematics services and infrastructures in the city (Graham, 1991).

This review of policy initiatives provides useful guidance for strategy development for areas in rural England. It is argued that three main elements need to be addressed if rural areas are fully to exploit telematics: first, awareness raising; second, building a cooperative spirit between SMEs to promote a networking culture; and third, providing the infrastructure and services that will be cheap, relevant and easy to use. In addition, locally tailored strategies are required to take account of differences in awareness, uptake and use (Gillespie, 1987). It should also be emphasized that telematics might not be relevant to all businesses. As Graham (1991, p. 126) states "it is vital not to use the technology for its own sake", whilst research by Sociomics/Arkleton Trust (Research) Ltd (1993) argues that digital-based telephony and related telephone and fax services, cellular mobile and paging services, and possibly ISDN are quite sufficient for the needs of most rural businesses.

Awareness-raising is an immediate priority for policy-makers in 'remote rural' areas such as north Lancashire, where levels of awareness and uptake of information and communication technologies are very low. The development of telecottages/electronic village halls could be considered as a way of achieving this goal. In the short term, proactive measures will be necessary. Visits to companies will be required so as to make enterprises aware of the ways in which telematics might help their business. Promotional campaigns through the local media would also help. As awareness and usage levels increase, policy-makers can then turn their attention to developing a networking culture through telematics.

The greater levels of awareness and use of telematics in 'accessible rural' areas such as south Warwickshire mean that different policies are required. Emphasis can be placed upon measures to encourage businesses to exploit more fully the potentials of telematics. Scope exists to build upon the established culture of networking in the region so as to widen access to markets and suppliers and, as a result, to increase

Business use of information technology 85

levels of interdependency among firms and thus integrate and stabilize the local economy. There is an important role here for agencies such as the Warwickshire Rural Enterprise Network in terms of establishing demand, formulating user requirements and developing local links. Such initiatives are likely to be highly sector-specific (Goddard and Gillespie, 1986) but as they develop could have significant trickledown effects on other sectors. It is also important (as in the Manchester example) that organizations such as TECs, schools and colleges become involved in providing general training.

Having raised awareness and developed a telematics networking culture, the demand for telematics services should increase. It is important then that businesses have the access to the appropriate infrastructure and technology to meet their needs. The development of the Manchester HOST showed what can be achieved with a mixture of public and private funds. Clearly, however, small rural authorities will not have the resources to develop such a system. One way forward is for the Manchester-type systems developed in urban areas to be used as the 'anonymous mother' for smaller applications in rural areas (Graham, 1991). As such, rural areas can benefit by having access to the services without having to develop a full-blown system. This again requires that barriers of competition are overcome, not only between firms, but also between local authorities and between regions.

Conclusion

This paper has demonstrated that significant disparities exist in the uptake and use of new technologies between rural areas in England, particularly in respect of the more advanced telematics services. A number of factors are responsible, including: infrastructure, investment costs, business size, sectoral distribution, awareness and training. It is suggested that business culture, particularly the way in which rural SMEs integrate with other firms outside the local area, is a major explanation of the observed differences in uptake of new technologies between the two regions. The findings indicate a need for local policy intervention, a bottom-up approach that needs to raise usage levels generally and exploit the specific potentials of telematics that exist in individual local areas.

Acknowledgements—The authors gratefully acknowledge the helpful comments of two anonymous referees and the financial support of the European Commission for the SARBA project. However, the views expressed in the article are those of the authors themselves.

References

Bryden, J., Black, S. and Rennie, F. (1993) *Final Report on the Evaluation of Community Teleservice Centres in the Highlands and Islands.* Arkelton Trust (Research) Ltd, Oxford.

Capello, R. and Nijkamp, P. (1994) Borders and barriers in telecommunications systems, In: *New Borders and Old Barriers in Spatial Development*, pp. 209–227, P. Nijkamp (Ed.). Avebury, Aldershot.

Clark, D. (1979) The spatial impact of telecommunication, *DoE Research Report* 24. HMSO, London.

Clark, D., Ilbery, B. and Berkeley, N. (1995) Telematics and rural businesses: an evaluation of uses, potentials and requirements, *Regional Studies*, 29, 171–180.

Commission for the European Communities (1988) *The Future of Rural Society,* Supplement 4/88. Office for Official Publications of the European Communities, Luxembourg.

Dabinett, G. and Graham, S. (1994) Telematics and industrial change in Sheffield, UK, *Regional Studies*, 28, 605–617.

Driver, S. and Gillespie, A. E. (1993) Information and communication technologies and the geography of magazine print publishing, *Regional Studies*, 27, 53–64.

Giaoutzi, M. and Nijkamp, P. (1988) *Informatics and Regional Development*. Avebury, Aldershot.

Gibbs, D. and Leach, B. (1994) Telematics in local economic development: the case of Manchester, *Tijdschrift voor Economische en Sociale Geografie*, 85, 209–223.

Gillespie, A. E. (1987) Telecommunications and the development of Europe's less favoured regions, *Geoforum*, 18, 229–236.

Gillespie, A. E. and Williams, H. (1988) Telecommunications and the reconstruction of regional comparative advantage, *Environment and Planning A*, 20, 1311–1321.

Gillespie, A. E. and Robins, K. (1989) Geographical inequalities: the spatial bias of the new information technologies, *Journal of Communication*, 39, 7–18.

Gillespie, A. E., Coombes, M., Raybould, S. and Bradley, D. (1991) *Telecommunications and the Development of Rural Scotland*. A study for Scottish Enterprise by the Centre for Urban and Regional Development Studies, Newcastle-upon-Tyne.

Goddard, J. B. and Gillespie, A. E. (1986) Advanced telecommunications and regional economic development, *Geographical Journal*, 152, 383–397.

Graham, S. (1991) Telecommunications and the local economy: some emerging policy issues, *Local Economy*, 6, 116–136.

Graham, S. (1992) Electronic infrastructures and the city: some emerging municipal policy roles in the UK, *Urban Studies*, 29, 755–781.

Grimes, S. (1992) Exploiting information and communication technologies for rural development, *Journal of Rural Studies*, **8**, 269–278.

Hepworth, M. E. (1987) Information technology as spatial systems, *Progress in Human Geography*, **11**, 157–180.

Hepworth, M. E. (1989) *Geography of the Information Economy*. Belhaven, London.

Hepworth, M. E., Green, A. E. and Gillespie, A. E. (1987) The spatial division of information labour in Great Britain, *Environment and Planning A*, **19**, 793–806.

Ilbery, B., Clark, D., Berkeley, N. and Goldman, I. (1995) Telematics and rural development: evidence from a survey of small businesses in the European Union, *European Urban and Regional Studies*, **2**, 55–68.

Keeble, D., Tyler, P., Broom, G. and Lewis, J. (1992) *Business Success in the Countryside: The Performance of Rural Enterprise*. Department of the Environment, HMSO, London.

Morgan, K. (1990) Shaping the infrastructure: large firms, advanced networks and the dilemmas of freedom. Paper presented at the ESRC Programme on Information and Communications Technology Infrastructure Conference, 1–2 March, Cambridge.

Moss, M. (1987) Telecommunications, world cities and urban policy, *Urban Studies*, **24**, 534–546.

Parker, E. B., Hudson, H. E., Dillman, D. A. and Roscoe, A. D. (1989) *Rural America in the Information Age: Telecommunications Policy for Rural Development*. University Press of America, Lanham, Maryland.

Qvortrup, L. (1989) The Nordic telecottages, *Telecommunications Policy*, **March**, 59–68.

Robins, K. and Hepworth, M. (1988) Electronic spaces: new technologies and the future of cities, *Futures*, **April**, 155–175.

Rural Development Commission (1989) *Telecommunications in Rural England*. Rural Development Commission, London.

Schmandt, J., Williams, F., Wilson, R. H. and Storer, S. (1991) *Telecommunications and Rural Development*. Praeger, New York.

Sociomics/Arkleton Trust (Research) Ltd (1993) *Employment Trends Related to the Use of Advanced Communications*. Report to the Commission of the European Communities, DGX111.B. Office for Official Publications of the European Communities, Luxembourg.

[31]

Pergamon

Journal of Rural Studies, Vol. 12, No. 3, pp. 231–244, 1996
Copyright © 1996 Elsevier Science Ltd
Printed in Great Britain. All rights reserved
0743-0167/96 $15.00 + 0.00

S0743-0167(96)00025-3

Local Purchasing Schemes and Rural Development: an Evaluation of Local Exchange and Trading Systems (LETS)

Colin C. Williams

Centre for Urban Development and Environmental Management (CUDEM),
Leeds Metropolitan University, Brunswick Building, Leeds LS2 8BU, U.K.

Abstract — Through a critical review of economic base theory, this paper argues that the ability to prevent income leaking out of an area is as important to rural development as the capacity to generate external income. The problem at present, however, is that few effective policy instruments exist to thwart such seepage. Here, therefore, an innovative approach to facilitate local purchasing amongst rural dwellers is evaluated: Local Exchange and Trading Systems (LETS). Reporting empirical evidence from both a national survey of United Kingdom LETS and a membership survey of Totnes LETS in Devon, this paper finds that LETS are rapidly growing in rural areas and are not only encouraging local purchasing but are also rebuilding local social networks and enabling some of those marginalised from employment to gain access to work and credit. As such, they amalgamate both economic and community development. To further improve their effectiveness, several barriers to their development are identified and solutions offered to how these may be overcome. Copyright © 1996 Elsevier Science Ltd

Introduction

The aim of this paper is to critically review the importance of local purchasing for rural development and to evaluate an innovative means by which this might be achieved: Local Exchange and Trading Systems (LETS). LETS are local associations whose members list their offers of, and requests for, goods and services in a directory, and then exchange them priced in a local unit of exchange (e.g. acorns in Totnes, favours in Calderdale). To maintain a record of the exchanges, cheques written in the local currency are sent to a treasurer who functions in a similar manner to a normal bank, sending out regular statements of account to the members. No notes or coins are issued and neither is any interest charged or paid. As such, the local currency functions as a 'scoring system', much like matchsticks in baby-sitting circles. It has no 'value' outside of the local system. The local currency accumulated by members can only be used to buy other local goods and services offered on the system. LETS, more-

over, are a source of interest-free credit since members can spend local currency before earning it.

During the past decade, this new tool to aid local purchasing has rapidly spread throughout the rural areas of most English-speaking industrialised nations. By late 1994, Australia had 171 LETS, 59.6% of which were in rural areas, New Zealand had 54 systems, 40% of which were rural and the United Kingdom had 275 systems, of which 45.7% were in rural areas.* They are also now spreading to rural areas in other advanced economies including Denmark, Finland, France, Germany, The Netherlands, Norway, Spain and Sweden (LetsLink UK, 1994b).

The potential of this form of not-for-profit community enterprise has been quickly recognised by policy-makers. The U.K. government in their White Paper on rural development have advocated LETS as a way of 'encouraging local initiative and voluntary action' (DoE/MAFF, 1995, p. 17); 64% of U.K. local authorities have expressed an intention to develop LETS in their area (Gibbs *et al.*, 1995), and the Australian government have legitimised LETS by exempting local currency earnings from the means-test for benefits in the 1995 Social Security

---

*This data is derived from surveys of LETS in Australia and New Zealand conducted in 1995 by the author which are unpublished at the time of writing.

Rural Planning and Management

Colin C. Williams

Act. However, and despite this recognitiion of their potential in policy fora, there have been few empirical investigations of LETS.* This paper, therefore, attempts to fill this gap in the knowledge by evaluating the potential of LETS as a tool for promoting rural development.

First, therefore, this paper outlines the economic rationale for local purchasing. Through a critical review of economic base theory, the capacity to prevent income leaking out of an area will be shown to be as important to rural economic development as the ability to generate external income. This is then followed by an analysis of existing approaches for preventing the seepage of income out of rural areas. Highlighting that they are both undeveloped and ineffective, attention then turns towards evaluating the LETS approach to local purchasing. To do this, the paper reports the results of two surveys. On the one hand, a survey of LETS in the U.K. conducted by the author in April 1995 will evaluate the magnitude and character of LETS in rural areas. On the other hand, a membership survey of Totnes LETS in Devon undertaken by the author in February 1995, will be employed to evaluate the impacts of LETS schemes. The finding is that LETS are rapidly growing in rural areas and are not only encouraging people to engage in local purchasing, but are also rebuilding local social networks and helping some of those excluded from employment to gain access to work and credit. However, several barriers are identified which are constraining their effectiveness as tools for rural development. In a final section, therefore, these barriers are outlined and solutions offered to how these can be overcome.

The economic rationale for local purchasing

The orthodox approach to rural economic development is to increase the amount of external income flowing into a locality. The rationale for such a perception lies in 'economic base' theory (Glickman, 1977; Haggett *et al.*, 1977; Wilson, 1974). Assuming that an area needs to attract external income in order to grow, economic base theory divides any economy into two sectors: 'basic' industries which bring money into the economy from outside and are seen as the 'engines of growth', and 'dependent' industries which serve the local market and are perceived as 'parasitic' activities, contributing little if

anything to the economy since they merely circulate money within the local area (Kaldor, 1966).

Conventionally, so far as rural areas are concerned, primary and manufacturing sector firms have been regarded as basic industries whilst tertiary activities have been seen as dependent industries, reliant upon the primary and manufacturing sectors which attract external income (Clout, 1993; Redwood, 1988). However, over the past decade or so, this view of the service sector has been convincingly discredited. Rural producer services have been shown to export and are now widely accepted as 'basic' sector activities (Glasmeier and Borchard, 1989; Glasmeier and Howland, 1994; Polese, 1982; Smith, 1984; Smith and Pulver, 1981; Stabler, 1987; Stabler and Howe, 1988; 1993; Williams, 1994a; 1996a).

Furthermore, the basic sector of rural economies is now recognised to be composed not only of export industries, which include primary, manufacturing and a range of producer service activities which sell their products to customers outside the local area, but also those activities which induce external money into a locality, by drawing consumers into an area in order to spend their money (Farness, 1989; Williams, 1996a). Tourism is one such notable industry (Keane and Quinn, 1990; Nilsson, 1993). Another is the cultural industries sector (Williams *et al.*, 1995). Since each fulfils the same function of bringing external income into an area, both are accepted as basic activities.

However, this rethinking of the activities which contribute to rural development has not ended here. Recognising that economic growth is not so strongly correlated with external income generation as many previously assumed (Giarantani and McNelis, 1980; Mandelbaum and Chicoine, 1986; McNulty, 1977), the focus upon the basic sector alone in rural economic development has recently come under increasing scrutiny. It has been argued that what is needed for an economy to grow is not an increase in external income *per se* but, rather, a rise in net income. Net income, to explain, is determined by total external income, times a multiplier (which is larger the more self-reliant the economy), minus total external spending. The growth of any economy has thus been asserted to be dependent not only on attracting external income but also preventing the leakage of money out of the area (Persky *et al.*, 1993; Williams, 1994a; 1996a).

Accordingly, locally-orientated activities have been asserted to play an important additional role in encouraging economic growth in their role of preventing seepage of spending out of the local economy (Persky *et al.*, 1993; Williams, 1994a; 1996a).

---

* Notable exceptions include an analysis of LETS in southeast England in terms of their inclusivity and how they facilitate locally-defined systems of value-formation (Lee, 1996) and a case study of Calderdale LETS as a potential tool for informal economic development (Williams, 1996b).

This can be accomplished in two ways. First, locally-orientated activity can prevent money from draining out of the locality by supplying facilities which negate the need for the local population to travel outside the area to obtain a good or service. Second, locally-orientated activity can change the expenditure patterns of local businesses by raising the share of their expenditure spent in the locality.

The difficulty at present is that the positive role that locally-orientated activities play in economic growth as leakage preventers is frequently under-emphasised. As Persky *et al.* (1993) assert, most development agencies pursue export-led development policies by cultivating basic activities with little regard for the extent to which seepage of income is taking place. The consequence is that many rural economies leak like a sieve. Indeed, so rarely is this considered important that evidence on the extent to which rural economies leak is very rare. One exception is Polese (1982), who finds that over half of regional service demand in a rural area of Quebec is satisfied by imports.

Not only is there a lack of attention given to stemming the leakage of income out of rural localities, but there is also a shortage of effective policy instruments. On the one hand, and to encourage rural businesses to purchase local goods and services, import substitution policies can be pursued, for example by local sourcing campaigns which attempt to put local businesses in touch with each other, exemplified by the Better Made in Britain Bureau's Regional Audit of Industry (REGAIN) initiative. However, such initiatives have been largely unsuccessful because it is not solely a matter of imperfect information on the availability of local goods and services which prevents local purchasing. Businesses work within the constraints of the logic of the market where availability, quality and price are the major determinants of the suppliers used, none of which are addressed by current local sourcing initiatives (Williams, 1994b).

The principal method to encourage rural consumers to buy locally, on the other hand, has been the 'use it or lose it' approach, which has usually been applied to rural retail outlets. This method, however, suffers from several intransigent problems. First, the diversity of the goods and services available in rural areas is typically lower than in urban centres, so people still tend to go to urban areas to acquire them. Second, the costs of the goods and services are generally higher in rural areas, which reduces the tendency of rural people to buy goods and services locally. Consequently, when these problems of diversity and price are coupled with lifestyle

changes, such as greater car ownership, women's insertion into employment and heightened consumer demand for more sophisticated products, the result is that rural dwellers prefer to drive to an urban retail centre less frequently to choose from a wider range of goods where prices are lower (DoE/MAFF, 1995). Finally, even if people do buy locally, the businesses may often be owned externally and/or the goods and services sourced from external suppliers, so a share of the profits and income will quickly leak out of the area. It will not be re-circulated within the rural economy. The result is a low local multiplier effect within rural areas.

Given the lack of attention in conventional rural economic development efforts to stem the leakage of income from rural economies, and the shortage of effective policy instruments to remedy such seepage, attention turns towards evaluating an alternative means by which local purchasing might be facilitated.

LETS: a new approach to local purchasing

LETS, to repeat, are local associations whose members make offers of, and requests for, goods and services and then exchange them priced in local currency. In theory, this alternative means of enabling local purchasing overcomes many of the above problems with existing policy instruments. First, conventional approaches to local purchasing have low multiplier effects because, even if a person purchases locally, either the business is often externally owned so some of the money will leave the area, or the income will be used to purchase further inputs which are themselves produced outside of the area. In a LETS, however, the local currency can only be used to purchase further goods and services within the system. None of it can leave the locality nor can it be used to purchase goods and services outside of the area since it has no 'value' external to the local association. The effect is that it creates a 'closed system' so that none of the local money leaks out of the area (Davis and Davis, 1987).

The second problem with the above approaches to local purchasing is that the price of goods and services are often higher in rural areas, which reduces the tendency to buy locally. Those involved with LETS development, in contrast, frequently claim that such a situation does not occur on LETS. In this parallel economic system, if the costs of local goods and services are higher, so too will be the price which a person receives for their goods and services. Moreover, it is claimed that goods and services are differently priced according to the financial circumstances of the purchaser (Lang,

1994). LETS, therefore, are asserted not to suffer from the problem of conventional buy local campaigns that the prices will necessarily be higher.

A third and final problem with local purchasing is that the range of goods and services is less in rural areas than in their urban counterparts. This 'push' factor discourages local purchasing, and when combined with 'pull' factors in the form of the lifestyle changes documented above, leads rural dwellers to purchase goods and services outside of their locality. LETS, however, operating as a parallel economic system, are asserted to increase the range of goods and services available to people within their locality, which increases their opportunity to choose to buy locally (Davis and Davis, 1987).

Consequently, LETS have been widely advocated as a means by which local purchasing can be encouraged (Croft, 1995; Dobson, 1993; Greco, 1994; Lang, 1994; Offe and Heinze, 1992; Seyfang, 1994; Williams, 1996b). However, LETS are not only considered an economic tool. They are also viewed as a vehicle for community-building. Recognising that 'community' needs to be actively created and reproduced (Bauman, 1990; Bulmer, 1989; Crow and Allen, 1994) and that exchange is the principal mechanism in advanced societies through which social networks are developed and articulated, LETS are viewed as providing a formal structured framework within which social networks can develop through the medium of exchange (Brandt, 1995; Dobson, 1993; Greco, 1994; Seyfang, 1994; Williams, 1996b). As such, the LETS approach is seen to integrate the twin pillars of both economic and community development, which so often remain disparate activities in rural policy-making.

Whether LETS achieve this in practice is now considered. First, the national survey findings will document the nature and extent of LETS in U.K. rural areas and, second, an analysis will be undertaken of one particular rural LETS in Totnes to investigate its economic and community-building impacts.

LETS in U.K. rural areas

LETS are a recent phenomenon. Although the first U.K. LETS was formed in 1985 in Norfolk (Lee, 1996), it is only in the 1990s that the idea has begun to take-off. In early 1992, just five LETS were operating in the U.K. but there were 275 by December 1994 (LetsLink UK, 1994a) and 350 by June 1995 (LetsLink UK, 1995).

In April 1995, a postal questionnaire was sent to the 275 schemes listed in the December 1994 UK LETS directory (LetsLink UK, 1994a) in order to examine their magnitude and character: 90 responded (32.7%). Of the 81 useable responses, 37 defined themselves as located in rural areas (45.7%). Comparing these responses with those listed in the LETS directory, moreover, reveals that they are representative of not only the urban/rural distribution of LETS but also their regional distribution. Little, if any, bias in the response rate occurred. Examining these returns, therefore, LETS are revealed to have commenced in rural areas and then quickly spread to towns and villages and only then, cities (see Table 1). Indeed, LETS remain a strongly rural phenomenon. Hence, the popular prejudice which often assigns cities with a hegemonic status as the birthplace of innovations is not applicable to LETS.

Examining why these rural LETS were formed, 86.9% cite the economic reason of seeking greater local economic self-reliance in their rationale, 56.5% a community-building motivation and 26.1% a social equity rationale of enabling the poorer groups in rural society to get by, thus reinforcing the above assertion that they are seen as vehicles for both economic and community development.

Rural LETS in the U.K. have an average of 73.0

Table 1. Year LETS established: by geographical area covered

	Whole city	Whole town	Neighbourhood	Rural area
1995	–	2	1	4
1994	2	9	4	12
1993	4	9	3	11
1992	3	2	2	1
1991	–	2	1	2
pre-1991	–	–	–	2
% of LETS	11.1	29.6	13.6	45.7
% of all members	22.6	25.8	11.7	39.9

Source: author's survey.

Local Purchasing Schemes and Rural Development   235

Table 2. Turnover of rural LETS: by year established and membership size

	% of rural LETS	Average no. of members	Average turnover (£)	Average turnover/ member (£)
Year established				
1995	13.8	28.0	4	0.14
1994	41.4	69.1	4057	58.71
1993	31.0	54.9	3955	72.04
pre-1993	13.8	159.0	17,000	106.92
No. of members				
Under 50	46.4	31.0	1119.40	36.11
50–99	39.3	74.1	2613.33	35.27
100–199	7.1	103.0	9500.00	92.23
Over 200	7.1	209.5	20,000.00	95.46
All rural LETS	100.0	73.0	5526	75.70

Source: author's survey.

members (compared with 85.6 for all U.K. LETS) and a mean annual turnover of £5526 (£6006 nationally), giving an average annual level of trade per member of £75.70 (£70.16 nationally), assuming parity between the local and national currency.* Rural LETS, therefore, have a lower turnover and membership level than LETS nationally but a higher level of trade per member. Assuming that these responses are representative, then the 160 rural LETS in the U.K. will have a membership of about 11,700 (0.1% of the rural population) and a total turnover of just over £0.88 million.

There are major variations, nevertheless, in the size of rural LETS. Older ones tend to have higher memberships, turnovers and average trading levels per member (see Table 2). Moreover, the larger the number of members, the higher is the turnover and the levels of trade per member. This is a direct reflection of the time that they have had to establish themselves. The implication is that as rural LETS mature, the level of local purchasing that they facilitate will rise.

Indeed, given that 86.2% of all rural LETS are

* Lang (1994) asserts that only 65% of LETS are calibrated to sterling. This later survey finds that over 96% of LETS responding tie their local currency to sterling. This may be because many recently created LETS are calibrated to sterling. Informal feedback from non-respondents, however, suggests that it is also because parts of the questionnaire (e.g. on turnover) seemed inappropriate to LETS using time-based accounting, causing a low response rate from such systems. Future research will thus need to monitor carefully whether LETS are calibrated to sterling and be more open to the various ways in which work and credit are valued. The vast majority of respondents to this survey, nevertheless, embrace parity between the local currency and sterling, adopting a 1:1 ratio, whilst those with different ratios have been converted to sterling equivalents when evaluating trading levels.

growing, with just 10.3% in a stable state and 3.4% contracting, LETS look set to increase the level of local purchasing yet further in the immediate future. Those contracting are those which have failed to achieve what appears to be a 'critical mass' of 50 members, which is required for offers and requests to correspond and for people to gain confidence in the LETS. Those with larger memberships, meanwhile, display relatively high and expanding turnovers since the range and spatial density of goods and services available broadens and deepens as membership levels rise, enabling members' offers and requests to be more easily matched.

Indeed, the geographical dispersion of the members does influence the effectiveness of rural LETS. Rural LETS based on a village, for example, have an average annual level of trade per member equivalent to £79.80 whilst this is £58.70 in LETS with more spatially diffused memberships covering a broad rural area. This is because much of the trade on LETS is in consumer services which conventionally tend to be purchased in close proximity to the home (e.g. baby-sitting). The implication, therefore, is that rural areas with dispersed populations, rural dwellers in remote locations and those without access to a car may all be relatively disadvantaged when seeking to trade on LETS.

Who, however, participates in rural LETS? To understand this, what is first required is an anlysis of the ways in which they advertise themselves. Although no rural LETS claim that specific groups are explicitly targeted, there is evidence of much unintentional targeting. At their outset, the vast majority adopt a strategy of pursuing the line of least resistance in their membership drives. This consists of aiming their publicity at groups likely to be interested in the idea, especially environmental groups. Following this, most groups then rely on 'word-of-mouth' as the main means of diffusing the concept.

As LETS do not record any details of their membership beyond their name, address and level of trading, it is difficult to construct any picture of their membership profiles. However, as LETS are entities where people have relatively good knowledge of each others' circumstances, this survey asked LETS coordinators to make personal estimates of their membership profile. Of course, the legitimacy of such data is open to question. However, it is the only information currently available. As Table 3 displays, 76.9% of members in rural LETS were defined as 'greens' by the coordinators and there were relatively high estimated proportions of women (58.2% of members), incomers (44.4%) and the unemployed (20.4%). These latter groups probably all join LETS for similar reasons. For incomers, the LETS represents a means of bolstering their social networks and integrating into a community. Equally, for women, on whose shoulders the burden for forging social networks often lie, and whose unpaid work is often unrewarded and undervalued in the conventional economy, LETS provide a framework for attaching greater value to their work and for developing social networks. For the unemployed, meanwhile, LETS provide not only a vehicle by which they can engage in productive activity in order to demonstrate their worth through meaningful activity and boost their self-esteem, but also a tool for increasing their sources of aid. This is because social networks tend to swiftly deplete following redundancy (Dawes, 1993; Griffin *et al.*,

1992; Morris, 1993) and frequently, the unemployed tend only to mix with other unemployed (Morris, 1994; 1995).

There is evidence, however, of some significant differences in the composition of rural LETS (see Table 3). Those more recently formed are less dominated by greens and incomers and increasing numbers of the unemployed and women have joined them compared to older systems. This is perhaps because as LETS have spread, and have been the subject of widespread media attention, a wider range of people, especially those marginalised from employment, have started to see the benefits of such schemes to their lives and have thus joined in greater numbers. Earlier LETS, however, have remained a relatively exclusive club for a certain type of 'alternative' person (Lee, 1996) and have found it difficult to shake off that image and become more inclusive.

Membership of LETS, nevertheless, is not only confined to individual members. Recently, there has been a concerted effort to encourage formal sector businesses to join. As a consequence, just under 2% of the membership of rural LETS are now formal sector businesses. Indeed, rural LETS have an average of 1.36 businesses (see Table 4). Larger rural LETS, moreover, have relatively more business members than smaller LETS. This is an iterative process in the sense that larger memberships attract businesses, and vice versa. On the whole, these businesses are consumer services, such as clothes shops, food stalls, greengrocers and restaurants and cafes. To a lesser extent, they are producer services and mixed producer/consumer

Table 3. Membership profile of rural LETS: coordinators' estimates

Year established	% of membership who are:			
	Women	Unemployed	Incomers	Greens
1995	62.0	30.0	23.0	66.3
1994	59.2	29.0	23.4	76.8
1993	56.2	10.5	43.1	75.6
pre-1993	55.3	8.3	50.0	91.3
All	58.2	20.4	44.4	76.9

Source: author's survey.

Table 4. Business membership of rural LETS

No. of businesses	% of rural LETS	Average no. of members	Average turnover	Average turnover/ member
0–2	24	48.8	491.12	10.06
3–4	7	80.8	5766.28	71.36
5+	6	123.0	12,874.99	104.67

Source: author's survey.

services, such as solicitors, advertising agencies and printing firms.

Having provided this overview of the growth, magnitude and character of rural LETS in the U.K., attention now turns towards an evaluation of their economic and community-building impacts.

A case study of Totnes LETS

Totnes, a small town in Devon with 4257 inhabitants located between the Dartmoor National Park and the tourist coastal area of Torbay, has recently been referred to as 'a town with an uncanny attraction for New Seekers' (Margolis, 1995, p. 8). So, although the geography of the 'alternative/green culture' has yet to be written, Totnes may well be considered one of its centres. It is the home of 'Green Books', a rapidly expanding publishing house, and the Schumacher College, one of the principal institutions internationally for the teaching of 'green' philosophy.

Given that a great many LETS members are greens/alternatives, it is unsurprising to find that Totnes is the largest rural LETS in the country. It is also relatively mature. Totnes LETS was formed in October 1991 by eight people of mixed gender and ages. This larger, mature LETS was thus chosen for analysis as indicative of the tentative potential impacts of other rural LETS as they mature and grow. In February 1995, a postal questionnaire was sent to all 250 members of Totnes LETS: 63 responded (25.2%). Moreover, and as will be shown below, these respondents are representative of the membership, at least in terms of the level of trading undertaken, which is the sole indicator available with which to assess their representativeness, since records are not kept on any other details in this or any other LETS.

To examine the nature and extent of this local purchasing system, the survey results are here analyzed in terms of who belongs to this LETS, the magnitude and nature of the goods and services purchased, who does the work and what they charge, and members' views on its impact on their quality of life.

---

* It should be noted that Totnes LETS has a relatively high proportion of women members compared with the national average according to LETS coordinators' estimates. In this sense, it is atypical. Nonetheless, LETS have a high variance in their membership profiles, a product of the fact that LETS vary widely in the way in which they are embedded in different social networks in different localities.

Who belongs to Totnes LETS?

The vast majority of members responding are 'incomers' rather than indigenous to the area: 73% had moved to Totnes during the past 8 years. Just one respondent had lived in Totnes all of their life. Neither do members have extensive kinship networks in Totnes and the surrounding area. Not one respondent had any grandparents, uncles or aunties living in the area, and very few had any parents, brothers or sisters, or cousins in the locality. Totnes LETS, therefore, seems to be used to construct social networks by incomers who lack robust informal sources of support.

Are LETS, therefore, mere playthings for the bored affluent middle classes? To answer this question, there is a need to move beyond the simplistic dichotomy of rural dwellers as either locals or incomers, as displayed in Newby's (1979) notion that English rural communities are 'encapsulated' communities in which a minority of farm-based workers have found themselves surrounded by newcomers with different attitudes. Given that numerous studies have shown the need to further disaggregate the fractions within rural communities (Cloke and Thrift, 1990; Rogers, 1993), Table 5 examines the gender, age, household income and job status of respondents. This displays that Totnes LETS is over-represented relative to the population as a whole by women, those aged between 30 and 44 years old, low-income households and the unemployed and self-employed.* Consequently, one cannot simply read-off from their incomer status that they are also affluent and middle class. The vast majority are not. Take, for example, job status: 63.5% of respondents are either unemployed or 'self-employed'. The large proportion of 'self-employed' is because many respondents reject the notion of defining themselves through their employment status. Instead, they define themselves in terms of their perceived role/s and usefulness in the community (e.g. self-employed physiotherapist, community activist, counsellor or shiatsu prac-

Table 5. Characteristics of Totnes LETS members

Gross household income:		Gender:	
Under £4999	31.7%	Men	27.0%
£5–9999	30.1%	Women	73.0%
£10–14,999	15.9%		
£15–19,999	12.7%	Age:	
£20–29,999	7.9%	Under 18	0.0%
Over £30,000	1.6%	18–29	11.1%
		30–44	58.7%
Job status:		45–60	27.0%
Employee	36.5	Over 60	3.2%
Self-employed	44.5		
Unemployed	19.0		

Source: author's survey.

titioner), despite many being officially unemployed and claiming benefit. If job status leads to difficulties in determining the nature of the membership, however, household income brings greater clarity.

In the South-West in 1992, just 20.9% of households had a gross weekly income under £125 (Regional Trends 1994, Table 8.2). Yet in 1994, 31.7% of the LETS respondents' households had a total household income (before tax) of less than £96 per week. Only 9.5%, moreover, live in households where the total annual household income is over £20,000 whilst in the South West as a whole, 26.5% had a gross annual household income over £19,500 in 1992. Respondents, therefore, are disproportionately from the lower-income groups in the locality whilst the relatively wealthy are heavily under-represented. Indeed, the vast majority of the un-employed and 'self-employed' respondents live in 'low-income' households (defined here as earning less than £5000 p.a. gross). They are not the unemployed spouses of people in well-paying jobs. Consequently, Totnes LETS is not a hobby for the bored middle-classes.*

Nevertheless, although the poor and unemployed are over-represented on this LETS, it is only a particular section of this social group who join: 50% of respondents in low-income households and 50% of unemployed respondents are graduates. Totnes LETS, therefore, currently appeals to what can be called the 'disenfranchised middle class': those un-employed as a result of the decline in the middle-mass of jobs as the labour force has increasingly polarised between low- and high-wage jobs (Pinch, 1993; Sassen, 1991; Williams and Windebank, 1995). They join because they have the cultural or edu-cational capital, even if they lack the 'material' capital, and are thus more likely to feel able to appropriate LETS for achieving their own needs than other sections of the unemployed. However, this is not a reason to reject LETS. This 'disenfran-chised middle class' is suffering material deprivation to the same extent as any other segment of the unemployed and poor.

This is not to deny of course, the need for a wider share of the unemployed to be brought into LETS. There are, after all, far more socially excluded who have not joined LETS compared with those who have become members. Indeed, the social exclusion of this much larger group is very different in kind

from that of the 'disenfranchised middle class' since they will possess fewer personal transferable skills, greater demoralization with their situation and less self-confidence. Not only will this prevent them from joining LETS, but so too will the powerful influence of this disenfranchised middle class in local dis-courses around LETS since this broader mass are both outside of the relevant social networks and they may well perceive LETS as something for people other than themselves.

Nevertheless, when the reasons for joining Totnes LETS are explored amongst those who have en-rolled, 51.6% of respondents cite economic reasons in their rationale for joining, 30.6% cite social reasons and 30.6% ideological reasons. Of those in low-income households, 72.2% cite economic motivations and 50.0% social reasons. Totnes LETS, therefore, especially amongst the poorer respondents, is more frequently seen as an economic tool than a community-building facility. Women, however, who dominate the membership of Totnes LETS, are more likely than men to cite both economic and social reasons, whilst men are more likely to cite ideological motivations. This perhaps reflects that women join Totnes LETS for the practical reason of meeting their needs and wants whilst men view it more as an ideological tool (e.g. for challenging the dominance of capitalism). Hence, not only is membership of LETS skewed towards certain sections of the population but the rationale for participating is more often than not economically motivated.

What is the magnitude and character of members' purchases?

The 63 survey respondents had purchased the equivalent of £9964 over the past year, given the parity between the 'acorn' and the national cur-rency. This is an average of £153.39 per member. The total trade in the past year on Totnes LETS, therefore, can be estimated at £39,539. As the coordinators of Totnes LETS have independently assessed trading to be 40,000 'acorns', it can be assumed that the respondents are representative of the membership, at least in terms of the level of trading undertaken.

To examine LETS trade as a proportion of total household income, respondents were asked which income brackets their total household income (before tax) fell into using £5000 increments. Taking the middle income figure for each income bracket, the average household income (before tax) of respondents is £9722. Assuming that each household has just one LETS member, their LETS purchases

---

* Totnes LETS, however, is not joined solely by individual members. Five businesses also belong: 2% of the total membership. These are mostly consumer services and include a printing firm, clothes shop, paint shop and a book publisher, each of which sell their goods for a mixture of local and national currency.

represent 1.6% of total household income. Members in low-income households, meanwhile, had spent an average of £186.50 on the LETS during the past year. Even assuming the maximum possible average household income of £4999 for these households, this is the equivalent of 3.7% of total household income. In reality, it is probably somewhere between 3.7 and 7.5%, given that not all of these households will earn the maximum of £4999 in this income bracket. For many households,-therefore, their LETS spending made a significant additional contribution to their purchasing power.

The most commonly bought item on the LETS was food, bought by 40% (50% of respondents in low-income households), followed by clothes purchased by 34% (40% of low-income households) and to a lesser extent improvement and maintenance work (e.g. plumbing, carpentry and roofing) acquired by 31% (35% of low-income households). Only a small proportion of purchases were 'luxury' items. Totnes LETS, therefore, is being used to meet basic needs and wants.

This is perhaps unsurprising when it is recognised that the poor and unemployed have little access to credit. With the flight of financial institutions to more affluent populations, often in urban areas (Leyshon and Thrift, 1993; 1995), and the lack of informal sources of support, as discussed above, the only other option open to the poor and unemployed is to use 'loan sharks' at rates of interest considerably higher than formal sector rates. LETS, however, represent a means by which they can receive interest-free credit and this case study reveals that it is indeed being used for this purpose.

Take the example of 'Cathy', an unemployed single-parent with two young children under five years old who is claiming income support. She had spent the equivalent of £100 on the LETS during the past year but had not sold anything. This 'credit' had been used both to provide childcare and house cleaning at a rate of 4 acorns per hour. She intended to 'pay back' what she owed in the future when she would have more time available. 'Jane' another single mother, again on income support, but with four children, had used 160 acorns worth of credit to pay for house cleaning and 7 acorns for a massage. Without the LETS, both claimed that this work would not have been undertaken. Moreover, both assert that it had improved their material standard of living and enabled them to bolster the network of people that they could draw upon for help. Such anecdotal examples are evidence that LETS can operate in a manner which provides credit to those who need it so as to enable them to purchase local goods and services.

Who does the work and what do they charge?

LETS are not only a means by which members can purchase locally. The other side of the coin is that they are also a vehicle for meeting local needs and wants. To examine who does the work and what price they charge, Table 6 examines the frequency and extent of trade by household income. This shows that lower income households sell a wider range of goods and/or services than higher income households and receive a higher average price per transaction. However, both the average price per hour of services and the mean price received for the hire or sale of goods rises as household income increases. This means that members in lower income households or their capital goods are hired by the purchaser for longer periods to do jobs, thus revealing the way in which buyers facilitate a redistribution of income. This reinforces Lang's (1994) assertion that many LETS members do indeed know the economic situation of others in LETS and use positive discrimination policies when charging so as to facilitate income redistribution.

Totnes LETS thus overcomes the problem of orthodox 'buy local' campaigns in rural areas where goods and services tend to be higher priced by redistributing income in this manner. Even if prices are higher, then so too is the price received by sellers. The consequence is that local goods and services are affordable to all. Indeed, no LETS member claims that they cannot afford the goods and services on Totnes LETS.

Perceived impacts of Totnes LETS

Table 7 reveals the impacts of this local purchasing scheme on the members. Nearly a third of respondents believe that the LETS has helped them to improve their material standard of living, with members in lower income households being more likely to state this than those in higher income households. However, given that the rationale for participating is more often than not economically motivated, there are many who join for economic reasons who do not feel that it has improved their material standard of living. This is because 64.7% of respondents felt that their requests for goods and services had not been met immediately and only 59.7% were satisfied with the range of goods and services on offer. Totnes LETS, therefore, is not perceived by many members to be of a sufficient magnitude for it to have a significant impact on their material standard of living. So far as community-building is concerned, nevertheless, there is a greater level of satisfaction. Totnes LETS has enabled over two-thirds of members (68.4%) to

Table 6. Trading on Totnes LETS: by household income

	<£5000 (n = 20)	£5000– 9999 (n = 19)	£10,000– 14,999 (n = 10)	£15,000– 19,999 (n = 8)	£20,000– 29,999 (n = 5)
Mean no. offered	3.58	3.57	3.60	2.55	2.80
Mean no. sold	2.05	1.55	1.40	0.89	1.6
Mean no. times sold	11.61	8.86	22.7	9.56	9.56
Total price	3534	2631	2235	696	568
Mean income p.a.	176.7	138.5	223.5	87.0	113.6
Average price per transaction	16.02	15.62	9.84	8.09	11.36
Services sold (mean price/hour)	5.65	5.75	8.30	14.14	10.67
Goods sold/hired (mean price)	18.04	21.39	22.01	23.71	28.30

Source: author's survey.

Table 7. Impacts of Totnes LETS on members' quality of life: members' views

% of respondents	Develops wider network of people you can call on for help	Develops wider network of friends	Develops deeper friendships	Improves your material standard of living	Use skills you would not otherwise use
All members	68.4	40.0	8.0	32.7	38.2
Unemployed	66.7	41.7	10.0	33.3	50.0
Self-employed	65.4	37.5	0.0	32.0	28.0
Employed	73.7	42.1	21.4	33.0	41.7
Below £4999	83.3	41.2	12.5	38.9	35.3
£5000–£9999	55.5	41.2	5.9	50.0	41.2
£10,000–£14,999	55.5	44.4	0.0	12.5	40.0
£15,000–£19,999	85.7	14.3	0.0	14.3	42.8
£20,000–£29,999	60.0	60.0	25.0	0.0	25.0

Source: author's survey.

develop a wider network of people they can call on for help, although rather fewer accept that it has helped them generate more friends and even less deeper friendships. It appears, therefore, that at least in the early stages, Totnes LETS has provided contacts to call on for help but has not yet succeeded in converting such contacts into friendships. Moreover, Totnes LETS does appear to be re-integrating the unemployed (or at least a particular section of this group) into the community by widening the network of people that they can all on for help.

In sum, as a local purchasing scheme, Totnes LETS not only provides economic and social benefits to its members but also helps some of those who are relatively deprived to partially mitigate their circumstances. Nevertheless, the number and range of people who currently join LETS, as well as the magnitude of the local purchasing, remains restricted. To help overcome this, the next section identifies the barriers to participation in LETS and suggests ways in which they could be overcome.

Barriers to participation in LETS

These empirical findings reveal that although LETS do provide a facility to encourage local purchasing, this is perhaps more limited than some might have hoped. On the one hand, this is because LETS are a new phenomenon and are in their infancy. On the other hand, however, it is due to several additional problems which will need to be overcome for LETS to have more significant impacts. Five potential barriers are here identified which hinder the rural population's participation in LETS:

- whether one exists in their locality
- whether they know about it
- whether they perceive it as something for them

- whether they feel that they have anything to offer and anything which is worth their while requesting, and
- whether they are able to work on the LETS free from government constraints.

Each will be considered in turn.

First, there is the issue of whether a LETS exists in all localities. Although there are now 350 LETS in the U.K., many rural localities still have no LETS. Take, for example, Cornwall. Only 20% of the county's area is covered by the existing LETS. Therefore, there is no access to a LETS for those living in the vast majority of the county. To some extent, this will be resolved without intervention from formal sector institutions as LETS continue to spread. In some communities, however, especially the more deprived, there will be a need for capacity-building to enable them to help themselves (Murray and Dunn, 1995). Organisations such as rural local authorities and the Rural Community Councils are well-placed to bring this to fruition in the U.K.

Assuming that one exists in a locality, a second barrier to people's participation is whether they know about the LETS. In this regard, the approach to marketing LETS requires careful reconsideration. No rural LETS in the U.K. adopts a strategic approach to this issue. Instead, there is an unintentional targeting, especially in their formative stages, with LETS pursuing the line of least resistance by focusing upon environmental groups and then, once the membership is of a sufficient size, allowing 'word-of-mouth' to be the principal means of encouraging people to join: 58.1% of all members of Totnes LETS had heard about it through 'word-of-mouth'. The result is that mostly 'greens/alternatives', and particularly the poor and unemployed within this group, become members. This fosters an image of LETS which leads many to feel excluded. They perceive LETS to be for people 'other' than themselves (Lee, 1996). This is the third barrier to participation: even if a LETS exists and people know about it, they may not perceive it as something for them. Consequently, more strategic and focused publicity campaigns are required specifically tailored to different target groups.

Even if people perceive it as something for them, there is then the issue of whether they view themselves as having anything to offer and whether there is anything worth their while requesting. On the former issue, methods need developing to help people explore what they have to offer and the skills which they possess, rather than just ask members to list their offers, as is the case at present. So too is training required on LETS to enhance local levels of skill and empower people to provide inputs to the local economy beyond the LETS (see Williams, 1996b). On the latter issue, the range of goods and services on the LETS will need to be broadened and deepened to make them more attractive to potential members and engender widespread local purchasing. This is because, as indicated above, not only are offers and requests frequently not matched but members are spatially dispersed which leads to problems in gaining access to what are often consumer services with a small market area. Indeed, there is some evidence that although Totnes LETS functions beneficially for members living in Totnes itself, it does not for those in surrounding areas. As one respondent states, 'I do not live in Totnes and because of that nobody wants to trade with me. It is okay for people in Totnes itself but those of us who live out of town feel a bit marginalised'. There is thus much work to be done in empowering people to feel that they have something to offer and enabling them to have their requests met.

Once these barriers to people's participation are overcome, then a final hurdle which will need to be tackled is government policy towards LETS. At present in the U.K., the Inland Revenue state that if an exchange is clearly of a commercial nature, where a person is self-employed and offers a good or service connected with their normal business, then tax will be liable in the normal way. Exchanges not connected with a person's normal business, but offered and supplied regularly so as to amount to a business in itself, are also commercial and therefore are tax liable. Isolated or fairly infrequent exchanges where typically a person is doing a favour for a friend are not liable for taxation. In practice, however, most LETS work is disregarded for income tax purposes.

Current social security regulations, in contrast, are less clear about how working on LETS affects benefit. The DSS (which decides policy) and the Benefits Agency (which administers payments) assert that LETS credits constitute earnings (although there are discrepancies in how this is applied by local benefit offices). Any income over the disregard limit is thus asserted to affect benefit levels. So, as policy stands, those already in employment can participate in LETS without too much fear of recourse whilst those claiming benefits are more strictly monitored and controlled. The impact is that the unemployed are constrained to a greater extent than the employed. Present government regulations are simply bolstering existing social disparities and restricting local purchasing amongst those most in need.

Here, therefore, it is argued that U.K. government

242   Colin C. Williams

policy towards LETS should follow the approach adopted in Australia where those working on LETS as part of their main formal occupation are taxed on their earnings, similar to the U.K., but unemployed people can earn LETS currency without it affecting their benefit payments. This is a product of the 'Deahm Amendment' to the 1995 Social Security Act passed in the Australian Federal Parliament on 1 March 1995 which asserts that LETS earnings are exempt from any means-test for social security subject to three restrictions: that claimants continue to look for appropriate employment; that any national currency earnings on LETS (where a job is completed for a mixture of local and national currency) is declared and will be counted as income for means-testing purposes; and that the LETS is a non-profit community-based system.

If implemented in the U.K., this would allow those most in need to engage in local purchasing. It would also provide them with a competitive advantage on LETS when bidding to do work since those in higher waged formal jobs would have to charge higher prices for their work because they have to add the tax rate to their price, whilst the poor and unemployed would not.

Conclusions

Through an analysis of economic base theory, this paper has critically reviewed the orthodox perspective that rural development is contingent upon the export of goods and services. In so doing, it has revealed that a rise in net income is required for an economy to grow, not an increase in external income alone. Net income, to reiterate, is determined by total external income times a multiplier (which is higher, the more self-reliant the economy), minus total external spending. Recognising this, the growth of any economy is thus dependent not only upon outward-orientated activities which attract external income but also locally-orientated activities which prevent the leakage of money out of the area.

The problem, however, is that such locally-orientated activities are frequently under-emphasised in rural development discourse and there is a shortage of effective policy instruments to prevent seepage of spending out of rural economies. Neither local sourcing campaigns for businesses, nor the 'use it or lose it' approach for encouraging consumers to purchase locally, resolve the lack of diversity and relatively high cost of goods and services in rural areas. Neither do they address the fact that even if people do buy locally, the business may be owned externally and/or the goods and services sourced externally, resulting in profits and income leaking out of the area.

Given the lack of attention in conventional rural economic development efforts to stem the leakage of income from rural economies and the shortage of effective policy instruments to remedy such seepage, this paper has evaluated LETS as an innovative way to enable local purchasing and thus rural development. Analysing the results of both a national survey of LETS coordinators and a membership survey of the Totnes system, LETS are shown to be rapidly growing in rural areas where they are encouraging people to trade locally and to use local labour and also are rebuilding local social networks and helping some of those marginalised from employment to gain access to work and credit. As such, the LETS approach is argued to be effective in integrating the twin pillars of both economic and community development, which so often remain disparate activities in rural policy-making. However, at present, their achievements remain small-scale and, as revealed in the case of Totnes LETS, confined to a relatively limited group of rural dwellers. For improvements in their impacts on rural development to be achieved, therefore, it has been argued that: more LETS need to be created; they must be marketed to encompass all social groups; the goods and services offered need to be broadened and deepened such as through skill recognition and enhancement schemes; and current government policy needs to be modified to conform with the alterations made by the Australian government regarding tax and social security legislation towards LETS activity. If these changes are made, then LETS will become a powerful new weapon in the armoury of rural policy-makers and impact upon a broader mass of the rural population than at present.

Acknowledgements — I would like to thank Richard Knights of Totnes LETS for providing access to the membership and the anonymous referees for their insightful comments on an earlier version of this paper. As usual, however, the normal disclaimers apply. Any faults or omissions are mine alone.

References

Bauman, Z. (1990) *Thinking Sociologically*. Basil Blackwell, Oxford.
Brandt, B. (1995) *Whole Life Economics: Revaluing Daily Life*. New Society Publishers, Philadelphia.
Bulmer, M. (1989) The underclass, empowerment and public policy. *In The Goals of Social Policy*, pp. 245–257, Bulmer, M., Lewis, J. and Piachaud, D. (eds). Unwin Hyman, London.
Cloke, P. and Thrift, N. (1990) 'Intra-class conflict in rural areas'. *Journal of Rural Studies* **3**, 321–333.
Clout, H. (1993) *European Experience of Rural Development*. Rural Development Commission, London.
Croft, J. (1995) Buy local campaigns and LETSystems. *Ozlets News* **8**, 13.
Crow, G. and Allen, G. (1994) *Community Life: an*

Introduction to Local Social Relations. Harvester Wheatsheaf, London.

Davis, H.C. and Davis, L.E. (1987) The Local Exchange and Trading System: community wealth creation within the informal economy. *Plan Canada* 15, 238–245.

Dawes, L. (1993) *Long-term Unemployment and Labour Market Flexibility.* Centre for Labour Market Studies, University of Leicester.

Department of Environment/Ministry of Agriculture, Fisheries and Food (1995) *Rural England: a Nation Committed to a Living Countryside.* HMSO, London.

Dobson, R.V.G. (1993) *Bringing the Economy Home from the Market.* Black Rose Books, London.

Farness, D.H. (1989) Detecting the economic base: new challenges. *International Regional Science Review* 12, 319–328.

Giaratani, F. and McNelis, P. (1980) Time series evidence bearing on crude theories of regional growth. *Land Economics* 56, 238–248.

Gibbs, D., Longhurst, J. and Braithwaite, C. (1995) Towards sustainable development: integrating local economic development and the environment. Paper presented at European Regional Studies Association Conference, Gothenburg, May.

Glasmeier, A. and Borchard, G. (1989) From branch plants to back offices: prospects for rural services growth. *Environment and Planning A* 21, 1565–1583.

Glasmeier, A. and Howland, M. (1994) Service-led rural development: definitions, theories and empirical evidence. *International Regional Science Review* 16, 197–229.

Glickman, N.J. (1977) *Econometric Analysis of Regional Systems: Explorations in Model Building and Policy Analysis.* Academic Press, London.

Greco, T.H. (1994) *New Money for Healthy Communities.* Thomas H. Greco, Tucson.

Griffin, G., Wood, S. and Knight, J. (1992) The Bristol labour market. Employment Department Research Paper no. 82, Centre for Labour Market Studies, University of Leicester.

Haggett, P., Cliff, A.D. and Frey, A.E. (1977) *Locational Analysis in Human Geography.* Edward Arnold, London.

Kaldor, N. (1966) *Causes of the Slow Rate of Growth in the United Kingdom.* Cambridge University Press, Cambridge.

Keane, M.J. and Quinn, J. (1990) Rural development and rural tourism. Research Report No. 5, Social Sciences Research Centre, University College Galway.

Lang, P. (1994) *LETS Work: Rebuilding the Local Economy.* Grover Books, Bristol.

Lee, R. (1996) Moral money? LETS and the social construction of local economic geographies in south east England. *Environment and Planning A* 28.

LetsLink UK (1994a) *Directory of LETS in the UK.* LetsLink UK, Warminster.

LetsLink UK (1994b) *Directory of International Contacts.* LetsLink UK, Warminster.

LetsLink UK (1995) LETS soars to 350 and more. *LetsLink!* 3, 7.

Leyshon, A. and Thrift, N. (1993) The restructuring of the UK financial services industry in the 1990s: a reversal of fortunes? *Journal of Rural Studies* 9, 223–241.

Leyshon, A. and Thrift, N. (1995) Geographies of financial exclusion: financial abandonment in Britain and the United States. *Transactions* 20, 312–341.

Mandelbaum, T.B. and Chicoine, D.L. (1986) The effect of timeframe in the estimation of employment multipliers. *Regional Science Perspectives* 12, 37–50.

Margolis, J. (1995) Looking for enlightenment. *The Sunday Times* 9 April, 8–9.

McNulty, J.E. (1977) A test of the time dimension in economic base analysis. *Land Economics* 53, 358–368.

Morris, L. (1993) Is there a British underclass? *International Journal of Urban and Regional Research* 17, 404–412.

Morris, L. (1994) Informal aspects of social divisions. *International Journal of Urban and Regional Research* 18, 112–126.

Morris, L. (1995) *Social Divisions: Economic Decline and Social Structural Change.* UCL Press, London.

Murray, M. and Dunn, L. (1995) Capacity building for rural development in the United States. *Journal of Rural Studies* 11, 89–97.

Newby, H. (1979) *Green and Pleasant Land? Social Change in Rural England.* Hutchinson, London.

Nilsson, P.A. (1993) Tourism in peripheral regions: a Swedish policy perspective. *Entrepreneurship and Regional Development* 5, 39–44.

Offe, C. and Heinze, R.G. (1992) *Beyond Employment: Time, Work and the Informal Economy.* Polity, Cambridge.

Persky, J., Ranney, D. and Wiewel, W. (1993) Import substitution and local economic development. *Economic Development Quarterly* 7, 18–29.

Pinch, S. (1993) Social polarization: a comparison of evidence from Britain and the United States. *Environment and Planning A* 25, 779–795.

Polese, M. (1982) Regional demand for business services and inter-regional service flows in a small Canadian region. *Papers of the Regional Science Association* 50, 151–163.

Redwood, A. (1988) Job creation in nonmetropolitan communities. *The Journal of State Governments* 61, 9–15.

Rogers, A. (1993) *English Rural Communities: an Assessment and Prospect for the 1990s.* Rural Development Commission, London.

Sassen, S. (1991) *The Global City: New York, London, Tokyo.* Princeton University Press, Princeton.

Seyfang, G.J. (1994) The Local Exchange Trading System: political economy and social audit. MSc thesis, School of Environmental Sciences, University of East Anglia.

Smith, S.M. (1984) Export-orientation of non-manufacturing business in non-metropolitan communities. *American Journal of Agricultural Economics* 66, 145–154.

Smith, S.M. and Pulver, G.C. (1981) Non-manufacturing business as a growth alternative in nonmetropolitan areas. *Journal of the Community Development Society* 12, 32–47.

Stabler, J.C. (1987) Non metropolitan population growth and the evolution of rural service centers in the Canadian prairie region. *Regional Studies* 21, 43–53.

Stabler, J.C. and Howe, E.C. (1988) Service exports and regional growth in the post-industrial era. *Journal of Regional Science* 28, 303–316.

Stabler, J.C. and Howe, E.C. (1993) Services, trade and regional structural change in Canada. *Review of Urban and Regional Development Studies* 5, 29–50.

Williams, A., Shore, G. and Huber, M. (1995) The arts and economic development: regional and urban–rural contrasts in UK Local Authority policies for the arts. *Regional Studies* 29, 73–81.

Williams, C.C. (1994a) Rethinking the role of the service sector in local economic revitalisation. *Local Economy* 9, 73–82.

Williams, C.C. (1994b) Local sourcing initiatives in West Yorkshire: an evaluation of their effectiveness. In *Reinventing a Region: the West Yorkshire Experience*, Haughton, G. and Whitney, D. (eds). Avebury, Aldershot.

Williams, C.C. (1996a) Understanding the role of consumer services in local economic development. *Environment and Planning A* **28**, 555–571.

Williams, C.C. (1996b) Informal sector solutions to unemployment: an evaluation of the potential of Local Exchange and Trading Systems (LETS). *Work, Employment and Society* **10**, 341–359.

Williams, C.C. and Windebank, J. (1995) Social polarization of households in contemporary Britain: a 'whole economy' perspective. *Regional Studies* **29**, 727–732.

Wilson, A.G. (1974) *Urban and Regional Models in Geography and Planning*. John Wiley, Chichester.

Pergamon

Journal of Rural Studies, Vol. 14, No. 2, pp. 167–184, 1998
© 1998 Elsevier Science Ltd. All rights reserved
Printed in Great Britain
0743-0167/98 $19.00 + 0.00

PII: S0743-0167(97)00055-7

Local Responses to Central State Restructuring of Social Housing Provision in Rural Areas

Paul Milbourne

Countryside and Community Research Unit, Cheltenham and Gloucester College of Higher Education, Swindon Road, Cheltenham GL50 4AZ, UK

Abstract — This paper examines local impacts of recent central state restructuring of social housing provision in rural areas. Positioning such changes within a context of wider discussions on local government restructuring and regulation theory, attention is focused on some key local responses to social housing restructuring in two areas of rural Wales in the early 1990s. In this section of the paper consideration is given to the increasing residualization of the local social housing sector, changing systems of social housing allocation and management, and the localized mediation of central state restructuring of social housing through different housing agencies. ©1998 Elsevier Science Ltd. All rights reserved

Introduction

Local Authority activity in housing introduced a new element into the landscape of the village which is now taken for granted. (Rogers, 1976, p. 94)

While few researchers of British rural housing would disagree that post-war housing legislation up to the late 1970s was characterized by state intervention in the housing markets of all but a few rural areas, it is clear that, over 20 years after this statement was made, council housing may no longer represent a lasting aspect of the rural housing scene. Indeed, within four years of Rogers' chapter appearing in an edited volume on rural planning problems, the first major piece of housing legislation introduced by the recently elected Conservative Government — the 1980 Housing Act — was receiving Royal Assent. This Act signalled the start of a widespread assault on the council rental sector of the housing market, which, to date, has included a large-scale sell-off of local authority (and more recently housing association) properties to tenants, dramatic cuts in council housebuilding programmes, transfers of council stock to other social landlords, and a generally more restricted role for the local authority as an enabler rather than provider of social housing. Indeed, the ferocity of this attack on the social housing sector by central government has led certain commentators (Murie, 1982; Saunders, 1984) to suggest that collective housing provision now needs to be viewed as representing merely a transitional phase between different forms of private housing provision, while others (for example, Spencer, 1995; Stoker and Mossberger, 1995) have located social housing decine within a wider context of regulation theory and emerging post-Fordist systems of welfare provision in 1990s Britain.

While central state restructuring of social housing provision has been the subject of a large number of studies over recent years (Balchin, 1995; Cole and Furbey, 1994; Doling, 1993; Power, 1993), relatively few have been grounded at the local level, and fewer still have considered local outcomes in rural spaces. However, it can be suggested that these wider processes of restructuring have impacted differently on particular rural spaces, reflecting historical patterns of social rental provision, local state political structures and housing policies, the nature of local (private) housing markets, the mix of agencies able to provide new forms of social housing, and so on. This paper focuses on these local outcomes of central state social housing restructuring in areas of rural Britain, and in particular on the Housing Acts introduced by the Thatcher governments over the 1980s. It begins by providing a brief historical overview of changing social rental housing provision in rural Britain, and locating such changes within a wider context of local government restructuring, political economy and regulation theory. Local outcomes of social housing restructuring are then examined in the second part of the paper by drawing on research conducted in two districts of rural Wales in the early 1990s. Here attention is focused on changing local levels and geographies of social housing provision, the residualization of the council housing sector, restructuring of social housing management and allocation systems, and the mediation of central restructuring of social housing through key local agencies.

Changing social housing provision in rural areas

1919–1979: 60 years of state intervention

The historical development of social housing in rural areas can be seen as closely linked to general patterns of housing change initiated, in the main, by central government legislation. Although rural local authorities possessed powers under the 1890 Housing Act to provide rental properties, the tenure situation in rural Britain at the end of World War I remained overwhelmingly dominated by the private rental sector (Rogers, 1976). Such domination though, began to change during the inter-war period, as the introduction of several pieces of housing legislation initiated a large-scale intervention by the local state into most rural housing markets. Rogers (1976), for example, has reported that some 164,000 properties were constructed by local authorities in rural England between 1919 and 1943 — representing one-fifth of all new properties built — which raised the social rental sector's share of these housing markets to around 10% of all provision by the end of this period.

While the bulk of this inter-war housing legislation was concerned to address general housing issues and problems, associated mainly with inadequate housing conditions, attention was also directed specifically towards problems of poor housing conditions and tied accommodation in rural areas. This limited concern for sets of rural problems, however, became largely subsumed within wider programmes of urban reconstruction introduced by the 1945–1951 Labour administration (Rogers, 1976), although Phillips and Williams (1984) have suggested that additional subsidies continued to be paid on new public house building schemes in rural areas. Indeed, while the urban-focused nature of post-war central state housing policies cannot be

denied, council provision did become an established part of housing markets in almost all urban *and* rural areas in the immediate post-war period. Such state intervention continued through the 'consensus years' of the 1960s and 1970s, with macro-economic policies associated with successive Conservative and Labour administrations concerned with increasing levels of owner-occupied and public sector housing as central to their housing policies.*

By the late 1970s, though, a growing number of housing researchers working in rural areas began to highlight problems associated with social housing provision in particular parts of the British countryside. Shucksmith (1981), for example, reported that, even with such widespread state intervention, levels of public housing construction in many rural districts had tended to remain well below the national average over the post-war period (see also Clark, 1982; Dunn *et al.*, 1981), as a result of central government policies — with housing funding favouring those higher density construction schemes characteristic of urban areas, and the 1947 Town and Country Planning Act restricting the vast majority of both public and private housing developments to a small number of key settlements in rural areas. Newby (1979), though, has suggested that it has been the nature of local political structures that has led to these lower rates of social housing provision in rural Britain, with the domination of conservative councillors resulting in a lack of political will to raise taxes for council housebuilding programmes,[†] while links with landowning and agriculture amongst certain councillors meant that they were also reluctant to weaken their power bases within local housing markets as landlords of tied accommodation. This said, Dickens *et al.* (1985) have highlighted how, in rural areas such as Norfolk, earlier this century, the establishment of social housing was actually initiated by landowners who were concerned that a shortage of suitable rental accommodation in the county would be detrimental for agricultural production. However, both the

---

*Balchin (1995) has reported that rates of owner-occupation expanded from 29–55% between 1953 and 1979, and local authority provision from 25–32% over the same period. However, it should be noted that the emphasis switched to providing an increased provision of privately owned properties throughout this period, and this was particularly the case with Conservative government policies.
†Hoggart (1993), though, has highlighted how the differential between urban and rural authorities in terms of public sector housing constructions has reduced considerably since the late 1980s, since council house building programmes have been reduced dramatically in all geographical areas in the post-1979 period, thus removing the influence of local politics on levels of council housebuilding.

Newby and Dickens *et al.* studies have pointed to the ways in which central state policies have become mediated through different local agencies, resulting in very different housing outcomes in different rural areas.

Differential (urban–rural) local outcomes of central government policy have also been highlighted by Phillips and Williams (1982a,b) in relation to the distribution of council housing in many rural areas. Drawing on a study of council housing in rural Devon undertaken in the 1970s, they have suggested that a number of local factors can influence the allocation of such accommodation in rural areas. Firstly, the spatial distribution of social housing in many rural areas is characterized by concentrations of provision in a small number of larger settlements which has meant that opportunities to enter the sector are more restricted in village locations. Furthermore, Phillips and Williams have suggested that the composition of local political structures plays an important part not only in determining the nature and scale of council house provision, but also in influencing policies towards homelessness and particularly definitions of intentional homelessness. A third local specificity has concerned the allocation of local authority housing in those rural areas which are characterized by large numbers of agricultural workers who are treated preferentially outside of standard systems of allocation.

The post-1979 period: the forced retreat of local state housing intervention

By the early 1980s, new housing research agendas were beginning to emerge, linked mainly to the impacts of central state restructuring of social housing provision. Following the election of a Conservative administration in 1979, committed to policies aimed at increasing levels of competition, deregulation and privatization, and reducing levels of funding of the welfare state, social housing witnessed an increasingly widespread assault on its previously assumed integral position within housing programmes. New housing agendas were dominated by the goal of increased property ownership, with the key tenets of the early Thatcherite housing legislation characterized by:

> …the reduction of council stock, the expansion of owner-occupation, the decrease in capital spending by, and housing subsidies to, local authorities, and the maintenance of mortgage tax relief. (Cole and Furbey, 1994, p. 197)

The first piece of housing legislation introduced by the 1979–1983 Thatcher Government — the 1980

Housing Act — involved the large-scale sell-off of council homes to tenants at substantially reduced prices. By 1987, in excess of one million local authority properties had been sold in Britain, a figure which represented more than one-sixth of the 1980 stock (Cole and Furbey, 1994). In addition to tenants being given the right to buy their homes at a generous discount, central government also began to cut back on the financial resources and powers which enabled local authorities to intervene within housing markets. Authorities were prohibited from spending capital receipts accrued from sales on the construction of new social housing, and their housing role was reduced by the Housing Act (1988) from that of *provider* to one of *enabler* of social housing. Responsibility for providing new social housing was placed solely with housing associations, with increased levels of government funding provided through the Housing Corporation,* although the overall level of central funding for social housing was reduced substantially. In numerical terms, restructuring of the social housing sector resulted in an *absolute* reduction in public expenditure on housing of some 60% in real terms between 1979 and 1994, and a *relative* fall from 7–2% in housing's share of the public expenditure budget over this same period (Balchin, 1995).

While such central state restructuring has impacted on social housing provision in all parts of Britain, two particular sets of local outcomes have been highlighted in rural areas — the impacts of Right-to-Buy sales in villages in 'popular' areas of the countryside; and the limited ability of smaller housing associations active in many rural areas to provide social housing as set out in the 1988 Housing Act.

During the run up to the 1980 Housing Act receiving Royal Assent, concern was expressed by several important rural organizations that Right-to-Buy sales could remove the entire council housing stock from many smaller villages where stock levels were relatively low and alternative housing opportunities more difficult. An amendment to the Act was subsequently introduced[†] which allowed rural authorities to restrict sales in certain designated (tourist) parts of the countryside by awarding them powers to re-purchase ex-council

---

*Tai Cymru provides funding to Welsh associations and housing associations in Scotland receive finance from Scottish Homes.
[†]While the politics behind the introduction of this amendment have not been examined by researchers, this particular example of lobbying may provide an illustration of the power held by a small number of influential rural agencies in Britain.

properties. However, relatively few rural authorities were granted such powers of re-purchase, and those that were received no additional central funding. As such, most rural authorities have been powerless to prevent the loss of council housing stock in villages (and towns) within their areas, and a study of early local authority sales in rural Oxfordshire (Beazley *et al.*, 1980) has pointed to (better quality) council houses being purchased by (more affluent) tenants at faster rates in smaller villages than towns. Indeed, historical patterns of provision, in combination with such uneven spatial impacts of sales in the early 1980s led Dunn *et al.* (1981) to predict an increasing residualization of the rural council sector in many villages and a growing gulf between local authority provision in rural and urban areas. By the early 1990s, research findings confirmed these predictions, with the Department of the Environment (1993) reporting that the average level of council provision in rural authorities was around half that recorded in urban areas (10.7% compared to 21.8%), while Cloke *et al.* (1994a,b) have highlighted a similar level of local authority provision — 11% — in studies of 16 areas of the English and Welsh countryside.

It is also far from clear how effective housing associations have been in providing social housing in rural areas. With the historical urban roots of the association sector, and economies of scale associated with new schemes, larger housing associations have tended to be restricted to urban, and particularly, metropolitan areas in Britain. Hoggart (1993), for example, has reported that housing association new constructions in rural districts have reamined at around half the level recorded in metropolitan areas over the 1980s. Such low levels of new association provision in rural areas have been recognized recently by the Housing Corporation which has funded 9100 association properties specifically in areas of rural England between 1990 and 1995 (Balchin, 1994), and by Tai Cymru, which has focused one-quarter of its housing programme and funded around 6000 properties in rural Wales since 1989 (Welsh Office, 1995).

While there have been relatively few studies conducted since the mid-1980s which have examined the activities of housing associations in areas of the British countryside, earlier studies have pointed to the flexible (although partial) role performed by such associations in meeting housing needs in the countryside (see, for example, Cloke and Edwards, 1985) and providing support for rural economies (Young, 1987). However, Richmond (1984) has suggested that even those associations operating in rural areas have tended to restrict their activities to larger settlements and the needs of particular

groups, and have also allocated their properties on a somewhat *ad hoc* basis.

Theorizing social housing restructuring in rural areas: political ideology, changing local governance and regulation theory

The processes of restructuring of the social housing sector outlined thus far within this paper have been subject to considerable discussion over recent years concerning the factors underpinning such changes and the position of social housing within wider systems of welfare provision and political economy. While clearly such discussion has been focused on national and, indeed, international processes of restructuring, it can be suggested that the issues raised have important implications for the study of social housing restructuring in areas of rural Britain.

A number of studies have examined (historical) processes of social housing provision in Britain from a political economy perspective (see, for example, Dickens *et al.*, 1985), although it has been the staged withdrawal of the state from the provision of social housing (and other welfare services) that has sparked considerable debate over recent years. In the early 1980s, Murie (1982) and Saunders (1984) suggested that public housing in Britain needed to be viewed as a transitional phase of provision between different forms of private housing. Each proposed a three-fold periodization of housing in the twentieth century, with the early years dominated by the private market and particularly the private landlord, and state intervention limited to the regulation of the market. The failure of the private market to provide adequate and affordable accommodation for workers, though, in combination with pressure from working-class organizations, produced a socialized mode of consumption in which the state provided essential elements of consumption, such as housing:

> The development of council housing...redistributed housing resources in the interests of the working class and has served the interests of capital and the 'social order' by minimising the effects of the restructuring of the private market. (Murie, 1982, p. 35)

By the 1980s, Saunders (1984) has argued that in the process of overcoming contradictions between low wages and adequate housing provision amongst the workforce, socialized housing generated a further contradiction for the central state:

> that between the socialised costs of welfare provision and the availability of government revenues. It is this contradiction which became increasingly manifest through the 1970s in the form of 'fiscal crisis', and the

response has been a marked shift in recent years towards a new third phase in the form of a privatized mode of consumption. (p. 210)

While most housing commentators would concur with such a three-fold periodization of British local state housing, more recent debates concerning state intervention in, and withdrawal from, housing markets have focused on the political ideologies associated with successive Conservative governments in the 1980s and early 1990s. Spencer (1995), for example, has suggested that the recent restructuring of social housing provision needs to be understood within a wider context of central state ideologies which have favoured competition, markets and consumer choice; increased control of the local state by central government; and the private provision of welfare services. Indeed, Cole and Furbey (1994) have argued that central government has tended to use the social housing sector as a testing ground for its wider political project of dismantling the welfare state:

> In this process, the vulnerability of council housing as an insecure foundation of the welfare state — in terms of its origins, limited coverage, cost and exposure to market processes — was clearly demonstrated ...housing bore the brunt of the Conservative government attack on the welfare state during the 1980s; and council housing conveniently served as a symbol of the negative features of the public sector — inefficient, bureaucratic, remote, mismanaged and wasteful. It was a good place to begin a long-term process of structural transformation without provoking intense public resistance. (p. 7)

Other authors have located the restructuring of social housing (and other welfare) provision outside of central government policies and within the wider sphere of national and international political-economy. Hoggett (1987), for example, has viewed the Keynesian welfare state as a form of social regulation during a period of Fordist mass production and consumption from the 1930s to the early 1970s, with Cochrane (1994) suggesting that it was 'inflexibly geared towards the output of a few standardized products with economies of scale constantly emphasized' (p. 83). Both Hoggett (1987) and Stock and Mossberger (1995) have proposed that as Fordist modes of production and consumption have become replaced by those labelled as post (or neo-)Fordist, structures of local government have inevitably reflected these changes — they have become decentralized, more responsive, flexible and informal, with 'learner and flatter' managerial structures providing a more differentiated product.

Furthermore, a large number of local government responsibilities have been transferred to a range of private sector and quasi local government organizations which have been viewed by central government

as operating more efficiently in economic terms. In the context of social housing provision, Kennedy (1991) has suggested that housing associations provide a good example of such a public–private transfer. Central control of association funding through the Housing Corporation, Tai Cymru and Scottish Homes has meant that central government has been able to influence their activities. Indeed, the reduced level of central state funding, together with mixed public–private funding packages, have acted to produce a social housing *market*, in which many associations have come to resemble small businesses competing against each other for an ever decreasing level of central funds, with a series of recent mergers producing a small number of 'super' associations able to wield considerable power within the social housing sector. From this perspective then, social housing represents a commercial product, regulated by a quasi-governmental agency, which is manufactured and sold in different packages by different associations.

Finally, in this section on the theorization of social housing restructuring, the changing role of the local state in providing key aspects of welfare has been viewed by certain commentators as less concerned with the *imposition* of restructuring by the central state and more with 'the product of social *struggle* in an unstable society' (Stoker and Mossberger, 1995, p. 211, my emphasis). Such a regulationist approach has considered the ways in which central state restructuring has resulted from, and been mediated through and contested by, the actions of key agencies at the local level. Indeed, Stoker and Mossberger (1995) have referred to the 'vertical' imposition of central state restructuring of local governance resulting in complex 'horizontal' processes which reflect particular circumstances in different localities. An example of these 'vertical' and 'horizontal' interactions has been provided by Dickens et al. (1985) who have pointed to the ways in which varying local political-economic processes resulted in different levels of social housing provision in different localities in early twentieth century Britain, while the political influence of key rural organizations — such as those that lobbied ministers during debates on the 1980 Housing Bill — might be seen as a further instance of such interactions.

In the second part of the paper these interactions between 'vertical' and 'horizontal' processes of central state restructuring of social housing provision are investigated within the context of two areas of rural Wales in the 1980s and early 1990s. While providing more recent information on the changing level and nature of social housing provision in the countryside, this section of the paper positions such changes within a wider theoretical context of changing structures of local governance and regulation theory. As such, consideration is given to the ways in which wider processes of restructuring have been mediated through, and occasionally contested by, key local agencies. The remaining parts of the paper therefore explore the following four issues within the two study areas:

- changing levels and local geographies of social housing provision;
- the localized residualization of social housing;
- local state responses to central state restructuring of social housing provision;
- changing systems of management and allocation of social rented accommodation.

Local responses to social housing restructuring in rural Wales

The research on which this second part of the paper forms part of a wider study of housing change and conflict in areas of rural Wales in the 1990s (see Milbourne, 1997). In the context of this paper, a key part of the research involved an examination of the changing provision, management and allocation of social housing in these two areas of the Welsh countryside, based on three clear stages of enquiry:

- the collection and analysis of 'official' documentation and statistics on the changing levels and local geographies of social housing provision;
- semi-structured interviews with housing managers in local authorities and housing associations — which explored managers' perceptions of changes, practices of housing allocation, and problems being encountered in providing social housing;
- a survey of 83 current social housing tenants and ex-tenants who had purchased their property under the Right-to-Buy scheme — which examined the changing characteristics of households and properties remaining within the social sector.

Before proceeding to discuss key findings from this research, though, it is useful to provide some brief background information on the two case-study areas included within the research. Within the wider research project mentioned previously, the two study areas of Aberystwyth and Newtown were selected as being indicative of two high growth areas — in terms of both employment and population totals — located in contrasting parts of rural Wales.

The Aberystwyth study area is situated in Ceredigion in the western part of mid-Wales (Fig. 1). The key providers of social housing in the area, at the time of fieldwork, were Ceredigion District

Council,* which managed 1750 properties and four small-scale housing associations, which together controlled 92 units of social accommodation. Settlement structure and provision of social housing is dominated by the university town of Aberystwyth — which represents the main centre of population, employment and social housing provision. The key villages within the study area are located within commuting distance of Aberystwyth, with other smaller settlements lying in the more eastern parts of the area (Fig. 2).

The Newtown study area is situated in the eastern part of the mid-Wales, within Powys[†] (Fig. 1). In addition to social housing being provided by Montgomeryshire District Council and two small-scale housing associations, the Development Board for Rural Wales (DBRW) has been a key player in constructing low-cost accommodation for sale and rent in the area, particularly in Newtown. Settlement structure and social housing provision is dominated by the town of Newtown — the largest settlement, located in the eastern part of the study area — which has expanded rapidly in terms of housing provision (private and social), population and employment over recent years. Another key settlement and concentration of social housing is the smaller market town of Llanidloes, situated in the west of the area, while smaller villages are located mainly in western and northern parts (Fig. 2).

Changing local levels of social housing provision

The central government assault on the social housing sector over the 1980s and early 1990s has resulted in dramatic reductions in council housing provision in each local area, with stock levels falling by slightly less than one-quarter in the Aberystwyth area and by around one-fifth in the Newtown study area between 1981 and 1991 (Tables 1 and 2). By 1991, local authority housing accounted for only 12% of all dwellings in the former area, and 22% in the Newtown study area.[‡] While housing associations in each area have received increased levels of funding from Tai Cymru over recent years, enabling impressive rises in stock holdings (the number of association dwellings in the Aberystwyth area

*Following local government reorganization in April 1995, Ceredigion District Council became a unitary authority.
†Prior to April 1995, Montgomeryshire District Council had jurisdiction over the Newtown study area.
‡This higher level of public sector rental properties in the Newtown area relates to the large number of rental properties provided by the DBRW, although, by the early 1990s, its housebuilding functions had been restricted and tenants had been given the right to purchase their properties.

doubled and stock levels quadrupled in the Newtown study area over the 1980s), their impact on these local housing markets has been minimal — making up only 1.6% of all dwellings in the Aberystwyth study area, and 2.2% of housing in the Newtown area. Indeed, in overall terms, the number of units of social rental accommodation declined by 17.9% in the Aberystwyth area and by 14.6% in the Newtown study area between 1981 and 1991. Furthermore, notwithstanding the rising level of association stock, the social rental sector in these areas remains dominated by the local authority,

which, in 1991, accounted for seven and ten times the levels of association stock in the Aberystwyth and Newtown areas respectively.

With this decline in social housing, it is clear that these local housing markets have become increasingly dominated by the private sector over recent years — private housing accounted for almost 90% of total dwellings in the Aberystwyth market, and slightly more than three-quarters of all properties in the Newtown area in 1991. The vast majority of this private sector growth has involved owner-occupied

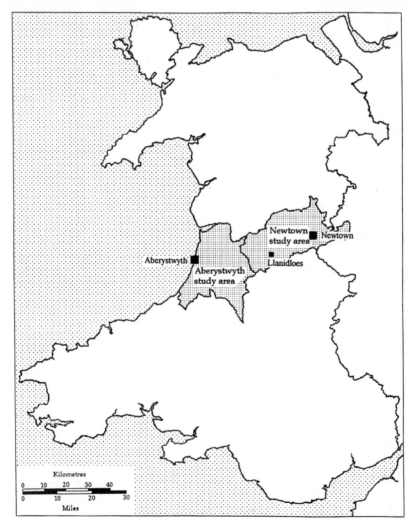

Figure 1. The location of the Aberystwyth and Newtown study areas.

174   Paul Milbourne

housing — which increased its stock holding by in excess of 50% and one-third in the Newtown and Aberystwyth study areas respectively over the 1980s — although a growth in certain parts of the private rental sector is also evident.

While the two local authorities have continued to provide a small amount of social rental housing in the early 1990s (approximately 7% of total new builds), their position as the main providers of new social rental accommodation in the local area has been overtaken by housing associations over recent years (Table 3). Indeed, whereas associations were responsible for only 29% and 35% of new social housing completions in the Aberystwyth and Newtown areas respectively in 1985–1986, their share of social housing new builds had risen to 65 and 58% respectively by 1990–1991. However, while

Figure 2. The distribution of wards in the Aberystwyth and Newtown study areas.

Social Housing Provision in Rural Areas   175

Table 1. Changing patterns of household tenure in the Aberystwyth study area, 1981–1991

	Year					
	1981		1991		% Change	
Tenure	No.	%	No.	%	1981–1991	
Owner-occupied	6095	62.4	8203	70.5	2108	34.6
Local authority/new town rented	1804	18.5	1375	11.8	−429	−24.5
Housing association rented	92	0.9	191	1.6	99	107.6
Private rented — furnished	629	6.4	1084	9.3	455	72.3
Private rented — unfurnished	855	8.8	612	5.3	−243	−26.7
Private rented — with job	287	2.9	167	1.4	−120	−41.8
All properties	9762	100.0	11,632	100.0	1870	19.3

Source: Censuses of Population, 1981, 1991.

this reduced level of recent local authority provision in each area was slightly above average levels for Wales as a whole, local housing associations were providing only about half the national level of new social housing provision (Table 3).

The uneven impacts of social housing restructuring

The overall contraction in, and restructuring of, social rental housing provision, have not impacted evenly on localities in each study area. Indeed, while previous programmes of council housebuilding were focused mainly on the main settlements in each area, recent trends of council house sales and housing association programmes have acted to accentuate this gulf in social housing provision between smaller villages and main towns in each area.

Council house sales under the Right-to-Buy provisions of the 1980 Housing Act accelerated in the early-to-mid 1980s before settling down at a reduced level towards the end of the 1980s and into the 1990s. Between 1980 and 1990, Ceredigion District

Council had sold slightly more than one-quarter of its housing to tenants in the Aberystwyth area and almost one-third of the Montgomeryshire council house stock had been purchased by tenants in the Newtown study area over this same period (Table 4). Levels of sales, though, have witnessed considerable variation within each area — ranging from no houses sold in one village to the sale of the entire council stock in another.* Notwithstanding such variations, the general pattern of council house sales would appear to confirm findings from other studies (Beazley et al., 1980), with the highest proportion of sales taking place in the smaller village locations. Table 4, for example, highlights that in each study area local authority sales were greatest (in proportional terms) in those localities that contained under 50 council houses in 1980.

Given the limited local authority new build activity over the 1980s and early 1990s, it is hardly surprising that the overall level, and localized patterns, of decline of the public sector stock have mirrored

---

*In certain communities, rates of sales have been effected by the location of units of elderly sheltered accommodation, which have been excluded from Right-to-Buy sales.

Table 2. Changing patterns of household tenure in the Newtown study area, 1981–1991

	Year					
	1981		1991		% Change	
Tenure	No.	%	No.	%	1981–1991	
Owner-occupied	4160	50.1	6430	63.9	2270	54.6
Local authority/new town rented	2823	34.0	2238	22.2	−585	−20.7
Housing association rented	58	0.7	222	2.2	164	282.8
Private rented — furnished	108	1.3	197	2.0	89	82.4
Private rented — unfurnished	844	10.2	679	6.7	−165	−19.5
Private rented — with job	308	3.7	295	2.9	−13	4.2
All properties	8301	100.0	10,061	100.0	1760	21.2

Source: Censuses of Population, 1981, 1991.

Rural Planning and Management

Paul Milbourne

Table 3. New property constructions in Ceredigion and Montgomeryshire, 1990–1991

	Ceredigion (%)	Montgomery-shire (%)	Wales (%)
Private companies	80.4	83.9	74.8
Housing associations	12.7	9.3	20.1
Local authorities	6.9	6.7	5.1

Source: Welsh Housing Statistics, 1991, 1992.

those of sales. Between 1981 and 1991, local authority stock decline by 20.7% in the Newtown area and by 23.8% in the Aberystwyth study area, with levels of stock reductions generally greater, in proportional terms, in the smaller rural communities — over 40% losses in stock were recorded in the wards of Llanfarian and Melindwr and Trefeurig in the Aberystwyth study area (Table 5) and the outlying Newtown area wards of Kerry, Llangurig, Llandinam, Dolforwyn and Berriew (Table 6). As such, the residual local authority housing stock in each area has become increasingly concentrated in the main settlements, with the town of Aberystwyth

Table 4. Council house sales in the Aberystwyth and Newtown study areas, 1980–1990

Number of council properties in 1980 in settlements containing...	Aberystwyth area		Newtown area	
	No. of settlements	% Sold	No. of settlements	% Sold
< 20 properties	10	31.1	10	45.4
20–50 properties	6	38.1	3	42.6
51–150 properties	8	22.8	6	38.7
> 150 properties	1	25.5	2	27.0
Total sales	25	26.1	21	31.5

Source: Ceredigion District Council and Montgomeryshire District Council housing departments (personal correspondence).

Table 5. The distribution of social housing in the Aberystwyth study area, 1991

	Housing association properties				Local authority properties						Social rental properties	
	1991				1991			Change in in local authority provision 1981–1991		Change in social rental provision 1981–1991	
	No.	% of all housing in ward	% of all housing assoc. provision in study area	Change in housing assoc. provision 1981–1991	No.	% of all housing in ward	% of all local authority provision in study area	No.	%	No.	%
Aberystwyth	138	3.6	72.3	63	759	19.5	55.2	−213	−21.9	−150	−13.4
Borth	4	0.5	2.1	1	35	4.4	2.5	−16	−31.4	−15	−27.8
Ceulanamaesmawr	3	0.4	1.6	1	66	9.3	4.8	−4	−5.7	−3	−4.2
Faenor	23	3.3	12.0	21	60	8.7	4.4	−16	−21.1	5	6.4
Llanbadarn Fawr	7	1.3	3.7	6	55	10.1	4.0	−17	−23.6	−11	−15.1
Llanfarian	0	0.0	0.0	−2	19	4.2	1.4	−33	−63.5	−35	−64.8
Llanrhystud	2	0.4	1.0	1	19	3.9	1.4	0	0.0	1	5.0
Llansantffraid	2	0.2	1.0	1	61	7.2	4.4	−9	−13.0	−8	−11.3
Lledrod	0	0.0	0.0	−3	117	9.1	8.5	−28	−30.4	−31	−20.9
Melindwr & Trefeurig	3	0.2	1.6	1	62	4.9	4.5	−45	−42.1	−44	−40.4
Tirymynach	7	1.2	3.7	7	76	12.8	5.5	−45	−37.2	−38	−31.4
Ystwyth	2	0.3	1.0	2	46	7.0	3.3	−3	−6.1	−1	−2.0
All wards	191	1.6	100.0	99	1375	11.8	100.0	−429	−23.8	−330	−17.4

Source: Censuses of Population, 1981, 1991.

Social Housing Provision in Rural Areas 177

Table 6. The distribution of social housing in the Newtown study area, 1991

	Housing association properties				Local authority properties					Social rental properties	
	1991				1991			Change in in local authority provision 1981–1991		Change in social rental provision 1981–1991	
	No.	% of all housing in ward	% of all housing assoc. provision in study area	Change in housing assoc. provision 1981–1991	No.	% of all housing in ward	% of all local authority provision in study area	No.	%	No.	%
Berriew	1	0.2	0.5	0	47	9.4	2.1	−33	−41.3	−33	−40.7
Caersws	0	0.0	0.0	0	107	18.6	4.8	−42	−28.2	−42	−28.2
Carno	4	0.6	1.8	−1	65	9.4	2.9	−32	−33.0	−33	−8.2
Churchstoke	7	1.4	3.2	5	60	11.8	2.7	−20	−25.0	−15	−18.3
Dolforwyn	0	0.0	0.0	−1	39	4.7	1.7	−43	−52.4	−44	−53.0
Kerry	3	0.5	1.4	2	49	7.7	2.2	−41	−83.7	−39	−42.9
Llandinam	1	0.3	0.5	1	8	2.5	0.4	−14	−63.6	−13	−59.1
Llangurig	0	0.0	0.0	0	5	1.9	0.2	−14	−73.7	−14	−73.7
Llanidloes	29	2.5	13.1	29	275	24.0	12.3	−119	−30.2	−90	−22.8
Newtown	175	4.2	78.8	127	1574	37.4	70.3	−222	−12.4	−95	−5.2
Trefeglwys	2	0.4	0.9	2	9	1.8	0.4	−5	−35.7	−3	−21.4
All wards	222	2.2	100.0	164	2238	22.2	100.0	−545	−20.7	−421	−14.6

Source: Censuses of Population, 1981, 1991.

accounting for 55.2% of all local authority housing in the Aberystwyth study area in 1991, while 82.6% of council provision in the Newtown area was situated in Newtown and Llanidloes (Tables 5 and 6).

This increasing 'urbanization' of local authority housing stock is also evident within the housing association sector. Association building and acquisition activities in each area over the 1980s and early 1990s have been focused predominantly on the three main settlements, with 63.6% of the 99 new units provided in the Aberystwyth area located in Aberystwyth, and 95.1% of the 164 additional Newtown area units provided in the towns of Newtown and Llanidloes (Tables 5 and 6). However, it should be stressed that even in these settlements the housing association sector accounted for less than 5% of all properties. Indeed, in the remaining non-urban wards of each area the impact of association activity has remained minimal — with five wards recording no association provision in 1991, while in a further 11 wards association provision accounted for less than 1% of all housing (Tables 4 and 5).

Bringing together these two components of social housing change, it is clear that the dramatic reduction in local authority building programmes, Right-to-Buy sales and the increased provision of housing association properties have not only resulted in an overall reduction in social rental housing in all bar two wards, but have also acted to 'urbanize' social

provision in each study area, with the final two columns of Tables 4 and 5 highlighting greater rates of social housing decline in smaller communities.

The residualization of the social housing sector: council house sales and rent increases

In an attempt to explore the decline of social housing stock in greater depth, a survey was conducted of 29 ex-tenants who had purchased their properties under the Right-to-Buy scheme and 54 tenants presently residing in the social housing sector.* As such, the survey allows a comparison to be made between some key characteristics of current and ex-tenants and their respective properties in the two study areas.

Key findings from the survey would appear to indicate a clear residualization of the social housing stock in each area, not just in terms of the dwindling size of this stock, but also in terms of the types of tenants and accommodation remaining within the social housing sector. As might be expected, it has been those households most able to purchase that have bought their properties, with remaining tenant households characterized by lower levels of income,

*This survey of social housing forms part of a wider survey of 400 households resident in the two study areas (see Milbourne, 1997).

Table 7. Income, employment and age characteristics of ex- and current social rental tenants in the Aberystwyth and Newtown study areas

	Ex-tenant	Current tenant
Annual incomes (full-time male earners)*		
< £5000	17.6	25.0
£5000–7499	23.5	16.7
£7500–9999	5.9	41.7
⩾£10,000	52.9	16.6
Socio-economic groups (all workers)		
professional	13.5	10.5
intermediate non-manual	43.2	36.8
skilled manual	21.6	15.8
semi-skilled manual	10.8	26.3
unskilled manual	10.8	10.5
Age(s) of head(s) of household		
15–24 years	6.0	11.8
25–44 years	32.0	29.4
45–59 years	38.0	24.7
⩾60 years	24.0	34.1

*Note: the number of female full-time workers was too small to be included in this table.
Source: author's survey.

Table 8. Property characteristics of ex- and current social rental tenants in the Aberystwyth and Newtown study areas

	Ex-tenant	Current tenant
Property location		
main town	17.2	57.4
village	82.8	42.6
Property size		
one bedroom	0.0	3.7
two bedrooms	7.1	37.0
three bedrooms	89.2	53.7
four bedrooms	3.6	5.6
Property type		
detached house	10.7	7.4
semi-detached house	67.9	37.0
terraced house	10.7	33.3
bungalow	7.1	18.5
flat	3.7	3.6
Property age		
pre-1990	0.0	1.9
1900–1945	7.4	9.3
1946–1960	70.4	31.5
1961–1970	11.1	48.1
1971–1980	11.1	3.7
1981–present	0.0	5.6

Source: author's survey.

higher proportions of workers in manual occupations and higher percentages of elderly persons than purchasing households (Table 7). Furthermore, Right-to-Buy sales have been concentrated amongst larger, better quality properties located in smaller villages, with over two-thirds of all sales involving three- or four-bedroom semi-detached houses built in the immediate post-war period and situated on smaller estates in villages (Table 8).*

The fact that the residual social housing sector is becoming increasingly characterized by low-income and elderly households may well indicate that sales will never again reach those levels recorded in the mid-1980s. Indeed, the survey revealed that around 70% of current social tenants do not want to purchase their properties in the near future, with the main reasons behind this disinclination to buy being a perception that the household would not be able to afford the likely purchase price of, or obtain a mortgage on, the property, and a feeling that the household was 'too old' to change its housing circumstances.

*A similar pattern of sales emerges from an analysis of sales of DBRW properties to tenants which were initiated in the early 1990s, with three-bedroom houses making up 60% of the Board's stock in 1990 but 81% of sales between 1990 and 1991, while flats and maisonettes accounted for only 2% of sales but 15% of all DBRW housing.

A further aspect of the residualization of social housing in each area has concerned the increasing costs associated with renting such accommodation, which has tended to create difficulties for those tenants who are ineligible to receive housing benefit payments. Indeed, recent central government housing and fiscal policies, aimed at introducing market rents into the social housing sector, have acted to increase average levels of local rents in both the local authority and housing association sectors. Between 1981 and 1991 average local authority rental levels increased by 131%, while housing association rents rose by 69% in the 1985–1991 period. Furthermore, the introduction of mixed funding for new housing association schemes have acted to make average association rent levels more expensive than those in the local authority sector, with mean association rents in the rural counties of Dyfed and Powys being 28 and 14% higher respectively than council rents in 1991 (Welsh Office, 1982, 1986, 1992).

New partnerships of provision: local responses to central state restructuring

By the late 1980s and early 1990s, the impacts of central state social housing restructuring on local housing needs were becoming clear. The number of households registered on local authority waiting lists showed increases over the late 1980s of 13% in the Newtown study area and 19% in the Aberystwyth area. Furthermore, levels of 'official' homelessness increased by more than 250% between 1985 and 1991 in the Aberystwyth study area, and a rise of 600% in households accepted as homeless was recorded in the Newtown study area* (Welsh Office, 1992). Articles in local newspapers began to highlight individual cases of housing need and the failure or inability of the local state to respond to such need. In July 1989, the Aberystwyth area local newspaper ran an editorial on the subject of the local needs for social housing:

'A new buzz term is currently being banded about by politicians and others — 'social housing'. It presumably lacks the stigma of good, old-fashioned 'council housing' and embraces, we suppose, private-sector rented accommodation too. Whatever our views on this latter-day jargon, it is an expression much in the news at present. Scarcely a single local authority meeting goes by when the acute shortage of social housing is not raised as a vital topic. And however you define the term, one thing is abundantly clear. There is not enough of it'. (Cambrian News, 7 July 1989, p. 24)

It was also clear, though, that many local authority councillors and members in each area were equally frustrated by the imposition of this new system of providing such social housing and the restricted role placed on local authority intervention within local housing markets. Two extracts taken from reports of meetings of the Ceredigion housing committee in the period immediately after the 1988 Housing Act becoming law illustrate these localized tensions concerning changing systems of provision:

Councillor A: People have been coming up to me wanting to know where they can live. These are young people looking for housing, many of whom have been on the waiting list for a long time.

Chief Executive: The Council would love to pursue its former programme of council housing, but the Government has changed the law. Instead of being the providers we are now only to assist in the provision, with housing associations being the main providers. (Ceredigion District Council housing committee meeting, December 1988)

We want money to build. We have architects and land we want to build on. But the legislation has got to be passed to allow us to do this. Housing associations are only scratching the surface. We should demand that local authorities get back this house building function

*These figures relate to the associated pre-1995 districts of Ceredigion and Montgomeryshire. District-level figures on homelessness were first published by the Welsh Office in 1985.

again, with amended legislation. (Councillor B, housing committee meeting, March 1990)

Accepting its new role as social housing enabler rather than provider, each local authority over this period began to increase its links with other 'social landlords', and particularly local housing associations, and entered into a series of partnerships in an attempt to meet local housing needs. In a 1991–1992 housing strategy document, for example, Montgomeryshire District Council stated that, while it wished to remain as the main provider of social housing in its area of jurisdiction, the authority also recognized the need to work with other agencies which were 'reputable, locally-based, accountable, have shared objectives with the Council and [form] part of a strategic approach [to the provision of social housing]' (p. 2). Partnerships with local associations in the post-1988 period have usually consisted of the local authority offering parcels of its land, at below market levels, to local associations for new social housing schemes in exchange for nomination rights on a proportion of the newly constructed units. An example of such a scheme, reported in the Aberystwyth local newspaper in the early 1990s, is outlined below. The article also illustrates the small-scale nature of these partnership schemes and the high level of local authority influence over nominations:

Land owned by Ceredigion District Council at Blaenplwyf may soon be sold for housing development at below District Valuer's price. CT Plumlumon, the Aberystwyth-based housing association, wants to build four houses, two bungalows and six flats on council-owned land. Nine units will be allocated to applicants on the council's waiting list and three to people on the housing association list. (Cambrian News, 9 March 1990)

Although partnerships between the local authorities and housing associations have resulted in the provision of new units of social housing in each area, the small-scale nature and limited years of operation of the local association sector have meant that most of these local associations possess neither the financial resources nor management experience for them to be involved in larger-scale schemes. Furthermore, interviews with managers of these associations revealed other problems concerning their activities in rural parts of each area. The limited availability and high cost of land for development in many villages, together with the fact that Tai Cymru funding was generally not available for renovating existing properties, meant that the bulk of their activities was focused on larger settlements, and particularly the towns of Newtown and Aberystwyth. More generally, though, interviews with housing association managers revealed that existing levels of central funding from Tai Cymru were inadequate for them to meet local housing needs, while the changing nature of this funding — with an increased emphasis on mixed public–private funding packages — meant that additional costs associated with new repayments schemes were being transferred to new tenants:

> Yes, we are encountering problems developing units at affordable rents with current grant rates from Tai Cymru. (association A)

> Our difficulties involve having to increase rents on new schemes and maintaining standards of design and specification whilst keeping houses affordable. We also have rising waiting lists, with demand far greater than supply. (association C)

> Sites are expensive and mixed funding has meant that rehabilitation is no longer an option. Rent levels have risen sharply due to mixed funding and high interest rates. (association D)

Finally, in this section on local state responses to central state restructuring, it should be stated that such changes have not merely been imposed on these study areas. Indeed, while it is clear that the two local authorities have been increasingly restricted in terms of the scope of their operations, action has been initiated by each in an attempt to offset (if not reverse) the effects of central government housing policies. In 1989, for example, Ceredigion District Council led a delegation of 12 district councils in rural Wales which called on the Welsh Office to release an additional £100 million of central funds to finance a new programme of council housing building in the Welsh countryside. Although this request proved ultimately unsuccessful, the Welsh Office did release an extra £1 million capital allocation to help rural local authorities purchase properties and land from the private sector in order to meet local needs in areas characterized by a high incidence of second homes. This said, one-third of Ceredigion's allocation of £90,000 was expended on the purchase of just a single property.

In addition to efforts to secure previous powers to build social housing, each local authority, like others in rural Wales, have actively used (and misused) the planning system in an attempt to provide additional units of social accommodation. In the mid-1980s, for example, Gwynedd County Council overtly challenged existing central state planning legislation by bringing social and cultural considerations into planning decisions on new housing developments. More recently, a Welsh Select Affairs Committee report (House of Commons, 1992/3) has criticized a number of local authorities in rural Wales for granting planning permission on new residential developments in non-designated areas. Indeed, Ceredigion's Director of Planning stated in May

1989 that the Council's elected representatives had acted illegally in that:

> from time to time permissions have been issued in locations which conflict with national and local planning policy on the basis of what has been regarded as being overwhelming local need. (p. 1)

With the introduction of new planning guidance by the Welsh Office in 1989, such permissions for new housing in cases of local housing need were to be permitted, but only on smaller sites adjoining existing settlements. As such, rural authorities were awarded new rights to intervene in the open housing market which enabled them to develop and implement local needs housing policies based on the provision of affordable private ownership, rather than social rental, housing opportunities. In developing such policies, each of the study authorities has considered wider linguistic and cultural factors alongside issues of local housing need. The Montgomeryshire plan, for example, stated that:

> throughout Montgomeryshire the protection and promotion of the Welsh language and culture will be a proper planning consideration in determining all applications for housing development. (p. 7)

Within these local needs land policies, suitable for development outside of designated planning areas was identified by the local authority and negotiations were entered into with landowners. Suitable land was then offered to local building firms, at below market prices, which could then construct houses at lower costs. However, only those households which could satisfy a local residence requirement and also demonstrate a recognized housing need were eligible to purchase such dwellings. The Ceredigion plan further stipulated that such housing would be restricted to those persons aged under 40 years and that dwellings could only be used as a sole residence. New occupants of this low-cost housing were required to enter into occupancy agreements which restricted future sales to those persons who also satisfied these occupancy requirements. As such, these housing needs schemes involved the local authority working with new sets of partners in the private sector, both in the capacity of securing new sites for development and reassuring the funders and builders of such housing of its financial viability. As Ceredigion's Director of Planning suggested:

> landowners, builders and building societies or banks may be reluctant to either release land, construct or finance the construction of dwellings on these terms. (1989, p. 2)

In fact, the power of these authorities to intervene in the open housing market is very much dependent on the co-operation of these private sector agencies, and the refusal of building societies to lend on properties involved in the Ceredigion low-cost housing scheme forced the authority to remove its original previous ownership restriction.

Changing systems of managing and allocating social housing

Given the new powers awarded to housing associations by central government and the sector's growing importance as provider of social housing in each study area, it is important to consider the ways in which systems of management and allocation of social housing operated by local associations compare with those characteristic of the local authority system. Indeed, it has been suggested previously that there exist some key differences between the two systems of social housing activities.

Although the issue of management structures was not pursued in any great depth within the research, it is clear that the relatively small scale nature of local housing association operations has meant that the sector is characterized by much more decentralized and flexible structures of management than the local authority in each area. This said, in the early 1990s, Montgomeryshire District Council reviewed its housing management structure and implemented a more decentralized system of management which involved the establishment of six Area Lettings Sub-Committees composed of officials and elected members for these areas. Furthermore, the authority began to experiment with schemes aimed at increasing the participation of council tenants in housing management issues.

While associations can be seen as more decentralized and flexible agencies for managing and allocating social housing in these study areas, it remains the case that they are also less accountable to local citizens than the local authority. Each association was managed by a committee of around nine members who served in a voluntary capacity and were drawn from various positions within the local community. However, members were invited, rather than elected, on to these committees, and the Local Government and Housing Act (1989) restricted representation of local authority officials or councillors to a maximum of 20%. Furthermore, these committees played a relatively minor role in the day-to-day operations of associations, with decisions on allocations taken solely by members of staff, and only reviewed on a general basis by committee members 'to ensure that tenancies have been made in line with laid down policy'.

Such processes of allocation contrast with those practiced by the two local authorities. Here, although waiting lists were managed by housing department staff, decisions on individual allocations were taken by a group composed of both officers and elected members, with this group able to award up to 8% of available points to applicants which it deemed as 'particularly deserving cases'. Indeed, in the case of the Montgomeryshire allocation system, the allocation group possessed additional powers in deciding on tenancies:

> Allocations will normally be made to the applicant with the highest number of points whose family is suitable for the accommodation. However, the Area Lettings Sub-Committee shall have discretion to select any applicant from the 10 highest pointed applicants in Llanidloes, Machynlleth, Newtown and Welshppol, and the 5 highest pointed applicants elsewhere, should they judge-...that the applicant in question has the greatest need of housing...the Area Letting Sub-Committee shall [also] use their judgement to determine priority amongst applicants with equal points.

With the exception of one association, social rental housing managed by each authority and association was available to all groups experiencing housing need who had been resident in the local area for a minimum period (usually 2 years), although recent reductions in council stock and the relatively small amount of association properties meant that the points system operated by each association and local authority took on a greater role in deciding allocations. Indeed, local authority managers suggested that these factors acted to discourage certain groups — young single people and childless couples were two groups cited — from applying for council accommodation.

An analysis of the points system operated by the two local authorities, in fact, reveals an allocation system which places much greater emphasis on factors concerning environmental health — such as overcrowding and the lack or sharing of key facilities — than on those of income levels and the availability or affordability of other housing options in the local area. Table 9, for example, highlights that the factors of overcrowding and inadequate amenities together account for 37 and 43% of all points respectively in the Ceredigion and Montgomeryshire allocation systems, while financial considerations only feature to a minimal degree in Montgomeryshire (and here only a maximum of 2 points are available). Furthermore, while each system utilizes a common set of eight factors which award points to applicants, it is clear that the relative weightings attached to these factors mean that applicants with similar characteristics will have different probabilities of being re-housed by the two authorities. For example, the Montgomeryshire system allocates a

Rural Planning and Management

Paul Milbourne

Table 9. A breakdown of the points system operated by Ceredigion and Montgomeryshire housing departments

	Maximum number of points awarded			
	Ceredigion		Montgomeryshire	
	No.	%	No.	%
Commonalities				
Overcrowding on bedroom standard	6	1.6	6*	4.5
Statutory overcrowding	10	16.4	5	3.8
Shared facilities	5	8.2	10	7.6
Inadequate or lacking facilities	5	8.2	27	20.6
Local connection	5	8.2	25	19.1
Family separation	5	8.2	10	7.6
Discretionary power	5	8.2	10	7.6
Tied tenancies	5	8.2	10	7.6
Differences				
Property in bad state of disrepair	5	8.2	0	
Period on waiting list	10	16.4	0	
Children in flats	0		3	2.3
Applicants in caravans	0		2	1.5
Financial circumstances	0		3	2.3
Applicants leaving care	0		10	7.6
Medical points	0		10	7.6
Maximum number of points available	61	100.0	131	100.0

*Based on 3 children sharing with adult(s).
Sources: Ceredigion District Council and Montgomeryshire District Council housing departments.

maximum of 19% of all available points for the length of residence in the district compared to upto only 8% of points in Ceredigion.

While local associations also award the vast majority of points to those applicants who are living in accommodation characterized by inadequate physical conditions, account is also taken of issues of the availability and affordability of other housing options within the local area. One association stated that it aimed to cater for those 'young people setting up home for the first time', with consideration given to 'the affordability of other solutions to the [applicant's housing] problem [and] the possibility of obtaining an alternative property'. A similar situation existed with association C, which assessed:

an applicant's ability to find alternative accommodation — whether the applicant has priority on the local authority waiting list, the applicant's ability to purchase suitable alternative accommodation, or secure shared ownership property

with another association, B, attempting to restrict its accommodation to those who were considered to be in 'low-income' households, by discriminating against 'applicants in well-paid employment or with a large capital sum after property sale', and advising such applicants on their remote chances of being re-housed by the association.

Conclusion

This paper has explored local impacts of, and responses to, central state restructuring of social housing in rural areas generally, and within two particular parts of the Welsh countryside over the 1980s and early 1990s. In doing this, it has attempted to position social housing changes within a context of wider discussion on local government restructuring, political ideology and regulation theory. Indeed, the paper has highlighted the ways in which social housing has been used by successive Conservative governments over the 1980s as a 'testing ground' for their attempts to 'roll back the welfare state', while drawing on a regulationist perspective, it has also considered how such central policies have been mediated though, and in certain cases contested by, the actions of different clusters of housing agencies at the local level.

It is clear that central state restructuring of social housing has impacted directly on these, and other, areas of the British countryside over recent years, with local housing authorities no longer able to intervene directly within the local housing market through new housing constructions, and local housing associations forced to compete in an increasingly market-driven financial environment. The social housing sector has become increasingly residualized over the 1980s and early 1990s, and it can be suggested that, with historically lower levels of council housing provision in rural areas, together with the more recent restricted activities of smaller rural housing associations, the degree of social housing residualization in areas of the countryside is now much more pronounced than in many urban housing markets.

A second aspect of residualization identified within the paper relates to the changing composition of households and stock within the social housing sector. As Right-to-Buy sales have been dominated by younger, more affluent tenants purchasing the larger, better quality social properties, so the gulf has widened between those households reliant on this restricted pool of social accommodation and those able to enter owner-occupation. Furthermore, this trend has been accentuated by recent rises in social rental levels, associated with changing central funding mechanisms, which have acted to exclude many low-income households who are ineligible for state benefits on grounds of (un)affordability.

A final component of social housing residualization, and one which can be seen as particularly characteristic of many rural districts in Britain, concerns the increased spatial residualization of social housing provision which has taken place over the 1980s and early 1990s. Indeed, the paper has highlighted how past and present patterns of social housing provision, together with recent Right-to-Buy sales, have resulted in an 'urbanization' of the residual social stock, with households resident in many of the smaller villages in each of the study areas faced with limited opportunities for entering the social housing sector.

Alongside a consideration of the residualization of the social housing sector, the paper has also explored the different ways in which central housing policy has been mediated through key housing agencies at the local level. It has highlighted how the two main social landlords — local authorities and housing associations — have experienced sets of problems in responding to their new positions within the social sector. The two local authorities in the study areas have attempted to maximize their more restricted roles through the increased use of partnerships with housing associations and other private sector agencies, while local associations have been forced to rely on these local authorities in order to secure development land at below market levels. Indeed, it can be suggested that, in these two rural areas at least, the local housing authority maintains a powerful position as both enabler and (indirect) provider of social housing opportunities.

As a greater number of agencies have become involved in providing social housing in these study areas — including the local authority, housing associations, landowners, building firms and building societies — so routes for potential tenants into the social housing sector have become much more differentiated. In fact, the paper has pointed to a wide range of procedures in operation which determine which groups of the local population can enter these different components of the social housing sector — differences in the composition of groups allocating social housing, in the weightings attached to criteria such as 'localness' and 'affordability' within allocation procedures, and in the role played by the private sector in influencing local needs housing policies.

In addition to this local mediation of central policy, the paper has also considered the role of these housing agencies in contesting the outcomes of central government social housing restructuring in rural areas. At a national level, attention has been focused briefly on the role played by the 'rural housing lobby' in securing amendments to national housing and planning policies, while the Welsh study has highlighted tensions amongst local authority officers and councillors concerning their restricted powers, efforts to secure previous levels of powers and resources through the lobbying of central government, and the use and misuse of the land-use planning system in an attempt to meet local housing needs. It remains to be seen how the processes of central state restructuring of social housing outlined in this paper, and explored within the context of two areas of rural Wales, have impacted on, and been mediated through and contested by social housing agencies in, other parts of the British countryside.

Acknowledgements — The research on which this paper is based was funded by a University of Wales studentship. I would also like to thank the editor and two anonymous referees for their constructive comments.

References

Balchin, P. (1995) *Housing Policy: An Introduction.* Routledge, London.

Beazley, M., Gavin, D., Gillon, S., Raine, C. and Staunton, M. (1980) The sale of council houses in a rural area: a case study of South Oxfordshire. Working Paper No. 44, Oxford Polytechnic, Department of Planning, Oxford.

Clark, G. (1982) *Housing and Planning in the Countryside.* Wiley, Chichester.

Cloke, P. and Edwards, G. (1985) Cymdeithas Tai Dyffryn and local authority housing provision in mid Wales. Working Paper No. 8, Department of Geography, Saint David's University College, Lampeter.

Cloke, P., Goodwin, M. and Milbourne, P. (1994a) *Lifestyles in Rural Wales.* Welsh Office, Cardiff (unpublished).

Cloke, P., Milbourne, P. and Thomas, C. (1994b) *Lifestyles in Rural England*. Rural Development Commission, London.

Cochrane, A. (1994) *Whatever Happened to Local Government?* OU Press, Buckingham.

Cole, I. and Furbey, R. (1994) *The Eclipse Of Council Housing*. Routledge, London.

Department of the Environment (1993) *The 1991 English House Condition Survey*. HMSO, London.

Dickens, P., Duncan, S., Goodwin, M. and Gray, F. (1985) *Housing, States and Localities*. Methuen, London.

Doling, J. (1993) British housing policy: 1984–93. *Regional Studies* 27(6), 583–588.

Dunn, M., Rawson, M. and Rogers, A. (1981) *Rural Housing: Competition or Choice*. Allen & Unwin, London.

Hoggart, K. (1993) House construction in nonmetropolitan districts: economy, politics and rurality. *Regional Studies* 27(7), 651–665.

Hoggett, P. (1987) A farewell to mass production? decentralisation as an emergent private and public paradigm. In Decentralisation and democracy, eds P. Hoggett and R. Hambleton. Occasional Paper 28, SAUS, Bristol.

House of Commons (1992/3) Welsh Affairs Committee Third Report, *Rural Housing 2*. HMSO, London.

Kennedy, R. (1991) *London: World City moving into the 21st Century*. HMSO, London.

Housing Act (1988) HMSO, London.

Local Government and Housing Act (1989) HMSO, London.

Milbourne, P. (1997) Housing conflict and domestic property classes. *Environment and Planning A* 29, 43–62.

Murie, A. (1982) A new era for council housing. In *The Future of Council Housing*, ed. J. English. Croom Helm, London.

Newby, H. (1979) *Green and Pleasant Land?* Hutchinson, London.

Phillips, D. and Williams, A. (1982a) Local authority housing and accessibility: evidence from South Hams,

Devon. *Transactions of the Institute of British Geographers* NS 7, 304–320.

Phillips, D. and Williams, A. (1982b) *Rural Housing and the Public Sector*. Gower, Aldershot.

Phillips, D. and Williams, A. (1984) Public-sector housing in rural areas in England. In *The Changing Countryside*, eds G. Clark *et al.* GeoBooks, Norwich.

Power, A. (1993) *Hovels to High Rise: State Housing in Europe Since 1850*. Routledge, London.

Richmond, P. (1984) Alternative tenures in rural areas: the role of housing associations. In *The Changing Countryside*, eds G. Clark *et al.* GeoBooks, Norwich.

Rogers, A. (1976) Rural housing. In *Rural Planning Problems*, ed. G. E. Cherry. Leonard Hill, London.

Saunders, P. (1984) Beyond housing classes: the sociological significance of private property rights in the means of consumption. *International Journal of Urban and Regional Research* 8, 202–227.

Spencer, K. (1995) The reform of social housing. In *Local Government in the 1990s*, eds J. Stewart and G. Stoker. Macmillan, London.

Stoker, G. and Mossberger, K. (1995) The post-fordist local state: the dynamics of its development. In *Local Government in the 1990s*, eds J. Stewart and G. Stoker. Macmillan, London.

Shucksmith (1981) *No Homes For Locals*. Gower, Aldershot.

Welsh Office (1982) *Welsh Housing Statistics*, HMSO, London.

Welsh Office (1986) *Welsh Housing Statistics*, HMSO, London.

Welsh Office (1992) *Welsh Housing Statistics*, HMSO, London.

Welsh Office (1995) *A Working Countryside for Wales*. HMSO, London.

Young, R. K. (1987) Housing Associations: their role in the rural context. In *Rural Housing In Scotland: Recent Research and Policy*, eds R. MacGregor, D. Robertson and M. Shucksmith. Aberdeen University Press, Aberdeen.

[33]

 Pergamon

S0966-6923(96)00002-6

Journal of Transport Geography, Vol. 4, No. 2, pp. 93–106, 1996
Copyright © 1996 Elsevier Science Ltd
Printed in Great Britain. All rights reserved
0966-6923/96 $15.00 + 0.00

Rural transport problems and non-car populations in the USA

A UK perspective

Stephen D Nutley

School of Environmental Studies, University of Ulster, Coleraine, County Londonderry BT52 1SA, Northern Ireland

The UK and the USA are compared with respect to the transportation problems experienced in rural areas by disadvantaged population groups. While this has been a popular subject in the UK, there appears to be little interest in the USA, where it is particularly neglected by geographers. This is primarily due to the assumption of universal car ownership in the USA. Hence the question arises of whether rural transport problems can be 'solved' by very high car ownership rates. The first part of this article is a brief review of the relevant US literature, drawing attention not only to the objective differences from the UK, but also to divergent perceptions of the issue. This is followed by a summary of statistical indicators for the USA, concentrating on car ownership patterns and their relationships with the rural condition and the poverty factor. Copyright © 1996 Elsevier Science Ltd

Keywords: rural transport problems, non-car populations, USA

The study of rural areas by transport researchers appears very much a minority interest in relation to the overall body of transport literature, although the degree of emphasis varies from one country to another. International comparisons may therefore be instructive, not only on the basis of objective analysis of transport consumption in rural areas and the governing policy framework, but also on the basis of the level of interest shown and perceived importance of the rural sector. The aim here is to compare the UK with the USA, on the grounds that there are very significant differences between the two countries in the geographical characteristics of rural areas, in the transport resources available, and in the attitudes of the public, institutional decision makers and academic analysts. Perceptions of transport-related 'problems' and policy 'solutions' invite comparison. These have to be appraised in the context of different levels of economic development between the UK and the USA, and in particular one factor – car ownership rates – has to be emphasized as the most crucial in determining passenger transport conditions in the rural regions of both countries.

These objectives will be developed further below. In the UK the distinctive problems of rural areas with respect to passenger transport and accessibility were recognized early and have attracted a lot of attention from geographers and other professional commentators. Compared with the urban norm, rural environments demonstrate an absence of significant congestion, parking and pollution problems, higher car ownership rates due not to wealth but to greater need and lack of alternatives, much lower levels of public transport due to the economic problem of serving a highly dispersed pattern of demand, longer distances to middle- and high-order centres of economic activity, and a greater social gulf between car owners and non-car owners with the latter possibly exhibiting problems of isolation and hardship (Moseley, 1979; Nutley, 1992). Long-term trends are for increasing car ownership, declining public transport and local service outlets, and increasing social polarization. At this level of generalization, such conditions are applicable also to the USA and other developed 'western' countries.

More specifically, the potential interest value of a

UK–US comparison is stimulated by two factors. The first is the significantly higher car ownership levels in the USA relative to the UK, and the second is the apparent lack of attention paid to rural transportation issues by academic geographers in the USA as opposed to the popularity of the subject in the UK. This latter point is examined in a comparative review of relevant literature, as much to discern differences in perception of the problem as to describe objective realities. In the light of the much greater weight of geographical research on the subject in the UK, the approach taken inevitably is to examine the situation in the USA *from a UK perspective*. This is followed by some basic empirical measures of aspects of rural transportation in the USA and some elementary statistical relationships, interpreted in the light of British research. To facilitate comparisons, data are taken from the US population census of 1990 and the UK census of 1991, even though in some cases more recent data are available.

Rural transportation is seen as a 'problem' by UK geographers essentially because of the difficulties of mobility, accessibility and isolation suffered by those people without the regular use of a car. The car ownership rate is therefore vital, and most British studies use this as the starting point for analysis. In 1991 the overall national figure was 66.6% of households with at least one vehicle or 364 cars per 1000 people; the US equivalents for 1990 were 88.5% or 577. Basic comparative data are provided in *Table 1* as an initial point of reference. Unlike in the USA, the UK census has no official definition of 'urban' and 'rural', and suitable data have to be obtained from local government units believed to be wholly or mainly rural or from contemporary surveys in rural case study areas. Distinctions are powerfully reinforced by looking at multiple car ownership. British research emphasizes that transport difficulties in rural areas are experienced by persons within single-car households who do not have access to the vehicle when required, and hence car ownership must be related to numbers of people rather than families. Differences in the prevalence of two- and three-car households, persons/car and vehicles/household, are remarkable. The two-car family is normal in the USA, and in rural areas even more so. It might be noted that households with only one car appear as a

minority group, with the rural figure lower than the national (the reverse of the UK situation), possibly supporting American authors' views that to have only a single vehicle is a symptom of disadvantage. There are also grounds for believing that with car ownership levels so high overall, urban–rural disparities are much lower than in the UK.

International differences are inevitably reflected in mobility patterns. Modal choice demonstrates not only higher car ownership in the USA but also wider public transport availability in the UK. As a basic indicator, *Table 2* gives some journey to work data, although national averages are heavily urban biased. For rural areas, the massive automobile dominance in the USA is expected, while public transport has collapsed to the extent that only 0.6% use it for their work journey. UK equivalents are generally higher but variable; public transport is more important for non-work purposes, and its level of service is a vital measure of potential mobility for non-car populations. Non-use of public transport can be ascribed to either (a) consumers exercising free choice and opting for a more convenient alternative, or (b) the almost complete absence of suitable services. In the UK the correct interpretation is (a); in the USA it is more likely to be (b). Inter-state variations in public transport use are very great. Perhaps surprisingly, the proportion of work journeys over 45 minutes is little greater in rural areas; the average journey time is 22 minutes against the urban 19 minutes. Neither is there much sign of greater car sharing – the main response to rural problems is simply higher car ownership.

UK car ownership continues to increase steadily, although it will never reach American levels, which are astoundingly high from a British viewpoint. Despite much research on the problems of rural immobility, the assumption persists that rising car ownership must reduce the scale of the problem by reducing the numbers of people affected. There is a danger that it lowers political concern and recognition of the problem, and encourages the myth that only a 'declining minority' of the population is in difficulties. Rising car ownership certainly undermines the demand for public transport and other alternatives and raises their unit

Table 1 Basic comparative data on car ownership

	USA (1990)	USA rural	UK (1991)	UK rural (estimates)
% households with				
No car	11.5	5.9	33.4	20 to 32
One car only	33.8	26.8	43.5	40 to 50
2+ cars	54.7	67.3	23.1	20 to 35
(of which) 3+ cars	17.3	25.1	4.0	3 to 8
Persons/car	1.57	1.43	2.65	2.3 to 2.8
Cars/household	1.67	1.97	0.94	0.9 to 1.1

Table 2 Basic comparative data on travel to work

	USA (1990)	USA rural	UK (1991)	UK rural (estimates)
% travel to work				
Solo car driver	73.1	75.8	54.1[a]	45 to 60[a]
Car sharing	13.4	14.7	8.0[b]	7 to 12[b]
Public transport	5.3	0.6	15.8	2 to 8
Walk	3.9	3.0	12.1	10 to 20
No journey	3.0	4.8	5.1	5 to 15
% car users sharing	15.4	16.3	12.8	10 to 20
% journeys >45 mins	12.5	13.5	n.a.	n.a.

Notes: [a]all drivers; [b]all passengers.

costs, thus leading to greater social polarization between 'car' and 'non-car' groups. While government institutions in the UK accept that rural car ownership will never reach anything close to 100%, and that there will always be a car-less population, this might in future be confined to the elderly and poor only. With these exceptions, a common assumption is that car ownership, in a congestion-free rural environment, *does* generally solve the problems of living in low-density regions.

It might be asked whether countries with very high car ownership rates experience any significant problems of rural mobility. Hence the interest in a UK–US comparison. In the USA the conspicuous lack of concern for such issues is undoubtedly due to the assumption that 'everyone has a car' or at least that everyone has a vehicle for use nearby. The only significant recognition of non-car populations in the USA refers to poor segregated inner-city zones. Paaswell (1973), for example, comparing problems of 'the carless' in the UK and USA, considered urban areas only. One irony of this is that in terms of relative distances and access to facilities, rural inhabitants face much greater spatial barriers than city dwellers. In comparison with the UK, population densities are much lower and distances much longer in the rural USA; can it be simply assumed that these are cancelled out by the lower cost of gasoline? In addition to seeking evidence on the situation of non-car groups in rural America, and transportation alternatives, it is also appropriate to look for mobility difficulties among the car-owning majority.

A UK view of the US literature

Not only does the literature convey a significantly lower level of interest in rural transportation in the USA, compared with the UK, but the work published has not been by geographers. US contributions by transport and management specialists, economists and sociologists lose much in their neglect of the spatial dimension, and show no awareness of important geographical concepts – such as accessibility – which are emphasized in UK studies. To ensure comparability, the following review will be confined to books and articles in mainstream journals, and will ignore 'semi-published' items such as local authority reports, technical papers and theses.

In the UK, recognition of a 'rural transport problem' dates from the early 1960s, a period characterized by severe cuts in local bus and rail services (Thomas, 1963). Interest and concern expressed through academic studies was strongest in the period 1970–85, partly reflecting greater local authority and government involvement, but has slackened since 1985 as attention shifted to the effects of bus deregulation. The most prominent book-length treatment of the subject has been by Moseley (1979), while a more recent general review is given by Nutley (1992). A good indicator of

the depth of interest is the publication of collected conference papers (such as Cresswell, 1978; White, 1978; Halsall and Turton, 1979; Cloke, 1985), although coverage is often very selective. Rural geographers have also identified transport as an important concern, and general texts usually devote a chapter to the issue (Pacione, 1984; Phillips and Williams, 1984; Robinson, 1990). Essentially, UK research is founded on the detailed analysis of local case studies, *inter alia*: Moseley *et al* (1977), Banister (1980), Stanley and Farrington (1981) Smith and Gant (1982), Nutley (1983), Kilvington and McKenzie (1985), Moyes (1989), Bell and Cloke (1990), Nutley and Thomas (1992), Jordan and Nutley (1993).

US literature on rural transportation is rather fragmented and struggles to establish a foothold within transport studies, reflecting the weak perception of the problem. It includes recognizable clusters of interest on economic and policy matters, such as the future of rural freight railroads, and on social concerns such as the plight of the elderly in small communities. There are very few book-length works on the subject. Much useful historical and background information is given in Maggied (1982), although the book is mainly a case study of rural Georgia. Its title, *Transportation for the Poor*, betrays a common assumption that the only reason for non-car ownership in the USA is poverty, but it also claims that low-income car owners experience problems in remote areas. Focusing on working people, the basic thesis is that there are close relationships between poverty, limited personal mobility and access to workplaces. This is related to the theme of rural economic decline, despite counter-urbanization, throughout much of the USA. A chapter on historical development of the problem claims the linkage between rural poverty and relative immobility was not recognized until the late 1960s. Government action was primarily focused on agriculture and freight rates. A review of US federal and Georgia state legislation between 1960 and 1980 found that macro-policies on economic development and transportation continued to miss the target of rural mobility, and cuts in federal programmes were anticipated from the Reagan administration after 1980.

Deregulation of the transport industries in the USA occurred between 1976 and 1982, and as in the UK the effects were expected to be felt most negatively in rural areas. Service standards available to small communities have been examined by Due *et al* (1990), with reference to buses, railroads, trucking services and airlines. This is a more transport- and policy-orientated approach, although with some concern for the impact on consumers and the viability of settlements. A notable feature of analysis is the inventory approach, less common in UK studies, where lists are compiled of the proportion of towns of a certain size with or without services of a certain type. The general conclusion is that the impact of deregulation has been variable, with smaller places losing out and others benefiting; trucking and air services have gained more than bus and rail. It is also argued that policy changes have only accelerated pre-existing economic and social trends in rural regions. The effect on local economies is a distinctive concern. In *Profitability and Mobility in Rural America* (Gillis, 1989), 'mobility' is interpreted mainly in terms of freight transport for agricultural and manufactured products, and is linked explicitly to the prosperity or viability of smaller communities.

In pursuing a UK–US comparison, an obvious point for consideration is the great differences in the character of rural areas, not least the scale factor between the two countries. Almost everywhere in the UK except northern Scotland is functionally tied to the economies of large cities, and nearly all rural districts have a growing ex-urban population. Especially in lowland England, rural population densities are relatively high, and most small settlements have their quota of middle-class commuters. These trends are reflected in transport resources and travel patterns. Greater distances in the rural USA, despite very high car ownership, must produce problems of relative isolation. However, this is not generally recognized as a significant issue by rural geographers (eg Bohland, 1988). The main exception is Lonsdale and Holmes's (1981) volume on the plains, mountain and desert 'sparselands' of the western USA. In reviewing transport issues, Briggs (1981) finds no general solution in state intervention or subsidy but prefers pragmatic, locally adaptable measures. Other economic sectors face the same problem of high costs in low-density areas, even if transport is not mentioned explicitly, eg Moriarty (1981) on health and education services. The changing functions of small towns and villages are a persistent theme (Johansen and Fuguitt, 1981, 1984), but unfortunately retail and other commercial services are analysed without reference to transportation facilities. Decline in commercial outlets among the smaller places is partly ascribed to increased mobility of the population. Amongst the very large literature on 'rural America', sociological works sometimes recognize transport as an important issue (Saltzman and Newlin, 1981; Kaye, 1982).

The assumption of near-universal car ownership has provoked a number of papers drawing attention to those minority groups who are lacking private transportation and suffer problems of immobility. Early recognition came from Briggs and McKelvey (1975) who defined the 'transportation disadvantaged' as 'the poor, young, elderly and disabled'. While the nature of problems experienced by these groups is familiar to UK observers, it is remarkable that in the USA it is widely believed that lack of a car is due *only* to age, poverty or disability. A more complete categorization of automobile-deprived groups is provided by Kidder (1989). The elderly, youth below driving age, the physically handicapped and persons without cars because of low incomes are commonly recognized. In

addition there are 'persons in families where the number of individuals with travel demands exceeds the number of vehicles available'. In the UK this is the largest problem group, but its numerical significance in the USA is difficult to estimate. Apart from the elderly, adults without a driving licence are very few. Kidder's other categories are small minorities, although impossible to enumerate: persons whose cars are not functioning, persons who fear to drive long distances, persons without the mental capacity for driving. This suggests that the demand for transport alternatives is fragmented and specialized.

The elderly have received most attention. Unlike their counterparts in the UK, the American older generations have lived all their lives with the automobile and many remain 'reluctant drivers' for lack of an alternative (Kihl, 1993). Basic health and welfare needs may be met by 'human service agencies', and in many areas these provide the only public transport. Otherwise, for discretionary travel there is a patchwork of local schemes using 'shared-ride' cars, taxis and vans (mini-buses) depending upon the availability of private enterprise, voluntary effort and suitable funding programmes. These, however, seem able to satisfy only a small proportion of the potential demand (Notess, 1978; Kihl, 1992).

From this point, it is more convenient to continue the review under the headings of specific topics which demonstrate clear differences between the USA and UK.

The case study approach: mobility and accessibility

The very strong input by geographers in UK research on rural transportation is reflected in the central role of the case study, an approach which is very rarely seen in the US literature. This is linked in the UK to a focus on the key concepts of *mobility* and *accessibility*, which are intrinsically spatial in nature. Both are usually orientated towards assessing the 'problems' of non-car users as disclosed by travel patterns in a specific area, or by the level of accessibility to local facilities. It is essential that measures of travel habits and access opportunities are disaggregated by journey purpose or type of facility sought, such as shops, schools, work, bank, doctor, etc, and also by subgroups of the population and their home locations. Only analysis at this 'grass-roots' scale exposes the specific problems experienced in everyday life. Studies of travel behaviour (*actual mobility*) are normally achieved by household questionnaire surveys in relatively small case study areas. Accessibility can be calculated from secondary data on population attributes, public transport schedules, and the results of local fieldwork, perhaps using the techniques of 'time-geography'. The access levels achievable in any area might then be assessed against optimum standards of 'need' defined on a normative basis.

Examples of mobility studies in rural districts of the UK include Banister (1980), Smith and Gant (1982), and Nutley and Thomas (1992). Accessibility at the local scale, and pertinent analytical techniques, are demonstrated in Moseley et al (1977), Nutley (1983), Kilvington and McKenzie (1985), and Jordan and Nutley (1993). The case study approach is also used to examine the quantity and quality of public transport services after policy changes such as deregulation (eg Bell and Cloke, 1990).

Comparable work in the USA is almost completely absent. The concepts of mobility and accessibility are recognized in no more than general terms, and there is a reluctance to work at the local scale, perhaps reflecting the lack of participation by geographers. Maggied's (1982) study of rural Georgia, at county level, is of a higher scale order. This does, however, include a closer look at two representative counties, the purpose of which is to demonstrate that a hypothetical bus service from outlying settlements would be far too time-consuming and expensive to provide a realistic journey-to-work facility. Otherwise, an isolated example is the limited exercise by Koushki and Berg (1982) to redesign a local bus service in upper New York State to enhance its cost-effectiveness.

The poverty factor

An emphasis on poverty as a critical factor in non-possession of an automobile and in defining the transportation disadvantaged is a peculiar feature of the US literature. It was mentioned above that, together with age and disability, low income is assumed to be the only reason for an individual to have no car. Low incomes are also associated with those households with only one car instead of the 'normal' two. While incomes are undoubtedly a factor in UK car ownership, there are other reasons for being without, like perceived lack of need, adequate public transport, the fact that most elderly people have never been car owners and the readiness of family members to share a single vehicle.

In the rural USA, poverty and immobility reinforce each other. Maggied's (1982) hypothesis is that remote rural areas generate excessive car dependence and long-distance commuting; persons lacking a car or those attempting to run a car on a low income have great problems of access to workplaces; such people are forced to take low-paid jobs nearby, withdraw from the labour market or leave the area; this perpetuates low personal incomes and relative immobility. This seemed to be endorsed by the results of a factor analysis applied to the rural counties of Georgia.

The problems of car owners

In the UK it is generally assumed that with few exceptions car owners in the countryside have no significant problems of mobility. Various sections of the American literature, however, cast doubt on the validity of this in a US context. Elderly car owners have

already been mentioned, who fear to drive long distances, to drive at night, in winter, or to enter congested towns, but who in the absence of alternative transport become 'reluctant drivers'. Maggied (1982) explains how most of the rural poor feel obliged to get cars, yet these are invariably old and in poor condition, require a lot of maintenance, cover high mileages and are very expensive to keep running. There are many complaints that the accumulated costs of motor transport in the rural USA have a severe impact on personal finances and local economies (Saltzman and Newlin, 1981; Gillis, 1989). This is extremely ironic from a British viewpoint where the cost of petrol/gasoline is about three times higher! Another point is that the one-car household in the USA is seen as a potential problem. While in the UK a car is still widely seen as a household asset to be shared among family members, in the USA it is an individual possesion, such that having 'only' one car in the household is indicative of hardship. Single-car households can be associated with other indicators of disadvantage (see below), and this variable is used by Rucker (1984) in compiling an index of need.

Buses and deregulation

Public road passenger transport in the USA is associated overwhelmingly with long distance, limited stop services (which in the UK might be known as 'express coaches') operating inter-city routes and calling at small towns within the rural hinterlands; this is dominated by the Greyhound company. Little attempt is made to serve areas of more dispersed settlement. These, and also many small towns, may have no public transit except for school buses, human service agency vehicles and taxis. Historically, although most towns had a railroad, much of rural America passed from horse-drawn vehicles directly to the automobile age, with no intervening public transport phase. This contrasts radically with UK experience, where until about 1960 all rural areas enjoyed relatively abundant passenger rail and bus services. Despite subsequent decline, a tradition and expectation of public transport survives, and basic coverage is still good. Only about 5% of the rural population is beyond reach of a bus route, and hence UK researchers are more concerned with standard of service and accessibility provided. Bus transit in the USA, on the other hand, has declined to such low levels (Briggs, 1981; Burkhardt, 1981; Kihl, 1990) that the priority has been to establish how many communities have a service at all.

The inventory approach is common. A 1978 survey found that, of a sample of places with populations of 2500–10 000, 57% had no inter-city bus service, 66% had no specialized transport and 21% had no taxi. Of places with populations under 2500, the corresponding figures were 89%, 84% and 91% (Jackson and McKelvey, 1978). After deregulation in 1982, even more routes and stopping places were abandoned (Kihl, 1985, 1988, 1990); 20% more communities had lost service by 1984. It is arguable that such changes only continued established trends and that the numbers of people affected were small, but there is no doubt that demand comes mainly from the more disadvantaged sectors of society and their need remains. As in the UK, a more strategic view of deregulation outweighs its effects on rural areas, and the overall verdicts are generally positive (Button, 1987, 1990; Phillips, 1990). Contrary to most predictions, bus deregulation in the UK appears not to have damaged service levels in rural areas (Bell and Cloke, 1990; Astrop, 1993; White, 1995), but whether there is any useful analogy between the UK and USA must be open to question.

Bus systems of a more localized nature, like the village–town routes common in the UK, depend upon the vagaries of federal and state subsidy provisions. Services are highly fragmented and variable, include welfare and volunteer schemes of a 'paratransit' type, and local feeder links in coordination with Greyhound (Fravel *et al*, 1990; Walther, 1990). Demand remains low and specialized; Maggied (1982) is adamant that public transport cannot solve the journey-to-work problem in remote areas.

Paratransit

Known in the UK as 'unconventional modes', or where volunteer labour is used 'community transport', a wide range of alternative systems has been developed to offer solutions to the rural transport problem, but largely in a supplementary role (Nutley, 1988a, 1988b, 1990). In the USA, however, 'paratransit' has been predominantly urban in orientation, motivated by the cost and aggravation of driving in congested cities. Nevertheless, Saltzman (1976) has claimed: 'virtually the only existing public transportation in rural areas consists of paratransit modes: taxis, car pools, jitneys, and demand-responsive and subscription buses.' This may depend on a generous definition of paratransit, or perhaps rural operations are less well known. Smith (1979) describes a volunteer driver car-based transport system in Wisconsin, of a type common in the UK, but it is unknown how widespread are such schemes in the USA. In the early 1980s there was some interest in postbuses (Adams, 1981; Fleishman and Burns, 1981), citing Scotland as an exemplar, but they are prohibited by US regulations. Many systems aimed at elderly and disabled passengers have paratransit characteristics, and in order to make the most of available vehicles and funding, much importance is attached to inter-agency coordination and 'brokerage' (Kidder, 1989; Kihl, 1993). Central government in both the UK and USA have sponsored paratransit experiments, and subsidy programmes are still available. A listing by the Community Transportation Association of America (1989) reveals that 27% of funded schemes are 'rural'.

Local economic impact, roads and freight

One aspect of rural transportation that receives little mention in the UK is the degree of adverse economic impact suffered by outlying districts. Economic disadvantage is certainly perceived, if not proved, by organizations in 'peripheral' areas such as the Scottish Highlands and Northern Ireland, but this is usually regarded as a regional, rather than a rural, issue. Perhaps it is the scale and distance factors in the USA which cause rural development to be linked more explicitly with transport infrastructure. The profitability of farms, businesses, and ultimately whole communities, is seen to be strongly related to the availability of suitable trucking and railroad services and the freight rates charged (Gillis, 1989). Very many rural roads and bridges are inadequate to cope with the increasing size of trucks; many county roads are unsurfaced. Weak local economies lack the tax base to finance improvements (Baumel *et al*, 1989). Major highways have been built in development areas under federally assisted regional development programmes, especially in Appalachia (Anon, 1981–82, 1985), with associated claims of job creation. However, the emphasis on highway construction has been criticized for not meeting the requirements of smaller communities, by neglecting local access and more basic mobility needs.

Previously thought to depend on the common carrier obligation to ensure road freight service for otherwise unprofitable shipments, rural areas seem not to have suffered unduly from the 1980 deregulation of the trucking industry. Various surveys agreed that motor carrier services remained stable or improved, but with some increases in freight rates (Allen, 1990). As with agricultural shipments (Cornelius, 1989), the benefits of deregulation are greater for larger loads and places with competing carriers; isolated producers still have problems.

Railroads

While the closure of uneconomic railway lines in rural areas has been a contentious issue in both the UK and USA, the crucial difference is that the arguments are centred upon passenger and freight services respectively. The rail closures issue in the UK depends on the context of a dense network of passenger services until the early 1960s and rural populations' reliance upon it, the political economy and ideologies of state-run industries and the question of subsidizing uneconomic lines, and the impact on vulnerable groups of users (Hillman and Whalley, 1980; Kilvington, 1985; Whitelegg, 1984, 1987). In the USA most rail passenger services outside urban commuter zones had been withdrawn prior to the formation of Amtrak in 1971. The latter now runs only a basic intercity network stopping at very few rural small towns; scheduling and marketing are aimed at the demands of the major terminal cities.

For US rural areas, the railroad is effectively a freight mode only. Major issues are the quality of rail freight service to rural communities, the effects of the regulatory reforms of 1976 and 1980, and railroad 'abandonments'. While passenger and other unprofitable services were allowed to decline, railroad companies did not generally attempt to abandon complete lines until the 1976 legislation made closure procedures easier (Due, 1990; McFarland, 1991). Although small communities have become less dependent on railroads, threats of line abandonment are usually resisted because of fears for the impact on local business. Earlier studies have suggested relatively little adverse impact as alternative transport, mainly by truck, was adequate (Allen and Due, 1977), but the current prospects for rail cuts are more severe. Where there remains some business potential in, as well as need for, railroad operation, an alternative is to form new operating companies to take over redundant lines. This has been a growing trend in the USA since the early 1970s. Infrastructure may be purchased by state and local governments, and operations contracted to new railroad companies formed by local business interests such as freight consignors (Due, 1984, 1985); some subsidies are available. In the 1980s an extension of this trend was for major rail carriers to sell off larger, less profitable, sections of their networks to new 'regional' railroad companies (Rockey, 1987; Rakowski and Dobie, 1991).

Air services

Air transport is not normally on the agenda for UK rural areas, it being relevant only in exceptional environments like the Highlands and Islands of Scotland. Greater distances in the USA have created a demand for air services from relatively small towns, although traditionally these were sustained mainly by regulation and subsidy. Dedicated commuter airlines were more successful (Briggs, 1981). Deregulation in 1978 has proved generally beneficial to the air transport industry, but the effects on services to small rural towns have been highly variable. Minimum service levels were specified for locations deserving 'essential air service', and subsidies provided for some, but many marginal places have still suffered reductions in traffic (Crum, 1990).

Statistical indicators for the USA, 1990

At this stage there is a need for evidence of a more systematic, empirical kind to discern the extent of, and variations in, transport-related problems in the rural USA. Owing to space constraints it is feasible to examine only those indicators derivable from the 1990 population census. The information already summarized in the above literature review refers almost entirely to before 1990. As in the UK census, transport-related variables are confined to two topics – car

ownership and the journey to work. Analysis is limited to the 48 co-terminous states, and it was not possible to examine data below state level. A particularly convenient attribute of the US census – absent in the UK – is the official definition of 'urban' and 'rural' areas. The latter are all zones remaining after the exclusion of census-defined 'urbanized areas' and outlying places with over 2500 people. The lack of a UK equivalent makes it impossible to pursue UK–US comparisons of 'rural' in any formal statistical sense. Furthermore, the US census includes some economic data and has an official 'poverty level', so that low-income households can be enumerated.

Patterns

Basic patterns of car ownership are mapped in *Figures 1* and *2*. Higher incidences of relative disadvantage are generally to be found in the east, especially the south-east, and the south, with West Virginia, Mississippi and Louisiana appearing consistently in the 'worst' category. The most exceptionally high rates of car ownership exist in the western and northern regions, with Colorado and Wyoming appearing 'best' on both maps, followed by other west coast, desert and mountain states. The north-east displays a highly variable pattern, perhaps reflecting different degrees of urban influence on the rural areas; very few households are without vehicles, but multiple car ownership is less popular. A few other states deserve comment. Florida also has very few non-car households but low multiple ownership; this is possibly related to a high proportion of elderly people together with low average household sizes. Arizona and New Mexico contravene the 'western' pattern with significantly lower car ownership and higher poverty rates, perhaps associated with strong concentrations of Hispanic and Native American populations.

The domination of the 'non-car' sector by disadvantaged groups is demonstrated in *Table 3*. There is ample justification here for US authors' concentration on the poor and the elderly as problem groups, although it is surprising that ethnic minorities have had so little attention in the literature. In rural areas, the lower proportions of disadvantaged groups that remain carless suggest the indispensability of a vehicle despite low incomes, while the proportion of non-car households that are elderly or poor are even higher. Non-white populations are less prominent in rural areas and have a more variable distribution.

Relationships

At the scale-level of the 48 states, the scope is limited for detecting realistic relationships among variables with high degrees of explanation. Such a low level of resolution would be expected to conceal most of the undoubtedly complex relationships that exist. Below the state only the urban/rural distinction is considered, but accumulated literature suggests a viable hypothesis that this is the most basic determinant of car ownership and journey-to-work differences.

Correlation coefficients, for example, are unlikely to be conclusive at this scale, but nevertheless do show some points of interest. At state level, households with no car correlate strongly with population density ($r = 0.75$), suggesting lack of a car is mainly an urban condition, but it is particularly notable that single-car households *also* correlate positively with density ($r = 0.46$), whereas multi-car households definitely do not. Within rural areas, however, population density has no significance, indicating that the decisive factor is the urban or rural location. Most remarkable is that correlation coefficients for single-car households consistently have the same sign as those for 'no car', and the opposite sign to those for multi-car households. This strongly supports US writers' belief that to have only one car in the family is a problem condition. At state level, low car ownership does not correlate consistently with disadvantaged groups, except for '% non-white', but expected relationships are much clearer

when rural areas are considered separately. The elderly, however, cannot be identified as a problem group by this method.

Other correlation analyses show few verifiable relationships. It is impossible, for example, to confirm the expected association between the disadvantaged groups and travel to work by public transport; the latter is too scarce in rural areas to support statistically significant results. One interesting finding is that the disadvantaged groups do seem to be associated with the use of car sharing.

In order to test the relative importance of the rural/urban distinction as opposed to other factors emphasized in the literature such as elderly populations and poverty, an analysis of variance (ANOVA) was conducted (*Table 4*). The aim was to discover whether dependent variables of car ownership, travel to work and disadvantaged groups have greater variation between urban and rural areas than among the US states. In almost all cases they do, with very high F-ratios. Other possible explanatory factors can be tested

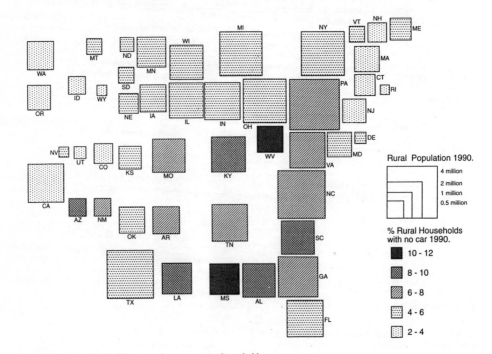

Figure 1 Car ownership in USA – rural areas: non-car households

Note: Key to states: AL Alabama; AR Arkansas; AZ Arizona; CA California; CO Colorado; CT Connecticut; DE Delaware; FL Florida; GA Georgia; IA Iowa; ID Idaho; IL Illinois; IN Indiana; KS Kansas; KY Kentucky; LA Louisiana; MA Massachusetts; MD Maryland; ME Maine; MI Michigan; MN Minnesota; MO Missouri; MS Mississippi; MT Montana; NC North Carolina; ND North Dakota; NE Nebraska; NH New Hampshire; NJ New Jersey; NM New Mexico; NV Nevada; NY New York: OH Ohio; OK Oklahoma; OR Oregon; PA Pennsylvania; RI Rhode Island; SC South Carolina; SD South Dakota; TN Tennessee; TX Texas; UT Utah; VA Virginia; VT Vermont; WA Washington; WI Wisconsin; WV West Virginia; WY Wyoming.

Table 3 Car ownership by disadvantaged groups, USA 1990

	Urban		(n = 49)	Rural		(n = 48)
	US mean	Mean of the states	c.o.v. %	US mean	Mean of the states	c.o.v. %
% all households no car	13.3	11.8	49.8	5.9	5.5	41.0
% households						
Over age 65, no car	24.9	23.4	28.4	14.4	13.3	34.3
Below poverty level, no car	41.0	38.0	31.7	23.1	20.4	29.4
Non-white, no car	25.3	23.1	41.7	16.4	12.5	49.7
% no car households						
Over age 65	41.4	46.2	15.4	55.7	57.2	15.8
Below poverty level	39.4	44.2	21.5	52.7	49.0	26.8
Non-white	44.0	34.5	59.5	24.2	20.6	100.1

Note: c.o.v. = coefficient of variation.

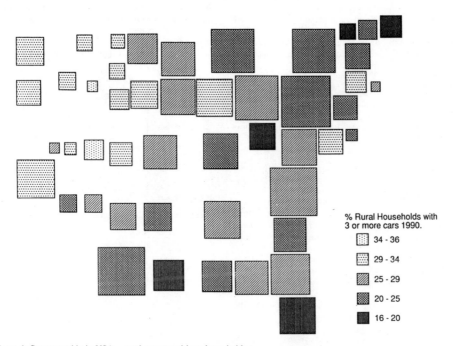

% Rural Households with 3 or more cars 1990.

- 34 - 36
- 29 - 34
- 25 - 29
- 20 - 25
- 16 - 20

Figure 2 Car ownership in USA – rural areas: multi-car households
Note: Key to states as for *Figure 1*.

in the same way. Using '% households below poverty level' and '% households non-white' as independent variables produced very much lower F-ratios, although still generally significant. This can be checked by a two-way ANOVA, using as independent variables 'urban/rural' together with 'poverty' or 'non-white'. In the great majority of cases most variation is attributable to 'urban/rural', the only exceptions being car sharing, walking to work and 'no phone', which are more strongly associated with 'poverty'. It may be noted that the 'over age 65' variable does not display any significant relationships in the correlations or ANOVA because, first, it has little spatial variation, and second, it is not in itself a problem condition but only when qualified by other factors.

Geographical patterns of car ownership rates,

Table 4 Analysis of variance by urban/rural areas, USA 1990

Analysis of variance
Dependent variables × urban/rural areas (n = 97)

	F-ratio (d.f. = 1,95)	
% households with		
No car	48.9	U
One car only	258.5	U
No car or one car	163.1	U
2+ cars	163.1	R
3+ cars	158.2	R
Ratio hhs 2+/1 or 0 cars	183.1	R
Persons/car	42.3	U
Cars/household	148.4	R
% travel to work by		
Solo car driver	0.004[a]	
Car sharing	11.4	R
Public transport	15.8	U
Walking	5.3	U
No journey	41.6	R
% car users sharing	6.5	R
% work journeys >45 mins	24.6	R
% households		
Over age 65	1.1[a]	
Below poverty level	0.001[a]	
Non-white	15.4	U
With no phone	7.9	R
% unemployed	0.28[a]	

Notes: [a]not significant at 95% level; U variable mean greater in urban areas; R variable mean greater in rural areas.

mapped in *Figures 1* and *2*, might be examined for relationships with other variables with a spatial expression. The map pattern of car ownership in the UK, for example, strongly suggests the influence of two factors – rurality and income (Nutley, 1992). Hypothetical relationships are depicted in *Figure 3*. While rural areas have higher rates than urban, this is mediated by income, leading to the relationship drawn in *Figure 3a*. The rural effect might be extended such that car ownership is proportional to 'degree of rurality', measured by a surrogate such as declining density of population or increasing distance from major cities. This would suggest the relationship in *Figure 3b*. The UK situation firmly supports (a) but not (b).

Applied to the USA, the 48 states are plotted on *Figures 4* and *5* using as dependent variable the ratio of households with two or more cars to those with one or none. While at first sight there is little pattern, a tentative interpretation is offered in *Figures 6a* and *b* respectively. There is no resemblance to the model in *Figure 3*, but the poverty factor and the urban/rural distinction are still detectable. Regarding *Figures 4* and *6a*, low car ownership can be identified first with high levels of poverty where three states (West Virginia, Mississippi and Louisiana) stand out on the upper right of the graph. A cluster of states with weaker car ownership ratios can also be identified with more urbanized populations on the lower left of the figure

(New York, New Jersey, Massachusetts, Rhode Island, Illinois, Florida, Nevada and Arizona). Comparing *Figures 5* and *6b*, referring to rural areas only, the poverty factor is again evident for a group of states on the lower right of the graph (West Virginia, Mississippi, Louisiana, Alabama, Kentucky, Arkansas, Arizona and New Mexico), which are also characterized by relatively low population densities. Over the graph as a whole, density of rural population (or degree of rurality) has no significance, with clusters of high car ownership being found at the top and bottom of the range. In the centre-bottom of the figure, a group of states with the lowest densities and high car ownership suggest a remoteness factor (Washington, Oregon, California, Idaho, Montana, Wyoming, Utah, Colorado, Nebraska, Iowa and Kansas). On the top left of the figure, a distinct group of four states with high rural densities and high car ownership (Connecticut,

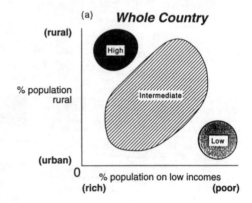

Figure 3 Car ownership related to rurality and income: hypothetical relationships
Note: (a) whole country; (b) rural areas.

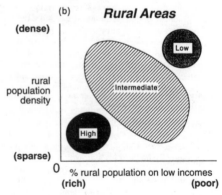

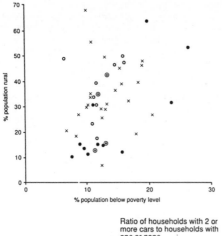

Ratio of households with 2 or
more cars to households with
one or none.

   ⊚ 1.81 - 2.10
   o 1.51 - 1.80
   × 1.21 - 1.50
   • 0.91 - 1.20
   ⊚ 0.60 - 0.90

Figure 4 USA 1990 – car ownership related to rurality and income/poverty

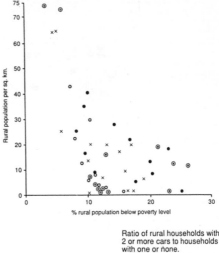

Ratio of rural households with
2 or more cars to households
with one or none.

   ⊚ 2.81 - 3.20
   o 2.41 - 2.80
   × 2.01 - 2.40
   • 1.61 - 2.00
   ⊚ 1.20 - 1.60

Figure 5 Rural areas, USA 1990 – car ownership related to rurality and income/poverty

Rhode Island, Massachusetts and New Jersey) suggests an affluent commuting population.

Concern for transportation disadvantage and reduced mobility suffered by certain populations might suggest the utility of a composite measure of 'need', as has been done in the UK. The only useful attempt in the US literature is Rucker's (1984) 'index of unmet need' applicable at state and county level using 1980 data. Its main practical advantage is that it uses only data from the population census, but it is entirely relative, as each unit area is assessed against the US mean for the variables used. Briefly, the results for 1980 showed significantly higher indices (greater need) in rural than in urban districts, higher scores in the south-eastern states, higher scores for blacks and a deterioration since 1970. An attempt was made to improve Rucker's index using more appropriate variables suggested by the above analysis, and 1990 data, but the mapped results display a pattern not dissimilar from that in *Figure 1*.

Conclusions

From a UK perspective, does a much higher car ownership rate, such as that experienced in the USA, 'solve' the rural transport problem? There is no doubt that the widespread perception in the USA is that it does. Everyone is assumed to have a car. No 'problem'

is acknowledged to exist, except by local interest groups. The academic coverage reflects this. The answer can only be that problems are solved for those who have cars (and sections of the literature cast doubt on this), isolating those who have not. In this sense there is little difference from the UK, but when numbers suffering hardship fall below a certain point they become politically invisible, as seems to be the case in the USA. Other factors are obviously relevant, such as the tradition of public responsibility for social welfare, or the expectation of individual self-reliance. However, it seems important to point out that a small minority in percentage terms, such as rural non-car owners, in the USA comprises very many people – about 18.5 million.

There are few lessons here for the UK (or western Europe) except that growing car ownership will further marginalize the have-nots. It is possible that these might reduce to 'elderly and poor' only, although in the UK this might mean 20% of households against 5% in the USA. Otherwise, there is no reason to believe that the UK will emulate the USA. Fundamental geographical and economic differences between the two countries, the forecast peaking of UK car ownership at lower levels, the survival of rural public transport and

Rural Planning and Management

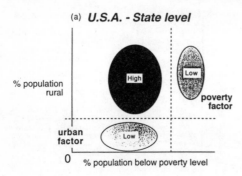

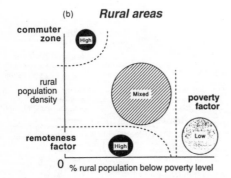

Figure 6 Schematic representation of car ownership related to rurality and income/poverty
Note: (a) USA 1990; (b) rural areas.

population growth in almost all rural areas will ensure this. Given the much greater attention to the problem in the UK, it might be asked whether any techniques or policies are realistically transferable to the USA. First, it would be of great interest to see the results of geographical case studies, equivalent to those common in the UK, examining at the local scale detailed patterns of mobility and accessibility in the rural USA. These would yield information (apparently unavailable at present) on how car-less or low-income rural residents respond to their relative immobility, and the degree of hardship suffered.

As far as policy is concerned, the only recommendation that seems realistic at this high level of generalization is that further provision of conventional public transport for local journeys in rural areas is unlikely to be successful, but in an overwhelmingly car-dependent society there needs to be a means of extending the

benefits of the automobile to those people currently deprived of one. Maggied (1982) seriously proposes the supply of cars to low-income families at public expense. Nevertheless, the most general 'solution' which seems feasible for rural districts of the USA would be the widespread organization of automobile-based paratransit systems.

The overall situation described for the USA can be expected to be typical of affluent, spatially extensive countries such as Canada and Australia (Lonsdale and Holmes, 1981). High average incomes and favourable economic conditions have encouraged car acquisition and use as the perfect answer to the need for mobility in environments of low population density and long distances, fatally undermining whatever public transport may have previously existed. It could be said that the UK situation is symptomatic of a 'European problem' which is substantially different. Higher rural densities have encouraged public transport to develop and survive, meeting a demand ensured by less widespread prosperity and slower growth in car ownership. Hence the tradition of public service and (relatively) larger dependent populations have perpetuated a greater awareness of the issue. In either scenario, however, problems are experienced on an individual or household basis at the local scale, and analysis and policy should be conducted at that level.

Acknowledgements

I would like to thank the Geography Department and the Library of Kent State University, Ohio, for providing facilities during research for this article.

References

Owing to the nature of this article it is more appropriate to give separate lists for the USA and UK. The US list is intended to be comprehensive while the UK list is a selection of the most important items.

United States

Adams, DE (1981) 'Post-bus for rural passenger transportation and rural mail delivery: an idea whose time has come' *Transportation Reseach Record* **797** 76–79
Allen, BJ (1990) 'Small community trucking service' in Due *et al*, *op cit*, 46–72
Allen, BJ and Due, JF (1977) 'Railway abandonments. Effects upon the communities served' *Growth and Change* **8**(2) 8–14
Anon (1981/2) 'Appalachian highways are catalysts of change' *Appalachia* **15** (2/3) 8–17
Anon (1985) 'Two decades of change in the region' *Appalachia* **18**(3) 41–88
Baumel, CP, Schornhorst, E and Smith, WD (1989) 'Alternatives for solving the local rural road and bridge problem' in Gillis, *op cit* 25–42
Bohland, JR (1988) 'Rural America' in Knox, PL, Bartels, EH, Bohland, JR, Holcomb, B and Johnston, RJ *The United States. A Contemporary Human Geography* Longman, Harlow, 151–187
Briggs, R (1981) 'Federal policy in the US and the transportation problems of low density areas' in Lonsdale and Holmes, *op cit*, 238–261

Briggs, R and McKelvey, D (1975) 'Rural public transportation and the disadvantaged' *Antipode* 7(3) 31–36

Burkhardt. JE (1981) 'Rise and fall of rural public transportation' *Transportation Research Record* 831 2–5

Button, KJ (1987) 'The effects of regulatory reform on the US inter-city bus industry' *Transport Reviews* 7 145–166

Button, KJ (1990) 'Transport deregulation in advanced capitalist nations– the case of the USA' in Bell, P and Cloke, PJ (eds) *Deregulation and Transport. Market Forces in the Modern World* David Fulton, London, 141–155

Community Transportation Association of America (1989) *A Directory of UMTA-funded Rural and Specialized Transit Systems* Urban Mass Transit Administration, US Department of Transportation, Washington, DC

Cornelius, JC (1989) 'Deregulated agricultural transportation: problems and issues' in Gillis, *op cit*, 73–91

Crum, MR (1990) 'Small community air service' in Due *et al*, *op cit*, 112–179

Due, JF (1984) 'New railroad companies formed to take over abandoned or spun-off lines' *Transportation J* 24(1) 30–50

Due, JF (1985) 'The surprising roles of the state and local governments in preserving rail freight service' *State Government* 58 7–13

Due, JF (1990) 'Small community rail service' in Due *et al*, *op cit*, 8–45

Due, JF, Allen, BJ, Kihl, MR and Crum, MR (1990) *Transportation Service to Small Rural Communities. Effects of Deregulation* Iowa State University Press, Ames

Fleishman, D and Burns, I (1981) 'Can the postal bus play a role in providing rural transportation?' *Transportation Research Record* 831 90–97

Fravel, FD, Hayes, ER and Hosen, KI (1990) *Intercity Bus Feeder Project Program Analysis* Urban Mass Transit Administration & Technology Sharing Program, US Department of Transportation, Washington, DC

Gillis, WR (ed) (1989) *Profitability and Mobility in Rural America* Pennsylvania State University Press, University Park

Jackson, AF and McKelvey, DJ (1978) *An Inventory of Transportation Services in Places of less than 10,000 Population outside of Urbanized Area* Urban Mass Transit Administration, US Department of Transportation, Washington, DC

Johansen, HE and Fuguitt, GV (1981) 'Changing functions of villages in sparsely populated areas: the American West' in Lonsdale and Holmes, *op cit*, 148–168

Johansen, HE and Fuguitt, GV (1984) *The Changing Rural Village in America*, Ballinger, Cambridge, MA

Kaye, I (1982) 'Transportation' in Dillman, DA and Hobbs, DJ (eds) *Rural Society in the US. Issues for the 1980s* Westview, Boulder, 156–163

Kidder, AE (1989) 'Passenger transportation problems in rural areas' in Gillis, *op cit*, 131–145

Kihl, MR (1985) 'The impact of bus deregulation on small towns' *Transportation Research Record* 1012 65–71

Kihl, MR (1988) 'The impacts of deregulation on passenger transportation in small towns' *Transportation Quarterly* 42 243–268

Kihl, MR (1990) 'Small community bus service' in Due *et al*, *op cit*, 73–111

Kihl, MR (1992) 'Marketing rural transit among senior populations' *Transportation Research Record* 1338 60–64

Kihl, MR (1993) 'The need for transportation alternatives for the rural elderly' in Bull, CN (ed) *Aging in Rural America* Sage, Newbury Park, 84–98

Koushki, PA and Berg, WD (1982) 'Improving rural mobility – a practical approach' *Transportation Quarterly* 36 631–642

Lonsdale, RE and Holmes, JH (eds) (1981) *Settlement Systems in Sparsely Populated Regions. The United States and Australia* Pergamon, New York

Maggied, HS (1982) *Transportation for the Poor. Research in Rural Mobility* Kluwer Nijhoff, Boston

McFarland, HB (1991) 'Railroad abandonment policy in the 1990s' *Transportation Practitioners Journal* 58 331–340

Moriarty, BM (1981) 'Existing and alternative methods of providing health care and education services in sparselands of America' in Lonsdale and Holmes, *op cit*, 295–321

Notess, CB (1978) 'Rural elderly transit markets' *American Institute of Planners J* 44 328–334

Paaswell, RE (1973) 'Problems of the carless in the United Kingdom and the United States' *Transportation* 2 351–371

Phillips, KB (1990) 'Intercity bus deregulation: origins and consequences' *Transportation Practitioners Journal* 57 351–363

Rakowski, JP and Dobie, K (1991) 'The new regional railroads: management perceptions and apprehensions' *Transportation Practitioners Journal* 58 137–149

Rockey, CF (1987) 'The formation of regional railroads in the United States' *Transportation J* 27(2) 5–13

Rucker, G (1984) 'Public transportation: another gap in rural America' *Transportation Quarterly* 38 419–432

Saltzman, A (1976) *Role of Paratransit in Rural Transportation* Transportation Research Board Special Report 164, 137–142

Saltzman, A and Newlin, LW (1981) 'The availability of passenger transportation' in Hawley, AH and Mazic, SM (eds) *Nonmetropolitan America in Transition* University of North Carolina Press, Chapel Hill, 255–284

Smith, RL (1979) 'Evaluation of rural volunteer driver transportation systems in Wisconsin' *Transportation Research Part A* 13 309–315

Walther, ES (1990) *Coordination of Rural Public Transportation Services in three Southeastern States* Urban Mass Transit Administration & Technology Sharing Program, US Department of Transportation, Washington, DC

United Kingdom

Astrop, A (1993) *The Trend in Rural Bus Services since Deregulation* Project Report 21 Transport Research Laboratory, Crowthorne

Banister, D (1980) 'Transport mobility in inter-urban areas: a case study approach in south Oxfordshire' *Regional Studies* 14 285–296

Bell, P and Cloke, PJ (1990) 'Bus deregulation in rural localities: an example from Wales' in Bell, P and Cloke, PJ (eds) *Deregulation and Transport. Market Forces in the Modern World* David Fulton, London, 100–121

Cloke, PJ (ed) (1985) *Rural Accessibility and Mobility* Institute of British Geographers Rural Geography Study Group, Lampeter

Cresswell, R (ed) (1978) *Rural Transport and Country Planning* Leonard Hill, Glasgow

Halsall, DA and Turton, BJ (eds) (1979) *Rural Transport Problems in Britain: Papers and Discussion* Institute of British Geographers Transport Geography Study Group, Keele

Hillman, M and Whalley, A (1980) *The Social Consequences of Rail Closures* Report 587, Policy Studies Institute, London

Jordan, C and Nutley, SD (1993) 'Rural accessibility and public transport in Northern Ireland' *Irish Geography* 26 120–132

Kilvington, R (1985) 'Railways in rural areas' in Button, K and Pitfield, D (eds) *International Railway Economics* Gower, Aldershot, 271–296

Kilvington, R and McKenzie, R (1985) *A Technique for Assessing Accessibility Problems in Rural Areas* Contractor Report 11, Transport and Road Research Laboratory, Crowthorne

Moseley, MJ (1979) *Accessibility: the Rural Challenge* Methuen, London

Moseley, MJ, Harman, R, Coles, O and Spencer, M (1977) *Rural Transport and Accessibility* 2 vols, University of East Anglia, Norwich

Moyes, A (1989) *The Need for Public Transport in mid-Wales: Normative Approaches and their Implications* Rural Surveys Research Unit Monograph 2, University College of Wales, Aberystwyth

Nutley, SD (1983) *Transport Policy Appraisal and Personal Accessibility in Rural Wales* Geo Books, Norwich

Nutley, SD (1988a) ' "Unconventional modes" of transport in rural Britain: progress to 1985' *J Rural Studies* 4 73–86

Nutley, SD (1988b) ' "Unconventional modes" of transport in the United Kingdom – a review of types and the policy context' *Transportation Research Part A* 22 329–344

Nutley, SD (1990) *Unconventional and Community Transport in the United Kingdom* Gordon & Breach, London

Nutley, SD (1992) 'Rural areas: the accessibility problem' in Hoyle, BS and Knowles, RD (eds) *Modern Transport Geography* Belhaven, London, 125–154

Nutley, SD and Thomas, C (1992) 'Mobility in rural Ulster: travel patterns, car ownership and local services' *Irish Geography* 25 67–82

Paaswell, RE (1973) 'Problems of the carless in the United Kingdom and the United States' *Transportation* 2 351–371

Pacione, M (1984) *Rural Geography* Harper & Row, London 281–300

Phillips, D and Williams, A (1984) *Rural Britain. A Social Geography* Blackwell, Oxford, 130–152

Robinson, GM (1990) *Conflict and Change in the Countryside* Belhaven, London, 351–363

Smith, J and Gant, R (1982) 'The elderly's travel in the Cotswolds' in Warnes, A (ed) *Geographical Perspectives on the Elderly* Wiley, Chichester, 323–336

Stanley, PA and Farrington, JH (1981) 'The need for rural public transport: a constraints-based case study' *Tijdschrift voor Economische en Sociale Geografie* **72** 62–80

Thomas, D St J (1963) *The Rural Transport Problem* Routledge, London

White, PR (ed) (1978) *Rural Public Transport. A Selection of Papers from Rural Public Transport Seminars held at the Polytechnic of Central London 1972–76 with Bibliography* Polytechnic of Central London, London

White, PR (1995) *Public Transport. Its Planning, Management and Operation* 3rd edn, UCL Press, London, 142–160

Whitelegg, J (1984) 'Closure of the Settle–Carlisle railway line. The case for a social cost-benefit analysis' *Land Use Policy* **1** 283–298

Whitelegg, J (1987) 'Rural railways and disinvestment in rural areas' *Regional Studies* **21** 55–63

Part IV
Institutions for Rural Development:
Joined-Up Governance

[34]

Pergamon

HABITAT INTL. Vol. 22, No. 4, pp. 347–354, 1998
© 1998 Elsevier Science Ltd. All rights reserved
Printed in Great Britain
0197-3975/98 $19.00 + 0.00

PII: S0197-3975(98)00026-5

Guest Editorial
Creating Institutions to Ensure Sustainable Use of Resources

DAVID J. BRUNCKHORST
University of New England, Australia

ABSTRACT

The foundation for a sustainable future is the continuance of ecological processes and functions across landscapes dominated by human activity whether hunter-gathering, agriculture, pastoralism, suburban living or wilderness recreation. Actions to sustain ecological systems, flows and functions must be integrated across regional landscapes. Such regions encompass natural areas, human living places and a mosaic of other land uses. No matter where on the globe, future sustainability will depend on the system of resource governance that mediates the relationship between the society and the economy on one hand, and continuance of ecosystem functional processes on the other. Methods need to be developed that recognise and account for the scales of influence that interconnected social and ecosystem functional elements have on one another. It will then be possible to demonstrate how ecosystem functional capacity might dictate resource governance. Real applications of this thesis will include urbanisation policies, urban infrastructure and planning and more thoughtfully integrated development aid programs. © 1998 Elsevier Science Ltd. All rights reserved

Keywords: ecosystems; landscapes; governance; sustainability; resources

INTRODUCTION

In less than a century, human population and its requirements for space, materials, goods, and amenities have increased by more than five-fold. Symptoms of environmental degradation, such as loss of species, loss of soil and decreasing water quality are increasing. Arguably more serious are the growing signs of functional problems in the operation of many ecological systems. Declining productivity, land salinisation, blue-green bacterial blooms in rivers and dams are symptoms of breakdown of ecosystem processes and function. Less obvious, but possibly more disturbing because they are mysterious to the general public, are the expanding hole in the ozone layer, global warming and acid rain. Ecosystem function, which flora and fauna alone cannot undertake, is of primary importance in sustaining both species,

Correspondence address: Department of Ecosystem Management and Institute for Bioregional Resource Management, University of New England, Armidale NSW 2351, Australia. E-mail: dbrunckh@metz.une.edu.au.

Rural Planning and Management

D. J. Brunckhorst

and functional processes and interactions (Naeem *et al.*, 1994; Walker, 1995; De Leo and Levin, 1997).

The foundation for a sustainable future is the continuance of ecological processes and functions across multiple spatio-temporal scales (Noss, 1983; Norton and Ulanowicz, 1992; Brunckhorst, 1995, 1998). It is also becoming evident that actions to sustain ecological systems, flows and functions must be integrated across regional landscapes. Such regions encompass natural areas, human living places (that include rural or oceanic production), and a mosaic of other land uses (Slocombe, 1993; Brunckhorst and Bridgewater, 1995).

Society must make a fundamental shift in the way it views and uses natural resources if it is to ensure an ecologically supportable future. Novel and radical approaches are needed if humanity is to find realistic solutions to social and environmental sustainability issues that the citizenry can adopt and adapt with matching civic skills and knowledge. An increasing number of authors in a variety of journals (for example in *Habitat International*: Choguill, 1993; 1996; Harpham and Boateng, 1997; Moore and Ahmed, 1997; Brown and Wolfe, 1997; Brunck-horst, 1998), are turning their attention to ecological sustainability issues related to land use, urban infrastructure and services, and development aid programs. This timely shift might be seen as consideration of 'biocultural appropriateness' for institutional, urban and agricultural capacity building programs in the developing world.

Securing the quality of life for future generations is one of the key goals of ecologically sustainable development (di Castri, 1995). Securing the ongoing functional processes of ecosystems and landscapes is a necessary condition for maintaining biodiversity, sustainable resource use, economies and human quality of life values. But changing technology or amounting masses of biological data will be ineffective in halting destruction of natural capital if the expectations of society are inconsistent with the relationship that people have with their environment. Not only must environmental degradation be minimised or stopped, considerable ecological restoration is likely to be needed. This might require social transformations towards a restorative economy where investment in biodiversity protection and environmental restoration provides, amongst other benefits, the natural 'growth capital' for future sustainable and restorative industries (Hawken, 1993; Brunckhorst *et al.*, 1997).

There is still too little understanding of the relationship between society (or local communities) and ecosystems at the scale of regional landscapes (bioregion). No matter where on the globe, future sustainability will depend on the system of resource governance that mediates the relationship between the citizenry and the economy on one hand, and continuance of ecosystem functional processes on the other (Brunckhorst, 1998). Methods need to be developed that recognise and account for the scales of influence that interconnected social and ecosystem functional elements have on one another. It will then be possible to demonstrate how ecosystem functional capacity might dictate resource governance (Brunckhorst, 1995, 1998; Brunckhorst and Rollings, in press). Real applications include urbanisation policies, urban infrastructure and planning and more thoughtfully integrated development aid programs.

Political economy or socio-ecological harmony?

Current institutions seem to be a long way from dealing with these extremely difficult issues but, while scientific knowledge is inadequate, urgency is growing. Our understanding of political economies and economic 'growth' appear to undermine moves towards an economically and ecologically sustainable society. The model most frequently used in decision making gives predominance to economic rationale, arguing that the environment can be 'looked-after' when the economy is good (Fig. 1).

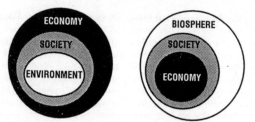

Fig. 1. A model based on Biosphere functional capacity promotes sustainable futures over economic rationalism. Economic rationale is the dominant model for decision making in most industrialised countries (LHS). It proposes that the environment can be looked after best when the economy is good. The model required for an ecologically supportable future views the economy as a component of human society, which is in turn part of the ecological systems of the entire biosphere (RHS).

The models of political economy or rational economics are fundamentally flawed and the inverse is required (see Caldwell, 1970; Bromley, 1991; Choguill, 1993; Harpham and Boateng, 1997; Brunckhorst, 1998). The required model for decision making must view economics as a subset of society, which in turn is a part of the biosphere (Fig. 1). The foundation of such a model is that environmental productivity, in the form of sustainable ecological function, is the determinant of social values and economic aspirations. Without environmental health there can be no economic or social sustainability.

Sustainability at a temporal scale that includes future generations as stakeholders in current decision making requires long-term vision and social flexibility (Courrier, 1992; Smil, 1993; Norton and Dovers, 1996). It also requires strategic integrated planning, policy development and implementation *across* traditional jurisdictional boundaries and narrowly focused programs. Policy and management responses will need a systems approach that reflects the complexity of the natural world and the cultural values associated with it. There is little likelihood of coherent policies emerging from the traditional compartmentalised approach in which different departments or different levels of government each handle different, small parts of a problem. Yet ongoing institutional flexibility and adaptation is possible because systems of rules and institutional operation are cognitive constructions not limited by physical reality as are ecosystems. Therefore, society and its institutions *are* infinitely adaptable in theory, but not often in practice. It remains to be seen if the social transformations towards a sustainable future are of the order that can shift governments and all sectoral interests to such a long term commitment. The future role of policy and administration at all levels of government (as well as the private sector) will be critically important to how sustainable our future might turn out to be.

ECOLOGICALLY COMPATIBLE RESOURCE GOVERNANCE

To be effective in achieving sustainable resource use, resource governance systems have to be compatible with the character and dynamics of the ecosystems involved, and with the social, cultural and institutional norms of the society to which resource users belong. Multi-scale and cross-scale spatial and temporal elements of ecological and social functions and their influence on the landscape need to be mapped and analysed together. Where resources are a part of broader scale systems, such features and activities might be organised into an operational hierarchy where the scale of governance is matched to the scale of the resource,

ecosystem function and associated externalities — the essence of adaptive management (Walters and Holling, 1990; Brunckhorst and Rollings, in press).

   A generalised view of the spatial scale of a variety of biophysical and societal
features is given in Fig. 2 (after Slocombe, 1993). The landscape-regional scale
draws together these (multi- and cross-scale) attributes so that human needs and
activities are reconciled and integrated with ecological structural and functional
processes. I refer to this scale of management as a 'bioregion' (Fig. 2). Hence, a
bioregion, "biocultural landscape" or "life region" integrates human governance
within ecological law. It is an area exhibiting "soft perimeters" characterised by its
drainage, flora and fauna, climate, geology, human culture and land use.

Institutional barriers

Many practical solutions to the sustainable use of natural resources are constrained
by institutional impediments, narrowly focused scientific research and entrenched
or compartmentalised systems of resource governance by the citizenry, property
rights, land ownership and use (Ostrom, 1990; Slocombe, 1993; Kim and Weaver,
1994; Holling and Meffe, 1996). Implementing ecosystem management approaches
are not simply impeded by a lack of data of ecosystems and their function at
various scales, but a lack of research and development for use of existing knowledge
(Brunckhorst, 1995; Brunckhorst *et al.*, 1997). Barriers to integration and communication or extension across institutions, to the rural community, municipal government and other land managers, and the general public often stem from inflexible or
narrowly focused management cultures and jurisdictional barriers. Enormous
benefits and efficiency gains will accrue through better communication and information transfer, a freeing up of institutionalised domains and programs and,
improved cross-jurisdictional responsibility for land use management. This is

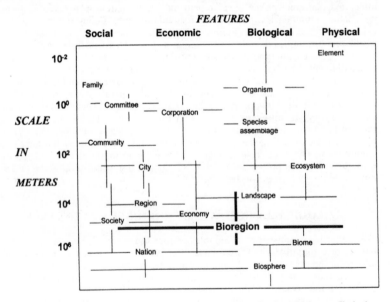

*Figure 2. A generalised view of the spatial scale of a variety of biophysical and societal features. The landscape-
regional scale draws together these (multi- and cross- scale) attributes so that human needs and activities are reconciled
and integrated with ecological structural and functional processes. Adapted after Slocombe 1993.*

perpetuated by the current system of governance where political expedience and bureaucratic inertia favour the modification of existing institutional forms rather than developing new ones (Caldwell, 1970; Brown and MacLeod, 1996; Norton and Dovers, 1996).

Institutional inadequacy stems from relying on entrenched, institutional forms to solve a new class of problems. For example, in Australia and the USA, our inherited European styles of agriculture and institutions, such as property rights, do not match the biophysical and climatic nature of our lands. This remains an exceedingly hard lesson to learn. Property rights and ownership issues in industrial nations are also major barriers to the pursuit of sustainability at the necessary, cross-jurisdictional, landscape scale. One example stems from the dual entities of rural areas which are agricultural land with freehold title, a commodity on one hand and, a set of interconnected ecosystem functions across a landscape with no regard to ownership boundaries on the other hand (Ostrom, 1990; Reeve, 1992; Reeve, 1997). However, consideration of the critical interplay between ecosystem function, institutional forms and functions, culturally defined land tenure, land use, and resource governance has been lacking in theoretical and applied research.

Community, civic and institutional adaptation to a system of ecologically sustainable resource governance will determine whether the functioning of the economy and actions of people erode the natural processes on which society relies, or remain within the limits necessary to sustain the functional integrity of ecosystems and ecological processes (see Ostrom, 1990; Young, 1992; Bromley, 1991, 1992; Brunckhorst *et al.*, 1997; De Leo and Levin, 1997; Reeve, 1997). It is apparent from this developing body of work that, to ensure resources are used sustainably, resource governance systems must have a number of key capacities (adapted after the above authors, particularly Ostrom, 1990):

1. *Spatial Information* — the ability to spatially define ecosystem structure and the way in which ecological processes provide resource-capability function across landscape regions.
2. *Functional Influences* — the ability to identify and monitor, in a spatial context, the interaction between resource use, the social system and ecosystem functional processes in terms of their extent, magnitude and direction.
3. *Coordinated Resource Governance Policy* — the ability of the local community or citizenry to arrive at rules for resource use through some form of collective action, which is based on a spatial understanding of landscape ecological functioning across their bioregion.
4. *Flexible Adaptation* — the ability to adapt these rules in response to new knowledge about the ecosystems, to changing demand for resources originating from exogenous economic forces, and to climatic and other biophysical sources of stress.
5. *Enforcement by Community Established Governance* — the ability to ensure that the rules for sustainability within the functional capacity of bioregions are adhered to by resource users.

The above attributes are manifested differently according to the social, cultural, institutional and historical differences in the societies to which resource users belong. In industrialised, capitalist societies the resource governance system provides access to resources by individuals and corporations through the institutions of property rights and ownership. Enforcement is provided by contract and statute law, adaptability is mainly achieved through the functioning of markets (science and technology to a lesser extent), coordination is achieved through democratic processes, monitoring is undertaken by the state, and information is constrained within scientific institutions. In traditional societies, the system of resource governance usually occurs within social, cultural and behavioural norms. Adherence to rules may be self-enforcing through individuals' fear of censure by elders or peers, coordination may be achieved through the processes of small group dynamics, monitoring may be by the resources users themselves, and understanding rests with traditional and/or religious beliefs (Reeve, 1997). Clearly there are lessons and perhaps new directions for application in urban and rural municipal planning, design and management of infrastructure and services as well as how western nations should approach development aid programs in less developed countries and traditional societies. Resource governance systems to be crafted to fit both the biophysical and socio-cultural-economic contexts within which they must function.

In essence, there is a need to combine three types of spatially distributed information that are essential building blocks for the design of sustainable resource governance systems. These are:

1. the spatial domain and effect of institutional and social structures;
2. the distribution of social, cultural, environmental and political values held by those with interest in particular resources;
3. the functional, ecological-connectivity and ecosystem processes between landscape components.

The third type of spatial information (above) refers to the extent of functional flows or ecological-connectivity across the landscape (Forman, 1995; Brunckhorst, 1995). In the case of dryland salinity, for example, a landscape component in a discharge area would carry information on which land elements in recharge areas had the potential to affect the level of the water table below that land element. Watersheds or catchments provide a different kind of example; that of a linear conduit. Along rivers ecological services are provided (cleansing, detoxification, nutrient uptake). Human inputs (factories, farms, sewerage) or other landscape functional elements (forests, clearings) can have positive or negative influences. No governance is needed when all ecological elements of the landscape (or river) can effectively buffer negative influences. Governance is required when the system starts acting as a conveyor of negative influences (externalities). This type of information essentially maps the extent of the externalities of land use or sphere of functional-influence, is essential to determining which landholders should participate as stakeholders in particular resource governance systems.

Maintenance of ecological function across regional landscapes has been identi-fied as a key requirement if we are to achieve sustainability. Ecosystem function itself stems from the interaction within and between structural components of the landscape that is driven by inputs. An integration between these components will provide flexibility with regard to the functional redundancy within ecosystems while maintaining important broad-scale ecological processes and landscape integr-ity (de Leo and Levin, 1997). When combined with social functions across the landscape, such a method may be employed to identify landscape associations that will form the basis for restructuring resource governance in that region.

This final requirement leads us towards the design of more efficient, adaptable and ecologically sustainable systems of resource governance that support the requirements of society but also match and sustain the functioning of ecological processes and services at a landscape or bioregional scale (Fig. 2; Brunckhorst and Rollings, 1998). Therefore we need some rationale to identify socio-ecological management zones that make sense in terms of sustaining ecosystem function across landscapes and, which local people identify with (or, with which they hold a bio-cultural identity, see Brunckhorst, 1995; Brunckhorst and Bridgewater, 1995; Walton and Bridgewater, 1996).

Studies of cities, urban infrastructure and services, rural (and indigenous) com-munity development, and development-aid projects should therefore be approa-ched from a regional-landscape context that addresses both, landscape ecological processes (services) and social processes and functions. This might best be accom-plished if social science and policy studies are conducted in tandem with large-scale ecological research. The information generated from policy studies can then be incorporated into other models of the interactions among socio-economics, policy decisions and ecosystem functions. The complementary nature of these efforts will also be important to identifying key issues, related scientific questions and, readapting or refining management strategies.

We must start facing the 'too-hard-basket' issues that we have avoided for too long. I wish to encourage innovation in theory and research to find practical solutions to social and environmental sustainability issues that institutions and citizens can adopt, and adapt with matching civic skills and knowledge. Realising the potential of our future sustainability will depend on a system of resource governance that mediates the relationship between society (including the economy), and endurance of ecological processes and services across human dominated landscapes.

Acknowledgements — My thanks to Charles Choguill for suggesting this guest editorial and for comments and suggestions on an earlier draft. Thanks also to Phil Coop, Ian Reeve, Nick Rollings and Richard Thackway for discussions and input. Opinions and shortcomings remain mine.

REFERENCES

Bromley, D. W. (1991) *Environment and Economy: Property Rights and Public Policy*. Basil Blackwell, Oxford, UK.
Bromley, D. W. (1992) *Making the Commons Work. Theory, Practice and Policy*. Institute for Contemporary Studies Press, San Francisco.
Brown, D. F. and Wolfe, J. M. (1997). Adjusting planning frameworks to meet changing needs in post colonial countries: the example of Belize. *Habitat International* 21(1), 51.
Brown, J. and MacLeod, N. (1996) Integrating ecology into natural resource management policy. *Environmental Management* 20(3), 289–296.
Brunckhorst, D. J. (1995) Sustaining nature and society — a bioregional approach. *Inhabit* 3, 5–9.
Brunckhorst, D. J. (1998) Comment on 'Urban governance in relation to the operation of urban services in developing countries' by Trudy Harpham and Kwasi A. Boateng. *Habitat International* 22(1), 69–72.
Brunckhorst, D. J. and Bridgewater, P. B. (1995) Coastal zone conservation — sustaining nature and society. In *Recent Advances in Marine Science and Technology '94*, eds. O. Bellwood, H. Choat and N. Saxena, pp. 87–94. PACON International and James Cook University.
Brunckhorst, D. J., Bridgewater, P. and Parker, P. (1997) The UNESCO Biosphere Reserve program comes of age: learning by doing, landscape models for a sustainable conservation and resource use. In *Conservation Outside Reserves*, eds. Hale and Moritz, pp. 176–182. Centre for Conservation Biology, University of Queensland Press.
Brunckhorst, D. J. and Rollings, N. M. (in press) Mapping ecological and social functions: I. Influencing resource governance. *Natural Areas Journal* 19.
Caldwell, L. K. (1970) The ecosystem as a criterion for public land policy. *Natural Resources Journal* 10(2), 203–221.
Choguill, C. L. (1993) Sustainable cities: urban policies for the future. *Habitat International* 17(3), 1–12.
Choguill, C. L. (1996) Ten steps to sustainable infrastructure. *Habitat International* 20(3), 389–404.
De Leo, G. A. and Levin, S. (1997) The multifaceted aspects of ecosystem Integrity. *Conservation Ecology* 1(1), 3 (URL:http://www.consecol.org/vol1/iss1/art3).
di Castri, F. (1995) The chair of sustainable development. *Nature and Resources* 31(3), 2–7.
Forman, R. T. (1995) *Land Mosaics: The Ecology of Landscapes and Regions*. Cambridge University Press, New York.
Harpham, T. and Boateng, K. A. (1997) Urban governance in relation to the operation of urban services in developing countries. *Habitat International* 21(1), 65–77.
Hawken, P. (1993) *The Ecology of Commerce: How Business Can Save the Planet*. Weidenfeld and Nicolson, London.
Hin, D. H. K, Chong, R. T. Y., Wai, T. K. and Briffett, C. (1997) The greening of Singapore's national estate. *Habitat International* 21(1), 107.
Holling, C. S. and Meffe, M. (1996) Command and control and the pathology of natural resource management. *Conservation Biology* 10(2), 328–337.
Kim, K. C. and Weaver, R. D., eds (1994) *Biodiversity and Landscapes: a Paradox of Humanity*. Cambridge University Press, New York.
Kyung-Hwan, K. (1997) Improving local government finance in a changing environment. *Habitat International* 21(1), 17.
Moore, D. R. and Ahmed, N. (1997) Proposal for the development of an indigenous materials and methods-oriented design data aid for design professionals practising in developing nations. *Habitat International* 21(1), 29.

Naeem, S., Thompson, L. J., Lawler, S. P., Lawton, J. H. and Woodfin, R. M. (1994) Declining biodiversity can alter the performance of ecosystems. *Nature* **368**, 734–736.

Norton, B. G. and Ulanowicz, R. E. (1992) Scale and biodiversity policy: a hierachical approach. *Ambio* **21**(3), 244–249.

Norton, T. W. and Dovers, S. R. (1996) Uncertainty, ecology, sustainability and policy. *Biodiversity and Conservation* **5**,1143–1167.

Noss, R. F. (1983) A regional landscape approach to maintain diversity. *Bioscience* **33**(11), 700–706.

Ostrom, E. (1990) *Governing the Commons. The Evolution of Institutions for Collective Action.* Cambridge University Press, Cambridge.

Reeve, I. J. (1992) Sustainable agriculture: problems, prospects and policies. In *Agriculture, Environment and Society: Contemporary Issues for Australia*, eds Lawrence, G., Vanclay, F. and Furze, B. pp. 208–223. MacMillan, Melbourne.

Reeve, I. J. (1997) Property and participation: an institutional analysis of rural resource management and landcare in Australia. In *Critical Landcare*, eds S. Locke and F. Vanclay, pp. 83–96. Centre for Rural Social Research, Wagga Wagga.

Slocombe, D. S. (1993) Implementing ecosystem-based management: development of theory, practice and research for planning and managing a region. *BioScience* **43**(9), 612–622.

Smil, V. (1993) *Global Ecology: Environmental Change and Social Flexibility.* Routledge, New York.

Walker, B. (1995) Conserving biological diversity through ecosystem resilience. *Conservation Biology* **9**(4), 747–752.

Walters, C. J. and Holling, C. S. (1990) Large-scale management experiments and learning by doing. *Ecology* **71**(6), 2060–2068.

Walton, D. W. and Bridgewater, P. B. (1996) Of gardens and garders. *Nature and Resources* **32**(3), 15–19.

[35]

Journal of Environmental Management (1996) **46**, 119–137

Landcare in Australia: Does it Make a Difference?

Allan Curtis and Terry De Lacy

The Johnstone Centre, Charles Sturt University, Albury, N.S.W. 2640, Australia

Received 29 *December* 1994

Victorian landcare groups are increasingly seen as the key element of an emerging Australian success story. The assumptions underlying landcare are that limited funding of group activity will produce more aware, informed, skilled and adaptive resource managers with a stronger stewardship ethic, will increase the adoption of sustainable practices, and will assist the move to more sustainable resource use. A survey of all landholders in 12 subcatchments of north-east Victoria was undertaken in 1993 to assess the impact of landcare participation upon key programme outcomes. Information from the northeast survey indicated that landcare participation had a significant impact upon landholder awareness of issues, level of knowledge and adoption of best bet practices. This information, and earlier research by the authors, suggests that landcare group activity has made an important contribution towards sustainable resource management. However, research findings also suggested a number of flaws in programme logic. Given the low levels of profitability amongst landholders, the vast scale and intractable nature of key issues and the considerable off-site benefits of remedial action, it is problematic whether limited funding of a community development process will effect behavioural changes that are sufficient to make a difference at the landscape level. Programme emphasis upon developing landholders' stewardship ethic also appears misplaced in that there was no significant difference in the stewardship ethic of participants and non-participants. Indeed, to the extent that landcare focuses upon changing individual behaviour rather than societal barriers to rural development, landcare is open to the criticism that it places too much responsibility upon individual landholders.   © 1996 Academic Press Limited

Keywords: landcare, community participation, rural development, sustainable agriculture, Australia.

1. Introduction

Landcare is seen as an emerging Australian success story and involves a considerable investment of public and private resources. Until recently, there has been little work to assess landcare programme effectiveness, in particular, the assumptions underlying programme logic. Indeed, this research and other work undertaken by the authors (see Curtis *et al.*, 1993c, 1994*a–c*, 1994*d,f*) formed an important element of the Commonwealth Department of Primary Industries and Energy (DPIE) 1994 review of

119

Rural Planning and Management

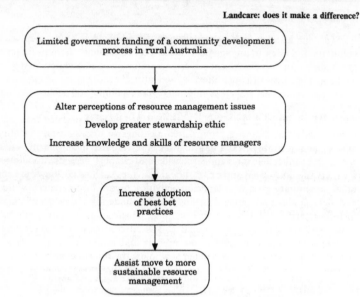

Figure 1. Assumptions underlying community landcare programmes in Australia.

the Decade of Landcare. Research reported in this paper employed a model of the landcare programme logic (Figure 1) to assess programme impact within one region. The intention was to provide information useful to key stakeholders by exploring the theoretical assumptions underpinning the landcare programme (Chen, 1990; Chen and Rossi, 1983; Rossi and Freeman, 1985). The emphasis was therefore upon formative evaluation that would enlighten stakeholders and assist programme improvement (Cronbach *et al.*, 1980).

2. Background

The landcare programme emerged as a distinctive entity in the state of Victoria during 1986 (Campbell, 1991*a*) and has been embraced by governments, farmer organisations and conservation groups throughout Australia as offering a model for effective community action to manage land degradation and assist the move to more sustainable resource use. Indeed, by July 1994, there were an estimated 2000 Australian landcare groups (including 500 Victorian landcare groups with two new groups formed each week for the previous 3 years). After lobbying from major farmer and conservation groups, the Commonwealth government committed spending of A$360m in the *Decade of Landcare* programme announced as part of a major environmental statement by the Prime Minister (Hawke, 1989): landcare was now a national programme. Landcare is intended to achieve more sustainable use of Australia's farming lands (DCE, 1992) and to enhance biodiversity (Farley and Toyne, 1989). Whilst governments espoused a "landcare programme" that embraced all facets of sustainable resource use, it was the emergence, growth and activity of these voluntary groups which captured public attention and distinguished landcare from previous efforts to achieve more sustainable resource use.

Most landcare groups have developed in rural areas and group membership is voluntary and open to any member of the local community. Groups frequently operate at catchment or sub-catchment scales and are involved in a variety of activities related to the management of issues affecting agricultural production and biodiversity, such as water quality decline, soil erosion, ground water salinity, soil acidity, vegetation decline and introduced pest animals and weeds. Reports by Campbell (1991b, 1992), Curtis and De Lacy (1994a) and Curtis et al. (1993a, 1994a–d) revealed that, amongst their various activities, landcare groups hold meetings to discuss issues, identify priorities, develop action strategies and debate a range of resource management issues with guest speakers; conduct field days and farm walks and establish demonstration sites; undertake a variety of educational and promotional activities such as hosting tours and involving other community groups in landcare activities, organise conferences, write newsletters and field guides and prepare media releases; undertake a range of onground work including seed collection and tree planting, constructing salinity and erosion control structures, coordinating pest animal and weed control activities, erecting fencing to control stock access to creeks and streams and establish wildlife corridors; groups coordinate planning activities related to whole farm or property planning and catchment planning; and some members are involved in the preparation of submissions for government funding.

Campbell (1989), Woodhill (1990), Edgar and Patterson (1992) and Curtis et al. (1993b) discussed the benefits of landcare participation from the landholder perspective in terms of landholders being able to share problems and ideas and, in doing so, gain support and encouragement to push ahead; work together to tackle common problems more effectively; have opportunities for learning about land management and to plan at property and catchment levels so that resource management is based upon a shared understanding of important physical, social and economic processes operating within and beyond the farm gate; obtain financial and technical assistance from government that they would be unlikely to receive as individual landholders; and have increased opportunities for social interaction with other members of their local community. Edgar and Patterson (1992) indicated social learning and social interaction, which was likely to be facilitated by involvement in landcare groups, and was an important ingredient in developing greater awareness of land degradation issues and in promoting better land management. Whilst participants could learn from one another, it was also suggested that peer pressure might encourage the adoption of improved practices and overcome the problem of free-riders in voluntary approaches to common-pool natural resources management.

Evaluators can turn to a number of sources in their effort to unravel programme theory: they can approach programme staff, clients and other stakeholders for their views, they can review literature on the programme under scrutiny or similar programmes, examine programme documentation, and observe programme operation. Shadish et al. (1991, pp. 236–237) suggest this process occurs as part of an "Evaluability assessment" which is ". . . a tool to help ameliorate the problems of lack of definition, clear logic, and management . . .". Evaluability assessment aims to explore both programme implementation and clarify program intent (Shadish et al., 1991). Given the lack of explicit programme goals, the diversity of stakeholder opinions about landcare programme objectives, and the heterogeneity of programme implementation at the local level, the authors have devoted considerable energy to unravelling programme logic. To a large extent, this task was accomplished using information collected through the state-wide group activities report process (Curtis et al., 1993a,c), the authors' knowledge

of landcare group activities in north-east Victoria and personal contacts with stakeholders at local, regional, state and federal scales. The key assumptions underlying
community landcare (Figure 1) are that, with the limited government funding of a
self-help programme, landcare group action will facilitate a process of community
participation that will mobilise a large proportion of the rural population and produce
more aware, informed, skilled and adaptive resource managers with a strong stewardship
or land ethic, and thereby result in the adoption of improved management practices
and assist the move to more sustainable resource use.

3. Methodology

During autumn 1993, a 16 page survey was mailed to all rural property owners in 12
small catchments in north-east Victoria: nine catchments where landcare groups had
been operating for more than 2 years and three catchments where no landcare group
existed (Curtis and De Lacy, 1994*b*).

The north-east regional survey attempted to:

- Assess the impact of landcare participation, including length of membership and
  intensity of participation, in making a significant difference to the adoption of
  best bet practices likely to:
    (i) enhance the economic viability of landholders; and
    (ii) enhance catchment protection and the conservation of biodiversity, through
        community development processes that make a significant difference to
        landholders':
        (i) awareness of land degradation issues;
        (ii) development of a stewardship ethic; and
        (iii) level of knowledge of resource management topics.
- Explore whether there are inconsistencies between aspects of landcare programme
  logic and the practice of landcare. In particular, to explore:
    (i) the linkage between attitudes towards stewardship and the adoption of
        conservation practices by landholders.
- Explore the characteristics of landcare participants and non-participants. An
  important step in assessing the impact of landcare was to determine the extent
  participants and non-participants were similar on key social and farming variables
  (see Curtis and De Lacy, 1994*b*).

The intention was to assess the impact of landcare in a single region by comparing:

1. Landcare respondents with non landcare respondents in landcare areas.
2. All respondents in landcare areas with all respondents in areas where landcare
   groups did not exist.

The north-east study was a cross-sectional, non-randomised study of individuals and
properties at January 1993. The researchers proposed to overcome some of the limitations
of cross-sectional, non-randomised studies through the inclusion of the non-landcare
areas as a control group and by applying bivariate and multivariate statistical procedures
to control for the impact of a range of independent variables likely to affect key
outcomes. However, the potential for multivariate analysis to accomplish such a task
is limited by a researcher's ability to identify relevant variables and include them in a
study. Despite the most conscientious efforts, the limitations of this cross-sectional

study in identifying causal relationships must be acknowledged: factors other than landcare participation may explain significant differences identified.

The decision to run with a regional case study reflected the authors' view that regional differences limited the effectiveness of surveying across a number of regions. Apart from the obvious biophysical variations, there are considerable regional variations in farm enterprises and profitability, access to off-farm work and administrative arrangements that affect landcare activity. Access to a region where a large number of groups had been operating for a considerable time was an important factor in the choice of the north-east region, as was the authors' knowledge of the region, landcare groups and agency staff. To enable sufficient time for landcare group activity to affect landholder perceptions, attitudes and actions, only areas where groups had been operating for more than 2 years were included in the nine landcare areas surveyed. At April 1993, these nine areas had groups which had been operating between 6 and 10 years. Information available to the researcher from the group activities reports (Curtis *et al.*, 1993a,c), and from personal contact with group leaders and agency staff, indicated the groups surveyed had received government support slightly above the mean of A\$10 657 (Curtis and De Lacy, 1994a) for Victorian groups. Given the information above, it appeared reasonable to claim that, if landcare groups were not effective in the north-east, it was unlikely landcare groups would be effective elsewhere. The three non-landcare areas were selected to provide a spread of land types, agricultural enterprises and distances from regional centres that approximated these characteristics in the landcare areas surveyed.

Survey methodology conformed with Dillman's (1978) Total Design Method in that the survey questionnaire was a small (B5) booklet with a distinctive, authoritative cover which was posted with an accompanying covering letter and stamped return envelope. A small thank you/reminder card was posted between 8–10 days after the first mail out and a second mail out to all non-respondents occurred 6 weeks after surveys were initially posted. With 352 responses from the 593 land holders in the nine landcare areas, a 59% survey response rate was achieved in the landcare areas. With 48 responses from the 110 land holders in the three non-landcare areas, a 42% response rate was achieved.

The literature on voluntary groups, community participation, the adoption of agricultural innovation and landcare were examined in an effort to identify key social and farming variables that might assist the understanding of landcare participation and the impact of participation upon landholder perceptions of land degradation issues, development of a stewardship ethic, knowledge of resource management and adoption of best bet practices. As Rogers (1983, p. 242) explained, "We know more about innovativeness...than about any other concept in diffusion research." Buttel *et al.* (1990), Pampel and Van Es (1977), Rogers (1983) and Nowak (1987) explored the adoption of agricultural/conservation innovations and discussed the findings of a large number of adoption studies. Earle *et al.* (1978), Vanclay (1986, 1992), Vanclay and Cary (1989), Wilkinson and Cary (1992) and Mues *et al.* (1994) provided the nucleus of a considerable body of research into the adoption of agricultural innovations in eastern Australia. Reeve and Black (1992) and Black and Reeve (1993) provided a thorough review of much of the literature on the adoption of agricultural/conservation innovations and the only published large scale study investigating factors affecting landcare participation. However, not all landcare members are farmers and landcare group activities extend beyond those related to the adoption of agricultural or conservation practices, such as conservation tillage. Landcare groups are another voluntary community group and the vast body of literature on voluntary groups provides information for those attempting to unravel the reasons for landcare participation. Brudney (1990), Curtis and Noble (1988), Humble (1982), Isley and Niemi (1981), Moore (1985), Pearce (1993) and Smith (1975, 1981) discussed the motivations and characteristics of volunteers and the nature of volunteer organisations.

As might be expected, these different sources are often contradictory. However, a number of commonly applied social and property variables which might assist understanding of the nature and impact of landcare participation were identified. Given the vast number of potential sociological, psychological and institutional variables that might explain landcare participation, it is probable that key variables were not included in the study. Questions seeking information about the following variables were included in the north-east sustainable farming survey booklet:

Personal characteristics independent of landcare participation:

- Age
- Sex
- Education
- Length of farming experience
- Length of residence in area (indication of geographic mobility)
- Involvement in other community groups
- Type of off-farm employment
- Extent of off-farm employment (hours worked)
- Amount of off-farm household income
- If the participant has a spouse, then the spouse's education, occupation, extent of influence upon decision-making within farm and household and extent and type of off-farm employment

Personal characteristics hypothesised as not independent of landcare participation:

- Perceived knowledge of land degradation processes and sustainable agricultural practices relevant to north-east Victoria
- Belief about extent of land degradation on property
- Belief about environmental and economic impact of land degradation on property
- Attitude—stewardship ethic
- Attitude—importance of community co-operation in managing land degradation
- Importance of sources of information about sustainable farming practices
- Landcare membership
- Length of landcare membership (relative to period of time group operating)
- Intensity of participation in landcare activities
- Reasons for joining or not joining landcare

Farming variables independent of landcare participation:

- Farm size (all land owned by household in local area)
- Arable farm size (calculated by subtracting area of remnant vegetation from farm size)
- Land type as a percentage of the total area: steep to moderate slopes; length of frontage to rivers and named creeks; amount of remnant vegetation (accounted for in arable farm size)

- Type of agricultural production
- Did the farm make a profit?
- Net farm income (taxable)

Farming variables not independent of landcare participation:

- Amount of perennial pasture at January 1993
- Perennial pasture established in previous 2 years
- Number of soil tests conducted in previous 2 years
- Number of trees planted in previous 2 years
- Length of fencing erected to control stock access to water courses, native bush/ trees or to protect new plantings of trees in previous 2 years
- Area limed in previous 2 years
- Involvement in property management planning

A number of best bet practices were identified which are the focus of considerable landcare group activity and which appeared to be the most useful strategies for effectively managing the major issues confronting Victorian landholders. Whilst there are regional differences in the severity of resource management issues, the strategies likely to manage these effectively are reasonably consistent across the state. The best bet practices included in the north-east study were:

- Perennial pasture establishment
- Tree planting
- Fencing for landcare activities such as controlling stock access to streams, protecting new and remnant vegetation
- Soil testing
- Liming to control soil acidity
- Whole farm planning or property management planning

4. Findings: does landcare participation make a significant difference to behaviour?

4.1. A COMPARISON OF LANDCARE AND NON-LANDCARE PARTICIPANTS IN LANDCARE AREAS

4.1.1. *Awareness of land degradation*

One of the key assumptions underlying the landcare programme is that landholders who are more aware of land degradation issues are more likely to adopt best bet practices that will assist the move to more sustainable resource management, and that community development processes within landcare can enhance landholder awareness. In his discussion of farmers' concern about land degradation, Vanclay (1992) noted that farmers' perceptions of the severity of land degradation on their properties affected the likelihood of their taking action to prevent it.

Using Likert-type response categories, respondents to the north-east survey were asked to indicate both their perception of the extent key land management issues were a problem on their property and the impact of these issues upon a range of economic and environmental values. Bivariate analysis (Curtis and De Lacy, 1994b) established that landcare and non-landcare participants were engaged in similar types of farming enterprises and their properties were similar in terms of farm characteristic likely to affect the occurrence and severity of land degradation in north-east Victoria. Bivariate analysis (Table 1) indicated that landcare respondents had significantly higher levels of awareness for almost all of the key land management issues listed, and for an index measuring overall awareness of land degradation. Landcare respondents also had a significantly greater concern for all of the listed potential economic and environmental impacts of land degradation on their property (Table 2). Indices measuring overall concern for both economic and environmental impacts were calculated for use as summary measures in other bivariate and multivariate analyses. Multivariate analyses were conducted using landcare outcomes as the response variables in either logistic or linear regression models with landcare membership as one of the explanatory variables. Results of multivariate analyses are summarised in Figure 2. A significant positive relationship was observed between landcare participation and concern about both the economic and environmental impacts of land degradation issues ($P = 0.0057$; $P = 0.0546$, respectively).

4.1.2. *Development of a stewardship or land ethic*

Until recently, the accepted view (Roberts, 1992) was that landcare participants would develop a stronger land ethic, landcare activity would foster the strengthening of the land ethic of others, and a stronger land ethic would affect the behaviour of land managers. For Vanclay (1992, p. 97), "Stewardship refers to the notion that farmers are stewards of the land and that farming is a way of life that places implicit responsibility on farmers to look after the land for future generations." Vanclay (1986) developed a stewardship/land ethic attitudinal scale utilising a series of statements with five point Likert-type response categories. After appropriate statistical tests for scale reliability and validity, respondents scores for each scale item were computed to provide an index score for each respondent. Vanclay's (1986) stewardship scale has been adapted for this research project in north-east Victoria. Using statistical procedures for constructing attitudinal scales outlined by De Vaus (1991), three items were eliminated to arrive at a scale of six items with item-to-item Spearman rank correlation coefficients ($P > 0.3$) and a standardised item alpha using an SPSS of 0.6479 (slightly below the accepted 0.70 standard). Given that the stewardship scale meets requirements for uni-dimensionality, has been used previously, and a number of relationships were found to be as hypothesised, the authors were confident of scale reliability and validity.

Analysis of survey responses revealed no significant differences in the scores of landcare and non-landcare respondents in landcare areas (Table 3) or between landcare areas and non-landcare areas on the stewardship/land ethic index. These results were consistent with Vanclay's (1986, 1992) findings that scores on the stewardship ethic do not discriminate between adopters and non-adopters of new agricultural practices. Vanclay (1986, 1992) concluded that most farmers have a strong stewardship ethic and that other factors related to resource availability, farmers' assessment of risk and other aspects of particular innovations are more important barriers to the adoption of agricultural innovations. The possibility that the stewardship ethic scale was flawed and failed to identify differences which actually exist was also considered. Statistical tests for scale validity and reliability were conducted and have been reported above. Vanclay (1992) discussed the issue of social desirability affecting participant's responses and concluded this should affect responses from respondents equally. Further bivariate analysis using variables such as age and education, which might reasonably be expected to discriminate respondents, produced a number of significant relationships. As expected, younger and more educated respondents (Table 4) and women (Curtis *et al.*, 1994e)

TABLE 1. Awareness of land degradation issues on own property—all respondents in landcare areas, north-east Victoria, April 1993 (N = 352)

Issue	Issue a problem in Landcare (%) N=270			Issue a problem in Non-landcare (%) N=77			Chi-square P
	Large areas	Significant in some areas	Not/minor areas	Large areas	Significant in some areas	Not/minor areas	
Salinity landcare (N=246) non (N=70)	3	8	88	1	6	93	0·0789
Soil erosion landcare (N=254) non (N=72)	8	28	64	5	18	77	0·0685
Tree decline landcare (N=249) non (N=71)	18	23	59	6	6	88	0·0002
Water logging landcare (N=247) non (N=68)	14	26	60	10	10	80	0·0042
Soil acidity landcare (N=242) non (N=65)	38	17	45	12	22	66	0·0012
Rabbits landcare (N=252) non (N=73)	12	19	69	13	11	76	0·0403
Weeds landcare (N=269) non (N=74)	33	28	39	34	15	51	0·0615
Decline in soil fertility landcare (N=245) non (N=68)	28	15	57	15	23	62	0·0008
Soil compaction landcare (N=242) non (N=63)	12	25	63	7	19	74	0·0229
Index score for all issues[1]	Mean rank 165			Mean rank 205			Z-3·0445 0·0012

[1] For Likert-type response categories, (1) more important rating than (5), hence lower score on mean ranking indicates a higher ranking for that variable.

TABLE 2. Concern about the impact of land degradation issues—all respondents in landcare areas, north-east Victoria, April 1993 ($N=352$)

Concerned that land degradation will	Extent of concern Landcare (%) $N=270$			Extent of concern Non-landcare (%) $N=77$			MWW
	Very	Some	None	Very	Some	None	1-tailed P
Reduce current farm income landcare ($N=243$) non ($N=73$)	21	48	31	13	29	58	0·0002
Threaten long term farm viability landcare ($N=250$) non ($N=70$)	29	38	33	17	26	57	0·0004
Reduce attractiveness of area as place to live landcare ($N=250$) non ($N=70$)	22	36	42	10	30	60	0·0013
Reduce current property values landcare ($N=50$) non ($N=70$)	17	43	40	7	39	54	0·0061
Threaten long term property values landcare ($N=248$) non ($N=70$)	23	41	36	9	40	51	0·0015
Detrimental effect upon neighbouring farms landcare ($N=248$) non ($N=70$)	13	30	57	10	17	73	0·0129
Contribute to decline of habitat and wildlife landcare ($N=246$) non ($N=69$)	17	32	51	7	25	68	0·0036

	Central tendency		Central tendency		
	Mean	Median	Mean	Median	MWW
Index score for concern economic impact issues[1]	11·28	12·00	12·53	14·00	0·0015
Index score for concern environmental impact issues[1]	5·89	7·00	6·39	7·00	0·0092

[1] For Likert-type response categories, (1) more important rating than (5), hence lower score on central tendency indicates a higher ranking for that variable.

scored significantly higher on the stewardship ethic scale and these findings appeared to validate it. Indeed, the scale discriminated respondents on many of the variables for which there had been significant differences between landcare and non-landcare respondents.

4.1.3. *Level of knowledge of land management topics*

Another assumption underlying landcare is that, through the process of community development, land managers will become more informed, skilled and adaptive and this will assist the move to more sustainable resource management. Using Likert-type response categories, survey respondents were asked to assess their knowledge of topics which have been the focus of landcare group activity attempting to manage the key

A. Curtis and T. De Lacy   129

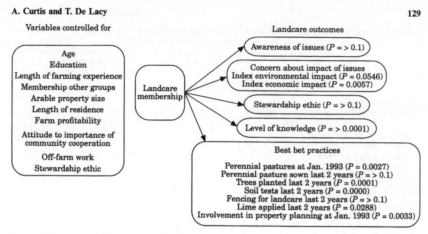

Figure 2. The impact of landcare membership on key outcomes using multivariate analysis to control for selected variables.

TABLE 3. Stewardship ethic scale scores—all respondents in landcare areas, north-east Victoria, April 1993 (*N*=352)

Group	Index scores for 6 item scale range 1–30 (%)					
	6 to 10	11 to 15	16 to 20	21 to 25	26 to 30	Mean
Landcare (*N*=268)	0·5	2·5	18	46	33	23·45
Non-landcare (*N*=75)	3·0	2·0	24	39	32	22·91

Mann–Whitney U Wilcoxon signed ranks test, $Z = -0·64341$, $P = 0·2600$ (not significant).

resource issues in the north-east. An examination of Table 5 revealed that landcare participants reported significantly higher levels of knowledge for all land management topics listed. Using multivariate analysis to control for a range of variables (Figure 2), a significant positive relationship ($P=0·0001$) was established between landcare participation and scores on the index measuring respondent's level of knowledge for all topics listed in Table 5.

Survey respondents were also asked to assess the impact of various information sources upon their level of knowledge for the topics listed in the previous question. Information in Table 6 provided considerable evidence to support claims that landcare group participation has an important impact upon landholders' level of knowledge. Table 6 shows landcare participants reported that landcare groups, field days, friends, relatives and neighbours, education courses, government department staff, farmer organisations and private farm consultants had a significantly higher impact upon their level of knowledge than did non-landcare respondents. Landcare groups received the

TABLE 4. Stewardship ethic and other social and farming variables—all respondents in landcare areas, north-east Victoria, April 1993 ($N = 352$)

Variable	$N=$	Stewardship ethic score			Kruskal–Wallis H		
		Low <20	Medium 21 to 25	High >25	Chi-square	df	P
Age	340	197	162	164	7·2776	2	0·0263
Highest level of schooling	336	144	173	180	8·5824	2	0·0137
Property size	337	208	166	146	19·1589	2	0·0001
Extent of off-farm work	176	74	86	97	4·6010	2	0·1002
Concern land degradation as an issue, index score[1]	348	180	169	17	0·8477	2	0·6545
Community co-operation attitudinal scale	348	120	17	217	45·0710	2	0·0000
Intensity of participation in landcare activities[1]	258	133	129	127	0·2097	2	0·9005
When joined landcare[1]	259	137	129	127	0·6909	2	0·7079

[1] For Likert-type response categories, (1) more important rating than (5), hence lower score on mean ranking indicates a higher ranking for that variable. For all other variables, higher scores on mean ranking indicates a higher ranking.

TABLE 5. Level of knowledge of resource management topics—all respondents in landcare areas, north-east Victoria, April 1993 ($N = 352$)

Land management topics	Level of knowledge Landcare (%) $N=270$			Level of knowledge Non-landcare (%) $N=77$			Chi-square (P)
	High/ very high	Fair	Low/ none	High/ very high	Fair	Low/ none	
Processes leading to soil erosion	62	31	7	44	39	17	0·0077
Property management plans on land classes	34	35	31	8	27	65	0·0000
Rabbit control methods	72	18	10	59	25	16	0·0495
Role perennial pasture in lowering water tables	46	31	23	21	40	39	0·0001
How to establish perennial pastures	44	36	20	39	19	42	0·0000
How to collect samples for soil tests	54	24	22	32	26	42	0·0029
Processes leading to soil acidification	30	40	30	22	27	51	0·0014
Role of minimum tillage maintaining soil structure	44	35	21	28	36	36	0·0040
Role of tree removal in raising water tables	67	21	12	45	33	22	0·0011

TABLE 6. Impact of information sources upon level of knowledge—all respondents in landcare areas, north-east Victoria, April 1993 ($N=352$)

Sources of information	Impact upon knowledge Landcare (%) $N=270$			Impact upon knowledge Non-landcare (%) $N=70$			Chi-square (P)
	High/ very high	Fair	Low/ none	High/ very high	Fair	Low/ none	
Friends, relatives and neighbours	62	26	12	53	29	18	0·0291
Radio and television	45	33	22	50	36	14	0·8098
Newspapers and magazines	72	23	5	69	25	6	0·9939
Education courses	60	13	27	40	11	49	0·0026
Banks and financial advisers	9	12	79	6	7	87	0·4666
Field days	70	19	11	54	18	28	0·0089
Landcare groups	84	13	3	36	25	39	0·0000
Government department staff	55	27	18	29	34	37	0·0004
Farmer organisations	37	28	35	30	17	53	0·0040
Farm suppliers and stock agents	32	30	38	30	17	53	0·6106
Private farm consultants	17	17	66	11	11	78	0·21843
	Central tendency			Central tendency			
	mean	median		mean	median		MWW
Knowledge key land management topics-Index[1]	2·605	2·444		3·158	2·444		0·0000

[1] Lower score for high/very high.

highest rating (84% as important/very important influence) from landcare respondents and 36% of non-landcare participants reported landcare groups were an important/very important information source affecting their level of knowledge. Table 6 also shows that newspapers and magazines (69%), field days (54%), friends and neighbours (53%) and radio and television (50%) received the highest ratings from non-landcare respondents as information sources with an important/very important influence upon their level of knowledge. Landcare groups in Victoria have been very active in publicising landcare and field days are a popular activity (Curtis and De Lacy, 1994*a*), and it is likely that groups are making an important contribution to enhancing the knowledge and skills of land managers through these activities as well as through contact between members, friends, relatives and neighbours.

4.1.4. *Adoption of best bet practices*

Table 7 shows that landcare participants reported significantly higher levels of adoption for all best bet practices included in the survey with the exception of perennial pasture established in the past 2 years. Further analysis revealed that "early joiners" (a measure of length of membership) and those who had greater intensity of landcare participation had significantly higher levels of adoption for almost all best bet practices (Curtis and De Lacy, 1994*b*). Using logistic regression to undertake multivariate analysis controlling for a range of variables (Figure 2), a significant positive relationship was observed

TABLE 7. Adoption of best bet practices—comparison of landcare and non-landcare respondents in landcare areas, north-east Victoria, April 1993 ($N=352$)

	Mean rank for each variable		MWW
Best bet practices	Landcare $N=270$	Non-landcare $N=77$	1-tailed (P)
Perennial pasture at Jan 1993 ($N=305$)	157·6	130·4	0·0115
Perennial pasture, past 2 years ($N=323$)	144·2	134·4	0·1799
Trees planted past 2 years ($N=322$)	174·5	104·4	0·0000
Soil tests past 2 years ($N=352$)	162·5	107·7	0·0000
Fencing for landcare past 2 years ($N=322$)	163·8	106·2	0·0000
Lime applied past 2 years ($N=278$)	142·3	125·1	0·0449
Involvement in whole farm planning ($N=352$)	Chi-square: 13·16552, df 4·01049		

between landcare participation and establishment of perennial pastures at January 1993 ($P=0·0027$), involvement in farm/property planning at January 1993 ($P=0·0033$), planting trees in the past 2 years ($P=0·0001$), undertaking soil tests in the past 2 years ($P=0·0000$), and lime applied in the past 2 years ($P=0·0288$). Multivariate analyses failed to establish any significant relationships between the length of landcare membership and adoption of best bet practices ($P>0·05$), but established significant positive relationships between the intensity of landcare participation and the undertaking of soil tests and the application of lime in the past 2 years, and involvement in farm/property planning at January 1993 ($P<0·05$). Despite the acknowledged difficulties of unravelling causal relationships within a cross sectional study, the weight of evidence from the north-east regional study that suggested that landcare participation makes a difference to the adoption of best bet practices is substantial.

4.2. A COMPARISON OF ALL RESPONDENTS IN LANDCARE AREAS WITH ALL RESPONDENTS IN NON-LANDCARE AREAS

4.2.1. *Respondents were very similar on independent social and farming variables*

Bivariate analysis of information provided by respondents revealed few significant differences between respondents from landcare and non-landcare areas for the range of independent social and farming variables included in the survey (Curtis and De Lacy, 1994*b*). Respondents from landcare areas reported significantly higher participation in other community groups and significantly lower proportions of their properties with steep slopes (Curtis and De Lacy, 1994*b*). Despite these differences, respondents from landcare and non-landcare areas were homogenous for the range of independent social and farming variables included in the survey. To the extent that this is the case, and despite landcare affecting respondents in non-landcare areas, the comparison of

TABLE 8. Key landcare outcomes—comparison respondents in landcare and non-landcare areas, north-east Victoria, April 1993 (*N*=400)

Key outcomes	Mean rankings on outcome		Mann–Whitney (W)	
	Landcare *N*=352	Non-landcare *N*=48	*Z*	1-tailed *P*
Concern land degradation as an issue-index score[1] (*N*=400)	200 (*N*=352)	201 (*N*=48)	−0·0293	0·4883
Stewardship ethic scale (*N*=400)	199 (*N*=348)	196 (*N*=48)	−0·1632	0·4352
Knowledge key land management topics-index[1] (*N*=390)	188 (*N*=343)	247 (*N*=47)	−3·3659	0·0004
Perennial pasture at Jan 1993 (*N*=344)	175 (*N*=305)	155 (*N*=39)	−1·1969	0·1157
Perennial pasture, past 2 years (*N*=323)	166 (*N*=286)	131 (*N*=37)	−2·3888	0·0085
Trees planted, past 2 years (*N*=366)	188 (*N*=322)	152 (*N*=44)	−2·1015	0·0178
Soil tests, past 2 years (*N*=340)	175 (*N*=303)	130 (*N*=37)	−2·8316	0·0023
Fencing for landcare, past 2 years (*N*=344)	174 (*N*=306)	161 (*N*=38)	−0·8055	0·2103
Lime applied, past 2 years (*N*=313)	159 (*N*=278)	142 (*N*=35)	−1·2021	0·1147
Involvement in whole farm planning (*N*=362)	185 (*N*=321)	158 (*N*=41)	−1·7375	0·0412

[1] For Likert-type response categories, (1) more important rating than (5), hence lower score on mean ranking indicates a higher ranking for that variable. For all other variables, higher scores on mean ranking indicates a higher ranking.

respondents from landcare and non-landcare areas provided an excellent opportunity to assess the impact of landcare group participation and activity upon key outcomes expected from landcare activity.

4.2.2. *Significant differences between respondents for key landcare outcomes*

Information summarised in Table 8 highlighted the significantly higher scores of respondents in landcare areas for a range of anticipated outcomes of landcare group activity. Again, the complexity of causal relationships and the limitations of a cross-sectional study must be acknowledged. With 48 respondents from non-landcare areas, there were insufficient observations to give robust results from multivariate analyses. However, given that respondents in landcare and non-landcare areas are very similar on a range of independent variables that should have predated landcare, it seems reasonable to attribute much of the differences highlighted in Table 8 to landcare group participation and activity.

Whilst information in Table 8 indicated respondents in landcare areas were not significantly more aware of land degradation on an index score, analysis of results for component issues revealed landcare area respondents were significantly more aware of salinity, soil fertility decline, soil compaction, soil acidity and weeds (MWW, $P<0·05$), with no significant difference in awareness of soil erosion, tree decline, water logging and rabbits (Curtis and De Lacy, 1994b). This information suggested respondents in landcare areas had a greater awareness of less obvious issues (weeds are the exception). Comparison of respondents in landcare and non-landcare areas revealed no significant differences in the holding of a stewardship or land ethic (Table 8).

5. Conclusion

Despite the complex nature of causal relationships in the social sciences and the difficulties of attempting to assess the impact of landcare participation upon expected outcomes using a cross-sectional, non-randomised study, the weight of evidence in this study indicated that landcare participation makes a significant difference to a range of outcomes related to landcare participation. Whilst landcare and non-landcare participants in landcare areas were different on key social and farming variables, bivariate analysis established that landcare participants:

- were significantly more aware of land degradation issues;
- reported significantly greater levels of knowledge of resource management topics;
- had significantly higher levels of adoption of almost all best bet practices surveyed.

Furthermore, bivariate analysis revealed significant positive relationships between the length of membership and intensity of participation in group activities and a range of expected landcare group outcomes. Multivariate analyses confirmed that landcare respondents were significantly more concerned about the economic impact of land degradation issues, more knowledgeable on some resource management topics, reported significantly higher levels of perennial pasture establishment and involvement in farm/property management at January 1993, and were significantly more involved in tree planting, conducting soil tests and applying lime in the past 2 years. Multivariate analyses also confirmed that landcare participants who were more intensively involved in landcare group activities were significantly more involved in farm/property management planning at January 1993 and conducting soil tests and applying lime in the past 2 years.

Respondents from landcare and non-landcare areas were not significantly different on most of the social and farming variables that should have predated landcare. Further analysis revealed respondents in landcare areas:

- were significantly more aware of many land degradation issues, particularly those that are less obvious;
- reported significantly higher levels of knowledge of resource management topics; and
- had significantly higher levels of adoption of almost all best bet practices surveyed.

Over 80% of landcare participants, 39% of non-landcare respondents in landcare areas and 37% of respondents in non-landcare areas indicated that landcare groups were an important/very important influence upon their level of knowledge of listed resource management topics. Field days were rated as an important/very important influence by 70% of landcare respondents and 54% of non-landcare respondents in landcare areas. This information suggested that the involvement of landcare groups in various educational and promotional activities and the interaction of members with friends, relatives and neighbours were important elements of the community development process within landcare and had enhanced the effectiveness of landcare group activity.

Whilst the weight of evidence in this research suggests that landcare participation makes a significant difference, it is important to establish whether best bet practices are being adopted at a rate which will have an impact at the landscape level. This task was beyond the scope of this study. Indeed, further research is required to develop biological indicators of sustainable resource management at the catchment level and standards to indicate the extent to which best bet practices need to be adopted to effect improvements over time. However, the authors used the extent of non- or very low adoption of best bet practices as a preliminary and very crude measure of the extent to which practices are being adopted at levels likely to make a difference to the landscape in the north-east over the next 10 years. Survey analysis revealed that over 50% of landcare respondents had never been involved in whole farm planning/property planning, and 44% had planted no more than 100 trees over the same period. Given that landcare participants have adopted best bet practices at significantly higher rates than non-landcare participants and that 30% of properties in the north-east (62% across Victoria—Mues *et al.*, 1994) do not have a landcare participant, a substantial proportion of Victorian landholders appear to be undertaking limited amounts of landcare work. It is probably fair to conclude that, with limited resources, landcare group participants are undertaking substantial landcare work and have "pulled down" considerable additional resources for landcare in local communities (Curtis *et al.*, 1993c). However, given the number of landholders not adopting best practices it would be difficult to sustain an argument that practices are being adopted at rates likely to produce major benefits at the landscape scale during the 10-year period of the Decade of Landcare Plan. Furthermore, much of the fencing and tree planting work undertaken by landcare group participants in the north-east would appear to be underpinned by government assistance through the National Landcare Program and the Murray-Darling Basin Commission's Natural Resources Management Strategy. Information provided by the Victorian group activities report process (Curtis *et al.*, 1993c) supported these findings in that groups had successfully undertaken a vast array of community development activities; however, only 20% of streams in landcare areas had been fenced to control stock access, 45% of groups reported that government assistance with materials and funds to manage land degradation was inadequate, and there was a significant positive relationship between group performance on an index of work undertaken and the amount of government funding received.

A central element of the landcare model outlined earlier (Figure 1) is the assumption that changes in attitudes, particularly the development of a stronger stewardship ethic, would produce significant changes in the management practices of landholders. Clearly, this research indicated that there were no significant differences in the stewardship/land ethic of landcare and non-landcare participants. Indeed, a persuasive argument can be advanced that much of the appeal of landcare is that it reflects values already widely held in the rural community, including a strong stewardship ethic. Attempts to manage land degradation by changing landholder attitudes appear misguided.

Given the intractable nature of many natural resource management issues, the marginal viability of many farms, and the considerable off-site benefits of many best bet practices, it is problematic whether limited funding of a community development process will effect behavioural changes sufficient to achieve sustainable resource management at the landscape level. To the extent that landcare focuses upon changing individual behaviour rather than societal barriers to rural development, landcare is open to the criticism that it places too much responsibility upon individual landholders. Indeed, it can be argued that farmer organisations and government have embraced landcare as a strategy to deflect criticisms of structural impediments to sustainable resource management and defer taking hard decisions about farm and regional viability, land tenure systems, allocations of river water for irrigation and vegetation clearing.

As a programme that involved only limited funding of a community development process, landcare has probably exceeded any realistic goals established at the start of the Decade of Landcare. However, as the middle of the Decade of Landcare is approached, it is time to adopt a different landcare model. It is time to acknowledge that changing attitudes is not the key to changing resource management practices. Whilst funding of community development processes is a fundamental element of landcare and must be maintained, additional resources are required to increase land-holder adoption of best bet practices and landcare group activity needs to be more closely integrated within regional landcare planning processes. Arguments that increased funding to landcare is a handout to land managers ignore the community benefits of important landcare work such as revegetation, fencing water courses and establishing perennial grasses on steep hills. They fail to acknowledge that most land degradation problems have been inherited from previous generations, they deny the responsibility of government when government policies have contributed to many land degradation issues, and fail to grasp the important link between the conservation of native flora and fauna and the condition of privately owned agricultural land. It is time to build upon the successes of landcare. Legislative initiatives in New South Wales, Queensland and Victoria have established or are about to establish integrated catchment management processes in which representatives from regional communities have a key role in natural resource management decision-making. These regional bodies can provide the missing links in landcare, linkages between landcare groups in regional communities, and a regional perspective that is becoming essential for the effective management of key resource management issues. Whilst a mix of measures may be employed, regional catchment boards provide the best mechanism by which additional resources can be targeted through regional plans to produce maximum effect, to provide accountability for funds expended, to support existing programmes such as regional development and to enhance the community development processes initiated by landcare.

References

Black, A. W. and Reeve, I. (1993). Participation in landcare groups: the relative importance of attitudinal and situational factors. *Journal of Environmental Management* **39**, 51–57.

Brudney, J. L. (1990). *Fostering Volunteer Programs in the Public Sector: Planning, Initiating and Managing Voluntary Activities*. San Francisco: Jossey-Bass.

Buttel, F., Larson, O. and Gilespie, G. Jr. (1990). *The Sociology of Agriculture*. New York: Greenwood Press.

Campbell, A. (1989). Landcare in Australia—an overview. *Australian Journal of Soil and Water Conservation* **2**, 18–20.

Campbell, A. (1991a). Community participation—a new frontier in land management. Paper presented to International Conference on Sustainable Land Management, Napier, New Zealand.

Campbell, A. (1991b). *Landcare—Testing Times. National Landcare Facilitator 2nd Annual Report*. Canberra: Department of Primary Industries and Energy.

Campbell, A. (1992). *Taking the Long View in Tough Times. National Landcare Facilitator, 3rd Annual Report*. Canberra: NSCP.

Chen, H. T. (1990). *Theory-driven Evaluations*. Newbury Park, California: Sage.

Chen, T. T. and Rossi, P. H. (1983). Evaluating with sense: the theory-driven approach. *Evaluation Review* **7**, 283–302.

Cronbach, L. J., Ambron, S. R., Dornbusch, S. M., Hess, R. D., Hornik, R. C., Phillips, D. C., Walker, D. F. and Weiner, S. S. (1980). *Toward Reform of Program Evaluation*. California: Jossey-Bass.

Curtis, A. and De Lacy, T. (in press). Landcare evaluation in Australia: towards an effective partnership between agencies, community groups and researchers. *Journal of Soil and Water Conservation*.

Curtis, A. and De Lacy, T. (1994). *Landcare: Does it Make a Difference*. Albury, NSW: Johnstone Centre.

Curtis, A., Birckhead, J. and De Lacy, T. (in press). Community participation in landcare policy in Australia: The Victorian experience with regional landcare plans. *Journal of Society and Natural Resources*.

A. Curtis and T. De Lacy 137

Curtis, A., Davidson, P. and McGowan, C. (1994). *Women's Experience and Participation of Landcare in Northeast Victoria.* Albury, NSW: Johnstone Centre.

Curtis, A., De Lacy, T., Keane, D. and Boughey, S. (1994). *Landcare in Tasmania: Getting the Job Done.* Albury, NSW: Johnstone Centre.

Curtis, A., De Lacy, T., Keane, D. and Daly, J. (1994). *Landcare in Queensland: Getting the Job Done.* Albury, NSW: Johnstone Centre.

Curtis, A., De Lacy, T., Keane, D. and Lang, R. (forthcoming). *Landcare in South Australia.* Albury, NSW: Johnstone Centre.

Curtis, A., De Lacy, T. and Klomp, N. (1993*a*). Landcare in Victoria: are we gaining ground? *Australian Journal of Soil and Water Conservation* 6(2), 20–28.

Curtis, A., De Lacy, T. and Klomp, N. (1993*b*). Assessing the effectiveness of landcare groups: the Victorian experience. *Regional Journal of Social Issues* 27, 80–92.

Curtis, A., Keane, D. and De Lacy, T. (1994). *Evaluating the Work of LCDCs in WA.* Albury, NSW: Johnstone Centre.

Curtis, A., Tracey, P. and De Lacy, T. (1993). *Landcare in Victoria: Getting the Job Done.* Albury, NSW: Johnstone Centre.

Curtis, M. and Noble, J. (1988). *Volunteer Management: A Resource Manual.* Adelaide: The Volunteer Centre of South Australia.

Department of Conservation and Environment (1992). *Victoria's Decade of Landcare Plan.* Melbourne: DCE.

De Vaus, D. A. (1991). *Surveys in social research.* Sydney: Allen and Unwin.

Dillman, D. A. (1978). *Mail and Telephone Surveys. The Total Design Method.* New York: Wiley.

Earle, T. R., Rose, C. W. and Brownlea, A. A. (1978). Socio-economic predictors of intention towards soil conservation and their implications for environmental management. *Journal of Environmental Management* 9, 225–236.

Edgar, R. V. and Patterson, D. (1992). The evolution continues—Victorian landcare groups. In *Proceedings Volume 1 of the 7th International Soil Conservation Organisation Conference—People Protecting their Land, 27–30 September 1992*, Sydney, Australia.

Farley, R. and Toyne, P. (1989). A national land management programme. *Australian Journal of Soil and Water Conservation* 11(2), 6–9.

Hawke, R. J. L. (1989). *Our Country, Our Future.* Statement on the environment by the Prime Minister of Australia. Canberra: AGPS.

Humble, S. (1982). *Voluntary Action in the 1980s: A Summary of the Findings of a National Survey.* England: The Volunteer Centre.

Isley, P. J. and Niemi, J. A. (1981). *Recruiting and Training Volunteers.* New York: McGraw-Hill.

Moore, L. F. (1985). *Motivating Volunteers: How the Rewards of Unpaid Work Can Meet People's Needs.* Vancouver: Vancouver Volunteer Centre.

Mues, C., Roper, H. and Ockerby, J. (1994). *Survey of Landcare and Land Management Practices.* Canberra: ABARE.

Nowak, P. J. (1987). The adoption of agricultural conservation technologies: economic and diffusion explanations. *Rural Sociology* 52, 208–220.

Pample, F. Jr. and van Es, J. C. (1977). Environmental quality and issues of adoption research. *Rural Sociology* 42, 57–71.

Pearce, J. I. (1993). *Volunteers: The Organizational Behavior of Unpaid Workers.* New York: Routledge.

Reeve, I. and Black, A. W. (1992). Interpreting consistent and inconsistent attitudes to land degradation: an application of cluster and discriminant analysis. Paper presented to Third National Social Research Conference. University of Western Sydney: Hawkesbury (unpublished).

Roberts, B. (1992). *Landcare Manual.* Sydney: New South Wales University Press.

Rogers, E. M. (1983). *Diffusion of Innovations.* 3rd edn. New York: Free Press.

Rossi, P. H. and Freeman, H. E. (1985). *Evaluation: A Systematic Approach.* Beverly Hills, California: Sage.

Shadish, W. R. Jr., Cook, T. D. and Leviton, L. C. (1991). *Foundations of Program Evaluation: Theories of Practice.* Newbury Park, California: Sage.

Smith, D. H. (1975). Voluntary action and voluntary groups. *Annual Review of Sociology* 1, 247–270.

Smith, D. H. (1981). Altruism, volunteers and volunteerism. *Journal of Voluntary Action Research* 10, 21–36.

Vanclay, F. (1986). Socio-economic correlates of adoption of soil conservation technology. M.Soc.Sci. Thesis, University of Queensland, St Lucia.

Vanclay, F. (1992). The social context of farmers' adoption of environmentally-sound farming practices. In *Agriculture, Environment and Society* (G. Lawrence, F. Vanclay and B. Furze, eds.) Melbourne: Macmillan.

Vanclay, F. M. and Cary, J. W. (1989) *Farmers' Perceptions of Dryland Soil Salinity.* School of Agriculture and Forestry, University of Melbourne.

Wilkinson, R. L. and Cary, J. W. (1992). *Monitoring Landcare in Central Victoria.* School of Agriculture and Forestry, University of Melbourne.

Woodhill, J. (1990). Landcare—who cares? Current issues and future directions for landcare in New South Wales. A discussion paper from the 1990 review of landcare in NSW. University of Western Sydney, Hawkesbury.

[36]

Journal of Environmental Planning and Management, 40(3), 293–313, 1997

New Zealand's Planning Revolution Five Years On: A Preliminary Assessment

B. J. GLEESON* & K. J. GRUNDY†

*Urban Research Program, Research School of Social Sciences, The Australian National University, Canberra, ACT 0200, Australia.

†Department of Geography, University of Otago, PO Box 56, Dunedin, New Zealand

(Received June 1996; revised December 1996)

ABSTRACT   *It is now five years since New Zealand radically changed its environmental planning regime by introducing the Resource Management Act 1991 (RMA). The RMA swept away the entire tradition of town and country planning which New Zealand had inherited from Britain, replacing this with an integrated framework for resource management that attempts to emphasize efficiency, sustainability and public participation in the new system of development control. These new emphases of the RMA reflect the agendas of New Zealand's green and New Right lobbies which gained political influence during the 1980s. However, the green and neo-liberal agendas which the RMA attempts to embrace are potentially contradictory. In this paper we investigate this potential contradiction through a preliminary assessment of the first five year's of the new legislation's implementation. In particular, we focus on the operational success, or otherwise, of three 'efficiency' innovations of the RMA, and consider the consequences of these for the environmental and public participation ideals of the legislation.*

Introduction: After Revolution

It is now five years since New Zealand radically transformed its planning system by replacing a plethora of environmental acts and statutes with a single Resource Management Act (1991) (hereafter, the RMA or 'the Act').[1] The principal legislation replaced by the RMA was the Town and Country Planning Act 1977, a planning framework that closely paralleled the traditional British form of development control (Memon, 1993).[2] The enactment of the resource management legislation in 1991 was certainly not a reformist gesture by central government, aimed at improving upon an existing planning framework. On the contrary, the RMA swept away entirely a long established tradition of town and country planning which New Zealand had inherited from its colonizer Britain (Memon & Gleeson, 1995).

These fundamental changes were driven by, and reflect, ideological premises which are quite different to those that underpinned the earlier 'town and country' approach to planning. The RMA can be best understood as an uneasy compromise between two quite distinct, and in many instances, contradictory socio-political forces: the neo-liberal New Right and the environmental movement (Grundy & Gleeson, 1996). Along with Maori (New Zealand's indigenous people) these political forces have played critical roles in the convulsive and far-ranging changes which have occurred in New Zealand society since 1984 (see Kelsey (1995) for an exhaustive review of this restructuring process).

The decade of political, economic and social upheaval which followed the election of the Fourth Labour Government in 1984 saw New Zealand transformed from a welfare-corporatist state (indeed, a paradigmatic form) into a neo-liberal, post-welfare society (Johnston, 1993). As Kelsey (1995) explains, the political economic restructuring programme was largely directed by New Right interests, centring on a powerful set of bureaucrats (notably in Treasury), politicians and business people. Like their counterparts in other English-speaking countries, New Zealand's New Right activists have consistently advocated minimal government and market-based resource allocation (see, for example, McArthur & Porter, 1991). During the 1970s and 1980s, New Zealand's planning regime came in for sustained criticism from New Right theorists and business interests (e.g. Proctor, 1985; Moriarty, 1986; Copeland, 1987; Treasury, 1984, 1987; Wheeler, 1987). The Resource Management Act is deeply embedded in this radical political economic restructuring, and reflects in part the New Right's insistence upon efficient, market-based resource management.

However, there have been other socio-cultural changes to New Zealand society since the early 1980s that have impacted upon public policy, and planning in particular. Important amongst these has been the rise of environmental consciousness nationally, reflected in the proliferation of green political lobby groups (Buhrs & Bartlett, 1993; Memon, 1993). Green groups have also influenced the process of planning reform by insisting upon a broader environmental ambit for public development control and greater opportunities for public participation. Again, the RMA reflects in part these green aspirations for more environmentally sustainable resource usage (Buhrs & Bartlett, 1993).

Previous analyses have pointed to these deep ideological tensions within the RMA which have arisen because the legislation was influenced by two lobby groups with different, even antagonistic, political ideals (e.g. see Gleeson, 1995; Grundy, 1995a; and Memon & Gleeson, 1995). Gleeson (1995), for example, pointed to the potential for one key 'efficiency' innovation in the RMA, the provision allowing greater non-notification of consent applications (s. 94), to undermine the Act's much trumpeted enhancement of public participation. But to date there has been little scholarly assessment of how the legislation has fared since its implementation in 1991.[3] To a large extent this dearth of empirical analysis of the RMA's implementation is readily understandable given both the recency of the legislation and the considerable confusion which the convulsive planning changes have engendered within both local government and the planning profession. Reflecting these considerations, the environmental analysts Papadakis & Rainbow (1996, p. 128) declared recently that "it is too early to judge the outcome of the reforms" to New Zealand's planning legislation.

None the less, it is possible in the light of experience measured thus far to offer some preliminary assessments of certain of the RMA's innovative features. Our interest here is in the progress of the 'efficiency' provisions which were embodied in the RMA as a response to pressure from New Right interests for a liberalized environmental planning system (Memon, 1993). In particular, these features of the new Act were supposed to reduce time and price frictions within the planning process whilst none the less safeguarding the Act's avowed commitment to environmental sustainability and community participation in public decision making (Robertson, 1993; Dormer, 1994). In this paper we shall examine three such innovations with a view to assessing: (1) how well the efficiency goal has been realized in implementation; and (2) the consequences of these new provisions for the Act's other major ideals of sustainability and public participation.

The evidence submitted in these assessments is admittedly limited to our own modest primary investigations (undertaken with other colleagues) and various, limited secondary analyses. Our conclusions are therefore speculative and intended to provoke both debate and questions for new research into the progress of New Zealand's radically innovative planning legislation.

The structure of the paper is as follows. We explain the innovatory nature of the RMA by first identifying the main aspects of the Town and Country Planning Act 1977, leading then to a discussion of the resource management law reform process which culminated in the drafting of the new legislation. We then outline the Resource Management Act, focusing on its aims and those sections which distinguish it from the previous legislation. From this an analysis is made of three aspects of the Act which reflect the attempts of the neo-liberal interests who influenced its framing to both reduce government intervention in the land economy and introduce market principles into environmental regulation. These aspects relate to spatial regulation, consent notification and transaction costs. The paper concludes by reflecting upon the relevance of New Zealand's planning experiment for other developed countries.

The Town and Country Planning Legislation

What was New Zealand's planning legislation prior to the RMA and why did it so concern the powerful New Right during the 1980s? The previous system can best be characterized as 'town and country planning', meaning a form of planning that derived directly from that which has been practised in Britain during this century (see Cullingworth, 1985). Broadly speaking, the approach involves the regulation and control of urban development and the protection of valued rural landscapes. The main instrument of town and country planning has been the land use plan, usually administered by local authorities. Such plans have normally been based around prescriptive zoning schemes which have attempted to direct the spatial pattern of rural and urban land uses (Memon, 1991).

Under the Town and Country Planning Act 1977 the purpose of land use planning was stated as:

> ... the wise use and management of the resources, and *the direction and control of the development of a region*, district, or area in such a way as will most effectively promote and safeguard the health, safety, convenience, and the economic, cultural, social, and general welfare of the people and the amenities of every part of the region, district, or area. (s. 4— emphasis added)

In addition, section 3 of the Act listed matters of national importance that were required to be recognized and provided for in planning documents formulated under the legislation. These included, once again, the wise use and management of New Zealand's resources, together with a number of specific principles as to how this was to be achieved. These were largely concerned with the direction and control of urban and rural development, along with some conservation issues and the relationship of Maori to their ancestral lands.

These principles, contained in sections 3 and 4, were to be realized through the provisions of a district scheme. Matters to be included in district schemes were prescribed in the Act. These prescribed matters covered a range of social, economic, spiritual, recreational, conservation and aesthetic considerations.

One can see from this very brief analysis of Town and Country Planning Act 1977 that the statute had potential for a comprehensive approach to local planning, including potentially wide-ranging socio-economic initiatives. This largely went unrealized however. Local government planning remained focused on land use control and infrastructure provision. The methodology for land use regulation, based on zoning, became very prescriptive (Memon, 1993).

Thus, town and country planning increasingly becoming a target of private sector dissatisfaction during the 1970s and the 1980s. Business groups complained about problems arising from the bureaucratic hurdles they encountered when seeking multiple consents from several different central and local agencies. They complained of an inflexibility of planning schemes, too generous public participation provisions in the decision-making process, and the delaying tactics employed by some community groups. Planning was perceived by many developers and New Right interests (such as the government Treasury) as an unnecessary intervention in the marketplace and an unwarranted intrusion on private property rights (Grundy, 1995b).

In addition, there were also environmental organizations and Maori people who were critical of planning for different reasons. These groups complained about the inadequate recognition of environmental and indigenous values in relation to economic considerations; of adversarial decision-making procedures; expansive hearing costs; lack of access to information; and the excessive discretionary powers accorded to central government bureaucrats and local councils.

The Resource Management Law Reform Process

In response to this dissatisfaction, and in its zeal to restructure every aspect of New Zealand society, the Labour Government of the 1980s established a resource management law reform process in 1987 beginning with a review of the Town and Country Planning Act (Hearn, 1987). The reform process was co-ordinated by a Core Group of bureaucrats based in the newly-created Ministry for the Environment, and input was sought from a wide range of contributors, including politicians, officials and public interest groups (see Memon, 1993, for a comprehensive review).

It is important to appreciate that the new Act, which emerged from this reform process, is as much a product of an 'econocratic' analysis of resource management issues, as it is of political direction and negotiation. In short, economists heavily influenced the final version of the legislation which emerged from the reform process. The important Core Group—particularly its Treasury representative—advocated neo-liberal economics, and focused on the problem of environmental externality in the context of property rights arrangements.

Treasury's overriding objective throughout the exercise was to limit the scope of the proposed Act, and focus it as a means of controlling externalities, by providing clear property rights to natural resources. It was critical of the broader purposes of the proposed legislation which were favoured by the Ministry for the Environment and environmental organizations. These broader purposes included concerns for sustainability and the needs of future generations, which Treasury regarded as being based on vague values. The Treasury feared that such broad ideas were unsuitable for public policy (especially planning) and, if adopted in the new legislation, could lead to arbitrary decisions by the local authorities and the Planning Tribunal (Fletcher, 1991).[4] Contrary to the Ministry for the Environment, Treasury was determined to resist any prioritizing of environmental control in planning, and was opposed to the notion that economic activity should be constrained in order to promote sustainable development. Treasury argued that such a presumption would threaten economic efficiency, and that the protection of the environment should simply take its place alongside other objectives and should be given no special status (Memon, 1993).

At the same time, New Zealand's growing environmental movement played an influential role during the reform process. Environmentalists sought both an expanded environmental mandate for planning and the explicit inclusion of ecological values in the new legislation. The environmental movement had been gathering strength since 1972 when the world's first green party, the Values Party, was formed and confounded pundits by winning 5% of the national vote in the 1975 elections (Rainbow, 1993). Environmental groups were influenced by, and strongly advocated for, the principles of sustainability espoused by the World Conservation Strategy (International Union for the Conservation of Nature (IUCN), 1980) and the report of the World Commission on Environment and Development, *Our Common Future* (WCED, 1987). Both the WCED report and the Conservation Strategy were strongly promoted by environmental interests within and outside the Labour Party and were influential in the formulation of the resource management legislation. The subsequent wording of the RMA reflects both the principles and verbiage of these documents (Grundy & Gleeson, 1996).

A critical moment in the reform process was the replacement of the Labour Government in 1990 by a National Party heavily influenced by New Right pressure groups and ideology. Because of both a lack of time and internal dissension within its ranks during its final days in office in 1990, Labour was unable to pass its version of the new Act. The Business Round Table (a powerful junta of corporate interests) and the Maruia Society (a neo-liberal environmental group) appear to have influenced to a very significant extent the approach of the new National Government to the Bill. The Business Round Table was concerned by the apparent green bias of Labour's draft Bill and made no secret of its objections. At the same time, the Round Table now appeared to regard the environmental cause as legitimate (or at least, inevitable) and recognized a need to come to terms with the environmental movement, rather than to simply oppose it (Memon & Gleeson, 1995).

In the event, the Resource Management Act was passed by the new National Government in late 1991. The new legislation swept away the entire town and country planning regime in law, and replaced some 54 Acts and 20 regulations with a single comprehensive resource management statute.

298   B. J. Gleeson & K. J. Grundy

The Resource Management Act 1991

Synopsis

The former town and country planning framework sought explicit direction of the spatial pattern of rural and urban land uses. By contrast, the new regime established by the Resource Management Act seeks only the regulation of the environmental effects of resource development, rather than control of the nature of land uses. The Act also extends the traditional environmental scope of planning by providing an integrated focus on a wide range of natural resources (land, air, water and geothermal). Developers now must seek formal planning consents from local government for the use of any such resources. The Act also enshrines the principle of sustainability as its guiding purpose; this is, as Alexandra (1994) notes, a world first for planning.

As has been earlier intimated, the RMA attempts to address in a single legislative framework the potentially contradictory objections of environmental and neo-liberal lobbies towards the antecedent planning regime. Some comments now follow on six specific features of the RMA which reflect in different ways the distinctive agendas which both pressure groups brought to the resource management law reform process.

Purpose

Section 5 establishes the principle of sustainable management as the central goal and purpose of the Act. Although derived from the principle of sustainable development advocated in the IUCN's Conservation Strategy and the WCED's Brundtland Report, the Resource Management Act's purpose is rather more limited. In the Act, sustainable management refers primarily to the control of bio-physical resources and the built environment, thereby limiting planning's capacity to intervene in the social and economic affairs of New Zealand society (Memon & Gleeson, 1995).

At the time of the new legislation's enactment, the Minister for Environment, Simon Upton, complained (in our opinion, unjustifiably) that the previous town and country planning legislation "allows, indeed encourages, almost limitless intervention for a host of environmental and socio-economic reasons" (cited in Fookes, 1992, p. 1). The Minister announced that the new Act was "not designed or intended to be a comprehensive socio-planning statute" and that it had only one objective—"to promote the sustainable management of natural and physical resources" (ibid.).

Sustainable management, as defined in section 5 of the Act, contains three requisites:

(a) sustaining the potential of natural and physical resources to meet the reasonably foreseeable needs of future generations; and
(b) safeguarding the life-supporting capacity of air, water, soil and ecosystems; and
(c) avoiding, remedying, or mitigating any adverse effects of activities on the environment.

These three distinct, but cumulative, imperatives must be secured if a resource use is to be considered sustainable. However, notwithstanding the wide legislative definition given to environment, these imperatives primarily relate to the bio-physical environment. The new legislation thus eschews any substantial consideration of socio-economic concerns in its purpose. (See comments of the Deputy Secretary for the Environment (Gow, 1991) on this.)

Moreover, the definition of sustainable management originally proposed for the new legislation (during the reform process) insisted that present resource use should not compromise the needs of future generations. In this definition, 'needs' were not specified and the implication was that these could include both the social and bio-physical requirements of future generations. By contrast, the final definition of sustainable management effectively desocializes future generations, limiting their 'reasonably foreseeable' needs (and therefore the obligations of present resource users) to natural and physical matter. This deliberate dilution of the concept of sustainability is attributable to the influence of New Right interests on the formulation of the new legislation (Banks, 1992).

Also, the notion of social equity, which was a key concern of the Brundtland Report (see Beder, 1993), has been deliberately avoided in the Act's definition of sustainable management. In framing the Act, the Government declared that it was rejecting the Brundtland approach to sustainability on the ground that this embraced "a very wide scope of matter including social inequities" and that it was "inappropriate for legislation of this kind to include such goals" (Ministry for the Environment (MfE), 1991a, p. 1). The greatly reduced emphasis on social objectives in the new planning legislation has forced councils to pursue such concerns through other statutes, especially the Local Government Act.

Methodology

The focus of the new legislation is to be on controlling externalities arising from economic activities rather than the regulation of activities themselves. The stated intent of the Resource Management Act envisages a move away from the prescriptive, zonal-type regulation of activities predominant under the previous legislation to a more flexible, effects-based market allocation mechanism. Simon Upton, Minister for the Environment, in his Third Reading Speech in the House on the Resource Management Bill, said of the Legislation:

> ... the Government has moved to underscore the shift in focus from planning for activities to regulating their effects ... We run a much more liberal market economy these days. Economic and social outcomes are in the hands of citizens to a much greater extent than they previously have been. The Government's focus is now on externalities—the effects of those activities on the receiving environment. (Upton, 1991, p. 3019)

This philosophy is manifest in the new Act by the legislative wording requiring the consideration of effects of activities rather than the direction or control of activities themselves (s. 5). This is supported by the empowering provisions of the Act relating to district plan preparation, which again reiterate the importance of controlling effects rather than activities.

In addition, policy statements by politicians and government officials further reinforce this point. For example, the MfE, in a published guideline for district plans, states:

> The Act ... places emphasis on effects and results rather than the control of specific activities. The emphasis has been moved from planning controls which, in the past, sought to direct activities. The principle now is that regulations must be focused and people should be able to do what they want, provided any damaging effects on the environment are avoided or minimised to levels determined by the community ... the focus of the Act is on controlling the adverse effects of resource use in a district to achieve sustainable development. (MfE, 1991b, p. 6)

Environmental Assessment

Section 88 of the Act mandates environmental assessment for all development proposals, from home improvements to major mining operations. In practical terms, this means that every resource consent application must be accompanied by an environmental impact assessment. This surely distinguishes the Act from other planning legislation and is certainly one of the main achievements of the new Act for environmentalists.

The fourth schedule of the Act outlines the matters that must be taken into account in the preparation of the environmental assessments which must accompany resource consent applications. These assessments must address a comprehensive set of social and bio-physical criteria which are laid out in the fourth schedule. In addition, the Act provides a sweeping definition of 'effects' (s. 3), which embraces *inter alia* the temporal and cumulative dimensions of impacts arising from resource use.

The Resource Management Act thus requires the assessment of the environmental consequences of proposed activities to be an integral part of the resource planning, management and decision-making process. Moreover, planning and consent authorities now have the responsibility for establishing and administering the procedures used. This has imposed a considerable burden on local authorities, and not surprisingly, there are already wide differences in approach seen between different councils.

Morgan (1993), in an evaluation of environmental assessment under the Act, found that the quality of assessments being produced varied enormously. This he saw as a reflection of the shortage of skills among council staff and consultants. In addition, the Parliamentary Commissioner for the Environment (a public watchdog on environmental matters) found that some councils had responded reasonably well to their requirements under the Act. However, this was contrasted with a poor understanding by the public of what was required, and more importantly, what the objective of an assessment was (Parliamentary Commissioner for the Environment, 1995).

Section 32: Cost Benefit Analyses

Section 32 of the Act requires assessment of the "likely benefits and costs of the principal alternative means" for all policy and plan preparation under the Act (though these evaluations need not be purely economic). Also, explicit consideration must be given to alternative methodologies for achieving the purpose of the Act (see MfE, 1993). This requirement relates to national policy statements (issued by the Minister for the Environment), New Zealand coastal policy statements (issued by the Minister of Conservation), regional policy statements and plans (issued by regional councils) and district plans (issued by district and city councils).

This requirement involves policy makers in a critical assessment of the objectives, policies and rules which they intend to implement to achieve the purposes of the Act. They must address the necessity of taking any action, they are obliged to consider using means other than those traditionally employed, and they must engage in a process of explicit reasoning as to the advantages and disadvantages of all the available alternative means of achieving their objectives (Wheen, 1995).

This, not surprisingly, reflects Treasury's desire to maintain, indeed enhance, instrumental rationality in planning procedures, and to coerce councils into considering the use of economic instruments and market-based incentives rather than regulation. However, it appears that Treasury's hopes are not being realized in practice—Dormer (1994) notes that most of the section 32 analyses conducted in the first few years of the RMA's operation were far from rigorous. Doubtless many councils simply cannot afford the expense of such exhaustive evaluation procedures.

Notification Provisions

Section 94 of the Act expands the circumstances in which developers can avoid the public notification of their consent applications.[5] Non-notification may occur where a council is satisfied that the criteria prescribed in section 94 are met. There are two tests effectively: (1) the adverse effect must be minor; and (2) written approval has been obtained from all those whom the council thinks will be adversely affected, unless it considers it unreasonable in the circumstances to obtain the written approval of every such person.

The non-notification of resource consents is assumed to increase efficiency in the planning process. Section 94 allows developers to seek written approval for their resource proposals from anyone "who may be adversely affected" by their proposal. It is assumed that written approvals will establish for councils that a development enjoys the support of a community and that consideration of the relevant consent application should therefore proceed without public notification. The provision is premised on the assumption that non-notification can save social costs and time. More particularly, non-notification serves the economic interests of the developer by possibly preventing the wider community from knowing about a resource proposal which may be controversial and likely to arouse opposition.

Potentially affected parties surrender certain key rights within the statutory planning process when they give written assent to a development proposal. In particular, such parties relinquish their right to object to a proposal at the initial consent consideration stage. Section 94 stipulates that the council shall take no account of the effect on people who have rendered written approval when it considers whether the impact of a consent proposal will be minor or not.

Administration

Lastly, the Resource Management Act together with a concurrent restructuring of central and local government (see Memon, 1993) established a new adminis-

302   *B. J. Gleeson & K. J. Grundy*

trative regime for planning in New Zealand. A hierarchical, three-tier planning structure involving (in descending order) central, regional and local governments was established. This hierarchy is based on the assumption that decisions should be made as close as possible to the appropriate level of community of interest where the effects and benefits accrue.

Central government's principal role is to oversee and monitor the Act. It also retains direct management responsibility for the allocation of public energy and coastal resources, and the control of hazardous substances. In addition, central government can influence resource management through: statements of national policy to guide local government activities; call-in procedures for proposals of national significance; and the setting of national environment standards by regulation for noise, contaminants, water, soil and air quality.

To date, central government has been noticeably reticent in exercising these options: there have been no statements of national policy (apart from the mandatory New Zealand Coastal Policy Statement released by the Minister of Conservation); there have been no national environmental standards provided; and the call-in procedure has been used only once (for a North Island power station proposal—see Grinlinton, 1995). This, it would seem, is a reflection of the Government's view of its role in resource management procedures: that is, one of minimal intervention.

The 13 regional councils have a pivotal role in the new resource management administration. Regional councils have been given primary responsibility for the management of water, soil, geothermal resources and pollution control. In addition, regional councils will have responsibility for regional aspects of natural hazard mitigation, soil conservation and hazardous substances. They also have joint control (with central government) over resource management issues in the coastal marine area. Each council must produce a policy statement and a coastal plan to provide strategies for managing its region's natural and physical resources.

The 74 territorial authorities (district and city councils) have the primary responsibility for the control of land use, including subdivision and noise, and for the control of the surface of rivers and lakes. They also complement the role of regional councils on some issues such as natural hazard mitigation and hazardous substances. District and city councils have to prepare district plans which can contain rules to mitigate, avoid or remedy environmental effects. District plans must be consistent with national policy statements, New Zealand coastal policy statements, regional policy statements and regional plans (MfE, 1991c).

Other innovatory features of the new Act include: enhanced public participation procedures; a greater sensitivity to Maori environmental values; strict time limits for all stages of the planning process; and the extension of planning regulation to the public sector (Memon, 1993). In summary, the Act includes wider and stronger powers to manage environmental impacts. In some respects, though, depending on the attitude of local authorities, its provisions could prove less protective of the environment than previous planning law. This is because the Act is much less prescriptive than its predecessor; within very wide boundaries, people can do what they like, so long as they have regard to environmental effects.

However, virtually all environmental standards and guidelines from earlier legislation have been discarded in the Act. The only minimum standards provided are for water use classification. It is up to the MfE and individual local authorities to develop appropriate environmental standards as a basis for regulating environmental impacts and promoting sustainability. To date, no national standards have been produced. The absence of national environmental standards has the potential to result in uneven regulation between local authorities and may also inhibit the evaluation of environmental assessments.[6]

The Market and Planning

The discussion will now consider three aspects of the Act's implementation. The theme that links these aspects is the new relationship between planning and the market which the Act sets out to achieve.

Spatial Regulation

As explained above, the Act prescribes that planning shift regulatory emphasis from the control of land uses to the management of the external effects of resource development. This, not surprisingly, has led some commentators (e.g. Dawson & Sheppard, 1994) to say that zoning —the instrument of land use control in town and country planning—must be abolished in favour of some other loosened form of regulation which seeks only to ensure that resource activities meet certain environmental standards. This thought has caused great excitement amongst business interests which anticipated the ability to co-locate previously isolated activities such as industry and residential uses (Dormer, 1994), thus overturning an entire tradition of careful zoning which sought the separation of incompatible land uses.

To some extent, such a re-thinking of spatial regulation was entirely warranted given the enormous changes since the early days of planning to the technological processes of industrial and resource extraction land uses. The externalities generated by many industrial and agricultural land uses have certainly changed since the nineteenth century. In many cases industry has become cleaner, whilst many forms of agriculture produce new forms of 'environmental risk', as Beck (1992) terms it. The dictum that industry and residential housing were utterly incompatible uses, for example, had not been re-examined since its first pronouncement in the nineteenth century by reformers who were reacting to the horrors of the industrial city.

(These comments focus on land use controls administered by district councils rather than water and air regulation by regional bodies. However, all externalities can be attached to some geographic activity and hence the comments on the compatibility, or otherwise, of land uses are generally applicable to other resources.)

This assumed new flexibility in planning regulation pleased New Right interests who saw it as part of a broader project to restructure and loosen all forms of state regulation of private activity so that New Zealand may better compete in the globalized capitalist economy. But, despite the hyperbole, it appears that spatial regulation—that is, some form of zoning—remains and, indeed, is really unavoidable. In a Business Round Table commissioned study of the RMA's first few year's of operation, Dormer (1994) examined the progress of councils in liberalizing their development controls. He was forced to make the gloomy report that "the record so far is not good", noting that, "Plans and Policy

Statements are still overly restrictive" (ibid., p. 19). The continuing attachment of local government to zoning controls was further confirmed in a study by Ballantyne & Bang (1995).

The first new sets of district plans to appear under the Act reveal that councils remain very much attached to zoning (that is the promulgation of distinct land use activity areas) as the principal form of planning control (see Hook, 1994). It is, however, obvious now that the new Act has encouraged a loosening of zoning, revealed as a tendency for district councils to reduce the number of distinct zones; for example, collapsing multiple residential zones into one or two broad zones with general environmental objectives.

Many councils feel compelled for the first time in the new district plans to defend, through explicit rationale, their continued use of zoning as a planning tool. Whangarei District Council provides an interesting rationale for the retention of zoning controls in its recent draft plan (Whangarei District Council, 1993). This council explains that zoning, as a form of regulation, has a certain currency and understanding with the general public that makes it a politically attractive form of control over private activity (see also Miller, 1994). This rationale also states that zoning can be reformulated so as to become a regulation of outcomes from resource use, rather than a control on the nature of activities themselves (a claim which is open to challenge). The shorthand version of this extended rationale could be stated as: "zoning is a form of regulation that is both politically viable and administratively efficient".

Many councils have adopted the general principle that any activity can be allowed in any area, but that each development proposal must be assessed on its individual merits to see whether the environmental costs outweigh the benefits. Other councils are adopting less exclusive notions of zones as simply areas in which a certain activity, such as residential living, is the predominant, rather than the exclusive, form of land use. The Whangarei Plan, for example, simply has three broad category zones now for urban areas—residential, commercial and industrial—and only one rural zone.

The contradiction, of course, for neo-liberalism in the 'loosened' form of zoning is that the case-by-case assessment of land use consents requires an enormous administrative effort. Also, the setting of environmental performance standards for such general zones is a considerable analytical and political challenge. It is possible, therefore, that many councils who have been enthusiasts for the new liberalism in regulation will, in time, come to see it as an unwieldy mode of control; they may eventually return to the more familiar pastures of prescriptive zoning.

The city council of one major South Island city, Dunedin, released its first draft plan under the new Act in 1995 (Dunedin City Council, 1995). The plan adopts the now practically obligatory rhetoric of less control and more flexibility in land use planning. But this surface rhetoric is deceiving. The plan reduces the number of zones to eight, but then divides these into a further 14 specific regulatory units. Above these zones and sub-zones is imposed a new layer of 'overlying provisions', relating to specific issues such as heritage and the natural landscape.

It could be argued that Dunedin's draft plan is a very sensible attempt to preserve and enhance the various features of Dunedin's variegated built environment. However, the Minister for the Environment disagrees and, in late 1995, submitted to the plan approval process, claiming that its provisions are 'too interventionist' (Hill, 1996). The Minister, interestingly, is also in disagreement with the Planning Tribunal, which in its recent decisions has tended to allow a broad and more interventionist interpretation of section 5, the sustainable management aim (see Grundy & Gleeson, 1996).

The Minister would prefer an interpretation that merely requires local government to manage present day externalities arising from resource use (Upton, 1995b). The Tribunal, conservationists and many councils prefer a broader view of the principle which would allow councils more scope to plan for the allocation of future resource patterns, thereby securing environmental quality for future generations (see Grundy, 1995c). This is a serious ideological difference that will eventually have to be resolved at the political level.

Another major South Island city, Christchurch, has pursued an effects-based system of regulation more rigorously than many other district councils. Its experience is revealing. In 1994, a senior Christchurch City Council planning officer reflected on the difficulties of the effects approach:

> One of the major concerns of the approach is the administrative and enforcement difficulties forseen. Both administrators of plans and the public are used to it being reasonably clear at the outset whether a particular proposal will be permitted. The effects-based approach requires a more rigorous testing of each proposal and the provision of adequate information to do so. (Carter, 1994, p. 8)

In summary, the stated requirement of the Act that councils manage the effects of resource development rather than their uses is leading to various interpretations and zoning practices at the local level in New Zealand. The Act has encouraged a geographically diverse regulatory regime, which may cause investment uncertainty and thus become a source of frustration to development capital.

Consent Purchasing (Section 94)

The second area of the Act's operation to be examined here is section 94, the non-notification provision. There is mounting evidence that councils and businesses have availed themselves of this provision to avoid the public notification of consent applications (see Gleeson, 1995). The Business Round Table has noted approvingly the decline in publicly notified consent applications (Dormer, 1994). However, the 1994 report of central government's Ombudsman (a public policy 'watchdog' who reports directly to Parliament) notes with concern that some local authorities were interpreting the provision too liberally and allowing non-notification in some instances without the written consent of potentially affected parties (Office of the Ombudsman, 1994). This same concern was echoed by the Parliamentary Commissioner for the Environment (1995).

For council planners, there are significant technical difficulties associated with section 94. These arise in part from the generality of the tests laid down by section 94. The planner is placed in the potentially difficult position of having to decide for each consent application whether the proposal passes the two tests required for a non-notified procedure. This requires decisions to be made, within tight time frames, and often within a context of considerable political pressure,

306   *B. J. Gleeson & K. J. Grundy*

about environmental development proposals which may involve considerable technical and socio-political complexity.

The first challenge which confronts the planner is the determination of the potential 'impact area' (externality field) of the subject proposal. As location geographers have long been aware, determining spatial externality fields is an exceedingly complex, and often highly subjective, exercise. The planner must then identify those individuals who have property interests within the external- ity field. This is by no means a straightforward and rational procedure (see Dormer, 1994, pp. 6–7, for comments on this). Identifying such interests involves interpreting the meaning of the phrase "every person who ... may be adversely affected by the granting of the resource consent". The vague wording of the legislation fails to establish clearly whether 'affected parties' are only those people with property interests which fall within the immediate externality field of a proposal. In many instances, communities might challenge too restrictive definitions of both the project externality field and the parties located within this. The Act does not tell us, for example, whether the workers who are employed within a project impact area (but are not property owners there) are 'potentially affected parties'.

After these difficult evaluations, the planner must then decide whether the 'net impacts' (i.e. exclusive of any impacts upon those who have rendered written approval) are 'minor'. Here the planner must decide the potential scale of environmental effects of a proposal, involving often complex *ex ante* evalua- tions of social, cultural and bio-physical impacts. In this respect, the Act asks much of planners whose training in formal environmental assessment proce- dures may be minimal at best. Given the nature of professional training, one must doubt the ability of many planners in contemporary New Zealand councils to make highly complex decisions about the nature and extent of environmental impacts within the streamlined consent approval time frame established by the Act (Dormer, 1994).

Moreover, there is increasing evidence that developers are using financial recompense and other, non-fiscal forms of compensation to obtain the written approval of potentially affected neighbours. This amounts to the purchase of approval and the process may be described as a 'compensation market' where the sellers are potentially 'adversely affected' parties, the buyers are resource applicants, and the commodity traded is 'written approval'. A 1994 study found widespread evidence of such compensation markets in New Zealand's 20 largest urban district councils (see Gleeson, 1995). The operation of such compensation markets recently moved a senior Planning Tribunal member, Justice Treadwell, to remark that "resource consents can to a degree be bought" (Treadwell, 1994, p. 4). Indeed, Treadwell concluded that "whether a consent from an affected person is obtained by unconscionable means is immaterial" (BP Oil NZ Ltd v. Palmerston North City Council W64/95). What he means is that written approvals can be sought from affected parties by any means, as long as they are legal methods; morality or political concerns are, as he says, 'immaterial' considerations.

Dormer (1994, p. 67) notes that, from the point of view of business, "the increased availability of non-notification procedures has been a distinct advan- tage". But what about from other social viewpoints? The potential equity implications of such compensation markets which appear to have flourished under the Act might include:

(1) empowerment for knowledgeable property owners who might bargain from powerful positions as 'adversely affected' parties for compensation;

(2) alternatively, neighbours may not always be fully aware of the consequence of their sale of written approval; viz., perfect information will probably not prevail—parties may not fully comprehend either the full nature of the effects (nor might developers) and/or the legal implications of rendering written approval;

(3) payments may be made to property owners, rather than property occupiers, meaning that those people who will suffer environmental harm will not be compensated;

(4) 'intergenerational' inequity: compensation is a one-off payment which does not compensate for long term impacts in terms of environmental disadvantage. Subsequent owners may receive a form of compensation through reduced property values (which will lower land prices to them), but they will not be compensated for amenity loss;

(5) developers may be encouraged to prey on economically deprived areas and communities which may be vulnerable to market compensation for repositories of 'locally unwanted land uses'.

The above list is hardly exhaustive. One might also add Altvater's (1993) observation that money can never be an adequate compensation for environmental degradation or risk (either to humanity or nature). It might suggest some caution is needed by councils in the application of section 94. Such caution, of course, is based on the assumption that social equity remains a concern for planning. New Right interests will doubtless argue that the Act provides little support for such a supposition and that planning should be seen merely as a safeguard for a narrowly conceived environmental sustainability which places little emphasis on social concerns.

Transaction Costs

The final area of implementation that will be commented upon here relates to transaction costs, the old demon of neo-classical economics. Conventional economic theory warns against the growth of transaction costs in markets—the price of 'middlemen's' services, including charges for government services, such as resource consent fees (Mansfield, 1985). (Transaction costs supposedly inhibit the volume of a good traded—e.g. improved land—and, more to the point, profit.)

It was certainly an aim of New Right lobby groups, including the government's Treasury, to develop a resource management system that would reduce both time and price frictions for developers (Memon, 1993). To some extent, the reduction of time-costs has been achieved (partly through instruments such as Section 94). Dormer's report to the Business Round Table notes approvingly that, "it is possible to obtain development approvals for major projects within time frames that could hardly have been achieved in days gone by" (Dormer, 1994, p. 67). Unfortunately, there has not been a systematic and rigorous assessment of the gross and distributional changes in financial transaction costs since the enactment of the new legislation. However there is a rising tide of anecdotal and partially documented evidence to suggest that the Act may have reduced expenses for some resource users—notably big business—whilst inflating costs for smaller interests.

308   B. J. Gleeson & K. J. Grundy

Several smaller business sectors, such as farming and property development, have complained about rising consent application costs. This inflation (confirmed by Dormer's (1994) study) is doubtless due in part to the enhanced requirements in the consent procedures (notably the requirement for environmental assessment) which are affecting both applicants and councils. Many farmers, in particular, who may not be enjoying the benefits of non-notification, see the Act as environmentally zealous and too costly (Gray, 1993). In reality, many farmers are being forced by the new regulatory emphasis on environmental quality to internalize previously socialized costs of their activities by new standards for water quality and soil management (Dormer, 1994; Chapple, 1995).

Just as worryingly for green and community groups has been a recent trend in Planning Tribunal decisions to award legal costs against interest groups who have appealed council consent approvals or the conditions attached to consents. In 1995 a local environmental group in the Coromandel Peninsula of the North Island had NZ$20 000 in legal costs awarded against them after the group appealed a council decision to grant a variation in the applicant's consent conditions regarding toxic discharges to waterways from mining operations (Peninsula Watchdog Group Inc v. Waikato Regional Council A14/96). Also in 1995, the Tribunal awarded NZ$37 000 against local Maori and environmental groups who applied for an enforcement order to halt a fast ferry operation which they argued was damaging to fragile ecology of a coastal area in the South Island (Marlborough District Council v. New Zealand Rail; Save the Sounds—Stop the Wash v. New Zealand Rail W40/95).

The threat of costs, together with the expense of presenting a case (for legal representation and expert witnesses) is proving prohibitive to many environmental and public interest groups (see Coromandel Peninsula Watchdog, 1995; Tiller, 1995).[7] Many community groups will not now consider Tribunal appeals and some have argued that the planning system favours large developers who can prevent opposition to consent proposals simply by threatening costly legal proceedings. These groups now complain that "big business can virtually buy its resource consents" (Chapple, 1995, p. 18). It is possible that the costs threat will encourage community groups to seek mediation and other non-statutory processes in order to avoid formal court proceedings—however, the success of such strategies will remain dependent upon the willingness of consent applicants to explore extra-juridical avenues for dispute resolution.

Finally, the costs of public consultation in planning have been rising. The new draft district plans being released for public comment are being priced at extraordinarily high levels (a consequence of the neo-liberal central state's insistence that all public services be charged at their 'true cost'). Dunedin's new draft plan (1995), for example, is priced at NZ$465 per copy: a huge cost for individuals or community groups. The price caused some Dunedin community groups to argue that the council was making "a mockery of the concept of public consultation" which the new Act was meant to enshrine (Hill, 1995, p. 4).

In summary, the rise in many transaction costs—especially for small businesses and community groups—which the Act has encouraged has generated some general criticism in the national press (e.g. *Otago Daily Times*, 12 September 1994, p. 4; Chapple, 1995). If the Government responds to this problem, it will probably lower costs by reducing regulation, rather than by providing extra fiscal and administrative support for councils and community groups.

Outlook and Lessons for Other Countries

What Lies Ahead

The future course of planning under the Act is clouded by confusion and conflict over certain of its key provisions. In particular, the precise meaning of section 5, sustainable management, is far from clear and it is here that the central political struggles over the Act will continue to occur. These struggles will be between those social interests who favour a broader interventionist role for planning, as an activity which secures the needs of both present and future generations, and those on the Right who wish to see planning reduced to an externality management function, the monitoring of bio-physical 'bottom lines'. This conflict flows from the broader struggle to define the ambiguous notion of 'sustainability' (see the debate on this between Grundy, 1995a, 1995c, 1995d; and Upton, 1994, 1995a, 1995b, 1996).

Second, the operation of certain 'innovations' of the Act which are intended to streamline planning, such as Section 94, may prove politically contentious in the future, especially if regressive social equity effects can be demonstrated. There is a need for thorough investigations on the social justice implications of many of the Act's new provisions, but the present Government is hardly disposed to this sort of research and funding will be hard to come by in the foreseeable future.

Third, the issue of costs is a real one that threatens the socio-political legitimacy of the Act. On the one hand, the Act's stricter environmental requirements have led to an increase in consent costs for many, notably those resource users who cannot avail of the non-notification provisions. On the other hand, many larger business interests are obviously saving money through both the non-notification provisions and the shorter time frames that the Act allows decision makers. Also, and critically, some businesses are saving time and money by threatening any potential opponents with expensive legal procedures and the recent attitude of the Tribunal has been to award these costs against appellants, usually community groups with limited resources. This undermines the public's faith in the Act's claim to enhance community participation in planning. There are already environmental groups claiming that the legislation is "a rich man's Act" (Coromandel Peninsula Watchdog, 1995, p. 1). This is new rhetoric in New Zealand planning.

There are many other outlook issues. The final one that we will mention is the critical under-resourcing of both levels of local government. This inhibits the ability of councils to implement the worthy environmental ideals of the Act, and encourages them to inflate transaction costs, such as consent application fees.

What Can Be Learned from New Zealand?

What lessons can other developed nations take from the New Zealand experience? First, there seems to be a general tendency in many countries for state urban and regional planning to be subsumed within a broader project of environmental management. This is encouraging a struggle to redefine the purpose of planning, and in New Zealand, that has principally been between those who see the market as the principal mode of social and natural transformation and those groups who are suspicious of capitalism's new green image (see Altvater, 1993). In New Zealand this broader socio-political struggle between a

310   *B. J. Gleeson & K. J. Grundy*

fragmented environmental movement and a far more cohesive business sector threatens to result in the replacement of planning by environmental management, a liberalized and desocialized regulation of bio-physical processes.

New Zealand's planners have tended to be reactive observers of this radical change in their institutional framework. We therefore strongly urge overseas planning communities to be active in the debates that are occurring around environmental management, as these go to the very heart of planning. Change is coming, and it is up to planners to defend the worthy ideals that have motivated their profession in the past. A broad ideal shared by planning professions in most Western countries is surely the pursuit of a fair spatial arrangement of society's benefits and burdens. In the new environmental management framework, such an ideal may simply be ignored or abandoned altogether.

Business is learning that being green requires more than a change in rhetoric and product labelling, and supposedly business friendly environmental frameworks, such as the Resource Management Act, are actually increasing the weight of regulation and the level of costs in many respects. Moreover, the Act teaches us that the sort of regulatory flexibility demanded by neo-liberal and business interests may actually increase both the size of the administrative apparatus of planning and transaction costs. (There is a distributional issue within capital here, which is difficult to clarify before new research is undertaken.) Also, this flexibility for certain developers may have regressive social equity effects.

Much more specifically, we think New Zealand's experience shows that some form of spatial regulation is unavoidable in planning. We should therefore oppose ludicrous appeals to altogether abolish zoning, or allied regulatory mechanisms.

Finally, the New Zealand case also demonstrates the need for the proper resourcing of environmental and social objectives in planning. This means that regulators must be properly trained and supported in environmental assessment and that the participation of community groups in planning is secured, either by strict limits on the amount and costs of litigation or through public resourcing of legal aid.

Notes

1. The long title of the legislation is: "An Act to restate and reform the law pertaining to the use of land, air, and water".
2. Other legislation repealed by the RMA included the Rivers Control and Soil Erosion Act 1941, Water and Soil Conservation Act 1967, Harbours Act 1950, Clean Air Act 1972 and the Noise Control Act 1982. The RMA also absorbed the Environmental Protection and Enhancement Procedures.
3. Some of the limited commentaries produced thus far on the implementation of the Act include Dormer, 1994; New Zealand Tourism Board, 1994; Olson, 1994; Pfahlert, 1994; New Zealand Local Government Association, 1995. There is, however, a major research programme commencing in 1996 entitled Planning under a Co-operative Mandate which will examine, over three years, policy statements and plans formulated under the Resource Management Act. This research will be conducted by a team from Massey University and the University of Waikato (see Dixon, 1996). In addition, the Office of the Parliamentary Commissioner for the Environment is conducting a series of investigations into the effectiveness of local government planning and management under the new legislation. This is an on-going project and thus far has produced a report on the environmental assessment procedures being conducted under the Act's mandate (Parliamentary Commissioner for the Environment, 1995).

4. The Planning Tribunal is a judicial body which hears appeals, makes enquiries and issues enforcement orders under the Act.
5. Section 94 applies to permissions sought for discretionary, controlled and non-complying activities.
6. The Ministry for the Environment has released a series of non-statutory, non-binding guidelines; however, these documents are primarily practice guides and have no legal or enforceable status. They have also recently released a comprehensive discussion paper on the development of environmental standards and guidelines, hopefully as a precursor to the establishment of national standards (MfE, 1995b).
7. It is important to note that the draft legislation prepared under the previous Labour Government had provision for publicly funded legal support for community groups. This provision was removed by the National Government when enacting the current legislation.

References

Alexandra, J. (1994) *New Zealand Legislates for Sustainable Development: Lesson for Australia* (Melbourne, Australian Conservation Foundation).

Altvater, E. (1993) *The Future of the Market: An Essay on the Regulation of Money and Nature after the Collapse of 'Actually Existing Socialism'* (London, Verso).

Anderson, A.J. (1991) The chronology of colonization in New Zealand, *Antiquity*, 65, pp. 767–95.

Ballantyne, B. & Bang, B. (1995) Satisfaction and ideology: the Resource Management Act three years on, *Environmental Perspectives*, May, pp. 1–4.

Bang, B. (1992) Aspects of local government planning in New Zealand: a study of the Dunedin City Council, unpublished PhD thesis (Dunedin, University of Otago).

Banks, G. (1992) The Resource Management Act, in: S. Britton, R. Le Heron & E. Pawson (Eds) *Changing Places in New Zealand: A Geography of Restructuring* (Christchurch, New Zealand Geographical Society).

Beck, U. (1992) *Risk Society: Towards a New Modernity* (London, Sage).

Beder, S. (1993) *The Nature of Sustainable Development* (Newham, Scribe).

Buhrs, T. & Bartlett, R.V. (1993) *Environmental Policy in New Zealand: The Politics of Clean and Green* (Auckland, Oxford University Press).

Carter, J. (1994) In the spirit of the Resource Management Act? An effects-based approach, in: *Proceedings of New Zealand Planning Institute Conference* (Auckland, NZPI).

Chapple, G. (1995) Clean, green and expensive, *The Listener*, 22–28 July, pp. 18–20.

Copeland, M. (1987) Planning in a free market, paper presented to the *New Zealand Planning Institute Conference* (Tauranga).

Coromandel Peninsula Watchdog (1995) Resource Management Act Special, unpublished newsletter, August (available from PO Box 51, Coromandel, New Zealand).

Cullingworth, J.B. (1985) *Town and Country Planning*, 9th edition (London, Allen & Unwin).

Dawson, S. & Sheppard, A. (1994) Zoning—transformed or merely recycled?, *Resource Management Law Association Newsletter*, September, pp. 5–7.

Dixon, J. (1996) What makes a good plan?, *Planning Quarterly*, 120, pp. 6–7.

Dormer, A. (1994) *The Resource Management Act 1991: The Transition and Business* (Wellington, New Zealand Business Roundtable).

Dunedin City Council (1995) *Draft Dunedin District Plan* (Dunedin, Dunedin City Council).

Fletcher, R. (1991) Treasury's late blind-side run, *Terra Nova*, July, pp. 16–19.

Fookes, T. (1992) *Social and Economic Matters—Some Thoughts on How These Can Be Dealt with under the Resource Management Act* (Wellington, Ministry for the Environment).

Gleeson, B.J. (1995) The commodification of resource consents in New Zealand, *New Zealand Geographer*, 51(5), pp. 42–48.

Gow, J.L.A. (1991) Resource management law reform in the context of other reforms, in: R. K. Morgan, P. A. Memon & M. A. Miller (Eds) *Implementing the Resource Management Act: Conference Proceedings* (Dunedin, University of Otago, Environmental Policy and Management Research Centre).

Gray, J. (1993) Councils 'over-regulating' says Maf policy adviser, *Otago Daily Times*, 15 November, p. 14.

Grinlinton, D. (1995) The Taranaki power station—atmospheric discharges and the Resource Management Act, *Resource Management Bulletin*, 1(8), pp. 1–3.

312   *B. J. Gleeson & K. J. Grundy*

Grundy, K.J. (1995a) In search of a logic: Section 5 of the Resource Management Act, *New Zealand Law Journal*, February, pp. 40–44.

Grundy, K.J. (1995b) Re-examining the role of statutory planning in New Zealand, *Urban Policy & Research*, 13(4), pp. 235–247.

Grundy, K.J. (1995c) Rural land use and the Resource Management Act, *Planning Quarterly*, 120, pp. 24–6.

Grundy, K.J. (1995d) Still searching for a logic: a reply to the Minister for the Environment, *New Zealand Law Journal*, April, pp. 125–126.

Grundy, K.J. & Gleeson, B.J. (1996) Sustainable management and the market: the politics of planning reform in New Zealand, *Land Use Policy*, 13(3), 197–211.

Hearn, T. (1987) *Review of the Town and Country Planning Act* (Wellington, Department of Trade and Industry).

Hill, F. (1996) Draft City Council Plan flawed say government departments, ORC, *Otago Daily Times*, 18 April, p. 4.

Hook, J.R. (1994) A comparative study of land use planning under the Resource Management Act 1991 and the Town and Country Planning Act 1977, unpublished MA thesis (Dunedin, University of Otago).

Horsley, P. (1989) Recent resource use conflicts in New Zealand: Maori perceptions and the evolving environmental ethic, in: P. Hay, R. Eckersley & G. Holloway (Eds) *Environmental Politics in Australia and New Zealand* (Hobart, University of Tasmania).

International Union for the Conservation of Nature (1980) *The World Conservation Strategy* (Switzerland, IUCN, UNEP, WWF).

Johnston, R.J. (1993) The rise and decline of the corporate-welfare state: a comparative analysis in global context, in: P. J. Taylor (Ed) *Political Geography of the Twentieth Century: A Global Analysis* (London, Belhaven).

Kelsey, J. (1995) *The New Zealand Experiment* (Auckland, Auckland University Press).

McArthur, A. & Porter, M. (1991) Economics and the environment: the New Zealand debate, in: P. Ackroyd (Ed) *Environmental Resources and the Market Place* (Sydney, Allen & Unwin).

Mansfield, E. (1985) *Microeconomics: Theory/Applications* (New York, Norton).

Memon, P.A. (1991) Shaking off a colonial legacy?—town and country planning in New Zealand, 1970s–1980s, *Planning Perspectives*, 6, pp. 19–32.

Memon, P.A. (1993) *Keeping New Zealand Green: Recent Environmental Reforms* (Dunedin, University of Otago Press).

Memon, P.A. & Gleeson, B.J. (1994) Reforming planning legislation: a New Zealand perspective, *Urban Policy & Research*, 12(2), pp. 82–90.

Memon, P.A. & Gleeson, B.J. (1995) Towards a new planning paradigm? Reflections on New Zealand's Resource Management Act, *Environment and Planning B: Planning and Design*, 22, pp. 109–124.

Miller, C. (1994) Plan making in practice, in practice makes perfect, in: *Proceedings of the Resource Management Law Association Conference* (Auckland, RMLA).

Ministry for the Environment (MfE) (1991a) *Resource Management Information Sheet Number Six* (Wellington).

MfE (1991b) *Resource Management: Guidelines for District Plans* (Wellington).

MfE (1991c) *Resource Management: Guide to the Act* (Wellington).

MfE (1993) *Section 32—A Guide to Good Practice* (Wellington).

MfE (1995a) *Discussion Document on Contaminated Sites Management*, (Wellington).

MfE (1995b) *Principles and Priorities for the Development of Environmental Guidelines and Standards: An Issues and Options Paper* (Wellington).

Morgan, R.K. (1993) An evaluation of progress with implementing the environmental assessment requirements of the Resource Management Act, *EPMRC Research Paper Series No. 2* (Dunedin, University of Otago, Environmental Policy and Research Centre).

Moriarty, M. (1986) Alternative approaches to planning in a free market economy, paper presented to the New Zealand Planning Institute Seminar on Planning in a Market Economy (Auckland).

New Zealand Local Government Association (1995) *The Resource Management Act 1991: Four Years Down the Track* (Wellington, New Zealand Local Government Association).

New Zealand Tourism Board (1994) *Tourism Investment and the Resource Management Act 1991: Discussion Document* (Wellington, New Zealand Tourism Board).

Office of the Ombudsman (1994) *Report of the Ombudsman/Te Kaitiaki Mana Tangata* (Wellington).

Olsen, O. (1994) Resource Management Act three years on: how the Act is working in practice, paper presented to the Resource Management Law Association Conference, October (Wellington).

Palmer, G. (1987) *Unbridled Power? An Interpretation of New Zealand's Constitution and Government* (Auckland, Oxford University Press).

Papadakis, E. & Rainbow, S. (1996) Labour and green politics: contrasting strategies for environmental reform, in F. Castles, R. Gerritsen & J. Vowles, (Eds) *The Great Experiment: Labour Parties and Public Policy Transformation in Australia and New Zealand* (Sydney, Allen & Unwin).

Parliamentary Commissioner for the Environment (1995) How well are effects assessed under the RMA?, *Resource Management Bulletin*, 14, pp. 182–183.

Pfahlert, J. (1994) How the RMA is working in practice—an industry perspective, paper presented to the Resource Management Law Association Conference, October (Wellington).

Proctor, R. (1985) The purpose and style of district planning: an economist's view, *Proceedings of District Planning Forum* (Wellington, Ministry of Works and Development)

Rainbow, S. (1993) *Green Politics* (Auckland, Oxford University Press).

Robertson, W.A. (1993) New Zealand's new legislation for sustainable resource management, *Land Use Policy*, 10(4), pp. 303–311.

Statistics New Zealand (1994) *New Zealand Official Yearbook* (Wellington, Statistics New Zealand).

Tiller, J. (1995) Interest groups beware of costs! *Planning Quarterly*, December, p. 4.

Treadwell, (1994) Address to Nelson Conference, *Proceedings of NZ Planning Institute Conference* (Auckland, NZPI).

Treasury (1984) *Economic Management* (Wellington, New Zealand Government Printers).

Treasury (1987) *Government Management* (Wellington, New Zealand Government Printers).

Upton, S. (1991) Third reading debate on the Resource Management Bill, *Debates 516* (Wellington, New Zealand Government Printers).

Upton, S. (1994) The Resource Management Act—section 5: sustainable management of natural and physical resources, address to the Resource Management Law Association Conference, October (Wellington).

Upton, S. (1995a) Section 5 of the Resource Management Act, *New Zealand Law Journal*, April, pp. 124–125.

Upton, S. (1995b) The problem of rural subdivision, address to the New Zealand Planning Institute Conference, May (Taupo).

Upton, S. (1996) In search of the truth, *Planning Quarterly*, 120, pp. 2–3.

Whangarei District Council (1993) *Whangarei District Plan: Proposed Hikurangi Section* (Whangarei, Whangarei District Council).

Wheeler, B. (1987) *Changing the Ground Rules of the Planning System* (Wellington, Ministry of Works and Development).

Wheen, N.R. (1995) The Resource Management Act 1991 and water in New Zealand: impact and implications, unpublished MA thesis (Dunedin, University of Otago, Faculty of Law).

World Commission on Environment and Development (1987) *Our Common Future* (Oxford, Oxford University Press).

Worley Consultants Ltd (1992) *Potentially Contaminated Sites in New Zealand: A Broad Scale Assessment* (Wellington, Ministry for the Environment).

[37]

 Pergamon

Journal of Rural Studies, Vol. 14, No. 1, pp. 27–39, 1998
© 1998 Elsevier Science Ltd
Printed in Great Britain. All rights reserved
0743-0167/98 $19.00 + 0.00

PII: S0743-0167(97)00045-4

Reconfiguring Rural Development in the UK: Objective 5b and the New Rural Governance

Neil Ward and Kate McNicholas

Department of Geography, University of Newcastle upon Tyne, Newcastle upon
Tyne NE1 7RU, UK

Abstract — A new form of rural governance is emerging in more peripheral parts
of the UK. As European Structural Fund monies come to play a greater role in
financing development projects, so new ways of making decisions about rural
development are being initiated. The rural development component of the Structural Funds (Objective 5b) requires that development objectives be prioritized by
means of a 'programming approach' which brings together a wide range of actors
in new institutional arrangements. This reconfiguration of rural development is
examined in this paper using case study material from the Northern Uplands —
the largest Objective 5b area in England. The paper concludes by drawing out a set
of further research questions the Objective 5b programme raises regarding the
tensions between centralization and localization, the role of rural communities in
their own governance, and the new techniques and technologies of rural governance. © 1998 Elsevier Science Ltd. All rights reserved

Introduction

The late 1990s are seeing significant changes in the
design and implementation of rural development
programmes in large parts of the UK's more peripheral rural regions. Primarily as a result of the
increasing importance of the European Union (EU)
Structural Funds, local, regional and national actors
are being required to work in new ways to plan for
and administer rural development programmes.
What might be termed a new mode of local governance is being established which requires the building
of new institutional forms and the forging of new
relationships between various rural development
actors.

The term 'local governance' has recently been
considered by Goodwin and Painter (1996) (see also
Jessop, (1995)). They argue that the concept of
'governance' is broader than that of 'government'
because it encapsulates not just the formal agencies
of elected local political institutions, but also

central government, a range of non-elected organisations of the state (at both central and local levels) as

well as institutional and individual actors from outside
the formal political arena, such as voluntary organisations, private businesses and corporations, the mass
media and, increasingly, supra-national institutions,
such as the European Union (Goodwin and Painter,
1996, p. 636).

The concept of governance, they argue, focuses
attention on the relations between these various
actors, with a shift from government to governance
implying 'not only that these other influences exist
but also that the character and fortunes of local
areas are increasingly affected by them' (p. 636).

This paper takes this broader notion of governance
as its starting point for an examination of the
administration of the Objective 5b component of the
EU's Structural Funds in the UK. It also engages
with a recent literature on governmentality — the
techniques and technologies of governance —
informed by the writings of Foucault (1991) (see
also Barry et al. (1996)). This literature is concerned
with the question of how the state thinks about, or
reflects upon, the legitimate scope of government. It
focuses upon how the state 'problematizes' the
social and economic world within its territory and

how these 'problematizations' are responded to; in other words, how the state first *represents* and then *intervenes in* the domains it seeks to govern. After first outlining the recent history of European rural development policy and its relationship to rural policy developments in the UK, the paper will examine the implications of a greater European role in rural development policy in the Northern Uplands Objective 5b area in northern England. In particular, it focuses on the arrangements for fostering community development in the region and shows how, through the use of new technologies of governance, rural communities (and rural regions) are being required to 'think themselves into existence' as a precursor to state intervention.

The European Structural Funds and rural development

The 1980s saw a set of significant structural transformations which altered the context for, and goals of, policy for Europe's rural areas. Traditionally, European rural policy has been equated with agricultural policy; the Common Agricultural Policy (CAP) represented by far the most important measure in both political and budgetary terms. However, the arrival of food surpluses by the 1980s shifted the political emphasis from increasing food production to curbing it, at the same time as new concerns arose about protecting the rural environment from the excesses of intensive agricultural practices. It was in the context of the challenges for rural Europe posed by these shifts, that the European Commission sought to re-examine EU policies for rural areas, and in 1988 published a communication entitled *The Future of Rural Society* (Commission of the European Communities [CEC], 1988). One important outcome of the document was its advocacy of a strengthened rural development component of what was to become a reformed and much expanded package of Structural Funds. The overall justification for the Structural Funds was the strengthening of economic and social cohesion (i.e. reducing the gap between the most and least affluent regions of the member states). The funds ran, in their revised form, for an initial 'programming period' from 1989 to 1993. Their operation during this first phase was reviewed and the funds were further enlarged for a second period (1994–1999) such that they now account for about 30% of the EU's overall budget.*

In *The Future of Rural Society* (CEC, 1988), the Commission laid out its new approach to the use of Structural Fund monies for rural development. They were to be targeted in a more spatially and themat-

ically focused manner than had previously been the case and were to be more carefully directed towards *specific* problems and *specific* areas (see Bachtler and Michie, 1994; Bachtler and Michie, 1995; Wishlade, 1994). A set of 'objectives' were formulated to guide the distribution of funds, one of which, Objective 5b, was intended to target 'specific problems in more limited rural areas', involving 'a more flexible approach when identifying and tackling rural problems' (CEC, 1988, p. 61). Areas would be designated as qualifying for Objective 5b funding if they had: a below average level of economic development, employment dominated by the agricultural sector, and poor levels of agricultural incomes. Secondary criteria also included: problems of peripherality, depopulation, and a susceptibility to economic pressures in the face of further CAP reforms.

A development plan was to be devised for each area designated under Objective 5b with details worked out through negotiation between the Commission, the national government and local bodies working in partnership. Actors and organizations from the target local area were to be given the opportunity to make an input into policy design under a new model termed 'local rural development' (Ray, 1996). The Commission, in *The Future of Rural Society*, argued that rural development policy:

> must...be geared to local requirements and initiatives, particularly at the level of small and medium-sized enterprises, and must place particular emphasis on making the most of local potential...Local rural development does not mean merely working along existing lines. It means making the most of all the advantages that a particular local area has: space and landscape beauty, high-quality agricultural and forestry products specific to the area, gastronomic specialities, cultural and craft traditions, architectural and artistic heritage, innovatory ideas, availability of labour, industries and services already existing, all to be exploited with regional capital and human resources, with what is lacking in the way of capital and co-ordination, consultancy and planning services brought in from outside (CEC, 1988, p. 48).

This new approach to rural development has initiated the forging of new relationships between the sub-State and supra-State levels of government. In

---

*Three Structural Funds have evolved from a modest initial European regional policy originally devised in the mid-1970s (see Preston, 1994). These are: the European Regional Development Fund (ERDF) which funds projects such as employment creation through industrial investment, infrastructure improvements and general local economic development schemes; the European Social Fund (ESF) which is used to support training and job creation programmes; and the European Agricultural Guarantee and Guidance Funds (EAGGF) which help finance the 'modernization' of farming practices, the promotion of agricultural processing, marketing, farm tourism and environmental protection.

the British case, new links have had to be established between local authorities and the regional branches of the central State on the one hand, and the EU on the other. The institutions of the EU set the criteria for eligibility for Objective 5b designation and the European Commission has had the power to approve (or, by implication, to propose modifications or to reject) Objective 5b draft programming documents from the rural localities. At the same time, however, actors at the local level were seemingly to gain a greater input into the policy process. The Commission envisaged the creating of 'a network of rural development agencies (or agents) to play a stimulating, mobilizing and co-ordinating role' (CEC, 1988, p. 62), and argued that

> the involvement of local and regional authorities and other social, local and regional economic interest groups in the identification of problems and the quest for solutions limits the number of errors of diagnosis that are all too common when planning is carried out from the outside (p. 62).

Thus these new and substantial funds for rural development were to be administered by an approach which stressed the building of new links between different levels of government — from local authorities, through regions and national governments, to the Commission in Brussels. In addition, the approach required that dialogue and partnerships be developed in localities between different sectors and groups of actors, including local government, business interests, rural development and training agencies and voluntary and community groups.

Rural policy and rural communities in the UK

In parallel with the emergence of this new approach to European rural development, British rural policy had similarly arrived at something of a cross-roads by the late 1980s. Pressures from within the UK to seek reform of the CAP mounted at the same time as an acute development boom, particularly concentrated in southern England, accentuated the pressures for the release of rural land for development. A dominant discourse of 'protecting' a 'threatened' countryside emerged as a host of policy contradictions came to light in the rural sphere and calls were increasingly made for a new strategy for the countryside. The government responded to these concerns with publication in October 1995 of the English White Paper titled *Rural England: A Nation Committed to a Living Countryside* (DoE/MAFF, 1995) along with similar papers for Scotland and Wales (see Lowe (1996) for a discussion).

The rural, rather than narrowly agricultural, focus of the exercise required that the government come to grips with the particular circumstances, opportunities and problems of people who live and work in rural areas. Indeed, the extent to which the White Papers covered issues of rural community development was notable and broadly welcomed by many rural community and voluntary groups (Action with Communities in Rural England, 1996; National Council for Voluntary Organisations, 1996). All three rural White Papers share a specific vision of rural communities with a strong emphasis on 'self-help'. The English White Paper, for example, states that:

> Self-help and independence are traditional strengths of rural communities. People in the countryside have always needed to take responsibility for looking after themselves and each other. They do not expect the Government to solve all their problems for them and they know that it is they who are generally best placed to identify their own needs and the solutions to them. In any case local decision-making is likely to be more responsive to local circumstances than uniform plans. Improving quality of life in the countryside starts with local people and local initiative (DoE/MAFF, 1995, p. 16).

As a result, the English White Paper proposes a much more active role for parish councils in the management of local affairs, both through the delegation of some responsibilities from district and county councils and also through the taking on of new responsibilities (in the areas of crime prevention and community transport, for example). At the same time, the government's role is seen as 'to listen to what people in the countryside have to say' (DoE/MAFF, 1995, p. 10) and 'to work in partnership with local people rather than imposing top-down solutions' (p. 16).

Recent policy statements from both the British government and the European Commission therefore appear in harmony insofar as they proclaim the virtue of 'bottom-up' models of rural development which 'empower' local communities to define their own needs and prioritize development schemes and projects. Differences in the 'British' and 'European' approaches are discernible, however. These arise, in part, as a result of the specific nature of the two state actors — one a long-established unitary nation-state which has experienced two decades of neo-liberal political governance, the other a supra-national inter-governmental body and neo-federal state in the making. For example, in the British case, the preoccupation with 'community' in rural policy and its associated emphasis on 'self-help' and voluntary community work represents, according to Murdoch (1997), a shift in the contours of state action — a new mode of governmentality (following

Foucault, 1991; Rose, 1993, 1996a,b). This shift is part of wider retreat of the welfare state and the seeming erosion of concern for governing through some notion of a 'national society'. In the European case, rural policy has to be seen in the context of the European integration project and state- and institution-building. In this sense, Objective 5b serves as an interventionist, distributive mechanism administered through a centralized bureaucracy as an emerging supra-national, neo-federal state seeks to 'increase its say' in a wider range of policy areas.

Despite the differences in these two discourses — the British retreat from welfarism and and 'state intervention' and the European interventionist project of integration and state-building — we can see that the emphasis on localness, community, empowerment and partnership are common to both. In the next section we turn to a discussion of these linked notions and the relationship between community, governance and governmentality.

Community and rural governance

The emphasis in recent policy pronouncements upon self-help and active citizenship within rural communities resonates, we would argue, with what many have seen as the essential characteristics of British rural community life. Sociological and anthropoligical studies in Britain have identified sets of characteristics that are sometimes claimed to distinguish rural communities from their urban counterparts. Williams (1956) and Frankenburg (1966), for example, both identified strong kinship networks, consensual social relations, an emphasis on face-to-face interactions and small geographical scales of community life as particularly distinctive to rural communities.

As early as the 1950s, however, rural sociologists were interested in the impacts on rural communities of social and demographic changes that have since come to receive a great deal more attention. Williams (1956), for example, saw the mobility of middle-class in-comers as a threat to the structure of rural community life. As an example, he pointed to the changing nature of village organizations, which were moving away from informal meetings towards a more structured and formal approach. He saw the Women's Institute as typical of this trend. By the 1960s, it was being suggested that in-comers may be having a more deep-rooted impact upon the make up of rural communities (Pahl, 1965). The middle-class influx into the countryside occurred in part because of a desire for a particular form of community — a parody of the traditional forms of community — one that Lowe *et al.* (1995) have

called a 'civilized retreat'. When such idealized communities were not necessarily found, middle-class in-comers tried to create them, demanding the co-operation of working-class locals. In an era of globalization with its associated economic, social and ontological insecurities (Giddens, 1990), several commentators have suggested that the strong desire for stability and security and the associated return to localism have resulted in a redefinition of community, often along more exclusionary lines, as those that have the means to do so 'seek to retreat from the modern world by selectively excluding its influence' (Murdoch and Day, 1997).

The type of community that middle-class in-comers wished to be part of, with its village associations and mutual responsibilities, is a forerunner of the present emphasis on self-help and active citizenship in rural policy. The belief that rural communities are somehow self-supporting remains popular — demonstrated, for example, in the language of 'facilitating', 'supporting', 'consulting' and 'empowering' that can be found in the British rural White Papers (and underpinned by the English rural White Paper's claim that 'self-help and independence are traditional strengths of rural communities' (p. 16)). The British government is not alone in propounding the advantages of community-led development for rural areas, and other organizations also subscribe to this notion of rural communities as particularly predisposed towards self-help. Both Action with Communities in Rural England (ACRE) and the National Council for Voluntary Organisations (NCVO) have endorsed the government's support for voluntary work, stressing both its historical significance for the sustainability of rural communities, and the sheer amount of personal effort that continues to be exerted (ACRE, 1996; NCVO, 1996), with ACRE also referring to the particular 'culture of coping' (p. 69) to be found in rural areas. These organizations, while approving of the English White Paper's community focus, also stressed the need to strengthen formal community support in rural areas, arguing (in the NCVO's case) that these are weaker than in urban areas. The National Federation of Women's Institutes (NFWI) sums up the link between rural community characteristics and issues of governance in its response to the English rural White Paper when it claims 'our experience of the positive aspects of country life, such as a strong community spirit, self-sufficiency and an ability to adapt to change, suggest that people living in rural areas should not and need not be marginalised in decisions about their future' (NFWI, 1996, p. 165).

The recent re-emergence of the term 'community' amongst politicians and commentators has taken on a new salience through the vocabulary of community care, community policing, community workers and so on (see Crow and Allan, 1994). For Rose (1996a), an exponent of the Foucauldian governmentality approach, the notion of 'community' has come to involve a 'new way of demarcating a sector for government' (p. 332), with 'community' coming to replace 'society' as the very *object* of government intervention. In short, the emphasis on community is bound up with a new mode of governmentality — a new way in which the state reflects upon the legitimate scope for, and objects of, state action.

Governmentality, for Rose, consists of 'the deliberations, strategies, tactics and devices employed by authorities for making up and acting upon a population and its constituents to ensure good and avert evil' (Rose, 1996a, p. 328). Scholars have discerned periodic shifts in the prevailing mode of governmentality, particularly around the mid-19th century with the emergence of so-called 'managed liberalism' — a mode of governmentality in which the state became 'a centre that could programme — shape, guide, channel, direct, control — events and persons distant from it' (Rose, 1996b, p. 40). Under this mode, people and activities were to be governed through invoking social norms — that is to say, governed through society. More recently, Rose believes that, in response to the failure of government to achieve its objectives, we have seen the emergence of a range of rationalities and techniques that seek to govern without governing *society*. The subjects of government come to be seen in new ways, with people conceived of as individuals who are to be *active* in their own government (see also Kearns (1992) and Kearns (1995) discussion of the notion of 'active citizenship'). Burchell (1996, p. 27) refers to this process as the autonomization of society. Under advanced liberalism, 'individuals are to be governed through their freedom, but neither as isolated atoms of classical political economy, nor as citizens of society, but as members of heterogeneous communities of allegiance, as 'community' emerges as a new way of conceptualising and administering moral relations among persons' (Rose, 1996b, p. 41).

The new governmentalities that can be identified around the notion of 'community' replace old forms of governing which concerned the welfare of a 'national society'. New governmentalities seek ways of governing by instrumentalizing the self-governing properties of individuals and communities. But for the state to 'act upon' a particular individual, population or territory, it first needs to 'render visible' that which is to be acted upon. It needs to develop knowledge about the subjects of government. Murdoch and Ward (1997) have used such an argu-

ment to examine how the British agricultural sector was 'brought into being' through the collection of statistics as a precursor to a highly interventionist state agricultural policy. The population, their circumstances and 'problems' had to become 'knowable' and to be reconfigured as a sector to facilitate state action. In the sections that follow, the arrangements for Objective 5b policy in the UK are outlined and the 'mentality' of Objective 5b is examined from the perspective of governmentality.

Objective 5b and the Northern Uplands

Under the first round of spatial designations after the 1988 reforms of the Structural Funds, Dyfed-Gwynedd-Powys in Wales, the Scottish Highlands and Islands, Dumfries and Galloway and parts of Devon and Cornwall were designated as Objective 5b areas in the UK. In early 1994, further designations were secured for a second programming period and 11 rural areas in the UK now qualify for Objective 5b funds for the period 1994–1999 (see Fig. 1

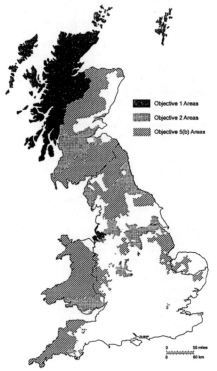

Figure 1. Map of the Objective 5b areas of the UK.

and Table 1). In addition, the Scottish Highlands and Islands became redesignated as an Objective 1 region. The English Objective 5b areas are in East Anglia (covering parts of the Fens, central rural Norfolk, rural east Suffolk and Lowestoft), the South West (which covers all of Cornwall, much of north and west Devon, West Somerset and the Isles of Scilly), the Northern Uplands (see below), the Marches (in the West Midlands), Lincolnshire and, finally, the Midlands Uplands (comprising parts of western Derbyshire and north-eastern Staffordshire). The Welsh area is known simply as 'Rural Wales' and the Scottish areas are Rural Stirling and Upland Tayside, North and West Grampian and the Borders. Together these 11 Objective 5b areas cover almost 70,000 square kilometres, contain more than 2.8 million people and are eligible for about £680 million of Structural Fund monies over the 6-year period from 1994 to 1999.

For individual grant applications to attract funding under Objective 5b, rural development projects must include one or more of a number of specific objectives. These include support and assistance for businesses, agricultural and fishery diversification, the development of tourism and cultural activities, and the conservation and enhancement of the environment. The strategic programme for each Objective 5b area is drawn up in the form of a Single Programming Document by central government through its Government Regional Offices (or the Scottish or Welsh Office). A group of local 'partners', including local authorities and local rural development organizations, are invited to comment on the draft document. In turn, implementation of the programme involves government departments and statutory agencies, the European Commission and 'a wide range of local organisations, including local authorities, TECs [Training and Enterprise Councils], higher and further education sectors,

environmental bodies and the private and voluntary sectors' (DoE/MAFF, 1995, p. 44). Grants paid from the Structural Funds under Objective 5b can only cover part of the costs of a project, normally up to half, with the remainder having to be found by the applicant. Often this is achieved through securing 'matching funds' from other domestic sources including the Rural Development Commission programmes, local authorities and the private sector. These funding arrangements therefore require co-operation between different actors and agencies within Objective 5b areas.

In January 1994, the Northern Uplands (covering parts of rural Cumbria, Lancashire, Northumberland, County Durham, North Yorkshire and Humberside) attained Objective 5b status, thus qualifying for some 108 million ECU (around £90 million) over 6 years. The Northern Uplands (Fig. 2) represents a very large and diverse rural region compared to England's other five designated areas. It is centred on the northern part of the Pennines, but embraces the Lake District, the Forest of Bowland and some lowland and coastal parts of Northumberland, North Yorkshire and Humberside. The designated area covers 14,286 square kilometres and has a resident population of 374,000 (Government Office for the North East [GONE], 1994, p. 7). The rural economy of the region has traditionally been dominated by agriculture, forestry and extractive industries, although latterly the impact of tourism has become increasingly important in some areas.

Despite the diversity of the economy and character of the Northern Uplands, the Single Programming Document (SPD) for the area is required to draw together the main problems and challenges for the area as a *whole*. The SPD for the Northern Uplands in its analysis of the region's fortunes concludes that

Table 1. The Objective 5b regions of the UK

Region	Area (square km)	Population	Funds [million ECU (£m)]
Rural Stirling and Upland Tayside	6900	71,000	25 (21)
North and West Grampian	4193	149,000	40 (33)
Borders	4714	103,881	30 (25)
Dumfries and Galloway	6400	147,800	47 (39)
East Anglia	2410	230,770	60 (50)
Lincolnshire	3094	190,878	53 (44)
Marches	3200	148,000	41 (34)
Midlands Uplands	1000	41,305	12 (10)
Northern Uplands	14,286	374,000	108 (90)
South West	7350	775,304	219 (183)
Rural Wales	14,271	623,828	184 (153)
Total UK Objective 5b regions	67,818	2,855,765	819 (682)

Source: SPDs, Conversion £1 = 1.2 ECU.

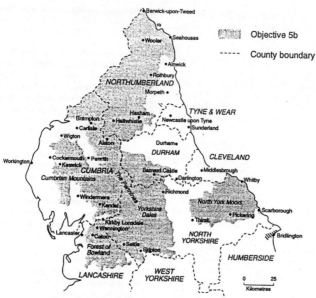

Figure 2. Map of the Northern Uplands Objective 5b area.

it is 'an area characterised by harsh climate, remoteness, rurality, indifferent communications and difficulties of access to the labour market' (GONE, 1994, p. 22), and suffers economically as a result of declining employment in agriculture, coal mining and defence-related industries.

Two strategic goals are identified for the region in the SPD: the creation of a sustainable economy, and the creation of sustainable communities. Flowing from these goals, four priorities were established: (i) economic development and diversification, (ii) tourism, (iii) community development, and (iv) environmental enhancement and conservation.*

---

*These priorities for the Northern Uplands region are very similar to those in the other Objective 5b regions. For example, the priorities for the other English Objective 5b areas are as follows; East Anglia, (i) business development; (ii) agricultural and fisheries diversification; (iii) the development of human resources; (iv) the development of tourism and culture; and (v) research and development and technology transfer; The Marches, (i) business development and diversification, (ii) local communities and countryside, (iii) tourism and related activities, and (iv) farm related development; the South West, (i) SME and business development, (ii) tourism, (iii) agriculture, (iv) community regeneration, (v) environmental management; Lincolnshire, (i) agricultural diversification and development, (ii) tourism, (iii) business development, (iv) human resources and communities; the Midlands Uplands, (i) promoting growth and diversification of the rural economy, (ii) community economic development.

Tranches of money from each of the Structural Funds to meet each priority were allocated, based on the perception of relative needs as stated in the SPD. Table 2 illustrates the weighting of funding across the four priorities for the Northern Uplands area. Overall, almost 44% (£35.9 million) of funds were allocated to economic development and diversification, 20% (£16.6 million) to environmental enhancement and conservation, 19% (£15.4 million) to tourism and 15% (£12.1 million) to community development. Additional monies are also allocated to 'technical assistance' which covers the administration, evaluation, information and publicity measures for the programme.

The Northern Uplands SPD acknowledges that 'the problems of the economy and the environment of the Northern Uplands cannot be divorced from the development of its communities' (GONE, 1994, p. 33). Indeed, the claim that 'economic development can only be based on strong, vibrant communities' (p. 80) provides the main justification for those monies given over to community development. The main community development problem is seen as being the 'outmigration of the young as a result of the lack of employment opportunities, low wages and the lack of affordable housing' (p. 33). Because of the emphasis on 'community' in contemporary governance highlighted above, it is worth turning to the SPD's treatment of community development in the Northern Uplands in more detail.

34   Neil Ward and Kate McNicholas

The strategic goal of creating sustainable communities spawns a set of measures under each of the four
priorities in the SPD. The ECU 15.92 million
(approximately £12 million) given over to the
community development priority forms the smallest
of the four priorities in money terms but still represents unprecedented funds for rural community
development in the region. The SPD sets out the
main elements of the Northern Uplands community
development strategy for the period 1994–1999 as:

● making the case for the revitalisation of rural
  communities as an important end in its own right,
  and as an integral part of economic development;
● identifying and addressing the social problems
  facing rural communities;
● forging partnerships between the organisations
  with an interest in community development which
  are operating, or could be operating, in the
  Northern Uplands;
● looking for synergy from the various programmes
  operating in the Northern Uplands, and looking
  to ensure that the 5b programme makes a genuinely additional contribution.

(GONE, 1994, p. 81).

To qualify for funds for community development,
the SPD states that individual projects that come
forward for support 'should, where relevant, be
identified as part of the process of "village appraisal
or similar studies" (GONE, 1994, p. 81). These
studies assess the economic, social and training
needs of individual villages or groups of communities in the designated area.

A set of physical indicators are set out against which
performance of the programme's community
development priority is to be assessed. These are
that: 100 village appraisals are to be carried out; 30
community facilities are to be enhanced and established; and 280 training places per annum are to be
provided (GONE, 1994, p. 81).

New governmentalities and new forms of rural governance

For the tranche of public funds flowing from Objective 5b to be of lasting benefit, new economic, social
and administrative linkages are required in the rural
north such that a shifting pattern of governance can
be identified. This is the case for the programme in
general (with its emphasis on partnerships and local
consultation), but is particularly so for the
community development priority.

For the programme as a whole, a host of different
actors in the Northern Uplands region have had to
come together to assist in the production of the
SPD. In doing so, they have been required to spell
out the needs, problems and potential for the
region. Although the Government Office for the
North East had lead responsbility for producing the
SPD, it benefitted from input from district and
county councils, two other Government Regional
Offices, the Ministry of Agriculture, Fisheries and
Food, the Rural Development Commission and
business groups. Thus through a complex process of
consultation and negotiation, the SPD document
was produced and the locality and its problems
came to be 'rendered visible' (as a precursor to state
intervention in the form of the distribution of
development funds). A detailed regional analysis in
the SPD captured, in statistical form, the shape and
structure of the Northern Uplands — a spatial unit
that prior to its designation under Objective 5b did
not exist.

These partnership arrangements have extended
beyond the mere drawing up of the SPD and now
also help guide the implementation of the
programme. EU policy requires that the distribution
of funds be overseen by a Programme Monitoring
Committee comprising the various partners in the
regions and representatives of central government
and the European Commission. For the Northern
Uplands region this requirement spawned a large

Table 2. The weighting of Objective 5b funding for the four priorities in the Northern Uplands

	ERDF		EAGGF		ESF	
	%	mecu*	%	mecu	%	mecu
1. Economic development and diversification	47.5	30.78	25	6.75	60	9.72
2. Tourism	22.5	14.58	15	4.05	10	1.62
3. Community development	12.5	8.09	20	5.40	15	2.42
4. Environmental enhancement and conservation	15	9.72	37.5	10.12	0.5	2.02
5. Technical assistance	2.5	1.62	2.5	0.68	2.5	0.41

Source: GONE, 1994, p. 28.
*mecu = million ECU.

and unwieldy body. Unique amongst the British Objective 5b areas, the Northern Uplands areas covers territory administered by three Government Regional Offices (for the North East, the North West and Yorkshire and Humberside), and no less than six county councils. Therefore, in order to improve monitoring of the Programme and render proceedings more responsive to local concerns and interests, part of the work of the Programme Monitoring Committee was devolved in 1996 to newly created Local Implementation Plan groups (LIP groups) at the sub-regional level. Although originally envisaged as operating as pairs of counties working together in LIP groups (North Yorkshire and Humberside, Cumbria and Lancashire, and Northumberland and County Durham), monitoring the programme has, in some cases, in effect been devolved to the individual county level with, for example, the partners for County Durham and Northumberland meeting separately with only nominal representation on each others LIP group meetings. These meetings allow the various partners an opportunity to comment on bids for Objective 5b funds and to make recommendations to the government office on which proposals best fit with the strategic objectives of the Programme and should be funded. Decisions on funding have been subject to final ratification by the relevant sectoral departments in London.* It is the SPD that therefore provides the 'template' for the Northern Uplands region, defining what the most pressing problems are and prioritizing what should be done to address them. More astute applicants for Objective 5b monies will tailor their project proposals to fit the various development requirements spelt out in the SPD.

Thus, from the above account of the administration of the Objective 5b programme, it can be seen how a large and diverse rural region, and a multi-dimensional strategy for its socio-economic development, becomes encapsulated in a single document of 180 pages. This document then structures the nature of development projects in the area. At a smaller scale, the level of individual rural communities, the Objec-

tive 5b programme generates a similar process of representation through document production as a result of the emphasis on linking applications for Objective 5b funding for community development with community needs identified in village appraisals. Village appraisal reports also help render communities and their development needs visible and thus able to be acted upon. Of course, this 'action' may involve no more than seeking to 'instrumentalize' a community's 'self-governing properties'.

Village appraisals have become an increasingly important element of rural community development in recent years. Moseley estimated that appraisals have been conducted in at least 1500 rural communities in Britain since the early 1970s, but a set of policy developments in the 1990s have prompted a marked growth in the number of appraisals being carried out. Implementation of Local Agenda 21 schemes in the aftermath of the Rio Summit on sustainable development often incorporates some form of appraisal or audit as a means of fostering community participation, and in the field of town and country planning, local authorities are increasingly accepting that 'local communities can and should be encouraged to play an active role in crystallising opinion and in galvanising people to take appropriate action themselves' (Moseley *et al.*, 1996, p. 310). Similarly, the English rural White Paper argued that 'mechanisms such as village appraisals and local housing need surveys can help communities define their priorities, identify what they can do to meet them and target limited resources effectively' (DoE/MAFF, 1995, p. 17).

Appraisals serve as a stocktaking exercise. They are usually audits of the resources and services available to communities and are combined with social surveys of the communities' needs and aspirations with a view to identifying desirable and potential improvements in local facilities and amenities and thus the life of the community. Typically, appraisals are managed and conducted, if not initiated, by members of the local community such as, for example, those active on parish councils. Questionnaires are delivered to every household and responses are analysed to help prioritize plans for community development and physical planning in the village. The growing interest in such exercises on the part of a number of statutory agencies has been accounted for by three factors:

First is the information that they provide on local needs, resources and priorities; professionally organised social surveys on a comparable scale would be prohibitively expensive. Second is their stimulus to self-help, be it in the form of community transport provision, good neighbour schemes or practical environmental action on whatever. Third is the legitimation that they confer on

---

*These complex arrangements for decisions about funding have not been above criticism. For example, one representative from the Association of County Councils complained to the House of Commons Environment Committee about the slowness and bureaucracy of the whole process, adding that accountability 'to a dozen partners and then three or four tiers of decision-making' was deterring some groups from applying for funds (House of Commons Environment Committee, 1996, p. xlv). The Secretary of State for the Environment explained to the Committee, however, that 'all decisions on Objective 5b are being referred to Whitehall because the project is new and there is no established framework of precedent which would ensure consistency in judgement' (p. xlvi).

policy decisions which in part reflect them (Moseley et al., 1996, p. 312).

It is the Rural Community Councils who, in recent years, have been most active in promoting the utility of village appraisals for rural communities, not least because of the perceived value of the appraisal process as a means of community development in itself. Appraisals can, it is argued, enhance the skills, awareness and confidence of the members of the community involved (Lumb, 1990; Roome, 1990). However, while Rural Community Council staff may suggest that rural community activists consider embarking upon a village appraisal and can subsequently offer advice and guidance on how the exercise might best be carried out, such staff are keen to stress that the impetus for an appraisal has to come from within the community. Village appraisal committees are then usually established to manage the exercise, design questionnaires, co-opt volunteers and so on.

The emphasis placed in the Northern Uplands SPD on linking applications for Objective 5b funds for community development to village appraisal exercises has proved to be an important spur to many rural communities in the region and a host of appraisals have been embarked upon since the region was formally designated as an Objective 5b area. The Community Council of Northumberland, for example, expects around 35 appraisals to be completed by the end of 1997 and has established a small research unit to advise village appraisal committees and assist in the analysis of questionnaire data.

A recent study by Moseley and colleagues (1996) examined the output of 44 village appraisals carried out in Gloucestershire and Oxfordshire between 1990 and 1994 to assess the extent to which recommendations and action points contained in the appraisal reports had subsequently been implemented and to identify those factors which either enable or constrain successful implementation. The counties studied do not fall within Objective 5b areas and may exhibit a different complexion of community concerns compared with the more peripheral location of the Northern Uplands. (The dominant and most widespread concern, according to the study, was an 'anti-development' interest in restraining speculative housing development). However, the study's conclusions provide some useful pointers to the nature and output of the village appraisal process. It suggests that:

> First, more than anything else, dynamic and motivated individuals are crucial if things are to happen; second, if careful and early attention is not paid to how follow up may best be achieved, then relatively little may result;

third, it is important that there is enthusiastic endorsement of the proposals contained in the appraisal reports by both the parish council and the wide community; fourth, realism as regards political realities and financial resources is crucial (Moseley et al., 1996, p. 324).

In general, the carrying out of village appraisals may help galvanize the local people involved to go on and do other things, with participants reporting to the researchers, for example, that 'a new community identity has been created' through the process of carrying out a village appraisal (Moseley et al., 1996, p. 325). There is some evidence from the Northern Uplands that local community activism has indeed been stimulated by the appraisal process. For example, one village appraisal committee, upon successful completion of its appraisal, decided that rather than dissolving itself with its task complete, it would instead become a village action group to help press for implementation of the recommendations made in the appraisal report.

We have seen in this section how the Objective 5b Programme, when viewed from the perspective of those theorists interested in the techniques and technologies of governance, provides a good example of an emerging, 'advanced liberal' mode of governmentality with its emphasis on governing *through* communities rather than a more universal and welfarist notion of a *society*. The new institutional networks and procedures that have been put in place as a result of the Europeanization of rural development policy for Britain's more peripheral rural regions in many ways resonate with the British government's approach as outlined in the rural White Papers by seeking to empower rural communities and individuals by 'instrumentalizing' their self-governing properties. In keeping with the line of analysis developed by governmentality theorists such as Rose (1993, 1996a,b), we can see how, prior to 'acting upon' a population or locality, the state has first to render the population or locality and its problems visible and calculable. Thus the Single Programming Document helps to bring into being the Northern Uplands as a 'problem-region' (or at least a region in need of assistance through funds targeted at specific development objectives). Similarly, and serving as an excellent example of how the self-governing properties of individuals or communities can come to be instrumentalized through such an approach, rural communities are themselves encouraged to appraise their own development needs and potential and so prioritize what might be achieved under conditions of finite resources. It is in the interplay between, on the one hand, the style and strategic approach of the EU to local rural development, filtered through national government and regional concerns (in the form of SPDs) and, on the other, the expression of community aspirations

from the bottom up through village appraisals, that new development initiatives in the Northern Uplands are being forged.

Discussion

The preceding sections have documented two trends: the rising importance of Objective 5b of the EU's Structural Funds in the financing of rural development initiatives in the UK; and the increasing emphasis, at the European, national and local levels, on the role of rural communities, particularly through voluntary efforts and 'self-help' schemes, in providing the initiative and impetus for the development of rural localities. The coincidence of these two trends has important implications for social science research into rural governance.

Not only is the nature of rural development policy being reconfigured, but so too are the institutional and administrative arrangements for policy design and delivery. New forms of decision-making involve a complex network of actors extending well beyond the traditional conduits of local policy — local authorities — and include a host of non- or quasi-state bodies at the local, national and supra-national levels (John, 1996). These innovative networks have emerged as part of the shift from local govern*ment* to local govern*ance* more generally within the UK (Jessop, 1995; Goodwin and Painter, 1996). The process has been compounded by the rising importance of EU Structural Fund monies in British regions and in some rural localities. Indeed, it was partly in response to the administrative requirements for distributing Structural Fund monies that the British government established its Government Regional Offices (GRO) in April 1994, the continental ideal of a 'Europe of the regions' having no formal institutional expression in England prior to then. Now the GROs are coming to be important players in the implementation of rural development policy. A strong regional role is likely to continue with the Labour government's proposals to establish regional development agencies in England.

The new rural governance is also in keeping with recent British government concerns, as expressed in the rural White Papers, to foster self-help and active citizenship in rural communities. As such it confirms the account offered by Foucauldian governmentality theorists of a move to an advanced liberal mode of governing *through communities* rather than through some notion of a unified 'society'. Ironically, however, while the shift to advanced liberalism has been equated by commentators with a retreat in state intervention and spending (i.e. Murdoch's

charge (1997) that governing through rural communities represents the government's efforts to 'cover its tracks as it creeps away from its responsibilities'), the coincidence of this shift with European redistributive efforts to promote cohesion through enhanced Structural Funds has meant that, for some more peripheral rural regions at least, significant new monies for development schemes are becoming available.

In the light of these new institutional arrangements and new monies, it is instructive to question the distribution of power within the networks of rural governance. It would appear that, initially at least, the arrangements for Objective 5b follow established trends within the British state, namely the concentration of power in Whitehall (see Jenkins, 1995) despite a rhetoric of decentralization and empowerment of individuals and communities. From the perspective of local communities, the requirement that applicants for Objective 5b funds fit their proposals into the measures laid down in the Single Programming Documents, obtain matching funds, and then negotiate a complex set of bureaucratic decision-making procedures has proved a deterrent to many rural groups. This was a common complaint expressed to the House of Commons Environment Committee inquiry into rural policy which also found that the metropolitan-based GROs, as important gatekeepers in the Objective 5b funding process, are too urban-orientated, lack an appreciation of rural development issues, and so are conceptually as well as geographically far removed from rural realities. For rural community groups, this problem is compounded when GROs are obliged to refer Objective 5b funding decisions to Whitehall for the perusal of Ministers.

A central concern here involves the seeming contradiction between the project of European integration and the rising purchase of the concept of subsidiarity. The Structural Funds are by no means the only policy area where the tension is apparent (for example, see Ward *et al.* (1995) for a discussion of EU environmental policy in this light), but locality-based studies of the Objective 5b process offer the potential for further examination of these issues through the prism of regional and rural development policy. As we have seen, recent EU policy statements have emphasized themes of partnership, local involvement and democratic accountability and yet, perhaps paradoxically, regions such as the Northern Uplands find not only the European Commission in Brussels having an increasing strategic influence upon the scale and direction of its rural development initiatives but also Whitehall having the final say over which individual projects are approved for funding (see John, 1996).

38   Neil Ward and Kate McNicholas

The new perspectives generated by the governmentality approach and its application to a more Europeanized system of rural development in the UK can help in understanding the rise of 'community' in local governance. Through the process of SPD formulation at the regional level, and the village appraisal process at the local level, new 'spaces for action' are being created. Both the 'Northern Uplands region' and individual rural communities are being required to 'think themselves into existence' using particular methodologies as a precursor to rural development funding. In the case of village appraisals, the appraisal report helps construe what the community is, and what it can become. The process provides an excellent example of governing through communities in ways which 'activate' the community. From these new perspectives, new research questions emerge that have particular pertinence for the study of local rural development initiatives. The first of these is the question of how the notion of 'community' is constructed, by state agencies. Second is the related question of whether particular constructions of 'rural communities' in specific localities involve not only different representations of rurality (Halfacree, 1993; Murdoch and Pratt, 1993) but also particular ideas about who counts as part of 'the rural community' and what counts as the community interest. For as Murdoch and Day (1997) have pointed out, communities can be as much about exclusion as inclusion (see also Young, 1990). The drawing up of regional Single Programming Documents or village appraisal reports provide a useful empirical starting point for addressing these questions. These technologies of the new rural governance capture and inscribe rural areas and rural communities in statistical and documentary form, first rendering them visible, defining and ordering their 'problems' and thus rendering them governable.

Acknowledgements — The authors would like to thank Philip Lowe, Jonathan Murdoch and the staff of Newcastle University's Centre for Rural Economy for their helpful comments on a draft of this paper.

References

Action with Communities in Rural England (1996) Memorandum of evidence. In House Of Commons Environment Committee *Rural England: The Rural White Paper*, Third Report, Vol. II, pp. 57–63. Minutes of Evidence, Session 1995–6, HC Paper No. 163-II. HMSO, London.

Bachtler, J. and Michie, R. (1994) Strengthening economic and social cohesion? The revision of the Structural Funds. *Regional Studies* 28, 789–796.

Bachtler, J. and Michie, R. (1995) A new era in EU regional policy evaluation? The appraisal of the Structural Funds. *Regional Studies* 29, 745–751.

Barry, A., Osbourne, T. and Rose, N. (ed.) (1996) *Foucault and Political Reason: Liberalism, Neo-liberalism and Rationalities of Government*. UCL Press, London.

Burchell, G. (1996) Liberal government and techniques of the self. In: *Foucault and Political Reason: Liberalism, Neo-liberalism and Rationalities of Government*, ed. A. Barry, T. Osbourne and N. Rose, pp. 19–36. UCL Press, London.

Commission of the European Communities (1988) *The Future of Rural Society*, Commission Communications, 29 July COM(88) 371 final, Brussels: Commission of the European Communities.

Crow, G. and Allan, G. (1994) *Community Life: An Introduction to Local Social Relations*. Harvester Wheatsheaf, Hemel Hempstead.

Department of the Environment/Ministry of Agriculture, Fisheries and Food (1995) *Rural England: A Nation Committed to a Living Countryside*. HMSO, London.

Foucault, M. (1991) Governmentality. In *The Foucault Effect*, ed. G. Burchill, C. Gordon and P. Miller, pp. 87–104. Harvester Wheatsheaf, London.

Frankenburg, R. (1966) *Communities in Britain: Social Life in Town and Country*. Penguin, Harmondsworth.

Giddens, A. (1990) *The Consequences of Modernity*. Polity Press, Cambridge.

Goodwin, M. and Painter, J. (1996) Local governance, the crisis of Fordism and the changing geographies of regulation. *Transactions of the Institute of British Geographers* 21, 635–648.

Government Office for the North East (1994) *Northern Uplands Objective 5b Programme 1994–99 – Commission Decision and Single Programming Document*. Government Office for the North East, Newcastle upon Tyne.

Halfacree, K. (1993) Locality and social representation: Space, discourse and alternative definitions of the rural. *Journal of Rural Studies* 9, 23–37.

House of Commons Environment Committee (1996) *Rural England: The Rural White Paper*, Third Report, Session 1995–6, HC Paper No. 163. HMSO, London.

Jenkins, S. (1995) *Accountable to None: The Tory Nationalization of Britain*. Penguin, London.

Jessop, B. (1995) The regulation approach, governance and post-Fordism: alternative perspectives on economic and political change. *Economy and Society* 24, 307–333.

John, P. (1996) Centralization, decentralization and the European Union: The dynamics of triadic relationships. *Public Administration* 74, 293–313.

Kearns, A. (1992) Active citizenship and urban governance. *Transactions of the Institute of British Geographers* 17, 20–34.

Kearns, A. (1995) Active citizenship and local governance: Political and geographical dimensions. *Political Geography* 14, 155–175.

Lowe, P. (1996) *The British Rural White Papers*, Centre for Rural Economy Working Paper Series No. 21, University of Newcastle upon Tyne.

Lowe, P., Murdoch, J. and Cox, G. (1995) A civilised retreat? Anti-urbanism, rurality and the making of an anglo-centric culture. *Managing Cities: The New Urban Context*, ed. P. Healey *et al.*, pp. 63–82. Wiley, London.

Lumb, R. (1990) Rural community development: process versus product. In *Rural Development: Problems and Practices*, ed. H. Buller and S. Wright, pp. 177–190. Avebury, Aldershot.

Moseley, M., Derounian, J. and Allies, P. (1996) Parish appraisals — a spur to local action? A review of the

Gloucestershire and Oxfordshire experience 1990–1994. *Town Planning Review* 67, 309–329.

Murdoch, J. (1997) The shifting territory of government: Some insights from the Rural White Paper, *Area*, 29, 109–118.

Murdoch, J. and Day, G. (1997) Middle class mobility, rural communities and the politics of exclusion. In *Migration and Rural Areas: Issues and Prospects*, ed. P. Boyle and K. Halfacree. Wiley, London.

Murdoch, J. and Pratt, A. (1993) Rural studies: Modernism, postmodernism and the 'post-rural'. *Journal of Rural Studies* 9, 411–427.

Murdoch, J. and Ward, N. (1997) Governmentality and territoriality: The statistical manufacture of Britain's 'national farm'. *Political Geography* 16, 307–324.

National Council for Voluntary Organisations (1996) Memorandum of evidence. In House of Commons Environment Committee *Rural England: The Rural White Paper*, Third Report, Vol. II, pp. 157–159. Minutes of Evidence, Session 1995–6, HC Paper No. 163-II. HMSO, London.

National Federation of Women' Institutes (1996) Memorandum of evidence. In House Of Commons Environment Committee *Rural England: The Rural White Paper*, Third Report, Vol. II, pp. 160–165. Minutes of Evidence, Session 1995–6, HC Paper No. 163-II. HMSO, London.

Pahl, R. (1965) Class and community in English commuter villages. *Sociologia Ruralis* 5, 5–23.

Preston, J. (1994) *Spicers European Union Policy Briefings: Regional Policy*. Longman, Harlow.

Ray, C. Local rural development and the LEADER 1 Programme. In *The Rural Economy and the British Countryside*, ed. P. Allanson and M. Whitby, pp. 150–166. Earthscan, London.

Roome, N. (1990) Community action as a mechanism for rural policy. In *Rural Development: Problems and Practices*, ed. H. Buller and S. Wright, pp. 151–164. Avebury, Aldershot.

Rose, N. (1993) Government, authority and expertise in advanced liberalism. *Economy and Society* 22, 283–299.

Rose, N. (1996a) The death of the social? Reconfiguring the territory of government. *Economy and Society* 25, 327–356.

Rose, N. (1996b) Governing 'advanced' liberal democracies. In *Focault and Political Reason: Liberalism, Neo-liberalism and Rationalities of Government*, ed. A. Barry, T. Osbourne and N. Rose, pp. 37–64. UCL Press, London.

Ward, H., Buller, H. and Lowe, P. (1995) *Implementing European Environmental Policy at the Local Level: The UK Experience With Water Quality Directives*, Volumes I and II, Centre for Rural Economy Research Report, University of Newcastle upon Tyne.

Williams, W. (1956) *The Sociology of an English Village*. Routledge and Kegan Paul, London.

Wishlade, J. (1994) Achieving coherence in European Community approaches to area designation. *Regional Studies* 28,(1), 79–87.

Young, I. M. (1990) The ideal of community and the politics of difference. In *Feminism/Postmodernism*, ed. L. Nicholson, pp. 300–323. Routledge, London.

Name Index

Runge, F. 53
Rushton, K.M. 212
Russell, N. 308, 362–3
Ruttan 166
Ruttan, V.W. 322
Rutten 72
Ryan, J.G. 98

Sabel, C.F. 25, 29
Sachs, W. 26
Sadangi, B.N. 115
Sader, S.A. 167
Sadler, B. 293–4
Sadler, D. 447, 454
Sahn, D.E. 87, 94, 96–7
Saith, A. 87, 90–91, 103, 106, 111
Salant, P. 23
Salbitano, F. 477
Saltzman, A. 584–6
Sampson, R.N. 488
Sargent, D. 302
Sarris, A. 87, 115
Sassen, S. 556
Sattler, F. 322
Saunders, C. 55, 387
Saunders, D.A. 206, 478
Saunders, P. 563, 566
Savadogo, K. 107
Saville, N.M. 206, 208
Sax, J. 144
Sayer, J. 466, 474
Schaller, N. 307
Scheffer, M. 213, 215
Schillizzi, S. 305
Schindegger, F. 21
Schmandt, J. 537
Schmid, A. 130, 165
Schimidt, H. 333
Schofield, C. 473
Schoonmaker, P. 477
Schopfhauser,W. 491
Schotman, A. 206
Schreiber, G.A. 68
Schroeder, R.L. 228
Schüle, W. 464
Schultes, R.E. 473, 478
Schultink, G. 319–20, 335
Schumacher, E.F. 321
Schütz, P. 329
Schweigl, U. 329
Scoones, I. 471
Scott, J.M. 225
Scurlock, J.M.O. 488
Sebastian, I. 274

Secaira, E. 168
Segal, A. 413
Segerson, K. 150
Selman, P.H. 204, 215–17
Semple, H. 464
Sen, A. 156
Serageldin, I. 147
Sethuraman, S.V. 103
Seyfang, G.J. 552
Shadish, W.R. 607
Sharma, N.P. 472
Shaw, G. 513
Shaw, M. 12
Shaw, P. 206
Sheldrake, R. 321–2
Shepherd, G. 469
Sheppard, A. 634
Sherwood, A. 362–3
Shoard, M. 243
Shortle, J. 52–3
Shucksmith 564
Shucksmith, M. 11, 14, 16
Shugart, R.H. 206
Siddall, R. 449–50, 454
Sigelko, W. 173
Silvander 380
Simberloff, D. 204, 207, 225
Simon 72
Simpson, I.A. 307
Sinclair, A.R.E. 418
Sinclair, G. 251
Sinden, J.A. 136
Sindiga, I. 416
Singh, I. 91, 100
Singh, R.P. 115
Skeratt, S. 362
Skinner, J.D. 419
Slade, R. 105
Slatkin, M. 206
Slee, B. 511–12
Slocombe, D.S. 598, 600
Smil, V. 599
Smith, A. 115, 129–30
Smith, D.H. 610
Smith, J. 583–4
Smith, P. 351
Smith, R.L. 586
Smith, S. 384, 550
Snowdon, P. 511
Soete, L. 57
Søgaard, V. 532
Solow, R. 302
Sombroek, W.G. 481
Soulé, M.E. 206–7, 210, 214, 225